A History of Sociological Analysis

A HISTORY OF SOCIOLOGICAL ANALYSIS

Tom Bottomore & Robert Nisbet

EDITORS

RAWAT PUBLICATIONS
Jaipur and New Delhi

ISBN 81-7033-896-4

Indian Reprint, 2004

First published in the United States by Basic Books,
A subsidiary of Perseus Books L.L.C.

Published by
Prem Rawat for **Rawat Publications**
Satyam Apts., Sector 3, Jawahar Nagar, Jaipur - 302 004 (India)
Phone: 0141 265 1748 / 7006 Fax: 0141 265 1748
E-mail : info@rawatbooks.com
Website: rawatbooks.com

Delhi Office
4858/24, Ansari Road, Daryaganj, New Delhi 110 002
Phone: 011-23263290

Printed at Chaman Enterprises, New Delhi

Contents

INTRODUCTION

TOM BOTTOMORE and ROBERT NISBET

THE IDEA of this book arose mainly from the long-standing interest of both editors in the diverse ways in which sociology has been shaped as an intellectual discipline, but it was inspired more immediately by reflection upon the contribution made to the history of economics by J. A. Schumpeter's *History of Economic Analysis*. Contemplating the existing histories of sociology, we realized that despite many illuminating studies of particular thinkers or episodes, there was lacking a comprehensive work which would show, with the same wealth of detail as Schumpeter's book, how sociological analysis has developed; how the various theoretical schemes have been elaborated and modified; what relation they bear to each other; how theoretical debates have arisen, been pursued, and eventually been resolved or put aside.

When we came to consider how such a history might be written, it seemed evident that the exceptionally broad scope of sociological analysis—claiming as it does to comprehend social life "as a whole"—and the very great diversity of theoretical orientations, which if anything has increased in recent years, made desirable a collective work in which particular types of theory would be examined in a thorough fashion by scholars having a special interest and competence in each area. But we also thought it essential to complement these studies of what may be called "theoretical schools" with two other major kinds of contributions: one concerned with the various methodological orientations of a very general character which have coexisted throughout the history of our discipline, found expression in diverse theoretical schemes, and given rise on occasion to important methodological debates; the other concerned with a number of broad theoretical issues—the significance of power and stratification, the relation between sociological analysis and practical social life—with which all the major schools of sociological theory have had to grapple. Finally, we considered it useful to include, as a type of case study, an account of some aspects of the history of sociological analysis in the United States, where sociology developed more rapidly and extensively than anywhere else and in consequence has had a major historical influence.

This initial conception of the book rested also upon a fairly rigorous distinction between sociological analysis and social thought in a broader sense. Our intention was not to present, even very briefly, a historical panorama of the development of thought about society and to set sociology in this context, but rather to delineate the emergence and development of a "new science" which has been one major element in the history of the modern social sciences since the eighteenth century. Our contributors have not wholly ignored precursors, but they, like ourselves, have concentrated their attention firmly upon sociology as a theoretical and empirical science which has assumed a definite shape only during the past two centuries and more especially in the present century. This distinction, between social thought—the history of which is coterminous with the history of humanity—and sociological analysis, is examined in various ways in the early chapters of this book but requires at least a preliminary exposition here. Like Schumpeter in his discussion of economics, we have to pose the question of whether sociology is a science; and like him again, we have to recognize that the very idea of sociological analysis, of a sociological science, is in some respects obscure, partly hidden by the dust and smoke of many battles, some of which rage unabated to the present day. This is not the place to enter in detail upon controversies in the philosophy of science which concern the nature of science in general, its demarcation from nonscience,[1] and the particular character and problems of the social sciences, some of which are considered from various aspects in later chapters with reference to particular theoretical views and are dealt with more directly in the chapter on positivism. Here we can approach the question by noting some of the features which constitute sociological analysis as a systematic form of inquiry, possessing a distinctive, though varied, array of concepts and methods of research.

The break in social thought which produced sociology may be interpreted in various ways, and it was certainly the product of many different influences, but one of its most important features was undoubtedly the new and more precise conception of "society" as an object of study, clearly distinguished from the state and the political realm in general,[2] as well as from a vague universal history of mankind and from the particular histories of "peoples," "states," or "civilizations." The idea of "society" was elaborated in analyses of social structure, social systems, and social institutions which formed the central core of sociological theory at least from Marx onward; and all the diverse schools of thought which are considered in this volume are so many attempts to define the fundamental elements of social structure—both those which are universal and those which have a particular historical character—and to provide some explanation or interpretation of the unity and persistence of societies, as well as of their inner tensions and their potentialities for change.

Constituted as a scientific discipline by this definition of its object, sociology, however vast, unwieldy, and liable to extremely varied conceptualizations, has developed in what may be regarded as a fairly normal way through the continued elaboration of alternative paradigms and theoretical controversy among their advocates, through the accumulation of an ordered body of knowledge resulting from empirical research directed by one or another paradigm, and through the specialization of research. In this progress, comprising what claims to be a detached and critical construction and evaluation of theories and an objective collection and arrangement of empirical data, there are, to be sure, a number of unsatisfactory features. One is the coexistence over long periods of a multiplicity of paradigms, without any one of them being clearly predominant; hence it might be said, on one side, that no sociological theory ever properly dies but becomes "comatose" and is always capable of subsequent revival; and on the other side, that there are no real "scientific revolutions" in which a reigning paradigm is unmistakably deposed and another becomes sovereign. A second feature is the closeness of the scientific knowledge produced by sociology to ordinary common-sense knowledge, which is sometimes proclaimed in an extreme way by references to the "obviousness" of sociological theories and investigations when stripped of their protective layer of jargon.[3]

These two characteristics account for much of the dissatisfaction that sociologists themselves sometimes feel about the state, and the progress, of their discipline. Nevertheless, they should not be exaggerated. The findings of sociological research are not always truisms; indeed, they may be opposed to common-sense everyday beliefs about a particular matter, or may support one "obvious" conclusion against another that is contradictory but equally "obvious" and widely believed, or may provide knowledge of phenomena that have not been properly noticed by common sense at all. More important for the subject matter of this book is the fact that sociological analysis, to whatever extent it has its original source in a common-sense understanding of human interaction, not only contributes a more systematic, comprehensive, and rigorous understanding, but transforms our knowledge of the social world by new conceptualizations of it. Marx's analysis of commodity production, Max Weber's study of the relation between the Protestant ethic and capitalism, Durkheim's conception of the bases of social solidarity, and the structural analysis of kinship, all provide new knowledge which did not previously form part of the common-sense view of the world and some of which indeed, later became incorporated, in various ways, into everyday knowledge.

The problems posed by the multiplicity of paradigms in sociology—amply revealed in the present volume—may be considered from several aspects. Obviously, various competing paradigms emerge within a definite intellectual arena, and to that extent at least they presuppose a broad, though implicit rather than distinctly formulated, agreement upon what constitutes the specific domain and problems of sociology. So far as this is *not* the case—and there are manifestly wide-ranging controversies about the nature and validity of sociology as such, or of any general social science—then we cannot claim that there is some universally accepted conception of the object of sociological analysis which provides the context for every theoretical dispute. This uncertainty, the lurking presence of radically opposed, or incommensurable, images of man and society in the background of diverse theoretical schemes, presents major difficulties with regard to resolving disagreements, moving from one paradigm to another, or evaluating scientific progress in sociology.

Is it indeed possible to speak of progress at all? We would certainly want to claim that the initial development of sociology represented a distinct progress in the study of human society by its clearer definition of the object of study and its formulation of new themes and problems for analysis. And from the midnineteenth to the early twentieth century—in the works of Marx, Weber, and Durkheim—there appeared bold theoretical constructions, incisive statements of sociological method, and major studies of fundamental elements in the social structure which together established sociology as a rigorous mode of scientific inquiry and brought about a great expansion of empirical social investigations. There can be little doubt that these achievements represent a considerable advance beyond the more speculative constructions of Saint-Simon and Comte, or of the conservative thinkers of the early nineteenth century, however important they may have been as precursors. Edward Tiryakian remarks that Durkheim's life project was to establish sociology as a rigorous science, and the he "provided the discipline with its first comprehensive scientific paradigm,"[4] but this might also be said in only slightly different terms about the work of Marx, which has long demonstrated—notwithstanding occasional periods of "dogmatic slumber" among Marxists themselves—that capacity to generate new research problems and to provoke scientific controversies which is one indication of the fruitfulness of a scientific paradigm.

However, it may seem that a more important question to ask with respect to the progress of sociological analysis is whether there has occurred, since that brilliant age in which the foundations of the discipline were laid, any definitive advance in the construction either of a general theory or of more limited theories about particular social phenomena, and in the criticism and rejection of older theories. In our view, this question is one of great complexity and cannot be answered in any simple way. On one side it is quite evident that the kinds of sociological analysis embodied in the works of Marx, Weber, and Durkheim still possess authority and influence and are far from having been discarded. One aspect of this situation is that there has not yet emerged in the twentieth century any new paradigm which clearly advances beyond those which were produced in what has been called the "golden age" of sociology. The nearest approach to such a paradigm is probably the structural-functionalism of the 1940s and 1950s, but this did not accomplish a comprehensive reconstruction of sociological theory, for although it incorporated (especially in the work of Talcott Parsons) some important theoretical concepts from Weber and Durkheim and attempted to go beyond them in formulating a new conceptual scheme, it did not confront directly either the Marxist theory or some other, less prominent types of sociological thought, or try to include them in its synthesis. This example does indicate, however, one of the ways in which sociological theories are constructed and reconstructed, for the rise and subsequent decline of structural-functionalism can be seen as an oscillation between two contrasting emphases in the study of human society—upon structural continuity, interconnectedness, cultural unity; or upon discontinuity, propensity to change, conflicting interests and values—in the course of which, nevertheless, a greater conceptual clarity and systematization may be achieved.[5] As a whole, though, the process may appear to be cyclical rather than linear; and in the specific case of functionalism the difficulties and criticisms which led to its decline—but not demise—were closely associated with the revival of Marxism as a major sociological theory, not with the emergence of a novel theory or more general paradigm which would give an entirely new orientation to sociological analysis.

Even if, as this discussion suggests, we cannot demonstrate the occurrence, at least in recent times, of any major paradigm changes which have transformed the whole field of inquiry, there remains the possibility that significant progress has taken place in the development of some particular theories. Undoubtedly, as many of the following chapters show, there have been advances in clarifying and reformulating fundamental concepts, in eliminating those which did not stand up to critical examination (for example, some organic analogies), and in revising propositions derived from specific theories. But there has also been a tendency for work within any particular theoretical framework to develop in much the same way as that which is concerned with more general paradigms; namely, to produce alternative conceptions which then coexist without any effective resolution of the differences among them.

A good example is furnished by the development of Marxist thought in recent decades; characterized certainly by very intense theoretical debates, by some noteworthy reinterpretations of Marx's method, and by much illuminating conceptual analysis, these studies have led to the formation of a number of sharply demarcated Marxist "schools" rather than to the consolidation of a single, scientifically more advanced Marxist theory.

Similar difficulties in tracing a distinct line of advance appear if we move from the examination of specific theoretical schemes such as Marxism or functionalism to a study of the diverse, and successive, ways of analyzing particular social phenomena. As Frank Parkin observes with respect to social stratification, the theory of the subject ". . . has no history in the sense of a cumulative body of knowledge showing a pattern of development from a primitive to a more sophisticated state of affairs," and ". . . most of what counts today as class or stratification theory has its origins almost exclusively in the writings of Marx and Engels, Max Weber, and the Pareto-Mosca school."[6] In this case, therefore—and this applies also to other fields of inquiry which are considered elsewhere in this volume—the contribution of later thinkers seems to have been limited to modifying in various ways the major theories formulated at an earlier time, and to introducing new elements which need to be taken into account, as for instance the significance of ethnicity and gender in social stratification. In the main, such progress as there has been has involved the refinement and amendment of existing theories without any notable theoretical innovations or the subsumption of rival theories in a broader conception. At the same time it can reasonably be claimed that some kinds of analysis have been shown to be unfruitful and have been largely discarded, so that as Parkin remarks, ". . . it is difficult to envisage the rise of any new equivalent to the Warner school of stratification."[7]

But if, as the preceding discussion suggests, there have not been any successful scientific revolutions in sociology during the past half century, there have undoubtedly been quite pronounced variations in the ways of approaching the subject matter, and in the kinds of problems that are singled out for attention, as is indicated, for example, by the rise and fall of functionalism and by the growing influence in recent years of Marxism and phenomenology. We need to ask, therefore, how such variations occur, and in particular, to consider whether these movements of thought do not have their source at least as much in the changes taking place in the social and cultural environment as in the theoretical debates and discoveries within sociology as a scientific discipline.

One way of posing this question is to ask whether the history of sociological analysis is not, after all, simply a history of ideologies, depicting the varied and changing attempts to express in a body of social thought, or a world view, the economic, political, and cultural interests of different social groups engaged in practical social struggles. Some such conception appears to be held implicitly or explicitly by a number of scholars engaged in studies of the history of sociology or the philosophy of the social sciences, but a proper consideration of this question requires in the first place some discussion of the concept of ideology, itself susceptible to diverse interpretations. In Marx's theory ideology refers to those symbols and forms of thought, necessarily present in class-divided societies, which distort and conceal real social relationships and in this way help to maintain and reproduce the rule of a dominant class. Yet there are also countervailing forces, most particularly in the modern capitalist societies, one of them being the capacity of dominated classes to resist, in some measure at least, and through an understanding of their own everyday experience, the influence of the prevailing ideology; and another being the progress of science, including social science, which makes possible the disclosure of the real state of affairs that ideology conceals. The contrast between ideology and a universal human reason or understanding, especially the contrast between ideology and science (as the most developed form of reason), is an essential element of Marx's theory. This is demonstrated most fully in his analysis of commodity production, the whole object of which is to show, by a scientific investigation, the real social relationships in capitalist society that lie behind the appearances expressed in ideology. From this standpoint a description of sociology—a presumptive science of society—as nothing but ideology makes no sense. All the sciences, and every other manifestation of intellectual and cultural life, may be influenced by ideology, but there is nonetheless a relatively autonomous and authentic growth of scientific knowledge. Above all, it is the development of social science which enables us to distinguish what *is* ideological and to criticize it.

There is, however, another conception of ideology, elaborated most fully by Karl Mannheim, according to which the social sciences are inescapably ideological. What they produce is not scientific theories which can be tested and rationally evaluated, even though they contain such elements as empirical data and rational systematization, but doctrines, which formulate the interests and aspirations of various social groups, among them nations, ethnic groups, and cultural groups, as well as social classes. From this point of view, the movements of thought in sociology depend upon developments in society and culture, and the waxing and waning of sociological theories have to be accounted for by the varying fortunes of different social groups in their ceaseless competition and conflict. Such ideas are by no means alien to some kinds of Marxist thought: Gramsci and Lukács both conceive Marxism as a world view, as the historically developing consciousness of the working class, not as a science of society; and the thinkers of the Frankfurt school, in a very different fashion, criticize sociology itself—in the form which it has assumed as one element in the growth of modern science—as a "positivist" ideology which has its source in the specific social relationships established in capitalist society, while taking their own stand upon a "critical theory" which involves not only a general criticism of ideologies but also the assertion of a distinct philosophical conception that relates all social inquiry to the aim of human emancipation.[8]

As this discussion has briefly indicated, the idea that sociological analysis is essentially ideological has been presented in quite diverse ways, ranging from a sociology of knowledge to a Hegelian-Marxist philosophy of history. But these conceptions are themselves problematic—thus, a sociology of knowledge presupposes a nonideological sociology, while a philosophical theory of history raises all the problems of teleology—and none of them has shown convincingly that a valid distinction cannot be drawn between ideological thought and a science of society. What they have undoubtedly achieved is to make us more clearly aware of the various ways in which ideology, in whatever manner it is conceived, may enter into sociological paradigms, and hence of the need to consider theories and paradigms not only from the point of view of their internal coherence and development, but also in relation to their wider social context.

This view, applied to the history of science generally, has become more familiar since the work of Kuhn,[9] and it obviously has a special relevance for the social sciences because of the distinctive character of their connection with the interests and values that arise in practical social life. The history of any science is important in providing a better understanding of its theoretical development, and hence of current theories, in stimulating new ideas, and in conveying the sense of a continuing activity of inquiry through which there occurs a gradual, or occasionally sudden and dramatic, growth of knowledge. Quite often it is through a reexamination of earlier attempts to solve a particular problem that new advances are made. These considerations quite evidently apply to the history of sociological analysis, but in addition there are other benefits to be gained. First, a historical study that takes into account the social and cultural context in which a particular body of theoretical ideas has developed should enable us to discriminate more precisely between the evolution of the theoretical concepts and propositions themselves, and the influence upon them of various social and cultural interests—or in other words, to distinguish between the scientific and the ideological content of a system of sociological thought. Second, because the objects of sociological analysis include not only universal characteristics of human societies but also historical and changing phenomena, a history of the various approaches and theories reveals the extent to which many of them, at least in some aspects, have a restricted and specific scope inasmuch as they deal with the facts and problems of particular historical periods. In this respect, however, there may be quite substantial differences between theories in different areas of sociology. For instance, it may be suggested that the continuing importance of nineteenth-century theories of class and stratification is due to the fact that there has been relatively little change, over a long period, in the phenomena with which they deal, whereas theories of development have gone through a number of transformations in the space of a few decades, not only as a result of the controversies between Marxist and other theories, but also because the conceptions of uninterrupted economic growth prevalent in the 1940s and 1950s which influenced sociological theorists have been strongly criticized and to some extent replaced by a preoccupation (whether well or ill founded) with the "limits to growth"; and in this way the facts and problems with which a sociological theory of development has to deal have themselves changed.

In the following chapters our contributors examine particular theories and paradigms, broadly speaking in the manner outlined here, paying attention both to the inner development of theories as a result of criticism and innovation and to the impact of changing social and cultural circumstances. They also discuss, in some chapters, the problems that emerge in trying to evaluate and decide among rival theoretical schemes; such discussion has been central to sociology since Comte. But there are two trends in the recent development of sociological analysis that merit preliminary attention at this stage. First, there is the growth and consolidation, during the past two or three decades, of an international scientific community within which, in spite of the diversity of viewpoints upon which we have insisted, the active exchange and criticism of ideas and research findings have the effect of defining more clearly the boundaries of the discipline and the set of problems that constitute its subject matter. To this extent at least it may be claimed that there is now a single discipline, a realm of scientific discourse outside of which sociological analysis cannot properly be pursued at all; and this discipline—at once the product and the binding element of a community of scientists which sets itself distinct and specified aims—constitutes a relatively autonomous sphere which is perhaps increasingly resistant to purely ideological influences.

A second trend is closely associated with this development; namely, the movement away from "national" schools of sociology, and from the creation of highly individual sociological systems, which were characteristic of an earlier period. Of course, some elements of the previous conditions remain. Even though there are no longer any very distinctive "national" schools of sociology, there is still a "regional" preeminence of European and North American sociology in the discipline as a whole. But who can foresee with any confidence what further transformations of sociological analysis will occur as it develops in the context of different cultural traditions and other civilizations? Equally, much sociological analysis still has its main source in the work of the founding fathers; that is to say, in particular, individual, intellectual creations. But there is today no Weberian or Durkheimian sociology, and even in the case of Marx a considerable gap exists between Marx's own theory of society and the varied forms of present-day Marxist sociology, with the development of the latter, we would dare to suggest, embodying advances in "sociological" rather than "Marxist" thought.

Our claim, then, is that sociological analysis can be seen to have attained a measure of scientific maturity, that its development exemplifies in a more general way those characteristics which are mentioned by Leszek Kolakowski in his discussion of the place of Marxism in the social sciences: ". . . the concept of Marxism as a separate school of thought will in time become blurred and ultimately disappear altogether, just as there is no 'Newtonism' in physics, no 'Linnaeism' in botany, no 'Harveyism' in physiology, and no 'Gaussism' in mathematics. What is permanent in Marx's work will be assimilated in the natural course of scientific development."[10] But we advance this view only tentatively, well aware that some of our contributors, and perhaps a larger proportion of our readers, would be disinclined to accept it, at any rate without numerous qualifications; and also aware that there are still large and difficult questions about the relation of sociology considered as a science to more philosophical forms of thought about society. In effect, there are two separate but interwoven strands of discussion in this volume, and also in our introduction: one concerned with the development of different theories and paradigms in a discipline whose location in the ensemble of human knowledge is largely taken for granted, and the other dealing with the very nature and foundations of the discipline, its title to a separate existence. What we have attempted to do is to present as comprehensive an account as possible of these debates, albeit with a stronger emphasis upon the first; and while we recognize that there are some gaps in this account—in particular, we have not been able to deal as fully as we wished with the sociological theories of culture and of knowledge—we nevertheless believe that this book does provide the necessary means for assessing and comparing different theoretical orientations, for considering how far and in what ways sociological analysis has advanced, and for understanding the historical development of major controversies about the basic concepts of sociology.

NOTES

1. Some of the general issues and disagreements are well conveyed in the volume edited by I. Lakatos and A. Musgrave, *Criticism and the Growth of Knowledge* (Cambridge: Cambridge University Press, 1970).

2. See the discussion of this distinction between the political and the social in W. G. Runciman, *Social Science and Political Theory* (Cambridge: Cambridge University Press, 1963) chap. 2.

3. For example, A. R. Louch, *Explanation and Human Action* (Oxford: Basil Blackwell, 1966) p. 12, discussing some aspects of Talcott Parsons's "general theory," comments: ". . . what's the news? Parsons's elaborate structure turns out to be a way of classifying the various interactions among individuals and groups, and any surprise arises only in that what we know already about human activities can be rephrased in this terminology and classificatory system." In more general terms, Isaiah Berlin, in an essay on Vico's idea of social knowledge, refers to that knowledge "which participants in an activity claim to possess as against mere observers . . . the knowledge that is involved when a work of the imagination or of social diagnosis, or a work of criticism or scholarship or history is described not as correct or incorrect, skillful or inept, a success or a failure but as profound or shallow, realistic or unrealistic, perceptive or stupid, alive or dead." Isaiah Berlin, "A Note on Vico's Concept of Knowledge," *New York Review of Books*, XII: 8 (1969).

4. See p. 188 herein.

5. See chapter 9, herein.

6. See p. 599 herein.

7. See p. 603 herein.

8. For further discussion of these ideas see chapter 4 herein.

9. See Thomas Kuhn, *The Structure of Scientific Revolutions*, 2d ed. (Chicago: University of Chicago Press, 1970).

10. Leszek Kolakowski, *Marxism and Beyond* (London: Pall Mall Press, 1969) p. 204.

A History of Sociological Analysis

1

SOCIOLOGICAL THOUGHT IN THE EIGHTEENTH CENTURY

ROBERT BIERSTEDT

THE HISTORY OF IDEAS, except in its hidden origins, always begins *in medias res*. All ideas have ancestors, and no one can write of the rise of sociological ideas in the eighteenth century without folding a seamless tapestry and concealing most of the panorama it would otherwise display. There was no sociology as such in the eighteenth century because there was no such word. No one coined it until the nineteenth century, and Auguste Comte, who did so, thought of himself as making a sharp break with the past. He therefore adopted his curious doctrine of "cerebral hygiene," reading only poetry during the composition of his *Positive Philosophy*, in an effort to prevent the ideas of his predecessors from contaminating his own. It was a futile effort. Sociology may have only a short history, but it has a very long past. One may be sure that ever since the dawn of reason the restless and inquisitive mind of man not only cast itself into the heavens and pried into the entrails of the earth (the expression belongs to George Berkeley), but also asked questions about man himself and his societies. For it is of the nature of man, as Aristotle observed, to live in groups, and only a beast or a god is fit to live alone. The nature of these groups, whether marital pairs or friends or rulers or slaves, thus became a concern of the philosophers of the West.

No period of history, in fact, has been free of sociological speculation, and few periods have offered so much of it as the eighteenth century. Crane Brinton may exaggerate a bit, as he himself concedes, when he writes, "There seem to be good reasons for believing that in the latter part of the eighteenth century more intellectual energy was spent on the problems of man in society, in proportion to other possible concerns of the human mind, than at any other time in history."[1] Indeed, Brinton goes so far as to say that the word *philosophe,* not translatable into modern French, might best be rendered as *sociologue.* Certainly the word cannot be translated as "philosopher" in the contemporary meaning of that word. The first *Dictionary of the French Academy,* which appeared at the end of the seventeenth century, gave it three definitions: "(1) a student of the sciences, (2) a wise man who lives a quiet life, and (3) a man who by free thought (*libertinage d'esprit*) puts himself above the ordinary duties and obligations of civil life."[2] Since most of the Philosophers were hostile to religion, especially established religion, the word *philosophe* came to carry the connotation of a man of letters who is a freethinker. Most of them were dedicated, if not to atheism, at least to deism.[3] Atheism, as Robespierre explained, was aristocratic and not something one discussed before the servants.[4] "Do you know," wrote Horace Walpole from Paris in 1765, "who the *philosophes* are, or what the terms means here? In the first place it comprehends almost everybody, and in the next, means men who are avowing war against popery and who aim, many of them, at the subversion of religion."[5] From his vantage point in the twentieth century Robert Nisbet writes that the eighteenth century was one of a relentless attack upon Christianity and that that, in fact, was what the French Enlightenment was all about.[6]

One does not expect the eighteenth century to show a differentiation of the social sciences into such separate disciplines as anthropology, sociology, social psychology, economics, political science, and jurisprudence.[7] It is too early, in fact, to exhibit such a thing as social science. There is no article with that title in the great *Encyclopedia* of Diderot and d'Alembert. Furthermore, the social thinkers of the century were to a large degree moral philosophers rather than social scientists, interested not in the study of society for its own sake but in the reformation of society for the benefit of mankind.[8] They were also political scientists rather than sociologists, interested in the origin and usages of government rather than in the structure of society. It is doubtful if the latter expression would have had much meaning for them. In any event, these Philosophers were men of reason and men of enlightment. Indeed, Enlightenment became the name of the age.[9] The virtues they respected were skepticism, rationalism, naturalism, humanism, toleration, and freedom of thought. The vices they detested were ignorance, superstition, intolerance, and tyranny, and of course they all sought to expose the follies of their predecessors.[10] Condorcet wrote of the age "when the human spirit moved in its chains, relaxed all and broke some; when all old opinions were examined and all errors attacked; when all old customs were subjected to discussion; and when all spirits took an unexpected flight towards liberty." And Holbach used strong language to say "Now is the time for reason, guided by experience, to attack at their source the prejudices of which mankind has so long been the victim . . . For, to error is due the slavery into which most peoples have fallen . . . To error are due the religious terrors that shrivel men up with fear or make them massacre each other for illusions. To error are due inveterate hatreds, barbarous persecutions, continued slaughter, and revolting tragedies."[11] The motto of these enlightened Philosophers was *Sapere aude*—dare to know.

No one can do justice to the ideas of the Enlightenment, and no summary can suffice. But four propositions, perhaps, can capture the temper of the times better than others. There was first of all the replacement of the supernatural by the natural, of religion by science, of divine decree by natural law, and of priests by philosophers. Second was the exaltation of reason, guided by experience, as the instrument that would solve all problems, whether social, political, or even religious.[12] Third was the belief in the perfectibility of man and society and, accordingly, the belief in the progress of the human race.[13] And finally there was a humane and humanitarian regard for the rights of man, and especially the right to be free from the oppression and corruption of governments—a right claimed in blood in the French Revolution. It should not be supposed, of course, that the Philosophers were unanimous in their views. Pierre Bayle (1647–1706), for example, one of the earliest of their number, subtle enemy of the Church,[14] and brave defender of tolerance against the Jesuits, entertained a redoubtable skepticism about the idea of progress and thought that reason could easily be as deceptive as the senses. Nevertheless, these four propositions by and large contain the principal themes of the Enlightenment.[15]

The most important of these propositions, almost without question, is the first. It would be impossible to overemphasize the role of the scientific revolution in Western history. The spark that ignited it was struck in 1543 by the publication of Copernicus's *On the Revolution of the Celestial Orbs*,[16] and by 1687, with the publication of Newton's *Principia Mathematica*, it was in full flame. In the 144 years between the world became a different place. It even changed its position in the cosmos, surrendering its location in the center and moving to an orbit around the sun. Surely this is the most spectacular period in the entire history of science—and the most spectacularly successful. Without it there would have been no Enlightenment.

One would like to retell the story in detail but a rapid survey will have to serve. First, of course, was Copernicus, who was on his deathbed when a copy of his great book was brought to him. It contained the fraudulent preface by Osiander, a Lutheran divine who, fearful of the effect the book would have, suggested that the propositions in it were hypotheses only, set forth to facilitate calculation and not to be accepted as true. It was Kepler who exposed the fraud in 1597, but many continued to believe that Copernicus did not accept his own conclusions.[17] Then there was Tycho Brahe, who patiently watched and charted the stars from his observatory, Uraniborg, on the island of Hveen, between Denmark and Sweden. Then came Kepler himself, with his three laws, the first of which "corrected" the orbit of the earth from a circle to an ellipse, with the sun as one of the foci. It is Kepler who has been called the Wordsworth of astronomy because three-quarters of his work is rubbish and the remaining quarter priceless.[18] Then there was Galileo, who discovered the law of the pendulum and the law of freely falling bodies, the first by watching a lamp swing in a little chapel in the cathedral at Pisa and the second by dropping light and heavy objects from the Leaning Tower next door.[19] As the world knows, he was summoned to the bar of the Inquisition first in 1616 and five times in 1633. He had been warned on the earlier occasion but nevertheless proceeded to publish, in 1632, his *Dialogue on the Two Principal Systems of the Universe.* In this *Dialogue* there are three speakers: the first, Salviati, defends the Copernican system; the second, Sagredo (actually a Copernican), poses as an impartial referee; and the third, whom Galileo could not refrain from calling Simplicio, supports the Ptolemaic view. It was too much for the Church. He was required to recant, threatened with torture if he refused to do so, and sentenced to life imprisonment—a sentence that was enforced with some leniency in that he was permitted to receive foreign visitors, one of whom was John Milton. That he did not in fact change his mind is clear from his marginal notes in a book by the Jesuit Antonio Rocco (1633) in which he castigates the Ptolemaic author as "an ignoramus, an elephant, a fool, a dunce, a malignant, an ignorant eunuch, and a rascal."[20] The Inquisition, as Preserved Smith wryly remarks, made many hypocrites but few converts. Galileo was neither. He was, as Condorcet said, the greatest genius Italy gave to science.

We come finally to the man whom John Locke called "the incomparable Mr. Newton." The *Principia Mathematica* was the culmination of the science of the century and a half before, and seldom, if ever, has civilization been the beneficiary of so great a book. Edmund Halley said that of all mankind Newton was closest to God; Isaac Barrow, his mathematics teacher at Cambridge, called him an unparalleled genius; Leibniz, whose independent discovery of the calculus Newton acknowledged, said that his work in mathematics was equal in value to all previous work in that science; Hume praised him as the "greatest and rarest genius that ever rose for the ornament and instruction of the human species;" and Voltaire carried his fame to France,[21] where La Grange described the *Principia* as the greatest production of the human mind. It was La Grange too who regarded Newton not only as the greatest genius who ever lived but also the most fortunate. Why the most fortunate? Because there is only one universe and it can therefore be given to only one man to discover its laws! Later on Kant will pay Condorcet his highest compliment by calling him the Newton of the moral world and still later Saint-Simon will call his tricameral legislature "the Council of Newton." It may be, as one historian complains, that tributes to Newton became monotonous, but one cannot end this story without quoting the lines Alexander Pope intended as his epitaph:

> Nature and Nature's laws lay hid in night:
> God said, Let Newton be! and all was light.[22]

Science was now on the ascent and religion on the decline. It was not only "fluxions" and inverse squares and the laws of motion and the law of gravitation but a discovery more potent by far than any of them—the scientific method itself—which influenced the Enlightenment and which, in fact, created it. We are perhaps a little jaundiced by it now because it has not done justice to sociology in the twentieth century, but without it the human mind would still be mired in superstition, revelation, and authority. As Preserved Smith writes, in concluding his masterful treatment of the Copernicans:

> There has never been a greater revolution in the history of thought than that marked by the establishment of the Copernican astronomy. The abandonment of a geocentric universe of matter was logically followed by the relinquishment of an anthropocentric universe of thought. But the importance of the new idea lay less in the changed picture of the world, vast as that change was, than in the triumph of that great instrument for probing nature, science. To a reflecting mind—and there have been a few such in every generation—no victory could possibly have been more impressive than that of science in this battle with the senses, with common opinion, with inveterate and all but universal tradition, and with all authority, even that claiming to be divine revelation.[23]

The victory had another effect. It turned inquiry off of divine things and on to human things. Pope's couplet has become a cliché but it is indispensable nevertheless:

> Know then thyself, presume not God to scan,
> The proper study of mankind is man.

The philosophers took him seriously.

It is obviously impossible, even if one were equipped to do so, to treat the social thought of an entire century in the space of a single chapter. There are too many names and the discussion could easily degenerate into an annotated bibliography. Nor shall we treat the social sciences separately. As mentioned before, they were not differentiated in the eighteenth century and indeed did not emerge in that century. We shall make every effort to sift out those ideas that are sociological in character, and not economic or political or ethical or otherwise specialized in twentieth-century disciplines. The history of political theory, for example, has been competently and often brilliantly written. We shall thus avoid theories of the origin of the state, of the nature of government, and of various forms of government. Other social sciences, somewhat on the periphery, like geography and demography, will remain untreated.[24] The great historians of the century will also be omitted, and thus there will be nothing of Gibbon and Turgot. Hume will appear not as historian, moralist, or epistemologist, but as sociologist. We shall be alert, in short, for ideas about society itself, including its manners and customs, and shall ignore government, law, the marketplace, and other institutions. We shall present a small and highly selective portrait gallery of those who wrote of society in the eighteenth century and whose works, accordingly, belong to the library of sociology. For reasons of convenience we shall discuss them country by country.

France

We may begin with Montesquieu, the subject of Durkheim's Latin dissertation and almost without question the greatest sociologist of the eighteenth century. He was born Charles Louis de Secondat, Baron de La Brède et de Montesquieu, at La Brède, near Bordeaux, on January 18, 1689. The story is told that a beggar at the gate of the estate was brought in to serve as his godfather in the hope that the child would never forget the poor when he grew up. He was educated at a college near Paris, returned to Bordeaux at the age of sixteen in order to study law, and received his degree three years later, in 1708. After four more years in Paris he again returned to Bordeaux in 1713, the year of his father's death. The following year, at the age of twenty-five, he was appointed a counselor at the Parliament of Bordeaux and two years later inherited from his uncle both a fortune and the presidency of the Parliament. The uncle had purchased the presidency, and it was a practice that Montesquieu, who later sold it, was to defend on the ground that it induced men of wealth and family to undertake tasks they would not otherwise perform. Montesquieu's interests in the law, however, diminished as they grew in science. He joined the Academy of Bordeaux; indulged in laboratory experiments; wrote papers on physics, physiology, and geology; and planned a "geological history of the earth," which, however, was never written. During the years 1720–31 he traveled in Austria, Hungary, Italy, Germany, and Holland and spent the last eighteen months of that period in England. He came to think of himself as a man first and a Frenchman second, and desired to view all peoples impartially. He was well known in the salons of Paris, was elected to the French Academy in 1728 and the Royal Society of London in 1730. He divided the remainder of his life between his estate at La Brède, where he built an English garden, and Paris. In Paris he became the victim of an epidemic and died there on February 10, 1755, at the age of sixty-six.

The publication at the age of thirty-two of his *Persian Letters* brought him immediate fame. Indeed, eight editions were exhausted in its first year. In this book he utilized the device, not original with him, of viewing French life and French institutions through Oriental eyes. It gave him an opportunity to describe the customs of his own society as if they were exotic and extraordinary. His Persians, of course, were more European than Persian because he knew little of Persia except what he had gleaned from reading. One of the reasons for the book's popularity was that he described seraglio life in Isfahan from the point of view of one of the women inhabitants, whose conception of paradise was a place where every woman had a harem of handsome men to serve her. In any event, in this guise Montesquieu's two "Persian" interlocutors were able to comment with impunity on the manners and morals of the French; talk deceptively about the powers of a magician named Pope, who persuades his followers that bread and wine can be turned into flesh and blood; profess a pained astonishment at the horrors of the Inquisition; and argue indirectly for religious toleration: "If unbiased discussion were possible, I am not sure, Mirza, that it would not be a good thing for a state to have several religions. . . . History is full of religious wars; but . . . it is not the multiplicity of religions that has produced wars; it is the intolerant spirit animating that which believed itself in the ascendant."[25]

In this book Montesquieu also wrote on the family, the only social institution that he did not condemn. He treated it also as the only one that does not proceed from a contract; indeed, it precedes all contracts. As for marriage, it is made intolerable by the prohibition against divorce; monogamy and polygamy both fail to win his praise; and incest does not disturb him. His general attitude toward life, finally, is one of melancholy: Men should be bewailed at their birth and not at their death, and every man has the right to suicide because life is an agreement made without his consent.

In his second book, *Considêrations sur les causes de la grandeur des Romans et de leur dêcadence* (1734), Montesquieu joined the ranks of those who have tried to explain the decline and fall of the Roman Empire. In examining the course of Roman history he became a philosopher of history and one from whose ken Providence was politely excluded. The principal cause of the fall was the location of the rule of a large empire in one central place, thus destroying the strength of the provinces. To this were added numerous secondary causes, but always Montesquieu has in mind the transformation of the republic into a monarchy and the dire consequences that ensued. The scholarship of the book is often faulty—the commentators agree that he relied too literally upon Livy—but it is also a masterpiece of French prose. Montesquieu not only excluded the Deity from the historical process but reduced the role of the individual as well. Writing like an earlier Tolstoi, Montesquieu suggests that the individual is but an instrument of what he called the "general movement." If Caesar and Pompey had not done what they did to lead the Empire to ruin, others would have come along to take their places. In his own words:

> It is not Fortune who governs the world, as we see from the history of the Romans. . . . There are general causes, moral or physical, which operate in every monarchy, raise it, maintain it, or overthrow it. All that occurs is subject to these causes; and if a particular cause, like the accidental result of a battle, has ruined a state, there was a general cause which made the downfall of this state ensue from a single battle. In a word, the principal impulse draws with it all the particular occurrences.[26]

Clearly Montesquieu would not have agreed with Pascal's notion that if Cleopatra's nose had been shorter the whole face of the earth would have been changed. Montesquieu is seeking general causes in order to make history intelligible and thereby also asking sociological questions. Furthermore, in these two early works he had a concept of society and not merely of government. As Plamenatz puts it: "We already find him looking at a people, not as a multitude of individuals under one government, but as a community distinguishable from others by their manners and institutions. All institutions, political, religious, domestic, economic, and artistic, are, in his eyes, intricately related to one another."[27]

Montesquieu worked on his great book, *The Spirit of the Laws,* for twenty years and was often tempted to abandon it. He persevered, however, and it was published unsigned, as were his earlier books (the French clergy were still dangerous), in 1748, with the subtitle "On the Relations Which Must Exist between the Laws and the Constitution of Each Government, the Manners, Climate, Religion, Commerce, etc." A more sociological concern can hardly be imagined. It appeared in two volumes containing no fewer than thirty-one books, each book containing from twenty to thirty chapters, few of them longer than ten pages and some less than a full page. It has no organization whatever. Montesquieu himself was aware of this defect and wrote in his preface, "I have followed my object without any fixed plan—I have known neither rules nor exceptions; I have found the truth, only to lose it again." Students of Montesquieu have even tried to rearrange the material into a more acceptable order. In what follows we shall try to winnow out those matters that seem appropriately sociological and ignore the political theory. We shall especially be interested in his emphasis upon climate and its influence on slavery, on the relations between the sexes, and on the customs and morals of a nation; the interrelationships between commerce, morality, and poverty; and his observations on money, population, and religion.

Montesquieu gives a great deal of attention to the role of climate in determining the spirit of the laws or more broadly, as we would say today, the culture of a people. The geographical interpretation of society is not, of course, original with him. Indeed, it is as old as Hippocrates, and Bodin in the sixteenth century anticipated Montesquieu in the eighteenth. Montesquieu is not so extreme as Cousin will be in the nineteenth century,[28] but his intent is clear. He wants to relate climate to temperament and temperament, in turn, to customs, laws, and forms of government. For example:

> People are more vigorous in cold climates. Here the action of the heart and the reaction of the extremities of the fibres are better performed, the temperature of the humors is greater, the blood moves more freely towards the heart, and reciprocally the heart has more power. This superiority of strength must produce various effects; for instance, a greater opinion of security, that is, more frankness, less suspicion, policy, and cunning. In short, this must be productive of very different tempers.[29]

And again:

> In cold countries they have very little sensibility for pleasure; in temperate countries, they have more; in warm countries, their sensibility is exquisite. As climates are distinguished by degrees of latitude, we might distinguish them also in some measure by those of sensibiltiy. I have been at the opera in England and in Italy, where I have seen the same pieces and the same performers; and yet the same music produces such different effects on the two nations: one is so cold and phlegmatic, and the other so lively and enraptured, that it seems almost inconceivable.[30]

If we travel toward the North, Montesquieu thought, we meet people with many virtues and few vices; we meet the opposite if we travel to the South. In latitudes between the inhabitants are inconstant in their manners, and climate "has not a quality determinate enough to fix them." When the climate is too hot the body is deprived of vigor and strength and this may in turn account for the immutability of manners and customs over long periods of time.

Agriculture is the principal occupation of man, but too warm a climate induces him to shun this kind of labor. "Monkery" rose in the warm countries of the East because there they are more inclined to speculation than to action. Customs pertaining to the use of alcohol are also regulated by climate:

> The law of Mohammed, which prohibits the drinking of wine, is, therefore, fitted to the climate of Arabia: and indeed, before Mohammed's time, water was the common drink of the Arabs. The law which forbade the Carthaginians to drink wine was a law of the climate; and, indeed, the climate of those two countries is pretty nearly the same.[31]

In cold countries, on the other hand, the climate practically forces the people into intemperance. "Drunkenness predominates throughout the world in proportion to the coldness and humidity of the climate." Climatic factors also, of course, exercise their influence upon the laws. And finally on this subject, Montesquieu propounds the thesis that the institution of slavery is also the consequence of climate:

> There are countries where the excess of heat enervates the body, and renders men so slothful and dispirited that nothing but the fear of chastisement can oblige them to perform any laborious duty: slavery is there more reconcilable to reason; and the master being as lazy with respect to his sovereign as his slave is with regard to him, this adds a political to a civil slavery.[32]

On the other hand, he is not altogether sure about this and is willing to entertain the thought that slavery is unnatural:

> But as all men are born equal, slavery must be accounted unnatural, though in some countries it be founded on natural reason; and a wide difference ought to be made between such countries, and those in which even natural reason rejects it, as in Europe, where it has been so happily abolished.[33]

At the end of the following chapter he writes, rather touchingly:

> I know not whether this article be dictated by my understanding or by my heart. Possibly there is not that climate upon earth where the most laborious services might not with proper encouragement be performed by freemen. Bad laws having made lazy men, they have been reduced to slavery because of their laziness.[34]

It is painful to have to acknowledge, however, that in one chapter he defends Negro slavery as natural.

Climate also has something to do with the relations between the sexes. In hot countries the female sex becomes marriageable as early as eight or nine, and old at twenty. It is natural then that in these countries men leave one wife to take another, and this is the reason that Asian countries permit polygamy whereas the colder European countries do not. This in turn has consequences for religion. It explains why Mohammedanism, which approves of polygamy, was easily established in Asia but found no foothold in Europe. Similarly, "There are climates where the impulses of nature have such force that morality has almost none."[35]

It would be a mistake to suggest that Montesquieu has only the temperature in mind when he advances his geographic theses. He considers also the nature of the soil, the availability of water, the distance to the sea, the presence of natural harbors, and the distribution of land and water masses. He almost certainly had Britain in mind when he wrote the following famous passage:

> The inhabitants of islands have a higher relish for liberty than those of the continent. Islands are commonly of small extent; one part of the people cannot be so easily employed to oppress the other; the sea separates them from great empires; tyranny cannot so well support itself within a small compass: conquerors are stopped by the sea; and the islanders, being without the reach of their arms, more easily preserve their own laws.[36]

It would also be a mistake to suggest that Montesquieu emphasized geographic factors to the exclusion of others. So far as the "general spirit of mankind" is concerned, not only climate but also religion, laws, governmental maxims, precedents, morals, and customs play their part. The rule of climate loosens as civilization advances. Nevertheless, "The empire of the climate is the first, the most powerful, of all empires."[37]

As one might suppose, Montesquieu, albeit in an unsystematic fashion, touches on many more social phenomena than the ones mentioned in the preceding paragraphs. They include laws (both those that are legislated and those that govern man as a physical being), religion, commerce, manners, customs, education, agriculture, music, crime, punishment, poverty, luxury, population, marriage, divorce, suicide, the family, war, money, usury, festivals, and many others. He is full of attractive observations, such as that the Venetians are so parsimonious that only courtesans can make them part with their money; and epigrams: "Everything ought not to be corrected."[38] He is vitally interested in the relation between customs and laws, and suggests that it is bad policy to try to change by law what ought to be changed by custom.[39] He is rich in erudition, not all of it reliable. But above all, he is a sociologist in the contemporary meaning of the word. He excluded the supernatural from the explanation of human societies and advanced the comparative method for the study of social institutions. Raymond Aron regards him as much more a sociologist than Auguste Comte (without demeaning Comte) and as one of the discipline's greatest theorists. It is obvious to him that the aim of *The Spirit of the Laws* is the aim of sociology itself—the aim, quite simply, to make history intelligible.[40] And Durkheim observes that, in instituting sociology, his successors "did little more than give a name to the field of study he inaugurated."[41]

Voltaire (1694–1778) will occupy less of our attention than Montesquieu primarily because it is difficult to think of him as a sociologist. Skeptic, wit, poet, playwright, correspondent, historian, pamphleteer, and, above all, militant rationalist—it is impossible even to think of the eighteenth century without mentioning the man whose literary and philosophical effusions, as Georg Brandes said, summarized it. He detested Christianity because of its unreasonable belief in the supernatural and because of its promotion of social injustice. He was the Bertrand Russell of his century, but both something more and something less. He disliked the Jews largely because he held them responsible for Christianity. He thought of the Middle Ages as barbaric and railed against intolerance everywhere. He believed that political and religious oppression were incompatible with civilization, and he expressed these views with such vigor and clarity that he became the most influential writer of his age. He was capable of scalding his opponents with such expressions as scoundrel, toad, lizard, snake, spider, viper, knave, spy, and hound. One looks in vain in Voltaire for a systematic treatment of anything, including society. He was, as someone has said, a conversationalist in print.

Like Turgot, he believed firmly in the unity of mankind. No matter how much men may differ in outward appearance in different parts of the earth, they are nevertheless the same in feeling and desire. He admired the English, as his *Lettres sur l'Anglais* (1733) attest, but he offered no systematic account of English culture or English government. He noted especially that it was a free country and that the Englishman, as a free man, could go to heaven by any route that pleased him. Newton, for example, was not only fortunate enough to be born in such a country, but also to be born in a time when "*les impertinences scolastiques*" were banned and when reason alone was cultivated.

Voltaire had no particular political preference and was content to point out that the rich preferred an aristocracy, the people a democracy, and kings a monarchy. Climate may have something to do with manners and customs, but it cannot explain the great events of history. In his *Essai sur les Moeurs* (1765) he contrasts nature and custom: "There are two empires, the Empire of Nature, which unites all men on the basis of certain common principles; the Empire of Custom, which, covering as it does manners and customs, spreads variety through the world."[42] The natural order thus stands opposed to the social order, and he uses the former to attack the imperfections of the latter. It is foolish to believe that man ever lived alone, deprived of society. Indeed, the instinct of man and a natural benevolence toward others of his kind induce him to live with them in groups. Man has two sentiments, commiseration and justice, without which there would be no society. Voltaire was no champion of social equality: there will always be cooks and cardinals in this world, and equality is therefore an illusion. He did not go nearly as far as some of his contemporaries in the direction of cultural relativism. He knew of no country that would regard it as respectable to steal from a man the fruits of his labor, to tell a lie that would injure him, to turn against a benefactor, to slander or murder.

Finally, Voltaire wanted to know the steps by which mankind had moved from barbarism to civilization. He called for the writing of history not in terms of military victories and defeats but in terms of great ideas. Although he wrote, in addition to his histories, some observations on history, they do not add up to a philosophy of history.[43] We remember his cynicism on history as written—"a pack of tricks we play upon the dead"—and his pessimism on history as lived—"a long succession of useless cruelties." If climate has something to do with "the empire of custom," so too do chance and accident. In the long run, society, including its manners, morals, laws, sciences, and arts, is made by the interaction of men and their environments.

There was bound to be a reaction to a world that tried to see itself in the hard, cold, and often harsh light of reason alone, and it came with Jean Jacques Rousseau (1712–78). Rousseau was born in Geneva to a family of French origin who had lived in that city for almost two hundred years and who were among the few who had the right to use the title "citizen" after their names. His mother died about a week after his birth, and his childhood became a precarious one. The story is told, of course, in his *Confessions*. His entire life was a peripatetic and often pathetic one. He had a lifelong liaison with Thérèse Levasseur, an uneducated hotel worker who bore him five children, all of whom were consigned to a foundling home—a custom, he was assured, that was quite common at the time.

In 1749, the Academy at Dijon announced an essay contest on the question, "Whether the restoration of the arts and sciences has had the effect of purifying or corrupting morals." He submitted an essay entitled "A Discourse on the Moral Effects of the Arts and Sciences" and it won the prize. In it he contended that civilization has been a corrupting influence and that ignorance has unfortunately been succeeded by skepticism.

> The daily ebb and flow of the tides are not more regularly influenced by the moon than the morals of a people by the progress of the arts and sciences. As their light has risen above our horizon, virtue has taken flight, and the same phenomenon has been constantly observed in all times and places.[44]

The god who invented the sciences, according to ancient tradition, was an enemy to the repose of mankind. Rousseau concurs.

Here, surely, is a sociological thesis. Not only is it a sociological thesis, but Rousseau supplies empirical evidence to support it—in Egypt, Greece, Rome, and Constantinople, where exactly this happened—and in those nations like Persia, Scythia, and Germany where, "being preserved from the contagion of useless knowledge," it had not. Indeed, Sparta had the virtues that Athens lacked, and Socrates, if he were alive, would despise the vain sciences of the eighteenth century and "lend no aid to swell the flood of books that flows from every quarter."[45] Honest men are satisfied with the practice of virtue; they become undone when they try to study it. This implies in addition that it is better to live in society than to analyze it and suggests that if sociology had been among the sciences of his time, Rousseau would have condemned it with the others. Nevertheless, in his own essay he wants to see what inductions he can make from history. Some of them are mistaken, as when he confuses Socrates' profession of ignorance with praise of ignorance. Others are questionable.[46] But the thesis is clear. The rise of science coincides with the decline of morality. Rousseau even hurls maledictions at the art of printing and approves of the burning of the Alexandrian library.[47]

Rousseau's second essay, submitted to the Dijon Academy a year later, was entitled "What Is the Origin of Inequality among Men, and Is It Authorized by Natural Law?" It begins with an echo of Pope that the most useful and yet imperfect of the sciences is that of mankind and a bow to the admonition of the Delphic oracle to "Know thyself." The setting of the essay appears in its second paragraph:

> I conceive that there are two kinds of inequality among the human species; one, which I call natural or physical, because it is established by nature, and consists in a difference of age, health, bodily strength, and the qualities of the mind or of the soul: and another, which may be called moral or political inequality, because it depends on a kind of convention, and is established, or at least authorized, by the consent of men. This latter consists of the different privileges which some men enjoy to the prejudice of others; such as that of being more rich, more honored, more powerful, or even in a position to exact obedience.[48]

The philosophers who have inquired into the foundations of society have all found it necessary to go back to the state of nature, but none of them, according to Rousseau, ever got there. All of them have assigned to nature attributes that could have had their source only in society. Indeed, it is doubtful if a state of nature ever existed in any historical sense.[49] As to the early life of mankind, there is a hint of natural selection in Rousseau.[50] He speculates on the origin of language and, comparing it with the origin of human society, asks himself whether society preceded language or language society—a question he fails to answer. By examining with care and in detail what the state of nature must have been, he is able to conclude that the differences among men in that state are small and that natural inequalities are greatly increased by the inequalities of social institutions.

It is this second *Discourse* which contains the famous passage: "The first man who, having enclosed a piece of ground, bethought himself of saying 'This is mine,' and found people simple enough to believe him, was the real founder of civil society." Think only of how many crimes, wars, horrors, and misfortunes would have been avoided if no one had listened to "this impostor." As the human race increased, so in proportion did human cares. The influence of soils, climates, and seasons had its effect in introducing differences among men, especially in their occupations. Communities and languages first appeared on islands because men were collected together there and had more opportunity for interaction. Slowly they began to perceive relations that could be denoted by such terms as great, small, strong, weak, swift, slow, fearful, bold, and so on. They also began to perceive situations where they might rely upon others and situations which might give rise to suspicion of others. Slowly, and in the abundance of time, husbands and wives, parents and children, began to live under one roof and form a family, and "every family became a little society." Then men and women assembled together in larger groups, and ceremonies began:

> Whoever sang or danced best, whoever was the handsomest, the strongest, the most dexterous, or the most eloquent, came to be of most consideration; and this was the first step towards inequality, and at the same time towards vice. From these first distinctions arose on the one side vanity and contempt and on the other shame and envy: and the fermentation caused by these new leavens ended by producing combinations fatal to innocence and happiness.[51]

Men thus began to injure one another, and this led some writers to suppose that primitive man was cruel. Cruelty, however, came later. "Nothing is more gentle than man in his primitive state, as he is placed by nature at an equal distance from the stupidity of brutes, and the fatal ingenuity of civilized man."[52] This is the state in which men were meant to continue, and in it they were free, happy, honest, and healthy. Metallurgy and agriculture produced a great revolution; iron and corn civilized man and ruined humanity. As Locke had noted earlier, property can come only from labor, and since the strongest and the most skillful accumulate the most, the inequalities among men increase. It is easy, says Rousseau, to imagine the rest. Terrible disorders accompanied the destruction of equality. Dominion and slavery, rapine and violence, appeared on earth, and perpetual conflict.

In this situation someone must have come along and persuaded men to join together for mutual protection. They were easily seduced, and all "ran headlong to their chains," thinking it was better to sacrifice some of their freedom in order to safeguard the rest. "Such was, or may well have been, the origin of society and law." One community made others necessary, and so societies multiplied. In a pessimistic appendix Rousseau again contrasts the state of nature with the state of society, the savage with the citizen, and leaves no doubt about which of the two he prefers. It is right to be an enemy of civilization. Man is by nature good, and only his institutions have made him bad.[53]

In an article entitled "A Discourse on Political Economy," published in Diderot's *Encyclopedia* in 1755, Rousseau moderates his view of society and civilization and defends such institutions as government, law, property, and inheritance. The inheritance of property from parents to children is proper both because the children probably contributed something to its acquisition and because it is fatal both to morality and to the Republic to have a constant shifting of people with respect to rank and fortune. Here too he writes of "the advantage that every person derives from the social confederacy." Although it requires only brief mention, Rousseau wrote a long letter to d'Alembert in 1758 which contains an inchoate sociology of entertainment. Monarchies can afford the luxury of the theater, but for republics and small cities it is better to encourage festivals, parades, athletic contests, and other outdoor activities.

Émile, Rousseau's treatise on education, appeared in 1762. We need only observe that with this book the discipline of child psychology is born. It is of more than incidental interest to note, however, that the cultural relativism of Montesquieu is not for Rousseau:

> Cast your eyes over every nation of the world; peruse every volume of its history; in the midst of all these strange and cruel forms of worship, among this amazing variety of manners and customs, you will everywhere find the same ideas of right and justice; everywhere the same principles of morality, the same ideas of good and evil.[54]

There is in the heart of every man an innate principle, and this Rousseau calls conscience. For sociologists there is the admonition that in order to study society we must study men and in order to study men we must study society. Which to do first is a question to which the next two centuries failed to find an answer.

In the same year (1762) that Rousseau published *Émile* he also published *The Social Contract,* only a fragment of the master work he intended to write on political institutions. Much of it is devoted not to sociological concerns but to problems that are today assigned to political science and political philosphy—the nature of sovereignty, the process of legislation, the forms of government, the marks of a good government, the electoral process, and the means of strengthening constitutions. Everyone knows the famous words with which chapter I begins: "Man is born free; and everywhere he is in chains." In this, as in Rousseau's earlier writings, civilization is a bane, the state of nature a boon. How can men, through government, be guaranteed the liberty that they enjoyed in their natural state? At some point obstacles to the preservation of life become greater than the resources for overcoming them. Then men enter into a contract with one another, creating a collective body and receiving from this act a unity and a common identity. What they appear to have surrendered in the contract they regain in the exchange. As Rousseau says in italics, "Each of us puts his person and all his power in common under the supreme direction of the general will, and, in our corporate capacity, we receive each member as an indivisible part of the whole."[55]

The concept of the general will has created endless difficulties of interpretation. It differs from the will of all. It is a kind of public entity, the unity of all persons, those of the generations now alive and of generations both past and future. It bears a close resemblance to Durkheim's *conscience collective.* It imposes the same sacrifices upon all citizens and is the ultimate safeguard of their liberties. It protects each individual from every other individual, it protects him from the abuse of power by a monarch, and it literally forces him to be free. To surrender to the impulse of appetite is slavery, but to obey a law we prescribe for ourselves is liberty.

One passage is almost pure sociology, in that Rousseau emphasizes the superiority of custom to law and recognizes the power of public opinion:

> Along with these three kinds of law [political, civil, and criminal] goes a fourth, most important of all, which is not graven on tablets of marble or brass, but on the hearts of the citizens. This forms the real constitution of the State, takes on every day new powers, when other laws decay or die out, restores them or takes their place, keeps a people in the ways in which it was meant to go, and insensibly replaces

authority by the force of habit. I am speaking of morality, of custom, above all of public opinion; a power unknown to political thinkers, on which none the less success in everything else depends. With this the great legislator concerns himself in secret, though he seems to confine himself to particular regulations; for these are only the arc of the arch, while manners and morals, slower to arise, form in the end its immovable keystone.[56]

Rousseau also recognizes that once customs have become established it is useless to try to change them.[57]

The difficulties and inconsistencies in Rousseau's work have been noted and argued by numerous critics. He himself suggested that *The Social Contract* should have been rewritten and that those who claim to understand it are more clever than he. But there is no doubt of its importance, and that of his earlier discourses, to both political philosophy and sociology.[58]

A few words may be said about Diderot's monument, the great *Encyclopedia* of the century, published in seventeen volumes of text and eleven of plates during the years 1751–72. Whether it was forward looking or backward looking, whether its articles were original or mere compilations and borrowings, whether its authors were geniuses or quill drivers, are questions that need not be answered here.[59] Its editor and a number of its authors were accused of atheism. There is no mention of the creation story, for example, in the definition of Man ("Noun Masc.") as "A sentient, thinking, intelligent being, moving freely over the earth. He is above all other animals and exercises dominion over them; gregarious in his habits, he has invented various arts and sciences, and has virtues and vices peculiar to his species." The word "society" appears and among its meanings is a union of several persons for some objective, with family and village as examples. "Society" is also treated in the contemporary sense of an association or organized group. We are informed that man is made to live in society because he lacks the proper equipment for living alone. We seek the company of those like us (*nos semblables*) and can be happy only with them. The word "social" is referred to as a new word, one that designates the qualities that make men useful to their fellows. It might be said that the *Encyclopedia* replaced the word "divine" by the word "social," but only with a bit of exaggeration. There is no genuine conception of a sociological discipline in it. The notion that in order to study humanity we should start with the group rather than the individual fails to receive recognition. The *Encyclopedia,* in spite of its difficulties with the censors, cannot be counted as one of the steps in the advancement of sociological knowledge—or even of sociological speculation.

The role of the Philosophers in bringing about the momentous events of the French Revolution, like the role of ideas in social change in general, has been the subject of extended debate. In 1770, nineteen years before the storming of the Bastille, the *avocat général* Séguier wrote, "The philosophers have with one hand sought to shake the throne, with the other to upset the altar. Their purpose was to change public opinion on civil and religious institutions, and the revolution has, so to speak, been effected. History and poetry, romances and even dictionaries, have been infected with the poison of disbelief. Their writings are hardly published in the capital before they inundate the provinces like a torrent. The contagion has spread into workshops and cottages."[60]

The last of the Philosophers not only influenced the Revolution, he participated in it and gave his life to it. His name was Marie-Jean-Antoine-Nicolas Caritat, Marquis de Condorcet. Born in 1742 of a poor noble father and a wealthy bourgeois mother he, who was later to become a militant opponent of priests, was educated by them in Jesuit schools. At the age of sixteen he brilliantly defended a thesis in mathematics; choosing mathematics as his career, and at nineteen went off to pursue it in Paris where, under the tutelage of d'Alembert, he attended the salons, at one of which he met Turgot, who was to become one of his closest friends. He published his first book, on the calculus, in 1765, at the age of twenty-two; and this, together with additional papers, won him election to the Academy of Science at twenty-six, a body he later served as permanent secretary until his death. He was elected to the French Academy in 1782. He also had a public career as inspector of the Mint in Turgot's Ministry; member of the legislative assembly and chairman of its Committee on Public Instruction; and later a member of the National Convention in 1792, where he was chairman of a committee to draft a constitution. He became a victim, however, of the hostility between Girondin and Jacobin, wrote a bitter pamphlet against the Jacobins which was denounced as seditious; and the Convention voted for his arrest. He found refuge in the pension of a gallant woman, Madame Vernet, where he hid for nine months and, with only a few books and notes, wrote his *Sketch of the Intellectual Progress of Mankind*. The danger to Madame Vernet in harboring him grew so great that he finally left in disguise, was soon apprehended by the police, and placed in a cell of the prison of Bourg-le-Reine, where he was found dead the following morning—April 8, 1794.

Condorcet's views on social questions were so advanced that many of them would meet opposition by twentieth-century conservatives. He was an early opponent of slavery, wrote a pamphlet *Reflections on Negro Slavery* (1781), and served as president of a society called Friends of the Negro. He was a powerful advocate of the rights of women and thought they should have all the opportunities open to men, including access to public office. He supported universal suffrage, universal free education, the separation of church and state, religious liberty for all sects without exception, social welfare and social security for the poor, due process of law for everyone, a unicameral legislature, a world court with authority to adjudicate international disputes, free enterprise, civil marriage and divorce, and birth control. He opposed—along with slavery—war, capital punishment, primogeniture, and the cruel penalties meted out to prostitutes and homosexuals. Even for the Enlightenment, he was an enlightened man.

As a mathematician Condorcet hoped to apply mathematical methods to the study of society. To him "social mathematics" meant political arithmetic or, as it came to be known, statistics. In a discourse presented to the French Academy he said:

> Considering the nature of the moral (social) sciences, one cannot help seeing that, if based like the natural sciences, on the observation of facts, they would follow the same method, acquire a vocabulary equally precise, and attain an equal degree of certitude. One, not of our species, would be able to study human society as unemotionally as we study the society of beavers or of bees. A great difficulty arises in the fact that the observer is part of what he observes, and truth cannot be judged by those who are prejudiced or corrupt. That is why the progress of the social sciences has been slower than that of the physical sciences.[61]

The last two sentences especially have a contemporary ring to them. If he was less successful in carrying out his designs, he nevertheless attempted to use the calculus of probability—a subject to which he himself made contributions—to test the justice of court decisions, to examine the degree to which legislative decisions correspond with the wishes of the electorate, and to find a superior electoral system. He was sensitive to the relationship that various factors in society have to one another—the relationship that sex, temperature, climate, profession, government, and "ordinary habits" have to the duration of life; the various factors that influence the death rate; the causes and effects of changes in population; and the composition of the population according to age, sex, and occupation. In all of these respects he anticipated Quételet.[62]

Although Condorcet ranged over the entire field of what we today call the social sciences, his greatest work, *Sketch for a Historical Picture of the Progress of the Human Mind,* is sociological in intent and emphasis. It is sociological in the same sense that the work of Comte is sociological. It is more than that. It is a paean to progress, to the uses of reason, to the perfectibility of mankind, and to the happiness of the human race. But it is sociological specifically in that it is not a history of any particular city or nation or empire but rather a study of the progress of humanity or, as we should be more likely to say today, of society. Progress is subject to the same general laws that can be discerned in the development of individual faculties, and it is indeed "the sum of that development realized in a large number of individuals joined together in society."[63]

Condorcet will thus instruct us in the ways that we can insure that progress will continue:

> Such is the aim of the work that I have undertaken, and its result will be to show by appeal the reason and fact that nature has set no term to the perfection of human faculties; that the perfectibility of man is truly indefinite; and that the progress of this perfectibility, from now onwards independent of any power that might wish to halt it, has no other limit than the duration of the globe upon which nature has cast us.[64]

Not for Condorcet is Voltaire's view that history is nothing but a mass of crimes, follies, and misfortunes. He is even optimistic about the military use of gunpowder. By permitting combatants to fight at a great distance it will reduce the number of casualties.

The book is divided into ten chapters, corresponding to the ten epochs or stages through which mankind has passed (the titles are his own): (1) Men are united in tribes; (2) Pastoral peoples: The transition from this stage to that of agricultural peoples; (3) The progress of agricultural peoples up to the invention of the alphabet; (4) The progress of the human mind in Greece up to the divison of the sciences about the time of Alexander the Great; (5) The progress of the sciences from their division to their decline; (6) The decadence of knowledge to its restoration about the time of the Crusades; (7) The early progress of science from its revival in the West to the invention of printing: (8) From the invention of printing to the time when philosophy and the sciences shook off the yoke of authority; (9) From Descartes to the foundation of the French Republic; and (10) The future progress of the human mind. The last chapter differs from the others in that it looks ahead, with utopian vision, to the future.[65]

Condorcet's optimism was sometimes tempered by his recognition that prejudice and error would on occasion destroy the gains that knowledge had created, that the enlightened might be only a small minority in a much larger world of the ignorant, and that progress could be arrested for shorter or longer periods. Sometimes chance factors would retard or accelerate "the regular march of nature." Like the philosophers of the British empirical tradition, and especially Locke, Condorcet was conscious of the importance of language in the process of inquiry:

> One of the essentials for any sound philosophy is to produce for every science an exact and precise language in which every symbol represents some well defined and circumscribed idea; and so by rigorous analysis to guarantee that every idea is well defined and circumscribed.[66]

He is especially eloquent on the changes that have been brought into the world by the invention of printing. It has introduced into society a new force, the force of public opinion, which is especially able to protect the truth against error. "We now have a tribunal whose scrutiny it is difficult to elude, and whose verdict it is impossible to evade."[67]

In recognizing the fact that population was increasing, Condorcet asks himself whether it might be increasing too rapidly and whether it might finally outrun the food supply. Will this not result in a diminution of happiness, a true retrogression? To this, two answers may be given. The first is that the use of machinery will increase the productivity of the land. No one can foresee how the ingenuity of man will enable him to convert the resources of nature to his use. The second is birth control. If the time comes when an abundant population has an insufficient food supply, and if at the same time reason has conquered the absurd superstitions that corrupt the moral code, then men will know that they have a duty to those as yet unborn not to give them existence at the expense of the destruction of those who have already been given life. Malthus, four years later, devotes a chapter of his *Essay on Population* (1798) to Condorcet and attempts to refute his optimism, but he misses Condorcet's point on birth control. Indeed, the subtitle of Malthus's *Essay* is "With remarks on the speculations of Mr. Godwin, M. Condorcet, and other writers." Malthus, however, belongs to the nineteenth century.

Saint-Simon and Comte both appreciated Condorcet, but neither exempted him from criticism. Saint-Simon said, "It was Condorcet who was first to conceive the idea of writing a history of the past and future of general intelligence. His project was sublime." He quickly added, however, that its execution was worthless. Saint-Simon objected to the *Sketch* on three grounds: (1) Condorcet maintained that language was present at the very beginning, whereas it could have appeared only after a long process of development; (2) he presented religion as an obstacle to human welfare when in fact it once served as an integrating factor in society; and (3) his view of the unlimited perfectibility of mankind was erroneous.[68] Comte was more positive than Saint-Simon. He called Condorcet his spiritual father, referred to the introduction and the last chapter of the *Sketch* as immortal, and wrote, "After Montesquieu the most important advance in the fundamental conception of sociology was made by the unfortunate Condorcet in his memorable work, the *Esquisse*." Comte felt nevertheless that, although Condorcet had provided a concept of progress, he failed to develop a theory to account for it. The true law that he wanted to discover, a law like the law of gravitation, eluded him. For Condorcet, of course, Newton was always present as the standard by which the progress of the other sciences should be judged and as the inspiration to find in society the operation of the same universal laws that governed the motions of the physical universe.

Italy

> In the night of thick darkness which envelops the earliest antiquity, so remote from ourselves, there shines the eternal and never failing light of a truth beyond all question: that the world of human society has certainly been made by men, and its principles are therefore to be found within the modifications of our own human mind. Whoever reflects on this cannot but marvel that the philosophers should have bent all their energies to the study of the world of nature, which, since God made it, He alone truly knows; and that they should have neglected the study of the world of nations, or civil world, which, since men have made it, man can truly know.[69]

These are the words of an Italian original, Giambattista Vico, Italy's greatest sociologist and one of the most original in the history of the discipline. If, by some fluke of circumstance, he had happened to coin the word "sociology" as a label for his enterprise, he and not Comte would today be regarded as the founding father, and the discipline would be a hundred years older than it is.

Vico was born in Naples in 1688 and died in that city in 1744. For almost all of his adult life he occupied a poorly paid professorship of rhetoric in the University of Naples; indeed, so poorly paid that he had to supplement his income by private tutoring. When it came time to publish his book no papal or other subsidy was forthcoming and he had to pawn his most prized possession, a ring, in order to pay the printer.

The year was 1725, and the name of the book was *Principi di una scienza nuova d'intorno alla commune natura delle nazioni* [Principles of a new science concerning the common nature of the nations] now known universally as *Scienza Nuova* or *The New Science*. It was a book he continued to revise until his death, and it is a book that touches on every one of what we today call the social sciences. But above all, it is a sociological theory of the rise and fall of nations. It is the story of the genesis of society and the eons-long transition to civilization, a process that begins with religion and ends with the arts and sciences.

Inasmuch as the Inquisition was still unpleasantly conspicuous in Naples, Vico had to preserve the Garden of Eden, but after the Flood men were in a bestial state, scattered "through the forest of the world," terrified by thunder and lightening, and shamed into seeking the shelter of caves for their carnal intercourse. Thus families arose, and then communities. The order of things was first forests, then hovels, then villages, then cities. Societies begin with religion, which is also a response to fear. "Varro diligently collected no fewer than twenty thousand names of Gods known to the Greeks. These names indicated the needs of life, natural, moral, economic or civil, from the primeval age onward.[70] Social classes arise early in the historical process. Refugees seek protection from settled families and receive it in return for their labor. We thus have two classes, heroes and fugitives, as later, in Rome, we have patricians and plebeians.

Vico, attributing the idea to the Egyptians, finds three stages or periods in the histories of human societies, thus anticipating Turgot, Saint-Simon, and Comte. The first is the age of the gods, in which men live under divine governments and are ruled by auspices and oracles. The second is the age of heroes, when patrician is in conflict with plebeian, the former wanting to preserve society, the latter to change it. The third is the age of men, when men rocognize their equality and are able to form first a commonwealth and then a monarchy. Vico, like Comte, sees triads everywhere. In language the progression is from the sacred to the symbolic to the "vulgar." Homer, for example, mentions a language older than his own, which must have been the language of the gods. There are similarly three ways of apprehending the world—the animistic, the mythopoeic, and the scientific; and three kinds of customs—religious, punctilious, and humane. Law was first divine, as in the Mosaic code; then heroic, as in Lycurgus; and then human, when reason developed. Each stage is an organic unity and carries with it in its progression language, art, government, and religion, each of them changing in phase with the others. In the third stage also societies moved from poetry to prose, and from custom to law—almost, one is tempted to say, from *Gemeinschaft* to *Gesellschaft*.

The third stage, however, is no more permanent than the first and second. The age of men decays when men cease to respect the law, when license impairs equality, and when philosophy succeeds religion. A new barbarism appears, and the cycle begins again. Thus history is a series of cycles, *corsi e ricorsi*, repeating itself forever. Societies, of course, may succumb to conquest from outside, and they may at times be arrested in their progression through the three stages. But on the whole their histories exhibit the cyclical pattern. These are the stages through which both Rome and Europe passed. It is an error, furthermore, to suppose that culture arose in one society which then transmitted it to others. Each society evolved its own institutions in isolation from the others. We may assume therefore that if identical ideas develop in societies that have had no contact with one another, they must have some basis of truth, and no tradition can be wholly false.

Trained on Tacitus and the medieval Aristotle, Vico early on rejected Descartes and embraced Francis Bacon. For Vico it is not mathematics but history and, by inference, not deduction but induction, that tells us truly about the nature of the world. Although making many obeisances to Providence, and never failing to emphasize the significance of religion in human societies, Vico nevertheless gave a scientific cast to history. It is not Providence but the mental states of man that determine the course of human events. The explanation of history, and of society in general, is to be sought in man himself, and history thus has a base in psychology. Each society has its own immanent destiny, and the causes of its changes are natural rather than providential. In this he strikes a new note, and one that wins him a place among the sociologists of the Enlightenment. If Voltaire was the Bertrand Russell of the eighteenth century, Vico was its Oswald Spengler.

The story of the reception of the *Scienza Nuova* is a curious one. One would ordinarily expect so innovative an achievement to have had an immediate effect upon Vico's contemporaries in France, Germany, England, and, above all, Italy. Except for a small group in Venice, nothing of the kind happened. There was a brief and negative comment in the *Acta Eruditorum* of Leipzig, but otherwise the book was completely ignored. As H. P. Adams writes, "It was as if a great ship had been built, capable of navigating all the oceans of the world, and was left moored in the dock of the shipbuilder to be visited occasionally by a few friends of the inventor, and mentioned in their correspondence by one or two superior persons who recognized not so much its value as the cleverness that must have gone to its construction."[71] According to Adams, Montesquieu visited Venice in 1728, was persuaded to buy a copy of *Scienza Nuova* by a literary figure named Antonio Conti, but did not, when in Naples the following year, try to meet Vico. Using Benedetto Croce as authority, Max H. Fisch says that Montesquieu may have met the author during his stay in Naples and possibly received from him a copy of the first edition, which is still preserved in Montesquieu's library at La Brède. René Wellek tells us that Montesquieu entered in his journal, when in Venice, his intention to acquire the *Scienza Nuova*, but may not have done so, and Wellek flatly contradicts Fisch and others: "There is no copy of the volume in the catalogue of Montesquieu's library nor is it among the books today preserved at La Brède."[72] Goethe bought a copy of the book in Naples in 1787 and lent it to his friend Jacobi. John Stuart Mill, in an 1844 letter to Auguste Comte, confessed that he had not read Vico; and it was in that year that Comte read him, two years after the last volume of *The Positive Philosophy* was published. There is a brief discussion of him in *The Positive Polity* and his name was duly entered in the Positivist Calendar. The American George Frederick Holmes, then teaching at the University of Virginia, wrote to Comte in 1852 that Vico had a greater claim than Condorcet to be his (Comte's) precursor.[73] Vico, in short, was not discovered until the nineteenth century. Benedetto Croce attributes the absence of recognition in his own time to his "singular and perhaps unique position in the history of philosophy, an anachronism by virtue of his excess of genius."[74]

Scotland

David Hume (1711–76), one of the most amiable of men and greatest of philosophers, is known as epistemologist, moralist, political theorist, and historian. Skeptical of the validity of causal inference, which he attributed entirely to custom rather than to reason, he was also sensitive to the role of custom and convention in other areas of the life of the mind. Custom indeed is the great guide of human life. It renders our experience useful and leads us to expect that the future will be like the past. If there is a preestablished harmony between the course of nature and our ideas, it is again due to custom: "Custom is that principle, by which this correspondence has been effected; so necessary to the subsistence of our species, and the regulation of our conduct, in every circumstance and occurrence of human life."[75] Here indeed is an inchoate sociology of knowledge. Hume also attacked the doctrine of natural law and insisted that what we mean by the right and the good are derived from the conventions of society. Rules—or what we should today call norms—are necessary both for the satisfaction of individual interests and for the stability of society. Society is possible without government, but we see it in this way only under primitive conditions. The weakness of men is that they seem to prefer an immediate good to a more remote one, and this tendency it is possible for the institution of government to palliate but not to cure.

Hume's closest approach to an appreciation of sociology, without of course the name, occurs perhaps in the following passage:

> It is universally acknowledged that there is a great uniformity among the actions of men, in all nations and ages, and that human nature remains still the same, in its principles and operations.

And continuing later in the paragraph:

> Would you know the sentiments, inclinations and course of life of the Greeks and Romans? Study well the temper and actions of the French and English: You cannot be much mistaken in transferring to the former *most* of the observations which you have made with regard to the latter. Mankind are so much the same, in all times and places, that history informs us of nothing new or strange in this particular. Its chief use is only to discover the constant and universal principles of human nature, by showing men in all varieties of circumstances and situations, and furnishing us with materials from which we may form our observations and become acquainted with the regular springs of human action and behaviour.[76]

One must, of course, make allowance for the diversity of character, prejudices, and opinions, and for differences of age and sex, but on the whole there is a uniformity of dispositions among men.

In discussing the origin of justice and property, Hume has occasion to speculate on the origin of society. Nature has been cruel to man in giving him more needs than he has the means to satisfy, and it is therefore only in society that "his infirmities are compensated."[77] Conjoined to these necessities is another, which is the first and original principle of society: "This necessity is no other than that natural appetite betwixt the sexes, which unites them together, and preserves their union, till a new tye takes place in their concern for their common offspring. This new concern becomes also a principle of union betwixt the parents and offspring, and forms a more numerous society."[78]

Hume, incidentally, believes that a state of nature is an idle fiction. In an essay entitled "Of the Original Contract" he says it is useful only in that it shows how justice arises as a result of human convention. He is willing to concede that at the very beginning, when government had its "first origin in the woods and deserts," some kind of social contract must have been involved, under conditions "so clear and obvious that it might be esteemed superfluous to express them." But all governments known to history have been founded on force rather than consent.[79] This essay induces Peter Gay to say that "Hume seeks to convert not merely moral philosophy, but political philosophy, into sociology."[80]

In an essay entitled "Of National Characters" Hume discusses in considerable detail the influence of geographic factors in society and doubts, in contrast to Montesquieu, that "men owe any thing of their temper or genius to the air, food, or climate." Indeed, in a learned disquisition on the subject he offers no fewer than nine reasons why the geographic interpretation is unacceptable. It is possible that in northern latitudes men have a propensity to the consumption of alcohol whereas in southern they prefer love and women, but even in this respect moral causes may be as important as physical ones. Hume wrote many other essays on matters that may be deemed sociological—on taste and passion, on superstition and enthusiasm, on the dignity or meanness of human nature, on civil liberty, on the rise and progress of the arts and sciences, on polygamy and divorce, on the standard of taste, on money, on interest, on customs, on the population of ancient nations, on impudence and modesty, on love and marriage, and on suicide. Finally, his

Natural History of Religion, with its use of comparative materials, is clearly a contribution to the sociology of its subject.

Claims that Adam Ferguson (1723–1816) is the real father of sociology are now so numerous that, like tributes to Newton, they have become monotonous. He was an important member of a circle of luminaries that included the better-known David Hume and Adam Smith, a group that created, along with those in other arts and sciences, the Scottish Enlightenment. Indeed, we are reminded that the Edinburgh of the time, known as "the Athens of the North," vied with Paris and surpassed London and Philadelphia as a center of culture and learning.[81] In many respects eighteenth-century Scotland had closer ties with France than with England. In any event Ferguson, the Scotchman most typical of the whole race, as he was referred to in the *Edinburgh Review*,[82] served as chaplain to the Black Watch Highland Regiment, left the Church of Scotland under circumstances still mysterious,[83] succeeded Hume as the keeper of the Advocates' Library, and became first Professor of Natural Philosophy and then Professor of Pneumatics and Moral Philosophy at the University of Edinburgh, posts he held from 1759 until his retirement in 1785. He published his *Essay on the History of Civil Society* in 1767 and later (1792) his lectures, under the title *Principles of Moral and Political Science.* He also wrote a *History of the Progress and Termination of the Roman Republic,* which he published in 1782.

Ferguson believed that society is the natural state of man and that the proper study of mankind is the study of groups rather than individuals. "Mankind are to be taken in groups . . . and every experiment relative to this subject should be made with entire societies, not with single men."[84] And again, "Mankind have always wandered or settled, agreed or quarrelled, in troops and companies."[85] The human mind itself, in a proposition related to one of Hume's, is dependent upon society for its development:

> The atmosphere of society, from the whole, we may conclude is the element in which the human mind must draw the first breath of intelligence itself: if not the vital air by which the celestial air of moral sentiment is kindled: we cannot doubt but it is of mighty effect in exciting the flame; and that the minds of men, to use a familiar example, may be compared to those blocks of fuel which taken apart are barely to be lighted; but if gathered into heaps are easily kindled into a flame.[86]

And again:

> From society are derived not only the force, but the very existence of man's happiest emotions; not only the better part, but almost the whole of his rational character. Send him to the desert alone, he is a plant torn from its roots: the form indeed may remain, but every faculty droops and withers; the human personage and the human character cease to exist.[87]

In studying society it is necessary to avoid inventions, conjectures, and speculations (he has Rousseau in mind) and rely instead upon observation. Indeed, moral philosophy must rest on scientific foundations and use empirical evidence from geography, psychology, the history of language, and population. But he did not try to deduce the structure of society from psychological principles.

Influenced, like all of his contemporaries, by Montesquieu, Ferguson recognized the importance of geography but rejected any single-factor theory of social change. He has his three stages—savage, barbarous, and "polished"—and they enable MacRae to treat him as an evolutionary thinker before Darwin. He also rejected any notion of men living in a state of nature: if we seek a state of nature we shall find it where we are, all around us, in the British Isles no less than at the Cape of Good Hope. And, more sophisticated than many of his nineteenth-century successors, he rejected the organismic analogy:

> The human frame has a general course; it has, in every individual, a frail contexture, and a limited duration; it is worn by exercise, and exhausted by repetition of its functions: But in a society, whose constituent members are renewed in every generation, where the race seems to enjoy perpetual youth, and accumulating advantages, we cannot, by any parity of reason, expect to find imbecilities connected with mere age and length of days.[88]

Ferguson emphasized both the uniformity and the diversity of human societies. Social evolution is not purposive: societies "stumble upon establishments, which are indeed the result of human action, but not the execution of any human design." They borrow customs from one another, but only when the receiving society is ready for the exchange. Social evolution is not linear but cyclical. Ferguson often asks himself why nations cease to be eminent and offers no wholly satisfactory explanation except that there is a decline in virtue. Virtue thrives in times of struggle and succumbs to vice when the goals are won.

Anticipating Simmel by about a century and a half, Ferguson argued that social conflict had its uses and was, indeed, essential. "He who has never struggled with his creatures, is a stranger to half the sentiments of mankind." Men positively enjoy conflict and happily embrace occasions of opposition. Aggression is invigorating. War contributes to the cohesion of civil society; without it society would have no form: "It is vain to expect that we can give to the multitude of people a sense of union among themselves, without admitting hostility to those who oppose them," and "Athens was necessary to Sparta, in the exercise of her virtue, as steel is to flint in the production of fire." We could hardly have more lucid expressions of the in-group/out-group principle. On another matter Ferguson recognized, as did Condorcet—and both before Malthus—that the means of subsistence would limit population growth. "Men will crowd where the situation is tempting, and, in a few generations, will people every country to the measure of its means of subsistence."

Finally, Ferguson wrote on the division of labor and, like sociologists after him, appreciated both its advantages and disadvantages. It is necessary to progress and to the cultivation of "the arts of life." In savage and barbarous societies men have to do too many things to be able to do any of them well. With the division of labor they can separate the tasks, grow proficient at them, and become in consequence more productive. But the division of labor, as Marx (who admired Ferguson) recognized, also induces alienation. It is thus both a blessing and a curse. It divides the community and threatens its integration—thus creating the sociological problem that Durkheim was to try to solve a century later. We can easily agree with Peter Gay that "Ferguson's pages on the division of labor are a minor triumph of eighteenth-century sociology."[89] If we add to these pages the many he wrote on other sociological subjects we have not a minor triumph but one of major proportions. There is a contemporary flavor about Ferguson, and we can talk about him in a language that is as appropriate to our own time as to his.

As Donald MacRae suggests, if there is any economics in Ferguson, it served his sociology. For Adam Smith the contrary was the case. His sociology served both his ethical theory, in *The Theory of Moral Sentiments* (1759), and his economic theory, in *The Wealth of Nations* (1776). The latter, of course, is one of the great books in the history of economics. In introducing "the invisible hand," it laid the foundation for laissez-faire capitalism and became, although not immediately, one of the most influential books ever written in the social sciences. It even created what the Germans called "the Adam Smith problem," because his ethical theory seemed to support altruism; his economic theory, egoism ("It is not from the benevolence of the butcher, the brewer or the baker that we expect our dinner, but from their regard to their own interest."). But we cannot claim it for sociology. Except for its early chapters on the division of labor, it belongs entirely to economics.

A tour of eighteenth-century Scotland would be incomplete without a mention of John Millar. He was born on June 22, 1735, in Kirk o' Shotts, a few miles east of Glasgow on the Edinburgh road; entered the Old College (the University of Glasgow) at the age of eleven; studied there for six years and attended the lectures of Adam Smith who later became a close friend; was admitted to the bar at Edinburgh in 1760; and in 1761, at the age of twenty-six, was appointed Professor of Civil Law at the University of Glasgow, a chair he occupied with distinction for forty years until his death on May 30, 1801. He wrote two major works, both widely acclaimed during his lifetime, then neglected, and more recently rediscovered as serious contributions to sociology. The first of them, *The Origin of the Distinction of Ranks,* carries the informative subtitle: *An Inquiry into the Circumstances Which Give Rise to Influence and Authority in the Different Members of Society.* It appeared in 1771 and went through four editions. The second, *An Historical View of the English Government from the Settlement of the Saxons in Britain to the Accession of the House of Stewart (sic),* appeared in 1787 and also went through several editions, with supplements.[90]

Millar's thought, like that of Ferguson, fits clearly into a sociological frame. He is interested in manners, customs and institutions as they come to govern the social relations of mankind. Although he is appreciative of the contributions of such legislators to the human race as Lycurgus, Solon, and King

Alfred, he nevertheless gives greater weight to custom than to individuals in the formation of the law. In response to Montesquieu he rejects an emphasis upon climate as a causative factor in social change and observes that it can hardly explain the differences to be discerned in countries that share the same general location—Sparta and Athens; Spain and France; Greece and Turkey; and, for that matter, England, Scotland, and Wales. Furthermore: "The different manners of people in the same country, at different periods, are no less remarkable, and afford evidence yet more satisfactory, that national character depends very little upon the immediate operation of climate.[91] Inequalities among men, which result in ranks, Millar attributes to differences in ability and achievement and, curiously, to the desire to honor superiors. He is far from wanting to do away with these inequalities; indeed, a classless society is a vain hope.[92] Upper classes have been known to be both parasitic and endowed with qualities of leadership; lower classes both stupid and endowed with an animated intelligence.

Millar wrote perceptively on the division of labor and recognized the effect an excess of it would have upon the human spirit. He anticipated the nineteenth century in finding four stages in the course of social evolution—hunting, pastoral, agricultural, and commercial. In society there is a natural progression from ignorance to knowledge, from the rude to the polished, a uniform process which can neither be successfully resisted nor prematurely accelerated.

John Millar was thus a sociologist in all but name. Robert M. MacIver refers to him as a seminal thinker and sociological pioneer.[93] He fully shared the antiecclesiastical sentiments of his enlightened contemporaries and was himself one of the leading figures of Scotland's Augustan Age.[94]

Germany

Although not then a nation, Germany too had its Enlightenment in the eighteenth century. Inspired by a combination of English deism and French free thought, it contained on its roster such illustrious names as Goethe, Kant, Lessing, Schiller, Herder, and Frederick the Great himself. Indeed, Frederick left some seven volumes of history, out of a total of thirty volumes, all in French; and in his *L'Histoire de mon temps* he recorded not only the military and political events of his reign but its science, philosophy, literature, and art as well. Lessing wrote a book on the education of the human race[95] which was in effect a philosophy of history, and in which he regarded Christianity as representing only one stage in history, to be succeeded by a stage, already attained by some individuals, in which reason will rule. But only Herder can conceivably be called a sociologist, and even then one is being too generous with the label.

Herder (1744–1803), more romantic than rationalist, was more pious than his French and Scottish contemporaries, and Providence has a place in his scheme of things. The rationalists had little but scorn for the Middle Ages; Herder, on the contrary, praised them as a period of imagination, simplicity, and peace. In his first book on the philosophy of history—*Auch eine Philosphie der Geschichte* (1774)—he argued against the idolatry of reason and admired the classical civilizations of Greece and Rome. His *magnum opus* appeared in four volumes, 1784–91, under the title *Ideen zur Philosophie der Geschichte der Menschheit.*[96] In the preface he explains that he did not intend, in his earlier work, to apply such figurative terms as infancy, childhood, manhood, and old age to all nations or to imply that the whole "history of cultivation" could be traced with certainty. The thought occurred to him, however, that since everything else in the world has its philosophy and science, so also there ought to be a philosophy and science of that which concerns us most, namely, the history of mankind itself. Can it be that God, who has regulated everything else in nature, has left the course of history to chance?

The book is perhaps best described as a universal history. It begins with the creation of the earth and its place in the solar system and treats the vegetable and animal kingdoms, the structure of plants and animals, the instincts of animals, the differences between men and animals, and man's capacity to reason. The author proceeds to discuss the physical characteristics of peoples in various parts of the world and exhibits an especial appreciation of the influence of climate in shaping different races. On this subject, however, he is not dogmatic:

> It is true we are ductile clay in the hand of climate; but her fingers mould so variously, and the laws that counteract them are so numerous, that perhaps the genius of mankind alone is capable of combining the relations of all these powers in one whole.[97]

He insists—indeed it is the title of one of his chapters—that "Notwithstanding the Varieties of the human Form, there is but one and the same Species of Man throughout the Whole of our Earth."[98] One must not say that there are four, or five, races of mankind, because "complexions run into each other." One is warned not to go too far in comparing man with ape, however, and thus there is little anticipation of Darwin here.[99]

Unlike Hobbes, Herder does not regard man as an unsocial being, much less a beast of prey. He recognizes that man is dependent upon others for the development of his faculties:

> Conceived in the bosom of love, and nourished at the breast of affection, he is educated by men, and receives from them a thousand unearned benefits. Thus he is actually formed in and for society, without which he could neither have received his being, nor have become a man.[100]

Peace, not war, is his natural state, although the latter is sometimes "the offspring of necessity." Nature drives man to woman, "a creature dissimilarly similar to "himself", and whose passions are as unlikely to come into collision with his, as is consistent with the end of their forming a union together.[101] Herder suggests that "the softer sex" possesses virtues not granted to man and that she rules him by her kindness. Male virtues are courage, paternal love, and friendship, and friendship is "the noblest tie of man."

Much of the book is orthodox historiography. Herder describes in detail the history of China and Japan, Babylonia and Assyria, the Medes and the Persians, the Hebrews and the Egyptians, Greece and Rome, the German and Slavic nations, the barbarian kingdoms, the progress of Christianity, the Crusades, and the history of Europe. He tells us that every historical event must be seen as a natural phenomenon and, when this is done, "the causes why it could not be otherwise will commonly appear."[102] One can only wish that this were indeed the case. One may say, incidentally, that there is in Herder no conception of classes of events; of repeating patterns; of what we mean, in short, by social institutions. In one passage he has a distant glimpse of what sociology might do. Since man is a part of creation, it follows that he must obey laws "not less beautiful and excellent than those by which all the celestial bodies move."[103] The laws to which he gives expression, however, are simplistic and even insipid.[104] If we are disappointed in the answers he gave to the questions to which he addressed himself, we have to say on a positive note that the questions themselves were genuinely sociological in character. In any event, his influence upon the historiography of von Ranke and Mommsen and upon the philosophy of history of Kant and Hegel cannot be gainsaid.

Conclusion

The reader of this chapter has doubtless noticed that there is no section on sociological thought in England in the eighteenth century. Odd as it may seem, there is no figure in that country, in the entire period from Locke to Malthus, who had anything like the stature of these two writers, and few whom one could name with confidence as having a primary interest in the nature of society. Bacon, Hobbes, and Locke—to say nothing now of Newton—powerfully influenced the French Philosophers, but the successors to Locke in the British empirical tradition were George Berkeley, an Irishman, and David Hume, a Scot. David Hartley published his *Observations on Man: His Frame, His Duty, and His Expectations* in 1749; but he, like Condillac across the Channel, belongs to psychology rather than to sociology. Earlier in the century Shaftesbury, in his *Characteristics of Men, Manners, Opinions, and Times* (1711), argued that society is based upon man's natural sociability; but he was more interested in ethics and aesthetics than in the manners of his title. Mandeville, author of *The Fable of the Bees* (1714), to which he added an appendix in 1723 entitled "A Search into the Nature of Society," insisted that private vices are public goods, found the origin of society in the appetites of men, and anticipated Social Darwinism.[105] Bolingbroke wrote *Letters on the Study and Use of History* (1735), told us that "History is philosophy teaching by example," and asked us to inquire into the causes and consequences of historical events. And Burke, more practitioner than philosopher, believed that God is responsible for social order, decided that since man is a social animal the family is the proper unit of study, and defended social inequality on the ground that it is inevitable. But none of these is a major representative of sociological thought. The same may be said of Blackstone and Bentham, whose work appeared later in the century, and of Gibbon, whose book conferred majesty upon English historiography.

On the western side of the Atlantic Franklin and Jefferson were both men of the Enlightenment, both had strong French connections, and both were at least equal in genius to the greatest of their French contemporaries. Franklin wrote some *Observations Concerning the Increase of Mankind, Peopling of Countries, etc.*, in 1755, in which he set forth the demographic proposition that immigration to a country would not in the long run increase the population because it would depress the natural rate of increase and suggested that a single country, England for example, would be sufficiently prolific to populate the entire earth in the absence of other inhabitants. Jefferson had thoughtful comments on social phenomena, including population, stratification, and various social institutions. His *Notes on the State of Virginia*, intended to be a statistical survey, turned out to be a lively treatment of many aspects of American life and society.[106] But again, one would not contend that the literary contributions of Franklin and Jefferson belong to the area of sociological inquiry.

As in the case of Vico in Italy and Ferguson in Scotland, there is no continuity in the development of sociological thought in the English and American thinkers of the eighteenth century. They had no immediate successors, and thus the story is one of saltations and retreats, of books whose sociological significance is discovered only after long periods of neglect. The French case is different. Here we have a direct line from Montesquieu, Rousseau, and Condorcet to Malthus, Spencer, and the Social Darwinists, on the one hand, and to Saint-Simon, Comte, and, later, Durkheim, on the other. We have, in short, a line of inquiry that will become a discipline and a tradition when the word "sociology" issues, freshly stamped, from the mint of Comte.

NOTES

1. Crane Brinton, "The Revolutions," *Enclyclopedia of the Social Sciences* (New York: Macmillan Co., 1930) vol. 1, p. 129.

2. Quoted in Preserved Smith, *A History of Modern Culture* (New York: Henry Holt & Co., 1934) vol. II. pp. 355–56. D'Alembert defined a philosopher as one who torments himself while he is alive in order to be remembered after he is dead!

3. On the deism of the period, especially that of Bolingbroke, Pope, Voltaire, and Lessing, see Paul Hazard, *European Thought in the Eighteenth Century,* J. Lewis May, trans. (New Haven: Yale University Press, 1954). Hazard warns us: "There was not one deism, but several, all different, all mutually opposed, and even at daggers drawn with one another. Pope's deism is not Voltaire's, and Voltaire's was worlds away from Lessing's." The English deists of the seventeenth century—including such figures as Lord Herbert, Tindall, Toland, Wollaston, Collins, and Chubb—also exhibited a diversity of views. In the main, however, they all wanted to construct a natural religion on the basis of reason alone. Their deity, whose creation of the universe they were willing to concede, was thereafter relegated to the position of observer of the operation of natural laws. Addison, incidentally, called himself a freethinker on the ground that "atheist" was old-fashioned.

4. Carl Becker, *The Heavenly City of the Eighteenth-Century Philosophers* (New Haven: Yale University Press, 1932) pp. 31, 157.

5. Quoted in Smith, *A History of Modern Culture,* vol. II, p. 356.

6. Robert Nisbet, *The Social Philosophers* (New York: Thomas Y. Crowell, 1973) pp. 217–18.

7. The expression "political science," however, was apparently first used in 1701, in a letter from Leibniz to Bishop Burnett. In 1726 Jonathan Swift, in *Gulliver's Travels,* wrote of the failure of the Brobdingnagians to "reduce politics to a science, as the more acute wits of Europe have done." After Hume the expression became common currency. Smith, *A History of Modern Culture,* vol. II, p. 191.

8. One does not imply, in saying this, that the two concerns are incompatible.

9. It was Immanuel Kant who translated the often used *lumières* as *Aufklärung,* defined it as "the liberation of man from his self-imposed minority," and suggested that man had come of age in the generation preceding his own. Immanuel Kant, *Was ist Aufklärung?* (1784); Smith, *A History of Modern Culture,* vol. II. p. 359.

10. Nisbet reminds us, however, that they were often as intolerant as their sacerodotal opponents and that two of them, Marmontel and d'Alembert, even appealed to the censor to silence Elie Fréron, journalist, historian, and critic. Nisbet, *The Social Philosophers,* p. 218. Even Locke, champion of toleration, declined to extend it to atheists, Unitarians, Jews, and Catholics.

11. Condorcet's words appear in *Éloge de Buffon,* Holbach's in the preface to his *Systême de la Nature.* Both are quoted in Smith, *A History of Modern Culture,* vol. II, pp. 358–59.

12. One now forgotten figure went so far as to proclaim the divinity of reason: Johann Christian Edelmann, *Die Göttlichkeit der Vernunft* (1741.)

13. The classic work on this subject is J. B. Bury, *The Idea of Progress* (New York: Macmillan Co., 1932) with an introduction by Charles A. Beard. We shall touch upon the idea only indirectly because it is treated in detail in another chapter in this book.

14. Few would believe the miracles in the Bible had they not so distinguished an author!

15. See Peter Gay's two-volume work, *The Enlightenment: An Interpretation* (New York: Alfred A. Knopf, 1967, 1969).

16. Vesalius's *On the Structure of the Human Body* appeared in the same momentous year; and Cardanus's *The New Art* (on algebra), two years later.

17. It is possible that the preface had the beneficial effect of removing obstacles that would have impeded or prevented publication of the book.

18. It was Kepler too who, like some of his twentieth-century successors in the social sciences, entertained an exaggerated view of the efficacy of mathematics. His income failed by far to equal his fame, and when his first wife died he decided to choose another by ranking all of the ladies of his acquaintance on a scale in accordance with numerical values assigned to their qualities. The rest of the tale also belongs to Preserved Smith: "This method of choosing a wife seems so prudent that it must have come to him as an inexplicable contrariety in the fitness of things that the lady clearly proved by his calculations to be the most eligible declined the honor, and he was obliged to go further down on the list before the equation of mathematics and matrimony was solved." Smith, *A History of Modern Culture,* vol. I, p. 27.

19. The work of Lane Cooper has thrown considerable doubt on the authenticity of the latter experiment, as it has on the "Eppur si muove," which Galileo supposedly whispered after his final conviction by the Inquisitorial Court. There is no reference to the experiment in any of Galileo's published work and, interestingly enough, the correct view of the matter—that bodies of unequal weight would fall with the same velocity in a vacuum—may be found in the *De*

Rerum Natura of Lucretius. See Lane Cooper, *Aristotle, Galileo, and the Tower of Pisa* (Ithaca: Cornell University Press, 1935).

20. Smith, *A History of Modern Culture*, vol. I, p. 53.

21. Both in his *Lettres sur l'Anglais* (1734) and his *Éléments de la Philosophie de Newton* (1738).

22. To which, incidentally, there is a twentieth-century emendation:

> And so it was; until the Devil, crying Ho,
> Said, Let Einstein be, and restored the status quo.

23. Smith, *A History of Modern Culture*, vol. I, p. 58. It is worth mentioning, perhaps more than incidentally, that Copernicus was a Pole, Brahe a Dane, Kepler a German, Galileo an Italian, and Newton an Englishman.

24. Geography, which includes both exploration and cartography, developed rapidly in the seventeenth and eighteenth centuries. See Preserved Smith, *A History of Modern Culture*, vol. I, chap. V, and vol. II, chap. III. On demography and statistics see A. Wolf, *A History of Science, Technology, and Philosophy in the Eighteenth Century*, 2d ed. revised by D. McKie (London: George Allen & Unwin, 1952). On demography see also *The Determinants and Consequences of Population Trends* (Population Studies no. 17) (New York: United Nations, 1953).

25. Letter LXXXVI. Montesquieu, *Persian Letters*, John Davidson, trans. (New York: M. W. Dunne, 1901) pp. 166–67.

26. Montesquieu, *Considérations sur les causes de la grandeur des Romans et de leur décadence* (1734), chap. xvixi.

27. John Plamenatz, *Man and Society: Political and Social Theory: Machiavelli through Rousseau* (New York: McGraw-Hill Book Co., 1963) vol. 1, p. 256. See the entire chapter on Montesquieu, pp. 253–98, although most of it deals with his political theory.

28. "Yes, gentlemen, give me the map of a country, its configuration, its climate, its waters, its winds, and all its physical geography; give me its natural productions, its flora, its zoology, and I pledge myself to tell you, *a priori*, what the man of that country will be and what part that country will play in history, not by accident, but of necessity; not at one epoch, but in all epochs." Victor Cousin, *Introduction á l'Histoire de la Philosophie*. Quoted by Lucien Febvre, *A Geographical Introduction to History* (London: Routledge & Kegan Paul, 1925) p. 10. One is also reminded of Hegel's impatient "refutation": "Do not speak to me of geographical determinants. Where the Greeks once lived the Turks live now. That settles the question."

29. Montesquieu, *The Spirit of the Laws* (1748), book XIV, chap. 1. Translated by Thomas Nugent, (New York: Hafner Publishing Company, 1949).

30. Ibid., book XIV, chap. 1.

31. Ibid., book XIV, chap. 10.

32. Ibid., book XV, chap. 7.

33. Ibid., book XV, chap. 7.

34. Ibid., book XV, chap. 8.

35. Ibid., book XVI, chap. 8.

36. Ibid., book XVII, chap. 5.

37. Ibid., book XIV, chap. 14. On Montesquieu on climate in general, including the sources of his ideas, see Robert Shackleton, *Montesquieu: A Critical Biography* (Oxford: Oxford University Press, 1961) pp. 302–19. See also Plamenatz, *Man and Society*, vol. I, pp. 257–60; and Raymond Aron, *Main Currents in Sociological Thought*, Richard Howard and Helen Weaver, trans. (New York: Basic Books, 1965) vol. I, pp. 33–38.

38. Montesquieu, *The Spirit of the Laws*, book XIX, chap. 6.

39. One is reminded of Aristotle, who wrote that "a law derives all its strength from custom," and of the famous question of Tacitus, "*Quid leges sine moribus?*"

40. Aron, *Main Currents in Sociological Thought*, vol. I, pp. 13–14.

41. Emile Durkheim, *Montesquieu and Rousseau, Forerunners of Sociology* (Ann Arbor: University of Michigan Press, 1960) p. 57. See also Werner Stark, *Montesquieu: Pioneer of the Sociology of Knowledge* (Toronto: University of Toronto Press, 1961).

42. Voltaire, *Essai sur les Moeurs* (1765), Chapter cxcvii (Paris: Editions Garnier Frères, 1963), Tome II, p. 810.

43. Voltaire's book *The Philosophy of History* (1766) is better described as universal history. To him the expression meant history as written by a Philosopher or freethinker. An English

edition appeared in the same year (1766), translator unknown. A reprint of this edition was published in 1965 (London: Vision Press, Ltd.).

44. Jean Jacques Rousseau, *The Social Contract and Discourse* trans., and with an introduction by G. D. H. Cole (London: Everyman's Library, J. M. Dent & Sons, 1947) p. 123. The Council of State that banned Diderot's *Encyclopedia* in 1759 was of the same opinion: "The advantages to be derived from a work of this sort, in respect to progress in the arts and sciences, can never compensate for the irreparable damage that results from it in regard to morality and religion." Quoted in Will and Ariel Durant, *The Story of Civilization*, vol. IX, *The Age of Voltaire* (New York: Simon & Schuster, 1965) p. 642.

45. Rousseau, "A Discourse on the Moral Effects of the Arts and Sciences," in *The Social Contract and Discourse*, p. 127.

46. As when he writes: "When the Goths ravaged Greece, the libraries only escaped the flames owing to an opinion that was set on foot among them, that it was best to leave the enemy with a possession so calculated to divert their attention from military exercises, and keep them engaged in indolent and sedentary occupations." Ibid., p. 135.

47. It is of incidental interest to note that Rousseau in this essay uses the word "society" as a synonym of "this herd of men." In other places it is synonymous with "the body politic."

48. Rousseau, "What Is the Origin of Inequality among Men, and Is It Authorized by Natural Law?" in *The Social Contract and Discourse*, p. 160.

49. Durkheim clearly perceived the point: "The *state of nature* is not, as has sometimes been said, the state in which man lived before societies came into being. The term might indeed suggest a historical period of the beginning of human development. This is not what Rousseau meant. . . . Natural man is simply man without what he owes to society, reduced to what he would be if he had always lived in isolation. Thus the problem is more psychological than historical, namely to distinguish between the social elements of human nature and those inherent in the psychological make-up of the individual." Durkheim, *Montesquieu and Rousseau*, p. 66.

50. Rousseau, "The Origin of Inequality," p. 164.

51. Ibid., p. 197.

52. Ibid., p. 198.

53. Rousseau sent a copy of the *Discourse on Inequality* to Voltaire and received a charming reply. It reads, in part: "I have received, Monsieur, your new book against the human race. I thank you for it. You will please men, to whom you tell truths that concern them, but you will not correct them. You paint in very true colors the horrors of human society; . . . no one has ever employed so much intellect to persuade men to be beasts. In reading your work one is seized with a desire to walk on four paws. However, as it is more than sixty years since I lost that habit, I feel, unfortunately, that it is impossible for me to resume it." Quoted in Will and Ariel Durant, *The Story of Civilization*, vol. X, *Rousseau and Revolution* (1967) p. 31.

54. Rousseau, *Émile*, Barbara Fox, trans., Everyman's Library (London: J. M. Dent, 1930) p. 251.

55. Rousseau, *The Social Contract*, In Everyman's Library edition, book I, chap. VI.

56. Ibid., book II, chap. XII.

57. Ibid., book II, chap. VIII.

58. Rousseau's opposition to capital punishment is worth noting: "The State has no right to put to death, even for the sake of making an example, any one whom it can leave alive without danger." Ibid., book II, chap. V.

59. "Quill drivers" is a favorite expression of Paul Hazard. See his chapter "The Encyclopedia" in *European Thought in the Eighteenth Century*, pp. 199–214. On the *Encyclopedia* also, see René Hubert, *Les Sciences social dans l'Encyclopédie* (Paris: 1923; Genève: Slatkine Reprints, 1970). I am indebted to Tom Bottomore for this reference to Hubert.

60. Quoted by J. B. Bury, *The Idea of Progress*, p. 203. Aided, it might be said, by the increase in literacy; the popularity of reading; the growth of scientific academies, journals, and museums; and by the fact that the Philosophers had surrendered Latin for the vernacular. See Preserved Smith, *A History of Modern Culture*, vol. II, pp. 126–40, and also his chap. XI, "The Propaganda of the Enlightenment," vol. II, pp. 355–67. Nineteen editions of Voltaire's works were printed between 1740–78 and the number of his readers was estimated at 200,000.

61. Quoted by J. Salwyn Schapiro, *Condorcet and the Rise of Liberalism* (New York: Harcourt, Brace & Co., 1934) p. 117.

62. On Condorcet's mathematics see Gilles-Gaston Granger, *La Mathématique Sociale du Marquis de Condorcet* (Paris: Presses Universitaires de France, 1956).

63. Condorcet, *Sketch for a Historical Picture of the Progress of the Human Mind*, Library

of Ideas edition, Stuart Hampshire, ed., June Barraclough, trans., (London: Weidenfeld & Nicolson, 1955) p. 4.

64. Ibid.

65. It should be mentioned that the book was only a prospectus for a much larger work that Condorcet intended to write.

66. Condorcet, *Sketch for a Historical Picture*, p. 44.

67. Ibid., p. 100.

68. Schapiro suggests that Saint-Simon misunderstands Condorcet on this point. Condorcet maintained that progress accompanies the increase of knowledge, not that the capacity of the human mind to acquire knowledge increases. *Condorcet and the Rise of Liberalism*, p. 263. The quotations from Saint-Simon and Comte are both from Schapiro.

69. Vico, *The New Science*, Thomas Goddard Bergin and Max Harold Fisch, trans., (Garden City, New York: Anchor Books, Doubleday & Co., 1961) pp. 52-53.

70. Ibid., p. 27.

71. H. P. Adams, *The Life and Writings of Giambattista Vico* (London: George Allen & Unwin, 1935) p. 172. See also Paul Hazard: "It was not until later that his appeal was heard and answered. For the moment it awakened no echo; no converts, no disciples followed in his train." Hazard, *European Thought in the Eighteenth Century*, p. 37.

72. René Wellek, "The Supposed Influence of Vico on England and Scotland in the Eighteenth Century," in *Giambattista Vico: An International Symposium*, Giorgio Tagliacozzo, ed. (Baltimore: Johns Hopkins Press, 1969) p. 223; and see the entire essay, pp. 215–23. This book, with its forty-one contributors, is itself a testimony to Vico's contemporary importance. See also in this volume Werner Stark's essay "Giambattista Vico's Sociology of Knowledge," pp. 297–307. The third edition of *The New Science* appeared in 1744, when Rousseau was serving as secretary to the French ambassador in Venice, then a mart for books, but no one apparently knows whether he encountered it in any of the stalls.

73. Holmes, who taught at the University from 1857–97, purchased Comte's *Cours de philosophie positive* in May of 1848 and, as his marginal notes attest, read it the same year. In 1852 he published two papers on Comte, both in the *Methodist Quarterly Review*. Comte, in turn, considered Holmes his most worthy American critic. See Richard L. Hawkins, *Auguste Comte and the United States, 1816-1853* (Cambridge: Harvard University Press, 1936) pp. 99–142.

74. Benedetto Croce, "Vico," *Encyclopedia of the Social Sciences* (New York: Macmillan Co., 1934). See also Croce, *The Philosophy of Giambattista Vico*, R. G. Collingwood, trans. (1913), (New York: Russell & Russell, 1964). Curiously, there is no mention of Vico in Peter Gay's two volumes on the Enlightenment.

75. David Hume, *An Enquiry Concerning Human Understanding*, sect. V, part II, p. 44.

76. Ibid., sect. VIII, part I, p. 65.

77. David Hume, *A Treatise of Human Nature*, book III, part II, sect. II.

78. Ibid.

79. David Hume, "Of the Original Contract," in *Hume's Essays* (London: George Routledge & Sons, no date) pp. 322–38.

80. Peter Gay, *The Enlightenment*, vol. II, p. 335.

81. Donald G. MacRae, "Adam Ferguson, Sociologist," *New Society* (24 November 1966) pp. 792–94. This essay, slightly revised, is reprinted in *The Founding Fathers of Social Sciences*, Timothy Raison, ed. (Baltimore: Penguin Books, 1969). See also MacRae, *Ideology and Society* (London: Heinemann, 1961) chap. XII.

82. William C. Lehmann, *Adam Ferguson and the Beginnings of Modern Sociology* (New York: Columbia University Press, 1930) p. 16, note 4.

83. But see David Kettler, *The Social and Political Thought of Adam Ferguson* (Columbus: Ohio State University Press, 1965) pp. 47–49.

84. Adam Ferguson, *Essay on the History of Civil Society*, 2d ed. (London: Printed for A. Millar and T. Caddell, 1768) p. 6.

85. Ibid., p. 23.

86. Quoted in Kettler, *The Social and Political Thought of Adam Ferguson*, p. 193.

87. Ibid., p. 195.

88. Quoted in Lehmann, *Adam Ferguson and the Beginnings of Modern Sociology*, pp. 149–150.

89. Peter Gay, *The Enlightenment*, vol. II, pp. 342–43.

90. Details of Millar's life and writings may be found in William C. Lehmann, *John Millar of*

Glasgow: His Life and Thought and his Contributions to Sociological Analysis (Cambridge: At the University Press, 1960). Lehmann reprints the third edition of *The Origin of the Distinction of Ranks* in this book, together with excerpts from other writings.

91. John Millar, Introduction to the third edition of *The Origin of the Distinction of Ranks*.

92. As an author in the *Edinburgh Review* wrote about him, Millar "looked with profound contempt at those puerile schemes of equality that threatened to subvert the distinctions of property, or to degrade the natural aristocracy of virtues and of talents." vol. III, p. 158; quoted in Lehmann, *John Millar of Glasgow*, p. 67.

93. Robert M. MacIver, foreword to Lehmann, *John Millar of Glasgow*, p. xii.

94. For other figures of the Scottish Enlightenment, including Thomas Reid, Francis Hutcheson, Dugald Stewart, Lord Kames, and Lord Monboddo, see Gladys Bryson, *Man and Society: The Scottish Inquiry of the Eighteenth Century* (Princeton: Princeton University Press, 1945); and Louis Schneider, ed., *The Scottish Moralists: On Human Nature and Society* (Chicago: University of Chicago Press, 1967).

95. Gotthold Ephraim Lessing, *Der Erziehung des Menschengeschlechts* (1780).

96. Johann Gottfried von Herder, *Ideen zur Philosophie der Geschichte der Menschheit*, translated into English in 1800 by T. Churchill, with the title *Outlines of a Philosophy of the History of Man*. Quotations are from the two volumes of the second London edition, 1803.

97. Ibid., vol. I, p. 311.

98. Ibid., vol. I, p. 293ff.

99. Although, unfortunately and inconsistently, Herder permits himself to say that nature placed the Negro close to the ape. Ibid., vol. II, p. 274. Collingwood accuses Herder of racist thinking, an accusation Manuel regrets. R. G. Collingwood, *The Idea of History* (Oxford: At the Clarendon Press, 1946) p. 92; Frank E. Manuel, editor's introduction to Joann Gottfried von Herder, *Reflections on the Philosophy of Mankind* (Chicago: University of Chicago Press, 1968) p. x.

100. Herder, *Ideen zur Philosophie der Geschichte der Menschheit*, vol. I, p. 376.

101. Ibid., vol. I, p. 378.

102. Ibid., vol. II, p. 187.

103. Ibid., vol. II, p. 269.

104. As an example: "The progress of history shows, that, as true humanity has increased, the destructive demons of the human race have diminished in number; and this from the inherent natural laws of a self-enlightening reason and policy." Ibid., vol. II, p. 281.

105. Mandeville also wrote a piece in favor of prostitution as part of the self-regulating machinery of society: *A Modest Defense of Publick Stews* (London: Scott & Browns, 1724), 78 pp.

106. See C. Randolph Benson, *Thomas Jefferson as Social Scientist*, (Cranbury, N.J.: Fairleigh Dickinson University Press, 1971).

2

THEORIES OF PROGRESS, DEVELOPMENT, EVOLUTION

KENNETH BOCK

I

THERE IS a broad and complex array of ideas about social and cultural change that can, on historical grounds, be most conveniently designated as the idea of progress. Efforts to distinguish progress, development, and evolution are interesting in the abstract,[1] but the distinction has not actually been made in the general course of humanistic inquiry, and much confusion has resulted from presumption that it has. This is particularly true when the relationship of social and organic evolution is discussed. A similar difficulty is introduced when the nineteenth-century "development hypothesis" of biology is confounded with contemporary notions of social development as well as with some of the current efforts to explicate changes taking place in "underdeveloped" countries. In the interest of both convenience and clarity, therefore, the generic term "idea of progress" will be used here to name a definite and pervasive theoretical orientation in sociological analysis.

Often in our struggle with the history of sociological theory, we find ourselves confronted with the expression or presentation of an idea that turns to be far more complicated than the idea itself. Excess of verbiage, tireless reiteration, and endless variations on an actually simple theme can transform a common-sense notion of little theoretical import into an apparently deep and sophisticated insight. So, we often find ourselves engaged in the unrewarding and disheartening task of tearing aside verbal veils to reveal banalities.

When we approach the idea of progress we are in just the opposite situation: here is an apparently simple and straightforward notion that, upon closer examination, involves us in some of the most vexing problems of modern Western social thought. In his still classic history of the idea, Bury defined it economically as the belief that "civilisation has moved, is moving, and will move in a desirable direction,"[2] but he found himself laboring in nineteen chapters of tight exposition and interpetation to get at the implications of that bare declaration. What at first appears to be merely a naive expression of faith in a better future for man in society—an attitude of optimism—turns out to be a complex and subtle web of ideas with far-reaching methodological and substantive consequences for social science and social philosophy.

When Professor Bierstedt remarks, then, that progress may not be a sociological problem at all, that the idea of progress is hardly even an idea, and that a belief in progress is a matter of optimism rather than of fact or truth, he is surely not referring to the same idea that intrigued Bury.[3] Nor can it be some vague optimism about life that Teggart had in mind when he said that "The difficulties which the humanist must meet at the present time arise from his acceptance of the idea of progress as the directive concept in the study of man."[4] The idea of progress, when seen as something more than a normative concept, has been central to the formation of sociology as a discipline and continues to shape profoundly the issues and outlooks of this and related social and cultural sciences.

A difficulty here, of course, arises from the fact that progress is an omnibus term that has been used to refer to a whole galaxy of ideas, not all of them consistent with one another, and advanced in varying combinations.[5] What it is that is said to progress, where and when the progress is supposed to have occurred, and which criteria are used to distinguish progress are by no means agreed upon by progress theorists from era to era. Again, the causes of progress, its successive manifestations, and its ultimate goals receive different specifications among different thinkers. Basic questions about the shape of progress—its linearity—are answered variously. Ways of picturing or demonstrating progress range from mere idyllic imagery and empty declarations of faith to the construction of detailed and intricate sequences based on types drawn from history, archaeology, and ethnography and tied together by elaborate laws of change. And yet amid this diversity there are basic elements that do form a unity that we can usefully call the idea of progress. It is these elements that we should identify when we seek an understanding of the part played by theories of progress in the history of sociological analysis.

One obvious impediment to the detection of more fundamental implications of the idea of progress is that it has usually been regarded as, above all, a value judgment about history. The word "progress" carries chiefly normative connotations for most of us, and the most notable efforts to trace the history of the idea have been marked by a concern to distinguish it from beliefs about decadence or regression, or about cycles. Or the differences and similarities of an idea of secular progress and the idea of Providence have been examined. The intermittent waxing and waning of optimism and pessimism in the Western world are of dominant concern. This is understandable. The intellectual tradition that concerns us here was repeatedly (though not always) expressed in the seventeenth and eighteenth centuries in a context of enthusiastic avowals of inevitable improvement in one or another facet of human life. Our immediate inheritance of the tradition is in that context.

The questions of whether there was a movement in human history in the direction of valued goals, and the question of how such a movement was facilitated and impeded, are important and legitimate. The moral philosophy out of which humanistic disciplines have emerged can, in this respect, hardly be denied. And such questions cannot be ignored in a discussion of the part played by theories of progress in sociological inquiry. But, partly because these questions have hitherto dominated discussions of the idea of progress and have been treated competently, and more important, because this has been at the expense of other aspects of the idea, those other aspects are chosen for emphasis here.

The idea of progress—that congeries of ideas whose classic expression we find in Aristotle and Augustine, in Fontenelle and Saint-Pierre, in Condorcet and Comte, in Spencer and Tylor—contains a detailed and comprehensive image of change. It involves specific orientations to history as a record of events. It points to a definite and singular interpretation of social and cultural differences and designates a use of differences in constructing theories of social and cultural change. It postulates a nature of things, asserts a universalism, and creates a system of correspondences that presents us with a rich and detailed picture of how things work in human affairs. It identifies as a real entity a category of the accidental, the fortuitous, the abnormal or unnatural. It provides an intricate method of hypostatizing or reifying entities whose careers in time can be traced. It is shot through with primitive organic notions of being and becoming.

It is chiefly with these features of the idea of progress that this chapter will deal.

II

Bury identified the idea of progress as a strictly modern product that emerged in the seventeenth century and reached full expression in the eighteenth. He contrasted it with the idea of cycles characteristic of Greco-Roman antiquity and with the medieval European idea of Providence.[6]

The essential ingredient of an idea of cycles is the view that history repeats itself in an endless succession of upward and downward phases, a perpetual coming to be and passing away of forms which are in themselves eternal. The

Greeks saw this process in all nature, not just in the vicissitudes of human history, and from the earliest accounts known to us they described it as a biological process of birth, growth, decline, and death. Bury has been generally followed in the judgment that such a perspective precluded absolutely a belief in an indefinite improvement in human life and established a block to any meaningful historical vista, including an idea of progress.

The Christian idea of Providence denied cycles, postulated a definite beginning and ending to human terrestrial history, and pictured the intervening period as a working out of the drama of salvation. Again, Bury's case for the distinctiveness of the idea of progress has been widely accepted. He argued that the providential view of history is restricted to a relatively short time span at the end of which the drama is completed and the scene of worldly progress is destroyed, whereas secular progress is conceived to have more remote beginnings and an indefinite future. The point was also made that the idea of Providence, insofar as it envisions progress at all, sees it not as an improvement in temporal affairs, but only as a realization of the Kingdom of God or the achievement of a state of grace.

But Bury's opinion has also been challenged on both counts. It is argued that, despite their preoccupation with cycles, the Socratics and such later figures as Lucretius and Seneca saw some advance in the past, and that the obvious concern of both the Greeks and Romans with improving their present condition—administering to the body politic—could rest only on a belief in at least the possibility of a better future.[7] With respect to the idea of Providence the claim is made that it was only with the advent of a prospect for salvation that the dreary scene of cycles could be escaped; that the ecumenical outlook of Christian doctrine was the key to a conception of mankind as a entity advancing through history; and that elements of this-worldliness in Christianity encouraged an amelioration of the human scene by alteration of men's behavior toward one another. More important, perhaps, theologians and philospophers have argued that the secular idea of progress is only an unstable version of the idea of Providence because any conception of movement toward the good stands in urgent need of criteria of goodness, and only religions can supply these on an absolute and unchanging basis. The modern, secular idea of progress is accused of leading us on a rudderless voyage that has carried us to a point where we identify as betterment the crassest and most dangerous forms of material innovation.[8]

These are fascinating problems in the history of ideas, not just because they call for a careful reading of what Plato or Marcus Aurelius or the early Church fathers had to say about the future, but because they call to our attention rich cultural settings in which the question of the relationship between historical perspectives and ethical systems can be explored.

The bare question of how far back the idea of progress can be traced or what its origins might have been is a tedious one, however, and need not detain us here. But there is another side to this matter that should not be obscured by giving our total attention to the question of whether the Greeks believed in betterment or whether meaning in history could be discerned only with the coming of the Christian vision. However these questions might be answered, it is useful to take notice of the fact that both the Greeks and the early Church fathers did have definite ideas about processes of change in time and about how we should study them. These ideas persist in the Western intellectual tradition and are basic to the modern idea of progress. Because the ideas are didactically presented in the early writings and are discernible, perhaps, only by implication in later and contemporary versions, it serves a purpose to look, however summarily, at a couple of examples from the earlier literature before proceeding to a history and analysis of the more immediate sources of progress theories in sociological study.

Aristotle is the most significant case in point. In the *Physics*, Aristotle took "nature" as his subject of study, and his first step was to define nature as "the principle of movement and change." (This was not a definition out of the blue, of course; centuries of Greek speculation on problems of being and becoming had preceded Aristotle, and the substance of the discussion was known to him.) Nature has other attributes: "nothing natural or accordant with nature is without order; for nature is the universal determinant of order." Nature, then, is orderly change. Moreover, "the natural process . . . [is] . . . guided by a purpose." Nature is change that takes place in an orderly way for a purpose. The exposition continues:

> . . . natural things are exactly those which do move continuously, in virtue of a principle inherent in themselves, towards a determined goal; and the final development which results from any one such principle is not identical for any two species, nor yet is it any random result; but in each there is always a tendency towards an identical result if nothing interferes with the process.

All things in nature, there, change continuously in an orderly and teleological fashion as a consequence of properties contained within them, and these properties vary from one kind or species to another. Change occurs as a product of something that is there before the thing begins to change. Finally, Aristotle notes that all this goes on in natural things only if nothing interferes. Not everything that happens, happens naturally, then; and if nature is our subject it becomes a matter of importance to distinguish between the natural and whatever else is going on. Aristotle attacks the problem:

> Of things that exist, some exist by nature, some from other causes. "By nature" the animals and their parts exist, and the plants and the simple bodies (earth, air, fire, water)—for we say that these and the like exist "by nature." All the things mentioned present a feature in which they differ from things which are not constituted by nature. Each of them has within itself a principle of motion and of stationariness (in respect of place or of growth and decrease, or by way of alteration).

Natural things have an innate impulse to change and so are to be distinguished from products of art—"a bed and a coat and anything else of that sort." And there is another difference, for in addition to art as a producer of not natural things, there is, according to Aristotle, "chance and spontaneity." Some things always come to pass in the same way, he observed, others for the most part; these things come to pass "by necessity." Things that do not come to pass in this way are "by chance;" what does not come to be "by rule" is by chance. Monstrosities occur in nature, but these are like mistakes in art. Inanimate things and the lower animals cannot do anything by chance. Chance follows from the actions of men as moral agents when what they intend to result from their actions is not what actually results.

The natural, for Aristotle, is not just an average or a mean that might be arrived at by observing and counting; it is not defined by regularity of occurrence. Nature has a certain *quality:* orderly, purposive, continuous, inherent change. When change occurs in any other way, it is not in nature. And that is of crucial importance, since Aristotle observed that what is by chance cannot be studied by science. The world of human experience in particular, therefore, is composed of happenings comprehensible by science and happenings incomprehensible to science.[9]

There is a neatness to all this that explains the strong hold that Aristotle kept on medieval and modern minds. The scheme contains a solution to the problem of being and becoming, of permanence and change, or, if you will, of order and progress. Nature is presented as a principle of orderly development for the realization of certain classes of ends. There is purpose in existence. Change proceeds within a static framework of species or kinds that contain as potential a whole range of orders which in themselves are eternal. Order and purpose and real things exist in the world despite the fact that the world is characterized by change.

The implications of all this for a study of society become plain when Aristotle inquires into the origin and development of the state, for the state is regarded as being in nature. The clearest view of the state must be sought in its "first growth and origin," because its seed form contains all the potentialities of what it is to become; the essence of the state is discernible in its origin. As with other things in nature, the state passes through certain stages in its development: in the beginning there are man and woman, and their relationship arises out of a "natural instinct to leave behind one another being of the same sort"—in the abstract, a desire for self-sufficiency. They form the first partnership, the family, and the state is such a partnership, and "every partnership is formed with a view to some good." Several families unite to form the village, and several villages come to form the city-state, which permits the first partnership to attain at last "the limit of virtually complete self-sufficiency."

> Hence every city-state exists by nature, inasmuch as the first partnerships so exist; and . . . the city-state is the end of the other partnerships, and nature is an end, since that which each thing is when its growth is completed we speak of as being the nature of each thing, . . . Again, the object for which a thing exists, its end, is its chief good; the self-sufficiency is an end, and a chief good. From these things therefore it is clear that the city-state is a natural growth, and that man is by nature a political animal, and a man that is by nature and not merely by fortune citiless is either low in the scale of humanity or above it. . . .

It is also clear to Aristotle, by the same argument, that the state is "prior by nature to the individual," for an individual cannot be self-sufficient except in the state. Again, a man who is incapable of entering into the state partnership, or who does not need to, "must be either a lower animal or a god."[10]

Obviously, Aristotle was aware of the possibility that "fortune" could "interfere" with the natural process of city-state formation for certain men, and his own experience in Athens no doubt inclined him to regard such recalcitrants as lower animals rather than gods. The point here, however, is that the process that Aristotle regarded as natural was not what he observed going on in the world, and so he had to relegate that "going on" to his category of the accidental. The natural process of social change that his science discovered, therefore, was a statement of what he thought *best* for men in their historical experience. He hypostatized a "city-state" and depicted its hypothetical career in time. Actual histories of peoples were set aside as irrelevant to the discovery of natural processes of change.

It is not difficult to read a doctrine of progress as improvement into this. Granted that Aristotle and his contemporaries saw all processes of coming to be in nature followed by processes of passing away, in picturing the upward phase of the cycle they were delineating a process of realization of an end, and in Aristotle's conception of final causes the "end" of anything in nature was the achievement of what was "best" in it, not the death or disappearance of it. In his account of the origin and growth of the state Aristotle is obviously talking about something of which he would approve: the realization of a *desideratum* in human affairs. If such a state was also going to decay in time, well, that could be said of any lion or olive tree or horse or any other natural thing as well. The world was full of things perfecting themselves eternally. That is hardly a dismal view, and, as the Greeks might have observed, it avoids the bothersome point of asking perfection to improve itself. So far as the broad historical picture was concerned, if one lived in the ascendancy phase of the cycle there was the prospect of participation in perfection. If one lived in the descending phase, then there was the glory of the past and the certainty of eventual good tidings again. The question of whether antiquity believed in progress is, from this point of view, not significant.

But apart from questions about betterment through time, what we do find in Greek thought exemplified by Aristotle is a clear and detailed prototype of the eighteenth-century Western European theory of progress, and it will here prove useful for identifying the salient characteristics of that theory and tracing their ramifications into contemporary social theory.

Before leaving the Greeks it is appropriate to recall that they and the Romans commonly indulged in building conceptual culture series that were taken to represent time sequences in an abstract culture history. Aristotle himself, though his account of the political process is usually quite general, did not hesitate on occasion to recover the early history of advanced Hellenic peoples by pointing to barbarian institutions in his own day.[11] A more striking instance of this practice is furnished by Thucydides who, when he found himself without evidence on the early history of Greece, turned to barbarians and "backward" Greeks in his own day for a picture of what things must have been like in Athens long ago. Thus piracy must have prevailed, because that is the condition among certain "tribes" now. Bearing of arms must have been common, for the practice is to be observed in primitive parts of the country now. "And the fact," Thucydides sums up, "that the people in these parts of Hellas are still living in the old way points to a time when the same mode of life was once equally common to all." How is it that some peoples lag behind this way? Thucydides' answer is clear: "Various . . . were the obstacles which the national growth encountered in various localities."[12]

It is important to notice at this point that Thucydides was not only talking about culture progress but was seeking to demonstrate it by devices that were allowable only on the basis of propositions about natural change such as those found in Aristotle's theory. Use is made of the ideas that there is such a thing in nature as society or culture; that it undergoes a growth that is the same wherever it is found, because the same potential is in every instance of it; that obstacles or impediments or interferences alter the natural process in various places, so that we see peoples in various stages of "*the* national growth." The panorama of progress is thus spread out before us in the present.

Among the early Christian writers, St. Augustine offers us the clearest example of using Greek ideas in the construction of a philosophy of history that would serve in many ways as a model for eighteenth-century progress theorists. In his *City of God* Augustine took a biblical historical record of discrete events, rationalized it, gave it meaning and purpose, and presented the whole in a systematic account that would meet the pagan theory of cycles on its own ground and replace it. History was conceived as a process of change that manifested the will of an orderly and purposive God. The end of history was the realization of the City of God or the principle of the good in a chosen portion of the human race. What was to be in the end was present in the beginning, for the principles of good and evil were in Adam's seed. The process could be depicted in stages that were marked off by events drawn from sacred history—from Adam to Noah, from the Flood to Abraham, from Abraham to David, and so forth. The change was conceived as an education of the human race which "has advanced, like that of the individual, through certain epochs, or as it were, ages, so that it might gradually rise from earthly to heavenly things, and from the visible to the invisible."[13]

Augustine thus retained the Aristotelian view that the reality to be studied is orderly and purposeful change that proceeds gradually and continuously through a series of steps or stages to an end that was immanent in the beginning or origin. But Augustine managed as well to stay within this conceptual framework while dealing with what he accepted as a series of unique events, and he did so by resorting to a force behind all history, productive of all happening. In his case the force was God's will, which his faith and reason let him know. Later thinkers were to rely on other historical motors—geographic environment, human nature, the Spirit or Geist, the economic factor—but the form of the inquiry remained the same and the resulting picture of a progress or advance or development was changed only in content.

III

The modern theory of progress took shape in the Quarrel between the ancients and the moderns, or at least it is convenient in restrospect to trace in that context the confluence of ideas that we see brought together ultimately in the work of Turgot and Condorcet.

The issue in the Quarrel was how the artistic, philosophical, and scientific works of modern Europe compared with the works of the Greeks and Romans of antiquity. Although the question had been asked throughout the Renaissance,[14] that part of the Quarrel relevant to our present interest falls in the second half of the seventeenth century.

As a purely literary debate the Quarrel was at first marked by expression of mere opinion concerning the relative merits of the old and new, but the moderns soon undertook to show not only that more recent productions were superior to older ones, but that they *must* be. Their argument took the form of a scientific demonstration quite in keeping with the revolution in learning that was under way in Europe, and some powerful ideas were enlisted in the task.

Bodin and LeRoy, while coming very close to asserting a kind of institutional progress in human affairs, had suggested in the sixteenth century that the powers of nature had been uniform through all time. Francis Bacon, calling for a "great instauration" of learning, had found occasion to criticize scholastics for their reverence for antiquity, to observe that the "wisdom which we have derived principally from the Greeks is but like the boyhood of knowledge," and to suggest that, had not many obstacles been raised, the advance of knowledge would have been much greater. In René Descartes's *Discourse on Method* these implications are made quite explicit in the course of an effort to deal with the old problem of order and change.[15] Instead of concerning himself with disputes about what had happened at the time of the Creation, or at any time in the past, Descartes set himself the task of discovering, through reason, "what would happen" if God created a new world. Given matter and motion, a pure chaos, Descartes was able to reveal the laws that God had put into nature to bring order out of chaos by a process of coming to be. Here was a magnificent "conjectural history" for the *philosophes* to emulate. In addition, Descartes saw the need to invest the object of his speculation with qualities that made it accessible to reason (what Aristotle had categorized as "natural" or "of necessity"), and he accordingly asserted that the laws put into nature by God operated constantly through time and uniformly through space.[16]

It was on this basis that the moderns came to argue that, since nature is regular and uniform in her working, men of equal ability must have been produced in all ages; and that, by sheer accumulation of equal products of equal resources, there must have been an advance or progress in knowledge. The forms that this argument took and the metaphors used deserve careful attention if we are to appreciate what was involved in the grand eighteenth century "science of man and society" that followed and in the sociological distillate, the nineteenth. Auguste Comte was fully justified in the importance he attributed to the Quarrel and its contribution to the foundation of his new science.[17]

Fontenelle's "On the Ancients and the Moderns" (1688) summarized the thesis for progress. The case rests on the constancy and uniformity of nature's powers. Were the trees greater in ancient times? If not, we should not suppose that Homer and Plato were superior to seventeenth-century men. (All nature is one; there are corresponding levels in nature.) The Augustinian comparison of the life of the race and the life of an individual man is renewed in an elaborate analogy.

> A good cultivated mind contains, so to speak, all the minds of preceding centuries; it is but a single identical mind which has been developing and improving itself all this time. Thus this man, who has lived since the beginning of the world up to the present, had his infancy, when he occupied himself merely with the most pressing needs of existence; his youth, when he was fairly successful in imaginative pursuits, such as poetry and eloquence, and when he even began to reason a little, though with less soundness than fire. He is now in his prime, when he reasons more forcefully and has greater intelligence than ever before; . . .

But the analogy is not carried to its logical conclusion: "The man in question will have no old age." In fact (and here Fontenelle anticipated biological theories of man's organic progress), the man will become endowed with greater and greater intellectual powers.[18]

In another of his essays, "Sur l'Histoire," Fontenelle recommended a way of arriving at a true picture of the progress that takes place. It is possible, he said, simply by regarding human nature, to conjecture all history, past, present, and future. Human nature consists of certain qualities, and these result in certain facts or happenings. By studying history in this way, one gets to the basic source of things. In fact, the issue in the Quarrel could never be settled by reference to the facts of history itself. But by getting at the underlying principles (in human nature), one gets a "universal view" of all that *could have been*. Thus the details, the events of history, become a sort of diversion that may be noted or omitted according to taste. Events and chance sometimes contribute to the orderly succession of changes that form the substance of human history, but we should attend mainly to the customs and usages of men that result from the human mind and passions. It is not on the fact themselves that we must rely, but on the "spirit" of the facts.[19] Such is the final Cartesian reaction to the poor little conjectural science of history.

Fontenelle's views, which appear in substantially the same form in Pascal, Perrault, and other leading champions of the moderns' cause, constitute a basic conception of how things work in human experience and how we can reconstruct that experience. Given a condition of knowledge in ancient Greece and Rome and a condition of knowledge in seventeenth-century Europe, the question of which was superior was converted into a question of how the latter developed out of the former in accordance with laws of change that guaranteed the superiority of the product. This was not just a matter of things improving through time; more fundamentally, it was a case of an entity that had a career in time, that had unfolded a certain potential and realized itself in time. The condition observed in modern Europe was judged to be *different* from the condition noted in ancient Greece, and the difference was explained as a difference in degree of development. Development of what? Not anything Greek and not anything European, for as Fontenelle was at pains to point out, the moderns did not rest their case on an examination of the history of any people. In order to connect modern Europe with ancient Greece it was necessary to postulate some thing that was present in both places and times, some thing that had a life of its own, some thing that passed one stage of its life in early Greece and another stage in seventeenth-century Europe. For Fontenelle, as for most of the moderns, the thing postulated was "the human mind," which seemed appropriate since a change in the condition of knowledge was being discussed. Occasionally the reference was to "man" or "the human race," and in the eighteenth and nineteenth centuries a great number of different developing entities were identified for the purpose of sketching much more elaborate progressive series. But this made no difference in the form of the inquiry or the kind of result.

"The human mind," then, is presented by the moderns as having changed in time, and the change is represented as growth: it is slow and gradual and marked by stages or phases rather than events. Events are only manifestations of the growth process. The change is seen as development in the precise sense of an unfolding or coming to be of what is potential in the thing changing. Change is immanent. As Leibniz so appropriately put it, ". . . each created being is pregnant with its future state, and naturally follows a certain course, if nothing hinders it."[20] Change is also regarded as "natural" in the sense that it is to be expected, it is normal, it is characteristic of things, it is necessary in the Aristotelian sense. The moderns were under no obligation to *account for* the change they depicted, therefore, but instead were concerned with explaining stagnation or retrogression or any deviation from the growth of the human mind that they envisaged. And there were deviations, indeed, to be explained. The awful spectacle of medieval decline following the grandeur of the Greco-Roman world confronted every progressivist argument. And in the Quarrel itself, there were enemies of progress, the champions of the ancients, the stubborn adherents to a dated, an infantile intellectual phase. How were such phenomena to be explained if an immanent principle of progress was at work, if God had put into nature laws that operated constantly and uniformly to realize the full potential of the human mind?

Fontenelle posed this question in its broad form by asking how different conditions of human life could be explained. If nature's powers are constant, then instances of a thing she produces should be the same everywhere and at all times. But peoples are not the same from time to time or place to place. Even if we are talking about the human mind as something that comes to be in time and so must be expected to appear in different forms at different times, the question still presses as to why all peoples at any given time do not present the same aspect. If differences are defined as differences in degree of development of the same potential, then what calls for explanation is the variation in speed of change (development of the human mind) from time to time and place to place. Fontenelle's tentative answers have an ad hoc quality and are not convincing. Time, he says, produces differences in men's experiences. Contact with other minds has its effects. Different climates might be responsible. Governments can impose different conditions of life, and bad governments are always a threat to normal progress. Special events such as wars could explain lapses such as the Middle Ages. And, as the moderns in the Quarrel tended generally to point out, "Nothing is such an impediment to progress, nothing hinders mental development so much, as excessive admiration of the ancients." All of this is negative, however: changes remain unexplained and differences are presented as the consequences of fortuitous circumstances or events.[21] Uniformity of the human experience is thus preserved.

It is clear, then, that Fontenelle and the moderns were not saying merely that Western Europeans had learned something from the ancient Greek and Roman literature and had added to it so that, by the seventeenth century, Frenchmen and Englishmen, for example, were better informed than Aristotle had been. In the course of making the point they had elaborated a theory about human progress, as evidenced by mental development, which said that in *any* such temporal relationship of two branches of the human race, the later in time *must* have advanced in mental development beyond the earlier in time. And an adjunct to the theory stated that when such advance did not take place, or when it was slowed, or when actual retrogression occurred, that was because special circumstances prevailed that constituted obstacles or impediments to the process. But beyond an occasional unsystematic effort to associate these mishaps with human passions or other antirational forces, there was, as in Aristotle, no *theory* of obstacles, because they lay in a realm of chance and beyond the purview of science.

IV

The idea of progress formulated during the Quarrel was a conception of the way in which *knowledge* had grown, not of the advance of society. The moderns sought a reform in knowledge and in methods of inquiry, not a reform of society. But the consequences for social and cultural life of a development of the human mind were soon subject to speculation. Francis Bacon had pointed out earlier that knowledge was useful here in this life and that by knowing nature we could imitate and control her to our benefit. This view was exploited early in the eighteenth century by such figures as the

Abbé de Saint-Pierre. Human reason, he said, could remake knowledge and so remake the conditions of life. That had, in fact, happened in a procession of Iron, Bronze, and Silver ages. In the beginning men had been ignorant and poor, as the savages in America and Africa were now. Then they had acquired government, an effective institution for gaining security, rule by law, and the conditions under which material invention flourished. Now man had entered a third great era, in which advance in reason would improve the art of government, abolish wars, and foster material progress. Saint-Pierre saw a thorough amelioration of human life in the offing once sovereigns were persuaded to follow the dictates of reason (as spelled out in Saint-Pierre's "projects") and humanity had learned to avoid such obstacles to progress as wars and bad rulers. He represented "humanity" throughout his writings as an entity which, like an individual organism, grows to perfection, but, unlike other organisms, never dies.[22]

Saint-Pierre's reference to contemporary savages as representative of an early condition of mankind was to be greatly expanded in subsequent portrayals of progress. The stages of advance documented by the moderns, and connected by a theory of change, had actually been only two in number—the ancient and the modern. Eighteenth-century Europeans discovered many more stages and populated them with exotic peoples, real or imagined, drawn from around a world they were coming to know by their ventures in trade, colonization, and conversion. The European discovery of the world was intimately connected with the formation of an idea of progress in a way that had come to be almost taken for granted. What Western man was confronted with at this time was a startling and puzzling array of cultural differences that called for explanation. Why this bewildering variety in a Cartesian world of constancy and uniformity? Whence the "godless savage" in a common humanity descended from Adam's seed? These questions were often asked, and tentative answers offered: God delighted in diversity and had filled the world with a profusion of all possible things and gradations. The physical environment shaped peoples and their ways differently. Various races had either been created separately or had deteriorated to their present condition. The vicissitudes of history, such as calamities or the chance contacts of isolated peoples, accounted for the different circumstances in which instances of humanity were found.[23]

A far simpler solution to the problem, and one that was in keeping with the Cartesian world picture as well as Scripture, was to deny the differences—to assert the basic likeness of people everywhere and to attribute apparent differences to various degrees of achievement in a uniform process of development. As Carl Becker has pointed out,[24] the task then became one of detecting among the varieties of human experience the true or natural condition and course of history and depicting them by an arrangement of selected types. Although there were those, like Rousseau, who questioned civilization itself, and many others who were deeply concerned about the obstacles and pitfalls that had hindered normal improvement, European scholars generally accepted the belief that Europe represented the point of greatest advance to date and that other tribes and nations represented the steps through which progress had made its way.

One of the first systematic expositions of this orientation to cultural differences was made by Turgot in a series of remarkable essays composed when he was a student at the Sorbonne in 1750 and 1751.[25] Following Bishop Bossuet (who had taken Saint Augustine as a model), Turgot worked with the notion that there is universal history of mankind in which a gradual unfolding of human potential passes through certain stages, epochs, or eras. Where Bossuet used the idea of Providence to give unity to his presentation, Turgot turned to the idea of progress. He had no doubt that humankind in its totality advanced continuously, though slowly, to greater perfection. While natural phenomena move in fixed cycles, mankind goes through a succession of novel stages, each linked to all those preceding in an unbroken series of cause and effect. The unity of the process is preserved, again, by regarding humanity as "one vast whole" and by repeating the familiar analogy between the history of the race and the growth of an individual man.

Turgot's theory of progress included the important and influential idea that all institutions, every part of culture, advance side by side. Mankind progresses as an organic whole: religion, morals, the arts, knowledge, and political institutions all change at the same time and are linked together in such a way that when one changes they all change, and in accordance with the same principle. This makes it possible, in seeking a configuration in historical events, to attend chiefly to only one aspect of the human scene—for example, the development of science or modifications of economic production—in order to discern a guiding or controlling thread in the whole process.

Although his work in universal history remained only a sketch and the details were not worked out, Turgot sought the basic cause of motion or progress in human nature itself. Human nature is made up of both reason and passions, so the triumph of reason and resulting growth of knowledge do not follow the simple path suggested by the moderns' argument. Error and evil have, indeed, marred man's past, and we should not suppose that a sudden flash of light now or at any time in the past demarks progressive from unprogressive epochs. Continuity, for Turgot, is the hallmark of history; the past was quite necessary to the present state of advancement. There has been a continuous linkage of the generations and a growing up or education of the human race—a favorite metaphor of both the French and German enlightenments.

If there is such a thing as human nature, if it is the same everywhere, and if it has undergone continuous development through time, then it followed for Turgot that any given condition of mankind represents a stage in the universal development. Every nuance of savagery and civilization are, in fact, observable in the present, and these picture for us every step taken by the human mind—"the history of all the ages." Present differences among cultures are to be regarded, then, as differences of degree, not of kind. The origins, early stages, and later epochs in the history of humanity can be recovered by a conceptual arrangement of these differences. If we ask how the historical condition of one people can be used to document a stage in the history of another people, or in universal history, the answer is that man is man wherever and whenever we find him. The human mind, as Turgot put this basic principle of theories of development, "contains everywhere the germs of the same progress." Any natural human condition must, therefore, be referable to a single line of progress.

It is clear that although Turgot uses seventeenth-century language in speaking about the progress of the human mind, the focus of his attention was on social institutions, and his stages of advance are demarcated by institutional changes. Condorcet's classic presentation of the theory of progress[26] at the close of the eighteenth century is also nominally concerned with development of mind but is actually an account of social or cultural change, and now with conscious attention to substantive and methodological detail. He was specific about the content of progress: reason would come to dominate the passions, society would then be reorganized for continuous growth on a rational basis, and the result would be equality—equality of achievement among nations; equality in wealth, education, and social status among all men—and freedom as a consequence. Condorcet was confident that the revolution in France would be instrumental in furthering these ends, and he left no doubt that the progress that had been going on had been leading to the kind of society represented by France in his own time.

In sketching the course of that progress Condorcet was as candid about his method as he was about the source of his criteria of progress. History as it was generally presented was of no use to him. His object was to discover "the various epochs through which the human race *must have* passed," not the actual events in the experiences of a particular people. In order to do this, Condorcet saw more clearly than most of his successors in the tradition that he had to create conceptually an entity that had undergone progress. He achieved a preliminary unity by the usual device of drawing a parallel between the development of the human mind and the individual mind—seeing the progress of each as subject to the same general laws. In laying out the concrete stages of progress, however, Condorcet constructed what he called "the hypothetical history of a single people" by choosing certain happenings from the histories of various peoples and comparing them and then combining them in a progressive order.

The actual stages formed in this way indicate what is involved in the method: (1) Hunting-and-fishing horde (appearance of the family and language); (2) Pastoral (beginning of private property); (3) Settled agriculture to appearance of alphabetical writing (appearance of government); (4) Greece; (5) Rome; (6) Early Middle Ages; (7) Late Middle Ages; (8) Invention of printing to Descartes. (9) Descartes to the revolution of 1789 (Newton in science; Locke and Condillac in human nature theory; Turgot and Rousseau in social theory). The first three stages are constructed by arranging selected contemporary societies (of a "savage" or "barbarous" status) in an order suggested by a priori ideas about human nature and how it develops. Then follows an ancient, medieval, and modern history of the human mind that is achieved by moving from one space to another in order to get the hypothetical history of an abstract people. The only suggestion of reality in the picture is Condorcet's undisguised effort to show that all of human history has been a prelude to the emergence of the French people as the supreme product to date of the progressive principle. Besides that, the sketch is only an arbitrary arrangement of cultural conditions presented as a fictitious history of a fictitious people. To call the arrangement arbitrary is not quite accurate, of course, for it is evident throughout that Condorcet enters upon his task with a finished conception of what the course of "human history" has been—and should have been.

Condorcet's strong optimism and his certainty about the future were accompanied by a clear recognition that progress had not, in fact, been smoooth or easy. What *must* have happened had not actually happened, just as Aristotle's realm of necessity by no means comprised the whole universe of happening. Condorcet thus observed that stagnation, fixity, and stability are often characteristic social states and that people are habitually opposed to changing their ways. The revolution in France had, indeed, been necessary just because of a persistent clinging to outworn institutions like the monarchy and the Church. Condorcet attributed this unprogressiveness in man to such factors as habit, tradition, a natural aversion to the new, indolence, and superstition. But Condorcet did not dwell on these matters, for his stated aim was to outline the natural or normal course of progress; persistent or retrogressive forces could then be identified as obstacles to progress and dealt with as such.

Again, as he set down the steps in the steady course of progress, Condorcet was quite aware that the actual historical process had been punctuated and affected by great events such as wars, migrations, and conquests, but he called this the "hazard of events" that confused his story from the fourth epoch on, and such events were not considered in formulating the picture of natural progress.

These apparent contradictions in Condorcet—an affirmation and denial of the inevitability of progress, an acceptance and rejection of historical events as the stuff of the progressive process—are quite common among even the more extreme theorists of progress, and this has bolstered a view that none of these theorists actually entertained the simplistic idea of progress identified, for example, by Bury. The question can become tiresome, but the point would seem to be that once the concept of a normal unfolding of potential in man or society or culture is abandoned in qualifications based on the observation of particular historical conditions and events, then it becomes necessary to account for progress (however defined) in terms of observed circumstances of time and place. And this the progress theorists did not do, because such a procedure ran entirely contrary to their conception of scientific method.[27]

While Turgot and Condorcet can be taken to epitomize the theory of progress in the French Enlightenment, it is difficult to uncover the equivalent figures in the German Enlightenment. It is hard, indeed, to attribute to the

German philosophers of history of this period anything like the idea of progress being discussed here. There is, to be sure, the concept of a "universal" history (although even that appears to come and go in the contradictory facets of Herder's rich vision); and there is, perhaps, an ultimately dominant assertion of the possibility of progress. If we attend only to Leibniz, the components of the seventeenth-century theory of progressive change remain clear: change is gradual, continuous, immanent, and universal, and the whole universe is always improving. But, as Frank E. Manuel[28] has made clear, German progressists were concerned with the question of *moral* improvement, and that preoccupation rendered the crude and facile construction of stages of scientific or material progress an irrelevant enterprise.

Thus, in Herder's *Outlines of a Philosophy of the History of Man* the entity that is developing or realizing itself in time is "humanity," a rather vaguely defined quality that took form only as a contrast to a present barbarism. In Herder's treatment not only is the subject of progress clouded in heavy religious overtones, but the locus and tempo of the process itself emerge with nothing like the simplicity and clarity of Condorcet's scheme. For in Herder universal history does not necessarily imply a unity in history. While humanity is the end, its manifestations in the historical cultures are represented by Herder as so distinctive and really incomparable that the progress theorist's favorite device of reconstructing universal history by an arrangement of cultural differences would appear to be ruled out. Rather, we get a picture of a great array of tribes and nations, each possessing what Spengler was to call a "culture soul," each working out the potential of its soul (if nothing interfered) in a cyclical process of rise and decline, where decline implies exhaustion instead of degeneration. Herder, on occasion, is firm in his belief that humanity will triumph; but that question seems hardly worth pursuing through the murky labyrinths of his writings. What is interesting to notice in Herder is the destructive results for the classical theory of progress that follow upon the adoption of a pluralistic view of history. His work becomes a shambles, hardly comprehensible.[29]

Kant does not present the same kind of difficulties, but his is not the usual eighteenth-century theory of progress. The trappings are there: the idea that universal natural laws are at work in human history as they are elsewhere; the belief that change is immanent, and that in the human scene this means that the species as a whole slowly and continually advances toward a full unfolding of its original potential implanted by God; even an elaboration of the notion that all this takes place because of antagonistic components at the very heart of the system. *The Idea of a Universal History from a Cosmopolitical Point of View* contains all this plus an agreeable acceptance of the belief that we can look forward to a time (though it is distant) of greater perfection in the arts and sciences, an increase in happiness, and even a better moral order. But it takes no especially careful reading of this, and of his essay "On the Saying: That a Thing May Be Right in Theory, but May Not Hold in Practice," to find that Kant was not trying to tell us what had happened in history, much less what was going to happen. It was not his aim (as it was with so many of the *philosophes)* to pursue the study of history by the method of natural science and so lay bare the iron law of progress. A Kepler or a Newton of historical scholarship might come along later and do this, Kant observed, but it was not his object "to supplant the empirical cultivation of history." That had been exactly Condorcet's object, as it was to be Comte's.

Kant is clear enough about his object: to construct a philosophy of history that presents a picture of what might possibly have gone on in the past and might possibly continue to go on in the future and what is morally acceptable to an active man with an innate sense of duty. What he was saying was, admittedly, assumption; and there was no point in verifying the assumption by reference to historical fact. Kant hoped for some beneficent side effects from such a philosophy, but he had nothing of the prophet's certainty, and he was very far from seeking to reveal the laws of history that men might grasp and use to control affairs for the enhancement of their wealth and happiness.

When we cross the Channel to examine Enlightenment theories of progress we leave behind many of these complications and enter an intellectual climate much more like that of the *philosophes*—the *philosophes* had, of course, helped to shape it—a climate in which a sociology founded upon the idea of progress would soon be welcomed more warmly than in its birthplace and certainly less critically than in Germany. If we look for example to the Scottish Enlightenment and the remarkable effort to shape a science of man and society, many facets of the progressist view stand out in sharper image, indeed, than in the French versions. At the same time, the Scots in many instances were equivocal on so many key ingredients of the idea that a rejection of the whole orientation seems to be implied.

Thus Frederick J. Teggart found in David Hume what amounts to an antithesis of the idea of progress—a denial of the naturalness of social or cultural change, a denial of its ubiquity in both time and place, and thus a denial of its immanence. Hume instead posited a general inertia or stability as characteristic of the human condition and saw this as subject to rather common gradual modifications and to infrequent changes consequent upon breaks or interruptions in established orders.[30] More recently, Stocking has shown that the ambiguities in Lord Kames's *Sketches of the History of Man* indicate not only inconsistency but a fundamental questioning of inevitable progress and a confrontation of conjectural history with real histories that revealed, on occasion, the superior savage and the decadent modern.[31]

The equivocalities of the Scots can be accounted for, in part at least, by their characteristically inductive and empirical approach to the problem of progress. For someone like Kames, the painfully obvious corruptions and putrefactions that seemed to accompany "civil" society could only with great difficulty be relegated to a category of the accidental or the impedimenta to progress. Yet, what is so obvious in this respect among the Scottish moral philosophers is by no means uncharacteristic of progress theorists generally. Condorcet's recognition of persistence and German concern with the problem of moral progress have been noted. And among the *philosophes* the reality of evil and the stubborn fact that peoples show little inclination to change their ways were not ignored. There is something of Rousseau in most theorists of progress. They were profoundly dissatisfied with their own societies, and they pointed to past evils even when they recognized the past as a necessary step to a better future. The analogy between a society and an organism has, since Plato posed as physician to the body politic, invariably been accompanied by the conviction that society is sick. In their biological metaphors progressists used both immaturity and disease to account for imperfection—either an imperfection awaiting perfection or disease standing as an obstacle to or aberration from the normal course of improvement. The enlightened in both France and Scotland were concerned with pointing to particular circumstances that impeded progress, but, like Aristotle, they had no *theory* of accidents, and they were inclined to see orderly change in the direction of fulfillment as an inherent natural principle.

The way in which Adam Ferguson met such questions and at the same time sharpened and gave substance to Turgot's outline can, with reservations, be taken as typical of the Scottish Enlightenment's conception of progress and method of depicting it. Ferguson certainly stands as a model for nineteenth-century sociologists and anthropologists in their study of change (as well as in so many other areas of their concern).[32]

In his *Essay on the History of Civil Society* Ferguson was plainly aware of exceptions to progress in human experience. A strong case could be made that he did not regard progress as the rule at all. He devoted a major portion of the work (part fifth) to the "decline of nations," and he noted that stagnation was common—most notably in India and China. But stagnation was accounted for largely by the influence of climate and "situation," and decline, he said, was caused by ". . . those revolutions of state that remove, or withhold, the objects of every ingenious study or liberal pursuit; that deprive the citizen of occasions to act as the member of a public; that crush his spirit; that debase his sentiments, and disqualify his mind for affairs."[33] Ferguson was typical of the Scots in his view that a preoccupation with commerce and decline of national spirit threatened his own civil society as it had so many others.

But decline, he argued, is not inevitable, and it does not occur "on account of any incurable distemper in the nature of mankind, but on account of their voluntary neglects and corruptions." On the contrary, human nature, like all "natural productions" is progressive both in its activities and in its powers. "Not only the individual advances from infancy to manhood, but the species itself from rudeness to civilisation."[34]

> [Man] would always be improving on his subject, and he carries this intention wherever he moves, through the streets of the populous city, or the wilds of the forest. . . . He is perpetually busied in reformations, and is continually wedded to his errors. . . . But he does not propose to make rapid and hasty transitions; his steps are progressive and slow. . . . It appears, perhaps, equally difficult to retard or to quicken his pace. . . . we mistake human nature, if we wish for a termination of labour, or a scene of repose.[35]

For Ferguson, then, there is a principle at work tending to produce advancement, and it was with the sketching of that tendency—the "natural history" of mankind, or of civil society—that he, as a moral philosopher, was concerned. That there are frightful diversions from the realization of the potential in human nature is true, but there is the history of civil society, and it is the object of the philosopher to discover it. That there are situations in which men are placed that impede the development of what is immanent in man is true, but "if we mean to pursue the history of civil society, our attention must be chiefly directed to such examples [of peoples in temperate climates] and we must here bid farewell to those regions of the earth, on which our species, by the effects of situation or climate, appear to be restrained in their national pursuits, or inferior in the powers of mind."[36]

How is the history to be constructed? Ferguson was explicit on the question of method to a degree equaled by few of his predecessors or successors. His point of departure was a firm rejection of the aims and procedures of traditional historians. While the Greek and Roman historians "understood human nature" and could display its features, they were, in Ferguson's judgment, ill succeeded by early European historians who, hampered by monkish tradition, paraded an arbitrary selection of facts, confused narration with true history, and, in their preoccupation with "events and the succession of princes," lost sight of the "active spirit of mankind" and those "characteristics of the understanding and the heart" that alone made history interesting and useful. Only Caesar and Tacitus were to be consulted about the early history of man, therefore, although contemporary society might be explored by more enlightened historical study.[37]

The natural historian, then, must look to human nature in order to discern the lines along which civil society comes to be. Ferguson was more careful in this endeavor than most of his contemporaries in either France or Britain, and the result was a rather sophisticated psychology. Introspection took a backseat to shrewd observations of his fellows, to whatever he could find in the now burgeoning descriptions of contemporary non-European peoples, and to the wisdom of those "sublime and intelligent" Greeks and Romans. He strenuously objected to speculations about a remote state of nature, specifically eschewed Rousseau's imaginary reconstruction in the *Discourse on the Origin of Inequality,* and determined to stay "within the reach of our own observation, and in the records of history."[38]

Ferguson's objective, as he put it, was to find out "what the mind of man could perform" and to look for that in "the history of mankind." He took his clue from Thucydides, who, "notwithstanding the prejudice of his country against the name of *Barbarian*, understood that it was in the customs of barbarous nations he was to study the more ancient manners of Greece." He continued:

> The Romans might have found an image of their own ancestors, in the representations they have given of ours; and if ever an Arab clan shall become a civilised nation, or any American tribe escape the poison which is administered by our traders of Europe, it may be from the relations of the present times, and the descriptions which are now given by travellers, that such a people, in after ages, may best collect the

accounts of their origin. It is in their present condition that we are to behold, as in a mirror, the features of our own progenitors; . . . If, in advanced years we would form a just notion of our progress from the cradle, we must have recourse to the nursery; and from the example of those who are still in the period of life we mean to describe, take our representation of past manners, that cannot, in any other way, be recalled.[39]

In addition to Caesar and Tacitus, Ferguson consulted such works as Charlevoix's *History of Canada*, Lafitau's *Moeurs des Sauvages [Customs of Savages]*, D'Arvieux's *History of the Wild Arabs*, and Abulgaze Bahadur Chin's *History of the Tartars*.

By these means Ferguson reconstructed the savage and barbarian stages that led to the formation of civil society. This last stage was represented basically by the European society known to him through history and recent observation. Again, he saw it as by no means perfect, and subject to all sorts of hazards, but it was, nevertheless, a product of a process of progressive change, a development from what had been in the past, and fundamentally, an expression of human nature in its latest manifestation. But it was not just European society; it was civil society, a condition, barring impediments, to which every people would come by the same process. The constant that made this possible, if not inevitable, was human nature. Ferguson was clear on the point: human nature was everywhere the same, and it always had been. The products of human nature changed by accumulation, and the powers of human nature increased, but all of this was incipient in every population, past and present, and in every babe born today and yesterday.[40]

In view of the controversy in recent years over the necessary implication of unilinear change in eighteenth- and nineteenth-century progressist or evolutionary theory, it is instructive to notice the way in which Ferguson dealt with this matter in the context of his own conception of social history. It was not a question of whether all peoples had progressed at all times; Ferguson, along with essentially all other progress theorists, knew, of course, that that had not been the case. But the uniformity of human nature dictated that where progress did occur, it always followed the same path, for social advance was a product of human nature manifesting itself in favorable circumstances. Still, did not nations borrow from or stimulate one another, and might not this account for their similar developmental paths? And if such were the case, would not the progressive sequence by complicated by whatever historical contacts various societies happened to have enjoyed? Could not certain societies have skipped stages by these means, and would this not have rendered progress a haphazard process consequent upon events rather than a smooth unfolding of potential in human nature? At this point Ferguson found a way to recognize what was later to be called diffusion or borrowing in culture growth and reconcile it with what was called independent invention. The key ideas was that, "If nations actually borrow from their neighbors, they probably borrow only what they are nearly in a condition to have invented themselves."[41] Thus the integrity of a hypothetical history of a hypothetical people was kept intact; the picture of social progress as slow, gradual, continuous, and uniform was maintained; the methodology of using the history of one people to document the history of another people remained justified; and above all, the unity of mankind and of progress was preserved. All this was an important and profoundly influential legacy to the nineteenth century.

V

In light of the background sketched so far, it should be evident that the positive theory of progress that Auguste Comte made the basis of his sociology was, at least in its essentials, only a masterful summation of lines of thought that extend far back in the history of Western speculation on the problem of order and change. It is especially useful, however, to look at Comte's version, not only because of its continuing influence in sociology and related disciplines, but because Comte, while he did not question the idea of progress, presented and used it in such an open, thorough, and systematic fashion that he exposed its assumptions and implications as few believers had before.[42]

It is through Comte's orientation to the traditional study of history that the substance of his theory of change can best be understood. Like his acknowledged mentors, Condorcet and Ferguson, Comte saw the work of ordinary historians as a literary endeavor resulting in the production of annals that pictured human experience as a scene of miracles and the doings of great men. The mischief in this "superficial philosophy" was that it created an impression that chance played a significant role in human affairs and thus impeded the "discovery of those laws which regulate the social development of the human race," the laws that show "by what necessary chain of successive transformations the human race, starting from a condition barely superior to that of a society of great apes, has been gradually led up to the present stage of European civilisation."[43]

Comte was asking an historical question, then, but it was not possible, he believed, to answer it by reference to historical events. The materials gathered by historians were relevant—they furnished a "tolerable equivalent for the preliminary collection"—but they had to be used "philosophically." Even Condorcet, who had seen that civilization was subject to laws of progress, had remained "within the circle of literary historians" by supposing that he could demarcate his epochs of advance by particular events.[44]

Historical study, then, if it was to be positive, must, according to Comte, be pursued in the abstract. This meant that Condorcet's artifice of creating a hypothetical history of a hypothetical people was to be used, and even within that framework attention could be confined to intellectual history inasmuch as the intellect had been the source and controller of progress. Reference to particular events was to be avoided or, at most, made for purposes of illustration or embellishment. Given this conception of his task, and on the basis of the "tolerable" data grubbed out by less gifted historians, Comte was able to proceed immediately to the formulation of his basic law of history—the advance of all knowledge through theological, metaphysical, and positive stages.[45]

What is interesting and instructive about Comte is that he was quite aware of some basic propositions that must be accepted before he could proceed in this manner, and he was unusually explicit about most of them. The division of the historical world into realms of chance and necessity was more or less taken for granted by this time; Comte did not give the matter the careful attention that Aristotle had. Nor did the fact of progress itself detain him, since "All men who possess a certain knowledge of the leading facts of history . . . will agree in this, that the cultivated portion of the human race, considered as a whole, has made uninterrupted progress in civilisation from the most remote periods of history to our own day."[46] The incidence of stagnation or retrogression in history did not bother Comte as it had Ferguson or Kames or Hume, for the fact that there had been progress despite human activity designed to impede it proved to Comte that a powerful progressive force must be at work in history.[47]

But Comte was open and didactic about the propositions underlying the comparative-historical method of the new science of sociology. If progress can be referred to the human race "as a whole," if the hypothetical people designated by Condorcet can be hypostatized, if we can construct a single social or culture series as a historical proposition, then it is necessary to assume that all peoples had the same history and passed through the same progressive stages. Comte clearly affirmed the point: ". . . the progress of society, depending as this does on the permanent nature of mankind, must be at all times essentially the same; the differences consisting simply in greater or less rapidity." It was, in fact, the "remarkable identity" in the development of different nations that testified to the force of a uniform principle of progress deriving from basic laws of human nature. That was why the customs of nineteenth-century savages were almost identical with those of ancient Greece and the feudalism of contemporary Malays closely resembled that of eleventh-century Europeans.[48]

If uniformity in evolution should lead us to expect cultural similarities, then what of the obvious global array of cultural differences presented at any given time? What Comte saw in the present was an absolute panoply of different cultures.

> . . . in the present condition of the human race, considered as a whole, all degrees of civilisation coexist on different points of the globe, from that of the New Zealand savages to that of the French and English.[49]

The point was, then, that differences represented degrees of development along a single line—as one might observe in a pasture differences among foals, one-year-olds, two-year-olds, and mature horses. Given a progressive rather than a cyclical interpretation of history, however, Comte had to attribute the temporal coexistence of differences in culture to accident. It is not in the *nature* of any culture to be different from any other culture.

Differences are not even to be understood in terms of climate, race, political situation or other external factors. Progress is determined; it cannot be reversed, stages cannot be skipped. The variations we see, then, must be explained by "*causes accidentelles ou passagéres*," factors which, Comte insisted, could affect only the speed of evolution and were exactly analogous to maladies in the individual organism.[50]

It was only after Comte had established, to his satisfaction, that social change is a product of forces internal to society and deriving from human nature; that change is therefore continuous, normal, and uniform in time and place; and that differences among peoples must therefore be explicable only as differences of degree of development consequent upon accidental intervention—only then could he suggest a "comparative method" for conceptually arranging an array of cultural differences in a single series that would portray the advance, progress, development, or evolution of civilization. It is important to notice that the empirical facts of cultural differences could not, in themselves, suggest such an operation. Comte seems not to have been aware of that.

But he did recognize that use of the comparative method required something more as prelude: it needed the guidance of a very general conception of what the course of human history had been. For Comte, the substantive components of the idea of progress served the purpose. He observed that the comparative method in itself—the method that the biologist used to arrange a static series of organisms in accordance with criteria of complexity—could produce only a coexistent cultural series. If the series was to be temporalized—made into a consecutive series—something had to be known about what had actually happened in time. For this purpose, Comte said, the historical method must be used, and it was this method that was to characterize and distinguish the new science of sociology.[51]

The historical method did not mean to Comte, as we have seen, what it meant to traditional historians. It involved a philosophical view of human experience that would produce a general picture of what the course of history had been. Comte had such a picture in mind from the start of his inquiries, and his venture in the intellectual history of Europe merely confirmed it. His intention to pursue the historical portion of his work further was never realized.[52] It is difficult to avoid the conclusion that Comte had simply inherited an idea of progress that provided both the criteria for his use of the comparative method and the theory of history that was to have been confirmed by the historical method. Comte's claim that the historical method substantiated the results of the comparative method—converted the coexistent cultural series into a consecutive series—is intellectual gimmickry. The assertion that "the connections established by the succession of epochs can be verified by a comparison of places"[53] is circular. The coexistent series was actually constructed on criteria provided by a theory of change or succession; that theory of change could not be used to confirm the coexistent series as a consecutive series.

Comte's procedure reveals clearly that the attempt to depict a process of cultural change by an arrangement of cultural types requires a prior theory of change. The significance of the work of progress theorists such as Comte lay not in the peculiar operation of reifying cultural items and conceptually manipulating them into ideal series. It lay rather in their uncritical acceptance of a theory of change that they inherited without examination. The question of whether "savages" represent an early stage of civilization is trivial compared to the question of whether social change is a normal, uniform, and continuous manifestation of forces resident in a social entity as such.

Throughout the nineteenth century questions were frequently raised about the mechanics and limitations of the comparative method but much less often about the developmentalist postulates underlying it. Despite his ranging sophistication, Herbert Spencer seems to have followed rather closely the Comtean developmentalist hypothesis, yet with a significant difference. If Comte's idea of progress had taken on a deterministic flavor and had lost the active and revolutionary tone of the Enlightenment vision, at least he still spoke in terms of concrete advances in knowledge and of a growing preponderance of altruism over egoism. For Spencer, if the conception of progress was to be converted into a scientific law, it had to be stripped of its happiness component and dissociated from mere measurements of growth in territory or population, accumulation of knowledge, greater satisfaction of human wants, or moral advance.[54]

The essential nature of progress "in itself" was discovered by Spencer to be a development of the heterogeneous out of the homogeneous, a process of differentiation. He first ran across this principle, not in relation to the study of human history—Spencer thought even less of history in the traditional sense than had Comte—but in the work of a German embryologist, von Baer. With a sensitivity to "levels of correspondence" in nature that would have pleased seventeenth-century philosophers, Spencer saw this process as "the history of all organisms whatever"; and society was, of course, an organism.

> . . . this law of organic process is the law of all progress. Whether it be in the development of the Earth, in the development of Life upon its surface, in the development of Society, of Government, of Manufactures, of Commerce, of Language, Literature, Science, Art, this same evolution of the simple into the complex, through successive differentiations, holds throughout. From the earliest traceable cosmical changes down to the latest results of civilization, we shall find that the transformation of the homogeneous into the heterogeneous, is that in which progress essentially consists.[55]

Given the universality and uniformity of change throughout all nature, including society, Spencer proceeded without question to the familiar observation that the stages of change in civilization "as a whole" could be documented by reference to existing savage and barbarous peoples, to extinct civilizations, and finally to contemporary Europe.[56] The entire movement is from the homogeneous to the heterogeneous, from the simple to the complex, from the undifferentiated in form and function to the differentiated.

Throughout his work on social or civilizational change Spencer did little more than enlarge on the details of a process that was in its fundamental aspects the same as that pictured by the *philosophes* or, indeed, by Aristotle. Only on occasion did he stop to notice the fact that the system did not actually explain change or account for social or cultural differences. After Darwin had made it clear that if we seek to envisage organic evolution as a whole we must recognize its divergent and redivergent character, Spencer noted that the same was true of social progress. This meant, he thought, that we must recognize the existence of social "types" or "species" or "genera" and that we cannot view different forms of society as different stages in the evolution of a single unity. The reasons for differences were still obscure to Spencer; he had no theory of differences. He noted simply that the environment differed from place to place and had its effect on social life, that the size of societies was often altered by annexation or loss of territory, and that racial mixtures introduced by conquest change the average character of the units of societies.[57]

Emile Durkheim agreed with Spencer on this point, observing that societies do not differ only in degree but also as to type or species. In his search for the "normal," therefore, he felt that there were distinct normalities not only for the different species but for different stages in the growth of a given species.[58]

Spencer and Durkheim did not carry this discussion to a theoretical conclusion, however. For Spencer, the appearance of differences occasioned by extrinsic influences did not in itself constitute a problem for investigation. Rather, these facts "obscured" the results of comparisons aimed at revealing the "normal" course of evolution, confused the picture, and made it difficult, if not impossible, to draw conclusions about special cases. General conclusions could be positively established, however, and Spencer thought that, happily, these were the most valuable.[59] In any event, there is no evidence that Spencer attempted any systematic delineation of divergent paths of evolution. When he discussed the future of domestic relations, for example, he noticed some "surviving inferior types" but focused attention deliberately on "types carrying further the evolution which civilized nations now show."[60] Repeatedly in his later writings he asserted the effect on social type of racial type, but this comes to nothing more than an expression of doubt that inferior human types will ever become civilized. Spencer's object was always to mark out *the* normal path of social progress. He wrote about the genesis of primitive ideas, not the geneses.[61] When he looked at domestic institutions, it was to sketch the course of their development, and he did so by juxtaposing marital and sexual customs of Bushmen, Chippewas, Eskimos, Aleuts, Arawaks, Veddahs, etc. His conclusion was that *the* genesis of the *the* family "fulfills the law of Evolution under its leading aspects."[62] When he classified societies as simple or compound aggregates, it was clear enough that the "first" were "simple" and the later were complex. There was no hesitation about populating his classes with contemporary primitives, primitives as they existed upon first contact with Europeans, ancient extinct civilizations, early historical stages of modern existing civilizations, and modern civilizations as they existed in the present. That cannot be done without assuming a unilinear evolutionary process, however "general" it might be conceived to be. The generalizations that emerged from the classification were statements about universal processes of change:

> The stages of compounding and re-compounding have to be passed through in succession. . . . In this order has social evolution gone on, and only in this order does it appear to be possible. Whatever imperfections and incongruities the above classification has, do not hide these general facts—that there are societies of these different grades of composition; that those of the same grade have general resemblances in their structures; and that they arise in the order shown.[63]

For Spencer, social and culture differences simply represented various stages of evolution; the data his associates gathered for him served to "illustrate social evolution under its various aspects."[64] If social evolution has been other than unilinear, certainly the other lines were not described to us by Herbert Spencer.

Durkheim approached the problem of cultural differences from a broader perspective by identifying comparable social units that could be viewed as lying somewhere between the unique historic societies that engaged the attention of traditional historians and the ideal singular humanity whose career the philospher of history endeavored to sketch.[65] It can hardly be said that he succeeded in this task, or even that he seriously undertook it. His classification of social types remained incomplete and was never filled in with actual peoples. Even in his discussion of the methodology involved it is apparent that Durkheim followed Spencer in viewing his types or species as steps in an evolutionary process of compounding. Thus, he identified the horde as the simplest society and marked it as "the seed from which all social species have developed."[66] Given that origin (Durkheim was not sure that it had ever existed), he proceeded to identify succeeding "simple polysegmental societies," "polysegmental societies simply compounded," and "polysegmental societies fully compounded." He represented these stages by examples drawn from savage, barbarous, and more advanced peoples taken out of temporal context. It is clear that Durkheim placed his social types—his different societies—on a "genealogical tree."[67] In his substantive work it is again evident that Durkheim's distinction of types of social solidarity was not simply an operation to demonstrate the variety of social life; organic solidarity succeeded mechanical solidarity in time, and it developed out of the earlier state. The mechanism by which this is brought about, a growing division of labor, was regarded by Durkheim as "a fact of a very general nature," applicable "to organisms as to societies." Societies conform to this law, "yielding to a movement that was born before them, and that similarly governs the entire world."[68] It would be difficult to find in all the progress literature a more impressive assertion of the universal operation of nature's laws. Again, in his work on religion, Durkheim was looking for the common or characteristic elements of religious life and for *the* genesis of the fundamental categories of thought; and he believed his search would be rewarded by looking at a single people.[69]

The procedure outlined by Auguste Comte for documenting progress was widely followed throughout the remainder of the nineteenth century. Cultural anthropologists, folklorists, and students of comparative institutions of all kinds undertook to trace the origin and development of the family, marriage, law, religion, art, magic, music, the division of labor, property, the state, poetry, morals, science, technology, and society itself.[70] This literature is not all of a piece, and the task of finding lines of development in culture history was attended by serious problems. The nagging question to which Tylor addressed himself directly—whether cultural similarities should be attributed to diffusion or to independent invention—was a persistent difficulty. The attempt to derive institutions and culture traits from universal psychic courses had its adherents and critics. The individual or collective origins of items such as poetry and property were debated. Clergymen joined slave traders in arguing that savagery was a product of degeneration, and evolutionists tried to restore the integrity of the developmental series through the use of survivals. Parallelism in culture development—the unilinearity of culture change—was attacked and defended by a variety of arguments, but with little attention to relevant historical evidence. The extent to which archaeological evidence could be used to buttress the image of an evolutionary series was a special concern. The old question of whether change in a single object of society or culture might be a clue to change in general was raised again and again. And there was, of course, continued discussion of the proper criteria to be used in converting coexisting cultural differences into a consecutive or time series.

A major disagreement among progress theorists of the late nineteenth and early twentieth centuries that has attracted special attention was over the question of the inevitability of progress and the need for or appropriateness of human participation in the process. Those who merely reiterated eighteenth-century laissez-faire doctrine were now identified as "social Darwinists."[71] An elaborate case for active intervention in progress was made by the American sociologist Lester F. Ward, who argued that evolution became "telic" at the level of human society and involved conscious proposing and choosing by man.[72]

Beneath these superficial rumblings in the progressist camp, however, a strong persistence of the basic idea is evident.[73] Change is accepted as natural, to be expected, a characteristic of the social or cultural as such. Change is depicted as slow and gradual and continuous. In all the series of social or cultural forms constructed the growthlike quality of the process is emphasized. While tempo can vary, succession is fixed. The process is represented as directional; there is an end toward which it is drawn. And, despite recognition within the progressist school of diffusion or borrowing, the immanent quality of change is retained. Societies or cultures and their parts are viewed as entities with growth potential. The need for finding origins (much of the developmentalist literature never got beyond the origin stage) is dictated by the judgment that the essence to be realized in time resides in the seed. There is a designation, a hypostatization, of things—society, culture, law, property, and so on—that are regarded as having had a history that is to be comprehended in terms of this developmental process. Finally, the opinion is usually, but by no means always, expressed that the progress or development or evolution depicted in this way involves a betterment of the human condition. But even with Spencer it was important, as we have noted, to dissociate progress from considerations of happiness or interest; and as the quest for an objective science of man gathered strength, the beckoning vision of the good society becomes less and less a part of the modern idea of progress.

VI

The problem of cultural differences, the Marxist theory of progress, and the role of Darwin in the history of the idea of progress are topics deserving special consideration, however brief that must be in the present context.

A

It has been noted that Europeans, when confronted with a world populated by radically different societies carrying disturbingly different cultures, characteristically denied the basic reality of those differences and interpreted them as representations of stages in the development of society or culture as such. The Cartesian dictum on the uniform operation of nature's laws suggested not only the slow and gradual quality of change, but also directed inquiry to a search for universals—the essential nature of religion or music or morals. Undeniable variations among these entities were then compared for the purpose of arranging them in a presumed time series leading to the high point represented by the European variety. The serviceability of this world view to a people interested in establishing its own superiority and in justifying its use of the rest of the world is clear enough. Looking at the idea as an analytic tool, however, it should be noticed that it makes comparison a procedure for homogenizing the world. An explanation of differences is rendered impossible, and they must be treated as incidental products of special, fortuitous, or accidental conditions and events. Seeing cultural differences as alternative ways of life consequent upon concretely different historical experience is precluded, and, indeed, the attempt to do so is then viewed as a surrender to historical empiricism and an abandonment of the social-scientific enterprise.

This function of the idea of progress is cast in relief when we recall that Comte's version of the comparative method is quite different from other uses of comparison. Thucydides' comparison of barbarians and Athenians for the purpose of documenting early stages in an Athenian history assumed to be a model of "the national growth" stands in sharp contrast to Herodotus' patient and laborious attention to specific events in the histories of peoples with a view to explaining differing customs among them.[74] More to the immediate point, at the same time that Comte's successors were scouring the world for exotic items torn out of context to recover the origin and development of cultural abstractions, other students of comparative law and comparative religion were proceeding along distinct lines of inquiry. Aware of the large body of assumption that underlay developmentalist schemes and of the traps in the "comparative method" that Boas pointed out,[75] Stanley Arthur Cook felt obliged to remain close to his rich body of historical data on religions covering a period of four thousand years. When he came to test current theories on the evolution of religion, theories that depended heavily on a doctrine of survivals, he found that the processes they described bore little resemblance to what he had learned from a comparison of actual histories.[76] Frederic William Maitland, the jurist, saw as clearly as anybody in his time that developmentalism rested on a biological analogy that led to a search for the "normal." When the sequence of stages constructed with that end in view turned out to be contradicted by historical evidence at hand, developmentalists, he noted, explained the discrepancy as an incidence of the "morbid" or "abnormal." Maitland preferred to rely on the documentary evidence available to him, but this did not keep him from making comparisons. The comparisons, however, were of histories, not of types, and the object was to shed light on what to look for in any particular history as well as to detect what might be common to histories when compared.[77] "History," he remarked, "involves comparison."[78]

The case of Henry Sumner Maine is particularly revealing in this regard. Although Maine sometimes wrote in terms of broad generalities and seemed clearly to be reconstructing historical processes by reference to occurrences in widely separated places and times, it should not be forgotten that he was dealing always with a group of peoples whose histories were actually commingled and, as a group, distinct from the histories of other peoples. To Maine, an arrangement of institutional types drawn from the whole storehouse of history and ethnography was an interesting intellectual exercise, but the results were never to be confused with actual history; he doubted that they had any use at all. For Maine, as for Max Weber later, comparison primarily served the purpose of illuminating a particular situation or historical individual by drawing attention to the *differences* that it exhibited among a cohort of *comparable* cases. At the same time, in Maine's case, the similarities could be revealed that made comparison possible in the first place.[79]

Scholars such as these are distinguished from progress theorists by a rejection of the beliefs that change is naturally ubiquitous, that it is uniform and immanent, and that historical processes should be sought in the life courses of social or cultural universals.

B

It is difficult to place the work of Karl Marx in the history of the idea of progress. Because Marx gave us a vision, if not a prophecy, of a better society, even though the vision is not detailed, it is easy to see in Marxism, as Ginsberg has,[80] a modern embodiment of the belief in progress. The value question is accepted, and the call to action is as clear as Lester Ward's. Although there is evidence that Marx would have nothing to do with such a bland and bourgeois notion, his concern and hope for what he openly regarded as a likely improvement in the human situation places him in at least a broadly defined group of believers in progress as betterment.

When it comes to the idea of progress as the complex of ideas about the nature and course of change that we have been discussing here, the inclusion of Marx in the developmentalist fold is another matter. Finding a pigeonhole for Karl Marx, however, is not important. His equivocality on the point can better be examined with a view to fixing the distinguishing features of the idea of progress and their consequences for historical study.

For all his startling originality, Marx was not, of course, unaffected by the intellectual climate of his day. Given the pervasiveness of the idea of progress, it would be surprising if we did not find traces of evolutionism in his writings. They are not hard to find.

First, Marx and Engels were obviously interest in describing historical stages. In *The German Ideology* they discerned stages in the development of forms of ownership—tribal, ancient, feudal, and capitalist. Asiatic, ancient, feudal, and modern modes of production were delineated by Marx in the *Critique of Political Economy*, and the subject was pursued in greater detail in *Pre-Capitalist Economic Formations*. It is by no means clear from these discussions what the universe of discourse is—to what entity these stages refer—but the suggestion is strong that ownership and production were regarded as universal categories that had *a* history that could be constructed by an arrangement of forms chosen from various times and places. This apparent hewing to developmentalist lines of historical reconstruction is reenforced by Marx's and Engels's enthusiastic reception of Lewis Henry Morgan's evolutionary classic, *Ancient Society*, and Engels's essential duplication of that work in his *Origin of the Family, Private Property and the State*.[81] To note that Marx did not believe that every society necessarily passed through each of the specified stages of development is only, of course, to identify a standard evolutionist position.

Second, Marx on occasion used the traditional language of progressists in describing historical process. Society was treated as a whole: "The history of *all* hitherto existing society is the history of class struggles."[82] Bourgeois society was repeatedly pictured as only the "most highly developed and most highly differentiated" form, so that it can be used as a key to "all the past forms of society" in much the same way that "the anatomy of the human being is a key to the anatomy of the ape." It followed for Marx, then, as it did for Comte, that if he attended only to the "more developed" country, the one in which the "natural laws" of capitalist production had operated typically, normally, and free from disturbance—that is, if he looked only to England—he would discover "tendencies working with iron necessity toward inevitable results" and show to "less developed" countries their future as it was mirrored in the "more developed."[83]

All of this is sound evolutionist doctrine. One can visualize Turgot and Condorcet and Ferguson nodding with approval.

However, as Bober and others have pointed out, this might be rhetoric, and Marx certainly took occasion later to qualify it. He cautioned against generalizing his account of the rise of capitalism in Western Europe into "a historico-philosophical theory of the general path imposed by fate on all peoples regardless of their historical circumstances," and said that Russia, for example, might be excluded from a picture that he meant to draw in broad sketches for England and Western Europe only.[84] If the first volume of *Capital* and Marx's more limited studies of other European countries are taken in that sense, their historical object can be likened more to Henry Sumner Maine's purpose in seeking similarities and differences among a commingled set of histories. That interpretation, of course, demands an unusual limitation of Marx's theory of history and abstention from tortuous efforts to apply it to situations unknown to or unanticipated by him. The theoretical and, as Marx might have observed, the practical consequences of the limitation are considerable.

C

Confusion of the idea of social progress, development, or evolution with the theory of organic evolution has wrought great confusion in the history of social theory, and the consequences have never been in stronger evidence than today.

It should be apparent from the kind of historical evidence considered here that the conception of a long, gradual process of social and cultural change considered as differentiation, a movement through defined stages from the simple to the complex, has marked Western social thought throughout and dominated the great eighteenth-century program to establish a science of man and society. To suggest that it was Charles Darwin and his concept of natural selection that were responsible for the assumption of a historical perspective in the humanistic disciplines in the second half of the nineteenth century is to ignore the long tradition of evolutionist thought in social theory which preceded adoption of such a point of view in biology. It must be recalled not only that cultural developmentalists such as Tylor and McLennan, though quite aware of Darwin's work, pointed to the simple fact that they were engaged in a different sort of study, but that the tradition in which they worked had a history independent of the line of thought culminating in Darwinisn. Auguste Comte insisted on the fixity of species, but he saw social forms as products of continual flux. Herbert Spencer, two years before the publication of *The Origin of Species,* had serious doubts that there had been a movement in time from simpler, homogeneous plants and animals to the production of complex, heterogeneous organisms. He had no doubts, however, that society had evolved in that way. Aristotle had taken a basically similar view of the matter. If we look only at that aspect of Darwin's work that involved a temporal or historical approach to the data at hand; that accepted change as in the nature of things; and that envisaged change as slow, gradual, and continuous—free of leaps and of divine intervention—it is difficult to avoid the judgment that in these respects Darwin owed much more to the humanists who had gone before him than he left to those who followed. And it takes no very careful perusal of *The Descent of Man* to see how heavily Darwin depended on the anthropologists of his day.[85]

The question of priority is not important, however. What should be noted is the unfortunate misinterpretations of both Darwin and the social evolutionists that result from attempts to conjoin the two, and the often confused and abortive efforts that are then made to provide by this union a basis for biosociology or sociobiology. The idea of progress and its modern expression in social evolutionism require for implementation, as we have seen, the conceptual establishment of an entity that is progressing or evolving. Assertions by Spencer and Durkheim about divergence and redivergence notwithstanding, such an idea is incompatible with the progressist formula. A "whole" must be maintained.[86] That is what is entirely lacking in the Darwinian picture. Darwin, occasional rhetoric apart, was not concerned with the evolution of life or of the organic, or even of a thing called species. Darwin observed that variations were present among individuals in a population of a given kind of organism; that, in conditions where survival is difficult, individuals with certain variations leave more progeny; and that, if such variations are heritable, change in the character of the population will ensue. What the concrete results of these happenings had been over the long course of time could not, of course, be predicted by the theory of evolution, and any attempt to put such a picture together by an arrangement of living and fossil forms from stratigraphic evidence was confronted with the enormous complications introduced by the phenomena of divergence and redivergence. Such an arrangement was not of much interest to Darwin and his successors, however. It was not a central problem for them in the sense that it was for the social evolutionists.

When the actual procedures of the latter are recalled, it should become evident that they were concerned with a process that they regarded as strictly analogous to the growth of an individual organism, not the history of kinds or populations of organisms. The simple hylozoism of the Greeks remained substantially unchanged in the more elaborate forms taken in the eighteenth and nineteenth centuries by the analogy between the growth of an individual man and the progress or development of the human race. The cruder forms of the analogy were elaborated only in degree by sophisticated presentations of an "ontogeny-recapitulates-phylogeny" hypothesis. When, therefore, efforts were made after Darwin to graft ideas of organic evolution onto existing ideas of social or cultural evolution, the results were sometimes what biologists call systems of autogenesis, orthogenesis, or, perhaps more to the point, preformism.[87] That, in effect, left the traditional idea of social progress intact. It is probably correct to say, however, that the reaction of social evolutionists to Darwin (after the early candid disclaimer of relationship) has more often been on the level of a superficial use, or abuse, of terminology. Thus, variation is seen as invention, selection (a loaded word that Darwin came to regret) is taken at its face value of choices being made, struggle and survival blend nicely with old patterns of laissez-faire philosophy, and fitness is applied to any current conception of requisites met by the progressive or modern society.[88]

There can be little doubt that Darwin's immense success gave credence to social evolutionism and encouraged its pursuit. The support, however, was actually on the surface level of language, where it was misleading, or at the very general level of endorsing a time-ordered approach to nature, where it was superfluous. Darwinian organic evolutionism simply dealt with a different kind of problem in a radically different way; effective communication between organic and social evolutionists was precluded.

This is not to say, of course, that biological and sociological inquiries must go their separate ways in the study of social change or in other studies concerning human populations. Social behavior, its evolution, and the interconnectedness of organic and cultural changes are topics that have more recently attracted the attention of both biologists and social scientists, with interesting results. That is another matter, however, and not on the level of analogy.

VII

Although it was a dominant guiding perspective for sociology and social science generally in the nineteenth century, the idea of progress or evolution did not, as I have noted, escape challenge. Accounting for cultural differences has always been a difficult problem for evolutionists. When racial explanations were offered in the first half of the nineteenth century, they were found wanting by scholars like Maine and Theodor Waitz[89] who, under the circumstances, were compelled to deal directly with the question. The kind of answer they presented, couched as it was in terms of certain events in the histories of peoples, lacked the theoretical neatness of evolutionist doctrine, and its appeal was not widespread.

From other quarters,[90] largely within the ranks of anthropology, some of the assumptions underlying the use of the comparative method were challenged. Difficulties associated with the conversion of coexistent series of culture items into consecutive series in the absence of historical date were pointed out—as they had been earlier by Comte. Evidence was gathered that denied the uniformity of social and cultural processes through time and space. There was a growing self-consciousness about the ethnocentric character of the European developmentalist scheme. The reaction, led by Boas, was a return to a diffusionist outlook in an attempt to account for cultural similarities or to reconstruct history by the use of similarities attributable to contact and borrowing. Here the results for historical reconstruction were tenuous, and while the study of diffusion in itself seemed to stand as a substitute for the study of independent invention, it did not provide an alternate theory of change incompatible with evolutionism.[91]

As a result of this kind of criticism, the classic form of nineteenth-century evolutionism was in serious trouble in the nineties, and by the 1930s had been pronounced dead. (The belief in progress as improvement had suffered a similar fate, but under different circumstances.) It was not, however, driven from the field by another theory of social or cultural change. It is more accurate to say that the apparent bankruptcy of evolutionism discouraged construction of such a grandiose theory of change and that further theoretical work was concentrated around a related theme in the tradition of Western social thought: functionalism.[92]

Although it has undergone considerable refinement in the twentieth century, functionalism is not a recent product.[93] Above all, it is a mistake to regard it as a reaction against or vanquisher of a progressist or evolutionist view. It would be difficult to find a classic exposition of social evolutionism that is not accompanied by a strong and strikingly "modern" functional analysis. Certainly the writings of Ferguson, Comte, and Spencer dealt as much with the structural and functional relationships of social and cultural items as they did with sequential relationships. The reason seems clear enough: if change is a product of forces within society— i.e., if change is *immanent*—then the lines and direction of change are to be discerned in the nature of society itself. This was precisely Aristotle's strategy in reaching a picture of how the state has come to be in time; he had first to discover what the function of the state is. So among modern functionalists, Malinowski argued that before we can understand how cultural phenomena have come to be, we must know the "nature" of culture. It was clear to Radcliffe-Brown that "we cannot successfully embark on the study of how culture changes until we have made at least some progress in determining what culture really is and how it works." Or, as Talcott Parsons put it later, for construction of a sound theory of social change, "it is necessary to know what it is that changes."[94]

If there has been any conflict between evolutionism and functionalism, then, it would appear to consist of functionalist-evolutionists in recent years telling earlier evolutionist-functionalists that they had not carried out the functional portion of their work with sufficient care. The inference seems to be that when this deficiency has been corrected, we can return to the difficult problem of social evolution. The return seems to be taking place today.

The "revival" of evolutionism is marked by a rather close adherence to the nineteenth-century format. In many distinguished cases there has been no pretense of reviving, or of purifying, but simply a faithful continuation of an honored traditon. V. Gordon Childe, Robert MacIver, and Leslie A. White and his school have self-consciously followed the lead of Herbert Spencer or Lewis Henry Morgan and have denied any "neo" quality to their evolutionary schemes.[95]

Where the restoration of evolutionism starts from a structural-functionalist position, there is an impressive reiteration of the central tenets of conventional developmentalism.[96] The normality and ubiquity of change are reasserted now in a context of denial that functionalism had ever impeded the study of change. The immanent or endogenous source of social change is announced as a principle discovered in the preparatory work of structural-functional analysis. Differention in form and function and movement from the simple to the complex are re-presented as the fundamental processes of change. Gradualness and continuity of change are avowed as principles and demonstrated in social or cultural series constructed. The evolutionary process described is the process that produced Western European or "modern" society and culture. Other societies, although many of them exist in the present, are designated as "premodern." (Occasional references to "postmodern" societies would have intrigued Oswald Spengler.) Development is spoken of as a uniform process, and societies that have had a different experience are described as *under*developed. The requisites, or, in the Aristotelian sense, *necessary* features of society are arranged in a series taken to represent the coming-to-be of society through time; the process of social evolution is thus considered as a uniform unfolding or realization of the nature of society.[97] The analogy between society and an organism is now presented in the intricate language of microbiology, and new levels of correspondence in nature are revealed.

The emergence of this modern idea of progress or evolution from functionalism could hold our promise for a reformation in theory of social and cultural processes. In their concern with the problem of social order, structural-functionalists have called attention to and have tried to account for the historical realities of persistence or stability in human societies. This represents a clear departure from the customary evolutionist explanation of "stagnation" in terms of the accidental or abnormal. More important, it would appear to press hard for an explanation of change, an accounting for change instead of the traditional assertion of its naturalness and omnipresence. If stabilizing and boundary-maintaining processes operate so forcefully in societies, then breaks in the cake of custom that Bagehot spoke of must be consequent only on the occurrence of exceptional and distinct patterns of events. Efforts to locate the sources of change within society, in inherent strains or tensions, for example, can end only with the old picture of continuous and uniform change that leaves social and cultural differences unexplained. What is *characteristic* of societies and cultures cannot explain the erratic incidence of changes consequent upon kinds of events. Escape from the uniformitarianism of the idea of progress is prerequisite to an accounting for change and difference.

NOTES

1. See, for example, Morris Ginsberg, *The Idea of Progress: A Revaluation* (London: Methuen, 1953) pp. 41–42; Robert M. MacIver and Charles H. Page, *Society: An Introductory Analysis* (New York: Rinehart, 1949) pp. 521–22.

2. J. B. Bury, *The Idea of Progress: An Inquiry into Its Origin and Growth* (London: Macmillan, 1928) p. 2.

3. Robert Bierstedt, *Power and Progress: Essays on Sociological Theory* (New York: McGraw-Hill, 1974) pp. 284, 294.

4. Frederick J. Teggart, *Theory and Processes of History* (Berkeley and Los Angeles: University of California Press, 1941) p. 219.

5. For an appreciation of the wide-ranging forms that the modern idea of progress has assumed, see W. Warren Wager, *Good Tidings: The Belief in Progress from Darwin to Marcuse* (Bloomington: Indiana University Press, 1972) pp. 3–10 et passim.

6. Bury, *The Idea of Progress*, pp. 1–36. Other basic histories and analyses of the idea of progress include Jules Delvaille, *Essai sur l'histoire de l'idée de progrés jusqu'à la fin de xviiie siécle* (Paris: F. Alcan, 1910); R. V. Sampson, *Progress in the Age of Reason* (Cambridge: Harvard University Press, 1956); Frank E. Manuel, *The Prophets of Paris* (Cambridge: Harvard University Press, 1962) and *Shapes of Philosophical History* (Stanford: Stanford University Press, 1965); Sidney Pollard, *The Idea of Progress: History and Society* (London: C. A. Watts, 1968); Carl L. Becker, *The Heavenly City of the Eighteenth-Century Philosophers* (New Haven: Yale University Press, 1932). Useful sourcebooks have been compiled by Frederick J. Teggart, *The Idea of Progress: A Collection of Readings*, rev. ed., with an introduction by George H. Hildebrand (Berkeley and Los Angeles: University of California Press, 1949) and A. O. Lovejoy and George Boas, *Primitivism and Related Ideas in Antiquity* (Baltimore: Johns Hopkins Press, 1935).

7. For a thorough exploration of this question, see Ludwig Edelstein, *The Idea of Progress in Classical Antiquity* (Baltimore: Johns Hopkins Press, 1967). Manuel, in *Shapes of Philosophical History*, pp. 68–69, has, quite appropriately, observed that "The origins of the idea of progress have often been pushed too far back in time, usually on the basis of a few engaging images pulled out of context." But the reference here is properly to the idea of progress as improvement rather than to the basic theory of change that it contains.

8. On the relation between the idea of Providence and the idea of progress, see John Baillie, *The Belief in Progress* (London: Oxford University Press, 1950); Christopher Dawson, *Progress and Religion* (London: Sheed & Ward, 1929); Ernest Lee Tuveson, *Millennium and Utopia* (Berkeley and Los Angeles: University of California Press, 1949); Karl Löwith, *Meaning in History* (Chicago: University of Chicago Press, 1949); Reinhold Niebuhr, *Faith and History* (New York: Charles Scribner & Son, 1949).

9. Aristotle, *Physics*, trans. by R. P. Hardie and L. K. Gaye, in *The Basic Works of Aristotle*, ed. by Richard McKeon (New York: Random House, 1941) book II, chaps. 1–3, 4, 8. See also *Metaphysics*, trans. by W. D. Ross, ibid., book I, chap. 3; book V, chap. 2; book VIII, chap. 4; book XI, chap. 8.

10. Ibid., *Politics*, trans. by Benjamin Jowett, book I, chap. 2.

11. Ibid., and book II, chap. 8.

12. Thucydides, *The Peloponnesian War*, trans. by Benjamin Jowett, in *The Greek Historians*, ed. by Francis R. B. Godolphin (New York: Random House, 1942) book I, chaps. 1–6.

13. St. Augustine, *The City of God*, trans. by John Healey (Edinburgh: J. Crant, 1909) book X, p. 14.

14. Something like the Quarrel had gone on in Italy in the sixteenth century. See Warren D. Allen, *Philosophy of Music History* (New York: American Book Co., 1939).

15. For Descartes's argument re the uniformity of nature's laws, see his *Discourse on Method*, trans. by John Veitch (New York: J. M. Dent & Sons, 1934) pp. 33–36.

16. This background to the Quarrel and citation of the relevant literature is covered in Bury, *The Idea of Progress*, chaps. 1–3. On the Quarrel itself see, in addition to Bury, H. Rigault, *Histoire de la querelle des anciens et de modernes* (Paris, L. Hachette, 1856); R. F. Jones, *Ancients and Moderns* (St. Louis: Washington University Press, 1936).

17. Bury, in *The Idea of Progress*, p. 78, notes Comte's attention to the implications of the quarrel.

18. Excerpt in Teggart, *The Idea of Progress*, pp. 176–87.

19. Bernard Fontenelle, *Oeuvres*, nouvelle ed. (Amsterdam: François Changuion, 1764) vol. IX, pp. 246–54.

20. Gottfried Leibniz, *The Monadology, and Other Philosophical Writings*, trans. by Robert Latta (Oxford: Clarendon Press, 1898) p. 44, note 1; as cited by Teggart, *Theory and Processes of History*, p. 91.

21. Excerpt in Teggart, *The Idea of Progress*, pp. 177–78, 187.

22. See Bury, *The Idea of Progress*, chap. VI, for a summation of Saint-Pierre's voluminous writings.

23. I have reviewed the eighteenth-century problem of cultural differences and the fascinating literature dealing with it in *The Acceptance of Histories* (Berkeley and Los Angeles: University of California Press, 1956), pp. 67–75. For a more detailed examination of the question, and particularly of efforts to reach racial explanations of cultural differences, see George W. Stocking, Jr., *Race, Culture, and Evolution* (New York: Free Press, 1968).

24. Becker, *The Heavenly City of the Eighteenth-Century Philosophers*, chap. III.

25. See "Tableau philosophique des progrès successifs de l'esprit humain," "Plan d'un ouvrage sur la géographie politique," and "Plan de deux discours sur l'histoire universelle," in *Oeuvres de Turgot et documents le concernant*, Gustave Schelle, ed. (Paris: F. Alcan, 1913) vol. I.

26. Condorcet, *Esquisse d'un tableau historique des progrés de l'esprit humain*, in his *Oeuvres complètes* (Paris: Henrichs, 1804) vol. VIII.

27. Becker, in *The Heavenly City of Eighteenth-Century Philosophers*, pp. 66–60, 87, saw the *philosophes'* distinction between the natural and unnatural as part of their solution to the problem of evil and their search for the normal as an effort to distinguish what is right from what is. He also noted the idea of obstacles in this connection, pp. 110, 134–35. It seems clear, however, that Condorcet, like Aristotle, was also concerned with separating the normal or generalizable from the exceptional or unusual in order to arrive at a "true" picture of what had really happened in human history. That is what the ordinary historian, focusing on trivia of "times when and places where," could not offer him.

28. In what follows on the German Enlightenment I depend heavily on Professor Manuel's *Shapes of Philosophical History* for guidance.

29. I do not mean to say that Herder's writing is unclear only because his theme is unfamiliar to us. He assumed contradictory—or at least irreconcilable—positions as he wrote his way through his problems. Revealing selections from Herder are presented in Teggart, *The Idea of Progress*, pp. 308–20.

30. Teggart, *Theory and Processes of History*, pp. 180–83. Teggart attributes a similar perspective to Turgot, ibid., pp. 183–85.

31. George W. Stocking, "Scotland as the Model of Mankind: Lord Kames' Philosophical View of Civilization," in Timothy Thoresen, ed., *Toward a Science of Man* (The Hague: Mouton, 1975) pp. 65–89.

32. The classic study of this quest for a science of man is Gladys Bryson's *Man and Society: The Scottish Inquiry of the Eighteenth Century* (Princeton: Princeton University Press, 1945). On Ferguson in particular see William C. Lehman, *Adam Ferguson and the Beginnings of Modern Sociology* (New York: Columbia University Press, 1930).

33. Adam Ferguson, *An Essay on the History of Civil Society*, 5th ed. (London: Printed for T. Cadell, 1782) p. 384.

34. Ibid., pp. 403, 1. See, generally, part fifth, sections III–V.

35. Ibid., pp. 11–12.

36. Ibid., p. 219.

37. Ibid., pp. 143–44.

38. Ibid., pp. 3, 8–9.

39. Ibid., pp. 146–47.

40. "The seeds of every form are lodged in human nature; they spring up and ripen with the season." Ibid., p. 223.

41. Ibid., pp. 303–06. Notice that it would be difficult to test this proposition.

42. It is after Comte's exposition and use of the idea of progress as both a philosophy of history and the basis of sociological method that penetrating critiques of progressist, developmentalist, and evolutionary schemes make their appearance in European scholarship. See, for example, George Cornewall Lewis, *A Treatise on the Methods of Observation and Reasoning in Politics*, 2 vols. (London: J. W. Parker and Son, 1852) and the reactions of historians such as Goldwin Smith, *Lectures on the Study of History* (Toronto: Adam, Stevenson & Co., 1873) and Charles Kingsley, *The Limits of Exact Science as Applied to History* (London: Macmillan, 1860).

43. Auguste Comte, "Plan of the Scientific Operations Necessary for Reorganizing Society,"

and "Philosophical Considerations on the Sciences and Savants," reprinted in *System of Positive Polity,* trans., by John H. Bridges et al. (London: Longmans, Green and Co., 1875–77) vol. IV, pp. 557–59, 587–88, 599. Much of the basis for Comte's later work is laid in these early (1822, 1824) essays.

44. Ibid., pp. 570–72.

45. Auguste Comte, *Cours de Philosophie Positive,* 4th ed. (Paris: Ballière et fils, 1877) vol. IV, pp. 328, 458–59; vol. V, pp. 6–7, 12–17, 570. The law of the three stages is presented in essential outline in Comte's 1822 essay, "Plan of the Scientific Operations . . . ," pp. 547–49.

46. Ibid., p. 555.

47. Ibid., p. 556. This intellectual *tour de force* highlights a historical determinism in Comte that Gertrud Lenzer, ed., *Auguste Comte and Positivism* (New York: Harper & Row, 1975) "Introduction," has documented persuasively. Ginsberg, *The Idea of Progress,* pp. 24 ff., sees Comte differently and is less sure of Marx's escape from determinism. Comte himself argued that although progress is inevitable it proceeds by rather violent perturbations around a mean line, and that these can be reduced by acting intelligently on the knowledge of what the line is. Comte, "Plan of the Scientific Operations . . . ," pp. 560–61.

48. Comte, "Plan of the Scientific Operations," pp. 537, 556–57. That such similarities might result from contact or diffusion occurred to Comte, of course, but he accepted Ferguson's resolution of the problem. Comte, *Cours de Philosophie Positive,* vol. IV, p. 289.

49. Comte, "Plan of the Scientific Operations . . . ," p. 585.

50. Comte, *Cours de Philosophie Positive,* vol. IV, 284–85; 309, vol. V, pp. 6–7.

51. Ibid., vol. IV, pp. 321–24, 135–36.

52. Comte had intended to use his *System of Positive Polity* to present historical data in support of the broad generalizations offered earlier in the *Cours de Philosophie Positive.* He decided, instead, to let the latter rest on his "authority" and to leave "verification . . . to the public." Comte, *System of Positive Polity,* vol. III, p. xi.

53. Comte, "Plan of the Scientific Operations . . . ," p. 585.

54. Herbert Spencer, "Progress, Its Law and Cause," in his *Essays: Scientific, Political, and Speculative,* (New York; D. Appleton and Co., 1899–1904) vol. I, pp. 8–9.

55. Ibid., p. 10. Note Spencer's easy use in the same paragraph of "progress," "development," and "evolution" to designate the same process. For his insistence on society's organic quality and his refusal to see this as a matter of metaphor, see Spencer, *The Study of Sociology* (New York: D. Appleton and Co., 1874), p. 330.

56. Spencer, "Progress, Its Law and Cause," pp. 19–35. The cause of progress is depicted in a similarly abstract fashion: it results from the fact that every cause produces more than one effect. Ibid., pp. 37–38.

57. Spencer, *The Study of Sociology,* pp. 329; *Principles of Sociology* (New York: D. Appleton and Co., 1901–07) vol. II, pp. 242–43; vol. III, p. 331. Spencer also suggested that retrogression had possibly been as frequent as progression. But he makes this observation in a context of concern about the "lowest types" now known to us being truly representative of "primitive" man. Spencer, Principles of Sociology, vol. I, p. 95.

58. Emile Durkheim, *The Division of Labor in Society,* trans. by George Simpson (New York: The Free Press, 1964) pp. 71, 433, 435; *Rules of Sociological Method,* 8th ed., trans. by Sarah A. Solovay and John H. Mueller (Glencoe, III.: The Free Press, 1938) pp. 56, 64, 77, chap. IV.

59. Spencer, *Principles of Sociology,* vol. II, p. 243.

60. Ibid., vol. I, p. 764.

61. Ibid., vol. I, pp. 432–34.

62. Ibid., vol. I, pp. 614–622., 757.

63. Ibid., vol. I, pp. 550–56. It is worth noting that when Spencer also tried to classify societies as militant or industrial, he sought to place those types in a temporal succession and was seriously embarrassed by contrary historical evidence, which in this case pressed more clearly than in the case of the more abstract series. Ibid., vol. I, pp. 564–74, 579, 581, 585, 587.

64. Herbert Spencer, *Descriptive Sociology,* div. III, no. 1, part I-C: "English" (London: Williams and Norgate, 1873) pp. iii-iv; *An Autobiography* (London: Williams & Norgate, 1904) vol. II, p. 261.

65. Durkheim, *Rules of Sociological Method,* p. 77.

66. Ibid., pp. 81–83.

67. Ibid., pp. 84–85.

68. Durkheim, *The Division of Labor in Society,* pp. 40–41.

69. See Durkheim's pointed remarks on this matter in *The Elementary Forms of Religious Life,* trans. by Joseph Ward Swain (New York: Free Press, 1965) pp. 462–63.

70. The literature is vast and rich. Some outstanding examples: Edward Burnett Tylor, *Primitive Culture* (London: J. Murray, 1871); Lewis Henry Morgan, *Ancient Society* (New York: Henry Holt and Co., 1877); John Ferguson McLennan, *Studies in Ancient History* (London: Macmillan, 1886); Charles Letourneau, *Property: Its Origins and Development* (London: W. Scott, 1892); John Lubbock, *The Origin of Civilization and the Primitive Condition of Man*, 6th ed. (London: Longmans, Green, 1911); A. Lane-Fox Pitt-Rivers, *The Evolution of Culture and Other Essays* (Oxford: Clarendon Press, 1906); Andrew Lang, *Custom and Myth* (London: Longmans, Green, 1884); Edward Westermarck, *The History of Human Marriage*, 5th ed. (New York: Allerton Book Co., 1922). This and related literature were treated in a sophisticated manner by Robert H. Lowie, *The History of Ethnological Theory* (New York: Farrar & Rinehart, 1937).

71. See Richard Hofstadter, *Social Darwinism in American Thought, 1860–1915* (Boston: Beacon Press, 1955).

72. See, for example, Ward's *Dynamic Sociology* (New York: D. Appleton and Co., 1883).

73. The hold that the idea of progress had on sociologists and anthropologists at the close of the nineteenth century is obviously testified to by the incredible influence of Herbert Spencer. Casual acceptance of the idea as an intellectual orientation to be taken for granted is strikingly evident, for example, in the collection of readings compiled by Harvard professor of political economy Thomas Nixon Carver, *Sociology and Social Progress* (Boston: Ginn & Co., 1905). There, Comte and Ward, Fiske and Buckle, Spencer and Kidd, are presented to college students as standard fare addressed to the "problem of human welfare," and to supplement their elementary textbook. See also, A. J. Todd, *Theories of Social Progress* (New York: Macmillan, 1918).

74. For examples of Herodotus' procedure see *The Persian Wars*, trans. by Rawlinson, in *The Greek Historians*, book I, pp. 131, 155–57, 171, 173; vol. II; pp. 22, 30, 49–51, 79, 91; vol. III; pp. 12, 16, 20; vol. IV; 46, 67, 76, 106, 180, 189; vol. V; pp. 58; vol. VI; pp. 58–60.

75. Franz Boas, "The Limitations of the Comparative Method of Anthropology," *Science*, vol. 4 (December 18, 1896) pp. 901–08.

76. Stanley Arthur Cook, *The Study of Religions* (London: A. and C. Black, 1914).

77. See, especially, Maitland's remarkable essay on "The Body Politic," in *The Collected Papers of Frederic William Maitland*, ed. by H. A. L. Fisher (Cambridge: The University Press, 1911) vol. III.

78. Ibid., vol. I, p. 488.

79. Kenneth Bock, "Comparison of Histories: The Contribution of Henry Maine," *Comparative Studies in Society and History*, vol. 16 (March 1974) pp. 232–62.

80. Morris Ginsberg, *The Idea of Progress*, p. 36.

81. Karl Marx and Friedrich Engels, *The German Ideology* (New York: International Publishers, 1947) pp. 9–16; Karl Marx, *A Contribution to the Critique of Political Economy* (Chicago: Charles H. Kerr, 1904) p. 13; *Pre-Capitalist Economic Formations* (London: Lawrence & Wishart, 1964); Friedrich Engels, *The Origin of the Family, Private Property and the State in the Light of the Researches of Lewis Henry Morgan* (New York: International Publishers, 1942)—see especially the preface to the fourth edition in which Engels places his work in the tradition of nineteenth-century developmentalism.

82. Karl Marx, *Manifesto of the Communist Party*, in Lewis Feuer, ed., *Basic Writings on Politics and Philosophy: Karl Marx and Friedrich Engels* (Garden City, N. Y.: Doubleday, 1959) p. 7, my italics.

83. Marx, *Critique of Political Economy*, p. 300; Karl Marx, *Capital* (Chicago: Charles Kerr, 1906), vol. I, p. 13.

84. Cited in M. M. Bober, *Karl Marx's Interpretation of History*, 2nd ed., rev. (Cambridge: Harvard University Press, 1948) pp. 41–42.

85. The line of argument presented here was developed by Teggart in 1925. See his *Theory and Processes of History*, pp. 110–11. See also Kenneth Bock, "Darwin and Social Theory," *Philosophy of Science*, vol. 22 (April, 1955) pp. 123–34. Darwin's efforts to see man in relation to other animals had, of course, been anticipated in the eighteenth century. For James Burnett's (Lord Monboddo) preoccupation with this theme, see Bryson, *Man and Society*, pp. 66–77. An elaborate parody of the argument appeared in 1818 in Thomas Love Peacock, *Melincourt, or Sir Oran Haut-ton*.

86. Serious efforts to escape this difficulty with the concept of multilinear evolution have been made by Julian H. Steward, *Theory of Culture Change* (Urbana: University of Illinois Press, 1955), and with a designation of lines of general and special evolution, by Marshall D. Sahlins and Elman R. Service, eds., *Evolution and Culture* (Ann Arbor: University of Michigan Press,

1960). In both cases, however, it would appear that the tendency is to create a residual category for diversity while maintaining the universal.

87. Theodosius Dobzhansky, *Mankind Evolving* (New Haven: Yale University Press, 1970) pp. 10, 24–25. In this connection, Dobzhansky remarks that Sahlins's and Service's "general evolution" as a concept resembles the hypothesis of autogenesis or orthogenesis in biology.

88. See, for example, Talcott Parsons and Robert F. Bales, *Family, Socialization and Interaction Process* (Glencoe, Ill.: Free Press, 1955) pp. 395–99; Wilbert Moore, *Social Change* (Englewood Cliffs, N.J.: Prentice-Hall, 1963). After publication of Darwin's *The Origin of Species* in 1859 the literature of cultural anthropology, evolutionist sociology, and social Darwinism was marked with Darwinian terminology, but there was no real change in ideas, and the mechanisms of Darwinian evolution were, of course, never detected in social or cultural processes.

89. Theodor Waitz, *Introduction to Anthropology*, ed. by J. Frederick Collingwood (London: Longman, Green, Longman, and Roberts, 1863) esp. pp. 10–16. For Maine on the race issue, see Bock, "Comparison of Histories."

90. Boas, "The Limitations of the Comparative Method"; Alexander A. Goldenweiser, *Early Civilization* (New York: A. A. Knopf, 1922) pp. 23–27; "Four Phases of Anthropological Thought," *Publications of the American Sociological Society*, vol. 16 (1921) pp. 52, 61.

91. Leslie A. White effectively disposed of the argument that diffusionism had killed evolutionism, and he was one of the few observers in the 1940s to note that the idea of evolution was still dominant in anthropological thinking—even among those who had pronounced it dead. See his "Diffusion vs. Evolution: An Anti-Evolutionist Fallacy," *American Anthropologist* vol. 47 (July–September, 1945) pp. 339–56; "History, Evolutionism, and Functionalism," *Southwestern Journal of Anthropology*, vol. 1 (Autumn, 1945) pp. 221–48.

92. The relationship of evolutionist and functionalist theories of change was noted by Robert A. Nisbet, "Social Structure and Social Change," *Research Studies of the State College of Washington*, vol. 20 (June, 1952) pp. 70–76, and explored in greater detail in his *Social Change and History* (New York: Oxford University Press, 1969). More recently the connection has been thoroughly analyzed, with special reference to the literature on differentiation, development, and modernization, by Anthony D. Smith, *The Concept of Social Change: A Critique of the Functionalist Theory of Social Change* (London: Routledge & Kegan Paul, 1973). My comments here depend also on Kenneth Bock, "Evolution, Function, and Change," *American Sociological Review*, vol. 28 (April, 1963) pp. 229–37.

93. This was noted long ago by Lowie, *The History of Ethnological Theory*, chap. XIII.

94. Bronislaw Malinowski, "Culture," in *Encyclopaedia of the Social Sciences* (New York: Macmillan, 1935) vol. 4, p. 624; A. R. Radcliffe-Brown, "The Present Position of Anthropological Studies," *The Advancement of Science: 1931* (London: British Association for the Advancement of Science, 1931) p. 22; Talcott Parsons, *The Structure of Social Action* (Glencoe, Ill.: Free Press, 1949) p. 450.

95. V. Gordon Childe, *History* (London: Watts & Co., 1947) *Social Evolution* (London: Watts & Co., 1951); Robert M. MacIver and Charles H. Page, *Society: An Introductory Analysis* (New York: Rinehart, 1949); White, "Diffusion vs. Evolution"; Sahlins and Service, *Evolution and Culture;* Robert L. Carneiro, "Scale Analysis as an Instrument for the Study of Cultural Evolution," *Southwestern Journal of Anthropology*, vol. 18 (Summer, 1962) pp. 149–69.

96. For examples, see the extensive literature reviewed by Smith, *The Concept of Social Change*. A fair assessment of the influence of evolutionism in the literature of development or modernization appears in Herbert R. Barringer, George L. Blanksten, and Raymond W. Mack, eds., *Social Change in Developing Areas* (Cambridge, Mass.: Schenkman, 1965) and S. N. Eisenstadt, ed., *Readings in Social Evolution and Development* (Oxford: Pergamon Press, 1970). Parsons and Moore have been most forthright in stating their positions; see Wilbert Moore, "A Reconsideration of Theories of Social Change," *American Sociological Review*, vol. 25 (December, 1960) pp. 810–15; *Social Change;* Talcott Parsons, "Some Considerations on the Theory of Social Change," *Rural Sociology*, vol. 26 (September, 1961) pp. 219–39; "Evolutionary Universals in Society," *American Sociological Review*, vol. 29 (June, 1964) pp. 339–57; *Societies: Evolutionary and Comparative Perspectives* (Englewood Cliffs, N.J.: Prentice-Hall, 1966); *The System of Modern Societies* (Englewood Cliffs, N.J.: Prentice-Hall, 1971); Talcott Parsons and Victor Lidz, *Readings on Premodern Societies* (Englewood Cliffs, N.J.: Prentice-Hall, 1972).

97. The implications of this procedure are clearly revealed in Leslie A. Sklair's *The Sociology of Progress* (London: Routledge & Kegan Paul, 1970), a most interesting attempt to graft the idea of progress onto functionalism and thus pursue Hobhouse's and Ginsberg's quest for a rational ethic without the oppressive weight of uniformitarianism.

3

CONSERVATISM

ROBERT NISBET

I

GUNNAR MYRDAL, in his *An American Dilemma*, sets forth aptly the principal contribution of conservatism in the early nineteenth century to sociology. "The conservative wing," writes Myrdal, "profited from its 'realism.' In its practical work it abstained from speculating about a 'natural order' other than the one that existed; it studied society as it was and actually came to lay the foundations for modern social science."[1]

The conservatives (whom I shall identify presently) were in no sense dispassionate in their approach to problems, much less scientific. In all of them there was a strong element of the polemical. They wrote acknowledgedly in support of a type of social order that, in the judgment of others of their day, history was rapidly passing by. They were profoundly opposed to the natural-law individualism of the French Enlightenment and Revolution, and also to such doctrines as equality, freedom, and popular sovereignty. But, as Myrdal notes, in the process of opposing the whole philosophy of the natural order, the conservatives were led to rest their emphasis upon the institutional order. And in the process of *defending* on moral grounds a set of traditional institutions—family, religion, local community, guild, social class—the conservatives succeeded in *identifying* these institutions; that is, thrusting them into the foreground of intellectual contemplation where they could become the objects of liberal, even radical, ideological regard and also, most to the point here, the empirical elements of sociology and other social sciences. The widespread interest throughout the nineteenth century in social institutions like kinship, locality, occupational association, social class, and religion in its varied forms cannot be understood in historical terms except by reference to the conservative writings at the beginning of the century in which these institutions were given high *moral* prominence.

Karl Mannheim in his classic study of German conservatism has called attention to another important aspect of this intellectual movement, one as evident in French, English, Swiss, and Spanish conservatism as German.[2] This is the *style* of conservatism. As Mannheim points out, the concept of style has as much relevance to intellectual as to artistic history. Just as we distinguish among styles in the history of painting or sculpture or music, so are we obliged to distinguish among styles when we direct attention to political, social, and moral thought. The style of conservatism, in its concern for problems of order and freedom, was as different from that of liberalism or radicalism as the style of romanticism was different from, say, classicism.

There are several ways of characterizing the conservative style, and we shall touch upon all of these at a later point in this chapter. For the moment it suffices to refer only to methodological style. It is the very obverse of the style of thinking that had dominated the Enlightenment and, before it, the Age of Reason in the seventeenth century. That style had been strongly Cartesian in nature, born of Descartes's emphasis upon what he had called "clear and simple ideas" and upon the kinds of conclusions which could be reached, not by direct empirical observation of things, but by rigorous, deductive procedures akin to those found in geometry. Vico at the beginning of the eighteenth century had protested strongly, even passionately, against this Cartesian method so far as the study of mankind was concerned. This protest is at the heart of his notable *New Science* (1725). But Vico and his ideas were largely overlooked in the eighteenth century. Not until the nineteenth century, after the conservative movement was well under way, would Vico come into his own.

The conservative style or method was empirical, historical, and wedded to observation of what could in fact be seen and described. Not man in the abstract sense, not "natural" man, not man as he might be envisaged in either a state of nature or an ideal society, but man in the historically concrete, man as Frenchman or Englishman, as peasant or aristocrat, as churchman, businessman, soldier, or statesman: this is the object of the inquiries, tracts, essays, and philosophical works of the conservatives. From the conservatives' point of view the Enlightenment's emphasis upon abstract man, conceived as stripped of the identity history, time, and place had given him, was false in itself, and, worse, responsible for the terrible wave of disorganization which the conservatives one and all saw rolling over Western society.[3]

There is one other major characteristic of conservatism that should be cited in light of the influence it would have throughout the century, on liberals and radicals as well as conservatives. Stated succinctly, this is the typology of traditionalist and modernist. There are various ways of stating the typology: in Sir Henry Maine, "status" vs. "contract"; in Tocqueville, "aristocratic" vs. "democratic"; in Marx, "feudal" vs. "capitalist"; in Toennies, *Gemeinschaft* vs. *Gesellschaft;* in Weber, "traditional" vs. "rational-bureaucratic"; in Simmel, "rural" vs. "urban"; and so on. Few perspectives are more dominant in nineteenth-century sociology than this one, this typological contrasting of two structurally distinctive, and historically successive, forms of social order. From this typology a large number of ancillary concepts arose which continue to this day.[4]

Behind the emergence of the typology lies the conservative contrasting of, on the one hand, the *ancien rêgime,* with its strong medieval roots, its organization primarily in terms of land, family, class, religion, and guild; and, on the other hand, the kind of society, so much more individualistic, impersonal, and contractual, that the twin forces of revolutionary democracy and industrialism were introducing into turn-of-the-century Western Europe. The conservatives, from Burke on, were fascinated by this contrast. They saw the decline of Western Europe essentially in these terms. Again we are able to say: the conservatives, in the process of damning the modern regime and of glorifying the feudally-rooted *ancien rêgime,* managed to give clear if biased institutional identity to each, identity that would, in typological form, figure prominently in the sociology of the nineteenth and also twentieth centuries.

In a later section I shall deal in more detail with the specific themes and perspectives of conservatism as it took shape during approximately a quarter of a century in several countries in the West. What I want to turn to now is first the principals, the leading figures of the conservative movement, and then the crucial contexts in which this anti-Enlightenment took form and acquired influence.

II

Who were the conservatives?[5] The first and in many ways the seminal figure was Edmund Burke (1729–97).[6] His influence upon those who were to become acknowledged traditionalists and conservatives during the third of a century following Burke's death was immense, reaching every country in Western Europe. Indeed, until the very end of the century there were those in all Western Countries who declared their indebtedness to Burke's ideas on law and society.

Burke probably did not ever consider himself a conservative. He was, after all, Whig, not Tory, in party affiliation. He adored the memory of the English Revolution of the preceding century, believing it the foundation of English liberty. Beyond this, he was a strong supporter of the American colonists' claims (though he disapproved of their declaration of war on England), a bitter enemy of the British East India Company for what he regarded as its depredations upon the traditions and historic rights of India, and, finally, a staunch sympathizer with the Irish people in their resistance to British domination. By Dr. Johnson's standards indeed, Burke (whom Johnson admired and also liked) was altogether too much the liberal.

But it is history in the long run that establishes the roles of the great. Burke, his Whiggish inclinations notwithstanding, has to be seen as the father of modern political and social conservatism. This is the result of his momentous attack on the French Revolution, an event which he saw in the shape of not freedom, but absolute power, destructive and despotic. Moreover, Burke said, the French Revolution, if allowed full sway, would destroy not only French traditional society but that of all European, and eventually all other, societies. For, as Burke emphasized, the French Revolution was unlike all other political revolutions in history in that it made, not a single nation its object, but all mankind.

Burke was assuredly not without bias and prejudice in his attack upon the French Revolution. He is occasionally wrong in statements of fact. Some of the passages in the *Reflections* evince more sentimentality than sense. But this has to be said of Burke: he was the first to sense a character of the French Revolution that his liberal contemporaries utterly failed to see, a character that the Jacobins themselves would proclaim to the whole world within a year of the writing of the *Reflections:* "the universal mission of the French Revolution," the mission of liberating not just the French people from the chains of the past, but in time all peoples everywhere. It was this fact, as Burke realized, that gave affinity to the French Revolution and the great universal religions in history.

This was the perception, I would say, that made Burke the progenitor of a body of thought that would come to flower in several countries: Germany, England, Switzerland, and Spain, as well as France itself. Not all European conservatives would give Burke his due (though many did) for being the first to sense the real character, the real mission of the French Revolution, but it is hard to find one of them whose writings do not reflect Burke's seminal impact. His *Reflections,* written in an astonishingly short time in 1790, became within five years one of the most widely read books on the Continent as well as in England. Liberal though Burke, with some reason, believed his mind to be, the fact remains that he is the authentic father of modern European conservatism. He must also be seen as one of the key influences on the creation of what came to be called "the historical school" in the study of political, legal, social, and economic institutions. There is a straight line—and an acknowledged one—from Burke through Sir Henry Maine in midcentury down to the historical-institutional studies of such later minds as Maitland, Vinogradov, and Pollock.

Turning to France,[7] there are four individuals worthy of note here. All were members of or closely related to the French aristocracy and in some degree suffered the impact of Revolutionary legislation on property and status. All were members of the Roman Catholic Church. Finally, all were ardent monarchists, deeply opposed to democracy and other elements of modernity.

Joseph de Maistre (1754–1821)[8] was the most brilliant and versatile of the four. Diplomat, avowed servant of the Church as well as monarchy, and brilliant polemicist, he found time to write a succession of influential books, among them *Considerations on France* (1796), *An Essay on the Sources of Political Constitutions* (1814), and *On the Papacy* (1819).

Louis de Bonald (1754–1840),[9] was probably the most learned and also the most profound philosopher among the French conservatives. However, unlike de Maistre's, Bonald's style tends to repel by virtue of its relentless turgidity. Very probably he is, of all the conservatives, the one whose writings left the greatest impact on the minds of the early French sociologists, for he is broadest in his treatment of the structural elements of the social order. His masterwork, at least from the sociological point of view, is *Theory of Political and Religious Authority* (1796). Others which should be mentioned are: *Primitive Legislation* (1802), a frequently devastating rebuttal of the philosophy of natural rights and the state of nature; *Analytical Essay on the Natural Laws of the Social Order* (1800); and *Philosophical Researches* (1818).

Hugues Felicité de Lamennais (1782–1854)[10] had by all odds the most dramatic personal life. A devout priest in the beginning, offered, it is said, a seat in the Sacred College at Rome by virtue of early writings, he yet became the subject first of Church censure, then excommunication for his increasingly liberal and secular views. However, until about 1825 Lamennais was unqualifiedly conservative: royalist, deeply traditionalist, and ultramontane Catholic. His major work in his conservative period is *Essay on Indifference in Religion* (1817). It is at once philosophy of history, theology, and what might be called Catholic sociology of knowledge.

Francois Rene de Chateaubriand[11] (1768–1848) is best known for one book: *The Genius of Christianity* (1802). It was written shortly after his reconversion to Roman Catholicism after a career in which liberalism and secularism were the dominant elements of his thought. Strongly influenced by Burke's *Reflections* and, perhaps more directly and immediately, by the works of de Maistre and Bonald, this book is the source of the intellectual revival of Roman Catholicism in the early nineteenth century, giving the religion a luster in the minds of the educated that it had not had for a long time. What Chateaubriand does is to portray Christianity, and particularly Roman Catholicism, not primarily in terms of creed and faith but, rather, as community. His emphasis throughout is on the conservative and protective character of religion conceived as liturgy, communion, and also as art, literature, and social community. The book was an immediate best-seller and, as both Saint-Simon and Comte acknowledged, exerted considerable effect upon their minds.

In Germany four names must be mentioned, all important in the development and spread of conservative ideas in the study of law, culture, and society.[12]

Justus Möser (1720–94) is undoubtedly the crucial and seminal influence here, and also the one major thinker who may be said to have preceded Burke in expressing a number of the tenets of conservative philosophy. Goethe was an admirer and, in one work, a collaborator of Möser. Möser's *Patriotic*

Discourses (1774–86), a multivolume collection of essays, is a treasury of his principal ideas, among which are a systematic and relentless attack on natural-law rationalism, analytical individualism, and faith in rational-prescriptive law over historically evolved custom and tradition, and, in positive terms, a clear development of the theory that the only vital constitution for any country is unwritten, the product of history and institutional continuity.

Adam Müller (1779–1829) had found his way to Burke very early, and his admiration for Burke's fundamental principles was very great. Müller's *Elements of Statecraft* (1810) is the best single expression of his general ideas, and it had a strong influence in both philosophy and practical politics for a generation after his death.

Friedrich Carl von Savigny (1779–1861), member of an ancient and wealthy German family, was among the very first of his class to become a respected teacher and scholar. His reputation was established in 1814 with the publication of *A Defense of Historical Tradition in Government*. Here, in addition to an assault on natural-law thought, we find a criticism of Roman Law which was achieving great influence in academic circles and a defense of the *Volksgeist*—not different from Burke's emphasis on the historical spirit of each people—as the only valid source of law and government.

However, Georg Wilhelm Friedrich Hegel[13] (1770–1831) is by far the most influential force in the development of German conservatism. He had had his liberal-radical period as a youth, during which his admiration for the French Revolution was great. Throughout the greater part of his career, however, traditionalism was dominant. His *Foundations of the Philosophy of Law* (1821), written while Hegel was a professor at the University of Berlin, is ample testament to a view of society hardly different in its fundamentals from that of Burke (whom Hegel had come to admire) or of Bonald. From Hegel, as from Burke in England, stretched a succession of followers, or at least of those deeply influenced intellectually, throughout the century—and it included, paradoxically, minds oriented to the Left as well as to the Right. If his dialectical method, his insistence upon the historical and also upon the social nature of man, and his interest in institutions served conservatism, these elements of thought could also be bent, as Marx was to demonstrate, to serve radicalism.

In Switzerland, two conservatives must be mentioned. The first, Johannes von Müller[14] (1752–1809), is much more historian than philosopher or protosociologist. His influence upon the great Ranke is a matter of record. But his Pietistic involvement and also his frequently expressed admiration for paternalistic Roman Catholicism, along with an uncompromising regard for the Middle Ages, serve to suggest the conservative thrust of his mind. He had the same dislike of individualistic-secular rationalism that all the other conservatives had.

Much more important sociologically, however, is Karl Ludwig von Haller (1768–1854).[15] Deeply conservative, an ardent admirer of Burke and the French conservatives, Haller was also one of the genuinely great social scientists of the century, as is evidenced by his masterwork, *Restoration of the Social Sciences* (1816–34). He is little known today even by social scientists. Even in his lifetime he achieved only a modest part of the recognition due him. He is, however, one of the most original minds of the century, resembling Frederick Le Play in the sheer volume and diversity of his empirical materials and Max Weber in his theoretical acumen and historical sweep. Social scientist he was indeed, but along with this went a deeply rooted conservatism of philosophical and political principle.

The final two conservatives to be mentioned here are Spanish:[16] Juan Donoso y Cortés (1809–53) and Jaime Luciano Balmes (1810–48). Neither can rank intellectually with some of the other European conservatives—Burke, Bonald, Hegel, Haller—but both are minds of excellence all the same, and their influence in Spain was great. Both were Roman Catholic, of course, strongly committed to monarchy and the Church, but they exhibit a strong devotion to social institutions generally, and to their autonomy that bespeaks the kind of liberal perspective to be found in much of Burke's work, which both of these Spanish thinkers knew in considerable detail. Indeed, to a considerable degree both can be seen in the tradition of the late medieval conciliar movement in Spain. Donoso y Cortés's major work is probably his early *On Absolute Monarchy in Spain*, broadly sociological in nature. Balmes's *Protestantism Compared with Catholicism* makes a case in behalf of the linkage between Protestantism and destructive economic individualism.

III

Having now identified the principals of early nineteenth-century conservatism, it will be useful to offer a few observations concerning the contexts—intellectual, historical, and social—in which their lives and philosophical careers must be seen.[17] We will then pass directly to the dominant themes of conservatism.

I have already referred to conservatism as the anti-Enlightenment. Had the Enlightenment not existed in eighteenth-century Western Europe, it is hardly an exaggeration to say that one would have had to be invented, so far as the conservatives were concerned. For it is impossible to understand their major ideas and values except as direct responses to the challenges of such minds as Voltaire, Rousseau, Diderot, and other radical minds of eighteenth-century France. There is not one crucial proposition regarding man, society, religion, and morality to be found in the Enlightenment that is not directly attacked by the conservatives. It would be hard to find a better illustration anywhere of Sir Isaiah Berlin's observation that in intellectual history ideas do not beget ideas as butterflies beget butterflies, but are rather responses to recent or contemporaneous intellectual challenges. The rationalist ideas born of the Enlightenment provided much of the challenge for the conservatives.

But ideas are only part of the story. There are also events and changes in the political, economic, and social scene. Highest among these so far as the minds of Burke, Bonald, Haller, and others were concerned, was the French Revolution. Nearly all of the conservatives were, as I have noted, either themselves part of the Catholic-monarchical-aristocratic complex that the Revolution had descended upon with such impact after 1791, or else they had become convinced supporters of that complex. It is easy today for historians to debate the question of whether the Revolution did in fact make as much difference institutionally in France as longtime belief has had it. Quite possibly France was already undergoing most of the great changes in property, law, government, and religion which after the Revolution tended to be ascribed to this event alone. After all, we have the word of the greatest of the historians of the Revolution, Tocqueville—himself shaped in considerable degree by conservative thought—that the Revolution of 1789 was hardly more than the consequence of historical tendencies several centuries old in France.[18]

All of this may be accepted, at least in some degree. But what cannot be overlooked or swept under the rug is the clear fact that large numbers of human beings, intellectuals included, *believed* that the French Revolution was not only of immense significance but even, in Burke's words, unique in all history so far as its impact upon mind and society was concerned. For all of the conservatives—and this was just as true among German, Swiss, Spanish, and English conservatives as French—the Revolution was hardly less than a cosmic event. The deeply religious Bonald saw it as God's direct punishment of mankind for its assimilation of all the heresies which had become part of the European mind after the Reformation. It was at once, Bonald declared, the outcome of the Enlightenment and God's curse upon the Enlightenment.

For all the conservatives, the Revolution's Reign of Terror was the perfect epitome of the larger event: the annihilation through force of life, property, authority, and just liberty. Exaggeration notwithstanding, it has to be said for the conservatives that they, beginning with Burke, were the first to go directly to the *legislative* aspects of the Revolution. I refer to the succession of laws passed which touched upon almost every aspect of political, religious, economic, and social life.[19] I am obliged to be brief here. It will suffice to refer to laws which profoundly affected the family, establishing divorce for the first time, giving sons independence of fathers at age twenty-one, and abolishing the ancient laws of entail and primogeniture; laws which affected the fabric of social status through abolition of the aristocracy and enactment of the famous principle of careers open to individual talents, thus enjoining equality of opportunity before the law; laws which first fettered the Church, then nationalized it, and finally, in the dechristianization decrees of 1793–94, abolished it; laws which abolished the guilds in industry, a feat that had eluded the best efforts of even the most despotic of French kings from the sixteenth century on; laws which replaced the multiplicity of weights, measures, and standards that had come out of the Middle Ages with a unified decimal system, one that has remained to this day and, indeed, has spread to many other parts of the world and is still spreading; laws which transformed the educational system, putting all education in the hands of the government in a single system reaching from primary schools all over France all the way to the capstone of the system, the University of Paris; laws which literally reformed language, moral convention, and, far from least, the Gregorian calendar; and finally, laws which sought a total remaking of the French government, from the smallest locality up to Paris, which was deemed the omnipotent center of all French political life.

Few of these laws ever were actually put into effect, though some were. A number of them died before the Revolution was over, casualties of the large-scale war revolutionary France was obliged to wage with other European countries over the issue of the Revolution. Others attained real impress only after Napoleon instituted his own, highly bureaucratized, despotic form of government. The Church rather quickly reestablished itself in economic and spiritual, if not legal, substance; the greater number of aristocrats recovered their expropriated lands; and in many ways life in France could appear much the same after the Revolution as it had been before. In due course monarchy, aristocracy, and clericalism regained a significant degree of the influence they had enjoyed in the *ancien régime*.

But all this notwithstanding, the impact of the Revolution on *ideas* was massive. And it is ideas that we are concerned with. From the point of view of most intellectuals in Western Europe, those of radical or liberal as well as conservative disposition, the Revolution in France was an epochal event, one that had impressed itself on the whole Western world. No modern event, with the possible exception of the later Bolshevik Revolution in Russia, has ever had greater, more focused, and more lasting effect upon ideas—philosophical and literary as well as political, social, and economic—than the French Revolution. Again we may say, in seeking to understand the tenets of conservatism, had there not been a French Revolution, one would have had to be invented.

Much the same has to be said of the other great revolution at the end of the eighteenth century: the industrial.[20] The deep traditionalism of such thinkers as Burke, Bonald, Hegel, and Donoso y Cortés was almost as violated by the new forms of economic life which were appearing on the scene, chiefly in England, as by the French Revolution and the Enlightenment. Apostles of a stable, rooted, and hierarchical society, enemies of any form of individualism that tended to separate man from his primary social contexts—starting with family, village, and parish but including social class and other close forms of association—it was perhaps inevitable that the conservatives would look dourly upon not only the factory system but also those other manifestations of the new economic order—such as increasing substitution of money, credit, shares of stock, and financial position generally for the older bases of status and authority in the social order—which could be seen transforming so much of Western society at the beginning of the nineteenth century.

Conservatism had in it, then, extreme dislike of economic modernity; that is, industrialism and finance capitalism. Nothing resembling socialism can be seen in or deduced from conservative writings, but it would be gross caricature to ascribe to these writings defense of or justification for the new forms of economic enterprise, the new patterns of ascendant finance, and the whole spirit of economism which we think of as capitalist. For the conservatives, capitalism was but the economic face of popular democracy. From both, it was thought, there would emanate dislocation, fragmentation, and atomization of traditional society.

It is this character of conservatism that frequently gives it the cast of a kind of radicalism. After all, the single greatest issue of nineteenth-century social thought and social action was the economic system, with the national state a close second. This new economic system had its full share of apologists. But such traditionalists as Burke, Bonald, Haller, and Donoso y Cortés were not among them. Not without reason have they been called "prophets of the past."

IV

It will be clarifying at this point to examine in some detail the ideas of one of the major conservatives by way of suggesting the range and diversity of conservative thought at its best and also some of the more distinctive insights which were to find their way in one form or other into sociology. Bonald is, I think, the best choice. He was without question deeply learned, and the mere fact that Comte seems to have admired Bonald above any of the other French conservatives makes him an appropriate choice here.

In almost every important respect Bonald is the complete antithesis of Rousseau. Nor was this fact lost upon Bonald. Rousseau is the brooding eminence, the specter that hangs over countless pages of Bonald's works. Bonald had the insight even by 1796, when the first of his major works appeared, to recognize Rousseau's intellectual stature, however evil Bonald thought this stature to be. Rousseau had constructed a political and social theory out of the elements or values of individualism, popular sovereignty, equality, a generally romantic envisagement of human nature, and a belief that nothing need prevent what he called "the soul of the legislator" from effecting a radical and complete reconstitution of society and human nature. Not until Proudhon and Marx would philosophers as deeply radical as Rousseau make their appearance in European social thought.[21]

It is important to observe how Bonald's philosophy of society differs from

Rousseau's.[22] Not the individual but *society* is Bonald's point of departure: society created directly by God. It is society that shapes the individual, not the individual that gives shape to society. Authority, not individual liberty, is the dominant objective of social life; only under the authority of family, local community, church, and guild is it even possible for human beings to thrive. Hierarchy is the essence of the social bond, and all talk of equality is idle and iniquitous. The authority of the political state descends from God, who is alone sovereign in the world; to speak of the state's authority as rising from some contract among individuals in a state of nature is as logically absurd as it is without foundation in recorded history. Forced change of social institutions, as in revolution, under the inspiration of individual reason is calamitous and in the long run self-defeating, for true change is the result of slow, long-term processes of history wherein the wisdom of humanity reveals itself. The idea of natural rights is false and preposterous; individuals have duties—to family, church, community, and other groups.

Those are among the more positive perspectives we find in Bonald's system of thought. Their medieval roots are evident. Nor did Bonald seek to hide his admiration for the Medieval Age—its pluralism emanating from "the doctrine of two swords"; its organic functionalism resulting from the belief that each major group or institution served a purpose that could not rightfully be contravened by any other agency; its combined localism and universalism, with the national-secular state accordingly diminished in power; its embedded respect for social class and estate; and its pervasive emphasis upon duty and membership rather than upon freedom and individualism. Bonald not only admires the Middle Ages; there is also his pronouncement that Western society can save itself, can recover from its sickness only by returning to medieval principles of society. What John Morley has written of the conservatives is especially applicable to Bonald:

> The problem which presented itself was not new in the history of Western civilization. The same dissolution of bonds which perplexed the foremost men at the beginning of the nineteenth century had distracted their predecessors from the fifth to the eighth. . . . The practical question in both cases was the same: how to establish a stable social order which, resting on the principles that should command the assent of all, might secure their lives. . . . Why, many men asked themselves, should not Christian and feudal ideas repeat their great achievement, and be the means of reorganizing the system which a blind rebellion against them had thrown into deplorable and fatal confusion.[23]

In what follows here, then, it is well to bear in mind that behind Bonald's analysis of the social order and the individual's relation to it lies a philosophy of history in which the Middle Ages is the high point of the development of civilization, with the Reformation, Age of Reason, Enlightenment, and French Revolution all chapters in the decline of Western society from its medieval heights. Now let us look at Bonald's specific propositions on man and society.

His point of departure, in any sociological sense, is his attack upon individualism and his elevation of society to the position of primacy. *Man exists only for society; society shapes him to her own ends.* This is the keynote of Bonald's social theory. Where the eighteenth century had tended to derive society from man's impulses, passions, and reason, Bonald takes society as the aboriginal force (created by God) and the vital context of the individual's formation and development. "Not only is it not true that the individual constitutes society; it is society that constitutes the individual, by socialization (*par l'education sociale*).[24] The individual by himself is helpless and sterile in contribution. The individual creates or discovers nothing. "Truth, like man and like society, is a seed that grows in the succession of ages and of men, always ancient in its beginnings, always new in its sequential developments." The life of man becomes only what society makes it; society, like a mother, "receives the germs of talent from nature; she develops them, making her members artists, poets, orators, moralists, scientists."[25]

In his desire to prove the inconsequentiality of the individual and the omnipotence of society, Bonald presents us with a long and complex theory of language.° There are neither words nor ideas naturally in the individual. Only in society are ideas and symbols to be found, and these become communicated to the individual. Ideas, Bonald argues, are possible only in a thinking being, but since thinking is impossible apart from language, it is obvious that we could not have the thought of language without having language itself. We may rule out the gesture theory, he continues, as well as any belief that ideas grow out of laughing, weeping, loving, or hating. No *idea* is, or can be, conveyed in this fashion;—only emotions. Language could have arisen only out of *thought*. But since thought is impossible without language, its invention—with due respect to eighteenth-century theorists on the subject—was not within the finite individual's powers. Apart from society's shaping, instructing, and forming influence upon individuals, words and ideas are simply inconceivable. God is the author of society. But society is the author of man. The insoluble paradox of thought and language—neither being possible except with the other—proves decisively that society precedes the individual, and that for society to exist, there must be a sovereign, creative God. "If God did not exist, this great conception [language] could never have been given to the mind of man; and this language, which by demonstration man could not himself have invented through his individual powers, is . . . decisive proof of the existence of a Being superior to man."[26]

Bonald's theological-sociological theory of language is not an end in itself, but only a kind of paradigm through which to combat individualism of any kind. He extends his philological analysis to morality. The source of all morality lies not in individual instinct or reason, but in society and its disciplines over the individual. The Enlightenment was false in its belief that from embedded passions in human nature such as altruism or compassion, human morality can be deduced. Neither altruism nor compassion is possible in man apart from prior exposure to the constraints of moral authority. In

° Bonald's stress upon society is every bit as encompassing as Durkheim's was to be. Bonald, however, never lets us forget his conviction that society's priority and omnipotence are made possible only by God. Durkheim, needless to say, does not hypothesize God.

short, in morality, as in language, there is the necessary anteriority of society and God.[27]

There is also the anteriority of authority. As I have already observed, "authority" is without doubt the central concept in Bonald's thought. Nothing could have seemed more important to Bonald, and to all of the other conservatives as well, than the restoration of authority to a civilization that seemed as shattered as European society did in its conventions, beliefs, and institutions at the beginning of the nineteenth century. It is this perception of the problem of authority, of the need for some new authority to replace the false idols generated by the Enlightenment and the Revolution, that is fundamental in Bonald's thought. So was it in the writings of others of the time—Saint-Simon, Comte, Fourier—by no means traditionalist in their aspirations. The great appeal Bonald could have for Comte lies foremost in Bonald's distinctive rendering of what he believed to be *the* European crisis: individualism. It was Comte who referred to individualism as "the disease of the Western world," but the phrase could have come directly from Bonald.

Bonald's sociology of authority is pluralist in its foundations. Inasmuch as sovereignty is the possession of God alone, no single institution on earth may claim it—not even the political state. "Authority," he writes, "in all societies divides itself between family and state, between religion and government, and excess on one side works to the disadvantage of the other."[28] This, for Bonald, as for all the conservatives, had been the political enormity of the French Revolution: the assumption by the state alone of authorities naturally resident in family, church, and other institutions.

Bonald's major work on authority is *Theory of Authority*.[29] The book is divided into three equal parts: "Political Authority," "Religious Authority," and what he calls "Social Education." The last is a general category covering the authorities and socializing effects upon individuals of family, school, guild, and like associations. This book, published in 1796, is probably the first significant *pluralist* work to be written after Bodin's *Republic* (1576), although that work, for all Bodin's attention to the rights of families, communities, guilds, and other social groups, clearly vested absolute sovereignty in the national state. One has to go back to the Middle Ages to find a sociology of power like Bonald's, one proceeding from ascription of absolute sovereignty to God alone, then insisting upon division of earthly authority among political government, church, family, and other associations. Granted that the primary motivation for Bonald's attack upon the secular national state and its claim of sovereignty was the Roman Catholic church. It was Bonald's—and the other French conservatives'—desire to see ultramontane Catholicism again flourish; Catholicism governed solely from Rome, and unchecked by any national sovereignty. But whatever the motivation, the effects are the same in Bonald's theory: critical attack upon the idea of unitary political sovereignty and insistence upon pluralization of authority in society. Authority, he tells us, normally and legitimately, divides itself into multiple forms.

In Bonald's thought, are the beginnings of structuralism. They flow naturally from his relentless antagonism toward individualism—whether social, moral, or analytical. The last is important. "Society is formed by itself." Its elements cannot be individuals but must be social—that is, also must be societies. "It is a body in which the elements are 'natural societies,' that is, families; and in which individuals are but members."[30] Gone from Bonald, thus, is any iota of Enlightenment or Age of Reason analytical individualism. In those ages, as Sir Ernest Barker has well stated it: "Individuals alone possessed reality; all else was ephemeral; institutions were but shadows cast."[31] Not so in Bonald. To seek to decompose society into individuals is as absurd as to decompose the living into the nonliving, space into lines, lines into points. Comte would draw much of his own insistence upon the irreducibility of the social into the individual—indeed, his own full-blown hostility to individualism in any form—from Bonald.

It is Bonald's critical attitude toward political state and individual alike that leads to his interest in intermediate associations. The Revolution had worked severely against church, parish, guild, and other forms of association intermediate to individual and state; it had done this in the name of fraternity, which for the Jacobins had meant *political* fraternity and which, following Rousseau's injunction in his *Social Contract* (1762), they had determined to maintain in pure form by abolishing most existing intermediate groups and then prohibiting any new ones. (The same law of June 1791 that abolished the guilds contained a provision banning any new forms of economic association numbering more than sixteen individuals.)

But for Bonald "constituted"—that is, legitimate—society is simply impossible without layers of association between man and state. Such intermediate social-economic groups (and for Bonald the model for these is the medieval guild) not only are limits upon the power of the political government, but "they have another advantage in conferring the sense of belonging upon men when fortune and status are condemned to obscurity, and in giving men, by union, the sense of importance in life."[32] Durkheim at the end of the century would give strictly secular expression to a proposal very much like Bonald's—that of "occupational associations," first advanced in the final pages of *Suicide,* and restated at length in the preface to the second edition of *Division of Labor.*

Characteristically, Bonald repudiates a system of territorial representation in government. Medievalist to the core, he prefers the more functional system of representation, one in which the larger associations of the social order—estates, church, guilds, universities, and other major social structures—are the bases of political representation in parliaments. Clearly, he would like to make membership in these structures hereditary, in the interest of stability and continuity, but feels that this would be impossible given the inroads of individualism in modern life and thought. The important point for Bonald, though, is eradication of the large territorial aggregates of individuals, which tend to be meaningless in social terms, and which had come to serve as the bases of representation in government. Each of the great *corporations* would be at once, then, political, social, educational, and moral. Each would have its own *constitution particulier,* which would "properly regulate the duties of the corporation toward the state, those of the family toward the corporation, and those of the individual to the family."[33] Clearly, Bonald's ideal society is a society of societies, ranging from the small to the large. What is anathema for him is anything suggesting individualism, a condition that he regarded as utterly pathological insofar as the requisites of society are concerned.

Needless to say, there is much in Bonald's writing about religion—meaning, of course, Roman Catholicism. There is no mistaking Bonald's dislike of Protestantism in any form. It is to the Reformation that he traces a great many of Western society's ills, including political absolutism, under which religion lost out to state power—and also the whole spirit of individualistic aggrandizement, of greed, and of sacrifice of the spiritual to the material. Bonald is not, of course, the first to see the historical relation between the rise of Protestantism and the spread of the commercial ethic, but no one before him had seen the relation more encompassingly—and also bitterly—than Bonald.

The single worst individual feature of the Revolution had been its exploitation, then spoliation, of the Church. Under the Revolution there had flourished the idea that the political state, rooted in popular sovereignty, is qualified to govern the Church. For Bonald, however, this is worse than heresy; it is monumental stupidity. "Religion should constitute the state, and it is opposed to the very nature of things that the state should constitute religion."[34] Bonald stays just short of advocating theocracy, but it is evident that he would prefer this to its opposite. What he insists upon at a minimum is the Church's absolute freedom, its corporate freedom, within the state. Moreover it, joined only by the family, must be the sole avenue to education in the social order, for only the Church can see to it that education is moral as well as intellectual. He distinguishes between *éducation* and *enseignment* and declares that the best the state can ever accomplish is the latter—that is, mere technical instruction. True education involves qualities and contexts inseparable from religion and family.

The reader is bound to be struck by the social, even sociological, cast of Bonald's treatment of religion. Religion is faith, yes, but more important it is a form of society, of community. He declares that the word "religion" comes ultimately from the Latin verb *religare,* meaning "to bind together." The sin of Protestantism, he argues, is its effort to locate religion in the individual, in his faith, which must always be precarious when separated from social organization. Religion for Bonald is first, last, and always a form of society; *the* form of society, with all else social cast in religion's image when properly constituted. Inevitably, therefore, we find much attention given by Bonald to the key religious groups—parishes, churches, and monasteries, of course, but also the assemblage of juridical, educational, charitable, and artistic groups which, when the Church had been at its height, flourished.[35] Without doubt it was Bonald's study of authority—published in 1796, with its rich inquiries into the social-cultural nature of religion—that inspired Chateaubriand, perhaps led to his reconversion, and almost certainly led to his *Genius of Christianity,* a work also steeped in regard for the communal and structural, as well as the aesthetic, in religion.

Hardly less than the Church, the family engages Bonald's moral and sociological attention. It, not the individual, is for Bonald the molecule of society. No charge against Protestantism is more serious for Bonald than the Reformation's legitimating divorce. By making divorce legal, by placing the power of granting divorce in the political state and in effect destroying the sacramental nature of marriage, Luther and Calvin weakened the family and, with this, society. What the Reformation began, the Enlightenment and then the Revolution continued. Bonald is also grim in his account of the results which may be expected from the Revolution's abolition of primogeniture and entail—vital economic bulwarks, he tells us, of family stability—and its separation of son from family through its grant of political independence to all males at age twenty-one.[36]

Bonald is, in his way, the student of the family as well as its advocate. His analysis of the political and moral nature of domestic society clearly anticipates Comte's. And much of Frederick Le Play's monumental study of the family is hardly more than a comparative documentation based upon fieldwork of insights which this incontestably conservative mind drew from his reading of Bonald. Bonald's principal observations on the family relate to its necessary structural autonomy in the social order and, most important, its functional freedom from the state. It is nothing less than the patriarchal family, indeed the medieval family, that he takes as his model. In the father is normally vested all authority, and this authority should be *perpêtuel,* terminating only with death. The child must always be under the authority of parents—"*mineur dans la famille, meme lorsqu'il est majeur dans l'Etat.*" The ancient rule of *droit d'ainêsse* must prevail so far as the bequeathing of property is concerned; otherwise economic fragmentation of the family will follow, itself the precursor to social fragmentation. The tie between child and parent must not be abridged by state action, however benevolently inspired, for the family is the earliest and the most successful school of social education. Bonald conceives the family explicitly as monarchy, with the father in the role of king and the child as *le sujet.* The family is, in sum, a small society in itself, "a society for the production and development of individuals" just as the state is a society for the conservation of families.[37]

Polemical (and in retrospect romantic) though Bonald is on the family, it cannot be denied that he sees clearly the indispensability of both economic and structural safeguards to the family's vitality in a social order. The Revolution's abolition of the *droit d'ainêsse* [right of the oldest] and its enjoining by law of *égalité du partage* [equality of division] had almost immediate consequences in the fragmentation and dispersal of family unity and authority. The hateful military conscription of the Revolution was only possible, Bonald insists, through prior weakening of the autonomy of the family. Military conscription fell most heavily, he notes, on those families where both economic and social solidarity were strongest. Any restoration of the strength of the family, and thus of the social order as a whole, was contingent upon restoration of economic liberty—that is, autonomy—to the family.

As I have said, Bonald is the student as well as advocate of the family. This is nowhere more evident than in his extraordinarily perceptive essay "On the Agricultural and the Industrial Family."[38] This essay may well be seen as a forerunner to what later came to be called rural-urban sociology. To be sure, conservative bias is evident throughout. Bonald does not like industrialism or urbanism; these forces, like democracy and liberalism, he deems destructive of the social fabric. But what is explicit in Bonald becomes implicit, as many a reader has noted, in the later succession of works (in Europe as well as the United States) which dealt with rural and urban contexts of association.

City and factory are the family's enemies, Bonald believes. The higher mobility, the tenuous character of the wage system, and the sheer congestion all work to the disadvantage of the family and its necessary roots. Separating members of the family economically, as the factory system does, prevents or erodes rapport within the family. The urban family tends to be weak socially by virtue of its precarious economic foundations. The rural family enjoys greater security from the accidents of circumstance, whether physical, as in injury or death; geographic, as in famine or cataclysm; or political-military, as in time of war. Bonald has a sophisticated view of the difference between a mere gathering together of individuals, as in a city or workhouse, and an actual uniting of individuals. Industry and commerce, he writes, bring human beings together without actually joining them; rural life, on the other hand, disperses people but succeeds in giving them a higher sense of relatedness to one another.

Finally, it should be said that Bonald has a keen, however biased, view of the political contexts of stable family systems. High among his indictments of democracy is that pertaining to the individualizing effects democracy, with its mass electorates and citizen-atoms, has upon the family, and indeed upon the social order as a whole. He is frank and resolute in his preference for monarchy, for, on the evidence, monarchy is more likely than democracy to respect the individual's social, especially family, ties. "Monarchy considers man in his ties with society; a republic considers man independently of his relations to society."[39]

It is not, however, a centralized, despotic monarchy that Bonald seeks. Deeply committed though he was to authority and the necessity of its restoration in Europe, he saw the destructive effects the absolute, centralized state—monarchy included—could have upon social ties. There must be decentralization, and this is possible only on the basis of strong local government. For Bonald, the historic *commune* is the proper basis of government. The Revolution had come close to destroying this historic local unit in its efforts to remake totally the political structure of France. But the *commune* is fundamental. It is the true political family.[40] Finally, it is necessary if there is to be an absence of the bureaucratic centralization which, Bonald thought, was fast ruining order as well as liberty in France. Centralization, he warns, is "ruinous for the administration and fatal to the polity."[41]

Prophet of the past: this Bonald assuredly was. Emile Faguet later referred to Bonald as "the last of the scholastics." It is impossible to dispute that characterization, whether it is Bonald's intellectual content, historical thrust, or simply style of writing we have in mind. A medieval scholastic adrift in the waters of nineteenth-century modernity—I cannot better describe Bonald. And yet we are still obliged to credit him with a certain impact, even a relevance, that strict antiquarianism rarely has. I have already indicated how deep were Saint-Simon's and Comte's admiration for Bonald, along with that of other conservatives. He was, obviously, a key figure in the renascence of medievalism in the early nineteenth century that was to have significant if not decisive effect upon Europe, its life, and, its thought. A reactionary in the literal sense of the word, his writings on religion and its necessary freedom from the political sphere, on the family and its required autonomy from political interference, as well as on the indispensability of solid economic foundation; his emphasis upon localism and decentralization, an emphasis as medieval as anything else in Bonald; all of this was not without discernible effect upon others in the century whose ideas were liberal, even radical. Bonald's insistence upon the analytical indissolubility of *sociêtê* and of its priority to the individual and the psychological may have been set forth primarily as a proof of God's existence and sovereignty, but such a proposition took on, as propositions so often do in the history of ideas, a force of its own—one that became the very basis of Durkheim's system. His repudiation of individualism on ethical, political, and economic grounds—but also, much to the point here, on methodological-analytical grounds—is a cardinal aspect of the sociological tradition, especially in France, but also in other parts of the West to some degree. I shall have more to say later about the impact of Bonald and of conservatism on sociological thought. Here it suffices merely to bring out clearly the sociological—as well as polemical-reactionary—content of much of Bonald's thought. "The last of the scholastics" he may have been, but the history of social movements as well as of ideas teaches us that more often than not some kind of renascence underlies eruptions of the seemingly novel.

V

Having looked in some detail at the ideas of one of the principal conservatives, let us turn now to a few of the larger themes or propositions on man and society which we find in the writings of the conservatives and which have most clearly affected the development of sociology.[42] In the next section we shall have an opportunity to see concretely how these propositions, or modifications of them, entered into the mainline of European sociology.

The Priority of the Social

This is perhaps the single most important contribution of the conservatives. It springs of course from their relentless assault upon the individualism of the Enlightenment and the Revolution. From the time Burke wrote his *Reflections on the Revolution in France*, in 1790, we are in the presence of profoundly antiindividualistic ideas. For Burke it is as irrational as it is immoral to seek to construct a social order out of the assumed rights of individuals or their assumed capacity for effecting a political order through rational contract. If there is a contract, Burke concludes, it is one through all time, one that is inseparable from the historical development of institutions. Society for Burke is a "partnership," but it is a partnership of the dead, the living, and the unborn. Bonald, de Maistre, and the youthful Lamennais are even more insistent upon the independent reality of the social. As we have seen, Bonald declares the aboriginal existence of society. There has never been a state of nature; there has never been a social contract by which human beings were brought from a "state of nature" into political or any other kind of society. Society has existed since man has. Society is eternal. In Bonald's explicit phrasing: "Man does not create society; it is society that creates man." Individuals as we know them, as they have existed from the beginning, are inseparable from the shaping social contexts of family, clan, community, and association. Reversing Pope's celebrated aphorism, the proper study of man is mankind—or, as Bonald and the other French conservatives had it, *société*. The individual, wrote the youthful Lamennais, is but a fantasy, the shadow of a dream. Hegel was equally critical of individualist-rationalist attempts to reduce the social to a mere collocation of individual drives or acts of reason. In the intensity, then, of their hatred and repudiation of the Enlightenment and the Revolution, the conservatives were led to formulation of an antiindividualistic view of society, one in which the metaphysical reality and also priority of the social is made fundamental.

The Functional Interdependence of Social Elements

It would be extreme, even incorrect, to attribute an organismic view of society to all of the conservatives. But what is not extreme or incorrect is ascription to them of a perspective that saw all social elements related in some degree to one another; a perspective that also saw a genuine function or purpose in each of these social elements, however difficult it might be for ordinary observation to detect this purpose or function. It was, of course, the spectacle of legislation of the Revolution riding roughshod over traditional institutions that generated this conservative response. For the revolutionists, as for the *philosophes* before them, a great deal of what existed in the form of custom, belief, and institution was expendable in the name of reason. Burke finds this attitude repugnant in the extreme, and although he does not seek to deal with the matter in any systematic fashion, his belief in the underlying wisdom of institutions and of what he calls "prejudices" is evident on a great many pages. He had objected to spoliation of Indian and Irish customs in the name of English common law; he objects equally to spoliation of traditional French customs in the name of mankind or reason.

In Germany, Möser, no less affronted by the modern rationalist philosophy that sat in judgment on history, wrote: "When I come across some old custom or old habit which simply will not fit into modern ways of reasoning, I keep turning around in my head the idea that 'after all, our forefathers were no fools either' until I find some sensible reason for it. . . ."[43] In an essay called "The Moral Point of View," Möser demonstrates that the real value of a social structure or belief cannot be ascertained from the utilization of abstract, general principles drawn from natural-law philosophy. Everything carries within itself the governing purpose or function. The interconnectedness of things is, of course, a fundamental principle in Hegel's philosophy—social as well as natural. His rationalism, unlike that of the Age of Reason or Enlightenment, is founded upon the reason that lies, often undiscerned, in history itself, and in the institutions which are the products of history. The degree of this objective or functional rationalism varies from conservative to conservative. But there is not one in whom a substantial faith does not lie in the utility of social forms as history has produced them, even when individual observation may fail to detect this utility. Nor is this attitude the result of quiescent traditionalism or simple antiquarianism. It is much more positive than that; it is rooted in the belief that history is much more than a random string of events, acts, and personages—is, in fact, a slowly evolving form of reason that expresses itself in customs and conventions. The conservatives did not doubt the existence of individual reason; they were simply more impressed by the prerational foundations of reason, and these foundations for the conservatives were unqualifiedly social.

The Necessity of the Sacred

If, as many modern historians of the subject have argued, the essence of the Enlightenment was its systematic assault upon Christianity, and in some degree all religion, we are justified in saying that the essence of conservatism, or certainly a large part of this essence, was conviction that no society, community, or group can exist apart from some kind of religion. The contempt for Christianity we find in Voltaire, Diderot, Rousseau, and others in the eighteenth century has its fitting counterpart in the great religious renascence of the early and middle nineteenth century, one that took many forms, ranging from simple revivalism to the sophisticated theologies of Lamennais, Döllinger, and Newman. And this renascence of interest in religion is closely connected with the writings of the conservatives. From Burke's insistence in his *Reflections* on the indispensable role played by Christianity in the development of European culture to Hegel's measured assertions of the complementary roles of politics and religion in his *Philosophy of Right*, there is a common belief in the necessity of religion as a vital context of individual life.

There is, moreover, a strong interest among the conservatives in the structural and symbolic elements of religion, those which provide supports for belief. Chateaubriand's study of Christianity may be an extreme instance of this, but it is by no means aberrant so far as conservative stress upon religious symbolism and community is concerned. From the conservative viewpoint the crime of the Reformation lay in its effort to isolate individual faith, to wrench it from the supporting ties of religious community and authority—*visible* community and authority. Lamennais's "Essay on Indifference" was written precisely around this theme; and closely related is Lamennais's argument in the same work that Protestant isolation of the individual from Church discipline paved the way for modern political despotism. There can be no society without a governing sense of the sacred; and there can be no persisting sense of the sacred without society. This is a fair characterization of the conservative view of religion.

Intermediate Association

I refer here to the groups and communities which lie intermediate to individual and state. It would have been strange had the conservatives not given attention to this sphere of association, for both the Enlightenment and the Revolution had come down hard on it, in philosophic text and legislative enactment. It is hard to find attitudes of other than contempt or hatred for family, traditional village, monastery, guild, and other reminders of the Middle Ages and of the *ancien rĝime* in the writings of the *philosophes*. Rousseau was but one of the rationalists who recorded his distrust of "partial associations" in the body politic. By many of these philosophers such groups were deemed as restrictive of individual liberty and as inimical to equality as they were harmful to the expression of any rational political authority in the state. As I have noted, much of the concrete legislation of the Revolution—on the patriarchal family, the ancient commune, the guilds, and so on—was directed to these social bodies.

From the conservative point of view, however, the abolition or sharp curtailment of intermediate associations in the social order spelled the creation of the atomized masses on the one hand and, on the other, increasingly centralized forms of political power. Burke made plain his distrust of the "geometrical" system of the Revolutionary legislators with its inevitable dislocation or atomization of the historic groups and associations which are, Burke tells us, "inns and resting places" of the human spirit. He ridiculed an administrative system which, with an absolute Paris at the center, would seek to govern in all the details of French social, economic, educational, and cultural life. What Burke began, the other conservatives, without exception, continued. Bonald called for the reinstituting of the guilds and also the old provinces and the historic communes. And, as we have seen, he was almost passionate in his support of a strong family system and Church. Lamennais, while still a loyal servant of the Church, founded, with Montalembert and Lacordaire, a journal called *L'Avenir,* and high among the stated purposes of the journal were first, restoration of the local commune; second, complete freedom of association; and third, decentralization of administration in France. So do we find strong emphasis upon intermediate association in Hegel. His whole treatment of "civil society" in *Philosophy of Right*, with its stress upon family, marriage, town, and what he calls "corporation" (analogous to the traditional guild), reflects this interest. Haller gives a great deal of attention to the subject in his monumental work on the reform of the social sciences, in which he pleads not only for the revival of valuable older intermediate associations but for new ones as well. In Spain Donoso y Cortés in a series of works put forward a proposal for a pluralist-associationist structure of the state that is difficult to separate at times from the syndicalist program.

Looking ahead, indeed, to the anarchist-syndicalist and the several variants of guild-socialist programs which would flourish in the late nineteenth century in so many parts of Europe, it is tempting to stress a certain modernist character in the conservatives; proposals for intermediate association and its role in government. But in truth, there was little modernity, if any at all, in the motivations of the conservatives here or elsewhere. The medieval flavor of what they proposed is far more evident. After all, the Middle Ages, by virtue of relatively weak central power in the state, and by virtue also of an indistinct concept of the individual and his rights, were rich in intermediate associations, ranging from partriarchal family through village community, guild, monastery, and university to the great profusion of mutual-aid groups which thrived in the absence of a strong political state. In sum, here as in other places, the essential motivation for the conservatives came from the past, not the future.

Hierarchy

Needless to stress, there is no tincture of egalitarianism in conservative thought. Burke and Haller perhaps excepted, it would be difficult to find in the conservatives regard even for legal equality or what had come to be known as equality of talents in open careers. Burke, himself a profound believer in social class, especially the landed class, was willing to speak for a sufficient degree of mobility, through which individuals from the lower ranks could rise as high as talent carried them. But such mobility should not be too free, he argued. And as far as political establishment of equality in society was concerned, he stood firmly on his belief that "those who attempt to level never equalize."

For Bonald, with his dedication to an essentially organic, feudal society, any thought of equality was utterly out of the question. Social classes must be real, and there should be a strong element of the hereditary in them. In Bonald's view, hierarchy of functions, authorities, and individual statuses is as much a part of "constituted" or "legitimate" society as "hierarchy" of neurophysiological functions is in the human body. He avails himself of the old Western principle "the great chain of being," conceived by the ancient

Greeks and given great importance in Christian-medieval thought, and points to the inevitable gradations which exist in the universe, from the smallest organism all the way up to the sovereign God.

Hegel, though by no means as dogmatic on the subject as Bonald, has nevertheless a strongly developed view of the value of social classes in society. Subdivision of civil society into distinct strata is, he writes, a necessity. "The family is the first precondition of the state, but class divisions are the second."[44] Adam Müller, in his *Elements of Statecraft*, had a full decade earlier given full value to social classes as necessary to a stable political order and as bulwarks against the kind of individualism that had sprung from the Reformation and that threatened the social bases of Western society.[45]

There are two other reasons for conservative regard for social class; each of which has an importance that goes beyond mere traditionalism. The first lies in fear of the "masses," the "incoherent, distracted multitude" of Burke's fancy. What he abhorred, as did all the conservatives, were those reformers and revolutionists who would seek "to tear asunder the bonds of the subordinate community and to dissolve it into an unsocial, uncivil, unconnected chaos of elementary principles." Closely related to fear of the masses and their potential turbulence is conservative dread of the kind of direct, centralized, omnicompetent power that is based upon the masses, which can thrive only in the absence of well-formed social classes and other forms of intermediate association. True social interdependence is not only horizontal but also vertical: this was a firm conservative principle.

The Specter of Social Disorganization

We commonly credit Saint-Simon and Comte, and also in some degree Fourier, with the first apprehensions of the kind of disorder that springs from dislocated social and moral roots. And without question the vision, and theory, of social disorganization is to be found in the writings of these men. Saint-Simon's New Christianity and Comte's Positivism—and then his newly-coined "sociology"—were expressly created as necessary means of repulsing the forces of anarchy which each thought were creeping day by day into the very recesses of society and the human mind in Western Europe.

But here as in so many other instances initial credit must be given to the conservatives. There is, in the first place, their very philosophy of history. For a Bonald, a Haller, or a Balmes, modern history represents in signal ways an actual decline, not progress: Renaissance, Reformation, Age of Reason—these are but so many steps or stages in this decline. History, far from possessing the organizational, progressive character ascribed to it by Condorcet and Kant, to name but two, is in fact susceptible to decay and disorder, to disorganization. The Revolution seemed to the conservatives hardly more than a dramatic, terror-ridden culmination of disorganizing forces which had been present in Western Europe from the late Middle Ages on. Saint-Simon would divide all history into "organic" and "critical" periods. For him the Middle Ages had been an organic society. However, all that intervened between the medieval and the contemporary eras was, for Saint-Simon, "critical," meaning disorganized, negative, and even nihilistic. As Saint-Simon freely acknowledged, this view of history had roots which came directly from the writings of de Maistre, Bonald, Chateaubriand, and other "traditionalists" in France.

It was not new to see disorder. After all, for Rousseau in his *Discourses* or Condorcet in his *Sketch on Human Progress*, the regime around them was nothing if not disordered, made so by human iniquity, superstition, and ignorance. What was needed was at once rational political authority and individual liberation from the torments of the *ancien régime*. But in conservative writings after the Revolution—indeed, beginning in 1790 with Burke—we have something rather different; the view that disorganization of family, community, class, and the sacred is an inexorable accompaniment of all that advocates of modernity were hailing: city, industry, technology, democracy, and equality. For better or worse, right or wrong, there is a deeper, more tragic contemplation of man and his problems in conservative writing. The kind of pessimism we associate in the nineteenth century with Tocqueville in his latter years, with Burckhardt, Nietzsche, and others in a line that continues down to Spengler, Berdyaev, and Sorokin in our own century, is a pessimism that is grounded in the view of history as a process of disorganization.

Everywhere the conservatives looked in the period that followed the French Revolution they saw, or believed they saw, uprooted kinship ties, dissolved communities, shattered classes and estates, and broken moral values, all without exception consequences of Enlightenment liberalism and Revolutionary democracy. The nearest they dared come to optimism was, as in the works of Bonald, Haller, and Hegel, in their positive prescriptions for the reestablishment of those institutions which had been destroyed or weakened by the acids and poisons of modernity.

Historicism

The final theme I wish to consider from conservative writing is in some degree implicit in the foregoing sections. It nevertheless deserves distinct identification here. "Historicism" is not, alas, a very precise word. It has been used to cover just about everything from strict historiography of the kind written in the nineteenth century by Ranke, Mommsen, Motley, and others dedicated to exact rendering of time, personage, and place, to what we more commonly refer to as social developmentalism, with or without evaluative implications of long-term progress or amelioration. As Popper and others have used the word "historicism," it has the added flavor of necessity or determinism. Thus, from Popper's point of view, both Hegel and Marx are "historicists."[46] Each, Popper tells us, used past, present, and also in some degree future as a scheme for setting forth a developmental construction of mankind that was at once immanent, directional, and made necessary by either spiritual (as with Hegel) or material (as with Marx) forces. From this rather broad and flexible point of view, then, "historicism" can be seen as conservative, liberal, or radical in thrust.

It is, however, most often to the conservatives, or at very least, to those concerned to show the roots of the present in the past, that the word seems to be directed in our histories of social thought. When we speak of the "historical school" in, say, German economics in the nineteenth century, we refer to writers who, departing in substantial degree from abstract Ricardian economics, attempted to show the *historical-developmental* nature of the economic system that Ricardians were prone to explain in terms of abstract, timeless forces in human nature. Similarly, the "historical school" of law in England, with Maine, Maitland and Vinogradov prominent, sought to show that modern political sovereignty and its attendant legal system cannot adequately be understood in terms of natural rights or universal interests or psychological forces embedded in human beings, but must be seen in terms of historical development. That is, understanding of the past is held vital to explanation of the present.

It is this emphasis on the historical past that has greatest relevance to the conservatives. For veneration of the past, and of the institutions and values descended from the past, is the very essence of conservatism, as we have already seen. The conservatives opposed strenuously, even bitterly, the rationalist view which had flourished in the Enlightenment, especially in France, and which had in effect declared the irrelevance of the heritage of the past so far as social reform and social reconstruction were concerned. Few things agitated Burke more than the idea that reason alone, proceeding logically and deductively, was sufficient to create or reform a state—or any other large social structure. From Burke's point of view—one that extends to all of the conservatives without exception—past and present are a seamless web. We are essentially what historical tradition has made us. Change is not impossible, or even undesirable; after all, there had been the Revolution of 1688 in England, a revolution Burke adored. But this revolution had been of a purely political character; it had not sought to disarrange or destroy social, moral, and spiritual ties; moreover, that revolution had justified itself by its restoration to Englishmen of rights once possessed but taken away by wielders of "arbitrary power."

This is, in sum, what the historicism of the conservatives was: a respect for, even a dedication to the past on the ground that apart from our recognition of this past, no understanding of the present, or foresight into the future, is possible. Because of their disavowal of all so-called natural rights, of anything resembling a state of nature, and because of their profound skepticism with regard to the capacities of individual reason in constructing societies and states, it was almost inevitable that the conservatives would turn to history, or rather to the lines of continuity and tradition which joined past and present. They did this on moral-political grounds; these were surely their primary motivations. It was the *ancien régime* and, before it, the Middle Ages, they venerated. But it cannot be denied that in their pursuit of moral-political objectives, in their roles of "prophets of the past," the conservatives were responsible also for a methodology, a framework of dealing with human behavior in terms of its institutional roots in the past, that could be, and was, used by others later in whom conservative disposition was a good deal less apparent. Between Haller's, Burke's and Bonald's frankly conservative attention to institutional roots and continuities in the economic, legal, and political spheres, and the kind of scholarly attention we find given to these matters later in the century by Maine, von Gierke, and Fustel de Coulanges, there are assuredly differences of a moral and technical kind. But there is nevertheless a straight line from the first to the second group.

VI

Let us turn now to some of the demonstrable influences of conservatism upon the rise and development of sociology in the nineteenth century. These influences are primarily to be seen in France and Germany, the two countries in which sociology prospered earliest in Western Europe. I focus here on France, partly because it was in France that sociology came first into being as an acknowledged, systematic, and identified discipline, and partly because, thanks chiefly to the work of Karl Mannheim, we already have an easily accessible body of work on German thought.

Both Saint-Simon and Comte were strong in their praise of what Comte called "the retrograde school"—that is, Bonald, de Maistre, Lamennais, and Chateaubriand. This "immortal school," Comte tells us, will always deserve the gratitude and the admiration of Positivists. Comte declares that the conservatives were the first in Europe to appreciate the true nature of the crisis that was overwhelming Western society. They—particularly Bonald, as their philosophical eminence—actually used Positivist principles, Comte tells us; and, Comte adds magnanimously, the origin of "social statics" (one of the two great divisions of Comte's sociology, the other being "social dynamics"), is to be found in Bonald's analyses of social order and stability.[47]

That all of this is not empty praise by Comte is made quickly evident. We need merely read his youthful *Essays*, written in the 1820s when Comte was first giving serious thought to the moral crisis of the postrevolutionary period, to see how substantially his analysis, indeed his philosophy of history, follows that of Bonald, de Maistre, and the young Lamennais. For Comte, too, the origins of the crisis lie in the individualism ("the disease of the Western world"[48]) that the Reformation introduced and that the Age of Reason and the Enlightenment brought to crisis point. In Comte's *Essays* is clearly stated (as would be restated in Comte's later works) his animadversion to the basic principles ("dogmas," Comte calls them) of Enlightenment and Revolution: popular sovereignty, equality, individual liberty, and the whole negative view of family, religion, local community, and intermediate association which had been so much a part of the writings of the *philosophes* and of the enactments of Revolutionary legislators.[49]

Clearly, Comte was no liberal, much less a radical, by the standards of the day. His views would remain basically the same on these matters throughout his life, in his notable and widely praised *Positive Philosophy* (1830–42) and in his ambitious, extraordinary, if less widely hailed, *Positive Polity* (1851–54). To suggest, as a few writers have, that is was Comte's short mental breakdown in early middle age, his disastrous first marriage, and then his devoutly platonic union with Clothilde de Vaux afterward, not to mention the visible growth of his sense of messianism during the final years of his life, which together account for his expressed dislike of Enlightenment and Revolution, is to overlook the early and continuing place this dislike has in his thought.

To be sure, in two major respects Comte differs with the conservatives. First, he is no Catholic. Although born in a devout Catholic and royalist family, Comte himself abandoned the Catholic faith at an early age (although, such is the power of early belief in one's life that his *Positive Polity*, which is in part a constructed positivist utopia, was called, with considerable reason, "Catholicism minus Christianity" by one critic). The conservatives in France had advocated rebuilding Western society through revival of feudal-Catholic principles. Comte, recognizing the identical crisis, advocates instead a new body of intellectual-spiritual principles—those of Positivism. But he is frank in declaring that Positivism will only be doing for the modern world what Catholicism had done for the medieval, and in several places he enjoins Positivists to look to the Catholic Middle Ages as a structural model for what Positivism, with its "new" principles, will be able to do for the future.

The second difference between Comte and the conservatives lies in Comte's acceptance of the value of the Enlightenment in at least two respects: first, despite his dislike of Rousseau, Voltaire, and their fellow *philosophes*, whom in one place Comte refers to as "*docteurs en guillotine*" and in another refers to their ideas as "*sauvage anarchie*,"[50] Comte nevertheless ascribes to them an indispensable negative value. Had it not been for their "metaphysical-critical" principles—false though they are as possible supports of a truly stable society—the moribund Catholic-feudal system could not have been destroyed, with the ground thus left clear for the principles of Positivism. And paralleling this favorable judgment of the Enlightenment is Comte's clear insistence that the second of his two great divisions of sociology, "social dynamics," owes just as much to such Enlightenment minds as Turgot and Condorcet as "social statics" owes to the postrevolutionary conservatives such as Bonald.

In final effect, sociology was, Comte thought, based upon an amalgamation of ideas of the Enlightenment and ideas of the conservatives. In some degree this is certainly true. But it is a rare reader of the *Positive Polity*—which Comte himself regarded as his masterwork, the only one to which he gave the subtitle "treatise on sociology"—that does not come away with the belief that in Comte's mind Conservative-Catholic values ultimately triumphed. It is worth repeating in this connection that throughout the nineteenth century, indeed into the early twentieth, Comte remained, despite his formal abjuration of Catholicism, a favorite, much quoted writer by French political conservatives, including Charles Maurras.

What is more to the point here, however, is the very evident impact of conservative ideas, especially those of Bonald, on Comte's detailed treatments in the *Positive Polity* of family, marriage, locality, social class, religion, and functional association. His treatment of the nature of language as a socializing influence upon individual development is in striking accord with Bonald's. For Comte, as for Bonald, the family—the true, the legitimate family—must be patriarchal in character; there is to be no divorce. Paris, he tells us, will succeed Rome as the spiritual capital of the future Positivist humanity. Religion—that is, Positivism—will coexist with political government as one of the two supreme powers over individuals. Society will be structured in clear-cut, functionally oriented social classes, with the uppermost being the intellectual-scientific-religious stratum, the business-professional just below it, and the bulk of the population spreading out below these two. There is no pretense of equality in Comte's order, any more than there is of individual liberty. The latter, in matters of social organization and government, is quite as absurd as the thought of individual liberty in mathematical domains. No one is "free," he writes, to believe other than that two times two is four. So with human society once it has come under the suzerainty of the wisest, of those deeply educated in the principles of Positivism, of sociology. Finally, for Comte, society is *Le Grand Etre!*[51]

VII

If there were but the work of Comte to offer as evidence, the impact of the conservatives on sociology in France and also other parts of Europe would be significant enough. For, all his idiosyncracies and obsessions aside, Comte remained a highly respected name throughout the century to such imposing thinkers as John Stuart Mill and Herbert Spencer, criticize him though they did in one respect or another. For a long time indeed "Comte's science" was a synonym for sociology. His fundamental categories of social status and social dynamics proved lasting ones, and we have the word of Durkheim and his followers at the end of the nineteenth century on the continuing impact and relevance of Comte's major ideas, especially those, inherited from Bonald, affirming the absoluteness and the irreducibility of society, and with this the insubstantiality of all individualistic ideas.

But there are other than Comtean evidences of the appeal the conservatives had, through however subterranean channels. There is the work of Frederick

Le Play, one of the most neglected sociological minds of the nineteenth century. He did not call himself, or think of himself, as a sociologist, for that word was stamped with Comtism, which Le Play—like Karl Marx—disliked. But his monumental *European Workers* (1855) is the first empirical, quantitative, comparative study of European family systems—and of their environing contexts in community and class—ever written. It had, by virtue of its budget-oriented method of study, and its confinement of data to what could be empirically observed and analyzed in Europe, almost immediate influence everywhere in Europe.

Of Frederick Le Play's conservatism of mind there can be no doubt whatever. The literary critic–historian Sainte-Beuve called him "A Bonald, revived, progressive, and scientific,"[52] and the characterization fits. From one point of view, Le Play's vast study, made over a period of years, is hardly more than a detailed, empirically broadened fulfillment of ideas contained in Bonald's aforementioned prescient essay on the social contrasts of rural and urban families and their contexts. Behind every bit of Le Play's study of the working-class families of urban and rural Europe, behind his celebrated differentiation of family types as "patriarchal," "stem," and "unstable," lies a set of moral-political principles which would be hard to separate from those of Bonald and de Maistre—except perhaps with respect to industry and the factory system, which Le Play unlike his predecessors had come to accept, subject only to a kind of feudalization of structure. Le Play is deeply monarchist, Roman Catholic, and altogether traditionalist in moral philosophy. His widely read *Social Reform in France* (1864)[53]—a work, the author tells us, specifically based upon the conclusions resulting from his earlier study of European family organization—is as much a conservative as a sociological classic. Precisely the same emphasis upon a strong, autonomous Church; a stable, rooted, family; abolition of divorce; a combination of localism and federalism, with marked decentralization of administration; a retreat of centralized political power from all areas of social organization; and, not least, a substantial reduction of *individualisme* in economic, social, and cultural spheres is to be found in Le Play's prescriptions, as in the earlier Bonald's. For the ideas, indeed the whole cast of mind, of the Enlightenment, Le Play's antipathy is at least as great as Bonald's and Comte's. And his admiration for the Middle Ages is also as great as his forerunners'.[54]

There is in Le Play the same distrust of the centralized political state that we have seen in the conservatives and the same desire to see restored a rich variety of intermediate association. "The suppression of all intervention of the state . . . must be the point of departure for social reform."[55] This is in a sense the dominant theme of Le Play's sociological proposals. From such suppression alone, he believes, can there take place the revival of family, religious, and local life so necessary to a healthy, stable society. He divides intermediate associations into two large groups: *communautes* and *corporations*.[56] He envisages these as supplements to the family. The first are equivalent to the guilds of the Middle Ages, and of many ancient societies also. They are not regarded by Le Play as useful in industrial society, once the family has been reformed and industry conceived as a complex of families rather than of individuals. *Corporations*, however, do have a place in contemporary society. There are many kinds of these, at least in possibility, ranging from mutual-aid and charitable societies among the poor to literary, scholarly, and scientific societies. It is the mark of a vigorous, creative society when the latter are flourishing.

The effect of conservatism upon Alexis de Tocqueville is beyond question, although he is chary of specific reference to any of the conservatives and regards himself as more of a liberal in his practical politics than a conservative.[57] Indeed his prefatory remarks in *Democracy in America* (1835, 1840) are addressed to those conservatives who continue to imagine that the *ancien régime* can somehow be reestablished. From Tocqueville's point of view democracy and equality are tidal forces in modern European history; they cannot be arrested, only, he hoped, guided in such a way that liberty would not be destroyed. Tocqueville, in a celebrated speech in the Chamber of Deputies, in January 1848, actually predicted the revolution which broke upon France shortly after, and he played a prominent role as a liberal on the Constitutional Commission. If he could not accept the more radical forms of social democracy proffered, neither could he bring himself to alliance with the far Right.

The conservative influence upon Tocqueville's thinking is manifest in both *Democracy in America* and *The Old Regime and the French Revolution*, as well as in his *Notebooks* and various other works, including his final *Recollections* of the Revolution of 1848. There is in the first place his obsession with equality and its potentially destructive effect upon liberty. More dispassionate, temperate, and perhaps also divided in mind than such conservatives as Bonald and de Maistre, Tocqueville can on occasion see a good side to equality and actually praise it. But, as every student of Tocqueville knows, he takes, on balance, a deeply pessimistic view of the long-term impact of equality upon freedom. Equality he thought, would, unless checked constantly by major institutional forces, gradually lead to a leveling of the population, a creation of the undifferentiated mass, and a form of despotism totalitarian in character.

The conservative distrust of the political state, especially the centralized state, is also apparent in Tocqueville. So is the conservative fear of industrialism, the factory system, and of technologically based division of labor. And on the positive side, we find in Tocqueville a full measure of conservative veneration for family, local community, regionalism, division of political power, religion as the necessary basis of society, complete autonomy of religion from the state, and, far from least, veneration for profuse, voluntary, intermediate association. Of all checks upon the spreading power of the state, none is more important, Tocqueville thought, than complete freedom of association. Earlier, as I have noted, the conservative Lamennais had made this insistence upon freedom of association, along with a reinstituting of strong local government and of decentralization of government, key elements of policy in his journal *L'Avenir*, founded several years before Tocqueville made his memorable voyage to the United States.[58]

On the Enlightenment and the *philosophes*, Tocqueville's attitude, while more restrained than what is to be found in the works of the conservatives, is nevertheless critical, even vitriolic. This is especially noticeable in his study of the French Revolution and its background. We find there the same general views on the ideas of the *philosophes* and of the legislators of the Revolution that Burke had expressed in 1790—views which we know Tocqueville to have been thoroughly familiar with. He finds them guilty of a gross simplification of social reality that proceeds from natural-law principles; of a political zeal that is ordinarily to be found, he tells us, in religionaries; and of a contempt for the institutional complexities of experience, the result of passion for general ideas and abstract principles.[59]

In summary, Tocqueville probably deserves the label of "liberal" if only for his unswerving consecration to liberty. That value is for Tocqueville the touchstone of all assessments of state and society. But his liberalism has little in common with the individualistic thought of the Enlightenment, or the acceptance of the idea of direct use of central political power in the name of social reconstruction we also find in the Enlightenment. Tocqueville's liberalism is manifestly tempered by conservative recognition of the priority of authority, community, and hierarchy to any genuinely free political society. There is little if any relation between Tocqueville's view of the grounds of freedom and the *philosophes'* views during the Enlightenment.

Returning to sociology in the systematic sense of the word, it is impossible to miss the vitality of conservative concepts, chiefly as transmitted by Comte, in the nineteenth century in France. From Comte to Durkheim, the single most influential and also distinctive school of sociology in France is that resting on the priority of society to the individual and the derivation from the social order of all essential characteristics of individual personality and of culture.[60] Eugene de Roberty (1843–1915), Russian born, German educated, spent many years in France, and his *Sociology* (1880) had significant influence upon the field even though he himself was never able to succeed in founding a school of disciples. In his major work there are abundant references to not only Comte's but to Bonald's ideas.

We must also mention Alfred Espinas, one of the most neglected of pre-Durkheimian sociologists. He preceded Durkheim in appointment at Bordeaux and also at the Sorbonne, though, like Roberty, he failed to establish a lasting school. The Bonald-Comte stress upon the priority of society, and upon the impossibility of explaining social behavior in terms of forces or processes drawn from the individual or from direct interactions of individuals (as Tarde sought to do)—all of this is overriding in Espinas. His interest in the social organizations of the subhuman species, made manifest in his *On Animal Societies* (1877), was predicated entirely on the desire to show that all the really essential attributes of human society—solidarity, dominance of the social bond over individual will, the social basis of individual reactions to the natural world, and so on—are to be found in the social organizations of animals.

Espinas's repudiation of individualism on both moral and methodological grounds is total, indistinguishable in its fullness and intensity from the repudiation we found in Bonald and Comte. His remarkable *The Origins of Technology* (1897) demonstrates the relative ineffectuality of individual invention as such, compared with the contextual and even supervening influences which are social in nature. What Durkheim showed, in exactly the same year, in *Suicide*—the triumph of the social over the individual in the incidence of suicide—Espinas demonstrates with respect to technology and invention. Espinas's *Social Philosophy in the Eighteenth Century and the Revolution* (1898) is one of the most thorough and also perceptive criticisms of Enlightenment individualism that has ever been written. His indebtedness to the conservatives is clear throughout.

With Durkheim I shall be brief here, inasmuch as his thought is the subject of a separate chapter in this book.[61] Writing a full century after the eruption of the conservative anti-Enlightenment in Western Europe, he is proof of the continuity and persistence, as well as the power, of the ideas contained in that eruption. Durkheim was not, by political-moral predilection, a conservative. He was a Dreyfusard and had given himself without qualification to the cause of Captain Dreyfus following the latter's imprisonment on charges of having given French army secrets to the Germans. Certainly there is nothing in Durkheim's writing or personal life to suggest the slightest sympathy with any conservative movements. Durkheim was eminently secular in mind (an avowed nonbeliever), liberal in political sympathies, and antagonistic to the royalist-aristocratic-clerical views of contemporaneous traditionalists.

It is another matter, however, when we turn to his major sociological principles. Precisely as had the conservatives and then Saint-Simon and Comte, Durkheim begins in his first major work, *The Division of Labor* (1893), with the crisis in Western, as well as French, morality and social organization. This sense of moral crisis remained vivid in his mind to the end of his life, as did the principle that, at bottom, all social phenomena are moral in substance. Only through a reestablishment of moral consensus, a consensus joined to a recovered intellectual solidarity, can genuine social reform occur. For Durkheim, as for his predecessors a century earlier, the evidences of moral crisis are found in increasing rates of internal conflict, political and economic, and also of anomie.

In his *The Rules of Sociological Method* (1895) the priority of society to the individual as a sociological principle, has an emphasis that not even Bonald could have improved upon. The coerciveness of the social over the individual, the priority of collective representations to individual, and the necessity of sociological explanations being invariably social, not individual nor psychological—these propositions, which first made their appearance in conservative thought, are the very stuff of Durkheim's methodological treatise.

Suicide (1897) carries on and documents the argument of the *Rules*.

Lamennais, in an essay on suicide (1819), had written, while still a Catholic conservative that man's loss of social order leads to intolerable anguish and estrangement. "Alone in the midst of the universe he runs, or rather he seeks to run, into nothingness." Tocqueville two decades later expressed much the same view in *Democracy in America,* noting the rising tendency toward suicide in France as the close contexts of community broke down under the ravages of hedonistic individualism. Let us acknowledge Durkheim's superior methodology in *Suicide;* this work rests nevertheless upon the view of the individual's organic relation to society that Lamennais had set forth in 1819.

There is finally Durkheim's masterpiece, *The Elementary Forms of Religious Life* (1912). It is ironic that this book, dedicated to the proposition that religion is an inescapable element of social life, functionally indispensable to the social bond, should have been written by an avowed nonbeliever, by one whose only real passion was science and the scientific analysis of social phenomena. There is further irony in the fact that Durkheim's very interpretation of religion draws heavily from the stream of religious analysis that had begun in France with such minds as Bonald and Chateaubriand. This interpretation is social, collective to the core. Not in individual faith, belief, or communication with a god does Durkheim find the substance, the origin, of religion. Religion—that is, the sacred—is inconceivable apart from society, just as society is religion's other face. Bonald could not have improved upon that—or upon Durkheim's hostile references to Protestantism and its historic insistence upon the primacy of individual faith. It is to the rationalist students of religion that Durkheim directs some of his strongest blows—for their efforts to derive religion from superstition, from irrationalities, and other strictly mental phenomena. There is a functionality about religion, a proffer of community and the sense of membership, that is both vital to the individual and to society itself.

So deep runs Durkheim's antipathy to individualism that he seeks, even as had Bonald, to demonstrate the origin of language, of mind itself and its categories of thought, from society rather than from individual thought. Like Bonald, Durkheim can write that "society is a reality *sui generis*; it has its own peculiar characteristics, which are not to be met with again in the same form in all the rest of the universe." It could be either Bonald or Burke rather than Durkheim who, in his study of religion, wrote of collective representations: "they are the result of an immense cooperation, which stretches out not only into space but into time as well; to make them a multitude of minds have associated, united, and combined their ideas and sentiments; for them long generations have accumulated their experiences and knowledge. A special intellectual activity is therefore concentrated in them which is infinitely richer and more complex than that of the individual."

Nor, finally, can we miss the flavor communicated by Durkheim's single, major reform proposal for the France of his day: the creation of guildlike occupational associations within which industry would be conducted, but also a great deal of political, social, and cultural life as well. These intermediate associations, described by Durkheim in the concluding pages of *Suicide* and then at greater length in the preface to the second edition of his *Division of Labor*, are renderings of the earlier conservative proposal for *corps intermediaires*. In words which might have sprung from Burke, Bonald, Hegel, or any of the other conservatives, Durkheim tells us that the destruction of the guilds by the French Revolution had created an intolerable vacuum in the economic order, giving rise in time to augmenting rates of strife, breakdown, and of individual isolation from society.

In sum, conservatism, as it took shape philosophically in reaction to both the Revolution and the Enlightenment—and also, as I have noted, to the new industrial system—had profound effect upon the creation and the development of sociology in the nineteenth century. In its repudiation of the Enlightenment's cherished natural order, of asserted natural law and natural rights, and in its polemical emphasis upon the historically developed institutions of man, conservatism called attention to a sphere of society that had been largely neglected for two centuries. What the conservatives identified by way of praising for political-religious reasons, others, commencing with Saint-Simon and Comte, made the basis of a new science of society.

NOTES

1. Gunnar Myrdal, *An American Dilemma* (New York: Harper & Row, 1944; new ed., 1962) vol. 2, p. 1047.

2. Karl Mannheim, "Conservative Thought," in Paul Kecskemeti, ed., *Essays on Sociology and Social Psychology* (New York: Oxford University Press, 1953) pp. 74–164. Mannheim's work was written originally in German, in 1927. It is almost entirely concerned with nineteenth-century German conservatism.

3. Mannheim, "Conservative Thought," p. 116–19, gives strong emphasis to this contrast between the Enlightenment and conservatism.

4. See Robert Nisbet, *The Sociological Tradition* (New York: Basic Books, 1967) especially chaps. 1 and 2, for fuller treatment of this vital typology.

5. No single, systematic work exists on the conservative anti-Enlightenment of 1790–1830; nothing that deals with this movement in any way comparable to the countless treatments of the Enlightenment; nothing that seeks to do justice to the time period or to the geographical distribution of the conservative movement; nothing that concerns itself at length with the central, unifying ideas of the movement. There are, fortunately, some excellent works on the emergence of conservatism in individual countries—chiefly France and Germany—as well as on the primary figures involved, and I shall refer to these appropriately in the notes that follow. Mannheim, "Conservative Thought," is the most useful interpretation of German conservatism. I have dealt with French conservative thought in a succession of articles commencing in 1943, all of which are noted in Nisbet, *The Sociological Tradition*, which also deals with European conservatism as a background to the emergence of sociology, with principal emphasis given to the French and English.

6. The literature on Burke's political and social thought is of course vast. Two recent works of originality and interest are Ruth A. Bevan, *Marx and Burke: A Revisionist View* (La Salle, Ill,: Open Court, 1973) and David R. Cameron, *The Social Thought of Rousseau and Burke* (Toronto: University of Toronto Press, 1973). Gerald W. Chapman, *Edmund Burke, The Practical Imagination* (Cambridge: Harvard University Press, 1967) should also be consulted. Finally, I recommend for its thoroughness B. T. Wilkins's *The Problem of Burke's Political Philosophy* (Oxford: Oxford University Press, 1967).

7. Roger Soltau, *French Political Thought in the Nineteenth Century* (New Haven: Yale University Press, 1931) is probably the best treatment of conservative, among other types of, political and social thought. See also J. T. Mertz, *History of European Thought in the Nineteenth Century* (London, 1914) especially vol. 4. Emile Faguet, *Politiques et Moralistes du Dix-Neuvième Siècle* (Paris, 1891–1900) 3 vols., has some penetrating accounts of individual French conservatives and their ideas. So does Charles Sainte-Beuve, *Causeries du Lundi* (Paris, 1885) 16 vols. George Boas, *French Philosophies of the Romantic Period* (Baltimore: Johns Hopkins Press, 1925) is valuable. A recent, moderately useful work is J. McClelland, ed., *The French Right* (London: Jonathan Cape, 1970) which carries the story from de Maistre down to Charles Maurras.

8. An excellent study of de Maistre is Claude J. Gignoux, *Joseph de Maistre, Prophête du Passé, Historien de l'Avenir* (Paris: Nouvelles Editions Latines, 1963). See the penetrating article by Elisha Greifer, "Joseph de Maistre and the Reaction Against the 18th Century," *American Political Science Review* (September 1961).

9. The best single full-length study of Bonald remains Henri Moulinié, *Bonald* (Paris, 1915). The comparisons with Comte and other sociologists are excellent. My own "Bonald and the Concept of the Social Group," *The Journal of the History of Ideas* (January 1944) deals with his wider social influence in the nineteenth century. A recent important study emphasizing the religious basis of Bonald's thought is Gianfranco Merli, *De Bonald: Contributo alla Formazione del Pensiero Catolico nella Restaurazione* (Torino, 1972).

10. See Robert Nisbet, "The Politics of Social Pluralism: Some Reflections on Lamennais," *Journal of Politics* (November 1948). Peter N. Stearns, *Priest and Revolutionary: Lamennais and the Dilemma of French Catholicism* (New York: Harper & Row, 1967) is a fascinating and important account of Lamennais's extraordinary spiritual and intellectual evolution and his effect upon his contemporaries.

11. The best single study of the political and social aspects of Chateaubriand's life and thought is Charles Dedeyan, *Chateaubriand et Rousseau* (Paris, 1973). The author is better on Chateaubriand than on Rousseau.

12. Karl Mannheim, "Conservative Thought" serves admirably for ordinary analysis of the ideas of Adam Müller and Möser; Mannheim has caught the flavor of each successfully and related it to the mainstream of German conservative thought. I recommend also David Y. Allen, *From Romanticism to Realpolitik: Studies in Nineteenth-Century Conservatism* (New York, 1971), though it is more oriented toward practical politics than to theoretical matters.

13. Shlomo Avineri, *Hegel's Theory of the State* (Cambridge: Cambridge University Press, 1974) is strongly recommended. So is Raymond Plant, *Hegel* (Bloomington: Indiana University Press, 1975). Also Walter Kaufmann, ed., *Hegel's Political Philosophy* (New York: Lieber-Atherton, 1975). It is legitimate to stress the proto- or potential radicalism of the young Hegel and his influence on Marxism, but it must not be forgotten that Hegel was, in his mature, great years of teaching and writing, conservative, and was recognized as such throughout educated Germany.

14. On Müller see Karl Mannheim, "Conservative Thought," and, for a more detailed treatment of his historical-social ideas, Karl Schueck, *Studien uber Johannes von Müller* (Heidelberg, 1912). Also Karl Henking's monumental study, *Johannes von Müller* (Stuttgart, 1909–28) 2 vols.

15. Sad to relate, there is no even adequate study of Haller's remarkable system of social and political thought. His *Restauration* has not been translated—not even sections of it, to my knowledge—and he receives short shrift in the standard histories of political thought. The best study I have been able to find of Haller is W. H. von Sonntag, *Die Staatsauffassung Carl Ludwig von Haller* (Jena, 1929). The most recent study I have been able to find is Mario Sancipriano, *Il Pensiero Politico di Haller e Rosmini* (Milano: Marzorati, 1968). It is, however, uneven in quality so far as Haller is concerned.

16. On Donoso y Cortés see Carl Schmitt, *Interpretacción a Donoso y Cortês* (Madrid: Rialp, S.A., 1964); also an extraordinarily good appreciation in *The Dublin Review* (Spring 1947). No good study of Balmes has been done in modern times. Probably the best appreciation to this day is Ade de Blanche-Raffin, *Jacques Balmes, sa vie et ses Ouvrages* (Paris, 1849), a work written in sympathetic but not uncritical spirit. Given the relevance of both Donoso y Cortés and Balmes to current trends of liberalized conservatism in Spain, we can hope for increased attention to these two thinkers, the more especially since the collected works of both have become easily available in Spain.

17. A more extended account of these contexts will be found in Nisbet, *The Sociological Tradition*, especially the first two chapters, but *passim*. For different but valuable treatments of

the scene, intellectual and social, in which conservatism rose, see Raymond Williams, *Culture and Society: 1780–1950* (Garden City, N.Y.: Doubleday Anchor Books, 1960) and E. R. Hobsbawm, *The Age of Revolution* (New York: Mentor Books, 1964). For the German scene, see Klaus Epstein, *The Genesis of German Conservatism* (Princeton: Princeton University Press, 1966). For the French, see Stanley Mellon, *The Political Uses of History: A Study of Historians in the French Restoration* (Stanford: Stanford University Press, 1958).

18. Alexis de Tocqueville, *The Old Regime and the French Revolution* (Garden City, N.Y.: Doubleday Anchor Books, 1955), *passim*. See also Norman Hampson, *A Social History of the French Revolution* (London: Routledge & Kegan Paul, 1963) for its balanced insights, and also Franklin F. Ford, "The Revolutionary-Napoleonic Era: How Much of a Watershed?" *American Historical Review* (October 1963)

19. On this vital aspect of the Revolution, the best works are still Philippe Sagnac, *La Législation Civile de la Revolution Française* (Paris, 1898) and Etienne Martin Saint-Leon, *Histoire des Corporations de Métiers* (Paris, 1898). Robert R. Palmer, *Twelve Who Ruled* (Princeton: Princeton University Press, 1941) is also useful in this context.

20. Williams, *Culture and Society*, is particularly good on the impact, especially in England, of the Industrial Revolution on literary and social thought. See also Ronald Walter Harris, *Romanticism and the Social Order: 1780–1830* (New York: Barnes & Noble, 1969) for a useful treatment.

21. Moulinié, *Bonald*, draws in considerable detail this contrast between Bonald and Rousseau, and other members of the Enlightenment as well. On this same contrast see also the study of Bonald by Harold Laski, *Authority in the Modern State* (New Haven: Yale University Press, 1919) chap. 2.

22. All citations and references following are from Bonald, *Oeuvres Completes* (hereafter *O. C.*), Abbé Migne, ed. (Paris, 1859–64) 3 vols.

23. John Morley, *Critical Miscellanies* (London, 1888) vol. II, p. 303. As typical examples of Bonald's own admiration for the Middle Ages and his belief that this age should serve as the model for the reconstruction of his own, see Bonald, *O. C.*, vol. I, pp. 248, 262, 723, and 1336–39. It was Faguet, *Politiques et Moralistes*, vol. I, p. 70, who referred to Bonald as "the last of the scholastics."

24. Bonald. *O. C.*, vol. I, p. 123.

25. Bonald, "Reflections sur l'histoire de Bossuet," *O. C.*, vol. III, p. 983.

26. Bonald, "Economie Sociale," *O. C.*, vol. I, p. 115.

27. Bonald, "Legislation Primitive," *O. C.*, vol. I, pp. 1074–75.

28. Bonald, "Pensées sur les divers sujets," *O. C.*, vol. III, p. 1281.

29. *La Théorie du Pouvoir* is found in Bonald, *O. C.* vol. I, pp. 134–950. The treatment of political power occupies p. 134–456; of religious power, p. 458–719; and of social education, p. 742–950.

30. Bonald, *O. C.*, vol. I, p. 163.

31. See Barker's introduction to his translation of Otto von Gierke, *Natural Law and the Theory of Society* (Cambridge: Cambridge University Press, 1934) 2 vols. p. XLIX.

32. Bonald, *O. C.*, vol. I. p. 1374.

33. Bonald, "Théorie du Pouvoir," *O. C.*, vol. I, pp. 262ff. Also "Mélanges," *O. C.*, vol. III, p. 1279, where Bonald elaborates on the benefits, social and psychological, to the individual members of the functional corporations; and "Economie Sociale," *O. C.*, vol. I, p. 1040, for further observations on the value of occupational-intermediate associations.

34. Bonald, "Économie Sociale," *O. C.*, vol. I, p. 1260.

35. Bonald, "Théorie du Pouvoir," section on "*pouvoir religieuse*," *O. C.*, vol. I, p. 458–719.

36. Bonald, "Principe Constitutif de la Société," *O. C.*, vol. I, pp.39–50; also "Économie Sociale," *O. C.*, vol. I, pp. 993ff, and "Divorce," *O. C.*, vol. II, p. 97.

37. Bonald, "Mélanges," *O. C.*, vol. III, pp. 1282–83. Bonald denies the right of the state to conscript for military service—a practice that had begun with the Jacobins in the Revolution—on the ground that it is an infringement of family government and patriarchal supremacy.

38. This interesting and seminal essay is to be found in Bonald, *O. C.*, vol. II, pp. 238ff. One of Bonald's stronger attacks on industrialism, especially English, is in "Mélanges," *O. C.*, vol. III, pp. 1336–39.

39. Bonald, "Théorie du Pouvoir," *O. C.*, vol. I, p. 358.

40. Bonald, "Sur les Élections," *O. C.*, vol. II, p. 1319.

41. Bonald, "Discours Politiques," *O. C.*, vol. II, p. 1074.

42. I have dealt in more detail with these and other themes, found alike on conservatism and nineteenth-century sociology, in Nisbet, *The Sociological Tradition*. The principal works of the

conservatives in which these constitutive themes are to be found are: Burke, *Reflections on the Revolution in France;* Bonald, *Oevres Completes;* Lamennais, *Essay on Indifference;* Chateaubriand, *The Genius of Christianity;* Hegel, *Philosophy of Right;* Haller, *Restoration of the Social Sciences;* and de Maistre, *Considerations on France*. All of these, and other works, are more explicitly identified in the second section of this chapter.

43. Cited by Karl Mannheim, "*Conservative Thought,*" pp. 140, 143.

44. Hegel, *Philosophy of Right,* Trans. by T. M. Knox (Oxford: Oxford University Press, 1942) p. 271. Hegel, on p. 154, has a passage reminiscent of Bonald's earlier work and anticipatory of Simmel: "The town is the seat of the civil life of business. There reflection turns in upon itself, and pursues its atomizing task. . . . The country, on the other hand, is the seat of an ethical life resting on nature and the family. Town and country thus constitute two moments, still ideal moments, whose true ground is the state, although it is from them that the state springs."

45. See Mannheim, "*Conservative Thought,*" pp. 157ff.

46. Karl Popper, *The Open Society and its Enemies* (London: Routledge & Kegan Paul, 1945) vol. 2. Also Karl Popper, *The Poverty of Historicism* (New York: Harper Torchbooks, 1964); see also Nisbet, *Social Change and History* (New York: Oxford University Press, 1969), especially the final three chapters.

47. Auguste Comte, *Systéme de Politique Positive ou Traitê de Sociologie,* 4th ed. (Paris, 1912) vol. III, pp. 605, 614. See also the *Opuscules* (the early essays), which form an appendix to the *Systéme,* p. 157. Additional praise of Bonald and the French conservatives by Comte is found in the *Systéme,* vol. I, p. 64; vol. III, p. 615; and vol. II, p. 178. It is no wonder that the continuing line of French conservatism through the century invariably praised Comte, although he had formally renounced Roman Catholicism, which most French conservatives espoused.

48. Comte, *Systéme,* vol. III, pp. 551–52.

49. Comte, *Systéme,* vol. I, pp. 361, 159ff.

50. Comte, *Systéme,* vol. I, p. 74.

51. One has to read Comte's *Positive Polity* much more critically and discerningly than his earlier *Positive Philosophy.* The earlier work was in effect a call to science, the science of society, and it is filled with the methodological and theoretical steps necessary to achievement of a science. But the *Positive Polity* is much more complex. The careful reader will find astute analyses of the structure, functions, and fundamental processes of family, religion, education, social class, and government, but these are set almost invariably in the larger context of a near-messianic account of positivism—now regarded less as science than as the new religion of mankind, the worship of society, *le Grand Etre.* Side by side one will find in the *Polity* adjuration respecting the precise form positivist liturgy should take and a sophisticated dissection of ritual and liturgy in the life of man. On the whole, despite the fact that the subtitle of the *Positive Polity* is "a treatise on sociology," it is a work in sociological religion, millennialist in inspiration. Boas, *French Philosophies of the Romantic Period,* pp. 292–93, does not exaggerate, it seems to me, in his stress on the Catholic-revival roots of Comte's work. "Positivism is Catholicism of the Bonald-Maistre type expressed in more or less novel and secular language. . . . That Bonald and Maistre found pretended corroboration for their ideas in the teachings of the Church, verified by observation, whereas Comte found his verification in pretended observation alone, is an accident of biographical importance only." As I say, I regard Boas as correct in his assessment of Comte—the Comte, certainly, of the *Positive Polity*—and yet there is no hiding from the profound influence Comte had on a succession of sociologists culminating in Durkheim.

52. Charles Sainte-Beuve, *Nouveaux Lundis* (Paris, 1867) vol. IX, p. 180.

53. This is, without any question, the best work in which to find the whole of Le Play's social and political thought. Although prescriptive in intent, there is a large amount of descriptive-analytical writing, and the early chapters on method are admirable. I find it extraordinary that Le Play has never been translated—apart from some long sections in Carle C. Zimmerman and Merle E. Frampton's *Family and Society* more than a generation ago—or made the subject of a full, critical study—beyond what is contained in the brief work by Dorothy Herbertson, "*The Life of Frederick Le Play,*" reprinted as section 2 of vol. 38 of *The Sociological Review* (1946).

54. Frederick Le Play, *La Réforme Sociale,* vol. I, pp. 55ff. Le Play distinguishes between the genuine feudalism of the Middle Ages, which he admires, and its corruption under the monarchical *ancien régime.* He does not, as did Bonald, de Maistre, and even Burke, confuse the two.

55. Le Play, *La Réforme,* vol. II, p. 371. In all important respects Le Play was decentralist and pluralist in politics. There is, for all his deep-seated Catholic traditionalism, much in common with Proudhon when it comes to the relation of social groups to political power.

56. See Le Play, *La Rêforme*, vol. II, chap. 42, for his distinction between *communautes* and *corporations*.

57. The conservative-liberal conflict in Tocqueville's mind is no more apparent to us, his readers, than it was to Tocqueville himself. Throughout his life, as we know from letters to friends, from his memoirs of the Revolution of 1848, and from his own participation in the Revolution, he agonized over his inability to find a secure place in either a party or recognized ideology that was acceptable to his mind. In a letter to Henry Reeve, friend and English translator of Tocqueville, in 1837 (prior to the publication of part II of *Democracy in America*), Tocqueville wrote: "People ascribe to me alternately aristocratic and democratic prejudices. If I had been born in another period, or in another country, I might have had either one or the other. But my birth, as it happened, made it easy for me to guard against both." It is probably better to put Tocqueville in the liberal tradition than in the conservative. But where he cannot be accurately placed is in the social democratic movement that was becoming strong by the end of the Revolution of 1848. The conservative undertones of Tocqueville's treatment of the earlier French Revolution and of the period of thought leading up to it are only too evident. And his long, brooding critique of democracy and its erosive effects upon culture, mind, literacy, genius, as well as, in the long run, freedom, which fills part II of *Democracy in America* is eminently Burkean and Bonaldian in character. As I say, it is Tocqueville's passion for liberty that comes closest to separating him from the conservatives, in whom authority was a more dominant concept.

58. The conservative elements of *Democracy in America* are most pronounced in Tocqueville's eloquently expressed fear of the majority and of public opinion in part I of that work, and in his analyses of the destructive effects of equality and worship of majority upon culture, individual psychological stability, pluralism, and liberty in part II, as well as in his treatment of the crippling effects of technology and industrialism upon the worker and his aristocratic strictures upon money and the kind of social class produced by money.

59. See Tocqueville, *The Old Regime and the French Revolution* especially pp. 140ff.

60. The best treatments of this tradition in French sociology are Pitirim Sorokin, *Contemporary Sociological Theories*, (New York: Harper & Brothers, 1928)—see the chapter on "sociologism"; Emile Benoit-Smullyan, *The Development of French Sociologistic Theory and Its Critics* (1938, in microfilm, University of Wisconsin Library, still unpublished so far as I am aware, which is regrettable; and Howard Becker and Harry Elmer Barnes, *Social Thought from Lore to Science* (New York, 1938) 2 vols.—see the chapter on French sociology in vol. 2. The failure of such sociologists as Roberty and Espinas to acquire followings among students and thus exert greater impact upon the social sciences in France than they actually did—and, conversely, the success of Emile Durkheim, among others, in achieving marked success along this line—is the subject of Terry N. Clark's *Prophets and Patrons: The French University and the Emergence of the Social Sciences* (Cambridge: Harvard University Press, 1973). When all is said and done, however, I think the single most striking fact about the so-called "sociologistic" tradition in nineteenth-century France is its continuity, an almost inexorable continuity, from the time it came into existence in the theological-political tomes and tracts of Bonald and his associates down through Durkheim and his illustrious student followers such as Mauss, Fauconnet, Davy, Halbwachs, and others.

61. I have dealt at some length with Durkheim's sociological conservatism in Robert Nisbet, *The Sociology of Emile Durkheim* (New York: Oxford University Press, 1974); see also Nisbet, "Conservatism and Sociology," in *The American Journal of Sociology*, (September 1943) and Nisbet, "The French Revolution and the Rise of Sociology." Steven Lukes, in his authoritative biobibliographical study, *Emile Durkheim: His Life and Work* (New York: Harper & Row, 1972) says of Durkheim on p. 546: "He was in many ways both a moralistic conservative and a radical social reformer, who would qualify, on most definitions, as a socialist of sorts. His conservatism was sociologically based but rested ultimately on a view of human nature as being in need of limits and moral discipline." The real impact of conservatism on Durkheim, though, has less to do with any set of attitudes Durkheim had respecting individual and society in the contexts of contemporaneous politics than with the *constitutive concepts* of his sociology. Such ideas as the *conscience collective*, the absolute priority of society to individual, the basis of religion and morality in social discipline, the occupational groups intermediating between individual and state, the view of religion as functionally necessary to all forms of social life, the exteriority of social facts, the role of the state as destructive of *social* solidarity, and, not to be missed, the utter antipathy toward individualism of any kind—such ideas came to flower in the writings of the conservatives at the beginning of the century, in polemical-political context, to be sure, and they are the very elements of Durkheim's sociology.

4

MARXISM AND SOCIOLOGY

TOM BOTTOMORE

The Formation of Marx's Thought

For more than a century there has been a close, uneasy, contentious relationship between Marxism and sociology. The closeness is due to the fact that Marx's theory was intended, like sociology, to be a general science of society, and that it was similarly directed, in particular, toward gaining an understanding of the changes in society resulting from the development of industrial capitalism and from the political revolutions of the eighteenth century. Its scope and ambitions were quite evidently the same as those expressed in the sociological systems of Comte and Spencer, and to some extent it drew upon the same intellectual sources, among them the histories of civilization, the theories of progress, Saint-Simon's analysis of industrial society, and the new political economy. On the other side, the unease and contention arise, as will be discussed more fully later, from the ways in which sociology and Marxism developed historically in largely separate spheres, from the direct conflict of theoretical views, and from the underlying, persistent uncertainty and controversy about whether Marxism is to be conceived as *one* sociological theory among others or as a unique body of thought, a complete intellectual world of its own, which constitutes a radical alternative to any kind of sociology as a means of understanding, and orienting action in, human society.

In the present chapter I shall not concern myself directly with this last question, which I have discussed elsewhere,[1] but shall assume that Marxist theory deals with a specific and circumscribed set of problems which also constitutes the subject matter of various sociological theories, regardless of the diversity of their conceptual schemes and methodological principles. From this point of view the differences between Marxism and sociology may appear no greater than those which exist between rival theories within what is commonly accepted as the field of sociological analysis. Moreover, as will be shown in due course, there are many connections and agreements, as well as mutual influences between some versions of Marxist theory and some theoretical positions in sociology. In what follows, therefore, my intention is to set out the principal elements of Marx's own theory,[2] regarded as one of the principal types of sociological analysis, and then to follow its later development, the reinterpretations or creative innovations that have occurred, and the ways in which Marxist thinkers have responded both to critical attacks and to the new problems posed by changing historical circumstances.

Marx's theory is, in the first place, a remarkable synthesis of ideas derived from the philosophy, the historical studies, and the social sciences of his time, the formation of which can best be followed in the *Economic and Philosophical Manuscripts* of 1844.[3] Here Marx begins to define the most fundamental concept in his theory, that of "human labor," which he later will develop in an array of related concepts. "The outstanding achievement of Hegel's *Phenomenology*," Marx says, "is, first, that Hegel grasps the self-creation of man as a process, . . . that he therefore grasps the nature of *labour*, and conceives of objective man . . . as the result of his *own labour*."[4] In these manuscripts we can see how Marx transforms Hegel's conception of "spiritual labor" by introducing the quite different notion of labor to be found in the works of the political economists—labor in the process of material production, labor as the source of wealth. It is not that Marx here, or in his later writings, restricts the idea of labor simply to material production as has sometimes been suggested, for he always retains the broader notion of labor as human activity, in which material and intellectual production go on together. Man does not only produce the means for his physical existence, he creates at the same time, in a single process, a whole form of society. It is true, nonetheless, that the distinctiveness of Marx's concept consists in his emphasizing the importance of labor in the economic sense (the developing interchange between man and nature) as the foundation of all social life. Hence it may be argued, as it was by Karl Korsch, that Marxism should be regarded as political economy rather than sociology;[5] and it is certainly the case that Marx's theory is distinguished from many other sociological theories by the fact that it situates human society firmly in a natural world and analyzes all social phenomena in the context of the (historically changing) relation between society and nature.

There is a second transformation of Hegel's thought that Marx undertakes in the *Economic and Philosophical Manuscripts;* namely, the conversion of the idea of alienation into an economic and social concept by an analysis of the "alienation of labor" as it can be grasped in the writings of the political economists. Like labor itself, the alienation of labor is for Marx a process which takes place, not exclusively in the intellectual or spiritual realm, but in the world of man's physical existence and material production. "Alienated labor" is work which is imposed upon some men by others, "forced labor" as opposed to free creative activity; and it is furthermore a kind of labor in which what is produced by the worker is appropriated by others, the "masters of the system of production."

From these two concepts, not fully elaborated in the manuscripts of 1844, but also expressed in other writings of Marx during that period, we can derive the main elements of his whole theory of society. To begin with, labor, in its principal form as the interchange between man and nature, is conceived as a historically developing process in which man changes himself and his society in the course of changing nature. This conception then leads naturally to the idea of stages in the development of labor and production, characterized by the prevalence, in different historical periods, of specific modes of production and corresponding forms of society. Moreover, this historical process has a progressive character; humanity moves from a condition of almost complete dependence upon given natural forces and resources through successive phases of increasing control over nature, so that it is possible for Marx to refer, in later discussions of the social history of mankind (in the *Grundrisse*)[6] to "progressive epochs in the economic formation of society" and to "higher forms" of society. This development of social labor, however, does not occur in the form of a cooperative, communal effort to improve the productive forces and so to dominate nature more effectively. The conception of "alienated labor" already introduces the idea of the division of society into two major groups, the relation between which determines the general character of economic and political life. Later (in *Capital,* vol. III)[7] Marx expresses this view in the following way: "It is always the direct relation between the masters of the conditions of production and the direct producers which reveals the innermost secret, the hidden foundation of the entire social edifice, and therefore also of the political form of the relation between sovereignty and dependence, in short, of the particular form of the state. The form of this relation between masters and producers always necessarily corresponds to a definite stage in the development of the methods of work and consequently of the social productivity of labour."

In the *Economic and Philosophical Manuscripts*, therefore, we find—whatever else may be derived from them in the way of a "humanist" social philosophy—the broad outlines of Marx's sociological theory, in which the basic concepts of labor, private property, mode of production, forms of society, stages of development, social classes, and class conflict are either directly expressed, or at least intimated, in an exposition, however fragmentary, which reveals the actual development of Marx's thought, through an encounter between Hegelian philosophy and political economy, in the process of converting and reconstructing philosophical ideas into the concepts of a theory of society which was described by Marx himself in the preface as "the fruit of an entirely empirical analysis." These manuscripts, of course, have their place in a larger body of work produced during the seminal years of 1843–45, and Marx's concept of social class, for example, was elaborated in writings which owe much to the studies of the modern proletariat by the French socialist thinkers. By 1845 Marx had reached a point in the development of his ideas at which he could formulate in precise terms the main principles of his theory: "This conception of history, therefore, rests on the exposition of the real process of production, starting out from the simple material production of life, and on the comprehension of the form of intercourse connected with and created by this mode of production, i.e., of civil society in its various stages as the basis of all history, and also in its action as the state. . . . it does not explain practice from the idea but explains the formation of ideas from material practice, and accordingly comes to the conclusion that all the forms and products of consciousness can be dissolved, not by intellectual criticism . . . but only by the practical overthrow of the actual social relations which gave rise to this idealist humbug; that not criticism but revolution is the driving force of history. . . . It shows . . . that at each stage of history there is found a material result, a sum of productive forces, a historically created relation of individuals to nature and to one another, which is handed down to each generation from its predecessors, a mass of productive forces, capital, and circumstances, which is indeed modified by the new generation but which also prescribes for it its conditions of life and gives it a definite development, a special character. It shows that circumstances make men just as much as men make circumstances." (*The German Ideology*, 1845–46)[8] The formation of this theoretical scheme is explicitly assigned by Marx to the period 1843–45 and is described as the "guiding thread" in his subsequent studies in a much later text, where there occurs a famous passage expressing in the same terms his general conception: "In the social production which men carry on they enter into definite relations that are indispensable and independent of their will; these relations of production correspond to a definite stage of development of their material powers of production. The totality of these relations of production constitutes the economic structure of society—the real foundation, on which legal and political superstructures arise and to which definite forms of social consciousness correspond. The mode of production of material life determines the general character of the social, political and spiritual processes of life. . . . At a certain stage of their development, the material forces of production in society come into conflict with the existing relations of production, or—what is but a legal expression for the same thing—with the property relations within which they had been at work before. . . . Then occurs a period of social revolution." (Preface to *A Contribution to the Critique of Political Economy*, 1859)[9]

After the mid-1840s it is clear that the direction of Marx's intellectual interests changed considerably, but this reorientation can be understood in different ways. Louis Althusser has argued that in about 1845 there occurred an "epistemological break," which separates the young Marx, the propounder of a "humanist" and "historicist" ideology still profoundly marked by the ideas of Hegel and Feuerbach, from the mature Marx, the creator of an original and rigorous science of society.[10] But this view (even if we ignore the fact that in spite of the frequent references to "scientificity" in Althusser's work the distinction between science and ideology is never clearly and convincingly established) is difficult to sustain when the content and arguments of Marx's later writings, especially the *Grundrisse,* are compared closely with the earlier texts. It is more plausible, I think, to state that Marx, after having sketched the general outline of his theory, then turned to a more detailed and thorough analysis of the capitalist mode of production which was intended to be only the starting point for a study of capitalist society as a whole in the context of an overall process of social development.

In fact, Marx sets out, in the introduction to the *Grundrisse*, a vast program of studies which confirms this view. Here he restates firmly his conception of the historical development of production, while noting that "all epochs of production have certain common characteristics"; analyzes the relation between production, distribution, exchange, and consumption; examines the method of political economy and sets out the elements of his own method. Finally he presents, in the form of notes, some of the major issues that would have to be confronted in any attempt to demonstrate in a detailed manner, the connection between modes of production, forms of society and the state, and cultural phenomena, or to interpret the historical development of societies in relation to the concept of progress. Moreover, the *Grundrisse* contains a long section on precapitalist economic formations which is Marx's most extensive and systematic attempt to discuss the problems of historical development.[11]

It is evident that Marx was unable to complete his ambitious project and that his major works from the late 1850s until his death were largely devoted to an economic analysis, which itself remained incomplete, of capitalism as a specific mode of production. Nevertheless, he never entirely abandoned his studies of the diverse historical forms of society, and especially in his last years (between 1880–82) he wrote extensive commentaries on the writings of scholars who were investigating in diverse ways the social and cultural history of mankind, among them L. H. Morgan, J. B. Phear, H. S. Maine, and John Lubbock.[12] Hence Marx's studies in his mature years have two aspects: one, the refinement of his theoretical analysis of modes of production through an intensive study of modern capitalist production and a critical examination of the theories of his predecessors and contemporaries in political economy; the other, a continuing effort to locate the capitalist mode of production and capitalist society in a historical scheme of social development, which he outlined in his early work but also tried to elaborate and improve in sections of the *Grundrisse* and in his notes on Morgan and others.

The advances which Marx made in his economic analysis have been ably discussed by Martin Nicolaus in an essay devoted to the *Grundrisse,* "The Unknown Marx."[13] The *Grundrisse* shows the development of Marx's thought on three principal questions. First, he elaborates the analysis of money and exchange which he began in the *Economic and Philosophical Manuscripts* and formulates a conception of money as a "social bond" which expresses the historically produced social relationships of capitalist society; but he now makes this account of market relationships subordinate to an analysis of capitalist production and the process of capital accumulation, or the self-expansion of capital. Second, in analyzing production he makes use of the new concept of "labor power" (in place of the term "labor" in his earlier writings) to describe the commodity which the worker sells in return for his wages, and he brings to light the unique quality of this commodity; namely, that it is capable of creating values where they did not exist, or of creating greater values than are needed to sustain it—which is to say that it creates surplus value, the source of capitalist profit. And finally, Marx discusses more fully in the *Grundrisse* than in his other writings the conditions under which capitalism will break down. Here, it seems to me, two kinds of factors are invoked, one negative, the other positive. In the first place, Marx argues that "capitalism contains a specific barrier to production—which contradicts its general tendency to break all barriers to production—[namely] *overproduction*, the fundamental contradiction of developed capitalism." Marx goes on to characterize this overproduction in various terms, but his view can largely be summed up in the statement that it involves the "restriction of the production of use-value by exchange-value"; that is to say, the limitation of production occurs because the products (commodities) cannot be exchanged, and hence the surplus value which they contain cannot be realized. Or as Marx expresses it in *Capital*, vol. III: "The ultimate cause of all real crises is always the poverty and restricted consumption of the masses, in contrast with the tendency of capitalist production to develop the productive forces in such a way that only the absolute power of consumption of society would be their limit." This analysis provides the main content of Marx's general proposition that the transition to a new form of society begins when a contradiction or conflict develops in the existing society between the forces of production and the relations of production (which in the case of capitalism are constituted by money and exchange; in short, by the market). But the second, positive factor in the breakdown of capitalism is the creation, by the development of capitalism itself, of economic conditions in which a collective, or communal, direction of the process of social labor is already partly attained. In some remarkable passages at the end of the *Grundrisse* Marx expresses this idea: "To the extent that large-scale industry develops, the creation of real wealth comes to depend less upon labour time and the quantity of labour expended than upon the power of the instruments which are set in motion during labour time, whose powerful effectiveness is likewise unrelated to the labour time directly involved in their production, but depends rather upon the general state of science and the progress of technology, or the application of this science to production. . . . With this transformation, what appears as the mainstay of production and wealth is neither the labour which man directly expends, nor the time he spends at work, but his appropriation of his own general productive powers, his understanding and mastery of nature; in short, the development of the social individual. . . . The development of fixed capital indicates the extent to which general social knowledge has become a *direct productive force*, and thus the extent to which the conditions of the social life process have themselves been brought under the control of the general intellect and reconstructed in accordance with it." The breakdown of capitalism and the transition to a new form of society are seen by Marx, in the *Grundrisse,* as a complex and protracted process in which economic crises and political struggles, but also the growth within capitalism of an alternative economic system and the awakening of "all the powers of science and nature, of social organization and intercourse," all play a part.

How, then, does Marx's analysis of capitalism, and especially of the capitalist mode of production, which constitutes by far the greater part of his life's work, fit into the general theory of society which he outlined in his youth? As I have already indicated, there was no period in which Marx was not concerned in some way with the question of the historical development of society, conceived as a succession of distinct modes of production and social formations, and he returned to the study of such historical issues in his general discussion of precapitalist economic formations, particularly in the *Grundrisse,* in his writings on the "Asiatic mode of production," and in his observations on early tribal and peasant societies based upon his reading of the work of Morgan, Maine, and other scholars dealing with the early history of institutions. The conclusions of these studies are by no means as clear as those resulting from his infinitely more thorough analysis of capitalism, and they have been interpreted in a variety of ways by later writers. Thus for example Eric Hobsbawm, in his introduction to *Pre-Capitalist Economic Formations,* suggests that "the general theory of historical materialism requires only that there should be a succession of modes of production, though not necessarily any particular modes, and perhaps not in any particular predetermined order"; and in considering this particular text he argues that Marx is not dealing with chronological succession or with the evolution of one system out of its predecessor, but rather with analytical stages in the general development of societies after the break-up of primitive communal society.[14]

These general difficulties concerning the precise scheme of social development that Marx was attempting to formulate are enhanced by the fact that he did quite evidently want to emphasize the uniqueness of the capitalist mode of production and capitalist society in relation to all previous modes of production and social formations. This contrast is expressed in various ways. For example, Marx's analysis suggests that whereas in a capitalist society the appropriation of surplus value takes place by more or less purely economic means (and therefore has to be revealed by penetrating the secret of commodity production), in all earlier societies it required some kind of noneconomic coercion.[15] Again, if in capitalist society the fundamental contradiction is between the forces of production and the social relations of production constituted by exchange and money, a problem arises concerning the nature of the contradictions in previous forms of society and the manner in which a transition from one to another occurs. This question is also connected with the problem of social classes. In a broad sense Marx's theory postulates a universal division of society into classes (after the epoch of primitive communal society) in terms of the "masters of the system of production" and the "direct producers"; but in another sense classes are regarded as a distinctive feature of capitalist society, and Marx himself observed, in *The German Ideology*, that "The distinction between the personal and the class individual . . . appears only with the emergence of class, which itself is a product of the *bourgeoisie*." At all events, it can be argued that in Marx's terms the role of social classes is exceptionally important in capitalist societies, where class relations are the principal expression of the contradiction between forces and relations of production; whereas in earlier societies the dominant social relations may be those of kinship, religion, or politics; may not express contradictions; and may presumably constitute societies which do not undergo any development.

This exposition of Marx's theory suggests a variety of problems, not only in the analysis of the main tendencies of development in capitalist societies, but still more in the construction of a general theory of social development or "science of history." Increasingly, the latter question seems to be approached by Marxist thinkers in terms of a three-stage model: an original, small-scale form of communal society; followed by the development of diverse social formations which are so many different "exits" from this communal form, some successful and others less so (in the sense of making possible a further development); and finally the emergence, in one region of the world, of capitalism as a very distinctive type of society embodying hitherto undreamed of potentialities for development.[16] But as will be seen later the study of these problems has given rise, in recent years, to a wide variety of reformulations and extensions of Marxist theory.

The Development of Marxism, 1883–1917

During his own lifetime Marx's social theory received little attention from other scholars. The greatest interest was shown in Russia, where the first translation of *Capital*, vol. I appeared in 1872 and was followed later in the year by a substantial and generally favorable review in the St. Petersburg journal *Vestnik Evropy*, which Marx himself commented on in the preface to the second German edition of *Capital* in 1873. In Germany, as Marx noted bitterly, his work was largely ignored, except by socialist writers, most notably Joseph Dietzgen, who published a series of articles on it in the *Volkstaat* (1868); but in 1879 Marx's economic theory was more extensively discussed in the second edition of a textbook of political economy by Adolph Wagner, *Allgemeine oder theoretische Volkswirthschaftslehre, Erster Theil, Grundlegung* (General or Theoretical Political Economy, Part I, Foundations), on which Marx made a series of "marginal notes" in 1879–80 with a view to publishing a critical essay on the book.[17] From this time on Marx's theory attracted increasing attention,[18] and soon after his death it began to exert a growing influence, both intellectual and political, in two different ways which have continued to mark its development up to the present time; in the labor movement and in the academic social sciences.

Thus "Marxism" became, as Marx intended, in some sense, that his work should become, the pre-eminent social theory or doctrine of the working-class movement. It established itself most strongly in this form in the German Social Democratic Party, whose leaders, as a result of the rapid growth of the socialist movement, and also through their close association with Engels, became the principal intellectual and political heirs of Marx and largely dominated the international labor movement up until 1914. But the SDP, because of the particular political conditions in Germany, took on, as Peter Nettl has noted,[19] the character of "a state within a state," and as such it developed on a large scale its own independent cultural and educational institutions, party schools, publishing houses, and journals. Though not isolated to the same extent, socialist movements and parties in other countries also developed their ideas largely outside the official academic world; and the exposition and discussion of the Marxist theory took place mainly in books and journals published by socialist parties and groups.[20]

The first major debate within Marxism—the "revisionist controversy"—arose in the German Social Democratic Party, and quickly spread to other socialist parties, after the publication of Eduard Bernstein's *Die Voraussetzungen des Sozialismus und die Aufgaben der Sozialdemokratie* (1899).[21] Bernstein presented two main arguments in his book, both concerned with the claim of Marxism to be a social science. First, he insisted that if Marxism is a science, its results must ultimately be testable by empirical evidence, and that regarded in this way some parts of the Marxist theory needed to be revised, because the trends of development in the Western capitalist societies were diverging from those foreseen by Marx; in particular, the structure of capitalist society was not being simplified into a relation between two main classes but was becoming more complex, the middle classes were not disappearing, a polarization of classes was not taking place, misery was not increasing but diminishing, and economic crises were becoming less rather than more severe. Second, he argued that Marxism as a positive science needs to be supplemented by an ethical theory, but he discussed this question only briefly and did little more than assert the existence and importance of an "ideal" element in the socialist movement.[22]

Bernstein's book especially animated a controversy about the Marxist theory of crisis and the breakdown of capitalism, but it also helped to set in motion a broader reassessment of Marx's theory in relation to the economic and social changes that were taking place in the European societies, and to the new movements of thought in philosophy and the social sciences. On the question of crisis Kautsky replied to Bernstein by reasserting the orthodox Marxist view of the "inevitable" economic breakdown of capitalism, and by turning the issue into one of defending the revolutionary core of Marxism (conceived in this deterministic manner) against reformism; but the problems were later analyzed in a more profound way in Rudolf Hilferding's *Finance Capital* and Rosa Luxemburg's *The Accumulation of Capital*.[23] These two works both attempted to develop Marx's analysis of capitalism in the light of changes which had occurred since his death and, in particular, sought to explain the continued expansion of capitalism by the phenomenon of imperialism. But whereas Luxemburg concluded that capitalism would ultimately suffer an inevitable economic collapse when it had finally absorbed all the precapitalist economies and the precapitalist enclaves within capitalism, Hilferding argued that capitalism, in its more organized form, as finance capitalism, had the ability to overcome or moderate economic crises, and that it would be overthrown and replaced by socialism, not as a consequence of economic collapse, but as the result of the political struggle of the working class.

The wider debate about Marx's theory took place in many different forms—for example, in the writings of Sorel during the 1890s, in which he attempted to set out the principles of a "materialist theory of sociology,"[24] and in the essays Croce wrote in the same period on historical materialism[25]—but the most systematic effort to present Marx's ideas in a new form, to investigate new problems, and to discuss critically the recent developments in philosophy and the social sciences, is undoubtedly to be found in the writings of the Austro-Marxists. Their intellectual orientation was described in the following terms by Otto Bauer: "What united them was not a specific political orientation, but the particular character of their intellectual work. They had all grown up in a period when men such as Stammler, Windelband and Rickert were attacking Marxism with philosophical arguments; hence they were obliged to engage in controversy with the representatives of modern philosophical trends. If Marx and Engels began from Hegel, and the later Marxists from materialism, the more recent 'Austro-Marxists' had as their point of departure Kant and Mach. On the other side these 'Austro-Marxists' had to engage in controversy with the so-called Austrian school of political economy, and this debate too influenced the method and structure of their thought. Finally, they all had to learn, in the old Austria rent by national struggles, how to apply the Marxist conception of history to very complicated phenomena which defied analysis by any superficial or schematic use of the Marxist method."[26] Their principal works—Otto Bauer's study of nationalities and nationalism, Max Adler's sustained inquiry into the methodological foundations of Marxism as a science of society, Renner's analysis of legal institutions, and Hilferding's investigation of the recent development of capitalism—were so many attempts to establish Marxism as a system of sociology by formulating precisely its basic concepts and method and carrying out, in the framework of this paradigm which guided all their research, studies of the most important empirical realities of their time.[27]

During the first decade of the twentieth century, therefore, diverse schools of thought emerged within the socialist movement as a result of controversies about the interpretation of Marx's theory, attempts to revise or elaborate it in response to criticisms and to the appearance of new phenomena, and the development of empirical studies in the field of sociology and social history. Broadly speaking, three main tendencies can be distinguished: the orthodox

Marxism of the German Social Democratic party, represented above all by Kautsky, which expressed a somewhat mechanical conception of the development of the capitalist economy toward an inevitable breakdown, a development reflected more or less automatically in the class struggle and the final victory of the working class; the revisionist view of Bernstein, which largely rejected the ideas of economic breakdown and of increasingly bitter class struggle and saw the advent of socialism as the culmination of a process of gradual permeation of capitalist society by socialist institutions and ideals; and Austro-Marxism, which developed a much more sophisticated sociological theory, took account of the growing complexity of capitalist society and the changing conditions of the class struggle, but maintained, though in a qualified way, a revolutionary outlook and emphasized the importance of the active intervention of a mass working-class movement, politically conscious and organized, in order to attain socialism. Also in this decade, however, there emerged another body of Marxist thought—that of Lenin and the Bolsheviks—which subsequently had an immense influence upon the whole character of Marxism; and this will be examined in the next section.

In the period following Marx's death his theory, although it spread most rapidly in the socialist movement, also began to have an impact upon the academic social sciences, especially economics and sociology. Tönnies, in the preface to *Gemeinschaft und Gesellschaft* (Community and Association) (1887), acknowledged his indebtedness to Marx, whom he described as a "most remarkable and most profound social philosopher," as the discoverer of the capitalist mode of production and a thinker who had attempted to give expression to the same idea that Tönnies himself was trying to express in new concepts.[28] At the first international congress of sociology in 1894 scholars from several countries (including Tönnies) contributed papers which discussed Marx's theory; and it was during the 1890s that Marxism began to be taught in a number of universities (notably by Carl Grünberg[29] at the University of Vienna and by Antonio Labriola[30] at the University of Rome), began to inspire new kinds of research, and began to be discussed more seriously in academic publications. The first substantial critical studies appeared at this time, one of the earliest being R. Stammler's attempt to turn Marx's theory on its head by showing that legal norms constitute the indispensable foundation of the system of production, and by substituting for the materialist conception of history a social teleology based upon Kantian ethics.[31] Another important work of criticism was Böhm-Bawerk's *Zum Abschluss des Marxschen Systems* (The Conclusion of the Marxian System) (1896), written from the standpoint of the Austrian marginalist school of economics, which raised objections to the labor theory of value as the foundation of Marx's analysis of capitalism, but was in turn criticized by Rudolf Hilferding in a monograph, *Böhm-Bawerks Marx-Kritik* (1904), where the "subjectivist" approach of the marginalist school was rejected.[32] In France, Durkheim discussed the Marxist theory in a review of the French edition of Labriola's book on the materialist conception of history in the *Revue philosophique* (1897) and in subsequent reviews of various Marxist studies which he published in the early issues of the *Année socioloqique.* Among many other studies that appeared during this period mention should be made of the major analysis of Marx's sociological method and hypotheses by T. G. Masaryk, professor of philosophy in the Czech University of Prague, *Die philosophischen und soziologischen Grundlagen des Marxismus* (The Philosophical and Sociological Foundations of Marxism) (1899), and the short critical exposition of Marx's theory by E. R. A. Seligman, *The Economic Interpretation of History* (1902; rev. ed. 1907).[33]

By the first decade of this century Marxism was firmly established as an important social theory which was widely debated in the socialist movement and in the academic world, and it began to inspire much new social research.[34] Perhaps the most important characteristic of the Marxist theory as it appeared at this time was its very broad scope, illustrated by the fact that the various expositions and criticisms of it were undertaken by scholars working in such diverse disciplines as economics, anthropology, history, and jurisprudence. Labriola emphasized this feature when he wrote that "The various analytic disciplines which illustrate historical facts have ended by bringing forth the need for a general social science, which will unify the different historical processes. The materialist theory is the culminating point of this unification."[35] From this vantage point it is not difficult to understand why Marxism should have had such a profound influence on the establishment of sociology itself—which aims at the same kind of unification—as an academic discipline and more generally as a new intellectual framework for comprehending the social world. Nowhere was this influence more apparent than in German-speaking Europe. Austro-Marxism developed specifically in the form of a sociological theory,[36] and it indeed constituted the major part of Austrian sociology in the first three decades of this century.[37] In Germany, Marxism was an important influence upon Tönnies's thought, as I have indicated, and upon Simmel, most evident in his major study of the social relationships which develop with the transition from a natural economy to a money economy;[38] its subsequent influence in the writings of Korsch, Lukács, Mannheim, and the thinkers of the Frankfurt Institute of Social Research will be examined in later sections of this essay. But the strongest impact of Marxist thought at the time when sociology was being formed as an academic discipline is undoubtedly to be seen in Max Weber's writings. It is not simply that Weber, in his best-known study, *The Protestant Ethic and the Spirit of Capitalism* (1904) set out to show the limitations of the Marxist account of the origins of capitalism, and that more generally, in his sociology of religion, he undertook what he called "a positive critique of the materialist conception of history," but that in all his work, from his early study of Roman agrarian history to the diverse analyses incorporated in *Economy and Society* (1922); and the outline of a general economic history written at the end of his life, he frequently took as his starting point problems or conclusions which had been formulated by Marx. Indeed, it might be argued that the greater part of Weber's sociology can be read more properly as a prolonged and varied commentary upon the Marxist theory—dealing with the origins and prospects of capitalism, social classes, the state and politics, and problems of method—though written from the standpoint of a very different world view,[39] than as an original, systematic theory of society.

Thus, in the three decades since his death Marx's theory had undergone a notable development, being extended, and in some respects revised, to take account of the changes in capitalism; creating whole new fields of research; and entering profoundly—in the continental European countries, though not in the English-speaking world,[40]—into the construction of sociology as a general science of society. This process was interrupted by the first world war; and although some of the earlier styles of thought persisted after the war, they did so in vastly changed circumstances, which gave rise to quite new directions in Marxist theory.

The Bolshevik Hegemony, 1917–56

The Russian Revolution of 1917 and the establishment of the first "workers' state," and on the other side, the failure of the German revolutionary movement in 1918–19, opened a new era in the development of Marxism. The center of gravity of Marxist studies now moved to Eastern Europe, the institutionalization of Marxism as the ideology of a political regime began, and this official Marxism gradually acquired a preponderant influence in the development of Marxist thought. Soviet Marxism[41] began from the ideas of Lenin; and Lenin's interpretation of Marxism, which has to be seen in the context of political circumstances in the period from the beginning of the century to 1917, involved above all a new reassertion of the practical, revolutionary significance of Marxism against the growth of revisionism and reformism in the European socialist movement.

The principal elements in Lenin's version of Marxism—concerning the role of the party, the peasantry as an ally of the proletariat, and the conditions of working-class political struggle in the imperialist stage of capitalism—reveal clearly this practical intent. Lenin did not set out to reexamine in any systematic way the Marxist theoretical system, but instead adopted a conception of Marxism as "the theory of the proletarian revolution" and devoted his efforts to working out, and embodying in an effective organization, its implications for political strategy. Thus, in his analysis of imperialism[42] he drew largely upon the studies made by J. A. Hobson and Rudolf Hilferding, and his general characterization of imperialism did not differ greatly from Hilferding's except that he drew more revolutionary conclusions; namely, that capitalism had entered a "moribund" phase, creating more favorable conditions for its overthrow, but also that it had produced a division in the working-class movement between a reformist and revolutionary tendency which demanded an intensified effort to strengthen revolutionary parties and to combat reformism. Again, in his discussion of the peasantry, first in the case of Russia and later in relation to the colonial countries,[43] Lenin was not primarily concerned with elaborating a Marxist theory of the peasantry as a social class or of the stages of social development, but with analyzing the revolutionary potential of the peasantry in backward countries and the means by which some sections of the peasantry could be brought into a political alliance with the working class, or rather, with the revolutionary party of the working class. Lenin's most distinctive contribution to Marxism, indeed, was his conception of the party, based upon a distinction between the working class, which in his view could never attain spontaneously anything more than a "trade-union consciousness" (i.e., a preoccupation with economic demands), and the revolutionary vanguard of fully class-conscious workers and intellectuals, which brought socialist ideas to the working-class movement from outside and assumed the leadership of the whole movement of the oppressed (both workers and peasants) by virtue of its total commitment to revolutionary Marxism and its organization as a centralized and disciplined political party.

Leninism, as a doctrine and political movement to which others besides Lenin (notably Trotsky)[44] also contributed, brought into existence a new type of political system and a new kind of party which have had immense consequences for political life and for the development of Marxist thought in the twentieth century. In the first decade after the revolution there was considerable development of Marxist scholarship, in diverse forms, just as there was a burst of creativity in literature and the arts. David Riazanov, the founder of the Marx-Engels Institute in Moscow, began his remarkable collection of the published writings, manuscripts and letters of Marx and Engles in preparation for the monumental critical edition of their works, *Karl Marx/Friedrich Engels: Historisch-Kritische Gesamtausgabe*, (Historical-Critical Edition of the Complete Works of Karl Marx and Friedrich Engels) the first volume of which appeared in 1927, but which remained incomplete as a result of Riazanov's arrest and disappearance in 1931. Also during these years Nicolai Bukharin made important contributions to the theoretical controversies that were taking place in the social sciences and published in 1921 his *Historical Materialism: A System of Sociology* which, although it was intended mainly as a textbook, also introduced "innovations" to meet criticisms of Marxist theory by other social thinkers.[45] Indeed, some of the most interesting sections of the book are those in which Bukharin examines and criticizes the ideas of Max Weber, Michels, and Stammler, or comments on recent studies influenced by Marxism. But, by the later 1920s, the growing ascendancy of Stalin put an end to these theoretical debates and the possibility of any serious advances in Marxist social science. Thereafter, Soviet Marxism became an increasingly rigid and dogmatic ideology, not in the sense of an entirely arbitrary justification of the regime, but as a doctrine which reflected the actual development of Soviet society—the process of achieving "socialism in one country," or more simply, rapid industrialization—at the same time as it helped to sustain the Stalinist regime.[46] Its intellectual consequences were to inhibit, throughout a large part of the international socialist movement, any creative and original Marxist thought, and in particular to obstruct any development of a Marxist sociology, whether in the form of theoretical analysis or empirical research.

The first world war, and the revolutionary situation in Europe in the immediate postwar years, produced other significant changes in Marxist thought, resembling those which became embodied in Leninism, but having a more profound theoretical character. Their most distinctive feature was the stronger emphasis upon class consciousness and political activism, rather than the economic development of capitalism, as the principal factors in the transition to socialism. Two books, published in 1923, exemplified and contributed to this intellectual reorientation: Korsch's *Marxism and Philosophy* and Lukács's *History and Class Consciousness.*[47] In both works the idea of Marxism as a positive science of society—as sociology—was rejected; instead, it was conceived as a "critical philosophy" which expressed the world view of the revolutionary proletariat just as, according to Korsch, German idealist philosophy had been the theoretical expression of the revolutionary bourgeoisie. Lukács, in the opening pages of his book, defines Marxist theory as "essentially nothing more than the expression in thought of the revolutionary process itself," and he then goes on to argue, in a way which provides a theoretical-philosophical foundation for Lenin's conception of the party, that Marxism is the "correct class consciousness of the proletariat" which has as "its organizational form, the communist party."[48]

A similar view of Marxism was formulated by Antonio Gramsci, though it became widely known only at a later time when his writings in prison were published after the second world war.[49] Gramsci also rejected any conception of Marxism as a science of society or a sociological theory; Marxism—the "philosophy of praxis"—" 'is sufficient unto itself' . . . contains in itself all the fundamental elements needed to construct a total and integral conception of the world, a total philosophy and theory of natural science, and not only that but everything that is needed to give life to an integral civilization."[50] In this case, too, Marxism was presented as a philosophical world view which guides the proletariat in its political struggle to create a new society and a new civilization.

These developments in Marxist thought, although they were largely influenced, as I have indicated, by the political conditions in Europe after the first world war, also occurred within a more general movement of thought, beginning in the 1890s, which has been described as a "revolt against positivism."[51] Croce's discussion of Marxism as a method of historical interpretation, closely related to Hegel's philosophy of history,[52] and Sorel's rejection of the idea of historical inevitability and his insistence upon the character of socialist thought, including Marxism, as a moral doctrine which primarily brought to the world "a new manner of judging all human acts,"[53] are important elements in this movement. There also emerged, soon after Korsch and Lukács had published their reinterpretations of Marxist theory, a group of thinkers associated with the Frankfurt Institute of Social Research, who in due course worked out in a much more elaborate fashion the conception of Marxism as a "critical philosophy" which they opposed to sociological "positivism."[54] In the early years of the institute's existence, under its first director Carl Grünberg, its work spanned empirical and theoretical studies, and it could be regarded as having embarked upon a course similar to that taken by the Austro-Marxists (with whom Grünberg was closely associated); namely, to reexamine the foundations of Marxist theory, to discuss critically new ideas and doctrines in philosophy and the social sciences, and to use a Marxist method in the investigation of new or hitherto neglected phenomena. But this is not what happened when a distinctive "Frankfurt School" began to take shape in the late 1920s and early 1930s. Its leading thinkers, Adorno and Horkheimer, became preoccupied with methodological questions, and in particular with the opposition between Marxism as a critical philosophy deriving from Hegel and the positivism of the social sciences, which they increasingly identified with the whole development of science and technology since the Enlightenment. This opposition as a central object of theoretical concern is expounded in Marcuse's *Reason and Revolution* (1941), which provides in many respects the best statement of the ideas of the Frankfurt School as they had developed in the 1930s. Marcuse here formulates very sharply the contrast between critical reason, "which had been intrinsically connected with the idea of freedom," and positivist sociology, which was to be "a science seeking social laws" and hence eliminating the possibility of changing the social system.[55]

Although the thinkers associated with the Frankfurt Institute developed their ideas in the same intellectual context as did Korsch and Lukács and, to a large extent, Gramsci—that is to say, in a criticism of positivism and a reinterpretation of Marxism as the heir to classical German philosophy—these ideas came to maturity in conditions which were very different from those of the immediate postwar years. By the late 1920s left-wing intellectuals in Germany were confronted, in the political sphere, by a choice between Soviet Marxism, which had already entered its dogmatic, Stalinist phase, and the reformism of the Social Democratic Party. Most of the members of the Frankfurt School rejected both options and chose the path of keeping alive the critical spirit of Marxism, as they conceived it, outside the sphere of party politics. Increasingly, therefore, Marxism became for them a criticism of ideology, or a general criticism of bourgeois culture, addressed to an audience of intellectuals and students. Another circumstance also impelled them along this path—namely, the apparent weakness of the working class in the face of the rise of fascist movements—which led them to argue that the struggle for socialism could not be carried on successfully unless the working class developed a "conscious will" for a liberated and rational society;[56] and it was evidently the responsibility of intellectuals to provide the criticism and the liberating ideas which might eventually shape this will.

In some respects Korsch and Lukács had to face similar problems. Both were in opposition to some aspects at least of Bolshevik orthodoxy, and their books were condemned as "revisionist" and "idealist" at the fifth Congress of the Communist International in 1924. Lukács repudiated his work and remained a member of the Communist party, but in spite of his concessions to Stalinism it seems unlikely that he changed his fundamental views, and after 1956 he expounded them again in a manner which encouraged a more critical attitude in the political regimes of Eastern Europe. Korsch, on the other hand, was expelled from the German Communist Party in 1926; he then participated in various left-wing movements until his exile in the United States after 1933, when he ceased to be active in politics. During these years his conception of Marxism gradually changed, and he ceased to regard it as the philosophy of the working-class movement, emphasizing instead its achievements as a social science. In his book on Marx as a sociologist, published in 1938, he gave a clear indication of how his own ideas had changed when he wrote: "In the subsequent development of Marxism, the critical materialist principle that Marx had worked out empirically . . . was elaborated into a general social philosophy. . . . From this distortion of the strongly empirical and critical sense of the materialistic principle it was only a step to the idea that the historical and economic science of Marx must be based on the broader foundation not only of a social philosophy, but even of a comprehensive materialist philosophy embracing both nature and society, or a general philosophical interpretation of the universe"; and he summed up his own view by saying: "The main tendency of historical materialism is no longer 'philosophical,' but is that of an empirical scientific method."[57]

The writings of Korsch, Lukács, Gramsci, and the members of the Frankfurt Institute do not, of course, exhaust the work of Marxist thinkers outside, or partially outside, the orbit of Soviet Marxism during this period. The Austro-Marxists continued to develop Marxism as a social science, in close association with political action, until 1934 when Austrian Social Democracy was destroyed by fascism. In Germany, Marxism was one major influence on the work of Karl Mannheim, and we can see in his writings, as in those of Max Weber earlier, an attempt to define the contribution of Marxism to sociology—and more specifically to the sociology of knowledge and culture[58]—without accepting it as a world view.

Yet in spite of all these reexaminations and reinterpretations of Marxist thought, especially in the decade of the 1920s, I do not think it can be said that during this period from 1917 to 1956 the influence of Marxism upon sociology, or the development of the Marxist theory of society, was as vigorous or extensive as in the preceding and succeeding periods. One reason for this was the political dominance of Soviet Marxism, which pushed other versions of Marxism into a marginal position (or suppressed them altogether, as in the case of Lukács's *History and Class Consciousness*), with the result that they were, generally speaking, little known and largely ignored. But another major factor was the triumph of fascism in Europe. In Italy Gramsci propounded his ideas in conditions which precluded any extensive discussion or development of them (many of his most fundamental notions are formulated in notes and essays written in prison); in Austria the Austro-Marxist school was dispersed; and in Germany every kind of Marxist study and debate came to an end in 1933. It was another twenty years before the Marxist theory could again be adequately expounded and critically examined.

The Renewal of Marxist Thought

During the past two decades there has been a notable revival of Marxist thinking in the social sciences. The reasons for such a development are diverse. Most important perhaps is that the Bolshevik dominance over Marxism came to an end with the revelations about the Stalinist regime, the political and intellectual revolts in Eastern Europe, and the emergence of a less monolithic, more critical view of Marxist theory, encouraged further by the rise of alternative centers of Marxist political practice, especially in China. Largely as a result of these changes a transformation of Marxist thought has also occurred in Western Europe, partly through the rediscovery and renewed discussion of earlier thinkers—among them Trotsky, Korsch, Lukács, Gramsci, and the Frankfurt School—whose work had been neglected or consigned to oblivion during the period of Stalin's rule, partly through the formulation of new Marxist conceptions influenced both by fresh ideas in the social sciences and philosophy and by the changing character and problems of societies in the second half of the twentieth century. This Marxist revival has been stimulated too by the publication, translation and wider diffusion of important manuscripts of Marx which had previously been little known, especially the *Economic and Philosophical Manuscripts* (1844) and the *Grundrisse* (1857–58).[59]

The political and intellectual movements of the past twenty years have produced, therefore, a great burgeoning of Marxist scholarship, as well as many new attempts to rethink the whole Marxist theory of society, particularly in relation to the general development and results of the modern social sciences, with respect both to their substantive achievements and to their methodological orientations. Marxism no longer has the appearance, within the social sciences, of a body of thought which has long since been surpassed, or which can be set aside as a social doctrine expressing mainly value judgments and political aspirations. Marxism is not, as Durkheim once characterized socialism, simply a "cry of pain."[60] What is perhaps most striking in the recent development of the social sciences is that Marxist ideas have regained an important influence everywhere; in economics, where Marxism is now recognized as a major theory of economic growth[61] which has contributed much, in particular, to the study of the "developing" countries; and in anthropology, where, as Raymond Firth has noted, contact with Marx's ideas was long avoided;[62] as well as in sociology, political science, and history. In sociology especially, Marxist theory has emerged, though in diverse forms, as a major paradigm capable of accomplishing the aim which Labriola described as the establishment of a general social science which would "unify the different historical processes" and bring together in a systematic form the results of the more specialized social sciences.[63]

In this recent development two principal orientations of Marxist thought have emerged which I shall refer to as "structuralist Marxism" and "critical theory." The former owes its distinctive character to the work of Louis Althusser[64] on one side and to modern structuralist anthropology, itself strongly influenced by structural linguistics,[65] on the other. Althusser's own concerns are primarily epistemological; he sets out to establish a theory of knowledge in opposition to empiricism, to make apparent the "immense theoretical revolution" that Marx accomplished, and to show the "scientificity" of Marx's mature theory in contrast with "ideological" thought.[66] However, in the course of this philosophical analysis he brings into prominence especially that aspect of Marx's theory which lays stress upon structural analysis: according to Althusser, Marx's theory "reveals the existence of *two problems* . . . Marx regards contemporary society (and every other past form of society) both as a *result* and as a *society*. The theory of the mechanism of transformation of one mode of production into another, i.e., the theory of the forms of transition from one mode of production to the succeeding one, has to pose and solve the problem of the *result*, i.e., of the historical production of a given mode of production, of a given social formation. But contemporary society is not only a result, a product; it is *this* particular result, *this* particular *product*, which functions as a *society*, unlike other results and other products which function quite differently. This second problem is answered by the theory of the structure of a mode of production, the theory of *Capital*."[67]

The structuralist version of Marxist theory has been expounded with great clarity, and its uses exemplified from anthropological studies, by Maurice Godelier.[68] In *Perspectives in Marxist Anthropology*[69] he distinguishes between functionalist, structuralist, (i.e. the structuralism of Lévi-Strauss) and Marxist approaches and presents Marxism as a particular form of structuralism, characterized by two main principles: first, that "the starting point in science is not to be found in appearances," but in the inner logic of a structure which exists behind the visible relations between men:[70] and second, that "a materialistic approach which takes Marx as its point of departure, cannot consist merely of a lengthy enquiry into the networks of structural causality without eventually seeking to evaluate the particular and unequal effect that these different structures may have on the functioning—i.e. particularly the conditions of *reproduction*—of an economic and social formation. In analyzing the hierarchy of causes which determine the reproduction of an economic and social formation, materialism takes seriously Marx's fundamental hypothesis on the determining causality 'in the final analysis' for the reproduction of this formation, of the mode or modes of production which comprise the material and social infrastructure of this formation."[71]

This general approach, therefore, takes as its principal object of study—a "theoretically constructed" object—the mode of production of material life and the corresponding social formation, which is conceived as a hierarchy of structures. From this point of view the analysis of structure has priority over historical analysis; in Godelier's words "whatever the internal or external causes or circumstances . . . which bring about contradictions and structural changes within a determined mode of production and society, these contradictions and changes always have their basis in internal properties, immanent in social structures, and they express unintentional requirements, the reasons and laws for which remain to be discovered. . . . History, therefore, does not explain: it has to be explained. Marx's general hypothesis concerning the existence of a relation of order between infrastructure and superstructure which, in the final analysis, determines the functioning and evolution of societies, does not mean that we may determine in advance the specific laws of functioning and evolution in the different economic and social formations which have appeared or will appear in history. This is because no general history exists and because we can never predict what structures will function as infrastructure or superstructure within these different economic and social formations."[72]

The structuralist approach, with some variations and differences of emphasis, has inspired much recent Marxist inquiry. Thus, besides the work of Godelier, mention should be made in particular of the studies of political power and social classes by Nicos Poulantzas,[73] which define the fundamental concepts of "mode of production" and "social formation" and distinguish different structures or "levels"—economic, political, ideological, and theoretical—that are combined and articulated in a specific way in each historically determined social formation; of the analysis of precapitalist modes of production, and of the relation between mode of production and social formation, by Hindess and Hirst,[74] who formulate a particularly strong antihistoricist view, rejecting entirely the conception of Marxism as a "science of history";[75] and of the investigations by Pierre Bourdieu and his colleagues of ideological structures and their relations with economic and political structures in the process of reproduction of a particular social formation.[76] These works, and others of a similar kind, have brought a new theoretical and methodological sophistication to Marxist studies, have emphasized (and in many cases sought to exemplify) the predominantly scientific character of Marxist thought, and in light of this, have adopted a more flexible and tentative approach to the problem of the relation between infrastructure and superstructure. The Marxist structuralists insist that the different structures which constitute any given social formation all have a certain autonomy, and that while the economic structure (the mode of production) has to be conceived as ultimately determinant, other structures may nevertheless be *dominant* in constituting and reproducing a particular form of society; furthermore, it is the developent of contradictions both within and between the different structures, not simply the effects, conceived in a mechanical way, of purely economic contradictions, which lead eventually to the breakdown of an existing social formation and the emergence of a new one. Hence, it is argued, the state and the "ideological apparatus" (through which a dominant cultural outlook is reporduced) undergo a partially—and even largely—

independent development and have a major influence upon the evolution, the persistence or decline, of a particular social formation. The Marxist notion of "crisis" has been reinterpreted in accordance with these views, and Althusser has introduced the term "overdetermination" to express the idea of a confluence of separate lines of development, and a conjunction of crises occurring more or less independently in different spheres of society, which result in a revolutionary transformation.

It may be objected that some of the more abstract recent writings on infrastructure and superstructure do not advance much, if at all, beyond Engels's very general observations on the "relative autonomy" of the superstructure;[77] although in the works of Godelier there is a more empirical, and illuminating, analysis of ideology, especially myth, in relation to the economic structure of primitive societies.[78] Nevertheless, there remains a largely unresolved general problem concerning the exact degree of autonomy that is to be attributed to the various spheres of society, and the precise meaning of the claim that the functioning and development of a society as a whole are determined "in the final analysis" by the economic structure. It will be useful, in this context, to consider the ideas of some of the thinkers associated with the other broad tendency in present-day Marxist thought, namely, "critical theory"; for in spite of the very different character of their basic conceptions they agree largely with the structuralist Marxists in distinguishing three principal, quasi-independent spheres of social life—economic, political, and ideological—among which there is a complex interaction, rather than a simple unilinear determination by the economic structure. Thus, Jürgen Habermas in his *Legitimation Crisis* (1977) examines the manifestations of economic, political, and ideological crisis in late capitalist societies, as well as diverse interpretations of such crises, and argues that since the economic system has surrendered part of its autonomy to the state, an economic crisis cannot, in these conditions, directly provoke a crisis of the whole social system. The responsibility for dealing with the crisis is assumed by the state, and a crisis of the whole system could only develop if there were a political crisis and an ideological crisis in which the cultural system became incapable of providing the necessary motivations for the maintenance and reproduction of the existing society. In Habermas's view, therefore, the fundamental, increasingly difficult problem of late capitalist society is that of providing an adequate, persuasive *legitimation* of the social order.[79] Similarly, Claus Offe, in his studies of the state, and of one pervasive ideology which he calls the "achievement principle,"[80] gives preeminent importance, "in an era of comprehensive state intervention"—when it is no longer possible to speak reasonably of " 'spheres free of state interference' that constitute the 'material base' of the 'political superstructure' "—to the ideological justifications of the social system: "The late capitalist welfare state bases its legitimacy on the postulate of a universal participation in consensus formation and on the unbiased possibility for all classes to utilize the state's services and to benefit from its regulatory acts of intervention."[81]

In the studies by Habermas and Offe, it will be seen, there is a move away from the idea of determination by the economic structure, even "in the final analysis," while the state and ideology seem to be treated as the main determining forces; although it might still be argued—employing Godelier's distinction—that their *dominance* is the consequence of a particular mode of production—namely, that of advanced capitalism, which in this sense remains *determinant*. At all events, the concentration in these studies upon the critical analysis of ideology shows their affiliation with the Marxism of the Frankfurt School, but there is also a more marked divergence from Marx's own theory and a more direct criticism of certain aspects of it. This appears very clearly in Wellmer's exposition of critical theory, where he develops an argument against the "objectivism" and the "latent positivism" of Marx's theory of history, which are held to result from the undue emphasis that Marx placed upon the process of labor and material production as opposed to social interaction (or in Habermas's terminology upon "instrumental" as opposed to "communicative" behavior), and from the epistemological implications of this view—namely, that the fundamental processes constituting, or transforming, particular forms of society can be analyzed with the precision of natural science and formulated as laws.[82] According to Wellmer, this conception—strongly though not exclusively present in Marx's thought—furnishes the starting point for a technocratic interpretation of Marxism, to which he opposes a conception of Marxism as a theory of the development of a critical consciousness which aims at emancipation. His view is summed up in a discussion of the necessary conditions for a transition from capitalism to socialism; after observing that "history itself has thoroughly discredited all hopes of an economically grounded 'mechanism' of emancipation," he goes on to argue that it is necessary "to take into account entirely new constellations of 'bases' and 'superstructures,' " that "the criticism and alteration of the 'superstructure' have a new and decisive importance for the movements of liberation," and that "to reformulate Marx's supposition about the prerequisites for a successful revolution in the case of the capitalist countries, it would be necessary to include socialist democracy, socialist justice, socialist ethics and a 'socialist consciousness' among the components of a socialist society to be 'incubated' within the womb of a capitalist order."[83]

Although there are considerable differences among individual thinkers, some of the general conceptions which characterize critical theory are evident. In the first place, there is an emphasis upon consciousness and intentional activity as a major element in constituting, reproducing, or changing a particular form of society. For critical theory it is not the case that "being determines consciousness," particularly in the sense that consciousness is only a determined reflection of the conditions of material prodcution. Consciousness is not simply an outcome of the human interaction with nature, but it is a distinct and independent capacity to use language, to communicate with others, to create symbols and engage in symbolic thought. From this aspect critical theory has to be seen as one of the schools of "interpretative sociology," analyzing the social world by the interpretation of "meanings," not by the investigation of causal relations, and hence rejecting not only

Marx's "latent positivism," but also the notion of "structural causality" which is central to the thought of the Marxist structuralists. It is evident, furthermore, that the sources of critical theory include, besides Marxism, German philosophical idealism and especially phenomenology,[84] as may be seen in the work of Jürgen Habermas[85] and in Sartre's attempted conjunction of existentialism and Marxism in order to comprehend the relation between the intentional actions of individuals (human "projects") and the unintended, in some way determined, consequences of the behavior of groups and classes.[86]

This commitment to an interpretative method is a major element in the preoccupation of critical theorists with cultural criticism or "ideology-critique"; for insofar as the social world is conceived as a tissue of "meanings," the reproduction or transformation of any particular social world becomes a matter of sustaining or modifying, in the consciousness of individuals, the dominant mode of representation of that world—the established interpretation of its reality and legitimacy—which is expressed in a system of cultural values and in ideologies (social, philosophical, and religious doctrines, legal systems, educational practices). From these concerns have emerged such analyses of late capitalist society as Habermas's study of science and technology as ideology, or of the problems of legitimation,[87] and Marcuse's account of the domination of these societies by neopositivist philosophy and technological rationality.[88] This emphasis, in critical theory, upon the shaping power of ideologies and, in a more general way, upon the character of social struggles as a conflict of ideas, a contest among different interpretations of the social world, has itself attracted criticism from both Marxist and non-Marxist social scientists, who point to the existence of a quasi-causal relationship between men and the physical world (upon which Marx himself insisted) and to the neglect, by critical theorists, of the elements of power (in the last resort, physical coercion) and material interests in social life which are held to be connected with this human dependence upon, and interaction with, the natural environment.[89] Here, the idea of material causality, formulated by the structuralist Marxists, offers a clear alternative mode of analysis.

A third distinctive feature of critical theory, again setting it in opposition to structuralist Marxism, is its conception of social theory as being primarily concerned with historical interpretation. Social life is seen as a historical process—and progress—in which reason, in its critical form, is able to recognize and seize upon the opportunities for liberation which exist in any given condition of society; or as Marcuse argues, to form historical projects which can advance rationality and freedom beyond the level so far reached.[90] This teleological view, which posits a more or less determinate and intelligible historical process in which the human species, as the historical subject, advances toward the end after which it has always striven—namely, emancipation and the comprehensive organization of social life in accordance with universal reason—has its roots in Hegel's philosophy; and as I showed earlier in discussing the work of Lukács, Korsch, and the thinkers of the Frankfurt School in the 1920s, it has long inspired one major version of Marxism, critical theory being only its most recent expression. From the standpoint of those who consider Marxism a science this teleological conception is quite unacceptable, and their criticisms may be summed up in Godelier's observation, quoted earlier, that history does not explain, but has to be explained; that is to say, accounted for in terms of efficient causes.

It will be apparent from the foregoing review that much recent Marxist scholarship has been devoted especially to problems of method, and this is very similar to the situation which prevails in sociology as a whole. Indeed, it is evident that the debates within Marxism and within sociology cover much of the same ground, being preoccupied with questions about the nature of a general social science, its scientific standing, and its relation to philosophy; and they also draw upon many of the same sources, among them phenomenological criticisms of the idea of a social science, theories of language, and structuralist doctrines. Hence it may be said that there is now a closer relation between Marxism and sociology, and even a merging of ideas, in their concern with problems in the philosophy of science. To a great extent this concern revives, though in different terms, the preoccupations that dominated the *Methodenstreit* in Germany in the nineteenth century, and especially a critique of positivist views such as was formulated by Dilthey and subsequently examined by Max Weber.[91] And just as Lichtheim remarks in an essay on the intellectual return "from Marx to Hegel" that "if then we find that contemporary thinking reproduces the problematic of an earlier historical situation—namely that out of which Marxism arose—we are entitled to suppose that it does so because the relationship of theory to practice has once more become the sort of problem it was for Hegel's followers in the 1840s"[92] so we might say that the methodological preoccupations of recent sociology arise in large measure from a situation of cultural and political uncertainty which has some resemblance to that of the period from the 1880s to the first world war.[93]

However, it would be wrong to leave the impression that Marxist scholarship in the past two decades has been more or less exclusively concerned with the reinterpretation of Marx's own texts and with methodological issues set in the context of wider discussions of the philosophy of the social sciences. As I have already indicated, there have been important substantive investigations: in anthropology, especially by Godelier; and in such studies of the state and of social classes as those by Offe and Poulantzas. There has also been an attempt, notably in the studies by Perry Anderson,[94] to investigate large-scale historical problems with the aid of new theoretical conceptions. Perhaps the most impressive contribution by Marxists is to be found, however, in that large and growing area of study which has come to be known as the "sociology of development." It is not too much to say that in this field both the theoretical framework and research strategies have been radically transformed by Marxist criticism of the predominant model of the 1950s, which was expressed particularly in the notion of "modernization," and by the elaboration of new Marxist concepts.

Three important ideas have been formulated in the course of Marxist discussions of development, which themselves are quite diversified and have not produced anything like an "orthodox" Marxist view. First, it is insisted that the economic and social development of nonindustrial countries cannot be adequately comprehended solely in terms of factors internal to those countries, but have to be analyzed in the context of a world economy which is predominantly capitalist. Second, from this standpoint a distinction is made between metropolis/satellite, or center/periphery, and it is argued that the peripheral countries are either actively "underdeveloped" by the capitalist centers or are subjected to a process of "dependent" and distorted development. Analyses of this kind are presented in Paul Baran, *The Political Economy of Growth* (1962); in A. Gunder Frank, *Capitalism and Underdevelopment in Latin America* (2d ed., 1969);[95] and, particularly with reference to the theory of "dependent development," in the writings of a number of Latin American economists and sociologists.[96] The debate about underdevelopment and dependency has also revived discussion of the Marxist theory of imperialism and has led to various attempts to revise and reformulate the theory to take account of postwar phenomena such as the dissolution of the colonial empires and, on the other side, the rapid growth of multinational corporations.[97] Finally, in the same context, Marxists have given much attention to the concept of a "postcolonial mode of production" as a framework for analyzing, within the world economy, the social structure and especially the character and actions of social classes in those nonindustrial countries which have emerged from colonial rule.[98]

There has been, of course, much recent work in other areas of social life—for example, studies of the family influenced both by the concern with "cultural reproduction" and by feminist criticisms of Marxist theory, and studies in the field of criminology—but it is primarily in the analyses of "late capitalism" and of "development" that the concepts of a new Marxist sociology, or "political economy," are being worked out, though as I have shown, in quite varied forms. In concluding this brief historical account it will perhaps be useful to reconsider, in light of this diversity and effervescence of present-day Marxist thought, the distinctive character of Marxism which I sketched at the outset—namely, its dual existence as a theory of society embedded in the intellectual and scientific life and institutions of modern societies, and as the doctrine of a social movement. Obviously, this connection between theory and political practice remains (and I would argue indeed that a similar, though often less obvious and less systematic, relation to practical life exists in the case of all social-science theories), but some important changes have occurred. The development of Marxism as a theory is now accorded a greater independence from direct political concerns and is more clearly located in the context of a general development of sociological theory, as is evident from the relations that I have shown to exist between recent Marxism and other movements of thought in the social sciences and in the philosophy of science. There is now no "orthodox" Marxism which can claim to generate infallibly a "correct" political (or party) view of aims and strategies in practical life. On the contrary, the diversity of theoretical stances, the acknowledgment of unresolved theoretical problems, and the recognition of the complex and partly indeterminate character of historical development have begun to produce a more tentative attitude to political action, in which many different considerations, not necessarily encompassed by the theory itself, have to find a place. Thus the idea of a large degree of autonomy in both scientific work and political action is now widely accepted. But still it may be said that this process of liberation of Marxist thought from dogmatism has itself to be seen in its social context; and from the standpoint of one type of Marxist theory it might well be regarded as an element in that general movement of human emancipation which Marx himself defined in such original and dramatic terms.

NOTES

1. Tom Bottomore, *Marxist Sociology* (London: Macmillan, 1975).

2. In speaking of Marx's theory, I do not mean to deny the importance of Engels's contribution to the general development of Marxist thought. But the fundamental and distinctive elements of this intellectual system were, as is universally acknowledged, the creation of Marx himself, and Engels's collaboration—except at the very beginning of their association, when he was largely responsible for directing Marx's attention to the writings of the political economists and economic historians, partly through his essay "Outline of a Critique of Political Economy," which was published in the *Deutsch-Französische Jahrbücher* (1844)—involved for the most part the application of these theoretical ideas to particular problems concerning the history of societies, or the development of the labor movement, and the exposition in more popular terms of the Marxist theory. After Marx's death Engels became, as we shall see, not only the editor of Marx's manuscripts, but also the first of many interpreters and systematizers of his ideas.

3. These manuscripts were first published in 1932, and several English translations are now available. In the text I shall quote from my own translation in T. B. Bottomore, *Karl Marx: Early Writings* (London: Watts & Co., 1963).

4. Bottomore, *Early Writings*, p. 202.

5. Karl Korsch, *Karl Marx* (London: Chapman & Hall, 1938).

6. The manuscript now known as the *Grundrisse* was written by Marx in 1857–58 and first published as a whole in 1939–41. The English translation, by Martin Nicolaus, was published in 1973. (Harmondsworth: Penguin Books, 1973).

7. *Capital*, vol. III was published by Engels from Marx's manuscripts in 1894. There are several English translations; the passage cited here is taken from T. B. Bottomore and Maximilien Rubel (eds.), *Karl Marx: Selected Writings in Sociology and Social Philosophy* (London: Watts & Co., 1956) pp. 112–13.

8. The manuscript of *The German Ideology*, written by Marx and Engels in 1845–46, was first published in 1932. The English trans. cited here is taken from Bottomore and Rubel, *Karl Marx: Selected Writings*, pp. 70–71.

9. The passage cited here is taken from Bottomore and Rubel, *Karl Marx: Selected Writings*, pp. 67–8.

10. Louis Althusser, *For Marx* (London: Allen Lane, 1969).

11. This section of the manuscript has been published separately in an English translation, with a very useful introduction by Eric Hobsbawm, under the title *Pre-Capitalist Economic Formations* (London: Lawrence & Wishart, 1964).

12. Marx's excerpts and critical comments have now been transcribed and edited, with an introduction, by Lawrence Krader, *The Ethnological Notebooks of Karl Marx* (Assen: VanGorcum & Co., 1972).

13. Reprinted in Robin Blackburn, ed., *Ideology in Social Science* (London: Fontana/Collins, 1972) pp. 306–33.

14. Hobsbawm, *Pre-Capitalist Economic Formations*, pp. 19–20, 36–37.

15. Cf. Perry Anderson, *Lineages of the Absolutist State* (London: New Left Books, 1974) p. 403: "*All* modes of production in class societies prior to capitalism extract surplus labour from the immediate producers by means of extra-economic coercion. Capitalism is the first mode of production in history in which the means whereby the surplus is pumped out of the direct producer is 'purely' economic in form—the wage contract: the equal exchange between free agents which reproduces, hourly and daily, inequality and oppression. All other previous modes of exploitation operate through *extra-economic* sanctions—kin, customary, religious, legal or political."

16. This last conception is by no means irreconcilable with some elements in Max Weber's account of the origins and development of capitalism; or to put the matter in another way, Weber's thesis can be partly assimilated into, and partly complements, Marx's analysis.

17. An English translation of these "marginal notes," which throw additional light on Marx's methodological views, together with a useful commentary, is to be found in Terrell Carver, *Karl Marx: Texts on Method* (Oxford: Basil Blackwell, 1975).

18. See, for example, the laudatory essay by E. Belfort Bax, "Karl Marx," in *Modern Thought*, December 1881.

19. Peter Nettl, "The German Social Democratic Party 1890–1914 as a Political Model," *Past and Present*, April 1965, pp. 65–95.

20. For example, in Karl Kautsky's journal *Neue Zeit*, in the *Marx-Studien* and *Der Kampf* of the Austro-Marxists, and in Sorel's *Le Devenir Social* to which most of the leading European Marxists contributed during its brief existence from 1895–98.

21. An English translation, under the title *Evolutionary Socialism*, was published in 1909. (Reprinted New York: Schocken Books, 1961).

22. I shall not attempt to discuss here the problems of Marxist ethics. There is a good account of the context of Bernstein's ideas—of his "positivism" and his views on ethics, both influenced by neo-Kantianism—in Peter Gay, *The Dilemma of Democratic Socialism* (New York: Columbia University Press, 1952). An excellent recent study of Marxist ethics is S. Stojanovic, *Between Ideals and Reality* (New York: Oxford University Press, 1973).

23. Rudolf Hilferding, *Das Finanzkapital* (1910, not yet published in English); Rosa Luxemburg, *The Accumulation of Capital* (1913; English trans., London: Routledge & Kegan Paul, 1951).

24. See especially Sorel's essays on Durkheim, "Les théories de M. Durkheim," in *Le Devenir social*, April and May 1895.

25. See the English translation of some of these essays collected in Benedetto Croce, *Historical Materialism and the Economics of Karl Marx*, with an introduction by A. D. Lindsay (London: Howard Latimer, 1913).

26. Bauer's essay, "What is Austro-Marxism?" published in 1927, is translated in full in Tom Bottomore and Patrick Goode, *Austro-Marxism* (Oxford: Oxford University Press, 1978), which contains a selection from the principal writings of the Austro-Marxists, together with an introductory essay on the formation and the principal ideas of the Austro-Marxist school.

27. The works referred to are: Otto Bauer, *Die Nationalitätenfrage und die Sozialdemokratie* (1907); Max Adler, *Der soziologische Sinn der Lehre von Karl Marx* (1914), *Soziologie des Marxismus* (2 vols., 1930–32; enlarged ed. with a third volume, 1964), and many other works; Karl Renner, *Die soziale Funktion der Rechsinstitute* (1904; rev. ed., 1928); Rudolf Hilferding, *Das Finanzkapital* (1910). Only Karl Renner's book has so far been translated into English, under the title *The Institutions of Private Law and Their Social Functions* (London: Routledge & Kegan Paul, 1949), but selections from the others are published in Bottomore and Goode, *Austro-Marxism*.

28. English trans., *Community and Association* (London: Routledge & Kegan Paul, 1955). Much later, in 1921, Tönnies published a study of Marx [English trans., *Karl Marx: His Life and Teachings* (East Lansing: Michigan State University Press, 1974)] in which he reiterated the importance of Marx's influence and in the second part of the book examined some of the economic and sociological problems that arise in Marx's theory.

29. Carl Grünberg, who has been called "the father of Austro-Marxism," taught economic history and the history of the labor movement at the University of Vienna from 1894 to 1924, when he became the first director of the Frankfurt Institute for Social Research. He is now chiefly remembered for the periodical *Archiv für die Geschichte des Sozialismus und der Arbeiterbewegung*, which he founded (in 1910) and edited, to which many distinguished Marxist scholars contributed.

30. Antonio Labriola taught philosophy at the University of Rome from 1874 to 1904,

published the first Italian translation of *The Communist Manifesto* in 1890 and a collection of essays, *The Materialist Conception of History*, in 1896.

31. Rudolph Stammler, *Wirtschaft und Recht nach der materialistischen Geschichtsauffassung.* Stammler's book was itself criticized at length by Croce, in one of the essays collected in *Historical Materialism and the Economics of Karl Marx;* by Max Weber, in an essay published in 1907, "R. Stammlers 'Ueberwindung' der materialistischen Geschichtsauffassung," reprinted in *Gesammelte Aufsätze zur Wissenschaftslehre* (1922); and by Max Adler, in "R. Stammlers Kritik der materialistischen Geschichtsauffassung," reprinted in *Marxistische Probleme* (1913).

32. English translations of Böhm-Bawerk's book and Hilferding's rejoinder have been published together in a volume edited by Paul Sweezy (New York: Augustus M. Kelley, 1949).

33. For a more detailed account of the reception and discussion of Marxism as a sociological theory, see T. B. Bottomore and M. Rubel, eds., *Karl Marx: Selected Writings in Sociology and Social Philosophy* (1956), Introduction, part II.

34. Besides the studies already mentioned that were undertaken by the Austro-Marxists, there were such works as M. Tugan-Baranovsky, *Geschichte der Russischen Fabrik* (in Russian 1898; rev. German trans., 1900) and E. Grosse, *Die Formen der Familie und die Formen der Wirtschaft* (1897), as well as the publications of Carl Grünberg in the field of agrarian history and labor history, where the influence of Marxism was obviously very great. Some idea of the extent of Marxist research, especially in the general field of social history, can be gained from Grünberg's *Archiv* from 1910 onward.

35. A. Labriola, *Essays on the Materialistic Conception of History* (English trans., Chicago: Charles H. Kerr, 1908) p. 149.

36. In addition to the writings of Max Adler see those of Otto Neurath, who formed a link between Austro-Marxism and the Vienna Circle, especially his monograph *Empirical Sociology* (1931; English trans. in O. Neurath, *Empiricism and Sociology*, (Dordrecht: D. Reidel Publishing Co., 1973).

37. See the illuminating essay by John Torrance, "The Emergence of Sociology in Austria 1885–1935," in *European Journal of Sociology*, XVII, 2 (1976), pp. 185–219.

38. Georg Simmel, *Philosophie des Geldes* (1900; English trans. London: Routledge & Kegan Paul, 1978). See also the discussion of Simmel's relation to Marx by Albert Salomon, "German Sociology," in Georges Gurvitch and Wilbert E. Moore, eds., *Twentieth Century Sociology* (New York: 1945).

39. This is well brought out in Karl Löwith, "Max Weber und Karl Marx" (1932), part of which is translated in Dennis Wrong, ed., *Max Weber* (Englewood Cliffs, N.J.: Prentice-Hall, 1970).

40. Marxism played only a small part in the development of American sociology, either at its beginnings or later, while in Britain, where sociology itself scarcely began to develop until after the second world war, Marxism had only a modest intellectual (or political) influence at any time. It is only since the 1960s that this situation has begun to change.

41. The most systematic theoretical study of Soviet Marxism is Herbert Marcuse, *Soviet Marxism* (London: Routledge & Kegan Paul, 1958). See especially chap. 2, "Soviet Marxism: The Basic Self-Interpretation."

42. V. I. Lenin, *Imperialism, the Highest Stage of Capitalism* (1916) in *Collected Works* vol. XIX (London: Lawrence & Wishart, 1942).

43. For Lenin's views and later developments, see Hélène Carrère d'Encausse and Stuart R. Schram, *Marxism and Asia* (1965, English trans., London: Allen Lane, 1969).

44. Trotsky, like Lenin, was primarily concerned with asserting the possibility of a socialist revolution in a backward country. He developed this idea in his theory of the "permanent revolution" [first formulated after the revolution of 1905 and expounded again in the introduction to *Permanent Revolution*, (1920)] which also introduced the idea that "for backward countries the road to democracy passed through the dictatorship of the proletariat."

45. This English translation of the book appeared in 1925. On Bukharin's contribution to Marxist theory, see Stephen F. Cohen, *Bukharin and the Bolshevik Revolution* (London: Wildwood House, 1974), especially chap. 4, "Marxist Theory and Bolshevik Policy: Bukharin's *Historical Materialism.*"

46. See the discussion in Marcuse, *Soviet Marxism.*

47. Karl Korsch, *Marxismus und Philosophie* (1923; English trans., London: New Left Books, 1970); Georg Lukács, *Geschichte und Klassenbewusstsein* (1923; English trans. London: Merlin Press, 1971). For further critical discussion of the ideas of Korsch and Lukács, see Bottomore, *Marxist Sociology*, chap. 3, and *Sociology as Social Criticism*, (London: George Allen & Unwin, 1975) chap. 7; and George Lichtheim, *Lukâcs* (London: Fontana/Collins, 1970).

48. Lukács, *History and Class Consciousness,* p. 75. Lukács's argument is based upon a distinction between what he calls "psychological" class consciousness (the actual consciousness which workers have in particular historical situations) and an "imputed" or "possible" rational consciousness (i.e., Marxism). Much later, in the preface which he wrote in 1967 for the new edition of the book, Lukács again insisted strongly upon the importance of this distinction, which he now associated explicitly with Lenin's distinction between "trade-union consciousness" and "socialist consciousness."

49. See Antonio Gramsci, *Selections from the Prison Notebooks,* ed., trans., and with an introduction by Quintin Hoare and Geoffrey Nowell Smith (London: Lawrence & Wishart, 1971).

50. From Gramsci's critical notes on Bukharin's *Historical Materialism,* in *Selections from the Prison Notebooks,* p. 462. Lukács also criticized Bukharin in much the same terms in a review published in 1925 [English trans. under the title "Technology and Social Relations," in *New Left Review* (1966)] in which he argued that the dialectic can do without sociology as an independent science.

51. See H. Stuart Hughes, *Consciousness and Society* (London: MacGibbon & Kee, 1958), especially chap. 2.

52. Benedetto Croce, *Historical Materialism and the Economics of Karl Marx.*

53. In his preface to Saverio Merlino, *Formes et essence du socialisme* (Paris, 1898).

54. The institute was created in 1923, as the outcome of a "Marxist Work Week," held in 1922, at which one of the principal subjects of discussion was the conception of Marxism expounded in Korsch's forthcoming book *Marxism and Philosophy.* On the history of the Frankfurt Institute, see the very comprehensive study by Martin Jay, *The Dialectical Imagination* (Boston: Little, Brown and Company, 1973).

55. Herbert Marcuse, *Reason and Revolution: Hegel and the Rise of Social Theory* (New York: Oxford University Press, 1941) p. 343.

56. This view was expressed particularly by Horkheimer, in a series of articles published in the mid-1930s and reprinted in *Kritische Theorie* (2 vols., 1968).

57. Korsch, *Karl Marx.* The quotations are translated from the revised German edition of the book (1967) pp. 145, 203.

58. See, in particular, Karl Mannheim, *Ideology and Utopia* (1929; English trans., New York: Harcourt, Brace and Company, 1936).

59. See notes 3 and 7 herein.

60. Emile Durkheim, *Socialism* (New York: The Antioch Press, 1958).

61. See the discussions in David Horowitz, ed., *Marx and Modern Economics* (1968).

62. Raymond Firth, "The Sceptical Anthropologist? Social Anthropology and Marxist Views on Society," in *Proceedings of the British Academy,* LVIII (London: Oxford University Press, 1972).

63. See p. 128-29 herein.

64. See especially Louis Althusser and Étienne Balibar, *Reading Capital* (London: New Left Books, 1970).

65. In particular, the work of C. Lévi-Strauss. See his *Structural Anthropology* (London: Allen Lane, 1968), the short study of his ideas by Edmund Leach, *Lévi-Strauss* (London: Fontana/Collins, 1970), and for a more general view, David Robey, ed., *Structuralism: An Introduction* (Oxford: Oxford University Press, 1973). See also chapter 14, "Structuralism," especially pp. 000, herein.

66. With what success is a matter of dispute. My own judgment is that Althusser fails completely to establish two of the main points of his argument—namely, the existence of a total "epistemological break" between the "young Marx" and the "mature Marx," and the precise criterion for distinguishing between science and ideology—and that his general discussion of problems in the philosophy of science is obscure, muddled, and unfruitful. See the criticisms along these lines by Leszek Kolakowski, "Althusser's Marx," in *The Socialist Register* (1971). pp. 111–28.

67. Althusser and Balibar, *Reading Capital,* p. 65.

68. Maurice Godelier, *Rationality and Irrationality in Economics* (London: New Left Books, 1974) and *Perspectives in Marxist Anthropology* (Cambridge: Cambridge University Press, 1977). Although much of Godelier's work is in the field of social anthropology as traditionally conceived, his methodological writings and many of his substantive analyses belong equally to the domain of sociological thought.

69. See especially the introduction and the first essay, "Anthropology and Economics."

70. Godelier, *Perspectives in Marxist Anthropology*, p. 24. "A mode of production is a reality which 'does not reveal itself' directly in any spontaneous and intimate experience of those agents who reproduce it by their activity ('indigenous' practices and representations), nor in any enquiries in the field or the knowledgeable external observations of professional anthropologists. A mode of production is a reality which requires to be reconstructed, to be reproduced in thought, in the very process of scientific knowledge. A reality exists as 'scientific fact' only when it is reconstructed within the field of scientific theory and its corresponding application."

71. Godelier, *Perspectives in Marxist Anthropology*, p. 4.

72. Godelier, *Perspectives in Marxist Anthropology*, p. 6.

73. Nicos Poulantzas, *Political Power and Social Classes* (London: New Left Books, 1973) and *Classes in Contemporary Capitalism* (London: New Left Books, 1975).

74. Barry Hindess and Paul Q. Hirst, *Pre-Capitalist Modes of Production* (London: Routledge & Kegan Paul, 1975) and *Mode of Production and Social Formation* (London: Macmillan Press Ltd., 1977).

75. In the concluding section of *Pre-Capitalist Modes of Production*, p. 321, Hindess and Hirst write: "It is not supposed that more developed modes (in our sense of the term) succeed less developed ones, or that there are *any* necessary relations of succession between modes of production. . . . The concepts of the modes of production developed here do not form a history in thought, mirroring in their succession the evolution of the real. . . . We reject the notion of history as a coherent and worthwhile object of study."

76. See especially Pierre Bourdieu and Jean-Claude Passeron, *Reproduction* (London: Sage Publications, 1977).

77. See, for example, Kolakowski's comment in "Althusser's Marx" that "the whole theory of 'overdetermination' is nothing but a repetition of traditional banalities which remain exactly on the same level of vagueness as before."

78. See especially Godelier's *Perspectives in Marxist Anthropology*, part IV.

79. Jürgen Habermas, *Legitimation Crisis* (London: Heinemann, 1976).

80. Claus Offe, "Political Authority and Class Structures: An Analysis of Late Capitalist Societies," *International Journal of Sociology*, II:1 (1972) pp. 73–105; and *Industry and Inequality* (London: Edward Arnold, 1976).

81. Offe, "Political Authority and Class Structures."

82. Albrecht Wellmer, *Critical Theory of Society* (New York: Herder & Herder, 1971).

83. Wellmer, *Critical Theory of Society*, pp. 121–22.

84. See the discussion in William Outhwaite, *Understanding Social Life* (London: George Allen & Unwin, 1975), particularly chap. 5, where the relation between Marxism and the "interpretative" tradition in the social sciences is examined. See also the remarks on Marxism and phenomenology in chapter 13, pp. 000, herein.

85. Especially *Zur Logik der Sozialwissenschaften* (Frankfurt: Suhrkamp Verlag, 1967) and *Knowledge and Human Interests* (London: Heinemann, 1972).

86. Jean-Paul Sartre, *Critique of Dialectical Reason* (1975), and *Search for a Method* (New York: Alfred A. Knopf, 1963). Originally published together as *Critique de la raison dialectique* (Paris: Gallimard, 1960).

87. Jürgen Habermas, "Science and Technology as Ideology" in *Toward a Rational Society* (Boston: Beacon Press, 1970); and *Legitimation Crisis*.

88. Herbert Marcuse, *One-Dimensional Man* (London: Routledge & Kegan Paul, 1964).

89. For a critical discussion of this question, see Brian Fay, *Social Theory and Political Practice* (London: George Allen & Unwin, 1975), pp. 83–91 and chap. 5.

90. Marcuse, *One-Dimensional Man*, chap. 8.

91. On this point, see further the discussion in chapter 7 herein.

92. George Lichtheim, *From Marx to Hegel and Other Essays* (London: Orbach & Chambers, 1971), p. 14.

93. Some characteristics of that period are examined in Hughes, *Consciousness and Society*.

94. Perry Anderson, *Passages from Antiquity to Feudalism* (London: New Left Books, 1974) and *Lineages of the Absolutist State*.

95. Paul Baran, *The Political Economy of Growth* (New York: Monthly Review Press, 1962); A. Gunder Frank, *Capitalism and Underdevelopment in Latin America* (New York: Monthly Review Press, 1969).

96. Among others, F. Cardoso and O. Sunkel. For a general account, see T. Dos Santos, "The Crisis of Development Theory and the Problem of Dependence in Latin America," in H. Bernstein, ed., *Underdevelopment and Development* (Harmondsworth: Penguin Books, 1973),

pp. 57–80. The concept of "dependency," although it originated in Latin America, can obviously be applied elsewhere, and its value in the analysis of problems in the development of Middle Eastern countries is examined in a forthcoming book by Bryan Turner, *Marxism and the End of Orientalism*. See also Colin Leys, *Underdevelopment in Kenya* (London: Heinemann, 1975).

97. For a general view, see R. Rhodes, ed., *Imperialism and Underdevelopment* (New York: Monthly Review Press, 1970).

98. For a short account of the "postcolonial mode of production," see Turner, *Marxism and the End of Orientalism*.

5

GERMAN SOCIOLOGY IN THE TIME OF MAX WEBER

JULIEN FREUND

FROM the early nineteenth century, the idea of a science of society was on the agenda in Germany as well as in the other European countries. The upheavals provoked all over Europe by the French Revolution could not fail to strike the imagination of those in quest of a new social stability. In Germany as elsewhere, there was no agreement on the status of this new science. Would it be a social science in the normative sense of the term, whose task it would be to regenerate society, for instance following Karl Marx's project; or, would it be a positive discipline, dedicated essentially to as objective as possible an analysis of social phenomena, in the context of a "science of society," which Lorenz von Stein wanted to establish? It seems to me that the definitive adoption of the term sociology (invented by Auguste Comte) by all those interested in the analysis of society tipped research toward the latter definition, that prescribed by von Stein. Credit must be given to the obstinacy of certain scholars, like Durkheim, Max Weber, Simmel, and Pareto, for the establishment of a scientific sociology, even though the success of this formula remained fragile because of the overwhelming influence of the normative conception of sociology, essentially in the political form of Marxism. Even today, the question is still debated, to the extent that Marxism has succeeded in establishing itself in the universities and research centers. It must be hoped that scientific sociology will be able to integrate what is valuable in Marxist methodology, leaving to the general domain of politics the task of deciding the future of Marxist philosophy. However, one thing is certain: the conception of sociology as a positive science—not merely normative—has won recognition in the republic of knowledge. A large part of the credit belongs to German sociology, which did not hesitate, thanks to Weber, Simmel, and Sombart, to carry the criticism of Marxism into the university in order to determine its limitations and its validity. To neglect the debate provoked by Marxism in the period we are considering would be to misapprehend the conditions of sociological analysis of that time. It was even one of the characteristics of this period. The fact that this debate continues in our own time is no reason to neglect the fact that Marxism was already in the center of academic discussions at the beginning of this century and that Weber tried to resolve it no less than did Durkheim or Pareto.

There is no doubt that Positivism, which as philosophy is as debatable as Marxism, contributed largely to defining the scientific status of nascent sociology. Indeed, Positivism spread rapidly in various countries, in England under the influence of John Stuart Mill, in Germany thanks to the establishment of positivist circles such as the "Club of Suicides" to which W. Scherer, H. Grimm, and especially the young Dilthey belonged. Dilthey later was to transform the entire epistemology of the human sciences *(Geisteswissenschaften)* thanks to his distinction between explanation and understanding and his theory of interpretation. We know how much this methodological breakthrough was to influence German science following the work of Windelband and Rickert, and later that of Max Weber. Anyway, to grasp all the implications of German sociology in the period of Tönnies, Simmel, Sombart, and Weber, we must understand the hesitations concerning social science during the time when sociological analysis definitively established itself in Germany. The very term sociology took a while to gain acceptance there, for it met competition from other terms, in particular that of "science of society" *(Gesellschaftswissenschaft)*. In fact, it was less the positivist philosophy of Auguste Comte that played the determining role, than the methodological views of Buckle, developed in the latter's famous *History of Civilization in England.*[1] Without going into the details of the birth of German sociology, we must nevertheless highlight two factors which influenced that discipline at the time, for they were to condition the originality of later research in the time of Max Weber.

1. Although at its inception German sociology was very sensitive to foreign influences, it nevertheless took its foundations as much from categories proper to German thought—in particular, the distinction, inherited from Hegel, between state (*Staat*) and society (*Gesellschaft*—which the influential minds of the period (for example, Lorenz von Stein) used from the methodological point of view as much as from that of the object of social science. This distinction is one of the original characteristics of German sociology, for it is rarely found in the works of the sociologists of other European countries. In general, it introduced a gap between society, conceived as an organic reality, and the state, a mere artificial and conventional creation. But other interpretations of this opposition exist as well, for example that of Lorenz von Stein, little known abroad but of decisive influence in Germany. In his view, the state is the field in which citizens freely express their choice, so that the

state as an institution is the source of all liberty, while society is the field of economic activity, which is the source of dependence and servitude. Whatever the merits of this distinction, it is basic to important currents of German sociological thought. For instance it functioned more or less directly in the distinction established by Tönnies between "community" *(Gemeinschaft)* and "society" (*Gesellschaft*), which Max Weber subsequently took up, albeit by introducing a dynamic process into this rather static opposition, in the form of a distinction between *Vergemeinschaftung* and *Vergesellschaftung*.[2] At any rate, it does not seem possible to me to form a clear idea of the development of nascent German sociology if one does not understand the dichotomy, classic for the Germans, between state and society.

2. More so than the incipient sociologies of other countries, early German sociology was influenced at the start by psychologism and, to a lesser degree, by historicism. Indeed, German sociology developed at first under the term of *Völkerpsychologie,* whether in the form which Lazarus and Steinthal gave it, or that prescribed by W. Wundt. These authors essentially thought of society within the category of the people, with the latter taken to constitute a reality at once spiritual and collective, in the spirit of the German philosophical tradition of the *Volksgeist,* of which Hegel and Savigny were the theoreticians at the beginning of the nineteenth century. Society became so to speak the equivalent of the collective psychology which, according to Wundt, for example, should consist of studies of social phenomena, such as customs, languages, myths, or religions, based on the laws established by general psychology, which was in turn inspired by individual psychology. Psychologism at that time was so influential in Germany that the sociologist A. Schäffle, for example, who in his early works had defended a rather organic conception of society, came to support the psychological interpretation in his last works. It is likewise known that Dilthey, who was one of the first to insist on the importance of history in the interpretation of social phenomena, nevertheless believed that the foundation of history, and consequently that of the *Geisteswissenschaften* (human sciences) was psychology, in the sense that history is psychology in "becoming." If psychologism directly influenced the conception of sociology which people had at this time, historicism's influence was only indirect to the degree that the specialists in economics, whether those of the first historical school of Roscher and Knies, or the second, dominated by Gustav Schmoller, were led to focus their attention on social phenomena to better understand the evolution of economic facts. It was above all due to Max Weber, who went from economics (the subject he taught at the university) to sociology, that the views of the historical school penetrated sociology more fully, but with the correction that Windelband and Rickert subsequently contributed through their work in epistemology centered on the role and meaning of history in knowledge in general.

This is not the place to undertake in detail the study of the diversity of the conceptions elaborated by the first German sociologists. All in all, this sort of exercise belongs more to a history of ideas than to a survey of the principles of sociological analysis. Indeed, most of these authors tried mainly to define a priori, often from a philosophical perspective, the idea that one *ought* to have of sociology, but they themselves hardly practiced sociological analysis as such in a concrete manner. Nevertheless, it was necessary to quickly mention their views, for, on the one hand, they conditioned the special way sociology was conceived in Germany, and on the other hand, familiarity with their work brings with it a better understanding of the sociologists of the great period of German sociology in the time of Max Weber. Therefore, it must not be forgotten that other researchers, less well known, made important contributions in the same period, both from the viewpoint of the general vision of sociology (for example, Sombart, Vierkandt, Gumplowicz, von Wiese, Oppenheimer, and Alfred Weber) and more specific viewpoints (Plenge in the sociology of organization, Michels in the sociology of political parties, or Ehrlich in the sociology of law). However, we will limit ourselves to the scrutiny of the major figures. Tönnies, Simmel, and Max Weber, because their works still influence the orientation of sociological research today and are still topical.

Ferdinand Tönnies (1855–1935)

The principal work of Tönnies, *Gemeinschaft und Gesellschaft* (Community and Society), belongs to the German tradition of distinguishing between State and society—there are numerous references in it to this opposition—but brings to it considerable and even substantial changes. This is the only work of Tönnies which we shall consider, in the definitive version of the 1912 edition which brought glory to its author. Therefore we shall leave aside the history of the genesis of this book, originally presented as a doctoral thesis in 1881 and reworked in 1887, mentioning only that its early concept focused the problem on the philosophy of culture, its later one, that of 1887, on the distinction between communism and socialism, and finally the last one, that of 1912, limited itself to making of these two notions "two fundamental categories of pure sociology." Nor shall we elaborate upon the nuances, let alone the complications, which Tönnies later brought to bear on this fundamental work, in particular in his *Einführung in die Soziologie* in 1931. The fact remains that the 1912 edition of *Gemeinschaft und Gesellschaft*, translated into most foreign languages, remains his fundamental text if one takes into consideration the literature which it stimulated among German as well as foreign sociologists.

It was in Germany where this work first provoked lively discussions. Some criticized the psychological foundation which Tönnies brought to his distinction between community and society and thinkers like Staudinger or an H. Freyer tried to give it a more objective characteristic of two organizational structures.[3] Others asked themselves if these two categories account for the totality of social reality, some thinking with H. Schmalenbach that a third category, that of the *Bund*[4] ought to be introduced, others believing with Th. Geiger that what is involved is merely two complementary aspects of the same sociological reality, that of the grouping of *Samtschaft*,[5] still others like Vierkandt holding that in fact only the community predominates.[6] I have already noted that Max Weber finds another interpretation, by opposing to the static division of Tönnies the dynamic one of *Vergemeinschaftung* and *Vergesellschaftung*. Abroad, the debates were just as intense, if one refers to the works of G. Gurvitch or Monnerot in France, and the works of Kimball, Young, Gillin, Parsons, MacIver, and others in America. It would be simply tedious to draw up a list of the sociologists who took up, one way or another, directly or indirectly, the distinction established by Tönnies. He formulated and even inaugurated a typology of social relations which no sociologist can henceforth ignore, if he does not wish to pass for an amateur in the science in which he claims to be a specialist. Indeed, all the discussions on the opposition between competition and accommodation, conflict and association, cooperation and hostility, fusion and tension, integration and dissolution, solidarity and rivalry, communion and revolt, and all the other forms of social concord and discord, bring us back, directly or indirectly, to the work of Tönnies. It must not be forgotten that among his contempories he was one of the first to rehabilitate the work of Hobbes, which everyone had read in order to criticize it, but without taking from it the insights which it held for the sociologist.[7] Tönnies was a socialist, but he always knew how to guard the rights of science, unlike the agitators of our time. He put a question to sociological science which the latter has never been able to overcome, except by subterfuges and intellectual subtleties which willingly sacrifice scientific research to the phoniness of popular success.

Yet, despite the precautions which Tönnies took—the work is not an "ethical or political treatise"[8]—it was not only the object of partisan interpretations, but his work has been used to theoretically legitimize various practical positions in Germany. It was first put to use by the communitarian romanticism of the Right, and at least indirectly it influenced certain currents in national socialism. Today it is used to justify the communitarian nostalgia of various orientations of the Left. At bottom, the work of Tönnies is typical in the way a purely sociological study can be received in contradictory manner by the most diverse opinions, in spite of its author's protests. Once published, the immediate intentions of the author of a work are more or less lost. However, we will be interested here not in the diverse practical uses which may have been made of *Community and Society*, but in the importance this work has had for sociological research.

Like that of most minds of his time, Tönnies's analysis has a psychological basis, in the form of an opposition between two types of will—organic will (*Wesenswille*), and reflective will (*Kürwille*)—it being understood that in his opinion every manifestation of social reality represents a will. That is his basic postulate. This distinction is founded on the fact that will either implies thought, that is to say the latter is the expression of an originating will, or thought contains will, in the sense that the latter is the product and the consequence of a previous thought.[9] Organic will is the one which determines thought; on the contrary, reflective will is determined by thought.

Organic will is the profound will of being, the one that expresses the spontaneity and the movement of life itself. As such, it is the source of all creation and all individual originality. It is immanent and consubstantial with being and, at bottom, as complex as life itself. Having its origin in the past, it is a motivated and surging will, which manifests itself in pleasure, habit, and memory. Reflective will on the contrary expresses man's capacity to produce an artificial world, following the directives of thought, which conceives a goal abstractly and gives itself the appropriate means of realizing it. Knowledge therefore precedes will, for instance in the case of premeditated decision. It is a question of a calculating and speculating will, one that tries especially to foresee. For this reason it faces the future, but by constructing relations exterior to beings. It is a superficial will, because it is directed by the categories of usefulness and happiness. It no longer functions as a spontaneous impulse, but as a motor powering a machine or a mechanism.

According to Tönnies, this psychological distinction between the two wills conditions the two ways in which men form social groups: either they form a community, based on organic will, or a society, based on reflective will.[10] These two categories constitute the fundamental ideas of what Tönnies calls pure sociology. By this must be understood the general theory of the two possible ways in which men establish relations between themselves. Therefore, the task is not to describe positively or casuistically social reality, examining one after the other the diverse and multiple ways men have grouped themselves together since the beginning of history: such a study would simply be endless. The task is rather to account for theoretically, in a sense close to Max Weber's ideal type, the two essential ways men customarily group themselves together, taking into consideration the fact that in reality these two ways act upon each other reciprocally, according to whether the one conditions the other or is conditioned by it. There are nevertheless grounds for a reservation; these reciprocal relations can be positive and constructive, or negative and destructive. However, Tönnies considers only the positive aspects and neglects the negative aspects.[11] It is one of the weaknesses of his analysis, for there are, for example, decaying communities which sociological research ought not to write off, if it claims to reject the moral or ideological a priori's of the researcher. Furthermore, although he rejects this claim, Tönnies at least seems to give the impression of favoring community, for he concentrates on the negative aspects of society.

This impression is confirmed by the very first pages of book I where he opposes the two notions. Community, he explains, answers the needs of "real and organic life," whereas society is on the order of "artificial and mechanical representation," which at any rate must be understood as "a pure juxtaposition of individuals independent from one another." Indeed community is the place of trust and intimacy, society that of what is public and anonymous, to the point where "one comes into society as into a foreign country." He further emphasizes this difference by insisting that "community is the true and lasting common life; society is only temporary. And to a certain degree one can understand community as a living organism, society as a mechanical and artificial aggregate." In other words, community is seen as the true essence of social cohabitation (coexistence), whereas society is merely an appearance. Thus Tönnies agrees that there may be bad societies, whereas the idea of a bad community "rings like a contradiction."[12] The sociologist therefore does not escape showing a preference tinged by ideology. What are the characteristics of the two categories?

Community is rooted in the "primitive and natural state" of the individual, because its source is in the vegetative life of the incipient being, as well as in that of the elementary groupings of social life, such as the relationship between mother and child, between man and woman, and between brothers and sisters. The maternal relation is the most profound, the fraternal one the least, because it does not display the instinctive spontaneity of the first which has the sexual relationship between the two. These three relationships are based psychologically on pleasure, habit, and memory, natural to organic will, which expresses itself in the possession and enjoyment of common goods. Sociologically, these relations determine three types of community, that of blood or kinship community, that of place or neighborhood community, and that of friendship or spiritual community. Yet it would be mistaken to believe that community is only of the village type: it also defines a way of organizing urban life, inasmuch as certain cities used to form "a living and common organism." Juridically, the basis of communitarian life is custom, which on the one hand conditions a particular social consensus between its members, which Tönnies calls comprehension or concord; and on the other hand gives rise to judicial and religious functions proper. In the village the essential relation is that of the home and the field, in the city that which unites crafts in corporations or guilds. The sum of these relations forms a typical style of life, which Tönnies sometimes calls communism, taking the term not in its Marxist connotation, but rather in the sense of primitive communism.

Community develops a specific political regime, which Tönnies calls ducal, but unfortunately he does not analyze it in detail except to remark upon its affinities with the religious spirit. This is equally true of cities, which he considers religious communities. He lays more stress upon community economics. In the village community the center of the economy is the house, with its outbuildings, movable and immovable, property. It is a mainly domestic economy, self-sufficient, and exchange isn't used. As for the communitarian urban economy, it practices exchange, but only to the extent that the latter is necessary in the relation between the various trades. There is no question of exchange for profit, for the craft is an art, practiced for one's dignity and not for the sake of enrichment, which is alien to it. Thus one sees, without further elaborations, why Tönnies finds community to be the place where morality is concretely and affectively lived, dominated as it is by the search for ethical value which becomes identified with the living unity which forms the community.

Society is by nature artificial, because everyone in it lives for himself, "in a state of tension towards all the others."[13] Without doubt men coexist within a society, but they remain separated organically from one another, in spite of the relations which they may forge. Each one strives to keep the other off his property, which explains why no one will do anything for anyone else except to return a service at least equivalent to one which he has himself obtained. Social relations are therefore founded upon calculation and speculation, so that all goods are negotiated in the course of an exchange or a transaction. Every good becomes a value; because it is measured capacity to be useful or efficacious, it becomes a commodity. The possibility of exchanging equivalent goods requires that value be considered as having an objective quality, translated into money terms. This quality belongs to no one in particular, but it has the advantage of permitting the division of goods into equal parts, allowing equivalent exchanges. The point is even reached when exchanges of pure matter are made, with no intrinsic value and perfectly impersonal, such as paper money. In the words of Adam Smith, everyone in society is considered a merchant. At any rate, society is dominated by abstract reason, and it is understandable that in these conditions the supreme forms of abstraction—science, technology, and machinery—should be privileged. Tönnies writes, for example, "The superior scientific concept, whose name no longer corresponds to something real, resembles money. For example, the concept of the atom or of energy."[14]

Considered from a political viewpoint, society is founded upon contract, that is the legal and abstract conventions whose unity is made by the State. Tönnies's interest in Hobbes, the theoretician of the State conceived as resulting from a social compact and giving rise to a conventional society called "civil society," is understandable. If he takes up the classical opposition in German thought between State and society, it is in order to join these two concepts and oppose them both to the new category of community. The point to remember is that society is the reign of associations pursuing different or even divergent interests, whose relations among themselves are strictly legal. Thus it progressively dissolves communitarian bonds and increasingly follows its own principle by dissolving these communitarian bonds more systematically. From the economic point of view, society gives priority to commerce, with all its corollaries: competition, the market, trade, and credit, with the understanding that this process is not limited to the exchange of material goods, but also takes over the domain of ideas. Everything becomes a commodity, products as well as labor, that is, everything reduces itself to a process of purchase and sale. Henceforth, the "supremacy of the land" is replaced by "industrial supremacy," which degrades communitarian relations in favor of an immense worldwide market with monopolistic tendencies. Founded on division, beginning with division of labor, society is bound to reproduce further divisions, for example between social classes. Its principle is no longer concord, but struggle. "As a collectivity on which system of conventional rules is imposed, society is thereby inherently unlimited; it is continuously smashing its real or fortuitous frontiers. And since each person seeks in society his own advantage and approves of others only to the extent and for the amount of time that they seek the same advantages as himself, the relation of all to all, above and beyond convention, . . . can be seen as covert hostility or as latent warfare, setting aside agreements of wills as so many pacts and peace treaties."[15]

This opposition between community and society informs Tönnies's vision of the historical future. He considers socialism to be the achievement of mercantile and technocratic society, and at the same time an appeal for a return to community. The class struggle, particularly the antagonism between capitalism and proletariat, constitutes the supreme form of antagonisms proper to society, but as such it also carries with it the hope of an imminent end to the anarchy which is characteristic of society and a rediscovery of the organic bonds which characterize communitarian life. The triumph of society, with its cosmopolitanism—the reign of public opinion—indicates its forthcoming dissolution, thanks to the expected reawakening of the vitality which is peculiar to organic will.

Georg Simmel (1858–1918)

Simmel occupies a special place in the sociology of his time. Since with his student days, he was in contact with one of the essential currents of early German sociology, the *Völkerpsychologie* of his teachers Lazarus and Steinthal, whose influence, often in an indirect form, can be found even in his latest work. His early writings displayed an acceptance of Positivism, influenced, however, by Spencerian evolutionism and Darwinian pragmatism. He was preoccupied with the establishment of an empirical sociology, although he never undertook research in that line. He remains above all a philosopher. With his *Philosophie des Geldes,* published in 1900, his thinking took another turn. Simmel focused his attention on the problem of value and he came close to the neo-Kantian Baden School, represented by Windelband, Rickert, and Max Weber. It was during this period that he published his principal sociological work, called simply *Soziologie* (1909), which made him known in sociological circles while at the same time making him one of the precursors of social psychology. From then on he concentrated on his philosophical studies, his sociological research, and his meditations upon aesthetics, represented by his writings on Rodin, Rembrandt, and Goethe. Simmel was a prolific writer. A new phase was apparent on the eve of the first world war, when under the influence of Bergson, he moved finally toward what has been called *Lebensphilosophie*, even though the central concept of this new reflection was culture.

Simmel occupies a special place in German and even European sociology because while being one of the founders of the new science, he conceived it in his own way, without ever separating it from philosophy. At bottom, sociology was for him in a new way to philosophize, because it opened up new paths of metaphysical reflection. Further, aestheticism pervades his sociological studies, for he was one of the rare sociologists of his time, as well as ours, to call attention to the subtle, so to speak fleeting and impalpable, aspects of social relations, such as courtesy, coyness, attire, faithfulness, or gratitude. One can regret that he has hardly been followed in this orientation, since sociologists still prefer the study of big facts like the State, power, social class, ideology, and distribution of wealth, and neglect those expressions, filled with subtlety, which make meetings between human beings so charming. It is easy to understand that all of Simmel's sociological writings continue to surprise us today. On the one hand he created a general theory of sociology, known as formal sociology, which von Wiese was later to develop by elaborating upon it in a more conceptual and complete way; on the other hand, he is the author of brilliant sociological essays, which are remarkable for their analytical sharpness but have no systematic connection, although they bear upon a number of notions fundamental to all sociology, such as foreigness, conflict, secrecy, or even the role of number or the sociology of the five senses. It is from this double point of view that Simmel's sociological analysis must be assessed.

Formal Sociology

Simmel was the founder of formal sociology, and he is still one of its most qualified representatives. How should one understand this current in sociological thought which directly or indirectly influences the orientation of various contemporary sociologists?

Simmel starts from three observations. The first is that individuals act upon diverse motives—interest, passion, will-to-power, etc. The analysis of these phenomena belongs to psychology. The second observation is that the individual does not explain himself only by reference to himself, but in relation to interaction with others as well, be it his influence upon them or theirs upon him. The analysis of these relations belongs to social psychology, which therefore studies the varied ways individuals cooperate or compete concretely within diverse social groups, which can be ephemeral meetings such as a walk or durable organizations like a political party. The third observation is that human activities develop in forms, within social configurations like the State, the Church, or the school, or according to general forms like imitation, competition, hierarchical structures, etc. The object of sociology is the analysis of these forms. Thus it seems to him that sociology is an autonomous and specific science, on the same order as psychology or chemistry. Yet, it is always being denied that it is a science, essentially for two reasons.

First of all, the fact that it is a recent science is held against sociology. Why create a new science, since its subject matter consists of forms which have been known as long as societies have existed? Would it not be useless, repeating the work of disciplines which have always been interested in these forms? Simmel does not deny the merit of this objection, but he notes that until the present these forms have not been explored systematically and scientifically as such, but only in relation to something else. The problem of traditional sciences was precisely not to study these forms to know their variety or their possible combinations. Certainly, the subject matter of sociology is not new, but it offers a new way—neglected until the present—to study known phenomena. Now, any science defines itself less by its subject matter than by the specific and particular point of view which it uses to consider phenomena that may be the subjects of other sciences as well, with their own way of considering them. The other objection bears upon the distinction between form and content. Is this distinction not artificial? Simmel notes that every science selects from reality, creating, in consequence, an abstraction. No science of the whole of reality exists, only specialized disciplines which are distinguished from one another by the specific types of abstractions which they create. He would be the first to grant that form and content cannot be separated empirically, but once that much is recognized, it is up to psychology to analyze the content of the motives which lead an individual to act, and to sociology to study the social forms within which this content acquires shape and meaning. Thus, sociology neither avoids content, nor repudiates the inevitable link between form and content, but, by virtue of its selective abstraction, it is not psychology. Indeed, a motive or content like jealousy or the will-to-power does not develop for its own sake, but in a social context. Like all the authors of his time, Simmel gave the greatest credit to psychology, because sociology is in no position to explain the concrete and particular attitude of an individual within a group; on the other hand, psychology cannot explain a structure or social form like the State, for the latter is something more and something other than the sum of the individuals that make it up. It is in this sense that Simmel writes: "Socialization is the form which develops in a thousand different ways, in which individuals make up a unity on the basis of felt interests or conscious or unconscious temporary or lasting ideals determined by a cause or by an end, in which they realize these ideals."[16] It is therefore only for the sake of methodology and scientific efficacity that sociology makes an abstraction of content, just as other sciences make abstractions of other things.

With the ground thus cleared, the nature of this science of social forms must be defined. To explain it, Simmel is quite willing to make comparisons with geometry, in the limited degree to which all comparisons are valid. Geometry did not discover spheres, for long before the invention of geometry men used marbles, bowls, balls, balloons, or simply apples, but geometry is the abstract science of the spherical form, that is, it studies the properities of spheres as such, or of any other form. In the same way there exist social forms having institutional characteristics which antedate the birth of sociology, like the State, the trade guild, or the family, which determine whether reciprocal action between individuals will be competitive, solidary, or hostile. Without these forms, individuals could not display the content of the feelings which arouse them. In other words, individual inclinations, passions, interests, or aspirations become concrete in the midst of reciprocal action only by taking specific forms. Inversely, it would be a mistake to conceive of society as an entity existing for itself, independent of the concrete relations which define the contents. However, as a science sociology creates abstractions from these contents in order to focus its attention on forms and structures, leaving to other sciences the task of analyzing the contents. Its relation to material content is "like that of geometry with regard to physico-chemical sciences of matter: it considers form, thanks to which matter generally takes an empirical shape—consequently, a form that exists in itself only as an abstraction."[17] In this sense, one can say that according to Simmel sociology is a geometry of social forms.

However, this comparison with geometry is suggestive rather than explanatory. Indeed, social form does not obey purely geometric laws, because the same content or interest may express themselves in various social forms, while inversely, different patterns may adopt the same social form. Simmel explains this in the following way: "Hierarchy, competition, imitation, division of labor, division into parties, representative institutions, simultaneous internal cohesion and a break with the outside world, as well as innumerable other analogous phenomena, can be found in the state as well as in a religious community, in a conspiratorial association as well as in an economic organization, in an art school as well as in a family. Interests which give rise to socializations may be diverse in their content, but they may take on similar forms. Inversely, the same substantial interests may express themselves in different forms of socializations; for example, economic interest may express itself as well in a competitive system as in one that is planned by the producers, whether they are divorced from other economic groups or in association with them; the substantial elements of religious life may remain the same and yet may require a communitarian form, which is sometimes liberal and sometimes centralized."[18] Thus it appears to be clear that these forms are not substantial, but rather they are the result of processes engendered repeatedly by the diverse interactions of individuals in order to express the content of their interests, their passions, and their aspirations. Yet, these forms persist independently of the individuals who integrate into them and express themselves through them, since the State and the family, competition and solidarity, remain forms which transcend them. Sociological science is possible because they have a certain formal autonomy.

In one way society is the creation of men, since it "exists only where many individuals interact,"[19] but at the same time, these interactions can express themselves only through a limited number of forms, even though they are historically variable. Thus, there always will be families, even though the status of the family may vary according to countries and periods. This is what Simmel explains with regard to the notion of competition: "We find innumerable cases of competition in the most diverse areas, such as politics and economics, religion and art. Starting from these facts, one may determine what is the meaning of competition as a pure form of human behaviour, under what conditions it is born and develops, how it is modified under the influence of different objectives, what simultaneous formal or material social factors cause it to be accentuated or down-played, how competition between individuals differs from that which opposes one group to another—in short, what it is as a form of relation among men, which can be charged with all kinds of interests even while the similarity of its manifestations, in spite of an unlimited diversity in its contents, means that it belongs to an area having its own law and justifies studying it abstractly."[20]

Whether or not we desire it, our attitudes inevitably take on pre-existing forms, or create new ones. If we are or become Catholics, we adopt certain rituals, just as we do if we become Methodists or Buddhists. Neither personal religiosity, nor a particular religion, whether it be monotheistic or polytheistic, can avoid forms. And this applies equally to any other human activity, be it political, economic, artistic, or simply worldly. Daily life itself is governed by a succession of forms—our professions, our meals, our social activities. Without forms, there is simply no society. "In every known society," writes Simmel, "there exist a great number of forms which bind us together, that is, socialize us. And even if one of the them falls into disuse, society continues to stand. . . . But if one imagines an absence of all forms, society would not exist."[21] It is in this sense that sociology is the science that abstractly analyzes social forms, with the understanding that these do not merely make society, but *are* society." [22]

Applying the Theory: an Example

It never occurred to Simmel to make a systematic exhaustive catalogue of every possible social form—such a project may even be unrealizable—and he was satisfied with showing the way by analyzing a few particularly typical forms. It is not possible here to review all these analyses. We shall choose only one, which illustrates clearly his general theory while opening new perspectives to sociological exploration. It is taken from chapter II of his *Soziologie*, called "Die quantitative Bestimmtheit der Gruppe" ("The quantitative Determinants of the Group").[23] There are in effect two ways of using number in sociological research: the first, by far the most common and the most utilized, is sociometrics, or the use of quantitative methods (statistics, graphs, factor analysis, etc.); the second, pioneered by Simmel, studies the cleavages which numbers bring to social groups, thereby defining them to a certain extent. In other words, when one passes from one number to another, one is in new forms with new boundaries and new significations clearly distinct from other forms.

Using many examples, Simmel demonstrates the role which number plays both in the way a group perceives itself and in the way it is perceived from the outside. Number plays the role of group organizer. The structures of a group of five or six members are very different from those of another one with hundreds of members. Furthermore, the chances and forms of conflicts vary according to the size of the group. Strikes are far less common in a small craft shop with thirty workers than in a factory employing thousands of people. Until the present time, the communal spirit of the communistic type has developed only in small groups, never in vast, anonymous collectivities. An intimate party and a reception with hundreds of guests are two entirely different things. The status of a millionaire living in a small city differs from that of one living in a megalopolis, and it varies also according to whether he is the only millionaire in the area or whether there are others living there. Similarly, the sociological results of moral turpitude in a community where everybody knows everybody else differ from the results they have in a large area. It is impossible to conspire secretly with a mass of individuals. Number is the basic difference between majority and minority. For the same reasons, aristocracy is not democracy. In earlier times, number was even synonymous with political leaderhip—as in the Council of the Fifteen in Strasbourg, the Six of Frankfurt, the Eight of Florence, the Hundred of Barcelona—and they were designated by no other name than the number. Number is the basis of the division of an army into corps, brigades, regiments, battalions, companies, and so forth.

More examples are unnecessary. It is clear that number determines whether certain social forms are possible and creates differences in the internal structures and characteristics of groups. For this reason Simmel regretted the neglect of this essential factor in the analysis of groups and certain social forms, for not only does it condition problems which are sociologically different and cause substantial modifications, but the numerical growth of a group gives it new characteristics and causes it to lose other ones. Thus, social forms have different specific aspects when they go above or below certain numerical levels.

Simmel did not merely gather examples to demonstrate his idea, but continued his analysis to show the importance of number in the sociological differentiation between forms. Number one, or unity, is the principle of solitude. As an absolutely original form, the latter has specific properties not found in other forms. However, it must suffice to mention it, for its sociological signification is only indirect. There is a veritable cleavage between unity and duality, for the dyadic form acquires particular and new characteristics which are not found in unity. It is the form of intimacy and of the couple, the two members being numerically equal so that their relations are those between individuals.

Going from number two to number three a new cleavage takes place, for the triadic form also has particular characteristics and brings about new relations which are not possible in unity or duality.[24] Thus only when there is a third can there be a majority and a minority, as in the example of $A + B$ in relation to C, and internal reversals are possible depending on whether A and B are allied against C or B and C against A. It follows that the unity of a triad transcends its members, and differs in this from the unity of a dyad which prohibits alliances. Let us take an even more characteristic example: marriage. In a couple the arrival of a third member—child or lover—not only modifies the individual attitude of each member, but brings with it a completely new kind of relation. Simmel also shows that monogamy is an absolutely original sociological form, for it exclusively requires a couple with two persons. As soon as polygamy introduces a second wife, that is a third person, the polygamous form is not fundamentally changed by the man bringing in a third or a seventh wife. The sociological cleavage between monogamy and polygamy comes with the arrival of a second wife, that is of a third person. Following Simmel's suggestions, other sociologists, starting from the concept of the third person, have analyzed diverse forms of alliances which are possible, which is essential to the sociological understanding of conflict.[25]

In the same way, Simmel showed that the alliance between France and Russia prior to World War I was politically crucial, for it completely changed the European political chessboard. Indeed, the situation would hardly have been modified by any further alliances of one of these countries with another nation, because henceforth Germany was threatened by a war on two fronts. It seems to me that Simmel put his finger on a fundamental sociological phenomenon: series really begin only with the number three, which means that the list of numbers after three, that is 4, 5, 6, 7, etc., are merely additions to 3. There is a gap in numerical forms from 1 to 2 and from 2 to 3, but between 3 and 8, 20, 30, etc., there is only a continuation. There is another formal gap when one passes from numerical continuation to indetermined or indeterminable numbers. Thus, a crowd or a mass is again an original sociological form with its own characteristics, because it can only be enumerated relatively.

While the triad person is a special sociological form, it gives rise, in addition, to equally original subforms, described by Simmel at length. In his view, the third person can:

1. Play the role of a neutral and impartial intermediary who keeps out of conflict. In this case he can be a mediator or a referee. The mediator only intervenes occasionally, on the condition of being acceptable to both parties, for example in a labor dispute. Without personally proposing a solution, he tries to gather the elements needed for a reconciliation. In case of success, the parties in question make reciprocal commitments, which means that the eventual agreement depends on their own good will and not on that of the mediator. In case of failure, the conflict continues. The referee, on the contrary, is a third person provided by the rules, for example in the case of a game of basketball or a boxing match, or by the institution, as with the judge in a trial. He is bound to the rules that make his position. While staying neutral, he intervenes to uphold the rule or the law, and he imposes his solution, that is, he has the power to end a litigation or a dispute. His decision is legitimate because the parties in question are committed in advance to respect it.

2. The third person can play the role of the third rascal or, in Simmel's phrase, the *tertius gaudens*. In this case, the third person does not personally get involved in the conflict, but tries to profit from it. When, in a parliamentary system, neither major party gets an absolute majority, the third person

can provide the balance and form a coalition with the party offering him the most benefits, sometimes out of proportion to his real strength. Or the third person may seek to strengthen his position at the expense of his two opponents, who bother and weaken each other. Or again, one of the two rival parties may try to aid the third person in order to block its rival.

3. Finally, the third person may play the role described by Simmel as *divide et impera*. In this case, he intervenes directly in the conflict, or even provokes it directly, in order to benefit from it or to better pursue his own goals. Or else he takes precautions in order to prevent rivals from arising, for example, by muzzling all opposition and suppressing all freedom of the press and of expression, or by making an alliance with one side in order to destroy the other, or again by spreading discord and suspicion in the rival camps in order to divert their attention from the objectives which he is himself secretly pursuing.

The thing to remember in this example of the role of number in sociology is Simmel's belief in the existence of specific and relatively autonomous forms, which one finds again and again in every society, and whose characteristics and combinations can be analyzed abstractly, independently of the variable content given them by each society and human activity. Thus, in theory one can tell in advance the limited possibilities of alliance within a given triad, basing oneself exclusively upon the interplay of the possible combinations, without the inductive work aimed at elaborating a classification on the basis of the observed diversity of empirical or historical material. He thought of formal sociology, in this sense, as a geometry of social forms.

Max Weber (1864–1920)

Weber, it will be recalled, came to sociology from economics. This is hardly the place to stress the fundamental influence which he had upon sociologists the world over, as well as upon many economists, historians, and philosophers, including those who opposed him. With Pareto, he is one of the leading figures in sociology at the turn of the century. At first, his thinking followed the traditional currents of German historicism and economic historicism, as is shown by his study of *Roscher et Knies und die logischen Probleme der historischen Nationalökonomie*[26] and the relations he formed in the *Verein für Sozialpolitik* with the young historical school, led at the time by Schmoller, and of philosophical historicism, whose principal representatives were his friends Windelband and Rickert. Actually, Weber very quickly went beyond historicism in the narrow sense of the term, not only because he wanted to develop as systematic a theory of sociology as possible (as is shown for example by the first chapter of *Wirtschaft und Gesellschaft [Economy and Society]*, called "Soziologische Grundbegriffe" ["Basic Concepts of Sociology"]), but also because his immense erudition—in history, economics, politics, law, art, literature, and religion—led him away at very an early stage from the narrow way of history so that he could set forth the general problems of sociology with as much breadth and rigor as possible, and outside any affiliation with a school of thought.

Generally, what is emphasized in Weber is the monumental edifice which he built, even though he died relatively young, or his impetuous temperament by which he imposed his positions on his contemporaries instead of convincing them. No doubt, those are two important traits of the man. However, I should like to point to something else often neglected, which is basic to the deeper understanding of his total view. He often repeated that every scientific work, no matter how prestigious is bound to grow old and be replaced. This means that sociology too is bound to the indefinite historical process and that, in consequence, no one can invent it again *ab ovo* in the sense that a sociologist could one day invent, in an original and pioneering way, the true and only sociological science. The study of society is as old as the study of nature, but it has been more or less scientific. Therefore Weber would not see in A. Comte—whom he liked no more than Hegel—the founder of sociology, except insofar as he invented the term. It means something else as well, in his view. There is a historical dimension to society itself, so that no one will ever reinvent it or create a new society, with no ties at all to any known societies. There is a philosophical or metaphysical content in the idea of alienation—as he says, it is a hypostasis—but its scientific value is only relative and limited sharply. At any rate, sociologists, as scientists, are in no position to construct a new society. If they tried to do this, they would forfeit the traits that make them scientists in favor of pseudoprophetic charlatanry.

At the outset, let me also make clear how original Weber's studies were. Most sociologists have based, or base, their fame on the fact that they are specialists in a well-defined problem area: organizations or music, action or social class, Judaism or Islam, sexuality or domination, etc. Weber analyzed all these questions in a masterly—if debatable—way, so that even today no specialist can avoid referring to his political sociology, his economic sociology, his religious sociology, his sociology of law, of art, of technology, etc. Furthermore, it can be said that he pioneered new studies on such fundamental notions as bureaucracy, urban affairs, legitimacy, patrimonialism, charisma, etc., and these analyses are still authoritative. However, sociologists like him, who have been able to build theoretical edifices representing the complex and varied system of relations between the various human activities, are especially rare, even very rare. Indeed, he wrote fundamental statements on the relations between politics and morality, politics and religion, politics and science, religion and economics, law and economics, politics, and religion, art and technology, science and art, art and morality, etc. Here his work was really prodigious. Not content to approach merely one type of these relations, he embraced them all.

Fortunately, he left us one of the threads of his thought and of his way of undertaking research in various human activities. We have it with reference to his economic concepts.[27] Three series of problems must be taken into consideration. First of all there are specifically economic questions which must be analyzed as such, for example financial techniques, price formation, business management, etc. A second series concerns the manner in which the economy is conditioned in various ways by other activities such as politics, religion, and technology. Thus Weber showed how modern capitalism was conditioned, in its inception, at least in part by the puritan spirit or by the new system of double entry bookkeeping. Today we are bemused by Puritanism, and forget all the other factors analyzed by Weber, especially in his *Wirtschaftsgeschichte (General Economic History)*.[28] Finally, the last series concerns the way the economy in turn conditions other activities, for example the reshaping of policy on the basis of economic considerations, or religious ascetism. One can do this with all other human activities and thus analyze phenomena which are essentially political (domination, power, political parties) or essentially religious (prayer, ritual, sacrifice). One can then analyze the way politics or religion conditioned the other activities, or certain of their aspects, and finally the way economics conditions politics and religion or certain of their aspects. This blueprint applies to the sociological analysis of any activity. This means that for Weber there is no activity which, from a scientific viewpoint, is in the last analysis the basis of the others. His break with Marxism on this point is complete. Indeed, this sort of statement belongs to the metaphysical sphere of hypostasis, because it can not be subjected to scientific demonstration. It belongs to faith or ideology. He never hesitates to challenge the partisans of this sort of theory: they only contribute pseudo-scientific arguments or twist science itself, giving it a vocation which is foreign to it and which it has not the means to fulfill.

It would be presumptuous to restate Weberian sociology in all its richness. By summarizing it under three headings, I think an idea of it can be conveyed which is both approximate and solid. First, Weber made a special study of the status of sociology within the general context of the human or cultural sciences, and he made use in this of all the resources of the critique of knowledge. Second, his works bring positive elements to all future studies, precisely because he had a general vision of the diversity of sociological problems. Finally, he defined the limits of sociological analysis with an almost ferocious rigour and lucidity.

Sociological Epistemology

Any budding science—like sociology in Weber's time—readily tends to define its methods a priori, before even having produced positive results that are scientifically valid. Comte, who never engaged in sociological research in the proper sense of the term, tried to impose a method in advance upon the discipline, above and beyond all scientific investigation. One of Durkheim's first concerns was to write his *Régles de la méthode sociologique*. Max Weber did not make this mistake. Indeed, before he approached the theoretical problem of methodology, he had already made an important field study.

Furthermore, methodology was neither his major nor his first preoccupation, as we shall also see. In any case, it is on the basis of his fieldwork experience that he examined the question of sociological methodology. Anyway, he had no superstition regarding method, since it was his opinion that a good method is one that proves fertile and efficient on the level of concrete work. Therefore, there is none that is more legitimate than the others, since the choice of one over another is determined by the chance to work and the choice of a subject matter. Because method is a technique of study, there can be neither dogmatism nor orthodoxy in this area. Still, he made a decisive contribution in this area on at least two points.

1. Weber introduced the interpretive method. Some historians of sociology even refer to it as his "interpretive sociology." Since this term has given rise to a number of misunderstandings, it is important to specify clearly Weber's thinking on this question. He was not the inventor of the interpretive method, nor even of the distinction between explaining (*erklären*) and understanding (*verstehen*). Droysen before him had tried to apply it to history, and Dilthey had made of it the cornerstone of the general methodology of the human sciences (*Geisteswissenschaften*). Weber's merit is to have elaborated this method conceptually with more rigor, applying it to sociology.

Unlike the naturalist, the sociologist does not work on inert matter, analyzing instead social relations and an activity (*Handeln*), that is to say forms of social behavior which are always evolving with the constant development of circumstances. Since man's activity never ceases, he is not a passive object. Now, human activities, which produce social relations, are affected by a quality absent in natural phenomena *meaning*. To act socially is, on the one hand, to take part in a conventional context of institutions, customs, rules and laws, created by men with certain ends in mind; second, to give oneself a goal or an end which justifies the activity, and finally, to appeal to certain values, aspirations, or ideals as motives for activity. Meaning plays a role on all three of these levels. Indeed, as soon as man creates conventions, he gives them meaning for the sake of the collectivity, in order to harmonize human coexistence as much as possible. To give oneself a goal is to direct activity in a definite way, which would be different if one had another goal. Finally, appealing to various and often antagonistic values and ideals is, on the part of every social agent, to give one's behavior a meaning which, in Weber's expression, is "subjectively directed." In sum, a social relation or activity is a combination of different meanings—individual and collective.

Given that social activity can have different meanings, distinctions must be made among them—all the more so since an individual is never isolated in that he acts in a vacuum and is also influenced by others' behavior. What, then, is social activity? "By activity," says Weber, "we mean human behavior (it matters little if it is an exterior or an interior act, the omission of an act, or the toleration of an act) which is given a subjective meaning by its agent or agents. By social activity we mean activity directed by the agents in reference to the behavior of others for the consequent orientation of its development."[29] Thus understood, the fact that activity includes a subjectively directed meaning allows it to fit into the situation: it can be for the sake of reparation or the maintenance of past acts (revenge or tradition), it can be the reply to an attack or simply a reaction, and finally it can be an anticipation of the future (a project) or an attempt to prevent it. An activity can also be directed toward others, be it a special person (love), or restricted group (a hunting club), a political collective (the State), or even humanity in its entirety. Generally, these two kinds of meaning are combined in an activity in diverse ways. Yet in all cases I assign meaning to activity, which would not exist without meaning; the latter is inherent in all activity. Even in a gratuitous or absurd act, I am not denying meaning, for by following the example of an officer entering the line of fire (to use an instance cited by Weber) I may influence the courage of the other soldiers.

These considerations are at the basis of the Weberian typology of social action. An action can, first of all, be traditional, recognizing by its meaning the sacredness of custom and of the past, and, in consequence, conforming to this sacredness. It can also be affective insofar as it is a present and immediate reaction to a given stimulus, by desire for pleasure or contemplation. Next, it can have a value-given rationality (*wertrational*), in that the agent believes that from conviction or out of a sense of duty he wants to serve a cause in the future, or a hope, whatever the conditions may be, simply because this cause seems good to him. Finally, it can have an end-given rationality (*zweckrational*), in that it aims for a limited objective on the basis of a calculation of the available means and attempts to foresee their possible consequences. Whatever the type of activity, it has consistency only to the extent that its individual or collective agent gives it meaning. Any phenomenology of action which avoids the notion of meaning misunderstands the nature of action and fails to fulfill the scientific requirements of analysis.

Given that the subject matter of natural science is without meaning (which is not to say it is absurd), its methodology cannot simply be transferred to the social sciences, where the problem of meaning plays a capital role. Natural, inert phenomena can be accounted for satisfactorily by causal explanations, that is by other, antecedent phenomena. An extra effort is required, however, to grasp social phenomena, because, to account for them, it is also necessary to understand their motives; that is, the reasons which have led men to act and the goals which they are pursuing. Every activity has an end—good or bad—which is not clarified by explanation. According to Weber, the comprehensive method is the best possible formula for the elucidation of the meaning of an activity. Consequently, when a political, economic, religious, or other phenomenon has been explained causally (by its physical, biological, climatological, geographic, or even psychological antecedents), there is still a remainder that is not covered by this kind of explanation. This is because human activity is based on *will*, on a capacity, therefore, for anticipation or resistance, which takes us beyond simple material conditions. Man does not act simply under the effect of a mechanical stimulus, but because he wants something for certain reasons. He has motives. For example, one can become a hunter for pleasure, out of a concern for exercise, because one has a taste for game, etc. All this eludes simple causality. Thus, the task of the comprehensive method is to fill the gaps which sheer explanation leaves in matters pertaining to human relations.

Weber was perfectly well aware of the weaknesses of this method. Since it is neither demonstrative nor experimental, its proofs are always more or less uncertain. It gives rise to an interpretation (*Deutung*), which means it is based on evaluations which require cross-checkings, comparisons, logically informed observations, and what he calls reference to values (of which more later.) It is therefore a matter of previously tested procedures. Thus Weber rules out Simmel's concept (which gave a psychological basis to understanding), and that of other theoreticians who put the accent on personal experience or the capacity to relive an event (*nacherleben*). He often said that it is not necessary to be Caesar in order to understand Caesar.[30] Like any other methodological process, understanding and interpretation must submit themselves to the uses of ordinary logic, not to the spontaneity of direct psychological experience. Yet, these methods are not limited to their areas of application, because their task is to interpret how and why an individual or a group evaluated a situation correctly or, on the contrary, demonstrate its errors. In short, since meaning is never given *in* the object, it is not a quality inherent to it; consequently, it cannot be grasped by a procedure designed only to study the qualities of things, their laws or their permanent characteristics. On the contrary, men give various meanings to the same things and the same meanings to different things. This diversity can be grasped only by the comprehensive method.

The greatest misunderstanding consists of imputing to Weber the idea that explanation and understanding are absolutely autonomous—even opposed—methods, when he never tired of repeating that they are complementary and can be used concurrently or even at the same time. Thus he often associates them in the same research project, either as interpretive explanation (*verstehende Erklärung*), or as explanatory interpretive (*erklärendes Verstehen*). In the same way, he says that understanding makes it possible for causal relations (*Kausalzusammenhänge*) to become at the same time significatory relations (*Sinnzusammenhänge*). The fact is that in sociology our knowledge is satisfied only if we have not only a causal explanation for a social relation, but an understanding of its meaning as well; that is, its motives or reasons and its purpose.

2. Weber's other contribution to methodology is his concept of causal pluralism, of which he was, with Pareto, one of the principal theoreticians. It complements his comprehensive method, which rejects as insufficient the blueprint of mechanical and unilateral causality. First he notes that in human activity cause and effect can be interchangeable, not only because a goal, once attained, can become the cause of a fresh undertaking, but because any proven means, because of its relative success, can transform itself into the cause of a fresh activity which was not originally foreseen. As a matter of fact, this sort of observation today seems banal, but it was not so in Weber's time. Perhaps we are unconsciously paying tribute to his epistemology, for he had

to oppose scientism, which placed all the emphasis on mechanical causality, giving no credit to ends. Weber's position is even shrewder, especially if one considers the reigning ideas at the time he wrote. He opposes the traditional idea of causality as sufficient reason. Not only does he reject the concept of an effect that can be set in a given moment, in conditions that can be identified, he holds that the origin of every effect is to be found in immeasurable eternity. Like the causal chain, the chain of effects is indefinite. What is more, causality is never more than a partial probabilistic explanation. Indeed, since reality is both extensively and intensively indefinite, we can never attain an exhaustive formulation of the world, even by way of causality. Even if the mechanism gave us such an illusion, there is still human volition, capable—at least in the area of social phenomena—of provoking decisive breaks in the causal chain. This is why Weber rejected emanationist theories which strive to reduce the totality of events to a single or fundamental cause, or which want to deduce them from the same cause. In his view there is no scientific value to the idea that development tends to incline a man or a group's judgment toward one cause over others, because it is merely a metaphysical and subjective view of things. Thus he dismisses both Binding, the lawyer, and Gomperz, the philosopher, who had made themselves the advocates of the preponderance of a certain type of causality over others. In the domain of the social sciences, there is no rigorous causality: it depends on the researcher's evaluation and the more or less good documentation of his information. An ignoramus and a specialist will establish different causal relations. It is not impossible that they should both be wrong, for science is not the universal judge.

However, the essence of his critique is aimed at the difficulty, often the impossibility, of finding a single antecedent cause for a social phenomenon, as causal monism would have it. In general, an event is explained by a plurality of causes, and it is up to the researcher to appreciate the weight of each one. He comes back to this several times in his study, unfortunately often badly interpreted, *Die protestantische Ethik und der Geist des Kapitalismus* (The Protestant Ethic and the Spirit of Capitalism). He shows that the accumulation of capital cannot be considered the only cause of modern capitalism, to the exclusion of the ascetic rationalization of economic life. He rejects both the idea that seeks to explain the Reformation exclusively by economic factors, and the contrary idea that the spirit of the Reformation is alone responsible for the birth of capitalism.[31] In his *Wirtschaftsgeschichte* he states that many factors, beyond economic ones, contributed to the appearance of this new economic formula: political, religious, technological, juridical, and other factors.[32] This concept of causal pluralism, which many sociologists, following Weber, share today, aids us in understanding two other points of his methodology.

First of all, there is the process of causal imputation (*kausale Zurechnung*). Once it is granted that the appearance of a social phenomenon depends on several causes, it is difficult to evaluate the importance of each one. The possibility of establishing a direct, necessary, and indisputable connection between an effect and all its causes is excluded. The only solution is to prove, with the aid of documents, that there is only a causal relation between a phenomenon or certain aspects of it and the antecedent factors, with no possibility of making a statement on the apodictic nature of the relation. It is therefore the researcher himself who uses his judgment to relate such and such a phenomenon to such and such a series of causes, rather than to another series of causes whose probability is relatively pertinent. Therefore there always is room for uncertainty, and imputation consists of attributing a certain phenomenon to certain causes, and it is impossible to establish a strict determinism in the course of events. "Not only," writes Weber, "is it practically impossible to make an exhaustive causal regression from a given concrete phenomenon in order to grasp it in its full reality, but this attempt is simply nonsense. We can only identify the causes for which there is reason to impute, in the specific case, essential elements of a development."[33]

Next, there is the category of "objective possibility," which is, all in all, the corollary of the preceding process. In order to estimate as adequately as possible the probable importance of a cause, imagine a chain of events excluding it and ask what *would* have happened without it. If the final event would have occurred anyway, it is highly probable that the abstractly excluded cause played only a minor or contingent role. But if the course of events *would* have been different, this cause probably had a decisive effect. Let us take two examples. The 1848 revolution in Berlin began after three gun shots. Suppress mentally these three shots: would the revolution have occurred anyway? Now the situation in Prussia and the rest of Europe, where revolutions had broken out in almost every capital, was such that almost any incident would have lit the fuse. There are therefore good reasons to say that these three gunshots were a merely incidental, not a determining, cause. Objectively, the revolution could have broken out without these gun shots. A second example: it is said that the Battle of Marathon saved Greek civilization. Let us suppose that instead of winning, the Greeks had been defeated: what then would have happened? The historical documentation that we have leads us to believe that had that occurred, the course of events would have been different. Consequently, the Battle of Marathon played the role of a capital cause in the development of Greek civilization. Thus, "objective possibility" allows us to make the most adequate possible causal imputation, within the limits of our knowledge.

While Weber's considerations on methodology in the social sciences are essential, his major effort in the area of the theory of knowledge nevertheless concerned a matter too often neglected by sociologists—sociological conceptualization. A science is valid because of not only because of its methods, but also because of the concepts which it develops. When its concepts are imprecise and equivocal, every confusion and misunderstanding is possible, and its results will lack the exactitude which is indispensable if they are to be operational. If a concept can be given several, contrary meanings, it loses some of its scientific validity. Therefore, a scientist worthy of the name must strive to develop the most rigorous concepts possible. Weber devoted himself to finding ways by which sociology might overcome this deficiency from which it badly suffers. We shall examine here the two principal ways he found: the ideal type and the reference to values (*Wertbeziehung*).

The essence of Weberian epistemology can be summarized in this sentence: "In order to untangle real causal relations, we construct unreal ones."[34] Science is not and cannot be a copy of reality, because reality is indefinite, whereas science is merely an ensemble of concepts always supported by fragmentary knowledge. In fact, every concept is limited to the extent that it apprehends only one aspect of reality, and the sum of all concepts is also limited, compared to the infinity of reality. The unknown and the unknowable will therefore always be unavoidable. Moreover, knowledge of reality is achieved through a transformation made by concepts. In other words, known reality is always a reality abstractly reconstructed by concepts. According to Weber, the ideal type is precisely one of these mental constructions which permit, in the social sciences, as rigorous an approach to reality as possible, but it is always limited to one or a few aspects of reality. His definition of the ideal type leaves no doubt on this question, inasmuch as he sees in it a pure mental picture or a utopia: "This mental picture," he writes, "brings together in a non-contradictory cosmos of *thought-out* relations specific historical relations and events. In its content, this mental picture has *utopian* characteristics, obtained by exaggerating *mentally* specific elements of reality."[35] In order to grasp well Weber's idea let us demonstrate, by means of an example, how an ideal type is made.

What is the scientific value of the concept of capitalism so often used by sociologists? In spite of their pretensions, it is just about nil. Indeed they usually characterize it vaguely and confusedly, mingling indistinctly investment theory and social doctrine, their political resentment as well as their personal partisan attitude, whether laudatory or prejorative. Everything is there except scientific rigor. If we want to form a scientifically valid concept of capitalism, we must at the outset silence our personal bias, for or against, in the axiologically neutral way which we discuss in forthcoming paragraphs. In the second place, we must know if we are discussing the economic system, the social doctrine, or the political theory. In the third place, we must distinguish among finance capitalism, commercial capitalism, and industrial capitalism. Finally, we must not confuse early capitalism and nineteenth century capitalism, or the latter and today's capitalism. When these distinctions are made, it is possible to construct various ideal types of capitalism, for example as social doctrine or as economic system, as finance capitalism or as industrial capitalism. Also, one can construct an ideal type of finance capitalism in the factory age or in the age of the multinationals. What is important is to avoid amalgamating these different perspectives. Let us say we have to analyze finance capitalism in the factory age. In this case, we select cautiously and broadly in the empirical reality of this period a number of given diffuse and discrete characteristics which we coordinate in a "homogeneous mental picture."[36] In this way we form a coherent concept of this type of capitalism in a given period. To be sure, it is an abstract picture, a pure conception nowhere to be found in empirical reality. It has nevertheless a double advantage: on the one hand, it gives us a rigorous concept free of personal bias; on the other hand we can measure how far or how close the financial institutions of the time were to this form, that is how far along the capitalist way they actually were. Analogous studies can be made of the other forms of capitalism mentioned above. Indeed, Weber writes: "It is possible, or rather it must be considered certainly possible, to sketch several, indeed a great many, utopias of this type of which *not one* would resemble another, and, more proof, *not one* could be found in empirical reality in a truly operative society, but of which *each one* can claim to represent the "idea" of capitalist civilization and of which *each one* can even claim to unite certain significant properties of our civilization in a homogeneous ideal picture, inasmuch as it has effectively selected them in reality."[37] Following these methods, one can even form an ideal type of capitalism in general.

For Weber, the ideal type was by no means an exclusive methodology, but only *one* among others used to make rigorous and scientifically valid concepts that could be used by researchers whose personal biases, in politics, economics, or religion, might be different. It is unfortunate that the specialists in the social sciences too often use vague and confused concepts, like socialism, imperialism, feudalism, or Catholicism, which at best have a conceptual significance only in their work, but which other researchers are prohibited from using as scientific communications requires. It is useless to hope that sociology will become a science in the full sense of the term as long as specialists reject the discipline of a rigorous conceptualization.

We have just seen that in order to make an ideal type, it is necessary to select the pregnant characteristics in reality and combine them in a homogeneous mental picture. This selection problem has a broader epistemological meaning, for it is encountered every step of the way in research, especially when, faced with a mass of collected data or documents, one has to put some aside as having secondary or insignificant importance, keeping those which appear important or essential. What criteria should be used to making this selection? According to Weber, there is no single, absolute or objective criterion. Observing a specialist's approach, one sees that he makes his choices according to a process which Weber calls the reference to values, following an expression of Rickert. At the same time, this accounts for the specialist's inevitable subjectivity. Indeed, the fact is that not everyone has the same idea of socialism, sectarianism, the State, business, etc. And since there is no universally accepted value system, authors have to refer to their own scale of values. It is precisely because historians are always referring to different values that they are always renewing the interpretation of history.

Thus, one thing is clear: facts are selected by reference to values, notwithstanding those who claim that Weber excluded values from scientific work. Therefore, it is possible and legitimate to write a history of capitalist economy while referring to socialist values, and vice-versa, just as it is possible to analyze skilled trades from a point of view favorable to the preservation of this kind of work. Weber even grants that an anarchist, by principle hostile to the law, can bring to light some aspects of the law of which we are unaware because of their very obviousness, precisely by referring to his own values. However, there is one condition that must be respected: the scholar must indicate clearly which values determine his choices, lest he deceive his readers. Since there is no universal system of values, it would be fraudulent for an author to pretend that his critique possessed universal validity. A critique of capitalism based on socialist choices is legitimate if the values referred to are made clear, for it is valid only from the socialist point of view. It cannot be valid from a different point of view. At any rate it cannot have universal validity. Weber calls obedience to this discipline intellectual probity. The general thesis of his whole epistemology comes from this: sociological research is valid only within the limits of the reference to values chosen each time by an author. "Ever new and variously nuanced cultural problems are constantly developing," says Weber, "and they are constantly troubling human beings. So that the sphere of everything which has meaning and importance for us, becoming a 'historical thing,' out of the inevitably infinite flow of unique things, is always changing. The intellectual relations we use to approach these things and grasp them scientifically also vary. Therefore, the starting points of the cultural sciences will always vary in the indefinite future—until a kind of Chinese stupor of the life of the mind disinclines men from asking inexhaustible questions of life."[38]

Sociological Research

As we have said, Weber is the author of a monumental body of work, in which he enters upon almost every one of the specialized branches of sociology. His own sociological research is therefore extremely varied, and only its general lines can be reviewed here. Most of it is based on documentary research, whether his studies on the agrarian system in antiquity, on the commercial societies in the Middle Ages, or his studies in the sociology of religion having to do with China, India, or ancient Judaism. However, it also should be noted that he was undoubtedly one of the first academic sociologists to have made real field studies, such as his report on the situation of agricultural workers in regions east of the Elbe. It is probably for this reason that his epistemological thinking was as profound as we have just shown it to be: he became acquainted with most of the procedures and techniques which sociologists are still using nowadays. From this perspective, one can speak of Weber's constant relevance.

Weber's work has a certain unity, even though his research covered every period from antiquity to the present and contains a number of surprising aspects, like his analyses of the psychophysics of industrial work or the stock market. This unity could be called the general reference to the values of his work. Not only was Weber deeply learned in economics and the law, he was also a solid historian and a great lover of literature, acquainted with poets and novelists. The more he wanted to make an abstract concept, the more he was interested in singular things. He connected the necessity for generalization in science and the importance of the singular in the following manner: "Only certain aspects of the always infinite diversity of singular phenomena—those which have a general significance for culture—are worth knowing."[39] This synthesis of the general and the singular is found again in the problem which makes the unity of his work: how to explore other civilizations in order to better understand the singularity of Western civilization. This is by no means to say that he subordinated his studies of other civilizations to his studies of ours, for he always emphasized the originality of each civilization. Rather, it is by contrast that he highlights things that are peculiar to European civilization. At no point does he display any condescension or scorn for allogeneous cultures. On the contrary, his analyses are made with the greatest respect, for example when he states that the tormented life of the Indians of the Great Salt Lake was undoubtedly as humanly valid as the life which the Mormons brought with them there in our times. Many other similar texts could be mentioned. It merely seemed necessary and useful to him to study the peculiarities of Western civilization from the sociological point of view.

A more or less rational economy and even certain forms of rudimentary capitalism are found in various civilizations, as are political power, methodical thought, music, customs, and elementary forms of law; but only the West developed a growth economy like contemporary capitalism, an experimental and mathematics-based science, a technology based on science, a homogeneous political structure like the modern State, a rational law, and musical harmony and orchestration. To be sure, some rationality is found in almost every civilization, but systematic rationalism, penetrating every sphere of human activity, is peculiar to the West, although today the rest of the world is adopting it. However, Weber displays no special admiration for these feats of Western civilization, for he also underlines their cost: disenchantment with the world. Indeed, we live in an intellectualized universe, dedicated to specialization and artificiality. We find our lives stripped of the charms of earlier times: poetry as well as the religious unity which strengthened the soul. This explains, on the one hand, the lethargy which many succumb to, fleeing from their responsibilities because they cannot meet the moral requirements of contemporary changes, and on the other hand, the need of youth to seek refuge in small communities, where it hopes to rediscover a breath of life, however weak.

Weber's research in political sociology bore essentially on four points. The first concerns the relations between violence and the State. The rationalization of the modern State consisted in confiscating the right of violence from individuals and subordinate groups (for instance feudal lords) for its own benefit. Whence Weber's definition of the modern State: "a human community which, within the limits of a specified territory . . . successfully claims for itself the monopoly of legitimate physical violence."[40] Second, he analyzed the phenomenon of domination (*Herrschaft*), primarily from the viewpoint of legitimacy: that is, the reasons which bring the governed to have confidence in political power. On this point, he established a typology of legitimacy which has remained famous: traditional domination, legal domination, and charismatic domination. The basis of the first is belief in the sanctity of current practices and in the legitimacy of those who come to power by virtue of tradition. This was the case in ancient monarchies, though today there is also a republican tradition. The second, legal domination, is based on belief in the validity of the rationally established law and in the legitimacy of those who come to power legally, usually through regular elections. Finally, charismatic domination is based on the devotion to one person of many others, who attribute to him talents or a special mission of holiness, of heroism, or of ability, as in the case of modern dictators, as well as prophets and demagogues of ancient times, or even revolutionary leaders. This is an ideal type typology, because one or another of these forms in its pure state is almost never found in history. Generally, every power combines these three forms of domination in various proportions.

The third point consists of the analysis of political parties, in which Weber was one of the pioneers. He was particularly innovative in making a distinction—later taken up by other writers—between elite parties and mass parties. However, it was a student of his, R. Michels,[41] who pursued this idea, showing how mass parties, under the cover of a democratic machine, are taken over by oligarchic leaderships. Weber's major contribution—this is the fourth point—is to have developed a sociology of bureaucracy, which is at the origin of every sociology of organizations. He was perfectly aware of the excesses the bureaucratic system could produce, if only because he foresaw that in Russia the dictatorship of the proletariat would transform itself into the dictatorship of the bureaucrats;[42] however, in keeping with the axiological neutrality, he grasped that this type of administration soon would dominate States as well as private enterprises, because it meets the requirements of modern rationalization. His description of bureaucracy remains valid, even though he did not perceive the growing importance of technocracy, which was practically inexistent in his time.

We shall consider together Weber's economic and religious sociologies, because he himself often studied them together, as one can see from the title of his immense sociology of religions: *Die Wirtschaftsethik der Weltreligionen.* Nevertheless, let us note in passing that he also studied the sociology of religion independently, with his analyses of religious behavior, the distinction between sacred knowledge and faith, the differences between religions of salvation and simply ritualistic religions, the analysis of religious types such as the sorcerer, the prophet, and the priest, as well as the various forms of asceticism, and the relations between religion and sexuality. He also developed an independent economic sociology, in which he examines the phenomenon by which needs are fulfilled, the structure of economic groups, and the problems of the distribution of wealth. However, it would be necessary to enter into too many details in order to account for the richness of these analyses in an intelligible manner. For the same reason, we must leave aside his work in comparative sociology, which is concerned with the economic aspects of the great world religions in China, India, and Judaism and Islam.

To give an idea of his unique investigative method, we shall nevertheless take some time to consider the work which brought him fame for the first time and in which he combined economic, religious, and moral sociological analyses: *Die protestantische Ethik und der Geist des Kapitalismus*. Weber knows that the development of capitalism is due in large part to an internal dynamic of the economy, whether due to the accumulation of capital at the end of the Middle Ages, or to the separation of the home and business budgets. However, this explanation is insufficient sociologically, for capitalism did not merely impose itself of its own will as a new, fully developed economic system. It was also the work of audacious entrepreneurs who over time progressively developed it. The new mentality of the backers of the new, still unnamed, economic system, is precisely what he meant by "the spirit of capitalism." This mentality was imbued with moral and religious beliefs, in particular the belief in predestination. The main lines of his thesis can be summarized as follows: the principal protagonists of incipient capitalism (not all of them) belonged to various puritan sects and, in accordance with their beliefs, they led a rigid personal and family life, in contrast to the Latin bankers who spent their profits on celebrations, good living, and patronage of the arts. Furthermore, success in business represented to them a sign of religious election. Since they could not personally enjoy their accumulated profits, what could they do with them but reinvest them in the business and make it grow? Basic to capitalism, therefore, was a shift in the direction of asceticism: in the Middle Ages it was other-worldly and limited to monks in cloisters; now it became this-worldly, since the capitalist entrepreneur lived like a monk in the midst of the social and economic world.

For three quarters of a century, Weber's thesis has provoked passionate debates. Some accuse him of attacking Catholicism while others, inversely, accuse him of discrediting Protestantism by tying it to capitalism. Others accuse him of having misinterpreted Calvin, still others claim that he wanted to refute Marxist materialism, while others still say he made Puritanism the single cause of capitalism. And so on. In fact, one has only to read Weber's work without bias to realize that all these criticism fall short of their mark, even though the study contains a number of errors. His was an undertaking of scientific research, in which he had no intention of bringing water to the mill of any theological apologetics. He states explicitly that Calvin is not the issue, but only certain interpretations of predestination several centuries later, offered by certain Calvinist sects (not all of them). He repeats constantly that Puritanism is not the sole cause of capitalism—his theory of causal pluralism prohibited this—but one cause only of certain aspects of capitalism. Finally, Weber is explicit in stating that he never meant to oppose a spiritualist interpretation of history to the materialist interpretation: both are possible and legitimate, but only within the limits of reference to the values which have been chosen.

We shall say only a few words on the other areas of Weber's research. In the field of the sociology of law, Weber strove to clarify, from the sociological point of view, the function of various types of law: private law and public law, positive law and natural law, subjective law and objective law, formal law and material law. He also followed the various phases of development from irrational to rational law, always in the spirit that dominates his sociological thinking: underline the growth of rationalization in societies. However, an original aspect of his analysis, used later by H. Marcuse, must be stressed: contrary to the opinion of many authors today, natural law is far from being exhausted, because its content is revolutionary. Opposing it to the established order of positive law, revolutionaries appeal to it at least indirectly. His sociology of art remained in outline stage, except for the long memorandum on music. Beyond that, his analysis deals essentially with the development of Romanesque art toward Gothic.

Finally, one must note that Weber was very interested in certain questions concerning sociology in general. He approached these questions from the point of view of the most rigorous possible definition of fundamental sociological concepts, those that are used commonly with no precise content and sometimes without clear distinctions, such as the notions we have of custom and tradition, or of convention and law. He puts himself to the task of characterizing them both by defining their general meaning and by scrutinizing, sometimes minutely, the shades of this meaning in particular contexts. Thus he defines concepts of social action, of social relations, of struggle, of groupings, of enterprise, of association, of institution, and of power. He did the same work on notions less often used, such as the notions of open relations and closed relations and hierocracy. While one can argue with this conceptualization, which takes up all of chapter I of *Wirtschaft und Gesellschaft*, the fact is that it remains an excellent tool for all those who try to advance in their undertaking rigorously, or who simply want to learn to analyze terms rigorously.

The Limits of Sociology

Like many new sciences—of which there are more all the time—sociology in Weber's time (and even earlier, if one thinks of Comte) made imperialist claims. It was it all the easier for it to think it could easily spread its jurisdiction to all fields inasmuch as its internal scientific foundations were poorly defined. It is to Weber's credit that he never succumbed to this, but delineated, with his usual rigor and lucidity, the limits of the new discipline. He did it with such clear-sightedness that it is difficult to criticize him, even in our time when sociology is accepted as a normal discipline in the university curriculum. At any rate, his own epistemology suggested such moderation to him, for he incessantly reaffirmed that a concept or a science can express only points of view that are more or less specific and in consequence limited in their relation to reality, and that the reference to values—principle of every selection in the social sciences—necessarily limited the presumptuous aims of the doctrinaires of universalism. In addition, Weber was sharply conscious of the incapacity of a science to make its own foundations scientifically. As a Kantian (Descartes had shown it previously), Weber knew that this was a philosophical problem, falling under what is known today as knowledge theory. As a matter of fact, Weber did not limit himself to this critical aspect of philosophy. He also formed a conception of the world inspired by Nietzsche, Tolstoy, Dostoyevsky, and Stefan George. From this awareness—sometimes in reaction against the authors he admired—he developed his fundamental philosophical hypothesis of the inevitable limits of all science, including, of course, sociology. He continued to work on this idea throughout his life and it led him to develop in his last years a new methodological principle—value neutrality (*Wertfreiheit*).

The world is given to a struggle between competing and antagonistic values, and this struggle can simply take the form of tensions or, in certain cases, it can degenerate into conflict. There is therefore a whole gradation of antagonism, since they may express themselves in the affable form of fraternal exhortation, or in the form of non-conformism, or it may take the form of a debate between ideas, of athletic competition, or, in extreme cases, lead to hostility and war. Its origin may be divergent aspirations of individuals, rivalries between groups or programs, or even cultural diversity. For example, it is impossible to determine that French culture is superior to German culture, and vice versa, "for there too different gods are locked in combat, undoubtedly for ever."[43] The grandiose pathos of Christianity was able to hide this fact for centuries, but in our time "the multitude of innumerable gods of antiquity are emerging from their graves, in the form of impersonal (because disappointed) powers, and they strive anew to dominate our lives, all the while taking up their eternal struggles."[44] The modern world is returning to polytheism, except that the gods are no longer called Jupiter, Apollo, Aphrodite, and Neptune, but, more impersonally, liberalism, socialism, sex, women's liberation, etc. Weber summarizes his thinking in this remarkable text: "If there is one thing today of which we are no longer ignorant, it is that something may be holy not only despite its not being beautiful, but also because and to the extent that it is not beautiful . . . In the same way, something may be beautiful not only in spite of not being good, but precisely in that which it is not good . . . Finally, folk wisdom teaches us that something may be true even though it is not, and precisely when it is not, beautiful, or holy, or good."[45] Science may well not be in accord with religion, art with morality, and politics with economics. Weber recognized that one could reject religion in the name of science, and science in the name of morality, since "scientific truth is only that which claims to be valid for all those who want truth."[46] One may thus reject scientific truth.

Despite the growth of rationality, there will always remain an irreducible basis of irrationality in the world, from which comes the unshrinkable power of beliefs and opinions. Value is not inherent in things, any more than is their meaning. They acquire value and meaning only from the strength of our convictions and by the degree of earnestness with which we conquer or defend them in the course of our actions. To affirm a value therefore implies necessarily the possibility of affirming other ones which may be opposed to it. Therefore it is impossible to demonstrate peremptorily the superiority of one value over other ones. A value can be preferred by an individual or a majority only on the basis of faith. Therefore, Weber does not believe in harmony, pre-established or man-made. The irreducible antagonism of values can only give rise to accommodations, compromises, or tolerance. Science does not have the power to settle between the points of view by which men struggle in the name of political, religious, or economic values.

Therein lies the foundation of what he calls value neutrality. Contrary to certain false interpretations according to which he wanted to exclude values, Weber recognized their primordial importance. They nurture every act and they dominate the struggles of the political, economic and religious worlds. Consequently, when a scientist analyses an act, he must take into account the values which it represents if he is to understand the meaning of this act, for wanting to do something is to give it a price or a value. Moreover, we have seen in the reference to values that value has a part in the scientific undertaking, particularly in the selection of data. What Weber rejects, in the name of value neutrality, is the possibility, for the sociologist or social scientist, of believing that a scientific hierarchy of values can be established, or of giving the impression that such a thing can be established. It is similarily impossible to judge between antagonistic values in the name of science, or to invest with scientific value one value over others. Only a compromise can temporarily reconcile opposed values, not a scientific demonstration. Antagonism between values is a problem which is beyond the competence of the scientist; therefore he is incapable of resolving it by the scientific method. However, it is permissible for any scholar, inasmuch as he is also a man, to take a position, like any other citizen, on political or religious affairs, and make known and defend his personal choices. But he commits a sin against the scientific spirit if he insinuates that, since he is a scholar, his partisan choice has scientific validity.

For example, let us take the famous distinction which Weber made between the ethic of conviction and the ethic of responsibility. One who acts according to the former wants the absolute victory of a cause, without concern for the circumstances and the situation or for the consequences. This is the case of one who applies rigorously the precepts of the Sermon on the Mount, who offers the left cheek when struck on the right one, and who, consequently, refuses to resist even that which he considers evil. Inversely, one who acts according to the ethic of responsiblity evaluates the available means, takes the situation into account, makes calculations with inevitable human failings, and considers the possible consequences. Thus, he assumes responsibility for the means, the shortcomings, and the foreseeable consequences, baneful or not. For Weber, both attitudes are equally legitimate and even laudable, opposed though they may be by the ultimate values motivating them. Thus an individual may adopt one or the other of these ethics in completely good faith. However, it is not the scientist's task to choose between them in the name of science, calling one scientific and the other not, because he is simply not qualified as a scientist to make a scientific judgment with regard to moral choice. Nor is he so qualified with regard to political or artistic choice; that is, with regard to peace, socialism, Christianity, or democracy, because his competence is not in the area of preferences. Of course, one can study scientifically a religion or an artistic style, but that does not give one the right to grant a scientific validity to one religion or style over others.

Science is not totally impotent in the field of action. Indeed, a scholar may suggest to a future man of action whether his project is coherent, if it has any chance of success, given the available means, or he may forewarn him of the eventual consequences.[47] But he can go no further without perverting science. The choice depends on the will and the consciousness of each: "An empirical science cannot teach anyone what he *should* do, but only what he *can* do and—if such is the case—what he *wants* to do."[48] The principle of value neutrality thus acquires its full meaning. On the negative side, it suggests to the sociologist that he ought not give others the illusion that he is competent in activities involving choice and decision, in consequence that he refuse to take part, *as a scholar,* in that which is beyond the competence of his science. On the positive side, it means that every science, including sociology, has limits; that is, a scientific proposition is valid for scientific reasons and not for external reasons of violence or moral or ethical rectitude. And just as science is competent only within its own limits and not in the domain of appreciative activities such as politics, art, and religion, these appreciative activities are not competent in the scientific domain.

It is easier to understand, under these conditions, why Weber rejected the scientific pretensions of totalist Marxism. It is not a question of hostility, since he was among the first to introduce Marxism into the university curriculum and since he broke more than one lance defending socialist academics, but simply of objecting to this doctrine's scientific pretensions. Given that Marxism is one of Weber's latent adversaries throughout his work, it seems useful to briefly analyze the relations between Weber and Marx, a task too often neglected until now, despite Löwith's study.[49] Weber first argues with Marxism for reasons of science, for "strict economic reductionism is in no way exhaustive, even in the matter of properly economic phenomena."[50] A great many Marxist concepts have no scientific rigor, and are merely metaphysical "ideas." Marx was free to prophesize, but science cannot guarantee the validity of any prophecy. Weber rejects the Marxist doctrine for reasons of personal preference as well. He does not believe a collectivist socialist economy can emancipate man, for economy has no capacity to play a role of global salvation, since like every activity it is limited by its means. It would lead rather to oppression of mankind under a bureaucratic machine. In any case, a fully collectivized economy would lead to anarchy worse than the market's, because of the bureaucratic excesses engendered by it. In addition, Marxist socialist revolutionaries tend to divide society abstractly in two opposed camps, whereas every concrete historical society is made up of a plurality of social strata, including various strata within the camps of the proletariat and the bourgeoisie. For Weber, revolution is usually a source of excitement for intellectuals. Anyway, believing that man can be radically transformed by revolution in the name of a concept as vague as disalienation is just an intellectual way of falling into the trap of the ideology of catastrophism. But Weber disapproves most of the Marxist intellectuals' intolerance, convinced as they are of knowing the truth, which they want to impose upon the rest of the population which at bottom they despise. They seemed to him "warriors for the faith," with whom discussion is impossible because their commitment to a social utopia makes them impervious to experience. Indeed, Weber often referred to his meetings with Marxist intellectuals, in particular Russian refugees in Germany, in whom he had only limited confidence, because it seemed to him they were more avid for power than willing to reflect upon the implications of political activity.

One can reproach Weber for having not always respected the imperatives of value neutrality. He would surely have been the first to admit it. Indeed, it is difficult for a thinker to avoid overstepping the limits of his competence, especially in speech. In reality, value neutrality is more a regulatory principle of the scientist's behavior (and as such it is not beyond abuse) than a constitutive principle of science itself. It would be rather preposterous for the sociologist to claim eventually to oversee physics or biology, in which he is not usually competent. Yet, these are sciences! All the more reason why he should be modest and prudent in nonscientific areas ruled by will, choice, and decision. The principle of value neutrality therefore has a double meaning: it asks the scholar to be conscious of the limits of his own discipline as well as those of science in general. A universal competence is in contradiction with the very notion of competence.

The Period of the Epigones

It cannot be said that Tönnies, Simmel, and Weber really dominated German sociology in their lifetimes, for their influence, with the exception of Tönnies', was most important after their deaths. In this period authors of less wide-ranging scope, primarily O. Spann,[51] were able to concentrate attention upon themselves. Spann's notoriety was then very great—greater, it must be said, for his political positions than for his strictly scientific work. His theory, which he called "universalism," was based on reciprocity between people. The latter found their true expression, however, only in a community at once organic and spiritual, characterized by a strong hierarchy. Despite the best intentions, W. Sombart, with his deeply analytical mind, failed to offer new views and had little influence on sociology, which in no way diminishes the merits of his other works, concerned with social economics. We may overlook O. Spengler, whose success was immense but whose work was not strictly speaking sociological, having much more to do with cultural philosophy.

The other German sociologists sought to develop their discipline in the directions pioneered by Tönnies and Simmel, sometimes combining the two orientations, sometimes using successively one after the other. Weber's influence was more widespread, for he reached minds as diverse as Jaspers, Schumpeter, Schütz, Michels, Hönigsheim, and C. Schmitt.

As we have already noted, Schmalenbach tried to complete or correct the distinction established by Tönnies, adding a third category, that of the league (*Bund*). The attempt had practically no success. As opposed to community, inspired by tradition, and to society, inspired by rationality, the league was supposed to have a more instinctive and sentimental basis. It would be a place for the expression of enthusiasms, of ferment, and of unusual doings. And yet, German sociology continued to think—albeit with diverse and sometimes confused variations—in the categories elaborated by Tönnies, the only ones which stayed meaningful. A. Vierkandt tried to reconcile Tönnies and Simmel, all the while attempting to develop a sociology that conformed to the philosophical temper of the times, which was phenomenology.[52] He takes up Tönnies's antithesis, but like Simmel he conceives the social to be the result of reciprocal actions. In fact, it is difficult to provide an account of Vierkandt's work as a whole, for it varied a great deal from his first study, *Naturvölker und Kulturvölker* (1896), to his last, *Familie, Volk und Staat in ihren gesellschaftlichen Vorgängen* (1936). His positions changed from one edition of his *Gesellschaftslehre* to another, since he finally made community the only fundamental category, society being only a degree of communitarian life. Th. Litt's work, *Individuum und Gemeinschaft*,[53] may be cited as belonging to an analogous current. It was very successful in its time. One might also mention the work of his student, Th. Geiger, *Die Gestalten der Gesellung*.[54] The first introduced into sociology the dialectic of I and thou, showing the appearance of the third to constitute the social bond. The second saw the group (*Samtschaft*) as the social form, presented under the category of *we*, which contains the means of going beyond the opposition between community and society, inasmuch as they complement each other in the group.

Nevertheless, there are a number of authors outside the mainstream, whose relatively original contributions should not be ignored. First, there is F. Oppenheimer, who sought his inspiration in French sociology—Comte and Proudhon—though he referred to Lorenz von Stein.[55] He worked toward a sort of sociological reconstruction of history by downplaying the law of primitive accumulation and putting the accent on factors like violence and justice. Léopold von Wiese undoubtedly had the most influence between the wars. To a certain degree he refers to Simmel's formalism, but he substitutes the notion of reciprocal relation for the notion of reciprocal action.[56] He also used the notion of a social process that takes account of social distance and social space. In his opinion, the object of sociology is not society as it is, but social life as it is developing, which engenders at the same time transitory relations and more lasting forms. His disciple, Plenge, developed this relational sociology in the direction of a theory of organizations.[57] Finally, one must note the historico-cultural theory of A. Weber, Max Weber's brother.[58] He introduced a division which was completely different from Tönnies's: the antithesis of civilization and culture. Civilization is the sphere of intellectual, rational, and technico-scientific relations, which can be transmitted. It obeys the laws of accumulation and evolution. Culture, on the other hand, is the sphere of affective relations: ethico-religious, mythical, and spiritual, which cannot be transmitted. It obeys the laws of originality and singularity.

Other authors concentrated their efforts on the development of specialized sociologies, the most noteworthy being Ehrlich in the sociology of law[59] and J. Wach in the sociology of religion.[60] However, special note must be taken of a branch of sociology which was to have a considerable impact, the sociology of knowledge (*Wissenssoziologie*). The names of Max Scheler and of Karl Mannheim merit particular attention. They made undoubtedly the greatest contribution in this period. Scheler is also known for having attempted a phenomenological sociology, in which he developed the idea that the various forms of human groupings are related to the forms by which consciences communicate. It is in the sociology of knowledge, however, that he really charted a new direction; indeed, partly in order to answer the question posed by the idea above. For every social unit there is a definite corresponding mentality, therefore a definite collective consciousness. For this reason, categories of thought vary with social grouping.[61] What do these thoughts represent? Today, we would call them ideologies. This question, and the question of utopia, was explored by Mannheim.[62] Yet for Mannheim, not everything is ideology, for there also are forms of thought which are governed by their own laws; for example, scientific research and technical knowledge. His distinction between ideology and utopia may be questioned from the scientific point of view; in his view, utopia is a collection of thoughts which takes exception to reality and tries to change it through action; ideology, on the contrary, is a totalistic way of thinking about a given situation—it may vary from group to group, but it must be, in the last analysis, inefficient. Mannheim deserves credit for having shown that ideological thinking does not obey criteria of truth and falsity, precisely because it is not a scientific theory, and especially for having accustomed the republic of sociologists to ideas that make up the immediate topics of sociological research, even if these have become clichés in the absense of critical sense. Lukács, his early work, could be classified under this heading also, but subsequently he parted company with German sociology.

Finally, the establishment of the Frankfurt School, in the 1930s, with Neumann, Adorno, Marcuse, and Horkheimer, must be noted. Its influence was felt chiefly after the Second World War. All things considered, however, even if this school contributed to the progress of sociological research, especially during its American period (that is, in exile), it still misled scientific sociology into an impasse. Its members took advantage of sociology's prestige to put across a primarily philosophical message. This is an example—rather typical nowadays—of the corruption of scientific sociology by ideas whose object is something other than strictly scientific research. This school provides an undeniable illustration of this phenomenon.

With the coming of Hitler to power night fell. Sociology nearly disappeared in Germany, partly because its chief representatives chose exile and emigration, and partly because the Nazi regime proved to be worse than distrustful of a discipline which displayed too critical a spirit.

NOTES

1. Though forgotten today, Buckle's work had a considerable influence on the pioneering minds of his time—which tends to prove that the history of ideas of the nineteenth century is incomplete—perhaps because it is still too close to us. For example, reading Buckle's work led the great German historian Droysen to at least partially revise his hermeneutical conception of history, and Dilthey was much impressed by it. Buckle's impact was determining not only in England and Germany; as evidence, one may cite Pareto's letter to Antonucci (December 7, 1907): "I read Buckle and it was like being struck by lightning. It seemed to me the *ne plus ultra* of reasoning applied to the social sciences." See A. Antonucci, ed., *Alcune lettere inedite di Vilfredo Pareto* (Rome, 1938), pp. 17–26, and G. Busino, *Introduction à une histoire de la sociologie de Pareto* (Geneva, 1968), 2d ed., p. 8.

2. For Lorenz von Stein, see his introduction "Der Begriff der Gesellschaft," in *Geschichte der sozialen Bewegung in Frankreich* (Hildesheim, 1959); for F. Tönnies, see his work *Gemeinschaft und Gesellschaft*, 1st ed., 1887; for Max Weber, see his *Wirtschaft und Gesellschaft* (Tübingen, Mohr), 3d ed., 1947, vol. I, p. 21.

3. K. Staudinger, *Kulturgrundlagen der Politik* (Jena, 1914); H. Freyer, *Soziologie als Wirklichkeitswissenschaft* (Leipzig, 1930).

4. H. Schmalenbach, "Die soziologische Kategorie des Bundes," in *Dioskuren* (Munich, 1922).

5. Th. Geiger, "Die Gruppe und die Kategorien Gemeinschaft und Gesellschaft," in *Viertelhahrschrift für wissenschaftliche Philosophie und Soziologie* (Leipzig, 1927).

6. A. Vierkandt, *Familie, Volk, und Staat in ihren gesellschaftlichen Lebensvorgängen* (Stuttgart, 1936).

7. F. Tönnies, *Hobbes Leben und Lehre* (Stuttgart, 1896).

8. *Communauté et société*, preface to 8th ed.

9. Ibid., book II, part 1, §§ i and ii.

10. Ibid., book II, part 3, § xxxix.

11. Ibid., book I, thème, § i.

12. Ibid., book I, thème.

13. Ibid., book II, part 2, § xix.

14. Ibid., book I, part 2, § xxi.

15. Ibid., book I, part 2, § xxv.

16. G. Simmel, *Soziologie* (Berlin, 1968), 5th ed., p. 5.

17. Ibid., pp. 9–10.

18. Ibid., p. 7.

19. Ibid., p. 4.

20. Ibid., pp. 10–11.

21. Ibid., pp. 8–9.

22. Ibid., p. 9.

23. Ibid., pp. 32–100.

24. I am personally one of those who hold that the third constitutes epistemologically one of the foundations of sociology, the latter being possible only on the basis of the number three,

because a group and the relations specific to a group require the presence of at least three members.

25. Th. Caplow, *Two against One. Coalitions in Triads* (Englewood Cliffs, N. J., 1968). These types of alliances may be given quasimathematical precision.

26. Max Weber, *Gesammelte Aufsätze zur Wissenschaftslehre* (Tübingen, 1951), 2d ed., pp. 1–145.

27. Ibid., pp. 162–63.

28. Max Weber, *Wirtschaftsgeschichte* (Berlin, 1958), 3rd ed.

29. Max Weber, *Wirtschaft und Gesellschaft* (Tübingen, 1947), 3d ed., vol. I, p. 1.

30. Max Weber, *Gesammelte Aufsätze zur Wissenschaftslehre*, p. 428 or 529.

31. Max Weber, *Gesammelte Aufsätze zur Religionssoziologie* (Tübingen, 1947), 4th ed., vol. I, p. 83.

32. Weber, *Wirtschaftsgeschichte*, p. 239.

33. Weber, *Wissenschaftslehre*, p. 178.

34. Ibid., p. 287.

35. Ibid., p. 190.

36. Ibid., p. 191.

37. Ibid., p. 192.

38. Ibid., p. 184.

39. Ibid., p. 178.

40. Max Weber, *Gesammelte politische Schriften* (Tübingen, 1958), 2d ed., p. 494.

41. R. Michels, *Zur Soziologie des Parteiwesens* (Stuttgart, 1909).

42. Max Weber, *Gesammelte Aufsätze zur Soziologie und Sozialpolitik* (Tübingen, 1924), p. 508.

43. Weber, *Wissenschaftslehre*, p. 588.

44. Ibid., p. 589.

45. Ibid., pp. 587–588.

46. Ibid., p. 184.

47. Ibid., pp. 496–497.

48. Ibid., p. 151.

49. K. Lowith, "Max Weber und Karl Marx," in *Archiv für Sozialwissenschaft und Sozialpolitik*, vol. 67 (1927). When one reads Weber's lecture on socialism in his *Gesammelte Aufsätze zur Soziologie und Sozialpolitik*, pp. 482–518, and considers that he could not know Marx's works published after his death, it can be said that he had a profound knowledge not only of Marxism but also of post-Marxism tendencies such as revisionism and anarcho-syndicalism.

50. Weber, *Wissenschaftslehre*, p. 169.

51. O. Spann, *Gesellschaftslehre* (Leipzig, 1923), 2d ed.; also *Der wahre Staat* (Leipzig, 1921).

52. A. Vierkandt, *Gesellschaftslehre* (Stuttgart, 1922; 2d ed., 1928).

53. Th. Litt, *Individuum und Gemeinschaft* (Leipzig, 1919).

54. Th. Geiger, *Die Gestalten der Gesellung* (Karlsruhe, 1928).

55. F. Oppenheimer, *System der Soziologie* (Jena, 1922–1929, 5 vols.).

56. Léopold von Wiese, *System der Soziologie als Lehre von den sozialen Prozessen und den sozialen Gebilden der Menschen* (Munich, 1933, 2d ed.).

57. Plenge, *Zur Ontologie der Beziehung* (Münster, 1930).

58. A. Weber, "Prinzipielles zur Kultursoziologie," in *Archiv für Sozialwissenschaft und Sozialpolitik*, vol. 47 (1920–1921).

59. Ehrlich, *Grundlegung der Soziologie des Rechts* (Munich–Leipzig, 1929).

60. J. Wach, *Einführung in die Religionssoziologie* (Tübingen, 1931).

61. Max Scheler, *Versuche zu einer Soziologie des Wissens* (Munich, 1924) and *Die Wissensformen und die Gesellschaft* (Leipzig, 1926).

62. Karl Mannheim, "Das Problem einer Soziologie des Wissens," in *Archiv für Sozialwissenschat und Sozialpolitik*, vol. 54 (1925) and *Ideologie und Utopie* (Bonn, 1929).

6

EMILE DURKHEIM*

EDWARD A. TIRYAKIAN

Introduction

Emile Durkheim is the crucial figure in the development of sociology as an academic discipline. Before Durkheim sociology was a provocative idea; by his professional endeavors it became an established social fact. Durkheim inherited a nineteenth-century sociological tradition, one with a distinctive French flavor of social realism and social reconstruction; much of contemporary sociology's framework reflects basic features which were imparted by Durkheim's refashioning of sociology into a systematic discipline. Two such features, "positivism" and "structural-functional analysis," have become in recent years targets of much criticism (ideological as well as conceptual); yet, at the same time, one can also say that Durkheim's visibility and esteem are presently at higher levels in both francophone and anglophone sociological circles than perhaps any previous period, including that of his own lifetime. Perhaps the quest for "roots of identity" is also operative in sociology, and Durkheim is surely, alongside Max Weber and Karl Marx, one of the deepest roots of the sociological imagination. Whatever the reason, every self-respecting sociologist has read at least *The Division of Labor* and *Suicide* as an undergraduate or graduate student, and quite likely most sociologists will also have read during their career *The Rules of the Sociological Method* and *The Elementary Forms of the Religious Life*. Each is a seminal study: the

* For their thoughtful comments and suggestions, I am indebted to the following readers of an earlier draft of this essay: James L. Adams, Thomas Beidelman, Phillip Bosserman, Georges Dumézil, Morris Janowitz, Gerald Platt, and particularly, Hermann Strasser. Some of the information presented in this essay was gathered under a research grant from the National Endowment for the Humanities.

first in industrial sociology, the second in deviance, the third in methodology, and the fourth in the sociology of religion and of knowledge. Each is a venture in sociological analysis which does not fade with time, in a discipline where most works disappear from reading lists within ten years after publication. How many other sociologists have three or four of their works read firsthand by succeeding sociological generations? Moreover, Durkheim is not only still widely read but he is also more and more commented and reflected upon by new generations of sociologists, who are also producing new collections of his writings, some seeing print for the first time. Truly, it may be said that the past ten years have seen the production of the most extensive and high-caliber Durkheimiana of any comparable period since his death in 1917.[1]

The understanding of such a major figure as Durkheim is, like any historical benchmark or event, not a once-and-for-all matter but rather more of an emergent process. Consequently, the essay developed in these pages does not claim to provide a comprehensive exposition of Durkheim's sociological analysis; it will be selective in its emphasis, while trying to give the reader a general orientation to Durkheimian sociology. I have been fascinated by Durkheim for twenty years, but I do not feel there is anything definitive in my present understanding of his writings; still, some things, some connections seem clearer to me now than previously, and these I propose to share with readers of this volume. In particular, I wish to advance as a thesis that Durkheim's sociological analysis, though it makes sense in itself, would better be understood as one component of a threefold life project.

Although the entelechy for this vast project cannot be documented in the form of a letter or journal entry kept by Durkheim, nonetheless there are sufficient indications to propose that his life project was constituted by three interwoven goals:

1. to establish sociology as a rigorous scientific discipline
2. to provide the basis for the unity and unification of the social sciences
3. to provide the empirical, rational, and systematic basis for modern society's civil religion

It may be asserted that Durkheim was successful in achieving the first. By the age of forty Durkheim had produced sociology's "manifesto" in the guise of the trilogy consisting of *The Division of Labor, The Rules of Sociological Method,* and *Suicide;* equally significant, he celebrated his fortieth birthday with the publication of the first volume of the *Année Sociologique*, a collective enterprise of the first real sociological school, whose formation was entirely due to Durkheim's intellectual charisma. When Durkheim began his teaching career in the 1880s, sociology was highly suspect in academic circles, in the Old as well as in the New World, for it ran counter to the dominant individualism of the nineteenth century. But Durkheim, in the pre-First World War French university setting which prided itself in intellectual elitism, became one of the most respected and influential members of the faculty of the prestigious Sorbonne; as symbolic of his conquest of the academic setting on behalf of the discipline which reflected so much his imprint, he was given the first chair of sociology in France in 1913.

The second component of the project entailed establishing the unity of the social (or cultural) sciences on a positivistic basis. Here Durkheim was heir to the Comtean idea of the essential unity of scientific knowledge, with sociology as the last emergent science, furnishing the pinnacle of man's cognitive mastery of the world. The social world was understood by Durkheim as a moral ensemble, with its structure and organization subject to rational understanding. But in the spirit of modern science, Durkheim saw that such an understanding was necessarily a collaborative undertaking, for science progresses only through a division of labor; the latter became for Durkheim both a moral principle and a scientific principle of essential importance for the modern world. *The Division of Labor* and the *Année Sociologique* are complementary in providing the theory and practice of what Durkheim thought of this fundamental principle of organization.

Social science deals with conventions, mores, ideals; in brief, Durkheim viewed it as investigating scientifically the normative infrastructure of human society. Economics, history, law, and religion are some of the familiar chambers of the human house, and sociology provides the thread of Ariadne which interrelates all the chambers. From Claude Bernard, the founder of modern physiology, Durkheim was well aware that the hallmark of science is experimentation and comparative analysis; however, direct experimentation (such as Bernard had done for experimental medicine with vivisection) is not possible in the social world. Nevertheless, the comparative analysis of social phenomena in a systematic, organized way was a project which Durkheim partially realized with the *Année Sociologique*. As Terry Clark has aptly commented,[2] this was in its operation a sociological laboratory as much as a journal, one in which recruits served an apprenticeship learning the craft of the new science; the paramount endeavor of this journal was to codify the forms and contents of sociology. Durkheim's academic collaborators in this project were not for the most part professional sociologists, yet they formed a highly integrated interdisciplinary team, sharing various academic and social bonds, and they translated to their own specialty areas the core sociological view obtained from Durkheim.[3] The *Année Sociologique* (still published today) reflected under Durkheim's editorship his acceptance of the essential unity of all social phenomena and his belief that their structural characteristics may be studied scientifically, objectively. But the journal was only a partial success in terms of unifying the social sciences, for the First World War terminated the life of its organizing spirit and decimated the ranks of the second generation of the project. Durkheim's successor and nephew, Marcel Mauss (1872–1950), was acknowledged as one of the great erudites of our century—"he knew everything," has been said of Mauss—but there was one thing which this genial man of genius did not possess, and that was the discipline and rigor of organization. Mauss himself did not complete his dissertation, and he was unable to carry on successfully the editorship of the

Année, which suspended publication after two issues.[4] Lacking a forum for its development and lacking effective instrumental leadership, Durkheim's project of the unity of the social sciences became stalemated in the interwar period.[5]

The third component of Durkheim's life project immerses us in the sociohistorical situation of the Third Republic and takes us into the sector of ideology and partisanship. This French regime, threatened with abortion at its start in the 1870s, was marked with political instability, like its two republican predecessors.[6] Modern France, from 1789 until today, seems to oscillate between the poles of republicanism and caesarism, punctuated with relatively brief but intense civil or near-civil wars. The French sociological tradition begun by Saint-Simon, followed by Comte, Le Play, and Durkheim, has a common denominator in its repugnance of political upheavals, of group struggles for power, of chicanery and civil strife; the tradition, in contradistinction to Marxist sociology, is to make sociology a healing and stabilizing science, one that will find a viable basis for restoring social consensus and for enhancing societal integration. This tradition seems, ultimately, to underscore the importance of morality as the cornerstone of social peace and justice. Thus, Saint-Simon, that fabulous visionary of modern society, saw at the end of a meteoric life that the industrial structure was incomplete without a normative component, and he wrote *The New Christianity* to establish the morality appropriate for the new dawning social order. The assessment that the social order needs an integrating morality to complement economic life recurs in the subsequent writings of Le Play, Proudhon, and Comte, irrespective of their divergent political leanings; it is a key aspect of nineteenth-century French social thought, *particularly of the liberal left.*[7]

Since morality figures prominently in Durkheim's writings, his sociological orientation has been characterized in some quarters as conservative.[8] Yet Durkheim was a trusted civil servant of the republican regime, which gave him the appropriate accolade of Chevalier de la Légion d'Honneur in 1907; he never frequented conservative circles and instead belonged to liberal voluntary associations (such as the Ligue des Droits de l'Homme). Moreover, it may be said that his most challenging assignment was to develop a scientifically grounded morality which would supersede once and for all the traditional Christian morality and the authority of the Catholic church which constituted a basic rallying point for every right-wing political movement that contested the legitimacy of the Third Republic. Consequently, the culmination of Durkheim's life project would entail providing France, as prototypical of modern society, with a civil religion which would be in accordance with the nature of things.

In this respect, Durkheim was the heir to a twofold patrimony. First, in carrying out this project he would assist in completing the Principles of 1789, which are those of modern liberal democracy. Durkheim viewed the French Revolution not as a calamity (which is the conservative outlook on this event), nor as a sham illusion (the radical outlook), but rather as a great promise lacking completion. The Revolution had installed a secularized religion complete with a cult,[9] but this had not taken root, essentially because of its imposition on society from above rather than its correspondence to felt collective religious needs. In an extensive review early in his career, Durkheim expressed the importance of sociology's concern for the Principles of 1789:

> What are the destinies of the revolutionary religion? What will it become? . . . There is indeed no question which should attract more the attention of legislators and Statesmen: do not all the difficulties in which nations find themselves at the present time stem from the difficulty in adapting the traditional structure of societies to these new and unconscious aspirations which have been tormenting societies for a century?[10]

Second, Durkheim was in this respect also heir to Comte's positivistic legacy. It should be borne in mind that Comtean positivism was more than a cognitive mapping of the world via the "positive" sciences; it was also intended as the formulation of a new world order, a rational, scientifically based "religion of mankind," complete with a calendar and the cult of the Great Being, which is mankind or human society writ large. The French Revolution and Comte, thus, were inspirational sources in the background of Durkheim's project to give sociology an ultimate pragmatic justification: sociology would uncover the appropriate integrative force for a secularized but moral social order. Consequently, the quest for a civil religion has to be kept in mind as one major factor if we are to make sense as to why Durkheim and so many of his ablest lieutenants devoted so much time and effort to the careful study of religious phenomena.[11] Such an effort would otherwise appear incongruous with the Durkheimians' sympathies for laicization, liberal republicanism, Jauressian socialism, and even anticlericalism.[12]

Durkheim's last work, *The Elementary Forms of the Religious Life* (hereafter cited as *The Forms*), while it may be considered the successful completion of Durkheim's sociology, left incomplete his global life project of providing the normative cement for modern secular society. France survived the holocaust of the First World War, and even had come together politically in 1914 with the "union sacré" in a rare moment of moral unification; but the Third Republic, morally shallow though economically sound, could hardly survive the peace that followed. Symbolically, Durkheim's erstwhile popularizer, Célestin Bouglé, who had become Director of the Ecole Normale Supérieure de Paris (the major spawning ground of the Durkheimian school), died as the Germans arrived at the gates of Paris in 1940. The Third Republic toppled over on the battlefield, but it had become inanimate before, perhaps more than anything else because, as Durkheim had surmised, an implosion follows a society which cannot fill its moral vacuum.

So much for an initial approximation of what marks Emile Durkheim in bold relief. Rather than present summaries of his works or a chronological and descriptive development of his sociology, I will structure this chapter in terms of three approaches. The first ingress will be a consideration of his Bordeaux beginnings and the societal context of France at the time. The second approach will be to treat some of the paramount intellectual influences which are reflected in his work and which provide structures to his analysis. The third and closing section will dwell on methodological aspects of Durkheim's sociology; I have come to the conclusion that if Durkheim may properly be seen as the monumental modernizer of sociology, it is above all because he provided the discipline with its first comprehensive scientific paradigm, one which entails more than a set of technical recipes but a whole method of approaching social phenomena. Even if he did not achieve the totality of his life project, the establishment of sociology as a rigorous science, with its own domain of inquiry and with an articulation of its major specialty areas, makes the figures of Emile Durkheim unique in the historical development of our discipline.

I

Among the routine affairs of the Faculty of Letters at the University of Bordeaux in the year 1887 was the election of its new dean from its ranks. Well liked and highly regarded by his colleagues, Alfred Espinas handily won the administrative nod. Ten years earlier he had created quite a stir by preparing the first doctoral dissertation in sociology, *Les Sociétés Animales*, which audaciously indicated the stimulus of Comtean positivism on the young scholar's approach to sociobiology; the thesis was accepted but only after deletion in the printed version of reference to Comte. In the 1870s the traditionalists still had enough sway in both the intellectual and the political arenas that secular doctrines, such as positivism, were ill viewed in university circles. But in the following decade the political climate in France began to shift leftward, with liberal republicans firmly in the saddle. The liberal left was the descendant of revolutionary Jacobinism: anticlerical, rationalistic, in favor of the centralization of political authority with Paris as the dominating hub of French political and economic life. Without too much distortion, one may compare the dominating liberal left of the Third Republic with New Deal Democrats in the United States; more extreme shades of the left in pre-First World War France were represented at different times by radical republicans and socialists of different convictions, such as Gambetta and Clemenceau on the republican left, and Guesde and Jaurès on the socialist side.[13] The major inspirational source and chief theoretician of the French left in the nineteenth century was Pierre-Joseph Proudhon, not Marx, who was to remain relatively insignificant in French socialist circles until the formation of the Communist Party and its takeover of the labor movement and *L'Humanité*. To the right and in opposition to a republican form of government were two major restorationist factions which became increasingly ineffective over time: the monarchists (whose split as to whether an Orléans or a Bourbon heir was the legitimate ruler prevented a restoration in the 1870s when the monarchists had control of parliament) and the Bonapartists. The right and the far left were in common agreement in opposing large-scale capitalism and the foreign policy of imperialistic expansion adopted by the liberals; they occasionally came together on various national issues,[14] but it was not an enduring alliance. The French parliament became a haze and maze of wheelings and dealings under the "opportunists"; ministries would be toppled but the middle-level bureaucracy would carry on, and after 1876 the republican cause was beyond danger of the repeat of a radical-inspired Commune uprising, a Bonapartist coup d'état, or a rural-based restoration.

But this statement is made with the wisdom of historical hindsight. The republican regime was to pass through two severe crises, one of which had no manifest effect on Durkheim, while the other proved to be an unanticipated boon to the fortunes of Durkheim and his school. The first was the abortive coup d'état of General Boulanger who, during Durkheim's first years at Bordeaux, nearly succeeded in seizing power in the French style of the military hero who regenerates his country from civil morass, in a tradition that extends from Joan of Arc through the Napoleons and on to Pétain in 1940 and De Gaulle in 1958. The second crisis, ten years after the Boulanger episode, was, of course, the Dreyfus affair, which brought out all the cracks and cleavages of French society on the eve of the twentieth century. Had the Dreyfusards not won out, the power structure of French higher education would have changed drastically and Durkheim would probably have languished on the banks of the Garonne rather than go on to flourish on the banks of the Seine.

Let us return to Espinas, who was more of a social historian than a sociologist, and who held a chair in philosophy. The University of Bordeaux had opened its doors to schoolteachers who needed academic credits to get certified, and Espinas had taken on the charge of offering them a concentrated course on pedagogy. This curricular innovation proved very successful, but this also meant that with Espinas assuming full-time administrative responsibilities in the coming year (1887–88), there was need to recruit from the outside a suitable replacement. The search did not take long, for Louis Liard, an ex-Bordeaux professor who had recently assumed charge of higher education in the Ministry of Public Education, knew just the right person for the vacancy: a young lycée instructor teaching at Troyes, a person who had just written some brilliant articles on recent trends in German social sciences.[15]

Liard was a progressive, a modernizer who with other liberal intellectuals had arrived at the conclusion that Germany's crushing of France in 1870 was because Germany had modernized its institutions more rapidly than France. In particular, German higher education had become part of the "German miracle" in overtaking France and England—helpless and overrun by Napoleon two generations before, Germany had become the most aggressive, vigorous modern country in the 1870s and 1880s. Behind its technology, its industrial growth, and its organizational discipline was its university system, which fostered new scientific and empirical approaches to the study of almost everything, including history.

One wing of Frenchmen coming from the eastern region which had suffered the German annexation of Alsace and part of Lorraine dedicated itself to the restoration of the "lost territories" and to keep firmly implanted in the national vision the plight of that part of the national soil desecrated by German rule; this wing was one important source of French nationalism during the Third Republic. Another wing from the same area had drawn a different lesson, namely that France must in turn modernize in the footsteps of Germany. To modernize entailed to secularize and dislodge Catholic authority from the public sphere, including the educational one (as Bismarck attempted to do with his *Kulturkampf*). The great figure for French domestic modernization was Jules Ferry, a man from the East, twice prime minister, who achieved great renown for his domestic reforms, particularly in educational legislation providing free and compulsory public education, and in giving schoolteachers a decent salary; like Lyndon Johnson nearly a century later, his important social reforms would be eclipsed by public reaction against his Indochina entanglements.

In the 1880s, then, the French Ministry of Education was a dynamic, reform-minded ministry, similar if one seeks comparison to HEW in the United States in the 1960s and 1970s. Travel awards were made available annually to a select number of very promising young scholars for a semester's study in Germany, so that they could bring back new ideas for renovating the French curriculum and mode of study, particularly in the matter of research. The young lycée teacher whom Liard found well qualified for the Bordeaux vacancy had been the recipient of such a fellowship and had made good use of his time at Marburg, Berlin, and Leipzig, being attracted at the last named to one of the great figures of modern social science, Wilhelm Wundt. The instructor, born in 1858 in a part of Lorraine that had escaped annexation, was David Emile Durkheim.

In addition to his publications in scholarly journals, Durkheim had other solid credentials. Like other public schoolteachers in France, his folder in the ministry included evaluation by his superiors.[16] Wherever he had been, Durkheim had received favorable recommendations; his teachers seemed to sense that much would be heard from him. And Durkheim was an alumnus of the elite-training Ecole Normale Supérieure de Paris, which produced some of the most important cadres of the Third Republic, its crack educators. Saint-Cyr (the French West Point) and the Ecole Polytechnique (the French MIT or Cal Tech) continued to be elite schools in the Third Republic, but it was during the regimes of the first half of the century that they had been the shining eyes of the government. The Ecole Normale came to have strategic importance for the republican regime since the latter saw the schoolroom as the ideal locale to conquer minds to the republican cause and wrestle them away from a traditional mentality.[17] It is with some truth that the Third Republic, assisted by its educational arm of the Ecole Normale, was to earn the sobriquet of "The Republic of the Professors," since so many of its major political personalities were academically trained intellectuals.[18]

Examining the dossier, Liard could readily see that Durkheim had done well at the Ecole Normale, as may be attested by the summary evaluation prepared shortly after his graduation by the director of the school, no less than the great historian Fustel de Coulanges:

> Excellent student; a very forceful mind both sound and original, with a remarkable maturity. He has a real aptitude for philosophical studies, especially psychology. His teachers think highly of him.
>
> The Ecole Normale has awarded him the Adolphe Garnier prize as the hardest worker and most deserving member of his class . . .[19]

One may note from this letter that "philosophy" in the French curriculum encompassed not only logic and metaphysics but also whatever might be seen as a source of reflection bearing on the human condition, including the nature of man and society. The stress on philosophy was not unrelated to republican ideology, for philosophy in the Third Republic occupied the privileged seat formerly held by theology. Durkheim was trained as a philosopher, published in leading philosophical journals (*Revue Philosophique, Revue de Métaphysique et de Morale*), participated in the distinguished Société Française de Philosophie (begun in 1901), and of course was concerned throughout his life with questions of moral philosophy.[20] The latter was an exceedingly popular subject throughout Durkheim's lifetime; it was not a mere academic topic but one which had ideological significance. An important problem for the Third Republic was that of getting legitimation. If the republic and the social order behind its polity were to become really accepted by Frenchmen, there was need for the state to have a moral authority for, as much as over, its citizens. Everyone saw that the Catholic church had provided the moral authority behind the monarchy, and because of this past association, the church (particularly the higher clergy) could not be entrusted with assisting the republic in its post–1870 nation-building endeavors. Conversely, the republic had as major proponents anticlerical Catholic liberals, Protestants, Jews, and Freemasons—and these could hardly qualify as faithful members of the papal flock.

The net result was that republican France was eagerly concerned with philosophy, with morality, and with moral education—not from intellectual disinterestedness but from practical considerations of finding a substitute for traditional Christian teachings, so as to legitimate itself and win the broader support of new generations of schoolchildren, wrestling them away from the moral authority of the Catholic church. There were two stark alternatives to finding a new moral cement for society: on the one hand, power without authority could become reality in a one-man takeover, as had befallen the First and Second republics. On the other hand, "power to the people" as a radical populist ideology (advanced on behalf of the Sans-Culottes by Hébert during the Revolution and by Vallès on behalf of the Communards in 1870) conjured the specter of proletarian uprisings, civil disorder, and violent strife.

Philosophy, the rational inquiry for cosmic and social order, was thus for the Third Republic the chosen alternative to either lawlessness or traditional dogmatism. Hence, that Durkheim was trained in and that he had taught philosophy since graduating from the Ecole Normale[21] was a further qualification for replacing Espinas in the teaching of pedagogy, for philosophy dealt more with the "real world" and was considered much more significant for affairs of state in 1887 than in 1977.

Pedagogy, teaching schoolteachers the principles of education, was thus the basic charge of Durkheim at Bordeaux. What else would he propose to teach, inquired the outgoing dean of the faculty. The young scholar did not hesitate in his reply: "My intention is to give a public course on *Social Science* . . . I propose to take as the theme of the course that of *social solidarity* . . ."[22]

And so Emile Durkheim became a member of the faculty at Bordeaux in the fall of 1887, got married in October to Louise Julie Dreyfus, and began teaching a special course in "social science." He would spend exactly half of his university career there, where he had been brought in to take over Espinas's teaching of pedagogy. Seven years later Espinas would be called to the Sorbonne, and this would create a vacant professorship. Durkheim's star continued to rise and within ten years of his entry at Bordeaux he, the son of an orthodox rabbi living in humble circumstances,[23] had scaled the academic height of getting created for him the first chair of social science. His father did not live to see Emile's later successes but his mother, Melanie Isidor Durkheim, must have felt great gratification that her son, the only Jew in his class (1882) at the Ecole Normale, had become a university professor; she died in 1901, the year before his being named to the Sorbonne. For in 1902 history repeated itself: Just as in 1887 Durkheim had been called due to a vacancy in pedagogy, so in 1902 Ferdinand Buisson, who had the chair of moral education, received a cabinet appointment in the new Combes government, and Durkheim was brought in from Bordeaux to substitute. His rise to the top of academic circles is indicative not only of his own sweeping accomplishments but also of the fact that the Third Republic was very propitious for Jewish intellectuals to distinguish themselves through talent—Durkheim's peer group in this respect included Henri Bergson, Lucien Lévy-Bruhl, Emile Meyerson, Léon Blum, Henri Berr, Léon Brunschvicq, and Xavier Léon, among others, many of whom were of families from Alsace or Lorraine.[24]

Perhaps this is an opportune time to consider his initial university teaching, because I find striking how well formed were his sociological ideas at the very start of his appointment, when he was barely thirty years old. Since his early courses contain previews of later analyses and are presently unavailable in English, I will concentrate on this formative period and forego the more standard coverage of the "later" Durkheim.

His first sociology course dealt, as he had promised, with the theme of social solidarity.[25] His second year at Bordeaux he offered "Introduction to the Sociology of the Family," and in his inaugural lecture[26] he traced what he had covered the previous year in dealing with the "initial problem of sociology" and advanced a program of study for the year's subject matter. His summary brings out that the initial problem which frames sociology, the question of social solidarity, is to know "what are the bonds which unite men, that is, what determines the formation of social aggregates."[27]

As would be typical of his later analysis, Durkheim eschewed a psychological answer to the question. There are different kinds of social solidarity, just as there are different kinds of society. Albeit our present incomplete state of scientific knowledge makes any classification somewhat arbitrary, yet two major social types are discernible in all societies, past and present. The former are "amorphous" societies lacking political organization, which range from roving bands of kinsmen up to groups living in urban settlements; the second type is characterized by political organization, or states, which appear with the city and culminate in the large contemporary nations. Each type of society, Durkheim continued, is marked by a different form of social solidarity: one due to the similarity of minds, to the community of ideas and sentiments, while the other arises from the differentiation of functions and the division of labor.[28] Under the influence of the former, individuals fuse into a mass, so to speak, whereas in the case of the latter each has his sphere of action although dependent on the specific contributions of others to the well-being of the whole.

Durkheim termed the former "mechanical" and the latter "organic," noting that these should be seen as analytical distinctions, although one predominates in primitive, the other in modern societies. The less extensive society is, the more similarities predominate over differences, the more like-minded individuals are; conversely, the more extensive society becomes (in population size and in social ties), the greater the competition between individuals for scarce resources, the more necessary is social differentiation for survival, so that "the division of labor becomes the primary condition of social equilibrium."[29] The major factor behind the transformations of social solidarity and behind all of history is thus "the simultaneous growth in the volume and density of societies."[30]

To reiterate, the above propositions were contained in Durkheim's initial course at Bordeaux in 1887–88. It already proposed the conceptualization, even down to the same terms, which would appear in 1893 as his major doctoral thesis, *The Division of Labor, Essay on the Organization of Advanced Societies*.[31] Durkheim's first year coincided with the publication of Ferdinand Tönnies's *Gemeinschaft und Gesellschaft (Community and Society)*. It is a bit as if Lamarck and Darwin (rather than Darwin and Wallace) had both brought out at the same time their respective theories of evolution, for like Durkheim, Tönnies dealt with two forms of social solidarity. Unlike Durkheim, however, Tönnies downgraded the social solidarity of modern large-scale society, which he saw as the temporary domination of capitalism stamping social relations with a cash nexus, an artificial sort of society unlike the more natural and earlier form of *Gemeinschaft*. Durkheim reviewed Tönnies in 1889[32] and took the occasion to note their agreement as to the nature, significance, and primacy of *Gemeinschaft*. But, he went on, the two differed in their evaluation of *Gesellschaft*. Tönnies saw in this type of society the progressive unfolding of individualism, and the society marked by it lacked internal spontaneity. What social life it had came from the external stimulus of the state; it was the kind of society thought of by Jeremy Bentham.[33] For him, Durkheim countered, modern societies have a life as organic and natural as earlier, less extensive societies. Modern and primitive society are two different types but they are types of the same kind. To demonstrate this, Durkheim went on, it would be necessary to write a book, one which would study inductively this modern form of society, that is, by studying the laws and customs associated with this form of societal structure, rather than the typological and deductive manner of German logicians.[34]

I find rather remarkable that this view of Durkheim's, written at the age of 31, is such an accurate announcement of his later work. He did expand his critique of Tönnies into a book, namely the *Division of Labor*, which is more than a rebuttal of Tönnies's view of modern society as *Gesellschaft* since it is also a critique of British utilitarianism associated with Bentham and advanced in sociological form by Herbert Spencer. Note also that he would in his dissertation, as he had proposed in his review, take up the legal system as a major correlate and manifestation of social solidarity, the latter being a primary condition of what might be termed *intersubjectivity*.

There is one more challenge which *Gemeinschaft und Gesellschaft* presented to Durkheim, namely the question of whether modern, large-scale society does have an internal spontaneity, that is, whether it has a genuine social solidarity capable of social renovation and regeneration. Tönnies's description of modern society, Durkheim noted, is a rather bleak portrait in terms of the richness of collective life:

> . . . the society which Mr. Tönnies describes is the capitalistic society of the socialists; indeed, the author frequently borrows from Marx and Lasalle the dark colors in which he represents that society.[35]

Durkheim saw Tönnies and the socialists in accord that the organization of modern society depends upon the state: the state is responsible for the administration of social life, for the enforcement of contracts and the limitation of individual wills whose unchained desires might, in the absence of genuine ties, result in a war of all against all. What for the German social thinkers—whether radical or moderate socialists—contained capitalism was and could only be state socialism; whether the state was the organ of the proletariat or of the bourgeoisie, the view of society is similar.

It may be mentioned in passing that Durkheim was ambivalent toward the state. He did view the central government as having played a liberating role in the historical process, that is, of liberating individuals from the yoke of tradition and ascription.[36] Undoubtedly this had some personal meaning for Durkheim, since it was the regime of the First Republic which had emancipated Jews from the restrictions of the *ancien régime*, as it did other groups such as slaves in the colonies and quasi-serfs at home. But Durkheim was also a follower of de Tocqueville in viewing a healthy democratic organization of society as consisting of viable and multiple intermediate groups between individuals and the state.[37] Individuals as such are not sufficient for social life to have stability and organization; the state qua centralized polity is at least one level removed from the everyday social world so that what it decrees is, in a sense, an external imposition.

Durkheim did not say this in so many words, but I think it is a reasonable extension of his thoughts to suggest that he felt those who place their hopes on the state to organize modern social life fail to realize that the state cannot decree or legislate the affective dimension of social organization, that is, the essential intersubjective affect which binds fellow societal members into solidary unions. Although very much a rationalist in his cognitive orientation to reality, Durkheim, as we shall pursue in a later section, actually gave a central place in his sociology to the role of affect in social life, including its role in regenerating social organization and cohesion. Relating these comments to his exchange with Tönnies, one may suggest that the challenge of providing a different interpretation of modern society than Tönnies had provided with his somber depiction of *Gesellschaft* would be a latent stimulus in Durkheim's sociological thinking for many years. Durkheim's rebuttal of Tönnies's notion that modern *Gesellschaft*like society is void of internal spontaneity is contained, I would propose, in *The Elementary Forms of the Religious Life* (1912). That seminal *magnum opus* contains among so many rich ideas the proposition of the autoregeneration of society, of periodic societal effervescence spontaneously recreating the sacred during the course of intense social interaction and thereby rebuilding social organization. May it not be suggested in terms of the present context that if Durkheim chose as source materials for the development of his theory those pertaining to a stateless or acephalous society (the Australian aborigines), this could be an indication of his refusal to see anything religious or mystical in the state, unlike the German tradition which goes back to Hegel for inspiration?

Let me return to the course on the family, which is worth further consideration as an early programmatic statement. After having summarized his first course of the previous year, Durkheim announced his plans for the coming year. First is mentioned what kind of course on the family he would have liked to offer. He would have wanted to focus on the contemporary modern family, the elements which structure it, how the state defines marital and kinship relations, and how the elements of the family function in interrelating its parts; the network of all these relationships comprise family life.[38] But, he added, such an anatomical (or structural) analysis is not an explanation: to explain, one must find the *raison d'etre* behind the relationship. Natural sciences discover the causes underlying relationships by means of experiments, which are unavailable to sociology. But as Claude Bernard indicated long before, Durkheim continued, what is essential in experiments is not the production of artificial phenomena by the researcher but rather the comparison of what is to be explained in different circumstances and in different forms—in other words, what counts in science is to be able to observe a given fact (*le fait étudié*) under varying conditions.[39] Varying the conditions enables the researcher to establish what is essential and what is contingent about a phenomenon; if variant forms of the phenomenon are produced naturally rather than in the laboratory, its comparative study may be termed indirect experimentation.[40]

And that, pursued Durkheim, is the method which would enable us to explain domestic relations. Thus, if we are interested in the conjugal bond, one would compare it in today's advanced societies with what it had been previously in patriarchal families, both monogamous and polygamous, in paternal and maternal clans, and all intermediary types. Although the conjugal relationship has undergone much evolution, it would not be difficult to find in all these different forms an identical or common ground. Furthermore, if one establishes which among the concomitant factors have not varied more, it will be possible to locate the condition that accounts for these fundamental characteristics.[41]

Unfortunately, Durkheim added, we lack at present systematic and reliable knowledge concerning the different forms of the family. So we must begin our work by classifying and describing major family types, group them in genus and species, and seek to the extent possible to find the causes which have led to their formation and survival.[42] Such a classification of things past will enable us to explain the present, the more comparative research unfolds, because the forms of domestic life, even the oldest and most distant from our own mores, have residues in the contemporary family. Higher social forms have evolved out of lower ones, hence the former is a résumé of the latter, after a fashion; the modern family contains the whole historical development of the family.[43]

The comparative analysis of the historical tableau of family development makes it easier to isolate and explain components of the contemporary family than starting our sociological analysis with today's family: by taking history as a whole we can discern individual family species and types easier than if we were to start with the contemporary scene where the threads are intertwined and jumbled up. But, affirmed Durkheim, no matter how far back into the past our analysis will lead, we shall never lose the present from view; even in describing the most elementary forms of the family, the endeavor is to arrive step by step at an explanation of our modern Western family.[44]

Let me point out here how Durkheim's approach to explaining domestic life anticipates, to the letter, his procedures *twenty-four years later* in giving a sociological account of religious life. For when in beginning *The Forms* he justifies approaching religion by a study of its very early versions, he announces: "primitive religions do not merely aid us in disengaging the constituent elements of religion; they also have the great advantage that they facilitate the explanation of it."[45] And shortly before that passage he indicates that although what was sought was an understanding of religion today, we must eschew beginning with a preconceived notion of what religion is or with an abstraction from our contemporary situation; rather, "what we must find is a concrete reality, and historical and ethnological observation alone can reveal that to us."[46]

I draw attention to this because of the striking continuity in Durkheim's approach to social phenomena. From the dawn to the dusk of his university teaching and research, he stressed a comparative method of analysis, one which sought to understand major facets of contemporary Western society by means of anthropological and historical data. To provide a linkage between these historical and ethnological strata, Durkheim retained an evolutionary position, one wherein the present represents the latest in a series of stages of development.[47]

Unlike earlier social evolutionists as well as many of his contemporaries, Durkheim did not take the last element in the social series—that is, contemporary institutions—to be morally superior to earlier elements. Primitive = inferior and advanced = superior are definitely *not* part of the Durkheimian evolutionary grammar. This is further indicated in the introduction to *The Forms* where he states:

> In reality, then, there are no religions which are false. All are true in their own fashion . . . when we turn to primitive religions, it is not with the idea of depreciating religion in general, for these religions are no less respectable than the others. They respond to the same needs, they play the same role, they depend upon the same causes.[48]

Durkheim had from the outset the vision that the vast panorama of social life constitutes, for the sociologist, a unified whole; in other words, for the sociologist interested in explaining modern conditions—whether it be the family, religion, or whatever—the past is prelude to the present, history and ethnology offer data that unlock the meaning of the present.[49] Sociological analysis, then, makes relevant what is distant from our modern society in time and social space. We might bear in mind that for Durkheim and his followers who formed the core of the *Année Sociologique* team, historical and ethnological materials, properly utilized, did constitute sociological "empirical data"; this in itself was not a methodological innovation, for Spencer had made use of these in his evolutionary sociology. However, Durkheim was to refine the comparative method by a much greater degree of rigor in the critical analysis of texts, and also by evolving a conceptual frame for the codification of data. Essentially, the framework of the *Année* represented in itself a theoretical conceptualization of the discipline, and from the first volume published in 1898 to the last one published under Durkheim's editorship, in 1913, modifications were made in the conceptualization in light of the data analyzed.[50]

In his "Introduction to the Sociology of the Family," Durkheim expressed himself on other methodological issues which would later guide him. The sociological method is one of induction resting on facts, but facts reported by travelers or temporary observers in a given society may be misleading; social observers see things through their ideological lens, whether of conservatism or radicalism.[51] What sociological analysis seeks to get at is the internal structure of the institution (such as the family), for this is what is of scientific interest, not superficial aspects which may catch the attention of concerned laymen; literary or moral accounts are not sufficiently objective documents. To go from surface, personal impressions of social phenomena to their basic structural aspects, one must find these in

> those ways of acting reinforced by practice which are called customs, law, mores. Here we are dealing not with simple incidents of personal life but with regular and constant practices, residues of collective experiences, fashioned by an entire train of generations.[52]

Anticipating the famous operational definition of social facts he was to offer seven years later in the *Rules of Sociological Method,* Durkheim then proposes that a custom may be recognized in being not only a habitual way of behaving but also one which is *mandatory* for all members of a society. It is not how often it occurs which gives salience to a custom but its moral imperative: a custom is a social rule which must be followed and which is endowed with the authority of some sanction. It is the existence of the latter which differentiates custom from simple habits.[53] So recognized, Durkheim adds, customs provide us recognizable facts analogous to those studied by the natural sciences.

Durkheim went on to indicate some of the anthropological and historical sources that can be used in examining the family (Bachofen, Lubbock, MacLennan, Morgan, Maine, Sohm, etc.). He was aware that mores and their further objectification in laws do not reveal all that is crucial about institutional life; legal features may survive by dint of habit and hide the fact that underlying conditions may have changed. So there is a degree of uncertainty and incompleteness about utilizing historical and ethnological sources to get at the dynamics of a social institution such as the family. But this methodological imprecision will be remedied when the sociologist comes to the contemporary family because we can use demography. Demography enables us to express contemporary incremental changes in social life;[54] unlike the single observer whose perspective may distort reality through his biases, demography embraces the totality of society. Durkheim (who understood demography in the broad sense of social statistics) found in the impersonality of numbers a guarantee of the genuineness and objectivity of the social phenomena they disclose. Statistical data, moreover, make manifest quantitative variations of social phenomena and allow their measurement. It is clear from this early text as well as from all his subsequent endeavors that Durkheim regarded quantitative and qualitative analysis as an integral whole.[55] There is no disjunction in Durkheim between "positivism" and "interpretive" sociology, any more than there is in Max Weber's sociological analysis.

I have been discussing Durkheim's "Introduction to the Sociology of the Family" as a text introducing Durkheim at the beginning of his sociological career. Taught in 1888, his course could be followed by sociologists today and not found seriously outdated in its basic approach: it is a *modern* sociology course, not in terms of factual information about the family, of course, but assuredly modern in terms of its conceptualization, its objectivity, and its comprehensive analysis of this basic social institution. And probably in terms of the treatment of the subject matter—since Durkheim felt a social institution has to be explained diachronically as well as synchronically—his course was a good deal more encompassing than most courses taught today under the rubric of "sociology of the family."

Durkheim's courses in general were very successful and drew an enthusiastic audience recruited from various faculties, a rather rare occurrence (then as now); his presence helped considerably in making intellectual sparks fly around the university.[56] Bordeaux readily accepted Durkheim, and although as a provincial university it may have lacked the prestige of Lyon, it would prove to be an excellent setting for the development of Durkheim's sociology. Within ten years of his arrival he completed his major thesis on the division of labor and his minor (Latin) thesis on Montesquieu, as well as the two other studies since become classics, namely *Suicide* and *The Rules of Sociological Method*. It was at Bordeaux where, beginning with Marcel Mauss, the first generation of the Durkheimian school began to gather. Bordeaux upgraded dramatically the caliber of its faculty during Durkheim's years, many of whose colleagues distinguished themselves sufficiently to receive the desired promotion to Paris.[57]

All in all, Louis Liard had been an astute marriage broker in bringing Durkheim to Bordeaux; Durkheim blossomed at the university (although one can say truthfully that he brought with him an already budding sociology), and he added great luster to the name of Bordeaux.

II

The second approach to Durkheim will be through selected major influences; these, together with the societal context, provide an important ground for his sociological analysis.

Obviously, Durkheim's self-awareness as a sociologist led him to a certain identification with the recognized founder of sociology, Auguste Comte, who died the year before Durkheim's birth.[58] But while Durkheim readily admitted that Comte founded sociology and established the basic sociological frames of social structure and social dynamics, there is a certain reserve and distancing in his discussion of Comte.[59] Moreover, one is hard-pressed to find the Comtean imprint visibly manifest in Durkheim's major works, since references to Comte are exceedingly few and far between. To be sure, Durkheim did owe to Comte more than the basic frames of structure and dynamics, and even more than the Comtean inspiration that social reality is an indissoluble whole: the essential feature for Comte of social phenomena, that which gives them an emergent property which cannot be reduced to less complex bioorganic phenomena, is the feature of social *consensus*, the intersubjective reality which Durkheim would study as solidarity. Also from Comte—though not from him alone—Durkheim saw social development in its virtual tendency as a development of egoism into altruism; if consensus tends to become the basis of social organization, if the rule of law progressively substitutes for military or despotic rule, it is because of the greater sphere of altruism.

Further, Comte's influence on Durkheim is present in Durkheim's acceptance of "positivism" understood in a double sense: (a) as the study of social phenomena in the same scientific and objective method as that used by the sciences in approaching the phenomena of nature; and (b) as opposed to the "negativism" of Enlightenment philosophy and its heirs which are not primarily interested in improving social conditions but more in dissolving institutions.

So, to understand the sociologist in Durkheim one must certainly begin with Comte.[60] And perhaps one should also end with Comte, for the bold thesis in *The Forms* that religion is no more and no less than the mirror of real society and that the divinity is the total society itself, hence that religion is both immanent (a natural phenomenon of society) and transcendent (since religion symbolically depicts the forces of society which transcend individuals and even subgroups of society)—this thesis is a reformulation of Comte's later years' proposition concerning the Great Being as the self-divinization of society.[61]

A more significant influence, in my judgment, was Henri de Saint-Simon (1760–1825), the brilliant, somewhat eccentric entrepreneur, who among other schemes and projects thought of a science of social phenomena, a science of "social physiology" which would gather scientific knowledge about social life. Such scientific knowledge, he foresaw, would be necessary to end the intellectual and moral chaos evident behind the turmoils of the French Revolution and its aftermath, with political constitution after constitution being drafted in vain by legislators who drew up their plans without knowledge of social conditions. Of various themes in Saint-Simon which find their later expression in Durkheim's writings, that of *crisis* merits special notice. Saint-Simon saw crisis as a moral condition of society in the state of "social disorganization" or destructuration, which is a transitory (albeit traumatic) state occurring between "social organization" and "social reorganization." There is a dissolution of organized knowledge involved in the broader normative crisis. The modern crisis is the latest in the historical process, for there have been other mutations, other disjunctures in the past when one form of social organization has perished and a new one has not yet become institutionalized.

Saint-Simon was heavily indebted to the analyses of two of his influential contemporary thinkers, Louis de Bonald (1754–1840) and Joseph de Maistre (1753–1821), who are important but often unrecognized precursors of structural-functional analysis.[62] Their diagnosis of the sociopolitical instability chronic since 1789 was that that it stemmed from the cleavage between Christian morality and civil society, from the separation of the spiritual and the temporal powers, which they considered as forming an organic whole.

Saint-Simon, while influenced by their diagnosis that a moral vacuum underlies social disorganization, did not follow them in seeking in medieval Europe the model of social reconstruction. He sought in the present society the seeds of tomorrow's social order, and in particular found these in the nascent industrial society characterized by the *productivity* of labor and capital. If productivity is the hallmark of industrial society, it signifies that old status distinctions based on ascriptive rank are of no import in relating men to one another. Each will be judged in terms of his contributions to the whole: "From each according to his abilities, to each according to his needs" is the formula of Saint-Simon.

All social classes in modern society[63] derive their social identity in terms of their social function, that is, in terms of their contribution to the societal beehive. And once the industrial order becomes fully institutionalized, so will the belief system of modern society become reorganized in terms of *scientific* knowledge, unified in terms of the knowledge of society and of nature. Every social order, every organized civilization, has an economic and a political integration to which corresponds an appropriate system of knowledge. Scientific knowledge and industry form the coupling of modern society in the same way as did theological knowledge and feudalism for medieval society.

Saint-Simon as a crucial modernizer of social thought, prophet of industrial technocracy, and charismatic head of a sect which was a forerunner of a sociological school, merits extensive treatment on his own in any study of the history of sociological analysis.[64] But it is Saint-Simon's influence on Durkheim which is the present subject of discussion. Durkheim had a thorough familiarity with Saint-Simon's ideas, and I do not find the element of ambivalence present which seems to be the case in his discussions of Comte. Durkheim certainly credited Saint-Simon with being the first to have a clear idea of the science of society.[65] More revealing is the extensive attention devoted to Saint-Simon and his school in Durkheim's course on socialism, which he taught at Bordeaux in 1895–96.[66]

More than half of Durkheim's study of socialism deals exclusively with Saint-Simon's doctrines. He begins by noting that the starting point of Saint-Simon is the notion that every social system represents the application of a system of ideas, which manifests itself in different institutions. A society is above all a community of ideas, of moral ideas linked together by the religion of the people; further, religion and science are not heterogeneous, for religion is popular science (a theme which Durkheim would come back to in *The Forms*). What binds men together in society is a common way of thinking, of representing the world; in every phase of history, men understand the world as a function of their scientific understanding, i.e., of knowledge which is taken to be certain. What unifies all partial understandings into a comprehensive knowledge is philosophy, which synthesizes the knowledge of all specific sciences.[67] Positive philosophy or the philosophy of science is encyclopedic, but unlike the critical philosophy of the Enlightenment, its spirit is one of reconstruction and organization. Such a synthesizing must be done periodically, since the particular sciences are constantly evolving; hence the scientific encyclopedia must be periodically upgraded.

In any case, adds Durkheim in explicating Saint-Simon's *Mémoire sur l'Encyclopédie* (ca. 1810), philosophy has a basic social function. In periods of normalcy, philosophy is the keeper of social consciousness, and in periods of crises—which Saint-Simon saw as an emergent system of beliefs seeking to displace an outmoded one—philosophy has the role of guiding the crystallization of the new. So Saint-Simon's philosophical and sociological studies, continues Durkheim, have the same object; philosophy was a natural complement of Saint-Simon's sociological interests.[68]

It might be suggested at this point that Saint-Simon's project for renewing the encyclopedia of science became Durkheim's own project the year after this course, when he began the preparation of the *Année Sociologique*, which in effect would be an evolving encyclopedia of the social sciences. And Durkheim could easily identify with Saint-Simon's stress on the unity of philosophical and sociological inquiry, both of which get fuller justification from seeking practical ends of improving social organization. After all, Durkheim never discarded his training in philosophy, which stood him well in directing sociological attention to philosophical issues.

But this just marks the beginning of Durkheim's affinity for, if not identification with, Saint-Simon. Durkheim was giving his course on socialism just a few years after having completed his dissertation. Although the emphasis of *The Division of Labor* was on the structural basis of integration in modern society, yet Durkheim ended his study aware that a new social equilibrium was far from institutionalized. He concluded by pinpointing what was unsettling social equilibrium, namely that "morality is going through a real crisis."[69] The diagnosis is worth noting:

> Our illness is not . . . as has often been believed, of an intellectual sort; it has more profound causes. We shall not suffer because we no longer know on what theoretical notion to base the morality we have been practicing, but because, in certain of its parts, this morality is irremediably shattered, and that which is necessary to us is only in the process of formation.[70]

I suspect that Durkheim had not undertaken to study Saint-Simon carefully while preparing his dissertation, because the latter's name is not to be found therein. It must have struck Durkheim when he did get to delve into Saint-Simon to see the correspondence between his *Division of Labor* and Saint-Simon's *L'Industrie* (ca. 1816–1818). For while Saint-Simon in this early period of his writings was dwelling on how the industrial order would provide a structural basis for the integration of modern society,[71] he also indicated that social organization could not transform itself successfully without a moral transformation. At present, the old moral system had been abandoned without a new one accepted in its place, hence the moral crisis of French society.[72] Durkheim also pointed out that Saint-Simon had initially believed that economic self-interest would suffice as a work ethic for the social order, but that he changed his mind. If anything, egoism or self-interest divides men more than it unites them; in fact, self-interest is a passion which, unless restrained, will lead to the dissolution of society rather than to its reinforcement.[73] We need not elaborate how this point coincided with Durkheim's own thinking in both *The Division of Labor* and *Suicide,* with the latter demonstrating in part that egoism is deleterious to individuals as much as to the organized societal community.[74]

Saint-Simon, Durkheim points out, saw that what had contained self-interest or egoism in a previous social order were traditional religious beliefs, which had lost their efficacy. This left society without a viable moral system to complement the socioeconomic structural system. Hence, no matter how well economically organized modern society becomes in an international more than a national social order,[75] this social organization needs a soul, a spirit in the form of common moral beliefs which will provide the moral unity to cement the economic unity.[76] Consequently, the last stage of Saint-Simon's thinking was to turn in *The New Christianity* (ca. 1825) to a consideration of the religion appropriate and necessary for modern society.

It is worth pointing out how similar to Saint-Simon's intellectual odyssey Durkheim's was to be, albeit at the time of *Socialism* he had just started renewing his interest in religion. The following passage in which Durkheim describes the last turn in Saint-Simon's writings could equally apply to a commentator viewing the apparent change from Durkheim's earlier analysis to its culminating point in *The Forms:*

> When one finds the opponent of the theological system, the founder of positive philosophy, demanding the establishment of a new religion, one is tempted to think that a revolution has taken place in his thinking and that he has abandoned his principles. This hypothesis is made plausible in that the *New Christianity* (1824) is his last work. . . . This interpretation is false. On the contrary, religious preoccupations were very keenly felt by Saint-Simon in all periods of his intellectual development. . . . Consequently, Saint-Simon never conceived positive and scientific philosophy as exclusive of every religious system. On the contrary he felt that one led to the other.[77]

It was the social ethic of Christianity which Saint-Simon stressed as the girder for the emergent industrial order. "Treat every man as your brother" is the Christian principle of altruism which in leading man to find himself one with others in God has both a this-worldly emphasis and an important social dimension. And Durkheim points out that although the new religion will have its cult and dogma, it is ethics which will be its central feature.[78] The new religion, which has an immanent, even pantheistic basis—for it finds God in everything which is real and does not find the divine in any extraterrestial setting or object of belief—has the task of providing the spiritual bond linking members of human society. It is religion for Saint-Simon (as it will be for Durkheim in *The Forms*) which gives to society the consciousness of its unity. If God is one with nature, the antithesis between science and religion disappears, for God is both the object of scientific investigation and of religious worship.[79]

Again, let me interject that this attempted reconciliation of science and religion is not only Durkheim's exposition of Saint-Simon but also will later emerge in *The Forms* as Durkheim's own intention. Saint-Simon was, I propose, extremely influential for Durkheim because of the former's perspective on religion which leads to a "rational justification of an ethics of solidarity," one which would not be an intellectual construct but would mesh in with major dimensions of modern society; its industrial economic nature, its democratic and cosmopolitan tendencies, and its psychological roots in Christianity. The stress on ethics in the last writings of Saint-Simon, on a morality of altruism, and on the immanence of religion are features which Durkheim could readily accept.

Durkheim tells us that Saint-Simon did not live to complete *The New Christianity,* and therefore we may say he left incomplete the civil religion and system of morality of modern society. That, ironically, is a further bond between them. What Durkheim could not know as he prepared his lectures on Saint-Simon was that twenty years later, he himself would die while working on his system of ethics, which would have been the culmination of his life project.[80]

In terminating his course (though not the subject matter, since he had the intention of extending his study to cover German socialism in following years), Durkheim brings out that in Saint-Simon one finds the seedbed of all major nineteenth-century intellectual currents: (a) the method of historical science; (b) positive philosophy, which is the major philosophical innovation of modern times; (c) socialism; (d) aspirations for religious renewal.[81] His summary evaluation of Saint-Simon could well serve as Durkheim's own epitaph:

> A mind eminently alive and keen to learn, curious about new trends, gifted with a sort of intuitive sympathy which made him sensitive to all the aspirations of his contemporaries, Saint-Simon succeeded in making of his work a sort of synthesis of all the tendencies of his period.[82]

Now let me turn to the second major influence on Durkheim, namely the philosopher Immanuel Kant, whose imprint left visible traces not only on Durkheim himself but on practically Durkheim's entire generation which attended higher education. I have indicated previously that philosophy for the Third Republic was of crucial significance in developing its ideology and its legitimation; Kant, I would argue, was above all other figures the philosopher who provided inspiration and stimulus for this development.

After the excitement of the Romantic movement (among whose children may be included Hegel, Lamennais, Schleiermacher, Schopenhauer, and the young Marx), the second half of the nineteenth century was marked by a more sober, rationalistic current. Kant was "rediscovered" as the major figure of modern philosophy, and in France this was particularly the case in republican circles, headed in philosophy by Charles Renouvier (1815–1903), whom Durkheim avidly read as a student, and by Durkheim's own teacher at the Ecole Normale, Emile Boutroux, the "philosopher of the Third Republic."

We may ask why this affinity between Kant and this regime. First, it will be recalled that one aim of Kant's *Critique of Pure Reason* was to rescue or salvage the certainty of knowledge from Hume's devastating skepticism. For the generation of Europeans who became adults in the mid-nineteenth century, the ascendance of science, particularly the acceptance of evolutionary theory, had shaken to the foundations the certitude of the stability of the world, a certitude formerly given by the religious interpretation of the universe. Between science and between the image of man as an economic actor motivated by economic self-interest, a generation of Europeans had experienced a drastic and traumatic passage "from the absolute to the relative."[83] The following generation—Durkheim's—became aware of the limitations of "relativism"; after the turmoils of the early 1870s, the nascent republican regime and its adherents were searching for an alternative to either moral anarchy[84] or to traditional Catholic morality with its other-worldly orientation.

Kantian philosophy provided an ideal fit on several dimensions. First, Kant's epistemology sought to restore the boundaries of absolute certainty provided by "pure reason." Second, it also had a crucial "practical" side in establishing the moral basis of action, and this without direct appeal to God, which suited ideally the republican temper for a "morale laïque." There is in Kant an expression of this-worldly Protestant asceticism,[85] which resonated very well with the world view of the effective leadership of Republican France. The Kantian themes of the autonomy of the will and "voluntarism," of the "categorical imperative," of the primacy of fulfilling one's "duty" without regard for material interest—these and others provided an injunction for a disinterested individualism compatible with a collectivity orientation. Stated differently, neo-Kantism had extraacademic appeal as a secular morality which would both legitimate the republican regime and provide mobilization for the diffusion of a social altruism that would appeal to the growing middle class, the major constituency of the Third Republic.[86]

The preeminence of Kant in the teaching of philosophy in secondary schools during Durkheim's formative years (and for the remainder of the century) is well shown in one of the most important documents about political life in France in this period. This is *The Uprooted*,[87] a political novel by Maurice Barrès, a contemporary (1862–1923) of Durkheim who also grew up in Lorraine (about thirty-five miles away from Durkheim), was exposed to the same secondary school education (at the lycée of Nancy), and who also like Durkheim eventually became an intellectual drawn to Paris. Yet, unlike Durkheim, Barrès became highly critical of secular education, which he saw as an alienating force that "uprooted" students from attachment to national traditions and their native soil; unlike Durkheim, Barrès was a spokesman for the right and became an antirepublican nationalist.

The novel, drawing from the author's experiences, essentially depicts a group of students initially in the last year of a provincial high school in Lorraine, who have as their philosophy teacher (named Bouteiller) one who is "a resolute Kantian"; after graduation, both the students and the teacher go on to Paris, and the novel, seizing upon actual events in French political life, interlaces their lives and fortunes. Let me select a few passages to indicate the salience of Kant in the philosophical training imparted to lycéens such as Barrès and Durkheim.

Quite early we are informed that, following Kant, Bouteiller held that "The world is like wax onto which our mind imparts its imprint like a seal. . . . Our mind perceives the world in terms of the categories of space, time, causality."[88] We are also informed that Bouteiller, "after a phase in absolute skepticism . . . believed with Kant and by appealing to the heart that he could reconstitute for his students the category of morality and an ensemble of certainties."[89]

At the end of the academic year, Bouteiller leaves his students with an overview of the most important points made in the course:

> We examined a crucial thought: how Kant ends in an absolute skepticism and then reestablished the principles of certainty by stating: "A reality exists, it is the moral law. . . . Remember the principle on which we established all ethics. . . . It is to act in such a way that our action can serve as a rule [for mankind in general].[90]

This is the message, I suggest, that Durkheim also received in his philosophy course at the lycée. He was not only thoroughly familiar with Kantian philosophy but also seems to have engaged in a lifelong dialogue with Kant whenever he, Durkheim, reflected philosophically. The preoccupation with morality and ethics, with a science of morality, as constitutive features of social life is an indication of Kant's imprint. Just as it may be argued that Marx's sociological analysis is thoroughly grounded in neo-Hegelianism, so one may argue that Durkheim's sociological analysis is neo-Kantianism in its philosophical grounding. Let us expand on this relation of Kant and Durkheim.

For Kant, there is a reality to morality which goes beyond the individual and which makes moral action binding on the individual; this is an a priori condition, yet Kant does not derive morality from God. Durkheim will readily accept the Kantian a priori as transcendental structure given to the faculty of understanding but he will modify the source of the a priori so as to validate these structures of reason. The transcendental source of the a priori of moral action, Durkheim would propose,[91] is society, whose existence is both anterior and posterior to that of any of its members. A moral fact (a societal norm) has two important attributes which give this phenomenon a specificity in regard to other behavioral rules of conduct. One of these is that it is *binding* on individuals, an attribute Durkheim takes from Kant.[92] To be sure, Durkheim then adds that Kant did not mention the second characteristic, namely that a moral action is desirable, a good thing for the individual to perform. Moral actions, like religious actions, he continued, have the twofold quality of being obligatory and desirable.

Durkheim's pronouncement on moral action is a condensation of materials he presented in his frequently given course, "Science of Education." One need only examine the first part of the posthumous publication stemming from the course, *Moral Education*,[93] to see how Kantian is the core of Durkheim's approach to morality. Although Durkheim faults Kant for neglecting that moral action gives personal satisfaction, this appears to be more of a mild rebuke since Durkheim's own discussion stresses the obligatory aspect of moral behavior much more than its eudaemonic side. More serious is Durkheim's criticism that Kant is not aware that morality, being related to society in its very essence, will show variability in time and space, since different societies and different historical periods in the same society call for different contents of morality. It will be recalled that for Kant an action is moral only when it can be made into a universal rule of conduct for mankind, irrespective of where and when. This said, Durkheim's argument in favor of moral relativism is one which should not be magnified. If different moral systems are appropriate for different societies, it is also the case that Durkheim felt there was one appropriate morality corresponding to the social organization of a given society at a given stage of its development.

Nowhere that I know of does Durkheim propose that different social strata, different social groups in the same society, may have different and appropriate moral codes of conduct hermetically sealed off from one another. This would have been tantamount to admitting that *anomie* was the normal and appropriate condition of modern society. If anomie,[94] taken in the sense of conflicting multiple normative paradigms present in the same society, is treated as a normal rather than as a transient pathological aberration of social organization, then what hope is there for national unity and the existence of a societal community? The societal community may evolve rather than stay fixed, leading to the evolution of moral representations, but Durkheim's social realism is anchored on the tenet that there is a societal community[95] beneath or behind all external or institutionalized aspects of social life.

Durkheim's realism can thus align itself with Kantian critical realism, which while making place for subjectivity (since the world is made intelligible by a priori structures of mind or consciousness) retains the facticity of a world that transcends the individual. For both Kant and Durkheim, morality is not the diminution of individual freedom in the face of transcendence; it is its very assertion.[96] In brief, Kantian moral philosophy, rationalistic to the core, must be seen as the guiding philosophical orientation for much of Durkheim's concerns as a sociologist and as an educator. Among these concerns were the form and emphases of secular education so as to promote civic consciousness, social solidarity, and commitment to democratic and republican institutions.

Durkheim also found in Kant a major epistemological stimulus and challenge. Kant's theory of knowledge gives centrality to the categories of mind which, so to speak, "program" our perception of the outer world. Durkheim could not accept that the categories—space, time, causality, totality, etc.—were rooted in the individual, that is, that they were functions of the individual mind. At the same time, Durkheim readily accepted Kant's positing of necessary a priori structures which render the world orderly. In effect, Durkheim sociologized the Kantian categories of understanding by arguing, in a seminal article published with Mauss,[97] that the very structures of logical thought are indeed a priori because they are collective, i.e., societal representations. In other words, Durkheim indicated in *Primitive Classification* that the cognitive mapping of the world is not a function of the individual mind but is rather rooted in a deeper substratum, social organization itself, or at least in the organization and adaptation of a given societal collectivity to its environment. Although Durkheim himself may not have realized the full import of this essay, I think it may be argued that his treatment of the social basis of classification is a major innovation or anticipation of phenomenological sociology: for if the modes of organizing and classifying objective reality are collective representations, then it follows that these a priori structures (similar to Husserl's noemata) are constitutive of the social world we seek to understand. *To understand the structure of a collectivity's classification of the world is, in effect, to understand its rules or principles of social organization*. This may well be considered as one of Durkheim's greatest insights and discoveries.[98]

It anticipates current research of the "ethnomethodological" school in sociology,[99] whose practitioners seem unaware of the implications of Durkheim's later analysis for phenomenological sociology, namely *Primitive Classification* and *The Forms*, which gives a sociological translation of Kantian theory of knowledge by grounding collective representations in the religious consciousness of the collectivity. Durkheim's "sociologism"[100] in this respect amounts to no less than an epistemological revolution from the traditional philosophical perspective that knowledge is a function of the individual knower, since Durkheim posits that knowledge is a function of a priori structures which are societal in origin and imparted to the individual in the socialization process. Hence, Durkheim is very far away from a caricatured image of him as the "positivist" of *Suicide* who relies naively on official statistics to explain an "objective" reality.

As I have recently argued elsewhere,[101] there are some intriguing bases of convergence between Durkheim and Edmund Husserl, the founder of modern phenomenological philosophy, born one year later than Durkheim: both sought a transcendental grounding of knowledge and reason, and both sought a transcendental consciousness which would not be "other-worldly." Durkheim found this transcendence in the *conscience collective*, "the highest form of the psychic life, since it is the consciousness of the consciousness."[102] Husserl initially found it in the transcendental ego; however, in his later years he seemed to gravitate more and more to the Durkheimian position. Husserl's concept of the *Lebenswelt*, or the life-world of experience, as the ultimate source of consciousness seems to me quite related to Durkheim's societal community as the source of the categories of understanding. And ultimately, the common ancestor to both Husserl and Durkheim is Kantian philosophy; this is reflected in the idealistic emphasis of Husserlian and Durkheimian realism. The phenomenological critique of reason undertaken anew by Husserl in his last major work, *The Crisis of European Sciences and Transcendental Phenomenology*,[103] and the sociological critique of reason undertaken in *The Forms* are complementary aspects of the Kantian legacy to reestablish the certainty and unity of knowledge.

If one recalls that Saint-Simon, the other towering influence on Durkheim, had sensed that social disorganization is a reflection of the social order having a lack of integration of knowledge and that this condition produced or was reflected in all major societal crises, then one may see that the influences of Kant and Saint-Simon reinforced each other by providing him with fundamental channels of global concerns for the more specific avenues of his sociological investigations.

I will not dwell long on other figures in this context of influences on Durkheim, particularly since he was such a great synthesizer and incorporated into his sociology strands from diverse currents and disciplines. I do feel, though, that Saint-Simon and Kant hold a unique status in providing the key to the unity of sociology and philosophy in Durkheim's overall world view. To be sure, some "lesser" influences need to be recognized: for example, Fustel de Coulanges, Durkheim's history teacher at the Ecole Normale, whose *Ancient City* undoubtedly sensitized Durkheim to both the importance of historical analysis for the sociological understanding of modern society and to the significance of religion as an institutional structure underlying evolving forms of social organization. Durkheim in the preface to the very first volume of the *Année Sociologique* stresses the need for the rapprochement of sociology and history and invokes Fustel de Coulanges's name to recall that the latter held that true sociology is history; nothing is less debatable, adds Durkheim approvingly yet relishing the last word, provided that history be done sociologically.[104]

Mention should equally be made of German social scientists, particularly Wundt and Schaeffle, both of whom he met on his visit of 1885–86; the "German influence" on Durkheim, while helpful at the beginning of his career, would later cause him some moments of anguish.[105] Later on, British social scientists, particularly those interested in the scientific study of "primitive religion," provided Durkheim with new perspectives and new sources of sociologically relevant data—here mention need be made of McLennan, Frazer, and above all, that remarkable Scottish scholar, W. Robertson Smith.[106] One could extend this list considerably, but I will terminate by mentioning just one more group of influences on Durkheim, namely his own students. There was a greater degree of collaboration between members of the school, such as joint essays and monographs, including joint authorship involving Durkheim, than the prevailing norm of "rugged individualism" elsewhere in the French university setting. Marcel Mauss, Henri Hubert, François Simiand, Maurice Halbwachs, Paul Lapie, Paul Fauconnet, Georges Davy, and Robert Hertz were among those of the first and second generation of his students who not only got their inspiration from Durkheim but who also provided him with important intellectual feedback as he evolved his sociological analysis. In this respect, Durkheim was in the same fortunate situation as expressed by the head of a later sociological school:

> Close association with advanced students of such caliber has been one of the most

rewarding features of my academic career. Such young minds cannot fail, it seems to me, to have a most stimulating effect on their teachers.[107]

III

Viewed as a whole set of interrelated professional activities,[108] Durkheim's sociological work or project amounts to nothing less than devising what the late philosopher of science Imre Lakatos termed "a scientific research program"[109] (hereafter designated as SRP). One can talk of an SRP as having three major parts: (1) a "hard core" comprised of what Lakatos terms "metaphysical beliefs"; (2) an intermediary "protective belt" of positive and negative heuristics; and (3) outlying theories for subdisciplines which make empirical statements, predictions, and interpretations of differentiated sectors of the real world. Theories have linkage to one another in terms of "adherence to metaphysical beliefs, *a priori* and hence irrefutable articles of faith, which, together with methodological rules contained in positive and negative heuristics, form the hard-core of the SRP."[110]

It may be argued that Durkheim advanced an early formulation of a scientific research program (SRP) for sociology from the onset of his university career. His initial courses at Bordeaux, as I have indicated earlier, clearly manifest that he had already formulated in his mind what needed to be done for sociology to become a scientific discipline; this initial vision got progressive refinement over the years, particularly as he attracted an actual school of students and colleagues who became, in effect, a scientific research team. In this vein, one may think of his dissertation, *The Division of Labor*, as providing an announcement of the SRP, of its logic of inquiry, and of its purpose. It contains "metaphysical beliefs" or what I prefer to call "presuppositions" and it advances a theory which Durkheim will subject to falsification. Durkheim's preface makes clear what is the goal of the investigation.[111] If solidarity is a central fact of social life, a social fact par excellence, it nonetheless cannot be studied directly (for subjective and intersubjective dispositions are not physical conditions); hence the need to operationalize solidarity so that it can be studied in its overt manifestations.[112] Consequently, Durkheim spends the first chapter of his dissertation outlining both his method of investigation and the theory which will be subject to falsification: given that systems of law may be taken as externalizations of the inner core of social reality (solidarity), it is predicted that as the inner core undergoes qualitative changes from "mechanical" to "organic" solidarity, there should be manifest shifts in the ratio of types of legal systems (chiefly civil and criminal law) as a proportion of the total legal corpus. There is no need here to go over the substance of the *Division of Labor* which follows the initial chapter. But since I am using this work as illustrative of Durkheim's SRP, let me dwell on it long enough to point out that it contains both positive and negative heuristics.

As Remenyi points out, the negative heuristics of any SRP make clear "the irrefutable metaphysical propositions of the programme,"[113] and thereby indicate what is legitimate and what is illegitimate in the way of scientific explanation. Durkheim does not make it explicit, but his chief negative heuristic is that the division of labor because it is a social fact cannot be accounted for in terms of the spontaneous economic exchanges between individuals; Spencer's accounting of the division of labor is the major target of Durkheim's criticism in chapter 7 of his treatise, and Spencer is for Durkheim representative of those seeking to explain social phenomena in terms of individuals rather than in terms of social structure. Durkheim makes very clear his opposition to an *exchange* model of society which would reduce social reality to *individuals* exchanging goods and facilities with one another:

> The division of labor does not present individuals to one another, but social functions.[114]

While *The Division of Labor* does have a methodology which distinguishes this early study, it is, of course, in Durkheim's following volume, *The Rules of Sociological Method,*[115] that he provides his audience with a comprehensive set of negative and positive heuristics. In effect, this was the first primer of "how-to-do sociology," and therefore of cardinal importance in the further articulation of his SRP. It made known to would-be researchers of social phenomena how to approach "social facts," how to recognize them, and how to go about explaining them. Providing a certain standardization of operating procedures is certainly basic to the institutionalization and rationalization of a scientific discipline; Durkheim's *Rules* furnished this to members of his "research team," and it also furnished a certain tone to sociological research which "modernized" sociology. By tone I mean the objectivity and rigor of analysis which is to be found in all of the works of the Durkheimians, even when they are dealing with topics of contemporary social concern. In part, this tone, which I am tempted to call "scientific asceticism," follows from an important negative heuristic of the *Rules*, namely that when dealing with social phenomena we must bracket common sense or laymen's understandings of the phenomena being investigated: as Durkheim states it, "All preconceptions must be eradicated."[116] After this negative heuristic, Durkheim proposes what is essentially a major positive one, namely that in beginning an investigation of social facts, the investigator must articulate an operational definition of what is to be investigated.[117] This is a positive heuristic in the sense that it leads to the externalization of the research program, that is, it leads to framing of theories which can make predictive statements or propositions that can be used to codify and interpret empirical social phenomena.

This by no means does justice to the *Rules* but may suffice to give the reader an indication of where this work stands in the totality of Durkheim's sociological analysis. It has not been uniformly accepted by sociologists and even in Durkheim's day it met with considerable objections and misunderstandings. It is for all that a key to understanding the logic of inquiry which runs throughout Durkheim's "empirical" studies (*Division of Labor*, *Suicide*, *The Forms*); it also served to orient the researchers of the *Année Sociologique* into producing an organized sociological research marked by the structural differentiation of subdisciplines from the central Durkheimian "hard core."[118]

For the remainder of this section I would like to discuss various elements of the "hard core" of Durkheim's sociology, that is, of the manifold yet interrelated set of presuppositions he entertains. Since these are often interrelated with theoretical propositions about how the social world operates, this discussion will enable us to approach some of the fundamental aspects of Durkheim's sociology we have not yet covered; at the same time, we shall also at various points seek to ground further Durkheim's analysis in the sociohistorical context of his situation.

Unlike Marxism, which presupposes that the social order is real but built out of exploitative relationships, hence fundamentally an abomination, Durkheimian sociologism presupposes that the social order is more in the nature of a social body (a metaphor probably suggested to him by Schaeffle). A slight modification of the traditional dictum "*mens sano in corpore sana*" results in what might well be taken as a basic Durkheimian perspective on the relation of individual to society: "a healthy mind in a healthy society." That is, for individuals to be truly free from the constraints of physical and biological nature so as to be fully functioning persons, they need to find themselves in a well-organized society. Social rules and discipline are part and parcel of social organization, for Durkheim, and social organization, far from being *alienative*, is integrative and congenial to mental health. In brief, social health and mental health intertwine and are contingent upon a well-regulated (i.e., normatively ordered) society. This presupposition of Durkheim's is certainly what much of the analysis and argumentation of *Suicide* is all about.

Durkheim's view of society in this respect may be linked with Claude Bernard's famous concept of the *milieu interne* as the key to the physiological organization of complex living organisms. It is the *milieu interne*—the blood system and its related fluids—which through its various functions, including the keeping of a constant internal temperature, enables complex organisms to improve their adaptability to the external environment and develop. Society is the *milieu interne* of human beings, and this in a double sense: (a) relative to the physical environment, society is a mediating system which enables us to sustain adaptation to nature; and (b) the social environment is also internalized by the individual in the socialization process, becoming the human component of the self, so to speak. Socialization for Durkheim is a learning process, chiefly one of learning the normative structures of the social environment.[119] Because of this internalization of society, which Durkheim treats as the reality behind the universal notion of the "soul," the "body-soul" dualism is an apprehension of reality which is borne out by sociological reflection.[120] But society exists not only in our minds:

It also has an objective existence, in the form of institutions and their embodiments (legal systems, market systems, etc.).

Far from seeing organized society as being fundamentally immoral, Durkheim presupposes its essential moral nature; in fact, morality and society are coextensive. Social life and social organization are made possible and reflect normative arrangements. Social institutions are aggregates of these normative arrangements, which are both prescriptive and proscriptive and which cross-cut social strata. Whatever its institutional arrangement and whatever its developmental stage, the social order as such is a real moral phenomenon.[121] We cannot say that everything we find in the social world today is moral, but that is not the same as the contention that morality lies outside social structures and social organization.

For Durkheim, then, morality is a social phenomenon and social phenomena have an intrinsic moral component; of course, as a corollary, what is immoral—that is, what strikes us as against the norms and standards or morality—is also a social phenomenon. Morality is not an intrinsic attribute of things, but a quality of behavior, of social action; morality refers to moral *action,* rather than being just an individual attitude or a state of mind. What is at the heart of the notion of social order is a moral or normative ordering of interpersonal conduct. Durkheim's analysis antedates current "role theory" or "role analysis," but certainly current microsociological perspective on the role is that of a social structure linking two or more actors in terms of reciprocal normative expectations which frame or "define the situation." This perspective is a continuation of the Durkheimian presupposition of the normative or moral basis of the social order.

Similarly, although Durkheim does not use the contemporary term "deviance," he certainly takes "crime" or "criminal behavior" to be intrinsically a social phenomenon, even "an integral part of all healthy societies."[122] Criminal behavior is negative moral behavior, but such behavior is normal to society in the sense that it is the laws of society, or the collective sentiments behind the laws, which provide the bounds of behavior; without such boundaries there would be neither moral nor immoral behavior. To be sure, Durkheim also advances two other pertinent propositions, which derive from the basic presupposition, namely that punishment is also a normal phenomenon of society and that criminality may have abnormal aspects, "when its rate is unusually high."[123] If morality (and immorality) are social phenomena, it follows that different societies will have different definitions of morality and immorality, and it also follows that the normative system and the system of penal sanctions of a given society are not static but are subject to evolutionary change as the social organization alters over time.

Durkheim's analysis not only postulates the essential nexus between morality and society, but also takes as a central presupposition that society is itself a reality sui generis. At the heart of this social realism is his notion that when individuals interact, the association generates ties or bonds (such as social institutions and social roles) which are real and which cannot be deduced from the property of the individuals. The whole is greater than the sum of its parts albeit the whole would not be without its parts: Durkheim did assert the latter, it should be kept in mind, as for example when he affirmed that society would not be without the individual, "the ultimate element of groups."[124] But Durkheim's sociology gives greater weight to the distinctness of social reality, which he saw as both transcendental to any given individual, yet immanent in the natural world, that is, not a "divine creation" nor an instrument of a divine will. Social reality, then, is both constituted by and constitutive of social interaction. The interaction process is not only generative of social reality but, under certain conditions, it is also regenerative of the social order: the latter contains Durkheim's theory of religion and social change, which shall be mentioned later.

Durkheim treats social reality as multilayered, extending on a continuum of innermost spontaneity and effervescence (from which core stem collective currents of enthusiasm, panic, pessimism, etc.) to progressively more institutionalized expressions of collective endeavors; thus, at the outermost layers are objectified cultural artifacts, from law courts to courtyards.[125] From the inner to the outer, from the center to the periphery, social life represents expressions of aggregated human consciousness or "conscience collective."[126] Durkheim is a dualist in regard to consciousness, since one source of consciousness is the individual (the body), while the other is the social; it might be pointed out that this twofold subjectivity is disclosed in ordinary language, since the subjective mode contains both the singular "I" and the plural "we." Further, consciousness is cognitive and affective, and social reality as a network of intersubjective consciousness may be thought of as hyperspiritual reality.[127] Durkheim means here that if human consciousness is a spiritual activity which produces ideational representations, then the consciousness of the whole (of social life) is hyperspiritual in the sense of being vaster and distinct from the individual psychic life, from the limited consciousness of any one individual. Psychic life, or consciousness, is cognitive in the sense that we map the outer world in terms of representations, conceptualizations, classifications of the external phenomena we encounter. A second core aspect of consciousness is that it is characterized by affective elements, that is, feelings and sentiments. Among these, Durkheim will give stress to the sentiment of "solidarity," which for him is a normal or natural sentiment, not one "alien" to human nature. In terms of the broader aspects of this discussion, what should be emphasized is that although Durkheim's own attitude toward the world was certainly rationalistic, he very much recognized the fundamental affectivity, or what I would like to call the "sentience," of social being.

This undercurrent of affectivity is a theme to be found in various of Durkheim's writings. We find it in *Suicide*, particularly in book III, chapter 1, where Durkheim speaks of "collective tendencies or passions" as "forces *sui generis*."[128] Some of these collective sentiments or feelings become institutionalized; others resist the frames of institutionalization but are no less efficacious in manifesting themselves as social forces upon individuals—whether we are talking about patriotism, humanitarianism, stock market mania or depression (bull- and bear-market mentality), or even "suicidogenetic currents." Everyday social life may be structured by articulated laws, by more informal precepts and rules of conduct, by moral principles which are still vaguer in terms of being rendered explicit in language but

> beneath all these maxims are actual, living sentiments, summed up by these formulae but only as in a superficial envelope. The formulae would awake no echo if they did not correspond to definite emotions and impressions scattered through society.[129]

So we can say that Durkheim sees the real depth layer (or its innermost core) of society as an intense foyer of affectivity: this is the heart of social life. And mediating between this foyer and the external physical environment is the system of collective representations, which not only represents the environment to men, but which also reflects the organization of the collectivity. How we view the world, in other words, is not simply what is given to us in perception but is also a reflection of our internal organization; and Durkheim will take the Kantian categories, as I mentioned earlier, and interpret them sociologically, so that the cognitive ordering of the world will be ingeniously reinterpreted as reflecting the underlying social ordering of the world. But in terms of the present discussion what is particularly of interest is that Durkheim finds the ties which bind or connect things are not only social in basis but also essentially affective. Passages in the seminal essay *Primitive Classification* are particularly instructive of his perspective:

> It is thus states of the collective mind which give birth to these groupings, and these states moreover are manifestly affective. . . . it is this emotional value of notions which plays the preponderant part in the manner in which ideas are connected or separated. . . . This is how it happens that things change their nature, in a way, from society to society; it is because they affect the sentiments of groups differently.[130]

And of course, Durkheim's perspective on society as a foyer of feelings and affectivity, which are at any period in different forms of institutionalization, reaches its most dramatic expression in *The Elementary Forms of the Religious Life*. The title could have just as easily read *The Fundamental Forms of Social Life*, for while manifestly a sociological exegesis of the ethnography of Australian aborigines, it is closer to being a general treatise on social structure and social change.

First, in terms of social structure, Durkheim extends the direction of his earlier essays, notably *Primitive Classification* and "De la définition des phénomènes religieux,"[131] to view collective sentiments as becoming embodied in symbols. Not lifeless symbols of intellectual construction such as "x = f(y)," but collective representations which designate and represent affective states—emblems, flags, religious creeds, prayers, and the like. Symbols and sentiments, as fundamental features of the societal community, are seen by Durkheim to be in a dialectical relationship:

> . . . the emblem is not merely a convenient process for clarifying the sentiment society has of itself; it also serves to create this sentiment; it is one of its constituent elements.[132]

Symbols, sentiments, and social life are thus closely intertwined. Social life, Durkheim argues, "is made possible only by a vast symbolism,"[133] and without symbols, "social sentiments could have only a precarious existence."[134] Symbols, understood as collective representations, are externalizations or vehicles which represent intersubjective feelings or collective sentiments. They represent them to later generations as well as to the generation of the collectivity whose interaction has given rise to these sentiments. Symbols therefore perpetuate the social order, for in the collective songs we sing on social occasions, the prayers we recite in unison, the national anthem we rise to hear, the initiation ceremonies we partake in, the "private jokes" we share with the group, the particular handshake of a group—these and myriads of others continue and reinforce the social solidarity.

A noteworthy sentiment or attitude, which for Durkheim is of immense importance since it is the ultimate foundation of group identity, is the religious sentiment, manifest in the feeling of the *sacred*. Durkheim entertains that human consciousness differentiates the world into two categories, the category of entities which are *sacred* and those which are *profane*. Durkheim's notion of *sacred* is strikingly similar to Weber's notion of *charisma;* the recipient of the attitude for Weber is a person and for Durkheim it is more in the nature of symbols or entities, such as the totem, but the attitude is the same. Basically, toward sacred entities we take an expressive orientation, we treat sacred things as ends in themselves, whereas toward profane things we take an instrumental or utilitarian orientation—that is, profane things are means and not ends of action.

Durkheim very clearly suggests, in chapter 7, book II, of *The Forms,* that social life has two main polar modes of activity: economic life and religious life. We may view the poles as standing on an affective continuum, with quality and quantity both being operative. Economic life is dull, monotonous: "it is generally of a very mediocre intensity," and it exercises centrifugal forces on the societal community which results "in making its life uniform, languishing and dull."[135] The religious life, generated by the coming together of the collectivity in a ceremonial and dramatic occasion, is an entirely different sort of affect; it is a *festival,* a period of *enthusiasm*. Collective sentiments of stimulation become magnified in the effervescence, the mundane world is transformed into an extraordinary world, one wherein individual boundaries break down, solidarity reaches a crescendo, in the process of which even antinomian behavior may take place.[136]

One may ask whether Durkheim's analysis is intended to go beyond the situation of primitive society, and the answer has to be in the affirmative. The year before the publication of *The Forms,* Durkheim presented at the Fourth International Congress of Philosophy a very well-received communication: "Value Judgments and Judgments of Reality."[137] Besides advancing the argument that society itself is the source of values, reflected in value judgments (whether they be aesthetic, religious, political, or economic in kind), Durkheim went on to propose that values reflect ideals generated by society. It is not the routinized, institutionalized, boundary-maintaining society he has in mind (the one appropriately analyzed as a system of organs or structures and their functions).[138] Rather, it is those extraordinary circumstances and periods that mobilize the whole of the societal community, which gathers together in "moments of effervescence." It is during these moments of dramatically intense interaction, moments of collective ecstasy it might be said, that the societal community generates or regenerates its ideals. Durkheim mentions such moments as the "movements of collective enthusiasm" of the twelfth and thirteenth centuries (which led to the European student population coming in droves to the University of Paris), the Renaissance and the Reformation, the French Revolution, and the great socialist agitations of the nineteenth century. At the peak of these periods, which are crisis periods for the societal community, there is a sharp qualitative and quantitative upgrading in the nature of social interaction; social distance breaks down, people exchange ideas, feel part of a whole, and forget their banal and selfish personal preoccupations. At the peak of these periods people live in the ideal, they live out the ideal collectively, in unison. And afterward—for such periods of crises and enthusiasm cannot be sustained—collective memories of these events may take the form of festivals, national holidays, and the like, which provide the occasion for the societal community to relive, at least in partial intensity, the great periods of social ideals.[139]

What Durkheim does not mention, in this suggestive model, is what may have been his own experiences. He would have been present, in all likelihood, or at least read about, the extravagant evening of May 31, 1885, when Victor Hugo's body was displayed at the Arch of Triumph; the next day the body of the poet, who had become a national symbol, collective representation of republican and humanitarian ideals, was taken on a triumphant day-long procession for a final burial in the Pantheon. Maurice Barrès, in *The Uprooted,* provides a description of that "happening," and between the Parisian populace of 1885 and the Australian aborigines interacting when a corroboree takes place (as described in the ethnographic accounts of Howitt, and Spencer and Gillen, which Durkheim used in his analysis of *The Forms*) the distance of civilization breaks down and we are confronted with a structurally similar scene of collective behavior:

> " . . . among this crowd hardly conscious of itself, some see glory and shiver with excitement; others, feeling death, hasten to live; others yet, elbowed by hobnobbing with their coreligionists, seek to fraternize. Better yet, they unify, this fantastic mixture of enthusiasts and profligates, of simpletons and good people, organizing themselves in a single formidable being . . .[140]

And Durkheim was also witness some years later to another period of collective effervescence, namely the upheavals of the Dreyfus affair in 1898–99 when Paris in particular was the scene of wild brawls and dramatic street demonstrations between the Dreyfusards and the anti-Dreyfusards; one important function of these demonstrations was to provide solidarity within different factions in each camp. For Durkheim and the Durkheimians, who were vanguards of the Dreyfusard movement, the "Affaire" had the serendipity of giving them greater legitimation in academic ranks. The common political struggle against the right led intellectuals such as Lucien Herr, Seignobos, Lavisse, Andler, Lanson, and others who had previously had strong reservations about the Durkheimian emphasis upon the primacy of the social over the individual, upon the salience of the "conscience collective," and other parts of his "sociologism," to reconsider their distrust and oposition to sociology. After all, participation in the same political movement and adherence to the same cause can make for bonds of solidarity which override intellectual divergences.[141] And so, when Durkheim years later reflected upon the integrative function of religion vis-à-vis the societal community, it might be kept in mind that he would have experienced on at least two momentous occasions the generation and regeneration of affective ties of solidarity bringing to the fore the consciousness of belonging to a powerful societal community. Each occasion was a secular event which nevertheless for its participants took on aspects of a religious gathering, a sacred occasion.[142]

Consequently, *The Forms* may be considered both a seminal study in the sociology of religion and also perhaps a prolegomenon of a religious sociology, that is, of a sociology seeking to formulate the religious parameters necessary for modern society. Durkheim has been aptly termed "the theologian of civil religion" by Bellah;[143] what should be understood as entailed in this designation is that Durkheim (unlike many theologians) did not belittle the affective dimension of the religious life, which he saw in his later years to be the fundamental structure of the societal community, including that of modern society.[144] Durkheim in his Bordeaux period had concentrated on demonstrating that social life is nothing if it isn't a moral reality; that an amoral or anomic society is one that breeds anarchy.[145] He had terminated his study on the division of labor by affirming that the malaise of the time is not due to intellectual criticism of the moral code of society (as conservatives alleged), but to that code having lost its meaning due to changes in the organization and the characteristics of the societal community. Sociology has the urgent task, nay the duty, of discovering the appropriate morality for modern society.[146] Durkheim advanced his analysis further in *Suicide* by showing how a phenomenon as seemingly irrational and individualistic as suicide had in fact irreducible sociological dimensions; when analyzed sociologically, differentials in suicide rates bear out moral aspects of the social milieu.[147]

The Forms should be seen as an extension of his analysis, linking morality, the affective grounding of the societal community, and religion; rather than a changing orientation in Durkheim's presuppositions, it is more in the nature of what Lakatos terms a "progressive problem-shift,"[148] which adds to the heuristic power of Durkheim's fundamental SRP. It is in this work that Durkheim outlines a theory of social change stemming from the moral regeneration of the societal community and expressed in some forms of collective behavior (which is hyperaffective, it may be said). The notion of "crises" is still present in *The Forms,* but there is a shift of emphasis. For whereas before "the Affaire" there is a certain ominous or pessimistic ring to Durkheim's use of "crisis," a sense of spiritual malaise and social pathology, after the Dreyfus affair was resolved in the triumph of secular republicanism over traditionalism, the notion of "crisis" in Durkheim's analysis becomes more associated with a spring thawing than with an approaching winter. The crisis of the Dreyfus events brought to a head various sores and accumulated tensions, although it left unresolved other aspects of "the social question," such as the relation between the working class and the new industrial bourgeoisie. Under the Combes ministry, the republican goal of the secularization of education was decisively implemented, and as further consequences of the resolution of the crisis, higher education reforms were adopted in 1902,[149] which in part were beneficial to Durkheim's advancement.

Thus, the period of the Dreyfus affair was not so much a period of crisis in a negative sense as a "crucial period," to borrow the expression of Georges Balandier. It was a period of passionate rhetoric, of violent agitation in which the two great moieties of French society—the left and the right—polarized, clashed headlong, and one emerged as the dominant faction for the remainder of the Third Republic. Such a period of effervescence may be thought of as a "moment of truth" for modern society, and it heightened Durkheim's awareness of the affective and symbolic dimensions of collective life, which bridge "modern" and "pre-modern" society. Extraordinary moments in collective life, such as those Durkheim would have witnessed in 1885 and 1898–99, would be experienced by a later French generation in May 1968, by an American generation in November 1963, by a Quebec generation in October 1970. In these and other instances, subjacent societal crises would erupt in an "event" whose significance for posterity all would feel, and whose meaning would be multivalent, so that in the words of sociologist Fernand Dumont, reflecting on his own society's critical days, "One event became an extraordinary symbol."[150]

In *The Forms,* then, "crisis" has become more of a catharsis, therapeutic for societal renovation and regeneration. That the Australian aborigines need periodic ritual gathering and effervescence to experience the intensity of religious life, and thereby to reaffirm both the identity of the societal community and the validity of its normative structures which guide everyday life, is a rather easy lesson to draw from an initial reading of *The Forms.* But that modern society is also subject to the same phenomenon of periodic regeneration in crucial situations, that modern society also needs to and does experience on rare but vital occasions its "moment of truth," is a subtler lesson which is nevertheless Durkheim's intention to convey.[151]

One may say that the *Année Sociologique* group formed a microcosm of the vaster regenerated social world which Durkheim prophetically envisaged in closing his great study of religion and society. The group met as a body in Durkheim's home on the occasion of the tenth anniversary of the *Année,* and after the holocaust of the war, the remnant of the group had ceremonial or ritual occasions in the form of monthly dinner meetings, which we may see as symbolic communal feasts. This professional group, the *Année* team, was, in effect, Durkheim's own chapel. Relationships in the group exemplified that egalitarianism based on merit which Bouglé saw as the principle of justice of modern society. A common cause, that of sociology as a science, unified the group and generated the energy and devotion for the prolific professional activities of the Durkheimians; it was, so to speak, a sociological cooperative.

The cooperative was formed before the Dreyfus affair but it was that crisis—really one of a civil war—which unified the bonds of the Durkheimian band. The First World War was one of the great moral tragedies of mankind's history, but in the midst of it, Durkheim saw an outcome which might be taken as a postscript to his earlier major studies. Writing to his friend Xavier Léon in March 1915, Durkheim assessed the national situation:

> Events have shown there still is a rich vitality in our country; the latter is worth much more than those who represent and direct it. When a strong sentiment unites it, the country demonstrates its energy. What we shall have to watch over when peace returns is to keep this moral thrust. It will not be easy, for all the mediocre parties will fall upon their prey. Salvation lies in socialism casting aside its outdated formulae or in a new socialism forming itself which would take anew the French tradition. I see so clearly what this could be![152]

So the war could have been a period of collective effervescence, a crucial period of destructuration and regeneration. Durkheim did participate in the war effort—his only son's death was an ultimate cause of Durkheim's own death in November 1917, a year before the armistice; Durkheim was also hyperactive in that period, much as he had been during the Dreyfus crisis nearly twenty years earlier. He served on various faculty committees to mobilize public opinion both in France and abroad in neutral countries (including the United States) on the side of the Allies, and among his so-called "war pamphlets," his essay "Germany Above All"[153] is an analysis of German value-orientations and national character through the use of German writings, notably those of Treitschke, whom Durkheim treated as a sort of collective representation of the spirit of imperial Germany. I draw attention to this seldom-studied writing of Durkheim because however much Durkheim had strong personal feelings—shall we say, existential concerns—about the subject, the analysis is still marked by the same objective approach to social facts which constituted a cardinal precept of Durkheim's methodology. Moreover, this little essay is also an innovative use in the study of "national character," and antedated by thirty years similar attempts during the Second World War of American social scientists (such as Ruth Benedict in *The Chrysanthemum and the Sword*) to decipher the cultural code of the wartime foe through the use of the latter's own writings. So, to the last, Durkheim stuck to the canons of his methodological principles.

To speculate on what would have happened to Durkheim had he survived the war and what would have happened to sociology if the Durkheimian school had not been decimated is a tempting invitation to engage in daydreaming. Unfortunately—or fortunately—it has no place in an essay designed to present actual features of Durkheim's sociological corpus. Perhaps after we have become thoroughly familiar with his writings and after we relate structural features of our own intellectual and societal situation to his own, then can we begin to reformulate what has to be done for sociology to renovate the Durkheimian project. Moralist, philosopher, even visionary, but above all a sociological scholar and teacher par excellence, Durkheim is an appropriate role model for those seeking to identify with the best that sociology has to offer. Appreciative of the contributions of the society of yesterday and sensitive to the needs of the society of the present, he was dedicated to the positive task of articulating the social order of tomorrow. Son of the Grand Rabbin des Vosges, Emile Durkheim found his roots in becoming the "grand rabbin" of modern sociology.

Bibliographical Note: Durkheimian Studies 1968–78

The past ten years have witnessed a marked increase in the sociological literature concerning Durkheim. Probably the single most important contribution is the comprehensive intellectual portrait by Steven Lukes, *Emile Durkheim, His Life and Work* (New York: Harper and Row, 1972), which is an indispensable source book containing a splendid bibliography by and on Durkheim. Other general studies of Durkheim worth noting are Robert A. Nisbet, *The Sociology of Emile Durkheim* (New York: Oxford University Press, 1974), particularly interesting in linking Durkheim to intellectual currents of the nineteenth and twentieth centuries; Dominick LaCapra, *Emile Durkheim, Sociologist and Philosopher* (Ithaca, N. Y.: Cornell University Press, 1972), which relates at various points Durkheim's thoughts with some present contemporary issues; and Ernest Wallwork, *Durkheim, Morality and Milieu* (Cambridge: Harvard University Press, 1972), which gives in-depth coverage to Durkheim's treatment of morality. Two essays devoted to Durkheim are excellent concise introductions: Talcott Parsons's presentation of Durkheim, prepared for *The International Encyclopedia of the Social Sciences* (New York: Macmillan and Free Press, 1968), vol. 4, pp. 311–20, which is a splendid analytical and theoretical treatment, and Lewis A. Coser's chapter on Durkheim in his *Masters of Sociological Thought* (New York: Harcourt Brace Jovanovich, 1977), pp. 128–74, particularly helpful on the social context of Durkheim.

Various collections of Durkheim's writings have appeared in this time period, the outstanding one being the three-volume set compiled by Victor Karady entitled *Textes* (Paris: Les Editions de Minuit, 1975). Omitted are the original essays published in the *Année Sociologique* and other works published in book form, but the set makes available articles, communications, and reviews which would otherwise be hard to find in any single library in the United States; in addition, letters of Durkheim published here for the first time make this set an important addition to our knowledge of Durkheim. More modest in scope but of uniformly high caliber are the edited volumes of Jean-Claude Filloux, *La Science Sociale et l'Action* (Paris: Presses Universitaires de France, 1970), which are valuable for their emphasis on Durkheim's political sociology, and by Jean Duvignaud, *Journal Sociologique* (Paris: Presses Universitaires de France, 1969), whose introduction points out emergent aspects of the *Année* and Durkheim's growing dynamic conception of sociology. Among volumes making available Durkheim's writings in English, one complementing Wallwork's study while containing an excellent introductory essay is Robert N. Bellah, *Emile Durkheim on Morality and Society* (Chicago: University of Chicago Press, 1973). In the same "Heritage of Sociology" series is a volume edited by Mark Traugott, which presents the reader with first translations of a number of Durkheim's writings under the title *Emile Durkheim on Institutional Analysis* (Chicago: University of Chicago Press, 1978).

Of numerous critical studies, P. Q. Hirst's *Durkheim, Bernard and Epistemology* (London and Boston: Routledge & Kegan Paul, 1975) is the most original albeit obfuscating; other critical works include Jean Baechler, *Les Suicides* (Paris: Calmann-Lévy, 1975); Leon Sheleff, "From Restitutive Law to Repressive Law," *Archives Européennes de Sociologie* 16 (1975) pp. 16–45; and Whitney Pope, *Durkheim's Suicide: A Classic Analyzed* (Chicago: University of Chicago Press, 1976).

One should also mention the recent formation of two Durkheim study groups in Europe, since these promise a sustained output of research and publications pertaining to Durkheim and his school. In Belgium a group started by Claude Javeau began in 1976 publication of *Cahiers Durkheimiens* (contact C. Javeau at Institut de Sociologie de l' U.L.B., 44 avenue Jeanne, B-1050 Brussels). In France, Phillippe Besnard (Maison des Sciences de l'Homme, 54 Boulevard Raspail, 75006 Paris) is coordinating a broader-based, international group which also began their activities in 1976 with the publication of a special issue on Durkheim appearing in the *Revue Française de Sociologie* 17 (April–June, 1976); besides excellent analytical studies by young Durkheimian scholars, the issue is an important research document containing unpublished letters of Durkheim, texts of Durkheim not previously commented upon, and a ten-page bibliography which updates that of Lukes (1972). The same journal is scheduled to publish in 1978 a special issue on the Durkheimian school, and to facilitate an international exchange of research interest on Durkheim and his group, Dr. Besnard is editing a newsletter, "Etudes Durkheimiennes."

The past decade is also noteworthy for a growing recognition of the school that formed around Durkheim. Terry N. Clark's *Prophets and Patrons: The French University and the Emergence of the Social Sciences* (Cambridge: Harvard University Press, 1973) contains excellent descriptive materials on the *Année Sociologique* group and its institutional setting before and after the First World War. Complementing it is an extensive research report prepared by Victor Karady, "Innovation, Institutionalization de l'Innovation et Naissance de la Sociologie en France," (mimeographed; A.T.P. du CNRS No. 6348, 1974); it provides excellent qualitative and quantitative comparisons of the *Année* group with competing sociological teams. A doctoral dissertation devoted entirely to the *Année Sociologique* under Durkheim's editorship merits recognition: Yash Nandan, *L'Ecole Durkheimienne et son opus: Une Etude Empirique et Analytique de l'Année Sociologique (1898–1913)*, available in microfiche (Paris: Microeditions du Centre National de la Recherche

Scientifique, 1975). Nandan has also compiled *The Durkheimian School: A Systematic and Comprehensive Bibliography* (Westport, Conn.: Greenwood Press, 1977). Still other pertinent studies include Thomas M. Kando's "*L'Année Sociologique*, From Durkheim to Today," *Pacific Sociological Review* 19 (April, 1976) pp. 147–74, and Edward A. Tiryakian, ed., *The Durkheimian School on Sociology and Social Issues* (Chicago: University of Chicago Press, forthcoming), also in the "Heritage of Sociology" series, under the general editorship of Morris Janowitz.

NOTES

1. See the bibliographical note at the end of this chapter.

2. Terry N. Clark, "The Structure and Functions of a Research Institute: The *Année Sociologique*," *Archives Européennes de Sociologie* IX (1968) pp. 72–91.

3. See Edward A. Tiryakian, ed., *The Durkheimian School on Sociology and Social Issues* (Chicago: University of Chicago Press, forthcoming).

4. In the mid-1930s, the *Année* became differentiated into five "series," known collectively as *Annales Sociologiques*, each having an editorial committee.

5. Of course, many Durkheimians survived the First World War—in fact, the last of the contributors to the first series of the *Année*, Georges Davy, passed away as recently as 1976—and unlike other schools drawn to a strong personality (like the Saint-Simonians, the Freudians, and the Marxists), the death of Durkheim was not followed by factional splits and conflicts over interpreting what the master had taught. Yet, no one stepped forth who could combine Durkheim's role as theoretician and intellectual leader.

Still, it might be pointed out that the Durkheimian project for the unification of the behavioral or social sciences was revived after the Second World War, with a somewhat different inspiration and orientation. I have in mind the development of the "theory of action" of Talcott Parsons in the 1940s and 1950s and the concomitant establishment of the Department of Social Relations at Harvard University in 1946. There are numerous points in common between the two schools, but these cannot be discussed within the confines of the present chapter.

6. Turnover in cabinet ministries was notoriously high throughout the Third Republic. A "Président du Conseil"—equivalent of prime minister—who survived as head of government for two years or more was a distinct rarity.

7. The three major sources of liberal left thinking in the Third Republic of Durkheim are republicanism, democratic socialism (exemplified by Jean Jaurès, A. Millerand, and Albert Thomas), and Freemasonry.

8. Lewis A. Coser, "Durkheim's Conservatism and its Implications for his Sociolotical Theory," in Kurt H. Wolff, ed., *Emile Durkheim 1858–1917* (Columbus: Ohio State University Press, 1960) pp. 211–32; Robert A. Nisbet, "Social Milieu and Sources," in Robert A. Nisbet, ed., *Emile Durkheim* (Englewood Cliffs, N. J.: Prentice-Hall, 1965).

9. Albert Mathiez, *La Théophilanthropie et le culte décadaire* (Paris: Alcan, 1903); Albert Mathiez, *Contributions á l'histoire religieuse de la Révolution française* (Paris: Alcan, 1906).

10. "The Principles of 1789 and Sociology," in Edward A. Tiryakian, ed., *The Phenomenon of Sociology* (New York: Appleton-Century-Crofts, 1971) p. 43. This was first published in *Revue de l'Enseignement* in 1890.

11. In his detailed examination of the *Année* published under Durkheim's editorship, Nandan found that out of a total of 2,073 reviews appearing in the twelve volumes, "Religious Sociology" constituted the single largest category, with total of 581, or 28 percent, of the entries. See Yash Nandan, *L'Ecole Durkheimienne et son opus* (Paris: Microéditions du Centre National de la Recherche Scientifique, 1975) p. 121.

12. In 1905, during the public debates over the controversial "loi Combes" (which led to the separation of church and state and the stripping of the Catholic church of its own schools),

Durkheim stated at a meeting of the progressive l'Union pour l'Action Morale, "The Church, from a sociological perspective, is a monster." He indicated that by this he meant the Catholic church, given its territorial vastness and multiple social constituencies, should have lost its intellectual and moral homogeneity long ago; the proposed legislation, he felt, would have the beneficial effect of stimulating the differentiation of the church. See *Libres Entretiens*, 13:7 (May 1905) pp. 368–70.

13. To extend the comparison, Jaurèssian socialism was structurally along the lines of the A.D.A. wing of the Democratic Party in the United States. Guesdian socialism, directly Marxist in doctrine, was outside the parliamentary pale of party politics.

14. Such as voting against credits for military expeditions to Madagascar, or denouncing the government over the Panama scandal, or even the Dreyfus affair where Guesde's Marxist-oriented group remained aloof from the Dreyfusard cause, which it saw as of no interest to the proletariat.

15. Durkheim later acknowledged that his Bordeaux appointment was due to Liard: see his article "L'Etat actuel des études sociologiques en France" (1895) in Emile Durkheim, *Textes* (Paris: Les Editions de Minuit, 1975) comp. Victor Karady, vol. I, p. 53 (hereafter designated as *Textes*, with appropriate volume following). Liard would be for the rest of Durkheim's career his staunch supporter in the important ministry; older than Durkheim, Liard outlived him. The two pieces that caught Liard's attention were Durkheim's "La science positive de la morale en Allemagne" (1887) in *Textes* I, pp. 267–343, and "La Philosophie dans les universités allemandes" (1887) in *Textes* III, pp. 437–86.

16. Durkheim's complete life dossier as a civil servant is available at the Archives Nationales in Paris. I have consulted this as well as his dossier in the Archives Départementales de la Gironde at Bordeaux.

17. The republican regime took this as a major domestic and colonial policy. In the latter, much of the ideology of colonization was an extension of the Ferry policy of modernization via secular education. Symbolic of this is the work of Georges Hardy, at the time Inspector of Education in French West Africa, *Une Conquête Morale: L'Enseignement en A.O.F.* (Paris: Armand Colin, 1917). Furthermore, the Ecole William Ponty at Gorée (Senegal), which provided Black French Africa with outstanding cadres and represented the pinnacle of "assimilation" policy, was patterned after the Ecole Normale.

18. See Albert Thibaudet, *La République des Professeurs* (1927; Paris: Editions André Sauret, 1973).

19. Letter dated October 14, 1882, in the Durkheim dossier in the Archives Nationales Such evaluations were to accumulate with consistency in Durkheim's dossier. Thus, in filing his report on Durkheim for the year 1899–1900, the Rector (chief administrative officer) of Bordeaux answered various categories as follows. Character, behavior and social habits: "Dominant traits: initiative and authority"; Sagacity and judgment: "A remarkably vigorous mind"; Teaching: "A powerful and systematic originality"; Administrative ability: "More of a head of a school (*chef d'école*) and theoretician than a man of practical details."

20. See Ernest Wallwork, *Durkheim, Morality and Milieu* (Cambridge: Harvard University Press, 1972); Robert N. Bellah, ed., *Emile Durkheim on Morality and Society* (Chicago: University of Chicago Press, 1973).

21. Durkheim was assigned as his first position after passing the *agrégation* to teach philosophy at the Lycée du Puy; he took up duties there on October 1, 1882, but before the end of the month was assigned to the more important lycée at Sens. In January 1884 he was shifted to St. Quentin, then took a year's leave during 1885–86, and was teaching at Troyes during 1886–87 when he got word of his appointment to Bordeaux. He took a small reduction in salary doing so, since as "professeur" at Troyes he was earning 4,100 francs, while his initial appointment at Bordeaux was as a lower-ranking "chargé de cours" with a salary of 4,000 francs.

22. Undated letter in Durkheim folder, Archives Départementales de la Gironde.

23. There is a letter in Durkheim's Paris dossier dated January 7, 1880, from the Grand Rabbin du Consistoire Central des Israélites de France to the minister of education asking for remission of the 400 francs required for a student's clothing and laundry at the Ecole Normale (during Durkheim's first year there) on the ground that Durkheim's father could ill afford this expense.

24. I bother to make this point because I think Lewis Coser in his otherwise splendid chapter on Durkheim errs in stating "A Sephardic boy could have moved by almost imperceptible steps into the world of French secular culture; an Ashkenazi boy like Durkheim could not" (*Masters of Sociological Thought* [New York: Harcourt Brace Jovanovich, 1977] p. 162). Unlike Germany and Austria, where Simmel and Freud had to contend with anti-Semitism which blocked university appointments, France readily made room for all those willing to serve the republican

cause; and moreover, unlike Teutonic countries, the doors of the lodges in France were open to Jews and provided them with significant behind-the-scenes support. See Philippe Bourdrel, *Histoire des Juifs de France* (Paris: Albin Michel, 1974) esp. pp. 162–225. To be sure, anti-Semitism did break out over the Dreyfus affair and had its vocal spokesmen in figures like Drumont and Maurras, but it had no influence inside the government and institutions of higher education, which remained solidly liberal. Perhaps Durkheim was subject to the "ordeal of civility," which is dealt with so sensitively by John M. Cuddihy in a recent work, *The Ordeal of Civility: Freud, Marx, Levi-Strauss, and the Jewish Struggle with Modernity* (New York: Basic Books, 1974) but all my indications are that he stepped with ease from his familial home in Epinal to his academic home in Paris and Bordeaux. If Durkheim, Brunschvicq, Lévy-Bruhl, Berr, and other Jewish intellectuals were such strong proponents of the Third Republic, it is surely in part because its government made them feel it had merited their trust and legitimation by giving full access to talent.

25. "Cours de science sociale. Leçon d'ouverture," reproduced in J. C. Filloux, ed., *La science sociale et l'action* (Paris: Presses Universitaire de France, 1970) pp. 77–110.

26. "Introduction à la sociologie de la famille," first published in 1888 and reproduced in *Textes* III, pp. 9–34, from which citations are here taken.

27. Ibid., p. 9. This basic theme of sociology is elegantly explored anew in Robert A. Nisbet, *The Social Bond* (New York: Alfred Knopf, 1970). It may be pointed out that the theme of "solidarity" was a cornerstone of republican social doctrine. Its first major exploration was by Henri Marion in *De la Solidarité Morale, Essai de Psychologie Appliquée* (Paris: Germer Bailliere, 1880). Marion's work articulated the republican temper and aspirations so well that a chair in moral education was subsequently created for him at the Sorbonne, the very chair which Durkheim would inherit from Buisson. The theme of solidarity became an unofficial synthesis of the sacred principles of "Liberty, Equality, and Fraternity," and at the same time as it figured prominently in Durkheim's *Divison of Labor* it was a subject of much public discussion and writing. See, for example, Léon Bourgeois et al., *Essai d'une Philosophie de la Solidarité* (Paris: Félix Alcan, 1907), for representative views.

28. "Introduction," *Textes* III, p. 10.

29. Ibid., p. 11.

30. Ibid.

31. *De la division du travail social. Etude sur l'organisation des sociétes supérieures* (Paris: Félix Alcan, 1893). The standard English translation by George Simpson is *The Division of Labor in Society* (1933: New York: Free Press, 1966).

32. An English translation of the review is presented by Werner Cahnman, along with the subsequent review of Durkheim's *Division of Labor* by Tönnies. See "Tönnies and Durkheim: An Exchange of Reviews," in Werner J. Cahnman, ed., *Ferdinand Tönnies, A New Evaluation* (Leiden: E. J. Brill, 1973) pp. 239–56.

33. Durkheim in Cahnman, *Ferdinand Tönnies*, p. 246.

34. Ibid., p. 247.

35. Ibid., p. 245.

36. Much of Durkheim's political sociology, and in particular his discussion of the eufunctional role of the state in establishing what would today be called civil liberties, will be found in his *Professional Ethics and Civic Morals* (London: Routledge & Kegan Paul, 1957). This is a posthumous collection of student notes based on a course he gave several times, "Physique des moeurs et du droit."

37. Compare Alexis de Tocqueville's *The Old Regime and the French Revolution* (1856) and his *Democracy in America* (1832) with Durkheim's *Professional Ethics*, especially chap. 9.

38. *Textes* III, pp. 11–13.

39. Ibid., p. 13.

40. Ibid., p. 14.

41. *Textes* III, pp. 11ff.

42. It may be pointed out that taxonomy was a basic aspect of Durkheim's sociological research.

43. *Textes* III, p. 15.

44. Ibid., p. 16.

45. *The Elementary Forms of the Religious Life* (1912; New York: Collier, 1961) p. 19.

46. Ibid., p. 16.

47. Robert Nisbet quite correctly makes Durkheim the bridge figure in sociology between classical nineteenth century developmentalism and contemporary neodevelopmentalism. See his essay "Developmentalism: A Critical Analysis," in John C. McKinney and Edward A. Tiryakian,

eds., *Theoretical Sociology: Perspectives and Developments* (New York: Appleton-Century-Crofts, 1970) p. 193. For a recent discussion of evolutionary thought in Durkheim, see Roscoe C. Hinkle, "Durkheim's Evolutionary Conception of Social Change," *The Sociological Quarterly* 17 (Summer 1976) pp. 336–46.

It needs to be pointed out that for Durkheim there is not one universal, unilinear evolutionary development, since he invokes the image of evolution as a tree, with multiple societal branchings. His position, I would suggest, is rather similar to that of Max Weber in seeing that civilizations, once formed, have their own internal logic of development.

48. *The Forms,* p. 15. Durkheim's respect for primitive religion has been shared by subsequent social anthropologists inspired by *The Forms;* a major figure in this respect is the late Evans-Pritchard, whose students at Oxford contributed to the changed Western perspective on non-Western and nonliterate societies, especially those of Africa, by their examination of the complex and rich religious life of such peoples.

49. At the same time, Durkheim does not have the covert admiration and respect for the past that Comte does.

50. The *Année Sociologique,* viewed as a sociological laboratory or scientific research institute, illustrates the cross-fertilization between theory and research discussed years ago by Robert Merton in chaps. 2 and 3 of his classic *Social Theory and Social Structure* (New York: Free Press, 1949). For a supplementary discussion of this see Jean Carbonnier's review of the volume of Durkheim's writings edited by Jean Duvignaud (*Journal Sociologique* [Paris: Presses Universitaires de France,]), in *Année Sociologique* 3e série: 20 (1969) p. 81.

51. To illustrate the point, Durkheim makes use of the missionary and the socialist, respectively ("Introduction," *Textes* III, p. 17).

52. Ibid., pp. 18–19.

53. "Ce qui la distingue, ce n'est pas la fréquence plus ou moins grande; c'est sa vertu impérative. Elle ne représente pas simplement ce qui se fait le plus souvent, mais ce qui doit se faire," Ibid., p. 19.

It is worth noting that in making the important differentiation of two kinds of social action, those that are morally imperative (which he calls "coutumes," or customs) from those that are merely typical or part of everyday life ("simples habitudes"), Durkheim is making the distinction that was the cornerstone of William Graham Sumner's influential conceptual distinction between "mores" and "folkways." Published in 1906, Sumner's *Folkways: A Study of the Sociological Importance of Usages, Manners and Morals* (Boston: Ginn) makes no reference to Durkheim. Reciprocally, the *Année* did not review Sumner's treatise but merely listed it among other titles of new publications in its section "Moral and Juridical Sociology," vol. 11 (1906–09) p. 279. The apparent unawareness of Durkheim and Sumner is noteworthy since both shared the same view of sociology as the "science of mores," finding in mores the appropriate domain of sociological investigation which provides sociology with phenomena as natural as those studied by the physical sciences; in fact, each separately proposed that the scientific study of customs, usages, and mores be designated by the name of "ethology." Needless to say, what is today accepted as "ethology" is a very different discipline from the one envisaged by Durkheim and Sumner.

54. "La démographie, en effet, parvient à exprimer presque aujour le jour les mouvements de la vie collective," "Introduction," *Textes* III, p. 23. In the division of labor which characterized the Durkheimian school, it was Maurice Halbwachs (1877–1945) who became the specialist in demography, although Halbwachs treated demography not as an end but as a means to develop the morphological matrix of social psychology. He thus drew inspiration from this early suggestion of Durkheim.

55. Under his editorship, the *Année* published two quantitative monographs in economic sociology: François Simiand, "Essai sur le prix du charbon en France au XIXe siècle," *Année Sociologique* 5 (1900–01), and Hubert Bourgin, "Essai sur une forme d'industrie: la boucherie à Paris au XIXe siècle," *Année Sociologique* 8 (1903–04). Further, as series editor for the Travaux de l'Année Sociologique, Durkheim was responsible for the publication of Halbwachs's doctoral dissertation, *La classe ouvrière et les niveaux de vie* (Paris: Alcan, 1913).

56. Thus Dean Espinas in his annual report for 1890 wrote with pride to the rector that several students, candidates for the *agrégation* examination in French grammar, had followed the course for candidates in philosophy, and many others were taking the course in psychology, while yet others had elected the one in social science (Durkheim's). At the same time, students in the natural sciences and in law had gotten together to sponsor a social-science colloquium, dealing in particular with political economy. "Rapport du Doyen," Archives Départementales de la Gironde, T108 (1876–95).

57. Besides Espinas and Durkheim, among Durkheim's faculty colleagues who would join the

elite ranks at the Sorbonne or the College de France were the historians Ernest Denis, Camille Jullian, and Imbart de la Tour; André LeBreton (a "Normalien" classmate of Durkheim) in French literature; and philosopher Octave Hamelin, a close friend whom Durkheim refers to in the introduction of the *The Forms* as his authority for treating time and space as categories of human understanding. A brief overview of Durkheim's situation at Bordeaux is presented by R. René Lacroze, "Emile Durkheim à Bordeaux," *Actes de l'Académie de Bordeaux*, 4e série: XVII (1960–61). Bordeaux: Hôtel des Sociétés Savantes, 1962.

58. Symbolic of this identification is the photograph of Durkheim taken in 1911 showing in the background a photo having the likeness of Comte. See Georges Davy, *Emile Durkheim* (Paris: Louis-Michaud, n.d. [c. 1911]) p. 9.

59. Durkheim credited Comte with having the idea that human societies, like the physical universe, are subject to natural laws (1904, *Textes* I, p. 166), but here as elsewhere (1903, *Textes* I, pp. 129–51; 1915, *Textes* I, pp. 109–18) Durkheim emphasizes that for Comte sociology was part of a philosophy of history, the crowning achievement of philosophical positivism to be sure, but *not* an empirical science. Comte's notion of progress and the law of three stages were not scientific inductions for Durkheim but rather a priori metaphysical principles; a further source of distaste was that Durkheim saw Comte's positivism as a one-man show, hence not really a science which, for Durkheim, is characterized by a division of labor and cumulative development. See in *Textes* I, p. 127–28, the relevant passage from the famous article (1903) by Durkheim and Fauconnet, "Sociologie et sciences sociales," originally published in *Revue Philosophique*, 55, pp. 465–97.

60. After all, Durkheim did declare on a public occasion in 1914: "J'ai souvent reconnu que je relevais de Comte," *Textes* I, p. 68.

61. See the insightful discussion provided by Célestin Bouglé, "Auguste Comte et le Grand Etre," in his *Cours de Sociologie Générale* (mimeographed; Paris: Centre de Documentation Universitaire, c. 1935) pp. 46–53.

62. Their designation as "reactionaries" places their works on the secular index. But if one can temporarily shelve one's political inclinations, de Bonald's *Du Divorce* (1805) and de Maistre's *Du Pape* (1819) have a surprisingly modern systems approach. Consider, thus, the opening statement of de Bonald's critique of divorce legislation:

> A chief source of errors, in dealing with a social question, is to treat it in isolation and without relation to other questions. Society itself is a set of relations and ties; in the social body, like in every organized body (that is, one whose parts are interrelated towards a determinate end), the ceasing of vital functions does not arise from the destruction of parts but from their displacement and from the disordering of their ties (*Du Divorce*, 2d ed. [Paris: Adrien Leclere, 1805] p. 1).

63. Saint-Simon's sociological analysis takes as its basic unit that of the social class, rather than the individual. Among other things, he is the pioneer of social stratification.

64. For a recent perspective, see Robert Alun Jones and Robert M. Anservitz, "Saint-Simon and Saint-Simonism: A Weberian View," *American Journal of Sociology* 80 (March 1975) pp. 1095–1123.

65. "La Sociologie" (1915) in *Textes* I, p. 110.

66. Marcel Mauss put together Durkheim's lecture notes and brought out *Le Socialisme* (Paris: Félix Alcan, 1928). The English translation, with an introduction by Alvin Gouldner, is *Socialism and Saint-Simon* (Yellow Springs, Ohio: The Antioch Press, 1958). Gouldner's comments bear more on differences between Durkheim and Comte than on the relation of Durkheim to Saint-Simon and Saint-Simonism. In the text, I am using the new French edition of *Le Socialisme* (Paris: Presses Universitaires de France, 1971). The preface by Pierre Birnbaum (pp. 5–26) is informative and insightful.

The stimulus for the course was student interest in the national political scene. In 1893 various socialist factions (excepting the Marxist one which refused to stand for election) had gotten a total of 50 parliamentarians elected and became a vigorous opposition bloc, although lacking ideological unity. It was logical for Durkheim to examine socialism as an instance of collective representations since several of his close friends, colleagues, and students (Jaurès, Herr, Mauss, Simiand, Lévy-Bruhl) were involved in the fortunes of socialism. Perhaps Durkheim in treating socialism objectively as a social fact may have intended to demonstrate that the sociological method could yield practical results: in the context of socialism, a rigorous sociological analysis might uncover the bases of unification for the various French socialist factions. It is interesting to note that just as he would subsequently in studying modern religion go back to its primitive source in totemism, so also in studying contemporary socialism Durkheim went back to its primitive expression in Saint-Simonism.

For a scholarly treatment of socialism in France in the 1890s, see Daniel Ligou, *Histoire du Socialisme en France (1871–1961)* (Paris: Presses Universitaires de France, 1962) chap. 4.

67. *Le Socialisme*, p. 120. Compare with Durkheim's statement in *The Division of Labor*, p. 364: "Philosophy is the collective conscience of science."

68. *Le Socialisme*, p. 122.

69. *The Division of Labor*, p. 408.

70. Ibid., p. 409.

71. Compare with *The Division of Labor*, p. 190: ". . . we may be permitted to predict . . . that a day will come when our whole social and political organization will have a base exclusively, or almost exclusively, occupational."

72. *Le Socialisme*, p. 190.

73. Ibid., pp. 191–92.

74. Note in particular the second section of Durkheim's chapter on anomic suicide in *Suicide* (New York: Free Press, 1963) pp. 246–54. In those pregnant pages, Durkheim anticipates notions of relative deprivation and the revolution of rising expectations.

75. Space consideration prevents a discussion of Saint-Simon's views, as presented and commented by Durkheim, concerning the dissolution of national political boundaries by the industrial order is the macro level and the breaking up of inherited private property at the micro level; both of these are necessary, argued Saint-Simon, if the full productive potential of the industrial order is to be realized. These Saint-Simonian themes are echoed in Durkheim's later teachings; for example, see the concluding chapter of *Professional Ethics and Civic Morals*.

76. *Le Socialisme*, p. 207.

77. Ibid., p. 208.

78. Ibid., p. 214.

79. Ibid., p. 218.

80. See Marcel Mauss, "In Mémoriam: l'oeuvre inédite de Durkheim et de ses collaborateurs," *L'Année Sociologique*, n.s. (1925), reprinted in Mauss, *Oeuvres*, comp. Victor Karady (Paris: Les Editions de Minuit, 1969) vol. 3, p. 475.

81. *Le Socialisme*, p. 219.

82. Ibid., p. 231.

83. I take this phrase from the novel of Maurice Barrès, *Les Déracinés*, which will be discussed shortly.

84. Anarchism was a strong, vocal intellectual current for at least the first thirty years of the Third Republic, even if its followers were relatively a very small number. One of its many sources of inspiration was Nietzsche. Among others, one of the first to militate for the rehabilitation of Captain Dreyfus was Bernard Lazare, a major figure in anarchist circles, and through Lazare and Lucien Herr, Durkheim (who, of course, had a strong distaste for anarchism as a doctrine) came to realize what was involved in the Dreyfus affair.

85. In support of this, there is no better authority than Max Weber: see footnote 58, chap. 5, of his famous essay, *The Protestant Ethic and the Spirit of Capitalism*, trans. Talcott Parsons (New York: Charles Scribner's Sons, 1958) p. 270.

86. See Jean-Pierre Azéma and Michel Winock, *La IIIe République (1870–1940)* (Paris: Calmann-Lévy, 1970) pp. 105–81, for an excellent discussion of social structure and political orientations in the period 1880–1918.

87. *Les Déracinés* is the first volume of a trilogy entitled *L'Energie Nationale* by Maurice Barrès, published in 1897. I will refer to it in the edition *L'Oeuvre de Maurice* Barrès (Paris: Au Club de l'Honnête Homme, 1965) vol. 3.

88. *Les Déracinés*, p. 20.

89. Ibid., p. 21.

90. Ibid., pp. 28f.

91. See, for example, his 1906 communication before the French Philosophical Society, "The Determination of Moral Facts," in Emile Durkheim, *Sociology and Philosophy* (1924; New York: Free Press, 1974) pp. 35–62.

92. Ibid., p. 36.

93. *L'Education Morale* (Paris: Félix Alcan, 1925, 1938). An English edition with a new introduction by Everett K. Wilson is available as *Moral Education, A Study in the Theory and Application of the Sociology of Education* (New York: Free Press, 1973).

94. The state of anomie is a major preoccupation of Durkheim in his studies *which precede the Dreyfus affair*. The resolution of that crisis and the subsequent strong ministries of Waldeck-

Rousseau and Emile Combes may have cleared the air of competing political paradigms, so to speak: the "morale laïque" and the republican cause had a decisive victory. Whether or not this accounts for it, Durkheim no longer used the term "anomie" after the turn of the century.

95. I take the notion of "societal community" from Talcott Parsons, since it is highly applicable to Durkheim's analysis of society. As Parsons expresses it:

The core structure of a society I will call the societal community. More specifically at different levels of evolution, it is called tribe, or "the people," . . . or, for the modern world, *nation*. It is the collective structure in which members are united or, in some sense, associated. Its most important property is the kind and level of solidarity—in Durkheim's sense—which characterizes the relations between its members (Talcott Parsons, "Social Systems," *International Encyclopedia of the Social Sciences,* [New York: Macmillan and Free Press, 1968] vol. 15, p. 461).

96. "The capacity for containing our inclinations, for restraining ourselves—the ability that we acquire in the school of moral discipline—is the indispensable condition for the emergence of reflective, individual will. The rule, because it teaches us to restrain and master ourselves, is a means of emancipation and freedom," *Moral Education,* pp. 48–49.

97. "De quelques formes primitives de classification. Contribution à l'étude des représentations collectives," *L'Année Sociologique* 6 (1901–02) pp. 1–72. English trans. with an introduction by Rodney Needham, *Primitive Classification,* (London: Cohen and West, 1963).

98. See Mary Douglas, *Implicit Meanings* (London and Boston: Routledge & Kegan Paul, 1975) p. 204.

99. See Harold Garfinkel, *Studies in Ethnomethodology* (Englewood Cliffs, N.J.: Prentice-Hall, 1967); Paul Filmer et al., *New Directions in Sociological Theory* (London: Collier-Macmillan, 1972); Roy Turner, ed., *Ethnomethodology* (Baltimore, Md.: Penguin Books, 1974); Aaron V. Cicourel, "Ethnomethodology," in his *Cognitive Sociology* (New York: Free Press, 1974) pp. 99–140.

100. For a brief exposition, see my *Sociologism and Existentialism* (Englewood Cliffs, N.J.: Prentice-Hall, 1962).

101. Edward A. Tiryakian, "Durkheim and Husserl: A Comparison of the Spirit of Positivism and the Spirit of Phenomenology," in Joseph Bien, ed., *Phenomenology and the Social Sciences* (The Hague: Martinus Nijhoff, 1977).

102. *The Forms*, p. 492.

103. Edmund Husserl, *The Crisis of European Sciences and Transcendental Phenomenology* (Evanston, Ill.: Northwestern University Press, 1970).

104. "Preface," *Année Sociologique* 1 (1896–1897) pp. ii–iii. For perceptive comments in this context, see Robert N. Bellah, "Durkheim and History," *American Sociological Review* 24 (August 1959) pp. 447–61; Robert Nisbet, *The Sociology of Emile Durkheim* (New York: Oxford University Press, 1974), pp. 258–60.

105. Writing in 1902, Durkheim mentioned that he owed much to the Germans, but five years later, when the Kaiser's policies had turned French public opinion against almost anything coming from across the Rhine, Durkheim defended himself from the accusations of Monsignor Deploige that he was one of those introducing into the Sorbonne German propaganda camouflaged as "sociology" (see *Textes* I, pp. 400–07, for Durkheim's declarations). During the First World War, a French senator on the occasion of a discussion on German espionnage made an allegation of Durkheim as a Sorbonne representative of the German "Kriegsministerium"; outraged, Louis Liard as Vice Rector of the Academy of Paris set the wheels in motion which led to the public rectification of this slander (Durkheim dossier in the Archives Nationales, letter of Liard dated March 27, 1916). I mention this since the German influence on Durkheim had political as well as intellectual ramifications.

106. For an excellent presentation of Smith and his influence on Durkheim's sociology of religion, see Thomas O. Beidelman, *W. Robertson Smith and the Sociological Study of Religion* (Chicago: University of Chicago Press, 1974). The reading of Smith's *Lectures on the Religion of the Semites* marked a turning point for Durkheim, not only because it suggested to him where one might go to find one of the main roots and foundations of Western religion and civilization, but also, I venture to say, because it enabled Durkheim to rediscover his own roots in orthodox Judaism with its rich symbolism and rituals. It is a great experience for an academic to rediscover intellectually that to which he has existential ties. Smith's *Lectures* may have been as pregnant for Durkheim as Baxter and Bunyan had been for Weber.

107. Talcott Parsons, "On Building Social System Theory: A Personal History," *Daedalus* 99 (Fall 1970) p. 842.

108. The major sociological activities of Durkheim were: (1) author of pioneering sociological investigations in such fields as industrial sociology (*Division of Labor*), deviance (*Suicide*),

methodology (*Rules*), sociology of knowledge (*Primitive Classification, Forms*), sociology of education (*L'Evolution pedagogique en France*), etc; (2) university professor offering first courses in sociology at university level and director of graduate training; (3) editor of the *Année* and series editor of its later "Travaux"; in effect, his editorial work was that of a laboratory director, enabling younger members of his team to get professional recognition and advancement as a result of publishing in a scholarly, high-quality series; and (4) a propagandizer for giving sociology legitimation in academic and intellectual circles by virtue of his participation in other learned societies and journals.

109. Imre Lakatos and Alan Musgrave, eds., *Criticism and the Growth of Knowledge* (London: Cambridge University Press, 1974) pp. 91–196. My attention to Lakatos has been drawn as a result of a remarkable study which demonstrates his applicability to the development of economics: Joseph V. Remenyi, "Core-Demi-Core Interaction in Economics" (mimeographed, Ph.D. thesis, Durham, N.C.: Duke University, 1976). Since I consider the conceptualization of Lakatos and Remenyi very fruitful for treating the Durkheimian school as a whole, a more adequate and elaborate discussion of this significant new approach, which I think is more comprehensive than the Kuhnian perspective, will be found in my introduction to *The Durkheimian School on Sociology and Social Issues*.

110. Remenyi, "Core-Demi-Core Interaction," p. 38.

111. "This book is pre-eminently an attempt to treat the facts of the moral life according to the method of the positive sciences," *Division of Labor*, p. 32.

112. ". . . solidarity . . . is a social fact we can know only through the intermediary of social effects," *Division of Labor*, p. 67.

113. Remenyi, "Core-Demi-Core Interaction," p. 39.

114. *Division of Labor*, p. 407. Needless to say, Spencerian sociology may seem outmoded today but the exchange model keeps surfacing, in such figures as George Homans, Peter Blau, Erving Goffman, and Claude Lévi-Strauss. Of course, Mauss's *The Gift* is an exchange model, one which may be viewed as exemplifying Durkheimian structural-functional analysis: economic exchanges are analyzed in terms of underlying normative, societal structures and in terms of their further consequences for social organization; the obligatory aspects of gift-giving, gift-receiving, gift-exchanging cannot be deduced from the volition of the specific actors. These aspects of the exchange are part of the psychosocial dimensions of role relationships and in turn are part of "the total social phenomenon." I mention this because Mauss's study, an exemplar in its own right of structural-functional analysis and prototypical of sociological exchange models, may also be seen as based or derived from *The Division of Labor*. Hence, rather than being treated in itself, it should be seen as one implementation of Durkheim's SRP. *The Gift* was first published in French in 1925, in *l'Année Sociologique*, 2e ser., vol. 1 (1923–1924) pp. 30–186. The English edition (full title: *The Gift: Forms and Function of Exchange in Archaic Societies*) was published by Free Press, New York, 1954.

115. *The Rules of Sociological Method* (1895, French; New York: Free Press, 1950).

116. *Rules*, p. 31. Durkheim suggests in so many words this is a negative heuristic when he comments "As it happens, this first rule for sociology is entirely negative. It teaches the sociologist to escape the realm of lay ideas and to turn his attention towards facts . . ." *Rules*, p. 34. I use the word "bracket" to suggest a similarity in Durkheim's procedure and that of Husserl's phenomenological method, both of which I consider to deal fundamentally with the analysis of structures.

117. "In order to be objective, the definition must obviously deal with phenomena not as ideas but in terms of their inherent properties," *Rules*, p. 35. This aspect of his methodological principles was followed by Durkheim in all his sociological studies (on suicide, religion, socialism, etc.).

118. In his own research, Remenyi has found it useful to modify the Lakatos conceptualization of the SRP by introducing the notion of "demi-core," which pertains to the presuppositions of a subdiscipline derived from the structural differentiation of the "hard core" of the discipline as a whole. This applies not only to his study of the development of economics but also to the development of sociology in the Durkheimian school.

119. "The aim of education is, precisely, the socialization of the human being," *Rules*, p. 6.

120. Durkheim's discussion of self, individuality, and personality—in a sense, a formulation of his microsociology—is largely developed in a late essay (1914), available in English as "The Dualism of Human Nature," in Wolff, *Emile Durkheim*, pp. 325–40.

Durkheim's conception of the dual aspects of the self and the two modes of consciousness arising from this (i.e., individual and collective or social consciousness) is structurally similar to George H. Mead's duality of the self, since the "I" has its base in the biological system and the "me" or "generalized other" develops from the internalization of the societal community.

Although cognizant of Comte, Mead seemed to have little exposure to Durkheim and was probably unacquainted with Durkheim's 1914 essay.

121. There is a twofold aspect to "moral": it should be taken as both that which is ethical or normative *and* that which is nonmaterial, i.e., psychological. To reiterate, for Durkheim, social life is psychological in the sense of being intersubjective, hence his willingness to state that sociology is a social psychology.

122. *Rules*, p. 67. See also Durkheim's "Deux Lois de l'Evolution Pénale," *Année Sociologique* 4 (1899-1900) pp. 65-95.

123. *Rules*, p. 66.

124. "Le Dualisme," in Wolff, *Emile Durkheim*, p. 206.

125. *Rules*, chap. 1. The examples suggested are my own.

126. For Durkheim's theory of mind, memory, and consciousness, see his "Individual and Collective Representations," in Durkheim, *Sociology and Philosophy* (New York: Free Press, 1974), pp. 1–34.

127. Ibid., p. 34.

128. *Suicide*, p. 307.

129. Ibid., p. 315.

130. *Primitive Classification*, pp. 85–86.

131. "De la définition des phénomenes religieux," *L'Année Sociologique* 2 (1897–98) pp. 1–28.

132. *The Forms*, p. 262.

133. Ibid., p. 264.

134. Ibid., p. 262.

135. Ibid., p. 246. In *Rules* (p. 114) Durkheim suggests that it even has a divisive element: ". . . purely economic relations leave men *estranged* from one another. . ." (emphasis mine).

136. *The Forms*, p. 247.

137. First published in 1911, and reproduced in *Sociology and Philosophy*, pp. 80–97. It might be mentioned that at this Bologna Congress were such outstanding figures of the intellectual world as Bergson, Mach, Lévy-Bruhl, Michels, Ortega y Gasset, H. Poincaré, Steiner and Windelband, among others. Durkheim had not attended the Third International Congress held at Heidelberg in 1908; Max Weber had attended that one but was not present at Bologna.

138. *Sociology and Philosophy*, pp. 90–91.

139. Ibid., p. 92. For a fascinating sociological presentation of the Paris May 1968 "events" which illustrates this discussion, see Alfred Willener, *The Action-Image of Society* (London: Tavistock, 1970).

140. Barrès, *Les Déracinés*, p. 333.

141. For an insider's perspective on the rapprochement of the Durkheimians and their university colleagues stemming from "the affaire," see Célestin Bouglé, "L'Année Sociologique," in *Pages Libres* 353 (October 5, 1907) esp. p. 347.

142. The Dreyfus affair was, for the opposite camps, a sacred combat between two polar sets of ideals. As to the Victor Hugo "happening," it should be recalled that Hugo remained anticlerical to his deathbed and that the Pantheon, where he was buried, became a sort of symbolic Valhalla of the Third Republic.

143. Bellah, *Emile Durkheim on Morality and Society*, p. xvii. It is because of Bellah's perceptive writings that I have come to realize the nexus between Durkheim's overall sociology and the theme of civil religion. See also Ruth A. Wallace, "A Source of Civil Religion: Emile Durkheim" (mimeographed; paper presented at the 1975 meeting of the Society for the Scientific Study of Religion).

144. Recall that in *The Forms* Durkheim takes religion to be "the serious life" (*la vie sérieuse*). However much of Durkheim's social realism has points in common with Marx's social realism, they ultimately stand in naked contrast as to what constitutes the infrastructure of social reality. For Durkheim, particularly the Durkheim of *The Forms*, it is in the religious life that the infrastructure of the societal community is to be found; the "deep structure" of social organization and societal change is to be found in the complexity of religion and its symbolism. For Marx, needless to say, the "serious life" is generated by socioeconomic relationships. Where Durkheim finds the infrastructure, there Marx finds the superstructure.

145. It might be borne in mind that at the very time that Durkheim was publishing *The Division of Labor* and *Suicide*, which give a prominent place to *anomie* as the pathological condition of social organization, France was rocked by a wave of violent *anarchism*. One may see a certain overlap between the two, since anomie and anarchy involve a repudiation or a breakdown of the regulations of social life.

146. "In short, our first duty is to make a moral code for ourselves," *The Division of Labor*, p. 409.

147. As an exemplar paradigm of modern sociological research, *Suicide* needs no introduction. Less obvious is that it constitutes a key part of the Durkheimian "manifesto" establishing the claims of sociology as an autonomous science. As any manifesto, consequently, it has a polemical aspect. It is patently a polemic against physical anthropology and biological racism. *Suicide* also contains an attack that Durkheim carried on for years against Gabriel Tarde (even after the latter's death) for his explanation of social behavior in terms of an individualistic microsociology; chap. 5 by its very title, "Imitation," makes clear who is the intended target of its criticisms. This was frankly recognized by one of Durkheim's ablest lieutenants, François Simiand, appraising *Suicide* in his "L'Année Sociologique 1897," *Revue de Métaphysique et de Morale* 6 (1898) pp. 608–53.

Ironically, the statistics Durkheim and Mauss used in drawing up the tables which helped make *Suicide* such a monumental monograph were provided to them by the Head of the Bureau of Legal Statistics in the Ministry of Justice: Tarde himself! For a discussion of the Durkheim-Tarde conflict see Terry N. Clark's introduction to Gabriel Tarde, *On Communication and Social Influence* (Chicago: University of Chicago Press, 1969) esp. pp. 7–18. Since the anti-Tarde polemic lasted so long, well after Tarde's death, and since Tarde's son, Alfred de Tarde, became active in conservative circles and attacked curricular and other reforms of "the New Sorbonne" which he saw as taking away the true French national spirit, I suspect that underlying or reinforcing the conflict were personal differences, perhaps political ones.

148. Lakatos and Musgrave, eds., *Criticism and the Growth of Knowledge*, p. 137. For a concise discussion of "progressive" and "degenerative" problem shifts, see Remenyi, "Core-Demi-Core Interaction," p. 40.

149. See Viviane Isambert-Jamati, "Une réforme des lycées et collèges. Essai d'analyse de la réforme de 1902," *Année Sociologique*, 3e série: 20 (1969) pp. 9–60.

150. Fernand Dumont, *The Vigil of Quebec* (Toronto and Buffalo: University of Toronto Press, 1974) p. 98.

151. "There can be no society which does not feel the need of upholding and reaffirming at regular intervals the collective sentiments and the collective ideals which make it its unity and its personality . . . . the old gods are growing old or already dead, and others are not yet born. . . . But this state of incertitude and confused agitation cannot last for ever. A day will come when our societies will know again those hours of creative effervescence, in the course of which new ideas arise and new formulae are found which serve for a while as a guide to humanity . . ." *The Forms*, p. 475.

152. Letter of March 30, 1915, to Xavier Léon, in *Textes* II, p. 478.

153. "*Germany Above All*": *German Mentality and the War* (Paris: Armand Colin, 1915).

7

POSITIVISM AND ITS CRITICS

ANTHONY GIDDENS

"POSITIVISM" has today become more of a term of abuse than a technical term of philosophy. The indiscriminate way in which the term has been used in a variety of different polemical interchanges in the past few years, however, makes all the more urgent a study of the influence of positivistic philosophies in the social sciences.

I shall distinguish two main ways in which "positivism" may be taken, one quite specific, the other much more general. In the more restrictive sense, the term may be taken to apply to the writings of those who have actively called themselves positivists or at least have been prepared to accept the appellation. This yields two major phases in the development of positivism, one centered mainly in social theory, the other concerned more specifically with epistemology. The earlier phase is that dominated by the works of the author who coined the term "positive philosophy," Auguste Comte. Although there are obvious contrasts between Comte's positivism and the "logical positivism" of the Vienna Circle, there are equally clear connections—both historical and intellectual—between the two. However, the term may also be employed more broadly and diffusely to refer to the writings of philosophers who have adopted most or all of a series of connected perspectives: phenomenalism—the thesis, which can be expressed in various ways, that "reality" consists of sense impressions; an aversion to metaphysics, the latter being condemned as sophistry or illusion; the representation of philosophy as a method of analysis, clearly separable from, yet at the same time parasitic upon, the findings of science; the duality of fact and value—the thesis that empirical knowledge is logically discrepant from the pursuit of moral aims or the implementation of ethical standards; and the notion of the "unity of science"—the idea that the natural and social sciences share a common logical and perhaps even methodological foundation.

In this chapter, I shall use the term "positivism" without qualification to refer, in the appropriate context, to the views of Comte and subsequently to those of the leading figures of the Vienna Circle—in other words, to those who have been prepared to call themselves positivists. I shall use "positivistic philosophy" to designate views that embody important elements among those mentioned in the second category. In this sense, positivistic strains are much more widely represented in the history of philosophy, overlapping with empiricism, than would be suggested if attention were confined to self-proclaimed "positivism."

However, I also want to distinguish a third category, which I shall call, for want of a better name, "positivistic sociology." We owe to Comte both the term "positivism" and the term "sociology"; in his writings, the two are closely conjoined, since the coming into being of sociology is supposed to mark the final triumph of positivism in human thought. The connection has been a fateful one for the subsequent development of the social sciences, for certain leading traditions in social thought over the past hundred years have been considerably influenced by the kind of logical framework established by Comte in his *Cours de philosophie positive*. As mediated by Durkheim, this framework is closely tied in to modern functionalism. But the influence of positivistic philosophy as defined above in sociology (and in Marxism) has ranged much more widely than this. Here sociology is conceived of as a "natural science of society" which can hope to reproduce a system of laws directly similar in form to those achieved in the natural sciences. In positivistic sociologies, at least, as formulated over the past four or five decades especially in the United States, all three senses of "positivism" I have just distinguished to some extent recombine. Several of the prominent members of the Vienna Circle emigrated to the United States and have exerted a strong influence over the development of philosophy there, particularly with regard to the philosophy of science. Their conception of the philosophy of science has in turn been appropriated, explicitly or otherwise, by many authors writing in the social sciences, and it has proved particularly compatible with the ideas of those drawing heavily upon the sorts of views expressed by Comte and by Durkheim.

In this chapter, I shall begin by discussing the positivism of Comte and its similarities to and differences from the logical positivism of the Vienna Circle. From there, I shall move to a consideration of two partly convergent critiques of positivistic philosophies more generally conceived: one, the so-called "newer philosophy of science," emanating mainly from within the English-speaking world; the other, "Frankfurt philosophy" or critical theory, originating primarily in long-established German philosophical traditions.

Auguste Comte: Sociology and Positivism

In crude summary, we may differentiate several major elements in the intellectual background of Comte's writings. One is the frontal assault on metaphysics undertaken in eighteenth-century philosophy, above all in the works of Hume and his followers in British empiricism, and sustained in different form in Kant's "critical idealism." Comte went further than such authors, not only in accepting the success of the destruction of transcendental illusions, but in formally embodying the metaphysical stage in the evolution of humanity as a phase superseded by the advent of positivist thought. In this respect, he accepted one of the fundamental aims of the writers of the Enlightenment, as he did important aspects of the rationalist critique of established religion. In Comte's scheme of history, the theological stage of thought is relegated to a phase prior to the metaphysical—both, to be sure, regarded as necessary stages in social evolution, but both being dissolved once and for all when positivism triumphs. If Comte himself came to the rediscovery of religion, it was because he combined these aspects of Enlightenment philosophy with a deep-rooted aversion to the methodical critique of inherited authority that was basic to the writings of the *philosophes*. Comte rejected the essential idea of "Enlightenment" itself: that the Middle Ages were also the Dark Ages, whose repudiation opens up the way to revolutionary changes in human intellectual and social life. In place of this Comte substituted a progressivism influenced by the "retrograde school" of authors—conservative apologists for Catholicism, reacting against Enlightenment radicalism and against the 1789 revolution which was its heir—such as Bonald, de Maistre, and others. Comte's positivism preserves the theme of progress but undercuts the radicalism with which this was associated in Enlightenment philosophy. "Progress" and "order" are more than reconciled: the one becomes dependent upon the other. Positive thought replaces the "negative" outlook of the *philosophes*, the perspective that a new dawn can be achieved through the shattering of the past.

Of course, Comte owed many of his ideas most immediately to Saint-Simon, who in turn was considerably indebted to Condorcet and Montesquieu, who both had tempered the enthusiasms of the Enlightenment with a rigidly applied version of the subservience of society to natural laws of development. Condorcet assigned to history the same kind of potentialities that Comte was later to allocate to the positive science of sociology, expressed in the famous phrase "*savoir pour prévoir, prévoir pour pouvoir.*" Condorcet looked to the past to supply the moving principles of evolution whereby the future could be made open to human intervention. Hence he took to task those who arrogantly supposed that it is possible to achieve social change in massive fashion *ex nihilo*. The progress of mankind achieves equilibrium in such a way that, while the pace of development can be speeded or retarded by active human intervention, it has the character of an autonomous force for betterment. I shall not take up the vexed issue of just how directly Comte plundered Saint-Simon's ideas in constructing his own system, a matter of great acrimony in the relations between the two thinkers after Comte broke away from the tutelage of his mentor. Whatever their immediate provenance, it can be remarked without undue simplification that Comte's writings constitute one direction of development out of Saint-Simon, that which gave "sociology" its name and established a logical framework for the supposedly new science. The other direction is that taken by Marx, in which elements of Saint-Simon's ideas are reconnected to revolutionary social transformation.[1]

That Comte entitled the first of his two major works *Cours de philosophie positive* should not blind us to the fact that the work actually declares an end to philosophy as previously practiced: as an independent enterprise separable from the achievements of science. "Positive philosophy" is perhaps not, as Marcuse suggests, a contradiction *in adjecto*.[2] But it does reduce philosophy to expressing the emergent synthesis of scientific knowledge. The "true philosophic spirit," Comte says, incorporates the "essential attributes . . . summed up in the word *positive*." These include, first of all, an orientation to "reality" and to "utility": the useless endeavors of speculative philosophy to penetrate behind appearances are disavowed. But the term also implies—in all the European languages, according to Comte—"certainty" and "precision," attributes which similarly distinguish the intellectual life of modern man from his predecessors. Finally, also suggested by the term are an "organic tendency" and a "relativist outlook." The former of these refers to the constructive character of the positivist spirit: by contrast, "the metaphysical spirit is incapable of organizing; it can only criticize." The latter seals the rejection of absolutism as characteristic of metaphysical philosophy: the laws that govern the covariance of phenomena always retain a provisional character, since they are induced on the basis of empirical observation, rather than being posited as "absolute essences."[3]

In the *Cours*, the relation between the various sciences is claimed to be hierarchical, in both an analytical and a historical sense, the second being explained in terms of the renowned law of the three stages of human intellectual development. Analytically, Comte makes clear, the sciences form a hierarchy of decreasing generality but increasing complexity; each particular science logically depends upon the ones below it in the hierarchy and yet at the same time deals with an emergent order of properties that cannot be reduced to those with which the other sciences are concerned. Thus biology, for example, presupposes the laws of physics and chemistry insofar as all organisms are physical entities which obey the laws governing the composition of matter; on the other hand, the behavior of organisms as complex beings cannot be directly derived from those laws. Sociology, at the apex of the hierarchy of sciences, logically presupposes the laws of each of the other scientific disciplines while similarly retaining its autonomous subject matter.

The logical relations between the sciences, according to Comte, provide the means of interpreting their successive formation as separate fields of study in the course of the evolution of human thought. The sciences which developed first—mathematics and astronomy, then physics—were those dealing with the most general or all-enveloping laws in nature that govern phenomena most removed from human involvement and manipulation. From there, science penetrated more and more closely to man himself, moving through chemistry and biology to its culmination in the science of human conduct—originally labeled "social physics" by Comte, then redubbed "sociology." The process is not achieved without struggle; scientific understanding lies at the end of the progression of intellectual life through the theological and metaphysical stages. Human thought as a whole, as well as each science taken separately, progress through the theological, the metaphysical, and the positive stages. In the theological stage, the universe is comprehended as determined by the agency of spiritual beings; this stage—*l'état fictif,* as Comte calls it—is "the necessary point of departure of the human intellect," and it reaches its climax in Christianity with its recognition of one all-powerful deity.[4] The metaphysical phase replaces these moving spirits with abstract essences, thereby clearing the ground for the advent of science, *l'état fixe et definitif* of thought. The enunciation of the law of the three stages, Comte says, is enough "that its correctness should be immediately confirmed by anyone who has a sufficiently profound knowledge of the general history of the sciences." (Comte later claimed to have achieved personal verification of the law of the three stages in his periods of insanity, which he had experienced, he claimed, as a regression back through from positivism to metaphysics to theology on the level of his own personality, in his recovery retracing these stages foward again.)

The task of the *Cours* is not only to analyze the transmutation of human thought by science, but also to *complete* it. For man's understanding of himself is still in substantial part in its prescientific phase:

> Everything can be reduced to a simple question of fact: does positive philosophy, which over the two past centuries has gradually become so widespread, today embrace all orders of phenomena? It is evident that such is not the case and that consequently there still remains the major scientific undertaking of giving to positive philosophy the universal character that is indispensable to its proper constitution. . . . Now that the human mind has founded astronomy, and terrestial physics—both mechanical and chemical—and organic physics—both botanical and biological—it remains to finalise the system of the sciences by founding *social physics*. Such is, in several capital respects, the greatest and the most pressing intellectual need today. . . .[5]

Positivism supplies a general ground plan for the formation of sociology; that is to say, the new science of society has to share the same overall logical form as the other sciences as it is cut free of the residues of metaphysics. But since the phenomena with which it is concerned are more complex and specific than the sciences lying below it in the hierarchy, it also has to develop methodological procedures of its own. Like biology, sociology employs concepts that are "synthetic" in character; that is to say, concepts which relate to the properties of complex wholes rather than to aggregates of elements as in the lower sciences. The two also share a division into statics and dynamics. In sociology, the first consists in the study of the functional interrelationship of institutions within society, the second in the study of the process of social evolution. The significance of dynamics in sociology, however, is more profound than in biology, because—via the law of the three stages—it examines the intellectual development of positive thought as a whole. Sociology relies on three methodological elements, each of which involves features that are particular to it: observation, experiment, and comparison. Comte holds that a commitment to the essential importance of empirical observation is not equivalent to an advocacy of empiricism. "No logical dogma," Comte says, "could be more thoroughly irreconcilable with the spirit of positive philosophy, or with its special character in regard to the study of social phenomena, than this."[6] Consequently, theory is basic to sociological investigations. On the other hand, the context of Comte's discussion makes it apparent that "empiricism" here is understood in a limited sense; his point is not that all observations of objects or events are (to use Popper's term) "theory impregnated," but that "scientifically speaking, all isolated, empirical observation is idle." "Scientific and popular observation," Comte says, "embrace the same facts"; but they regard them from different points of view, because the former is guided by theory whereas the latter is not. Theories direct our attention toward certain facts rather than others.[7] While experimentation in the laboratory sense is not possible in social physics, it can be replaced by indirect experimentation—that is, "natural experiments" whose consequences can be analyzed. But this is less important than the comparative method, which is the crucial foundation of sociological research.

Comte always intended sociology to be directed toward practical ends. If it is true that the strange extravagances of the immanent social future envisaged in the *Système de politique positive* are largely absent from Comte's earlier writings, it is still the case that the main elements of his political program already appear there. These are perhaps stated with greater clarity, in fact, in the *Cours* than they are in the later work. The overriding theme continues that of the intellectual diagnosis of the origins of positive philosophy: the mutual necessity of order and progress. For Comte it is precisely his insistence upon the conjunction of the two that allows positivism to supersede both the "revolutionary metaphysics" of the *philosophes* and the reactionary connotations of the Catholic apologists. The latter school wanted order but was against progress; the former sought progress at the expense of order. The "order" desired by the "retrograde school" was nothing but a reversion to feudal hierocracy; while the "progress" aspired to by the revolutionaries was nothing less than the subversion of any form of government as such. The sort of society Comte foresees as guaranteeing order and progress nonetheless places a heavy enough emphasis upon features that brook large in the writings of the members of the "retrograde school"—moral consensus, authority, and an antagonism to the "chimera of equality"—even if stripped of their specific association with Catholicism. At first sight the call to establish a Religion of Humanity seems quite inconsistent with the positive philosophy advocated in the *Cours*, and many commentators have supposed that there is a major hiatus between Comte's earlier and later works.[8] But it is perhaps more plausible to argue that the *Système de politique positive* brings fully into the open the latent substratum of the positive spirit: we see that science cannot, after all, provide its own commitment.

How, even so, can a perspective which insists that the course of human social development is governed by laws akin to laws of nature provide any leverage for rational human intervention in history? Doesn't this imply the adoption of fatalism in the face of the inevitable sweep of social change? According to Comte, the contrary is actually the case. For the rational facilitation of progress is only possible if the limiting conditions of intervention are known; the laws that control the movement of society are subject to considerable margins of variation in their operation, and such variation can be actively influenced by deliberate action.[9]

Comte's Influence: The Origins of Logical Positivism

Although his writings had rather little immediate influence in France, Comte's works attracted a considerable following abroad: in other European countries, the United States, and particularly Latin America. In Britain, the *Cours* acquired a notable admirer in John Stuart Mill, and Mill's *Logic* was in important respects its counterpart in English-speaking social thought. Many such followers were alienated, however, by the drift of Comte's thought in the later part of his career, as expressed in the *Systéme de politique positive,* which Mill called "this melancholy decadence of a great intellect." As a social movement, which Comte had all along tried to make it, positivism died with the withering of the groups of disciples who remained to celebrate the Festival of Humanity held in London in 1881. I shall not be interested here in trying to detail in what ways Comte's works were drawn upon by other authors, during his lifetime or after it: some prominent contemporaries, most notably Herbert Spencer, were anxious to claim a greater independence between their ideas and those of Comte than seems in fact to have been the case.[10] I shall consider the influence of Comte only from two aspects: the mode in which his writings were utilized by Durkheim and the extent to which Comte's views conform intellectually to the philosophical program developed in logical positivism.

The importance of the line of connection from Comte to Durkheim is easily attested. So far as social science in the twentieth century is concerned, the influence of Comte's writings derives less from their direct impact than from their reworking in Durkheim's version of sociological method. Durkheim's works have provided the proximate source of functionalism in both anthropology and sociology. But Durkheim's work has also had a more broad ranging and diffuse effect as a stimulus to those central traditions of contemporary social thought in which the goal of achieving a "natural science of society" is considered both desirable and feasible.[11]

In Durkheim, the methodological framework of Comte's positivism, which is sustained, is separated from the global theory of historical change, which is largely abandoned. Durkheim makes this quite explicit. Comte regarded

Condorcet and Montesquieu as forerunners who established the groundwork of the positivist spirit but nonetheless were unable to detach themselves adequately from the speculative philosophy of history. Durkheim has much the same view of the two former thinkers, but lumps Comte along with them as belonging to the prescientific phase in the history of sociology. The "law of the three stages," according to Durkheim, is proclaimed by fiat rather than corroborated empirically: a massive research undertaking, well beyond the capacity of any single scholar, would be required to document adequately such a principle of social change.[12] In this respect, Durkheim's comments concur with the judgement of Mill: "M. Comte, at bottom, was not so solicitous about completeness of proof as becomes a positive philosopher."[13]

Durkheim's discussions of social evolution and his diagnosis of the trend of development of modern industrial civilization owe as much to Saint-Simon and to the German "academic socialists" as they do to Comte. But the influence of Boutroux and others notwithstanding, it is undeniably the legacy of Comte that looms largest in the methodological scheme of sociology which Durkheim set out. While Durkheim does not endorse the "hierarchy of the sciences" as such, he insists perhaps even more strongly than Comte upon the autonomy of sociology as a distinctive field of endeavor. Like Comte, he holds that recognition of such autonomy does not imply that the study of human social conduct is logically discrepant from natural science; social facts have a moral dimension that is absent in nature, but they have "to be treated as things" in the same manner as natural objects. The aim of sociology is to arrive at the formulation of principles that have the same objective status as natural scientific laws. In Durkheim, a Baconian version of scientific method is perhaps more apparent than in Comte. Every science, Durkheim says, including sociology, advances only slowly and cautiously, through patient inductive generalization based on observed regularities in social facts. This is, indeed, why he is critical of Comte's claims to have established a positivist account of history. When Durkheim refuses the designation "positivist" in favor of "naturalism," he seeks to dissociate his general position from that of Comte while reaffirming the character of sociology as a natural science of society. Durkheim's account of the emergence of the scientific spirit, although not elaborated in anything like the historical detail attempted by Comte, actually follows the outline of Comte's discussion very closely. All thought originates in religion, Durkheim holds, (and he tries to explain how this should be the case in *The Elementary Forms of Religious Life*); it can be demonstrated that even the Kantian categories are first of all religious concepts.[14] The key differences between prescientific and scientific thought are methodological; "thought and reflection are prior to science, which merely uses them methodologically."[15] As religious concepts become secularized in the form of metaphysical philosophy, they become more precise, but they are finally rendered scientific only by being anchored in empirical observation and thereby transformed.

It is clear that Durkheim derives his conception of functionalist method from Comte and not from Spencer. Durkheim follows Comte closely in separating out functional explanation (statics) from historical explanation (dynamics), although he criticizes Comte along with Spencer for reifying "progress": treating the impetus to self-betterment as if it were a general cause of the evolution of society. As in Comte's writings, and of course in those of many other nineteenth-century writers also, Durkheim's stress upon the significance of functional explanation in sociology comes fairly directly from the model of biology, as does his acceptance of "holistic" concepts as basic to sociological analysis. However, the biological parallel also provides another very important element in Durkheim's works, bearing immediately upon the practical implications of social science. In claiming that the scientific study of society can provide the means of distinguishing what is normal from what is pathological in any particular type of society, Durkheim upholds the most intrinsic part of Comte's program for positivism. For just as natural science shows us that the development of knowledge can only be achieved incrementally, so sociology shows us that all truly progressive social change occurs only cumulatively. The mutual dependence of progress and order is as much a theme of Durkheim's writings as it is of Comte's writings. Durkheim's antagonism to revolution continues that of Comte and is likewise held to be grounded scientifically: political revolution expresses the inability of a society to generate progressive change, rather than itself providing a possible instrument of securing social transformation. However, while the form of the account is similar, the content is not wholly the same; that is to say, in identifying what is normal and what is pathological in contemporary society, and thus specifying the immanent trend of social development, Durkheim moves away substantially from Comte.[16]

In mentioning these respects in which Durkheim was indebted to Comte, I do not, of course, mean to claim that Durkheim's works can be regarded as little more than an extension of those of the earlier thinker. But I do hold that Durkheim's writings have been more influential than those of any other author in academic social science in the spread of "positivistic sociology" as I have defined that term. Through them, Comte's "positivism" has had a major influence upon the more diffuse development of such positivistic sociology. This is one line of filiation leading from Comte through to twentieth-century thought. The other is less direct, connecting Comte to the logical positivism of the Vienna Circle.

The principal mediator between Comte's positivism and the positivism of the Vienna Circle is normally held to be Ernst Mach, the physicist and physiologist. Mach, like Durkheim, rejected the label "positivist" and, unlike Durkheim, was not directly influenced by Comte save in minor respects.[17] The importance of Comte in relation to Mach is really in helping to further the intellectual currents that were in the background of Mach's work as a natural scientist. The following elements in Comte's thought are relevant in this respect:

1. The reconstruction of history as the realization of the positive spirit. In this scheme of things, religion and metaphysics have a definite place, but only as prior phases of mystification to be broken through by the advent of science.

With the development of the scientific outlook, the "prehistory" of the human species is completed; the positive stage of thought is not a transitional one like the other.

2. The final dissolution of metaphysics, closely linked to the idea of the supersession of philosophy itself. In Comte's positivism, science replaces philosophy: "positive philosophy" is the logical explication of the canons of scientific method. Metaphysics is not accorded the status of being open to philosophical discussion in its own right: it is consigned to the lumber room of history on the basis that the questions posed in metaphysical philosophy are empty of content.

3. The existence of a clear and definable boundary between the factual, or the "observable," and the imaginary, or the "fictitious." Comte does not provide an ontological justification of what counts as factual, but rather a methodological one.[18] It is in this regard, his disavowals notwithstanding, that Comte adopts the standpoint of empiricism. Systematic observation supposedly distinguishes positive science from other claims to knowledge, and such observation, according to Comte, depends upon the evidence of sense perception; this is the ground of certainty in science. The rationalist features of Comte's thought do not enter in at this level, but only at the level of the selective organization of facts within theories: theories provide for the *connection* of facts to universal propositions or laws.

4. The "relativism" of scientific knowledge. "Relativism" here is not used in the sense which it has subsequently come to acquire: the acceptance, in some form or other, of multiple worlds of reality. That is to say, it is again not an ontological term but refers to the thesis that science confines itself to explaining the interdependence of phenomena: it does not claim to discover essences or final causes. Scientific knowledge is never "finished" but is constantly open to modification and improvement.

5. The integral tie between science and the moral and material progress of mankind. Comte's adoption of the Baconian formula that the foreknowledge yielded by science makes possible technological control, the integration of "prevoir" and "pouvoir," expresses this exactly. This not only unifies science and technology but extends the realm of the technological to human social development itself; as Comte says quite explicitly, technology will no longer be exclusively associated with the physical but will become "political and moral."[19]

Each of these views reappears in Mach's writings, although not of course in identical form to their expression in Comte's works. There is nothing in Mach comparable to Comte's massive endeavor to synthesize scientific knowledge within a scheme that is simultaneously historical and analytical. But Mach was directly influenced by theories of evolution and saw in Darwin and Lamarck a basis for explaining the emergence of scientific thought from the entanglements of metaphysics. For Mach, the scientific outlook triumphs historically and finds its moral justification in facilitating the survival and welfare of the human species.[20] Mach uses the term "philosophy" with the same dual connotation as Comte. When he writes that he is not a philosopher and that science does not rely on any particular type or system of philosophy, Mach echoes Comte's theme of the abolition of philosophy. "Philosophy" here is used to mean transcendent or "metaphysical philosophy"; both Comte and Mach proclaim an end to philosophy in this sense. Where Comte and Mach speak of the retention of philosophy, on the other hand, it is as *philosophie positive:* philosophy here is the logical clarification of the bases of science. "There is above all *no* Machian philosophy," Mach emphasizes. There is at the most "a natural-scientific methodology and a psychology of knowledge," and these latter "are like all scientific theories provisional, incomplete attempts."[21] Mach's dismissal of metaphysics is as complete as that of Comte, although linked to a more thorough-going phenomenalism that Comte ever adopted:

> I should like the scientists to realize that my view eliminates all metaphysical questions indifferently, whether they be only regarded as insoluble at the present moment, or whether they be regarded as meaningless for all time. I should like then, further, to reflect that everything that we can know about the world is necessarily expressed in the sensations, which can be set free from the individual influence of the observer in a precisely definable manner. . . . Everything that we can want to know is given by the solution of a problem in mathematical form, by the ascertainment of the functional dependency of the sensational elements on one another. This knowledge exhausts the knowledge of "reality."[22]

For Mach, scientific knowledge is "relative" in Comte's sense; the object of science is to discover relations between phenomena. According to Mach, however, this carries the implication that theory has a purely heuristic role in scientific investigations. The precise identification of the mathematical functions that express the dependencies between phenomena in nature renders theory obsolete. In Mach's phrase, theories resemble dead leaves which fall away when the tree of science no longer has a need to breathe through them. Although this is distinct from Comte's view, it is not as far removed from it as may seem the case at first blush. In his discussion of the positive method of science, Comte commingles empiricism and rationalism: as I have already mentioned, however, he does so by treating theory as the mode of organizing fact in a way relevant to scientific procedure.

In Comte's positivism, no place is found for the reflexive subject; psychology does not even appear in the hierarchy of the sciences, and the notion of subjective experience is regarded as a metaphysical fiction. In this regard, Comte stands in direct line of descent from Hume. But this is a standpoint that is taken for granted in Comte's writings rather than defended in detail. Mach, however, confronts the issue directly, and his stand upon it is quite unequivocal. The self or ego does not exist as a unity; it is merely an aggregate of sensations. According to Mach, if this is accepted, it disposes of the accusation of solipsism that is frequently made against phenomenalism; since the self does not exist, there can be no question of the isolation of the self in the universe. Mach saw no discrepancy between this view and either the existence of morality or the role of science in furthering the betterment of humanity. It is antireligious insofar as it has the consequence that there can be no survival of the soul after death, since "I" has no unitary existence anyway—although in the latter part of his career Mach came to see affinities between his standpoint and the world view of Buddhism. Mach believed that his view, far from rejecting the ethical value of the individual personality, enhances it by preventing an overevaluation of the "self"; it places the emphasis on the moral welfare of mankind as a whole. This links back to Mach's conception of the relation between science and human progress: the triumph of the scientific spirit provides both a technological and a moral basis for the evolutionary advancement of man.

Mach's writings and teachings both helped to foster a climate of opinion in Vienna propitious for the development of what came to be known as logical positivism or logical empiricism (the latter being the term preferred by Schlick) and also directly influenced ideas of the most prominent members of the Vienna Circle.[23] But the logical positivists drew heavily upon other sources also, and in certain respects their work contrasts quite clearly with that of Mach. Beginning with the group formed in 1907 around Frank, a physicist, Neurath, an economist, and Hahn, a mathematician, the logical positivists sought to develop a view of science which would recognize the vital significance of logic and mathematics in scientific thought as systems of symbolic representations. This led them to acknowledge the central importance of language: a theme which connects their writings to the major thrust of development of philosophy as a whole in the twentieth century. One line of thought leading in this direction within the philosophy of science was that provided by Poincaré's conventionalism, sometimes referred to as the "new positivism." Schlick and others were critical of conventionalism but recognized the force of the claim that scientific theories embody linguistic conventions. The thesis that theories are languages for the representation of facts, stripped of some of the skeptical features of conventionalism, was taken over as a key element of logical positivism.

But in their approach to the mode of analyzing the content of such languages, the logical positivists were indebted to British philosophy. What has been called the "revolution in British philosophy,"[24] led by Moore and Russell, was initiated by them as a reaction to the Hegelianism of Bradley, McTaggart, and others. It was both a return to the traditions of British empiricism and a new departure. Russell himself did not set out to discredit metaphysics; rather, he believed that philosophy should become rigorous and precise and that the way to achieve this goal lay through the logical elucidation of the language in which scientific theories are couched. Philosophy is to reveal the logical structure which underlies the superficial play of appearances. Russell's object was not, like that of Husserl's transcendental reduction, eventually to recover the everyday world of common sense or of the "natural attitude," but to provide an account that would conform to established scientific knowledge. Russell's "logical atomism" had a strong influence on the young Wittgenstein, and it was partly through Wittgenstein's personal contacts with some of the Vienna Circle, and through his *Tractatus*, that these ideas were communicated. Wittgenstein's impact upon the members of the Vienna Circle has been so frequently emphasized, however, that it is worthwhile pointing out that Carnap, ultimately the most influential of the group, has acknowledged Frege and Russell as having had the strongest effect upon his philosophical development. He attended Frege's lectures in Jena and through them was introduced to the *Principia Mathematica;* Hahn had independently acquainted the members of the Vienna Circle with the latter work.[25]

In retrospect, it has become clear that the logical positivists read Wittgenstein's *Tractatus* against a Machian background which led them to disregard crucial features of it. The book is not an exposition which as a whole could be exemplified by any of the traditional tenets of empiricism; it is rather, as Wittgenstein remarked subsequently, a sort of "Platonic myth," a metaphor in its own right. This separates the early Wittgenstein decisively from the main line of development of logical positivism, even if Schlick and his associates saw themselves as continuing along the path Wittgenstein had opened up.[26] The *Tractatus* influenced the growth of logical positivism particularly with respect to the argument for the distinction between the analytic and the synthetic. There are no synthetic a priori judgments. Systems of logic or mathematics, deductively derived from axioms, are essentially tautological; any other general claim to knowledge is synthetic, which means that it can be counterfactually shown to be false.

Logical Positivism and Modern Empiricism

The members of the Vienna Circle in its early days saw themselves as the enthusiastic progenitors of a new enlightenment: as Feigl has described it, carrying on "in the spirit of Hume and Comte, but equipped with more fully developed logical tools."[27] In the writings of the logical positivists the differentiation of what is scientific and what is not became convergent with what is meaningful and what is meaningless. What became called the "Verification Principle" went through numerous versions, as the inadequacy of Schlick's original formulation—that the meaning of (synthetic) statements consists in the method of their verification—became very rapidly apparent. In these later versions, "testability" was substituted for "verification." Obviously it would be mistaken to hold that a statement is meaningful only when we have managed to test its validity; otherwise, with improvements in empirical techniques of validation, previously meaningless statements would suddenly become meaningful ones. So the Verification Principle was altered to hold that a statement is meaningful if there is some means of potentially testing, or "confirming," it. But various major difficulties still remained apparent, the most debated being the status of the principle itself. For if it cannot be subjected to the criterion of testability, if it cannot itself be tested, it should seemingly be dismissed as meaningless.

To attempt to get round this difficulty, the Verification Principle was declared to be a procedural rule, not itself a statement. This helped to indicate that what was at issue was, in some part, a problem of the nature of statements; that is, of what constitutes a statement. This can be illustrated by reference to another dilemma in the early formulations of the Verification Principle, concerning the breadth of its application. If taken as a criterion to be applied very generally to all kinds of moral prescriptions or aesthetic judgments, it has the consequence of eliminating these as meaningless, along with metaphysics and theology. But if it concerns only the meaningfulness of "statements," the implication could be drawn that it supplies a criterion of distinguishing statements from other kinds of judgments, commands, etc. The first, more "radical" version of logical positivism gradually became abandoned in favor of the second, more "liberal" one—especially in the hands of Carnap.[28] The view that the "pseudosentences" of metaphysics are meaningless came to be supplanted by the more sophisticated notion that metaphysical doctrines lack cognitive meaning, although they may have emotive meaning. To borrow an expression of Ayer's originally applied in a slightly different context, the metaphysician is treated less like a criminal than like a patient.[29]

The logical positivists initially classified most of the traditional ontological and epistemological dilemmas of philosophy as belonging to metaphysics, and hence as outside the scope of rational discussion. The disputes between phenomenalism, realism, idealism, and so on were dismissed as meaningless, since there is no way that they can be made to submit to any characterization of the Verification Principle. However, they believed that certain issues relevant to these long-established debates could be sustained, and resolved, if they were treated as debates about appropriate philosophical languages. In this way the back door was left ajar for the incorporation of features within the writings of the logical positivists that were denied public admittance at the front. Carnap's earlier work sets out a version of phenomenalism, although he claimed to be discussing only the relevance of "a phenomenalistic language" to scientific procedures. His major work in the first part of his intellectual career, *Der clogische Aufbau der Welt,* pursues the theme that the aim of philosophy is to express knowledge as a logical structure of basic certainties. Here Carnap advocates a phenomenalistic grounding of such certainties. The only sure knowledge is that which is immediately given as sense data; our knowledge of material objects is secondary and derived.[30] Neurath was mainly instrumental in persuading Carnap to abandon this position, the first of several substantial alterations the latter was to introduce into his views over the course of the years. In order to skirt the suggestion that he was again becoming involved in the sorts of epistemological debates that were prohibited, Carnap referred to his shift from phenomenalism to physicalism as a change of "attitude" and not one of "belief," since this would require a theoretical defense of the falsity of the first and the truth of the latter. However, it is clear enough that there was an underlying theoretical justification of the change which both Neurath and Carnap accepted: that whereas phenomenalism leads to solipsistic paradoxes, physicalism more readily provides for an intersubjective language in which reports of observations are communicated among observers.[31]

Neurath and Carnap developed their physicalist thesis in some part in direct opposition to the tradition of the *Geisteswissenschaften*, which insisted upon the existence of logical and methodological differences between the natural and the social sciences. Everything, Neurath held, occurs in nature, as part of the physical world. Carnap attempted to express this as a thesis about language; that is, to show that all knowledge can be reduced to the propositions of a physicalist language. This applies as much to our knowledge of minds as to that of happenings in nature. All statements in psychology, according to Carnap, whether they are about mental states of one's own or of others, can be translated into a language which refers to physical events in the body of the person or persons concerned. "On these grounds, psychology is a part of the domain of unified science based on physics. By 'physics' we wish to mean, not the system of currently known physical laws, but rather the science characterized by a mode of concept formation which traces every concept back to state-coordinates, that is, to systematic assignments of numbers to space-time points. Understanding 'physics' in this way, we can rephrase our thesis in a particular thesis of physicalism—as follows: psychology is a branch of physics."[32]

The members of the Vienna Circle were already divided quite considerably among themselves prior to their enforced scattering into exile and Schlick's death in 1936. Hahn, Neurath, and Carnap, the so-called "left wing" of the Vienna Circle, were the main figures in the shift away from the dogmatic views of the earlier days, whereas Schlick and Waismann were more inclined to hold fast to their established views. In later times, the core of the movement was continued in the United States and, to a lesser extent, in Britain. "Logical positivism" lost the clear-cut identity that it previously had and devolved into a more general stream of positivistic philosophy, finding ready contacts with, and having a great deal of influence upon, the traditions of empiricism and pragmatism already strongly ingrained in Anglo-Saxon philosophy. Among the members of the Vienna Circle, Carnap, Neurath, Frank, Gödel, and Feigl went to the United States, as did Reichenbach, von Mises, and Hempel from the Berlin group of philosophers who shared much in common with the former group and the Polish logician Tarski, whose ideas influenced both Carnap and Popper (who came to Britain after spending some time in New Zealand). The influence of these authors over the development of certain core areas of analytic philosophy in the English-speaking world has been very considerable indeed, although tempered in Britain particularly by the influence of "ordinary language philosophy" and the later Wittgenstein. I shall be concerned with two principal, and connected, aspects of the influence of the former group of authors: first, with respect to the philosophy of natural science, the dominance of what has been called the "orthodox" (by Feigl) or the "received" (by Putnam) model of science; and the elaboration, in the light of these views, of the thesis of the unity of science with respect to the logic of the social sciences.

The orthodox model of science derives from the liberalization of the original logical positivist doctrines, especially as led by Carnap; but it also preserves features that stretch back through to Mach's writings. Mach wanted to reduce experience to relations between simple elements. These elements are sensations, not statements about sensations such as appear in scientific theories. Hence Mach failed to recognize the difference between "formal" and "material" modes of speaking. Statements are frequently couched in such a form that they seem to concern experiences, while in fact they are assertions about other statements: these are called "syntactical sentences" by Carnap. Mach's positivistic philosophy was transformed into logical positivism by the treating of Mach's "elements" syntactically, as components not of experience but of a formal language in which experience is described. Mach's elements became "element sentences" or "protocol sentences"—the simplest sentences, not further reducible, in which the formal language is expressed.[33] A protocol sentence, as in legal transcription of protocols, is supposed to be a statement of experience immediately recorded. Carnap regarded the problem of the form of protocol statements as the basic issue in the logic of science, and his attempts to grapple with it provide the key to some of the major changes in his ideas from his early phenomenalist viewpoint onward. The original view of most of the Vienna Circle was that scientific knowledge rests upon a bedrock of indubitable fact, expressed in the immediacy of sensations as specified by Mach. This is the theme of the *Aufbau*. But just as Neurath rejected phenomenalism, he never accepted the existence of the bedrock of certainty as ordered by protocol statements. In his famous analogy, knowledge is like a ship that has to be continually rebuilt even while it remains afloat. Carnap was influenced by this and also came to acknowledge that the thesis that scientific theories could in a fairly simple sense be "reduced" to protocol statements had to be revised and made more elaborate.

Carnap was thus led to place a much greater emphasis than in his very early work upon the role of theoretical concepts in the advancement of scientific knowledge, upon the incompleteness of such concepts, and upon their differentiation from the language of observation protocols. Theoretical concepts, one part of the system of scientific knowledge, cannot be directly derived from, or reduced to, the other part, the language of observation. However, the theoretical language and the observation language are connected by "correspondence rules," whereby observations may be interpreted in light of theories, and vice versa. This conception is the core of the orthodox model. A science such as physics is conceived to be a calculus, in which axioms are the fundamental physical laws. The calculus is not directly interpreted but is a "free floating system" in relation to which other theoretical terms are defined. Some of the latter can be interpreted by semantic rules that relate them to a groundwork of observable fact; but interpretation of the theoretical terms is never complete. The theoretical cohesion of the system is provided by its hypothetico-deductive character, in which theorems can be deduced from the axioms and hence, via the rules of correspondence, particular observations can be "explained." This is some way from the original emphases of logical positivism insofar as the criterion of "testability" only applies in an immediate way at the level of the observation language—although in the final works of his career Carnap still expressed the belief that a means could be found for differentiating cognitively meaningful theoretical terms from meaningless ones.

The precise nature of correspondence rules has proved a controversial matter among positivistically-minded philosophers. The usual general picture of the relation between the observational and theoretical languages is something akin to Braithwaite's analogy: correspondence rules are the "zip" that fastens together theory and observation; the fastener progressively pulls the two elements of a system of knowledge together, as uninterpreted theorems are transformed into observation statements, expanding the empirical content of the theoretical constructs.[34] The allowing of a detachment between theoretical concepts and observation statements, representing the abandonment of the Verification Principle in anything at all close to its original form, has the virtue, Carnap claims, of allowing for the creative scope of scientific innovation and the wide explanatory power that abstract theory can possess.[35] On the other hand, since it has become generally recognized that observation statements are not unchallengeable, the implication might be drawn that the claimed differentiation between the theoretical and the observation language cannot be drawn clearly at all. For, as Feigl says, most positivistically inclined authors today, even those involved in or close to the original Vienna group, recognize that observation-statements cannot be entirely "theory-free."[36]

The dominant account of scientific explanation developed in modern empiricism is given clearest shape in a famous article by Hempel and Oppenheim.[37] It has stimulated a wide-ranging debate and a great deal of literature, in response to which Hempel has modified and elaborated upon his views as first set down. I shall only summarize the main features briefly here; since its possible application to the social sciences and history has provoked as much discussion as its relevance to natural science, it provides an appropriate transition point for moving on to an appraisal of the influence of positivistic philosophy in sociology. The core idea is that the most precise, scientific form of explanation, although not the only one, is "deductive-nomological" (this has also, following Dray, come to be called the "covering-law model" of explanation). Explanation of an event here involves reference to information supplied by two types of statements which are brought together. These are, first, general laws; and, second, statements that specify particular circumstances in which those laws have application. The statement referring to the event or phenomenon to be explained (the "explanandum") is deduced as a necessity from the conjunction of these two.[38] The objective testing of a scientific explanation hence involves empirical confirmation of the statement describing the initial or "boundary" conditions; empirical confirmation of the laws in relation to which the explanandum is deduced; and logical confirmation of the deduction made. According to Hempel, there is a symmetry, or a "structural equality," between explanation and prediction, since the logical form of the two is the same; a prediction consists in deducing a statement about a future rather than a past event. Deductive-nomological explanation is held to be integral to all "empirical sciences"; however, in the social sciences and history it is often less clearly manifest than in natural science. Hempel offers two reasons for this: the universal laws in question are frequently common-sense ones that are taken for granted implicitly rather than formulated as explicit statements; and, partly because of this, not enough is known about the empirical basis of such laws for us to be able to state them with precision. Historians mostly offer what Hempel calls "explanation sketches," in which the relevant laws and boundary conditions are only vaguely hinted at; explanation sketches can be made more complete, and thus in Hempel's words more "scientifically acceptable," through being filled out by empirical testing of the laws and conditions on which they are based.

This theory of explanation in social science is affirmed by Hempel in conscious contradistinction to the tradition of "interpretative understanding" of the *Geisteswissenschaften*—thus echoing one of the persistent themes of logical positivism. *Verstehen,* or what Hempel refers to as "the method of empathic understanding," is admitted as a component in the method of the social sciences only as a mode of suggesting hypotheses. It is not indispensable for social or historical explanation, and many hypotheses arrived at empathically have then to be established in deductive form and tested empirically. Hempel makes it clear that an empiricist criterion of cognitive meaning has to be applied in the same way here as in the natural sciences. Interpretations of "meaning" that are made in sociology and history "consist either in subsuming the phenomena in question under a scientific explanation or explanation sketch; or in an attempt to subsume them under some general idea which is not amenable to any empirical test. In the former case, interpretation clearly is explanation by means of universal hypotheses; in the latter, it amounts to a pseudo-explanation which may have emotive appeal and evoke vivid pictorial associations, but which does not further our theoretical understanding of the phenomena under consideration."[39]

Positivistic Philosophy and Modern Sociology

Of the members of the Vienna Circle, Neurath wrote most extensively on social issues and made the most sustained attempt to apply logical positivist views to sociology, which he approached from a self-professed Marxist standpoint. While Neurath was a strong supporter of, and a major influence upon, the thesis that the "scientific way of thinking" in philosophy marked the way ahead in the evolution of human thought, he was more inclined than the other members of the group to emphasize the importance of the social context of particular philosophical traditions in explaining the hold that such traditions may have over their adherents. Neurath was the main figure who kept logical positivism tied to the general interest in the promotion of social progress characteristic of Comte and of Mach. His Marxism, however, was unobtrusive theoretically, except with respect to his advocacy of physicalism; he rejected dialectical logic, the Hegelian legacy in Marx, no less completely than did his colleagues.[40]

For Neurath sociology is regarded as one segment of the division of labor in the totality of unified science; like every other science, it is "free of any world view."[41] He envisages the coming into being of a system of the sciences in which the laws of each particular science, such as sociology, will be connected with the laws of all the other sciences in a uniform logical structure. Laws, Neurath says, are abstract means of passing from observation statements to predictions; the concept of observation is in turn analyzed in terms of physicalism, involving a "social behaviorism." Neurath's behaviorism bears close affinities with operationalism, which of course has in various general respects run parallel to logical positivism as a whole. In deciding whether a term such as "religious ethos" may be legitimately employed in sociology, we have, according to Neurath, to infer the sorts of observation statements it presupposes as concrete modes of behavior. "Let him [the sociologist] not speak of the "spirit of the age" if it is not completely clear that he means by it certain verbal combinations, forms of worship, modes of architecture, fashions, styles of painting, etc."[42]

Neurath's writings seem to have had little direct influence in sociology as such. The influence of the writings of the logical positivists has been assimilated into sociology in a much more important and pervasive way through a general acceptance of the model of scientific explanation developed in the phase of the devolution of logical positivism into positivistic philosophy. Since this is so diffuse, it would be out of the question to inquire into it in any detail here. I shall therefore indicate some of the connections between positivistic philosophy and positivistic sociology by illustration. Illustrations are easy to find. One aspect of the broad influence which positivistic philosophy has enjoyed within the social sciences, in the English-speaking world at least, is reflected in the replacement of the term "method" by "methodology." The latter has come to mean nothing more than the analysis of procedures of research; it has little explicit relation to the broader process of reflection on the form and concerns of sociology, which is regarded as the proper task of the "philosophy of the social sciences." Methodology is often presumed to involve no particular philosophical commitments; but most of the leading texts offer a few positivistic trimmings to the package. Thus Lazarsfeld and Rosenberg, for example, quote Bridgman and Hempel with approval, accepting the positivist program of effecting the substitution of a precise, formal language of observation for everyday language as the first demand of a scientific sociology.[43]

Rather than attempting to multiply such examples, I shall concentrate upon indicating the direction of emphasis of three works which have been widely adopted within the mainstream of contemporary sociology. First, Ernest Nagel's *The Structure of Science,* which has served as a stock reference for innumerable sociological texts and discussions; second, Zetterberg's *On Theory and Verification in Sociology,* a representative and influential discussion of the methodology of social science; and third, Hempel's analysis of functionalism, which connects functional explanation to the deductive-nomological model, thereby reestablishing direct contact between "positivism" in its modern form and "positivism" in the tradition of Comte and Durkheim.

Nagel's book is explicitly indebted to Carnap and Frank (as well as to M. R. Cohen).[44] The work follows something of a Comtean outline: the discussion proceeds from mechanics through physics to biology and the social sciences. The account is anchored in terms of an exposition of deductive-nomological explanation, and the differentiation of languages of observation and theory connected by correspondence rules; biology and the social sciences are distinct from the rest of natural science insofar as the former may make use of teleological or functional explanations. Nagel denies that "teleology" is specifically dependent upon the activities of conscious, reasoning agents or that teleological explanation involves a presumption of final causes. The question of the "subjective" or "meaningful" character of human conduct is taken up at some length. "Interpretative understanding," according to Nagel, involves two characteristics: the assumption that one or more particular individuals are, at a certain time, in certain psychological states; and the assumption of a general principle or law stating the ways in which such states are related both to each other and to "overt behavior." Observational evidence is required for both of these, rather than any kind of empathic identification with the actors whose conduct is to be explained: "we can *know* that a man is fleeing from a pursuing crowd that is animated by hatred towards him is in a state of fear, without our having experienced such violent fears and hatred or without imaginatively recreating such emotions in ourselves—just as we can *know* that the temperature of a piece of wire is rising because the velocities of its constituent molecules are increasing, without having to imagine what it is like to be a rapidly moving molecule."[45] Like Hempel, Nagel accepts that empathy may play a part in the derivation of hypotheses; but such hypotheses have then to be tested by "controlled sensory observations."

Most of the generalizations in the social sciences, Nagel says, are statistical uniformities rather than universal laws. This, however, is not because of any specific features of human behavior as such but is primarily because of the relatively youthful stage of development of sociology, which has not yet developed the conceptual and observational precision necessary to determining exactly the limiting conditions of its generalizations; although he has strong reservations about existing functionalist theories in the social sciences, Nagel apparently believes that such precision may be achieved in principle, although there are various factors likely to prevent its full realization in practice. In any case, statistical rather than universal laws are typical of many areas of natural science. Statistical generalizations are complemented in the social sciences by functional ones, the latter explaining the maintenance of system states through regulative feedback. The advancement of functional explanations in sociology and anthropology is, as in the case of deductive explanations, hindered by the as yet diffuse character of most social-scientific concepts.

In Nagel's view, the fact that human beings can modify their conduct in light of their knowledge, including potentially their knowledge of generalizations made by sociologists, is not a major source of "difficulty" for social science. It is not in fact something which is unique to the social sciences: in natural science also the observation of a phenomenon can alter the character of that phenomenon. The very statement of the latter implies some awareness of the extent to which what is observed is altered by the process of observation; hence the effects produced by the interaction will either be small and can be ignored, or if large can be calculated and corrected for. The logical character of the "interference" is the same in nature and society, although the "mechanisms involved" are different.[46] The possibility of self-fulfilling and self-negating predictions in the social sciences similarly finds direct analogy in natural science. For example, a computer which guides the firing of a gun may be defective such that it just misses the target; however, the oscillations produced by the transmitting of the (erroneous) calculations could cause the gun to in fact hit the target just because it was originally aimed wrongly.

Nagel's work is consciously directed to a spelling out of "liberalized logical positivism"; that of Zetterberg, on the other hand, is more concerned with describing the conduct of research in sociology and the connection between such research and what he calls "theoretical sociology."[47] It is an attempt, Zetterberg says, to complement the insistence of authors such as Lundberg that sociology should match the scientific rigor of the natural sciences, with a fuller appreciation than Lundberg expressed of the basic importance of theory in science. Zetterberg pays due obeisance to the "humanistic content" of the social sciences, but the main emphasis of his argument is upon the continuity between physics, biology, and sociology. Explanation in sociology, if it is to advance beyond lay knowledge or lay beliefs, must assume the same deductive-nomological form which it has in natural science. "Theory" in sociology is often used very broadly as virtually equivalent to "social thought," Zetterberg says; in his usage, however, it means a set of deductively connected laws to which any particular event, within boundary conditions, can be referred. Zetterberg's description of the formalized language which sociology needs if it is to meet the demands of being an empirical science, in which he draws upon Hempel's analysis of cognitive meaning, implies a strict criterion of reducibility of theoretical terms to the terms of the observation language. In an ideal theory it would be possible to reduce the content of all second-order theoretical concepts to a set of "primitive terms," utilizing the procedures of formal logic. The primitive terms of theoretical sociology as a whole refer to observations of the behavior of actors in interaction.[48]

Zetterberg answers affirmatively the age-old question: are there sociological laws parallel to those discovered in the natural sciences? There are many such laws or theoretical propositions that have been turned up by social science; for example, "persons tend to issue prescriptions that maintain the rank they enjoy in their social structure" or "the more favourable evaluations rank-and-file members receive in a group, the more their ideas converge with those of other group members."[49] Two factors influence the specification of such laws in the sociological literature: the conditions of their application are often only vaguely indicated, and it is not made clear what procedures are necessary to confirm or "verify" them. Everyday life abounds with generalizations that people make of their own conduct or of the activities of others: the task of sociology is to test these so as to turn them from lay hypotheses into confirmed findings and laws, discarding those shown to be invalid. "I think sociology should make a more serious effort to incorporate in its theories the best thoughts (theoretical hypotheses) of the human conditions found in Homer, Dante, Shakespeare, Cervantes, Twain and other great writers, who now provide the lion's share of any educated layman's conception of the human drama. In the end, however, the outcome of the theoretical enterprise should be "high informative content, well backed by experience," that is, laws."[50]

Zetterberg's discussion touches only marginally on functionalism and does not elucidate the relevance of what he has to say for significance of functional explanation in sociology. Nagel has treated the question at some length; but here I shall consider the account provided by Hempel, which is concerned with connecting deductive-nomological to functional explanation.[51] According to Hempel, functional analysis is a form of teleological explanation, the latter referring not to the causes of an event but to the ends to which it is directed. Teleological explanation, however, has traditionally been impervious to empirical testing: Hempel quotes the example of entelechy, or "vital force," as a metaphysical principle which in biology has been involved in unacceptable teleological theories. The problem is to strip functional analysis away from any association with such nontestable vitalistic principles.

In biology, Hempel says, functional analysis is concerned with the explanation of a recurrent activity (e.g., the beating of the heart) in terms of its contribution to a state (e.g., the circulation of the blood through the body) of the organism required for the maintenance of life. In the social sciences, the objects of analysis are similarly patterned and repetitive modes of social conduct examined in relation to states of the larger social system. But what is the explanatory element in functional explanation? It is not to be found in the type of nomology characteristic of either deductive-nomological or inductive statistical explanation. There is a close similarity in logical form nevertheless. When, in giving physical explanations, we say that an ice cube melts because it was put into warm water, we are able to justify this as an explanation of the melting by reference to general laws of which the specific case is an instance. In a similar way, the "because" of functional explanation implies a principle such that, within specified conditions, a system will either invariably or with a high degree of probability meet the functional exigencies needed for its survival in the face of forces threatening to change it. That is to say, the general propositions involved in functional analysis refer to the self-regulation of biological or social systems; thus understood, they yield predictions which can be objectively tested.[52] This depends upon defining concepts like "system need" operationally. "It will no doubt be one of the most important tasks of functional analysis in psychology and the social sciences to ascertain to what extent such phenomena of self-regulation can be found, and can be represented by corresponding laws. Whatever specific laws might be discovered by research along these lines, the kind of explanation and prediction made possible by them does not differ in its logical character from that of the physical sciences."[53]

The three examples I have chosen here are arbitrary, insofar as they could have been replaced by many others expressing similar views—although each has been influential in its own right. I do not want to claim, of course, that the general standpoint they represent has ever become an unrivaled one, but it has undoubtedly been until quite recently the dominant approach in English-speaking sociology. This is not just because the main tradition has insisted that the social sciences should model their aspirations on the sciences of nature; rather, many authors in the former field have accepted, explicitly or implicitly, that "science" can be identified with the positivistic philosophy of science. Functionalism has played an important part in this, as the conceptual vehicle of the continuity between natural and social science; the division between the physical and the life sciences appears as great, if not larger, than that between biology and sociology.

The Postpositivistic Philosophy of Science

In the philosophy of science, as contrasted to the methodological self-understanding of the social sciences, the "orthodox model" has long since become subject to broad-ranging attack led by such authors as Toulmin, Feyerabend, Hesse, Kuhn, and others. While these writers disagree about the conclusions that should be drawn from their critical analyses of positivistic philosophy, it is clear that they have successfully displaced the orthodox model: it is an orthodoxy no longer. The work of Karl Popper, however, precedes theirs and in some part is one of their sources; a tracing of the critical views which Popper has expressed of logical positivism, as well as the evident themes which connect his writings to those of the Vienna Circle, necessarily precedes any commentary on the "newer philosophy of science" of the past two decades.

The relation between Popper's views and those of the leading members of the Vienna Circle, particularly Carnap, has been a controversial one from the beginning. Popper was not himself a member of the circle, but he had a close intellectual contact with it. His first and still his major work, *Logik der Forschung,* was discussed within the group and regarded as basically in accord with the perspective of logical positivism. Popper, on the other hand, emphasized that the work was radically critical of the philosophy of logical positivism and since its first publication has continued to stress the differences between his position and any kind of empiricism or positivistic philosophy.[54] The points at issue are not easy to disentangle. In assessing the differences between Popper's ideas and those of logical positivism, even in its more liberalized versions, one should mention the following of Popper's views as the most distinctive sources of contrast: his complete rejection of induction and his concomitant rejection of "sensory certainty," whether manifest as phenomenalism or physicalism; his substitution of falsification for verification, with the corresponding stress upon boldness and ingenuity in the framing of scientific hypotheses; his defense of tradition which, in conjunction with the operation of the critical spirit, is integral to science; and his replacement of the logical positivist ambition of putting an end to metaphysics by revealing it as nonsense with the aim of securing criteria of demarcation between science and pseudoscience. These differences are certainly considerable, and underlie Popper's continual insistence that not only is he not a "positivist," but he is one of its foremost critics in the philosophy of science. However there also some clearly apparent, major similarities between Popper's writings and those of the logical positivists. Popper shares the conviction that scientific knowledge, imperfect though it may be, is the most certain and reliable knowledge to which human beings can aspire; his endeavor to establish clear criteria of demarcation between science and pseudoscience shares much of the same impetus as the concern of the logical positivists to free science from mystifying, empty wordplay; and, like the logical positivists, his characterization of science is a procedural one: science is separated from other forms of tradition insofar as its theories and findings are capable of being exposed to empirical testing and therefore to potential falsification.

Popper's first formulation of the principle of falsification as the key to the demarcation between science and nonscience was arrived at, according to his own testimony, as a result of reflection upon the gulf between certain types of social theory—especially Marxism and psychoanalysis—and the physical sciences. The former, Popper came to the conclusion, had more in common with primitive myths rather than with science; they are more like astrology than astronomy.[55] The reason for this, according to Popper, lies less in their lack of precision, as compared to physics, than in what to their adherents is their most attractive characteristic: the range of their explanatory power. As total systems of thought, they gain their support from a quasi-religious experience of conversion or revelation, and, once converted, the believer is able to explain any event in terms of them. Since they can explain anything or everything, there is no source or type of empirical evidence that could be pointed to as a basis of showing the ideas involved to be mistaken. This stands in marked contrast to relativity theory in physics, which generated specific predictions about the movement of material entities and delivered itself as a hostage to the outcome of the testing of those predictions; such an element of risk is absent from theories such as Marxism and psychoanalysis, which protect themselves against counterfactual evidence. The distinctive characteristic of science, therefore, is that instead of merely seeking confirmation or verification of a theory, the scientist attempts to refute it. Confirmation, or what Popper has subsequently come to call "corroborating evidence," of a theory results from its successful withstanding of empirical assaults which have the aim of falsifying it. "One can sum up all this by saying that *the criterion of the scientific status of a theory is its falsifiability, or refutability, or testability.*"[56]

Popper's emphasis upon falsification stands in the closest possible relation to the critique of inductive logic with which he began his *Logik der Forschung.* A major tension had always existed at the heart of empiricist philosophies of science. Science was supposed to yield certain knowledge; on the other hand, the logical form of the induction of laws from observations precludes certainty. However many tests we may make confirming a theoretical proposition, there always remains the possibility that the next test will disconfirm it were it to be made; hence the validity of scientific laws can never be conclusively verified. Popper's response to this classical problem of empiricism is to deny the premise on which it rests; that is to say, he denies that science proceeds through induction at all, and he accepts that no abstract proposition in science can ever be finally verified. There is, as Popper puts it, an asymmetry between verification and falsification. No matter how many white swans we may observe, this does not justify the conclusion "all swans are white"; but while such a universal statement cannot ever be derived from singular statements reporting observations, it can be contradicted or shown to be wrong by singular statements.[57] Thus, although Popper's philosophy of science is skeptical in the sense that it accepts that no scientific law, even one which scientists may feel is completely and securely founded, can be conclusively proved; it insists that scientific advance is possible through the empirical refutation of hypotheses. The object of science is still conceived of in a traditional manner as the securing of abstract generalizations that are true insofar as they correspond to facts; but we can never be logically certain that we have attained truth, although we can approach closer and closer to such certainty by the elimination of false theories.

Just as scientific theories are not tested inductively, neither are they arrived at inductively; the manner in which a theory is discovered or invented has nothing to do with its scientific status, which depends solely upon its being able to specify falsifying conditions and being able to withstand empirical testing of those conditions. There is no "logic of discovery," since new ideas may be conceived as a flash of intuition or as the result of religious reflection or in many other contexts. Nor is there any "observations" which is prior to "theory" in the manner integral to the notion of inductive logic, and fundamental to logical positivism in the form of protocol statements. All observations are "theory-impregnated," and are interpretations of facts. There can be no foundation of certain or incorrigible knowledge upon which science builds, as logical positivism, and positivistic philosophy more generally, assumes. Scientific knowledge is built on shifting sand, and what is important is not where we begin but how far we are able to subject our conjectures to empirical tests and hence to rational criticism. This also supplies the guiding thread in Popper's social philosophy. An "open society" is one in which no single system of ideas is able to monopolize the social order—where freedom is ensured by the critical congrontation of deverse ideas and policies whose outcomes can thus be rationally assessed.

Popper has consistently attempted to separate his thought from the preoccupation with language characteristic of so much contemporary philosophy, holding that the latter obscures the true nature of the scientific enterprise, which is above all concerned with the relation between hypotheses and the world of real objects and events. Terminology, Popper says, does not matter, save insofar as clarity and unambiguousness of expression are demanded for the rigorous testing of scientific theories. The same ideas can be expressed in different words; all that matters is that they should be clearly expressed and formulated in such a way that the circumstances in which they can be declared to be falsified are known. Popper's philosophy possesses the boldness of formulation that he requires of science itself: the appeal of his substitution of falsification for verification derives in large part from the simple and incisive way in which it disposes at a stroke of the traditional dilemmas of induction. But the simplicity of the notion is belied by difficulties which it conceals, consideration of which forces us to confront more directly issues of language which Popper tends to dismiss as being at most of only marginal importance.

In the first place, the notion of falsification sits uneasily in Popper's writings with his commitment to a correspondence theory of truth. The aim of science, according to Popper, is more accurately described as concerned with "verisimilitude" rather than truth.[58] But the idea of verisimilitude is only defensible if we assume that there are a finite number of possible conjectures or theories about nature such that by progressively refuting them we come closer and closer to the truth. There seems no warrant for such an assumption, all the less so given Popper's injunction that it is incumbent on the scientist to look for "unlikely" hypotheses since these are the easiest to test. Second, the very idea of falsification, which looks so concise and clear presented as a logical solution to difficulties of induction, becomes quite murky when applied to the analysis of actual scientific activities of testing and the comparison of theories. Popper, of course, acknowledges that the logic of falsification is in some part separable from its implementation in scientific procedures. The universal statement "all swans are white" is in principle contradicted by the discovery of a black swan, but in practice matters are not so simple, because we have to decide, for one thing, what is to count as a black swan—that is, as a falsifying observation. It would be possible, for example, for someone accepting the universal statement "all swans are white" to discount any case of a black swan that might be found as not being a swan at all, hence placing it outside the scope of the law. Popper's response to such a tactic is to declare it unscientific, alien to the spirit in which science should be carried on. But this is not very convincing, and one could claim that here Popper is hoist with his own petard, because such an argument seems to do just what it criticizes: namely, to propose that any instance which does not accord with the thesis should be disregarded as "unscientific procedure." One of the consequences of Kuhn's work is to affirm that this will not do, and the same holds for that of Feyerabend and Lakatos—in spite of the fact that the latter author regards Popper as the main originator of what he calls "sophisticated falsificationism."

Kuhn's most important study, *The Structure of Scientific Revolutions,* has become very well known indeed, and there is no need to do more than refer in the most cursory manner here to its main themes. Kuhn's views may differ considerably in certain respects from those of Popper, but they also connect up closely with them, because both authors recognize the significance of the history of science for the philosophy of science (and vice versa). This has not been true, by and large, of the logical positivists, who have concentrated primarily upon producing abstract, formal analyses without giving any detailed attention to the historical study of the development of science. Hence, as Kuhn points out, they have tended to operate with accounts of scientific discoveries as finished achievements, as they are recorded in textbooks; but these no more satisfactorily describe the substance of what actually happens in science than tourist brochures describe the culture into which they initiate the traveler.[59]

Kuhn's work was partly stimulated by his awareness of a contrast between the natural and social sciences, not of the kind traditionally stressed in the *Geisteswissenschaften,* but concerning the lack of agreement among social scientists over the basic character of their intellectual endeavors. The social sciences, in short, lack "paradigms." Thus they do not show the characteristic pattern of development of the natural sciences, which is one of periods of relatively stable "normal science," involving puzzle-solving activities within the confines of a shared paradigm, interspersed with periods of revolutionary change as a result of which a new paradigm comes to supersede the old. Revolutions are written *out* of textbooks of science, or rather, never written *in* them; a textbook expresses a paradigm as the consolidated achievements of a particular science to date. Periods of revolutionary change in science are nonetheless a consequence of the activities of normal science, for it is through the puzzle-solving activities of normal science that contradictions or anomalies emerge within the existing framework of knowledge. A revolution in science is a change in world view, a gestalt switch; the conceptual transformation thus effected infuses "observation" itself. "Is sensory experience fixed and neutral? The epistemological viewpoint that has most often guided Western philosophy for three centuries dictates an immediate and unequivocal, Yes! In the absence of a developed alternative, I find it impossible to relinquish entirely that viewpoint. Yet it no longer functions effectively, and the attempts to make it do so through the introduction of a neutral language of observations now seem to me hopeless."[60]

The Structure of Scientific Revolutions has provoked a great deal of discussion, to which Popper, among many others, has contributed. In the course of this debate, Kuhn has attempted to clear up ambiguities in the original work and to elaborate upon it in various ways. I shall concentrate only upon issues relevant to the subsequent sections of this study. The most useful way to identify these is to indicate some of the differences of emphasis in Kuhn's work as compared to that of Popper. Three such differences are the following: (1) For Kuhn, "normal science" is integral to scientific progress, since the suspension of criticism involved in the common acceptance of a paradigm makes possible a concentration of effort upon clearly defined problems. Constant critical assessment of the most basic elements of a "disciplinary matrix" would prevent such a concentration of effort: this is just what occurs in preparadigmatic disciplines, such as the social sciences, in which the inability to agree over basic premises of the substance and method of inquiry blocks the development of knowledge in the form achieved in many areas of natural science. The sort of "permanent revolution" in science envisaged by Popper neither describes the actual conduct of science nor is a desirable framework for it; normal science is not merely deformed science. This view also separates Kuhn from Feyerabend's "scientific anarchism": a proliferation of basic theories is only to be striven for in times of revolutionary crisis. (2) Kuhn's writings demonstrate the hazards in transferring the idea of falsification to the actual practice of science. He says he takes the notion of "the asymmetry of falsification and confirmation very seriously indeed";[61] but "testing" has to be related to the conjunctions of normal and revolutionary science. Scientists working within a paradigm often either ignore or treat as consistent with their accepted theories findings that are subsequently—following the dissolution of the paradigm—recognized as imcompatible with or as refuting those theories. (3) Meaning variance, or the "incommensurability" of paradigms, appears as a fundamental problem in Kuhn's work in a way in which it does not in that of Popper; partly as a consequence of this, Kuhn finds Popper's account of verisimilitude unacceptable. Kuhn has consistently denied that he is a relativist, and it is quite obvious that he could not be one: for if the succession of paradigms is not regarded as "progressive," in some sense, the differentiation between preparadigmatic and postparadigmatic sciences effectively loses its significance: on the logical level, successive paradigms would only be "laterally" distributed, each equivalent to any other—the same situation that is claimed to exist in the social sciences. On the other hand, Kuhn has found some considerable difficulty in spelling out how scientific progress occurs through revolutions and what the consequences of the resolution of this problem are for a theory of truth.[62]

The Critique of Positivism in Frankfurt Philosophy

Since Hume, positivistic philosophers have generally adopted the stance that the sensory experience which provides the basis of scientific knowledge cannot be extended to encompass moral judgments or ethical values. Disputes concerning morality cannot be settled by appeal to intersubjectively available observations as debates over factual issues can. In the social sciences, this has long been the common assumption of most otherwise divergent schools of thought, including various forms of revisionist Marxism (such as that led by Eduard Bernstein). Perhaps the most well-known and influential exposition of the standpoint in sociology is that of Max Weber, who more than any other major writer pursued the implications of the "fact-value dichotomy" to its furthest limits and was prepared to accept these implications in full. For Weber, who drew his views on this issue from neo-Kantianism rather than from British empiricism, the findings of natural or social science stand in a purely instrumental connection to moral values. Science can show us which of a given choice of means is the most effective way of achieving a certain end and what the other consequences of achieving that end are likely to be; but it cannot give us the slightest degree of help in deciding to opt for that end itself (save insofar as that end might be in some part a means to other ends).[63] One consequence of this is that there can be no rational arbitration between the sets of "ultimate values" upon which the major world civilizations rest and which Weber set out to analyze in his studies of the "world religions"; such a clash of values is settled in the area of power struggles.[64]

The imposition of strict limits upon moral reason in positivistic philosophies is something which two generations of Frankfurt philosophers, from Horkheimer, Adorno, and Marcuse to Habermas, have been concerned to criticize. The critique of positivism in this respect has been one of the most central preoccupations of what has come to be called "critical theory." If there is a single dominating element in critical theory, it is the defense of Reason (*Vernunft*) understood in the sense of Hegel and classical German philosophy: as the critical faculty which reconciles knowledge with the transformation of the world so as to further human fulfillment and freedom.[65] Frankfurt philosophy attempts to follow Marx, and thereby to refurbish modern Marxism itself, by appealing to Hegel's transcendence of Kantian dualisms: not only that of pure and practical Reason, but that of the apperception of phenomena and the unknowable "things in themselves." Such dualisms are regarded as both the expression and source of a passive, contemplative attitude to knowledge, an attitude which reduces the practical import of knowledge to "technology" or "technique" robbed of the unifying potentialities of historical Reason. Whereas in Hegel, as Horkheimer puts it, Reason is seen to be inherent in reality, in Hume and in Kant, as well as in Cartesian philosophy, it becomes a "subjective faculty of the mind."[66] The individual subject is the sole possessor of reason, and the latter concept is taken to mean merely the calculative relating of means to ends.

The origins of the "Frankfurt School" were contemporaneous with those of the Vienna Circle, and the members of the former group sharpened their critical assessment of the influence of empiricism in the past by means of onslaughts upon its most prominent representatives in the present. In one such discussion, written in the late 1930s, Horkheimer connects logical positivism to the tradition of Hume and Locke but argues that the critical character which the writings of these authors possessed has been sacrificed by the modern logical positivists.[67] The skeptical empiricism of Hume was subversively directed against the prevailing dogmas in order to forge a new beginning in which rationalism would prevail over the forces of unenlightened mythology. In this sense, the Enlightment had a moral impetus which in actuality cut across the belief of Hume that facts could be separated from values. This is largely absent from logical positivism, which seeks only to complete and to sanction the domination of science as the contemplative reduction of experience to a logically coherent order of laws. This might be thought unfair to Neurath in particular and untrue to the Marxist leanings of various members of the Vienna Circle. But for Horkheimer such a consideration would be largely beside the point, because Marxism has not stood apart from the positivistic nature of much modern philosophy. On the contrary, the relapse of Marxism into positivistic philosophy is the origin of the twin characteristics of Marxism in the twentieth century: its quietism when in opposition (as in Germany) and its transformation into bureaucratic domination when in power (as in the Soviet Union).

The Frankfurt philosophers have attempted to diagnose the beginnings of "positivistic Marxism" in the writings of Marx himself. What for Althusser and his followers is an "epistemological break" separating the speculative, idealistic Marx from the first formation of scientific Marxism, for the critical theorists marks the phase of the incipient degeneration of Marxism into positivistic philosophy. The Frankfurt authors have differed among themselves about their evaluations of the nature and origins of positivistic Marxism, but their analyses—including that of Habermas in the "younger generation"—have major overall points of agreement. The critical inspiration of Marxism derives from the dialectic of subject and object and is lost where "materialism" means the denial of the active intervention of the subject in history, or the reduction of culture and cultural ideals to epiphenomena of physical events. Monistic materialism, which regards all change as the interplay of natural occurrences, converges directly with non-Marxist positivistic philosophy. Several of the critical theorists have had doubts about the use of the notion of labor in Marx's writings; insofar as this refers merely to the material transformation of nature, and the critique of contemporary society is tied to this, socialism comes to be conceived of merely as a technically more efficient version of capitalism. According to Habermas, in "turning Hegel back on his feet," Marx compressed two elements of Hegel's philosophy into one: man's reflexive awareness as the maker of history and the self-constitution of humanity through labor. When the former is reduced to the latter, the integral tie between history and freedom is dissolved.[68]

In critical theory, "positivism" has a much broader and more diffuse meaning than it does for most other writers, wider even than what I have distinguished as "positivistic philosophy." This use of the term has to be understood against the background of the attempts of the Frankfurt philosophers to effect an ambitious critique of the tendency of development of Western culture since the Enlightenment and, indeed, in certain basic respects since classical times. The progenitors of the Enlightenment set out to effect the disenchantment of the world, to replace myth by solidly founded knowledge, applying that knowledge practically in technology. In so doing they prepared the way for the domination of modern culture by technical rationality—the undermining of Reason against which Hegel struggled and which, with the disintegration of the Hegelian system, became largely lost to philosophy. In the name of freedom from the domination of myth, the Enlightment created a new form of domination, hidden from view by its own philosophy: domination by instrumental rationality. "Subject and object are both rendered ineffectual. The abstract self, which justifies record-making and systematisation, has nothing set over against it but the abstract material which possesses no other quality than to be a substrate of such possession. The equation of spirit and world arises eventually, but only with a mutual restriction of both sides. The reduction of thought to a mathematical apparatus conceals the sanction of the world as its own yardstick. What appears to be the triumph of subjective rationality, the subjection of all reality to logical formalism, is paid for by the obedient subjection of reason to what is directly given. What is abandoned is the whole claim and approach of knowledge: to comprehend the given as such; not merely to determine the abstract spatio-temporal relations of the facts which allow them just to be grasped, but on the contrary to conceive them as the superficies, as mediated conceptual moments which come to fulfillment only in the development of their social, historical, and human significance."[69]

Critical theory is a defense of just those traditions of philosophy which the logical positivists wished to show consist largely of empty metaphysics. Consequently, it is not surprising that the two schools have kept at arm's distance from one another, and their mutual influence has been slight indeed. However, in recent times, with the increasing strains to which the positivistic philosophy of science has been subject, the influence of the philosophy of the later Wittgeinstein and Austin's "ordinary-language philosophy" in Britain and the United States, and of hermeneutic phenomenology on the Continent, the situation in philosophy (as in social theory) has become much more fluid. Among the younger Frankfurt philosophers, Habermas has been particularly influential in connecting critical theory to each of the aforementioned types of philosophy, as well as to pragmatism—while sustaining most of its established themes. Habermas, together with Adorno, played the central part in the controversy over Popper's views that has come to be called (following the usage of critical theory rather than that of Popper) the "positivism debate" in German sociology. The debate is an odd one, insofar as none of the participants regard themselves as defending positivistic philosophy, much less describe themselves as positivists; given the standpoint of critical theory, however, in which the term "positivism" is applied very broadly to traditions of thought that would not ordinarily be thus designated, it is not difficult to appreciate that the contested meaning of the term is at the heart of the matters at issue, not merely a linguistic curiosity. The initial origin of the dispute was Popper's presentation of "twenty-seven theses" on the logic of the social sciences, at the meeting of the German Sociological Association at Tubingen in 1961; this was followed by a paper by Adorno. Popper and Adorno did not attack each other's contributions directly, however, and their confrontation only ramified into a wide-ranging debate through the subsequent interventions of Habermas, Albèrt, and others.[70]

In his paper, Popper reiterates his well-known view that the aim of the social sciences is the explanation of conduct through the "situational logic" of action; that is to say, through the rational reconstruction of the circumstances (goals and knowledge) under which individuals act, and of the consequences of their behavior. This is an "interpretative sociology," but not one, according to Popper, that retains any residue of the subjective, empathic qualities with which it has characteristically been associated. It is a "purely objective method."[71] As such, it differs in content but not in logical form from the methods of the natural sciences, which Popper elucidates in terms made familiar by the general corpus of his writings. He rejects what he calls "naturalism" in the social sciences on the same basis as he rejects "positivism" in natural science: naturalism supposes that sociology begins by collecting observations and measurements, inducing generalizations from these data which then become incorporated within theories. This derives from a mistaken (positivistic) philosophy of natural science: the "objectivity" of science lies in its critical method of trial and error. Popper thus affirms his support of "critical rationalism," meaning by this his advocacy of falsificationism as the most integral procedure of science.

Habermas's critique of Popper concentrates mainly upon the limits of Popper's critical rationalism which, according to the former, still contains a strong residue of positivistic philosophy. Popper's theory of science is an analytical, as opposed to a dialectical, one. Habermas suggests that the "objectivity" of natural science cannot be transferred directly to the social sciences, since the latter are concerned with a preinterpreted universe of occurrences; that is to say, with a social world in which the categories of experience are already formed by and in the "meaningful conduct" of human subjects. Hermeneutic understanding, involving the sustaining of communication between the social scientist and those whose conduct he studies, is an essential element of procedure in the social sciences and cannot be encompassed by simple appeal to the "observation" of events in nature, even if transposed as "situational logic." To conceive of the aim of sociology as that of discovering laws has the practical implication of making of it a social technology. "In contrast, dialectical theory of society must indicate the gaping discrepancy between practical questions and the accomplishment of technical tasks—not to mention the realization of a meaning which, far beyond the domination of nature achieved by manipulation of a reified relation, no matter how skilful that may be—would relate to the structure of a social life-context as a whole and would, in fact, demand its emancipation."[72] To accomplish this, a dialectical or critical theory must transcend the boundaries of critical rationalism as expressed by Popper.

The separation between fact and value, or cognition and evaluation, made in positivistic philosophies, Habermas says, condemns practical questions to irrationality, or to the "closed world" of myth which it is supposedly the object of positivism to dispel. Unlike most philosophers, Popper openly acknowledges this by declaring that his adherence to rationalism is an article of faith. This makes the adoption of rationalism an arbitrary initial decision. Some followers of Popper, notably Bartley, have accepted that there cannot be a deductive foundation for rationalism but have tried to ground critical rationalism by reference to itself; that is to say, by holding that the commitment to critical method as formulated by Popper can itself in principle be criticized.[73] But this will hardly do: Bartley is unable to specify the conditions under which the commitment to rationality would have rationally to be abandoned; this is because what is understood as "criticism" here is too narrow and is not grounded in the historical conditions of human social life and communication. Habermas points to the connection between Popper's adherence to a correspondence theory of truth and the thesis of the dualism of fact and value. Popper shields himself against some of the problems which the correspondence theory raises, when combined with his acceptance of the theory-impregnated character of observation statements, by stressing the difference between knowing what truth means and having a criterion for deciding the truth or falsity of a statement. According to the notion of falsification, we cannot have such a criterion or standard of truth; all we can achieve is the progressive elimination of false views. However, what this involves, Habermas says, is the surreptitious incorporation of standards of evaluation that are uncritically taken over from everyday life; the hermeneutic understanding of ordinary language and intersubjective experience is taken for granted. Critical discussion, as formulated by Habermas, involves three uses of language: the description of a state of affairs, the postulating of rules of procedure, and the critical justification of the former two.[74] Criticism thus cannot be terminated within the sphere of science itself but must concern itself with the standards or values which structure science as one mode of activity among others. So far as the historical context of modern science is concerned, positivistic acceptance of the dualism of fact and value leads to a failure to appreciate that technical rationality supports a system of domination as its legitimating ideology.

Neither Albert, defending Popper, nor Popper himself, in his commentary on the debate, accept that their views do place the sort of bounds upon critical rationalism that Habermas claims. According to Albert, the empirical sciences are able to deal with the type of experience Habermas allots to hermeneutics and can represent these as "facts" like any others. This is, for Albert, potentially a more profoundly critical standpoint than that of Habermas, since it is a more skeptical one, which finds its critical impetus in the premise that science often shows that assumptions made within the ordinary, day-to-day world are erroneous. Popper's theory of science as myth that is self-critical is the only way of avoiding the twin dilemmas of an infinite regress on the one hand, and the supplying of "foundations" through sheer dogma on the other.[75] Popper's critical rationalism, he repeats, is quite distinct from positivism in all major respects; the critical theorists use the term in such a lax way that they are able to blanket out these differences and hence obliquely charge Popper with some of the very same weaknesses that he has in fact shown to be characteristic of positivistic philosophy. In his comments, Popper concurs: "the fact is that throughout my life I have combated positivist epistemology, under the name of 'positivism.' I do not deny, of course, the possibility of stretching the term 'positivist' until it covers anybody who takes any interest in natural science, so that it can be applied even to opponents of positivism, such as myself. I only contend that such a procedure is neither honest nor apt to clarify matters."[76]

Comments on the Philosophy of Natural Science

It would obviously be completely out of the question to attempt in this essay a comprehensive discussion of many of the issues raised by the matters referred to in the previous sections. Hence I shall confine my comments to a few problems in two major categories: the philosophy of natural science and the relation between the natural and social sciences.

So far as the first of these is concerned, there are two issues raised by the postpositivistic philosophy of science that loom particularly large. One is the status of falsificationism, as elaborated by Popper and his disciples (particularly Lakatos), and more generally that of deductivist accounts of scientific knowledge, including within this the "deductive-nomological model"; the other is the problem of the "incommensurability" of paradigms such as derived from the writings of Kuhn.

Popper's "solution to the problem of induction," which he has relentlessly advocated from his earliest works, gains much of its attractiveness from its simplicity: the idea that it takes only a single disconfirming instance to falsify a universal statement. But the logic of falsification, he has to admit, is discrepant from the practice. Lakatos's studies, although nominally directed at supporting main elements of the Popperian standpoint, show how wide the discrepancy is. Lakatos distinguishes three kinds of falsificationism: dogmatic falsificationism and naive and sophisticated "methodological falsificationism." The first is the weakest, treating the logical form of falsification as equivalent to its practice: as if a simple observed event or unequivocally defined finite set of events provide the means of refuting scientific theories.

This is an empiricist version of falsificationism, in contrast to methodological falsificationism, which accepts the theory-impregnated character of observations. All testing of theories depends upon acceptance of a theoretical framework which, in any given context, represents unproblematic background knowledge.[77] Naive methodological falsificationism, however, still maintains the view that theories can be refuted, and therefore should be abandoned, in the light of "observations" thus conceived. This will not do because a defender of a theory can always, if he is prepared to be ingenuous enough, "rescue" it from any number of apparently contravening instances. Sophisticated methodological falsificationism recognizes this, and states that there is no falsification where the discarded theory is not replaced by a superior one, where superiority is indexed by the following factors: the second theory has surplus empirical content over the first, predicting facts excluded by or improbable in light of the theory it replaces; the second theory explains all that was explained successfully by the first; and some surplus content of the second theory is corroborated (in Popper's sense of that term). If these criteria are met in any given circumstance of the abandonment of one theory for another, we may speak of a "progressive problem shift." If they are not met, the problem shift is a "degenerating" one; it does not in effect constitute the falsification of the preexisting theory by the one which supplants it.

Lakatos's sophisticated methodological falsificationism is self-confessedly an attempt to reconcile a version of Popper's philosophy of science with some of the major difficulties created for the latter by the works of Kuhn and others. As such, as Kuhn points out, it actually expresses a standpoint quite close to that of Kuhn's own.[78] One of the consequences of Lakatos's emendation of Popper is to downplay the decisionism that brooks large in Popper's own writings (which Habermas emphasizes) and to provide standards for the critical comparison of theories; Lakatos argues that such standards, or "rules of acceptance and falsification," are in fact not provided, or at least are not made explicit, by Kuhn. But the question then arises whether Lakatos, having originally rejected justificationism in favor of fallibilism, has not in the end arrived at a justificationist position which can better be defended and expanded by discarding falsificationism altogether. For Lakatos admits: " 'Falsification' in the sense of naive falsificationism (corroborated counter-evidence) is not a *sufficient* condition for eliminating a specific theory: in spite of hundreds of known anomalies we do not regard it as falsified (that is, eliminated) until we have a better one. Nor is 'falsification' in the naive sense *necessary* for falsification in the sophisticated sense: a progressive problem shift does not have to be interspersed with 'refutations.' Science can grow without any 'refutations' leading the way."[79]

As Lakatos uses it, "falsification" (1) only applies to the "degenerating phase" of research programs (in other cases anomalies are largely ignored or accommodated to the existing theory) and (2) only is effective when a better theory supersedes the existing one. It is clear that here refutation no longer forms the main substance of falsification. Lakatos has to all intents and purposes accepted the two major flaws in falsificationism, where that term is used in a sense that still retains any connection with Popper's critique of inductive logic. The two objections to falsificationism are these. First, in deciding among theories, scientists do not do what Popper's account suggests; that is to say, look for the most bizarre, "unlikely" theory on the grounds that it is the most easily falsifiable. Nor could there be any defense of the thesis that they should do so. Popper's usage here seems to trade on two different senses of what is "unlikely." A theory may be "unlikely" insofar as it is highly innovative; or it may be "unlikely" in the sense that it appears very improbable in light of what is currently regarded as the relevant empirical evidence. Scientists would be wasting their time if they deliberately sought out as often as they could the latter type of unlikely hypotheses. The fact that they do not, however, indicates they operate with an implicit notion of inductive inference.[80] Second, as I have mentioned earlier, Popper's attempt to provide a plausible analysis of scientific progress in terms of "verisimilitude" is unsuccessful, since there is no reason to suppose, within Popper's epistemology, that there is a finite number of potential theories available to interpret any specific range of occurrences.

In rejecting falsificationism, we at the same time reject the Popperian criterion of the demarcation between science and nonscience and the rigid dislocation between the psychology of discovery and the logic of testing. But how can we do so without reverting to the ideas that Popper set out to criticize: those involved in positivistic philosophies of science? In attempting to provide the beginnings of an answer to this question, it is helpful to reconsider the problems that came to light with early formulations of the Verification Principle and subsequently with the liberalized version of logical positivism. The early formulations were based upon the thesis, which stands in direct line of descent from Hume and Mach, that the meaning of scientific concept can in principle always be reduced to empirical observations. The later differentiation between observation and theoretical statements abandoned this standpoint, replacing it with the notion of correspondence rules linking observations and theories; the liberalized model retains the same image of science as a hierarchy of statements built upon a secure foundation of observations. Some of the difficulties created by the distinction between observational and theoretical terms can, as Shapere has pointed out, be linked to this context in which the distinction was elaborated.[81] One such difficulty is that of the ontological status of "theoretical entities." What was no problem in the earlier phase of logical positivism emerges as a major obscurity in its liberalized version. A phenomenalist or physicalist standpoint connects observation terms unproblematically to entities that exist; but it is not clear in what sense a theoretical entity such as an "electron" exists or is some sort of handy fiction. The "surplus content" of a theoretical term—i.e., that which cannot be directly expressed in the observation language—is supposed to be created by the place of the term in the deductive hierarchy of statements. This seems to lead to the uncomfortable and unsatisfactory conclusion that, as there is a continuum from the observable to the unobservable, so there is from objects that exist to ones which do not exist.[82] A second related difficulty concerns the character of the deductive relations presumed to hold between the levels in the hierarchy of observational and theoretical statements as interpreted axiomatic systems. The "correspondence rules" that intervene between observation and theory are conceived of in a manner parallel to the interpretation of formal systems of mathematical logic, as rules of logical derivation. But logical connections of this sort are obviously different from the connections that may pertain between entities, such as causal relations; and hence we are again led to conclude that theoretical terms are linked to observational ones in such a way that the former do not refer directly to the properties of existent things.

The outline of an alternative scheme, involving a revised model of inductive inference, is suggested by the writings of Quine and has been elaborated in some detail by Hesse.[83] This draws upon Duhem's notion that scientific knowledge should be represented as a network of statements, while not accepting some of the aspects of Duhem's conventionalism.[84] Within this network, what is "observable" and what is "theoretical" can only be distinguished in a pragmatic and relative way. The connecting statements in the network are laws, but laws are treated as pertaining to finite domains; hence one of the classical dilemmas of inductivism, that one cannot move from particular statements to universal ones, is superseded, for all inductive inference involves movement from particulars to analogous particulars. Such a view of scientific laws, Hesse argues, does not imply that universal laws are statistical generalizations or that statistical generalizations are to be regarded as preferable to universal laws in finite domains.[85] Nor does it imply an instrumentalist account of science; rather it implies a realist one, in which the analogical character of theoretical innovation is made central. "Scientific language," as Hesse puts it, "is therefore seen as a dynamic system which constantly grows by metaphorical extension of natural language, and which also changes with changing theory and with reinterpretation of some of the concepts of the natural language itself." [86]

This view of scientific theory does away with the idea of correspondence rules. The network involves observational predicates, which are the "knots" that attach it to the object-world, but these are not a fixed and invariable foundation; where the knots are depends upon the state of development of the theory and the form of its language, and they may be altered in the course of its transformation, especially where the latter is of the "revolutionary" character described by Kuhn. Scientific theory does not involve two languages, a language of observation and a language of theoretical terms; rather, it involves two overlapping and intersecting uses of the same language. Nor is there an absolute differentiation between formal languages of science and natural languages, since the former proceed by metaphorical extension of the latter and of experiences originally organized by the latter in the "natural attitude." In everyday life—and in learning scientific theories—we manage to get to understand observational terms and use them in their relevant contexts, but only by at the same time coming to grasp more abstract terms to which their meanings are connected. If the mode in which this is accomplished conforms to the process suggested by Quine, then all descriptive predicates, however "theoretical," are learned in conjunction with definite stimulus situations, or through sentences that contain such predicates (or the two combined). No such predicates, however, are learned by empirical association alone; they do not form an "independent" class of observational terms such as is presupposed in positivistic philosophy. What counts as an observational term cannot be specified without presupposing a framework of accepted laws, which constitute the integrative elements of the network but which in principle and in practice can be radically changed. It is not possible to know, at any given point of time, which laws and predicates may have to be revised or discarded in light of research findings.

The network model of science provides a way of recognizing the poetics of theoretical innovation while at the same time offering a mode of distinguishing sense and reference with regard to "paradigms." Writings such as those of Kuhn, which show the importance of discontinuities in the development of science, push to the forefront two sorts of problems, each potentially posing dilemmas of relativism: one concerns how it is possible to make the transition from one paradigm to another, if they are distinct and different "universes of meaning"; the other concerns how it is possible to sustain a notion of truth, given that the succession of paradigms involves transforming what are recognized as "facts" within divergent systems of theory. The first, the so-called problem of "meaning variance," is in some part an outcome of exaggerating the internal unity of paradigms or of "frames of meaning" more generally.[87] If paradigms are treated as closed systems of concepts whose meanings are determined only by their mutual relation within the system, it becomes difficult to see how transference from one paradigm to another is achieved. The mediation of paradigms or frames of meaning should, however, be more aptly regarded as normal in human experience rather than extraordinary; becoming a scientist, for example, involves distancing oneself from common-sense views of the world as part of the process of mastering scientific theories. The capacity to shift between what Schutz calls "multiple realities," involving the control of allegory and metaphor, is a routine feature of everyday human activity, placed in relief insofar as it is consciously organized as a process of learning new frames of meaning, or one of becoming able to move from one paradigm to another within the context of scientific activity. In this view the mediation of radically discrepant paradigms, such as is involved in scientific "revolutions," is not qualitatively different from meaning transformations required in moving between quite closely related theories; the role of learning by analogy and metaphor is central to both.

The relativistic implications of Kuhn's writing with respect to truth have been a core issue in the debate surrounding his work from the first publication of *The Structure of Scientific Revolutions* up to the present time (although Kuhn himself has consistently rejected relativism in this sense). Such implications also emerge in the writings of some recent philosophers not concerned specifically with the philosophy of science—for example, in the works of Gadamer in hermeneutics and those of Winch in "post-Wittgensteinian philosophy"—and are one focal point in the respective controversies to which these have given rise.[88] The source of the strain toward relativism is easy to trace: it derives from the idealist leanings of these authors. If "paradigms" ("traditions," "language games") are treated as constitutive of an object-world, rather than as modes of representing or relating to an object-world, there are as many "realities" as there are frames of meaning. Kuhn has made it clear that he does not accept such a view, but without elaborating an account of what notion of truth should replace the versions of the correspondence theory of truth (including that of Popper) which he rejects.[89]

Hesse has suggested that the network model of science involves breaking with the time-honored dichotomy between correspondence and coherence theories of truth, borrowing elements from each while also discarding some of their traditional features; and that this position is most appropriately connected to a realist ontology. Acceptance of the theory-impregnated character of observations has seemed to some to foreclose altogether the possibility of doing what scientists usually claim to be doing; that is, comparing different theories in light of the evidence, since what counts as "evidence" is influenced by the theories themselves—the phenomena can always be saved by the interpretation and reinterpretation of observations. But in this view there lurks a strong residue of positivist philosophy; a purely instrumental account of science is the last refuge of the disillusioned positivist. Against such a standpoint we can pose two integral elements of scientific procedure. One is an insistence upon the significance of sanctioned standards of criticism which help to separate science—although not to demarcate it cleanly—from religious cosmologies. Acknowledgment of the importance of science as self-critique has no necessary connection with a falsificationist epistemology. Indeed, separating the one from the other helps to add force to Habermas's analysis of the shortcomings of Popperianism, by making it clear that the "critical tradition" of science presupposes normative standards that cannot be validated as such in terms of the procedures of scientific testing because they are the legitimating framework within which those procedures are organized. The second point is that the mediation of divergent theories, or paradigms, involves the conjunction of referential parameters which, given the normative orientation of science, always provide an "empirical intersection" subject to disputation with respect to truth claims. This follows directly from the network model of science. The mediation of paradigms is a hermeneutic task, in the sense that it involves the capability of moving between frames of meaning; but such a capability cannot be acquired purely on the level of intension, since the terms comprising the network are tied in in a complex (and variable) way to extensional predicates.

Since the correspondence theory of truth has been traditionally bound up with positivistic philosophies, critics of such philosophies have usually presumed that rejection of them necessitates discarding it also. There are several features of established correspondence theories of truth, however, which are the substantial part of the residue of positivistic philosophy and which can be separated out without disavowing the correspondence notion altogether.[90] One is the assumption that correspondence theory presupposes at least some statements which are founded upon indisputable observations: statements which are not open to revision. This can be traced in large part to the thesis that the meaning of terms employed in a theoretical language can either be expressed directly as empirical observations or must rest upon a foundation of such observations. The view of language which this involves is an impoverished one, and it muddies over the distinction between the relation of concepts within a theoretical network and the relation between statements involving those concepts and the object-world. The former relation can be illuminated, with respect to truth values, by the incorporation of coherence criteria, or "coherence conditions," as these are suggested by the network model. Such coherence criteria cannot be taken for granted here, as in the positivistic scheme, where the connection between concepts is implicitly explained through the operation of correspondence rules. The criteria can be specified as a set of conditions providing for the interrelatedness of concepts within the networks. The interrelatedness of the components of the network only concerns the object-world with regard to its production as a system of classification; as such this interrelatedness pertains to the network as an organizing medium whereby truth as a relation between statements and the object-world is made possible, but it does not provide the substance of that relation itself.

Two further assumptions deriving from the association of correspondence theory with positivistic philosophies are that advocacy of a correspondence theory presupposes the explication of "correspondence" in some more basic philosophical terms, and that such advocacy necessarily involves providing an account of the existence of the object-world itself. The first gets to the nub of the objections that are traditionally raised against correspondence theory, which concern the difficulty of defining what "correspondence" is.[91] The presumption that such objections have to be answered by specifying the nature of correspondence in terms of some other type of relation, however, is bound up with the positivistic view of the character of observation statements, since observation is taken as a more "primitive" relation than correspondence—that is, as one to which the latter can be in some way reduced. If we break with such a view of observation statements, we can also reject this mode of treating the correspondence relation; "correspondence" then becomes the more primitive term and as such is regarded as a necessary element of the extensional character of a knowledge claim.[92]

The assumption that a correspondence theory has to provide a justification of the independent existence of the object-world is similarly connected with the central concerns of positivistic philosophies, because these are directed toward tying the conditions of knowledge to sensory experience, the latter being taken (in phenomenalism) to actually consititute the object-world. Rejection of positivistic philosophy frees us from the obligation to ground a correspondence version of truth in such a justification, or at least indicates that an account of the concept of truth does not logically entail it. To propose that the network model of science may be conjoined to a realist epistemology is therefore not to claim that the latter is necessarily the only view which could potentially be reconciled with a reworked theory of truth of the sort suggested here. Moreover, this would involve in turn a detailed reworking of preexisting formulations of "realism."

The Natural and the Social Sciences

The foregoing discussion of the philosophy of natural science does not provide in and of itself an adequate scheme for a treatment of the connections and divergencies between the natural and the social sciences. It rather indicates some elements of an approach to epistemological problems that span whatever differentiations may exist between them. But the formulation of a postpositivistic philosophy of natural science undoubtedly has direct implications for social-scientific method, which has usually been analyzed against a background of positivistic philosophy, explicitly stated or implicitly assumed. This is not only true of that tradition of thought I began by discussing, which links Comte, Durkheim, and modern functionalism; it also applies to the "counter-tradition" associated with the notion of the *Geisteswissenschaften*.

The contrast between *erklären* [explaining] and *verstehen* [understanding], as portrayed by Droysen and Dilthey, is at the heart of the tradition of the *Geisteswissenschaften*. In establishing his version of this contrast, Dilthey opposed his views to those of authors such as Comte and J. S. Mill who emphasized the continuity of the scientific study of nature and society, stressing instead that the subjective, meaningful character of human conduct has no counterpart in nature. The natural sciences develop causal explanations of "outer" events; the human sciences, on the other hand, are concerned with the "inner" understanding of "meaningful conduct." But Dilthey also accepted important elements of the ideas of Comte and Mill, accentuating the need to make the human sciences as precise and empirical as the sciences of nature. The differences between the natural and the social sciences concern not so much the logical form of their investigations and their results, as the content of their objects of investigation and the procedures whereby they may be studied.

Some of the main tensions in Dilthey's writings (and in those of Max Weber) stem from his attempt to combine elements of positivistic philosophy with the idealistic conception of "life philosophy" taken from the earlier development of the *Geisteswissenschaften* tradition. The "understanding" of human action or cultural products is held to be, following Schleiermacher, a process of the reexperiencing or reenactment of others' inner experiences. But at the same time, this process is not one of mere intuition; it is one which must be made the basis of a scientific history and which consequently forms the centerpiece of the method of the human sciences. Dilthey's term *Erlebnis* [experience], as Gadamer has pointed out, expresses the strain between the positivistic and idealistic strands in his works.[93] Unlike the verb form *erleben*, the word *Erlebnis* only became common in historical works in the 1870s, largely because of Dilthey's use of it. The word is more restricted than the other German term that may also be translated as "experience," *Erfahrung*, and in Dilthey's writings is introduced as the specific focus of the process of interpretative understanding; in understanding the meaning of what another person does, we grasp the content of that person's "experience" of the world. *Erlebnis* constitutes the fundamental content of consciousness, which Dilthey sometimes refers to as "immediate lived experience"; it is prior to any act of reflection. The term thus ties together the influence of empiricism (only that which can be directly experienced is real) and the influence of life philosophy (the meaningful character of human life is given in the inner experience of consciousness).

The critical reponse to the *Geisteswissenschaften* tradition on the part of the logical positivists or those close to logical positivism has been a consistent one. *Verstehen* cannot supply the sort of evidence necessary to scientific research, since it depends upon some sort of empathic identification with others. The observation language of social science must refer to overt behavior, not to hypothetical states of consciousness. No matter how much one might try to provide a concrete specification of *Erlebnis*, the latter remains inaccessible to the intersubjectively agreed observations upon which all the sciences must depend. The value of *verstehen*, if it has any at all, is as a mode of suggesting hypotheses; but such hypotheses have to be tested against observations of behavior.[94] In this respect, the views of the logical positivists converge closely with behaviorism in the social sciences.

There are three ways in which this critique of *verstehen* can be assessed: one is in terms of assessing what "understanding" is; another is in terms of assessing what "observable behavior" should be taken to mean; a third is in terms of evaluating the significance of "subjective" elements in conduct. In Dilthey's works, particularly in his earlier writings, *verstehen* is represented as a procedure, or *the* procedure, whereby the human sciences gain access to their subject matter, and as founded upon some sort of empathic process of "reenactment." The notion that *verstehen* is primarily a mode of procuring data is also taken for granted in positivistic critiques. Thus Abel says that *verstehen* is an "operation" that produces "evidence" and goes on to claim that such an intuitional mode of procedure simply begs the question of whether the process of "understanding" that takes place is a valid one.[95] Such an objection has definite force if the notion of *verstehen* is represented as specific research procedure, and as involving some kind of empathic process; indeed, Dilthey did not successfully manage to reconcile subjectivity and objectivity in the manner in which he sought to do, within a framework strongly influenced by empiricism. But the dismissal of *verstehen* as a mere propaedeutic writes off major elements of the *Geisteswissenschaften* tradition; the preoccupation with the "meaningful" character of human conduct and culture that characterizes that tradition is abandoned in positivistic philosophy, which attempts to reduce this to the content of "empirical observation." Hence it is important to recognize that recent contributions from within the tradition, as revitalized by hermeneutic phenomenology, have reworked the notion of *verstehen* in such a way as to detach it from its dependence upon the idea of the "reenactment" or "reliving" of the experiences of others. Thus, for Gadamer, *verstehen* is to be treated not as a special procedure of investigation appropriate to the study of social conduct, but as the ontological condition of intersubjectivity as such; and not as founded upon an empathic grasp of the experiences of others, but upon the mastery of language as the medium of the meaningful organization of human social life.[96]

To associate the notion of *verstehen* with language as the medium of intersubjectivity offers direct points of connection with the postpositivistic philosophy of science. Recognition of the significance of frames of meaning, and of their mediation, appears both in Gadamer and in Kuhn, although in the writings of the former it is incorporated into a broad exposition of hermeneutics. Insofar as all "understanding" occurs through the appropriation of frames of meaning, it is no longer regarded as a procedure that distinguishes the social from the natural sciences, but as common to both. The question of the relation between the social and natural sciences can then be seen in a new light. Natural science involves the development of frames of meaning, organized as networks, and discontinuities in the progression of scientific theories pose hermeneutic problems similar to those relating to the mediation of frames of meaning in other spheres of activity. But the social sciences are concerned with a preinterpreted world, in which frames of meaning are integral to their "subject matter"—i.e., the intersubjectivity of practical social life. Social science thus involves a "double hermeneutic," linking its theories, as frames of meaning, with those which are already a constituent part of social life.[97] The ramifications of this, of course, are complex and difficult to trace, involving identifying the relations between lay beliefs and ordinary language concepts on the one hand, and the concepts and theories of the social sciences on the other.

Let us move to the problem of what the notion of "observable behavior" should be taken to refer to. It should be clear that what has already been said about the reformulation of the concept of *verstehen* connects with this, insofar as it helps to indicate the residual difficulties in the claim of positivistically minded critics that *verstehen* is no more than a preliminary source of hypotheses that then have to be matched against behavior. Abel explains this as follows: at the onset of a freezing spell of weather, a man sees his neighbor go out to his woodshed, chop some logs, carry them into the home, and light them in his fireplace. He understands what his neighbor is doing as "lighting a fire to warm himself because he feels chilly." But he cannot know, without further investigation, that this is correct; the neighbor may, for example, have lit the fire as a signal of some sort to someone else. Hence *verstehen* only provides a plausible hypothesis as to what happened.[98] This conclusion, however, begs one type of question by assimilating it to others. It presupposes that the observer already understands the ordinary language terms "freezing spell," "neighbor," "woodshed," etc. Because such understanding is taken for granted, the question of how it is accomplished is not distinguished from the issues of how behavior may be characterized and in what sense, if any, "subjective" elements are relevant to the explanation of human conduct in the social sciences.

The affiliation of positivistic philosophy with behaviorism stems from a common mistrust of features of conduct that are not "observable," where that term means "directly apprehended by the senses." Rejection of phenomenalism or physicalism frees us from some of the restraints of this view, which has never managed to come to terms with the difference between "behavior" and "agency"; that is, between involuntary reactions and acts that are "made to happen" by the individual. The notion of agency or action has been much discussed in the recent philosophical literature, in some substantial part as a result of the emphases of Wittgenstein's *Philosophical Investigations*. Some philosophers, particularly those strongly influenced by Wittgenstein, have argued that human conduct can be described on two discrete levels, one being that of "movements," employing something like the language of behaviorism, the other being that of "actions." To speak of "an arm moving up" is to describe a movement; to speak of "raising one's arm" is to redescribe the movement as an action. But this is misleading if it assumes that these are two alternative modes of description that are equally applicable to any specific form of human conduct. They are more appropriately seen as rival, rather than complementary, types of predicate; to refer to action as if it were merely (reactive) behavior is to *misdescribe* it. In the distinction between "movement" and "action" there is still a residue of the view that only "overt behavior" can be directly observed. But there is no warrant for this if the positivistic view be relinquished; we observe "actions" as directly as we do "behavior."[99]

This still leaves unresolved the status of "subjective elements" in action. Abel's example makes it clear that he is referring to the purposes for which an act may be undertaken: the actor in question lights the fire in order to keep himself from feeling chilly. He employs a behavioristic terminology in expressing this and holds that the event of lighting the fire can only be adequately explained when it is made part of a type of deductive-nomological scheme. The explanation takes the following form: low temperature reduces body temperature; heat is produced by making a fire; the "stimulus" (freezing weather) is connected to the "response" (lighting the fire) via the generalization "those feeling cold will seek warmth." This, as it were, formalizes the assimilation of reactive behavior and action. The scheme recognizes no difference between cases in which what Abel calls the "feeling states" of an individual are connected by some kind of mechanical effect, and those which are within the scope of his agency. Hence the treatment of purposive components of conduct is thin and barren: purpose or intention appears only as a "feeling state" tying stimulus to response. There is no place for a conception of the actor as a reasoning agent, capable of using knowledge in a calculated fashion so as to achieve intended outcomes.

This is one of the major points at which the line of thought running from Comte and Durkheim to modern functionalism, and modern positivistic philosophy as stemming from logical positivism coincide: in the absence of a theory of action. Each involves a deterministic form of social philosophy, although the logical positivists have regarded as suspect the proclivity of the former for "holistic" concepts such as "conscience collective," "representation collective," etc.[100] The writings of Talcott Parsons have played a major part in connecting Durkheim's works to modern functionalism. Parsons has specifically sought to break with some of the main emphases of positivistic philosophy; he has also formulated an "action frame of reference," originally established in order to incorporate an important element of "voluntarism" into social theory.[101] But the voluntaristic features of Parsons's scheme turn out to depend mainly upon the Durkheimian theorem that the collective values which facilitate social solidarity are also "internalized" as motivational components of personality. The attempt to provide a treatment of voluntarism in the context of a theory of institutions becomes reduced to an emphasis that social analysis needs to embody a theory of motivation, rather than providing a framework that relates motives to the rational monitoring of action.

A developed theory of action must deal with the relations between motives, reasons, and purposes, but must also attempt to offer, as functional theorists have always tried to do, an account of institutional organization and change. For if it is the case that functionalism, even in its most sophisticated form in Parsons's writings, has not been able to produce an adequate theory of action, it is also true that those schools of thought which have been most preoccupied with the philosophy of action, including particularly post-Wittgensteinian philosophy and existential phenomenology, have skirted problems of institutional orders and their transformation. I have suggested elsewhere, following Schutz, that the terms "motive," "reason," and "purpose" are misleading as employed in ordinary terminology because they presuppose a conceptual "cutting into" or segmentation of the uninterrupted flow of action; such a cutting into the ongoing course of action is normally made only when an actor is queried about why he acted as he did, when he reflexively categorizes a segment of his action, or when an observer does.[102] Thus it is more appropriate to regard the aforementioned three terms as processual ones; the subjective orientation of action can then be regarded as directed purposively in conjunction with ongoing processes of the motivation and rationalization of action. The latter implies that the socially competent actor routinely monitors his action by "keeping in touch" theoretically with the content of what he does; or, expressed in an alternative way, that when asked for an explanation of a specified "segment" of his conduct, he is able to provide one. The problem of connecting the subjective orientation of action to institutional structures has always appeared an enormously difficult one, but this is at least in some part because "structure" has usually been conceived of in a fundamental way as a *constraint* upon action. Durkheim explicitly makes this the defining property of social structure, separating "social facts" from "psychological facts"; if others have been less direct, they have accepted much the same notion.[103] But the structural properties of institutions are not just constraints upon action, they are enabling; a central issue facing social theory in this regard is that of developing a reformulation of the key concepts of "structure" and "system" in such a way as to acknowledge the enabling as well as the constraining aspects of institutional forms. In such a conception, the reflexive rationalization of action must be seen as operating through the mobilization of structural properties, and at the same time thereby contributing to their reproduction.[104]

Recognition of the central importance of such an approach to a theory of action involves repudiating the positivistic tendency to regard reflexivity as merely a "nuisance" and also has direct consequences for the question of the status of laws in the social sciences. Nagel's discussion of self-influencing predictions, referred to previously, is typical with respect to the first of these issues, insofar as reflexivity is treated only from the point of view of prediction and insofar as it is assumed that its influence is a "problem" for the social sciences. Even within these terms of reference, however, "self-fulfilling" and "self-negating" prophecies do not have, as he claims, direct analogies in the natural sciences. The point is the manner in which such things happen, not the fact of their happening, in society and in nature. That is to say, in the sphere of society, as contrasted to nature, self-influencing predictions occur because the predictions made come to be taken over and reacted to as part of the behavior of reasoning agents—as an element of the "knowledge" they apply in the reflexive rationalization of their conduct.

Human beings are reasoning agents who apply knowledge of their contexts of action reflexively in their production of action, or interaction. The "predictability" of social life does not merely "happen" but is "made to happen" as an outcome of the consciously applied skills of social actors. But the scope of the reflexive rationalization of action of concrete individuals is bounded, in several ways; each indicates specific matters of concern for social science. One concerns the formalization of the knowledge that is applied in action. In producing a grammatical English utterance, for example, a speaker demonstrates and draws upon knowledge of syntactical and other rules involved in speaking English; but he is not likely to be able to give a formal account of what those rules are, although he does "know" them—i.e., know how to use them. However, the application of such "knowledge" is made within a parameter of influences that are not part of the ongoing rationalization of his action. Such influences include not only repressions and unconscious elements of personality, but also external conditions, including the conduct of other actors. A third boundary of the reflexive rationalization of conduct is found in the unintended consequences of action. This connects closely to the second, insofar as the production and reproduction of institutional structures appear as the unintended outcome of the conduct of a multiplicity of actors.

A crucial point to recognize is that the boundaries between these three types of unacknowledged conditions of action are fluid, as is the scope of the rationalization of action in relation to them. We then have a basis for an analysis of the question of the status of "laws" in the social sciences. Zetterberg suggests that there is no shortage of generalizations in social science: the object of social science should be to make the formulation of generalizations more precise and to verify them in light of empirical research. Zetterberg's discussion follows the characteristic lines of positivistic sociology, in holding that such laws will derive from the progressive accumulation of research and should form a deductive hierarchy. Adoption of the network model of natural science involves rejecting his views. We can represent theories in social science, as in natural science, as networks involving laws or abstract generalizations. But in the second of these the network is not in interaction with the object-world it seeks to explain, whereas in the first it is. Generalizations in the social sciences are always in principle unstable in relation to their "subject matter"—i.e., social conduct and its institutional forms—insofar as their acceptance alters the relation between the rationalization of action and its unacknowledged grounds. This is distinct from the "technical" possibilities of intervention in nature offered by laws in the natural sciences. Knowledge of laws in natural science allows human beings to alter the empirical incidence of the circumstances under which they apply; or, if this be desired, to extend their range. But while knowledge of the laws allows for material transformation in such ways, this does not alter the causal connections involved in or underlying them. In the social sciences, on the other hand, the causal connections that are specified or implied in generalizations depend upon particular alignments of the rationalization of action and its unacknowledged conditions, and hence are in principle mutable in light of knowledge of those generalizations.

The degree to which this happens, and its consequences, are of course limited by practical circumstances. But however this may be, the implication is unavoidable that the relation of social science and its subject matter cannot be handled within a differentiation between "pure" and "applied" science. In a longer study, discussion of this would mean taking up in a direct way the character of social science as critique and offering an analysis of the thesis of the dualism of fact and value. For just as the idea of a transcendental language of observation turns out to be mistaken, so also is the idea of "ultimate values," upon which the notion of the fact/value dichotomy depends; what constitutes a factual statement, and what constitutes a judgment of value, is contextually variable.

NOTES

1. The influence of Saint-Simon over Marx is a matter of some controversy in itself. For a systematic treatment, see Georges Gurvitch, "La sociologie du jeune Marx," in *La vocation actuelle de la sociologie* (Paris, 1950).

2. Herbert Marcuse, *Reason and Revolution* (London, 1955) p. 341.

3. Auguste Comte, *Cours de philosophie positive*, vol. I (Paris, 1975) pp. 21ff.

4. Ibid., p. 21.

5. Ibid., pp. 28–29.

6. Ibid., vol. 2, p. 139.

7. Ibid., pp. 139–40.

8. See John Stuart Mill, *Auguste Comte and Posititvism* (Ann Arbor, 1961) pp.125ff.

9. Comte, *Cours de philosophie positive*, vol. I, pp. 44ff.

10. See Herbert Spencer, *Reasons for Dissenting from the Philosophy of M. Comte* (Berkeley, 1968). Mill comments on this in *Auguste Comte and Positivism*, pp. 5ff.

11. See Kurt H. Wolff, *Emile Durkheim et al., Essays on Sociology and Philosophy* (New York, 1964).

12. Emile Durkheim and Fauconnet, "Sociologie et sciences sociales," *Revue philosophique*, vol. 55 (1903).

13. Mill, *Auguste Comte and Posititvism*, p. 59.

14. Emile Durkheim, *The Elementary Forms of the Religioüs Life* (New York, 1965) pp. 170ff; Durkheim and M. Mauss, *Primitive Classification* (London, 1963).

15. Emile Durkheim, *The Rules of Sociological Method* (London, 1964) p. 14.

16. Ibid., pp. 48ff.

17. For a full-scale biography of Mach, see John T. Blackmore,' *Ernst Mach, His Work, Life and Influence* (Berkeley, 1972).

18. See Jürgen Habermas, *Knowledge and Human Interests* (London, 1972) pp. 74ff.

19. Comte, *Cours de philosophie positive*, vol. 2, pp. 16ff.

20. Ernst Mach, *The Analysis of Sensations* (Chicago, 1914) pp. 37ff.

21. Ernst Mach, *Erkenntius und Irrtum* (Leipzig, 1917) p. VII.

22. Mach, *The Analysis of Sensations*, p. 369.

23. See *inter alia*, Victor Kraft, *The Vienna Circle* (New York, 1953). Mach's theories also attracted the attention of prominent literary figures. Hofmannstahl, the poet, attended Mach's lectures, believing that if the world consists only of our sensations, it can be described more directly and thoroughly in poetry than in science. Robert Musil began his career as a philosopher, actually writing a doctoral thesis on Mach, before turning to the novel form.

24. A. J. Ayer et al., *The Revolution in Philosophy* (London, 1956).

25. Rudolf Carnap, "Intellectual Autobiography," in Paul Arthur Schilpp, *The Philosophy of Rudolf Carnap* (La Salle, 1963) pp. 12ff.

26. Stephen E. Toulmin, "From Logical Analysis to Conceptual History," in Peter Achinstein and Stephen F. Barker, *The Legacy of Logical Positivism* (Baltimore, 1969) pp. 31ff. Carnap later wrote on this point, "when we were reading Wittgenstein's book in the Circle, I had erroneously believed that his attitude towards metaphysics was similar to ours. I had not paid sufficient attention to the statements in his book about the mystical, because his feelings and thoughts in this area were too divergent from mine." Carnap, "Intellectual Autobiography," p. 27.

27. Herbert Feigl, "The Origin and Spirit of Logical Positivism," in Achinstein and Barker, *The Legacy of Logical Positivism*, p. 5.

28. See Rudolph Carnap's preface to the second edition of *The Logical Structure of the World* (London, 1967).

29. A. J. Ayer, editor's introduction, in *Logical Positivism* (Glencoe, Ill., 1959) p. 8.

30. Carnap, *The Logical Structure of the World.*

31. Carnap, "Intellectual Autobiography," p. 52.

32. Carnap, "Psychology in Physical Language," in Ayer, *Logical Positivism*, p. 197.

33. See Richard von Mises, *Positivism, a Study in Human Understanding* (Cambridge, Mass., 1951) pp. 80ff.

34. Richard Bevan Braithwaite, *Scientific Explanation* (Cambridge, 1968) p. 51.

35. See Carnap, "The Methodological Character of Theoretical Concepts," in Herbert Feigl and Michael Scriven, *The Foundations of Science and the Concepts of Psychoanalysis* (Minneapolis, 1956).

36. Herbert Feigl, "The 'Orthodox' View of Theories: Some Remarks in Defence as well as Critique," in M. Radner and S. Winokur, *Minnesota Studies in the Philosophy of Science*, vol. 4 (Minneapolis, 1970).

37. Carl G. Hempel and P. Oppenheim, "Studies in the Logic of Explanation," *Philosophy of Science*, vol. 15 (1948).

38. Carl G. Hempel, "Deductive-Nomological vs. Statistical Explanation," in Herbert Feigl and Grover Maxwell, *Scientific Explanation, Space, and Time* (Minneapolis, 1962).

39. Carl G. Hempel, "The Function of General Laws in History," in *Aspects of Scientific Explanation* (New York, 1965) pp. 240–41.

40. Carnap, "Intellectual Autobiography," p. 24.

41. Otto Neurath, "Sociology and Physicalism," in Ayer, *Logical Positivism*, p. 283; see also Otto Neurath, *Foundations of the Social Sciences, International Encyclopaedia of Unified Science*, vol. 2 (Chicago, 1944).

42. Neurath, "Sociology and Physicalism," p. 299.

43. Paul F. Lazarsfeld and Morris Rosenberg, "General Introduction," in *The Language of Social Research* (New York, 1955) pp. 2ff.

44. Ernest Nagel, *The Structure of Science* (London, 1961) p. X.

45. Ibid., p. 484.

46. Ibid., pp. 468–69.

47. Hans L. Zetterberg, *On Theory and Verification in Sociology* (Totawa, N.J., 1966).

48. Ibid., pp. 46ff. Compare Hubert M. Bialock, Jr., *Theory Construction* (Prentice-Hall, N.J., 1967) pp. 2ff and 10ff.

49. Zetterberg, *On Theory and Verification in Sociology*, pp. 81 and 85.

50. Ibid., pp. 102–3.

51. Hempel, "The Logic of Functional Analysis," in *Aspects of Scientific Explanation*.

52. Ibid., p. 317.

53. Ibid., p. 325.

54. See Popper's autobiographical article in Paul Arthur Schilpp, *The Philosophy of Karl Popper* (La Salle, 1974).

55. See, e.g., Karl Popper, "Science: Conjectures and Refutations," in *Conjectures and Refutations* (London, 1972) pp. 34–37.

56. Ibid., p. 37.

57. Karl Popper, *The Logic of Scientific Discovery* (London, 1972) pp. 41ff.

58. See, e.g., "Two Faces of Common Sense," in *Objective Knowledge* (Oxford, 1973) p. 57ff. For a critical discussion of Popper's use of Tarski's theory of truth, see Susan Haack, "Is It True What They Say About Tarski?" *Philosophy*, vol. 51 (1976). On "verisimilitude" see David Miller, "Popper's Qualitative Theory of Verisimilitude," *Int'l Journal of the Philosophy of Science*, vol. 25 (1974).

59. Thomas S. Kuhn, *The Structure of Scientific Revolutions* (Chicago, 1970) p. 1.

60. Ibid., p. 126.

61. See Thomas S. Kuhn, "Reflections on My Critics," in Imre Lakatos and Alan Musgrave, *Criticism and the Growth of Knowledge* (Cambridge, 1970) p. 248.

62. See Thomas S. Kuhn, "Second Thoughts on Paradigms," in Frederick Suppe, *The Structure of Scientific Theories* (Urbana, 1974). For Popper's most recent reflections on similar issues, see Karl Popper, "The Rationality of Scientific Revolutions," in Rom Harré, *Problems of Scientific Revolution* (Oxford, 1975).

63. Max Weber, *The Methodology of the Social Sciences* (Glencoe, Ill., 1949) pp. 13ff.

64. See Anthony Giddens, *Politics and Sociology in the Thought of Max Weber* (London, 1972).

65. Marcuse, *Reason and Revolution*, pp. 6ff.

66. Max Horkheimer, *Eclipse of Reason* (New York, 1974) p. 5.

67. Max Horkheimer, "Der neueste Angriff auf die Metaphysik," *Zeitschrift fur Sozialforschung*, vol. 6 (1937).

68. Jürgen Habermas, *Knowledge and Human Interests* (London, 1972) pp. 43ff.

69. Max Horkheimer and Theodor W. Adorno, *Dialectic of Enlightenment* (New York, 1972).

70. Theodor W. Adorno, et al., *The Positivist Dispute in German Sociology* (London, 1976). First published in German in 1969. A new controversy has now appeared, crossing some of the lines of the first, in which followers of Popper have moved to the offensive in launching an attack on the "politicization of science." For a discussion, see Ralf Dahrendorf, "Die Unabhängigkeit der Wissenschaft," *Die Zeit* (May 21, 1976) and the reply by Lobkowicz in the same issue.

71. Popper, "The Logic of the Social Sciences," *Positivist Dispute*, p. 102

72. Jürgen Habermas, "Analytical Theory of Science and Dialectics," Ibid., p. 142.

73. William W. Bartley, *The Retreat to Commitment* (London, 1964).

74. See Habermas, *Knowledge and Human Interests,* pp. 301ff.

75. Hans Albert, "Behind Positivism's Back?" in Adorno, *The Positivist Dispute in German Sociology,* pp. 246ff. See also, Hans Albert, *Traktat über kritische Vernunift* (Tübingen, 1968).

76. Popper, "Reason or Revolution?" *Positivist Dispute,* p. 299.

77. Imre Lakatos, "Falsification and the Methodology of Scientific Research Programmes," in Lakatos and Musgrave, *Criticism and the Growth of Knowledge,* pp. 106ff; see Imre Lakatos, "Changes in the Problem of Inductive Logic," in *The Problem of Inductive Logic* (Amsterdam, 1968).

78. Kuhn, "Reflections on My Critics," pp. 256ff.

79. Lakatos, *The Problem of Inductive Logic,* p. 121. See also footnote 4, p. 122; also p. 137, where "verification" is reintroduced, albeit reluctantly.

80. Mary Hesse, "Positivism and the Logic of Scientific Theories," in Achinstein and Barker, *The Legacy of Logical Positivism,* p. 96.

81. Dudley Shapere, "Notes Toward a Post-Positivistic Interpretation of Science," Ibid.

82. Ibid., p. 127.

83. See, *inter alia,* W. O. Quine, *From a Logical Point of View* (Cambridge, 1953); *Word and Object* (New York, 1960); *Ontological Relativity and Other Essays* (New York, 1969); Mary Hesse, *The Structure of Scientific Inference* (London, 1974).

84. See Pierre Duhem, *The Aim and Structure of Physical Theory* (Princeton, 1954); *To Save the Phenomena* (Chicago, 1969).

85. Hesse, *The Structure of Scientific Inference,* pp. 175ff.

86. Ibid., pp. 4–5.

87. See Anthony Giddens, *New Rules of Sociological Method* (London, 1976) pp. 142ff; see also Israel Scheffler, *Science and Subjectivity* (Indianapolis, 1967) pp. 80ff.

88. Karl Otto Apel, *Hermeneutik and Ideologiekritik* (Frankfurt, 1971); Brian Wilson, *Rationality* (Oxford, 1970).

89. See Kuhn, "Second Thoughts on Paradigms."

90. Hesse, *The Structure of Scientific Inference,* pp. 57ff.

91. See the Austin-Strawson debate, in George C. Pitcher, *Truth* (N.J.)

92. Hesse claims that this standpoint is consistent with Tarski's "semantic conception" of truth.

93. Hans-Georg Gadamer, *Truth and Method* (London, 1975) pp. 55ff.

94. Theodore Abel, "The Operation Called *Verstehen,*" *American Journal of Sociology,* vol. 54 (1948); Carl Hempel, "On the Method of *Verstehen* as the Sole Method of Philosophy," *The Journal of Philosophy,* vol. 50 (1953).

95. Abel, "The Operation Called *Verstehen.*"

96. Gadamer, *Truth and Method*; see also Idem: *Kleine Schriften* (Tübingen, 1967).

97. See Giddens, *New Rules of Sociological Method,* pp. 148ff.

98. Abel, "The Operation Called *Verstehen.*"

99. See John G. Gunnell, "Political Inquiry and the Concept of Action: A Phenomenological Analysis," in Maurice Natanson, *Phenomenology and the Social Sciences* (Evanston, 1973).

100. For a definition of "determinism" here, see Giddens, *New Rules of Sociological Method,* p. 85.

101. Talcott *The Structure of Social Action.* (Glencoe, Ill., 1949).

102. Giddens, *New Rules of Sociological Method*; Alfred Schutz, *The Phenomenology of the Social World* (London, 1972).

103. The idea of "structure," of course, appears in many varying contexts in modern thought. There are obvious contrasts between the mode in which the term is used in "structural-functionalism" on the one hand, and "structuralism" on the other. For relevant surveys, see Raymond Boudon, *The Uses of Structuralism* (London, 1971); Jean Piaget, *Structuralism* (New York, 1970); Peter M. Blau, *Approaches to the Study of Social Structure* (New York, 1975).

104. See my analysis offered in Anthony Giddens, "Functionalism: *aprés la lutte,*" *Social Research,* vol. 43 (1976).

8

AMERICAN TRENDS

LEWIS A. COSER

Moral Fervor and Social Reform

"In all seriousness, then, and with careful weighing of my words," wrote Albion Small, one of the founding fathers of American sociology, "I register my belief that social science is the holiest sacrament open to men."[1]

It is hard to believe that such a sentence could have been written by any of the major European exemplars of our discipline. It points to the distinctive marks of early American sociology. The evangelical passion and moralistic rhetoric that informs many of the writings of early American sociologists becomes understandable when it is realized that a very high proportion of them were sons of ministers or had themselves been ministers or studied in divinity schools. Of the early presidents of the American Sociological Society, Giddings, Thomas, and Vincent had been born in clerical homes, while Sumner, Small, Vincent, Hayes, Weatherly, Lichtenberger, Gillin, and Gillett pursued careers in the Protestant ministry before they became sociologists.[2] Analyzing the 258 responses to a questionnaire asking sociologists to provide autobiographical background information originally gathered by Luther Bernard in 1927, Paul J. Baker and his associates found that sixty-one sociologists had previously been in the ministry and an additional eighteen received formal training in divinity schools without pursuing a career in the Church.[3]

To be sure, some of these men, like Sumner and Ross, lost their faith after embarking on a career in sociology, often after exposure to the evolutionary thought of Darwin and Spencer. Others, however, like Small or Vincent, remained believing Christians throughout their lives. I have no numerical data on the personal beliefs of all the members of the sociological discipline during the first few generations, but perusal of many biographies leaves no doubt in my mind that Christian faith was widespread among those men—almost all from a rural or small-town background—who became sociologists in the period before the first world war.

A large majority of believing sociologists around the turn of the century were tied in one way or another to the Protestant social reform and Social Gospel movements that had developed very rapidly during the Progressive era. The Protestant denominations had largely been staunch supporters of the status quo in the first two decades after the Civil War, but by the turn of the century critical voices could be heard forcefully in all major churches. The orgies of speculation in the age of the robber barons, the mad scramble around the great barbecue, the violent repression of the emergent labor movement, the largely uncontrolled growth of cities, the closing of the frontier, the millions of new immigrants herded into appalling slums and mercilessly exploited in coal mines and sweatshops—these and many more harbingers of crisis and decay brought many formerly complacent clergymen, as well as other concerned citizens, into the Progressive movement. They were all eager to transform America into a country more nearly in tune with the moral message of Christian doctrine. "No other movement in American political history," writes Richard Hofstadter in reference to the Progressive movement, "had ever received so much clerical sanction."[4]

There is still another reason why increasing numbers of Protestant clergymen turned to reform around the turn of the century. Clergymen had lost much of the leading status they possessed before the Civil War in the rush for wealth and power that marked the post-Civil War period. No longer were they looked at with the same awe and reverence which had made them the unquestioned moral leaders of the community in colonial days and, largely, until the Civil War. New trends of secular ideas, especially evolutionary thought, now contested the previous preeminence of religious doctrine. While formerly men of the cloth had dominated all educational institutions, the boards of trustees of colleges and universities were now mainly comprised bankers, businessmen, and corporate lawyers. A divinity degree was no longer the accepted passport to administrative positions in the world of higher education. Moreover, and in tune with these trends, the salaries of the clergy began to compare unfavorably with those of members of other professions and often did not even keep up with the increasing cost of living. Thus, the rise of the Christian social reform movement can be understood, at least in large part, in terms of the new social and material interests and the status insecurities of the Protestant clergy. To quote Hofstadter again, the movement can be seen as an "attempt to restore through secular leadership some of the spiritual influence and authority and social prestige that clergymen had lost."[5]

Many of the Christian reformers were acutely aware that their newly awakened social consciousness needed to be informed by knowledge of social conditions and social problems which had up until recently not been in the intellectual baggage of Christian ministers. They therefore turned for assistance to various reform-oriented researchers, settlement workers, social welfare specialists, or muckraking journalists. A variety of networks came into being linking all these professions, religious or not, in the center and on the periphery of the Progressive movement.

The first and second generation of American sociologists were very much part of the growing reform movement. Whether directly tied to the Social Gospel and related developments or not, they saw themselves as reformers and addressed themselves largely to an audience of reformers. Moreover, their moral fervor, sustained by their immersion in the melioristic tradition, helped give their newfangled calling a legitimation which it might otherwise have lacked. As Vernon Dibble tersely put it, "sociology needed moralists to get started."[6]

Background of Reform

American sociology emerged as a self-conscious discipline in the nineties, but it had, of course, an earlier history. In their exhaustive study of the *Origins of American Sociology*,[7] L. L. Bernard and Jessie Bernard describe in great detail the predecessors of formal sociology in the nineteenth-century social-science movement.

This movement was strongly pervaded by a spirit of reform. Although those aiming at reform and those emphasizing scientific research did not long live in harmony with each other, it is indicative of the common roots of reform and sociology in America that the Massachusetts Board of Alien Commissioners, which was founded in 1851 "to superintend the execution of all laws in relation to the introduction of aliens into the Commonwealth and the support of state paupers therein,"[8] became some fifteen years later the nucleus of the American Social Science Association.

The American Social Science Association proclaimed as its objects "to aid the development of Social Science, and to guide the public mind to the best practical means of promoting the Amendments of Laws, the Advancement of Education, the Prevention and Repression of Crimes, the Reformation of Criminals, and the Progress of Public Morality, the Adoption of Sanitary Regulations and the Diffusion of Sound Principles on the Questions of Economy, Trade and Finance."[9] From its inception in 1865, it combined a spirit of reform with a zeal for scientific investigation. The "problem" emphasis met increasing opposition within the association during the seventies and eighties, especially after various social-welfare associations such as the National Prison Association and the National Conference of Charities and Correction broke away. Those of its members who were concerned with the academic respectability of social science attempted to dissociate it from immediate application in social work and other practical activities. Yet, as will be shown in the following pages, the reformist ethic so canalized the interest of the first generation of American sociologists that it constitutes an important element in the enhanced cultivation of sociology. The deep-rooted reformist interests of the day demanded in their forceful implications the systematic, rational, and empirical study of society and the control of a corrupt world.[10]

The predominance of the "problems" approach over the purely theoretical concern with sociology is clearly evident in the charter statements of the earliest departments of sociology. Thus, Columbia University's announcement of a chair of sociology stated: "It is becoming more and more apparent that industrial and social progress is bringing the modern community face-to-face with social questions of the greatest magnitude, the solution of which will demand the best scientific study and the most honest practical endeavor. The term 'sociology'... includes a large number of the subjects which are most seriously interesting men at the present time. The effective treatment of social problems demands that they be dealt with both theoretically and concretely." The newly established chair "will provide for a thorough study of philosophical or general sociology and of the practical or concrete social questions in their relation to sociological principles... special courses of instruction will be offered on pauperism, poor laws, methods of charity, crime, penology and social ethics."[11]

The Columbia statement, drafted by Giddings, gives perhaps more weight to theory than similar statements announcing other chairs.[12] As a historian of American sociology has said: "On the one hand, the development of sociology as a subject of instruction in American universities was influenced strongly by Spencer and to a lesser degree by several other European pioneers.... On the other hand, the sociology that was taught before 1920 in the colleges and Universities of the United States was even more strongly influenced and shaped by the humanitarian, philanthropic and social reform movements that were actively under way in the country during the nineteenth century.... It is certain that a large proportion of the courses being offered under the name of sociology... as recently as the second decade of the present century dealt mainly with 'social problems,' i.e., they covered such topics as poverty, crime and the treatment of the 'dependent, defective and delinquent classes.' "[13]

Even though American sociologists around the turn of the century attempted to achieve academic respectability by emphasizing the scientific and theoretical aspects of their work, their reformers' zeal was still not spent.[14] To a modern sociologist, noting the almost complete separation, if not opposition, between social science and reform today, the recurrence of reformist phrases in the writing of the fathers of American sociology is apt to signify merely customary usage. But such an interpretation is possible only if one neglects to translate oneself into the framework of late nineteenth-century values.[15]

As Albion W. Small and George E. Vincent stated in the first textbook of American sociology: "Sociology was born of the modern ardor to improve society."[16] Although sociology's early devotees attempted repeatedly to dissociate themselves from immediate reform, it crept in again and again through the back door.[17] Attempting to define "what is a sociologist?" Small could write in 1905 that "a great many people" consider sociology "to be absorbed in plans for improving the condition of wage earners, or for dealing with paupers and criminals," but that this was only a small part of the truth since the sociologist is concerned with the study of all social phenomena.[18] But the same Small had said earlier that "scholars might exalt both their scholarship and their citizenship by claiming an active share of the work of perfecting and applying plans and devices for social improvements and amelioration."[19] In *Adam Smith and Modern Sociology* Small stated unequivocally: "Sociology in its largest scope and on its methodological side is merely a moral philosophy conscious of its task."[20] He was to repeat later that "there is an irresistible conflict in modern society between presumptions of capital and the paramount values of humanity. Our academic social scientists would serve their generation to better purpose if they would diminish the ratio of attention which they give to refinements interesting only to their own kind, and if they would apply them to tackling this radical moral problem of men in general."[21]

Small, who for the many years of his editorship of the *American Journal of Sociology* mainly was preoccupied with problems of methodology, was also the author of *Between Eras—From Capitalism to Democracy*,[22] a series of conversations in fictional form in which he advocated a basic reform of capitalism and in which he called the present system of distribution a "rape of justice."[23] In his presidential address to the American Sociological Society meeting of 1913, Small, the respectable deacon of a Chicago Baptist church, stated emphatically: "The social problem of the twentieth century is whether the civilized nations can restore themselves to sanity after the nineteenth-century aberrations of individualism and capitalism."[24]

There will be occasion later in this paper to allude again to the mixture of reform rhetoric and scientific language in the writings of Albion Small's generation. Even though its reform orientation was conspicuous, sociology made rapid strides toward becoming an academic discipline.

Sociology Becomes an Academic Discipline

In spite of the strong appeal of Christian moralism and Progressive reform, sociology would not have been anchored in American society without a material basis. This was provided by the unprecedented growth of the system of higher education beginning around the turn of the century and by the receptivity of that system to the upstart discipline. The reason why sociology was known for many years all over the world as the "American science" is largely to be sought in its early institutionalization in a mushrooming American academy.

As Anthony Oberschall, following the lead of Joseph Ben David, has put it, "The wide resource basis and competitive nature of the rapidly expanding higher education system in the United States, together with the sponsorship and active backing of the new discipline by influential and organized groups who perceived sociology in their interests, were the crucial factors enabling the institutionalization of sociology in the United States. Moreover, the opportunity provided by sociology was exploited not just by intellectually dissatisfied and socially concerned scholars, but by a group of upward mobile men who otherwise could not have moved into university positions through the already established disciplines."[25]

Although colleges devoted to the instruction of future clergymen, other professionals, and members of the upper strata have flourished in America since the colonial period, the first full-fledged American university, Johns Hopkins, opened its doors only in 1876. Four years later Columbia College began to develop into a national university. The universities of Michigan and Pennsylvania followed soon after. In 1891 large endowments from private benefactors led to the creation of two new major universities, Stanford and the University of Chicago. Others soon followed.

Not only did the American university system expand by leaps and bounds within a relatively short period, but the new institutions, unencumbered by the century-old traditions of European universities, proved to be receptive to new disciplines, especially in the social sciences. As a result, young social scientists, whether trained in Europe (mostly Germany) or in the new graduate schools, commanded a premium on the academic marketplace. Those who did not find a niche in the most prestigious institutions of the East found opportunities farther west. The burgeoning demand for enlightenment about novel social conditions and for guidance along the road to reform allowed young social innovators and progressive social scientists to introduce reform-oriented courses and curricula with relative ease. Even though there were some ugly cases of restriction of academic freedom, the relative scarcity of trained social scientists created a sellers' market for these innovators, so that they had a good deal of leeway when it came to defining their subject matter and structuring the courses they offered.[26]

The first sociology course in the United States was taught by William Graham Sumner at Yale in 1875, despite the strenuous objections of Yale's president Noah Porter, who felt that Sumner's Spencerian orientation would do "intellectual and moral harm to the students." But soon after, many college presidents themselves began to offer courses in "sociology" as a replacement of their former courses in mental and moral philosophy. At the end of his first year as president of Colby College in 1890, Albion Small, for example, reported to the trustees that he had changed the subject matter of one of his key courses previously called "moral science." "Instead of attempting to trace the development of metaphysical philosophy," Small wrote, "he had introduced the class to modern sociological philosophy." His syllabus at Colby, which served him as a guideline later when he became the first chairman of the new Department of Sociology at the University of Chicago, fell into three parts: "Descriptive Sociology—The actual society of the past and present, the world *as it is*"; "Statical Sociology—The world *as it ought to be*"; and "Dynamic Sociology—The methods available for causing approximation of the ideal, the world *in process of betterment*."[27]

The early courses in sociology, whether offered by college presidents or young instructors, tended to be a motley assemblage of moral exhortation, factual description, social problems, conservative or reform-oriented Darwinism, Christian uplift, institutional economics, and concern with various forms of social pathology. But by 1900 a rudimentary differentiation began to set in.[28] Those instructors interested in sociological analysis or "pure sociology" began to separate themselves from their colleagues who were mainly concerned with social problems or "applied sociology." At the same time sociologists began to differentiate themselves from institutional economists and from historians and philosophers who previously had often taught generalized "sociology" courses. Around the time of the first world war, sociologists largely led by the Department of Sociology of the University of Chicago—which also published the only journal entirely devoted to sociology, *The American Journal of Sociology*—had developed a publicly recognized identity and visibility.

The main currents of ideas that animated the developing discipline are best dealt with in terms of the major contributions of those figures in the early history of American sociology who have left an enduring mark on the discipline. These ideas must, of course, be considered within the historical and social context in which the founders of American sociology did their work.

Sumner and Ward: Laissez-Faire vs. Meliorism

Although among their predecessors in the social-science movement the doctrines of Auguste Comte had by far the most potent influence, the generation of Sumner and Ward was under the spell of the work of Herbert Spencer and the social Darwinists. Not all of them accepted the main lines of Spencer's doctrine, but even those who opposed him in important respects felt the need to respond to his challenge.

Around the turn of the century the social Darwinist camp in America came to be largely divided between "conservative Darwinism," glorifying the captains of industry as the flowers of civilization and giving ideological support for an economic system of uncontrolled laissez faire, and "reform Darwinism." The latter tendency took major clues from Thomas H. Huxley, Darwin's ardent disciple, his "bulldog" as he was then called. In his "Evolution and Ethics" of 1893 Huxley argued that there were two distinct processes in which mankind participated, the "cosmical" and the "ethical." Evolution and the survival of the fittest belonged to the "cosmical" part of human destiny, but humankind in evolution had created an ethical process that deviated from, and worked counter to, the "natural" course of evolution, so that ethics need not take any lesson from biology.[29] To the reform Darwinists there was no disjunction between the findings of evolutionary theories and efforts at making the world over in the image of ethical ideas. Sumner was squarely in the first camp, while Ward, together with a number of other early sociologists, was in the second.

William Graham Sumner, 1840–1910

Sumner, the most outspoken disciple of Herbert Spencer in America, combined evolutionism, laissez-faire, and Malthusian pessimism with the ardor of a great Puritan divine. There were few men on the American scene who applied the Darwinian doctrine of the survival of the fittest more inflexibly to the human social realm than this Episcopal rector turned sociologist. One is tempted to sum up Sumner's whole social philosophy in one of his pragmatic sentences: "Society needs first of all to be free from meddlers—that is, to be let alone."[30] It is doubtful whether Sumner in his youth ever believed in the invisible hand of God as deeply as he later believed in the invisible hand of Adam Smith.

Sumner's father was a frugal, hardworking Lancashire immigrant mechanic, a devout Protestant who, if one is to believe Sumner's own portrayal, had a deep and passionate relation to but one social cause—that of abstinence. In his later life Sumner abandoned most of his father's religious beliefs but never the underlying "Protestant" attitude. Thrift, hard work, prudence, and abstinence remained his central virtues and values. His father would have approved most heartily when the son wrote, "Let us not imagine that . . . any race of men on this earth can ever be emancipated from the necessity of industry, prudence, continence and temperance if they are to pass their lives prosperously."[31]

When only thirteen or fourteen years old, Sumner, already an avid reader, came across Harriet Martineau's *Illustrations of Political Economy* at the library of the Young Men's Institute at Hartford, Connecticut. From this collection of didactic stories popularizing Ricardo and Malthus he imbibed free-trade principles, and learned "natural truths" such as "Restriction on the liberty of exchange—is a sin in government." Sumner said later on that "my main conceptions of capital, labor, money and trade were all formed by those books which I read in my boyhood."[32] When, after a brief career as an Episcopalian rector Sumner lost his religious faith under the impact of Spencer and Darwin and accepted a teaching position at Yale College, he kept his faith in free enterprise.

As generations of Yale College graduates consistently exposed to "Sumnerology" assumed their place in the banking and commercial world, as his class talks were reported fully in New York dailies and letter columns began to be filled with Sumnerian polemics, it became apparent that Sumner was by no means a dispassionate recorder and observer of the laws of evolution and competition. Fighting against protectionism and for free trade, attacking the imperialist tendencies behind the Spanish-American War, Sumner was suspect to a major part of the community of wealth and to the high and mighty. The Republican press and Republican alumni repeatedly tried to have him dismissed from Yale.[33] But Sumner was not to be dismayed. To him, the advocates of protectionism were not only in error, they were in sin, and he was convinced that "socialism was profoundly immoral." Even though he had been converted to evolutionism, the Christian moralism of his background informed much of his later writing.

Sumner saw himself as a sort of apostle to the gentiles—an old testament prophet who sorrowfully and wrathfully castigated his people for the errors of their ways. In an age of "foxes" Sumner was a "lion," passionately defending free individual enterprise at just the moment when it was rapidly displaced by huge trusts and corporate giants. He fought his losing battle with all the feeling of moral righteousness that underlay the reformist ardor of his colleagues on the left of center.

To Sumner, "the law of the survival of the fittest was not made by man and cannot be abrogated by man. We can only by interfering with it, produce the survival of the unfittest."[34] The history of humankind, Sumner taught, can be viewed as a perpetual struggle between individuals, classes and groups. In fact, Sumner's doctrine involved a kind of economic determinism considerably more dogmatic and unbending than that of Karl Marx. "The thing which makes and breaks institutions," he wrote, "is economic force, acting on the interest of man, and, through him, on human nature."[35] In his opinion, the "views of rights are thus afloat on a tide of interests."[36]

Sumner was impatient with those reformers who wished to correct the balance of natural forces as they worked themselves out in the harsh struggle for survival. "They do not perceive," he wrote, "that . . . 'the strong' and the 'weak' are terms which admit of no definition unless they are made equivalent to the industrious and the idle, the frugal and the extravagant. They do not perceive, furthermore, that if we do not like the survival of the fittest, we have only one possible alternative, and that is the survival of the unfittest."[37]

Had Sumner only produced secular sermons, impassioned pamphlets in favor of evolutionism, crusading philippics against moral crusaders, he would probably only be remembered as a not very original social Darwinist, a Spencer in American dress. In fact, fairly late in his life (1906) he published the one work, *Folkways*,[38] that left an enduring mark on the subsequent history of American sociology. In this work, his moralism is largely replaced by a pervasive moral relativism, yet his underlying laissez-faire stance remained virtually unchanged.

The subtitle of this work, "A Study of the Sociological Importance of Usages, Manners, Customs, Mores, and Morals," describes its content. Supporting his thesis with a vast array of ethnographic and historical materials culled from a variety of cultural contexts, Sumner attempted to develop a comprehensive theory of human evolution while also giving an account of the persistence of basic human traits.

Guided by instincts that humankind had acquired from its animal ancestors, Sumner argued, and by the tendency to avoid pain and maximize pleasure, the human race had gradually, through trial and error, developed types of group conduct, habitual ways of doing things, that maximized adaptation to the human environment and a successful outcome of the struggle for existence. These types of group conduct and habits operated below the level of conscious deliberation.

When these habitual ways of doing things, which Sumner calls "folkways," are regarded as assuring the continued welfare of the group, they become transformed into "mores." "The mores are the folkways, including the philosophical and ethical generalizations as to societal welfare which are suggested by them, and inherent in them, as they grow. They are the ways of doing things which are current in a society to satisfy human needs and desires, together with the faiths, notions, codes, and standards of well living which inhere in those ways. . . ."[39] The mores can make anything right. "What they do is that they cover usage in dress, language, behavior, manners etc., with the mandate of current custom, and give it regulation and limits within which it becomes unquestionable."[40] They are coercive and constraining. They dominate all members of society or groups, and they are enforced by sharp negative sanctions in case of infringement. Whereas sanctions against deviance from folkways may only be relatively mild—like gossip, for example—the sanctions upon infringing mores are severe precisely because they are thought to guarantee the welfare of the group.

Sumner's third key concept is "institutions." "An institution consists of a concept (idea, notion, doctrine, interest) and a structure. . . . The structure holds the concept and furnishes instrumentalities for bringing it into the world of fact."[41] Most institutions of the past have been "crescive"; that is, they have slowly grown out of folkways and mores. "Enacted" institutions, in contrast, belong to the modern world as products of rational invention and intention. Religion, property, and marriage are primarily crescive institutions, whereas modern banks and the electoral college are enacted institutions. But acts of legislation can succeed only to the extent that they have their roots in the mores. "Legislation has to seek standing ground on existing mores . . . to be strong it must be consistent with the mores."[42] Folkways, mores, and crescive institutions are based on sentiment and faith. Laws and enacted institutions, on the other hand, are conspicuously brought into being and embody positive prescriptions or proscriptions of "a rational and practical character."[43] But, and this is of the utmost importance to Sumner, laws "are produced out of the mores" which they codify. Hence any attempt to legislate against the mores is bound to fail. Stateways can never contradict folkways.

It should be apparent by now that although in *Folkways* Sumner subscribed to a consistent moral relativism, he still maintained his prepotent belief in laissez-faire. Any attempt to legislate against the mores, he argues, is bound to fail. The mores do change, but they change slowly, in tune with changing "life conditions," with changing adjustments of mankind to its surrounding environment, and mainly through trial and error. They roll along like a muddy river, and any attempt to influence them purposefully is bound to upset the cosmic applecart. Sumner must have chuckled beatifically in his heavenly abode when he learned of the attempts to legislate prohibition in America and their disastrous failure in the face of American drinking mores.

And yet, it would seem apparent that his conservative bias made him overlook the fact that while homogeneous societies may indeed be strongly resistant to attempts at deliberate change, this is by no means the case in societies that are heterogeneous, where the mores of groups or strata are in conflict and tension. In such societies, deliberate efforts can indeed subvert previous mores held on to by vested interests. Enacted legislation is vastly more powerful in such societies than Sumner was willing to concede. When news about the success of civil-rights legislation reached Sumner in heaven, his beatific smile must soon have been replaced by an expression of disbelief and pain.

Sumner's argument, when shorn of its all-embracing pretensions, may still be of considerable usefulness when one attempts to account for large areas of persistence even in a world subject to rapid waves of change. However, in addition to the general message of *Folkways*, this work also contains a number of other observations that have had an enduring influence on subsequent theorizing. Only a few can be mentioned here. Though he stressed that, impelled by the major human motives—hunger, love, vanity, and fear—men and women were most of the time engaged in conflict, he also highlighted what he termed "antagonistic cooperation." This term refers to "the combination of two persons or groups to satisfy a great common interest while minor antagonisms of interest which exist between them are suppressed."[44] That is, Sumner highlighted the important fact that conflict and cooperation are not diametrically opposed notions but are intertwined in a variety of concrete ways that can only be separated analytically.

Two related notions developed by Sumner are perhaps of even greater interest. Both of them have entered the common language. Sumner distinguishes between the "in-group" and the "out-group" and posits a dialectical relation between them. "A group of groups may have some relation to each other (kin, neighborhood, alliance, connubium, and commercium) which draws them together and differentiates them from others. Thus a differentiation arises between ourselves, the we-group, or in-group, and everybody else, or the others-groups, out-groups. The relation of comradeship and peace in the we-group and that of hostility and war towards other-groups are correlative to each other. The exigencies of war with outsiders are what makes peace inside."[45] In a related train of thought Sumner points to the tendency of a group to view itself as "the center of everything, and all others as scaled and rated with reference to it."[46] This tendency he termed "ethnocentrism." Both of these notions have led to an impressive amount of research since Sumner's days and have proved exceedingly fruitful guides.[47]

Even though Sumner's ingrained conservative stance has surely alienated many contemporary sociologists and has led them to neglect him, there is no doubt that he will continue to occupy an honored niche among the founders of our discipline. The crisp and pithy prose of the old curmudgeon from Yale can still be read with considerable profit, especially by those who persist in believing that if there were only a law most human problems could be legislated out of existence.

Lester F. Ward: 1841–1913

When discussing Ward's contribution to sociology, we enter a universe of discourses very much different from that of his contemporary, Sumner.

Like so many American reformers in the Progressive age, Ward was a son of the Middle Border. Born in Illinois in 1841 into the family of an itinerant mechanic and tinkerer, Ward passed his youth in dire poverty. Whenever some time was left over from his many jobs in mills and factories, he taught himself various languages, as well as biology and physiology, and finally succeeded in becoming a secondary-school teacher. After two years of soldiering in the Civil War, Ward moved to Washington and entered the civil service as a clerk in the Department of the Treasury. Continuing his struggle for learning, he went to evening-session colleges and managed within five years to take several diplomas in the arts, medicine, and the law. Still later, Ward continued his studies in the natural sciences and came to specialize in paleontology and botany. In 1883 he was made chief paleontologist in the United States Geological Survey. Only in 1906, near the end of his career, was he finally called to teach in the groves of academe—he accepted a chair in sociology at Brown University. He died in 1913.[48]

Though he wrote the first major treatise in sociology in America, *Dynamic Sociology,* Ward never had any formal instruction in the social sciences and was largely self-tutored. His ponderous manner of writing reflects his struggle to acquire his considerable learning in sociology. It is probably largely due to his lack of expository skills that Ward is hardly read today, while Sumner, a masterful stylist, still commands a considerable audience. And yet it would seem that in some ways Ward is a considerably more "modern" author than Sumner. While the latter hankered after a free-enterprise economy that was already largely disappearing during his lifetime, the former laid the foundations for what later generations called a welfare state.

Ward shared with Sumner an intense admiration for Darwin and for evolutionary science. One might even call him a social Darwinist, but only if it is understood that his allegiance to that doctrine was of the reform variety. Though detailed treatment of his work would probably focus on several other of his contributions to the emergent discipline of sociology, I shall limit myself here to only two of them: his evocation of the need for social planning and the emergence of a "sociocratic" society, and his break with the biologistic analogies of social Darwinism and of Spencer's doctrine.

Spencer and his cothinkers had argued for a monistic explanation of all human and natural phenomena. They believed that such concepts as natural selection, the survival of the fittest, or differentiation applied to the human and nonhuman field alike, that they were the master keys that would allow access to all the riddles of the universe. Their defense of laissez-faire economics followed logically, or so they thought, from the universal natural laws that they believed to be firmly established by evolutionary science. It is this major premise that Ward wished to refute. Since he was wedded by background and general orientation to a meliorist and reformist stance, he considered it of the utmost importance to be able to show that the laws of natural evolution did not apply to human development, there being "no necessary harmony between natural law and human advantage."[49]

Ward laid the foundation for a dualistic interpretation according to which natural evolution proceeded in a purposeless manner, while human evolution was informed by purposeful action. Nature proceeded according to the laws of "genesis," human evolution was guided by "telesis." By introducing this bifurcation, Ward undermined the Spencerian system which rested largely on biological analogies. He thus helped to emancipate the emergent social sciences from dependence both on biological processes and on laissez-faire principles. To Ward, nature's way was not the human way. As Hofstader puts it, "Animal economics, the survival of the fittest in the struggle for existence, results from the multiplication of organisms beyond the means of subsistence. Nature produces organisms in superabundance and relies upon the wind, water, birds, and animals to sow her seed. A rational being, on the other hand, prepares the ground, eliminates weeds, drills holes, and plants at proper intervals; this is the way of human economics. While environment transforms the animal, man transforms the environment."[50]

Given this basic bifurcation between human and nonhuman processes, Ward argued, Malthus's theory of population, which had been so instrumental in forming both Spencer's and Darwin's views, does not apply to the human race. "The fact is," he wrote, "that men and society are not, except in a very limited sense, under the influence of the great dynamic laws that control the rest of the animal world. . . . If we call biological processes natural, we must call social processes artificial. The fundamental principle of biology is natural selection, that of sociology is artificial selection. . . . If nature progresses through the destruction of the weak, man progresses through the protection of the weak."[51]

Having demolished, at least to his satisfaction, the case for "natural" laissez-faire, Ward then proceeded to argue for a sociology based on the analysis of changing human institutions in terms of theological progress. He conceded to the orthodox social Darwinists, and to the Austrian "conflict theorists" Gumplowicz and Ratzenhofer in particular, that in the past the struggle between races and classes had indeed marked the course of human history. He went even so far as to assert that, "When races stop struggling progress ceases."[52] Yet he was also at pains to point out the wastefulness of such struggles, and he expressed the hope, indeed the certainty, that in the future they would be eliminated through planned and purposeful action led by an enlightened government, a "sociocracy."

Welcoming all popular movements which in his day worked for reform, he saw in these movements the seeds of an emergent "people's government" that would set its course on a deliberate recasting of the social order. There are, to be sure, certain passages in Ward that remind one of Comtean delusions about the ability of scientist-kings to guide humanity into a socially engineered and managed paradise. But his propensities in this direction were held in check most of the time by his prepotent belief in education as the rational means of developing the intellect of even the humblest men and women. Education would enable them to participate consciously in the self-government of democratic citizens. He was convinced that " . . . the bottom layer of society, the proletariat, the working class . . . nay, even the denizens of the slums . . . are by nature the peers of the boasted 'aristocracy of brains,' "[53] if only they would receive proper instruction. The man who had sacrificed so much in order to acquire an education put an almost unlimited faith in the conscious enlargement of the mind of every man and woman. One may judge this overriding faith to have been somewhat naive, but one can hardly deny the nobility of this vision.

Ward was by no means always consistent. In particular, despite his stress on telic processes and the unique and artificial character of social organization, he repeatedly relapsed into Darwinistic language and cosmological speculations of an evolutionary nature. But it remains his great historical merit to have made the first major attempt in America to free sociological inquiry from its biological fetters and to have stressed that collective human purposes, informed by an applied sociology of social reform, might inaugurate a major new step in the direction of what at a later date Amitai Etzioni called "the active society."[54]

Ross and Veblen: The Emergence of Critical Sociology

While retaining many of their roots in the tradition of reform-oriented Darwinism and putting to their uses the melioristic message of Lester Ward, many leading sociologists of the succeeding generation, Edward Alsworth Ross and Thorstein Veblen in particular, articulated a more critical stance in reaction to the American scene in the Gilded Age. Ross, who would not give "a snap of his finger for the 'pussyfooting' sociologists,"[55] was involved throughout his career in the politics of radical reform, while Veblen during most of his life cultivated a weary and ironic aloofness from the sphere of politics; yet both were at one in expressing in their work a fundamental critique of major social tendencies in their America. They laid the foundations for a type of radical critical sociology that was to flower in a later age in the works of men such as C. Wright Mills.

Edward Alsworth Ross: 1866-1951

Like Ward, to whom he was tied by bonds of discipleship as well as kinship, Ross was a son of the Middle West. He was born on December 12, 1866, in Virden, Illinois, of parents who pursued a checkered farming and homesteading career in Kansas, Illinois, and Iowa. Both parents died at an early age, and so Ross was left an orphan when he was only eight years old. He was brought up by various relatives in the small town of Marion, Iowa. Given his unusual status, lacking a sense of family tradition or geographical roots, the young Ross seems to have felt very early that he had little in common with his small-town contemporaries. Selling some of the land he had inherited from his parents, the restive youngster managed to enroll at Coe College, a Presbyterian institution in Cedar Rapids which, despite its intellectual restrictiveness, helped open for him the doors of higher learning. He subsequently taught at the "collegiate institute" in Fort Dodge, Iowa. Although he started out as a staunch member of the local Presbyterian church, he soon lost his faith after immersing himself in the works of Spencer and Darwin. As was the custom for many young intellectuals of his generation, Ross then resolved to acquire a "real education" in Germany. Hegelian philosophy and other metaphysical systems proved uncongenial to the young midwesterner, and though he toyed for a while with the cultural pessimism of Schopenhauer and Nietzsche, Ross soon resolved that the cultural gloom of *fin-de-siécle* Europe was not for him. When he returned to America at the end of 1889, Ross was resolved to leave behind him the world of speculation and to immerse himself instead in action and reform. Working under Richard Ely at Johns Hopkins, he wrote a dissertation on public finance in the spirit of the new reform economics and then taught the subject at Indiana, Cornell, and Stanford. There he encountered the work of Lester Ward and resolved, largely under Ward's influence, to switch from economics to sociology. What appealed to him in Ward's system was the notion that society was not subject to "natural" laws but was an "artificial" creation subject to human control and direction. Thus sociology could be conceived as a guide to radical action and not only as a simple program of study. He decided, to use the words of R. Jackson Wilson, that "he could be objective and still passionate, scientist and still progressive, that social science could be both data and program, law and plan of action."[56]

Fired from Stanford after having offended the "vested interests" and the widow of the founder of the University, he moved to the University of Nebraska and finally to the University of Wisconsin, where for thirty years he combined a distinguished academic career with a free-lance calling as one of America's leading muckrakers and as a main exponent of the tenets of the Populist and later the Progressive movements. From the Free Silver Crusade of William Jennings Bryan, to the Bull Moose Campaign of Theodore Roosevelt, to Lafollette's Wisconsin progressivism, and to a great variety of other progressive causes, Ross was always to be found in the thick of battle. A friend and associate of radical reformers like Clarence Darrow, Jane Addams, Lincoln Steffens, Upton Sinclair, Ida Tarbell, and Justice Brandeis, but also of such somewhat more aloof liberal reformers as Justice Holmes and Dean Roscoe Pound, Ross became a most successful popularizer of a critical sociology. His more than two hundred magazine articles and twenty-four books (which had sold over 300,000 copies by 1936) gave him maximum exposure as an outspoken spokesman of action-oriented sociology.

Had Ross limited himself to his pamphleteering and his devotion to the literature of exposure, he would surely have merited more than a footnote in the history of American reform. His stature as a sociologist, however, rests largely on his seminal book, *Social Control* (1901), and its successors, *The Foundations of Sociology* (1905) and *Social Psychology* (1908).

In his theoretical work, Ross's main objective was to elucidate the ways in which societies control the behavior of their component members so as to make them accept social requirements. Having been inoculated in Germany against large-scale historical and philosophical speculations, Ross worked largely by way of description and enumeration, sticking "close to the facts." He initially set down a list of no less than thirty-three different ways in which he thought societies controlled their members. The list was pruned down later on, but it still is more a laundry list than an analytically rigorous classification. Nevertheless, it is clear that he was working his way toward a distinction between forms of social control that operate largely through external imposition and those that gain their effectiveness through "internalization" achieved in the course of interaction.

For Ross, the most prominent among those control mechanisms that work through external constraint and punishment is the law and the repressive mechanisms at its command. Custom, which in earlier times had preempted almost the whole area now dominated by law, still functions as an informal, though potent, adjunct to legal regulation in modern society, but it has a less repressive character. In the same way, institutionalized religious beliefs, a major means of social control in earlier societies, still operate in this way, although to a more limited degree.

In contrast to those regulative institutions that operate largely in terms of outside controls on component individuals, there are, according to Ross, means of control that become effective through persuasion instead of constraint. Here he discusses, among other things, public opinion, education, the emulation and imitation of extraordinary moral figures, and the creation of ideal images by artists who invite the public to live up to moral and aesthetic ideas.

Ross believed that the course of moral progress was marked by the gradual replacement of external constraint by inner disciplines that are rooted in social interactions and internalized in socialized individuals. The more democratic a community, the more it is able to turn from repressive controls to enlightenment and persuasion. Enlightenment, Ross believed, would help make people aware of the social origins of their moral being and of their social obligations as members of the democratic community.

Ross's deep-rooted antagonisms to the trusts, the malefactors of great wealth, and all the other objects of his wrath were rooted in his belief that their greed, their predacious appetites, and their grasping egoism hindered the emergence of the great democratic community that he hoped to see in America. In the last analysis, then, his sociological and his polemical writings were but different facets of his overarching desire to enlarge the scope of the good society. He taught that equalitarian social interactions in democratic communities, through the ideals, conventions, and institutions that they constitute and foster, have the "task of safeguarding the collective welfare from the ravages of egoism." The greater the ascendancy of the few over the many, on the other hand, the more distinct, close-knit and self-conscious the dominant minority, the more likely that social control will be coercive and authoritarian.

Ross significantly enlarged the sociological understanding of social control by pointing out that there exists a wide range of control mechanisms, and that law, which had earlier been seen as the only important mechanism, is only one of many, and possibly not even the most important one. He groped his way to a view that conceived of control as more internalized than externally imposed, but he never satisfactorily explained the precise manner in which external factors come to be incorporated into the personality. When it came to such issues, he most often had recourse to such ad hoc notions as imitation and habit. It is only in the work of Cooley and Mead, who will be discussed later, that such mechanisms are identified and explicated in a theoretically satisfying manner.

Thorstein Veblen: 1857-1919

Except for a short period near the end of his career, Veblen kept aloof from the political activities of the radicals of his day and cultivated instead a stance of amused detachment from the foibles of his contemporaries and the contentions of his America. Unlike E. A. Ross, he felt no need to enter the arena in which the political battles of his age were fought out. Yet his work is infused by a radical perspective more deep-going than that of almost all of his contemporaries. Though he liked to veil his highly charged radical value judgments by using a complicated, illusive, and polysyllabic style of exposition, the attentive reader soon discovers the subversive implications behind his allegedly value-neutral mode.

Much of Veblen's critical bite, as well as certain of his key observations, can be accounted for by the fact that throughout his life he remained a marginal native in American society, a stranger who spent most of his life accounting for the queer ways, customs, and institutions that ruled the lives of those who remained committed to the regular grooves and routines of American culture.

He was born of Norwegian parents on a frontier farmstead in Wisconsin, the son of the Middle Border like Ward before him or Vernon Parrington and

Charles Beard after him. But while these men may have felt somewhat alienated from the genteel culture of the East, they nevertheless came from old American Protestant stock. Veblen's parents, in contrast, were recent immigrants who lived in remote farming communities almost totally cut off from contact with the surrounding world of the Yankees. Having grown up as a marginal Norwegian, Veblen became a marginal student as well during graduate study at Johns Hopkins and Yale. He later moved on to a career as a marginal professor at the University of Chicago, Stanford University, and the University of Missouri, a marginal civil servant, and a marginal editor. Forever refusing to pay tribute to the pieties and routine requirements of the various institutions in which he found a temporary refuge and resting place, he indeed lived within American society without ever being of it. His amazingly acute insights into the cracks and fissures, the contradictions and failures, of American society were fostered by his vantage point as a stranger among natives.[57]

Veblen was trained as an economist, but much of his life was spent in an endeavor to undermine the assumptions of classical and neoclassical economics which dominated the academic world and which were part of the cultural fabric of American free enterprise. The tools he used in this endeavor were partly derived from Karl Marx, but mostly from the evolutionary thought of Darwin and his followers. But conservative Darwinists such as the erstwhile teacher Sumner extolled the captains of industry as the flowers of civilization; and the reform Darwinists were committed to a vision according to which, through unremittant reform efforts, America would gradually evolve into a community of brotherly benevolence. In contrast to them, Veblen was unremittingly critical of all structural and ideological assumptions of American society.

Far from being based on unchanging "laws," as the classics had taught, economic behavior to Veblen could only be understood in evolutionary and institutional terms. The evolutionary process involved selective adaptation to the environment. And this adaptation, in turn, was largely the result of technological development. In the last analysis, institutional change was rooted in the continuous improvement of the industrial arts. Ways of acting and ways of thinking that crystallize over time into institutional molds are sanctioned by communities and impressed upon their component members; they are rooted in technological soil even though they may attain a relative autonomy of their own. In particular, those who hold power in given communities are wont to defend the existing scheme of things in which they have a vested interest and so retard the progress that technology already makes possible.

Modern capitalist America, and the capitalist world in general, is characterized, according to Veblen, by an irremedial opposition between business and industry, ownership and technology, pecuniary and industrial employment—between those who make money and those who make goods, between workmanship and salesmanship. It is dominated by a leisure class that lives "by the industrial community rather than in it."[58] Not only does the leisure class exploit the underlying population, but the price system to which it is bound hampers the development of the industrial arts and sabotages the advancement of production and hence the forward course of mankind's evolutionary developments. Those who have been seen in the prevailing myths as the constructive builders of industrial America in Veblen's inverted vision turn out to be engaged in sabotaging the benevolent forces of technology through their malevolent backing of a price system that goes counter to the evolutionary scheme of things.

The price system in its turn gives rise to a competitive culture which forces all men and women to pay unremitting attention to their relative standing in relation to other persons. Bound to the Ixion's wheel of perpetual interpersonal comparison, people's self-esteem tends to be rooted in the impression they make upon their fellows and not on intrinsic achievement. Attempting to gain advantage in the continuous struggle for heightened self-evaluation, people engage in conspicuous consumption, conspicuous leisure, conspicuous displays of symbols of high worth so as to outrace their neighbors. It is not the propensity to truck and barter that animates people in the modern world, but the propensity to excel. The struggle for competitive standing is a basic datum if one is to understand the institutional framework of modern economic behavior.

The price system distorts the industrial process, and the competitive system distorts the human character. It subverts the instinct of workmanship, the inbuilt tendency to produce to the limits of one's capacity, the concern for a job well done. It induces a lag between technological and institutional developments.

Committed to an ethos of unremitting application to the tasks at hand, a somewhat "puritan" work ethic, Veblen was a kind of Benjamin Franklin living in the age of the Great Gatsby. He castigated the wasteful ways of the age of the robber barons and contrasted the rationality of the machine process to the irrational caprices of speculators, financiers, and other malefactors of great wealth. Behind an ill-fitting mask of scientific objectivity, he proceeded to shoot his poisoned analytical arrows in the direction of all sacred cows.

Yet it would be a mistake to see in Veblen only the grand critic. Had he been only that, he would not loom as large in a contemporary America, which in many ways has characteristics quite dissimilar from his own. His theory of the socially induced motivations for competitive behavior, certain elements of his technological interpretation of history, his institutional economics in general, and his concern with lags between technologocal and institutional development in particular, are likely to have enduring value even when the tooth of time will have rendered his particular critical positions obsolete. His sociology of knowledge, though rudimentary, still is worth rereading for its emphasis on the interrelations between people's thoughts and their position in the occupational order. And a student of modernization cannot afford to remain unaware of Veblen's writings about uneven developments, with Veblen's insistence that those who borrow from the predecessors in development realize advantages that result in the relative decline of those who have originally taken the lead. One could go on. Suffice it to say here that Veblen's was probably the most original mind of his generation, a mind whose critical bite and analytical perspicacity still fructifies contemporary social thought.

Cooley and Mead: The Rise of Pragmatic Social Psychology

Even though both Cooley and Mead considered themselves part of the Progressive movement and saw their work as contributing its share to the tradition of equalitarian and democratic reform, moral and political concerns were less central to their work than to that of most thinkers considered so far. Reforming intentions emanate from Mead's and Cooley's thoughts, but their quests for reform are not as salient on the surface as are those of men like Ward or Ross. This is why this brief account of their respective work will have little to say on this subject and will instead focus on their substantial contributions to a pragmatic social psychology. Cooley and Mead can be considered primarily as the creators of a view of the human personality that tries to overcome the Cartesian dualism of the thinking ego and the surrounding world. Instead, they view human actors as enmeshed in a network of interactions. Human actors emerge from biological roots, but their selves are formed through social experiences. Human personality, hence, cannot be understood except as part of a social process which shapes each person through communicative interaction in terms of his or her significant social matrix.

Charles Horton Cooley: 1864-1929

The shy, withdrawn, introspective, and bookish Charles Horton Cooley, who ventured but rarely from the confines of his study on the campus of the University of Michigan, lacked all the characteristics that the popular imagination usually associates with the sociologist's calling. He did no surveys, administered no questionnaires, and knew next to nothing about the seamier side of urban living. The only observational study he ever conducted was largely confined to his own small children. He was preeminently what is often sneeringly referred to as an "armchair sociologist." But the thoughts generated in the privacy of his study proved to have informed the minds of generations of followers who had themselves a more socially active conception of what it meant to be a sociologist.

Cooley was born on the edge of the campus of the University of Michigan where his father, a professor of law at that university, continued to reside after his election to the Supreme Court of Michigan. The Cooley family was well off and belonged to the small upper crust of Michigan's legal and social elite. While the young Cooley therefore did not suffer all the social and economic disabilities that marked the lives of so many of his contemporaries among sociologists, his early years were marked by impediments of a psychological nature. His father was a hard-driving, ambitious extrovert who seems to have overawed the son who, in order to protect himself from his father's imperious manner, withdrew into a shell of sickliness and passivity. He attempted to derive secondary gains from a series of ailments, some of which seem to have been psychosomatic. Long torn by an emotional dependence on a father from whom he was basically alienated, Cooley required an unusually long time to come into his own. It took him seven years to complete his B.A. in, of all things, engineering. His Ph.D. dissertation on "The Theory of Transportation," a pioneering study in social ecology, was written in a tough-minded, "realistic" style of which his father presumably approved, but which was fundamentally at variance with his own tender-minded and introspective approach which he later used. This dissertation, as well as a few other early contributions, grew out of two years Cooley spent in Washington working for the Interstate Commerce Commission and the Bureau of the Census, a role in which he found himself badly miscast. It was only after he returned to the University of Michigan in 1892, to begin a teaching career he pursued to the end of his life, that Cooley finally came into his own. Having no financial worries and living in an age in which the publish-or-perish philosophy had as yet made few inroads, Cooley could devote himself to a life of unhurried contemplation and leisurely study. His three major works, *Human Nature and the Social Order* (1902), *Social Organization* (1909), and *Social Process* (1918) grew slowly and organically from notes he took over long periods of time and were distilled from his informed reactions to a wide variety of stimuli received from his extraordinary range of reading.

Like all the sociologists of his generation, Cooley was influenced by Darwin, but he was much less interested in the social implications of Darwin's thought than in the intricacies of the interrelations Darwin had been able to discover in the world of biology. The sense of the organic unity and wholeness of life Cooley found in Darwin was also what drew him to Goethe and Emerson, from whom he gained philosophical sustenance throughout his life. But his greatest intellectual debt was undoubtedly to William James, from whom he not only derived his view of the mind as forever changing and expanding in terms of novel experience, but also, the notion of selves being constructed through a variety of transactions with the outside world. Another formative influence was that of the social psychologist Mark Baldwin, who in his pioneering studies of child development kept insisting that the personality of the child can only be studied in social terms. From such ingredients, and many others besides, Cooley developed his own distinctive theoretical contributions.

Stress on the organic link and indissoluble connectedness between self and society is the cornerstone of Cooley's teaching. As he put it, "self and society are twin-born."[59] A person's self, Cooley taught, grows out of commerce with others. The self is not first individual and then social; it arises dialectically through communication with others. There can be no isolated selves, since there can be no sense of "I" without the correlative sense of "thou." The self can be defined as a "looking-glass self" because it is reflexive and arises in the person's consciousness through an incorporation of the views of others in a process of communicative interchange. If there can be no "I" without a "thou," the human personality does not emerge in splendid Cartesian isolation from the world but arises in the process of social experience. Without roots in social life the human plant would wither.

Cooley's preoccupation with the "organic" relations between individuals and their society led him to try to identify those types of social formations that would be especially conducive to sustain vivifying connections between human actors. Many social interactions, he reasoned, are fleeting in character and leave little trace in the personality. In contrast, others, such as those within the family, among close friends, in children's play groups and the like, have an intimate character and seem to leave a profound impact on individual selves. Such intimate groups, which he called "primary groups," are breeding grounds for the emergence of human cooperation and fellowship. Here individuals are drawn away from the propensity to maximize their own advantages and are tied to others by sympathy and affection. In such groups, the "we" primes the "I," and diffuse solidarity replaces the search for specific benefits that marks social life in other spheres. To Cooley, then, society can become a part of individual selves only to the extent that communal bonds in primary groups assure that the individual experiences a sense of trusting concern from those in whom he is linked in such groups. There is no looking-glass self without primary groups and without a community.

More extended commentary would have to discuss in some detail Cooley's not inconsiderable part in the development of institutional economics, or his insistence that sociological method must be attentive to the subjective meanings human actors give to their actions. One would also have to develop a critical stance vis-à-vis Cooley's excessively mentalistic and introspective views of the social nature of the self. Here it must suffice to note that the "sage of Ann Arbor" contributed a general perspective on the interrelations between individuals and their society which, though refined, extended, and elaborated, still seems to dominate genuinely social psychological approaches in contemporary thinking.

Although, as has been shown, political considerations and macrosociological concerns played a less prominent part in Cooley's thought than was the case with other sociologists in the Progressive tradition, he remains part of that tradition. He was at one with the other proponents of Progressivism in believing that only a revival of primary groups, of brotherly communities, would be allowed to stem the tide of acquisitive individualism of his times which, if left unopposed, would destroy the fabric of communal solidarity on which he thought America's promise was built.

Had he only written the two crucial chapters on "the looking-glass self" and "the primary group," Cooley's name would loom large in any historical account of early American sociology. Since he contributed much more, he is surely to be considered a modern master.

George Herbert Mead: 1863-1931

Although they were linked by a close intellectual companionship, Cooley and Mead differed significantly in their backgrounds and personality. In contrast to Cooley, Mead became acquainted early in his life with hardship and want. His father taught theology at Oberlin, where his son was born and grew up. But when the boy was still an adolescent, his father died, and the family was forced to sell their house and to move into rented quarters. The young Mead waited at colleges tables to earn his board, and then moved on to teach school, to become a private tutor, and to do survey work for railroad construction in the Northwest. An omnivorous reader, Mead prepared himself during those embattled years for an intellectual career and managed finally, in 1887, to go to Harvard to study philosophy under Royce and James. Harvard liberated him from the remnants of his father's puritanism, and the combined influence of Darwin and James led him to develop a philosophical orientation that placed him squarely in the pragmatic tradition of his Harvard teacher. Further advanced studies in Germany, partly under the direction of Wilhelm Wundt, whose conception of the "gesture" influenced him deeply, completed his philosophical education. Returning to America, it was Mead's good fortune to secure a position at the University of Michigan, where Cooley, Dewey, and James H. Tufts also taught at the time. Although Mead spent only two years at Michigan, the association with colleagues equally drawn to pragmatism influenced his later intellectual development. When Dewey was called in 1893 to the new University of Chicago to head the philosophy department, he prevailed upon Mead to follow him there. Mead stayed at that university until his death almost forty years later.

While Cooley tended to look for protective cover behind the walls of the University of Michigan, Mead took his university appointment as a vantage point from which he could involve himself in the social life of the bustling, energetic, raw, and vulgar city in which the new University of Chicago was located. He immersed himself in various urban associations and, while never neglecting his teaching duties, joined Jane Addam's Hull House as well as the City Club of Chicago, an association of reform-minded businessmen. Together with the other eminent members of the department who collectively elaborated the foundations of pragmatic philosophy under John Dewey's guidance, Mead felt that it behooved pragmatic philosophers not to limit themselves to philosophical work but to study the manifold social problems of the city firsthand. They all wished to learn by doing good.

Mead was a superb lecturer who kept his audiences in thrall, and he was surrounded by admiring students throughout his career. Yet he found it very hard to put his thoughts on paper, so that most of his work now available consists mainly of lecture notes published posthumously by his students. This largely accounts for the fact that during his lifetime he was overshadowed by his friend John Dewey, who did not suffer from a writing block. Mead's reputation was largely established only after his death. In retrospect it would seem, however, that his contribution to philosophy and social psychology equals that of Dewey. When it comes to his impact on sociology, it was surely more deep-going than that of his friend. In fact, Mead has now become the sociologists' philosopher. In a discipline in which philosophy weighs lightly among intellectual baggage, there are probably few sociologists who do not have at least some familiarity with Mead's work.

Following James, and largely paralleling Cooley's thought, Mead insisted that consciousness must be understood as a stream of thought arising in the dynamic relationship between a person and his significant environment. Individuals are continually involved in a succession of joint enterprises with associates, and this forms and shapes their minds and selves. Reflexivity is the essence of the self. By introducing the distinction between the "I" and the "me," Mead wished to clarify the nature of the self. Both the "I" and the "me" relate to social experience, but the "I" is the response of the organism to the attitudes of others, while the "me" is the organized set of others' attitudes which the person assumes through communicative interchange. To put it differently, as a "me" the person is aware of himself as an object and reacts or responds to himself or herself in terms of the attitudes of others. The parallels between this conceptualization and Freud's and Durkheim's notion of internalization are readily apparent. Self-appraisal is the result of a felt perception of the appraisal of others in the person's significant environment. People are born into social structures not of their own making, they are constrained by the "generalized other," the norms, customs, and laws that channel their actions. All of these enter the "me" as constituent elements, yet the "I" always reacts to preformed situations in a unique manner. Hence, while human actors are always immersed in social experiences that fashion their selves, each individual "I," with its incalculable spontaneity, is constantly actively responding against society, so that the mature self transforms the social world even as it responds to its exigencies in socially patterned ways.

The capacity to shape the self in accord with the attitudes of others assumes the capacity to comprehend these attitudes through the ability to take the role of others. To visualize one's performance from the point of view of others, the person must develop the ability to conceive the attitude of these others in imagination and in symbolic form. The world of symbols is to Mead the world of human activity. While animals communicate by means of simple gestures involving direct responses to given stimuli, humans communicate *significant* gestures based on linguistic symbols carrying a content that is shared by different individuals. Such significant gestures allow "an arousal in the individual himself of the response which he is calling out in the other individual, a taking of the role of the other, a tendency to act as the other person acts." [60] Symbols as significant gestures allow individuals to direct their later conduct in terms of received responses. Human communicative processes involve the constant self-conscious adjustment of ongoing behavior to the conduct of others whose role one takes.

By rooting thought in communicative interaction and locating the self as an emergent in ongoing transactions between the person and the community, Mead prepared the ground for investigations of the concrete sociological links between social and thought processes. Providing a convincing answer to the earlier philosophical assumption of a radical disjunction between thinking and acting, he also furnished the rudiments of a sociology of knowledge that was more securely grounded in social psychology than was the case with the European tradition in that area. Advancing the idea that consciousness is an inner discourse carried on by public means, he set the stage for efforts to link styles of thought to social structures, and to ascertain the reciprocal relations between a thinker and his audience. More generally, Mead's work had led, or so one hopes, to the final demise within sociology of what Simmel once called the "fallacy of separateness"—the fallacy of considering actors as monads without windows, without reference to the interactions in which they are continuously engaged.

While Cooley's theorizing sometimes came perilously close to a subjectivistic and solipsistic view of society, Mead remained steadfast in his social objectivism. The world of organized social relationships was to him as solidly given in intersubjective evidence as the physical world. To him, society is not a mental phenomenon but belongs to an "objective phase of experience." Properly understood, his work lends no support to the subjectivistic biases that have afflicted many recent developments in the social sciences. This is why, one ventures to think, Mead's work will inspire much future work in sociology and social psychology when currently fashionable doctrines will have joined the solipsistic teachings of the good Bishop Berkeley in the cabinet of antiquity.

Mead was as solidly rooted in the Progressive tradition and its search for a more enduring community as Cooley was, yet he was more tough-minded than the latter. Mead was wont to cast a cold eye on efforts to make the world over tomorrow morning, but he never wavered from his deep-seated conviction that the future of humankind was tied to the urgent task of improving society. Mature individuals, he believed, can secure enduring and nourishing roots in the community of their fellows if that community in its turn is sustained by an ever-renewed quest for wider and deeper forms of democratic participation.

Thomas and Park:
Chicago Sociology as Exemplar and Pathsetter

It seems no exaggeration to say that for roughly twenty years, from the first world war to the mid-1930s, the history of sociology in America can largely be written as the history of the Department of Sociology of the University of

Chicago. During these years, the department set the general tone of sociological inquiries, published the only major journal of the discipline, and trained most of the sociologists who made a mark on the profession and who assumed the presidency of the American Sociological Society. Its members wrote the most influential monographs and textbooks.

The Chicago department had its beginning in 1892. Under the guidance of Albion Small it immediately assumed a preeminent place on the American sociological scene. Whereas other early departments, such as the ones at Columbia under Giddings and at Yale under Sumner, tended to be dominated by the strong personalities of founders who endeavored to impose their theoretical vision on their fiefdoms, Small seems from the very beginning to have been committed to a deliberately eclectic stance. Though personally working in the German historicist tradition in which he had been trained, he attracted other members of the department who had but little use for his style of inquiry, and who worked in the traditions of urban ethnography, social pathology, urban ecology, or social psychology. It was probably this commitment to let many flowers bloom that accounts in part for much of the success of his department. Another major reason for this success was the location of the department in the new metropolis of Chicago, that ambitious city with its mosaic of recent immigrant groups, that "Hog Butcher for the World," which had developed in little over a half century from a frontier outpost to America's second largest city. Chicago sociologists—and most of them had a strong empirical inclination—needed to walk only a few blocks from their protected surroundings on the sedate Midway to find their "social laboratory."

Whether from deliberate design or as a kind of ecological adaptation, fieldwork-oriented studies, mainly in Chicago, became the hallmark of the department's contribution, even though statistical investigations were to become prominent when William Ogburn joined the department in 1927. What fascinated most members of the department was the variety of urban life-styles, of urban organization and disorganization, of occupations and professions, whether licit or illicit, that could be observed in the "laboratory." The founders of the department were largely drawn to such studies by the reforming impulse they shared with so many other sociologists dealt with in these pages. The next generation, though still committed to reform, turned to various local elites and local professionals in city-improvement associations, race-relations commissions, and the like, in efforts to make sociology relevant to public affairs.[61]

While the first University of Chicago generation still had largely small-town and religious roots, the next was more urban, even cosmopolitan, in origin and orientation, and more professionalized. While the first generation worked in close collaboration with reform-minded social workers, the next generation, having developed a surer sense of professional identity, tended to compete with social work in its search for clients and audiences willing to profit from advice of those who now bathed in the glory of a newly acquired professional and institutionalized identity. The members of the second generation were still much committed to doing good but now tended to pursue their calling in a somewhat less exuberant, more restrained, more gentlemanly way, as professionals talking to other professionals.

Moving from the working style and the audience of the Chicago sociologists to the substance of their work, it must be stressed that their reputation as atheoretical fact finders and empty-headed empiricists is by no means deserved. The members of the early generation possessed well-furnished theoretical minds and were very much conversant with social theory, whether European or homegrown. Simmel, Durkheim, the Austrian conflict theorists, but also Marx (though not Weber) were part of the theoretical toolkits of most Chicago sociologists of the first generation, and also, though less uniformly so, of the second. A simple glance at Park and Burgess's influential textbook, *Introduction to the Science of Society* (1921), an attempt at codification of the Chicago department's approach to sociology, will readily show that its authors attempted to introduce their students to a great deal of sociological thought of a theoretical nature. They did not succeed in fully assimilating the theoretical structure of the various European social thinkers with whom they were familiar, but they benefited from them in bits and pieces and in tune with their specific research requirements.

W. I. Thomas and Robert E. Park straddled the first and second period of the development of sociology at the University of Chicago. Thomas joined the department in its early stages but was forced to leave it in 1918. Robert Park joined only in 1914 but served there until his retirement in 1933. Both of them singly or jointly helped train most of the major sociologists of the second generation, from Everett C. Hughes and Herbert Blumer to Louis Wirth, E. Franklin Frazier, Clifford Shaw, Leonard Cottrell, and a host of other, though not lesser, scholars.

William I. Thomas: 1863-1947

W. I. Thomas, the son of a Southern dirt farmer and Methodist preacher, had to travel a rocky road to reach the eminence he finally attained. Thomas has said that the social environment in which he grew up, twenty miles from the nearest railroad, resembled that of the eighteenth century. He subsequently moved to the University of Tennessee and later to metropolitan cities of the Middle West and the North so that he could say that he had lived "in three centuries, migrating gradually to the higher cultural areas." Thomas had originally contemplated a career in literature and the classics, and it was only after his stay in Germany, where he became familiar with the tradition of *Voelker-psychologie*—i.e., ethnography—that he resolved to devote himself to anthropological and sociological research. He became a graduate student in the new Department of Sociology of the University of Chicago in 1894 and stayed there as a key member of the faculty until 1918. He was fired on account of a minor infringement on the straight-laced sexual mores of the community of scholars and gentlemen.

This episode was one of the most shameful in the whole history of

American academic life. Thereafter, although he taught upon occasion, Thomas was forced to live as an independent research scholar without institutional affiliation. A man less vital, ebullient, and rambunctious might have been destroyed by this disgraceful event. Thomas, however, continued his life seemingly undisturbed and was nearly as productive in his later career as he had been at Chicago.

Thomas's work, as well as his teaching, was informed by an insatiable curiosity about the ways in which diverse persons and groups react in characteristic manners to their transportation from a rural origin to the wilderness of modern cities. His magnum opus, *The Polish Peasant in Europe and America,* which he coauthored with Florian Znaniecki, is informed by this curiosity, which probably had its roots in Thomas's own experience. Employing novel research methods, among which the collection of life histories and other personal documents were the most noteworthy, the authors attempted to give an exhaustive accounting of the transformation of life-styles, ways of looking at the world, modes of perceiving, and moral orientations that attended the move of peasants from their native village to the modern city. Thomas and Znaniecki attempted to show how different modes of social organization and social control generated different value structures in the significant environment of migrants from village to city, and how such value changes in turn called forth different personal attitudes. In attempting to do justice to both objective and subjective factors in the determination of human conduct, Thomas and Znaniecki insisted that only the conjoint interplay of individual attitudes and objective cultural values was adequate for an account of human behavior. The cause of all social phenomena, but more particularly of social change, which was the main object of their inquiry, was never, as they put it, "another social or individual phenomenon alone, but always a combination" of both.[62]

To these authors, the influence of objective factors upon human conduct assumes importance largely to the extent that they are subjectively experienced. It was certainly their peculiar genius to balance their emphasis on attitudes, subjectively defined meanings, and shared experiences with an equally strong emphasis on the objective characteristics of cultural values and their embodiment in specific institutions. This is why their work, while paying a great deal of attention to the subjective definitions that their life histories and other personal documents reveal, pays equally sustained attention to microsociological units, such as primary groups and families, and to the larger institutional settings, from churches to schools to clubs, in which these smaller units are embedded.

Despite the great diversity of topics discussed in the book, it gains its unity through its portrayal of the impact of urbanization and modernization in the contemporary world. The authors documented the replacement of traditional forms of social control by the looser and more tenuous controls that guide the conduct of modern men and women. They documented the sea change from a kin-dominated culture to one based on urban associations or loose neighborhood ties. Thomas and Znaniecki were of course not alone in this endeavor; in a sense, most modern sociology can be said to be embarked on that task. But whereas their predecessors provided mainly typologies or generalized descriptions, Thomas and Znaniecki sustained their thesis by way of a rich texture of concrete and vividly portrayed personal documentation and firsthand observation. It is generally agreed by now that their book, despite its many flaws, despite gaps between theoretical foundations and empirical findings, is the first great landmark of American research sociology.

Thomas's later work grew naturally out of the earlier collaborative effort. The stress he placed on the fact that all human subjective meanings come to be constructed by definitions through which the prism of the mind orders perceptual experience, already adumbrated in *The Polish Peasant*, was only fully developed later on. The most seminal sentence Thomas ever wrote in his later career runs: "If men define situations as real, they are real in their consequences." This phrase sums up his most deeply ingrained sociological conviction and his essential message: people do not only respond to objective features of a situation, but also, and often mainly, to the meaning a situation has for them, and this has social consequences. If people believe in witches, even though educated Westerners know that they do not exist, such beliefs have tangible effects. Once a Vietnamese is seen as a "gook" or a black as a "nigger" or a Jew as a "kike," he has been transmuted through the peculiar alchemy of social definitions into a wholly "other" who may now become a target of prejudice and discrimination, and even of murder. There are, of course, both benevolent as well as malevolent consequences of social definitions. In any case, it was Thomas's distinct merit to have pointed to the salient fact that definitions organize experience, and hence action. Even if some contemporary theorists have distorted Thomas's insight into the absurd proposition that only definitions count and that objective social conditions need not be attended to, it is certainly the case that Thomas's formulation remains one of the essential building blocks of contemporary sociology. In his own right, and through his influence on many social psychologists both within the Chicago tradition or, as in the case of Robert K. Merton, outside of it, Thomas's heritage has decisively influenced the course of American sociological theorizing and research.

Robert E. Park: 1864-1944

Few journalists prepare themselves for their job by taking an M.A. degree in philosophy at Harvard, fewer still gain a Ph.D. degree in Heidelberg under one of Germany's major philosophers, and still fewer, after years of newspaper reporting, become professors of sociology at a major university. Robert Park managed all that.

Park was born in Pennsylvania, the son of a prosperous businessman who, soon after the son's birth, moved to Minnesota, where the young Park grew up. Like Veblen, Ward, Cooley, and Mead, Park is a product of the Middle Border. Despite his father's opposition to book learning, Park enrolled at the University of Minnesota, transferring to the University of Michigan in his sophomore year. At Michigan, Park was influenced by the progressive atmosphere and by the pragmatic philosophy of his teachers, John Dewey among them. This is why, upon graduation, he decided not to join his father's business and to seek instead a career in which he could follow his concerns for reform. Having a strongly developed empiricist bent and distrusting systems of ideas, Park felt that intimate acquaintance with social problems was a prerequisite for attempts to resolve them. So he became a newspaperman, believing that a career in reporting would allow him to make firsthand observations. He worked for a dozen years on various newspapers in a number of cities, covering the urban scene, investigating city machines and the corruption they brought in their wake, and exposing the squalid conditions in immigrant ghettos and high-crime areas.

Always fascinated by the character of news and newsmaking, Park decided in 1898 to go to Harvard to acquire a wider philosophical background. After earning his M.A., he proceeded to Germany for further studies. These culminated in a Ph.D. dissertation on "The Mass and the Public" under the neo-Kantian philosopher Wilhelm Windelband. Returning to Harvard as an instructor in philosophy, he soon found that he was "sick and tired of the academic world" and resolved to return to the "real world" after six years in academia. Fascinated by race relations in America and elsewhere, he wrote a series of muckraking exposés of the Belgian colonial atrocities in the Congo, and he roamed around the South to acquaint himself with the conditions of black people. This led to his acquaintance with Booker T. Washington, the president of Tuskegee Institute, to whom Park served as an informal secretary and traveling companion for seven years. In 1914, at the age of fifty, Park decided upon an academic career in sociology, after having met W. I. Thomas, who invited him to give a course on "The Negro in America" at the University of Chicago. Though his position in the Chicago department was at first somewhat tenuous, Park became its outstanding member by 1920 and impressed his stamp on it throughout the twenties and early thirties.

Park was, above all, a great teacher who managed to inspire his students with his own enthusiasm for the study of urban phenomena and race relations. He wrote relatively little himself; his main contributions consist of journal articles and introductions to the books of his students. He wanted above all to train scholars who would be able to explore the social world, and especially the urban scene, with a precision and objectivity that only rarely could be found among his former associates in the newspaper world. In this he succeeded magnificently, as the long list of works written under his guidance on such topics as urban gangs, slums, taxi dance halls, and the gold coast and the slums eloquently testifies.

Although he concerned himself with apparently disparate topics, Park nevertheless followed a fairly distinct theoretical strategy. Social life, so he argued, should be conceived as governed by four major social processes: competition, conflict, accommodation, and assimilation. These processes accounted, for example, for the "natural history" of ethnic and racial groups attempting to carve a niche for themselves in the wider social order. Eschewing static approaches to society, Park defined sociology as "the science of collective behavior," thereby indicating his view that relatively fluid social processes rather than fixed social structures govern social life. He tended to conceive of society not as relatively stable but as an instrument of social control attempting to direct and challenge the process of collective behavior while, at the same time, responding to its challenge. In this view, the corporate existence of society is perpetually challenged by component groups and individuals, so that a permanent state of equilibrium is an asymptotic and utopian goal.

Taking a leaf from the Darwinian notion of the "web of life," Park focused on the process through which a biotic order emerges through competition, dominance, and succession among mutually interdependent groups. These groups are seen as carving out a niche for themselves through ecological adjustments and spatial accommodation. Park maintained that the processes characterizing the growth and development of plant and animal communities apply to human communities as well. But at the same time he argued that human communities differ from animal communities in that they are sustained in a culturally transmitted symbolic and moral universe that has no counterpart in other species. Human societies, to him, have a double aspect: they are made up of interdependent individuals and groups competing with one another for economic and territorial dominance and for favorable ecological niches; but they are also held together by symbolically affirmed solidarity, consensus, and common purpose. The social and moral order softens the impact of the competitive struggle for existence through social control, normative guidance, and involvement in transindividual tasks.

I shall not deal here with Park's conception of social role, social distance, marginality, or the social nature of the self. Many of these conceptualizations, though he gave them an original cast, owe a good deal to previous thinkers, particularly William James and Georg Simmel.

It would be exaggerated to claim that Park furnished a finished system of sociology. He never had such an intention. He was content instead to develop a series of general ideas and sensitizing concepts that could appropriately guide the empirical work of his students. Being especially attentive to the process of social change and to the emergence of novel social formations that upset or render obsolete previous adjustments and accommodations, Park's theoretical ideas were persuasive enough to develop a Chicago-based "school" of urban ethnography and human ecology that still inspires a great number of contemporary investigations.

Concluding Remarks

The later developments of American sociology are being dealt with in other chapters of this volume. The end of the Chicago dominance may conveniently be dated as 1935, when the American Sociological Society, previously largely, though not wholly, dominated by the Chicago department or Chicago-trained scholars, decided in a minor coup d'etat to establish its own journal, *The American Sociological Review*, thus serving the longtime formal and informal links of the discipline to the University of Chicago department. Two years later the appearance of Talcott Parson's *The Structure of Social Action* heralded the emergence of a theoretical orientation considerably at variance with that developed at the University of Chicago. This new orientation was largely to dominate American sociology for the next quarter of a century. Having gradually become institutionalized and largely professionalized in the years with which this essay has dealt, having passed through a period of incubation during the years of Chicago dominance, sociology could embark on its mature career.

NOTES

1. Quoted in Vernon K. Dibble, *The Legacy of Albion Small* (Chicago: University of Chicago Press, 1975) p. 54.
2. Anthony Oberschall, "The Institutionalization of American Sociology," in *The Establishment of Empirical Sociology*, Oberschall, ed. (New York: Harper & Row, 1972) p. 198. I have profited a great deal from Oberschall's brilliant account and have liberally borrowed from it both in regard to factual information and to interpretative schemes.
3. Paul J. Baker, Martha Long, and Susan Quensel, "The Pioneers of American Sociology," paper presented at the annual meetings of the American Sociological Association, New York, August 1973.
4. Richard Hofstadter, *The Age of Reform* (New York: Vintage Books, 1960) p. 152.
5. Hofstadter, *The Age of Reform*, p. 152. See also Oberschall, "The Institutionalization of American Sociology," p. 198.
6. Vernon Dibble, *The Legacy of Albion Small*, p. 153. The pages that follow are largely taken from an unpublished part of my Ph.D. dissertation entitled, "Toward a Sociology of Social Conflict," Columbia University, 1954. I have also drawn on this dissertation in other parts of this chapter.
7. L. L. Bernard and Jessie Bernard, *Origins of American Sociology* (New York: Thomas Y. Crowell, 1943).
8. Ibid., pp. 530–31.
9. Ibid., p. 562.
10. The closing sentences of this paragraph are adapted from Robert K. Merton's description of the Puritan ethic in its relation to the cultivation of natural science, "Puritanism, Pietism and Science" in *Social Theory and Social Structure* (Glencoe, Ill.: The Free Press, 1968) pp. 628–60. I believe that the relation between reformist ethic and social science is similar to that between the Puritan ethic and natural science.
11. Quoted by Howard Odum, *American Sociology* (New York: Longman, Inc.) pp. 60–61.
12. See F. L. Tolman, "The Study of Sociology in the Institutions of Learning in the United States," *American Journal of Sociology*, vol. VII (1902) pp. 797–838; and Ibid., vol. VIII (1902) pp. 85–121, 251–72, 531–58; and A. W. Small, "Fifty Years of Sociology in the United States," Ibid., vol. XXI (1916) pp. 721–864.
13. Floyd W. House, *The Development of Sociology* (New York: McGraw-Hill, 1936) pp. 220–25.
14. As John L. Gillin, writing on the development of sociology in the United States, remarks: "From one point of view the sociologists might be properly classified as the left wing of the new

economists." "The Development of Sociology in the United States," publication of the American Sociological Society, vol. XXI (1927) p. 6.

15. Again I have adopted two sentences by Robert K. Merton, "Puritanism, Pietism and Science," p. 631, on the relation of Puritan religion and science.

16. Albion W. Small and George E. Vincent, *An Introduction to the Study of Society* (New York: American Book Company, 1894) p. 77.

17. Lester Ward's reaction to attempts to dissociate sociology and reform is worth noting: When a social Darwinist, Henry J. Ford, attacked sociologists in *The Nation* for their espousal of reforms, Charles A. Ellwood felt the need to reply: "Mr. Ford does not distinguish (sociologists) from social radicals and revolutionaries. . . . Very few sociologists of reputed standing endorse the revolutionary ideas which he credits all with possessing. Free love, trial marriage, divorce by mutual consent, the contract theory of society, and other anarchistic ideas, so far from being endorsed by a majority of sociologists, have, perhaps, been more powerfully combated by them than by other classes of scientific men." Ford's *Nation* article, "The Pretensions of Sociology," is reprinted in the *American Journal of Sociology*, vol. XV (1909–10) pp. 96–104, and is followed by Ellwood's answer, "The Science of Sociology: A Reply," pp. 105–10. The same volume also contains further discussions by Small, a reply by Ford, and a rejoinder by Ward. This defense, Ward thought, was "more damaging to sociology than anything which Ford had said." Ellwood read the "social radicals and revolutionists" out of the field of sociology. See "The Letters of Albion W. Small to Lester F. Ward," Bernhard Stern, ed., *Social Forces*, vol. XV (1937) p. 324.

18. "What Is a Sociologist?" *American Journal of Sociology*, vol. VIII (1902) p. 471.

19. "Scholarship and Social Agitation," *American Journal of Sociology*, vol. I (1895–96) p. 581.

20. Albion W. Small, *Adam Smith and Modern Sociology* (Chicago: University of Chicago Press, 1907) p. 22.

21. "Socialism in the Light of Social Science," *American Journal of Sociology*, vol. XVII (1911–12) p. 819.

22. Albion W. Small, *Between Eras—From Capitalism to Democracy* (Kansas City: Intercollegiate Press, 1913).

23. Ibid., p. 353.

24. "A Vision of Social Efficiency," *American Journal of Sociology*, vol. XIX (1914) p. 440.

25. Oberschall, "The Institutionalization of American Sociology," pp. 188–89.

26. It is also true, however, as Mary O. Furner has recently shown in her fine study, *Advocacy and Objectivity* (Lexington: University of Kentucky Press, 1976), that they often trimmed their sails in order to gain academic respectability.

27. Dibble, *The Legacy of Albion Small*, p. 32.

28. Cf. Paul J. Baker, Mary Ferrell, and Susan Quensel, "Departmentalization of Sociology in the United States, 1880–1928," paper presented at the annual meetings of the American Sociological Association, San Francisco, August 1975.

29. Cf. Richard Hofstadter, *Social Darwinism in American Thought* (Boston: Beacon Press, 1955) and R. J. Wilson, ed., *Darwinism and the American Intellectuals* (Homewood, Ill.: Dorsey Press, 1967).

30. William G. Sumner, *What Social Classes Owe to Each Other* (New York: Harper, 1883) p. 120.

31. William G. Sumner, *The Challenge of Facts and Other Essays* (New Haven: Yale University Press, 1914) p. 38.

32. Harris E. Starr, *William Graham Sumner* (New York: Holt, 1925) p. 22.

33. Hofstadter, *Social Darwinism*, p. 64.

34. William G. Sumner, *War and Other Essays* (New Haven: Yale University Press, 1911) p. 177.

35. William G. Sumner, *Earth Hunger and Other Essays* (New Haven: Yale University Press, 1913) p. 314.

36. Sumner, *War and Other Essays*, p. 163.

37. Quoted in Hofstadter, *Social Darwinism*, p. 57 from Sumner's *Essays*, vol. II.

38. William G. Sumner, *Folkways* (Boston: Ginn & Co., 1907).

39. Ibid., p. 59.

40. Ibid., p. 521.

41. Ibid., p. 53.

42. Ibid., p. 55.

43. Ibid., p. 56.

44. Ibid., p. 18.

45. Ibid., p. 12.
46. Ibid., p. 13.
47. Cf. for example Robert A. Levine and Donald T. Campbell, *Ethnocentrism* (New York: John Wiley & Sons, 1972).
48. This account is largely based on Hofstadter, *Social Darwinism*, pp. 68–69.
49. Ibid., p. 72.
50. Ibid., p. 74.
51. Ibid., p. 79.
52. Lester Ward, *Pure Sociology* (New York: Appleton, 1903) p. 238.
53. Hofstadter, *Social Darwinism*, p. 83.
54. Amitai Etzioni, *The Active Society* (New York: The Free Press, 1968).
55. E. A. Ross, *Seventy Years of It* (New York: Appleton-Century, 1936) p. 180.
56. R. Jackson Wilson, "Edward Alsworth Ross: The Natural Man and the Community of Constraint," in Wilson, *In Quest of Community* (New York: John Wiley & Sons, 1968) p. 102. I have profited a great deal from this fine study.
57. Joseph Dorfman's monumental *Thorstein Veblen and His America* (New York: Viking Press, 1934) still remains the best intellectual biography of Veblen and an indispensable source. Compare also my chapter on Veblen in Lewis A. Coser, *Masters of Sociological Thought*, 2d ed. (New York: Harcourt Brace Jovanovich, 1977) pp. 263–302. The interested reader will find further references in this book.
58. Thorstein Veblen, *The Theory of the Leisure Class* (New York: Modern Library, 1934) p. 246. A fine sample of Veblen's major writings is to be found in *The Portable Veblen*, edited and with an introduction by Max Lerner (New York: Viking Press, 1948). This volume also contains a bibliographic listing of all of Veblen's works.
59. Charles H. Cooley, *Social Organization* (New York: Schocken Books, 1962) p. 5. For a biographical account see Edward C. Jandy's *Charles Horton Cooley: His Life and His Social Theory* (New York: Dryden Press, 1942). Albert J. Reiss, Jr., ed:, *Cooley and Social Analysis* contains a number of valuable analytical contributions, by Talcott Parsons among others. See also my chapter on Cooley in Coser, *Masters of Sociological Thought* pp. 305–330 on which I have drawn in these pages.
60. George H. Mead, *Mind, Self, and Society* (Chicago: University of Chicago Press, 1934) p. 73. This work is the major source for Mead's contributions to social psychology. See also Anselm Strauss, ed., *George Herbert Mead on Social Psychology* (Chicago: University of Chicago Press, 1964). Among the many commentaries on Mead's thought, Herbert Blumer's "Sociological Implications of the Thought of George Herbert Mead, *American Journal of Sociology*, LXXI:5 (March 1966) pp. 535–44, and Tomatsu Shibutani, "George Herbert Mead," in *International Encyclopedia of the Social Sciences* (New York: Macmillan Company, 1968) are especially illuminating. Here as elsewhere in this essay I have drawn heavily on Coser, *Masters of Sociological Thought*.
61. Cf. James T. Carey, *Sociology and Public Affairs: The Chicago School* (Beverly Hills: Sage Publications, 1975), as well as Robert E. L. Faris, *Chicago Sociology, 1920–1932* (Chicago: University of Chicago Press, 1970) and Edward Shils, "Tradition, Ecology, and Institutions in the History of Sociology," *Daedalus* (Fall 1970) pp. 760–825.
62. William I. Thomas and Florian Znaniecki, *The Polish Peasant in Europe and America*, vol. 1 (New York: Dover Publications, 1958) p. 44. This essay on Thomas is largely based on more extended treatment in Coser, *Masters of Sociological Thought*. See also Morris Janowitz's introduction to Janowitz, ed., *William I. Thomas on Social Organization and Social Personality* (Chicago: University of Chicago Press, 1966) and other sources cited in Coser, *Masters of Sociological Thought*.

9

FUNCTIONALISM

WILBERT E. MOORE

IT WOULD almost appear that functionalism has become an embarrassment in contemporary theoretical sociology. True, the functionalist perspective commonly figures in those guides to modern theory usable as textbooks,[1]—though certainly not as a model or standard for approximation, but rather as a position held with decreasing conviction, subject to attack or evasion. Robert Nisbet, in a context noting the conservative implications of functionalism, comments on its decline.[2] The decline is scarcely one of interest in the functionalist canon, for the leading sociological journals, to the extent that they contain prose exposition at all, continue to publish articles attacking what—from that indicator—may be called "bad old theory."

That the contemporary attacks on functionalism come commonly (though not exclusively) from sociologists with a self-identified "critical" or "radical" orientation is not surprising, given both the intrinsic relevance of value or ideological orientations to sociological theory at the level of concern with what we may call the "true nature of society," and the circumstance that sophisticated or vulgar neo-Marxist orientations have had a strong recrudescence among young sociologists. (Value assumptions, which turn out also to be assumptions concerning the proper mission of the sociological discipline, will perforce engage our attention at several junctures in this discussion.) The paucity of current theoretical writing presenting a spirited defense of functionalism may be interpreted in several ways which are not mutually exclusive: that the attackers have well and truly found their target, leaving functionalism as defeated bad old theory on both scientific and ideological grounds, sullenly cherished by a dwindling company of ineluctably aging and unreconstructed believers (and the continued attacks representing a kind of addiction to overkill); that the principal adherents and expositors of functionalism, represented, say, by the notorious "Harvard circle" at one time revolving around Talcott Parsons, have turned their primary attention to other sociological concerns; that the proponents of functionalism are out of fashion in the current climate of radical rhetoric, have lost their power or influence, and thus—to indulge in the kind of conspiracy theory much admired in radical circles—simply cannot get published.

To the first of these interpretations we may now respond "Well, yes and no" or, better, "Only partly," leaving the untangling of that unsatisfactory situation to the ensuing exposition. The third interpretation we may dismiss as about as fanciful and unverifiable as most conspiracy theories. In support of the second interpretation we may cite some examples which will still leave a somewhat mixed judgment. Talcott Parsons can probably be fairly described as an unrepentant functionalist,[3] but for a number of years he has been primarily concerned with developing a typology of societies from an explicitly evolutionary perspective,[4] and with power as a generalized medium of exchange, analoguous to money.[5] Kingsley Davis, author of a general textbook from a functionalist perspective,[6] coauthor with me of the enduringly controversial "functional theory of stratification,"[7] and author of a defense of functionalism in his presidential address for the American Sociological Association,[8] has for years been primarily concerned with clarifying and verifying the social determinants of human fertility and mortality.[9] Robert Merton, renowned for his formalization of functionalism,[10] has in recent years returned to his early interest in the sociology of science.[11] Marion Levy, whose work on *The Structure of Society*[12] explores the "functional requisites of any society" at a level offering greater articulation with universal structures than does Parsons's unduly abstract fourfold scheme,[13] has for years been primarily interested in the analysis of modernization.[14] Since his analysis is set in the framework of "comparative statics," he might also be characterized as an unrepentant functionalist. I have described my own position as a "chastened, penitent, and somewhat reformed functionalist," with explicit departures from functionalist faith in *Social Change*,[15] and a principal and self-critical interest in the global process of modernization.[16]

Lest a somewhat extended discussion of the history of functionalism and its current standing be regarded as an exercise in the futile attempt to resurrect dead doctrines, some further introductory comments are in order. I shall be noting in subsequent paragraphs the centrality of a systems perspective in all explicitly functional analyses, but also in much analytical work that may leave theoretical assumptions mainly unstated, and in some scholarly work that explicitly adopts some form of conflict orientation. This, it appears, is the tenable truth in Davis's insistence that functional analysis and sociological analysis constitute an equation.[17] Almost all of those statistical reports that now crowd the sociological journals represent attempts to measure mainly atemporal relations. The statistical analysis is fundamentally correlational, however refined by factor analysis, analysis of variance, path analysis, or regression equations. The manipulation of so-called empirical observations—a semantically improper bit of jargon substituted for the accurate terms numerical or quantitative—attempts verification of the assumption that various measures of patterned behavior and its consequences do not stand in random relation to each other—in other words, that they are parts of some sort of system. Though the theoretical innocence of some research practitioners is pristine and profound, they are unwitting functionalists. Durkheim's judgment that the canon of inductive logic most apt for sociology is that of correlation[18] appears amply fulfilled in the research literature, though the perpetrators may not have read Durkheim.

The agenda for the subsequent proceedings here are principally these: an examination of the origins of functionalism; functionalism viewed as a systems perspective; structural functionalism; functionalism as a neoevolutionary perspective, including the theory of modernization; and concluding comments concerning limitations and controversies with respect to functionalism, though some of these will necessarily intrude in the earlier exposition as it proceeds.

The Problem of Origins

In the moderately long history of social theory, genuine theoretical "breakthroughs" are rare. It is not mere modesty that has led the more conscientious innovators to recognize that they "have stood on the shoulders of giants." Any allegation of primacy in a fundamental idea is likely to provoke scholars into becoming detractors by assembling evidence of earlier anticipations and even articulations of the same ideas. Integration and formalization of prior insights are easier to document for claims of constructive novelty than are the component ideas. Conceptual innovations are of course easy. If they merely enrich the vocabulary of synonyms, their novelty is spurious. If they add defensible precision or identify distinctions that make a difference, the claim of clarification is enhanced. New observational instruments (the telescope, the microscope, the sample survey) are seemingly easier to document as to origin and consequence than are systems of ideas.

These stipulations and cautions are meant to be disarming, for I intend to view functionalism as a more or less systematic framework for social analysis and, with that qualification, to begin its history as recently as the latter part of the last century. My intent thus is not to deny that some of the fundamental ideas are of impressive antiquity in recorded "philosophies," and thus of probably even greater antiquity in unrecorded folk wisdom. Rather, by reliance on integration and formalization as comprising significant novelty, I hope to evade the requirement of tracing the origin of component ideas.

The central ideas of the functionalist perspective can be stated rather simply. Human social aggregates involve differentiated units which are interdependent. These units may be individuals, families and kinship structures, villages, or such analytical structures as age-sex categories or broader status groups. It has been customary for sociologists to view "societies," and anthropologists to view "cultures," as the most encompassing social aggregates or social systems, of which other concrete or analytical units thus become parts of subsets. (The circumstance that the contemporary world may offer few if any actual examples of genuinely self-subsistent social units is worth passing notice, but need not detain us here as long as most social aggregates are mainly contained within what we may cautiously want to call quasi-societies. The truly self-subsistent unit—that is, society—then becomes an analytical construct or "model.")

The combination of differentiation and interdependence permits asking two related questions: how is the interdependence of units effected? what contribution do the parts make to the whole?

The central importance of differentiation in the functionalist perspective warrants close scrutiny. There is no better place to start than with the classic work of Emile Durkheim, *De la Division du Travail Social*[19] (translated as *The Division of Labor in Society*). Durkheim, often credited with "founding" functionalism, devoted the greater part of his prolific scholarly writing to aspects of differentiation and integration. Yet in *Division of Labor* he began that enduring concern in a curious way: by positing a fictitious primitive state of social cohesion based on likeness rather than on interdependent differences. His concept of "mechanical solidarity" makes semantic sense only when placed in contrast to "organic solidarity," with its readily grasped connotations of differentiated parts that perform various interdependent functions in maintaining the viability of the complex organism as a whole. Durkheim did not succeed in making his state of mechanical solidarity quite credible, for actual examples of societies lacking internal differentiation were not available, and indeed it is highly improbably that such a primitive state among wandering prehistoric groups or bands ever could have existed. (As a minimum, age and sex are always relevant and necessary bases for differentiation, and others such as aptitudes and skills are highly probable.) The factual point is relatively unimportant, for Durkheim was using his fictitiously homogeneous society as an expository device for examining the sources of differentiation and the problem of maintaining cohesion of increasingly differentiated societies.

The theme of increasing differentiation was of course not original with Durkheim, as it was solidly based on evolutionary theories, particularly in their post-Darwinian versions and extensions.[20] Durkheim had the exceptional merit of not taking the process as a given, a datum; rather, he noted the importance of population growth and density as well as a rather unsatisfactory concept of "moral density," that came close to meaning "increasing normative complexity," which was what was to be explained. (To take increasing differentiation as a given seems still to mar the contemporary work of Parsons[21] and Smelser.[22]) The reality of fundamental social transformations accompanying the expansion of industrial capitalism was of prime concern to Saint-Simon and Comte,[23] with their quest for a rationally constructed new social order; to Marx,[24] with his concern for the radical alienation of the worker from the product of his labors; to Tönnies,[25] with his nostalgic regret for the loss of multibonded ties in the stable community as contrasted with the fragile structure of specialized associations; and to Weber,[26] with his nervous admiration for the bureaucratic state and bureaucratized work organizations generally. Though these well-remembered scholars, whose work spanned nearly a century, differed in many significant respects, they all reflected an underlying concern for the twin themes of differentiation and interdependence, of specialization and integration.

A secondary and somewhat muted theme underlies the preoccupation of these scholars with the new forms of social interdependence established by a highly rationalized economy and polity. That theme is order and change. It was the passing of old and putatively stable social orders that provoked scholarly concern. With the most notable exception of Marx, the scholars muted the theme of change by the expedient of constructing dichotomous types of social systems. Durkheim contrasted contemporary (and admittedly precarious) organic solidarity with "primitive" mechanical solidarity. Tönnies clearly regretted the passing of the ordered community with the establishment of rationalized forms of social organization. Weber compared rational-legal political systems with those deriving their legitimacy from unchallenged tradition. We shall later note that the before-and-after comparison still haunts the analysis of "traditional" and "modern" societies in contemporary scholarly work on the universal process of modernization.

It was, in effect, the emphasis on interdependence in social systems that partially diverted attention from the processes of their creation. The neglect of dynamics was of course not total. Comte adopted an essentially evolutionary view with his theological, metaphysical, and positivistic (scientific) stages of sociocultural systems. Marx developed a special variant of social evolution with his emphasis on technology, property systems, and class struggle. Weber was insistently historical in his perspective and notably emphasized the importance of changes in values and ideas as sources of structural transformation. Even Durkheim, as noted, made modest efforts to account for the phenomenon of increasing differentiation.

What these social theorists—and of course a number of others—had in common was the preception of the emergent reality of social systems. They were antireductionists. The position is again most articulately formulated by Durkheim in his famous assertion that social facts have a reality sui generis and his admonition that social facts are to be explained by other social facts[27] (and thus, not to be reduced to psychological states of the actors). This is closely akin to Marx's equally famous assertion, "It is not the consciousness of men that determines their existence, but, on the contrary, their social existence that determines their consciousness."[28] Neither Marx nor Durkheim had any enthusiasm for the vulgar hedonism or utilitarianism of classical economics. Durkheim's discussion of the "noncontractual elements in contract"[29] called attention to the normative order, the body of rules that comprised the "collective conscience." Marx and Durkheim differed as to whether the rules are to be regarded as manipulative or consensual, but not as to their superindividual quality.

It was Durkheim's correct perception that interdependence does not assure solidarity of the system as a whole that led him to explore the function of ultimate values, of beliefs held not subject to question.[30] In *The Elementary Forms of the Religious Life*[31] he made the assumption that a primitive or tribal society with the most rudimentary forms of survival technology would also have a religious system of the most elementary sort. Reflecting the evolutionary principle of progression from simple to complex structures, the argument also assumed a principle of social integration that would become a basic tenet of functionalism: that analytically distinguishable parts of any society or culture must be appropriate for the rest of the system. Ironically, Durkheim's assumption of "uniformity of simplicity" turned out to be simplistic. The aboriginal Australians, ethnographic reports on whom led Durkheim to their selection as a case, were later shown to have an exceptionally complex kinship system.[32] That complicating consideration had more devastating implications for oversimplified notions of social evolution—and, more than incidentally, for notions of technological determinism—than it did for notions of interdependence and integration. And Durkheim's conclusion that the object of religious worship is, at base, society itself remains an arguable interpretation of at least part of religious beliefs and practices.

Durkheim's concern with problems of social integration was early and enduring. Not only in the *Division of Labor* but also in subsequent books and essays[33] a great part of his work focused on the maintenance of the moral order, the avoidance of anomie—that is, rulelessness. Yet, curiously, his immediate associates and students did not deal with whole societies or cultures, but rather with aspects of cultures and their significance in a comparative perspective. Some, like Durkheim's own work on religion, reflected an evolutionary perspective. Thus, Durkheim joined Marcel Mauss in an essay on "primitive forms of classification."[34] Mauss also wrote a small book on the gift as a "primitive" form of exchange.[35] On the other hand, Arnold van Gennep's book on *rites de passage*[36] explored a structural universal in human societies without strong overtones of searching for origins.

The persistently comparative focus of Durkheim and his associates bespoke an effort to build a science of society, or at least of social phenomena, with ample attention to non-Western societies. It was almost certainly the evolutionary perspective that prompted attention to the growing volume of ethnographic reports on "primitive" societies, though one should not forget the influential work of Marcel Granet on China.[37] One enduring consequence of the comparative emphasis was the avoidance in the French academic establishment of a sharp distinction between anthropology, primarily concerned with nonliterate cultures, and sociology, primarily concerned with complex literate societies. The distinction has little intellectual merit—no more, say, than societies with or without money as a generalized medium of exchange, or those with or without a formalized system of government.

(Unfortunately for either a rigid evolutionary doctrine or a rigid functionalist view of systemic determinism, these—and other—discontinuities in the structural features of societies exhibit scant coincidence. The inventions of writing, of money, of government, of settled agriculture do have important systemic consequences. Those consequences are not total and definitive.)

There is a further irony. Functionalism mainly reached contemporary sociology by virtue of the work of British social anthropologists. In a university setting more hospitable to the analysis of exotic tribes than to the analysis of strictly Western cultures, some anthropologists abandoned the attempt to arrange cultures in a stringent evolutionary order. Rather, particularly following the work of A. R. Radcliff-Brown,[38] a new model of analysis appeared. A culture was to be viewed as an integrated whole. ("Culture" was taken in the inclusive sense of knowledge, beliefs, and rules of conduct, but also patterns of behavior and forms of social organization.) Conventions for "mapping" a culture were developed, with attention not only to forms but also to functions—that is, consequences of forms for other aspects of the culture.

Most of the cultures so studied were relatively small and only moderately contaminated by contemporary Western influences—of which, of course, the anthropologists themselves were a part. Mainly the resulting reports documented diversity among cultures as they traced systemic integration within them. The primacy of kinship within the patterns of organization, however, emerged with such clarity and uniformity that its centrality became a kind of conventional wisdom. The "explanation" of any belief, rule, structure, or practice was to be found either through linkages with other parts of the system—a view completely consistent with that of Durkheim—or in its contribution to the survival of the system and its members.

The attempt at deliberate exclusion of extraneous influences in order to reconstruct the culture in its "pure" form had as a cost of its benefits the neglect of adaptation to change. Yet there was a further, perhaps more signifcant, cost: the acceptance of the system as given and not as the product of some evolutionary process or of adaptation to prior external influences. Thus appeared one of the clearly identifiable weaknesses or ambiguities in functionalism. Does adherence to Durkheim's prescription that social facts are to be explained by other social facts imply that the qualifier "coexisting" be inserted before the explanatory facts, or may one properly attend to a system's history?

The Systems Perspective

Durkheim called the combination of differentiation and integration "organic" solidarity. After brief discussion of his choice of the term[39] he did not avidly pursue the metaphor of society as an organism. Others did. Particularly in the work of Herbert Spencer,[40] elaborate analogies between specialized units of society and parts of the human body were developed. Evolutionary doctrine provided a ready rationale for differentiation through genetic variability and for the use or function of organic parts by their contribution to the survival of the organism. With this comforting answer to the question "Why?" attention could be given to examination of interdependence and thus the question "How?" Around this organic metaphor the functionalist could develop a set of operating assumptions about social systems.

The two most fundamental assumptions, we have noted, are differentiation and integration. Two others were essentially derived from these. One is the "canonical" view that any observed cultural form or pattern of behavior must fit the system—that is, must have a function.[41] Thus survivals without current utility are discredited. It may be admitted, implicitly or explicitly, that the current function is not the same as the original or other prior use, but the "strict constructionist" in functional theory could not admit that an extant form or practice is simply accidental or a currently meaningless survival and thus unrelated to the system and essentially irrelevant. The system, in other words, is to be regarded as highly integrated, with no loose parts lying about. This is what Merton calls "the postulate of universal functionalism."[42]

The other derivative assumption is that forms fit functions. As Timasheff observes,[43] this comes close to being tautologous, as either the forms develop "to fulfill the function"—a teleological view much evident in the writings of biologists—or the function is simply the consequence of any form. If the vague term "form" is rendered as "structure"—a pattern of social behavior—then the relations among such structures and their consequences for integration or survival of a society or some lesser system do constitute significant questions. To those we shall return a little later.

Organic analogies were of course particularly appealing to the postDarwin social evolutionists. Herbert Spencer, as a voluminous expositor of that perspective, was not consistently cautious in remembering that an analogy is not an equivalency.[44] But the analogy has retained its appeal, while the evolutionary argument has been muted. Animal anatomy and physiology provide analogies or metaphors for the relation of parts to the whole in any "living" system, the biological whole comprising the skin-bound organism. Parsons, in a recent recapitulation of aspects of his theoretical position, unblinkingly uses a biological system analogy for the social system.[45] Since such analogies rarely if ever figured in his theoretical writing in earlier decades, it is not unlikely that they came to his attention by a familiar route. In relatively recent work he made a fairly extensive foray into a refurbishing of social evolution both as a taxonomic device for classifying societies and as a dynamic principle in accounting for their transformations.[46]

The use of organic analogies in sociological theory is not limited to explicitly functionalist perspectives. Ecology, as the study of the relationship of the organism to its environment or of the interdependence of living species, has been extended not only to the spatial distribution of human populations but also to interdependence (symbiosis) among differentiated activities.[47] True, human ecologists tend to adopt the view that they are dealing with a "natural" order that exists independently of mere socially invented norms and values. Their approach has even been characterized as devoting attention to the subsocial. Yet the exclusion of political and institutional variables is difficult and misleading. What is at issue is not the use of a systems perspective, but the properties of the systems. The ecologists do attend to problems of form conforming to use and the adapting of forms to changing circumstances of the system as an entity.

Central to the systems perspective is the problem of integration. How is order possible? Parsons started his early work, *The Structure of Social Action*,[48] with an analysis of Thomas Hobbes on the presocial "state of nature." Hobbes correctly perceived that in an aggregate of solely self-seeking human beings where other human beings become potential means to any individual's goals, force and fraud would turn out to be the most effective means of goal attainment. Parsons of course did not accept Hobbes's royalist solution of an absolute sovereign as viable, but derived from Durkheim, Weber, and Pareto the central importance of a value system and a normative order. Among that company, it was especially Durkheim who was attentive both to the problems of maintaining the moral integration of such specialized social units as religious or occupational groups and to the problems of integrating these into a more general fabric. And it was Durkheim, too, who was most sensitive to the fragility of that integration, though here his most lasting contribution was his discussion of anomie, the objective state of rulelessness (in a sense, Hobbes's state of nature).

Now, genuine states of anomie are likely to be rare and transitory, for a social situation without rules is likely to prove intolerable. Yet universal conformity to normative expectations is unlikely, on the evidence. This is what led Durkheim to comment on the "normality of crime."[49] From this Durkheim developed a special variant of a retributive theory of punishment. Punishment, Durkheim argued, was of crucial significance, not primarily for deterrence of future criminality by the malefactor, but as a reassertion of the moral sentiments of the community. Punishment is not meant for the criminal but for honest men.[50] And note, punishment serves not primarily as a deterrent by example but as an opportunity to reaffirm the moral code. By only a slight extension, one could argue from this the social utility of misbehavior. That is, by adding only the assumption of a probable atrophy of moral sentiments if they remain unchallenged, with seemingly slight deviations increasingly tolerated, gradual demoralization might ensue if conspicuous deviance did not occur and provoke the emotional reaction of the community.

Nonconformity or deviance has remained a theoretical problem with respect to integration. The social sources as well as social consequences of deviance were placed solidly within the functionalists' social-systems perspective by Merton's famous essay on "Social Structure and Anomie."[51] Accepting the fundamental tenet that both values and norms are essential for integration, Merton developed a classificatory scheme as follows:

	Cultural Goals	Institutional Means
Conformity	+	+
Innovation	+	−
Ritualism	−	+
Retreatism	−	−
Rebellion	±	±

Two points are noteworthy about this scheme. The first is a semantic one, but of some importance. None of these forms of deviance has anything to do with anomie, for both social goals and codes of conduct are stipulated. Merton's discussion focuses on the lack of close integration between goals and means as a source of deviance. Deviance then is not only a manifestation of disorganization by lack of consensual conformity, but derives from the failure of the system to provide uniformly appropriate connections between approved procedures and avowed purposes. It is a profound disavowal of a social integration model, for it goes beyond a mere recognition of the propensity to sin and identifies society as an instigator of sin. Social disorganization yes, but anomie it is not. (Merton offhandedly recognizes this conceptual problem in a later essay.)[52]

The other point raises a different problem with respect to the character of social systems. I said that in Merton's analysis both social goals and prescribed means are "stipulated." This assumes that wise and prescient formulators of values and rules of conduct have foreseen all contingencies and have a rule to cover any occasion (or that unconscious evolution has somehow produced the same comprehensive result, with no further adaptations in prospect). I have argued in *Social Change*[53] for the probability of "evasive innovation," of actors or groups finding ways to achieve accepted goals by neither following conventional procedure nor violating established prohibitions. If the types of deviance identified by Merton doubly impair an integration model (not every one conforms, and at least part of the nonconformity derives from inconsistencies in the structure itself), evasive innovation impairs notions of inherent fixity in social systems. Since innovation must be accepted, modified, or rejected, new rules are required: thus the principle of normative accumulation.[54]

We have arrived at a position some distance removed from a stable integration model of society maintaining an equilibrium among parts by various homeostatic mechanisms, such as the classical economists' model of a self-regulated market economy. But before we leave the troublesome problems posed by deviance and internal inconsistencies, we should attend to more orthodox functionalist interpretations of them.

Under the dictum that "if it exists and persists, it must have a system-maintenance function," attention turns to practices and structures that are condemned or at best viewed ambivalently. For example, Bronislaw Malinowski, solidly in the tradition both of Durkheim and his associates and of the

British social anthropologists, examined the uses of magic. Defining magic as the use of nonrational means for the achievement of practical, observable goals, he found that the Trobriand islanders did not substitute magic for the best experiential knowledge and rational techniques available.[55] (More than incidentally, he thus argued against the idea that the "primitive mind" is qualitatively different from the modern.)[56] Malinowski made analytical distinctions between religion (concerned with superempirical values and beliefs) and magic, as well as between magic and science (a more appropriate term would have been technology).[57] And he did not limit magic to primitives, but generalized that it could be expected in situations of uncertainty and need for control.

Kingsley Davis argued that prostitution is consistent with, rather than a threat to, the conventional structure of the family.[58] (This was an argument made by Bernard de Mandeville in *The Fable of the Bees,* published in 1714.)[59] Merton wrote kindly words about urban "machine politics" in terms of the access to a modicum of "justice" for the poor through the vote-assuring assistance of urban politicians.[60] Lewis A. Coser, building on the work of Georg Simmel, has documented some of the positive functions of social conflict.[61]

Certainly the most enduring controversy in contemporary functionalism has revolved around the Davis and Moore "functional theory of stratification."[62] The theory, properly called an "immodest" one by authors of a recent article,[63] argued that universally there is a differentiation of tasks or positions that are of unequal functional importance for the systems in which they are found, that there is an unequal availability of talented and trained persons to fill these positions, and consequently that unequal rewards are used to ". . . insure that the most important positions are conscientiously filled by the most qualified persons."[64]

Critics have properly objected to the term stratification, which seems best reserved for systems of differentiation that permit fairly distinct boundaries between strata and that are likely to be more or less hereditary. Davis and Moore were concerned with institutionalized social inequality, with or without hereditary strata. Critics have also properly noted that the authors paid no attention to tensions and to inequities within systems of social inequality. Yet much of the criticism has derived from an ideological position that espouses the ideal of equality and rejects a "functional" view of inequality as giving aid and comfort to the enemy.

In none of the controversy has the universality of inequality been challenged. Its inevitability is in dispute, along with the particular explanation advanced by Davis and Moore. Attempts at empirical tests of the theory have yielded "mixed notices."[65] In fact, a test at the level of generality assumed by the theory would require establishing an ordered array of essential functions, clear data on availability of persons with differential talent and training, and a measure of awards, financial and otherwise. And, since those in positions of power probably can exercise that power to "rig the system" in terms of levels of rewards, the definition of talent, and access to training, one would need to be wary of spurious confirmation of the theory as a sort of self-fulfilling prophecy.

These examples confirm the merits of looking beyond an aspect or segment of social systems to find system-supporting consequences that may not conform to conventional values and preferences—a demonstration that common sense may be wrong. It remains true, however, that complex societies offer ample evidence of lack of consistency and of system failures. Patterns of behavior may have truly negative consequences for system maintenance and effective operation. Merton suggested that such consequences be identified as "dysfunctions."[66] To keep the terminology symmetrical, Levy[67] suggested that "functional" be made a neutral designation, meaning only that patterns have consequences beyond themselves for other parts of the system or the system as a whole. If positive or supportive, the consequences are identified as "eufunctional"; if negative, "dysfunctional."

Complexity, however, does confound; mixed cases abound. If differential rewards serve as the motivational incentive to assure that important positions are conscientiously filled by appropriately competent performers, it remains true that known systems of social inequality exhibit counterproductive characteristics: for example, in Western societies, excessive inequalities give rise to differential hereditary opportunities to acquire skills and display competence, with negative motivational consequences for the least privileged segments of the population. If magic is the universal expedient for eking out the gap between rational control and certainty of outcome, magic imbedded in a predominantly religious context may impede a rational calculus of instrumental acts: for example, reliance on a Saint Christopher's medal for a safe journey to the neglect of the mechanical safety of an automobile and careful driving.

Determining the consequences—the functions—of an aspect of social reality thus often requires an appraisal or calculation of net balances. Such calculation will of course not be attempted if one starts with the unexamined assumption that systems are perfectly integrated—or nearly so, with the exception of random deviance.

System integration is put in further doubt if circumstances permit "subsystems" with sufficient degrees of independence or autonomy so that what is eufunctional or dysfunctional for the part does not have the same consequences for the broader society. Though Charles E. Wilson, a former chief executive of General Motors Corporation before he served a term as United States secretary of defense, expressed the opinion that what was good for General Motors was good for the United States, this view appropriately aroused considerable dissent. Corporate profit maximization at the expense of environmental pollution or bribing legislators or selling unsafe vehicles impairs other legitimate interests, public and private. Or let us take a somewhat more complex example. We know, by time-honored sociological principle, that up to some (poorly established) point, increased external threat or conflict increases the cohesion of social groups. Ideologically oriented dissident political groups are not only in conflict with the existing political regime, but often also with other dissident groups with differing ideological orientations. These latter conflicts have their expected favorable consequences for group solidarity, at the expense of a more broadly based opposition that might unseat the government. Knowledgeable officials perceive this reality, encourage the conflicts among dissidents, and thus follow another time-honored precept, "Divide and rule."

The almost surreptitious introduction of a conflict perspective into this discussion provides an opportunity to face that challenge to functional theory. Conflicts of course exist in complex societies. (They almost certainly exist in nonliterate societies also. Such conflicts tend not to be reported in the anthropological monographs, and we are permitted to suspect that they go unnoticed because of the observers' acceptance of an "integrated-system" model or are discounted as mere examples of relatively unimportant deviance.) The conflicts have multitudinous sources and manifestations. These include almost purely "ideological" disagreements, such as those of varying persuasions in their religious orientations and theologies and those that reflect differing views of an ideal society, ranging from nostalgic distortion of a simpler past to possible equally distorted visions of, say, a more equalitarian future. Conflicts of a more immediate and pragmatic character are also evident: between management and labor, between producers and merchants on the one hand and consumers on the other, between those who would extend the influence of government and those who would reduce it. To argue that some form of conflict—say between classes in the Marxist sense—is more fundamental than others either rests upon a doctrinal faith that unbelievers are not bound to accept or requires factual and logical demonstration that will meet the canons of empirical science.

Yet conflict clearly impairs any "consensual-integration" model of society. Even Parsons, commonly identified as the staunchest defender of "consensualism," writes into his social-system model the management of tensions.[68] Feldman and Moore have gone somewhat further, suggesting a tension-management model of society, noting the advantage of making order as well as disorder problematical.[69] Since no society, including allegedly "classless" ones, actually eliminates sources of conflict, tension management becomes a requisite part of any viable social system.

Parsons, in *The Social System,*[70] constructs a complex model of societies in which the social system provides a linkage with two other analytically distinct systems: personality and culture. To make these aspects of social phenomena analytically distinguishable implies that they may display independent variability. Parsons explores that variability primarily with reference to personality. Socialization, the combination of cognitive learning with the internalization of established norms and values, comprises, along with biological reproduction, the master process of social continuity. Adopting a modified Freudian perspective, Parsons explores the psychodynamic complexities of personality formation and differentiation.[71] To these we may add the certainty of genetic variability and structural differentiation (both among families and within them, as in birth order), which in combination assure that a "cookie-cutter" pattern of uniformity in socialized product will not occur. Personality differences thus become not only sources of variability and deviance, but also possible instigators of changes in patterns, norms, and values.

If culture is defined approximately as comprising various symbolic subsystems, such as language, normative codes, and articulated values, it obviously comprises an intrinsic part of any rounded description of a social order. Yet parts of cultural systems appear less closely linked than others to principal components of social structure. I have argued[72] that the supernatural components of religious beliefs as well as aesthetic canons and forms are such loosely linked cultural features. This is not to say that no connections can be established with, say, political and economic structures (a sociologist should, after all, be able to link anything with anything), but they may be tenuous and not highly determined or predictive in either direction. To take an extreme example, there appears to be no clear structural source of a five-note, seven-note, or twelve-note musical scale, and little structural consequence except in a strictly musical context. Similarly, except through explicit administrative rulings requiring that painting, sculpture, or the ballet must display "socialist realism," there appears little way to account, in terms of integrated systems, for the appearance of representational, geometric and formal, or purely abstract "art." The precise system-maintenance function of these products of human activity prove difficult to demonstrate, though the universality of aesthetic expression invites speculation regarding its sources and consequences.

Sorokin, it is true, attempted to demonstrate what we might call thematic consistency of cultural forms within each of his three major cultural types, the ideational, idealistic (later called integral), and sensate.[73] Though Sorokin criticized my assertion of looseness to fit between cultural forms and patterns of social organization,[74] his own work did not establish the kind of linkages that a strictly functionalist view of social systems would require.

One further difficulty with the functionalist view of social systems needs comment. The integration model, we have noted, neglected or minimized conflict. From a Marxist perspective the neglect was double: blindness to the reality of conflict and thus failure to perceive conflict as the source of systemic change. The problem is in fact more extensive. For example, though fertility and mortality patterns are not autonomous variables external to social systems,[75] the consequences of those patterns clearly do not establish stationary states. Further, no society can be fairly described as existing in an untroubled adjustment to its environment. Environmental challenges provoke innovative "coping" strategies, including attempted control or mastery, but these do not result in final solutions.[76] And lest that essentially technological interpretation of social change stand as uniquely significant, we must note strictly systemic sources of innovation. Perfectly integrated systems do not exist "in nature." To deviance and conflicts we must add the gap between ideal values, goals, and normative standards and actual practices and achievements. This gap, too, invites innovation, including attempts at tension management, but also including changes in political structure, economic systems, and modes of distribution of social position and benefits.

The functionalists, we have seen, have not totally neglected the individual motivational elements in social behavior, while generally avoiding reductionist "psychologizing" that would negate the emergent social reality intrinsic to the concept of systems. There has been, however, an apparently studied neglect of collective purpose, of public and private decision making on behalf of collectivities such as corporations, universities, or national states. Deliberate change—social planning—may not figure prominently in relatively uncontaminated tribal societies beloved of anthropologists, but it now comprises a major feature of the social landscape in virtually all contemporary political systems. How this reality affects the analysis of modernization will engage our attention later in this essay.

Structural Functionalism

Functionalism in sociological theory could, in most instances, also be called structuralism, though not in the special sense of the latter term as used, for example, by Claude Lévi-Strauss.[77] The primary key here has been the focus on a whole relatively autonomous social unit, whether called a culture by the anthropologists or a society by the sociologists. This "macro" focus has distinguished functionalism not only from various social-psychological concerns with the transactions between individuals and various social units, but also from various "process" orientations as represented by the German formalists such as Leopold von Wiese[78] or their American counterparts represented by Robert E. Park and Ernest W. Burgess.[79]

The "holistic" approach advocated and practiced by the social anthropologists attended to structural interdependencies but as a consequence did not encourage attention to structural commonalities across cultures. Meanwhile American sociology, which was expanding rapidly in colleges and universities beginning with the 1920s, became for a time almost exclusively concerned with the United States. This was not in the tradition of such earlier notable figures as William Graham Sumner, Lester F. Ward, Albion W. Small, or Franklin H. Giddings. By the mid to late 1930s, however, the enduring influence of these earlier scholars, increasing interaction with anthropologists, the concern of Talcott Parsons and his students with social analysis at a very high level of generalization, and no doubt other influences began to be reflected in the general textbooks on sociological principles. For a time after its publication in 1937 the single most popular introductory text was that by Robert L. Sutherland and Julian L. Woodward.[80] The authors organized the bulk of their material around major "social institutions" (an unfortunately ambiguous term), meaning the family, economy, polity, religion, education, and so on. The outstanding feature of this text was the introduction of each of these "core" topics with descriptive material from exotic (mainly tribal) societies.

That kind of reintroduction of a comparative perspective of course had the effect of emphasizing differences, differences that came to be known as "cultural relativism," which can be crudely rephrased as "We do it this way, they do it that way." For a considerable time the topics in textbooks became fairly standardized, but from the perspective of a generalist the complaint could be fairly made that any general theory of social structure was represented only by chapter titles, not by their contents. That is, the titles represented universal structural aspects of any society, but the contents emphasized the differences in the actual structures without attention to why these structures could be so conveniently grouped under standard rubrics.

Human Society by Kingsley Davis,[81] published in 1949, though not a best-selling introductory text, turned out to be an influential one. Davis adopted an explicitly functionalist perspective, relating the common structural aspects of society to the common problems of systemic integration and survival. Later text writers, with or without credit to Davis's work, tended to be not only comparative but also to make at least modest justifications for their topics and organization.

Davis's own exposition paid appropriate attention to systemic linkages, including such subtleties as the distinction between the part and the whole and the positive consequences of nominally disapproved patterns. Yet part of the language implies a virtually anthropomorphic view of society, which somehow chooses appropriate structures from among limited options. (The previously discussed essay on social inequality by Davis and me, published several years before his general work, cryptically refers to systems of social inequality as having "unconsciously evolved."[82] In *Human Society,* functions (eufunctional consequences of patterns of action) appear essentially to determine structures, though by mechanisms not fully articulated.

Even if the functions are stipulated as consequences necessary for the system to survive—a stipulation that we shall discuss in the next principal subdivision of this essay as implicitly reflecting an evolutionary perspective—the structural determinism can scarcely be regarded as complete and definitive. The documentation of historical and contemporary structural differences provides ample warning, even if those variable structures can be grouped around a limited number of categories that represent commonalities at a high level of abstraction. Here the focus on interdependent systems provides an escape from the position that one may expect merely eclectic combinations from the rather wide range of options available for any essential performance outcome. The situation, in other words, is not one in which the major requirements for any society to exist and persist would form column headings, under each of which a list of observed (and possibly even hypothetical) options would be listed, with the only requirement for constructing a society being that one option must appear from each list. It follows that actually observed societies should not display a kind of random or eclectic combination of structural elements, so long as each essential "function" is represented. Indeed, if we were to take seriously a model of society with "perfect" interdependence and integration, observation or stipulation of one major structural feature should permit reliable prediction of the appropriate item in every other list. This is the kind of assumption that underlies the explication of the social consequences of industrialization. A stipulation of the structure of economic production would make all other social structures highly determined dependent variables. This approximates the Marxist position but also that of many other analysts of modernization. From a strict functionalist perspective the selection of an independent variable is essentially arbitrary. Thus, it should be possible to derive all other essential structural features equally well from stipulation of the form of the political or the educational structure or the system of social inequality.

Three types of comparative structural analyses in a sense have put this form of the functionalist position to test. One type represents the extension of the Marxist interpretation to situations different from the dynamics of industrial capitalism, which was Marx's own concern. Here adherents to the Marxist tradition attempt to demonstrate the fundamental character of economic structure and the dependency of the noneconomic "superstructure."[83] Critics of that interpretation argue for the equivalence in importance of other structural features of society[84] and/or the partial indeterminacy (and thus independent variability) of other structural characteristics.[85]

A second type of comparative test of systemic determinacy is prominently illustrated by the use of the Human Relations Area Files, which represent a compilation of recorded observations, primarily of nonliterate cultures or societies studied by anthropologists, arranged topically (unfortunately, by a not very highly rationalized classification of categories). For example, George Peter Murdock has selected types of kinship organization and made correlational analyses of other structural features found with a given kinship type.[86] Stanley H. Udy, Jr., has used the same information source to determine the structural determinants of forms of work organization.[87]

The third type of test of structural interdependence is represented by the analyses of the structural consequences of industrialization or economic development. In anticipation of fuller discussion later, I have concluded in my own moderately extensive work in this field that industrialization—often used in an encompassing sense to represent extensive rationalization of the modes of economic production and distribution—has both structural preconditions and consequences. In the relationships between economy and society, and indeed in the precise forms within a rationalized economy, the viable structural characteristics are radically more limited than would be represented by a full list of options representing the range of human experience, but they are not fully determinate. For example, there is no case of even moderately successful economic development in the absence of both a stable political order and a widely shared ideology favorable to economic rationalization.[88] However, evidence makes clear that neither parliamentary democracy nor the "Protestant ethic"[89] is a uniquely requisite structural component for such an economic order.

The same "limited determinacy" emerges from the other types of comparative analysis just discussed. We thus once more find the utility of the systems perspective but the factual reality of looser, less fully cohesive systems than assumed by orthodox functionalism.

We have been exploring the extent to which parts of a social system determine the remainder—whether the selection of the part is merely convenient or arbitrary or is genuinely more fundamental than others, as in forms of economic determinism (or what might be called Weber's theological or ideological determinism in The Protestant Ethic). Other complications arise if one starts from the assumption of a kind of general functional determinism—that is, that various functions must be fulfilled if the society is to survive. The first point to be noted is that there is nothing inevitable about the survival of societies, as recorded history amply testifies and, by justifiable if speculative inference, unrecorded history would further confirm. The introduction of a value position—say, a just, humane, or even a totally compliant society—would argue that some societies should not survive or at least should not survive as presently constituted. Both positions reject the kind of "functional teleology" represented by the simplistic view that "if it exists it must be essential." That view is further undermined by the recognition of some structural indeterminacy, even when parts of the system are stipulated.

It was earlier noted that the idea that the "form must fit the function" verges on a tautology. There is of course a necessary consistency, which we may call "structural suitability." The evidence for some systemic looseness and indeterminacy leads to a parallel and cautionary idea, that of "structural substitutability."[90] Parts of systems may be subject to evolutionary, accidental, or deliberate change, perhaps resulting in an improved "goodness of fit" among structures or closer approximation to articulated ideals. Of course evolution and accident, being mindless, may have dysfunctional consequences, and errors in knowledge and strategies in planned change may also produce unanticipated and regretted results.[91] This view argues for the possibility—and probability—of piecemeal alterations in societies. The value-based view that the evils of a system are so pervasive and interconnected that only a radical and total transformation will suffice thus represents a more fundamental commitment to determinant integration than the modified structuralism that we have been discussing would warrant.

There is a further complication that must be noted. The stipulation of functions requisite for societal survival does not imply the necessity of a similar list of discrete and specialized structures. Here we encounter once more the degree of structural differentiation. The modest (though variable) degree of such differentiation, linked with the pervasive, multifunctional importance of kinship structures, especially distinguishes the nonliterate societies studied by social anthropologists, as compared with the highly differentiated structures of complex societies of the ancient and modern world. Yet even in complex societies the matching of structure and function is not precise. Levy distinguishes between "concrete" and "analytic" structures.[92] Concrete structures constitute membership groups (such as families or lineages) or aggregates (such as unorganized "classes"). Such memberships are in principle preclusive within their type. That is, one belongs to one kinship group and not others, one community and not others, one occupational group and not others. Analytic structures are essentially identified by their functions (consequences for the system). Thus the economic structure comprises all patterns relevant to the production and distribution of goods and services. Though there are predominantly economic organizations that are concrete structures—manufacturing corporations, collective farms, trade associations, retail stores—they neither comprehend the totality of the economy nor are they exclusively economic in either form or function. The economy is pervasive. No individual member of the society can avoid membership in the economy and stay alive. Virtually every group or association has its economic aspects. On the other hand, corporations or professional associations are also political bodies, being concerned with normative compliance and maintenance of order, as well as having a variety of other social consequences, such as their effects on members' families. Similar points are appropriate to the polity or to the structuring of social inequality.

This complication, though awkward for any attempt at tidy structural mapping in terms of a standard list of systemic consequences, constitutes one of the more impressive claims for the utility of the functionalist approach to comparative structural analysis. It permits posing the significant questions: how are goods and services produced and distributed? how are power and responsibility allocated? The answers to those questions permit the observation of the interdependence among differentiated structures, not only through transactions between them or their regulation by some overarching supervisory body such as the state, but also through their concrete interpenetration.

It is of course not necessary to start a "functional analysis" with fundamental functions. That starting point is especially appropriate for comparative structural or "cross-cultural" analyses, for the universal functions requisite to societal survival provide at minimum the standard categories for structural comparisons, though other uniformities such as magic and passage rituals or structurally distinctive recreational patterns[93] may supplement the more "fundamental" (and partially self-evident) necessities for systemic persistence. That approach also has the more than incidental benefit of providing generality in sociological theory in the textbooks that dutifully document diversity. The historic roots of functionalism are more partial: addressing the question of the "meaning" of cultural forms or behavior patterns in terms of consequences beyond the particular form or structure. Leaving aside the somewhat ambiguous meaning of cultural forms, for reasons already discussed, analysis may start with structures rather than functions. What do structures actually do? Schools are established to educate pupils, and they perform that mission with varying degrees of proficiency. They also serve, for younger children, as baby-sitters and day-care centers, as the context for possibly deviant peer-group socialization, as preliminary sorting mechanisms for adult social placement, and possibly as a devious or at least indirect and not very effective device for palliating racial and ethnic discrimination in housing and employment. For younger teenagers, schools keep their pupils off the streets during school hours and serve as "day reformatories" for juvenile delinquents not committed to official reformatories. For later teenagers and young adults the adult placement function becomes more precise; meanwhile staying in school delays entrance into the competitive and possibly overcrowded labor force, and in that sense at least represents a prolongation of infancy.

Hospitals provide another convenient example of multifunctionality. While at least nominally providing medical therapy for the sick or wounded, they must necessarily also provide custodial and hotel-and-restaurant services. They get the sick or dying persons out of the household and, especially for the moribund, provide a kind of emotionally sterile setting for death. Concentration of medical services in a separate establishment eases the problems of coordinating specialized services and has the more than incidental consequence of requiring the patient to get to the services rather than the physician or visiting nurse delivering the services to the patient's home.

The possible illustrations abound. "Service clubs" avow their aim of improving their communities, but their weekly luncheons provide opportunities for business and professional contacts and developing clienteles. Professional associations profess that they are designed to maintain and improve standards of professional competence and performance. They also serve to limit access to certification of proficiency and, by monopolizing the skill, can collectively enjoy monopolistic price fixing for their members' services to the laity.

Tracing the true consequences—the "outputs"—of organizations and other patterns of action or the ramifications of a seemingly minor innovation constitutes major claims for the functionalist version of a systems perspective. Like the various examples of the utility of derogated practices such as magic or corrupt urban government, the unadvertised and often unintended consequences of organized behavior go well beyond common sense or the unreflective experience of participants and lay observers. The sociological expositor, as teacher or writer, is permitted a feeling of mastery over mysteries that transcend concepts and classifications or mere surface descriptions rendered in an exotic tongue.

To accommodate and formalize this application of functional analysis to the relations among structures within societies, Merton suggested a conceptual distinction between "manifest" and "latent" functions.[94] Manifest functions comprise the overt purposes or missions of organizations, and latent functions the additional (or possibly substituted) consequences of the activities of the organizations. The substitution of latent functions for avowed goals may be unintended and harmless or benign in their consequences. Parent-teacher organizations, established to mediate and improve relations between families and schools, may have no detectable influence on those relationships but may survive because of the recreational and status-enhancing satisfactions that members derive from activities and offices. The possibility of latent functions may also invite intentional deception, however. Charity frauds, "front organizations" for espionage, nominally legitimate businesses as covers for organized crime, legislatures that serve the interests of wealthy campaign supporters or bribers instead of their ordinary constituents—these essentially constitute a disparity between the concealed real intentions of the active participants and the appearance of pursuing other goals viewed as proper by significant elements of "the public."

To call the concealed illicit outcomes latent functions may stretch the ordinary sense of the term, but since intentions and motives are implicit in the concept of manifest functions, there seems no bar to symmetry. Just as Levy added symmetry to Merton's discussion of dysfunction with the concept of eufunction, he has noted that Merton's dichotomy of manifest and latent functions is oversimplified. In order to take into account both the perception and the motivation of actors in any social system, he introduces the further categories of unintended but recognized functions (eu- or dys-) (UIR) and intended but unrecognized functions (IUR).[95] Useful examples of UIR consequences come readily to mind: schoolteachers may be all too aware that although they are supposed to train their pupils they spend a considerable amount of time and energy in being their custodians; hospital nurses are notorious for exhibiting greater interest in the maintenance of normal routines than in the specific relevance of procedures to individual patients. Useful examples of IUR consequences seem more difficult to identify. (Levy suggests the "compulsive striver" who does not recognize success when achieved.) Here the quest for classificatory symmetry may have exceeded utility. (A good rule-of-thumb caution to dedicated developers of conceptual taxonomies is that if one cannot think of a significant—perhaps hypothetical—example where the distinction makes a difference, the exercise is excessive.)

We must now revert to a recurrent query: just what is the relationship between structures and their consequences? One of the theoretical difficulties in strict functionalism, as several critics have noted,[96] is the expressed or implied argument that the functions determine the structures. Merton has been complimented on having made structuralism independent of functionalism by starting with structures and tracing their consequences for other structures and more encompassing systems, rather than starting from functions as a way of accounting for structures.[97] Certainly the notion of dysfunctions would scarcely arise if one started only with an integration model of consequences necessary for systemic operation and preservation, unless the ensuing empirical quest for the appropriate structures turned up disquieting surprises. And Merton's latent (including Levy's UIR) functions would be far more likely to be noted if one started from structures than if one started with a tidy list of expected or "necessary" consequences. The avoidance of functional determinism evades the teleological assumption that reality has a purpose—the kind of assumption that pervades biologists' writing on "Nature's purposes." Homans, for example, asserts the fallacy of explanation by "final causes."[98]

Yet the concept of manifest functions warns against outright rejection of purpose in human action. Of course the consequences determine (or at least radically delimit) the behavior patterns for their production if the consequences are intended and planned. (I am reminded of a comment by the late philosopher Ralph Barton Perry on the question of whether the ends justify the means. Asked Perry, "What else could?") If we were to start with a "completely planned" model of society, as some contemporary postrevolutionary national states have attempted to approximate, we should note the specification of collective and distributive objectives and the establishment of structures for their accomplishment. Ignorance and error would of course lead to partial failures (let us, preciously, call those latent dysfunctions) in implementation, leading to deliberate attempts to improve performance, including reduction of unanticipated negative side effects. Homans, as his work in general testifies,[99] manifests a regrettable failure to understand the reality of collective human purpose, the existence of which makes his strictures on "final causes" irrelevant.

Orthodox functionalism is not cleared of suspicion by hypothetical reference to a planned society, for the functionalists have operated from a generally implicit evolutionary model of systems that have persisted and maintained their structural integrity through a more or less prolonged process of natural selection. Integration models fail to fit reality for a variety of reasons already discussed. Yet interdependence and the problem of order are intrinsic to the human condition, so that some form and degree of integration are requisite not only to preserve "the system" but for bare biological survival.

The survival test, which has been the functionalists' alternative to the planned society as a way of making consequences the determinants of procedures, fits most of human societies for most of human history. Yet that test is shaky, partly for reasons of definition and identification. The patterns of behavior in a society, faithfully observed and measured in some particularity at a moment in time, will differ in significant ways from previous states of the system, even if those are recorded more crudely. Thus, a certain amount of abstraction, of attention to continuities rather than alterations, is necessary in order to claim that one is dealing with the "same" system. Further change is to be expected in future observations, because of intrinsic, though unplanned, sources of change, unforeseen disturbances, and deliberate problem solving and goal seeking. How rapid, extensive, "fundamental," and discontinuous would such change need to be for the analyst to admit that the system had not survived?

Failure of a society to survive as a more or less autonomous entity for reasons intrinsic to the system (failure of one or more necessary functions to be fulfilled) may be difficult to demonstrate. Within the range of our reliable knowledge, societies that have ceased to exist or have persisted only as subsets of more encompassing systems, falling on their evil fate as a consequence of conquest, novel diseases, or natural disasters. Since adequate protection against human and nonhuman enemies is bound to be a requisite for survival of any social system, the survival test does call attention to structural deficiencies: inadequate military preparedness; insufficient public health and medical technology; lack of anticipatory precautions against uncontrolled plagues of locusts, droughts or floods, earthquakes, and volcanic eruptions. Existing societies have either had the good fortune not to have faced potentially devastating adversity or have had means for coping. Those means are not without theoretical interest in terms of the operation of social systems.

A major part of the problem in both the exposition and the criticism of what Turner[100] calls "functional imperativism" has been the failure to take into account the level of generality or particularity involved in the functional analysis attempted. Survival requirements, viewed across the spectrum of human societies, must be stated fairly abstractly; thus they are not highly predictive of exact structural forms. Were the integration model of society more tenable, observation or stipulation of one or at most very few "fundamental" structures should be highly predictive of the remainder. Known societies are looser and more disordered, so that various system properties determine only ranges of variability in behavior patterns and formal organizations, not their exact form. The loss of information in the process of abstract generalization may unnerve those who prefer to study more concrete patterns and relationships, but that is a matter of taste and not of scientific virtue.

The Neoevolutionary Perspective

Despite the disclaimers of defenders of the faith, functionalism has mainly eschewed dynamics. The course of functionalist analysis, among both anthropologists and sociologists, veered from Durkheim's muted evolutionary orientation to "synchronic," cross-sectional analysis. Not only was the older evolutionism rejected, but also virtually all sequential patterns. (Short-term, repetitive cycles of activity marked by days, weeks, months, seasons, years, and even life cycles were of course noted when relevant, but these essentially comprise elements of order, having few if any enduring consequences for the shape of social systems.) The assumptions concerning interdependence and integration were principally responsible for paying scant attention to demographic variability, the propensity to adopt innovations promising to narrow the gap between the ideal and the actual—whether in dealing with nonhuman environments or in approximating ideal goals—and various essentially dialectical disharmonies intrinsic to organized societies.[101]

The explicit introduction of system survival as a test of necessary consequences of human action and the structural mechanisms for producing those results perforce appealed to an evolutionary perspective. The argument must essentially be that various behaviors appear in human aggregates, some of which support or improve the viability of those aggregates and others that do not. Through "natural selection" those that contribute to system operation survive, and others are rejected. The same argument can be made for whole societies, whether in competition with other societies or simply in coping with the challenges of the nonhuman environment.

In the early explicit formulations of what came to be called "functional requisite analysis" this evolutionary assumption was not articulated. Rather, as exemplified in Levy's analysis,[102] a society is essentially defined as a persistent and self-subsistent social system—that is, a system comprising a plurality of interacting individuals oriented primarily to the system, the individuals being at least in part sexually recruited, and the system being in principle self-sufficient for those individuals and capable of surviving beyond the life span of current individuals. Levy then proceeds to indicate the "requisite functions" for such a unit to exist and persist. The explanation of why societies exist at all requires certain stipulations regarding human nature and the relations between the organism and the nonhuman environment, which Levy incorporates as part of the explanation of the functional requisites.

Levy[103] incorporates all of what I should call the bioeconomic requisites for system maintenance under the single rubric of "provision for an adequate physiological relationship to the setting and for sexual recruitment."[104] He justifies this on grounds that the nonhuman environment, man's biological nature, and the existence of other societies constitute aspects of the "setting" of human action. In a sense, therefore, they are givens—data in the strict sense—though Levy does note that purely passive modes of adaptation are not to be expected and indeed are not possible if a society is to persist.

Because these relationships to the societal setting are not only analytically separable but also require concretely distinguishable patterns of action, their disaggregation as requisites seems sensible. Adequately motivated heterosexual copulation leading to reproduction is an evident requirement for persistence of the relevant population. And since the human infant at birth and for a considerable proportion of its life span thereafter is unable to sustain life unaided, reproductive behavior would simply result in total infant mortality without provision for care and nurturance. No society leaves either mating or infant care unregulated, and the cross-cultural variety of the relevant patterns precludes any reductionist assumption that the behavior is merely instinctual, "doing what comes naturally."

Food supplies are obviously necessary for biological survival, and in some physical settings clothing and shelter are also. High mortality rates from starvation or exposure can of course be sustained if fertility rates (and survival rates at least until the age of reproductive capacity) are high enough to maintain the population in approximate balance. Negative population growth obviously must lead to extinction if not reversed. Positive population growth requires changing environmental parameters by territorial expansion, changing the diet and/or the technology of food acquisition, or sooner or later reaching limits requiring higher mortality. (Human populations, given the biological capacity for calculated, purposive action, are never limited to merely "natural" restraints on growth through starvation. Rules on who may mate and under what circumstances, contraception, induced abortion, and infanticide provide possible remedies for excessive increase. Many orthodox functionalists, if they attend to the "demographic equation" at all, favor such structures as intertribal warfare or rules on eligibility for mating that seem not to be explicitly intended or recognized as limiting growth. Truly latent functions—consequences of patterned action—of course exist, but it seems unwise to underestimate calculated conduct, even in nonmodern societies.)

A further comment is necessary with respect to sustenance. In all societies there are consumers who are not producers: infants and young children certainly, and also those temporarily or permanently incapacitated, including the infirm aged, unless the disabled potential dependents are simply permitted to die from "natural causes"—that is, lack of food and protection from the elements. On the historical and ethnographic evidence, further task differentiation is virtually certain—at least on the basis of sex—and highly probable on the basis of genetic or trained differences in talents and skills. Thus effective sustenance must include patterns of distribution as well as production, and probably patterns of exchange.[105]

The nonhuman environment also offers a number of uncertainties and threats. The inorganic ambience may produce droughts, winds, boat-engulfing waves, floods, earthquakes and tidal waves, or volcanic eruptions. If one of these natural disasters simply obliterates a population, no great insight is required to conclude that the system has not adequately coped with its setting. Lesser and recurrent dangers are likely to provoke preventive and palliative measures, representing a mixture of rational and magical behaviors according to the technological and organizational sophistication available. The nonhuman organic environment may offer threats from wild animals requiring evasion, mastery, or simply accepting the risk if the incidence of death is manageable. The ingestion of poisonous plants and animals is likely to lead to trial-and-error learning. Protection against unseen enemies such as microbes and viruses is likely to be magical in the absence of requisite knowledge, though again latent structures such as eating only cooked food and attaching negative magical properties to human wastes and the corpses of the dead give support to notions of mindless adaptation.

A threat from other societies may or may not exist in particular circumstances. Where it does, negotiation, actual or ritual exchange, or essentially military patterns are probable. Failure of these accommodative structures results either in the elimination of society by death of its members or their incorporation into another society, possibly as slaves or otherwise subordinated units.

The remainder of Levy's functional requisites may be characterized as emergent social properties, less closely linked to mere biological survival than those just discussed. "Role differentiation and role assignment" rests upon at least the minimum task differentiation by age and sex, and the further importance of genetic variability in physical capacities and possibly in learning ability. Varieties of productive tasks must be performed, even at the simplest of technological levels, and supportive tasks in care for the unproductive. Randomness in task performance, even among those competent, yields only chaos. Any degree of specialization requires coordination in some form, with authority patterns being highly likely, particularly for any "emergency" task. Whether unequal rewards to induce crucially important and skilled or responsible performance are necessary remains theoretically in dispute, as we have discussed. They are factually universal.

Communication in the human species is mainly by way of symbolic language. The instruction of infants in the information requisite for participation in social interaction and the orderly and predictable conduct of interpersonal transactions depend in large measure upon language. In systems too large for each-to-every, face-to-face transactions, language provides the means for indirect communication throughout the system. (Other symbol systems, such as talking drums, essentially represent supplemental languages.) Simple signals, such as danger or food availability, may be "passed along" in other animal species, but symbolic language permits rather complex information, ideas, affective states, and value articulations to be shared. Learning a language permits not only a common understanding of what the symbols mean, but therefore "shared cognitive orientations" as to the perception of reality. This Levy adds as a further functional requisite, noting that not only common "definitions of the situation" are required to avoid endless, conflictful misunderstandings, but also common "explanations" for failures and uncertainties.

Next on Levy's list of functional requisites is "a shared articulated set of goals," but for reasons that will be discussed shortly, I believe that this system requisite is incorrectly placed in his sequence. Levy is essentially and correctly arguing that for any relatively (in principle, absolutely) self-sustaining aggregate within the human species, and beyond biological reproduction and "coping" with biological heredity, the nonhuman environment, and possibly other human aggregates, differentiation and consequent interdependence are intrinsic to the human condition. Yet nothing in human heredity would assure mutuality or care for infants and other physiological dependents. Purely self-serving action would assure Hobbes's war of all against all. Thus the first emergent property of human aggregates, requisite for their physical survival, comprises the elementary mechanisms of interdependence—communication and shared cognitive understandings. Mere cognitive commonalities, however, do not alleviate the probability of conflicting interests. Interdependence requires also, and crucially, rules governing interpersonal transactions; the approved, permitted, and prohibited forms of interpersonal and more complex transactions; the powers and duties, rights and responsibilities of interacting units. Thus the next emergent system property is that or order: rules, carrying effective negative sanctions if necessary, rendering social encounters in any and every differentiated context predictable.

Thus the fundamental social-system property of order (which of course has its counterpart in personality at the psychological level) comprises, in addition to role differentiation and role assignment, another five of Levy's requisites, which he chooses to distinguish: regulation of the choice of means, regulation of affective expression, adequate socialization, effective control of disruptive forms of behavior, and adequate institutionalization. Only two of these merit additional comment. The regulation of affective expression is a recognitition of human emotionality, which is as firmly based in human genetics as is the capacity for cognition and rational calculation. This is a reality commonly neglected in rationalistic theories of social action and social systems. Similarly with respect to socialization, the process of incorporating infants (or other neophytes) into socially patterned behavior involves more than cognitive learning, including mere knowledge of the regulatory codes. Ideally, both norms and values are internalized and become the individual's conscience. (Freud's term superego adds nothing to our understanding.) Factually, any known society is marked by some overt deviance and some difficult to determine proportion of "external conformity"—that is, adherence to rules because of fear of negative sanctions. No social system could survive the discovery that no one accepted the rules as personally binding, as a matter of moral rightness. Systems may persist, of course, without a high degree of normative consensus, if one segment of the population controls the rest through force and fraud, terror and deceit. But the costs of extracting reluctant compliance, the representatives of any system of authority will seek to secure "legitimacy" and thus conscientious compliance.

We come then to the troubled question of goals and values. Here it is useful to make an initial distinction between distributive or "like" goals and those attaching to the collectivity as such, or "common" goals. Distributive goals, even if nearly consensually shared, do not assure order if one actor's goals are achieved at the expense of others or if the means for their achievement are not readily and uniformly available. This, once more, is the fatal defect in speculative systems comprised only of self-seeking participants. Shared distributive goals simply raise once more the problem of order. Ultimate goals, particularly those attaching to collectivities such as whole societies, present other questions. Here the argument for the necessity of ultimate values, of beliefs and ideals held not subject to question, is essentially one of logical inference. Ultimate values and collective goals provide the rationale, the final answer to a succession of querulous "whys," for the normative order. Granted that some rules of mere administrative convenience may rely for their acceptance solely on that instrumental basis, and others that command moral allegiance rest, sooner or later in a possibly complex means-end chain, on ultimate virtues or collective welfare. The universality of nonrational bases for the legitimacy of any system for maintaining order, including the exercise of political authority, lends support to this argument. The argument as presented, however, rests on logical inference rather than inductive generalization.

The exact number of identifiable functional requisites distinguished is somewhat discretionary, since some may be subsumed under others—as I have just done with several of Levy's analytical distinctions, which he chose to make in order to highlight various nuances in a complex analysis; I have subdivided another one for the same reasons. Indeed, at that level I should add still another—namely, the maintenance of motivation. Early socialization cannot be assumed to endure indefinitely, particularly under changing circumstances, including the possible lack of reinforcement by the expectations of significant others. Maintenance of orderly compliance solely by resort to penalties for deviance is not essential to the inferential argument and certainly does not conform with observed reality. Positive rewards commonly ensue from normative compliance, and these constitute components of "social control" of generally greater efficacy than are repressive measures. The universality of recreational patterns and other releases from routine suggest a motivation-maintaining outcome.

It is also important to note the tactical costs and benefits of the number of system properties analytically distinguishable as essential to continued operation, after one has started from some general axiom such as: "If human beings are to survive and reproduce their successors, they can do so only as participants in social systems." (Various human-nature stipulations, including individual mortality, infant incapacity, lack of complex instincts, capacity for learning, and calculated problem solving of course lie behind this axiom.) A fairly extensive elaboration of requisite system properties has the advantage of reminding the analyst to look for the patterns of action, the structures, that serve each need. There are two difficulties, two types of costs, involved in this tactic of disaggregation. The first is that the same kind of analytical distinctions made among functions are unlikely to be reflected precisely in differentiated structures, as observed. All concrete structures such as organized membership units are in some degree multifunctional, partly because they too have system properties that must be fulfilled. From a functional-requisite perspective, all structures thus become analytic structures. A somewhat cautious scientist, intending observational tests of a deductively derived set of predictive propositions, would surely suggest or perform observations on concrete structures to determine their actual consequences for the encompassing systems in which they are encountered.

The second difficulty with extensive enumeration of analytically distinguishable requisites is that their interdependence may obscure their more general properties. Thus, in Levy's list of requisites, it is impossible to discuss meaningfully "adequate institutionalization" without reference to "socialization," and conversely. The analysis being strictly at what we might roughly call the social interdependence-and-order level of system properties, as distinct from the bioeconomic requirements for survival, the order in which requisites are identified becomes arbitrary, and indeed the attempt to map the territory in detail may lead to distinctions without fundamental differences. For example, "adequate institutionalization" includes and encompasses "regulation of the choice of means," "regulation of affective expression," and "effective control of disruptive forms of behavior." To repeat, the only advantage in the more extended list is to alert the theorist or observer to aspects of structured behavior that might be otherwise neglected.

Parsons, expectably, consolidates various analytically distinguishable system requisites into fewer categories than does Levy. In a first attempt at stipulating what he called "the functional prerequisites of social systems,"[106] Parsons acknowledged familiarity with the formulation of his former students[107] but also acknowledged a radical departure from it. He starts with his tripartite division of individuals as organisms and personalities, the "interactive system" (that is, the social system narrowly identified), and the system of cultural patterning. For the individuals he specifies nutrition and physical safety and personality stability. From the individuals the system needs positive motivation for required performance and the avoidance of disruptive behavior, effected through socialization, but this is supplemented by institutionalized social control. For the cultural system Parsons specifies language, relevant empirical knowledge, and "sufficiently integrated patterns of expressive symbolism and of value orientation."[108] He later adds "nonempirical existential ideas."[109] Partial closure of his tripartite system is achieved by noting that culture becomes part of personality through internalization.

A substantially more orderly, and even diagrammatic, presentation of system requisites soon appeared in Parsons's work jointly with Robert F. Bales and Edward A. Shils[110] and a little later in *Economy and Society,* written with Neil J. Smelser.[111] The functional requisites are now grouped under four headings: Adaptation, Goal Attainment, Integration, and Latency. The concepts are moderately self-explanatory except for the bizarre term "latency," which turns out to comprise pattern maintenance and tension management. By the time of the relatively brief essay, "An Outline of the Social System,"[112] latency has become simply pattern maintenance, with tension management being one set of mechanisms for that function. In his quest for abstraction through grouping, Parsons could go one step further, for at the level of generality at which he presents his argument, there is little merit in his distinction between pattern maintenance and integration.

Throughout his discussion of these functional requisites Parsons is punctilious in noting that exact correspondence between personality and the normative order and values attributed to the social system is unlikely; that deviance will occur; that conflicts (of both interests and ideologies) are an observed reality; thus, that norms and values themselves may not be fully integrated; and (less frequently) that change, for example in information levels, may be intrinsic to the system.

Certain advantages inhere in the comparative analysis of societies in terms of functional requisites. One such advantage clearly is the provision of observational categories or standardized questions: how does the system under observation provide for socialization? for role assignment? for maintaining motivation? Aside from the awkward circumstance that a neat correspondence between a requisite outcome and a specifically differentiated pattern of action is unlikely, the answers to the questions provide the opportunity to record the interdependent structures of social systems in a comparable way across the wide spectrum of organizational forms and degrees of differentiation. If the answer to a standard question, after careful probing, is that there is no provision for a stipulated requirement, the rules of the game permit only one of two conclusions: either that requisite has been falsely alleged to be essential, or the patterns under observation do not constitute a society as defined—that is, do not qualify as a self-subsistent social system.

The specification of the requisites for any society might be regarded as merely an enumerative definition of society, but the stipulation that the system is self-subsistent makes of properties of any such system genuine theories of society: for example, any society will have the structural means for producing rules that govern standardized interpersonal or intergroup transactions.

It may be noted that the explication of the functional requisites, starting from human-nature assumptions or axioms and proceeding logically and expeditiously to the properties of social systems, constitutes a deductive theory, so much admired by Homans,[113] and one attending to complex social reality that could not be derived from his psychological reductionism.

Derivation of the requisite system properties of any society has evolutionary implications only if one attempts to account for the survival of existing systems that closely approximate the model. The line of reasoning then becomes, if not the survival of the fittest, at least the survival of the relatively fit. In the vernacular expression, "They must be doing something right." More circumspectly, they must be doing things not fatally wrong. The term "natural selection" is an inviting one for a kind of process presuming wide variability in practices, some of which must have been lethal to systems in which they were adopted, leaving existing ones adequately adaptive.

Given the purposive, problem-solving orientation possible among human actors, no current social structure can be automatically assumed to have been created by purely random innovation, its successful persistence solely the consequence of chance avoidance of mindless forces of rigorous restraints on tolerable variation. The possibility of deliberate, even collective, problem solving and choice cannot be ruled out for any socially organized aggregate of the human species with approximately the same genetic capacity for "intelligence" that characterizes current representatives of the species. Written records attest to such deliberate actions in ancient civilizations. Not all of those policies now appear wise. The same can be said for executive, legislative, and judicial decisions in contemporary states. Societies dependent on oral traditions commonly attribute the origin of current practices to supernatural or at least superhuman figures in a vague and mythic past. (It has been suggested that it is the universal function of myths to account for meaningful uncertainties.[114]) These qualms about the application of doctrines of biological evolution to human social systems are fundamental, but they have not dissuaded the perpetrators.

Durkheim, we have noted, inferentially accepted evolutionism in his quest for the most "elementary" forms of religion in the one society, among those on which information was available to him, with the most elementary techniques of acquiring food. More significantly, he contrasted a contemporary, differentiated society with a mythical (or rather, heuristic) primal aggregate bonded by the likeness of its members, and he attempted to account for increasing differentiation especially to pursue its systemic implications.[115] This diachronic, or process, view of societies was not pursued by Durkheim, who became almost exclusively concerned with problems of interdependence and integration. The evolutionary perspective was essentially renounced by the anthropologists, who emphasized explanation of cultural or social traits and complexes in terms of current utilities, not in terms of origins.

Yet increasing differentiation became the basis for a persistent concern with "developmentalism," emphasizing orderly change in mainly orderly systems. Actually, as Szymon Chodak has shown,[116] directional change by incremental units is consistent with two explanatory stances in the social sciences. One is evolutionary, with systemic change the consequence of unsuccessful adaptation to the exigencies of a harsh and competitive ambience. The other is more or less explicitly goal directed, concerned with such problem solving as the quest for individual and collective security and with such "progressive" changes as improvements in material well-being and other aspects of "modernization."

What might be called "evolutionary functionalism" was first made explicit by Parsons in an essay published in 1964.[117] Here Parsons is less abstract with reference to requisite system properties, since hs is attempting to stipulate the prerequisites for "sociocultural development" rather than systemic survival as such. These prerequisites he identifies as: (1) communication based on symbolic language, (2) kinship organization based on the incest taboo, (3) at least a rudimentary technology, and (4) religion. These constitute "evolutionary universals" in the human species that substantially increase generalized adaptive capacity, as compared with other species, in cushioning the impact of natural selection. Parsons notes, however, that the relative advantage of these systemic emergents is less in terms of survival than in terms of the potentiality for further major developments. These universals, the argument proceeds, constitute necessary (but apparently not sufficient) conditions for other system properties. In an intermediate "stage" of development Parsons identifies stratification beyond the ascriptive statuses inherent in primitive kinship systems and cultural legitimation through institutionalized agencies that are independent of a diffuse religious tradition. He then adds four further structural complexes that are fundamental to the distinctive features of modern societies, constituting thus his third "stage" of development: bureaucratic organization of collective goal attainment, money and market systems, generalized universalistic legal systems, and democratic associations with elective leadership to establish policy orientations.

Parsons appears to be curiously oblivious to, or unimpressed by, conventional historical interpretation and social evolutionary doctrine. Ancient historians underscore the discontinuity in those societies that accomplished the invention of settled agriculture and the consequent availability of food surpluses to support not only other forms of physical production but also occupationally distinct "professionals" (especially priests and healers), governors, and perhaps other service producers. There is no reason to question the accuracy of that interpretation. It is perhaps significant that Parsons does not pursue the significance of technology beyond the minimum stipulated as a survival requisite for any society.

The other major neglected discontinuity in developmental stages, deriving from earlier social evolutionary theories, is that marked by the invention of written language. In the conventional American academic division of labor that difference has been made the primary basis for the distinction between anthropology and sociology. Though we have earlier noted that the absence of written language does not necessarily mean total "simplicity" of social organization, there is no doubting the significance of writing in allowing indirect communication without distortion by intermediaries, communication at a distance in time and space, reliable codification of rules despite possible turnover in those affected, and the assembly of reliable records as a supplement to human memory and as a protection against willful or merely nostalgic distortion of past events and circumstances. The neglect of these significant "developmental emergents" is made all the more puzzling by Parsons's final achievement of democracy. If intended as some sort of end point or climax in social development, it cannot fail to remind us of the ethnocentric interpretation of stages in social evolution among complacent late-Victorian scholars.

What Parsons does, in essentially his first attempt to deal with structural differences among societies, is to make a number of structural specifications much more precisely identified than those to be derived from his fourfold set of functional requisites. The way whereby those system-survival requisites are fulfilled distinguishes a limited number of classes of societies, with those in successive stages of development being marked by more highly differentiated, and thus somewhat more functionally specific, subsystems, displaying increasing autonomy within their specialized jurisdictions or spheres of competence.

Because of the central, and therefore controversial, position that Parsons has occupied in contemporary sociological theory for something over four decades, particularly as the expositor of the general properties of social systems, it is appropriate to note the changes evident in his recent work. Especially in the two relatively brief books elaborating his evolutionary classification of societies and the distinctive features of modern societies,[118] Parsons has made some notable departures from the main emphases in his previous theoretical work. He has been frequently criticized for equating theory with a conceptual scheme, so that much of his work has been definitional and taxonomic rather than propositional. True, he occasionally dealt with less abstract and less general topics, such as the professions, American kinship, or political situations of current interest.[119] Yet he gave little attention to the variability in the structural characteristics of whole societies until these more recent works, which thus feature more allegations of testable relations among variables as distinct from definitional distinctions among concepts.

A further notable departure is the explicit recognition—but only as a distinctive feature of modern societies—of organized goal setting, problem solving, and decision making. Parsons was always concerned with the motivated actor, and later with the intersections between the personality system and the sociocultural system. The (consensually held) ultimate values, the individual and societal goals requiring structures appropriate for their attainment, were more postulated than viewed as problematic and subject to contention and deliberate resolution. The structural mechanisms for collective goal setting now get explicit recognition and are interpreted as a kind of evolutionary emergent that permits further "development."

The evolutionary argument used by Parsons[120] can be stated rather simply.

Increasing structural differentiation requires new principles and forms of integration. The consequence is an increased survival capacity of the differentiated system in relation to its environment. Now this conclusion is far from self-evident truth. That organic evolution is directional, from simple to complex, is also part of biological doctrine, but that too will not withstand inspection. Simple organisms do survive as a species, and some have a greater antiquity, with little or no change by the fossil record, than later and complex structures have yet had a chance to demonstrate. Meanwhile, many species of complex animal organisms have become extinct without the evil depredations of human beings.

What is true is that technological superiority (which includes highly rationalized organizations) possessed by modern complex societies imperils less developed ones and has in fact mainly put the latter in one form or another of dependency—thus increasing their distance from true self-subsistence. The cumulative, and avidly fostered, useful knowledge with respect to the nonhuman environment has led to increasing environmental "mastery" rather than passive adaptation. Even environmental influences not yet subject to control, such as physiographic disturbances in the earth's surface, climate, and weather, are the focus of calculated coping procedures. Rational control of fertility and mortality results in less wasteful reproductive patterns and less erratic mortality conditions from infectious and contagious diseases.

Yet the superiority of highly differentiated societies is not without costs and hazards. Differentiation obviously requires integration if system properties are to be maintained. No trouble-free mode of integration exists. Between the poles of consensual adherence to norms and values and the coercive regimentation of the many by the powerful few, both of which are ideal typical and not actual alternatives, there are various somewhat disorderly mixtures. Moreover, a high degree of interdependence with structural integration through centralization of essential controls (including power, money, and information) has a higher vulnerability to attack through destruction of its center than does a less fully integrated system.

Let us revert to the question of increasing differentiation, on which brief comments were made early in this essay. In his fullest discussion of his version of social evolution, Parsons[121] seems to leave unexplained the initial emergence of differentiation beyond that biologically mandated by age and sex and that socially mandated by the universal incest taboo (which requires some differentiation between or within kinship systems). Once differentiation beyond kinship structures occurs (for whatever reason), it tends to be self-confirming, and may become self-expanding through the organization and institutionalization of change. Thus, after the emergence of what we may call "intermediate" differentiation, the process becomes the efficient cause of further development. In a later (1975) restatement of his evolutionary perspective, Parsons uses the analogy of genetic variability to assert that "some cultural values or norms arising in processes of social change do in fact become constitutive of concrete social structures, whereas others fail to do so."[122] The consequence for which he adduces this argument is with respect to "institutionalization," and thus he misses differentiation as the process crucial to his explanatory system.

Although Parsons extended his evolutionary view of variability among societies to the common structural features of modern societies, he has not been primarily concerned with "modernization" as that term has come to stand for the contemporary transformation of "traditional" or "underdeveloped" countries in the direction of the economic and other structural features of high-technology national units. That focus of interest among the social sciences, mainly since the Second World War, began for the most part with economists and was phrased in terms of "economic growth" or "economic development." Within the framework of a neoclassical orientation to markets and profits, backward economies were seen as possible candidates for incremental growth through capital expansion. Past failures to achieve such growth could then be seen in terms of one or more relevant inadequacies: of savings or their mobilization, of rationalized impersonal markets, of technology, of entrepreneurship. Economic growth then became the agency, indeed the cause, of other structural transformations characteristic of "advanced" societies.

Other social scientists became involved in the conversation, partly through the agency of the Committee on Economic Growth, chaired by the eminent economist Simon Kuznets, under the auspices of the (American) Social Science Research Council. That committee, established in 1950, sponsored a wide-ranging series of interdisciplinary conferences, with the contributed papers subsequently edited for publication in a number of influential symposia.[123] Later, UNESCO sponsored a series of regional conferences with a similar format.[124]

Anthropologists, political scientists, and sociologists explored the cultural and structural sources of "underdevelopment" or "backwardness," often in terms of the functional integration of traditional societies, which included the lack of improvement-oriented values. Attention was also turned to the sociocultural preconditions, immediate concomitants, and less closely linked structural consequences of economic rationalization or industrialization (commonly used in a fairly broad sense).[125] This focus on the prospects for developmental change seemed appropriate in view of the unmistakable facts that the political spokesmen for virtually every one of what the United Nations came to call the Less Developed Countries articulated goals of economic growth and other forms of modernization, and that, given the opportunity, people everywhere clearly did not let their traditional cultural values inhibit their desire for improved conditions of material well-being. (The economists appeared to be right all along in their assumptions concerning hedonic motivations, at least at the level of creature comforts, including health and longevity. Anthropologists and sociologists found their emphasis on cultural differences slightly tainted.)

The use of the term "modernization" symbolized the participation of social scientists besides economists in analyzing the general characteristics of modernity. Although economic development, including industrialization in the narrow sense of manufacturing, was taken to be a prime ingredient of modernity, wide-ranging structural features that set modernized societies apart from traditional or less developed ones were explored. Thus, modernized societies are characterized by such structural features as formal systems of graded education; mobile nuclear families, with extended kinship relatively weak and discretionary; political systems capable of mobilizing diverse and often divisive populations toward programmed change; modes of social participation in specialized associations, furthering shared economic or political interests or simply shared recreational and expressive activities; social placement and mobility closely linked to occupation; extensive reliance on formal modes of social control such as law enforcement and bureaucratic regulations rather than the customs of kinship organizations and communities.

These and other structural characteristics may be taken as an enumerative definition of modernity, with societies sharing those characteristics considered modernized. The contrast between that class of societies and others has led to a curious scholarly convention. That convention is to use, more often than not implicitly, a three-stage model of modernization. Stage one is the functionally integrated and therefore relatively static traditional society; stage two comprises the transitional processes of structural alteration in the direction of modernity; stage three is the functionally integrated fully, or at least "highly," modernized society. What I have called the "model modernized society" [126] thus becomes the destination toward which the "newly modernizing societies" are moving or seeking to do so through deliberate programs of change.

The neglect of the documented differences among so-called traditional societies is perhaps not a fatal defect if their commonalities are such as to make the recipe for modernization a standard one. In view of differing histories and current states, that could scarcely be the situation. The actual course of transition has received remarkably little attention, as the mode of analysis has been that of comparative statics—before-and-after comparisons—rather than factually based sequential models of structural change. And the common destination presents grave problems of both factual and theoretical import. Those problems must now be clarified.

The "model modernized society" rests upon two assumptions: that all industrial or highly modernized societies have sufficient structural commonalities to be treated as a class or type, and that such conspicuous (or subtle) differences as remain are either relatively unimportant or anachronistic.[127] What has come to be called "convergence theory" argues that members of the modernized class are on courses of change that will eventually eliminate their remaining significant differences. Since convergence theory is the actual source of what passes for modernization theory, this sophisticated form of functional teleology warrants close examination.

Several years ago I argued[128] that crucial differences were likely to remain, noting particularly the political (as distinct from the merely administrative) structure of the national state. I noted genuine differences in political ideologies and the bases for the claimed legitimacy whereby the governors govern. These differences are compounded by different historic paths to the present, leaving unresolved residual tensions requiring management, and the functional utility of nationalism—buttressed by the doctrine of national sovereignty—as a collective value for differentiated and often conflictful populations. Of course under imaginable but not highly probable conditions of common crisis or an imposed singular world state through conquest, the exigencies of the world political system might lead to convergence of a rather different sort than any of the less drastic courses of change now evident. (Of course the world does constitute a singular, if disorderly, system from some points of view. The growing factual interdependence and abrasive interaction among national states puts increasing strains on the model of societies as self-subsistent systems.)[129]

More recently it has seemed to me that the processes called modernization are best viewed as forms of rationalization of social structures.[130] These processes include monetization and commercialization of exchange, together with ledgered accounting, credits and debts; technification in the restricted sense of applying useful knowledge from physics, chemistry, and biology in physical production, transportation, communication, health services, and a myriad of other contexts; bureaucratization as a highly rationalized form of integration of specialized tasks; formalization of legal codes and procedures; and even a considerable, but still limited, degree of secularization with respect to conventional values and beliefs.

The limits to secularization are symptomatic of the limits to rationalization generally. In addition to the inescapable significance of human emotion and of affective patterns of interaction, there are collective or system-oriented limits to rationality. Rationality describes a calculated choice of effective means for given ends but is not the basis for the ends pursued. Except where the goal is intermediate and thus an appropriate means for some higher or at least subsequent goal, rational action or rationalized systems of action cannot determine the goals sought. Bureaucractic organization lends itself at least as well to warfare or internal repression as it does to producing cars or distributing welfare benefits. Max Weber's rational-legal basis for political legitimacy[131] cannot stand on the same footing of ultimacy as his traditional and charismatic types. This correct perception has been developed by Heinz Hartmann.[132]

We come then by this indirect route to a rediscovery of the importance of collective values and goal orientations in viable social systems. Those systems, however, are no longer self-equilibrating entities but rather systems in constant disequilibrium because of deliberate change, unintended consequences of change, and the very unequal susceptibility of segments of conventionalized behavior to the master process of rationalization.

Of course much of functionalism survives. This is especially noteworthy in the systems perspective, whereby structurally differentiated parts provide a substantial degree of determination of other (but not all) parts. It is also true of functional requisite analysis, which leads to some structural universals (such as the nuclear family—not discussed in this essay—or magic, myths, and *rites de passage*) and otherwise leads only to a tolerable range of expected consequences out of some combination of patterned behavior. The neoevolutionary perspective either yields a kind of mindless adaptation with trial-and-error acceptance of innovations that have useful emergent properties, or the emergence of institutionalized change, which makes the continued use of the evolutionary model of change highly dubious. Modernization is the first truly global process of structural change, and it is producing a world quasi-system of a complexity so far beyond the small, self-subsistent tribal group as to require theoretical models of a different, and not yet visible, order.

Much remains to be done by way of what might be called conventional comparative structural analysis, though at increasing risk of making erroneous assumptions about the stability of structures observed at a particular time that may in fact be in rapid transition. Comparative dynamics offers somewhat greater challenges for both conceptualizing and measuring sequential systems. (The refinements of measurement used in sociology are almost entirely sophisticated forms of atemporal correlations and might be said to be what static functionalism deserved.) Of course, through the discretionary division of labor within disciplines, many if not most sociologists may choose to work on small fields of observation with tidy techniques of testing hypotheses. Meanwhile, as the gross structural features of social life on this planet are likely to continue in rapid transition verging on turmoil, the challenge to those scholars who will not abandon a macrosociological focus will require innovative intelligence of a high order.

NOTES

1. See, for example, Jonathan H. Turner, *The Structure of Sociological Theory* (Homewood, Ill.: Dorsey Press, 1974).
2. Robert A. Nisbet, *Twilight of Authority* (New York: Oxford University Press, 1975) pp. 250–51.
3. Talcott Parsons, "The Present Status of 'Structural-Functional' Theory in Sociology," in Lewis A. Coser, ed., *The Idea of Social Structure: Papers in Honor of Robert K. Merton* (New York: Harcourt Brace Jovanovich, 1975) pp. 67–83.
4. Talcott Parsons, *Societies: Evolutionary and Comparative Perspectives* (Englewood Cliffs, N.J.: Prentice-Hall, 1966); Parsons, *The System of Modern Societies* (Englewood Cliffs, N.J.: Prentice-Hall, 1971).
5. Parsons, "The Present Status of 'Structural-Functional' Theory in Sociology."
6. Kingsley Davis, *Human Society* (New York: Macmillan, 1949).
7. Kingsley Davis and Wilbert E. Moore, "Some Principles of Stratification," *American Sociological Review*, vol. 10 (April 1945) pp. 243–49.
8. Kingsley Davis, "The Myth of Functional Analysis as a Special Method in Sociology and Anthropology," *American Sociological Review*, vol. 24 (December 1959) pp. 757–72.
9. Kingsley Davis, *Human Society*, pp. 555–86; Davis and Judith Blake, "Social Structure and Fertility: An Analytical Framework," *Economic Development and Cultural Change*, vol. 4 (1956) pp. 211–35.
10. Robert K. Merton, *Social Theory and Social Structure* (Glencoe, Ill.: Free Press, 1957) chap. I, "Manifest and Latent Functions," pp. 19–84.
11. Robert K. Merton, *The Sociology of Science: Theoretical and Empirical Investigations* (Chicago: University of Chicago Press, 1973).

12. Marion J. Levy, Jr., *The Structure of Society* (Princeton, N.J.: Princeton University Press, 1952) chap. IV, "The Functional Requisites of Any Society," pp. 149–97.

13. Talcott Parsons, Robert F. Bales, and Edward A. Shils, *Working Papers in the Theory of Action* (Glencoe, Ill.: Free Press, 1953) chap. 5, "Phase Movement in Relation to Motivation Symbol Formation, and Role Structure," pp. 163–269; Parsons and Neil J. Smelser, *Economy and Society* (Glencoe, Ill.: Free Press, 1956) pp. 13–29.

14. Marion J. Levy, Jr., *Modernization and the Structure of Societies* (Princeton, N.J.: Princeton University Press, 1966) 2 vols.; Levy, *Modernization: Latecomers and Survivors* (New York: Basic Books, 1972).

15. Wilbert E. Moore, *Social Change*, 2d ed. (Englewood Cliffs, N.J., 1974).

16. Wilbert E. Moore, *The Impact of Industry* (Englewood Cliffs, N.J.: Prentice-Hall, 1965); Moore, "The Singular and the Plural: The Social Significance of Industrialism Reconsidered," in Nancy Hammond, ed., *Social Science and the New Societies* (East Lansing: Social Science Research Bureau, Michigan State University, 1973); Moore, "Modernization as Rationalization: Processes and Restraints," in Manning Nash, ed., *Essays on Economic Development and Cultural Change in Honor of Bert F. Hoselitz*, published as supplement to vol. 25, *Economic Development and Cultural Change* (1977).

17. Davis, "The Myth of Functional Analysis as a Special Method in Sociology and Anthropology."

18. Emile Durkheim, *The Rules of Sociological Method*, trans. by Sarah A. Solovay and John H. Mueller (Glencoe, Ill.: Free Press, 1938). First published in French in 1895. See especially chap. VI, "Rules Relative to Establishing Sociological Proofs," pp. 125–40.

19. Emile Durkheim, *The Division of Labor in Society*, trans. by George Simpson (Glencoe, Ill.: Free Press, 1960). First published in French in 1893.

20. Robert A. Nisbet, *Social Change and History* (New York: Oxford University Press, 1972).

21. Parsons, *Societies: Evolutionary and Comparative Perspectives.*

22. Neil J. Smelser, "Mechanisms of Change and Adjustment to Change," in Bert F. Hoselitz and Wilbert E. Moore, eds., *Industrialization and Society* (Paris and The Hague: UNESCO and Mouton, 1963) pp. 32–54. In a later statement, however, Smelser does attend to the sources of differentiation. See Smelser, *Essays in Sociological Explanation* (Englewood Cliffs, N.J.: Prentice-Hall, 1968) chap. 8, "Toward a General Theory of Social Change," pp. 243–54.

23. For a brief overview of the voluminous writing of Claude-Henri de Saint-Simon, see the *Selected Writings*, ed. and trans. by M. H. Markham (Oxford: Blackwell, 1952). On Comte, see Auguste Comte, *System of Positive Polity* (London: Longmans, 1875–77) 4 vols.; originally published in French.

24. See especially Karl Marx, *Economic and Philosophic Manuscripts of 1844* (New York: International Publishers, 1964).

25. Ferdinand Tönnies, *Community and Society (Gemeinschaft und Gesellschaft)*, trans. by Charles P. Loomis (East Lansing: Michigan State University Press, 1957). First published in German in 1887.

26. Max Weber, *The Theory of Social and Economic Organization*, trans. by A. M. Henderson and Talcott Parsons (New York: Oxford University Press, 1947) pp. 329–41.

27. Durkheim, *The Rules of Sociological Method.*

28. Karl Marx, *A Contribution to the Critique of Political Economy* (Chicago: Kerr, 1913). First published in German in 1859.

29. Durkheim, *Division of Labor*, book one, chap. 7, "Organic Solidarity and Contractual Solidarity."

30. On this interpretation of Durkheim, see Talcott Parsons, *The Structure of Social Action* (New York: McGraw-Hill, 1937) pp. 409–29.

31. Emile Durkheim, *The Elementary Forms of the Religious Life* (New York: Macmillan, 1954). Originally published in French in 1912.

32. See W. Lloyd Warner, *A Black Civilization: A Social Study of an Australian Tribe* (New York: Harper, 1937).

33. See, for example, Emile Durkheim, *Suicide: A Study in Sociology* (Glencoe, Ill.: Free Press, 1951), first published in French in 1897; Durkheim, *On Morality and Society: Selected Writings*, ed. by Robert N. Bellah (Chicago: University of Chicago Press, 1973) contains both essays and selections from books; Durkheim, *Moral Education: A Study in the Theory and Application of the Sociology of Education* (New York: Free Press, 1961), lectures first published in French, 1902–06.

34. Emile Durkheim and Marcel Mauss, *Primitive Classification* (Chicago: University of Chicago Press, 1963), originally published in French in *L'Année Sociologique*, (1903).

35. Marcel Mauss, *The Gift: Forms and Functions of Exchange in Archaic Societies* (Glencoe, Ill.: Free Press, 1954), first published in French in 1925.

36. Arnold van Gennep, *The Rites of Passage* (Chicago: University of Chicago Press, 1960), first published in French in 1908.

37. Marcel Granet, *La Pensée Chinoise* (Paris: La Renaissance du Livre, 1934), reissued by Michel in 1950.

38. See especially A. R. Radcliffe-Brown, *Structure and Function in Primitive Societies: Essays and Addresses* (New York: Free Press, 1961), representing earlier work, 1923–49; see also a posthumous collection of essays on comparative social anthropology, edited by M. N. Srinivas: Radcliffe-Brown, *Method in Social Anthropology: Selected Essays* (Chicago: University of Chicago Press, 1958).

39. Durkheim, *Division of Labor*, book one, chap. 3.

40. See especially Herbert Spencer, *The Principles of Sociology* (New York: Appleton: 1925–29) 3 vols., originally published 1876–96.

41. See Merton, "Manifest and Latent Functions."

42. Ibid., pp. 30–32.

43. Nicholas S. Timasheff, *Sociological Theory: Its Nature and Growth* (Garden City, N.Y.: Doubleday, 1955) pp. 225, 243.

44. On Spencer, see ibid., pp. 30–42.

45. Parsons, "The Present Status of 'Structural Functional' Theory in Sociology."

46. Parsons, *Societies: Evolutionary and Comparative Perspectives;* and Parsons, *The System of Modern Societies.*

47. See Amos Hawley, *Human Ecology: A Theory of Community Structure* (New York: Ronald, 1950).

48. Parsons, *The Structure of Social Action*, pp. 89–94.

49. Durkheim, *The Rules of Sociological Method*, pp. 64–75.

50. In addition to ibid., see the discussion by Parsons in *The Structure of Social Action*, pp. 309, 318–19, 402–3.

51. Merton, *Social Theory and Social Structure*, chap. 4, "Social Structure and Anomie," pp. 131–60.

52. Ibid., chap. 5, "Continuities in the Theory of Social Structure and Anomie," pp. 161-66.

53. Moore, *Social Change*, at pp. 27–29.

54. Ibid., p. 27.

55. Bronislaw Malinowski, "Culture," in *Encyclopedia of the Social Sciences* (New York: Macmillan, 1930–34) vol. 4, pp. 621–45; Malinowski, *Magic, Science and Religion, and Other Essays* (Glencoe, Ill.: Free Press, 1948).

56. See especially Lucien Lévy-Bruhl, *Primitive Mentality* (New York: Macmillan, 1923).

57. Malinowski, *Magic, Science and Religion.*

58. Kingsley Davis, "The Sociology of Prostitution," *American Sociological Review*, vol. 2 (October 1937) pp. 744–55.

59. Bernard de Mandeville, *The Fable of the Bees, or Private Vices, Public Benefits* (Oxford: Oxford University Press, 1924) 2 vols. Originally published in 1714, with later editions by the author.

60. Merton, *Social Theory and Social Structure*, pp. 71–82.

61. Lewis A. Coser, *The Functions of Social Conflict* (New York: Free Press, 1956); Coser, *Continuities in the Study of Social Conflict* (New York: Free Press, 1967).

62. Davis and Moore, "Some Principles of Stratification."

63. See Leonard Broom and Robert G. Cushing, "A Modest Test of an Immodest Theory: The Functional Theory of Stratification," *American Sociological Review*, vol. 42 (February 1977) pp. 157–69.

64. Davis and Moore, "Some Principles of Stratification," p. 243.

65. In addition to Broom and Cushing, "A Modest Test of an Immodest Theory," see Mark Abrahamson "Functionalism and the Functional Theory of Stratification: An Empirical Assessment," *American Journal of Sociology*, vol. 78 (1973) pp. 1236–46; Burke D. Grandjean and Frank D. Bean, "The Davis-Moore Theory and Perceptions of Stratification: Some Relevant Evidence," *Social Forces*, vol. 54 (1975) pp. 166–80; K. C. Land, "Path Models of Functional Theories of Social Stratification as Representations of Cultural Beliefs on Stratification," *Sociological Quarterly*, vol. 11 (1970) pp. 474–84; Joseph Lopreato and L. S. Lewis, "An Analysis of Variables in the Functional Theory of Stratification," *Sociological Quarterly*, vol. 4 (1963) pp. 301–10; Arthur L. Stinchcombe, "Some Empirical Consequences of the Davis-Moore Theory of Stratification," *American Sociological Review*, vol. 28 (1963) pp. 805–8; Stinchcombe and T. R.

Harris, "Interdependence and Inequality: A Specification of the Davis-Moore Theory," *Sociometry*, vol. 32 (1969) pp. 12–23.

66. Merton, *Social Theory and Social Structure*, pp. 36, 51–53.

67. Levy, *The Structure of Society*, pp. 76–83.

68. See Parsons and others, *Working Papers*. . ., pp. 163–269; and Parsons and Smelser, *Economy and Society*, pp. 13–29.

69. Wilbert E. Moore and Arnold S. Feldman "Society as a Tension-Management System," in George Baker and Leonard S. Cottrell, Jr., eds., *Behavioral Science and Civil Defense*, Disaster Research Group No. 16 (Washington: National Academy of Sciences—National Research Council, 1962) pp. 93–105. Also, Moore, *Social Change*, pp. 11–12.

70. Parsons, *The Social System* (Glencoe, Ill.: Free Press, 1951) pp. 3–36.

71. See especially Parsons and others, *Working Papers*. . . .

72. Moore, *Social Change*, pp. 77–80.

73. Pitirim A. Sorokin, *Social and Cultural Dynamics* (New York: American Book Co., 1937–41) 4 vols., 1-vol. ed. (Boston: Porter Sargent, 1957).

74. Sorokin, *Sociological Theories of Today* (New York: Harper and Row, 1966) pp. 609–11.

75. Davis, *Human Society*, pp. 555–86; Davis and Blake, "Social Structure and Fertility."

76. See Moore, *Social Change*, pp. 13–22.

77. See Chapter 14 herein.

78. Leopold von Wiese, *Systematic Sociology: On the Basis of the Beziehungslehre and the Gebildelehre of Leopold von Wiese*, adapted and amplified by Howard Becker (New York: Wiley, 1932), originally published in German, 1924–29.

79. Robert E. Park and Ernest W. Burgess, *Introduction to the Science of Sociology*, 2d ed. (Chicago: University of Chicago Press, 1924).

80. Robert L. Sutherland and Julian L. Woodward, *Introductory Sociology* (Chicago: Lippincott, 1937 and later editions).

81. Davis, *Human Society*.

82. Davis and Moore, "Some Principles of Stratification," p. 243.

83. See for example Adam B. Ulam, *The Unfinished Revolution: An Essay on the Sources of Influence of Marxism and Communism* (New York: Random House, 1960); Irving M. Zeitlin, *Marxism: A Re-examination* (Princeton: Van Nostrand, 1967).

84. See for example Parsons and Smelser, *Economy and Society*.

85. See for example Moore, *Social Change*.

86. George P. Murdock, *Social Structure* (New York: Macmillan, 1949).

87. Stanley H. Udy, Jr., *Organization of Work: A Comparative Analysis of Production Among Nonindustrial Peoples* (New Haven: HRAF Press, 1959).

88. See for example Moore, *The Impact of Industry*.

89. See Max Weber, *The Protestant Ethic and the Spirit of Capitalism*, trans. by Talcott Parsons (New York: Scribners, 1930), first published in German in 1904.

90. Merton uses the term "functional alternatives." See Merton, *Social Theory and Social Structure*, pp. 33–36, 52.

91. See Robert K. Merton, "The Unanticipated Consequences of Purposive Social Action," *American Sociological Review*, vol. 1 (1936) pp. 894–904.

92. Levy, *The Structure of Society*, pp. 88–100.

93. See Wilbert E. Moore, "Recreation and Modernization: Themes and Variations," unpublished paper presented at American Sociological Association, New York, 1973.

94. Merton, *Social Theory and Social Structure*.

95. Levy, *The Structure of Society*, pp. 85–88.

96. See George Caspar Homans, "Contemporary Theory in Sociology," in Robert E. L. Faris, ed., *Handbook of Modern Sociology* (Chicago: Rand McNally, 1964), chap. 25, pp. 951–77, at pp. 963–67; Turner, *The Structure of Sociological Theory*, chaps. 3 and 4; Francesca M. Cancian, "Functional Analysis: Varieties of Functional Analysis," in David L. Sills, ed., *International Encyclopedia of the Social Sciences* (New York: Macmillan and Free Press, 1968) vol. 6, pp. 29–43—Cancian also reviews criticism by several philosophers of science.

97. See Peter M. Blau, "Structural Constraints of Status Complements," in Lewis A. Coser, *The Idea of Social Structure: Papers in Honor of Robert K. Merton* (New York: Harcourt Brace Jovanovich, 1975) pp. 117–38, at pp. 117–18.

98. Homans, "Contemporary Theory in Sociology," pp. 963–67.

99. See, in addition to the essay cited in ibid., Homans, *The Human Group* (New York: Harcourt, 1950); Homans, *Social Behavior: Its Elementary Forms* (New York: Harcourt, 1961).

100. Turner, *The Structure of Sociological Theory*, pp. 52–59. Turner follows Walter L.

Wallace in characterizing the theoretical position in the work of Talcott Parsons as "functional imperativism." See Walter L. Wallace, ed., *Sociological Theory* (Chicago: Aldine, 1969), "Introduction," pp. 37–43.

101. See Moore, *Social Change*, pp. 1–30, 68–70.

102. Levy, *The Structure of Society*, p. 113. See also the prior statement by David F. Aberle, Albert K. Cohen, Arthur K. Davis, Marion J. Levy, Jr., and Francis X. Sutton, "The Functional Prerequisites of a Society," *Ethics*, vol. 40 (January 1950) pp. 100–11.

103. Levy, *The Structure of Society*, pp. 151–97.

104. Ibid., pp. 151–57.

105. See Cyril S. Belshaw, *Traditional Exchange and Modern Markets* (Englewood Cliffs, N.J.: Prentice-Hall, 1965).

106. Parsons, *The Social System*, pp. 26–36.

107. Aberle and others, "The Functional Prerequisites of a Society."

108. Parsons, *The Social System*, p. 34.

109. Ibid., p. 35.

110. Parsons and others, *Working Papers. . . .*

111. Parsons and Smelser, *Economy and Society*.

112. Parsons, "An Outline of the Social System," in Talcott Parsons, Edward Shils, Kaspar D. Naegele, and Jesse R. Pitts, eds., *Theories of Society*, 1-vol. ed. (New York: Free Press, 1965), pp. 30–79.

113. Homans, "Contemporary Theory in Sociology."

114. See Neil H. Cheek, Jr., and William R. Burch, Jr., *The Social Organization of Leisure in Human Society* (New York: Harper & Row, 1976) chap. 8, "Myth and Realms of Social Conduct," pp. 180–94.

115. Durkheim, *Division of Labor*.

116. See Szymon Chodak, *Societal Development* (New York: Oxford University Press, 1973).

117. Talcott Parsons, "Evolutionary Universals in Society," *American Sociological Review*, vol. 29 (June 1964) pp. 339–57.

118. Parsons,*Societies: Evolutionary and Comparative Perspectives*; and Parsons, *The System of Modern Societies*.

119. Part of these ventures into "applied theory" figure in *The Social System*, and others in Parsons's midcareer collection of papers, *Essays in Sociological Theory: Pure and Applied* (Glencoe, Ill.: Free Press, 1949).

120. Parsons, *Societies: Evolutionary and Comparative Perspectives*.

121. Ibid.

122. Parsons, "The Present Status of 'Structural-Functional' Theory in Sociology," p. 77.

123. See for example Simon Kuznets, Wilbert E. Moore, and Joseph J. Spengler, eds., *Economic Growth: Brazil, India, Japan* (Durham, N.C.: Duke University Press, 1955); Wilbert E. Moore and Arnold S. Feldman, eds., *Labor Commitment and Social Change in Developing Areas* (New York: Social Science Research Council, 1960); Melville J. Herskovits and Mitchell Harwitz, eds., *Economic Transition in Africa* (Evanston, Ill.: Northwestern University Press, 1964); Neil J. Smelser and Seymour Martin Lipset, eds., *Social Structure and Mobility in Economic Development* (Chicago: Aldine, 1966).

124. See Bert F. Hoselitz and Wilbert E. Moore, eds., *Industrialization and Society* (Paris and The Hague: UNESCO and Mouton, 1963).

125. Moore, *The Impact of Industry*.

126. Moore, "Modernization as Rationalization."

127. Moore, "The Singular and the Plural."

128. Ibid.

129. Moore, "Global Sociology: The World as a Singular System," *American Journal of Sociology*, vol. 71 (March 1966) pp. 475–82.

130. Moore, "Modernization as Rationalization."

131. Weber, *Theory of Social and Economic Organization*, pp. 324–423.

132. Heinz Hartmann, *Funktionale Autorität* (Stuttgart: Ferdinand Enke Verlag, 1964).

10

THEORIES OF SOCIAL ACTION

ALAN DAWE

MARIANNE WEBER said of her husband, Max Weber, that he was "moved, above all, by the fact that on its earthly course an idea always and everywhere operates in opposition to its original meaning and thereby destroys itself."[1] No single statement could better epitomize the sociological course taken by the concept of social action, and by the attempts of its major exponents (including, ironically, Weber himself) to construct theories of social action. For the career of the concept is the career of a paradox, whereby the *idée fixe* of social action has always and everywhere generated its own negation by culminating in the concept of a dominating and constraining social system. And that is not merely the history of one concept in sociology. It is fundamentally the history of sociology itself.

Already I anticipate. But the anticipation serves to make both a programmatic and a substantive point about this chapter. The programmatic point is that what is presented here is necessarily my version of the sociology of social action. Or rather, it is the version to which I adhere, since I can hardly claim

A single contribution to a collaborative enterprise is not the occasion to acknowledge all one's debts of every kind. However, two intellectual debts have been of such importance to me in writing this chapter that they cannot pass unacknowledged. The first I owe to John Heritage, both for particular points noted in the text and for the immense encouragement and stimulation of the dialogue between us over a long period about many of the issues discussed here. In an otherwise bleak, faction-ridden, and closed-minded intellectual environmnent, his response and encouragement have been absolutely vital.

The second debt arises from the fact that a large part of this chapter is built around a radical revision of a thesis I presented some years ago about the opposition—decisive for the history of ownership of the entire sociological tradition it articulates. This does not absolve me from giving an adequate account of its meaning in the work of others, a duty especially required by a volume whose primary purpose is that of basic exposition. But, against that whole autocratic and profoundly positivistic school of "proper sociological" theorizing which legislates that there can only be one "authoritative" and "correct" account of, say, the work of Emile Durkheim or the meaning of class, I want to insist that there are many, as this volume amply testifies; which points to the fact that all such accounts are always particular interpretations, derived from one or another sociological tradition. They must be possible interpretations; that is, warrantable by reference to the evidence of the subject matter under examination. But when all the tests of sociological method are counted and done, there always remain more possible interpretations than one. In short, exposition is never totally separable from interpretation. And, for me, the whole idea of social action is archetypal of a particular approach to sociology and a concomitant perspective on the origins and development of sociological thought. It is only within the framework of this approach and perspective, therefore, that I can address the sociological career, status, and meaning of the concept.

The substantive point is that the idea of social action has been central to sociological thought less as a theory or set of theories in any formal sense than as a fundamental moral and analytic preoccupation. Indeed, sociology has no "theories" of social action. What it does have is a vast body of *theorizing about* social action: its nature, its sources, its consequences. And this theorizing around a single idea has, I shall argue, been decisive for and definitive of the entire history and nature of sociological analysis from its very inception. The argument begins with the familiar and elementary observation that sociology has been perennially concerned with the problem of the relationship between the individual and society; the problem being that of reconciling their competing claims. Of course, this will meet with instant denial, since sociology abounds with assertions that there is no such competition; that "the individual" and "society" are but two sides of the same coin. But it also abounds with obsessional returns to the leitmotiv of reconcilation, which testify to the uneasy intuition in the recesses of the sociological mind that, in some very deep sense, their claims remain in competition.[2] At the very least, there remains in sociological work a persistent tension between them and a

---

sociological analysis—between a sociology of social system and a sociology of social action. The revision lies in an argument that this opposition is, in fact, merely a derivative of a much more basic opposition between two conceptions of human agency, and thus of social action; and, therefore, that the divergence between the two sociologies begins within the social action framework itself. I owe the initial formulation of the distinction between the two types of action I use in this chapter, together with its initial elaboration in the context of the "two sociologies" thesis, to Pamela Nixon, whose idea it was and is. I therefore owe to her the seminal insight upon which the revised thesis is predicated. While I alone take the usual responsibility for the way in which I have developed it, the very great extent of this debt will become obvious from the citations of and quotations from her work in the text. It is a debt I acknowledge with profound gratitude.

reluctant recognition of that tension as constituting a problem of continuing and central concern.

But, of course, this concern and this tension are hardly unique to sociology. On the contrary, they run as a fundamental theme throughout all varieties of Western social, political, moral, and creative thought and work, from philosophy and ethics to the novel and the film. Nor should their centrality surprise us. For the problem of the relationship between the individual and society is an existential problem; a problem central to our everyday experience in vast industrial societies. We experience it every time we feel dominated as individuals by huge organizations, by multifarious networks of confusing and conflicting social expectations, by external demands and pressures of all kinds which seem to leave us no room at all for our individuality:

> I don't understand how come more guys don't flip. Because you're nothing more than a machine when you hit this type of thing. They give better care to that machine than they will to you. They'll have more respect, give more attention to that machine. And you *know* this. Somehow you get the feeling that the machine is better than you are. . . . If that machine breaks down, there's somebody out there to fix it right away. If I break down, I'm just pushed over to the other side till another man takes my place.[3]

We experience it every time we feel the encroachment on our personal lives of massive forces which seem to us abstract, shadowy, impenetrable, alien, and beyond our control. And we manifest our experience of the problem in our zealous and jealous guarding of our homes, our families, our privacy against an outside world we feel as a constant threat of invasion.

> Calmly in control of the administrative machine, working within the inflexible system, we walk the corridors somehow many, many removes from land and people. Nobody can get at us except through the organisation, and only then in an approved series of moves. Equally, we cannot get at anyone, cannot even write a simple report that is not ground through the mesh of six to eight approved censors and channels. . . . We work in a great no-man's land of the machinery of negotiations, consultations, meetings, paper as complex and inhuman, and for all I know maybe as necessary as a traffic intersection. . . . And on Friday night everybody tells everybody it is the weekend, and spends the evening on their private method of recovering their own personalities—children—liquor—the garden—the car.[4]

And in the end: "I'm just tired of this type of thing. I just think we ought to be just human."[5]

How many of us feel like this? How many of us feel caught up in a monstrous, impersonal machine whose workings we understand not at all, save that they are irrelevant to and destructive of our own purposes and aspirations as individuals? Yet precisely this same feeling also testifies to our experience of our own individuality. In every testimony to the experience of the dehumanizing pressure of modern industrial society, there is also a testimony to a contrary sense of self, of personal identity, of being human; of what it is or might be like to be in control of our own lives, to act in and upon the world, to be active human agents. So, in the name of our personal identities, our personal hopes and projects and longings, in the name of our *selves*, we resist: "Oh, I'll continue to cope. I'll continue to struggle against the machine."[6] Most of the time, our resistances are small, private, subterranean, residing only in half-hidden cracks in the institutional colossus which dominates most of our lives; but not always. Once in a while, they become overt, public, aboveground. Once in a while, they mushroom into movements of protest of all kinds. All are specific historical events with specific historical causes, contexts, and purposes; but all upsurges of human agency, all exertions of human control, all outbursts of human action. In one way or another, we all try ceaselessly to assert our creativity, our personal agency, our control over the world in the face of that monstrous, impersonal, impenetrable, and alien machine. And the sum? The machine, the bureaucracy, the system versus human agency, human creativity, human control: this is the contradictory modern experience running through all our lives in mostly minor and mundane, but occasionally major and dramatic ways. While we never cease to experience ourselves as acting, choosing, purposeful, aspiring human beings, we also never cease to be aware of the factory gates closing behind us, the office days that are not our own, the sense of oppression by organizations nobody runs, the "not-enough world" we are forced to inhabit most of the time.[7] On the one hand, we are "nothing more than a machine." On the other, against these massive odds, we persist in our stubborn refusal to be less than "just human." And, of course, this conflict is not confined to the world of work, central and dominating though that is. It spreads throughout our lives, into every area where we, with our sense of self and identity and individuality, confront the machine, the bureaucracy, the system which relentlessly denies these human attributes.

Thus dualism of social experience is central to our very existence in modern society. It is, therefore, central to all the forms of thought and work which articulate our experience of that society. For these forms of thought and work, from philosophy to the film, are creatures of their social, political, and moral context. As such, they are permeated by and expressive of our everyday experience of that context. So it is with sociology. It is as much a creature of the social world upon which it reflects as any other form of thought and activity. It, too, is expressive of everday experience in the societies in which it is one mode of articulation. Its thematic preoccupations are precisely those of the lives of the members of these societies—the lives about which we have just heard some voices from everyday life tell. Herein lies the point of listening to them: sociology is not the strictly detached, neutrally analytic discipline the imperatives of modern professionalism and academic institutionalization represent it to be. On the contrary, it is rooted in and articulative of the human social experience of which those voices speak. It is this which gives it its whole point and purpose, its meaning and its life.

It gives it, first, its fundamentally moral character. For, in articulating experience, it necessarily engages with the fundamentally moral texture of social life; with "life as it is lived . . . shot through with moral choices."[8] It gives it second, its equally fundamental character as a creative enterprise. For experience is not fully experience until it has been articulated, and thus grasped and known *as experience*. To the extent that sociology articulates experience, therefore, it plays a central role in creating it. Third, sociology's grounding in human social experience links it, in terms of thematic preoccupations, with other forms of thought and activity rooted in the same social, political, and moral context. And fourth, it links the world we live in today with the reflections on the worlds in which they lived of such figures as Marx, Weber, Durkheim or, more distant in time, Hobbes and Rousseau. For while not ignoring historical particularity, what makes their work live on is the continuing relevance of their concerns to our experience. When Weber speaks to us of his bureaucratic nightmare of a world, he is also speaking to us of our world. So, too, is Marx speaking to us of our world when he speaks of his world of alienation and dehumanization; and Durkheim, speaking of his and our worlds of anomie. Through the *creative* power of their thought and work, they reveal the historical and human continuity which makes their experience *representative* of ours.[9] The point is always the link with experience. It matters not at all whether it is Marx writing in the middle of the nineteenth century; or Parsons, Mills, Fromm, Goffman, Aron, Gouldner, Castaneda, whoever, writing in our own time. As long as they continue to speak to *our* experience of *our* lives and times, they live on. And this is why, and only why, we continue to listen to them. It is what gives the history of sociological analysis its whole and sole point and purpose. Such a history is idle chatter signifying nothing—which it so often is—if it is no more than a museum of ideas torn from their experiential roots. It can only have meaning and justification as an articulation of the history we live and make now.

And this it does. For the basic dualism of modern social experience, to which those voices from everyday life have testified, has been articulated in sociology in the form of a basic dualism of sociological thought and analysis on which the entire history of the discipline has turned. Throughout that history, there has been a manifest conflict between two types of social analysis, variously labeled as being between the organismic and mechanistic approaches, methodological collectivism and individualism, holism and atomism, the conservative and emancipatory perspectives, and so on. The debates about these issues are central and perennial in sociological discourse and, at root, they are all different versions of the fundamental debate about the abiding conflict between the domination of the system and the exertion of human agency. And modern sociology, for all the apparent experiential aridity of its professionalized language, has recast these debates and the conflict behind them into the most complete embodiment and articulation of the experience on which they are founded that they have yet received. For modern sociology centers on the opposition between a sociology of social system and a sociology of social action—which is precisely the opposition between the system and human agency of modern social experience.

The opposition between the two sociologies is central to any discussion of theories of social action, but in ways which have yet to be made clear and upon which a fuller elaboration of it depends. However, at this stage in the argument, it is essential to sketch in its outlines very briefly and simply. In a sociology of social system, then, social actors are pictured as being very much at the receiving end of the social system. In terms of their existence and nature as social beings, their social behavior and relationships, and their very sense of personal identity as human beings, they are determined by it. The process is one whereby they are socialized into society's central values and into the norms appropriate to the roles they are to play in the division of labor, the roles which give them both their self-identity and their social place and purpose in meeting the functional needs of the system. They are totally manipulable creatures; *tabulae rasae* upon which can be and are imprinted the values and behavioral stimuli necessary for the fulfillment of the functions and, therefore, the maintenance of what is thus a supra-human, self-generating, and self-maintaining social system, ontologically and methologically prior to its participants. As such, it provides for them definitions of their situations, relationships, purposes, and lives—their subjective meanings—and their consequent action and interaction. Social action is thus entirely the product and derivative of social system.

In total opposition to this, a sociology of social action conceptualizes the social system as the derivative of social action and interaction, a social world produced by its members, who are thus pictured as active, purposeful, self- and socially-creative beings. The language of social action is thus the language of subjective meaning, in terms of which social actors define their lives, purposes, and situations; of the goals and projects they generate on the basis of their subjective meanings; of the means whereby they attempt to achieve their goals and realize their projects; of the social action upon which they embark in the prosecution of such attempts; of the social relationships into which they enter on the basis of their pursuit of goals and projects; and of social roles, institutions, and the social system conceptualized as the emergent product of their consequent social interaction. Clearly the whole picture, especially that of the relationship between social action and social system, is in this perspective the exact opposite of that painted by a sociology of social system.

Equally clearly, to pose the opposition between the two sociologies as starkly and as simplistically as this is to beg a number of important questions about the relationship between social action and social system, the answers to which it is the task of the remainder of this chapter to explore. For the moment, however, it does have the point of making entirely evident the link between the two sociologies and the contradictory modern experience they articulate. The connection between the modern experience of the domination of the system and the social world portrayed by the sociology of social system is obvious. This is the world of "the inflexible system" in which "you're nothing more than a machine." The social world of modern social-system sociology is precisely the machine, the bureaucracy, the system; the vast, impersonal, impenetrable, alien machine of modern social experience, the alienated dimension of which its abstract, remote, lifeless, and impenetrable web of overpoweringly obscurantist and self-spawning conceptual systems thus articulates. The connection is equally obvious between, on the one hand, that other part of the modern experience which speaks to us of our own hopes and longings, our own purposes, our own agency, our own creativity; and, on the other, the sociology of social action, which rests upon and articulates precisely the central ideas and aspirations of human agency, human control, the self and socially creative capacities and potential of human beings. From this strand in the history of social thought comes this:

> *History* does nothing, it "possesses *no* immense wealth," it "wages *no* battles." It is *man*, real living *man*, that does all that, that possesses and fights.[10]

Thus spoke Marx, and it would be hard to find a more concise and more apposite evocation of the sociology, the experience, and the link between the two.

This would seem to bring us to the point where, for the purposes of this chapter, the focus should now be solely on the sociology of social action, with its grounding in the notion of human agency, to the exclusion of any further discussion of the sociology of social system, with its apparent irrelevance to that notion. However, this is far from being the case. For the situation is not simply that each sociology articulates one dimension of modern social experience, one of concern here, the other not. Rather, it is that the opposition and tension between them parallels the opposition and tension between the two kinds of experience. In other words, the contradiction between the two sociologies articulates the contradiction which is at the heart of the dominant modern experience and which permeates our lives as a constant existential tension of our time and place. From this emerges the analytic point that, on the basis of the experience they articulate, the two sociologies propose alternative versions of the relationship between social action and social system; which relationship, in whatever version, is central to any consideration of the concept of social action. And this, in turn, leads to a yet more basic point in the form of a further and fundamental relation between the two sociologies, this time not of opposition, though it is the basis for their opposition. This is best approached by looking first at their moral foundations, which, despite the apparent 'scientific objectivity' and 'value neutrality' of their languages, they do have; and which they must have, if the earlier claim about the fundamentally moral nature of the sociological enterprise is correct. In the process, we shall discover first that the moral foundations of the two sociologies are decisive for their languages and methods, as has always been the case throughout the history of sociology. We shall find, second, that they are the *same* moral foundations—the same traditions of moral concern and aspiration which have been decisive for and definitive of the entire sociological tradition from its very beginnings. And all this will lead to the conclusion that the two sociologies are both responses to the single most central problematic in this history of sociological analysis; that the concept of social action is the most basic and complete articulation of this problematic, which thus gives it a paradoxical centrality to both sociologies; and therefore that the real significance of each and the real relation between them is predicated upon this centrality.

Turning, then, to the moral foundations of the two sociologies, it is essential to make an initial general point. All sociological work, like all work of thought and imagination, is founded upon and derives its meaning from views of human nature, whether they are stated explicitly or remain implicit (and often unrecognized even by those whose work rests upon them). And whatever the status claimed for them where they are explicitly advanced—whether empirical, scientific, and universal or conjectural, hypothetical, and heuristic—their real nature and significance is ethical. They are ethical fictions, but fictions with point and consequence. For, whether in practice or analysis, they are acted upon *as if true,* and are therefore true in their consequences. That is, in that people act upon them, they create the worlds implied by and *confirmatory of* them. Again, this applies to both practice and theory, social action and social analysis; to the practical worlds created by social actors and the conceptual worlds produced by social analysts. In practice, of course, the point is rather more problematic. In the practical world, anyone who acts on the basis of a view of human nature which is at odds with that of the dominant culture and power structure is, to say the least, likely to have a hard time and to face immense obstacles in trying to create the world consonant with that view. And, in the world of analysis, given the relation between theory and practice whereby the former is inescapably embedded in and reflective of the latter, views of human nature and the analytic schema consequent upon them cannot simply be plucked from a conceptual void. They are inextricably tied to and articulations of the views available in the practical world. But neither of these qualifications undermines the general point. In fact, they underline it. For dominant cultures and power structures are as much the consequence of people acting on the basis of particular views of human nature as are attempts to create different social worlds and forms of social organization on the basis of alternative views of human nature. And the clash, in terms of actual conflict, between such alternatives and the social and political action consequent upon them has been productive of the history of the last three centuries or so, the history created by "*man,* real living *man,*" and thus generative of the social and political analysis of the last three centuries or so, which is but "real living *man*" reflecting on the history he has made in order to make more.

Views of human nature, then, are not merely ethical fictions, but ethical *prescriptions* with immense consequences for practice in the social world and for the theory which articulates that practice and thereby generates further practice. Moreover, they are prescriptions of a particular kind. Views of human nature are essentially views of human capacity and potential: human *being.* In the context of social practice and analysis, they thus lead to a view of the relationship between human being and social being, and thence to a view of the latter. In terms more straightforwardly related to sociological usage, the progression is from a view of man to a view of the relationship between man and society, and thence to a view of the nature of society. Further, from the point of departure in the initial view of man, the progression is entirely logical and, as such, retains at all levels its essential character as ethical prescription. This is not to deny the elements of analytic conceptualization, empirical proposition, and theoretical explanation involved in all inquiry into forms of the relationship between man and society, and into the nature and types of social organization. But it is to insist that these are grounded in and derive their meaning from the context of ethical prescription consequent upon the views of human nature on which they are necessarily founded. Put differently, all forms of thought and practice have to start somewhere, and so must rest on assumptions about the nature of their subject matter or projects, the "truth" or "self-evidence" of which has to be taken for granted if they are to proceed at all; in a word, upon axioms which cannot be questioned if the thought or practice based upon them is not to lose all viability. As we have seen, social thought and practice are inescapably rooted in the intrinsically moral character of social life. Hence the moral character of their basic axioms, the ethical prescription inherent in the necessarily taken-for-granted assumptions from which they proceed, and, therefore, in all that follows from those assumptions. In sum, views of the nature of man, of the relationship between man and society, and thus of the nature of society constitute "doctrines"[11] which define universes of meaning for specific sociological concepts, propositions, and theories. Further, doctrines penetrate and shape sociology at both the substantive and metatheoretical levels of analysis. For they entail not only theories of society, but, in consequence, characteristic approaches to the analysis of society; that is, concomitant sets of propositions about the language and method of sociology itself.

As we shall now see. For we have reached the point of being able to establish in outline the moral character of the two sociologies in terms of their views of human nature and the progression following from those views; that is, their basic character as doctrines. Taking the sociology of social system first, it is clearly a pessismistic view of man which leads to the conception of social actors as totally manipulable creatures, in which can be and are implanted the values and behavioral stimuli necessary for the stability both of their own personalities and the social system. But the pessimism is even more profound than this, for it is not merely that social actors have to be thus socialized because they could otherwise create nothing themselves. Rather, it is that they are viewed as beings who, if left to their own devices, can and will create self- and socially destructive anarchy and chaos. Just how, more precisely, their devices are viewed from this perspective will be examined later. The point now is that this has obvious consequences in terms of the logical progression from axiomatic views of human nature. Clearly, if man's nature is such that he can of his own volition create only self- and socially destructive anarchy and chaos, then for his own survival as an individual and social being and, above all, for the survival of society itself, he must be constrained into self- and socially constructive behavior by an entity external to and superordinate over him. Hence the view of the relationship between man and society as being one which people are at the receiving end of society, determined by it in terms of their subjective meanings and their consequent action and interaction, in terms of their very existence and nature as social beings, and their very sense of personal identity as human beings. Hence, too, in the same logical progression, the view of society as suprahuman, self-generating, and self-maintaing social system. In Durkheim's famous words, "society" is "a being *sui generis*,"[12] an idea which points straight to the metatheoretical conclusion of this entire progression.

Society as a reality sui generis is a *thing* like the *things* which comprise the subject matter of the natural sciences. It can therefore be studied as an object on a par with the objects of natural science, upon whose logic sociology can thus be modeled. So social systems can be conceptualized in terms of convenient analogies drawn from natural science, such as the organic or the cybernetic. Again, Durkheim has some famous words for it: "Consider social facts as things . . . as distinct from the consciously formed representations of them in the mind."[13] Here he makes the further point that human consciousness makes no difference to this process. For, though socialization and internalization may give it the appearance of constituting a distinctive subject matter requiring a distinctive mode of study, its source is still the external reality and constraint of society as "a being *sui generis*"; reality and constraint are all the more effectively reinforced precisely by the *appearance* of a distinctive human consciousness induced by socialization and internalization. The progression, beginning from the pessimistic view of human nature and entirely logical in its development through all levels of the doctrine known as the sociology of social system, is complete. Moreover, the pessimistic view of man makes clear the central problem, or moral and analytic concern, to which the doctrine is addressed: the problem of social order. How is society possible? How, given the basically self- and socially destructive nature of human beings, can social order exist at all?

Here we touch upon one of sociology's few orthodoxies, as witness the teeming multitude of texts at all levels on the nature and history of the discipline which take it as their ironically unproblematic point of departure. They testify to the virtually universal acceptance of the thesis that the problem of order is *the* central problem of sociology. There are, however, two versions of this thesis, one the logical version which proposes that the question of order is logically prior to all other questions on the grounds that we must first delineate a social *order* before we can say anything else about it. This version need not detain us long. For, if we are not to confuse the conceptual and the substantive levels of analysis, this can mean nothing more startling than that we impose a conceptual order on empirical data. We systematize, in sociological as in all other thought, including the everyday. On this level, order is axiomatic rather than problematic. Like the logically and functionally equivalent proposition "man is social," it is a conceptual precondition for the very existence of sociology. In its logical formulation, then, the problem of order is unexceptionable, but banal; and it is not a problem. The real problem on this level is not the *conceptual* existence of order, but the *kind* of conceptual order we employ in analysis. Which, of course, is one of the points at issue between the two sociologies.

Clearly, the "problem of order" thesis could not have retained its grip on sociological thought on such flimsy grounds as these. For a real explanation of its persistence, we must turn to the other version of it, which is infinitely more substantial and persuasive. Nisbet has provided a concise summary:

> The fundamental ideas of European sociology are best understood as responses to the problem of order created at the beginning of the nineteenth century by the collapse of the old regime under the blows of industrialism and revolutionary democracy.[14]

This is, as I shall argue shortly, only part of the history of the ideas in question. Nevertheless, there can be no doubt that there was a nineteenth-century conservative reaction centered on the problem of order and expressed, in the work of Bonald, de Maistre, Comte, Burke, Coleridge, Southey, and a host of others, with the urgency of people who actually lived through those cataclysmic times with such an immediacy as to feel that problem as a personal experience and articulate it as a representative experience. It was a reaction against the Enlightenment for its over optimistic celebration of human reason as the means and the measure of human progress, and for its wholesale critique of traditional institutions and values, which those who were part of the reaction saw as the necessary cement of society. It was a reaction against the French Revolution for its actual destruction of those institutions and values, for its allegedly anarchic belief in total equality, and for its work as the progenitor of the social disorganization, chaos, and tyranny which conservative commentators thought were about to spread from France across the whole of European civilization. And, above all, it was a reaction against the new industrialism for its destruction of the foundations of traditional communal bonds, its consequent production of a totally fragmented, disjointed, and anomic social and moral world, and for the sheer human misery on a visible, massive scale which everywhere followed in its wake. Thus, in opposition to what was seen as the subversive rationalism of the Enlightenment, the traumatic disorder of the French Revolution, and the amoral egoism of the Industrial Revolution, the conservative reaction sought the restoration of a supra-individual social and moral hegemony. In so doing, it created a language of moral authority—the group, the sacred, and, above all, the organic community—which at once defined the solution to the problem of order and, on the argument that this is *the* central sociological problem, the sociological perspective. There can be no doubting the impact of the conservative reaction on the development of sociology, or the significance for the discipline of the concern with the problem of social order. Hence the obvious link—the doctrinal link—between the modern social-system perspective and its origins in the classic tradition.

However, if the problem of order is *the* central problem of sociology, then the social-system perspective must be *the* sociological perspective. Yet, as we have seen, it is not. It now becomes necessary, therefore, to establish the distinctive moral character of the sociology of social action, again in terms of its view of human nature and the progression following from that view. So, just as the view of man at the root of the sociology of social system is a pessimistic one, the view of man at the root of the sociology of social action is an optimistic one. Man is taken to be an autonomous human agent, self- and socially creative, the active and only source of the production and development both of his own personality and of society. Far from being one of external constraint, therefore, the relationship between man and society is one of human control, in which society is the derivative of human agency; of the human capacity for the construction of meaning and action upon that meaning. Hence, by the same token and in the same logical progression, the view of society not as a supra-human, self-generating, and self-maintaining entity but as a humanly accomplished social world; a social system conceptualized as the emergent product of the social action and interaction of its members. This does not mean that this perspective denies the manifest existence of constraint. Rather, it locates constraint not in an entity external to and superordinate over man but, quite simply, in the actions of other actors; that is, in humanly constructed structures of power and domination. To paraphrase Sartre, constraint is other people.

As in the social-system perspective, so in the social-action perspective: the entire progression leads to a metatheoretical conclusion. Meaning and action are again the decisive terms. In that the social system is viewed as the emergent product of the social action and interaction consequent upon subjective meaning, the understanding of this meaning and its relation to action is, in contrast to its neglect by the social-system perspective, of vital heuristic importance in the social-action perspective. The human capacity for the construction of meaning is, therefore, held to constitute the crucial difference between the conceptualizing subject matter of sociology and the nonconceptualizing subject matter of natural science. Thus society is not a "thing," a "being sui generis," an object on a par with those of natural science. It is a distinctive kind of entity, its nature residing in its generation by social action and interaction on the basis of humanly constructed meaning. Hence the methodological rejection of the social-system use of natural-scientific models of systems, and the distinctive social-action approach to the nature of social inquiry: the "interpretive," *verstehende* or "understanding" mode of sociological analysis. The progression, beginning from the optimistic view of human nature and entirely logical in its development through all levels of the doctrine known as the sociology of social action, is once again complete.

Once again, too, the nature of the central problem, or moral and analytic concern, to which the doctrine is addressed is evident from its optimistic view of human nature. It resides in the idea of human control over the system, rather than social-system control over its human members. However, human control is precisely a *problem*, as witness its centrality to modern social experience; but not only to that experience. For the problem of human control is also a legacy of the same revolutionary period in history and ideas as the nineteenth-century conservative reaction, but a legacy of the movement of social, political, and moral thought to which the reaction was implacably opposed. That movement was the Enlightenment.

Just as historians of sociology have taken the reaction to be the seedbed of the discipline, so they have in consequence accepted its hostile characterization of the Enlightenment. In the main, they have continued to characterize it as shallow, frivolous, complacent, and, above all, blindly optimistic in its naive faith in mechanical reason, narrow empiricism, and the inevitable, unproblematic progress of humankind toward human perfectability.[15] For example, a recent and weighty discourse on sociological theory returns repeatedly and with breathtaking eccentricity, not to mention hysterical pessimism, to its obsessive and uninformed assault on "the hysterical optimism of the Enlightenment," in the course of which we are told that its "political theorists had imagined that what was happening in the world was clearly for the good in the best of all possible worlds," and informed of "the processes of exploitation, dehumanisation and tyranny which the Enlightenment had bequeathed to us."[16] Alas, poor Voltaire; he knew you ill. What is even more breathtaking, and depressingly significant as a measure of sociological conceptions of the Enlightenment, is that this absurdity can pass unremarked among the historians and theorists of sociology. Very occasionally, some of them will note in passing that the movement had something to do with human agency, human creativity, human release. But these are invariably mere asides in sociological commentaries which, on the whole and with only a modicum of greater erudition, essentially reproduce the popular caricature of it drawn by vulgarizing almanacs with mythmaking titles like the *Age of Reason* and the *Idea of Progress*.

This is not to deny that the caricature is built upon a germ of truth; all caricatures are. To an extent, the *philosophes* were optimistic and confident, they did pin their hopes on the human potential for progress, and they did place their bets on the revelatory power of science. But the hopes were never blind and the bets were always hedged. For they were also acutely aware of the likely limits of their science; of the probable scorn of future generations; of the suffering, barbarity, and inhumanity in the new world they saw rising around them; of the deep shadows the release of human potential might equally well cast; of the agonizing fluctuations between hope and despair, intellectual credence and emotional doubt. So, alongside the confidence there was also caution, misgiving, skepticism, and frequent descent into utter hopelessness. All these feelings vie with one another in times of epochal change and, in this, the *philosophes* were no different from anyone else who has ever lived through such times. They, too, could see the dark, as well as the light, at the end of the tunnel. In the end, they remained hopeful. But, because they were realists surrounded by manifest suffering and oppression, they were never sanguine.

All this has emerged from decades of serious scholarship by dedicated students of the Enlightenment, in light of which the conventional sociological portrayal is inexcusable nonsense, and the influence of that portrayal on accounts of the history and nature of sociology disastrous.[17] The fact is that the Enlightenment had a positive impact on the development of the discipline of a kind and a centrality hitherto unrecognized. And, although his own view of that impact is somewhat one-sided, Nisbet again provides the clue:

> The dominant objectives of the whole age . . . were those of release: release of the individual from ancient social ties and of the mind from fettering traditions.[18]

Whilst for Cassirer, the Enlightenment "joined, to a degree scarcely ever achieved before, the critical with the productive function and converted the one directly into the other."[19] The end, human liberation; the means, ceaseless *practical* criticism of a society and its institutions hitherto held to be inviolable because divinely ordained; the tools, a synthesis of rationalism and empiricism in a scientific method, the application of which allowed nothing to remain inviolable. Such criticism is indeed action in such a society—explosive action. Divinely ordered, universal situations became man-made, historical situations. Social relationships, institutions, and systems became the subject and object of human action. In a word, the Enlightenment postulated the human, as opposed to a divine, construction of the ideal. By uniting "the critical with the productive function," it fashioned the logical gap between the "is" and the "ought" into a weapon of social criticism, transforming it into the gap between the actual and the ideal, in which the attainment of the ideal entailed the creative imposition upon the actual of a human, as opposed to a supra-human, meaning.

Herein lies the formulation of both the problem and its solution. History, personality, society, community are essentially human accomplishments. Yet their human construction, as manifest and inalienable actualizations of human meanings, possibilities, and aspirations, remains an ideal because the actual is a situation in which they have escaped from human control into the reifications of divine authority, supra-human social systems, seemingly autonomous machines. The problem of control, then, is the problem of how human beings can *regain* control over what are, at root, their own social products; how they can "struggle against the machine" to create a world in which "to be just human." The solution lies in the unceasing attempt to exert human control through social action over existing institutions, relationships, situations, and systems in such a way as to bring them into line with human constructions of their ideal meanings. We arrive again at the decisive terms of meaning and action—which makes the positive impact of the Enlightenment on the development and nature of sociological thought entirely clear. It has bequeathed to sociology its second, distinct, and opposed central problem: the problem of control. By the same token, it has given birth to a second, distinct, and opposed sociology as, essentially, the doctrine constituting the answer to the problem: the sociology of social action. Once again, the link—the doctrinal link—between the modern social-action perspective and its origins in the classical tradition is obvious.

Two problems, two sociologies: thus far, the opposition between them still seems total and irreducible.[20] However, the next stage of the argument takes us behind their opposition to the single, fundamental problematic to which they are but contrary responses. This involves another and longer journey back in time to establish the ancestry of the views of human nature upon which they are based. For the crucial point now about these views is that they were not even conceivable in medieval society, and only became so by virtue of its demise.

In a brief account, compression is bound to attribute to medieval society more coherence and consistency as an entity than it really had, and to make the long, drawn-out, and piecemeal process of its disintegration appear more sudden and dramatic than it really was. Nevertheless, slow, halting, and fragmented though it may have been, the collapse of medievalism constituted a complete historical break between one world and another, with which it is no exaggeration to say that all forms of Western thought have been grappling ever since. The totality of the break is manifested in its cosmic inversion of the conception of the individual, the semantic history of which term has been traced, very aptly for present purposes, by Raymond Williams:

> "Individual" meant "inseparable," in medieval thinking. . . . Slowly, and with many ambiguities, since that time, we have learned to think of "the individual in his own right," where previously to describe an individual was to give an example of the group of which he was a member.[21]

This inseparability of the person from the group very much reflects the pattern of life in the typical medieval village.[22]

It was a closed and static community, penetrated by no new ideas, affected by no movement of any kind, subject to no geographical and social mobility whatsoever. Life was as regular and as predictable as the seasons. It was a small community, where everyone knew everyone else and where, therefore, everything everyone did was known to everyone else. It was a community in which all life from birth to death was lived in public, and there was thus no possibility even of conceiving of the distinction between the public and the private dimensions of life, which is so much part of the modern conception of the individual. Further, it was also an undifferentiated community, in which everyone depended upon the one group for the fulfillment of all their needs. In other words, there was no division of labor. And this, of course, is crucial, because upon the division of labor depends the differentiation of biography and experience productive of the sense of difference from others which is at the heart of the modern conception of the individual. Without it, experience, biography, and personal life remain undifferentiated from one person to another. Without it, therefore, there can be no conception of "the individual in his own right."

In short, medieval man lived within a fixed, static, and immutable world, unquestioningly accepting it and his place in it as preordained and aware of himself only as part of his group. Moreover, the world was thus given because it was divinely authored. The medieval conception of man was of a being who was but one manifestation of divine nature and will, inseparable and indivisible from it. Clearly, when the only world view available to the closed, static, undifferentiated community of the medieval village was that the essence of and the agency behind all things lay in divine creativity and authority alone, there was no room at all for any conception of a distinctive human nature and agency. Hence the impossibility of views of human nature in medieval society. And if there was ever any danger of such views emerging, it was easily countered by the feudal power of church and state in combination.

Except, of course, that it was not so easily countered; for medievalism had, in the end, to face new, growing, and fundamental challenges to every aspect of its social, political, and cultural existence. One challenge was itself theological. Protestantism was emerging and, while retaining the belief in a divinely ordained world, it viewed man as a creature alone in vulnerable individuality before an inscrutable God, who had written no script for him but had simply predestined him to salvation or damnation without him knowing or being able to influence his fate, and had thus left him to his own isolated, individual devices in the world. How this creature should act in the world in accordance with a divine will utterly inaccessible to his knowledge was now a matter for his own agonized judgment as an individual being; a problem which could only be resolved by individual *human* choice. As divine will became opaque, so human will emerged—but individualistically, and so with equivalent opacity between each individual and his fellows. The new problem of the opacity of divine will on a cosmic scale parallels exactly the new problem of what John Heritage has called "the opacity of motives" in the human world.[23] And it is becoming a human world, for the disjuncture between divine will and human knowledge created by Protestantism was one of the tentative first steps toward a new conception of a distinctively human agency. Another such step was taken by the fifteenth-century Renaissance. Here, speaking of God's briefing to Adam, but in a tone far more confident in its acceptance of human agency than a terrified Protestantism, is Pico della Mirandola:

> You alone are bound by no limit, unless it be one prescribed by your own will, which I have given you. I have placed you at the center of the world . . . so that you may freely make and master yourself, and take on any form you choose for yourself.[24]

Though the language is still religious, the message is radical and modern. God was at the center of the medieval world; man is at the center of the post-medieval world. Man and his world are whatever he chooses them to be, including whatever limits he chooses to place upon them.

But the message was not merely the consequence of changes in belief. The new doctrines which challenged medieval orthodoxy were themselves articulations of the profound challenges to the very fabric of medieval society arising from new social experience, practices, and organization. It was facing the incipient growth of the division of labor, of towns, of markets, of communications, of a money economy, and of entrepreneur capitalism. In short, it was facing differentiation of all kinds, and thus the variegation of biography and experience which gives rise to the sense of difference from others central to the modern concept of individuality. Crucial here is the possibility of mobility, for it creates the possibility of thinking in terms of achieving roles and statuses, rather than having them immutably ascribed from birth to death. In consequence, people can begin to conceive of themselves as active agents in the shaping of their own lives; as having personal attributes, capacities, and identities distinct from any particular social role; and thus as occupying not only a public, social, and communal sphere, but also a separate personal, individual, and private sphere of life, experience, and activity. They can conceive of themselves as "individuals in their own right." Slow, uneven, and beset by *felt* ambiguity and tension though the whole process was, there was no stopping it as, over time, it reached inexorably into every corner of human existence. The modern individual had been born, crying perhaps, but lustily as befits the indisputable inheritor of the earth. It is small wonder that the new ideas, world views, and conceptions of man articulated by changes in religious doctrine and belief fell on such fertile soil; and small wonder, too, that these changes had a profoundly secular significance and consequence.

One such consequence being, eventually, the emergence of sociology as one part of the long, arduous, and immense task of making sense of the new world, which is simultaneously the task of *making* the new world since the sense is made in order to live in it. The first step in making such sense, given that man could no longer be viewed as merely an icon of divine nature, was obviously to establish a view of his own distinctively human nature. The predication of sociology on views of human nature, therefore, constitutes much more than an analytic point about the logically necessary basis of the discipline. It locates it as the historical phenomenon it is, as one manifestation of "our long and uneven growth from the medieval world."[25] As views of human nature were inconceivable before the disintegration of medieval society, so, by the same token, was sociology.[26] And as views of human nature are articulations of the ambiguous experience of the post-medieval world, so, by the same token, is sociology. Further, we are now in a position to see the real essence of views of human nature, the deepest meaning of their character and decisive role in sociological analysis; and, from this, the single, fundamental problematic at the root of the entire sociological tradition.

The first problem in the task of establishing a view of a distinctively human nature was that its first term had already been defined by the very processes which had given rise to this possibility in the first place. In contrast to medieval man, modern man was individualistic man. But central to the experience of individualism—and, as we shall see, to its articulation—was its ambiguity. On the one hand, to recall Pico, man was now "at the center of the world," free to "make and master" himself and his world as he chose. Positively, he was autonomous human agent, the author and arbiter of his own world. On the other hand, he was abstracted from all communal bonds and group identifications; negatively, an individual alone, isolated not only from his god but also from his fellows. Medieval society had at least provided a communal foundation for the life, being and identity of its members, and this had been lost. So the task now was the creation of a new communal framework, socially and morally appropriate to the new individualism, which meant the search for an adequate basis for a genuinely moral individuality. But how this was to be established was itself problematic, again because of the ambiguous, positive, and negative experience of individualism. The modern individual is autonomous human agent with a world to win, but with only his own individualistic resources to draw upon.

From all this, the deepest meaning and significance for sociology of views of human nature is evident. They are, first and obviously, responses to the rise of individualism. Hence the abiding preoccupation of sociology with the historically consequential problem of the relationship between the individual and society. And hence its participation, manifestly central to sociological thought, in the search for the appropriate communal foundation for a genuinely moral individuality. But the rise of individualism on the ashes of a world conceived of as the creation and the legislation of divine agency is, more profoundly, the rise of human agency. So, second and fundamentally, views of human nature are responses to the rise of human agency. They *are* views of human agency; of the human capacity and potential upon which man and his world now depended. *In sum, the whole point of all of this is precisely human agency.* Views of human agency articulate the ambiguous experience of the modern individual as being, on the one hand, isolated and communally rootless and, on the other, as being necessarily self- and socially creative. Upon views of human agency and its impact depend views of the relationship between the individual and society. From views of human agency derive views of the appropriate communal foundation for a genuinely moral individuality. *Here, then, is the problematic around which the entire history of sociological analysis could be written: the problematic of human agency. And it is this which gives social action its status as the single most central concept in sociology; for it is the immediate and the definitive sociological translation and embodiment of the problematic of human agency.*

And it is this problematic which gives the concept of social action its paradoxical centrality to both of the two sociologies, and thus defines the real significance of each and the real relation between them. For the opposition between them now appears in a completely new light. In the first place, their concern with the relationship between the individual and society clearly points to their shared involvement in the search for the appropriate communal foundation for a genuinely moral individuality. Their different solutions to this problematic may still seem to indicate an opposition based on the affirmation by one and the denial by the other of autonomous human agency, and the consequent foundation of one on the concept of social action and of the other on its negation as a base concept. But this version of the opposition now emerges as superficial and misleading, and we can now go behind it to discover the second point of basic linkage between the two sociologies. For it follows from the predication of both upon views of human nature—that is, of human agency and its consequences—that *both not only entail but rest on views of man as autonomous human agent, and thus upon concepts of social action.* That this is true of the social-action perspective has already been made abundantly clear. But now it should be equally clear in the case of the social-system perspective. To recall the pessimistic social-system view of man, it is less one of an infinitely manipulable creature than one of a being who, *if left to his own unconstrained devices,* will create chaos and anarchy; which, of course, is as much a view of man as autonomous human agent as that to be found in the social-action perspective. The obvious difference is that man is viewed by one sociology as self- and socially creative, and by the other as self- and socially destructive. In other words, the real opposition between them lies not in the opposition between system and action; that is, between system and not-action on the one hand and between action and not-system on the other. Rather, it lies in their opposed responses to human agency and its consequences, and thus in their opposed conceptualizations of the source, characteristics, and outcome of social action, on the basis of which each has built its entire analytic, theoretical, and doctrinal apparatus. *In sum: sociological thought and analysis constitute one response to the ambiguous experience of the rise of human agency. Their history turns on the bifurcation of the ambiguity into two opposed concepts of social action, and thence into two opposed moral and analytic traditions, the sociologies of social system and social action. Their central problems of order and control constitute opposed formulations of human agency and its consequences, and their doctrinal answers to these problems opposed versions of the appropriate communal foundation for a genuinely moral individuality. At root, therefore, both sociologies are sociologies of social action.*

Thus the obvious step now is to look more closely at the two views of human agency and the two conceptions of social action at the root of the two sociologies. In the bifurcation into two sociological traditions of the ambiguous experience of the modern individual as being isolated and communally rootless but also an autonomous human agent, the social-system perspective has clearly latched onto the first and negative dimension, while the social-action perspective has fastened onto the second and positive dimension. In this respect, both traditions have their roots in relatively early post-medieval thought. We have seen how the behavior of medieval man had been characterized by ceaseless communality and visibility, universality, necessity, and therefore total predictability, whereas that of post-medieval man was individualistic, motivationally opaque, situational, contingent, and therefore totally unpredictable. One of two possible responses to this was to find some way of restoring the visibility, universality, necessity, and thus the predictability of human behavior. The other was to affirm, as the seedbed of human capacity and possibility, its new uncertainty, historical and cultural variability, contingency, and thus unpredictability. We shall see later the massive contradiction latent in the second response. For present purposes, however, the contrast points straight to two archetypal versions of the responses to the rise of human agency, and thus to the two archetypal conceptions of social action at the root of the two sociologies. These versions are those of, in the first case, Thomas Hobbes and, in the second, Jean-Jacques Rousseau.

Though mediated by the nineteenth-century conservative reaction, the problem of social order in sociology is classically defined in Hobbesian terms. And it is not surprising that this was the problem of prime and exclusive concern to Hobbes himself. Most immediately and urgently, he was producing his *Leviathan* in the aftermath of two civil wars in less than a decade. Beyond this, he was facing head-on the consequences, as he saw them, of the rise of modern individualism and the total break from all vestiges of medieval society. Once again, the link between experience and articulation, practice and theory is obvious. Hobbes was articulating the practical responses of his time to its historically contingent practical problems. In a situation of such total uncertainty, however, it is also unsurprising that the search for order should take the form of an attempt to restore to human behavior in general the universality, necessity, and predictability it had lost. What is undoubtedly a commentary on a society riven by civil war and thus by the apparently disastrous consequences of modern individualism, is also and crucially a social and political theory for which universality is claimed, and from which the commentary follows as a logically necessary sequence of propositions. This Hobbes constructed by means of the geometric mode of reasoning, with its ability to demonstrate complex and unlikely propositions from simple and apparently self-evident axioms, and Galileo's new laws of motion, especially the proposition that things moved naturally unless stopped artificially.

He begins by embracing completely the modern concept of the individual as the basis of his entire social and political theory; or at least, that part of it which emphasized the isolation of the modern individual from his fellows:

> A person is he, whose words or actions are considered, either as his own, or as representing the words and actions of another man. . . . When they are considered as his own, then he is called a *natural person:* and when they are considered as representing the words and actions of another, then he is a *feigned* or *artificial person.*[27]

In short, the "natural person" is the modern individual, abstracted from all social relationships, which are "artificial"—that is, the products of his artifice. At this point the laws of motion take over, for Hobbes now sets out to establish the nature of man as one form of body in motion, and the logical consequences of human motion for the social world. Thus man is a machine, conforming to the laws of motion. And the primary motions which drive the machine are the primary passions: the desire for power and the fear of death. Clearly, men moved by such passions are inherently competitive, all the more so because there is a natural scarcity of resources, particularly and by definition of power. They are also utterly egoistic. Individuals being the only "natural" entities, and individual passions being the basic motions, there is no moral order extrinsic to individual desire and judgments of desire. Thus egoistic passions are served by egoistic reason or "arithmetic reckoning," whereby individuals calculate the balance of their actions in terms of their consequences for the achievement of desires and the avoidance of fears. Further, nature has made them virtually equal in their physical and mental capacities to attain their ends. The whole adds up to a deadly competition, a ceaseless fight over scarce resources in which men are naturally enemies whose primary purpose, in the pursuit of their own ends, is constantly to defeat each other. Hence the famous Hobbesian "war of every one against every one," in which "force, and fraud . . . are the two cardinal virtues," and in which "there is . . . continual fear, and danger of violent death; and the life of man, solitary, poor, nasty, brutish and short."[28] In sum, Hobbes's "natural person" is amoral and utterly self-seeking. It is an unrelievedly bleak view of the human condition, thought not incomprehensible in a time of civil war (and, underlining the point about the relevance of past social thought to present concerns, not incomprehensible as a possible view of the world today).

Moreover, it poses the problem of order very sharply, for there seems no way in which such people can possibly secure either their own survival or that of society. On the face of it, Hobbes's solution seems somewhat surprising, since it requires the voluntary agreement of his egoistic, power-seeking individuals to surrender themselves and their powers totally to the absolute power of a supreme political sovereign. Moreover, the agreement is not just contractually binding, but is backed by sovereign force, since contracts without such backing are mere words. Though such a surrender would seem to be totally alien to the Hobbesian individual, it is utterly logical and necessary. In the most obvious sense, it is necessary because the "war of every one against every one," with its "continual fear, and danger of violent death," is no more in the interests of Hobbes's egoistic individuals than it would be in the interests of anyone. In short, the practical logic and necessity are those of sheer self-survival.

But, of course, they are not simply practical. They derive from Hobbes's own schema whereby he attempted precisely to impose logic and necessity on the new contingency of human behavior; and, in particular, from his formulation of the primary motions or passions, and of the calculative reason he made their servant. Thus, given the consequences of the desire for power, the fear of death becomes the overriding passion and the "reckoning" suggests the necessity, for survival, of the voluntary submission of all to the will of one. Leviathan remains the product of "arithmetic reckoning"—and not merely in its genesis, but in its characteristics. It is the "artificial person" created by and in the image of the "natural person." Thus it is a machine moved by the same primary motions or passions: the fear of social death and the desire for total power. And it must "reckon" in terms of expediency or calculatively on the basis of the "cardinal virtues" of "force, and fraud." In all these respects, society for Hobbes is both the social embodiment of the individual and the product of human agency; thus far, an aggregate of its members, the sum of its parts.

However, it does not stop there. Having surrendered his powers so completely to Leviathan, the individual is now subjugated to a force which is no longer his own possession but stands over and against him. In other words, force and the society which rests upon it have become, together, an emergent social product; that is, an entity no longer reducible to its individual elements, no longer merely an aggregate of those elements, and thus no longer reducible to the social contract from which it emerged. Paradoxically, what is merely the sum of its parts in that it is made by man is also made by man into more than the sum of its parts. To recall Pico, man has indeed "bound" himself by a "limit prescribed by his own will." In a later terminology, he has externalized and reified himself, to become dominated and controlled by what he originally created in his own image. In the even later terminology central to this chapter, he has engineered his own domination by a social system which, once generated, becomes self-generating, self-maintaining, supra-human, and superordinate. By virtue of its self- and socially destructive consequences, the contingency of his social action has led to the necessity of an externally constraining system.

Hobbes has embraced completely the modern individual as the basis of his social and political theory only to arrive at a conclusion which totally negates him. It is a prime example of the sociological course taken by the concept of social action, whereby it generates its own negation by culminating in the concept of a dominating and constraining social system; or rather, of one particular concept of social action. For the necessity of an externally constraining social system obviously derives from a particular view of human agency and a particular conception of social action. In other words, the view and the conception at the root of the sociology of social system should now be entirely clear. Hobbesian man is totally *instrumental* in calculation and action, a term which refers to his egoistic pursuit of his egoistic desires by means of an instrumental "reckoning" or reason and the use of instrumental "force, and fraud." It is this basic instrumentality of social action which creates the absolute need for an equally instrumental supra-human social system, the artificial means of stopping man's self- and socially destructive motions; which terminological reminder makes the point that this iron necessity resides in the iron logic of the Hobbesian schema, built upon the instrumental view of human agency and social action and, once that basic premise is accepted, spelling out its consequences in unassailable logical sequence. In sum:

> Hobbes's analysis thus stands as archetypal of the *instrumental* conception of *individualistic* social action and of the implications it entails for a social system which is *external* and *constraining* upon its individual members.[29]

And archetypal, too, of the doctrinal and self-fulfilling nature of such analysis; and, when acted upon, of such action. For it perceives instrumentality and its consequences by employing the instrumental mode of reasoning it attributes to its instrumental beings in its most instrumentally efficient form; the scientific mode of "reckoning" which, as Weber pointed out, constitutes the supreme manifestation of Western instrumental rationality. Thus it also constitutes a major component of the modern Western world view and, as such, is both a basis of action and the modern source of the predictability once provided by the world view of medievalism. Both in analysis and action, therefore, it must always involve what Hobbes, in his search for certainty in the wake of civil war and the collapse of medieval society, wanted it to achieve: the imposition of necessity on the fundamental contingency of post-medieval human behavior.

We are now in a position to see the real significance in the history of sociology of the nineteenth-century conservative reaction. Given the grounding of the social-sysem perspective in the concept of instrumental social action and its consequence conceptualization of the social system as being externally constraining upon its members, the history of sociological analysis now becomes a series of mutations in the notion of external constraint. Externality becomes internalization, constraint becomes a moral imperative, and the individual becomes the social self. And the first step in this process of mutation was taken by the reaction, which is thus not the source of the modern social-system perspective but the mediation between it and its origins in Hobbesian thought. There is a double irony in this, for the reaction was totally opposed to the mechanistic and individualistic social theory represented archetypally by Hobbes. It viewed society as a natural organism, not as an artificial mechanism, and its affirmation of the former was essentially an appeal to the moral authority of the organic community of medieval society against the modern individual, whom it saw in instrumental Hobbesian terms and thus as utterly devoid of any capacity for creating moral and social cohesion, as witness the traumatic social disruptions which gave rise to it. It thus wished theoretically and morally to negate the modern individual altogether. But, of course, there could be no practical negation of modern man, no practical return to medieval man. So the appeal to medievalism is not seriously an appeal for such a return, but rather an attempt to transplant one of its central features into a society which had long since moved irreversibly away from it. This could only mean the advocacy of a supra-individual structure of social and moral constraint as the only possible basis for social order. Herein lies the double irony. First, the reaction is once again proposing an externally constraining order, but in a way that strengthens Hobbes's equivalent proposal in that it is advocating, however embryonically, the internalization of constraint so that it becomes acceptable to those subject to it; which, of course, is far more effective than Hobbes's crude reliance on force. Bitterly opposed as it was to the kind of social and political theory of which Hobbes was an archetypal representative, the reaction has set the scene for the full sociological elaboration of his schema. It has given legitimacy to Leviathan. The second and related irony is that its Hobbesian revisionism entails the reinsertion into Hobbes's thought of precisely those medieval conceptions of moral authority with which he had broken so decisively. And at the root of it all is still the same basic concept of instrumental action.

Nobody articulated the second version of human agency and social action more clearly and more consequentially for the development of the social-action perspective than Rousseau, to whom sociology therefore owes as great a debt as it does to Hobbes; though, while it commonly acknowledges the latter, it dismally fails to recognize the former, no doubt because of its shallow characterizations of the Enlightenment and its "problem of order" orthodoxy. Like Hobbes, Rousseau saw the society around him in instrumental terms, as being predominantly characterized by "wants, avidity, oppression, desires and pride,"[30] and thus egoistic competition. But for him, this was existing society and no more. Hobbes's mistake had been to translate a historically located, contingent form of society into a universal and necessary human and social condition. Moreover, as the former, society was essentially man-made. And Rousseau was in no doubt as to how man had made it into an arena of "wants, avidity, oppression, desires, and pride":

> The first man who, having enclosed a piece of ground, bethought himself of saying "This is mine," and found people simple enough to believe him, was the real founder of civil society. From how many crimes, wars, and murders, from how many horrors and misfortunes might not anyone have saved mankind, by pulling up the stakes, or filling up the ditch, and crying to his fellows: "Beware of listening to this impostor; you are undone if you once forget that the fruits of the earth belong to us all, and the earth itself to nobody."[31]

But nobody pulled up the stakes. Instead, they planted more, enclosing not only their ground, but themselves; once again, imprisoning themselves within limits "prescribed by their own will." The prison was alienating civil society, but it was men who created and refined its powers, men who alienated themselves. If "Man is born free; and everywhere he is in chains,"[32] they are chains of his own making.

But, for Rousseau, he *is* born free. The problem, therefore, is how he can recover his natural freedom; in a word, the problem of control. And, of course, the very idea that he has become alienated from himself implies a particular view of human capacity and potential. It is that which seizes on the positive dimension of the ambiguous experience of the modern individual: autonomous human agency as a creative force. As such, it is utterly opposed to the view of human capacity of Hobbes, whose "natural person" and necessary Leviathan were, for Rousseau, merely theoretical articulations of alienated practice; that is, of the distortion of man's true nature by existing society. Rousseau's contrary version of man's true nature resides in his location of two innate human characteristics, the first of which is self-love. This sounds like a prescription for Hobbesian egoistic self-interest and, indeed, has become so in existing society. For it has become distorted into selfishness, the basis of envious comparison and competition, and the perversion of authentic self-love. Self-love becomes both fully authentic and the basis for Rousseau's alternative to existing society in combination with the second innate characteristic, compassion:

> The enthusiasm of an overflowing heart identifies me with my fellow-creature. . . . I care for him because I care for myself . . . extend self-love to others and it is transformed into a virtue . . . the love of others, springing from self-love, is the source of human justice.[33]

And it is the source of a community of regard for the equal authenticity of others and the completion by community of self-authenticity.

Rousseau furnishes both a striking image of and a detailed blueprint for such a community. The image is of the open-air public festival:

> Let the spectators become an entertainment to themselves; make them actors themselves. This way each one sees and loves himself in the others, and all will be better united.[34]

In evoking the spirit of the festival, Rousseau is illustrating the way in which, for him, people will come to *realize* the essential and creative interdependence of self and community, through autonomous and spontaneous participation in communal activity. He is thus responding to postmedieval human behavior by affirming its contingency and unpredictability as the seedbed of human capacity and potential. And in so doing, he is postulating that particular relationship between consciousness and action whereby, in an ongoing process, we express our being in action through which we develop our consciousness of it and its possibilities. This is, in other words, a remarkable anticipation of the Marxian notion of *praxis*. It also captures the particular notion of reason employed by Rousseau which, though more intangible and less precise, is much broader and richer than Hobbes's instrumental reason. For it refers to a concept of whole man and the total integration of all his faculties. Reason is the consciousness embodied and developed in action, whereby the feeling, thinking, acting, judging faculties of man become unified in him as a whole, integrated, self- and other-regarding, self- and other-related being.

At the heart of Rousseau's view of human agency, therefore, it is a particular view of the relationship between consciousness and action which takes that relationship, and therefore human behavior, to be essentially and creatively contingent and open-ended in terms of its attributes and possibilities. And, of course, it has to be viewed thus, not as enclosed within prior conceptions of necessity of any kind, if the *autonomy* of human agency is to be taken seriously. However, also at the heart of Rousseau's view of human agency is an ideal project, set against the actual, and in terms of which he has already programmed the project by his specification of the innate characteristics of man and of the generic relation between authentic self and authentic community. And the project is further programmed by the elaboration of the communal framework which he held to be the prerequisite for it to generate the human possibilities he attributed to it. This, of course, is to be found in *The Social Contract*, his detailed blueprint for authentic community.

Rousseau's version of the social contract is riddled with contradictions and has been the subject of much interpretive controversy. However, in the present context, there is one point that is clear, unequivocal, and entirely consonant with the whole thrust of his social and political thought:

> The problem is to find a form of association . . . in which each, while uniting himself with all, may still obey himself alone, and remain as free as before. This is the fundamental problem of which the social contract provides the solution.[35]

In our terms, the problem is to find a new and appropriate communal foundation for a genuinely moral individuality in that version of it I have called the problem of control. And Rousseau's organizational solution is essentially a city-state, on the model of the Greek *polis* and his own Geneva, and small enough to enable genuine participation by all citizens in decision making public assemblies. Included in their decisions would be, at frequent, regular, and fixed intervals, the renewal or abrogation of the social contract by the autonomous citizens party to it. The society of the contract is thus an authentic community of freely participating individuals in which men have regained control over their own action, purposes, situations, relationships, and lives; in which the social world has become again the visible product of the human construction of meaning and action upon that meaning, a manifest and ceaseless actualization through *praxis* of human capacities, possibilities, and aspirations; in which history, personality, society, community have become again the unconcealed human accomplishments they really are; in which it has become possible "to be just human."

In the terms central to this chapter, Rousseau has embraced completely the modern individual as the producer of his own social roles, institutions, and systems, and thus provides the inspiration and the archetypal articulation of the social-action conceptualization of the social system as being the derivative of self- and socially creative autonomous human agency. And the particular view of human agency and particular conception of social action at the root of the sociology of social action should now be entirely clear. Rousseauian man is self- and socially creative because he is fundamentally *moral* in reason and action, a term which refers to his extension of self-love to others through a moral *praxis* whereby he creates, evolves, and fulfills both moral self and moral community in generic relation. It is the basic morality of social action which is the seedbed of a humanly constructed and controlled social system. In sum:

> It is this view of human agency I propose to call, in contrast to instrumental action, *moral action* . . . the expression of a common humanity and a *moral* expression, which can therefore only find fulfilment through social relationships . . . such a moral community is wholly *contingent* upon reciprocal social relations.[36]

Or, to adapt the summation of Hobbes to Rousseau, the latter's analysis thus stands as archetypal of the *moral* conception of *communal* social action and of the implications it entails for a social system which is the emergent product of its members. We thus have the second of the two opposed responses to human agency and conceptions of social action which are the source of the opposition between the two sociologies.

However, we also have a massive contradiction *within* the second response, of seminal significance for the history of sociological analysis insofar as that history turns on its treatment of the problematic of human agency. It is the contradiction between, on the one hand, the affirmation of the contingency and open-endedness of human behavior as the seedbed of human potential, and, on the other, the prior referral of human agency to the program entailed in the specification of innate human characteristics, the generic relation between authentic self and authentic community, and the detailed blueprint of *The Social Contract*. The contradiction resides in the way Rousseau tries to make the relationship between consciousness and action he proposes—essentially that of *praxis*—do two jobs: that is, affirm human contingency *and* express his version of the human ideal. And it derives from the way in which his mode of analysis formulates the actual, the ideal, and the opposition between them. Here we can now see the profound consequences of the bifurcation, into two opposing responses, two opposing concepts of social action, and two moral-analytic traditions of social thought, of the ambiguous experience of the rise of human agency and modern individualism. For it means that the ambiguity is dissolved as an ambiguity—which is crucial.

Clearly, if there is to be any possibility of the transformation of the actual into the ideal, the seeds of the latter must be present in the former. Otherwise, it is neither conceivable as a possibility nor available as an alternative course of action. Equally clearly, the transformation must be generated and realized by human agency. Quite simply, there is nothing else; which means that human agency has to be autonomous and therefore contingent, both of which attributes are, in any case, intrinsic to the postulated ideal of moral action and moral community. However, both the presence of the ideal in the actual and the autonomy and contingency of human agency reside, not in one kind of action (moral) as opposed to the other (instrumental), *but in the ambiguity itself*. For it is in the very nature of ambiguity that it contains alternative conceptions of the social world and manifests alternative versions of human agency. It thus exhibits the presence of the ideal in the actual, and the autonomy and contingency of human agency in that the latter can generate and realize alternative possible social worlds on the basis of one or other dimension of the ambiguous actuality it has already created. And if this means accepting the uncertainty and the unpredictability of the direction it might take, then so be it. For one thing, there is no alternative; again, it is in the very nature of human agency that it is its own unpredictable, contingent master. For another, the consequences of refusing to accept this by attempting to impose an alien necessity upon it are disastrous *in terms of the realization of the ideal to which such attempts are geared*. To sheer away the *ambiguity* in the human experience of the rise of human agency is to destroy any possibility of seeing the seeds of the (moral-action) ideal in the (instrumental-action) actual, and of human agency creating anything but its own alienation and thus its own negation. It is to destroy human agency altogether—its autonomy, its contingency, its social creativity, its moral capacities and possibilities. *If there is one genuine necessity inherent in human agency and social action, it is the necessity of ambiguity*. To dissolve it is to produce one-dimensional theories which postulate a one-dimensional man and society, and can thus locate no viable agency whatsoever in the real world, as opposed to that of their desperate mythmaking, for the transformation of the actual into the ideal; can hear no voices speaking in the actual of the possibilities of the ideal, like the voices from everyday life we heard earlier.[37] But the one-dimensionality is not that of man and society, as those voices testify. It is that of the theories which portray them thus; the theories which bifurcate multivisioned ambiguity into single-visioned negation, thus severing human agency from its possibilities.

This is what Rousseau has done. In the end, unable to tolerate the ambiguity his affirmation of human contingency creates, he seeks certainty as much as Hobbes, who set out to recover it in the first place. So he translates the ambiguity into a total separation between its positive and negative dimensions, and thence into a stark contradiction between the actual and the ideal whereby the actual, seen one-dimensionally as the necessary and all-pervasive consequence of instrumental action, has to be opposed by a morally conceived ideal, which must be made to appear equally necessary if the necessity of the actual is to be dislocated. Two iron necessities, implacably opposed; and no possibility whatsoever of transforming the one into the other. For human agency, the only possible source of the transformation, has been negated at every turn. Instrumental action negates itself by the necessary production of its own alienation in a dominating and utterly imprisoning system. And there is no way out, because the system is the product of human agency in the first place. Having forged their own chains, men have in the process rendered themselves incapable of breaking them. By the same token, instrumental action negates any possibility of the moral action which sustains and is sustained by a moral community of autonomous, freely participating, authentic human beings. An alternative prior necessity thus has to be found for the latter, in terms of innate human characteristics, and thus an alternative view of *universal* human nature. But this itself negates moral action, again because such action is postulated as being in essence autonomously creative and, therefore, historically contingent action. Between the actual and the ideal, then, there is an unbridgeable gulf. But it has been created by the fallacy of the single vision; by the mode of analysis which has translated ambiguity into intractable contradiction because, in the process, it has destroyed its fidelity to the autonomous human agency that constitutes the only possible bridge. Rousseau has embraced Hobbes, inevitably to be negated by him. And, once again, this is archetypal. For it introduces the final paradox in the paradoxical career of the *idée fixe* of social action.

Thus far, we have traced the opposition between the sociologies of social action and social system back to its root in two concepts of social action. The archetypal formulation of instrumental action and its consequences has been located in the work of Hobbes; that of moral action and its consequences in the work of Rousseau. On this basis, we have discovered the paradoxical centrality of the concept of social action to both sociologies and, in consequence, that they are both very profoundly sociologies of social action. It has now become obvious, however, that the two concepts of social action together constitute the split nucleus of Rousseau's archetypal single vision. Hence, now, the paradoxical centrality of both concepts of social action to the single vision of the social-action perspective. That is, *the contradiction and opposition between the two responses to human agency, the two concepts of social action, and thus the two sociologies of social action and social system is in fact a contradiction and an opposition at the heart of the sociology of social action itself.* The contradiction and the opposition between instrumental action and moral action, and the consequences of each, are deeply embedded *within* the social-action perspective:

> That is to say, in presenting a *unitary* version of the social action perspective . . . a fundamental divergence *within* that perspective is ignored: a divergence between two versions of social action which thereby suggests a far more complex relationship between social action and social system than has hitherto been conceived.[38]

Very complex indeed. For we can now establish in the first place a much more precise characterization of the search for the appropriate communal foundation for a genuinely moral individuality. Clearly, to oppose moral action and moral community to instrumental action and instrumental society is to define the exact terms of that search as a response to the rise of human agency and modern individualism.

This, in turn, is to provide the history of sociological analysis with a very close and a very sharp focus. For it now becomes the story of successive attempts to solve the fundamental dilemma of how to get from instrumental action and society to moral action and community. But it is a more complex story than it earlier appeared to be. It is no longer a simple matter of the predication of the solutions proffered on the doctrinal perspectives adopted, such that those who, like Hobbes, start from instrumental action to formulate the problem as that of order and thus the solution as that provided by the sociology of social system; or those who, like Rousseau, start from moral action to formulate the problem as that of control and thus the solution as that provided by the sociology of social action. For the stark opposition between the actual and the ideal, and so the recurring theme of the negation of human agency, permeate all the thought and work addressed to the dilemma, from whatever doctrinal perspective and with disruptive consequences for the once neat and straight line from central problem to moral and analytic solution.

Thus, for example, Marx's perspective is clearly that which begins from the concern with the problem of control, and he sets up the opposition between the actual and the ideal in a way which, though more elaborate, is in its essentials and to a remarkable degree of obvious coincidence, the same as Rousseau's. To find the seeds of the ideal in the actual, he then combines the concept of *praxis* with that of the proletariat as a universal class which, in pursuing its real interests as a particular class, is thus taken to be pursuing the general human interest in the transcendence of alienation. The proletariat is therefore the embryo of the moral community to which its ultimately revolutionary action in pursuit of its own interests will eventually lead. Marx's obvious attempt here to unite an instrumental and a moral *praxis* ends in failure because, for all his complex economic, social, and political analyses, he leaves entirely unexplicated the cruicial transformation whereby the instrumental action of the proletariat in pursuing its particular class interests will become the moral action definitive of the moral community it is supposed to bring into being. Marx's proletariat is built in the image of that most instrumental of all beings, *homo economicus*, whose *praxis* is solely and irremediably instrumental. There is no reason whatsoever for supposing that instrumental *praxis* will generate moral *praxis* and every reason for supposing, from the logic of Marx's analysis, that it can only generate further, endless, and increasingly instrumental action. For the analysis once again places the actual and the ideal in familiar and total contradiction, and compounds the resultant negation of human agency by formulating the process of transition in the utterly instrumental terms of the actual.[39]

Equally, if we were to explore Durkheim's work fully, we would find a manifest concern with the problem of order and a consequent reification of society as being external to and constraining upon its members. Within this framework, however, we would also find a manifest concern with the creation of a truly moral individualism, as the necessary basis for moral solidarity, out of the egoistic individualism in terms of which he saw the society around him. But once again, the dilemma of how to get from the latter to the former remains unresolved, and they remain in utter opposition. The unsuccessful and prolonged attempt to overcome this opposition is at the root of the frequently noted shifts of emphasis, tensions, and contradictions in Durkheim's work.[40] And the same argument could be applied to a vast number of social thinkers and analysts, from both the classical tradition and modern sociology. However, the final task of this chapter is to examine briefly how the basic dualism and opposition between instrumental action and society and moral action and community manifests itself in the work of the two figures in the history of sociological analysis conventionally regarded as the major theorists of social action: Max Weber and Talcott Parsons.

The central and definitive preoccupation of Weber's work is with the processes of rationalization which have led modern industrial society into the "iron cage"[41] of a totally bureaucratized order. And there can be few passages in the whole of sociology which speak more directly to our modern experience of the domination of the machine, the bureaucracy, the system than his famous assault on that order:

> This passion for bureaucracy is enough to drive one to despair. It is as if we were deliberately to become men who need order and nothing but order, who become nervous and cowardly if for one moment this order wavers, and helpless if they are torn away from their total incorporation in it. That the world should know no men but these; it is in such an evolution that we are already caught up, and the great question is therefore not how we can promote and hasten it, but what we can oppose to this machinery in order to keep a portion of mankind free from this parcelling-out of the soul, from this supreme mastery of the bureaucratic way of life.[42]

In other words, "the great question" is the problem of control: from which follows Weber's insistence on the social action perspective consequent upon that concern:

> In general, for sociology, concepts such as "state," "association," "feudalism" and the like designate certain categories of human interaction. Hence it is the task of

sociology to reduce these concepts to "understandable" action, that is, without exception, to the actions of participating individual men.[43]

And here, even in language as abstract, formal, apparently neutral as this, Weber captures both dimensions of the contradictory modern experience. There is the emphasis on "participating individual men," which is one part of our experience of ourselves. But there is also the other part, that of being dominated by such entities as the "state" and the "association." Moreover, he opts for one against the other. For to "reduce" concepts referring to such dominating entities to "understandable action" is to take the side of human agency against those entities. It is to assert "the actions of participating individual men" against "the supreme mastery of the bureaucratic way of life."

It is in this context that Weber proposes his basic definition of sociology and its subject matter:

> We shall speak of "action" insofar as the acting individual attaches a subjective meaning to his behavior—be it overt or covert, omission or acquiescence. Action is "social" insofar as its subjective meaning takes account of the behaviour of others and is thereby oriented in its course.[44]

Social action is thus crucially tied in with the concept of social relationship:

> The term "social relationship" will be used to denote the behaviour of a plurality of actors insofar as, in its meaningful content, the action of each takes account of that of others and is oriented in these terms.[45]

Obviously, it becomes necessary to define the types of social action which are also, because they turn on modes of orientation to others, types of social relationship. For Weber, there are four types of social action and orientation: *instrumentally rational* (action geared to "the attainment of the actor's own rationally pursued and calculated ends"); *value-rational* (action "determined by a conscious belief in the value for its own sake of some ethical, aesthetic, religious or other form of behaviour, independently of its prospects of success"); *affectual* ("determined by the actor's specific affects and feeling states"); and *traditional* ("determined by ingrained habituation").[46]

All typologies are, of course, heuristic devices involving the conceptual and artificial abstraction of particular elements from given phenomena, which will concretely exhibit combinations of all the elements thus made to appear separate and unidimensional. Thus, as Weber acknowledges both directly and by his reference to them as ideal or pure types, actual social action and relationships will manifest in various combinations elements of all his types of action and orientation. It would seem to follow that they should be analyzed in precisely this way; that is, for the various ways in which they manifest such combinations. This, however, is not the course Weber takes. For it now emerges that his prime interest is in using his types of action to establish the nature of different types of social order. And this he makes possible by his conflation of the related but distinct concepts of meaning and action into modes of orientation to others. For obviously, if action is "oriented in its course" by "the behavior of others," the modes of "taking account of" that behavior become modes of social cohesion and consensus. But this is also to slip once again into the fallacy of the single vision. To have analyzed social action and relationships for the ways in which they manifested various combinations of all the types of action would have been to acknowledge and retain the ambiguity inherent in and essential to human agency. To translate types of action into types of social order is to translate their heuristic into a literal one-dimensionality. It is also to transform social actors and their subjective meanings, which were Weber's starting point, into mere reflexes of the social order. Instrumentally rational social action becomes instrumentally rational social system, the utterly dominating and constraining instrumental system of modern Western capitalism, which thus provides the subjective meaning and consequent action of its members for them. Hence Weber's "men who need order and nothing but order," an assumption he can make without referring to their own versions of their own meanings, purposes, and aspirations because these are provided by the system. Hence, too, Weber's reproduction of the familiar sociological distinction between industrial and preindustrial society, which clearly resides in what has now become the distinction between instrumentally rational and traditional social order.

Weber has begun with a putative sociology of social action, which he never develops beyond a few initial concepts because his particular use of those concepts leads him straight to a sociology of social system. There are a number of reasons for this. First, his thought is not unaffected by a concern with the problem of order, which is at odds with his concern with the problem of control. Politically, he saw the world in terms of a competition between power states and, being a German nationalist, he was intensely concerned with the unity and strength of the German state, which he regarded as having been undermined by the inadequacy of the political structure and leadership of Wilhelmine Germany. Indeed, this was another reason for his alarm at the spread of bureaucracy, since he took the overbureaucratization of the German political structure to be one cause of its weakness. From this concern, too, stems that part of his work which emphasizes and extensively explores the concept of legitimate authority. Second, he brought to sociology a scientific aspiration, which led him to give analytic primacy to the ideal type of instrumentally rational action. For such action was crucially concerned with the appropriate or the scientifically accurate relationship between means and ends and, as such, was the most easily understandable and explicable in the rigorous and exact terms scientific analysis demanded. Thus it became the yardstick for the analysis of actual courses of action, which were viewed in terms of their approximation to or deviation from it. The problem with this, of course, is that, while it may establish the existence and extent of such deviations, it provides no basis for their explanation.

However, the vital point underlying this is that, for Weber, action in modern Western capitalism would not in fact deviate significantly from the ideal type. For this is the society of the "supreme mastery of the bureaucratic way of life." Once again, the analytic prescription articulates the moral vision. And once again, we come to the gulf between the instrumental actual and the moral ideal, which constitutes the third and most basic reason for Weber's shift from a social-action to a social-system perspective. For him, too, the moral ideal lies in the exertion of human agency:

> Every single important activity and ultimately life as a whole, if it is not to be permitted to run on as an event in nature but is instead to be consciously guided, is a series of ultimate decisions through which the soul . . . chooses its own fate, i.e., the meaning of its activity and existence.[47]

But for him, too, human agency was utterly negated by the instrumental rationality and action dominant in modern society, which has transformed us into "little cogs in the machine."[48] Given this view of its total negation, it is hardly surprising that we find yet another instance of a stark and total distinction between the actual and the ideal, and the consequent analysis of the former in social-system terms. However, we also find another instance of this distinction as the product of the mode of analysis employed, in this case more than in any other, of Weber's particular conception and characterization of human agency and, therefore, the moral ideal. This becomes clear from his types of value-rational and affectual action; the link between them, and the way he uses them in analysis.

The whole tone of his definition of value-rational action, with its emphasis on the "conscious belief in the value for its own sake . . . independently of its prospects for success," indicates that its real significance lies, not in the value itself, but in its emotional basis. Hence the crucial link between it and affectual action, for the former is clearly rooted in "the actor's specific feeling states" which are definitive of the latter. It may be "distinguished from the affectual type by its clearly self-conscious formulation of the ultimate values governing the action and the consistently planned orientation of its detailed course to these values," but, as a manifestation of human agency, the vital point remains that "the two types have a common element, namely that the meaning of the action does not lie in the achievement of a result ulterior to it, but in carrying out the specific type of action for its own sake."[49] Indeed, as we shall see, the distinction Weber makes between the two lays the basis for the negation of human agency. For the moment, however, the point is that the fundamental meaning of the action lies in the emotional commitment to it. This becomes very clear from Weber's linked use of the two concepts. For they are at the root of his definition of charismatic authority and charismatic community.[50] Charismatic authority rests upon the recognition by the followers of a charismatic leader of his individual possession of extraordinary qualities, by virtue of which he commands their personal devotion and exemplifies the single-minded emotional commitment of the charismatic community to its pursuit of its chosen values, regardless of consequences. A movement based solely on emotional commitment, intense personal dedication, and constant exemplary display of its exclusive values, its extraordinary faith and its unshakable solidarity inevitably rejects all rules, possesses no hierarchy or formal organization, and manages its affairs in a totally ad hoc manner. The crucial consequence of this is that charismatic authority is completely antithetical to bureaucratic and traditional authority, both of which are essentially rule-governed and formally structured. Thus it is a revolutionary force: "In traditionalist periods, charisma is *the* great revolutionary force."[51] In Weber's sociology, charismatic movements are his great agency of historical and social change, sudden, overwhelming upsurges of human agency which, when successful and for as long as they last, are completely disruptive of existing, rule-embedded social orders.

Thus far, for Weber, human agency clearly has two fundamental characteristics. The first is its ineluctable individualism. The charismatic movement is defined in terms of personal devotion to an individual leader regarded as extraordinary. What is constantly at issue in the movement is individual proof, by the leader of his extraordinary individual qualities through exemplary act and revelation, and by the disciple of his total and exclusive dedication and worthiness, again through exemplary manifestation. The second characteristic of human agency, for Weber, is its equation with pure feeling. This is clearly the *sine qua non* of charismatic authority, which rejects all rules save the rule of intense, single-minded emotional commitment whereby separation from the world of mundane rationality is preserved, and which therefore demands the "sacrifice of the intellect."[52] The appeal is directly to the deepest emotional roots of individual human being. And this is clearly the source of Weber's moral ideal. It is a theme which pervades all his thought and work: his reflections on politics and science, his substantive analyses, his methodological essays. For him, "the soul chooses its own fate." For him, "nothing is worthy of man as man unless he can pursue it with passionate devotion."[53] For him, "the highest ideals, which move us most forcefully, are always formed only in the struggle with other ideals which are just as sacred to others as ours are to us."[54] For him, we are essentially beings "endowed with the capacity and the will to take a deliberate attitude towards the world and lend it significance."[55]

In that prescription resides his view of the essential contingency and the self- and socially creative core of human agency. And in the charismatic movement resides his version of its fullest development and ultimate expression. Indeed, for him the only possible hope of release from the "iron cage" of the modern bureaucratic order lay in another such movement; another spontaneous, overwhelming, and creative eruption of human agency led by another of the "human heroes" who alter the course of human history. But, of course, it was a vain hope. For charismatic movements do not and cannot last. By their very nature, they are doomed from the moment of their birth.

The problem is that, to the extent it is successful, grows in scale and impact, and has to face up to the prospect of permanence, the charismatic movement can no longer maintain itself on the basis of intense, spontaneous, single-minded emotional commitment. So, to preserve its original inspiration and intention, it has to embark upon the "self-conscious formulation" of its values and of the action required to realize those values; to add, in a word, the "rational" to "value-rational." But, in so doing, it completely changes its character. It becomes routinized; that is, rule-governed, hierarchical, and institutionalized, a process which typically begins with the problem of succession created by the disappearance of the original charismatic leader. It is a process to which Weber gives the appearance of an utter inevitability deriving from the inherent instability of a purely emotional commitment. However, at this point, there is a logical gap in his argument. That charismatic authority cannot last on the basis of emotional commitment alone is no doubt true. But it is not, in principle, inevitable that its routinization should proceed in the way Weber characterizes it, again with seeming inevitability. In principle, there is no reason why a movement whose members "live primarily in a communistic relationship with their leader" and each other[56] could not develop into a Rousseauian moral community. Yet, for Weber, this is clearly not a possibility. For he has a very definite conception of the motives behind the transformation of charisma, which he inserts into his argument at this point, and in which the inevitability of the direction routinization will take resides.

In effect, he invokes his notion of the "elective affinity" between ideas and interests, whereby "the followers 'elect' those features of the idea with which they have an 'affinity,' a 'point of coincidence' or 'convergence.' "[57] And he is in no doubt about the nature of this point of coincidence. The interests of the followers in the maintenance of the community beyond its initial uprising, especially of those whose own charismatic qualities have already given them some kind of leading role in it, are those of securing and stabilizing their own economic and social position. Thus, in the "self-conscious formulation" of its original intention and inspiration, they will elect those aspects of it which coincide with and advance these interests. This is the basis for the emergence of rules, offices, hierarchies, the institutionalized distribution of power and economic reward, and so on; in other words, of rationally accomplished and accountable behavior in a rationally accomplished and accountable social order. But the whole point of routinization is that, once accomplished, the social order generates its own dynamic and no longer needs the support of the emotional commitment to the movement of human agency which originally created it.

All this adds a further and decisive dimension to Weber's view of human agency. For it now becomes clear that there is a fundamental opposition between its two basic characteristics, and that in this opposition resides the inevitability of its routinization. As long as its individualistic dimension expresses itself solely on the level of its emotional dimension, the opposition remains latent; pure feeling swamps all. But it becomes manifest when feeling has to be "self-consciously formulated." At this point, the "rational" is added to the "value-rational" in such a way that the original emotional commitment, ultimate value, and communal solidarity dissolve into the election of those aspects of the commitment and the value which advance individual economic and social position, And this gives the "rational" a very precise meaning. It is clearly, unequivocally, and immutably instrumental.

Hence the familiar progression from instrumental action to routinization as a rule-governed, institutionalized social order which becomes externally constraining upon those whose action initially created it. It follows that Weber locates self- and socially creative moral action, not in the sphere of value-rational action, but in that of affectual action. Value-rational action, in that it crucially involves the addition of an immutably instrumental "rational," is the seedbed of the domination of instrumentally rational action and social order and, therefore, of the negation of human agency. Hence the reason for saying earlier that the fundamental meaning of action lies, for Weber, in the emotional commitment to it, and that to distinguish affectual from value-rational action on the grounds of the latter's "clearly self-conscious formulation" of ultimate value and concomitant action is to lay the basis for the negation of human agency. For it has now become clear that this distinction is fundamentally between moral feeling and instrumental reason.

But there is a twist to Weber's formulation of the latter and its consequences which carries the logic of his version of human agency to a paradoxical and bleak conclusion. First, as the corollary of its individualism, instrumental reason is clearly an inherent characteristic of human agency. Second, it is precisely what gives value-rational action its revolutionary impact, in that it gives rise to the instrumentally rational order whereby traditional order is overthrown[58]—which makes it both an inescapable stage in the exertion of human agency and the source of its negation. Thus, simultaneously and by the same token, human agency is both revolutionary and carries within it the seed of its own inevitable negation. It may create a new social order, but in the very process and by virtue of so doing, it also creates its own negation as human agency. The dualism and opposition between moral feeling and instrumental reason can have no other outcome. But, of course, it is Weber's dualism and opposition which produces the familiar progression from contingent and creative action to its negation by necessary and imprisoning social order. In particular, it is the product of an antinomy at the very heart of his moral vision: the antinomy between reason and emotion.[59]

Unlike Rousseau, with his conception of whole, integrated man and moral reason as the faculty whereby moral integration is achieved, Weber works with a conception of man, very familiar in Western thought, as being split between emotion and reason, such that emotional man is authentic moral man and reasoning man is inauthentic instrumental man. This has obvious romanticist connotations, but Weber is only part romantic. For, as we have seen, he views instrumental reason as an innate human faculty, not as a socially produced distortion. Thus the antinomy is not one between alternative possible social worlds. It is built into Weber's fundamental conception of human nature, *whereupon it is immediately dissolved as an antinomy*. For it is obvious from the whole thrust of his analysis of charisma that, of the two basic characteristics of man, he sees the drive toward instrumental reason as being the more powerful. So the antinomy dissolves into a progression from moral man to instrumental man, a sequence always culminating in instrumental reason, which is at once the articulation of the self-defeating characteristic of human agency and the negation of the morally creative characteristic. So it goes with all his antinomies, not merely analytically, but literally because that is how he sees the world of the "iron cage"; they become progressions from one to the other. Faith becomes reason, ultimate value becomes instrumental rationality, action as the exertion of "the will" becomes behavior as "an event in nature," the moral realm becomes the scientific realm, adequacy on the level of meaning becomes causal adequacy, the noumenal world becomes the phenomenal world.[60] Now there is no longer even the irreconcilable opposition between two single-visioned antinomies, the actual and the ideal. There is only the ultimate single vision of instrumental man in an instrumental world of instrumental rationality. Weber first bifurcates ambiguity into antinomy, and then dissolves antinomy into the triumph of the instrumental rationality whose "supreme mastery" he deplores, but whose "total incorporation" he can escape no more than anyone else. And *human agency becomes human bondage because of the very nature of human agency*. Such is his progress from "participating individual men" to "little cogs in the machine."

And, of course, he tells this story and charts this progress in his seminal study, *The Protestant Ethic and the Spirit of Capitalism,* in a way which places it here not merely as an illustration, but as the prime expression and summation of his view of human agency, its location in charisma, and its negation by its instrumental production of modern Western capitalism. There is no doubt that, while his model for the charismatic movement was the exemplary religious uprising of the kind led by the Judean prophets, he also saw the Protestant entrepreneurs as charismatic figures. They emerge as "human heroes" who very radically altered the course of human history. And Protestantism emerges as a charismatic movement of "revolutionary force" for the destruction of "traditionalist" social order and the genesis of capitalism in the modern West. The Protestant entrepreneurs were charismatic figures by virtue of their archetypal display of the two basic characteristics of charismatic human agency: extreme individualism and intense emotionalism. We have already seen that they were morally isolated individuals, left by an opaque divine will in ignorance as to whether they were of the elect or the damned and as to the behavior required of them in the world. At first, required behavior could be determined by the arbitrary revelations, through ad hoc edict and act, of Protestant charismatic authority, and manifested by followers through exemplary displays of intense emotional faith in that authority and its edicts. But, as the movement expanded in scale and influence and its increasing membership became more and more removed from the immediacy of charismatic authority, the Protestant entrepreneurs could no longer live with the emotional strain of their moral isolation and, above all, of not knowing whether they were of the elect or the damned.

They thus had an ideal interest in a "self-conscious formulation" of Protestant ultimate value and concomitant action which would ease their moral isolation and give them some sign that they could count themselves among the elect. But they also had a material interest in electing those aspects of original Protestant doctrine which had an "affinity" with their increasing economic and social position as entrepreneurs. Hence the detailed elaboration of rules for proper Protestant conduct by such people as Benjamin Franklin and Richard Baxter, which amounted to a daily exercise in moral accounting whereby each individual took solitary responsibility for and ceaselessly monitored his own conduct to insure its total fidelity to Protestant belief. In that this was a highly individual exercise, it provided for the continued viability and validity of Protestantism by articulating its distinctive and profound emphasis on individual responsibility before God. In that it was also a highly public (because routinized) exercise, it provided for the ideal interests involved, first and obviously, by easing moral isolation; and second, by instilling a comforting sense of being among the elect since, once established and conspicuous, strict adherence to the exercise and the rules it generated could be taken as a visible sign of election. And in that it emphasized those elements of Protestant belief which were consonant with the increasing economic activity of the entrepreneurs, at the expense of those which were not, it provided for their material interests. The gradual disappearance from Protestant commandment of the prohibition on usury, an economic practice essential to the expansion of capitalistic enterprise, is an obvious example.

The progress of Protestantism is obviously that of the charismatic movement in particular and human agency in general. It originates in emotional commitment and exemplary display, but also in extreme individualism. In time, its own growth in size and impact, the increasing instability of its emotional base, and the emerging ideal and material interests of its followers generate the detailed elaboration of rules for proper Protestant conduct—the addition of the Protestant "rational" to the Protestant "value-rational." These rules constitute the accomplishment by its followers of Protestantism as a "self-consciously" formulated doctrine and movement. By the same token, however, they constitute the accomplishment of its routinization. They thus accomplish, with "revolutionary force," a new social order; but also the negation of the human agency from which it and they began. For the individualistic "value-rational" of Protestantism becomes the "instrumentally rational" of modern Western capitalism. The latter therefore emerges as a humanly accomplished order. But, once accomplished, it no longer needs the support of the human agency, value, and commitment which created it. So, resting on its own "mechanical foundations," it destroys the agency, the value, and the commitment, and determines "the lives of all the individuals who are born into this mechanism . . . with irresistible force."[61] Once again, in its inherent, inevitable, inescapable, universal progress from moral feeling to instrumental reason, human agency revolutionizes the world, only to accomplish its own negation in the very process. And, in the final reckoning, that is all it can ever accomplish for Weber. No wonder he could see nothing ahead but "a polar night of icy darkness and hardness."[62] No wonder he was "moved, above all, by the fact that on its earthly course an idea always and everywhere operates in opposition to its original meaning and thereby destroys itself." It was his idea, his "self-concious formulation." The conclusion is obvious. No sociology of social action predicated upon a view of human agency as "always and everywhere" generating its own "opposition" can lead to anything but a sociology of social system. In such a sociology, "participating individual men" must always become "little cogs in the machine," forever dominated by the "supreme mastery of the bureaucratic way of life," while real people in the real world who "continue to struggle against the machine" once again disappear from view.

In the Herculean terminological labors of Talcott Parsons, the decree nisi between modern institutionalized sociology and the classical tradition seems to have become absolute. His unremitting pursuit of professional and scientific purity—"I stand squarely on the platform of science"[63]—appears to be so dominating a motive behind his work as to create a radical break between it and the traditional sociological concerns discussed so far in this chapter. Yet, though the influence of this motive can scarcely be dismissed, the original traditions provide the real key to his work in such a way that it would not be innaccurate to describe him as the last of the great founding fathers of sociology. First, and most obviously, there is the acknowledged centrality of his role in the development of social-action theory, which places him squarely in the tradition of sociology's abiding concern with the problematic of human agency. Second, and less obviously, it can be argued that the prime motivating dynamic behind all his work has been the search for ultimate value, as we shall see. Third, and consequently, that work constitutes a continuing exploration of the relationship between the actual and the ideal. And fourth, in its outcome, it arrives at the most elaborate formulation in sociology of the social-action and social-system perspectives, of the tension between them, and of the recurring transition from one to the other.

The complex and shifting Parsonian story begins with *The Structure of Social Action,* one major purpose of which was to overcome "the positivistic-idealistic dualism of modern social thought."[64] To simplify a multifaceted argument, the problem with positivism is that it discards as heuristically irrelevant all subjective meanings of social actors which do not accord with its own tenets and hypotheses about the social world. The world is as, and only as, positivism describes it, and human action, therefore, is merely a process of passive adaptation to it. The social actor is merely an objective product of his objective situation. The problem with idealism is that, in concentrating exclusively on ideal conceptions of the world, it goes to the other extreme, yet with a similar consequence for the characterization of social action. The social world is nothing but a universe of meaning in which all phenomena, including action, are emanations of all-pervasive ultimate value. Again, this is not a world of action, but merely one of passive orientation to pregiven meaning, which thus determines social action. For Parsons, both positivism and idealism nevertheless bequeathed elements essential to a viable conception of social action. Positivism reminds us that men act within existing situations which cannot simply be assimilated to their subjective definitions of them. Idealism reminds us that men act on their subjective orientations to value which are not simply a reflex of existing situations. But the exclusive emphasis on one or the other engendered by the "positivistic-idealistic dualism" has stood in the way of the development of any theory of action at all. Neither positivism nor idealism contains any notion whatsoever of people *acting*, not only for the reasons already explained, but because action "must always be thought of as involving a state of tension between two different orders of elements, the normative and the conditional.[65] The point of this tension is that it gives rise to the effort required to overcome "conditional" elements in order to bring them into line with the "normative." The expenditure of effort thus becomes a vital independent element in Parson's theory of action and, crucially, distinguishes action from both ideal meanings and actual situations. This avoids the conflation of action and meaning into the single concept of modes of orientation, the disastrous conseqences of which for a viable conception of social action we have already seen. By the same token, it locates action as the property and the product of "the independent agency of the actor."[66]

We now have all the elements of "the voluntaristic theory of action,"[67] which was Parsons's answer to "the positivistic-idealistic dualism." The elements of action, combined in a "basic unit" he called the "unit act" are, first, "an agent, an 'actor' "; second, "an 'end' ", a desired "future state of affairs toward which the process of action is oriented"; third, "a 'situation', comprised of 'conditions' over which the actor has no control, and 'means' available to him in the pursuit of his ends"; and fourth, "a 'normative orientation' on the basis of which he chooses means in relation to ends from the range of those available to him." This schema has important implications for the characterization and analysis of social action. It begins, first, with the subjective dimension of action; that is the starting point of action, and therefore of its analysis, is the subjective meaning attributed to it by the actor. Second, action always takes place over time. It is history—which leads to the third implication. It is utterly vital to Parson's thinking at this point that, while ideals or "desired future states of affairs" do not yet exist as actual situations, they *do* exist in that they constitute the motivating dynamic of present action. It is an integral and basic part of his conception and analysis of action that the actual is defined and acted upon by human beings in terms of their visions of the ideal. In short, Parsons is planting, firmly and as an analytic imperative, the seeds of the ideal in the womb of the actual.

Thus far, all this appears to lead to an obvious conclusion about the view of human agency at work in Parsons's thought: "man is essentially an active, creative, evaluating creature" who acts upon the actual in order to bring it into line with his "ends, purposes, ideals."[68] He is a being of choice who, through his own "independent agency" selects his own ends, his own "normative orientations" and makes his own decisions to act. He is thus a being of contingency:

> His voluntarism is primarily an expression of his antideterminism. . . . Parsons is

stressing the openness of social action and historical development. . . . The actor, in short, introduces a *non*predictable element.[69]

Above all, he is a moral being: the "relation of men to norms" is essentially "creative"[70] and, fundamentally, creative of moral community. For Parsons insists that it is only by conceiving of the actor as exerting his "independent agency" that it is possible to conceive of the emergence of "a community of values."[71] In sum, this appears to be the version of human agency predicated on conceptions of moral man, moral action, and moral community; the active, purposeful, self- and socially creative version set by Parsons against any conception from any sociological tradition of man as purely "passive, adaptive, receptive" creature;[72] and, of course, this is the version which leads straight to the social-action framework he spells out in logical consequence and precise detail. Thus the foundation seems to have been laid for the development of the elements of action into a conceptualization of the emergent *outcome* of *interaction*—that is, the social system—as the product of social actors creatively defining their actual situations in terms of their ideal ends on the basis of courses of action geared to the attainment of their ends, actively constructing their relationships with one another, and, in the course of their consequent interaction founded upon their "creative relation to norms," communally accomplishing the social world.

However, in *The Structure of Social Action,* Parsons has another purpose which, to say the least, massively complicates the issue and which, moreover, is primary: to solve the problems created for sociological analysis by utilitarian social thought. The main point about utilitarianism, of course, is that it is fundamentally an economic theory which attributes to social actors the single "normative orientation" of economic rationality. In the terms of this chapter, this is the instrumental rationality whereby, in their egoistic pursuit of private interest, people seek optimum gratification by means of an egoistic calculation of an optimum balance of ends, in relation both to other possible combinations and to the amount of effort required to achieve them. And in so doing, they accomplish the social world; for, according to utilitarianism, which is thus an action theory, the public good automatically emerges from the pursuit of private interest. There is, of course, no good reason why it should, and it is upon this that Parsons seizes. His argument at this point is again multifaceted, but it culminates in one central point of direct concern both here and to Parsons. The norm of economic or instrumental rationality may well enlighten self-interest, not in the direction of cooperation, but toward the realization that private interests would be most efficiently pursued by means of "force and fraud." In short, utilitarianism reproduces the Hobbesian problem of order inevitably posed by its own instrumental view of human agency. And Parsons makes it entirely clear that the whole point of confronting the doctrine lies in the centrality *to him* of the concern with the problem of order; which, of course, immediately involves him in contradiction. It is the massive contradiction between the "moral-action" view of human agency on which, as we have seen, the social action framework rests, and the "instrumental-action" version on which, as we have also seen, the concern with the Hobbesian problem of order rests. It is thus the contradiction between the opposed concerns with the problems of order and control, and thence between the opposed sociologies consequent upon these concerns.

It is not surprising that Parsons should have become enmeshed in the opposition between the two concerns. Despite his initial theoretical appeal to the European sociological tradition, to which it is central in any case, he is very much an American sociologist. And American sociology emerged in a social context in which the problems of order and control were socially, politically, morally, and therefore sociologically, central. After an initial and short-lived burst of Social Darwinism, it developed partly as a response to the rampant economic exploitation, the growth of urbanism and corporatism, and the emergence of machine politics of the late nineteenth and early twentieth centuries; hence the concern with the problem of control. On the other hand, it also developed partly as a response to the "great migrations" from Eurpope of the same period, which immensely exacerbated the classic American "melting pot" problems of social and cultural diversity; hence the concern with the problem of order. It is surprising, however, that Parsons should recognize neither of these problems as moral concerns turning on differing views of human agency. After all, his voluntaristic perspective rests on the proposition that "man is essentially an active, creative, evaluating creature." And, given this, it is even more surprising that he fails to recognize the existence of any central problem other than that of order at all. But, for him, this is not just the central, but the only problem. Only one inference is possible. Against the view of human agency on which his conception of social action rests, that at the root of his critique of utilitarianism is the egoistic, instrumental Hobbesian view.

And so it proves. Mainly through his discussion of Durkheim, whose central propositions he not only endorses, but develops, he spells out a version of the individual, the social, and the relationship between the two which is unmistakably Hobbesian: "since individual wants are in principle unlimited, it is an essential condition of both social stability and individual happiness that they should be regulated in terms of norms."[73] The Hobbesian view of the self- and socially destructive consequences of the unconstrained individual pursuit of private interest is obvious, as is the corollary that Parsons is here accepting the utilitarian view of the individual as an instrumentally calculative being. Morality, therefore, is necessarily a socially derived phenomenon. Everything individual is instrumental, everything social is moral. And, of course, there is no doubt about the necessary relationship between the two: the "integration of a social group consists in the common recognition on the part of its members of a single integrated body of norms as carrying moral authority," so that "a common value system is one of the required conditions for a society to be a stable system in equilibrium."[74] Between this and "the independent agency of the actor" which Parsons claims to be basic to the voluntaristic perspective, there seems to be no possible relation but one of utter and absolute contradiction.

However, for Parsons, the voluntaristic conception of action now assumes a central role in his proposed solution to the problem of order; but in a way which radically changes the meaning of its original formulation. The essentials of his argument at this point are, first, that the ideals embodied in the common value system still depend for their actualization on the expenditure of effort by social actors. Not only does this seem to reduce action from all the elements of the original action schema to the single element of effort, but it hardly seems to resolve the contradiction in which Parsons has become enmeshed. For what he is now saying is that social order depends upon the sharing of a common value system, but that this can only be accomplished by independent human agents. This merely underlines the contradiction. If human actors are independent, then in the context of Parson's location of the problem of order, we are back in the utilitarian position; they can create only the very opposite of a common value system. So the latter must come first. Social actors must be socialized into the common value system before they can act; that is, before they can expend the effort to actualize it instead of, as would otherwise be the case, actualizing a Hobbesian state of war. The common value system remains, therefore, pregiven to those subject to it. And the element of ends seems to be have been assimilated by the element of conditions of the situation, which determine the behavior of social actors. Yet Parsons has been insisting on precisely the distinction between ends and conditions in his critique of positivism and his formulation of the basic requirements of an adequate action framework.

Second, therefore, he redefines voluntarism in such a way that it becomes equated with "voluntariness," as distinct from "arbitrariness."[75] And this is a distinction between acting under the coercion of external conditions and acting out of a subjective sense of moral obligation. Both involve constraint, but in the second case, the notion is no longer really applicable because people acting from moral obligation do so willingly. The external "constraining element" is "independent of human will," whereas the internal "constraining element" is "an expression of human will."[76] Thus is the role of independent human agency preserved. It sounds like the miracle of advertising whereby one buys something willingly because, whatever it is, one has been persuaded that it is an utterly basic necessity of human existence; not an entirely frivolous point, because it captures something of Parsons's view of the source of this "voluntarism." People "voluntarily adhere" to the common value system because it is "in the Freudian term, 'introjected' " to form a constitutive element of the individual personality itself.[77] Now, therefore, the battle between the social "moral" and the individual "instrumental" depends on the effectiveness with which the former is implanted in the individual.

None of this, of course, does anything to save voluntarism in its original meaning. For it now no longer refers to independent human agency in any serious sense, but only to attitudinal orientation to pregiven meaning. Concomitantly, the analytic starting point is no longer "the point of view of the actor," since this can now be taken as given by the common value system and the "introjection" process. By the same token, it does nothing to save the distinction between the normative and the conditional elements of action. On the contrary, it completes its collapse. For the appeal to the process of introjection in no way changes the location of the common value system as prior to and constraining upon the social actor. It does, however, reinforce its constraint. Through introjection, the common value system becomes constitutive rather than merely regulative of the personality of the social actor, who thus becomes nothing more than a mere reflex of it. Once again, external constraint becomes all the more effective by losing the appearance of externality and taking on the *appearance* of a distinctively human consciousness. All this, of course, has drastic consequences for the basic conception of action with which Parsons started. The reference to the subjective dimension has gone. Because of the assimilation of ends to conditions of the situation, there is no longer any gap between the actual and the ideal, and thus no longer any notion of acting to transform one into the other; which means that the ideas of action as a process over time and action as crucially involving the expenditure of effort have gone. *The sum total is that, in terms of the initial premises on which Parsons founded it, the very concept of action itself has gone.*

All this stems from the total incompatibility of the two theoretical programs in *The Structure of Social Action*, despite Parsons's attempt to weld them into one on the basis of the voluntaristic theory of action.[78] Indeed, it is precisely the shifting meaning of voluntarism that reveals their incompatibility. The first program is the confrontation with "the positivistic-idealistic dualism" which, because of the "passive, adaptive, receptive" view of human agency at the root of both positivism and idealism, entails the construction of a theory of social action based on the counteraxiom that "man is essentially an active, creative, evaluating creature." The second program is the search for a solution to the Hobbesian problem of order, consequent upon the confrontation with utilitarianism. Here, the axiomatic point of departure is necessarily very different: the postulation of a common value system as the only possible basis for social order. Voluntarism thus loses the axiomatic status it had in the first program, becoming transmuted into attitudes inculcated by introjection. In the second program, therefore, Parsons abandons his initial theory of social action by destroying the premises upon which he built it.

In fact, in pursuing that program, he falls victim to the very failings his first program is intended to remedy. He first adopts a utilitarian concept of the egoistic individual, because the thesis that utilitarianism ignores the problem of order is dependent on that concept. In consequence, he gives priority to the common value system over the social actor and, in the process, collapses the distinction between the normative and the conditional elements of action. He thus becomes positivist in exactly the way in which he claims the failure to maintain this distinction entails. At the same time, however, he also contrives to fall into the trap of idealism. For the priority of the common value system means that the social actor now confronts a world constituted by pregiven meaning, to which he merely has to orient and of which his behavior is merely an emanation. Further, the idealist trap is related to the positivist trap. The point here is that, while the common value system exists for the actor as an internalized world of meaning, it must be treated by the observer as an observable empirical phenomenon if it is to have any place in social scientific knowledge. The incompatibility of the two programs is transparent. Idealistic, positivistic, both—the view of human agency is the same. The "active, creative, evaluating creature" of the first program becomes the "passive, adaptive, receptive" creature of the second.

In short, in his search for the source and nature of ultimate value, Parsons has gone off in two totally opposed directions. And they are, of course, very familiar directions and a very familiar opposition: the opposition between the "instrumental action" and the "moral action" views of human agency, and the consequent opposition between the concerns with the problems of order and control. In *The Structure of Social Action*, he conceives the embryos of both a sociology of social system and a sociology of social action, thus providing himself with alternative paths for his subsequent work. But there is no doubt which he is going to take. He has already defined his central concern as being with the problem of order, and the theoretical program focused on that has destroyed the program arising from his confrontation with "the positivistic-idealistic dualism." The conclusion of his first major work is inevitable:

> Sociology may then be defined as "the science which attempts to develop an analytical theory of social action systems in so far as these systems can be understood in terms of the property of common-value integration."[79]

And such, indeed, is Parsons's progress. For, by 1951, his fully fledged social system has emerged.[80]

In its combination of the concepts of central values, norms, roles, structure, function, equilibrium, and structural differentiation, it constitutes the fullest elaboration yet of the doctrinal and analytic consequence of the assumption of self- and socially destructive Hobbesian man. Taken together, these concepts portray a social system which both exercises the necessary external constraint over its members and is self-generating and self-maintaining. On the first count, central values, embedded in the cultural system of society, are the ultimate source of the moral authority which sets the social system over its members in such a way as to impose a consensual set of meanings and, therefore, order upon them. They are broad and generalized directives for action, which pattern for them a series of fundamentally moral choices all actors face in social life.[81] Choice, once the prerogative of the actor, is now the property of the system. Central values also pattern the specific norms governing specific situations and the modes of fulfillment of specific functions. They thus define the roles which, in institutionalized and integrated relationship, comprise the social system. Social actors are now the incumbents of roles which define, through socialization and internalization, not merely their behavior, but their self-identities. Hence the Parsonian hierarchy of the cultural, social, and personality systems.

On the second court, that of the self-generation and self-maintenance of the system, central values again provide the starting point. For, through the medium of the specific functional norms derived from them, they structure roles and subsystems into the total system by defining the network of activities necessary to meet the functional prerequisites for system survival. For Parsons, there are four such prerequisites which are also, in that action is geared to meeting them, the four basic dimensions of systems of action: *adaptation, goal-attainment, latency* or *pattern-maintenance,* and *integration.*[82] Each role and subsystem plays its part in the whole structure by the fulfillment of the particular functions assigned to it by its place in the process of meeting the four functional prerequisites. When survival is threatened by an environmental pressure or internal strain, the system adapts and adjusts at whatever institutional point necessary to restore and maintain its equilibrium. Moreover, it generates its own dynamic of change through the process of structural differentiation, which means simply a growing division and specialization of function of increasingly differentiated subsystems whereby one institution performing a number of functional tasks subdivides into a number of specialized institutions, each performing one of the functional tasks in question. For Parsons, this is the inevitable evolutionary development of societies into increasingly large-scale, complex, and technologically sophisticated units. In short, in the concept of structural differentiation, the idea of the system's self-generation and self-maintenance receives its clearest expression yet.

All this, of course, amounts to the culmination of the destruction of the whole Parsonian conception of social action in its original formulation. The unit act is replaced by the status role as the basic unit of analysis, and the latter is not a property of the social actor, but of the social system. The elements of action are explicitly narrowed down to modes of orientation to the situation. Ends are no longer part of the action frame of reference. Indeed, there are no longer any ends but one: the optimization of gratification, defined in terms of seeking approval and avoiding disapproval according to standards legislated, once again, by the common value system. And this, of course, is utilitarian man who pursues pleasure and avoids pain, the Parsonian twist being to define pleasure and pain in terms of conformity to and deviation from the common value system, thus creating a pliable creature for the inculcation of central values. In other words, Parson's social system constitutes the culmination of his acceptance of the utilitarian conception of the individual, the basic principles of which he uses, with breathtaking contrivance, to transform the utilitarian notion of free choice into its very opposite, and thus to make the utilitarian individual central, not to the problem of order, but to its solution. And this makes the point that the Parsonian social system is built on the model of the Parsonian social actor; which is to say, on the basis of the same instrumental "normative orientation." It is a system of action with, as we have seen, four subsystems of action. As such, "it" rationally pursues goals using efficient economic, political, and cultural means to meet its needs, insure its survival, and maximize its equilibrium. "It" is, in short, utilitarian man writ social. Parsons has imbibed utilitarianism to the extent of casting his model of the social system in its image. He has, one might say, turned it on its head, inverting its famous precept in classic fashion: "the pursuit of public interest automatically insures the private good." And this means that there is a remarkable symmetry between his solution to the problem of order and that of Hobbes himself. For exactly like Hobbes, who started it all, Parsons has used the same basic principles and concepts which articulate his view of the individual to construct his view of the social. By the same token, he has used the same basic principles and concepts which articulate his view of human agency to construct the apparatus of its negation. He has created his "artificial person" out of the materials of his "natural person," with all the consequences we have seen from the time of Hobbes onward. Three centuries later to the very year,[83] Leviathan has come home to roost—and crow in triumph.

It has been a long journey from Hobbes to Parsons. Yet it seems to have been no journey at all. For, in the conventional sense, sociology still has no theories of social action. Consistently, it has begun with the concept of social action and ended with its negation, paradoxically by its repeated translation of the concept from the level of the social actor to that of the social system. In the end, in Marx, in Weber, in Durkheim, in Parsons, it is always systems which act, disembodied systems torn from their roots in the human agency which created them. Human agency does not live in these systems, for they are not the systems of ordinary men who are "neither obsessed nor privileged with a single vision."[84] They are the systems born of the unworldly imperatives of certainty, of necessity, of a science which would persuade the world that only its "utterances were true to the practical bearing of life." [85] Over and again, it is the resort to science which has denied human agency, seeming to sever it from its potential, but really severing itself from "the practical bearing of life" that is its ground and only reason for being. For those for whom science was a new dawn and a new promise, it meant a new world view with which to give shape and possibility to their moral vision. We cannot blame them for bequeathing it to us. But this is one part of their legacy we must now discard, for its time is long past. The mechanistic, rationalistic science with which sociology still works became obsolete as soon as Einstein and Heisenberg revealed the relative, uncertain, provisional, contingent character of all humanly accomplished "knowledge," scientific or otherwise. Now, in a sociology shorn of the moral vision it once served, it is a vanity, a means of expropriating and molding social life and human experience to the persuasions and purposes of those who would secure their own place and character through it. In particular, the scientific imperative has become the professional imperative, so that fidelity to it affirms only our membership in the sociological community, and in a way that denies our membership in the human community. For, in our pursuit of academic acceptability and professional position, we insist on the strict separation of the two, thus missing the real pulse of living human agency which "does not wait upon the constructions of scientific reasoning."[86] Ordinary men are neither driven by nor "hasty with the imperatives of science,"[87] and are thus not forgetful, as sociology has become, of their capacities and possibilities; as those voices from everyday life we heard at the beginning of the journey testify. If it is to hear them again, if it is to respect and grasp and articulate the essential autonomy, contingency, and creativity of human agency, sociology must abandon its obsolete and imperious scientific pretension, which cuts us off from the world of which we are also members. We live in the world we also watch, and our living informs our watching. A science which divorces the two "always obliges us to forget what we know"[88] of the social world whose story it is our job to tell. If we cannot converse with ordinary men—with ourselves as ordinary men—we cannot begin to speak of "life as it is lived." We can only chatter to ourselves, idly, emptily, and unheard.

This suggests another metaphor for sociological analysis than that of science: the metaphor of the conversation:

> We are the inheritors, neither of an inquiry about ourselves and the world, nor of an accumulating body of information, but of a conversation, begun in the primeval forests and extended and made more articulate in the course of centuries. It is a conversation which goes on both in public and within each of ourselves. Of course there is argument and inquiry and information, but wherever these are profitable they are to be recognized as passages in this conversation, and perhaps they are not the most captivating of the passages. . . . And it is this conversation which, in the end, gives place and character to every human activity and utterance.[89]

Changes of metaphor are vital, for metaphor is at the root of the ways of seeing, in whatever mode and through whatever consequent conceptualizations, whereby we make sense of such a diversity of experience that it would otherwise be totally beyond our grasp. But the choice of metaphor is also vital, for some shed light, while others blind.[90] And the first thing the metaphor of the conversation enables us to see, where the metaphor of science blinds us, is the positive legacy of the journey from Hobbes to Parsons. To recall a point and a distinction I made at the beginning of the journey, sociology may have no theories of social action, but it does have a vast body of theorizing about social action. Theories of social action come and go, foundering on their own contradictions. But they are unimportant; transient "passages in this conversation" and by no means "the most captivating of the passages." Theorizing is "this conversation which, in the end, gives place and character to every human activity and utterance." It *is* human activity and utterance; human agency, active, creative, world-building. Theorizing about social action is man meditating on his prolonged awakening from the sleep of medievalism; reflecting upon his activity in and on the world in order to "make and master" himself; articulating the history he has made in order to make more. The theorizing, not the theories, has given us the imprecise, unrigorous, uninhibited speculations of indeterminate scope that are still at the heart of sociology because they are saturated in the diversity of human experience, rich in the expression of human aspiration, vast in the sense of human scope. Alienation, rationalization, anomie, metropolis, the sacred and the profane: these are the imaginative insights to which we return again and again when all the "well-defined propositions of limited scope"[91] are dead and gone, buried as rapidly as they appear in once-read and immediately forgotten professional journals and monographs. And we do so because they are given "root by reality" and born of "the passion for reality that is direct and unmediated."[92] We do so because they capture one or another dimension of our lived and living experience. It is when they are taken for all of our experience, the whole of our world, that they cease to be creative, life-enhancing, world-building insights and ossify into deadening theories and systems: "The system killeth, the insight giveth life."[93] "Assume *man* to be *man* and his relationship to the world to be a human one: then you can exchange love only for love, trust for trust, etc."[94] Thus Marx, and such insights and the life, the worlds, and the possibilities they encompass are killed by the degeneration into system.

But the metaphor of the conversation rescues the journey; and not merely as the journey of those who made and reported it publicly. For they made it in conversation with the life around them, of which they were part. Again, they were articulating the experience they both watched and lived. And insofar as, in their theorizing, they still articulate our experience, their journey is that of all of us in all our lives. The conversation thus dissolves the antinomy between the human social world and the peremptory legislations of a scientific sociology which rides roughshod over that world. For it is, first, a conversation between ourselves as members and ourselves as sociologists. But it also dissolves the antinomy between the individual and society. For, second, it is a conversation between ourselves as both members and sociologists and all other members we meet along all the roads we travel in our lives, whether "present to us here and now, or through their work and its legacy.[95] This is to say that it is through and through a communal enterprise and, therefore, that we must now discard another part of the traditional sociological response to human agency: the dualism of the individual and the social. Again, we cannot blame those caught up in the rise of individualism for bequeathing it to us. For them, it was a new experience, both intoxicating and terrifying. But, at root, there never has been an "individual in his own right," nor could there ever be. The change was never from community to individual. Behind that deceitful formula, it was fundamentally a change in the details of our inherently communal lives. When the masses of rural laborers migrated to the new towns and cities of the Industrial Revolution, they did not change from communal to individual beings. They changed from one kind of communality to another. Any moral imperative, any analytic schema which begins from the individualist abstraction is, on this most fundamental fact of the human. condition, foredoomed. As we have seen, it can lead only to the imperialism of "society" over "the individual" on the one hand; and, on the other, to the pervasive reifications of individual singularity, the private self, the solitary ego. At this juncture in the history of sociological analysis, we have come to the end of a long road. It is time the basic question changed, to take us beyond the two sociologies. It is not In which ways are we individual and in which ways social beings? Rather it is How do we communally provide for which versions of individuality?

The new question is unequivocally active. It captures the ceaseless activity of human agency and, above all, the active *communality* of the production of the social world. And the "we" points straight to the conversation, which thus becomes a metaphor not merely for the nature of sociological inquiry, but for the basically communal constitution of that world. Through the conversation between us—whether of word, gesture, glance, posture, work, play, pain, pleasure, sadness, joy, hate, love—*we* coauthor the social world as an active relationship between us; not "you" and "I" but "we" as active human subjects, producing it together in a way which provides for "you" and "I." This is true of any relationship, any activity, any world, no matter how passive and dominating it may seem to be. As soon as someone utters the first word, makes the first gesture, strikes the first blow, the other responds and the conversation is underway. And, unless people remain forever silent, expressionless, and motionless, response is always active, and thus participant in the meaning and the creation of the relationship, the activity, the social world. This means that the conversation is always open-ended, contingent, loaded with alternative directions and possibilities. Here is the locus of human agency, capacity, and possibility. No matter how predictable it may seem, the conversation is always a new accomplishment, whether an innovatory accomplishment or a reaccomplishment—"another first time." Indeed, predictability itself is a contingent human choice and accomplishment of one alternative possibility; and again, a communal achievement since, like every other possibility, it depends upon the communal sequence of utterance and response.[96] So, through the conversation, we both constitute and confirm our mutual sociality and individuality, and thus recover the primal sociality in which our individuality is grounded, once again despite the pervasive mystification of individualism. And once again, too, this sociality has nothing to do with the imperialism of "society" over "the individual:"

> The fundamental fact of human existence is neither the individual as such nor the aggregate as such. Each, considered by itself, is a mighty abstraction. . . . The fundamental fact of human existence is man with man.[97]

In short, "All real living is meeting."[98] The conversation of sociology is the narrative of the meeting. It is the measure and purpose of our task when we enter sociology because "it is the display of our shared lives, of our own growth, and the place others have in our lives without which we should be diminished and lonely."[99] It is a journey of the self through the world sociology seeks to grasp. And it is a journey of the relations between oneself and others whereby the self, in its particularities and generalities, is discovered as an element and an embodiment of the human community which embraces and authenticates it. It is a journey not merely through the world, but of the world. The conversation of sociology is the conversation of humanity in which sociology, by definition, is rooted.

A new metaphor, a new question. But surely this is not enough. Where is the delineation of a precise language and the specification of a rigorous method? The answer to this is that, as ever, it is the questions we ask that are all-important, for they incorporate the ways of seeing that define what we are looking for and how we talk about it. In other words, the language flows from the question and, since there is no distinction between the two, the conversation is the language and method. To specify its terms prior to holding it is to legislate those terms unilaterally, thereby translating dialogue into monologue; the conventional sociological monologue which thus rules out of sight, sound, and substance the human agency that is its only possible subject, and for which the conversation is the metaphor. It is in the very nature of conversation that it is open-ended, its terms those of contingent utterance and response. And, as far as sociology is concerned, the conversational sequence is that the social world speaks first. So, instead of the usual sociological procedure which makes its subjects its "respondents"—its objects—the conversation makes sociologists the respondents, to themselves as members and to all other members. The distinction is between using "respondents" as ciphers for our own membership of the sociological community, and always remembering that we are, first and last, beholden to the human community without which we would have no place. It is also between theory and method as abstracted procedure, artificially "controlled" by canons of inquiry which incarcerate us in an observational no-man's land, and theorizing as a richly empirical activity, naturally "controlled" by the contingencies of living in the social world whose story we are supposed to tell. And it is between engulfing that world and its members in our own persuasions and purposes, swallowing them up in categories expressive only of our own designs and concerns, and respecting their integrity and autonomy as separate and distinct beings with their own designs and purposes, which are the first utterances in the conversation. This is not to say that one's own concerns, one's own sociological vision, one's own allegiance to a moral axiom plays no part and has no validity in the conversation. It is, after all, a *dialogue,* and the concern, the vision, the axiom is still the presumption of active, communal human agency. But it is to make it absolutely clear that this does not and must not preclude a due regard for "the integrity of the phenomenon." Indeed, the sociological vision in question demands it, for the first term in its view of human agency is its autonomy. And this means three things.

It means, first, that the terms of our responses to the utterances of the social world will always be ad hoc and eclectic, suited to and generated by the particular "human activity and utterance" with which we are in conversation. This is scarcely new. A magnificent example of ad hoc sociology already exists in the great series of ethnographic studies of the Chicago school of urban sociology. Ad hocing and eclecticism, in terms of the generation of language and the range of materials drawn upon, is also the hallmark of Erving Goffman's "method" and, whatever view one may hold of his vision of the world,[100] it is difficult to name another sociologist today who communicates so strong a sense of so many dimensions of "life as it is lived." But, in any case, ad hocing is intrinsic to the practice of sociological inquiry. As we all know, it is only covered over afterward by the "authoritative" categories and devices of approved theory and method, the gloss of which invariably crumbles if examined at all closely. Second, it means that we are required to read interactional texts with the sensitivity and openness of the best of literary criticism to the literary text, letting them speak for themselves—listening to the voices from everyday life, or of Hobbes, Rousseau, Marx, Weber, whomever we are talking with—in all their human variety and ambiguity. Third, and above all, it means reading the texts, listening to the voices for the detail which, in its naive quest for the nirvana of the universal, it is sociology's persistent inclination to ignore. For people's lives reside in the details. So, therefore, does human agency. People's lives *are* the details, the fundamentally communal details, the materials with which they weave their lives, strand upon strand. So, therefore, is human agency:

> All over the great round earth and in the settlements, the towns, and the great iron stones of cities, people are drawn inward within their little shells of rooms, and are to be seen in their wondrous and pitiful actions through the surfaces of their lighted windows by thousands, by millions, little golden aquariums, in chairs, reading, setting tables, sewing, playing cards, not talking, talking, laughing inaudibly, mixing drinks, at radio dials, eating, in shirt-sleeves, carefully dressed, courting, teasing, loving, seducing, undressing, leaving the room empty in its empty light, alone and writing a letter urgently, in couples married, in separate chairs, in family parties, in gay parties, preparing for bed, preparing for sleep; and none can care, beyond that room; and none can be cared for, by any beyond beyond that room.[101]

All so alone, yet all assembling their lives out of its profoundly communal details. And that is the point. The experience is deeply and inherently ambiguous. On the one hand, it is that of individualism gone sour; no longer new, neither intoxicating nor terrifying, but a weary isolation and privatization "within their little shells of rooms" beyond which "none can care" or "be cared for." As such, it is a central experience of modern society, and prompts the question Agee asks: "How was it we were caught?"[102] It has also prompted every movement in recent years which has aspired to transcend it by seeking new forms of communality. On the other hand, it is both communal and accomplished as such. It is ceaseless activity, people doing things all the time. They accomplish privatization; but not only privatization. In their activity, there is constant contingency; a constantly contingent, accomplished arrangement and rearrangement of patterns and sequences, each holding an alternative possibility, an alternative life, an alternative world (the maintenance of the existing pattern, when chosen, again being merely one of those humanly accomplished and contingent alternatives). This is active human agency at work, always presenting itself with alternative patterns, alternative sequences, alternative possibilities. Herein lies the essential ambiguity, which is the only possible basis for human agency and accomplishment, for the translation of the actual into the ideal. The experience is both individualistic and communal, both locked within privatization and reaching beyond it, both living "within their little shells of rooms" and seeing each other "through the surfaces of their lighted windows," both "wondrous and pitiful." So, simultaneously, it prompts another question: "How it is that men belong to one another despite all differences?"[103]

A new metaphor, a new question; and the purpose, a perspective which retains the enduring vision of human agency as moral action and moral community. It also retains its grounding in and articulation of human social experience—the sour and weary modern experience of isolation and privatization "within their little shells of rooms," and the halting and diffuse emergence in recent years of the aspiration to transcend it. But, against all single visions, it insists on the ambiguity of the experience and the aspiration. For ambiguity remains essential to any serious conception of the self- and socially creative capacities and possibilities of human agency. It remains the only possible basis for the translation of the actual into the ideal. And, in any case, it will not be wished away by any single-visioned attempts to impose alien necessity on the contingency, autonomy, and diversity of human activity, utterance, and experience. Only by virtue of the ambiguity is it possible to envision a community of moral caring being created out of a community where "none can care." So it is the prime imperative of the sociology of the conversation that we ceaselessly listen to and converse with the voices from everyday life, wherever and however they are to be heard, including our own; that we listen for the detail, for every nuance, every inflexion, every change of tone, however slight, in the myriad ways in which people make their lives, in order to recognize and understand and articulate human agency at work. There is no other way. For, in the end:

> . . . life is never a material, a substance to be moulded. If you want to know, life is the principle of self-renewal, it is constantly renewing and remaking and changing and transfiguring itself, it is infinitely beyond your or my theories about it.[104]

To the sociology of the single vision, which would mold life in its reified and deified systems, that is a minor nuisance, easily ignored. To the sociology of the conversation, it is the whole point.

NOTES

1. Marianne Weber, *Max Weber: A Biography*, ed. Harry Zohn (New York: John Wiley, 1975) p. 337.
2. On the theme of reconciliation, two examples from recent sociology are, in their formulations of it, especially apposite in the context of this chapter. One is Percy S. Cohen, *Modern Social Theory* (London: Heinemann, 1968); the other, Peter L. Berger and Thomas Luckmann, *The Social Construction of Reality* (London: Allen Lane, The Penguin Press, 1967).
3. Studs Terkel, *Working* (London: Wildwood House, 1975) pp. 152–53.
4. Ronald Fraser, ed., *Work: Volume 2* (Harmondsworth: Penguin Books, 1969) pp. 172, 176.
5. Terkel, *Working*, p. 295.
6. Ibid., p. 287.
7. The phrase is Alvin W. Gouldner's; see Fraser, *Work*, p. 346.
8. Richard Hoggart, *Speaking to Each Other* (London: Chatto & Windus, 1970) vol. 2, p. 26.
9. For the full elaboration of the idea of sociology as one form of articulation of "the

representative experience," see my "The Role of Experience in the Construction of Social Theory" in *The Sociological Review* 21:1 (February 1973) pp. 25–55.

10. Karl Marx, *The Holy Family* (London: Lawrence and Wishart, 1956) p. 125.

11. Raymond Aron, *Main Currents in Sociological Thought: II* (London: Weidenfeld & Nicolson, 1968) p. v.

12. Emile Durkheim, *Moral Education* (New York: The Free Press, 1961) p. 60.

13. Emile Durkheim, *The Rules of Sociological Method* (Glencoe, Ill.: The Free Press, 1938) pp. 14, 28.

14. Robert A. Nisbet, *The Sociological Tradition* (New York: Basic Books, 1966) p. 21.

15. For an honorable, humane, and grossly underrated exception to these strictures, see Geoffrey Hawthorn, *Enlightenment and Despair* (Cambridge: University Press, 1976) chaps. 1 and 2.

16. John Rex, *Sociology and the Demystification of the Modern World* (London: Routledge & Kegan Paul, 1974) pp. 239–40, 253.

17. I attempt a more balanced assessment of the movement and its impact on the development of sociological thought in *The Two Sociologies* (New York: Harper & Row and London: Longman, forthcoming).

18. Nisbet, *Sociological Tradition*, p. 8.

19. Ernst Cassirer, *The Philosophy of the Enlightenment* (Boston: Beacon Press, 1955) p. 278.

20. What follows in the remainder of this chapter constitutes a radical revision of the original "two sociologies" thesis I presented in "The Two Sociologies" in *The British Journal of Sociology* XXI: 2 (June 1970) pp. 207–18, reprinted in Kenneth Thompson and Jeremy Tunstall, eds., *Sociological Perspectives* (Harmondsworth: Penguin Books, 1971).

21. Raymond Williams, *The Long Revolution* (London: Chatto & Windus, 1961) pp. 73–4.

22. For this account of medieval society, I lean heavily on unpublished work by my colleague, John Heritage.

23. See John Heritage, *The Sociology of Motives* (forthcoming).

24. Quoted in Ernst Cassirer, *The Individual and the Cosmos in Renaissance Philosophy* (Philadelphia: University of Pennsylvania Press, 1963) p. 85.

25. Williams, *The Long Revolution*, p. 74.

26. More accurately, views of human nature were recovered from antiquity by post-medieval social thinkers, having been buried during the Middle Ages by the doctrines of medieval religious orthodoxy.

27. Thomas Hobbes, *Leviathan*, ed. Michael Oakeshott (New York: Collier Books, 1962) p. 125.

28. Ibid., pp. 100–01.

29. Pamela Nixon, "Conceptions of Human Agency in Social Theory" (unpublished paper) p. 5.

30. Jean-Jacques Rousseau, *The Social Contract and Discourses*, trans. G. D. H. Cole (London: Dent, 1973) p. 45.

31. Ibid., p. 76.

32. Ibid., p. 165.

33. Jean-Jacques Rousseau, *Emile*, trans. Barbara Foxley (London: Dent, 1911) pp. 197, 215.

34. Quoted in Marshall Berman, *The Politics of Authenticity* (London: Allen & Unwin, 1971) p. 215.

35. Rousseau, *Social Contract*, p. 174.

36. Nixon, "Conceptions of Human Agency," pp. 6–8.

37. For modern radical as well as modern conservative social theory, modern man is fundamentally one-dimensional, and is therefore given no chance of liberation whatsoever. If you press a self-proclaimed modern "radical" beyond his optimistic promulgations of the necessity of revolution, you all too often find a modern pessimist, not to say cynic. And the vehemence of the promulgations is usually in direct relation to the depth of desperation born of the pessimism (and out of all relation to anything that is actually going on in the world outside his bible classes on *Das Kapital*). The pessimism is crucially the consequence of the failure to locate a plausible and viable agency of change, as witness the increasing desperation and implausibility of the search by radical theorists in recent years—the intellectuals for Mills, the students for Marcuse, the artists for Birnbaum. But the failure is once again not that of the one-dimensionality of modern man, but of the one-dimensionality of the theories which portray him thus.

38. Nixon, "Conceptions of Human Agency," p. 2.

39. Here I have in mind Marx's frequently noted reliance on the instrumental mode of scientific reasoning and, especially, upon some of the categories of classical economics.

40. Nixon, "Conceptions of Human Agency," presents a concise and penetrating analysis of these shifts as the consequence of the impact on Durkheim's work of the instrumental-moral dualism.

41. Max Weber, *The Protestant Ethic and the Spirit of Capitalism*, trans. Talcott Parsons (London: Allen & Unwin, 1930) p. 181.

42. Quoted in J. P. Mayer, *Max Weber and German Politics* (London: Faber, 1956) pp. 127–28.

43. H. H. Gerth and C. Wright Mills, eds., *From Max Weber: Essays in Sociology* (London: Routledge & Kegan Paul, 1948) p. 55.

44. Max Weber, *Economy and Society*, ed. Guenther Roth and Claus Wittich (New York: Bedminster Press, 1968) p. 4.

45. Ibid., p. 26.

46. Ibid., pp. 24–5.

47. Max Weber, *The Methodology of the Social Sciences*, Edward A. Shils and Henry A. Finch, eds. (New York: The Free Press, 1949) p. 18.

48. Quoted in Mayer, *Max Weber*, p. 127.

49. Weber, *Economy and Society*, p. 25.

50. For the full account of which the following is a summary, see Ibid., vol. 1, chap. 3, sect. 5.

51. Ibid., pp. 244–45.

52. Gerth and Mills, *From Max Weber*, p. 352.

53. Ibid., p. 135.

54. Weber, *Methodology of the Social Sciences*, p. 57.

55. Ibid., p. 81.

56. Weber, *Economy and Society*, p. 243.

57. Gerth and Mills, *From Max Weber*, pp. 62–3.

58. This is not to deny that Weber argues that routinization may take either a traditionalized or rationalized direction. But it is to query the logic of this argument, since so self-consciously individualistic a process as routinization, in Weber's account of it, must disrupt traditional society beyond any possibility of restoration. The logic, in other words, gives rather more weight to his somewhat contrary claim that "in traditionalist periods, charisma is *the* great revolutionary force." And it is, of course, the logic of his view of human agency, which is the basis for his otherwise unexplicated insertion into his argument of his conception of the motives behind the routinization of charisma.

59. See Alvin W. Gouldner, "Anti-Minotaur: The Myth of a Value-Free Sociology" in Jack D. Douglas, ed., *The Relevance of Sociology* (New York: Appleton-Century-Crofts, 1970) for the point that this antinomy—for him, the antinomy between faith and reason—lay behind the antinomy between the moral and the scientific realms. However, the most systematic elaboration I have come across in the literature on this fundamental characteristic of Weber's thought is in Pamela Nixon's "Weber and the Moral Realm" (unpublished paper), which draws out the strikingly symmetrical interconnections between all the Weberian antinomies and their grounding in the basic antinomy between moral action and instrumental action with revealing clarity.

60. The noumenal/phenomenal distinction is, of course, Kant's, and was basic to Weber's epistemology—and moral vision. But the point I am now making is that he could not maintain it. Nor can any of the latter-day proponents of the Weberian tradition who proclaim themselves to be Kantians, for the position is utterly untenable, and its maintenance another example of the way in which so much of modern sociology clings to the obsolete epistemological hang-ups of the eighteenth and nineteenth centuries, while discarding or being blind to the moral vision in which they were grounded and which is still vital and relevant.

61. Weber, *The Protestant Ethic*, pp. 181–82.

62. Gerth and Mills, *From Max Weber*, p. 128.

63. Talcott Parsons, "The Place of Ultimate Values in Sociological Theory" in *International Journal of Ethics* (now *Ethics*) 45: 3 (1935) p. 316.

64. Talcott Parsons, *The Structure of Social Action* (Glencoe, Ill.: The Free Press, 1949) p. 719.

65. Ibid., p. 732.

66. Ibid., p. 701.

67. Ibid., p. 11; and see pp. 44–6 for the account of the theory, of which this paragraph is a summary.

68. Parsons, "The Place of Ultimate Values," p. 282.

69. Alvin W. Gouldner, *The Coming Crisis of Western Sociology* (New York: Basic Books, 1970) pp. 190–01, 197.

70. Parsons, *Structure of Social Action*, p. 369.
71. Ibid., p. 399.
72. Ibid., p. 397.
73. Ibid., p. 382.
74. Ibid., pp. 389–90.
75. Ibid., p. 384.
76. Ibid., p. 380.
77. Ibid., p. 388.
78. I take this formulation of the frequently noted dualism of theoretical focus in Parsons's first major work from Ken Menzies, *Talcott Parsons and the Social Image of Man* (London: Routledge & Kegan Paul, 1977), though I develop the difference between the "two theoretical programs" somewhat differently.
79. Parsons, *Structure of Social Action*, p. 768.
80. For a full account of this see, especially, Talcott Parsons, *The Social System* (London: Routledge & Kegan Paul, 1951); and Talcott Parsons and Edward Shils, eds., *Toward a General Theory of Action* (New York: Harper & Row, 1951).
81. Here, the reference is to what Parsons calls the "pattern variables," a series of two-sided dilemmas about appropriate orientations to action all actors have to face and choose between. It is not necessary to spell them out here, but for a useful and concise summary of Parsons's latest version of them, see Guy Rocher, *Talcott Parsons and American Sociology*, trans. Barbara and Stephen Mennell (London: Nelson, 1974) pp. 36–9.
82. Again, it is not necessary to elaborate these here; and again, see Ibid., chap. 4, for a full exposition, which is as clear as can be expected in view of the obscurantism of the terminology Rocher has to penetrate.
83. *Leviathan* was published in 1651, *The Social System* in 1951.
84. John O'Neill, *Making Sense Together* (New York: Harper & Row, 1974, and London: Heinemann, 1975) p. 15.
85. Ibid., p. 16.
86. Ibid., p. 39.
87. Ibid., p. 11.
88. Ibid., p. 39.
89. Michael Oakeshott, *Rationalism in Politics and Other Essays* (London: Methuen, 1962) p. 199.
90. On the uses and abuses of metaphor in historical and social inquiry, see Robert A. Nisbet, *Social Change and History* (New York: Oxford University Press, 1969) chap. 8.
91. Stephen Mennell, *Sociological Theory: Uses and Unities* (London: Nelson, 1974) p. 138.
92. Nisbet, *Social Change and History*, p. 319.
93. Robert A. Nisbet, *Tradition and Revolt* (New York: Random House, 1968) p. 159.
94. Karl Marx, *Economic and Philosophic Manuscripts of 1844* (London: Lawrence & Wishart, 1959) p. 141.
95. O'Neill, *Making Sense Together*, p. 4.
96. This point owes much to my general discussions with John Heritage.
97. Martin Buber, quoted in Charles Talbot Gillin, "Freedom and the Limits of Social Behaviourism" in *Sociology* 9: 1 (January 1975) p. 36.
98. Ibid., p. 31.
99. O'Neill, *Making Sense Together*, p. 56.
100. For my view, see my "The Under-World View of Erving Goffman" in the *British Journal of Sociology* XXIV: 2 (June 1973) pp. 246–53.
101. James Agee and Walker Evans, *Let Us Now Praise Famous Men* (London: Peter Owen, 1965) p. 54.
102. Ibid., p. 81.
103. O'Neill, *Making Sense Together*, p. 10.
104. Boris Pasternak, *Dr. Zhivago*, trans. Max Hayward and Manya Harari (London: Collins & Harvill Press, 1958) p. 306.

11

EXCHANGE THEORY

HARRY C. BREDEMEIER

THAT people are interdependent with one another and therefore necessarily exchange things has probably not been a secret to anyone ever since there were people. And that the stability of any set of interdependencies calls for agreement on who does and should exchange what with whom for what reasons and on what terms has not been out of the consciousness of anyone who has ever thought much about the matter from Plato on, just to make a conventional choice of an early thinker. Moreover, that those issues involve the matters of power, bargaining power, deviance, justice, selfishness, altruism, stratification, efficiency, competition, cooperation, conflict, monopoly, strategies, tactics, morality—this also has hardly escaped the attention of anyone who has ever tried to write anything about human affairs. Those matters are the stuff of social science and social philosophy; and they are all straightforward implications of the fact of interdependence and its corollary, exchange.

In a sense we shall see to be significant, then, the history of exchange theory is the history of much of social science, since all the issues just recited are among the issues currently dealt with under the rubric of exchange theory. The analyses and researches carried out under that rubric have approached some of those issues in ways that are sometimes fresh and sometimes freshly parsimonious. In this chapter I shall sketch the more salient of those ways, linking them to earlier approaches as the occasion arises.

The Nature of the Theory

Either or both of two scenes may be taken as primal for contemporary exchange theory. One is B. F. Skinner in his laboratory trying to get a pigeon to peck a round dot; the other is Person in an office trying to get Other to give him some advice (Blau, 1964; Homans, 1961; 1974). A third would do as well, but part of the peculiarity of the history of exchange theory is that it is hardly ever included in the strictly "exchange-theory" literature as part of that literature's major dramas. This third would be Talcott Parsons's Ego interacting with Alter in some situation.*

Let us select the first scene to dwell upon, and justify the selection with a statement by James S. Coleman which has the added advantage of revealing something about a current view of the history of exchange theory. Coleman wrote in the introduction to his paper on "Collective Decisions" (1964:166):

> This paper constitutes an attempt to extend a style of theoretical activity which is quite new to our domain. It is a theory which rests upon the central postulate of economic theory [viz, individual rational decision making.] The introduction of this approach into sociological theorizing was carried out by Homans. Homans has since then led himself by degrees away from such an approach into that of operant conditioning.

The first historical note to be made about this is that the paper by Homans to which Coleman was referring appeared in 1958 in an issue of *The American Journal of Sociology* partly devoted to George Simmel, who had written an essay explicitly entitled "Exchange" in 1907. The relevance of the note is that Simmel had there dealt with many of the issues of contemporary exchange theory, as we shall see; but that Homans did not mention Simmel's work on exchange in that paper (nor, incidentally, in either edition of *Social Behavior*).

We shall return to the history after examining the Skinner scene. The reason for dwelling on that at the outset is to make clear the logic of exchange theory and to make clear exactly what it is a theory *of*.

Exchange Theory Explanations

Two recurring criticisms of contemporary exchange theory are that its explanations are tautologous and that it is erroneously reductionist.† The

* Other writers, some of whose work definitely belongs with the logic of exchange theory but who are curiously uncited in the main literature principally identified with that theory include Howard Becker (1960), Orville Brim (1956), Walter Buckley (1967), Kingsley Davis and Wilbert E. Moore (1945), Erving Goffman (1961), William S. Goode (1960), Hans Zetterberg (1962), and—last for dramatic effect, Robert K. Merton. To show in detail the affinity of Merton's work to the logic of exchange theory would require a long paper by itself. For present purposes, it must do to note illustratively that much of his analysis of the political machine is straight exchange analysis (1957:70 ff).

† Jonathan H. Turner's (1974) sympathetic discussion of these criticisms is among the best.

charge of tautology is that exchange theory explains an act by pointing to the reward which elicited it and defines a reward, or reinforcer, as that which elicited the act. The charge of reductionism is that explanation in terms of "psychological" processes of actors fails to take account of "emergent" levels of social reality. This, of course, concerns the venerable issue of society as a reality sui generis, needing to be explained by "social" facts.

Both criticisms reflect a misunderstanding of the fundamental logic of exchange theory, a misunderstanding that may stem in equal parts from less than careful writing and less than careful reading. The issues can be clarified by scrutinizing the theoretically primordial exchange: that between Skinner and his pigeons.

What Skinner Explains The first step is to be clear about what it is that Skinner explains and what it is that he discovers—two different issues. Suppose we observe that one set of pigeons consistently pecks round dots, never square ones; and another set does the opposite.* We seek to explain the difference. Skinner can explain it perfectly; he can account for 100 percent of the variance. He does so by drawing on certain knowledge that we, the initially puzzled observers, did not have. His explanation is that the first set of pigeons had adapted successfully to an environment which was so structured that pecking round dots was a constantly necessary (but perhaps only randomly sufficient) condition for getting something they wanted; and that the second set had adapted successfully to an environment structured in the obviously different way.

It is a valid explanation; it is not tautologous; it is not reductionistic; it is wholly transactional; it is essentially Darwinian in its logic. It does not point to anything about pigeons as "causes"; it does not point to a reward as the cause; it points to a *relationship* between the pigeons and their environments. Notice, furthermore, that the "knowledge" on which Skinner drew to erase our initial puzzlement was not a theory. It was factual knowledge. We have no "theory" yet.†

What Skinner Discovers Notice, secondly, that we have not yet pointed to any discovery Skinner makes in his laboratory. He most definitely did not discover why some pigeons peck round dots and others peck square dots. He makes that happen. What he discovers is another set of things altogether, such as that pigeons are creatures which value (a concept to be discussed in what follows) a certain rate of input of grain; that they have the perceptual ability to detect deficits and surfeits of grain and to discriminate between round and square dots; and that they have ability to peck. He also discovered, of course, that in adapting to environments which make a certain kind of pecking a constantly necessary but only randomly sufficient condition for successful

*I intend this primitive example to stand for all the difference between actors who do some *X* and actors who do not that are focuses of a very large part of sociological research, such as the differences between people who vote Democratic or commit suicide, and those who do not.

†Skinner's laboratory experiments are, of course, tests of a theory. We shall come back to that.

adaptation, pigeons will adapt by pecking in that certain way as if it were always necessary but only randomly sufficient.

The Pigeon-Skinner Exchange It is also important to notice a third aspect of the scene. This is, as has been noted in passing earlier, that Skinner and his pigeon are exchanging with one another. Homans noticed this (1958:508) but dismissed it, saying, "let us not dwell upon that, for the behavior of the pigeon hardly determines the behavior of the psychologist at all." But let us see.

Skinner wants a pigeon to do something—peck a round dot. The pigeon wants some food, as well as a lot of other things I shall come to. Under certain conditions, each gets what he or it wants. The emphasis is usually put on how Skinner gets what he wants, but it is essential to realize that one of the conditions under which Skinner gets rewarded by the pigeon is that Skinner does what the pigeon requires him to do—all of it. There is food at the end of those pecks, a reasonably warm and dry cage, no cats lunging, ample water, and on and on. Moreover, Skinner does not ask the pigeon to sing "The Star-Spangled Banner," and he does not try to pay off the pigeon with dollar bills or cheese.

More precisely, if Skinner started out with the hypotheses that the pigeon would respond to dollars or could be made to sing (or with the moral conviction that the pigeon should be such a creature), Skinner would be a frustrated psychologist. He would have to change—that is, to learn. His learning would take place in accordance with the same principles as the pigeon's, principles which are, not so incidentally, explicated in more detail than Skinner explicates them by someone often thought to be utterly incompatible with Skinner and Homans, Talcott Parsons. (1955)

Parsons and Skinner Boxes

The essence of Parsons's theory of socialization is that socializing agents make outputs of five kinds of things to socializees: information, permissiveness, denial of reciprocity, support, and contingent rewards. They demand in return certain behaviors and signs of certain attitudes from socializees. The details of the theory concern the different consequences of surfeits and deficits of those outputs at various points in a sixteen-step sequence of socialization.

The details are more than this chapter is entitled to deal with, but the theory is obviously an exchange theory. Moreover, in specifying the five critical socialization outputs, Parsons in effect makes explicit certain important aspects of a Skinner box which Skinner usually leaves implicit. The operant conditioning process begins with the output to the pigeon* of the information that, let us say, the childish habit of pecking at a tray of grain has to be put aside for the more adult behavior of pecking round dots. The pigeon

* The application here of Parsons's theory to Skinner's procedures is appropriate also to Robert L. Hamblins's theory (and demonstration) of "the humanization processes." See Hamblin, David Buckholdt, David Ferritor, Marton Kozloff, and Lois Blackwell (1971).

(I freely anthropomorphize for the sake of economy) shows signs of frustration and perhaps even aggression at this change of signals. Skinner now provides another Parsonian output, permissiveness: he does nothing. He also supplies a third, denial of reciprocity: he reciprocates neither the pigeon's "aggression" nor (let us be imaginative) the pigeon's importunities to return to the status quo ante. Skinner then clearly follows Parson's instructions and makes a fourth output, the reward of grain contingent on the pigeon's pecking the round circle.

There remains the Parsonian concept of "support." For Parsons (as for whom not?), a critical ingredient of socialization in the human case is the provision of diffuse acceptance of the socializee as a person, with only certain *behaviors* being rejected. This provision of support amounts to holding constant for the socializee the things that are most valued and important to him or her while single specific things are changed. What corresponds to this in the case of the pigeon is precisely the holding constant of the many things vital to the pigeon mentioned above: temperature, water, protection from cats, and so on.

By procedures formally parallel to those by which the pigeon learns, Skinner learns also; and it is such learnings that constitute Skinner's discoveries. Skinner's learning, and that of all of us, always starts, more or less explicitly but necessarily, with a certain conception of the nature of the environment (e.g., pigeons) to be adapted to. It is in this sense that Kenneth Boulding has remarked that most human experience is like a badly structured scientific experiment. One forms a notion that an environment is so structured that if one does *X*, it will do *Y*. One then does *X*. If the environment then does not do *Y*, one is often frustrated. People handle such frustrations in various ways we cannot here go into;* but one way is to formulate a different hypothesis. ("Maybe they prefer grain to cheese.") One then acts on that image; and so on.

One goes on in that way until either the environment does do *Y* or one gives up. In either case, one has learned; one has changed his or her conception of the environment or his or her technique for dealing with it or his or her desire for the *Y*.

That, very simply put, is the theory of adaptation which Skinner tests in his laboratory. And confirms.

Sometimes, of course, one does *X* and the environment responds with the expected *Y*. Then one's hypothesis has been confirmed. Or rather, as sophisticates say, it has not been disconfirmed; and this is one of the respects in which most human experience is a "badly structured" scientific experiment. We hardly ever push our notions still further; and, of course, scientific controls are ususally absent.

The basic point of all this is to clarify the sense in which the logic of exchange theory purports to explain actions. Its explanation, in the first instance, is an explanation of why *A* did *X*. For that explanation, the

* See Harry C. Bredemeier (1979).

"exchange" theorist in fact does not deal with exchanges at all; he or she deals entirely with elements *inside the actor*. That statement will now have to be unpacked at some length before we can get to two other things exchange theory attempts to explain—namely, how those elements got there, and how both of those matters (the internal nature of controls and the processes of their development) are related to *social* systems.

Individual Action

The fact that exchange theory starts with observations and assumptions about actors and acts is what leads George Homans to regret that the term "exchange theory" is ever used:

> Since much social behavior may . . . be looked on as exchange, some social scientists have tended to call the type of explanation we put forward "exchange theory." We believe this practice should be given up. It implies that exchange theory is somehow a distinct and independent theory, whereas in our view it consists simply of behavioral psychology applied to the interaction of men.

Homans's "whereas" clause is notoriously controversial. Its essential meaning can be stated without the red flag of Homans's language as the proposition that individuals will do what they can to optimize their adaptation. The three key terms are "what they can," "optimize," and "adaptation." Let us begin with the last.

The Concept of Adaptation

Adapting to an environment involves four processes: obtaining things from it, disposing of things to it, avoiding things that are in it, and retaining things inside the actor that might "escape" (e.g., secrets, blood).

Every actor (indeed, every living system) is characterized at a given time or over a specified period of time by the amounts of different kinds of things the actor is set to obtain, dispose, retain, and avoid. A large part of the differences among pigeons, panthers, Peter, and Paula are differences in the kinds and amounts of things they characteristically seek to obtain, avoid, and so on. Those characteristics comprise the controls which make an actor a controlled system, or a negative feedback system. In the recent vocabulary of William Powers (1974), people are characterized by "reference signals" (values, goals) which prescribe the desired rates of inflows and outflows of things; "perceptual signals," which tell them the actual rate of those inflows and outflows; and a "repertoire of actions" operating to keep discrepancies, or "error signals," at zero. Alfred Kuhn (1974) has a slightly different vocabulary for the same elements: selector functions, detector functions, and effector functions. Each set of terms refer respectively, for example, to the setting of a thermostat (reference signal, selector function); the thermometer registering the actual temperature (perceptual signal, detector function); and the operation of the furnace or air conditioner to keep discrepancies at zero.

When the nature of the things wanted by a person is established and the question is *how much* of it the person wants, we have Thibaut and Kelley's (1959) concept of the person's "comparison level" and Homans's *Q* – the quantity that would satisfy. Reference signals are arranged in a cybernetic hierarchy, such that for the sake of a higher one, lower-order ones will be instantly sacrificed. (If you value honesty above money, you will return the wallet you found.)

A Word about "Things" It will be convenient here to insert a word about the nature of the "things" one might seek to dispose or obtain at various rates; for much wordage in the exchange literature is generated by confusion on this score. The things are any of the things anyone has ever written about or imagined. To follow James G. Miller's (1965) overall classification, they include all forms of matter, from apples to zithers; all forms of energy from atomic to zealous; all forms of human services, from apple growing to zither playing; and all forms of information, from recipes for apple sauce to instructions in zither playing.

The Concept of Optimization A straightforward definition of rewards and costs follows from the basic concept of adaptation. Rewards are the onset of things peoples' reference signals drive them to obtain or retain (money, for example), and the offset of things to be disposed of (labor services) or avoided (electric shocks). Costs are the opposite. They are the offset of things to be obtained or retained (monetary fines) and the onset of things to be disposed of (having labor service rejected) or avoided (receiving electric shocks). Costs are also, obviously, punishments.

To say that people will do what they can to "optimize" their adaptation, then, is to say that they will do what they can to keep rewards high and costs low. They will do so by virtue of being open, controlled, negative feedback systems. In that strictly definitional sense, people are profit maximizers; optimum adaptation is adaptation that keeps rewards as high and costs as low as circumstances permit.

The Issue of Rationality

The sense in which exchange theory assumes people to be rational is simply that it defines rational decision making as the effort to get rewards and avoid costs, given the way the actor perceives the situation. George Homans's "rationality proposition" says it precisely (1974:43): "In choosing between alternative actions, a person will choose that one for which, as perceived by him at the time, the value *V*, of the result, multiplied by the probablility, *P*, of getting the result, is the greater." [*]

Notice again that Homans's proposition says nothing about "exchange". It

[*] For an application of this proposition to an astonishingly wide variety of behavior, see Robert L. Hamblin (1977).

concerns any adapting actor. Homans is saying what Simmel said two-thirds of century earlier, in a passage one can readily imagine following immediately after Homans's rationality proposition (1907; 1971:46):

> That being the case, the isolated economic man who surely must make certain sacrifices in order to gain certain fruits, behaves exactly like the one who makes exchanges. The only difference is that the party with whom he interacts is not a second free agent, but the natural order and the regularity of things, which no more satisfy our desire without a sacrifice on our part [i.e., without our foregoing *something*] than would another person.

Rational-choice theory (Anthony Heath, 1976) usually considers three different situations in which people might act. One is "riskless choice," in which the person knows for sure the rank order of his preferences, knows for sure what he can do, and knows for sure the consequences of his action. That is the condition in which you know that you prefer apples to oranges, know that you have money, and know that you can get the apples by handing the clerk some money. Rational-choice theory says simply that you will buy the apples, assuming that your only choice is between apples and oranges.

The second is risky choice, in which the person still knows her or his preference schedule and the nature of her or his resources but does not know for sure the consequences of an action. To use Heath's example, this is the condition in which your choice is between playing a game in which you get ten dollars if the coin comes up heads, zero if it comes up tails; and a game in which you get twelve dollars if you select the one of three face-down cards with an *X* on it, zero if you select either of the other two. The cost of playing either game is the same. Rational-choice theory says you will pick the first game. ($0.5 \times 10 > 0.33 \times 12$)

People as Calculators?

So far, we are comfortably in the realm of Max Weber's *zweckrationalitat*, with the addition of a little probability estimate. Weber, however, considered this only one basis of action; so we need to pause to consider the relation between his influential set of distinctions and these starting-point arguments of exchange theory.

The basic sticking point seems to be the inference from rational-choice theory that people are forever consciously assessing their preference schedules, figuring out consequences, calculating probabilities, and multiplying. Weber, on the other hand, recognized this as only one kind of action and distinguished it from traditional action, *wertrationalität*, and "affectual" or "emotional" action. The problem, however, is only apparent.

All that is being said by rational-choice theory is that, given the facts just described, a person will be better off by his or her own standards if he or she chooses the apples or the coin-tossing game. It says further that people would prefer to be better off than worse off, and that, *whatever* goes on in the actor's head, the actor who behaves in accordance with rational-choice theory will be more likely to adapt optimumly. "Tradition" may be the source of the preference for apples, and/or it may be the conscious grounds for choosing the coin-tossing game. In the latter case, rational-choice theory says that the tradition (more generally, any norm) which prescribes the choice that would be rational is more likely to contribute to optimum adaptation than another tradition or norm.

Wertrationalität was considered by Weber to be a third distinct basis of action. Aron's example (1970:221) is the usual one: "Rational action in relation to a value is the action of . . . the brave captain who goes down with his ship. The action is rational, not because it seeks to attain a definite and external good, but because to . . . abandon the sinking ship would be regarded as dishonorable. . . ."

Even for Weber, of course, this is a type of *rational* action; and it should be clear that the captain's action is entirely encompassed by Homans's proposition. The distinction Weber made hinges on the distinction between an "external" goal and some "internal" goal such as the image of self as being honorable. But it is not clear that such a distinction is fertile, at least with respect to the issue of rationality or exchange. As Simmel saw clearly, the value to a person of an apple or of the fifty–fifty chance of winning ten dollars is as internal a matter as the value of seeing oneself or being seen as honorable. Simmel made the point as follows (1907; 1971:44).

> . . . Exchange takes place not for the sake of an object previously possessed by another person, but rather for the sake of one's own feeling about an object.

Lest there be any mistake, Simmel a little later elaborated the point (1907; 1971:45):

> In dealing with the concept of exchange, there is frequently a confusion of thought which leads one to speak of a relationship as though it were something external to the elements between which it occurs. Exchange means, however, only a condition or a change within each of those elements, nothing that is between them. . . . When we subsume the two acts or changes of conditions which occur in reality under the concept of "exchange," it is tempting to think that with the exchange something has happened in addition to or beyond that which took place in each of the contracting parties.

Another way of seeing the relationship between *wertrationalität* and *zweckrationalitat* from the point of view of exchange theory is simply to recall that among a person's adaptive needs is the need to avoid certain kinds of information, such as the information that one is dishonorable.

Weber's affectual or emotional action may seem to be the type farthest removed from "rational" action as defined earlier. Weber himself considered such action as outbursts of anger as emotional or irrational. There are, however, at least three ways of making clear the link between emotional behavior and rational-choice theory. The most obvious is to note that the angry striking of another person, or the loving embracing of him or her, is as much incorporated in Homans's proposition as buying an apple. Either may readily seem to an actor to be the alternative for which the value of the result, multiplied by the probability of getting it (usually seen as one in emotional behavior), is the greater. Closely related is the observation that a major difference between emotional or "expressive" actions and instrumental ones is the elapsed time between the act and receipt of gratification. Emotional behavior is often "intrinsically gratifying," which means that the gratification is simultaneous with the act. Emotional behavior is behavior with respect to which the actor has a very high "time discount rate," the economist's way of saying that the actor is (in that situation) present oriented. But there is nothing in rational-choice theory which says future orientation is more rational than present orientation in all circumstances.

Finally, the emotions are tied to rational-choice theory—that is, to optimum adaptation—in a more detailed and evolutionary way by Alfred Kuhn (1974). Kuhn sees them as biological reinforcers of approach to rewarding objects (love) and avoidance or destruction of costly or punishing objects (fear, anger).

The fundamental point in all this, however, is that rational-choice theory, the basis of exchange theory, is indifferent to the nature of the rewards ("external" or "valued principles") and does not imply any conscious deliberation on the part of the actor.

Choice under Uncertainty

A third condition dealt with by rational-choice theory is that of the necessity for making choices under uncertainty. The actor might be uncertain about at least three elements in his or her situation: preferences, abilities, and probabilities of outcomes.

The theory recognizes that people often do not have clear preference schedules. The stereotypical child before the candy counter, quarter clutched in hand, and and paralyzed by the inability to forego all the goodies that the choice of any one would imply, is a good example. This is the condition of internal conflict, or dissonance. Here, rational-choice theory simply says that the choice that would follow from Homans's proposition—that is, the most profitable action—is to reduce decision costs as much as possible, as by handing the decision over to the nearest adult or closing one's eyes and pointing—as such a child, is, in fact, likely to do.

Even if one knows his preference schedule and knows the odds, one might be uncertain about his ability—the adequacy of his resources—for performing the action. If the first kind of uncertainty is the phenomenon of "ambivalence," this is a condition likely to generate "anxiety." To say what is rational here is, as always, to say what would maximize profits. In this case it is to weigh the benefits of trying and succeeding against the costs of trying and failing, and to choose whichever promises to yield the larger profit.

Finally, one might not be able to estimate the probability that the action will lead to a given outcome. We are often simply uncertain about how the other person (or any environment) will respond, or what he or she is going to do next. This, for laypersons, is the peculiar horror of coping with an insane person. It is the field of Von Neuman-Morganstern theory of games, the development of which is beyond the scope of this chapter. Under certain conditions, the rational choice is said to be the one which, regardless of the other person's action, will maximize one's minimum gain or minimize one's maximum loss. Sometimes there is not even a choice that would do that, however; and then theorists seem to divide as to whether the course of action that would in the long run maximize profits is (1) to act as if all outcomes were equiprobable or (2) to consider only the best possible and worst possible outcome and consult one's preference schedule as between them. (See Heath, 1976; Luce and Raiffia, 1957.)

In all of this, the point to be emphasized is that rational-choice theory, the starting point of exchange theory, is an effort to describe the choices that are most likely to optimize adaptation—that is, to maximize profits in the sense defined—and therefore to characterize peoples' actions in the long run.

That optimizing adaptation is in fact what people do, regardless of the words they use to label what they do, has always been the point of cynics such as La Rochefoucauld and Pareto. Independently of their debunking animus, the starting point of exchange theory is similar in saying that the immediate controls of a person's actions are inside the person. They are *his* or *her* conceptions of what is rewarding to *him* or *her*, and they are *his* or *her* perceptions.

In more detail, we can list eleven variables that the logic of exchange theory points to as controlling the probability that a person will engage in some action. Call the action *X*, and let it be anything from going down with one's ship to apple growing to practicing canoe magic. Five of the variables concern rewards, five concern costs, and one concerns abilities or resources.

A person is likely to do X *to the degree that:*

1. He perceives potential rewarding consequences.

2. The reference signal defining those consequences as rewarding is high in his hierarchy of reference signals. This is another way of stating, in the language of controlled systems, the point of Homans's "value proposition." (1974:25): "The more valuable to a person is the [expected] result of his actions, the more likely is he to perform the action." "Value" here, it should be repeated, refers not to a characteristic of the consequences, or of an object; it refers to a characteristic of the actor. It is something about such hierarchies that, as noted earlier, one discovers through such experiments as Skinner's or through one's offering first this, then that, to another person. We shall return to the concept of value later.

3. The error he perceives between his reference signal and his perceptual signal is great. This is a more general and positive version of the principle of diminishing marginal utility and of Homans's "deprivation-satiation" proposition (1974:29): "The more often in the recent past a person has received a particular reward, the less valuable any further unit of the reward becomes to him." That is, with additional receipts of rewards, the discrepancy between reference levels for them and perceptions of one's state regarding them decreases; and the individual becomes more likely to turn to *other* actions

which might promise to reduce larger discrepancies, so as to optimize adaptation.

4. His subjective probability estimate is high that doing *X* will in fact result in the rewards. Two more of Homans's basic propositions apply here by pointing to determinants of the value (in the quantitative sense) of this variable. The "success proposition" (1974:16) points to a historical determinant: "For all actions [ever] taken by persons, the more often a particular action of a person is rewarded, the more likely the person is to perform that action." The "stimulus proposition" (1974:22–23) points to a situational determinant: "If in the past, the occurrence of a particular stimulus or set of stimuli, has been the occasion on which a person's action has been rewarded, then the more similar the present stimuli are to the past ones, the more likely the person is to perform the action or some similar action."*

5. He thinks the reward will follow the act swiftly.

Those five variables concern rewards. But actors seek not only to obtain rewards, but to avoid costs. Two kinds of costs are ordinarily distinguished, the contemporary labels being disutility costs and opportunity costs. Simmel made the distinction in different words in his paper on exchange (1907; 1971:49–50):

> The sacrifice which we make of labor in exchange is . . . of two sorts, of an absolute and a relative sort. The discomfort we accept is in the one case directly bound up with the labor itself, because the labor is annoying and troublesome [disutility costs]. In the case where the labor itself is of eudaemonistic irrelevance or even of positive value, and when we can attain an object only at the cost of denying ourselves another [opportunity costs], the frustration is indirect.

Many actions involve disutility costs; all actions involve opportunity costs. So we need to add that a person is likely to do *X* to the degree that:

6. He is not aware of any costs of doing so.

7. Costs he does perceive rank low in his hierarchy.

8. The error he perceives between reference levels for the foregone rewards and perception of their possession is small. (He has a lot of what must be foregone).

9. He estimates the probability that the costs will really have to be paid as low.

10. He thinks the costs will be felt far in the future.

Although most of the exchange literature takes the matter for granted, it is clearly necessary to add one more variable. All of the foregoing ten variables could predispose a person to do something, but if he does not think the ability or resources required to do it are at hand, it will not be attempted. So a person is likely to do *X*, finally, to the degree that:

11. He thinks he has the resources or ability to do it.

* Note that, as Weldon T. Johnson (1977:56) has pointed out, these propositions of Homans's quoted so far "state some empirical regularities observed about forty years ago" (Thorndike, 1911; Skinner, 1938).

To the degree that those eleven conditions exist, a person is likely to attempt to do the X, whatever it is.* Exchange theory seeks to explain action, in the first instance, by ascertaining the values of those variables—all of them, to repeat, being inside the actor. Ascertaining their values requires testing hypotheses about them, roughly in the manner suggested earlier in which Skinner ascertains that pigeons have reference levels for certain rates of input of grain, lack the resources for singing, and so on.

In short, exchange theory explains peoples' actions by pointing to the actions' adaptiveness in a certain environment, given certain characteristics of the actors. Putting the matter in this summary way should alert readers immediately to the close logical relationship between exchange theory and "functional analysis." It is a relationship that has gone remarkably under-noticed, with the major exceptions being Alvin Gouldner's seminal paper on the norm of reciprocity (1960) and—an even greater exception—Walter Wallace's brilliant analysis of different theoretical approaches (1969). The relationship will also have to go unelaborated here.

How Control Elements Get There

The next question is, how do the control elements become what they are? Addressing that question takes us also to the third term in the proposition previously stated as basic to exchange theory, that people will do "what they can" to optimize their adaptation.

The things people can do fall into two major categories. One is to operate on their environment in such a way as to make it respond favorably; the other is to operate on themselves in such a way as to make adaptation optimum, *given* the environment. The two kinds of actions, of course, usually operate together: In the process of trying to get a response from the environment, we alter our approaches to it in response to its reactions to our initial approach —and so on.

It is the second kind of operation to which exchange theory looks in order to account for control elements being what they are. It looks, in other words, to the relationship between what was inside *A* yesterday and the structure of the environment in which *A* acted yesterday.†

On the Development of Values

It was necessary to wait until this point in the exposition to get to a clarification of the concept of "value" promised earlier. As used in the context

* We have been summarizing the determinants of the likelihood that a person will attempt to do some specific thing, *X*. Unfortunately for simplicity, there is always more than one way to skin a cat; and there are usually alternative actions, *M* . . . *Y* that can lead to the same consequence as *X*. The probability that one will do *X*, then, depends on a comparison of those eleven variables with respect to all alternative routes to the desired payoff of *X*. This is a general statement of Thibaut and Kelly's concept of a "comparison level for alternatives." Life is very complicated.

† If one wants to predict what *A* will do the day after tomorrow, one must ascertain what is inside *A* today and what tomorrow's environment will be like. If one wants to practice *Verstehen*, the eleven control variables discussed herein are the variables one needs to understand.

of exchange theory, a major clarification was provided by Simmel in his essay on exchange, a section of which is entitled, "The Process of Value Formation" (1907;1971:55).

The value to a person of an expected consequence of an act develops out of the person's previous interactions with environments. *Valuing things differentially is one of the major operations people perform on themselves to optimize their adaptation.*

For Simmel, the key was the fact that nothing is costless. Everything requires a sacrifice of something. Using this as a starting point, Simmel provided an analysis that is (but has not to my knowledge been recognized as being) a theory of the phenomena currently discussed (Collins and Hoyt, 1972) under the label of "cognitive-dissonance" theory or "forced-compliance" theory: (1907;1971:51):

> If we regard economic activity as a special case [*note bene!*] of the universal life-form of exchange, as a sacrifice in return for a gain, we shall from the very beginning intuit something of what takes place within this form, namely, that the value of the gain is not . . . brought with it, ready made, but *accrues* to the desired object, in part or even entirely *through the measure of the sacrifice demanded in acquiring it.* [Emphasis added.]

To say that something has a value is meaningless in any but a comparative frame of reference. Its value is what one will sacrifice for it. (More precisely, its maximum value is the maximum one will sacrifice for it.) We learn *that* different things have different values to us; we learn, out of our experiencing the fact that we cannot have them all, that each requires a sacrifice—a disutility cost and/or an opportunity cost. We learn *what* value different things have for us out of experiences in which our environments were such that we had to pay certain costs to get those things, if we were to get them.

If we observe that we sacrificed much for something, we learn that we valued that thing highly; we attach a high value to it. Simmel warns against the opposite interpretation (1907; 1971:59):

> The fact that with well-developed concepts of value and tolerable self-control, judgments about value equivalence precede the act of exchange must not delude us. The probability is that here, as so often is the case, the rational pattern has developed out of a process that is psychologically the reverse . . . and that it is the *experience* of trading on the basis of purely subjective impulse which has then *taught* us about the relative value of things. [Emphasis added.]

It is this point of Simmel's that is demonstrated in the many experiments showing that people who voluntarily incur larger costs for some object or some experience than do others for the same object or experience come to value the object or experience more than do the others. (See, for example, Barry E. Collins and Michael F. Hoyt, 1972.) The significance of the point for our immediate purposes is to show that one of the things people can do to optimize their adaptation is to change their values to accord with the adaptations they in fact make. The further significance (making the same point in a different way) is to show that it is out of exchanges that inner controls become what they are. The inner controls then govern the next adaptive act, which is met with some response from the environment; this response then helps to shape the controls that will govern the next adaptive act; and so on.

We are, in short, simply applying to the troublesome concept of "value" the same reasoning we applied earlier to the less troublesome phenomenon of pigeons pecking round dots. The reasoning is that all of the controls which are learned*—values, perceptual discriminations, behavioral repertoires—are what they are because previous efforts to adapt optimumly resulted in their being that way.

Aspects of Exchange

We shall have to take up the issue of values again when we turn from individual adaptation to the social problem of *coordinating* individual actions; but we are not quite ready for that yet. The path to it begins with the recognition that the "control elements" previously distinguished are said to control the likelihood that a person will *attempt* to do any *X*. Whether or not the person will *succeed* is another matter. It is a matter of power; and we must now consider the exchange-theory treatment of that ancient issue.

The basic elements of the issue can first be indicated with a nonsocial example. The control elements govern the likelihood that a person will attempt to go to Chicago from New York by jumping off the Empire State Building and flapping his or her arms. The resistance of gravity has something to do with whether or not the effort will be successful. *If* the resistance of gravity has been incorporated in the person's control elements, then as a control element it will also govern the likelihood of the effort—but only *as* a control element; and it is a big "if."

Power in Social Life

Max Weber's conception of power, which involves the same elements as our nonsocial example, may be the one most often quoted (1947:152): "The probability that one actor . . . will be in a position to carry out his or her own will despite resistance, regardless of the basis on which this probability rests." The phrase, "despite resistance," may, in the social case, have been a source of some confusion, at least hinting at physical coercion as the ultimate basis of power, although Weber himself had explicitly added, "regardless of the basis." Much depends on how one is to understand "resistance." In one sense, everyone "resists" paying any costs whatever, by definition, as just explicated.

* Those that are not learned—that are genetically given—are what they are for the identical reason supplied by Darwin, but applied to phylogenesis rather than to ontogenesis.

In that sense, all interactions are resisted; and person *A* can adapt to *B* only by overcoming *B*'s resistance. Person *A* does so in any of several ways we shall come to, only one of which involves the use of physical force.

A related confusion stems from the loose usage of "coercion." Simmel put the matter straight seventy years ago in his essay on "Domination" (1908; 1971:97–98):

> Within a relationship of subordination, the exclusion of all spontaneity whatever is actually rarer than is suggested by such widely used popular expressions as "coercion," "having no choice," "absolute necessity," etc. . . . Actually, the "absolute" coercion which even the most cruel tyrant imposes on us is always distinctly relative. Its condition is *our desire* to escape from the threatened punishment or from other consequences of our disobedience. More precise analysis shows that the super-subordination relationship destroys the subordinate's freedom only in the case of direct physical violation.

We still have some troublesome undefined terms here, however ("subordination," for example); and recent developments in exchange theory help to clarify them.

Alfred Kuhn (1974) Considerable clarification comes from Alfred Kuhn, an economist who thinks that sociology is potentially *the* basic social science (Kuhn, 1974:465). Kuhn follows most of Weber's conception by defining a person's power as the probability that he can adapt successfully—that is, get other people to comply. One's power is great to the degree that six things are true: (1) one's potential offerings are greatly valued by others; (2) there are many such others; (3) there are not many like one; (4) those others are willing and able to meet one's needs; (5) one is willing and able to make one's potential offerings available; (6) one's desire for what the others control is great.

Kuhn further clarifies matters by sharply distinguishing power in that precise sense from *bargaining* power. Bargaining power refers to the probability that a person can get the compliance of others *at little cost*, "on good terms." It varies directly with the first four variables just identified, and in that sense is the same as power; but it varies *inversely* with the last two, and in that sense is the opposite of power. Other things (the first four), being equal, you will have your way with others at little cost to yourself to the degree that you are *not* willing or able to meet the others' demands and do *not* much need the others' offerings—*if* you have your way at all, which, to the same degree, becomes less likely. As Kuhn observes, a not-so-obvious corollary is that the strongest competitor (with respect to the fifth and sixth variables) always has the least bargaining power.

Homans and Blau on Power Kuhn's conceptualization helps to clarify some of Homans's and Blau's discussions of power. Blau writes, for example (1964:118), that:

> By supplying services in demand to others, a person establishes power over them. If he regularly renders needed services they cannot readily obtain elsewhere, others become dependent on and obligated to him for those services, and unless they can

furnish other benefits to him that produce interdependence by making him equally dependent on them, their unilateral dependence obligates them to comply with his request lest he cease to continue to meet their needs.

Blau's reference to "their" obligation to comply with "his" request obviously says that "he" is dependent on them for something. They have power. They have less bargaining power than he, but this seems more sharply illuminated by Kuhn's formulation.

Homans's statement of this issue (1974:83) is that: "When A's net reward—compared, that is, with his alternatives—in taking action that will reward *B* is less, at least as perceived by *B*, than *B*'s net reward in taking action that will reward *A*, and *B* as a result changes his behavior in a way favorable to *A*, then *A* has exerted power over *B*." *B* has less bargaining power than *A* because *B* thinks he needs *A* more than *A* needs him.

Simmel Again But it must be repeated that, in Homans's little scenario, *B* is still better off than he would have been without complying with *A*—in *B*'s own terms. Simmel again had it right in his essay on exchange (1907; 1971:59):

> . . . no contracting party pays a price which to him under the given circumstances is too high for the thing obtained. If, in the poem of Chamisso, the highwayman with pistol drawn compels the victim to sell his watch and ring for three coppers, the fact is that under the circumstances, since the victim could not otherwise save his life, the thing obtained in exchange is actually worth the price. No one would work for starvation wages if, in the situation in which he actually found himself, he did not prefer this wage to not working.

Justice

We are now, obviously, moving close to the issue of the justice of exchanges. Curiously, for all of his concern with exchange, conflict, and domination, Simmel did not concern himself with this aspect. That is perhaps even more curious since his contemporaries, Weber and Durkheim, and his predecessor, Marx, very much did.

Weber and Justice Weber made the basic distinction between the two principles of justice in exchanges that divides thought today, as most recently illustrated in the disagreement between the two Harvard philosophers, John Rawls (1971) and Robert Nozick (1974). They are the principles of "entitlement" and of "fairness." Aron (1970:254) has summarized Weber's position as follows:

> . . . In Weber's thought the theory of justice involves a fundamental antinomy. Men are unequally endowed from the physical, intellectual, and moral standpoints. At the outset of human existence there is a lottery, the genetic lottery. [And, we would now add, an operant lottery.] . . . Since inequality exists at the outset, there are two possible orientations: one that would tend to obliterate the natural inequality through social effort [John Rawls]; and another that on the contrary would tend to reward everyone on the basis of his unequal qualities [Robert Nozick, 1974; Milton Friedman, 1962; Ayn Rand, 1964, et. seq.] Weber maintained . . . that between these two antithetical

tendencies . . . there is no choice governed by science; every man chooses his God or his devil for himself.

Durkheim and Justice It is too infrequently emphasized that justice, for Durkheim, was *the* problem of organic solidarity. Justice, in fact, is an important part of what the "conscience collective" is all about; and the "anomic" division of labor, as well as the other "abnormal forms" discussed in Book Three of *The Division of Labor*, (1933:407–409) is one in which justice is not seen to prevail:

> But it is not enough that there be rules; they must be just, and for that it is necessary for the external conditions of competition to be equal. . . . We know only too well what a laborious work it is to erect this society where each individual will have the place he merits, will be rewarded as he deserves, where everybody, accordingly, will spontaneously work for the good of all and each. . . . It has been said . . . that morality . . . is going through a real crisis. What precedes [i.e., the entire analysis of *The Division of Labor*] can help us to understand the nature and causes of this sick condition. . . . What we must do to relieve this anomy is to discover the means for making the organs which are still wasting themselves in discordant movements harmoniously concur by introducing into their relations more justice, by more and more extenuating the external inequalities which are the source of the evil.

Durkheim's language still leaves room for the debate between the Nozickians and the Rawlsians over the proper interpretation of "equality of external conditions," "merit," and "deserves," although the language of working "for the good of all and each" and Durkheim's later emphasis on the importance of moral regulation of peoples' demands for inputs and levels of outputs move him, I think, toward the Rawlsian position.

Homans and Adams on Justice and Equity Half a century later, under the more explicit rubric of exchange theory, we have George Homans and, perhaps somewhat less widely known to sociologists, J. Stacy Adams being directed by their analyses to the crucial role of justice. Although Homans does not approach the matter in exactly this way, his essential reasoning can be put in terms of the analysis of adaptation with which we began. Doing so will also serve the not insignificant purpose of helping to meet Talcott Parsons's criticism of Homans's treatment of justice. Referring to Homans's "assertion (*Social Behavior*, 1961, p. 75) of the need to assume a 'rule of distributive justice,'" Parsons says (1971:33): "This clearly is a factor altogether independent of the assumptions involved in the previous four propositions. Is this factor a simple assumption or does it derive from somewhere?"

It derives from somewhere, as follows.

People do not act unless it seems to them profitable to do so. Consequently, if *A* wants *B* to act in a certain way, *A* must make it profitable for *B* to do so. What is in fact necessary in human affairs comes in time to be recognized as necessary (which is very different from saying that what people recognize as necessary is in fact necessary!); and what is regarded as necessary tends in time to be elevated to the status of a norm, particularly if the necessary runs counter to desires. (There is no norm commanding people to breathe, but there is one commanding them not to commit incest.) Hans Kelsen has referred (1945) to this latter tendency as "the normative power of facticity"; and it is the essence of the Peter Berger and Thomas Luckman (1967) theory of institutionalization.

The norm evolves, then, that it is just for a person's rewards to be proportional to his or her costs; and for profits to be proportional to the stakes (investments) risked in engaging in the action. In short, if you want me to do something, then the more costly that something is to me and the more valuable the investments I have to make in doing it, the more highly you must reward me. If you must, you come to realize you must; and you come to regard it as "fair" that you should do so (particularly, to repeat, if you would rather not—and if there is not much else you can do about it).

So we have Homans's principle of distributive justice (which he himself traces to Aristotle). It is (1961:75) that "a man in an exchange relationship with another will expect that the rewards of each man be proportional to his costs—the greater the reward, the greater the cost—and that the net rewards or profits of each man be proportional to his investments—the greater the investments, the greater the profit."*

Adams formulated that principle in a slightly different way, saying that justice, or equity, prevails between *A* and *B* to the degree that the ratio of *A*'s outcomes to *A*'s inputs is the same as the ratio of *B*'s outcomes to *B*'s inputs.†

Blau on "Fairness" Peter Blau's approach to this issue is subtly different in a way that has general significance. He writes (1964:156) that his concept of "fair exchange" is similar to Homans's principle, but that there is a difference: "The main difference is that Homans does not emphasize explicitly that social norms, which function to promote socially significant investments, underlie this notion of fairness or justice; indeed, he seems to imply that it is a natural sentiment."

The point that has general significance is that it is not that Homans "does not emphasize explicitly" the "underlying" importance of norms; for Homans, norms do not "underlie" such notions as fairness; the notion of fairness *is* a norm, and it emerges from and rationalizes regularities of action.‡ In this, and contrary to conventional wisdom, Homans and Talcott Parsons are in fact alike. One of Parsons's earliest comments on Durkheim (1937:381) was on just this issue: "It is all very well to think of social rules as given facts to a single concrete individual. But to the sociologist they are not given data in the same sense—they are just what he is trying to explain."

In the context of the rule of distributive justice, Homans's account of the

* In the 1974 edition of *Social Behavior*, this formulation does not appear. The formulation presented there, however, has subsequently (1976) been said by Homans to mean the same as J. Stacey Adam's formulation, which is more closely related to Homans's 1961 formulation, and to which we turn immediately.

† This formulation has the arithmetic fault that if *A* steals five dollars from the till and gains ten, his ratio is the same as *B*'s, who puts in five and loses ten. Elaine Walster, Ellen Berscheid, and C. William Walster (1976) have corrected this.

‡ By "equal" Homans means, I think, simply that whatever the terms of the exchange turn out to be, each person can *no longer* affect *further* changes in the other's behavior.

norm is consistent with his basic theoretical principles. "Except for some philosophers," he writes (1976:244):

> an equitable distribution of rewards may simply be a distribution by relative power—provided only that the relative powers of the parties have managed to remain equal* and constant for some considerable period of time. An inequitable distribution may be no more than one that no longer reflects the actual distribution of power.

He had earlier (1974:250) made the point even more tersely: "The rule of distributive justice is a statement of what ought to be, and what people say ought to be is determined in the long run and with some lag by what they find in fact to be the case."

It is also this reasoning that leads to Homans's at first glance extraordinary inclusion in the concept of "investments" such qualities as sex, race, ethnicity, or age. If such qualities are seen to be regularly associated with superior power and bargaining power, their association will tend to be regarded as inevitable; and the seemingly inevitable in interpersonal relations tends to be institutionalized.†

This observation returns us to Durkheim. The breakdown of social order, or social "cohesion," with which Durkheim was always wrestling, was precisely the habit of the modern consciousness to regard less and less as "inevitable": not ways of thinking about the universe, not ways of technologically coping with it, and not traditional ways of deciding who should play what roles or how much is enough. Anomie is the deregulation of all such relations; "consciousness raising" is the Durkheimean anomie, institutionalized.

This does not, however, invalidate the general principle that equity or justice is felt to prevail to the degree that ratios of outcomes to inputs are felt to be equal. What caused the breakdown of coordination from mechanical solidarity to the "abnormal forms" of the division of labor was the failure of collective representations to evolve which stipulated what was to count as outcomes and inputs and how they were to be comparatively measured. As Homans put this aspect of the matter (1961:246–247):

> . . . All the arguments about surplus value from John Ball to Karl Marx are one long attempt to prove that what employers count as investments ought not to be so counted, and that therefore they get more than their fair share of economic enterprise and exploit the workers.

In dealing with these issues, Blau discusses at length *both* possible outcomes of the uneasy relation between power and justice. His summary statement is that (1964:74):

> In brief, differentiation of power . . . evokes contrasting dynamic forces: legitimating processes that foster the organization of individuals and groups in common endeavors; and countervailing forces that deny legitimacy to existing powers and promote

* Interestingly, Blau comes very close to making this point about Gouldner's theory of a norm of reciprocity. (See Blau, 1964:92.)

† The assertion of this sentence has been formally and elegantly elaborated by Joseph Berger, Morris Zelditch, Jr., Bo Anderson, and Bernard P. Cohen (1972:119–146).

opposition and cleavage. Under the influence of these forces, the scope of legitimate organization expands to include ever-larger collectivities, but opposition and conflict recurrently redivide these collectivities and stimulate reorganization along different lines.

On the issue of disagreements over the justice of relations among rewards, costs, and investments, Homans winds up essentially with Weber. However, by 1961, Weber's "God" and "devil" have become secularized: referring to his point about surplus value, Homans says (1961:247), "Of course, none of the arguments prove it; such things are not capable of proof: they are matters of taste."

Modes of Coordination

So far we have remained close to the microlevel of interpersonal interactions, which is where the bulk of the literature on "exchange theory" proper is to be found. But the logic of what we have said carries over to macrolevel concerns. The transition from micro to macro lies in the problem of *coordinating* rationally adaptive actors in the teeth of the fact that the controls of their actions are inside them. It is the *actor's* conceptions of how much of what is to be obtained or disposed that govern his or her behavior.

The essence of the coordination problem—"the problem of social order"—is shown in Prisoners' Dilemma, the general form of which is illustrated in figure 1.*

Figure 1. The Coordination Problem

		Column	
		1	2
Row	1	+5, +5,	−4, +6
	2	+6, −4	-3, -3

Column chooses either column 1 or column 2; Row chooses either row 1 or row 2. The first entry in each cell is the payoff to Row; the second, the payoff to Column. If Row reasons with self-oriented rationality, he recognizes that if Column chooses column 1, his choice is between row 1, which yields him five,

* Significant analyses of the coordination problem from strict exchange-theory perspectives are to be found in Garrett Hardin (1968), Mancur Olson (1965), and Thomas Schelling (1971). Talcott Parsons has also noted the significance of this, writing (1968:437) that "The theory of games can be said to have proved that a complex interaction system with no rules, but in which each unit is supposed to be 'rationally pursuing its self-interest,' *cannot* [Parsons's emphasis] be stable. . . . "

and row 2, which yields him six. Preferring six to five, he should choose row 2. If Column chooses column 2, Row's choice is between row 1, which costs him four, and row 2, which costs him three. Preferring to lose three rather than four, his best choice is again row 2.

Similar reasoning by Column leads him to choose column 2; they are maximally malintegrated; and each is worse off by eight than he could have been, had there been some way of coordinating their autonomous decisions. That "some way," however, has to be something that would precisely *prevent* the exercise of their self-oriented rationality.

What makes society possible is a solution to the dilemma. There are five possible solutions, each of them the focus of enormous amounts of sociological and more general social-scientific analysis. My purpose in reviewing them briefly here is to show the generality of the basic elements of exchange theory and to bring conceptually together schools of thought too often treated in isolation and sometimes even thought to be in conflict.

The five possible solutions amount to five different kinds of "collective conscience" or moral principles. In what seems often to be regarded as a discordant metaphor, they consist of five differently structured social Skinner boxes, stating what actors must do in order to adapt successfully. Each has its own advantages and disadvantages; each is a perfectly adequate solution under certain circumstances; and the circumstances under which each is adequate seem almost impossible to maintain—which is one reason human existence is necessarily troubled.

The five solutions are most clearly distinguishable by staying for a moment more on the level of dyads. The transition to the more complex societal level is made by introducing symbolic media as intervening exchanges between the exchanges of "things"; and we shall get to that soon enough.

We picture an actor, *A*, adapting to another actor, *B*. *A* needs *B* to behave in one or another of the ways already identified: to give something to *A*, accept something from *A*, leave something of *A*'s alone, or not inflict something on *A*. *A* asks *B* in one way or another to comply. We imagine *B* saying, "Why should I?"

Coercion

One possible answer by *A* is the use of coercion. Coercion is not, strictly speaking, a *social* mode of relationship, although here (as where not in our literature?) terms are often not used strictly. Pure coercion involves treating a person as a "thing" rather than as a cultural creature with his or her own definitions of the world, definitions which must be taken into account by the actor. It consists of treating a person by the laws of physics rather than the laws of sociality. One coercively gets a person to leave the room the same way one gets a bag of garbage to leave the room, by picking it up ("it" is appropriate here) and carrying or throwing it out. Coercion, the use of physical force or violence, is the rock-bottom way of adapting. For Simmel, the coercive form of robbery was probably one of the precursors of the more social forms to which we turn next; they evolved partly out of robbery as institutionalized stabilizations of the relationship expressed in that form of exchange. (The other probable starting point of institutionalized exchange modes for Simmel was the spontaneous gift. We shall return to that later. See "Exchange," 1971:63–68; "Conflict," 1955:115.)

The Market

Another answer *A* can give to *B*'s always latent question is, "Because if you do, I will give you something you value more than you value what I am asking you to sacrifice." This is the basis of that great coordinating institution, the market, the focus of most of the corpus of economic theory.

When people are related to one another in the market mode, they adapt by meeting one another's prices. Two subforms of market relations need to be distinguished: the pure "bargaining" form and the fixed-price form. In the bargaining form, *A* and *B* negotiate over terms, and the use of bargaining tactics and strategies are significant elements in mutual accommodation. They have generated the vast literature on game theory (see, for example, Schelling, 1963; Luce and Raiffa, 1957; Rapaport, 1960).

In the fixed-price form, the tactics and strategies of bargaining do not appear; but it remains true that *A* adapts only by making it worth *B*'s while to accommodate him or her, which is the essence of the market. In the classical market, the price a given actor faces and can charge is fixed, so far as he or she is concerned, by the forces of competition.

Tradition, Legal Systems, and Bureaucracies

A third answer by *A* to *B* is, "Because it is my right to tell you to do it, and your duty to do it." This is the common element in *two* of Max Weber's classical "types of action" and "types of domination" [as Aron (1970:284) translates *Herrschaft;* or "types of authority," as Parsons (1937:646) translates it.] They are "tradition" and "rational-legal."

It is clear from Weber's writings on these subjects and from the many who have interpreted and elaborated on them (e.g., Abel, 1975; Aron, 1975; Parsons, 1937; Nisbet, 1970) that in the case of both rational-legal and traditional bases of *Herrschaft*, people do as they do because it is their duty to do so. The distinction between "tradition" and the legal-bureaucratic cases parallels the distinction between the fixed-price and the bargaining form of the market: in the former of both pairs, the justification is essentially that "that is the way it is, and that is all there is to it." In the latter, there is more to it: with respect to the bargaining, the more is a matter of tactics and strategies; with respect to bureaucracies the more is an explanation that the act in question is one's duty, because the decision that it is has been made properly by persons authorized to make it, after due and rational consideration of alternatives.

The parallelism between fixed price and tradition, and between bargaining and legal-rational-bureaucratic is important to note. (We shall note similar parallels in the other modes of relations also.) Its importance lies in the predictability of behavior and in the speed with which relations and actions can change. When something is one's duty because management or the Supreme Court have said so, or when the terms of a transaction are subject to bargaining, predictability is much less certain, and matters may change relatively rapidly.

Solidarity *(Gemeinschaft?)*

Person *A* can offer a fourth answer to *B*'s "Why should I?"—and if it is accepted (an "if" that obviously applies to the other modes also), *A* will be successfully adapted, and the *A-B* system will be integrated. That answer is "Because you value my welfare, and your doing this will make me better off."

That is the essence of mutual adaptations when people are related "altruistically," or in diffuse bonds of solidarity. Whether the familiar concept of *Gemeinschaft* is fully appropriate here may be debatable. Certainly, part of what *Gemeinschaft* connotes to modern theorists is this mode of relationship, as suggested by Nisbet (1970:106):

> The kinship group serves as the archetype of *Gemeinschaft*. It is by all odds the oldest form, and its spirit, its sense of communal membership, even its nomenclature, tend to become the image of other, non-kinship types of *Gemeinschaft*. In any genuinely *Gemeinschaft* type of social grouping there is a profound ethic of solidarity, a vivid sense of "we *versus* they," and of commitment of the whole self to the *Gemeinschaft*.

Some of that language connotes relations of love, care, altruism, brotherhood and sisterhood, friendship; but some of it need not. And some of Nisbet's further examples (ethnic ghettos, totalitarian nations, Indian social castes) could as easily point to traditional "duties" as to bonds of caring or interpersonal altruism. *Gemeinschaft* groupings are instances of the integrative mode being discussed here, then, only to the degree that they imply the Ruth-Naomi or Damon-Pythias kind of concern.

In these kinds of solidarity relations, there are also two subforms, distinguished in terms of the predictability and stability of behaviors they generate. The more predictable and stable behaviors are those stemming from ascribed solidarity bonds (familial, for example); the less easily predictable and more rapidly changing ones are those based on achieved solidarities (for example, friendship and romantic love).

In either of those forms, it is this mode of interaction to which Blau seems essentially to be pointing as "social" exchange in distinction from "economic" exchange, a distinction which also looms large in Peter Ekeh's work (1974). As Blau puts it (1964:93): "The basic and most important distinction is that social exchange entails *unspecified* obligations [Blau's emphasis]." Solidary relations are "diffuse"; and Blau might, of course, just as well have gone on to say that they are also particularistic and affective.

Cooperation

Finally, *A* can answer *B*'s question with some version of: "Because what I'm asking you to do is, in view of the circumstances, the best way for you to achieve your goal, which I share." The essence of cooperation is that *A* and *B* do share a goal and that what they can legitimately call on one another to do are those things which would reasonably further achievement of that goal—not because they love one another, not because of duty, and not because *A* will pay *B* or vice versa. Rather, because, given their understandings of physical and social realities, those actions seem efficient.

Here too, one might distinguish between more and less predictable and stable behaviors. The more predictable and stable are those in which the expertise of an actor is institutionally established, so that when he or she says that an act will lead to the other actor's benefit, the advice is unquestioned. Professional-client relations (when both the professional's expertise and his or her collectivity orientations are trusted) are examples. The less predictable, more fluctuating cases are those in which *A* must *persuade B*, through argument, demonstration, or even experiment, that the action is efficient.

A Note on "Mechanical" and "Organic" Solidarity

It may be helpful to pause here briefly to consider the relationship between all this and Durkheim's famous distinction. What is worth noting is that in Durkheim's description of mechanical solidarity, one does not get any picture of what all those people are *doing*, except occasionally punishing one another "repressively." We must supply our own picture, which is not difficult. They are telling one another things, having sexual relations, handing one another things, "curing" one another, not often insulting one another; saying "heave ho" in unison, . . . they are exchanging.

Durkheim took all that for granted. His concern was with the difference between societies in which exchanges are coordinated in fixed ("traditional") ways and in which most people have essentially the same adaptive problems, have the same environments, and are governed by the same controls, on the one hand; and, on the other, societies in which those conditions are the opposite. As Aron puts it (1970:16), what is special about mechanical solidarity is that "It is *the details* of what must be done [the exchanges] and what must be thought [the controls] which are imposed by the collective conscience. [Aron's emphasis]"

To the degree that people stopped resembling one another, to that degree it became harder for them to practice *Verstehen* accurately, to empathize with one another, and, above all, to share a common conception of one another's costs, rewards, profits, investments, and risks. Those increasingly became, as Homans would say, matters of (greatly differentiated) "tastes"; and it became harder to maintain a common sense that justice prevailed.

Complexity and Intervening Media

Peter Blau sets the stage for a transition to exchange in large systems precisely (1964:253):

> The complex social structures that characterize large collectivities differ fundamentally from the simpler structures of small groups. A structure of social relations *develops* in a small group *in the course of* social interaction among its members. Since there is no direct social interaction among most members of a large community or large society, some other mechanism must mediate the structure of social relations among them. Value consensus provides this mediating structure. [Emphasis added.]

In thus turning to "value consensus," Blau turns, so to speak, from Homans to Parsons. Parsons's emphasis on shared values is well known; but it is one of the areas in which he has been misunderstood to an extraordinary degree. His position (1968:437) is that "The most important *single* condition of the integration of an interaction system is a shared basis of normative order."

We must distinguish among three critical kinds of value consensus. One is consensus on the kinds of qualities actors should have; another is consensus on the kinds of actions and consequences that are valuable; the third is consensus on the kinds of media that can serve as symbolic substitutes for the direct reinforcements to which Blau refers. We shall deal with the three kinds in order.

The Moral Sentiments

To dwell on the first kind of value consensus has been for a long time sociologically unfashionable to the point of being taboo. One has the impression that the fact that pioneer social scientist, Adam Smith, wrote and rewrote until his death *The Theory of Moral Sentiments* seems almost embarrassing—certainly quaint—to those who, indeed, have not repressed it altogether.

Smith, however, lavished at least as much attention on his treatise dealing with sympathy, propriety, gratitude, justice, beauty, beneficence, duty, self-respect ("self-approbation"), and morality and virtue in general as he did on *An Inquiry into the Nature and Causes of the Wealth of Nations*. The two books, to be sure, seem at first glance so different that some (for example, Jacob Viner, 1968:323) have found it hard to believe that they were written by the same person.

Smith's concern in both books, however, was precisely with the question of the values that could effectively coordinate interdependent people in the face of the fact that they are autonomous—that the controls are inside each of them. In *The Wealth of Nations*, as everyone knows, he focused on the market as a coordinating mechanism—and he was far from blind to all the "noncontractual elements of contract" that many of us associate with Durkheim. In the *Moral Sentiments,* as perhaps fewer appreciate, he focused on the moral qualities of peoples' characters that contribute to coordination.

Smith did not, of course, develop his theory of the moral sentiments from the perspective of exchange theory recognized today. But the logic of exchange theory forces us to the same concerns that preoccupied him in that great work. It does so in the following ways.

A Further Implication of Interdependence

Given the fact that the controls are in the person, and given the fact that the persons are interdependent, certain things follow directly. One is that it is part of everyone's experience that others respond favorably to one to the degree that they find one rewarding. They find one rewarding to the degree that one's actions have three characterisitics: (1) they are difficult to do (they involve such costs and/or such rare qualities that not many people can or will do them; (2) they are valued by those others; and (3) one does them competently (one overcomes the difficulty with "grace," "elegance," "aplomb," and similar styles—only not so much aplomb that others forget how difficult it is!).

Since that is so, one learns to value in oneself the ability to do well, valued things that are difficult. In short, out of the facts of interdependence and of being an optimum-adaptation-seeking controlled system comes the human need for self-respect. "Self-respect" is the obtaining and retaining of information that one is competently doing something that is valued and is recognized as difficult. The *processes* of the development of such a need in the individual are those analyzed by G. H. Mead and Charles H. Cooley. They are, in the context of developing a sense of self, the processes previously described here in the context of Skinner's developing a sense of what pigeons are like.

The *sources* of the need are the background reasons (not explicated by him) of John Rawls's insistence that self-respect is *the* "primary good" which people seek to maximize: self-respect, when validly grounded, is a universal means to optimizing adaptation.° For the same reasons, everyone comes to value in everyone else (and by Meadian-Cooleyan processes, therefore in oneself) certain qualities above others. Those fall largely into the two categories distinguished by Aristotle as the dianoetic virtues and the moral virtues.

The dianoetic virtues are the instrumental ones that enable one competent-

° The fact that the grounds of self-respect are so important creates a pressure to develop self-respect and to persuade others that one is entitled to it. Those pressures can lead to self-deception and to deception of others, as well as to the acquisition of competencies that are valuable to others and difficult. As Homans is (I think regretfully) fond of pointing out, the principles of human interaction are as accessible to people as to sociologists; and once perceived can then be manipulated to achieve optimum adaptation. Once consciousness gets to that point, we have added to the anomie of life the entire panoply of Goffmanesque gamesmanship and Garfunkelian techniques of ethnomethodology.

ly to do valued things that are difficult: strength, agility, intelligence, and developed skills of all kinds.

The moral virtues are the ones that enable people to rely on others. Aristotle's list is the one usually referred to as "the eight moral virtues": veracity, courage, gentleness, high-mindedness, justice, temperance, generosity, and friendship. They are qualities that, in whatever language, are universally important and difficult to develop. People who manifest them well are universally (1) admired and (2) likely to get treated well by others—that is, to adapt well.*

The instrumental and moral virtues, that is to say, tend to emerge as the focuses of value consensus *in societies which solve the coordination problem*. There is, of course, no necessity in nature that it be solved. Parsons's point may be interpreted as saying that one of the most important conditions for solving the coordination problem is consensus on the virtues as desirable human qualities. One of the further points Parsons has consistently emphasized and elaborated concerns a second kind of value consensus. This is consensus on the kinds of activities regarded as valuable. These, for Parsons, are activities contributing to adaptation, to pattern maintenance and tension management, to integration, and to collective goal attainment.

More recently, Russell Ackoff and Fred Emery (1972) have argued along similar lines that four "ideals" need to characterize societies that cope successfully with the problems of adaptation and integration: the pursuit of plenty; truth; beauty; and goodness, or justice.

The Collectivistic Tradition of Exchange Theory

The instrumental and moral virtues and the preoccupation with truth, plenty, justice, and beauty are emergents from the facts of interdependence and the autonomy of individuals. Those facts make it necessary (*if* coordination is to be achieved) that people will seek from others and hence try to offer others the qualities and performances that are necessarily esteemed in the pursuits that are necessarily valued.

As emergents, they confront individuals as givens. It is important to understand precisely what it means for individuals to be "confronted with emergents as givens." It means that any individual born and socialized into an ongoing society experiences it as a fact that other people will meet his adaptive needs only to the degree that he does things they regard as valuable. The things they regard as valuable are more likely than not (the exceptions being in those societies not dealing adequately with the coordination problem) to be competent and difficult contributions to the problems they face in pursuing plenty, truth, beauty, and justice. The most general things they will

* But, of course, it is other peoples' *beliefs* about one's possession of the virtues that contribute to one's adaptation; this too can be realized by people; and therefore here, too, anomie can be furthered by peoples' manipulation of the beliefs of others and by the others' recognition of the possibility that they are being manipulated.

regard as valuable are the instrumental and moral virtues. All those things are specified by the norms of the society.

If an observer looks at the scene at any given historical moment, he is likely to be struck first by the facticity of the norms. If his attention remains focused on that (as well it might, for the norms *are* the structure of the social Skinner box to which the individual must adapt), he is likely to join the company of analysts who are said to be in the "collectivistic" tradition of exchange theory. (See Peter Ekeh, 1974.) In that tradition, exchanges are what they are because the norms are what they are.

In that tradition, a major point is made (and often made with a strange tone of moral indignation against the likes of Blau and Homans) that people do *not* seek to maximize their profits in any "economic" sense; they rather seek to conform to the norms for "social" reasons. Their values are not, this tradition goes on, "utilitarian" values; they are "symbolic" values or "ceremonial" values (Ekeh, 1974:26, 45.).

The distinctions being groped for by this rather vague and sometimes polemical vocabulary are probably distinctions among the different modes of exchange sketched in the preceding passages. Markets, bureaucracies, solidary groupings, and cooperative teams are, indeed, different kinds of social structures, comprising different rules of the game under which exchanges take place. They require a third kind of value consensus, to which we turn next.

Parsons and the Media of Exchange

This third kind of value consensus, necessary in complex societies for the reasons Blau noted, is the focus of Parsons's concern with the media of exchange (1960; 1963).* His analyses of these issues are complex and difficult; what follows is a freehand summary of his contributions to this part of exchange theory. I think the summary is faithful to the main thrust of his analysis, but I have cast it to show its linkage to other areas of sociology in ways he does not.

The Market Mode and Money When people are coordinated in the market mode, part of the value consensus that provides the substitute for direct social interaction is a consensus on the symbol called "money" as a medium of exchange. Money, for present purposes, is two things: (1) It is a symbolic "certificate of claim" on all the goods and services (and information and energy) that are offered for exchange on the market. (2) It is an "immediate positive sanction"—a "generalized reinforcer"—for compliance. When *A* asks for *B*'s compliance on the market, he displays the bona fide nature of his claim by showing money, *and* he immediately rewards *B*'s compliance by giving *B* money.

The consensus on money as the mediator among *A*, *B*, . . . *N* is not, of course, the only value consensus required by the market mode of coordina-

*Jonathan H. Turner (1974:280) also notes this relationship between Blau and Parsons.

tion. Consensus is required on the principles of competition; on the values of universalism, performance, affective neutrality, and specificity; on the nature of contracts; on all of Durkheim's noncontractual elements of contract; on the entire "legal foundations of capitalism" spelled out by John R. Commons in a much-neglected classic (1924). The market is a complex set of moral principles—a very special "conscience collective"—on which there must be consensus, *if* the market is to operate as a coordinating mechanism.

Corresponding complexes of values are necessary for any of the other modes also; but I shall not call attention to them in the other cases. The focus must remain, for present purposes, on the symbolic media of each mode; for those, to repeat, are the substitutes for direct interaction of which Blau wrote, and they most directly involve "exchange" in the most narrow sense.

Money, then, is the symbol with which *A* certifies to *B* the legitimacy of *A*'s claim to *B*'s compliance, and it is the reward *A* gives to *B* for complying.

The Legal-Bureaucratic Mode, Insignia, and Respect In all the other modes of coordination or integration, a corresponding certificate of claim and an immediate reward are also necessary (*if* the mode is to operate successfully). In those nonmarket modes, however, the two functions (certification and sanctioning) are performed by different media, whereas money performs both on the market. Also, alas, the other media do not have the marvelous quantitative qualities of money, so analysis is much more difficult.

Put simply, when *A* and *B* are related legally or bureaucratically, *A* demonstrates his bona fides by showing some symbol of his *right* to *B*'s compliance (a badge, a uniform, an I.D. card, perhaps an "authorized signature"). He rewards *B* for *B*'s compliance with a symbol of *his* respect for *B*'s rights and *his* acknowledgement of *his* duties. The police officer with the search warrant (his certificate) carefully shows respect for the rights of the citizen he is searching—when this mode operates to produce equilibrium. We shall come soon enough to all the breakdowns.

The Solidarity Mode, Exposures, and Gratitude When A and *B* are related to one another particularistically, diffusely, affectively, and on the basis of qualities—when they care for one another as persons—then *A* gets *B*'s compliance by demonstrating his need. It is banal but necessary to point out that this also requires a shared symbolic universe and value system. *A* must communicate to *B* that he is in need, and that the need really is a need. (Or that must be "obvious" to *B;* but it is, of course, shared symbols and values that make such things obvious—when they are.) In that sense, *A* must expose himself and his dependency; but *A* must also reward *B* for meeting his needs—not with money, and not with respectful civility, but with "gratitude," the dictionary definition of which is apt: the expression of warm feelings of goodwill.

The Cooperative Mode, Expertise, and Goal Acceptance A and *B* may be related cooperatively. Then when *A* requests *B*'s compliance, what *A* must show first is that he knows what he is talking about when he says that *B*'s compliance is the effective and efficient means for achieving *B*'s goal. He must symbolize his expertise in the matter—or, again, that must be "obvious" to *B*. *A* must also immediately reward *B*. The reward is *A*'s complete acceptance of *B*'s goal. This too may sound banal; its fundamental importance—and precariousness—can, however, be indicated simply by pointing to the confidence game, *all* the elaborate rituals of which are designed precisely to symbolize both the con artist's expertise and his acceptance of the mark's goal.

The Coercive Mode and Weapons Finally, if *A* and *B* are related coercively, a symbolic medium is involved also. Weapons, from a clenched fist to "showing the flag" in a foreign port, are *A*'s symbols of his ability to use force. There is, however, no sanction: if *A* rapes *B*, *B* gets nothing for her "compliance"; *B* has been used as a thing.

"Stocks" of Ability to Adapt

In each mode, one's aggregate ability to adapt successfully—to get another person's compliance—is represented by his or her total "stock" of certificates. There are familiar concepts for them, and simply naming them is sufficient to tie the basics of exchange theory to a great part of the sociological tradition. In the market, one's stock is one's wealth; in legal-bureaucratic systems, it is one's authority; in solidary relations, it is the loyalty one commands; in cooperative relations, it is one's influence (authoritativeness); and in coercive relations, it is (in one of the too many uses of the term) one's coercive power. (The acronym is not bad: one's chances of successful adaptation in society depend on one's WALIP.)

The Breakdowns

The five forms of social relations we have reviewed are the alternative ways of structuring interpersonal exchanges. They all have difficulties. The difficulties are the focuses of another large proportion of the sociological literature. I shall call attention to them under two main headings, "deviance" and "disequilibrium." In doing so, I am further pursuing a main theme of this paper, namely that most of us have been talking (the logical implications of) "exchange theory" all the time.

Deviance

Since the five modes are all potentially effective ways by which *A* can adapt to *B*, the *A*'s of the world can be counted on to know it. No matter which one is institutionalized, then, any *A* who lacks the certificates or sanctions appropriate for that mode always has the option of trying one of the others. This is merely a corollary of Homans's rationality proposition.

Using Nonprescribed Modes That corollary implies certain kinds of behavior which universally (there is no "relativity" here) are regarded as "deviant" behavior. All that is necessary is to list as the columns of a table the five modes which might be institutionally prescribed and as the rows of the table the same five that might be actually used; and one has a twenty-cell attribute space of familiar deviant behaviors. (The diagonal cells, of course, are conformist behaviors. The intersection of the column labeled "market" and the row labeled "solidarity" is "nepotism"; and so on.)

Too Much and Too Little Another set of the behaviors universally labeled "deviant" are also logical corollaries of exchange theory. Norms always evolve (by the essentially exchange processes described by the nonexchange theorists, Berger and Luckman, 1967) about how much is enough: how much a person should produce and how much he or she should consume. In both cases (production and consumption), people can violate the norms either by too much or too little.

Too much productivity gets the label of rate busting; too little, the label of malingering.* Too much consumption gets the label of greed, avarice, or the like; too little, the labels of sucker, patsy, or their equivalents.

Social Problems From a slightly different perspective, these implications of exchange theory also generate in a logical way most of the laundry list of "social problems," in the narrow sense, that occupy another large proportion of sociological attention. The slight shift in perspective simply requires distinguishing between the point of view of those on the producing end of "too much" or "too little," and those on the receiving end. Thus, figure 2.

Figure 2. Social Problems

	Too Much Is Produced	Too Little Is Produced
From Point of View of Producer	Problems of Strain: Prices are too high; taxes are too high; work load is too heavy; etc.	Problems of Slack: Un- and underemployment; premature retirement; adolescent loose energies; empty nests; etc.
From Point of View of Consumer	Problems of Surfeit: Pollution of all kinds; overcrowding; obscenity; noise; etc.	Problems of Deprivation: Not enough food, clothing, shelter, respect, income, etc.

* For a thoroughly exchange-theory reanalysis of the famous Western Electric Hawthorne studies of output restriction, see H. McIlvane Parsons (1977). Parsons suggests a new meaning of the notion of a "Hawthorne Effect." See also Donald Roy (1952) who anticipated Parsons's critique of the Elton Mayo interpretation of those studies, also from what is (implicitly) an exchange-theory perspective. Robert L. Hamblin and Paul V. Crosbie (1977) apply an exchange-theory analysis to deviance in general and to Durkheimian and Mertonian "anomie."

Wrong Parties, Wrong Things Norms also develop by the same processes of who should exchange what with whom. Indeed, it is, at bottom, everyone's definition of the concept of "status" (in the Linton-Merton sense) that a status is a set of cultural prescriptions of how much of what the person in the status must, must not, and may exchange with his or her role partners (and, of course, how—that is, in which mode). "Incest" is the exchange of sexual services between people whose statuses say that that is taboo. "Trading with the enemy" is a similar case. "Pornography" (when its production or consumption is "deviant") is the exchange of information that is taboo, no matter who is involved.

Disequilibrium

The various "deviances" and "social problems" are two sets of breakdowns of coordination that have preoccupied sociologists and others, usually without having their processes explicitly linked to the elementary logic of exchange theory. Another set of breakdowns I here group together under the heading of different kinds of "disequilibrium," by which I mean nothing fancy at all. The disequilibrium most explicitly tied to exchange principles, not surprisingly, is the market disequilibrium of inflation and deflation. I shall sketch its essential forms and processes shortly and will then show the corresponding forms and processes in the other modes of coordination. Both discussions, however, will be facilitated by first putting the essence of all the disequilibriums in common, general terms—which are "exchange-theory" terms.

The General Problem We may conveniently collapse all the thousands of specialized statuses and roles comprising the division of labor in complex societies into two major categories: on the one hand, controllers of all forms of matter, energy, services, and information (butchers, bakers, bosses, and landowners); on the other hand, seekers of what they control. As controllers of goods and services (for short), people are seekers of the sanctions and certificates previously discussed; as seekers of goods and services, people are controllers, to varying degrees, of those sanctions and certificates.

The equilibrium problem is the problem of maintaining a balance between the ability and willingness of controllers of goods and services to make them available, on the one hand; and the ability and willingness of seekers of goods and services to offer sanctions and certificates for them, on the other. "Inflationary" disequilibrium, to use the most familiar concept, is the breakdown of that balance in which people as seekers of goods and services increase their competitive *offering* of sanctions, and people as controllers of goods and services increase their competitive *demanding* of sanctions—while people as controllers of goods and services do not increase their mobilization to produce.

Deflationary disequilibrium is the breakdown of balance in which people as seekers of goods and services decrease their competitive offering of sanctions, and people as controllers of goods and services decrease their competitive demanding of sanctions—while people as controllers of goods and services do not decrease their mobilization to produce.

More colloquially: One kind of breakdown (inflation) consists of more people demanding larger slices of a constant, or even shrinking, pie; the other (deflation) consists of fewer people accepting smaller slices of a potentially constant, or expanding, pie.

Market Disequilibrium In the market mode, those breakdowns, as noted, are the familiar plagues of inflation and deflation, or depression. The details of their causes and corrections are the foci of endless arguments, much of them needlessly obscurantist. Increased competition for scarce goods and services, increased competition for money, expansion of the supply of money, decreased willingness or ability to produce goods and services—these lead to inflation. The causes of those increases or decreases are obviously complex, but they lie in the determinants of peoples' control elements, as previously discussed. On the other hand, declines in peoples' willingness or ability to demand money, contractions in the supply of money, or increases in peoples' willingness or ability to produce—these lead to deflation; and the causes lie in the same places.

Legal-Bureaucratic Disequilibrium The corresponding kinds of disequilibrium in legal-bureaucratic integrative modes are equally familiar, but not usually seen as precise correspondences, and hardly ever seen in exchange-theory terms. What corresponds to inflation is bureaucratic rigidity and at the extreme, a police state. What corresponds to depression is anarchy. Thus:

When more people demand more goods and services as a matter of *right*, and the corresponding duties do not lead to the output of more goods and services, the limited supply must (as always) be allocated somehow; and (as always) it gets allocated to those willing and able to pay most. "Paying," in the legal-bureaucratic case, is a matter of demonstrating authority and showing respect and deference to those with authority. The inflationary spiral here is a spiral of increased competition for insignia of authority, increased red tape in the allocation process, and a move from respect and deference toward servility and fawning on the part of seekers; and from respect and deference toward arrogance and contempt on the part of controllers.

In the opposite disequilibrium ("deflation"), people insist less on their rights; are willing to produce for less display of right and respect; respect and deference give way to rudeness; what authorities say is "bullshit." "Duty" becomes one of the more odious four-letter words. At the extreme, there are no rights and duties; only liberties.

Solidary Disequilibrium The coins of exchange in solidary relations are pleas for help and expressions of gratitude, or return solidarity. ("None of your law and justice, but *help*," as Merton (1957:75) quotes Boss Martin Lomasny.) There is nothing above love and altruism, however, that necessarily prevents demands from rising or supplies from falling; and when more people want larger slices of a constant or shrinking pie, the coinage is necessarily debased.

Emotionality, communalism, expressiveness, the fashion of "letting it all hang out," are the signs of "inflation" in this mode. The demand grows for more effusive expressions of love, "warmth," and "spontaneity"; but, as in a market inflation, the feverish acceleration of impulsiveness and self-exposure consists, at least after a certain point, only of more wheel spinning, with no more real goods and services being produced. It is the social condition marked by sentimentality and maudlin romanticism.

In the other direction lies the condition in which there is a minimum of fellow feeling. People do not feel close enough to or secure enough with others to expose their dependencies, and it is hard to find people who will show gratitude, display loyalty, or express warm feelings of goodwill. Expressiveness is in short supply. What Simmel (1950:393) wrote of gratitude becomes the dominant view:

> . . . some people do not like to accept, and try to avoid as much as possible being given gifts. . . . As a rule, such people have a strong impulse to independence and individuality; and this suggests that the condition of gratitude easily has a taste of bondage.

Beyond indifference, reserve, and a passion for independence lies the "depression" of widespread distrust or even malevolence. Then it may be that what solidarity there is exists only within small circles, with everyone outside being regarded as "gooks," fair game for exploitation, perhaps even for its own sake (David Hapgood, 1974).

Cooperative Disequilibrium "Inflation" in this mode takes the form of an explosion of charismatic leaders and intense, if gullible and fickle, followership. The demand for assurance, advice, and direction rises, and gurus emerge to meet it, with rhetoric of millennarian optimism. It is the social condition of true believerism, credulity, panaceas, nostrums, and cults of the faithful, from vegetarianism to fifty-seven varieties of psychotherapy.

At the other extreme is the world of anomie and alienation, as Leo Srole (1956) and Herbert McClosky and John Schaar (1965) have elaborated the former concept and as Melvin Seeman (1959; 1975) has elaborated the latter. It is the social condition of widespread feelings of mistrust of leaders, meaninglessness, powerlessness, normlessness, cultural estrangement, isolation, skepticism, and cynicism.

Conclusion

Exchange (attempted, aborted, or accomplished) is intrinsic to social relations in the virtually self-evident sense that social relations consist of people offering or not offering things to one another and demanding, accepting, or avoiding things from one another. Exchange theory might be understood summarily as an effort to deal with Durkheim's problem (1914; 1973:152) of "homo duplex" by starting from that part of the duplex that "represents everything in relation to itself and from its own point of view," and then trying to show how such a being would be led in time, through the constraining facts of interdependence with other such beings, to that other part of the duplex, a being "which knows things *sub specie aeternitis* . . . , which, in its acts, tends to accomplish ends that surpass its own."

The path from that starting point to that end point begins by traversing at some length the nature of rational adaptation by a self-oriented being. It continues through a reconnaissance of an actor's process of learning what he values and what tactics and strategies are necessary to elicit the behavior desired from similar environing beings. At an important part of the path, a scenic overlook has been provided, directing attention to the high probability that such a being will learn to value sufficiently in himself the qualities and performances other people value in him.

That is the point in the theory's path at which the second part of "Homo duplex" enters the picture, the social part, which more or less controls (depending on the actor's prior experiences), the other part. From there, the path of the theory heads toward the evolution of norms that define the appropriateness of exchanging parties, the contents of their exchanges, and the institutional modes and attendant symbolic media under which the exchanges are coordinated. Once there, the theory cannot avoid dealing with the phenomena of deviance and the disequilibria seemingly endemic in a world in which the size of the pie to be divided is only uncertainly related to peoples' efforts to obtain slices of it. Both of those variables (contributions and demands) are affected by and affect peoples' perceptions of when justice prevails.

Along the path, there are memorials to Adam Smith, Emile Durkheim, Max Weber, and Georg Simmel. Too few travelers pause long enough at these memorials, perhaps because they are not so new as the ones to George Homans and Peter Blau. There is (logically) also one to Talcott Parsons, but people on *this* path seem to rush by it in a curious hurry. Recently, many sections of the path have been made four lane by Alfred Kuhn, and a few of the early sections have been illuminated by William Powers and by Anthony Heath. I have been a tour guide.

BIBLIOGRAPHY

Abel, Theodore, *The Foundations of Sociological Theory* (New York, Random House, 1970).

Adams, J. Stacy, "Inequity in Social Exchange," in Leonard Berkowitz, ed., *Advances in Experimental Social Psychology,* vol. 2 (New York: Academic Press, 1965) pp. 267–99.

Aron, Raymond, *Main Currents in Sociological Thought,* vol. 2., trans. by Richard Howard and Helen Weaver (Garden City, N.Y.: Doubleday Anchor Books, 1970).

Becker, Howard, "Notes on the Concept of Commitment," *American Journal of Sociology,* vol. 66 (1960) pp. 32–40.

Berger, Joseph, Morris Zelditch, Jr., Bo Anderson, and Bernard P. Cohen, "Structural Aspects of Distributive Justice," in Joseph Berger, Morris Zelditch, Jr., and Bo Anderson, eds., *Sociological Theories in Progress* (New York Houghton Mifflin, 1972) pp. 119–46.

Berger, Peter, and Thomas Luckman, *The Social Construction of Reality* (Garden City, N.Y.: Doubleday Anchor Books, 1967).

Blau, Peter M. *Exchange and Power in Social Life,* (New York: John Wiley & Sons, 1964).

Bredemeier, Harry C., *Human Beings and Human Societies* (Brentwood, Calif.: Alfred Publishing Co., 1979).

Brim, Orville, "Attitude Content Intensity and Probability Theory," *American Sociological Review,* vol. 20 (1956) pp. 68–76.

Buckley, Walter, *Sociology and Modern Systems Theory* (Englewood Cliffs, N.J.: Prentice-Hall, 1967).

Coleman, James S., "Collective Decisions" *Sociological Inquiry,* vol. 34 (1964) pp. 166–81.

Collins, Barry E., and Michael F. Hoyt, "Personal Responsibility for Consequences: An Integration and Extension of the 'Forced Compliance' Literature," *Journal of Experimental and Social Psychology,* vol. 8, no. 6 (1972) pp. 558–93.

Commons, John R., *The Legal Foundations of Capitalism* (New York: Macmillan Co., 1924, 1968).

Davis, Kingsley, and Wilbert E. Moore, "Some Principles of Stratification," *American Sociological Review,* vol. 10 (1945) pp. 242–49.

Durkheim, Emile, *The Division of Labor in Society* (New York: Free Press, 1933; first published in 1893).

Ekeh, Peter, *Social Exchange Theory: The Two Traditions* (Cambridge: Harvard University Press, 1974).

Emerson, Richard M., "Social Exchange Theory," in Alex Inkeles, James Coleman, and Neil Smelser, eds., *Annual Review of Sociology,* vol. 2 (Palo Alto, Calif.: Annual Reviews, 1976).

Friedman, Milton, *Capitalism and Freedom* (Chicago: University of Chicago Press, 1962).

Goffman, Erving, *Encounters* (Indianapolis: Bobbs-Merrill Co., 1961).

Goode, William S. "A Theory of Role Strain," *American Sociological Review,* vol. 25 (1960) pp. 194–202.

Gouldner, Alvin W., "The Norm of Reciprocity," *American Sociological Review,* vol. 25 (1960) pp. 161–78.

Hamblin, Robert L., David Buckholdt, David Ferritor, Martin Kozloff, and Lois Blackwell, *The Humanization Processes* (New York: Wiley Interscience, 1971).

Hamblin, Robert L., and John H. Kunkel, eds., *Behavioral Theory in Sociology* (New Brunswick, N.J.: Transaction Press, 1977).

"Anomie and Deviance," in Hamblin and Kunkel, pp. 361–84.

"Behavior and Reinforcement: A Generalization of the Matching Law," in Hamblin and Kunkel, pp. 469–502.

Hapgood, David, "The Screwing of the Average Man," *The Washington Monthly,* vol. 6, no. 8 (October 1974) pp. 35–40.

Hardin, Garrett, "The Tragedy of the Commons," *Science* vol. 162 (December 13, 1968) pp. 1243–48.

Heath, Anthony, *Rational Choice and Social Exchange* (Cambridge: At the University Press, 1976).

Homans, George, "Social Behavior as Exchange," *American Journal of Sociology,* vol. 62 (1958) pp. 597–606.

Social Behavior: Its Elementary Forms (New York: Harcourt Brace Jovanovich, 1961).

Social Behavior: Its Elementary Forms, rev. ed. (New York: Harcourt Brace Jovanovich, 1974).

"Commentary," in Leonard Berkowitz and Elaine Walster, eds., *Equity Theory: Toward a General Theory of Interaction, Advances in Experimental Social Psychology,* vol. 9 (New York: Academic Press, 1976).

Johnson, Weldon T., "Exchange in Perspective: The Promises of George C. Homans," in Robert L. Hamblin and John H. Kunkel, eds., *Behavioral Theory in Sociology* (New Brunswick, N. J.: Transaction Press, 1977) pp. 49–90.

Kelsen, Hans, *General Theory of Law and State* (New York: Russell & Russell, 1945).

Kuhn, Alfred, *The Logic of Social Systems* (San Francisco: Jossey-Bass, 1974).

Luce, R. Duncan, and Howard Raiffa, *Games and Decisions* (New York: John Wiley & Sons, 1957).

McClosky, Herbert, and John Schaar, "Psychological Dimensions of Anomie," *American Sociological Review,* vol. 30 (February 1965) pp. 14–40.

Merton, Robert K., *Social Theory and Social Structure* (New York: Free Press, 1957).

Nisbet, Robert, *The Social Bond* (New York: Alfred A. Knopf, 1970).

Nozick, Robert, *Anarchy, State, and Utopia* (New York: Basic Books, 1974).

Olson, Mancur, *The Logic of Collective Action* (Cambridge: Harvard University Press, 1965).

Parsons, H. McIlvane, "What Happened at Hawthorne?" in Robert L. Hamblin and John H. Kunkel, eds., *Behavioral Theory in Sociology* (New Brunswick, N.J.: Transaction Press, 1977).

Parsons, Talcott, *The Structure of Social Action* (New York: McGraw-Hill, 1937).

Family, Socialization, and Interaction Process (with Robert F. Bales) (New York: Free Press, 1955).

"On the Concept of Influence," *Public Opinion Quarterly,* vol. 27 (Spring 1963) pp. 37–62.

"On the Concept of Political Power," *Proceedings of the American Philo-*

sophical Society, vol. 107 (June 1963) pp. 232–62.

Sociological Theory and Modern Society (New York: Free Press, 1967).

"Interaction," *International Encyclopedia of the Social Sciences*, vol. 7 (1968) p. 437.

"Levels of Organization and the Mediation of Social Interaction," in Herman Turk and Richard C. Simpson, eds., *Institutions and Social Exchange* (Indianapolis: Bobbs-Merrill Co., 1971) pp. 23–35.

Powers, William T., *Behavior: The Control of Perception* (Chicago: Aldine, 1973).

Rand, Ayn, *The Virtue of Selfishness* (New York: American Library, 1964).

Rapaport, Anatol, *Fights, Games, and Debates* (Ann Arbor: University of Michigan Press, 1960).

Rawls, John, *A Theory of Justice* (Cambridge: Harvard University Press, 1971).

Roy, Donald, "Quota Restriction and Goldbricking in a Machine Shop," *American Journal of Sociology*, vol. 57 (1952) pp. 427–42.

Schelling, Thomas, *The Strategy of Conflict* (New York: Oxford University Press, 1963).

"On the Ecology of Micromotives," *The Public Interest*, no. 21 (Fall 1971) pp. 61–98.

Seeman, Melvin, "On the Meaning of Alienation," *American Sociological Review*, vol. 24 (December 1959) pp. 783–91.

"Alienation Studies," in Alex Inkeles, ed., *Annual Review of Sociology* (Palo Alto, Calif.: Annual Reviews, 1975).

Simmel, Georg, *Conflict and the Web of Group Affiliations*, trans. by Kurt H. Wolff and Reinhard Bendix (New York: Free Press, 1955).

On Individuality and Social Forms, ed. by Donald N. Levine (Chicago: University of Chicago Press, 1971).

Smith, Adam, *The Theory of Moral Sentiments*, ed. by D. D. Raphael and A. C. Macfie (Oxford: Clarendon Press, 1976; first published 1759).

Srole, Leo, "Social Integration and Certain Corollaries," *American Sociological Review*, vol. 21 (1956) pp. 709–16.

Thibaut, John W., and Harold H. Kelley, *The Social Psychology of Groups* (New York: John Wiley & Sons, 1959).

Turner, Jonathan H., *The Structure of Social Theory* (Homewood, Ill.: Dorsey Press, 1974).

Viner, Jacob, "Adam Smith," *International Encyclopedia of the Social Sciences*, vol. 14 (1968) p. 323.

Wallace, Walter L., "Overview of Contemporary Sociological Theory," in Walter Wallace, ed., *Sociological Theory* (Chicago: Aldine, 1969).

Walster, Elaine, Ellen Berscheid, and C. William Walster, "New Directions in Equity Research," in Leonard Berkowitz and Elaine Walster, eds., *Equity Theory: Toward a General Theory of Interaction. Advances in Experimental Social Psychology*, vol. 9. (New York: Academic Press, 1976) pp. 1–38.

Weber, Max, *The Theory of Social and Economic Organization*, ed. and trans. by Talcott Parsons (New York: Oxford University Press, 1947).

Zetterberg, Hans, *Social Theory and Social Practice* (New York: Bedminster Press, 1962).

"Compliant Actions," *Acta Sociologica*, vol. 2 (1957) pp. 179–201.

12

INTERACTIONISM

BERENICE M. FISHER
and ANSELM L. STRAUSS

WHAT IS INTERACTIONISM? Or, at least, what do contemporary sociologists refer to when they write about interactionists and interactionism? What about the interactionists themselves: do they agree on what and who they are and have been? Have the references to this tradition changed over the years, or once an interactionist always an interactionist? Those queries are necessary because sociologists, both inside and outside the tradition, seem to have somewhat different images in mind when writing about interactionism.

The terms of reference themselves yield a clue to explaining the variety of images. Sometimes the interactionists are called "symbolic interactionists," but sometimes just "interactionists" or "the Chicago school" or "the Chicago tradition." When Alvin Gouldner, a few years ago, spiritedly attacked Chicago-style interactionism (1973), it was especially Howard Becker and Erving Goffman who epitomized for him the fieldwork, urban sociology, and defend-the-underdog sociology which he believed was severely crippled by its avoidance of macrostructural emphasis in favor of its microscopic interactional one. On the other hand, commentators (Coser, 1976; Mennell, 1974; Zeitlin, 1973; Wallace, 1969), either critical of or sympathetic to interactionism, nowadays frequently use the term "symbolic interactionism." Usually they refer also to the writings of Herbert Blumer (1969) (who coined the term) as an authoritative spokesman both for the tradition and for its founding father, George H. Mead (another Chicagoan), who laid the basis for the characteristic interactionist perspective on society. Among the interactionists themselves there is a similarly bifurcated conception, suggested rather appropriately by the circumstances under which the Society for the Study of Symbolic Interactionism was recently founded. The impetus for its formation seems to have come primarily from several men and women whose avowed intellectual positions are grounded in the writings of Mead. Among those invited to join the society were some who stem rather less from Mead than from other Chicagoans like Everett C. Hughes and the earlier sociologists, Robert E. Park and W. I. Thomas. A substantial proportion of interactionists have remained outside the society, and perhaps a paraphrased comment by one represents a not unusual stance: "they seem too sectarian, there is much more to sociology than Meadian social psychology. And I don't like the term 'symbolic' interactionism anyhow."

There would, then, seem to be at least two interactionist traditions, each grounded in a different intellectual history. Alas, having asserted that, it is equally true that a great many interactionists have gone to school in an atmosphere that scarcely allowed them to distinguish between the two intellectual streams so characteristic of Chicago sociology between, say, 1910 and 1950. While some interactionists owe little or nothing to a Meadian perspective, the work of others is rooted both in Mead and in what is nowadays called the Chicago-style perspective, which derives, in fact, mainly from Thomas and Park. A younger generation, coming more lately to interactionism and in a period after the Chicago Department of Sociology had radically changed in character, seem to divide—some moving toward Meadian interactionism, others doing work in accordance with the spirit of Chicago-style sociology. Still others draw on both sources of interactionism (Petras and Meltzer, 1973).

Consequently, one can understand neither interactionism's history nor its contemporary developments without looking closely at the founders of this dual tradition, and especially, we believe, Thomas and Park. The origins of this tradition deeply affect the theorizing and researching of the tradition's contemporary practitioners, affecting too their strengths and weaknesses. On the other hand, people of different generations have faced different worlds, have had different sets of intellectual and social concerns. Hence Mead, Park, and Thomas have meant rather different things over the years; indeed, they have meant rather different things, even to sociologists of the same generation. To compound matters further, there were intellectual differences not merely between Mead and Park-Thomas, but between the latter. Understandably, there were also contradictions within the body of ideas of each man. The contradictions and differences entered into the tradition, not always or even usually perceived by the followers of the founding fathers.

A tradition like interactionism is, in our view, to be regarded less as a royal inheritance passed down through the generations than as a long-lived auction house. The continuity of the institution depends far more on whether buyers find any of its offerings attractive than on whether the items are sold in any logical order, or to preserve their earlier relationships. In those terms, the continuity of this (or any?) intellectual tradition may be crosscut not only by the differences and contradictions in its "core" of ideas, but by how successors have accepted one rather than another aspect of the thought of predecessors, have incorporated fragments into their thinking, or have accepted earlier differences and contradictions and attempted the working out of their implied problems.

A Brief Chronology*

The University of Chicago Department of Sociology was founded by Albion Small in 1892. W. I. Thomas, born in 1863 and living until 1947, first entered the department as a graduate student, moved onto its faculty in 1895, published his influential *Polish Peasant in Poland and America* (1918–20), and in 1918 was fired by the university administration for political and/or moral reasons. Park (1864–1944) was trained in philosophy at Harvard and in Germany, worked for many years outside of academia, in 1914 was brought by Thomas to Chicago, where he was enormously influential until his retirement in 1933. Largely under his aegis, Chicago sociologists became world renowned for empirical studies, especially of race relations and urban relations. A variety of methods were utilized, but (ecological methods aside) especially field observation, interviewing, and the gathering of case histories. Mead, then thirty-one years old, was brought to the Department of Philosophy by Dewey in 1894; but sociologists were soon learning social psychology from him. Mead's major impact on sociologists, however, began in the 1920s when his advanced social psychology course became very popular. E. Faris, of the sociology department, also taught social psychology, an amalgam of his own views plus those of Dewey and Mead. Mead died in 1931, but Faris and Herbert Blumer continued the Meadian-inspired tradition. Blumer also continued the Park-Thomas tradition, especially in race relations and collective behavior; as did Everett Hughes (mainly influenced by Park) in race relations and urban sociology.† During the 1930s and 1940s, both men transmitted their respective aspects of the Chicago tradition to their students. Among the better known are: Alfred Lindesmith (deviancy, social psychology); Arnold Rose (race, urban); Tomatsu Shibutani (social psychology, race, collective behavior); Howard Becker (deviancy, occupations); Orrin Klapp (collective behavior); Elliot Freidson (occupations); Melville Dalton (occupations); Fred Davis (occupations, urban); Joseph Gusfield (collective behavior, modernization); Ralph Turner (social psychology, collective behavior); Rue

*For historical details about the Chicago sociologists, see R. Faris (1970) and J. Carey (1975). For the American university during this period, see L. Veysey (1965); also see Rucker (1969).

†We shall not discuss E. Burgess and L. Wirth, influential from the 1920s and 1930s until the early 1950s. Another, non-interactional, tradition at Chicago was founded in the early 1920s by W. Ogburn and, later, S. Stouffer who emphasized especially statistics, the study of trends, and demography.

Bucher (occupations); Enrico Quarantelli (collective behavior); Simon Marcson (sociology of science); Anselm Strauss (social psychology, urban, occupations); Lewis Killian (race, collective behavior); Erving Goffman (social interaction); Kurt Lang and Gladys Lang (collective behavior); Gregory Stone (social psychology, urban). With the changed nature of the department by the mid-1950s, the scattering of its former graduates, and the explosion of university departments of sociology in that decade and the next, the interactionist tradition (changed and doubtless of combined with elements of other traditions) was no longer associated closely with Chicago itself.

Concepts and ideas associated with this tradition included especially: Thomas's "definition of the situation," "the four wishes," and the social organization-social disorganization scheme; Park's "race-relations cycle," "the marginal man," processes like conflict, accommodation, and assimilation, and the idea of the formation of institutions through collective behavior and social movements; Mead's concepts of "significant other," "generalized other," "roletaking," and the I-me phases of the self; Hughes's "careers," "dirty work," and other ways of looking sociologically at occupations, work, and professions; Blumer's methodological idea of "sensitizing concepts;" Goffman's innumerable and influential ideas and concepts about interaction; Strauss and his associates' (Glaser, Bucher, Schatzman) formulations of identity; Shibutani's about social control and "reference group;" Becker's about deviancy; and Lindesmith's about addiction. Edwin Sutherland's theories ("differential association") of criminality also belong to this tradition.

For a reviewer of such a tradition, the temptation is to give way to explicating some of its well-known concepts, noting the connections among them, detailing some features of the chief monographs, and dwelling on the main substantive areas in which the work has been done. We have not chosen to do this because a careful reading of earlier and later figures in the tradition suggests that the mainstream of Chicago interactionist thinking (that is, what interactionists did when doing their research) stems primarily from the writings and teachings of Thomas and Park. To understand this tradition, one has to look closely at Thomas and Park's work and at the assumptions which underlie the work. Then the writing and teaching of George Mead must be fitted into that mainstream. Here, we shall not give a complete answer to the Meadian side of the tradition (Fisher and Strauss), but we shall be much concerned with the mainstream itself including the way in which the successors to Thomas and Park built upon but departed from their work. More briefly, we shall indicate also how some of the Chicago interactionists, and others newer to interactionism, have interpreted and used Mead. In addition, we shall suggest how some of the major problems that still plague the interactionist tradition derive from the Thomas-Park side of interactionism. A corollary issue is how some of the current criticism of "symbolic interactionism" is quite aside from the point or is the result of how interactionists themselves have construed Mead. We shall end with a consideration of a few of interactionism's major problems as we interpret them.

Historical Background

The interactionist tradition has many points in common with older traditions of American sociology. All were, to varying degrees, the product of intense interest in social reform and drew on nineteenth-century evolutionary theory. All were influenced by various European intellectual theories remolded in American terms. If Chicago sociology has had a distinguished position, it has been its specific combining of social evolutionary theory with a strong emphasis on creative response to change. These combined themes also ran through the Progressive era of American history and through the pragmatic movement in American thought. Thomas, Park, and Mead were allied with both movements, but in different ways.

To understand how these men carved out their relations to social reform, it is necessary to keep in mind several points. Each came of age intellectually at the end of the nineteenth century, in a world characterized by massive immigration and domestic migration, and when urbanization and industrialization were proceeding rapidly. Each came from a provincial background, as did many academics of the time.

Many of the questions encountered by such provincial intellectuals when they finally reached the larger urban stage were new ones. There was little precedence for building a highly industrialized and urbanized nation-state on the basis of mass, heterogenous immigration. There was even less precedence for building national unity on such a base through democratic means. The historical precedents for democratically directed change were neither numerous nor, from the standpoint of many American intellectuals, very encouraging. The great influx of peasants into the United States aroused, among both the well-off and the educated, much fear of social (if not class) war and mob rule.

The notion that intellectuals should provide a helping hand in shaping national policy found strong support. Scholars who went abroad encountered examples of educated elites making often successful bids to shape national policies. The development of American universities reinforced the prospect of expert, intellectual influence. Industrialists and state legislators poured money into higher education: universities would train national and regional leadership, they would provide insight and solutions to pressing problems.

The University of Chicago was one of the most generously sponsored and intellectually ambitious of these new institutions (Storr, 1966). Located in a rapidly industralizing city, it seemed ideally suited to studying and influencing social policy. The Department of Sociology faced a world in which the imperative to study "social problems" was ready-made. What precisely was their nature and how should be studied were the questions for the new discipline. From the standpoint of progressive reformers, the great problem was the growth of what they saw as special interest: how national cohesion could be developed in the face of increasingly powerful and monopolistic business interests, a growing and sometimes militant labor movement, and the increasing size and organization of immigrant, ethnic groups. Was it possible to reconcile the claims of self-interested groups? The question of national destiny was basic to the problem of reform. That involved the meaning of both the nation and its history—of the would-be community and how it could change.

Assumptions: Change, Rationality, Creativeness, Association, Freedom, and Constraint

Thomas and Park sought to understand such change in its relation to the national community, and in so doing they took certain crucial matters for granted. They generally conceived of change as inevitable, progressive, and forwarded by a struggle between groups seeking survival and development. This struggle did not so much destroy values as transmute them; and the more self-conscious and rational human beings became, the more such transmutations could be progressively directed. Emphasis was on the possibility of building new social institutions—not on the processes of degeneration and decay that made rebuilding necessary.

The idea that the processes of social change would yield increasingly rational control over the course of change was, as for many other contemporaries, closely linked to the notion of increasing individualization. Its important feature was that it realized and reinforced the active aspect of human nature. The more that people were able to cut loose from established modes of existence, the better they could direct change toward progressive ends. Central to the meaning of change was the relationship of this possible, active social control to ends toward which such activity was to be directed. The essence of activity, and the individualization accompany it, was creativity. What was created was society.

Thomas's ideal individual was the "creative man," who builds new institutions from the old on the basis of discovered sociological knowledge. Park's creative individuals were the leaders of social movements and emancipated thinkers, who are able to grasp basic human nature and human processes in order to know the potentials and limits of change. All of these creative types are profoundly different from the acquistive individual of classical economics or the political animal of liberal theory. What is built is not economic or political or legal institutions in particular, but social institutions in general. The fulfillment of individual capabilities and the promotion of change through building viable institutions become one and the same.

This idea derived support from another central assumption: the power of association. Like social change, social organization had an intrinsic virtue. Institutions were themselves solutions to the problems posed by change.

Neither well-being nor further development were possible with continued conflict and group strife. Group life, and the social organization it entailed, guaranteed the peace necessary for the enjoyment of life and its progressive improvement. Customs constituted a kind of peace treaty by which people agreed to conform to certain modes of living. Whether institutions were developed consciously or unconsciously, they served the same general purpose.

Clearly, such social organization also implied potential limits to the rational direction of society. Thus the basic dilemma of sociology was the relation between these limits and the active participation of people in promoting progressive change. As Thomas queried: how much social order is compatible with individual development, and how much individualtiy is compatible with the limitations that social life necessarily imposes? Sociology, for Thomas and Park alike, was to explore the contradiction built into its very assumptions: to discover the scope of freedom of action, especially for promoting social change, in the face of the social limits that change itself rendered necessary.

The sociology of Thomas and Park can be seen as attempts to find a mode of explaining and promoting social change that would avoid both the image of unimpeded individual action and the idea of a totally constraining society. In social reformistic terms, the sociological viewpoint implied that action would have to thread its way between progressively liberal and moderately conservative solutions. In terms of building a new discipline, the approach implied that sociologists should study how people were both constrained by institutions and yet able to go beyond their limitations. This type of social science would provide a far more satisfactory base for social reform than the "deterministic" theories offer by other new university fields.

Some of these theories, like the genetic psychological explanations of human differences, confused contingent social arrangements with biological necessity and were used to reinforce conservative social movements for racial purity and the like. Other disciplines, like economics or politics, tended to assume behavior as either too unconstrained by patterns of association—supporting laissez-faire business ideologies, or naive reform, or revolutionary schemes to create worthwhile institutions or even good societies out of whole cloth. Legal and formal educational reforms often fell into the same error. Their exponents did not see that their simple pronouncement of ideal schemes or even their passage of these schemes into law were based not on investigation of the actual scope of freedom and constraint in given social contexts, but on mere wish or the hope of being able to realize absolute authority.

Thus, another set of antitheses lay at the basis of the sociological problem of social change. All disciplines contributed knowledge to the development of sociology, but only explanations that took the freedom-constraint antithesis as central could provide the knowledge necessary to understand and promote progressive social change. Similarly, although all reform attempts expressed the active aspect of human nature, only those based in a realistic understanding of social constraint had a chance of success. Solid sociological investigation and viable social reform would entail a careful seeking out of increased possibilities for action over and against constraint, a gradual pace for most directed change, an emphasis on knowledge of constraints—by both actors and social scientists—and a basic commitment to make that knowledge more self-conscious.

Thomas and Park: Variations on Related Themes

Although Thomas and Park shared many progressive assumptions about social change and how people could bring it about, their specific sociological responses to the world differed in important ways. In the following discussion, we have treated their arguments rather schematically, in order to emphasize both commonalities and differences as they ramify into contemporary sociological research. The four questions we consider are: (1) the *prospect* of social reform—the nature of social progress, when and where it could take place; (2) the role of *science* in social reform—what kind of knowledge would be of use, whether that knowledge existed, or whether and how a scientific domain could be built; (3) the *agents* of change—whether reform required leadership and, if so, what kind; and (4) the *mode* of social change—what instrumentalities were needed, whether these existed or had to be developed, and if so, then how.

The Prospect of Social Reform: Theories of History and Change

For Thomas, the problem of reform was integral to the problem of nation building. His response to threatened national disunity resembled today's arguments for modernization. His questions were: how quickly could changes take place and how radical could they be? His answers reflected a basic dichotomy that beleaguered much social evolutionary thought. He believed in a universal human nature. As for many enlightenment thinkers, this conviction was a moral and social as well as a scientific postulate. If human beings were all made of the same stuff, they could be treated as equals: democratic government was possible. Carried further, this logic posed a problem. If human beings were made of the same stuff, one could expect them to develop similarly. Historically, this implied that societies, too, would follow an identical path of development. At the most extreme, societies, like children, would follow parallel stages of development in an almost lockstep manner. If any given society was not moving on to the projected next stage, this posed a problem for social explanation.

Thomas's solution was that differences in the rate of social development were due either to variation in social conditions (which prevented or speeded up change), or to partial or temperamental differences between human types (not sufficient to claim species difference, but enough to slow down or speed up development). The sociologists' job was to investigate these questions.

They had to determine the extent to which social conditions shaped group development. When such conditions could not account for such development, then they could take up the contribution of biopsychological factors. Humans were primarily sociological creatures, unless proven otherwise.

The idea of social limitation was part and parcel of this picture of social evolution. Social change began with the facts of natural and social conflicts. Social conflict led to a series of crises and reintegrations, each of which—by virtue of its challenging human capabilities to survive—pushed social and individual effort forward. Depending on the particular natural or social conflicts which groups encountered, they would be forced to progress at greater or lesser speeds. Thus, at any given time in history, groups would be arranged along a progressive hierarchy, more and less advanced according to their particular histories. The early groupings would be based on "natural" affinities—biological, kinship, etc. Later groupings would be built upon these. The most advanced form of grouping would be the nation-state, containing within itself various subgroups. At any period, groups could be ranked in terms of how far they had progressed toward modern nationalization, and subgroups within each state or would-be state could be ranked along a similar scale. This evolutionary process was not predetermined in the sense of having rigid stages, but its general shape was set by natural and social variables. Thus, early group conflict was based on force. As groups developed, other key variables came into play. Economic emancipation gave people another tool for survival. So did education. The greater its success in the evolutionary struggle, the more easily a group could shift from coercive to persuasive means for dealing with other groups.

This shift was crucial for social reform and sociology alike. The shift implied the possibility of benevolence, and of movement toward a society based on voluntary cooperation. Benevolence resulted because more advanced groups could afford to make generous offers when dealing with others. Security and maturity naturally led to mutually beneficial altruism. Voluntary cooperation was the natural outcome of group interaction based on consent rather than force. As groups emancipated themselves from the level of mere survival, their members could consent to advantageous forms of interaction with others. The questions would then become: what forms of interaction were advantageous? To what kinds of exchange with other groups would given people consent?

Posing the problem of (advanced) change thus implied that an adequate theory of change must include a theory of social psychology. That latter would show under what conditions human nature led people to make given kinds of decisions and why. If sociologists could answer this, they could give educated elites the scientific underpinnings that social reform efforts required. Sociologists would provide the basic knowledge for the most progressive interchanges between groups.

Park's approach to the prospect of reform and the questions of history and social change shared much of the same evolutionary outlook as Thomas's, although Park was far less optimistic about directed reform. He was, however, by no means a simple skeptic; even his conservative streaks were not simply conservative. His general approach to the problems of change suffered from deep contradictions in his thought. One aspect of his thought came rather directly out of Sumner's evolutionism, for Park stressed both ceaseless change resulting from group conflict and the limited ability of people to direct such conflict. Park's later ecological writings extended this mode of thought: the struggle for space resulted in an endless series of conflicts and accommodations between groups. The world was one of ceaseless migration and, therefore, of new and renewed conflict. A certain possibility for progress was built into this process: ecological competition led to economic competition and to the political and moral ordering of social relations. But order and progress were not necessarily identical. New forms of order became more progressive as they reflected greater rationality. Association based on the division of labor was more rational than association based on racial groupings, promising greater societal integration. On the other hand, the current social order remained based primarily on division and antagonism between racial groupings. These were being broken down, in many places, by urbanization. Emancipated individuals were regrouping themselves into occupational specialities, but occupational groups themselves came into conflict, moving the evolutionary struggle into a new realm. The problem remained: how was it possible to incorporate genuine rationality and progress into social life? In answer, Park called on two other elements of his thought.

Park was an early and ardent admirer of Dewey, but he took only special aspects from Dewey's work, notably the idea that society was a matter of communication. Park employed this idea when his Sumnerian vision of endless change and conflict became a bit too much to bear. Association was based on communication, and communication contained the possibility of increased awareness. As long as communication continued, consensus and understanding could emerge. The end product would be a community of discourse—a democratic public—that could direct its own fate. This public required supportive social conditions and a level of general education that enabled communication over what provincial people might see as insuperable barriers. Yet, the community of discourse was always in the process of forming. The moment people began to speak to each other, progress through such means was possible. The problem of democracy was: under what conditions would who be able to speak to whom? The difficulties of the American attempt to build a viable nation-state were linked to the reality that so many barriers to communication existed. Racial and ethnic groupings constituted the foremost barriers. If the democratic public were to be constituted, some aspect of the general process of change would have to enable people to overcome such barriers.

To this problem, Park's third, Jamesian, strain provided a partial response, and this is also relevant to how Park sought to balance between his more cyclical and progressive views of history. Park constantly alluded to William James's essay on "A Certain Blindness" in human beings. The blindness referred to the inability of people to see behind the masks worn by others.

The problem was understanding how the person behind the mask had been shaped by the often brutal exigencies that group conflict imposed. People were not only blind but unaware of their own blindness. Their heritage of group life emphasized survival and the group customs that insured it. Only when people broke out of traditional life could they begin to confront strangers as individuals. How would they respond to such strangeness? The emancipated and mobile lives into which people were moving made individualized response possible, but the conditions under which mobility thrived—such as competitiveness and lack of customary ethics—boded ill for progressive response to such encounters. At this point, Park relied on a combination of compassion and knowledge. If people could understand what lay behind the masks, their natural sympathies would respond. Knowledge plus compassion would bridge the gap between conflict and community, making social change possible and diminishing the pain which the context of conflict imposed.

Park's outlook on reform reflected a highly muted and qualified optimism, in part because his Sumnerian picture led in two directions. It suggested considerable limits on how much reform-minded individuals or groups could intervene in patterns of group conflict. It also acted as a warning against attempts to block mobility for selfish purposes. Thus, Park could view the influx of Southern, rural blacks into the northern cities as inevitably causing race conflict without treating such clashes as opportunities to push programs for racial integration. The basic processes of social change were beyond legislation. People would handle the problems of conflict and accommodation far better than would unrealistic legislation.

Precisely at this point in his logic, Park tended to switch to the ideal of an emerging democratic community. The moment that communication began, community building was possible. Thus, the labor movement's articulation of labor's needs was a progressive step: grievances found a hearing through the newspapers and therefore made a real claim on the public's attention. In the end, people could not be made to read newspapers that did not interest them, that did not build toward a greater degree of communication. This fact fit in with Park's emphasis on people as knowers and learners. Their ability to understand and critically assess their world would grow even more as they emancipated themselves from the customary bounds of ethnic life. The final element in Park's prospect of reform was individualization; not the hobo (individualized but not connected with others) but the person pursuing a career, the entrepreneur in any arena of life, the independent intellectual. Such people forwarded change through the pursuit of their own lives and the relationships they naturally built with others.

The greatest differences between Thomas's and Park's ideas of the prospect of social change devolved upon their respective ideas of progress and their judgments concerning how directed such progress could be. Thomas believed firmly that history was progressive. This involved necessary links among improved prospects for survival, greater intellectual understanding, and greater social harmony. How quickly groups would move along this progressive path was conditioned by their particular situations and the particular social conflicts and encounters in which they engaged. As the struggle for survival naturally produced more advanced groups, it produced elites capable of helping others. Elite groups would wish to help others; other groups, in turn, would wish to accept such help. The workability of beneficent interaction depended upon a particular kind of enlightenment, among both the elites and those they would help, enlightenment that Thomas saw as problematic and yet necessary. The problematic element was evident: all members of elite groups were not benevolent educators, and all those who might learn from them were not receptive listeners. The necessary element rested on the power of truth to compel attention and on the ability of sociologists to find this truth. With the help of sociological knowledge, truly educated members of the elites would lead the way, while knowledge-hungry members of the lower groups would learn from them. Thomas was convinced that eventually all groups would converge on the ideal of social life implicit in the evolutionary process itself. Science did no more than reveal the conditions of forward movement, while the elites and others moved with inexorable logic toward that ideal.

Park avoided Thomas's obvious problems by switching back and forth between images of inevitable collision and images of cohesion and liberty. This accounts for the sometimes difficult character of Park's writing and the fact that readers often see it as a series of disconnected "insights" rather than a coherent "theory." On the contrary, Park's entire work is permeated by a sometimes overlapping and sometimes contradictory argument. In general, both his images of Sumnerian social change and Deweyan community prevented his emphasizing the role of leadership in directing change. But his interest in marginality and his focus on freedom in urban life together prevented his cautious optimism (we must see what the conflict of groups brings, what the public opinion will sustain) from lapsing into a doctrine of passivity. When Park wrote of individuals making their ways through a nontraditional world, he used the language of action and options. This is particularly true when he referred to intellectuals. The basic restlessness that set great social groups into motion found its epitome in the insatiable curiousity of thinkers and writers. Such people also constituted a kind of vanguard, but, in contrast to Thomas, it was less clear how they would connect their progressive knowledge to the problems of the people.

The Role of Science: Where Knowledge Comes From and How It Is Used.

Both Thomas and Park stressed the development of knowledgeable, rational control over social behavior. Sociological knowledge was to help provide such direction, but what this knowledge was and how it was to be acquired differed for them. For Thomas, the nature of sociology was closely tied to the educated elite and the job of convincing it that this science should provide the basis of their beneficent activities. This meant establishing sociology—rather than politics, economics, etc.—as the most generally useful and correct basis for social action. Sociology was unique in seeking to establish the scientific laws by which change took place. They could be established only by showing how specific social conditions promoted or hindered progress at given points in social development. This task divided into two parts. First, sociologists had to compare the entire range of societies to determine specific conditions (or variables) which contributed to development. Sociologists would draw information from a wide range of disciplines, in terms of its special relevance to progress. Such comparative studies were closely linked to the conviction that the proper unit of sociological investigation was society itself, the study of social wholes. Specific institutions (studied by the special disciplines) were merely parts of these social wholes. The superiority of sociology to specialized disciplines and to practical knowledge stemmed from this holistic view. That social problems could be attacked without attention to the larger social context was a great error made by practical reformers and misguided social engineers.

A second sociological task was the study of particular conditions relating to the creative participation (or its absence) of individuals vis-à-vis their group contexts. In contrast to comparative sociological analyses, which draw on institutional studies from a variety of disciplines, social-psychological study was the special province of sociology. Thomas faulted psychology for its individualistic and acontextual assumptions. The study of human "attitudes"—how people reacted to the institutional conditions they encountered—had to be pursued, both in terms of attitudes previously internalized (themselves a product of the interaction of the individual and society) and of actual conditions encountered.

This implied investigation into people's pasts as well as their presents—but pasts and presents viewed contextually. The relation of response to context, inner and outer, made the sociological life record (case study, life history) "the most perfect sociological tool." Thomas, in no sense, saw such material as exclusively "subjective"—for this would be to deny the genuine interaction between individual and society.

Moreover, human response is not necessarily faultless nor in itself complete. If responses were as knowledgeable and rationally correct as possible, sociology would be superfluous. The premise of social psychology is this: people's knowledge and capability to respond were constrained by their particular social conditions and by their social psychology. People were historically limited in what they could understand (for groups lower down, it was nearly impossible to understand the world as did more advanced groups). Also people's rationality was naturally limited by the affective needs built into human nature. Social-psychological sociology was to determine the internal limits and possibilities for personal change in the face of encountered conditions. Social psychology would discover how the inheritance of social life, custom, had become internalized in terms of attitudes; also how the human need for response, security, recognition, and new experience (the famous "four wishes") could be integrated into a balanced and personally viable reaction to social change.

Park's image of sociology was less utopian and less geared to the argument for scientific legitimacy, undoubtedly because of changes in the social scene when Park became the central figure in the Chicago department. The support of private philanthropy and civic reform organizations had become a matter of course for research: it was no longer necessary to convince the educated elite that sociology was of value. Also, students were being trained and sent out to social service and professorial jobs. The issue for sociology now was not "in what sense is sociology scientific?" but "how is sociology to be done?"

Park wrote virtually nothing about the scientific nature of sociology or its method. Yet, both his writings and the history of the department suggest an implicit model for training and activity. This activity followed a division of labor built into Park's own argument. Sociology consisted of analyzing the big picture, a job that required a wide scope of knowledge of the world, an acquaintance with various sociological and other relevant theories, and the quiet time to put these things together. Sociology also consisted of getting out the news, finding out what was going on in the world and communicating this to others—to the emergent democratic public. Finally, sociology involved a more personal intellectual quest after the truth, an attempt to understand "human nature" and "human processes" as they unfolded before the sociological eye. This quest was in a sense universal—shared by intellectuals of all kinds and by human beings cut adrift in the world and struggling to find their bearings.

Park's own life reflected all of these aspects. His academic writing consisted almost entirely in spelling out the big picture. He had little interest in marking out the boundaries of the sociological discipline: on the contrary, his essays integrate work from a wide variety of disciplines, bringing in philosophy, economics, psychology, biology, history—all in support of his very general argument about the importance of conflict and accommodation in social change. Although in this sense Park's writing is replete with theory, there is little air of abstractness about it. Rather, it is permeated with the flavor of the news and Park's actual experience as a news gatherer. Yet, Park's writing reflected his own special role of news integrater. Students became news gatherers, going out to study the city, ethnic life, etc. For them, getting out the news meant writing about these ongoing activities in a clear, theory-permeated way and communicating it in some form of publication. While work sometimes was commissioned or sponsored by specific reform groups, research also was news that should get out to the general democratic public.

Neither Thomas's nor Park's conception of sociology as a useful science was a simple one. Thomas's concern over establishing its value for reform leadership led to awkward binds that well might have diminished his influence on later sociologists. His argument for sociology was strongly linked to assumptions about a reform elite who would embrace sociological knowledge. Yet Thomas was far from sanguine about the rapid development of sociological laws: if slow in being developed, sociologists would have to assure reformers that science was still worthwhile. Perhaps sociologists could offer their intermediate findings while the laws themselves were being developed. This suggestion, of course, raised questions about what these findings were about and how they could be applied. "Findings" seem to have concerned better and more thorough knowledge of social conditions and attitudes and responses to them. This was precisely where reform knowledge was often limited and narrow. But the depth and nature of the research which sociologists offered almost defied application. Thomas proposed the development of social technologists in order that sociological knowledge be translated into programs for practical action. When the long-awaited laws would be discovered, such technologists could help to guide society toward its democratic ideal. What would happen to the interactionist view and to the democratic ideal itself was not seen as a part of the problem.

Park's contradictions were even more evident in the realm of sociological expertise. He wanted such expertise, yet denied it. The entire enterprise of a professional training department spoke for the role of sociologist as expert. However, Park himself had come to that role late, and the meaning of expertise in his own life remained ambiguous. Strong elements in each of his contradictory arguments spoke against the ideal of the expert. If human effort could do little to effect large-scale change, if public opinion emerged out of the natural communicative process, if the sociological quest was merely an extension of natural, human curiosity—who would need sociological experts? Yet Park participated in advising and guiding reform inquiry as the teacher of researchers, if not as a researcher himself. Numerous students followed careers in which expertise would be demanded. Park seems to have coped with these contradictions in two ways. First, he implied that sociological expertise involved a knowledge of social limits—how far reform could be pushed and where it would inevitably falter. Yet second, this conservative function was crosscut both by his imperative to get out the news and by his abiding conviction that emancipated people would act creatively. From the standpoint of sociological science, this image of human nature was left vague, simple, and highly individualistic.

The Agents of Change: Social Interaction and Leadership

There were problems not only about how sociological knowledge could be applied, but about who would do the applying. For Thomas, the ultimate consumers of sociological science would be the social reformers, the educated elite. This leadership was carefully distinguished from that involved in party politics or even legislative reform. The latter was often only superficial, gaining legal enactment without resulting in genuine social change. Social change itself involved transformations both in values (the character of institutions) and attitudes. Leadership in the direction of making these progressive changes flowed from the social evolutionary process. In early stages of development, when group life was focused on mere survival, strong leaders were needed. Later, more educated leaders provided a higher level of moral cohesion. Ultimately, leadership would no longer be necessary. Institutions and education would make possible a self-directing, cooperative people.

Thomas's evolutionism implied any leadership could succeed only when genuinely interactional. Leaders who did not truly interact with their followers would not long remain leaders. Leadership groups not speaking to the needs of those less advanced groups whom they proposed to lead were similarly constrained. Leadership also depended upon the constraints and potentials of the leaders themselves: some were external, others were internal; people unable to find a viable balance within themselves could not play the creative role that true leadership required. This was true both of leaders coming out of the elite group and leaders developing in the less advanced groups. If each produced the most balanced ("efficent") leadership, these leaders would be able to build a generally more progressive society. The argument implied that such interactions would always be mutually educational. The result was a continual pushing of all groups up the evolutionary ladder. If the process operated at its best, virtually no person or group would be left out.

Park's theory of leadership was predictably split along the lines of his general argument for social change. Occasionally, Park displayed a relatively heavy-handed reformism, suggesting a benevolent elite not unlike Thomas's. Most often, his treatment of leadership had a wry quality. Few political or reform leaders peopled his intellectual pantheon. Despite his evident admiration for intellectual figures—scientists, writers, poets—he clearly envisioned no direct role for intellectuals in progressive activity—quite the reverse. He was inclined to treat efforts to moralize or lecture directly to the people as fruitless. People themselves discovered "correct" behavior in the context of social experience, which was, in turn, shaped by the context of group conflict: the emergence of crowds, their formation into social movements, their eventual shaping into social institutions. Leaders were essentially at the focuses of such movements, rather than being their causes. Dominance came about through the pressure of groups within a limited social arena, through the competition first for space and later for other resources that forced social order on a given scene. This ordering was crucial if life was to continue. How democratic such ordering could be depended on the difficulty of social conditions met and the extent to which people could become self-conscious. There was nothing contradictory in the idea of democratic leadership; rather, its possibility flowed naturally from a concomitant idea that no leadership succeeds unless it speaks to the needs and conditions of the people.

In this respect, Park's basic argument concerning leadership was functional and deterministic. Yet, his concept of marginality also related to leadership. To see things broadly, people had to cut loose from customary moorings. The potential for leadership was greatest in groups which had become marginal, although some types of marginality were not sufficient: the hobo is the last frontiersman, and a kind of poet, but he cannot contribute to the progressive shaping of society because he has no roots. Without roots there are no relationships, and without a point of orientation there can be no progress.

Thomas and Park clearly converged in their general image of viable leadership: leaders had to understand followers to be effective and had to be sufficiently integrated and educated to have that understanding. Thomas's image went even further. He discounted the importance of conservative segments of the elite or radical segments of the lower classes, by definition unbalanced: such leaders might find followers, but these would automatically decrease as enlightenment increased.

Park did not fall into this trap, at least at its most obvious. Since ordering per se was inevitable, leaders always performed a kind of social service in helping to focus sentiment and movement. Moralistic condemnation of leaders did little to change the social scene: the popular support of leaders, of machine politicians by their immigrant electors, of union leadership by the members, were all socially and psychologically grounded. However, there were limits to how far Park was willing to carry this argument. When the direction of social movements became too uncomfortable—as with revolution—his leadership took on another look. Its legitimacy extended only as far as other, more responsible, leadership did not speak to the same (movement-expressed) needs. The definition of responsibility was itself referred back to the idea of a democratic public. So, Park was clearly begging the question. As with Thomas, why one definition of responsible leadership should be preferred to another remained somewhat problematic.

The Mode of Social Change: Arenas and Mechanisms

Thomas's and Park's images of reform implied notions of where, when, and how change takes place. "When" was contingent on both group conflict and encounter (isolation meant stasis), and on the level of development of conflicting groups (their strength, education, institutional development, leadership). "Where" was contingent on the same conflicts and encounters. The earliest arenas for change were bound to simple territories. As forms of association became more complex, territorial dominance led to the building of nation-states.

Thomas's notion of effective mechanisms for change related to this image of context of conflict and encounter. The two central mechanisms—education and institution building—had to be viewed contextually. Attempts to educate or to build institutions outside the context were bound to fail. It was easy to fault established reform programs on such grounds but more difficult to show how new programs should take context into account. Thomas's writing is far stronger in its indictment of misguided reform than in positive images of institution building and education. The institutions held up as models all stress education as a part of development, are as voluntary as seems possible, stress the creative potential of people, and are guided by educated leadership.

Park's image of the mode of social change was typically less direct and more contradictory. The widest arena of change was the world itself, the ebb and flow of migratory groups seeking geographic and social space. Within this context, nations and cities were built. The city was a special arena for change because it became the focus of these larger patterns of movement. The city was also the focus of opportunity and understanding. Those two features informed Park's idea of institution building and education. Institutions could be built much more freely in the urban context, but not in an unlimited way. Even the effectiveness of newspapers was limited: the most they could do was to offer the most enlightened (broadest) form of news consistent with peoples' lives.

Given Park's Sumnerian hesitancy concerning direct intervention in social change, his Deweyan penchant for community building via communication, and his Jamesian commitment to getting to know the strangers behind the masks—the urban newspaper was *the* ideal reform institution. In his writing, few other institutions received the same attention. Even explicitly educational institutions are treated in terms of their potential for getting out the news and building community. Educational institutions were important, but the most important education took place in life—urban life—itself. This applied to blacks, immigrants, the lower classes, and the elite: all making their ways in the context of modern opportunity. Taking advantage of the work opportunities that so present themselves (there is little suggestion that work institutions are purposefully built) opens the door to more learning than most schools. Park did not deny that these opportunities are differential: indeed, that was a necessary consequence of the ecological and economic struggle of social groups. The more broadly applicable point, however, is that experience and education are made possible by taking advantage of opportunity. Such self-education is the hope not only of immigrants and other newcomers, but of would-be helpers. Park's skepticism toward reform does not rule out the progressive work of agents like reform judges and enlightened social workers. On the contrary, they are an important part of the audience for the new sociology. However, he attributes most of their understanding to their experience in dealing with people and the insight they have gained thereby.

Both Thomas and Park struggled with the relationships between education and institution building as the central modes of reform. Thomas admitted that it was easier to attack problems educationally than to rebuild institutions. Since sociologists were learning so much and people becoming better and better educated, the relative lack of institutional reform could lead to despair. Assuming other conditions of progress had been met (a great and questionable assumption), the paucity of creative people could be disheartening. His only answer was more and better education.

Park's qualified expectations for education gave greater leeway in avoiding such problems. The relationship between individual enlightenment and social change remained indirect and unspecified. The only educational change promising clear results for reform was the newspaper, but the results were slow and indirect. More direct forms of institution-building were good and useful only if they stayed in touch with people. Occasionally, Park suggests more specific conditions for success, but he does not emphasize that "we" need to take these enterprises in hand or help guide them. Park's relevant "we," then, is the democratic public which is only slowly building.

Sociological Successors: Their Contradictory Inheritance

Thomas's and Park's arguments about change and the nature of sociology join, but also diverge, at crucial junctures. Their shared theory of social evolution, with its emphasis on crises and conflict, and their general framework of group encounter and interaction made for a profoundly processual outlook. Their mutual interest in adaptivity and social peace led them to focus on institution building, while their conviction that blind accommodation could be replaced by self-conscious direction led to a stress on creativity and education.

On the other hand, they differed in their specific interpretations. Thomas emphasized direct intervention and the role of elite groups in guiding change, while Park's more deterministic *and* democratic outlook made him leery of reformist efforts. Thomas was much more confident in the progressive potentials of the evolutionary process itself; Park's less progressive stance enabled him to fall back to images of ceaseless change, when the evolutionary process disappointed him once again. For Thomas, creativity and individualization were not merely consistent with, but intrinsic to, the development of a cooperative society; while Park's individual (although hopefully finding a better place as society developed) always stood a bit apart from social participation.

Because Thomas's and Park's students developed their work out of an already contradictory inheritance, it is difficult to treat them according to subtraditions; nor do we think such a distinction desirable. Thomas and Park each had his students. To some extent, they themselves were students of each other. Many of the next generation who did not work with Thomas (because of his early "retirement") nevertheless studied with his students, who were also Park's colleagues. Despite this complex interweaving of careers and ideas, one can distinguish the strands of Thomas's and Park's respective arguments as their work was variously interpreted and acted upon by their successors.

We have chosen four for brief analysis: Morris Janowitz, Herbert Blumer, Everett Hughes, and Howard S. Becker. We have selected only *certain* aspects of their work, and we also have tended to play down those aspects reflecting the impact of specifically other intellectual traditions: Janowitz's admiration of modern functionalist sociology; Hughes's penchant for anthropological functionalism; even Blumer's and Becker's involvement with Meadian thought. The impact of these other traditions, like the basic fact that the sociological successors have confronted a changing social scene, are far from irrelevant. They are precisely part of the point: how the successors struggled to make sense out of the inherited theories, and how they have recast them in that attempt.

Morris Janowitz has made a self-conscious effort to incorporate Thomas's comparative program (1966). Janowitz's analysis of Thomas's work is revealing: he sees Thomas as an early macrosociologist (paving the way for much later functional sociology!) whose excellent grasp of the scientific mission of sociology (the development of testable hypotheses about social change and the relating of social-psychological questions to sociology) is faulted by his ignoring of political and organizational dimensions. In fact, Janowitz's own research into political sociology relies on a social-change argument very much like Thomas's. Also, his work on community politics follows closely in Thomas's and Park's steps: the local community is a key arena for the confrontation of groups (1952). Participation is crucial (absentee owners are faulted here) and the sociologist's role is to facilitate and raise the level of these interactions. This the sociologist can do by virtue of a broader social view, but the group interaction itself will determine the direction of change.

Janowitz's image of the role of sociology is very close to Thomas's, despite criticisms of the latter's undeveloped notions of the relation between theory and practice. The very theory-practice dimensions that Janowitz misses in Thomas's thought are part of his most important inheritances from Thomas: the notion that in educating the elite, sociologists can indirectly and most effectively contribute to social progress; also, that creative potentials in human nature promote progressive thought and action and give practical form to sociological knowledge.

Both themes run through Janowitz's comparative study of the military in developing nations (1969). Like Thomas, Janowitz sees the problem of progressive change as the problem of transcending coercion, but this is given a sadly ironic twist in the history of newly emerging nations. The specialists in coercion themselves become the most advanced or potentially advanced of the social groups. Here, Janowitz both utilizes Thomas's interactional logic and veers away from it. The emerging military elites develop political consciousness of their leadership through a combination of structural and intellectual conditions. Social-science knowledge, as part of their education, can function in this respect. Moreover, within the military career route, there is a type of officer who forges ahead to become a policy-making, leadership type—like Thomas's creative man. Social science is also available to aid such leaders. This does not imply that sociologists become advisers to new national leaders—quite the contrary. Janowitz has argued repeatedly the fallacy of trying to become specialist advisers of particular social clients. The role of basic, academic sociology is teaching—teaching those in power, teaching the general public. This was the "enlightenment" ideal of Thomas and Park, and although it had to undergo changes to become more applicable, it is, Janowitz asserts, still the first mission of sociology.

The crucial point about Janowitz's reinterpretation of the ideal is his own

Chicagoan notion of an emerging democratic public to incorporate sociological knowledge. Despite qualified and critical assessment of Thomas's and Park's assumptions along these lines, his own argument for change is even more dependent on such a notion. The military elites in the study of emerging nations grasp their leadership role to the extent that they strive toward the popular goal of modernization. Yet, no suggestions are made concerning how the interaction between elites and their public helps to shape the nature of leadership. (Janowitz states that his investigation will focus on the internal determinants of leadership development, but that itself illustrates the point.) The public and its general wish for progressive change are assumed, while the assumption that progressive leadership, sociological knowledge, and popular will must come together in the end pushes the argument along.

In regard to this democratic community, however, Janowitz departs from Thomas's optimism, for he is somewhat fearful of its instability in the face of challenges to it. In an early paper on native fascist groups of the 1930s, he concludes they failed because of inadequate leadership—but a future economic crisis might bring danger from a more educated, hence more effective, fascist elite. The same threat-to-community theme appears in his study of the local community and its press. His central concern there is with the contributions made by the press and the local elites to the community's integration, despite the very Thomas-Park type of forces (industrialism and the city's large-scale organizations) making for disintegration (1952). It was perfectly consistent with his views that certain reform activities during the 1960s were interpreted as threats to the democratic social fabric. And he continues to demonstrate some of his anxieties about social order (1976). It is not that Janowitz is pessimistic about progress, but one must be constantly on guard against forces that imperil its possibility. The sociologist plays his part in keeping up and making more efficient our defense of democracy. Using Thomas's language of "institution building" but departing radically from Thomas's antipolitical bias, the social scientist is to help strengthen the parliamentary, electoral institutions. If those crumble, democracy disappears.

This assumption of a democratic community also characterizes the work of several key successors to Park. However, given Park's ambiguous treatment of leadership and his disconnected treatment of change, democracy, and individualization, the sociological outcomes have a different appearance. This can be seen, for example, by comparing Janowitz's general argument about the relation of sociology to the process of social change with that of Herbert Blumer. Thus, Blumer's argument on the nature of industrial relations also depends strongly on the image of a democratic society spontaneously producing constructive conflict (1947). However, none of these groups "leads" the other in the sense of being more advanced in progressive, evolutionary terms. Rather, the very fact that group conflict and accommodation continue to take place—the endless series of contracts to be negotiated and renegotiated—itself constitutes the democratic process. Creativity is a property of the process itself; organized labor or business can always make new demands, forcing the interaction among groups to move toward a more satisfactory resolution. The actions of individuals, such as the line worker (to whom "human-relations" experts were paying so much attention) are relatively unimportant to this process.

Blumer's shift of creativity to the level of group interaction represents a significant and not altogether simple interpretation of Park's own contradictory position. In part, Blumer's industrial-relations argument employs Park's Sumnerian side to argue against any form of determinism. The world is an open one, and the ceaseless round of group encounters and conflicts demonstrates as much. On the other hand, Blumer, like Park, is not ready to abandon the notion of democratic progress. The democratic public is built into industrial-relations encounters in the form of a refereeing government which keeps relationships within the bounds of public interest. The public might not always have or express an interest—hence, Blumer's strong arguments for the investigation of the nature and development of public opinion. In the end, Blumer is loathe to accept the possibility that the emerging opinion will be reactionary. This is especially true in the realm of race relations, where "subjective" reality—the idea that people are biologically distinct—contributes powerfully to the discriminatory patterns that prevail. Like Park, Blumer counts on migration, urbanization, and occupational specialization to break down the racial barriers and to make people more aware of their common interests (Killian, 1970) (Blumer in Lind, 1973).

Blumer's interpretation of Park involved an attempt to establish the potentials of group encounter and creative group response for the pursuit of progressive, democratic relationships. Everett Hughes's interpretation stresses, instead, the limits of group action in promoting progessive change. In this respect, Hughes adopts the more somber and skeptical end of Park's thought and emphasizes its implicit functional problem of how institutions maintain themselves as "going concerns" (1971). This problem is especially prominent in Hughes's writings of occupational life (1958, 1971). Beginning with Park's (and Durkheim's) interest in occupational specialization as the emerging form of association, Hughes focuses on how such occupational groups are limited in their attempts to carve out social territory and achieve status.

These limits are crucial in two respects. One concerns the potentials and limits of reformism. In Hughes's occupational investigations, his skepticism underlines the natural limits of doing good on the part of occupational groups. The greatest problem of any occupational group is survival in a competitive world. Group cohesion is the result and prerequisite of such survival. Hence, exclusionary policies, licensing, and standard setting are normal parts and constitute natural limits of occupational life. These limits cut both ways, especially in the human service occupations, with their basic problem of serving well. On one hand, the limits of good service preclude clients from membership, restrict their participation in how things should be done, and generally require a certain degree of distance between client and practitioner. On the other hand, these same limits presuppose the consent of clients—also free agents—insofar as they continue to support a given group of practitioners. Here is where Hughes's own version of the democratic public comes into play. The knowledgeable public supports the competitive system in which the occupations check each other and are continuously forced to adjust their standards to the actual conditions of group life. The knowledgeable public also grasps the limits of good service in general. It understands these limits better if probing sociologists get out the news of occupational life.

This same reasoning leads to a second concern: the possibility that a given group may gain so much power that its treatment of others may be unchecked. Hughes raised this problem, significantly not in the context of occupations in the narrow sense but in the context of politics. The Nazi phenomenon represented precisely that situation in which "doing for" became "doing to" without the check or sanction of a democratic public. Hughes's explanation of this situation fits well with Park's own contradictory argument. On the level of institution building, the viciousness of German oppression resulted from the development of a secret sect (the S. S.) which precluded public scrutiny or any checking and balancing of group interest. On the level of human understanding, the fact that persecution was applied to aliens or competitors, rather than "one's own" people, supported a kind of self-sustained big lie about the "dirty work" to which Germans tacitly consented. For Hughes, the lesson of Nazi Germany is less that it illustrates one extreme human capability than that it points to the limits of responsible occupational life. One of the major features of occupational life is that we get others to do our dirty work. This being so, we (democrats) must at least give such license with full knowledge and responsibility. While we may have to grant people the secrecy under which they do dirty work, we need also to maintain conditions under which the general character of their work can be monitored. Only the comparison of occupations and social movements can tell us where it is reasonable to draw our lines. The danger of sects is that they preclude such comparison: the sociological eye is blindfolded and the door to democratic discussion is shut.

Hughes's concern with full public participation as crucial to the democratic community finds a curious counterpart in Erving Goffman's notion that all human beings are vulnerable to the constraints of social interaction. Goffman is not always thought of as an interactionist, althought many people certainly do think of him as in that tradition. Perhaps they think so partly because he writes explicitly about selves, partly because he does such fine-grain analyses of interaction. Aside from his actual "training" in the Chicago department, where he was undoubtedly at least influenced by Hughes, certain persistent themes in his thought resonate with interactionist concern.

Chief among the themes is his strong, unmistakable, and reiterated antideterminist argument—or in our terminology, his wrestling with the problem of how to take constraints into account while still finding a central place for human freedom and creativity. In one of his first and best-known papers, "On the Characteristics of Total Institutions" (1961), Goffman might have been read as assuming a strong structural determinism, but during the same year he delivered another paper, "The Underlife of a Public Institution" devoted to showing how individuals in such institutions (i.e., in any institution) manage to avoid being completely controlled and coerced by the institutions—including being controlled internally through personal commitments to the institution (1961). In effect, Goffman turned the tables on any literal reading of his previous total-institutions paper by arguing that specific kinds of social structures provide the material for the evolution of specific kinds of selves; yet they do not wholly determine the individual's actions, and they certainly do not totally determine his evolving self.

Structural determinism here and in much of his other work is the theoretical position against which Goffman arrays himself, arguing essentially that structural conditions are necessary but not sufficient to explain human action. Goffman's readers will quickly recognize that central to that argument is his emphasis on interactional rules. These and other rules are essential to, but do not simply govern, individuals' behavior. Goffman is at pains to show how interactional rules are maintained, are sustained, provide orientation, are transgressed, are put into disarray, and are put together again as functioning guides. Right down to his last and most complex book, *Frame Analysis* (1974), Goffman is on clear record against regarding rules, norms, roles, or any other structural item as strictly determining behavior. ("One can never expect complete freedom between individual and role and never complete constraint." (1974:269) In the closing pages, Goffman takes the argument further than anywhere else in his writing, asserting not merely that situations are potentially problematic and that others' responses to one's actions are always potentially problematic, but that one's own self is also problematic. In short, the individual is sufficiently complex to allow for appropriate flexibility; yet the freedom is far from total, since the self is social, acting in reference to societal rules, or, in Goffman's elegant phrasing, "The player and the capacity which he plays should be seen . . . as equally problematic and equally open to a possible social accounting" (1974:270).

Another reiterated theme is the relationship of deviant or uncommon behavior to normality, a theme which without violence can be viewed in terms of Goffman's handling of the enduring Chicagoan concern with community. In brief, Goffman denies any psychiatric or trait-psychology explanation of seemingly nonnormal behavior. We have a great deal to learn from extreme behavior, for we are all human. The very essence of norms means that there can be failure to live up to them. We are all "normal deviants" (1963:130). Even the rule infractions exhibited by psychotics "are first of all guidelines (and their disruption) of social organization, the organized association of persons present to one another" (1967:148). (Goffman's writings, indeed, gave leadership in the 1960s to some sociologists who reacted vigorously against psychiatric explanations for mental illness, denying that the behavior of psychotics and neurotics gave evidence of illness, except as defined by psychiatrists and society.) Morally as well as rhetorically,

Goffman is on the side of the mentally ill, the stigmatized, and the deviant against the stigmatizers, the accusers, and the professional moralizers. Where this stance relates to the question of community is that the common grounds of community are the rules—the norms. These are not sustained automatically but through the continued actions of members of the community. The very existence of those rules means we can stray—and be accused of straying and so cast unjustly out of the community—but Goffman the moralist insists that we are all of us human. As a sociologist, he believes we can all learn from each other as members of that larger community. As an interactionist, he wants to make certain we are given the freedom, by rule and by morality, to shape our individual destinies.

Goffman's very general assumptions about the nature of community suggest that although the possibility of community was a strong and persistent theme in both Park's and Thomas's work, neither strains in the interactionist tradition led to a clear and satisfactory way of interpreting the progress of community in modern America. The contradictions involved in both these strains are reflected in the work of Howard S. Becker, who while questioning basic ideas of both pioneers, continues directly in their tradition (1970).

Becker's influential work on deviancy suggests his concern that an increasingly fragmented society, dominated by one or more powerful groups, cannot be reformed into a democratically guided community. The world of deviants is a world of separate groups, individuals huddled together for mutual protection, periodically colliding with more powerful groups that claim control over the same social space. On one hand, the level of integration between groups is low. On the other, the means by which groups attempt to aggrandize social space systematically punish and promote forms of deviance. This is where Thomas's interactional problem enters, in reinterpreted form. Thomas saw the problem of interaction between groups as one of reasonable balance or a just exchange in the direction of progressive change: groups would trade off consent for awareness. This interaction justified the leadership of educated elites. For Becker, the aggrandizing force of powerful groups leads to unjust results, especially any attempts to define the very being of other humans. Definition from above cuts them off from their rightful place in the human community and diminishes the possibility of building such a community. If a democratic society were possible, it would be open to incorporating the very deviant values which moral entrepreneurs and other powerful groups preclude and stigmatize. Although some enclaves in the society seem to be opening themselves up to interaction with deviant values (marijuana legislation), the notion of a fully integrated society, along the lines of its own professed values, is far from realized.

In some respects, Becker's conception of tolerance and social criticism is far closer to the adversary image in English liberalism than to Thomas's fully integrated and cooperative society. However, Becker's idea of deviant groups presenting options goes beyond the ideal of democratic process. The core of his argument is very close to Park's notion of the secret self, the person behind the mask. Significantly, this core becomes evident in the political-methodological criticism which Becker has received. The best known is Alvin Gouldner's (1973). The crux of Gouldner's attack is twofold: that the kind of "underdog" sociology promoted by Becker was merely an aid to the encroaching federal bureaucracy (showing them how local welfare agents mismanaged "underdogs"); and that by being generally sympathetic to powerless groups without either discriminating between greater or less suffering, or indeed responding with any real passion to the problem of suffering itself, Chicago sociology promoted a posture of cool, dispassionate sympathy convenient to those in power and comforting to guilt-ridden, liberal academics.

The logic of Becker's response (1973) to these criticisms reveals his debt to both Thomas and Park. The problem of knowledge is central to any progressive social change, and no amount of reformist or revolutionary passion can replace such knowledge. The problem of sociology is to establish the conditions of progress, and two of the central conditions are how people treat other people and what people know about themselves and others. Much mistreatment of other human beings is promoted, if not caused, by false perceptions of them, supported by the current "hierarchy of credibility." More important, groups of people are handicapped in acting on their own behalf because false self-concepts have been forced upon them by more powerful groups able to constrain their options for action. For these reasons, the power of sociology lies in its potential for revealing to victims and other supporters the actual source of their human response.

The positive role for sociological research is assured by the care and openness with which sociologists approach their problems. The guarantee of a true and helpful study of people is genuine contact with them, rather than abstract moralizing or theorizing about them. The guarantee against knowledge gathering that merely aids oppressors is to look at all the groups involved and their interactions, not merely at the groups interesting to administrators or people in power. So, if Chicago sociology has failed, it has failed in the sense of carrying out its own program—of taking a genuinely interaction standpoint. Only when we see the actual, mutual effects of groups upon each other can we judge the degree of harm they do to each other. There is nothing dispassionate about this interest, only the qualification that for intellect to be the tool it is capable of being, it must be employed as sharply and widely as possible.

In effect, sociology has the potential of testing the ethical judgments on which we all agree—thus Becker's image of the democratic society, the general universe of humanitarian ethics that "we" all share. Thomas's educated elite has been expanded to include all people of goodwill. Without such goodwill, the possibility of knowing the people behind the masks and understanding the damage as well as the benefits which interaction can bring is limited at best. So is the potential for a genuinely democratic society, which the successors of Thomas and Park have understandably been loathe to abandon.

The Meadian Aspect of Interactionism

Most treatments of interactionism as a school of sociological thought or a general intellectual position designate George Herbert Mead as one of its founding fathers. The ambiguous character of such terms as "Chicago School," "interactionism," or "symbolic interactionism," makes it difficult—and perhaps fruitless—to argue with such claims. Mead's importance as an intellectual figure and his association with a theory of "interaction" is well established. (Mead, 1932, 1934, 1936, 1938; Petras, 1968; Reck, 1964). Yet a careful reading of most of the sociologists identified with the tradition stemming from the University of Chicago suggests that the use of Mead's overall thinking has been either very partial or negligible. In the case of social researchers who have employed Meadian concepts directly or have drawn on Mead's theory of social psychology for a research framework, little if any connection is made to his broader philosophic or social reform concerns. In the case of sociologists who have included some aspects of Mead's social psychology in their sociological work, Mead's thinking tends to be inserted into an approach which draws far more heavily on Thomas and/or Park.

Certainly Mead would not have imagined himself as a founder of Chicago sociology, although he just as certainly knew his social psychology was relevant to the sociology being developed in the Department of Sociology. Mead was a professional philosopher and his investigations concerning the nature of the self stemmed from philosophic concerns. He was also a social reformer, but one who personally felt no need to develop a science of sociology.

Mead's view of social change had many points in common with Thomas and Park, but was essentially more optimistic than either and focused on the the progress of "civilization" as a whole. Since Mead's argument deserves special consideration (Fisher and Strauss), we shall only note here that Mead's view of social change required him to develop a social psychology which would entail the kind of civilizational development he wanted, one which he envisioned as moving in the evolutionary direction of shared universes of discourse of increasing scope and significance. This social psychology in its turn became the starting point for various kinds of social psychological and sociological work. Again, we do not think it useful to distinguish between subschools. Rather, we would like to ask in general terms: what did the Chicago sociologists gain from their contact with or immersion in Mead's social psychology?

The answer to that question must undoubtedly be a complex one. We offer here a few possible aspects of it. To begin with, Mead has offered different generations of interactionists some kind of philosophical underpinning through his social psychology. What kind? Surely not a metaphysics, a philosophy of science, a logic, or an epistemology in the usual sense. We speculate that his general views of evolution, social change, community, and the like, as expressed through his social-psychological writings and courses, were highly supportive of the general interactionist approach. More specifically, one can hazard that different generations of interactionists have tended to emphasize different aspects of his thought in contest with the ideas of other traditions. For instance, during the 1920s and 1930s the behaviorists were in an important rival position with respect to explaining human behavior, with implications for how to regard changing that behavior and society too. Earlier, Mead's lectures and writings possibly provided a counterpoise to instinctivist explanations. Later, they were certainly used against Freudian and other psychiatric or psychoanalytic interpretations of man and society. Thus, in the writings of Blumer (1962, 1969) we can see that those kinds of defenses against other intellectual perspectives and traditions are basically antideterministic (antibiological, psychological, social-structural determinism), as the interactionists sought to find a balance between constraint and freedom. One can also see this antideterminism clearly in the long-standing interactionist textbook, first published in 1949 (Lindesmith, Strauss, and Denzin, 1975).

As a slight digression from discussing Mead, it is worth briefly speculating how *any* psychology functioned for the Chicago interactionists, since theirs is one of the few traditions that assumed psychology important to the sociological enterprise. And unlike psychology—in America at least, where social psychology evolved derivatively and as a minor subfield—sociological social psychology, Chicago style, was central to the science (Karpf, 1932). We have suggested why, in discussing Thomas, for whom social psychology is sociology's prime territory, and Park, for whom social psychology is less explicit but very important because of his Deweyan and Jamesian sides. The interactionists relatively early on were teaching and writing textbooks for classes in social psychology. But the interesting question is whether they centrally used Mead's social psychology in their research. There are some explicit instances: Becker and his associates' use of Mead's concept of "perspectives" in their study of medical students (1961); Lindesmith's Meadian, linguistic, self-indicating approach to opiate addiction (1968); Davis's drawing on Mead's treatment of time and emergence (1963); Denzin's general adoption of Meadian psychology for studying children (1978). In addition, there have been studies which attempted to test the usefulness of specific Meadian concepts or draw implications in the way of specific testable hypotheses (Stryker, 1962). Currently, Mead is often footnoted in interactionist writings, but it is not always easy to see exactly why, except insofar as he is again functioning as a kind of philosophic underpinning for the researcher's general interactionist position.

In the 1960s, in common with other approaches, like neo-Marxism and phenomenology, interactionism gained increased visibility both in the United States and abroad, and the tradition also continued to be taught by succeeding generations of interactionists now located in numerous teaching and training sites. The Thomas-Park type of interactionism, without much admixture of Meadian psychology, continues in research areas like collective behavior,

(Weller and Quarantelli, 1973; Klapp, 1964, 1972; Shibutani, 1970), social movements (Gusfield, 1963; Turner, 1970); occupations professions (Bucher, 1970; Daniels, 1975; Faulkner, 1972; Olesen and Whitaker, 1968), urban relations (Kornblum, 1974; Gans, 1976; Lofland, 1973), race and ethnic relations (Shibutani, 1965; Killian, 1970). Some research practitioners, especially those recently trained, probably do not think of themselves as interactionists, although recognizing quite clearly their roots in Chicago-style literature. Interactionism increasingly has come to mean "symbolic interactionism," whose ceremonial but still vital founding father is George Mead (Blumer, 1969; Stone and Farberman, 1970). As we noted earlier, both critics and interactionists tend to take Blumer's version of Mead and of symbolic interactionism as representative of the interactionist position today. The special irony in this situation is that Blumer, as one can see from our earlier discussion, has inherited both the Meadian and the Thomas-Park strands of the Chicago tradition. When he writes of substantive matters such as race (Blumer in Lind, 1973), (Killian, 1970) or collective behavior (Blumer in Lee, 1951), there seems to be very little of Mead in his thought, for then he is a direct descendant of Park especially; but when he writes of social psychology or explicitly addresses "symbolic interactionist" issues, he explicitly presents an interpretation of the Meadian perspective (1969). From our own students, as well as from the tone of recent admirers of Blumer and Mead, it is clear that their writings speak to the "active-actor," voluntaristic theme which has played such an important role in the reaction against functionalism, survey research, quantification in social science—as well as in the reaction against such targets as university administrations, government, bureaucracy, and the like.

Criticism and Reactions

This voluntaristic emphasis is, of course, deep in both strands of Chicago interactionism. However, when interactionism is equated—as "symbolic interactionism"—with Meadian social psychology, it can be faulted for its underemphasis of the social structural (read "constraint") factors in favor of its overemphasis on voluntary action (read "freedom") (Bandyopathyay, 1971; Lichtman, 1970). If one bothered to read Mead closely, probably no such conclusion would be reached, especially if writings other than his *Mind, Self and Society* or his very specifically social-psychological papers were read. But that is the Mead which most critics know and with whom many younger interactionists have identified themselves. So we should not be surprised that in recent years there have been a variety of reactions to Mead and an interactionism which flies the Meadian flag. For instance—other than the criticism just noted—a truly effective Marxism needs a better social psychology, so perhaps Mead can be wedded to Marx, especially the "younger Marx" (Reynolds, 1973)? Or perhaps symbolic interactionism is just another brand of idealistic philosophy and hardly a sociology at all; or just another instance of bourgeois liberal thought, since it is idealistic, leaving out the essential elements (structural) in explaining social phenomena; or merely another brand of functionalism (Zimmerman and Wieder, 1970); Or it has not and cannot develop genuine, testable theory (Huber, 1973; Swanson, 1961), since everything is regarded as so "fluid" and open-ended.

Younger interactionists, facing these kinds of criticisms—and themselves products of an era which has impressed upon them the undeniable relevance of large-scale governments, coercive governmental action, powerful corporations, warfare, other forms of violence, and the like—cannot but feel vulnerable to the charge that they fail to take into adequate account social structural variables, that they are intent on their microscopic studies to the neglect of "macrosociology." So, while still attempting to retain whatever version of the Meadian perspective they hold, they are self-consciously engaging in macrosociological researches (Denzin, 1978; Farberman, 1975; Gerson, 1978). They are trying to get "politics" into the interactionist tradition, where they sense or believe that their predecessors neglected that vital dimension of social life (Hall, 1972). And they are reaching out for a joining of the "macro" and the "micro" by pointing to what they interpret as exemplifications of that in the Meadian tradition (Benson and Day, 1977; Maines, 1977); namely, to the work of people like Strauss, Bucher, Schatzman, and Glaser, with their emphasis on "negotiated order" and "structural process" (Strauss, 1963, 1964; Glaser and Strauss, 1968; Glaser, 1977) and their associated studies of organizations and to follow-up work done in that mode. Again, there is irony insofar as this research is as much a product of the Thomas-Park strand as the Meadian, and in fact exemplifies again how particular men and women have chosen from the interactionist auction house whatever elements of interactionism struck them as especially valuable, putting their purchases together in ways that would not necessarily be approved of, let alone be recognized, by the original owners.

Interactionists who owe little to Mead but much to Park or Thomas are not particularly affected by these kinds of criticism. However, some are still sensitive to the genre of attack which many years ago within the Chicago department itself, Samuel Stouffer and William Ogburn leveled at Blumer and other interactionists; namely, that sociology required statistical studies in order to test anything, otherwise it was just a variety of social philosophy. Then there was the judgment of Chicago-style interactionism by Edward Shils (1948), with which functionalist theorists like Robert Merton and Talcott Parsons certainly concurred, that Chicago was strong on empirical studies but woefully weak on theory. (Park was a brilliant, intuitive brain, but hardly a systematic theorist.) Undoubtedly many people who teach social theory or think of themselves as theorists regard interactionist research publications in exactly that light. Of course, the Chicago-style work can be attacked—or ignored—just as much as the Meadian-style writing, because it neglects or underplays the really important or relevant or powerful or essential explanatory variables. That criticism would be made no matter how macrosociological was an interactionist in his or her perspective. The argument then becomes one of "which structural variable?" rather than "no structural variables," unless, of course, the criticized writing was focused on something deemed too microscopic to the neglect of the larger structural picture. The earlier Chicagoans were subject to just this kind of criticism from people who emphasized economic or political variables, as well as from political radicals. The radicals could even be sociologists trained under Park who both criticized him and accepted more of his interactionist assumptions than they knew. The most outstanding instance is the black Marxist-sociologist, Oliver Cox (1948).

Combiners, Crossovers, and Borrowers

Cox's criticism reminds us that nobody who is trained in a tradition needs to carry it like the Holy Grail, either through life or through graduate school, pure and uncontaminated by other traditions. After all, students take courses and read books by people from many traditions, not a few of them recommended by professors who disagree with their own recommendations. Many Chicagoans have attempted to reconcile, or have implicitly combined, interactionism with other traditions, including systems theory (Klapp, 1972; Shibutani, 1968), psychiatric perspectives (Shibutani, 1961), and Radcliffe Brown–style anthropology (Goffman, 1959, 1972). Some men, like Dollard (1939), quite literally left interactionism—in Dollard's case for Freudianism and behaviorism. There has also been some interest displayed by interactionists in exchange theory (McCall and Simmons, 1966; Singelmann, 1972) and ethnomethodology (Denzin, 1969).

Sociologists also could discover interactionism after intense exposure to other approaches, finding something in it which spoke to their intellectual requirements. Gouldner's postfunctionalist encounter with interactionism, largely through Becker, is a significant instance, although Gouldner later passed quite out of the interactionist orbit. Much of the writing of Irving Horowitz reflects still another encounter, that of an outsider to the tradition who incorporates certain aspects of interactionism (1977). Barney Glaser's more personal encounter through collaborative work with an interactionist (1965, 1968) illustrates still another route to combining intellectual stances, in this instance something of Lazarsfeld and something of interactionism. Some of David Riesman's writings also reflect his many years of close association with Chicago interactionists, especially with Hughes (1958). A few sociologists in the phenomenological tradition have been especially interested in the

Meadian aspects of interactionism (Berger and Luckmann, 1966; Grathoff, 1970).

Of course, outsiders have always taken bits and pieces from the interactionist armamentarium, finding of use ideas like "the significant other" or "role taking" or whatever. Understandably, the originators of these ideas, if still alive, would not infrequently be scornful, angry, or perhaps amused at the reinterpretations of their concepts or ideas. Insiders can also go astray when judged by that impossibly rigorous standard of "original intention": impossible because traditions do get combined, whether consciously or not. That is the way of the intellectual world, is it not?

The most obvious recombining of ideas from different traditions, of course, is when people from different disciplines draw sustenance from each other. The interactionists have had their share in nonsociological education ("the definition of the situation," "significant other," and "role taking," for instance, have spread far beyond sociology). Of course, interactionists, in common with other sociologists, have written for external audiences. ["Awareness context" (Glaser and Strauss, 1965) is possibly as well known by health professionals as by sociologists, and "student culture" (Becker, 1961) was beamed at medical educators as well as at sociologists.] In fact, the interactionists have been especially prone to write for external audiences, since some of their central assumptions lead them frequently to address themselves to the enlightenment of special publics and sometimes to the general public.

Five Problematic Areas

The limitations of the interactionist perspective can be approached, we believe, by thinking about five problems raised by the Park-Thomas (and Meadian, as interpreted by the sociologists) inheritance, especially the general theory of social change and sociological progressivism. These problems share certain common features. They reflect the liberal-conservative bind entailed by arguing the virtues both of active, creative individuality and of secure, stable association. They also reflect the problematics of social change, the fact that—once the sociological enterprise was committed to accounting for the nature of change—sociologists had to reconcile their basic theories with what was happening in the world and account for when, where, and how changes took place in terms of a general notion of how change itself was constituted. Finally, the problems involved—especially in the Thomas-Park positions—often led to breaking the interactional frame as a consequence of responding to the dilemmas entailed by the position itself. This meant abandoning the central assumption that change is produced via the clash and encounter of groups—via the mutual effects and reactions of intersecting groups and the attempts to cope with such encounters.

The Problem of Progress

This problem is a direct product of the conflict between the image of increasingly active, creative, individual development and the conviction that institutional life will develop in progressive directions. The Chicago tradition reveals continual strain between the idea of people as potential decision makers and the notion that such decisions must lead ultimately to the general type of social improvement envisioned by the social theorist. This bind often led, and leads, interactionists to blur the question of value by building values into the very way that the problem of change is cast.

Both Thomas and Park recognized human responses were not always progressive but believed they would become increasingly so. They did, however, have difficulty in handling nonprogressive or retrogressive responses. Thomas's assignment of "progressive" or "not progressive" to the Polish peasant responses is ultimately arbitrary. Park's generally humanistic outlook caused him to pull back from many of the human responses that he discovered, and he had fallback positions that allowed him to handle seemingly undesirable ones. Revolution, war, and strikes were responses appropriate to conflict between groups, and there was always the potential, if not the inevitability, that progressive changes could result.

Chicago sociologists of early generations had to cope with the consequences of interactionist assumptions about change. They either had to show why human responses were not as progressive as might be expected or argue that, despite certain counterevidence, indeed they were. This latter alternative divided into two choices: first, recasting the time schedule for change, showing that it was still occurring, albeit more slowly; second, shifting the investigation to another part of the social scene, where responses seemed to be leading in more progressive directions. Thus, for studies of race and ethnic relations, there was a tendency to stress the length of time it necessarily took for barriers to be broken through—nevertheless, barriers would crumble eventually. The writings of Hughes and Blumer in the 1940s and 1950s and Shibutani (1965) reflect this carefully qualified progressivism.

Given the strains involved in applying the general argument in areas such as race, perhaps it is not surprising that many interactionists turned to deviancy and occupations and work. In doing so, they followed their predecessors' leads. Behind many of the occupational studies by Hughes and his students surely was the assumption that sociologists could research the conditions and potentialities of occupational worlds and get this news to their most advanced, reform-minded segments. Moreover, occupational life offered an arena in which creative potentials could be realized. Not that careers were untrammeled; rather, individual progress involved a struggle with social constraints. The predominant focus on individual struggle—implicitly progress being defined in terms of outcomes for individuals—meant that the larger context of social change (the interaction between conflicting or encountering groups and the mutual change that interaction effected) generally would be muted, and it was.

The Problem of Process

This problem is essentially that of accounting for the specific characteristics of change—its speed, scope, depth—and by what mechanisms these are affected. The relative lack of attention to such questions by Thomas and Park is linked to their assumption that change does take place—that because its ultimate mechanism is the encounter of social groups and their mutual modification, genuine change must be slow, wide, and deep. All the specific mechanisms helping to further such change—the most important being institution building, enlightenment, and science—flow from this ultimate source.

Recollect that Thomas and Park saw change as progressing toward an increasingly rational control over social institutions. In general, their lack of attention to the forms of institutionalization themselves, other than in relation to level of evolutionary development, has been consequential for their successors. Thus, neither founder systematically asked how the conflict and encounters among groups affected the internal organization of institutions nor how the internal organization affected the institutions' responses to the challenges of conflict and encounter. In this respect, neither man carried through the interactional implications of his own position.

A most important consequence for their successors is the split between the questions of how institutions come to be established and what they are like once established. This is well illustrated by the split between research on social movements and research on specialized institutions. Interactionists have rarely done both as part of the same analysis. The former type of research requires historical and documentary data; the latter type of research rests primarily on fieldwork and interview data.

The interactionist views of social change direct the attention of fieldworkers to those processes through which people respond creatively to the limitations of their institutional context. Hence, research into occupations is rich in the description of processes touching on that issue. This interest in the potential of people to shape their institutional context accounts for the interest in clients (including ones with little power) as well as practitioners, workers as well as managers. Institutional life is described not merely in terms of how groups higher up exert influence and power, but of how any group can respond to the limitations that its institutional position imposes: psyching out expectations, covering up mistakes, negotiating the division of labor. Because of the split between historical and fieldwork approaches, relatively little attention is paid to how these processes are affected by the broader processes by which the institutional context have been established and by which they continue to be affected. Such study is suggested by the basic Thomas-Park argument—and Mead's (1934) too—although these men themselves provided little direction in that regard.

The Problem of Consent

At issue in early interactionism is not the political democracy of election and legislation, but of active participation. Among the most important processes for study, therefore, are those involving consent or the increased potential for consent among people in a given situation. In general, as mankind progressed and the possibility of enlightened, creative response increased, the more genuinely consensual would human activity become.

To this view, two particular historical situations posed severe problems. First, people did not always consent to what others considered relatively progressive social life. Second, people could consent to institutional arrangements which had distinctly nonprogressive consequences. Concerning the problem of nonconsent, Thomas emphasized the role of an enlightened elite and Park that of marginal people. Also, nonconsenting people are actually seeking new forms of association with which to consent. These points are complementary: leaders seeking progressive solutions and followers seeking progressive leadership. Conversely, when leaders fail to lead progressively, their followers will let them know, either by refusing to consent to new social arrangements or by taking the reins themselves. This theme of self-willed followers fits in with the general image of creative response to social limitations and was translated into a variety of arenas by sociological successors. For instance, Park's wry remarks on the limits of leadership are developed by Hughes (1971) in his critical assessments of practitioner-client relationships, with the latter assenting to a certain amount of not fully acceptable procedure (secrecy, odd modes of action, parading of esoteric knowledge) in return for services performed.

The problem of consent to nonprogressive forms of association is difficult to solve within the older evolutionary approach. It counts on the struggle of groups to produce relatively progressive forms of association and on the increase of awareness and education acting as a brake, on both leaders and followers, against their turning in socially destructive directions. This also implies that altruism is likely to increase, because the conditions of association would foster doing good. Correspondingly, when people failed to live up to the potentials for good implicit in their general level of society, then public opinion would act as a corrective, through an awareness of the nature of association and its limits.

Later, such guarded optimism seemed to apply well to the emergence of modern occupations—for instance, doctors who served well through a combination of self, competition, and public control. But contemporary interactionists like Becker (1973) and Goffman (1961) suggest how the assumptions of increased altruism and the safeguarding power of public opinion have come to be questioned. The lack of direct focus, generally, on coercion and exploitation—except for creative and individual responses to it—suggests again how the earlier interactionist stances shaped the problem of consent for their successors.

The Problem of Limitations

The older interactionists' argument regarding the limits on human responses moves simultaneously in two directions: first, toward an image of fixed limits on activity, involving implicit or explicit agreements about how best to survive; second, toward an image of limits as testable through the interaction of creative people with what they find established. From this latter standpoint, the question of change becomes the question: how do groups test out the limits which the various conflicts and encounters of social life impose? How do they discover by what mechanisms the limits are best attacked?

To put the problem of limits thus is to pursue Thomas's and Park's basic question without its progressivist interest in education and its sociological bias against political organization. It is also to connect the problem of limits with the more recent interest of contemporary interactionists in limits other than those emphasized earlier. They, in common with noninteractionists, have tended to turn to the limiting character of those economic, political, or organizational elements previously treated either as givens or as intermediary factors in the development of association.

However, any critical recasting of the earlier argument will raise two issues rather than one. Interactionist studies both extend the range of limits [for example, see Kling and Gerson on how the computer industry shapes the realm of choices for a variety of occupations (1977)] and also raise the question of how such changes contribute to the possibilities of creative response—the possibility of new instrumentalities arising not only out of the new knowledge but out of new forms of organization, new kinds of technologies, new modes of symbolic interaction.

The contribution of the interactionist approach to limitations lies less, perhaps, in showing the varied types of constraints today than in exploring how the interaction between social groups both sets limits and provides the conditions under which they can be tested.

The Problems of Power and Equity

The Thomas–Park theoretical formulations had serious consequences for their abilities to address the problems of power and equity. For them, social limits were the product of conflict. Conflict required association, and viable association required customary limits on activity, which implied that power could never be exercised in an unrestrained way. Power was limited by the conditions of social conflict under which association was developed. This all implied that the only means for making power less crushing was for people to become increasingly self-conscious.

Power was ultimately the power of association to assure survival. The idea of "power over" was notably absent in the Park–Thomas treatment of advanced societies. Hence, economic or political limitations resulting from the power of association and its consequences were played down. Economic and political elements tended to be treated as middle terms, and their distinct contributions to the problems of power thereby were diminished.

The problem of equity follows directly from this treatment of power. For Thomas, the problems of fairness or justice would be resolved by promoting evolution to the greatest extent possible. Park generally appealed to greater humanity and rationality. Behind these convictions lay the implication that the evolutionary process itself possessed its own justice. Where social conflict did not simply destroy, it yielded some beneficial changes for all involved. These general conceptions posed problems for the future generations of interactionists. Few believed that the issues of equity were solvable in the political arena. The links between power and equity were regarded as a long-run consideration, dependent on the continual building and rebuilding of associations and institutions, as well as on increasing self-consciousness and education.

In coping with the evident contradictions that such interpretations of power and equity have entailed, more recent interactionists have nevertheless tended to stay within the same general framework. Men such as Becker or Freidson have become far more questioning of the "basic" power relations that exist between groups, but their images of power and the equity it can preclude remain remarkably constant. Thus the power of association is the last and best resort of deviants in Becker's writing (1973, also 1970). If deviants have power, it is through the power of association. If they get any greater equity, it is through a combined exercising of that power in the political arena (no longer ruled out) and educating of people to the realities and basic humanity of their lives (sociologists will get out the news). Freidson's critique of the medical profession suggests a similar combination (1970, 1975). The associated power of doctors can be oppressive but is also a necessary part of professional service. The public needs to constrain the profession and direct it toward legitimate public needs, but the power struggle between doctors and others will not disappear. The last and best resort for equitable medical care is a self-disciplined (made self-conscious) profession within the constraints that interaction with the public imposes. Thus, power is converted into a definite tool to achieve equity, and the limitations intrinsic to conflict are monitored or transformed.

The Problem of the Intellectual's Role

Central to the older interactionists' views of social change was the idea that (sociological) knowledge was at the core of whatever modern progress was possible. As noted earlier, and as the reputation of interactionism itself suggests, this idea had strong democratic implications. Knowledge was not for the exclusive use of elites, nor drawn from sources inaccessible to the people themselves. Good sociological knowledge was largely drawn from the worlds of the people themselves, and to be effective in any progressive sense it had to be gotten back to the people, through indirect if not direct means. Moreoever, this same knowledge stood as the best bulwark against the very dangers that change also involved: the temptation to push reform, revolution, or governmental authority outside the context of association and consent. As the later interactionists began to focus on more specialized problems and audiences, their notions about what kinds of knowledge were requisite and for what purposes became more narrow than the more generalized Park-Thomas conception that sociology's viability and legitimacy comes from the association of people themselves. Still, it is important to note that the fundamental rationale for interactionists' sociological accountability did not change, nor did the democratic idealism in which it was rooted.

Where the argument for responsibility got into trouble was not because of the interactionists' elitism but because of their separatism, in the sense that in dealing with the nature of sociology, interactionists tend to break their own interactional frame. While sociology was to be based on understanding how people wrestled with their social limitations, the sociological enterprise itself stood apart from conflict and encounters between groups. Sociology incorporated the people's ideas and values into its developing form of knowledge but did not itself get directly into the big picture of conflict and encounter. Sociologists as citizens certainly could participate in such associations, but the science had to stand aside to do its proper work. Beneath the argument for progressive change lay the assumption that if sociologists really did their jobs properly, then significant conflict between them and other forms of association and between them and the developing public would not be possible. "Which forms of association and which publics?" were other questions. Implicit here was the assumption that these were neither evil nor intentionally nonprogressive—like extreme reactionary groups or an elite planning a takeover of the state.

The contradictions between this view of sociology and the facts of disagreement, not only between schools of sociology but between sociologists and their presumed publics, were not easy to solve in the context of institutionalized sociologizing. Perhaps the greatest dilemma could be seen in the relation between sociological teachers and their students. The division of labor suggested in Park's development of field research implied that students would gather social experience and bring it back to be integrated into the body of sociological knowledge. Thus, Hughes argues in 1969 that teaching can be seen as a form of fieldwork: students go out into the world and bring back the sociological news to their teachers. Teachers become wiser and better sociologists, and thus wiser and better teachers of sociologists (1971). The entire association expands and progresses. But, near the end of Hughes's talk, there is a tellingly honest section in which he notes the degree to which students have been questioning the very institutions on which American society itself is based. This kind of response is neither precisely the constructive response of the Thomas variety nor the news-gathering activity that Park stressed. Rather—though Hughes himself does not carry the point this far—it is a questioning of the very bases on which interactionists, and many other sociologists, operate, and on which they assume the consensual basis of institution building or the enlightened and progressive potentials of human response. In this regard, interactionists suffered a sense of shock when students, during the 1960s, first challenged their objectivity and value, tending to discount the challenge simply as antirationalistic gesturing. Sociologists with strong from-and-to "the people" values, like the interactionists, perhaps suffered more than those social scientists who had elitist or skeptical perspectives.

But to put sociology itself into the interactional frame of group conflict and encounter would involve precisely such challenges to its theories of social change. How well the basic interactionist argument would fare in such a big picture would become part of the problem of social change itself.

BIBLIOGRAPHY

Baker, R., ed., "The Life Histories of W. I. Thomas and Robert E. Park," *American Journal of Sociology,* vol. 79 (1973) pp. 243–61.

Bandyopathyay, P., "One Sociology or Many: Some Issues in Radical Sociology," *Sci. Soc.,* vol. 36 (1971) pp. 1–26.

Becker, Howard S., et al., *Boys in White* (Chicago: University of Chicago Press, 1961; paperback, Transaction Press, 1976).

Becker, Howard S., *Outsiders: Studies in the Sociology of Deviance* (New York: Free Press, 1973 ed.).

Becker, Howard S., "Whose Side Are We On?" in Becker, *Sociological Work* (Chicago: Aldine, 1970) pp. 123–39.

Benson, J., and Day, R., "A Critique of the Theory of Negotiated Order," *Sociological Quarterly,* vol. 18 (1977).

Berger, Peter, and Luckmann, Thomas, *The Social Construction of Reality* (Garden City, N.Y.: Doubleday, 1966).

Blumer, Herbert, "Collective Behavior," in Lee, A., ed., *New Outline of the Principles of Sociology* (New York: Barnes & Noble, 1951, originally 1939) pp. 165–220.

Blumer, Herbert, "Reflections on Theory of Race Relations," in Lind, Andrew, ed., *Race Relations in World Perspective* (Westport, Conn.: Greenwood Press, 1973) pp. 3–21.

Blumer, Herbert, "Society as Symbolic Interaction," in Rose, A., ed., *Human Behavior and Social Processes* (Boston: Houghton Mifflin, 1962) pp. 179–92.

Blumer, Herbert, "Sociological Theory in Industrial Relations," *American Sociological Review,* vol. 12 (1947) pp. 271–78.

Blumer, Herbert, *Symbolic Interaction* (Englewood Cliffs, N.J.: Prentice-Hall, 1969).

Bucher, Rue, "Social Process and Power in a Medical School," in Zald, M. P., *Power and Organizations* (Nashville: Vanderbilt University Press, 1970) pp. 3–48.

Carey, James, *Sociology and Public Affairs: The Chicago School,* vol. 16, Sage Library of Sociological Research (Beverly Hills: Sage Publications, 1975).

Coser, Lewis, "Sociological Theory from the Chicago Dominance to 1965," *Annual Review of Sociology,* vol. 2 (1976) pp. 145–60.

Cox, Oliver, *Caste, Class and Race* (New York: Doubleday, 1948).

Daniels, Arlene, "Advisory and Coercive Functions in Psychiatry," *Sociology of Work and Occupations*, vol. 2 (1975) pp. 55–78.

Davis, Fred, *Passage through Crisis* (Indianapolis: Bobbs-Merrill, 1963).

Denzin, Norman, *Becoming a Child* (San Francisco: Jossey-Bass, 1978).

Denzin, Norman, "Interaction, Social Orders and Problematics in the American Liquor Industry," in Denzin, ed., *Studies in Symbolic Interactionism: An Annual Compilation of Research*, vol. 1 (In press).

Denzin, Norman, "Symbolic Interactionism and Ethnomethodology: A Proposed Synthesis," *American Sociological Review*, vol. 39 (1972) pp. 922–34.

Dollard, John, et al., *Frustration and Aggression* (New Haven: Yale University Press, 1939).

Farberman, Harvey, "A Criminogenic Market Structure: the Automobile Industry," *Sociol. Quart.*, vol. 16 (1975) pp. 438–57.

Faris, Robert, *Chicago Sociology*, 1920–32 (Chicago: University of Chicago Press, 1970).

Faulkner, Robert, *The Hollywood Studio Musician* (Chicago: Aldinc, 1972).

Fisher, Berenice, and Strauss, Anselm, "Dilemmas of Social Change: Chicago Sociology" (unpublished ms.).

Fisher, Berenice, and Strauss, Anselm, "George H. Mead, Chicago Sociology, and 'Symbolic' Interactionism" (unpublished ms.).

Fisher, Berenice, and Strauss, Anselm, "W. I. Thomas, Robert Park and the Chicago Tradition" (unpublished ms.).

Freidson, Eliot, *Doctoring Together* (New York: Elsevier, 1975).

Freidson, Eliot, *Professional Dominance* (New York: Atherton, 1970).

Gans, Herbert, *Levittown* (New York: Random House, 1967).

Gerson, Elihu, "Market Structure and Technical Work Organization," in Denzin, *Studies in Symbolic Interactionism: An Annual Compilation of Research*, vol. 1 (In press).

Glaser, Barney, *The Patsy and the Subcontractor* (New Brunswick, N.J.: Transaction Books, 1977).

Glaser, Barney, and Strauss, Anselm, *Awareness of Dying* (Chicago: Aldine, 1965).

Glaser, Barney, and Strauss, Anselm, *Time for Dying* (Chicago: Aldine, 1968).

Goffman, Erving, *Asylums* (New York: Anchor Books, 1961).

Goffman, Erving, *Behavior in Public Places* (Glencoe, Ill.: Free Press, 1963).

Goffman, Erving, *Frame Analysis* (New York: Harper & Row, 1974).

Goffman, Erving, "Mental Symptoms and Public Order," in Goffman, *Interaction Ritual* (Chicago: Aldine, 1967) pp. 137–48.

Goffman, Erving, *The Presentation of Self in Everyday Life* (Garden City, N.Y.: Doubleday Anchor Books, 1959).

Goffman, Erving, *Stigma* (Englewood Cliffs, N.J.: Prentice-Hall, 1963).

Goffman, Erving, *Strategic Interaction* (New York: Ballantine Books, 1972).

Gouldner, Alvin, "The Sociologist as Partisan," in Goulder, *For Sociology, Renewal and Critique in Sociology Today* (New York: Basic Books, 1973) chap. 2 (originally published in *Am. Sociol.*, 1968).

Grathoff, Richard, *The Structure of Social Inconsistencies* (The Hague: Martinus Nijhoff, 1970).

Gusfield, Joseph, *Symbolic Crusade* (Urbana: University of Illinois Press, 1963).

Hall, P., "A Symbolic Interactionist Analysis of Politics," *Sociol. Inq.*, vol. 42 (1972) pp. 35–75.

Horowitz, Irving, *Ideology and Utopia in the United States*, 1956–1976 (New York Oxford University Press, 1977).

Huber, J., "Symbolic Interaction as a Pragmatic Perspective: The Bias of Emergent Theory," *Am. Soc. Rev.*, vol. 38 (1973) pp. 278–84.

Hughes, Everett, *Men and Their Work* (New York: Free Press, 1958).

Hughes, Everett, *The Sociological Eye*, two volumes (Chicago: Aldine-Atherton, 1971).

Hughes, Everett. "Teaching as Fieldwork," *Am. Sociol.*, vol. 5 (1969), reprinted in Hughes, *The Sociological Eye*, vol. 2, pp. 566–76.

Janowitz, Morris, *Community Press in an Urban Setting* (Chicago: University of Chicago Press, 1952; 2d ed., 1967).

Janowitz, Morris, introduction to Thomas, William I., *On Social Organization and Social Personality* (Chicago: University of Chicago Press, 1966).

Janowitz, Morris, *The Military in the Political Development of New Nations* (Chicago: University of Chicago Press, 1964).

Janowitz, Morris, *Social Control of the Welfare State* (New York: Elsevier, 1976).

Karpf, Fay, *American Social Psychology* (New York: McGraw-Hill, 1932).

Killian, Lewis, "Herbert Blumer's Contributions to Race Relations," in Shibutani, T., ed., *Human Nature and Collective Behavior* (Englewood Cliffs, N.J.: Prentice-Hall, 1970) pp. 179–90.

Killian, Lewis, *White Southerners* (New York: Random House, 1970).

Klapp, Orrin, *Currents of Unrest* (New York: Holt, Rinehart & Winston, 1972).

Klapp, Orrin, *Symbolic Leaders* (Chicago: Aldine, 1964).

Kling, Bob, and Gerson, Elihu, "Social Dynamics of the Computer World," in *Symbolic Interaction: An Annual Compilation of Research*, vol. 1 (In press).

Kornblum, William, *Blue Collar Community* (Chicago: University of Chicago Press, 1974).

Lichtman, R., "Symbolic Interactionism and Social Reality: Some Marxist Queries," *Berkeley J. Sociol.*, vol. 16 (1970) pp. 75–94.

Lindesmith, Alfred, *Addiction and Opiates* (Chicago: Aldine, 1968).

Lindesmith, Alfred, Strauss, Anselm, and Denzin, Norman, *Social Psychology* (Hinsdale, Ill.: Dryden Press, 4th ed., 1975; original ed., 1949).

Lofland, Lynn, *A World of Strangers* (New York: Basic Books, 1973).

Maines, David, "Social Organization and Structure in Symbolic Interactionist Thought," *Annual Review of Sociology*, vol. 3 (1977) pp. 235–59.

Maines, David, and Denzin, Norman, *Work and Problematic Situations* (New York: T. Y. Crowell, 1978).

McCall, George, and Simmons, J., *Identities and Interactions* (New York: Grove Press, 1966).

Mead, George H., *Essays on His Social Philosophy*, Petras, John, ed. (New York: Teachers College Press, 1968).

Mead, George H., *Mind, Self and Society* (Chicago: University of Chicago Press, 1934).

Mead, George H., *Movements of Thought in the Nineteenth Century* (Chicago: University of Chicago Press, 1936).

Mead, George H., *The Philosophy of the Act* (Chicago: University of Chicago Press, 1938).

Mead, George H., *The Philosophy of the Present* (Chicago: Open Court, 1932).

Mead, George H., *Selected Writings*, Reck, Andrew, ed. (Indianapolis: Bobbs-Merrill, 1964).

Mennell, Stephen, *Sociological Theory* (New York: Praeger, 1974).

Olesen, Virginia, and Whitaker, Elvi, *The Silent Dialogue* (San Francisco: Jossey-Bass, 1968).

Park, Robert E., *The Collected Papers of Robert E. Park*, Hughes, E., et al., ed., three volumes (Glencoe, Ill.: Free Press, 1950–1955), vol. 1 *Race and Culture*, (1950); vol. 2 *Human Communities: The City and Human Ecology* (1952); vol. 3 *Society: Collective Behavior, News and Opinion, Sociology and Modern Society* (1955).

Park, Robert E., *The Immigrant Press and Its Control* (New York: Harper, 1922).

Park, Robert E., *On Social Control and Collective Behavior*, Turner, Ralph, ed. (Chicago: University of Chicago Press, 1967).

Park, Robert E., and Burgess, Ernest, *Introduction to the Science of Sociology* (Chicago: University of Chicago Press, 1921).

Petras, J., and Meltzer, B., "Theoretical and Ideological Variations in Contemporary Interactionism," *Catalyst*, vol. 7 (1973) pp. 1–8.

Reynolds, M., and Reynolds, L., "Interactionism, Complicity and the Astructural Bias," *Catalyst*, vol. 7 (1973) pp. 76–85.

Riesman, David, *Constraint and Variety in American Education* (Garden City, N.Y.: Doubleday, 1958).

Rucker, Darnell, *The Chicago Pragmatists* (Minneapolis: University of Minnesota Press, 1969).

Shibutani, Tomatsu, "A Cybernetic Approach to Motivation," in Buckley, W., ed., *Modern Systems Research for the Behavioral Scientist* (Chicago: Aldine, 1968) pp. 330–36.

Shibutani, Tomatsu, *Human Nature and Collective Behavior*, 1970.

Shibutani, Tomatsu, "Reference Groups and Social Control" in Rose, A., ed., *Human Behavior and Social Processes* (Boston: Houghton Mifflin, 1962) pp. 128–47.

Shibutani, Tomatsu, *Society and Personality* (Englewood Cliffs, N.J.: Prentice-Hall, 1961).

Shibutani, Tomatsu, and Kwan, Kian, *Ethnic Stratification* (New York: Macmillan, 1965).

Shils, Edward, *The Present State of American Sociology* (Glencoe, Ill.: Free Press, 1948).

Singlemann, Peter, "Exchange as Symbolic Interaction: Convergence Between Two Theoretical Perspectives," *American Sociological Review*, vol. 37 (1972) pp. 414–24.

Stone, Gregory, and Farberman, Harvey, eds., *Social Psychology Through Symbolic Interaction* (Waltham, Mass.: Blaisdell Publishing Co., 1970).

Storr, R., *Harper's University* (Chicago: University of Chicago Press, 1966).

Strauss, Anselm, Schatzman, Leonard, Ehrlich, Danuta, Bucher, Rue, and Sabshin, Melvin, "The Hospital and Its Negotiated Order," in Freidson, E., ed., *The Hospital in Modern Society* (New York: Free Press, 1963) pp. 147–69.

Strauss, Anselm, Schatzman, Leonard, Bucher, Rue, Ehrlich, Danuta, Sabshin, Melvin, *Psychiatric Ideologies and Institutions* (New York: Free Press, 1964).

Stryker, Sheldon, "Conditions of Accurate Role-Taking: A Test of Mead's Theory," in Rose, *Human Behavior and Social Processes*, pp. 41–62.

Swanson, Guy, "Mead and Freud: Their Relevance for Social Psychology," *Sociometry*, vol. 24 (1961) pp. 313–29.

Thomas, William I., "The Scope and Method of Folk Psychology, *Am. J. Soc.*, vol. 1 (1896) pp. 434–45.

Thomas, William I., and Znaniecki, Florian, *The Polish Peasant in Europe and America* (Boston: Richard Badger, 1918–1920; 2d ed., New York: Alfred Knopf, 1927; reprinted New York: Dover Publications, 1958).

Thomas, William I., *The Unadjusted Girl* (Boston: Little, Brown & Co., 1923).

Thomas, William I., *On Social Organization and Social Personality,* Janowitz, ed.

Turner, Ralph, "Determinants of Social Movement Strategies," in Shibutani, *Human Nature and Collective Behavior*, pp. 145–64.

Veysey, Lawrence, *The Emergence of the American University* (Chicago: University of Chicago Press, 1965).

Wallace, Walter, ed., *Sociological Theory* (Chicago: Aldine, 1969) pp. 34–36.

Weller, Jack, and Quarantelli, Enrico, "Neglected Characteristics of Collective Behavior," *American Journal of Sociology*, vol. 79 (1973) pp. 665–85.

Zeitlin, I., *Rethinking Sociology* (New York: Appleton-Century-Crofts, 1973).

Zimmerman, D., and Wieder, D., "Ethnomethodology and the Problem of Order: Comments on Denzin," in Douglas, J., ed., *Understanding Everyday Life* (Chicago: Aldine, 1970) pp. 287–95.

13

PHENOMENOLOGY AND SOCIOLOGY

KURT H. WOLFF

THIS CHAPTER is predicated on the assumption that for sociologists the significance of phenomenology is tantamount to its sociological usage. Furthermore, even within this restriction, phenomenology here refers to the philosophy of Edmund Husserl (1859–1938) and to Alfred Schutz's (1899–1959) effort to show the bearing of Husserl's phenomenology on social science. Excluded are such important philosophers as Max Scheler (1874–1928), Martin Heidegger (1889–1976), Jean-Paul Sartre (1905–), and Maurice Merleau-Ponty (1908–61). All of these men are phenomenologists, in various significant senses of the term. Scheler's impact on sociology, above all on the sociology of knowledge, has not significantly come from his phenomenology (Karl Mannheim in his analysis of the sociology of knowledge to the contrary notwithstanding).[1] Scheler, like Sartre and Merleau-Ponty, though in quite a different way, finds his thrust above all in events and processes of his time—Scheler in more religious, ethical, and "philosophical-anthropological" terms, Sartre and Merleau-Ponty in more political terms. Scheler is haunted by the decay of European man;[2] Sartre is not only a philosopher but also an activist (as well as a novelist and playwright); Merleau-Ponty has changed the character of the Husserlian enterprise by centering his phenomenology on the body;[3] and finally, Heidegger may be said to be the bridge between phenomenology and contemporary hermeneutics, represented by such thinkers as Hans-Georg Gadamer and Paul Ricoeur.

Phenomenology

At all times, in all societies or cultures, every new generation has been taught and is taught how to conceive of things; this teaching is a central part of socialization, or enculturation. Socialization is concerned with how to perceive and interpret the world, how "to be in the world." If any of us, provided we are unacquainted with phenomenology, were asked how "this table" appears to us, the question would hardly make sense; we might answer, "why, of course, the way a table appears" or "the way a table looks—don't we all know what a table looks like or how it 'appears'?" All of us have been brought up to understand the world and its parts in certain ways, ways we take for granted or think of as "natural." We approach the world with the notions about it that we have received in the process of socialization.

Phenomenology asks us *not* to take received notions for granted.[4] It asks us to *question* them—to question nothing less than our culture, that is, our way of looking at and being in the world in which we have been brought up. "We" here refers to all human beings, not merely to twentieth-century Americans or to Westerners or to members of industrialized societies, for *all* people are socialized and have been always and everywhere. This is an essential characteristic of man; *all,* except those biologically incapable of it, are socialized—in short, cultured—beings. For man's biological equipment alone does not enable him to survive birth; culture, as this term is ordinarily understood in modern social science, is (among other things) an equipment necessary for this.

How then can we be asked, as we are by phenomenology, to *question* our culture? Is this not like asking us to imagine—as best we can, which is not likely to be good—how we could get along without it? That is, how to get along, human beings that we are, as if we were *not* human beings, *not* socialized, enculturated, cultured. But the command to question culture is much less preposterous than these rhetorical queries suggest. For we must realize that what we are asked to do is to *question* our culture, to call it into question—not to reject or abolish it; we are asked to "bracket" it, to suspend it, to keep it in abeyance. And to do *this* is part and parcel of our culture itself—although here "ours" no longer refers to mankind but only to *Western* culture. To question itself, to be critical of itself, is a characteristic of Western culture, but *not* of all culture. Indeed, this self-questioning, self-critical feature of Western culture has characterized it at least since Plato, who himself made the distinction between mere opinion and knowledge, always urging knowledge over opinion—that is, what "one says" or what is taken for granted; and this feature has found its most spectacular expression in the development of a uniquely Western way of looking at the world: science. Science is the most obviously self-critical and self-questioning of intellectual activities, systematically searching for negative cases and for explanations, hypotheses, and interpretations precisely other than the ones that to the best of one's knowledge are true or certain. Science (at least "empirical" science) is that knowledge which is valid only "until further notice."

The founder of phenomenology as it has been understood since the turn of this century is Edmund Husserl. One of the slogans for which Husserl is best known is "Back to the things!" What did he mean by this slogan? For sociologists in particular, the most important meaning is to call our received notions, our culture, in question; to suspend it, "bracket" it, and thus find out how things themselves actually appear to us directly, rather than through the veil of our culture (including language and other symbolic structures). To register how things directly appear to us was for Husserl to register how they actually are. We cannot take it for granted that they are as we have been taught they are; we must question the way we have been taught to look at them. To find out how they appear to us when we "bracket" them is to begin to philosophize; and since this requires the most painstaking effort for an accurate description—that is, a description which takes as little for granted as is humanly possible—Husserl spoke of philosophy as "a rigorous science." Indeed, "Philosophy as a Rigorous Science" is the title of a famous essay of his (1910); at the same time, it is another way of saying "back to the things."

How to account for the fact that this conception of philosophy arose when and where it did—in the German-speaking world around the turn of this century—is a quite different question. Thus far we have tried to understand what phenomenology means, now we are asking not about meaning but about history: how is it that that meaning came into being when and where it did, rather than at another time or elsewhere? The former, the question about *meaning,* is one of *understanding* or *interpreting.* The latter, the *historical* or *genetic* question, is one of *explaining;* in contrast to the former, it is a *causal* question. The point here is only to clarify the distinction because its neglect is likely to lead to confusion and dead-ends; we cannot now answer the historical question—except quite tentatively by the whole chapter.

There is an intimate theoretical connection between the demand "back to the things" and the quest of *verstehende,* or "understanding" sociology, as implied in the definition by Max Weber, considered to be its founder: "Sociology (in the sense in which this highly ambiguous word is used here) shall mean: a science which wants interpretively to understand social acting and thereby causally to explain it in its course and its effects."[5]

What is significant in this definition is that for Max Weber sociology is an enterprise which both interprets or understands (namely, meanings) and (causally) explains (namely, events in time); moreover, which interprets in order to be able to explain; which, as it were, prepares by interpretation its candidates for causal explanation. That is to say, Max Weber thought that before we can ask causal questions calling for explanation, we must understand what we want to ask causal questions about; we must be able to interpret it. Thus, logically, understanding precedes explaining.

The intimate theoretical connection between Weberian sociology's demand to understand and the demand to go "back to the things" is that the latter is phenomenology's demand to understand. This similarity may account for the fact that it is *verstehende* sociology within sociology where phenomenology has had its impact.

Still, there are very important differences between these demands: (1) the second function of Weberian sociology, (causal) explanation, is absent from phenomenology; (2) this means at least a predisposition on the part of phenomenology to neglect history and time in the sense of historical time,[6] which, on the contrary, is an essential characteristic of Weber's sociology, and the absence of which was to some extent recognized and remedied by Husserl in his last major work, *The Crisis of European Sciences and Transcendental Phenomenology* (1935–39). On the other hand, the shortcomings of Weber's conception of understanding have been illuminated and remedied by Alfred Schutz's phenomenologically inspired insights.

The phenomenological notion of bracketing is of great significance for sociology. Bracketing may occur spontaneously when we no longer get along with our received notions but raise questions about them. When do our traditional, habitual, customary methodologies fail? For it is then that we may begin to wonder about them, in fact bracketing our notions. Among the types of occasions on which this happens are "extreme situations" in any of the numerous senses of this expression, including "extreme" confusion or puzzlement, but also inescapable fascination with something new. All of these terms, of course, have subjective referents—what is an extreme situation for one person need not be for another, what confuses one may not confuse or puzzle another, what fascinates me as something new may be indifferent or habitual to you. But once one is caught in confusion or puzzlement, taking things for granted no longer serves; wonderment may begin (rather than confusion or anxiety persisting), the hitherto accepted ordering of the world no longer avails—and here is the ever rediscovered root of philosophizing.

In the course of his continuing analyses, Husserl came, under the shadow of Hitler, to find that all of Western culture found itself in an "extreme situation," a situation out of which he hoped *his* philosophizing—phenomenology—might help to lead. This realization and this hope are among the most powerful and important elements of the previously mentioned *Crisis of European Sciences and Transcendental Phenomenology.*

Hegel's *Phenomenology of Mind* (1807), too, was written in a critical period—when the French Revolution, instead of bringing about freedom, had lead to a new despotism, Napoleon's. But there are more similarities between Hegel's *Phenomenology* and Husserl's phenomenology. Both are studies of consciousness—though not in the sense of empirical psychology, in which consciousness is analyzed in the ordinary, common-sense, everyday, "mundane" world.[7]

Yet students of Husserl who should know say that Husserl claimed not to have read Hegel.[8] At any rate, incomparably more significant for him was René Descartes, who had already figured importantly in the work of Husserl's teacher, the Austrian philosopher and psychologist Franz Brentano (1838–1917).[9] What did Descartes himself say? His question was what he must believe beyond all doubt. "Finally," Descartes wrote, as the same precepts which we have when awake may come to us when asleep without their being true, I decided to suppose that nothing that had ever entered my mind was more real than the illusions of my dreams. But I soon noticed that while I thus wished to think everything false, it was necessarily true that I who thought so was something. Since this truth, *I think, therefore I am*, was so firm and assured that all the most extravagant suppositions of the sceptics were unable to shake it, I judged that I could safely accept it as the first principle of the philosophy I was seeking.[10]

It can be argued that Descartes's question also was Husserl's, but it may be more conducive to a grasp of phenomenology if it is pointed out that such a formulation covers only a component of the whole—a very complex whole—of Husserl's work and of phenomenology altogether. Other questions concern circumstances in Husserl's biography without which phenomenology would have developed differently than it has. One of these circumstances is Husserl's study with Brentano, from whom he took—though greatly modifying—one of the concepts which was to become fundamental, that of the *intentionality* of consciousness (which had been an important idea in scholastic philosophy but had long been out of use). Most simply put, intentionality means that there is no consciousness except consciousness *of something* (thought of, love of, dream of, fear of, doubt of something or somebody, and so on), and *what* consciousness intends are intentions, or more precisely *noemata*, namely, that which *is* to consciousness. And always correlated with this *noematic* aspect of consciousness, which concerns the characteristics and dynamics of the *noemata*, there is the *noetic*[11] (from *noesis*), aspect which refers to the specific style of consciousness, to the ways in which consciousness *intends* (e.g., thinking, fearing, loving, hoping, desiring, suspecting, etc.).[12]

According to Schutz's interpretation of Husserl, the emphasis on bracketing, on "performing the phenomenological reduction,"[13] lies on the withholding of all judgments concerning the existence or otherwise of the world that we ordinarily take for granted as being there and being there just as it appears to us. What is left over from the reduction is our consciousness, with all its contents and activities ("cogitations").

My perception of this chair in the natural [= ordinary, everyday, unbracketed] attitude corroborates my belief in its existence. Now I perform the transcendental [= phenomenological] reduction. I refrain from believing in the existence of this chair [but I don't deny it either: I suspend judgment concerning its existence]. Thereafter the chair perceived remains outside the bracketing, but the perception itself is without any doubt an element of my stream of thought. And it is not "perception as such," without any further reference; it remains "perception *of*"—specifically perception of *this chair*. [That is, perception, as all of consciousness, is intentional, is "*of*." But it] . . . is not the corporeal thing "chair" to which my perception intentionally refers; but the intentional object of my preserved perception is "the chair *as I have perceived it*," the *Phenomenon* "chair *as it appears to me*," which may or may not have an equivalent in the bracketed outer world. Thus the whole world is preserved within the reduced sphere in so far, but only in so far, as it is the intentional correlate of my conscious life.[14]

Phenomena, e.g., the chair as it appears to me, suggest aspects of themselves other than the perceived ones. This is most easily understood in the case of bodily things, such as the chair: thus the side of it that I actually perceive suggests other sides, e.g., the front suggests the back; the left side, the right, and so on; but the same also applies to nonbodily (abstract, ideal, irreal) things—democracy, virtue, love. Aspects of something not perceived (or thought of, associated, or otherwise intended—"appresented") but suggesting other aspects of the same thing are, in their entirety, called the "*inner horizon*" of the phenomenon. But there also is an "outer horizon," which is the totality of other phenomena that are presently not attended to but which the phenomenon perceived may refer to (William James called it its "fringes"). Thus, the chair may refer to the rest of the furniture in my room, to other rooms, to the house in which they are found, to the street, to the community, and eventually to the universe:

> Every perception of a "detail" refers to the "thing" to which it pertains, the thing to other things over against which it stands out and which I call its background. There is not an isolated object as such, but a field of perceptions and cogitations. . . .[15]

As I "look at" (attend to) different aspects of the noema, different parts of its inner or its outer horizon, the noema itself undergoes or appears to undergo changes, while my noesis of it may remain the same. There thus are *noematic modifications*. But in addition there also are *noetic modifications*, changes in the noesis. Among these, one is of special importance: the noetic difference between the originary experiencing of something and all derived experiences (e.g., experiencing in memory). The special importance of this particular noetic modification lies in the fact that, on the one hand, it bears on the problem of *evidence* and, on the other, it may serve to introduce the notion of *inner time* (Henri Bergson's *durée*) and its chief divisions.

Very broadly speaking, in the conception of phenomenology, *evidence* (that something is so) is "the possibility of referring derived [such as remembered] experiences to an originary one;"[16] this gives special sense to Husserl's demand to go "back to the things" as directly as possible.[17] The second pertinence of the distinction between originary and derived experience is that within memory (which of course is a matter of inner time, rather than of "clock time"), it is important to distinguish between *retention*—the retention of that which happened "just now"—and *recollection* of what happened further back. (In grammatical terms—which presuppose predication, which does not apply to the present context [see further in this section]—the distinction corresponds roughly to that between the perfect and the pluperfect tense.) Divisions of the future corresponding to these of the past are *protention* and *anticipation*, which respectively refer to expectations of what is going to occur immediately and what will occur later on (grammatically, the distinction resembles, though even more loosely, that between the future and future perfect tense). Just as every perceived phenomenon has its inner and its outer horizon, so every cogitation is surrounded by retentions and protentions and points to other cogitations, past or still to come, by recollection or anticipation (where the latter is "empty," i.e., a cogitation anticipated only as to type, rather than as yet experienced in its concreteness or fullness).

It should be pointed out that there is an important difference between *getting acquainted with* a nonbodily, ideal object—e.g., a mathematical equation or distinctions between concepts like democracy and aristocracy or capitalism and socialism—and *knowing* it. The distinction can easily be brought home by an example from geometry: the theorem that the sum of the angles of a triangle must be 180 degrees. When we learned it, we took many mental steps to arrive at the equation and its proof; but now we simply "know" it, perhaps without being able to repeat the proof. We now can encompass the process, which consisted of many single steps (was arrived at "polythetically"), in a single glance ("monothetically"), for our knowledge of an object "is nothing else than the sediment of previous mental processes by which it has been constituted."[18]

Everybody knows about all that has been mentioned thus far, though perhaps not by the terms used in phenomenolgy: we know that it makes no difference whether the terms of an example I give in order to explain something refer to actually existing things or not ("let's assume for the sake of discussion"); or whether or not the 2 and the 2 that make 4 are existents; or whether, to take an example from quite a different sphere, the person portrayed in this painting is "real" or "imagined" (there are various meanings of the suspension of judgments concerning existence).[19] Furthermore, we would be greatly surprised if this house which we see from the front turned out to have no back (cf. inner horizon) or that, back or no back, it stood on nothing and were surrounded by nothing (cf. outer horizon). We also know the difference between a phenomenon (noema) and our approaching it (noesis); the multitude of ways a phenomenon may appear to us (noematic modifications) and of approaches toward it (noetic modifications); and the difference between inner time (*durée*) and clock time—an hour may "last" a moment or an eternity; or that between what "it was like" (originary experience) and what I recall of it (derived experience, memory). We know that my memory of something that happened just a moment ago (retention) differs from my memory of it a week, a month, a year, ten years later (recollection); the difference between "in just a minute" (protention) and "next year" (anticipation). We may also remember that $(a + b)^2 = a^2 + 2ab + b^2$ but not know why this is so (monothetic vs. polythetic); and we may or may not be able to reconstitute this formula (constitution). In phenomenology all of these and many other phenomena are lifted into awareness, named, clarified, and analyzed in incomparably greater detail than is possible here, where they can merely be introduced.

This also applies to the last two themes to be mentioned. The first is that of *prepredicative experience*. We are acquainted with it probably from experiences of shock and surprise, where we "didn't know what happened to us" and where, therefore, it took some time—anywhere from a moment to all the years past since—before (if ever) we could say what it was, that is, give what we experienced a predicate. Husserl has shown, however, that *all* experience has a prepredicative basis (because experiences to become predicable, need interpretation).[20]

The other is the concept of *eidos* and the difference between an *empirical* and an *eidetic approach*. The eidos (Greek for form, shape, idea, essence; *Wesen*) of something is the combination of features without which it would be something other than what it is. To find the eidos we imagine features taken away from it or added to it—we proceed by what Husserl calls "free variation in imagination." The phenomenologist, as Schutz puts it, "does not have to do with the objects themselves; he is interested in their [essential] *meaning*, as it is constituted by the activities of our mind."[21] The empirical approach, on the other hand, deals with things and aspects and relations among them, with induction and generalization.[22] One of the questions left open by the notion of eidos and hence by the eidetic approach concerns the relation between objects which have an eidos that is not subject to cultural variation of relativity (e.g., presumably, mathematical objects such as geometric figures or arithmetic and algebraic equations,)[23] and those which may be so subject (e.g., presumably, social and political objects such as family, state, democracy, equality). The question is related to certain criticisms of phenomenology, above all of the notion of eidos, or essence, which we shall now consider.[24]

Critiques of Phenomenology

The most persuasive of these criticisms have been advanced by members of the Frankfurt School,[25] especially Herbert Marcuse and Theodor W. Adorno. In his essay "The Concept of Essence,"[26] Marcuse gives a historical survey of this concept—from Plato through Aristotle, Thomas Aquinas, Descartes, Kant, Hegel, Scheler, positivism, and Husserl—that shows its ever-diminishing critical power, which it gains back only in materialist theory (Marxism). Beginning with Plato, essence and appearance or essence and existence were not only cognitively distinguished in various ways, the difference between them was understood also as a challenge to make either appearance or existence more nearly commensurate with essence; thus, the two concepts were normative or ought-concepts. With Descartes the problem of essence became a matter of the cognitive subject: the cognitive subject is man's essence. In Kant, the problem is located in the theory of pure (theoretical) and practical reason; but since reason enables man only to *begin* actions, which afterward are conditioned by the system of necessities in which they must move, Kant's doctrine mirrors the fate of a world in which rational human freedom always can take only the initial step freely, only to encounter afterward an uncontrolled necessity which remains contingent with respect to reason. Man's essence is thus imprisoned "in a past without future."[27] In

Husserl, finally, "essence" (or eidos) becomes that which remains invariant in whatever "free variation in imagination" (as we have seen). This constitutes a profound change:

All the decisive concepts which played a role in the theory of essence since its beginnings reappear here, and all in a characteristically changed form. Freedom has become a mark of pure fantasy, as the free arbitrariness of ideational possibilities of variation. The constant, identical, and necessary is no longer sought as the Being of beings but as what is invariant in the infinite manifold of representational modifications of "exemplars."

Possibility is no longer a force straining toward reality; rather, in its open endlessness it belongs to mere imagination.[28]

For Marcuse, "the receptivity of the intuition of essence replaces the spontaneity of the comprehending understanding that is inseparable from the idea of critical reason."[29] The door is open, Marcuse holds, to declarations (theoretically arbitrary but ideologically or politically expedient) that certain individuals, facts, hierarchies, and institutions are "essential."[30] By contrast, the historical theory of essence found in Hegel, but confined to the mind, was revived and revised as a materialist dialectic which recouped, as it were, the actual world that had been lost in idealist philosophy, positivism, and phenomenology and proclaimed it the task of philosophy to make the existence of this world come closer to its essence.[31]

Adorno, too, accuses Husserl of ahistoricity. Husserl is unaware of "borrowing" the power of logical absolutism (not to be confused with the psychological foundation of logic) from the objectivity—stressed, on the contrary, by Durkheim and other sociologists—of the social process which controls the individual, who cannot penetrate it.[32] Like Marcuse, Adorno criticizes Husserl's conception of a science which has a "precritical" (uncritical) relation to the things it studies (and which is not changed by the reduction): "the world of things is accepted as that as which it is given."[33] While the slogan "back to the things" sounds antiidealistic, Adorno writes, it represents the *height* of idealism, because the "things" are imprisoned in consciousness, or (we might say) are "not of this world." Adorno explains this and many other paradoxes in Husserl's work as "the expression of the insolubility of his problem," which is that "he rebels against idealistic thinking while attempting to break through the walls of idealism with purely idealist instruments, namely, by an exclusive analysis of thought and of consciousness."[34] Yet Adorno admits a "truth" in Husserl's philosophy:

. . . [the] struggle against psychologism [which] does not mean the reintroduction of dogmatic prejudices, but the freeing of critical reason from the prejudices contained in the naive and uncritical religion of "facts" which he challenged in its psychological form.[35]

Husserl, however, can also be read differently. A passage from him to which many could be added suggests how Marcuse's and Adorno's critiques might be revised:

. . . and the consciousness in which the givenness, the pure intuiting, as it were, of things comes to pass, is not . . . something like an empty box in which these givennesses simply are [contained], but the intuiting consciousness is, aside from attention, [the same as] acts of thinking [which are] formed in such and such ways, and the things, which are not the acts of thinking, are nevertheless constituted in them [and] attain givenness in them, and only so essentially constituted do they show themselves as what they are.

But are these not but miracles? And where does this object constituting begin and where does it stop? Are there actual limits [to it?] . . . [36]

This excerpt suggests that a more "Husserlian" reading of Husserl would find him above all somebody who wonders, a philosopher, whose fundamental attitude toward life or whose "being in the world" has, ever since Aristotle first formulated it, been said to be that of wondering—although to wonder is by no means incompatible with being critical, which, as Marcuse often reminds us, likewise has been a traditional and perhaps even slightly older conception of the philosopher's activity. But between the two, Husserl better fits the former description, and part of the objection advanced by Marcuse and Adorno (and many others) is that he is not more of the latter.

Nor can it be claimed, as it is by Adorno, that Husserl did not differentiate among phenomena or *noemata* inasmuch as he held the *epochê* to be applicable to all of them (cf. the end of the preceding section). Thus in *The Crisis*, Husserl tries, among other things, to determine the "general structure" of the life-world "to which everything that exists relatively is bound" but which "is not itself relative."[37] Irrespective of the degree to which he attained this goal, the intention is to establish a structure, which by definition would be differentiated, even though the question of whether the accomplishment of this task would have forced Husserl out of consciousness and into the material world is difficult to answer. What appears incontrovertible, however, is that the material world (of everyday life) was not only *not* Husserl's starting point for philosophizing (as it early came to be for Marx, for instance), but played only a secondary role (compared to his concern with problems of logic).

The critique of the Frankfurt School is based on a conception of history and, particularly, of the time in which Husserl and his critics wrote. According to this critique, Husserl used his talent in a less than optimal if not in fact mistaken way, a way, furthermore, which could be exploited by authoritarians and totalitarians (cf. the quotation from Heidegger in n. 30 below). And yet, there is Adorno's praise of him (as we have seen) for having freed "critical reason from the prejudices contained in the naive and uncritical religion of 'facts' . . ." with which there is little doubt that Marcuse and other critics would concur. It is as if, despite all his criticism, Adorno celebrated Husserl as a liberator. Are his criticism and his celebration such that their juxtaposition betrays no contradiction—yes, Husserl's was a false consciousness; yes, he was a liberator—or does the juxtaposition not rather suggest the critics' ambivalence, possibly less philosophical than biographical, toward idealism, and thus a projection of such ambivalence onto Husserl? The question can only be raised; its analysis would require a considerable study for which this is not the place.

Phenomenology and Marxism

Perhaps because some commentators consider phenomenology and Marxist thought among the most important or promising contemporary intellectual outlooks, they have tried to bring them together in efforts toward a synthesis between them in a mutual cleansing and heightening or in order to criticize one in the light of the other.

The earliest attempt may well stem from Tran-Duc-Thao, a Vietnamese philosopher. Tran-Duc-Thao claims that the problems raised by phenomenology can be resolved only by Marxism; he is better at criticizing phenomenology than in answering its questions, and for this purpose he appears to have had "dialectical materialism" at the ready all along. A quotation may suggest the tone of his book:

> If Husserl still remained in the tradition of idealistic rationalism that marked the belated flowering of the German bourgeoisie and its last progressivist fancies, his evolution did not, for that, bear less witness to a growing uneasiness concerning the *real foundation* of the meanings intended by consciousness. From the enjoyment of eternity in intuiting essences to the anguished problematic of the *Crisis of the European Sciences*, interpreted as the crisis of Western humanity, there showed itself the ever more profound feeling of the futility in which traditional values had floundered; and the famous slogan *"back to the things themselves!"* came to mean ever more openly a return to the palpable realities of the *life-world.*[38]

Later Wolfe Mays and Fred R. Dallmayr provide useful overviews of thinkers who try in different ways to relate phenomenology and Marxism. Mays[39] discusses Jean-Paul Sartre and his critics (Georg Lukács, Adam Schaff, Raymond Aron, Klaus Hartmann[40]), Maurice Merleau-Ponty and Lukács's critique of him, Tran-Duc-Thao, Enzo Paci, Pier Aldo Rovatti, Paul Ricoeur, and Efraim Shmueli).[41] The essential difference between phenomenology and Marxism, Mays concludes, is—very briefly—the former's emphasis on individual consciousness and the latter's on the social, even though in the later work of Husserl there is "an increasing concern with the relation of the individual with history."[42]

Fred Dallmayr[43] treats most of the thinkers discussed by Mays and, in addition, Gajo Petrović, Karel Kosik, Antonio Gramsci, Herbert Marcuse, Theodor W. Adorno, and Jürgen Habermas,[44] but the bulk of his essay is devoted, as its title promises, to Enzo Paci. It ends with Paul Piccone and John O'Neill;[45] and hopes for a settlement of the relation between Marxism and phenomenology from Giambattista Vico's distinction between "philosophy" and "philology":

What I wish to suggest for consideration is the possibility that phenomenology and Marxist theory might be related like "philology" and "philosophy," as these terms were used by Giambattista Vico. In his *New Science* [1725], Vico delineates the respective preoccupations as follows: "Philosophy contemplates reason, whence comes knowledge of the true; philology observes that of which human choice is author, whence comes consciousness of the certain. In its second part this axiom comprises among philologians all the grammarians, historians, and critics who concern themselves with the study of the languages and deeds of people."[46]

And Vico urges philosophers and philologians to pay attention to each other's findings lest they fail in their own endeavors. Thus Dallmayr implies that Marxism, the "philosophy," and phenomenology, the "philology," should do likewise, and each will be the better for it. To be plausible, this proposition ought to be tested against another understanding of the relation between the two—an understanding which, roughly, is Mays's but which Dallmayr explicitly rejects—"that phenomenology and Marxism might complement each other by focusing, respectively, on subjective and objective dimensions."[47] To this understanding we will have to come back.

In the meantime, the reader should be alerted to Mihály Vajda's lively and informed analysis of Marxism(s), phenomenology, and existentialism.[48] It consists of conversations on the historical meaning of the participants' clarity, ambiguity, or conflict regarding their Marxist, phenomenological, or existentialist outlooks. Because of its liveliness and the throng and sparkle of arguments and facets, to do justice to this study requires an analysis at another place than here.

Not necessarily because it is better but because it is closer to social science and can provoke a response that may lead to a surer grasp of phenomenology and Marxism in their relation to and bearing on sociology, David M. Rasmussen's "The Marxist Critique of Phenomenology"[49] warrants more detailed treatment.

First, Rasmussen describes Marx's work as a theory of society within the history of modern theories of society, with special emphasis on Hobbes and attention to Locke and Hegel. While nobody had ever met a Hobbesian or Lockean individual, Hegel tried to transcend speculation by arguing the individual's concrete realization in family, civil society, and state; Marx, finally, rejected all stipulation of an originary state of nature and instead started with a social state the purpose of which was not exchange, as in social-contract theory, but production, and this, like social life—in families, tribes, and larger groups—could actually be observed.

Second, Rasmussen analyzes phenomenology, which he claims has no theory of society. From the mundane point of view, he observes, the world is social, but in the phenomenological reduction it must be bracketed. Yet in the *Cartesian Meditations*, says Rasmussen, Husserl comes to acknowledge the influence the social and historical world might have on the phenomenological method itself.[50] "The final episode in Husserl's reluctant encounter with preconstituted social phenomena occurs in *The Crisis*."[51] And after examining Alfred Schutz's effort to analyze the social world phenomenologically ("perhaps the most significant attempt in the history of contemporary phenomenology"[52]), Rasmussen finds that it ends up "by appropriating social phenomena on the basis of a 'mere analogy' to phenomena occurring in original individual experience."[53]

Lastly, Rasmussen denies any essential relation between Marxism and phenomenology (Husserl was overwhelmingly engaged in the analysis of egological experience, that is, of the solitary ego; Marx, of modern society) and then deals with the position according to which the "Marxist critique of phenomenology finds its foundation in an historical analysis informed by social theory." In trying to account for the inability of phenomenology "to give a meaningful description of social phenomena,"[54] "one must turn to the socio-historical context in which phenomenology functioned," a context which

> . . . can only be explained by reference to the historical development of social theory itself and the historically specific problem developed in modern theory of society. Husserl's concentration on egological experience and his assumption that it alone is valid finds its prototype in the early formulations of modern theory of society [such as were discussed in the first part of his paper, notably Hobbes's, in the light of which it becomes understandable that] as soon as one attempted to ground socio-historical experience all the problems and contradictions of a modern theory of society which had now become part of the "life-world" of society [fundamentally the contradiction between (theoretical) speculation and (actual) history] would manifest themselves.

If phenomenology were to attempt an analysis of social experience commensurate with that it has achieved of individual experience, it would have to revise its concept of the latter profoundly, and this, Rasmussen believes, may still occur. In such an attempt, he concludes, phenomenology "must confront, not on ideological but on theoretical grounds, Marx's critique of modern theory of society which, to the extent that it relies on the primacy of individual experience, is also a critique of phenomenology itself."[55]

In commenting on Rasmussen's presentation, it must be recalled that modern social theory generally, and thus Marx's, "attempted to construct a theory of society," "to provide a theoretical foundation for an emerging social order."[56] But Marx also denounced the ravages of this emerging social order and used his understanding of its structure to persuade his fellow human beings of the necessity of its overthrow—with all the hubris of such a prophetic hope and longing. This was one response to early capitalism, Marx's "sociohistorical context." For Rasmussen, as we have seen, the "sociohistorical context," which contains social theory, is an indispensable source of insight into the failure of phenomenology to undertake an adequate analysis of social experience. Husserl was so influenced by modern social theory that he found it impossible to provide one of his own, to ground the problem of intersubjectivity other than through analogy. In his explanation, Rasmussen thus goes outside phenomenology, but not beyond social theory into society itself into the society in which Husserl and Schutz lived. And while one can make a case for arguing that during the greater part of his life Husserl was, as it were, contained by social theory, in *The Crisis*—indeed already in the *Cartesian Meditations* if not even before—he tried, if in vain, to break out of it.

The broader "sociohistorical context" of which the modern social theory to which Rasmussen refers is an aspect has among its innumerable participants Marx *and* Husserl—and Schutz and any other phenomenologists and existentialists one may want to think of, and many other people as well. Some of the names that have been given to this context are secularization, rationalization, the eclipse of reason, disenchantment, alienation, disillusionment, unmasking, twilight of the gods, God is dead, relativization, relativism, and quite a few more. It is usually assumed to be a Western phenomenon (long since exported, however) and to have begun with the simultaneous developments of Protestantism, modern capitalism, and modern science. Obviously, it is a far more comprehensive than theoretical context and process, of which theory of society, to repeat, is only a part, as is social science altogether. Among its numerous more recent aspects in everyday life or the "life-world," one stands out: totalitarianism. What holds all aspects together, no matter where they may be found or how otherwise heterogeneous they may be, is their being either expressions of the breakdown of believable tradition or efforts to overcome the unbearability of such a breakdown.

Seen in this light, Marx found it outrageous, we may say, that the Good, the True, and the Beautiful, the syndrome that epitomized the German-idealist-bourgeois tradition of the desirable life, had come to be at an infinite distance from the life that an ever-increasing number of people had to lead. This idealist tradition, in which he had grown up, thus was no longer believable to him, and he used its very conception of history, after he "put it on its feet," to prove the necessity of overturning the society in which the idea of the desirable life had become an obscene joke for more and more people, and to bring about a society in which it would no longer be ludicrous. In other words, his social theory was in the service of the revolution diagnosed as necessary, and this service consisted in the precise analysis of the foundation of the society that had to be overturned, that is, of its economic system.

Husserl in comparison appears as one far more victimized by this same, though meanwhile far more developed, society than Marx. For Marx, objects were unproblematic commodities, for instance, while for Husserl they were problematic and had to be "constituted" (or—but this amounts to the same thing—"reconstituted") by phenomenological reduction. Marx took the plurality of human beings for granted, while for Husserl (at least through the *Cartesian Meditations*) this plurality was not only a problem: ultimately, as we have seen, it remained unconstitutable. Perhaps the reason for this unconstitutability, which is so convincingly shown in Rasmussen's paper, was Husserl's lack of faith in the body as something which cannot be bracketed, his taking for granted, but obviously finding of no help, the tradition of identifying thinking with cognition or mind activity only, rather than with an activity that involves the whole person. It is as if instead of bracketing this tradition, Husserl brackets the body which this tradition ignores or denies as an affective certainty and thus as an epistemological source.[57]

With such a reading, Husserl does indeed bear witness to a far more advanced state of the atomization or alienation of society than Marx, and the advent of the many things which occurred between Marx and Husserl—again, more important than any, totalitarianism—is reflected by such an advance. But is the notion of critique, whether Marx's of phenomenology or phenomenology's of Marx, an applicable notion here?

Before confronting this question, we must ask how *we* could criticize either. In the context suggested, the standard for our critique could only be something like appropriateness or adequacy of reaction to modern industrial society. Marx was more outraged by it and in consequence devised and worked for an alternative, whereas Husserl was more victimized by it and in his victimization illuminated his, that is, potentially everybody's, loneliness, thus transcending his sociohistorical occasion, but failing to ground intersubjectivity or, as it were, to outwit this society. Marx transcended and tried to change it, fired by his moral outrage, while Husserl in his victimization and, thus, far more intimate identification with his society, erected a monument to the contemporary monadic, atomized, lonely individual.

To say this means that the historical circumstances of a particular kind of society at a particular time gave rise in Husserl to something atemporal, typical: a type of the contemporary human being—thus a type of human being. Up to a point, there is a parallel to Marx's recognition of capitalism as the expression of "the truth of human existence, albeit [and here the parallel stops] in an alienated form."[58] The parallel ends because neither in Husserl nor in the present discussion is there alienation (or false consciousness), because neither there nor here is there a standard by which to distinguish alienation from its opposite, autonomy, or false from true or correct consciousness. In his conception of history, Marx had such a standard; there is none in Husserl, or at least none that could be used to assess Husserl as a type of man against other such types. And if there is any here that could so serve, it is neglected in order to attend to the more urgent topic of this process itself by which the sociohistorical context is transcended.

This transcendence is an instance of a process at work in the origination of *any* object. For any object always outlasts its genesis and, furthermore, must also be understood in its own terms, not only in those of the occasion of its genesis or only in reference to it. Rasmussen's attention is directed above all, though not exclusively, at the object, Marx's and Husserl's theories, and this is also true of the other comparisons between Marxism and phenomenology that have been mentioned.[59] By contrast, the preceding comments have stressed occasion, origin, and context, because Marx's and Husserl's occasion, origin, and context also are our own.

And yet we also saw how both Marx and Husserl, though in quite different ways, transcended their occasions. In Husserl, one of the most poignant expressions of this transcendence is a passage in *Ideas* that deals with bracketing, which Husserl calls a "radical alteration of the natural thesis"; it "transvalues it in a quite peculiar way." And continues: "*This transvaluing is a concern of our full freedom, and is opposed to all cognitive attitudes* that would set themselves up as co-ordinate with the *thesis*. . . ."[60] One way of reading this is as the celebration of solitude that may remind one of Dilthey's celebration of historical relativism. Dilthey wrote:

> Anything beautiful, anything holy, any sacrifice, re-experienced and interpreted, opens perspectives which open a reality. And likewise, we then take in . . . the bad, the terrible, the ugly, as occupying a place in the world, as containing a reality that must be justified in the context of the world.[61]

Again there is no standard of assessment, and by now this may strike us as either innocent or frivolous—but like Husserl's *Ideas*, it was written before the First World War. What Husserl himself may be said to celebrate in the last passage quoted from him is the solitude in which loneliness is overcome, the freedom *from* others that is the positive side of the want of others, the freedom of the anonymity which modern industrial society, most obviously in the city,[62] offers as the liberation from the choking intimacy of the village's preindustrial security. Here then—once more, it was just before the First World War—Husserl evinces an exemplary type of human being; but later, perhaps beginning in the late twenties, in the face of the threat to European man, it is as if Husserl could no longer let his theory be without acknowledging, somehow, the everyday copresence of others, the human plurality. Still, being the person he was, having grown up when and where he did, stamped by his philosophical tradition in the circumstances from Imperial to Weimar to Nazi Germany, eventually even traumatized by them, as it were, in his atomized, then totalitarianized society, he was no longer able to recast his theory so as to make room for the Other.

On such a view, it is obvious, Marx cannot criticize him, any more than he can criticize Marx. Instead, there is for each of them, as well as for us, only the shock of recognition—of which it may be hoped that it is the beginning we cannot know of what.[63]

But we must finally come back to that understanding of the relation between phenomenology and Marxism—that they "complement each other by focusing, respectively, on subjective and objective dimensions"—which is rejected by Dallmayr but is germane to Mays, as well as to Rasmussen. It may be noted that there is a parallel between the two dimensions and what have often been located as the two main complementary thrusts in sociology itself: the objective and subjective points of view or approaches, usually associated with, respectively, Emile Durkheim and Max Weber.[64] This suggests a further implication of the four developments and their affinities. For phenomenology and "interpretive" sociology, human consciousness—something exclusively human, something man shares with no other inhabitant of the cosmos—is central. On the other hand, Durkheim's "social facts" are "exterior" to us and "exercise constraint" on us—like history for Marx; and both want to bring them under our control, Durkheim by their explanation through sociology and by attendant reorganization of society; Marx, through understanding the nature of history—in this respect paralleling Freud—and attendant action: revolution.[65]

Before we further explore the relation between phenomenology and sociology by examining some extant views of it, we must briefly expound Alfred Schutz's understanding of the relation because, as we have heard repeatedly, Schutz's effort to apply phenomenology to the analysis of the social world is—recalling David Rasmussen's assessment—"perhaps the most significant attempt in the history of contemporary phenomenology."

Alfred Schutz

The work of Alfred Schutz consists of one book and a number of posthumous volumes of collected papers and more or less complete book-length manuscripts,[66] but this work, let alone the growing literature on it,[67] cannot be expounded or criticized here, where the task is rather, as we said, to sketch as concisely as possible his understanding of the relation between phenomenology and sociology. Some part of such a sketch has in fact been done already: when we drew on Schutz to introduce some of the major concepts of phenomenology, their selection depended on his own, which in turn was influenced by his interest in assembling those concepts of phenomenology that he held to be most fruitful for social science. It was also pointed out that in his very effort to bring sociology and phenomenology together—in a way or ways that still need to be clarified—Schutz began by examining some of Max Weber's fundamental concepts, showed their need for more explicit development, and proceeded accordingly. This he did in his book of 1932, *Der sinnhafte Aufbau der sozialen Welt* [*The Meaning-Structure of the Social World*], translated in 1967 as *The Phenomenology of the Social World.*

In the various uses to which Schutz has been put in recent years, especially in the United States, his point of departure in Weber has more often than not been forgotten. For this reason, it is useful to quote the very beginning of Schutz's book:

> The present book is based on an intensive concern of many years' duration with Max Weber's writings in the philosophy of science (*wissenschaftstheoretischen Schriften*). In the course of these studies there formed in me the conviction that while Max Weber's problematic (*Fragestellung*) had definitively fixed the starting point of every genuine philosophy of the social sciences, his analyses were not conducted down into that depth layer from which alone many important tasks that grow out of the procedure of the human studies (*Geisteswissenschaften*) itself can be accomplished. Deeper-going considerations must deal above all with Weber's central concept of subjective meaning, which is merely a heading for a multitude of most important problems that Weber did not analyze in particular, although they certainly were not unknown to him.[68]

Thus, after detailed analyses of the implications of Weber's "central concept," Schutz comes to define the subjective meaning of a product (that is, of anything anybody has produced) as that which we speak of

> . . . when we have in view the meaning-context within which the experiences of the producer testified to by the product stood or stand, that is, when we can run over in simultaneity or quasi-simultaneity with our own *durée,* the polythetic Acts in which these experiences were built up in the projecter (*Setzenden*) of the product.[69]

This statement requires not only the clarification of several concepts—"meaning-context," "simultaneity" and "quasi-simultaneity," "Acts," "projecter"—but also the awareness or, better, "thematization" of problems that are merely summed up in these concepts. In regard to the first of them, *meaning-context,* Schutz says:

> We say of our meaningful experiences E_1, E_2, . . . E_n that they stand in a meaning-context (*sinnhaften Zusammenhang*) if these experiences constitute themselves, in polythetically articulated Acts, into a higher synthesis and we can look at it [this synthesis] in a monothetic glance as on a constituted unit.[70]

Simultaneity Schutz discusses thus:

> Not only does the self (*Ich*) experience his *durée* as an absolute reality (in Bergson's sense), just as the Other (*Du*) experiences his own as such, but the *durée* of the Other is also given to the self, just as is the self's to the Other, as absolute reality. This and nothing else—the phenomenon of growing older together—is what we want to understand by the simultaneity of two *durées*.[71]

"Simultaneity" thus presupposes a face-to-face relation; otherwise, my "tuning-in"[72] with another person—to whom I am writing a letter, whose writing I am reading, whose painting I am looking at, whose music I am listening to, always provided, of course, that my aim is to grasp his meaning-context in the above-defined sense—does not proceed in genuine but in "*quasi-simultaneity.*" Finally, "*Act*" with a capital *A* must be distinguished from "act." By "Act" Schutz means any unspecified activity, whereas "act" (*Handlung*) is the product of "action" (*Handeln*), which in turn is the process that leads to the act. "Projecter" was coined here for "person who projects" something. This is inseparable from Schutz's definition of "acting" as the activity preceded (logically) by "projecting": by "acting" he understands behaving toward a projected aim or project.[73]

Schutz also submits Weber's concept of "understanding"[74] to a careful analysis. To clarify his critique, a distinction must first be made between "subjective meaning," which we know by now, and "objective meaning." Again, in regard to a product, objective meaning can be predicated only of a product as such, "that is, the wholly constituted meaning-context of the product itself, the production of which in polythetically constitutive Acts in the Other's consciousness is ignored by us."[75] [It is the difference between analyzing a book, proposition, painting, or whatever, regarding its meaning—for me personally, for "our time," within the history of its genre, and so on (objective meaning); and trying to find out what you, who wrote this book, were thinking, feeling, attempting—what it was like for Rembrandt to paint this picture, and so forth (subjective meaning).] Schutz criticizes Weber for having failed to make this distinction, which is of special significance in the social sciences. Instead of using for illustrative purposes any example Schutz gives from various social sciences, it may be more important to realize that the student of the social sciences, especially cultural anthropology, social and clinical psychology, and sociology, is acquainted with Schutz's distinction through the well-known injunction to try to understand his subject matter—people, institutions, cultures, and so on—in their rather than in his or her own terms; it is necessary to break out of the "ethnocentric" perspective. But why should Schutz call his understanding of them in his own terms "objective"? He does not quite explain, but we may assume that "objective" stands for "generally accepted" and in this sense "objectively valid in the student's own society or culture," "common-sensical," "taken-for-granted," the result of the student's effort to make sense in some fashion or another—which, though it, too, may be difficult, is still less of an effort than *not* to assume that what is to be understood can easily be incorporated into the student's own universe of discourse (culture, stock of knowledge). In the context under discussion, Husserl's demand to go "back to the things themselves" spells: "get at the subjective meaning."

But whether we try to get at the objective or the subjective meaning, we must use *typifications*. Unless physically present with me (a *consociate*), I can understand the Other (whether he be a *contemporary* or a *predecessor*[76]) only as a more or less refined and articulated *type*—and the degree of such refinement and articulation ("concreteness," in German *Inhaltserfülltheit*, "degree of fullness with content"[77]) ranges all the way from "my friend who just left me" to "my mailman" to "*a* mailman" to "the post office staff" to "the post office" to "that institution" and so on. But what is important to observe (and criticize) here is that by Schutz's argumentation, I cannot know even my consociate, no matter how "well" I do, except as a type, no matter how refined or concrete; I shall never, in the literal sense of Schutz's definition, be able to attain what he means to himself: I can never achieve pure "subjective meaning," only an approximation—that is, a mixture—though perhaps extraordinarily weighted on the subjective side, between it and objective meaning. The reason is simple: he and I are not the same person. No matter how close I get to "what it feels like to be you," our nonidentity, the differences, the otherness, of our connotations and memories—in short, our biographies and bodies—prevents me from achieving more than an approximation, even if a close one. And while Schutz admits this, he seems not to have noticed the contradiction or at least inconsistency between the no more than asymptotic character of intersubjective understanding, on one hand, and on the other, his conception of subjective meaning which implies the possibility of "genuine," more than asymptotic intersubjective understanding. How can this be accounted for?

Schutz's conception of social science may provide an answer. In the *Phenomenology of the Social World*, we read:

Social science is through and through an explicit knowledge of either mere contemporaries or predecessors; it nowhere refers back to the face-to-face experience. . . . Science is always an objective meaning-context, and the theme of all sciences of the social world is *to constitute an objective meaning-context of subjective meaning-contexts in general or of particular subjective meaning-contexts.* The problem of every social science can therefore be summed up in the question: *How are sciences of the subjective meaning-context possible at all?*[78]

There is much more on the nature of social science in the *Phenomenology of the Social World*, but it is better for our purpose to examine it together with later formulations, especially that of Schutz's important paper, "On Multiple Realities" (1945).[79]

Schutz begins by citing William James's *Principles of Psychology* (1890) as the origin of the notion referred to in the title of Schutz's paper. James speaks of "subuniverses," such as "the world of sense or physical things (as the paramount reality), the world of science," that of ideal relations, and more.[80] Schutz develops "basic characteristics" that constitute the "cognitive style" of a world: (1) "a specific tension of consciousness," (2) "a specific *epoché*," (3) "a prevalent form of spontaneity," (4) "a specific form of experiencing one's self," (5) "a specific form of sociality," and (6) "a specific time perspective."[81] He shows the nature of these characteristics with respect to the "paramount reality"—that is, the world of everyday life (the mundane world, the world of the natural attitude); treats far more cursorily the "various worlds of phantasms,"[82] such as those of Don Quixote[83] or of fairy tales, the "world of dreams";[84] and then comes to the "world of scientific theory,"[85] on which he is again more detailed. In the present context, most important among the characteristics of the world of scientific theory is its epoché, which like the other characteristics differs from that of the mundane world. For Schutz's conception of social science, one feature of this epoché is especially significant; it is that in it "there is 'bracketed' (suspended): . . . the subjectivity of the thinker as a man among fellow-men, including his bodily existence as a psycho-physical human being within the world."[86] For in Schutz's view, this epoché is also that of *social* science, whose "principal subject matter" is "the whole intersubjective world [of the natural attitude] . . . and even the problem how the existence of fellow-men and their thought can be experienced in the natural attitude. . . ."[87]

The task, then, as already in the *Phenomenology of the Social World,* is how social science can grasp "man in his full humanity and the social relationships in which he stands with Others" when this world of everyday life "eludes the immediate grasp of the theoretical scientist."[88] This is Schutz's answer (very similar to that of his earlier book):

He has to build up an artificial device, . . . in order to bring the intersubjective life-world in view—or better, not this world itself, but merely a likeness of it, a likeness in which the human world recurs, but deprived of its liveliness, and in which man recurs, but deprived of his unbroken humanity. This artificial device—called the method of the social sciences—overcomes the outlined dialectical difficulty by substituting for the intersubjective life-world a model of this life-world. This model, however, is not peopled with human beings in their full humanity, but with puppets, with *types;* they

> are constructed as though they could perform working actions and reactions. Of course, these working actions and reactions are merely fictitious, since they do not originate in a living consciousness as manifestations of its spontaneity; they are only assigned to the puppets by the grace of the scientist.[89]

These constructs must accord with the postulates of (1) logical consistency, (2) subjective interpretation (the scientist must construct the model of a mind whose activity would account for the facts observed), and (3) adequacy (the actor in the life-world must be able to understand an act committed in the life-world in the way indicated by the construct).[90] The "puppets" are a variant of Max Weber's "ideal types" and are mainly of two kinds: "personal" and "course-of-action." [91] And these ideal types, the social scientist's typifications or constructs, are based on the common-sense typifications of everyday life and thus may be called "second-order" constructs.[92]

One last point must be mentioned before we can try to answer our question (how to account for the inconsistency between the no more than asymptotic nature of intersubjective understanding and the assertion of the possibility of getting at subjective meaning) and thus assess Schutz's conception of social science, including sociology. It concerns Schutz's own epoché, more particularly the question of whether his discussion is undertaken within the natural attitiude or within the reduced sphere. Fortunately, Schutz himself clarifies this. In a note appended to the first, introductory chapter of the *Phenomenology of the Social World,* he explains that chapter 2, "The Constitution of Meaningful Lived Experience in the Constitutor's Own Stream of Consciousness," a study of the phenomena of constitution in the internal time-consciousness of the solitary ego, is "carried out within the 'phenomenological reduction,' "[93] whereas the remaining chapters are analyses undertaken in the mundane sphere, for they require no such "transcendental knowledge," as only phenomenological bracketing can yield.

> However, since all analyses carried out within the phenomenological reduction hold true essentially also in psychological introspection, and thus within the sphere of the natural attitude, we shall have to make no revisions whatsoever in our conclusions concerning the internal time-consciousness when we come to apply them to the realm of ordinary social life.[94]

How then does Schutz's conception of social science (presented here in abridged and selective fashion) contribute to answering our question? The main point is that the social scientist, including the sociologist, does not *interact* with the people he studies but rather *observes* them.[95] Furthermore, he observes them in reference to his typology, checking them against his types and checking his typifications against his observations. He thus does systematically what is done common-sensically in a fashion determined by the concerns of mundane life (which, as we heard, are suspended in the scientist's epoché). But if the Other—we must repeat our question—cannot be approached except by typification, asymptotically, either in the mundane sphere or in the (social-)scientific epoché, how then can Schutz present subjective meaning without at the same time warning us against the assumption that it can be attained other than approximately? What access to the Other which would make this possible is hidden behind such an assumption?

Perhaps the Other's subjective meaning can be attained if the approach is not purely cognitive—as has been taken for granted by Schutz (as by Husserl) without ever being spelled out—but also affective. Love (and possibly hate) might get at the Other directly, at his eidos, where pure cognition cannot.[96]

If the conjecture is correct that at least for Schutz[97] if not for Husserl both individual analyzed and analysis are purely cognitive, there is in Schutz—although less than in Weber, whom Schutz set out to explicate and correct—a strong component of "Protestant asceticism" or the "Protestant ethic," which, however, is contradicted by the desire or longing to throw it off and give in to feeling. In the formulation of the theory, there is no room made for this countercurrent, except in the form of the inconsistency under discussion and such other features as are mentioned in the preceding footnote.[98] As Weber was an eminently political human being, so Schutz was an eminently musical one, but both found it necessary, indeed no more than moral, to keep their respective interests out of their theoretical approaches (though admitting them, if found elsewhere, outside themselves, as topics of analysis). Weber's "freedom from value judgments"[99] (taken for granted by Schutz) has its homologue in Schutz in the "prohibition" for the social scientist to interact with the people he studies. The very term "puppet" (Schutz's own, not a translation) proclaims his heroic abstinence from his, the sociologist's, interest in his fellow men. We shall see in the section on ethnomethodology a further development of and significant change in this asceticism.

The interpretation ventured does not affect an assessment of Alfred Schutz's great contribution to a grasp of the bases of social-scientific inquiry. He has convincingly shown the elliptic nature of Weber's "basic concepts" of sociology, as well as demonstrating, though more by implication that explicitly, our practically complete ignorance concerning the nature of such everyday trivia as talking, waking up, falling asleep,[100] and innumerable other activities.[101] It is in the analysis of phenomena of this kind that ethnomethodology has specialized.

But before we come to it, we must inspect some writing on the relations between phenomenology and sociology, in an effort to check and thus strengthen the conception of this relation which is emerging in the present study.

Phenomenology and Sociology

In a very useful effort[102] to "demystify" the work of "creative sociologists," Monica B. Morris puts together under this heading phenomenologists (Husserl and Schutz), but also Max Weber; existential phenomenologists (from Kierkegaard to Sartre, Merleau-Ponty, Heidegger, Scheler, and Karl Jaspers); the "sociology of the absurd" of Lyman and Scott;[103] Berger and Luckmann's sociology of knowledge;[104] Marxist sociologists (Sartre, Enzo Paci, the early Herbert Marcuse, and others); symbolic interactionists (above all, George Herbert Mead, Herbert Blumer, and Erving Goffman); and ethnomethodologists (Harold Garfinkel). What they share is a "humanistic-culturalistic" as opposed to a "positivistic-naturalistic" approach.[105] Their common assumptions are:

> that human beings are not merely acted *upon* by social facts or social forces; that they are constantly shaping and "creating" their own social worlds in interaction with others; and that special methods are required for the study and understanding of these uniquely human processes.[106]

"Uniquely human" recalls a comment made earlier in this chapter on the central place of human consciousness—"something exclusively human"—in phenomenology and "interpretive" sociology,[107] that is, in the subjective approach, which along with the objective are "the two main complementary thrusts in sociology."[108] While the subjective approach to sociology thus equals Morris's "creative sociology," the "objective approach" is not necessarily "positivistic-naturalistic" and surely was not in Durkheim or, and even more obviously not, in Marx.[109]

Very briefly[110] one of the earliest expressions of the subjective approach (or "creative sociology") was Thomas and Znaniecki's *Polish Peasant in Europe and America* (1918–20)[111]; some fifteen years after, in the early 1930s, George Herbert Mead's posthumously published writings, especially *Mind, Self and Society from the Standpoint of a Social Behaviorist* (1934), made Mead's teaching much more widely known than it had been when its recipients were his personal students only, and greatly promoted the growth of symbolic interactionism; meanwhile Talcott Parsons had brought out his translation of Max Weber's *Protestant Ethic and the Spirit of Capitalism* (1930)[112] which though it had been written and published in quite a different context some twenty-five years before (1904–05), now entered the subjective current.[113] There followed, in 1937, Parsons's own *Structure of Social Action* and thus the launching of the "action" frame of reference;[114] then, beginning in the 1940s, the first papers by Alfred Schutz (though they seem to have gone largely unnoticed, his work becoming more widely known with the posthumous publications from the early sixties on and through ethnomethodology); further translations of Weber in the fifties; at about the same time, Goffman's and Garfinkel's first publications,[115] and in the late sixties, various sociologies of everyday life.

In order to show the background against which the discussion of the relations between phenomenology and sociology should be seen, some historical versions of this discussion may be considered. Husserl himself conceived that—in light of a contrast that for him had animated all of modern philosophy and that in the subjectivistic formulation he considered characteristic of the epoch in which he wrote—the relation between phenomenology and social science was that between the "anthropologistic" (or "psychologistic") and the "transcendentalistic" tendency. The former argues that philosophy needs a subjectivistic foundation and that this foundation must be supplied by psychology; the latter, that a new science dealing with transcendental subjectivity must ground all sciences, including psychology. Husserl, of course, holds the "transcendentalist" view; he is convinced that he has demonstrated that the new science he has founded, transcendental phenomenology, must lay the foundation of the sciences.[116] This, as we shall see later, also is Alfred Schutz's position. But as Jürgen Habermas in his analysis of the phenomenological approach to sociology shows,[117] this approach—as exemplified for him mainly by Cicourel,[118] Schutz, Garfinkel,[119] and Goffman[120]—cannot do for sociology what it followers expect of it—precisely, an analysis of the constitution of the life-world.[121] The reason is that "the phenomenological approach remains within the limits of the analysis of consciousness";[122] these limits can be transcended only if this approach is replaced by the linguistic one, originating in Wittgenstein.[123]

Thus far, then, we have two tasks that phenomenology is asked to perform for the social sciences and thus for sociology: one, to lay its foundations, a task with which its proponents, Husserl and Schutz, claim it to be successful; the other, to analyze the constitution of the life-world, a task with which its formulator, Habermas, claims it must fail. But if the task of social science is defined as the study of the life-world, or, in more colloquial and only a little less specific terms, of social life—a proposition with which most social scientists won't find it difficult to concur—then the two claims turn out to be synonymous, while the assessments of the capacity of phenomenology to meet them are opposed. The reason is that the constitution of the life-world is understood differently in the two cases: for Husserl and Schutz as a matter of consciousness, which so overshadows everything material as to permit its neglect; whereas for Habermas consciousness is inseparable from material circumstances in which it is always embedded. The difference may be tagged—provided this is understood to mean no more than what has just been said—as that between an idealist and a materialist conception of the life-world, or social life. This alternative should be kept in mind as we inspect other discussions of the topic.

Hans P. Neisser[124] confesses not to have found in the "third book" of Husserl's *Ideas*[125] any "descriptive types of 'essence' that refer to more than formal structure."[126] Indeed, Neisser asks, if

> we take the fact of the social world of other human beings as the only suitable starting point of social science, as an invariant feature of a certain class of acts; can we obtain further eidetic propositions which would form the basis of social science? *I have not been able to find any.*[127]

This may mean only that if we don't bracket intersubjectivity, we won't and obviously cannot find any eidos, which by definition could only be the result of bracketing. On the other hand, it has often been remarked that Husserl failed to constitute intersubjectivity—that is, to *find* its eidos. Yet even without bracketing it, Schutz, a student of phenomenology, has made important contributions to social science in his articulation of some of Max Weber's basic concepts. Yet we have seen already (in the previous section) that this articulation, like the bulk of Schutz's *Phenomenology of the Social World*, is written in the natural attitude; according to Neisser, this book is "based much less on phenomenology than even the author assumed, and much more on empirical knowledge." "Naturally," Neisser observes,

> we have a considerable body of knowledge drawn from *common experience* and scarcely open to doubt—but this does not make it eidetic. Who, for example, would dispute the distinction between a contemporary social world (Umwelt) on the one hand, a future and a past social world (Vorwelt), on the other hand? Yet this distinction is based on the empirical facts of birth and death; how could it be maintained, if following Husserl's instruction we bracketed "cosmic time?"[128]

Neisser's title, "The Phenomenological Approach in Social Science," is misleading in the sense that at least for the author, there seems to be no such thing. And if by the phenomenological approach to social science is meant a phenomenological social science the foundation of which is the bracketing of intersubjectivity and therewith of all the social world, then such phenomenological social science or sociology has not yet come to be. But something else might be meant by it. Before we come to a defensible position on the question, let us inspect additional discussions of it.

First, we shall examine Maurice Natanson's introduction (cited in note 24), "Phenomenology and the Social Sciences," to the monumental work by the same title which he edited.[129] In a section of this introduction which deals with the phenomenological method, Natanson points out that phenomenology is concerned only with the genesis of meaning, not of being, and that "the recalcitrant ground for the reconstruction of meaning is the social reality men share in everyday life."[130] The exclusive concern with meaning—a matter of consciousness—we already saw, most recently in connection with Habermas's plea that if we would go beyond it, we must substitute the linguistic for the phenomenological approach. This is not, however, Natanson's conclusion, for he holds that the Cartesian split can be healed "by the recognition that the truth of intentionality brings the inquirer face to face with the naive world he took for granted in the natural attitude."[131] He had already quoted Schutz: ". . . the empirical sciences will find their true foundation . . . in the constitutive phenomenology of the natural attitude."[132]

Thus far, following Natanson, the relation between phenomenology and the social sciences is twofold: it liberates them from Descartes's dualism of mind-body or meaning-being, and it furnishes their foundation. But there is a third connection: a phenomenology *of* the social sciences. Its task is:

> to explore the history of the life-world, to uncover the sedimentation of meaning which accompanies the dialectic of the constitution of sociality, and to trace out the relationships between the constructs of man in daily life [Schutz's "first-order constructs"] and those employed by the social scientists [his "second-order constructs"]. Ultimately, the phenomenologist is concerned with displaying and illuminat-

ing the derivation of scientific abstraction from typification in the mundane sphere. The life-world is held to be the matrix from which all abstractive activity is generated.[133]

With Husserl, Natanson interprets phenomenology as a response to our crisis, among whose many facets are

> the acceptance of a formal account of man's social being in place of a rigorous examination of the immediate experiential world he inhabits, and the separation of reason from experience.[134]. . .
>
> In Husserl's image, knowledge divorced from its telos results in the shattering of reason and the deformation of the life-world. The social scientist cut off from his own philosophical roots finds himself a stranger to the life-world.[135]

Thus, it appears that the "crisis of European sciences,"[136] "the product of a loss of confidence in human reason,"[137] furnishes the basis for the three relations between phenomenology and the social sciences. Part of the crisis or of the origin of its crisis is the split between body and mind, which phenomenology is said to heal by illuminating the life-world instead of taking it for granted. It seems difficult to understand how in analyzing the life-world, the separation of meaning from being is transcended—unless it is meant as involving or leading to (but is this what Husserl meant? what Natanson means?) a kind of second innocence once the first, a "prelapsarian" one, has been lost. It is the innocence of Heinrich von Kleist's "puppet" whose "grace" outdoes that of even the most accomplished human dancer[138]—but for Kleist, the puppet has "no consciousness at all," and its equivalent is the god, the being who has "an infinite consciousness,"[139] not man, who ever since the Fall has been condemned to fallibility, that is, has been split—much longer than since Descartes's formulation.[140] But this can only be the *direction* in which innocence lies, not the innocence itself that has been alluded to, since phenomenologists are human beings, not puppets like the social scientists' ideal-types. The innocence of the phenomenologists who are somewhere between split men and puppets or gods can only be that of human beings who live not naively in the natural attitude but in as full an awareness of its constructed character as they can manage. But the mind-body split would appear to be healed by such awareness just as by any wholly absorbing activity or state, for then the split is neither thought nor felt or experienced.[141] It follows that the first relation between phenomenology and the social sciences—liberation from the Cartesian split—is neither exclusive nor direct (but it does reflect a longing born out of our crisis).

The second relation consists in founding the social sciences. Phenomenology does so by the same method which according to Natanson heals the Cartesian split: by illuminating the life-world, by analyzing everyday typifications, our spontaneous sedimentations, and whatever else we take for granted as participants, in any sense, in social life. But thus far, as the term "founding" itself suggests, we can also express this relation by saying that phenomenology is a meta-social-science (metasociology, metapsychology, and so on), not a part of it; and we could accept the claim of the second relation so understood—provided we abolish such terms as "phenomenological sociology" or "phenomenological psychology," for they suggest that there are varieties of social science itself which are phenomenological. But the matter is less simple than that, and the added difficulty arises from the ambiguous meaning of "empirical"—which the social sciences are held to be, while phenomenology, a philosophical undertaking, is not. Thus, Natanson writes:

> Phenomenology cannot present its method or its results in empirically verifiable terms because it does not accept empiricism as an adequate philosophy of the experiential world. . . . For example, the phenomenologist is deeply interested in the logic of prepredicative experience, in passive snytheses of meaning,[142] in the covert no less than the overt aspect of action, and in the many facets of intentionality which are involved in tracing out sedimentation of meaning. Empiricism begins where phenomenology leaves off—that is why it is pointless to ask the phenomenologist for some sort of equivalent for empirical verification.[143]

That most readers, including social scientists and philosophers, would agree—that is, would agree that phenomenology is not (for example) sociology but metasociology—is no reason not to question the overwhelmingly accepted meaning of "empirical."[144] And indeed, there is at least one contributor to the work which Natanson edited and for which he wrote the introduction under analysis who has a broader concept of the term. In his discussion of phenomenology and anthropology,[145] David Bidney writes:

> Husserl's pure, transcendental phenomenology posits that absolute, unconditioned intuition of essences is actually possible and is to be recognized as a fact of radical experience. As opposed to the positivistic empiricism of Hume and Comte, he would not limit immediate experience to sense perception. Intuition as an activity of knowing or comprehending the essence of phenomena and their essential relations to one another is also accepted and recognized as a fact of experience. Husserl, like James, whom he read,[146] is a radical empiricist who would not limit empiricism to the perception of atomic sense data.[147]

Indeed, we can hardly deny that performing the reduction, and engaging in the other activities of the phenomenologist listed by Natanson, in short, that thinking is experiencing. Is thus the very "illumination" of the life-world not an experience? The answer can be negative only if "experience" is taken in the restrictive, historically received but theoretically and systematically dubious sense in which the term figures in "empiricism"—but the "bracketing" of received notions (such as that of an empiricism of this kind) was indicated in the beginning of this chapter as essential to phenomenology. It goes without saying that "empirical proof" thus, too, needs revision—that is, expansion—as therefore does the conception of the social sciences, including sociology, altogether. What we deal with here is not so much the relation between phenomenology and sociology that has been claimed—phenomenology laying the foundation of sociology—as the relation which consists in the entailment of a changed structure of sociology itself, of a new consciousness, even a new "being in the world." The effort to trace its outlines obviously transcends the scope of this chapter.

The third relation is suggested as the phenomenology *of* the social sciences, including, of course, sociology. If we follow Natanson's formulation here, it appears that the phenomenology of the social sciences is not the search for their eidos but, at its core, the study of the processes that lead from mundane to scientific typifications (idealizations, abstractions). After the discussion of the second relation, it can be seen that agreement with the nature of the third depends on the answer to the second, based on his narrow conception of exp^rience, and with his argument of the first, according to which phenomenology it a metasociology. But if a conception of experience which includes the phenomenologist's own activities be accepted, then the distinction between first-order and second-order constructs, as well as between the experience and the analysis of the "history of the life-world" or "the sedimentation of meaning which accompanies the constitution of sociality"—and indeed of whatever other undertakings of the phenomenologist Natanson might have mentioned—looks less obvious and clear cut and instead becomes problematic, in need of fresh examination. Furthermore, it might appear more promising to undertake a *sociology* of the social sciences, as well as of phenomenology, the task of which would be understanding their rise, nature, vicissitudes socially and historically, in the natural attitude. Such a hypothetical promise does imply a difference between phenomenology and sociology, which the preceding discussion may have seemed to deny. Its articulation, and thus a more definite stand on the relations between the two, will be attempted at the end of this section, after we acquaint ourselves with further investigations of the topic.

One of these is Michael Phillipson's "Phenomenological Philosophy and Sociology," contained in a book on "new directions in sociological theory"[148] which appeared a year before Natanson's, and the argument of which

> . . . is that traditional empiricism fails to come to terms with the problems of empirically grounded concepts in the life-world. Concepts are irrelevant unless they are grounded in concrete experiences and unless they refer to the realities of men in their life-worlds. . . .[149]

This proposition is found in the discussion of phenomenology and the sociological study of substantive issues, which is rather inconclusive, whereas in the preceding analysis of phenomenology and sociological methodology (clarification and generation of concepts, and new directions for methodology) and elsewhere in the paper phenomenology appears to play the role, the problematic character of which has been suggested, of metasociology. The more we proceed with Phillipson's paper, the more reference is made, and not always explicitly, to ethnomethodology, even in the very vocabulary used, rather than to phenomenology, although it also continues to draw on Schutz; this is especially noticeable in the discussion of validity and the slight revision applied to Schutz's three postulates of an "objective explanation" ("logical consistency," "subjective interpretation," "adequacy"[150]). Again the long section on "Clarifying the Limits and the Relevance of Sociology" hardly demonstrates that to do so is a privilege of phenomenology; some of the limits and irrelevancies of sociology considered can be removed or attenuated by more careful attention to traditional scientific canons—and by the sociologist's moral and political discrimination among potential employers, or rejection of them, eventually by such changes as would decrease the occasions on which such discrimination or rejection are called for or, if still called for, requiring less trouble to apply. Phillipson frequently uses the expression "phenomenological sociology," but it is hard to understand what he refers to unless it be to a sociology that keeps phenomenological teachings in mind in theorizing and doing research. But this would be like justifying the label "biological sociology" by referring to a sociology that in its efforts to explain human behavior does so with an awareness of potentially relevant biological factors. However, "phenomenological sociology" also at least points to ethnomethodology, if, indeed, that is not its basic referent.

In an earlier section, "Phenomenology and Sociology: Essentialism versus Empiricism,"[151] Phillipson elaborates the distinction which, as pointed out when it appeared in Natanson's analysis, is widely shared: that in contrast to phenomenology, sociology is empirical, and that consequently "evidence" and "objectivity" have different meanings in the two enterprises. While the sociologist gathers evidence from sources "other than simply his own intuitive experience," in phenomenology evidence "is the self-giveness of an object in the experience of the phenomenologist."[152] And for the former, objectivity is said to consist in his "ability to demonstrate that his interpretation is consistent with men's experiences" (Schutz's postulate of adequacy), whereas the latter holds that "the descriptions of the essential features of the intentional objects of consciousness which are indubitable for the experiencing ego are by that very fact 'objective.' "[153]

A slightly different version of the relations between phenomenology and sociology comes from the chapter following Phillipson's, "Some Neglected Questions about Social Reality," by David Silverman.[154] Silverman singles out three contributions phenomenology has made to sociology: "the analysis of properties of common-sense thought," the insistence on the intersubjective character of social life—that is, on "the processual relationship between subject and object in the social world," and the recognition that the social order "in many respects is a negotiated order."[155] But phenomenology calls for a general redefinition of sociological problems—which Silverman illustrates with the example of "organization", where Egon Bittner has gone a long way to supply the remedy[156]—and it urges far greater than customary attention to everyday language—here, reference is above all to the work of Cicourel and of Garfinkel and Sacks.[157] By now, one relation between phenomenology and sociology may appear established: that phenomenology has enriched and can further enrich the sociologist's sensitivity, in both theory and research, to potential relevances. This, evidently, is not a monopoly of phenomenology but is important just the same.

In 1973, the year in which Natanson's large compendium was published, the first, and thus far still only, reader in "phenomenological sociology" appeared. It was edited by George Psathas and contains an introduction by him.[158] Psathas's fundamental hope for the influence of phenomenology on social science is expressed in the following sentence:

> When social science recognizes that the objective reality of society, groups, community, and formal organizations is subjectively experienced by the individual and that these subjective experiences are intimately related to the subsequent externalization and objectification procedures in which humans engage as they think and act in the social world, then a more informed and reality-based social science will result.[159]

It is difficult to quarrel with the proposition that a social science which acts on its awareness of experiencing individuals is more adequate than one which does not. But to do so is, again, an injunction not exclusively issued by phenomenology: it is fundamental to Max Weber and is at least implicit in Marx and in Feuerbach.[160] Psathas points to his own and Frances C. Waksler's ascertainment of the essential features of face-to-face interaction (contained in his volume[161]) as an example of an "eidetic analysis," [162] but it is hard to see that the authors did something other than constructing a Weberian ideal-type. To be sure, in both Weber's construction of ideal-types and Husserl's eidetic analysis "free imaginative variation" is involved—the difference lies in the epoché, which is mundane in the former case,[163] reduced in the latter.

True to its function, the work organized by Psathas contains a programmatic statement, by Helmut R. Wagner, on "phenomenological sociology." [164] It is based above all on Schutz, whose major contribution is, according to Wagner, the illumination of social structure in its derivation (through typifications and interactions) from its subjective basis. Together with its development through Berger and Luckmann,[165] Wagner finds this contribution promising for, among other things, a sociology of world views, which should attempt on the phenomenological level what Wilhelm Dilthey, seventy-five years ago, did from his general, humanistic perspective.[166] But although phenomenology is weaker on "genetic," or "dynamic," than on "static" inquiries, Wagner proposes a number of the former that he thinks would benefit from phenomenological treatment. These, stimulated by Schutz's concept of the biographical situation, are studies of the growth of sedimentation in the individual, including the way consciousness appears and develops. Here Wagner observes that Husserl dealt only with the adult individual; the study proposed, therefore, must also draw on child psychology, especially Piaget. Wagner suggests inquiries into a number of types of reaction to disturbances of the taken-for-granted, from minor ones [167] to those to which responses are a considerable change in life-style: serious psychic troubles, anomic suicide, becoming manipulators, and flight into drug use, communes, or violence and terrorism. No matter how meritorious, it is not clear what is phenomenological about such a listing, which rather is a kind of Mertonian typology.[168] Wagner's essay adds little to the clarification of the meaning of "phenomenological sociology."

Neither does Egon Bittner's "Objectivity and Realism in Sociology," [169] the title of which, unlike that of Wagner, however, obviously does not promise it.

But it is very pertinent in a reader in "phenomenological sociology," above all for two reasons: it contributes to a sociological analysis of the declining faith in the objectivity (in the positivistic sense) of social inquiry and of the growing interest in a subjective approach; and it provides a setting for ethnomethodology, the most widespread, articulated, and influential development of phenomenology, especially of Alfred Schutz's version (see the next section of this chapter). Bittner suggests one negative and three positive reasons for the decline of that faith: (1) disappointment with the results of its practice; (2) the growing and spreading conviction that only events, not meanings, that only temporal, not atemporal objects are subject to causal analysis;[170] (3) the recognition that aiming at positivistically understood objectivity "is merely a way of avoiding having to face the study of society,"[171] which cannot be undertaken other than from a point of view; and (4) the (related) demonstration, coming "from an extraordinarily rigorous program of empirical research known as ethnomethodology," that all "accounts" "(i.e., all manner of describing, analyzing, questioning, criticizing, believing, doubting, idealizing, schematizing, denigrating, and so on) are unavoidably and irremediably tied to the social settings that occasion them or within which they are situated."[172] That is, they have the property of "reflexivity."

> The absence of this feature [from accounts of accounts, and so on]—the feature of dependence of accounts, and incidentally of all expressions and of all practical action, on the natural habitat of their occurrence for recognizable meaning, a feature known as "indexicality"—tends to give representations of social settings the aspect of confabulation of fiction, an ever-present risk in narrative historiography. . . .[173]

"Reflexivity" and "indexicality," it should be noted, are related to Karl Mannheim's *Seinsverbundenheit* or "existentiality,"[174] of which they represent a more cogent recognition and give what may be called a more local referent. But they also thus repeat or perpetuate the problem of Mannheim's epistemological relativism,[175] which his sociology of knowledge and these concepts share with phenomenology and which can be argued to be an intrinsic facet or expression of our crisis.[176]

In obviously knowledgeable and sensitive pages of fieldwork, Bittner shows the relevance for it of reflexivity and indexicality: they give it greater "realism,"[177] whether the field-worker acts on them spontaneously or by explicit instruction.

These papers, and others in Psathas's volume which are also very much worth reading,[178] hardly change the understanding of the relations between phenomenology and sociology which we are in the process of forming.

Finally, in the same year (1973), Fred R. Dallmayr, whom we have met before, published a paper on phenomenology and social science.[179] After tracing the development from "pure" to "existential" phenomenology (roughly in the sense suggested in the very beginning of this chapter), Dallmayr expounds its impact on social scientists, most of them sociologists (from Max Weber through, among others, Adolf Reinach, Simmel, Alfred

Vierkandt, Scheler, Mannheim, Schutz, to ethnomethodologists, especially Garfinkel and Cicourel, to Berger and Luckmann, and to some related scholars); he concludes with brief "Comments and Appraisals," most of which deal with criticisms launched against phenomenology partly from insufficient knowledge, partly in consequence of its own deviations from Husserl's rigor, and he emphasizes that phenomenology does not do away with traditional science but complements it. And then Dallmayr makes a historical observation:

> In its effort to recover even the dark residues of reason for human dialogue, phenomenology appears as the proper heir of the European enlightenment—as Husserl has tried to show in the *Crisis of European Sciences*. To be sure, ambitions tend to be more subdued in our time; enlightenment in its present sense . . . [implies commitment] only to the elementary standards of common decency and social discourse. Due to their focus on human interaction, the social sciences are peculiarly destined to participate in this heritage.[180]

Again, this essay is useful as an overview and an appraisal of aspects of contemporary moods but does not further our understanding of the relations between phenomenology and sociology beyond that reached before.

We conclude this section with brief mention of Anthony Giddens's assessment of "interpretative sociologies," which deals with a number of recent trends—Schutz's "existential phenomenology," ethnomethodology, Peter Winch's "post-Wittgensteinian philosophy," and hermeneutics and critical theory (Hans-Georg Gadamer, Karl-Otto Apel, and Jürgen Habermas);[181] some of these, it may be recalled, are also treated by Monica Morris. Giddens presents a philosophically educated analysis of the convergences and differences among these articulations, which shows (among many other things) that Schutz (as we saw) found that he had to abandon (or found himself abandoning) Husserl's transcendental phenomenology when he undertook his "constitutive analysis of the natural attitude," and that both Schutz and ethnomethodology (as well as hermenuetics) suffer from (1) dealing with action only as meaning, rather than praxis, (2) ignoring "the centrality of power in social life," and (3) at least underplaying the fact that social norms are differently interpreted according to divisions of interest.[182] For Giddens, the subject matter of sociology is "the production and reproduction of society," entailing an examination of the limits of human agency, recognition of "the modes in which social life is 'observed' and characterizations of social activity established," and "the formulation of concepts within the meaning-frames of social science as metalanguages."[183] He concludes with the formulation of "rules"[184] (taking off ironically from Durkheim's term) which, however, express in concise form the import he wants his book to have in pointing toward a program for sociological research.[185] As to the question of the relations between phenomenology and sociology, it should be clear by now that the shape they took on the basis of Natanson's introduction has not changed; but the promise then mentioned must now be articulated (as we anticipated that it should be).

The promise referred to a sociology of both the social sciences and phenomenology, the desirability of which was suggested by an examination of Natanson's claims concerning the relations between phenomenology and sociology. To recapitulate these: the first claim was that phenomenology overcomes the Cartesian split (between body and mind, thoughts and objects, idealism and materialism) by—and this is the second claim—illuminating the life-world rather than taking it for granted; the third claim was that phenomenology also is the phenomenology of the social sciences in the sense, above all, that it analyzes the processes leading from mundane to scientific typifications. But we had to reinterpret the first claim as the expression of a longing for "wholeness" or "being" (for a "postlapsarian" innocence) born out of our crisis; and thus had to reject the second claim understood as the means to such wholeness. That is to say that phenomenology could not be seen either as healing the Cartesian split or as *therefore* founding the social sciences. There remained the third claim: phenomenology as the study of (above all) the ways in which everyday typifications become (social-)scientific ones. We found that the understanding of this third claim depended on the meaning of "experience," which we argued we could not accept in the sense in which Natanson (and most others) use it when they distinguish social science as empirical from phenomenology as nonempirical. [186] It was here that instead of accepting these claims, we suggested that a sociology of the social sciences and of phenomenology promised to throw some light on this thicket of problems.

In part, such a sociology was intimated by submitting that the longing for a post-Cartesian, or, better (to repeat) postlapsarian wholeness be understood as a response to the feeling of being split which may be the expression in the industrialized society of an aspect of the "human condition" that has found many other expressions, of which one of the most familiar is precisely, the idea of the Fall; but now the Eden to which we cannot return any more than Adam could to his is the preindustrial or pre-Enlightenment, or at least the prenuclear, age. What this view or kind of view urges is to replace, at least for an interim period, an "intrinsic" with an "extrinsic," more particularly sociological, analysis [187] of our topic—to replace attention to its story with the analysis of its statements—without thereby in the least committing the genetic or reductionist fallacy, that is, assuming that all there is to it *is* its genesis, origin, story, history, while there is nothing to its statements, propositions, truth claims and therefore nothing to their analysis. We now argue that the reason why there is such disagreement among the commentators on the relations between phenomenology and sociology as we have seen is that there no longer is a viable tradition which would insure commonly accepted and thus unproblematic meanings to the concepts pertinent in the discussion, such as "experience," "sociology" vs. "metasociology," "healing the Cartesian split," "life-world" and its "epochés" as opposed to several other epochés; "phenomenology" and "sociology" themselves, and probably additional ones. Such a realization may be a "shock of recognition," similar and indeed related to one signaled before[188]—a further instance of the problematic (and unpredictable) character of experience. Part of the (tentative) response to it is to reaffirm the formulation of phenomenology presented in the beginning of this chapter: a maximally bearable suspension of whatever received notions the individual who wishes to study and understand anything as best as possible can muster. It is clear that this is a recommendation for an epoché that takes even less for granted than the Husserlian reductions do, and the reason for this may well be that so much has happened, above all in the world outside philosophy, since Husserl wrote. Pending the exercise suggested, the question of the relations between phenomenology and sociology cannot be analyzed here beyond the point reached—except by every interested reader for himself or herself. We shall adumbrate it in the form of a suggestion concerning a certain attitude toward our time, following an exposition of aspects of ethnomethodology which, as we have seen, is regarded by many commentators as the kind of scociology that comes closest to deserving the name "phenomenological."

Ethnomethodology

An excellent connection between some of these reflections and ethnomethodology itself is provided by James L. Heap and Phillip A. Roth's "On Phenomenological Sociology" and by Burkart Holzner's comment and Heap's reply to Holzner.[189] On the basis of three texts (Tiryakian, Bruyn, and Douglas[190]) selected by Heap and Roth for reasons indicated, they find "phenomenological sociologists" have misunderstood and in effect used only metaphorically some of Husserl's key concepts, notably "intention," "reduction," "phenomenon," and "essence," and have thus shown that phenomenological sociology in a strict Husserlian sense—that is, eidetic sociology—is "highly questionable." However, they say:

> . . . we should realize that Husserl actually knew little of the concrete problems of the social sciences (cf. Schutz, 1962: 140 [[191]]). In fact some sociologies which have been called phenomenological are closer to the spirit, if not the letter of phenomenology than the pertinent statements of its founder. What distinguishes these sociologies from those we have criticized is that *the following involve and invoke no claim that what is done actually is, or is the same as, Husserlian phenomenology.*[192]

They distinguish four types of such "phenomenological sociologies." The first may or may not realize that "it makes use of a phenomenological perspective" [193] by stressing the subjective approach; here, by the authority of Natanson,[194] they mention W. I. Thomas, Cooley, Mead, and Max Weber. The second refers to Schutz's work and includes Berger and Luckmann, as well as Holzner.[195] The third is "phenomenologically founded on the structures of the life-world . . . [and] can be understood as a philosophically radicalized version of the type of ['reflexive'] sociology Gouldner (1970) called for;" [196] among the examples of this type are John O'Neill's *Sociology as a Skin Trade* and Aaron

V. Cicourel's *The Social Organization of Juvenile Justice.*[197] A fourth type, ethnomethodology, is treated separately because of its

> distinctive relationship to both sociology and phenomenology. It is a program of inquiry which combines certain phenomenological and sociological concerns while transforming them in such a way as to do violence to neither but, rather, to constitute for itself a unique and independent domain of study.[198]

Heap and Roth point out that they are dealing not with all "of what currently travels under the rubric of ethnomethodology" but are limiting themselves to Harold Garfinkel's program "as found in the writings of Wieder, and Zimmerman and Pollner (in Douglas, 1970)." [199] They observe that while in Schutz's work, intersubjectivity is "an ontologically given feature of the social world" (hardly—not even after what we have seen of Schutz herein), in ethnomethodology it figures as its *sense,* which is "contingently accomplished by members' situated practices" (just as in Schutz—hence it also makes little sense to say that as we move from Schutz to ethnomethodology, we find that "the a priori becomes a problematic feature of actual accomplishment"). In contrast to both Schutz and ethnomethodology, in the natural attitude intersubjectivity does not become thematic but "resides at its foundation as an unexamined but essential presupposition" [200] (here Schutz would agree.).

Overlooking some questions—notably how the a priori can be a matter of accomplishment and whether or not it is fair to impute such a view of it to ethnomethodology—we move to Holzner's comment, on which perhaps the most interesting remark to be made is that his advocacy of an even broader reading of "phenomenology" than Heap and Roth's bespeaks an eclecticism which is based on his faith that "empirical utility"[201] decides whether or not something serves sociology and which convinces him "that phenomenology contributes to scientific growth in sociology." [202] In comparison with Heap and Roth and with the ethnomethodologists, Holzner seems still to see the world in unbroken orderliness.[203] In reply to him, Heap pleads for insistence on Husserl's rigor and explicates something in Holzner's reaction of the kind that has just been suggested in very summary fashion: he seeks a certainty that Holzner appears not to need but which Heap finds in phenomenology, the only foundation of sociology which among all the "multiple approaches" invoked and advocated by his commentator is radical in a sense formulated by Gurwitsch[204]—that is, it is the only one that can account for its own possibility.[205] Again, in line with the purpose of this chapter, an examination of such a claim is secondary to the observation that all of these writings—Heap and Roth's paper, Holzner's response, and Heap's rejoinder—are "intrinsic"—limited to making statements and examining them on their validity—rather than "extrinsic"—that is, concerned with genesis, history, sociological analysis *of* their statements. Here, as by now has been pointed out more than once, the emphasis instead is on the latter; it is in this sense that we now consider ethnomethodology, which thus far has only been alluded to (in a probably frustrating manner). But the fastest route to doing so is by way of a short detour.

In a late secularized application of Protestant asceticism, Max Weber, its student, proclaimed with passion that science (which in the beginning of this chapter was called that "most self-critical and self-questioning of intellectual activities") was incapable of passing judgment on purposes, ends, aims, goals, or, as Weber called them, "values," including the scientist's own. These were outside scientific and rational assessment; each individual had to judge them according to his own "demon." Science could not decide what goals one should pursue, it could not tell what is good or bad, beautiful or ugly, just or unjust, right or wrong; every one of us is responsible for finding out. Weber did not seem to think of such a situation as a crisis for people or for science; but not much later Edmund Husserl wrote *The Crisis,* and it can be shown that one sense of the crisis referred to in the title is the incapacity of science to tell us what our ends are or should be, the incapacity of science to tell us what to do, how to live.

Another way of arguing such a conception of science is to say that science can tell us about what is but not about what ought to be; for example, it does not follow from the universal tabu of fratricide that I must not kill my brother. But there is a reason why it does not follow: the Ought does not follow from the Is because Ought and Is have been separated, divorced. Our conception is such that the Is contains no Ought. If we apply this generalization to the example just mentioned: the universal tabu of fratricide is a mere "fact," something which exists, is the case, *is,* but for me is exclusively a matter which I may or may not want to *know;* it concerns me exclusively as a cognitive subject, *not* as a moral subject; the fact carries no moral obligation for me; it is up to me whether I wish to draw moral conclusions from it, conclusions for my own moral conduct, and if so, what conclusions—for example, that I find I too ought to follow this tabu or on the contrary feel uncommitted by it and wish to follow my own "demon" or conviction, preference, taste, which may tell me to kill my brother or not to kill my brother.

What this separation of Is and Ought means is that others' doing or believing has no moral consequences for me, does not commit or oblige me. But this in turn means that I am morally split off from others, that everybody is split off from everybody else. It does *not* mean that there are no moral bonds at all, for in fact there are, as most or at least many people can testify; typically, they exist among persons intimately related, but also among members of groups and movements whose bond is solidarity or fraternity. Yet the feeling toward other human beings—and if an individual has no intimate relations and feels no solidarity or fraternity with members of any group, the feeling toward human beings altogether—is not one of moral commonality, but on the contrary, one of being alone via-à-vis a multitude of others toward whom one's attitude is purely cognitive, noncommittal and noncommitted, observing, calculating, instrumental, utilitarian, manipulatory. *This* is the situation, this is the kind of atomized society which finds expression in the philosophies of science, especially of social science, in theory of knowledge or epistemology (and elsewhere, within and outside philosophy), as well as—and this is especially pertinent for our topic—in recent conceptions and practices of sociology.

It is extraordinary to observe that the insistence on the understanding of social life from the point of view of the individual involved in it, the subjective point of view, should have been voiced at a time and by a thinker—Max Weber—when this subjective point of view was deprived, or was held to be deprived, of moral instruction by the community, which supported the individual only cognitively, teaching him the nature and ways of scientific knowledge, its achievements and limitations. That is, the insistence on the importance of *Verstehen,* "understanding," emerged when understanding carried no moral enlightenment because Is and Ought had been separated, human beings had been separated from one another. Reason had become, or been reduced to, the individual's capacity to assess means in reference to ends to be pursued, but reason could not, as we heard already in a different formulation, make even tentatively conclusive statements about the ends themselves. As it had become a purely subjective or individual faculty, reason had also become instrumental, utilitarian, calculating; the moral considerations or judgments which the individual in fact did have were not rational. In other words, reason no longer was an attribute of humanity or the cosmos; there no longer was what once had been called objective reason.[206]

Within sociology, the endeavor in which the atomization of society and the instrumentalization of reason have made themselves felt most strikingly is that of the so-called sociology of knowledge; their manifestation can be seen, though in different ways, in both of its most powerful founders and students, Max Scheler and Karl Mannheim, but in even more extreme form in Ernst Grünwald, Scheler's and Mannheim's junior by a generation. The guise the atomization of society and the instrumentalization of reason took in all three of these thinkers was, as it had been in historicism before, the problem of relativism to which all three addressed themselves but which they could not resolve. As developed by them, the sociology of knowledge had gone beyond its two major and quite heterogeneous origins, Marx and Durkheim, both of whom pursued a clear and clearly nonrelative end: a better society. No matter how different were their conceptions of this goal and the ways leading to it, it was this that their studies and their other activities were in the service of. Marx was of far greater importance for Scheler and Mannheim than Durkheim; and for Grünwald, in turn, Scheler and Mannheim superseded both Marx and Durkheim. In all of these developments that led to Scheler and Mannheim and Grünwald, problems discovered in the process of coming to terms with those raised by the originators (by Marx more than by Durkheim), became detached from the original attitudes with which they had been associated and which were eminently moral attitudes toward society. They became purely cognitive problems. Most pointedly, the problem of relativism was conceived by all three—Scheler, Mannheim, and Grünwald—as the problem of universal or absolute *truth* as opposed to relative *truth;* it was not conceived as the problem of *moral* relativism; nor did any one of the three[207] raise the question of the connection between epistemological and moral relativism.

The scholar who is generally acknowledged to have shown or at least attempted most to show the importance of (Husserl's) phenomenology for the social sciences, particularly sociology, Alfred Schutz, is at the same time the major source, if a single one must be named, of the approach which was called ethnomethodology by its founder, Harold Garfinkel. It is interesting to follow the development of the conception of the subject—which it is held to be the task of social science to understand—as one moves from Schutz to Garfinkel and to Garfinkel's associates and students. If the subject is predominantly cognitive in Husserl and, in the sense we have seen, in Max Weber and Schutz, in ethnomethodology it becomes what might be called selectively cognitive, namely, specializing in method; it becomes a methodological specialist. Garfinkel himself writes:

> When I was writing up these materials [interviews with jurors whose deliberations had, unbeknownst to them, been bugged and transcribed] I dreamed up the notion underlying the term "ethnomethodology." You want to know where I actually got the term? I was working with the Yale cross-cultural area files. I happened to be looking down the list without the intent of finding such a term . . . and I came to a section: ethnobotany, ethnophysiology, ethnophysics. Here I am faced with jurors who are doing methodology, but they are doing their methodology in the "now you see, now you don't" fashion. It is not a methodology that any of my colleagues would honor if they were attempting to staff the sociology department. . . .
>
> Now, how to stick a label on that stuff, for the time being, to help me recall the burden of it? How to get a reminder of it? That is the way "ethnomethodology" was used to begin with. "Ethno" seemed to refer, somehow or other, to the availability to a member of common-sense knowledge of his society as common-sense knowledge of the "whatever." If it were "ethnobotany," then it had to do somehow or other with his knowledge of and his grasp of what were for members adequate methods for dealing with botanical matters. Someone from another society, like an anthropologist in this case, would recognize the matters as botanical matters. The member would employ ethnobotany as adequate grounds of inference and action in the conduct of his own affairs, in the company of others like him. It was that plain, and the notion of "ethnomethodology" or the term "ethnomethodology" was taken in this sense.[208]

Ethnomethodology is not "a mysterious enterprise," "not a cult," not "directed to the solution of whatever it is that we think ails sociology."[209] Asked to indicate briefly what its task is, Garfinkel answered:

> . . . we are concerned with the how society gets put together; the how it is getting done; the how to do it; the social structures of everyday activities. I would say that we are doing studies of how persons, as parties to ordinary arrangements, use the features of the arrangement to make for members the visibly organized characteristics happen. That is *it* if you need it in a really shorthand way.[210]

To specialize in methodology leads to, if it does not entail, the neglect of other things, most importantly issues, or topics, or substance.[211] The methodology applies to ordinary people's "practical activities, practical circumstances, and practical sociological reasoning";[212] to "practical actions";[213] to everyday life, whose "formal structures"[214] it is the enthnomethodologist's task to identify, "while abstaining from all judgments of their adequacy, value, importance, necessity, practicality, success, or consequentiality. We refer to this procedural policy as 'ethnomethodological indifference'."[215]

A related indifference may be suggested in the following exchange between Karl Schuessler and David Sudnow:

SCHUESSLER: There is one general point I think might be discussed and that has to do with the ethics of observing people without their consent. I do not know whether or not you want to address yourself to that.

SUDNOW: I would rather not. I do not have those ethics.

SCHUESSLER: I think it is a point to be discussed. If you feel that way you are certainly in a distinct minority, I would think.

SUDNOW: Among ethnomethodologists, I would not be in the minority. . . . *Let me put it this way.* I am very much concerned with observer effects, and I would not want people to know I was filming them. I will show you what happens as soon as they know there is a camera around. . . . I do not enjoy filming people without their knowing about it, but the nature of the work I am now doing is such that I film three minutes. I am perfectly willing to go up to people after I have filmed them and tell them, "I've filmed you. Can I use your materials?" If I were to publish any of the films, I would feel obligated to do that. Furthermore, I would not publish films with the subjects identified.[216]

Here, evidently, "ethnomethodological indifference" means indifference to moral consideration that might interfere with the ethnomethodologist's own methodology—even though, as the last sentences of the quotation show, "indifference" is too strong a word, and "avoidance" might be better; at any rate, there is no *theoretical* inclusion of moral considerations in the conception of the research. This—as is well-known and is indeed an implication of the previously signaled separation of Is and Ought, of the instrumentalization of reason, of the reduction of the individual to a purely cognitive individual—is a feature ethnomethodology shares with contemporary social science and science generally.

Nevertheless, in Garfinkel's own early studies this indifference to or avoidance of moral considerations is conspicuous.

Students were instructed to engage an acquaintance or a friend in an ordinary conversation and without indicating that what the experimenter was asking was in any way unusual, to insist that the person clarify the sense of his commonplace remarks. . . . Undergraduate students were assigned the task of spending from fifteen minutes to an hour in their homes viewing its activities, while assuming that they were boarders in the household. . . . Students were instructed to engage someone in conversation and to imagine and act on the assumption that what the other person was saying was directed by hidden motives that were his real ones. . . . pre-medical students were run individually through a three-hour experimental interview. As part of the solicitation of subjects . . . , the experimenter identified himself as a representative of an Eastern medical school who was attempting to learn why the medical school intake interview was such a stressful situation. . . . I assigned students the task of bargaining for standard-priced merchandise. . . . Students were instructed to play ticktacktoe . . . they invited the subject to move first. After the subject made his move, the experimenter erased the subject's mark, moved it to another square and made his own mark but without giving any indications that anything about the play was unusual. . . . Students were instructed to select someone other than a family member, and in the course of an ordinary conversation and without indicating that anything unusual was happening to bring their faces up to the subject's until their noses were almost touching. . . .[217]

And here are some reactions:

. . . the scenes exploded with the bewilderment and anger of family members . . . frank displays of anger and "disgust.". . . Two of them [the premedical students] showed acute suffering as soon as it appeared that the interview was finished and they were being dismissed with no acknowledgment of a deception. . . .[218]

The overriding of moral concerns by the desire to design an experiment that would satisfy the investigator's interest hardly warrants the judgment (Gouldner's) that the "cry of pain, then, is Garfinkel's triumphal moment" and that "objectivity and sadism become delicately intertwined."[219] The "ethnomethodological indifference" which Garfinkel stresses does, though, extend to topics, problems, or issues[220]—in fact, Peter McHugh equates an "issue" with something that is "in need of description"[221] (rather than being a matter of worry, despair, resolution, delight—other than, again, in a methodological sense). The ethnomethodologist's world is a world of sheer cognition, a candidate for cognition; and the subject, to repeat—and this includes the ethnomethodologist himself—is a purely cognizing subject.

There is a difference, however, between Max Weber's "neutrality" and Garfinkel's "indifference." What this difference means might become clearer by a reference to the previously mentioned Ernst Grünwald.

The conclusion of a study of Grünwald's conception of the sociology of knowledge was:

that Grünwald wants—in the twofold sense of this term—a cosmology, universal truth, cognitive features common to all men, identical objects, points of view that could be understood with reference to an order of culture and history, and a science that can make testable claims about the origin of a given thought, about the relations between thought and social class, and about the existentiality of knowledge [the bearing of one's existence on one's knowledge]. His world is a world that exhibits these wants. . . .

This is not a world that is meaningless by a subtraction, piecemeal or progressive, of items—cosmology, truth, objects, and so on—but rather the world of a man who has lost his continuity with history and with his fellow men with whom he is involved in a common history. . . . This man was not alone in this, nor is he (cf., among many other indications, the contemporary literature on alienation, and the mass society, etc.).[222]

These wants and lacks were ascertained by inference;[223] they were not proclaimed as were both Weber's value neutrality and Garfinkel's indifference. But what Weber and Grünwald have in common is a struggle to attain what they wanted:[224] a world that made sense, a meaningful society, that is, a good society. But Weber, much more explicitly than Grünwald, was convinced that science, including social science, could not identify such a society, let alone bring it about. Not even the founders of sociology had thought sociology, or science generally, could bring it about, but they were convinced that it could show what such a society was like. Auguste Comte was so convinced, but he also believed that it took feeling and religion to make the good society a reality; and Karl Marx, too, believed that he had ascertained the structure of society but thought it took revolution to put it into practice. In Weber, "value neutrality" stands for the separation of Is and Ought and for the conviction that science, being exclusively concerned with the Is and competent regarding it alone, can say nothing on what a meaningful or good society ought to be (other than in the sense of the individual scientist's personal preference). By contrast, in Garfinkel and most if not all of ethnomethodology, "ethnomethodological indifference" stands for indifference toward the very question of Is and Ought, including the question of a meaningful or good society.

It was said that for Grünwald the world was meaningless. To arrive at such a claim, Karl Mannheim's "documentary method" had been used—the same method which Garfinkel refers to as his own: the search, as Garfinkel quotes Mannheim, for ". . . an identical homologous pattern underlying a vast variety of totally different realizations of meaning," or in Hans Peter Dreitzel's formulation: "the actors take each other's actions as an expression, a 'document,' of an underlying pattern."[225] But if the world is meaningless, there is *no* world, no common world, either natural or social.[226] This perhaps is the reason why some of the ethnomethodological studies and even theories strike some hearers or listeners as trivial[227]—and why the *presence* of a common world makes Georg Simmel's studies of such "trivia" as the ruin or the handle (to mention only two which are available in English) so exciting and revealing to many readers.[228] Simmel seems to be eager to tell us what he has found or is finding, taking it for granted that we live in a common world in which his discoveries also are our discoveries[229]—but what is the ethnomethodologist's attitude toward his fellowmen? Some of it we saw in the discussion of "ethnomethodological indifference": his overriding interest in their methodology and in his own methodology, at the expense of moral concern. Yet Garfinkel points out that traditional social science, including sociology, treats the member of society as "a judgmental dope of a cultural and/or psychological sort."[230] But does Garfinkel himself treat him differently? He asks: "How is an investigator *doing* it when he is making out the member of a society to be a judgmental dope? Several examples will furnish some specifics and consequences."[231]

There follow in the text quoted the "early studies" that were sketched previously and that led Gouldner to his imputation of sadism but that here were interpreted more nearly as expressions of moral indifference. If the traditional sociologist knows better than do the people whom he studies, the ethnomethodologist, if it is permissible to generalize from the Garfinkel passage just quoted, has no relation whatever to his "subjects," because, as we have seen already, they are exclusively cognitive; but this means they are not subjects at all, but agents—who, furthermore, "achieve," "accomplish," "work at" establishing and maintaining social order.[232]

The best summing up of the ethnomethodologist's lack of a world comes from two lines in Rainer Maria Rilke's poem, "The Panther":

> Ihm ist, als ob es tausend Stäbe gäbe
> und hinter tausend Stäben keine Welt.[233]

It remains to make clear what the nature of the foregoing presentation of ethnomethodology is: sociological; not substantive. To examine the substantive yield of the many studies that have been undertaken by ethnomethodologists or in the name of ethnomethodology[234] would require another and different undertaking. The task here has been to show ethnomethodology as a development of phenomenology, especially Schutz's, in sociology or social science— undoubtedly at this time the most widespread and influential in the English-speaking world.[235]

After meeting the Marxist critique of phenomenology, we came to the realization that Marx cannot criticize Husserl, nor Husserl, Marx; that a posture truer to them—truer to their essence, possibly—is the shock of recognizing the way in which and the extent to which each in his own way evinced features of his society even if he thought he was analyzing them (Marx) or was analyzing mainly other things (Husserl); and that the response to such recognition is shock and compassion, not only for Marx and Husserl but for us in our shock as well; thus we came to be united with them and, so to speak, with ourselves in a feeling of solidarity, a "we relation." But this shock is no paralysis: it is an inspiration to build on more solid grounds than even Marx's and Husserl's. In doing so in relation to Weber (rather than Marx), and with Husserl's help, Alfred Schutz has made it possible for us, who come after and thus can criticize him, to build on more solid grounds than Schutz did. It should be clear from the discussion of ethnomethodology that this is not what, by and large, the ethnomethodologists appear to have done. As Maurice Natanson expresses it:

> Schutz's conceptions of taken for grantedness and typification are features of a phenomenology of the natural attitude. . . . Garfinkel . . . avoids placing in question the ground on which confidence in any segment of reality is based. . . . Appearance to the contrary, Garfinkel reinforces rather than challenges the involvement of man in the natural attitude.[236]

To conclude with a mere suggestion of what an attitude toward our time might be that is historically more adequate than Marx's, Husserl's, Schutz's, and the ethnomethodologists': it is one of deeper radicalness in two quite different but mutually complementary senses: a more comprehensive grasp of the present situation of man and simultaneously a grasp of ever deeper levels of my and my fellowmen's stock of knowledge and experience.[237]

NOTES

Both in the reader's name and personally I wish to express my gratitude and indebtedness to Egon Bittner, Tom Bottomore, Robert S. Cohen, Hans Mohr, and Arthur S. Parsons for illuminating talks while I was preparing this chapter; to Richard Grathoff, Jonathan B. Imber, Marcene Marcoux, Arthur S. Parsons, and Richard M. Zaner for important comments on its first draft; to Jonathan Imber, in addition, for extraordinary bibliographical help; above all, to David M. Rasmussen for a keen analysis of that draft that resulted in most helpful improvements.

1. Scheler's major work in the sociology of knowledge itself, *Die Wissensformen und die Gessellschaft* (1926), still awaits English translation. Karl Mannheim, "The Problem of a Sociology of Knowledge" (1925), trans. Paul Kecskemeti, in *From Karl Mannheim*, ed. and with an introduction by Kurt H. Wolff (New York: Oxford University Press, 1971) pp. 79–104. For Scheler as a philosopher within the phenomenological movement, see Herbert Spiegelberg, *The Phenomenological Movement: A Historical Introduction* (1960) (The Hague: Nijhoff, 1969) vol. I, chap. V, pp. 228–70. For an overall "intellectual biography," see John Raphael Staude, *Max Scheler, 1874–1928: An Intellectual Portrait*, (New York: Free Press, 1967).

2. Cf. esp. (among works available in English) Max Scheler, *The Nature of Sympathy* (1913), trans. Peter Heath, with an introduction by Werner Stark (London: Routledge & Kegan Paul, 1954); "Phenomenology and the Theory of Cognition" (1913?), in Scheler, *Selected Philosophical Essays*, trans. and with an introduction by David R. Lachterman (Evanston, Ill.: Northwestern University Press, 1973) pp. 136–201; "Man and History" (1926), in Scheler, *Philosophical Perspectives*, trans. Oscar A. Haac (Boston: Beacon, 1958) pp. 65–93; *Formalism in Ethics and Non-Formal Ethics of Values: A New Attempt toward the Foundation of an Ethical Personalism* (1916), trans. Manfred S. Frings and Roger L. Funk (Evanston, Ill.: Northwestern University Press, 1973); *On the Eternal in Man* (1949), trans. Bernard Nobel (New York: Harper, 1960); *Man's Place in Nature* (1928), trans. and with an introduction by Hans Meyerhoff (Boston: Beacon, 1961). Among the most important analyses of Scheler with particular reference to phenomenology and social science are three studies by Alfred Schutz: "Scheler's Theory of Intersubjectivity and the General Thesis of the Alter Ego" (1942), in Schutz, *Collected Papers*, vol. I, *The Problem of Social Reality*, ed. and with an introduction by Maurice Natanson (The Hague: Nijhoff, 1962) pp. 150–79; "Max Scheler's Philosophy" (1956) in *Collected Papers*, vol. III, *Studies in Phenomenological Philosophy*, ed. I. Schutz, with an introduction by Aron Gurwitsch (The Hague: Nijhoff, 1966) pp. 133–144; and "Max Scheler's Epistemology and Ethics" (1957–58), ibid., pp. 145–78.

3. On Merleau-Ponty, see Spiegelberg, *The Phenomenological Movement*, vol. II, chap. XI, pp. 516–62; Joseph J. Kockelmans, ed., *Phenomenology: The Philosophy of Edmund Husserl and Its Interpretation* (Garden City, N.Y.: Anchor Books, 1967) pp. 349–408 (essays by Kockelmans, Merleau-Ponty, and Remy C. Kwant); John O'Neill, *Perception, Expression, and History: The Social Phenomenology of Maurice Merleau-Ponty*, (Evanston, Ill.: Northwestern University Press, 1970). The limitation indicated (which, it is hoped, becomes more plausible as the chapter proceeds) excludes considering Edward A. Tiryakian's effort to show the convergence of Durkheim and existentialism (recalling Talcott Parsons's twenty-five years before in regard to Durkheim, Pareto, and Weber). See Tiryakian, *Sociologism and Existentialism: Two Perspectives on the Individual and Society* (Englewood Cliffs, N.J.: Prentice-Hall, 1962), as well as "Existential Phenomenology and Sociology," *American Sociological Review*, vol. 30 (October 1965) pp. 674–88 [and reactions by Jiri Kolaja and Peter L. Berger, with Tiryakian's reply, ibid., vol. 31 (April, 1966) pp. 258–64]. It should be noted that the writings of the authors involved in this exchange proceed, as Karl Mannheim would have put it, "intrinsically" in their comments on each other's and third persons' statements, rather than sociologically, as is the effort of the present chapter. Cf. Mannheim, "The Ideological and the Sociological Interpretation of Intellectual Phenomena" (1926), trans. Kurt H. Wolff (1953), in *From Karl Mannheim*, pp. 116–31 (and cf. editor's introduction, pp. xxxviii–xli).

4. Such a formulation of the social origin, or the social component of the origin, of the manner in which things appear betrays a social-scientific perspective. Aside from the historical context in which Edmund Husserl called for going back *zu den Sachen* (to the things), as we shall see presently—that is, aside from his argument against reductionism ("something is nothing but

something else"), especially psychologism ("logical laws are nothing but psychological laws")—aside from this observation about the time in which phenomenology arose, a philosopher will be more nearly inclined to accept Husserl's view of phenomena as intuited essences, without dwelling on the historical circumstances in which such a view arose. See Richard Schmitt, "Phenomenology," *The Encyclopedia of Philosophy* (New York: Macmillan and Free Press, 1967) vol. 6, pp. 139–51.

5. Max Weber, *Wirtschaft und Gesellschaft* (1918–20) (Tübingen: J. C. B. Mohr [Paul Siebeck], 1925) p. 1. Cf. Max Weber, *Economy and Society*, ed. Guenther Roth and Claus Wittich (New York: Bedminster Press, 1968) p. 4.

6. On the contrary, phenomenology has made essential contributions to the analysis of the nature of time itself. The seminal work is Husserl's *Phenomenology of Internal Time-Consciousness* (1893–1917), trans. James S. Churchill (Bloomington: Indiana University Press, 1964).

7. See Herbert Marcuse, *Reason and Revolution: Hegel and the Rise of Social Theory* (1941) (Boston: Beacon, 1960) pp. 94–95, where Marcuse shows implicitly an affinity between Hegel and Husserl and explicitly how in fact Hegel led to Marx. In *Husserl: An Analysis of His Phenomenology* (essays originally published between 1949 and 1957), trans. Edward G. Ballard and Lester E. Embree (Evanston, Ill.: Northwestern University Press, 1967) Paul Ricoeur points out (pp. 206, 210) that the "sense of the negative," the tragic element in Hegel, is missing in Husserl. For a quite different comparison between Hegel's and Husserl's phenomenology, see William Ernest Hocking, "From the Early Days of the *Logische Untersuchungen*," in *Edmund Husserl, 1859–1959* (The Hague: Nijhoff, 1959) p. 7. On other theoretical affinities between Hegel and Husserl, see Enzo Paci, *The Function of the Sciences and the Meaning of Man* (1963), trans. and with an introduction by Paul Piccone and James E. Hansen (Evanston, Ill.: Northwestern University Press, 1972), e.g., p. 144. [For Hegel's own use of "phenomenology," see Walter Kaufmann, "Hegel's Conception of Phenomenology," in Edo Pivcevic, ed., *Phenomenology and Philosophical Understanding* (Cambridge: Cambridge University Press, 1975) pp. 211–30.]

8. Dorion Cairns, *Conversations with Husserl and Fink*, ed. Husserl-Archives Louvain, foreword by Richard M. Zaner (The Hague: Nijhoff, 1976) p. 22, from a conversation with Husserl and Eugen Fink, Husserl's research assistant and close associate, of 22 August 1931): "Hegel, he [Husserl] said, he had never read." This claim does not seem contradicted by the statement (ibid., p. 52, from a conversation with Husserl and Fink of 25 November 1931): "Though he [Husserl] recognizes Hegel as a forerunner and a genius. . . ." Indirect knowledge of Hegel might well have brought Husserl to this conviction. Also cf. such incidental references to Hegel by Husserl as, e.g., in *The Crisis of European Sciences and Transcendental Phenomenology*, trans. David Carr (Evanston, Ill.: Northwestern University Press, 1970), and Theodore W. Adorno, "Husserl and the Problem of Idealism," *The Journal of Philosophy*, vol. 37, no. 2 (January 4, 1940) p. 6.

9. For Brentano, too, see the indispensable sourcebook by Herbert Spiegelberg, *The Phenomenological Movement*, chap. I. For Husserl on Descartes, see especially *The Idea of Phenomenology* (five lectures given in 1907), trans. William P. Alston and George Nakhnikian (The Hague: Nijhoff, 1964) second lecture; *Ideas: General Introduction to Pure Phenomenology* (1913), trans. W. R. Boyce Gibson (New York: Collier Books, 1962) esp. secs. 31–35; "Phenomenology," *Encyclopaedia Britannica*, 14th ed. (1929), trans. Richard E. Palmer (1971), in Richard M. Zaner and Don Ihde, eds., *Phenomenology and Existentialism* (Capricorn Books, 1973) esp. pp. 57, 70; *Cartesian Meditations: An Introduction to Phenomenology* (ms., 1929), trans. Dorian Cairns (The Hague: Nijhoff, 1960) esp. par. 3; *The Crisis of European Sciences and Transcendental Phenomenology* pars. 16–21 and Beilagen V–X, not trans.—original, *Die Krisis der europäischen Wissenschaften und die phänomenologische Philosophie*, ed. Walter Biemel, (The Hague: Nijhoff, 1954) pp. 392–431. On Husserl's relation to Descartes, see especially two conceptions of very different provenience: Herbert Marcuse, "The Concept of Essence" (1936), trans. Jeremy J. Shapiro, in Marcuse, *Negations: Essays in Critical Theory* (Boston: Beacon, 1968) pp. 56–58, 60; and Aron Gurwitsch, "An Introduction to Constitutive Phenomenology" (1939), in Gurwitsch, *Phenomenology and the Theory of Science*, ed. Lester Embree, (Evanston, Ill.: Northwestern University Press, 1974) p. 186, n. 35.

10. René Descartes, *Discourse on Method* (1637), trans. with an introduction by Laurence J. Lafleur (New York: Liberal Arts Press, 1950, 1956) p. 21 (in the beginning of part IV, "Proofs of the Existence of God and of the Human Soul," showing a setting of the doubt wholly different from Husserl's). Also see Descartes, *Meditations Concerning First Philosophy* (1641), trans, with an introduction by Laurence J. Lafleur (New York: Liberal Arts Press, 1951) p. 29f. (in the

second Meditation, "On the Nature of the Human Mind, and That It Is More Easily Known Than the Body").

11. Both *noema* (plural: *noemata)* and *noetic* (the noun: *noesis)* and related terms derive from the Greek *noein*, to perceive, which in turn comes from *nous*, mind: *The American Dictionary of the English Language*, v. *noesis, noetic*.

12. These formulations gloss over profound and difficult problems. E.g., what, on the definition of consciousness as intentional, becomes of psychic states in which for the individual having them there is no intentionality, when, e.g., we are simply happy or (on the contarary) "know no way out" or are anxious (rather than afraid *of*), and the like? [Cf. Maurice Merleau-Ponty, *Phenomenology of Perception* (1945), trans. Colin Smith (London: Routledge & Kegan Paul, 1962) p. 121, n. 5, and p. 137; and Kurt H. Wolff, "Surrender and the Body" (1974), in *Surrender and Catch: Experience and Inquiry Today* (Dordrecht and Boston: Reidel, 1976) p. 205, n. 8.] To open up the general topic of intentionality, see Aron Gurwitsch, "On the Intentionality of Consciousness" (1940), in Kockelmans, *Phenomenology*, pp. 118–37, and Husserl's Theory of the Intentionality of Consciousness in Historical Perspective" (1967), in Gurwitsch, *Phenomenology and the Theory of Science*, pp. 210–40.

13. To open up the complex of problems associated with this notion, following readings may prove useful: Edmund Husserl, *Ideas*, chap. 6, "The Phenomenological Reductions" (secs. 56–62); Joseph J. Kockelmans, "What Is Phenomenology?" in Kockelmans *Phenomenology*, esp. pp. 27–32; Schmitt, "Phenomenology," esp. pp. 140–144; Spiegelberg, *The Phenomenological Movement*, vol. II, pp. 690–94.

14. Alfred Schutz, "Some Leading Concepts of Phenomenology" (1954), in Schutz, *Collected Papers*, vol. I, p. 107.

15. Ibid., p. 108.

16. Ibid., p. 109.

17. At the present juncture, this demand is phrased in a temporal frame, while in the beginning of this chapter,it was given a cultural interpretation.

18. Schutz "Some Leading Concepts of Phenomenology," p. 111. (From this observation, Husserl developed his theory of *constitution*.)

19. Cf. Schmitt, "Phenomenology" pp. 140–44.

20. From this Husserl concluded that thse analysis of predictions must go back to prepredicative experience, that is, that formal logic must be based on the logic of the processes which constitute prepredicative experience and which can be analyzed only in the phenomenological reduction [cf. Husserl, *Experience and Judgment: Investigations in a Genealogy of Logic* (1939), trans. James S. Churchill and Karl Ameriks (Evanston, Ill.: Northwestern University Press, 1973)]—thus Husserl's distinction between formal and transcendental logic [developed in *Formal and Transcendental Logic* (1929), trans. Dorion Cairns (The Hague: Nijoff, 1969].

21. Schutz, "Some Leading Concepts of Phenomenology," p. 115.

22. Still, the distinction between empirical and eidetic should not be confused with that between the natural or mundane and the reduced sphere: the two distinctions crosscut each other. Cf. ibid., p. 113.

23. Here it may be pertinent to realize that Husserl came to philosophy from mathematics—his doctoral dissertation of 1882 was in mathematics; his first work, *Philosophy of Arithmetic* (1891), trs. José Huertas-Jourda (The Hague: Nijoff, promised), caused, in turn, the mathematician Gottlob Frege to point out its psychologism—a variety of reductionism—against which (as indicated before) Husserl argued in his whole subsequent philosophy. [Cf. Frege's review of Husserl's *Philosophie der Arithmetic* in *Zeitschrift für Philosophie und philosophische Kritik*, vol. 103 (1894) pp. 313–32]

24. What precedes is meant as a bare first, and selective, introduction to phenomenology. It may be useful to list some introductory texts that lead further, beginning with certain encyclopedia entries: Marvin Farber, "Phenomenology," *Collier's Encyclopedia*, 1975, vol. 18; He. Sp. (Herbert Spiegelberg), "Phenomenology," *Encyclopaedia Britannica*, 1973, vol. 17; Dorion Cairns, "Phenomenology," chap. 28 pp. 353–64, in Vergilius Ferm, ed., *A History of Philosophical Systems* (New York: Philosophical Library, 1950); D. C. (Dorion Cairns), "Phenomenology," in Dagobert Runes, ed., *Dictionary of Philosophy* (New York: Philosophical Library, n.d.); W. Bi. (presumabably Walter Biemel), "Phenomenology," *Encylopaedia Britannica*, 15th ed., 1943–73, vol. 15; Richard Schmitt "Phenomenology"; Edmund Husserl, "Phenomenology" (1927), *Encyclopaedia Britannica*, 14th ed., 1929 (trans. and much abridged by Christopher V. Salmon; the whole article, which had gone through several versions, is translated by Richard E. Palmer in Zaner and Ihde, *Phenomenology and Existentialism)*; J. N. F. (Findlay), "Phenomenology," *Encyclopaedia Britannica*, 14th ed., 1929, vol. 17. A few addition-

al introductions may be added, but the reader must find out which of them and of the preceding ones offer the best access and in which order they should be followed: Schutz, "Some Leading Concepts of Phenomenology," whole (pp. 99–117); Maurice Natanson, "Phenomenology and the Social Sciences," in Natanson, ed., *Phenomenology and the Social Sciences* (Evanston, Ill.: Northwestern University Press, 1973) vol. 1, pp. 3–44; Herbert Spiegelberg, *The Phenomenological Movement,* vol. II, chap. XIV, "The Essentials of the Phenomenological Method," pp. 653–701; Joseph J. Kockelmans, ed., *Phenomenology;* Zaner and Ihde, *Phenomenology and Existentialism;* Richard M. Zaner, *The Way of Phenomenology: Criticism as a Philosophical Discipline* (New York: Pegasus, 1970); David Steward and Algis Mickunas, *Exploring Phenomenology: A Guide to the Field and Its Literature* (Chicago: American Library Association, 1974); Marvin Farber, *The Foundation of Phenomenology: Edmund Husserl and the Quest for a Rigorous Science of Philosophy,* (1943) (New York: Paine-Whitman, 1962); Aron Gurwitsch, "The Phenomenological and the Psychological Approach to Consciousness" (1955), in Gurwitsch, *Studies in Phenomenology and Psychology* (Evanston, Ill.: Northwestern University Press, 1966) pp. 89–106. Of Husserl himself, *The Idea of Phenomenology* and the *Cartesian Meditations* are perhaps best suited to provide access (probably only after some of the above secondary writings have been consulted). As a bridge to developments in an existentialist direction (Merleau-Ponty, Sartre, Heidegger), perhaps most useful is Maurice Merleau-Ponty, Sartre, Heidegger), perhaps most useful is Maurice Merleau-Ponty's preface to his *Phenomenology of Perception* (1945), pp. vii–xxi. Such developments are presented in several works already cited, notably in Spiegelberg, *The Phenomenological Movement;* Kockelmans; Zaner and Ihde; as well as in many of the encyclopedia entries. Finally, some readers may find access to Husserl's philosophy most congenial by gaining access to the philosopher himself. Here four works are especially recommended: Dorion Cairns, *Conversations with Husserl and Fink; Edmund Husserl, 1859–1959;* Herbert Spiegelberg, ed., "From Husserl to Heidegger: Excerpts from a 1928 Diary by W. R. Boyce Gibson," *JBSP: The Journal of the British Society for Phenomenology,* vol. 2 (January 1971) pp. 58–82; and Edmund Husserl, "Letter to Arnold Metzger" (September 1919), German-English ed. trans. Paul Senft, *The Human Context,* vol. IV, (1972) pp. 244–256 [an earlier German English ed., trans. Erazim V. Kohak, appeared in *The Philosophical Forum,* vol. 21 (1963–64) pp. 48–68].

25. For an excellent introduction to the "critical theory" of the Frankfurt School, also with reference to phenomenology, see Jürgen Habermas, *Knowledge and Human Interests* (1968), trans. Jeremy J. Shapiro (Boston: Beacon, 1971), "Appendix: Knowledge and Social Interests: A General Perspective" (1968), pp. 301–17, 348–49 [cf. John O'Neill, *Sociology as a Skin Trade: Essays towards a Reflexive Sociology* (London: Heinemann, 1972), "Can Phenomenology Be Critical?" esp. pp. 224–26]. One of the "founding" essays is Max Horkheimer's "Traditional and Critical Theory" (1937), In Horkheimer, *Critical Theory: Selected Essays,* trans. Matthew J. O'Connell and others (New York: Herder & Herder, 1972) pp. 188–243. For a history of the Frankfurt School, see Martin Jay, *The Dialectical Imagination: A History of the Frankfurt School and the Institute of Social Research, 1923–50* (Boston: Little, Brown, 1973); for quite a different interpretation, see Zoltán Tar, *The Frankfurt School: The Critical Theories of Max Horkheimer and Theodor Adorno,* foreword by Michael Landmann (New York: Wiley, 1977); for a succinct, highly informed sketch, see Jeremy Shapiro, "The Critical Theory of Frankfurt," *Times Literary Supplement,* 4 October 1974.

26. Herbert Marcuse, "The Concept of Essence." A position very close to Marcuse's (and Adorno's, which follows) is taken by Bob Scholte in his review of George Psathas, ed., *Phenomenological Sociology: Issues and Applications, American Anthropoligist,* vol. 78 (1976) pp. 584–89, esp. p. 586.

27. Marcuse, "The Concept of Essence," p. 54.

28. Ibid., p. 59.

29. Ibid., p. 62. Cf. Adorno, "Husserl and the Problem of Idealism," p. 17.

30. "Let not doctrines and 'Ideas' be the rules of your being. Today and in the future, only the *Führer* himself is German reality and its law': Martin Heidegger in the *Freiburger Studentenzeitung,* (3 November 1933), quoted in Herbert Marcuse, "The Struggle against Liberalism in the Totalitarian View of the State" (1934), in *Negations,* pp. 41, 275. [For Heidegger himself on the Nazi period, see his 1966 interview with *Der Spiegel,* published posthumously: "Only a God Can Save Us Now': An Interview with Martin Heidegger," trans. David Schendler, *Graduate Faculty Philosophy Journal,* vol. 6 no. 1 (Winter 1977) pp. 5–27; also the informative preface by the editors, ibid., pp. 2–4; and in the same issue, Herbert Marcuse and Frederick Olafson, "Heidegger's Politics: An Interview," pp. 28–40.]

31. See also Herbert Marcuse, "On Science and Phenomenology" (1964), in Robert S. Cohen

and Marx W. Wartofsky, eds., *Boston Studies in the Philosophy of Science. vol. Two: In Honor of Philipp Frank* (New York: Humanities Press, 1965) pp. 279–90. This paper deals with selected aspects of Husserl's *Crisis of European Sciences and Transcendental Phenomenology*. For a more comprehensive review of the English edition, see William Leiss's essay, written in a related mood, *Telos*, no. 8 (Summer 1971) pp. 109–21; [also see Paul Piccone's a bit violent attack on Leiss's review (and on the Frankfurt School) immediately following: "Reading the Crisis," ibid., pp. 121–39]. Of special interest with regard to one of the key concepts developed in the *Crisis* are David Carr, "Ambiguities in the Concept of the Life-World," chap. 8, pp. 190–211, in Carr *Phenomenology and the Problem of History: A Study of Husserl's Transcendental Philosophy* (Evanston, Ill.: Northwestern University Press, 1974); and "The Phenomenology of the Life-World," chap. 98, pp. 117–30, in Cornelis A. van Peursen, *Phenomenological and Analytical Philosphy*, (Pittsburgh: Duquesne University Press, 1972). For a more general analysis of the relations between critical theory and phenomenology, see Pier Aldo Rovatti, "Critical Theory and Phenomenology" (1972), trans. Tom Hull, *Telos*, no. 15 (Spring 1973) pp. 25–40—this article is written with the perspective of Enzo Paci; also Fred R. Dallmayr, "Phenomenology and Critical Theory: Adorno," *Cultural Hermeneutics*, vol. 3, no. 4 (July 1976) pp. 366–405.

32. Theodor W. Adorno, *Zur Metakritik der Erkenntnistheorie: Studien über Husserl und die phänomenologischen Antinomien* (based on a ms. written in 1934–37) (Stuttgart: Kohlhammer, 1956) pp. 86–87. In English, Adorno treats Husserl's spearation of psychology (genesis) and logic (validity) in "Husserl and the Problem of Idealism," pp. 9–12.

33. Adorno, *Zur Metakritik*, p. 141; also cf. p. 185.

34. Adorno, "Husserl and the Problem of Idealism," p. 17.

35. Ibid., p. 9. Less sensitive than Adorno, and less ambiguous, is Giorgio Baratta's more impatient critique which substantively, however, is very similar to Marcuse's and Adorno's. The phenomenological reduction, Baratta writes, is based on "neutral consciousness," which "is nothing but a mode of ideological consciousness" [*L'idealismo fenomenologico di Edmund Husserl*, (Urbino: Argalia, 1969) p. 228], and claims "that once again idealism has shown itself congenial to the defense and the sublimation of the constituted order" (p. 241; this is the end of the book).

36. Edmund Husserl, *Die Idee der Phänomenologie: Fünf Vorlesungen* (1907), ed. and with an introduction by Walter Biemel (The Hague: Nijohoff, 1950) pp. 71–72. Cf. Husserl, *The Idea of Phenomenology*, pp. 56–57.

37. Edmund Husserl, *The Crisis of European Sciences and Transcendental Phenomenology* (originally published 1954), p. 139.

38. Tran-Duc-Thao, *Phênomênolgie et matêrialisme dialectique* (1951) (Paris: Gordon & Breach, 1971) p. 15. (An English translation is scheduled for publication in the near future.) Cf. Silvia Federici, "Viet Cong Philosophy : Tran-Duc-Thao," *Telos*, no. 6 (fall 1970) pp. 104–17.

39. Wolfe Mays, "Phenomenology and Marxism" in Pivĉević, *Phenomenology and Philosophical Understanding*, pp. 231–50. Barry Smart, *Sociology, Phenomenology and Marxian Analysis* (London: Routledge & Kegan Paul, 1976) may be read as a plea for a "phenomenologized" Marxism as the basis of a science of society.

40. Georges Lukács, *Existentialisme ou Marxisme?* (1948) (Paris: Nagel, 1961) parts I and II, esp. part III, sec. 2, "Sartre contre Marx" [also see James Miller "Marxism and Subjectivity: Remarks on Georg Lukács and Existential Phenomenology," *Telos*, no. 6 (Fall, 1970) pp. 175–183; Adam Schaff, *A Philosophy of Man*, (London: Lawrence & Wishart, 1963); Raymond Aron, *Marxism and the Existentialists*, (New York: Harper & Row, 1969), a partly autobiographical, very readable discussion of Sartre and Merleau-Ponty—for Aron ,the common ground of Marxism and existentialism is "the calling into question of both the destiny of the individual and the historical destiny of mankind" (pp. 11–12, origin in italics)].

41. Tran-Duc-Thao, *Phênomênolgie et matêrialisme dialectique;* Enzo Paci, *The Function of the Sciences and The Meaning of Man;* Pier Rovatti, "A Phenomenological Analysis of Marxism: The Return to the Subject and to the Dialetic of the Totality," *Telos*, no. 5 (Spring 1970) pp. 160–73; Paul Ricoeur, *Husserl: An Analysis of His Phenomenology;* Efraim Shmueli, "Pragmatic, Existentialist and Phenomenological Interpretations of Marxism," *Journal of the British Society for Phenomenology*, vol. 4, no. 2 (May 1973); also see Shmueli, "Can Phenomenology Acomodate [sic] Marxism?" *Telos*, no. 17 (Fall 1973) pp. 169–180 (above all on Paci).

42. Mays, "Phenomenology and Marxism," p. 150.

43. Fred R. Dallmayr, *Phenomenology and Marxism: A Salute to Enzo Paci," in George Psathas, ed., Phenomenological Sociology: Issues and Applications*, pp. 305–56. Cf. also Dallmayr, "Phänomenologie und Marxismus in geschichtlicher Perspektive," in Bernhard Waldenfels, Jan M. Broekman, Ante Pažanin, eds., *Phänomenologie und Marxismus*, Band 1,

Konzepte und Methoden, Band 2, *Praktische Philosophie* (Frankfurt: Suhrkamp, 1977) vol. 1, pp. 13–44 (a very useful source book); and Dallmayr, "Marxism and Truth," *Telos*, no. 29 (Fall 1976) pp. 130–59.

44. Gajo Petrovíc, *Marx in the Mid-Twentieth Century* (Garden City, N.Y.: Anchor Books, 1967); Karel Kosík, *Dialectics of the Concrete*, trans. Karel Kovanda with James Schmidt (Dordrecht and Boston: Reidel, 1976); Antonio Gramsci *Il materialismo storico e la filosofia di Benedetto Croce* (Turin: Einaudi, 1948); Herbert Marcuse, "Contributions to a Phenomenology of Historical Materialism" (1928), trans, not indicated, *Telos*, no. 4 (Fall 1969) pp. 3–34; Adorno, *Zur Metakritik;* Jürgen Habermas, *Knowledge and Human Interests*, and other writings.

45. Enzo Paci, *The Function of the Sciences and the Meaning of Man;* Paul Piccone, "Phenomenological Marxism," *Telos*, no. 9 (Fall 1971) pp. 3–31; John O'Neill, "Can Phenomenology Be Critical?" (which Dallmayr does not identify).

46. Dallmayr, "Phenomenology and Marxism," p. 344.

47. Ibid., p. 344.

48. Mihâhly Vajda, "Marxism, Existentialism, Phenomenology: A Dialogue," *Telos*, no. 7 (Spring 1971) pp. 3-29.

49. David M. Rasmussen, "The Marxist Critique of Phenomenology," *Dialectics and Humanism*, vol. 2, no. 4 (Autumn 1975) pp. 59–70. (See also Jerzy Łoziński, "Some Remarks Concerning D. M. Rasmussen's 'The Marxist Critique of Phenomenology,'" ibid., pp. 71–75,—the main point of interest here is the effort to show that, contrary to Rasmussen's claim, Husserl's phenomenology does contain a theory of society.) Rasmussen's paper has been selected for our purposes also because it presents a more direct, concrete, and focused discussion of Marxism and phenomenology than do such far more comprehensive works, which are less immediately relevant for us here because they are comparatively multifocused, as Sartre's *Search for a Method* (1960), trans. and with an introduction by Hazel E. Barnes (New York: Knopf, 1963) or Karel Kosík's *Dialectics of the Concrete: A Study of Problems of Man and World* (1963).

50. Cf. the paragraph (38) of the *Cartesian Meditations* to which Rasmussen refers.

51. Rasmussen, "The Marxist Critique of Phenomenology," p. 66.

52. Ibid., p. 67.

53. Ibid., p. 69.

54. Ibid., p. 69.

55. Ibid., p. 70.

56. Ibid., p. 59.

57. In this capacity it functions in other recent thinkers, notably Nietzsche and Merleau-Ponty.

58. Shlomo Avineri, *The Social and Political Thought of Karl Marx*, (Cambridge: Cambridge University Press, 1968) p. 163.

59. As well as in still others, e.g., Michael Landmann, "Phänomenologie, Kierkegaard, Marxismus," *Neue Rundschau*, vol. 86, no. 3 (September 1975) pp. 461–72.

60. Husserl, *Ideas*, par. 31, title, and p. 98 (original italics).

61. Wilhelm Dilthey, *Der Aufbau der geschichlichen Welt in den Geisteswissenschaften* (1910), *Gesammelte Schriften*, vol. VII (Leipzig und Berlin: Teubner, 1927) p. 291. (Into the response to this passage plays the question, raised in connection with Adorno's critique of Husserl, whether it is appropriate to bracket any and all phenomena.) Unlike Adorno and like Dilthey, Z. Bauman praises Husserl for his "stubborn refusal to acknowledge the relevance of the cultural or social temporality" in his, the "most radical among all proud, self-sustained philosophical systems"; for being concerned there with "*Geltung*, not *Existenz*," for leaving "outside its field of vision, in the elusive penumbra of *epoché*, not only the unthought things but the thinking individual as well": "On the Philosophical Status of Ethnomethodology," *The Sociological Review*, new series, vol. 21 (1973) pp. 5–23; pp. 5–6.

62. Cf. Georg Simmel, "The Metropolis and Mental Life" (1902), trans. H. H. Gerth with the assistance of C. Wright Mills, in *The Sociology of Georg Simmel*, trans., ed., and with an introduction by Kurt H. Wolff, (Glencoe, Ill.: Free Press, 1950) pp. 409–24.

63. Not all, perhaps not many, phenomenologists would agree that the comment on Rasmussen's paper, and especially the last short paragraph to which this note is appended, is more nearly an instance of *practicing* phenomenology than anything else in the present chapter. The concern of this chapter suggests that analysis be halted at this point—except for suggesting that this "instance of *practicing* phenomenology" is so, not in Husserl's sense, but in the sense of a possible, and important, development of it. The relation between the two remains to be specified further, but in the meantime see Wolff, *Surrender and Catch*, esp. chap. 22, "Sociology,

Phenomenology, and Surrender-and-Catch" (1974), pp. 153–76, and pertinent topics in the indexes of the book.

64. Cf. Reinhard Bendix, "Two Sociological Traditions," in Reinhard Bendix and Guenther Roth, *Scholarship and Partisanship: Essays on Max Weber* (Berkeley: University of California Press, 1971) pp. 282–98. A conception of sociology (more particularly of the sociology of knowledge) which is explicitly based on the recognition of these two approaches and tries to do right by both of them is presented by Peter L. Berger and Thomas Luckmann in *The Social Construction of Reality: An Essay in the Sociology of Knowledge* (Garden City, N.Y.: Doubleday, 1966). [Also cf. the substantively more than theoretically or conceptually complementary book by Burkart Holzner, *Reality Construction in Society* (Cambridge, Mass.: Schenkman, 1968.)] And we already heard of Alfred Schutz's refinement of Max Weber and suggested that within sociology it is the *verstehende* variant which is most cognate with phenomenology. The tie is far less close between Marx and Durkheim and seems absent between Marx and survey research, the most prevalent contemporary form of the objective approach.

65. The question of whether "social facts" are exclusively human or in part of a kind which are also found among nonhuman animals and among things can only be recorded here; at any rate, history and economics (whichever be argued as Marx's focus) are mixtures of both exclusively human and shared elements. (on "man as a mixed phenomenon" cf. Wolff, *Surrender and Catch*, esp. p. 75.)

66. The book is *Der sinnhafte Aufbau der sozialen Welt* (1932, reprinted 1960) English title, *The Phenomenology of the Social World*, trans. George Walsh and Frederick Lehnert, with an introduction by George Walsh (Evanston, Ill.: Northwestern University Press, 1967). The posthumous works are the *Collected Papers*, vols. I, II *Studies in Social Theory*, ed. and introduced by Arvid Brodersen (The Hague: Nijhoff, 1964), and III; *Reflections on the Problem of Relevance*, ed., annotated, and with an introduction by Richard M. Zaner (New Haven: Yale University Press, 1970); Alfred Schutz and Thomas Luckmann, *The Structures of the Life-World*, trans. Richard M. Zaner and H. Tristram Engelhardt, Jr. (Evanston: Northwestern University Press, 1973). There also is a selection from Schutz's work, *On Phenomenology and Social Relations*, ed. and with an introduction by Helmut R. Wagner (Chicago: University of Chicago Press, 1970). Of theoretical, historical, and sociological interest is the correspondence between Alfred Schutz and Talcott Parsons of 1940–41; it issued from Schutz's response to Parsons's *The Structure of Social Action* (1937), which Schutz had studied before he came to the United States. Cf. Alfred Schutz, Talcott Parsons, *Zur Theorie sozialen Handelns: Ein Briefwechsel*, ed. and with an introduction by Walter M. Sprondel (Frankfurt am Main: Suhrkamp, 1977) (including Parsons's retrospective commentary of 1974; to appear under the editorship of Richard Grathoff at the University of Indiana Press in the spring of 1978 as *The Theory of Social Action: The Correspondence between A. Schutz and T. Parsons*). Cf. Schutz, "The Social World and the Theory of Social Action" (1940, 1960), *Collected Papers*, vol. II, pp. 3–19. Much is also to be expected of an intellectual biography of Schutz at which Helmut R. Wagner has been at work.

67. One of the earliest overviews in English—probably the first—is Alfred Stonier and Karl Bode, "A New Approach to the Methodology of the Social Sciences," *Economica*, vol. 4 (November 1937) pp. 406–24. Among obituaries, the few pages by Hans Jonas are especially noteworthy: "Alfred Schutz, 1899–1959," *Social Research*, vol. 26 (Winter 1959) pp. 471–74, while Aron Gurwitsch's "The Common-Sense World as Social Reality—A Discourse on Alfred Schütz," *Social Research* vol. 29 (Spring 1962) pp. 50–72 (reprinted as the introduction to Schutz, *Collected Papers*, vol. III, pp. xi–xxxi) offers an excellent introduction to the main body of Schutz's work. Similarly illuminating is Maurice Natanson's introduction to Schutz, *Collected Papers*, vol. I, pp. xxv–xlvii, as are his "The Phenomenology of Alfred Schutz," *Inquiry*, vol. 9 (1966) pp. 147–55, and chap. 6, "Phenomenology Applied," pp. 104–25, in his *Edmund Husserl: Philosopher of Infinite Tasks* (Evanston, Ill.: Northwestern University Press, 1973). Two commemorative publications are "Essays in Commemoration of Alfred Schutz," *Social Research*, vol. 37, no. 1 (Spring 1970) pp. 1–101, and Maurice Natanson, ed., *Phenomenology and Social Reality: Essays in Memory of Alfred Schutz* (The Hague: Nijhoff, 1970). Berger and Luckmann, *The Social Construction of Reality*, which was cited as an effort to synthesize Weber and Durkheim, draws decisively on Schutzian ideas. Two monographs are Robert Williame, *Les fondements phénoménologiques de la sociologie compréhensive: Alfred Schutz et Max Weber* (The Hague: Nijhoff, 1973), and the comprehensive and penetrating unpublished dissertation by Arthur S. Parsons, *Alfred Schutz and the Foundations of Phenomenological Sociology* (Waltham, Mass.: Brandeis University, 1977). Among the many studies of more particular aspects or relevances of Schutz's work, of special interest to sociologists are Erving Goffman's assessment of

Schutz's place in his own theoretical work [Goffman, *Frame Analysis: An Essay on the Organization of Experience* (New York: Harper & Row, 1974) pp. 5–8] and Aron V. Cicourel's analysis of the connection between Schutz and ethnomethodology [Cicourel, "Basic and Normative Rules in the Negotiation of Status and Role," in David Sudnow, ed., *Studies in Social Interaction* (New York: Free Press, 1972) pp. 229–58, esp. pp. 250–56].

68. Alfred Schutz, *Der sinnhafte Aufbau der sozialen Welt* (1932) (Wien: Springer, 1960) p. iii; cf. *The Phenomenology of the Social World*, p. xxxi. (The translation here is less idiomatic and more literal.)

69. Ibid., p. 150 (original in italics); English, p. 133.

70. Ibid., p. 80 (original in italics); English, p. 75.

71. Ibid., p. 113 (original in italics); English, p. 103.

72. See esp. "Making Music Together: A Study in Social Relationship" (1951), *Collected Papers*, vol. II, pp. 159–78.

73. Cf. *Der sinnhafte Aufbau der sozialen Welt*, sec. 9, pp. 55–62; English, pp. 57–63.

74. In the present chapter we came across it in Weber's definition of "sociology," quoted in the first section.

75. *Der sinnhafte Aufbau der sozialen Welt*, p. 150. (original in italics); English, pp. 133–34.

76. Cf. ibid., secs. 36, 37, 41.

77. Ibid., p. 220; English, p. 194; that these terms are used to characterize "ideal-types" rather than just types is irrelevant in the present context. In fact, Schutz's important development of Weber's "ideal-type" will be ignored here.

78. Ibid., p. 255; English, p. 233 (translation slightly modified).

79. Schutz, "On Multiple Realities" (1945), in *Collected Papers*, vol. I, pp. 207–59. Cf. Aron Gurwitsch, *The Field of Consciousness* (1953) (Pittsburgh: Duquesne University Press, 1964) pp. 294–304, "Schutz's Theory of 'Finite Provinces of Meaning.' ".

80. Schutz, "On Multiple Realities," p. 207.

81. Ibid., p. 230. The notions of "tension of consciousness," goes back to Bergson (cf. pp. 212–14). In "The What and Why of Experience: The Contrapunctal Relationship Between Cognitive Style and Systems of Relevance," *The Annals of Phenomenological Sociology*, vol. II (1977) pp. 107–33, Brenda Venable Powell has shown that Schutz's *Reflections on the Problem of Relevance* contains a different way (in terms of relevance rather than cognitive style) of identifying a world.

82. Schutz, "On Multiple Realities," pp. 234–40.

83. Cf. Alfred Schutz, "Don Quixote and the Problem of Reality" (1954), *Collected Papers*, vol. II, pp. 135–58.

84. Schutz, "On Multiple Realities," pp. 240–44.

85. Ibid., pp. 245–59 (end of paper).

86. Ibid., p. 249.

87. Ibid., p. 254.

88. Ibid., pp. 254, 255.

89. Ibid., p. 255.

90. Alfred Schutz, "Common-Sense and Scientific Interpretation of Human Action" (1953), *Collected Papers*, vol. I, pp. 43–44.

91. Ibid., pp. 19–27, and *Phenomenology of the Social World*, secs. 38 and 39.

92. Cf. "Common-Sense and Scientific Interpretation of Human Action," esp. pp. 7–27, 34–44.

93. *Phenomenology of the Social World*, p. 43.

94. Ibid., p. 44.

95. Cf. esp. ibid., chap. 4, secs. 36–38.

96. There may be a parallel to Kant's critical reason, which can get only at phenomenona, and his practical reason, which can get at (moral) noumena. And cf. Arthur S. Parsons, *Alfred Schutz and the Foundations of Phenomenological Sociology*, esp. chap. 1, "Egological Consciousness"; and "Constitutive Phenomenology: Schutz's Theory of the We-Relation."

97. It appears to gain support from Schutz's references (in the *Phenomenology of the Social World*) to Simmel's formal sociology and its development by Leopold von Wiese and from two other often recurring but theoretically quite unassimilated elements in Schutz's theory: the notions of "growing older together" (which we have encountered) and "the fundamental anxiety" ("the basic experience of each of us: I know that I shall die and I fear to die": "On Multiple Realities," p. 228, and in many other passages in Schutz's work). The "longing" presently to be mentioned may also be discerned in various papers in "applied theory," such as

"Making Music Together," "Mozart and the Philosophers" (1956), or "Tiresias, or Our Knowledge of Future Events" (1959), in *Collected Papers*, vol. II, pp. 159–78, 179–200, and 277–93

98. Further support comes from Schutz's incorporation of Bergson, next to Husserl and Weber probably the most important figure for his theorizing; the incorporation disregards Bergson's stress on noncognitive elements of intellection.

99. For a historical account of this notion, see Guenther Roth, "'Value-Neutrality' in Germany and the United States," in Reinhard Bendix and Guenther Roth, *Scholarship and Partisanship*, pp. 34–54; as well as Reinhard Bendix, "Changing Foundations of Scholarly Detachment," in Bendix, *Embattled Reason: Essays on Social Knowledge* (New York: Oxford University Press, 1970) pp. 62–92.

100. Cf. Barbara Deck, "Characteristics of Consciousness Falling Asleep," unpublished paper (Waltham, Mass.: Brandeis University, 1969).

101. Such as, e.g., pregnancy and childbirth. Cf. Louise Levesque, *There Is More to Childbirth than Having a Baby*, unpublished Ph.D. dissertation (Waltham, Mass.: Brandeis University, 1977), which contains carefully descriptive chapters on pregnancy and childbirth that are influenced by Schutz's phenomenology. In Schutz's own writing, cf. the papers cited at the end of n. 97, and Simmel's analyses mentioned in n. 228, as well as several contained in Donald N. Levine, ed. and with an introduction, *Georg Simmel On Individuality and Social Forms* (Chicago: University of Chicago Press, 1971), esp. those contained in part III, "Social Types" (The Stranger, The Poor, The Miser and the Spendthrift, The Adventurer ["The Adventure"], and many others, most not translated. [Altogether, Simmel's important phenomenological side awaits study. For beginnings, see James Schmidt, *From Tragedy to Dialectics: The Theoretical Significance of Lukács's Path from Simmel to Marx*, Ph.D. dissertation (Cambridge: Massachusetts Institute of Technology, 1974); and John O'Neill, "How Is Society Possible?" (1970), *Sociology as a Skin Trade*, pp. 167–76, revised as "On Simmel's 'Sociological Apriorities,'" in Psathas, ed., *Phenomenological Sociology*, pp. 91–106. Also see Rudolph H. Weingartner, *Experience and Culture: The Philosophy of Georg Simmel* (Middletown, Conn.: Wesleyan University Press, 1960) pp. 23–28. Karl Mannheim's relation to phenomenology has been analyzed even less. But cf. Paul Kecskemeti, "Introduction" to Mannheim, *Essays on the Sociology of Knowledge*, ed. Kecskemeti (London: Routledge & Kegan Paul, 1952) pp. 8–9 (cf. Wolff, "Introduction: A Reading of Karl Mannheim," *From Karl Mannheim*, p. xxv and n. 15; also the section on Alfred Schutz of this chapter, i.e., the passage to which n. 225 refers, and n. 225); and David Kettler, "Sociology of Knowledge and Moral Philosophy: The Place of Traditional Problems in the Formation of Mannheim's Thought," *Political Science Quarterly*, vol. 82 (September 1967) pp. 399–426, esp. pp. 414 and 420.]

102. Monica B. Morris, *An Excursion into Creative Sociology* (New York: Columbia University Press, 1977). The book performs a welcome service by its reliable expositions of the major components of "creative sociology" and of the critiques that have been advanced against them. Its "demystifying" effort is made in a spirit of reconciliation or mediation, but the study does not represent a sociological analysis of "creative sociology," nor does it claim to do so.

103. Stanford M. Lyman and Marvin B. Scott, *A Sociology of the Absurd* (Pacific Palisades, Cal.: Goodyear Publishing Co., 1970). This book opens thus:

A new wave of thought is beginning to sweep over sociology. Aspects of the wave have been given an assortment of names—"labeling theory," "ethnomethodology," and "new-symbolic interactionism":—but these do not cover its entire range of critique and perspective. A new name must be found to cover a concept which presents not only a unique perspective on conventional sociology but is also a radical departure from the conventional.

We feel an appropriate name is *The Sociology of the Absurd.*

The term "absurd" captures the fundamental assumption of this new wave: *The world is essentially without meaning.*" But since the sociology of the absurd "draws its philosophical inspiration from existentialism and phenomenology" (mainly Husserl, Schutz, and Merleau-Ponty), it might also be called "an existential phenomenology for sociology" (pp. 1, 2).

Animated by a similar outlook is the somewhat earlier *Sociology and Everyday Life*, Marcello Truzzi, ed. (Englewood Cliffs, N.J.: Prentice-Hall, 1968). The affinity of ethnomethodology will become clear in the following section.

104. Berger and Luckmann, *The Social Construction of Reality.*

105. Morris, *An Excursion into Creative Sociology*, p. 4. This contrast must not be confused with that between the objective and subjective approaches mentioned at the end of the section on Phenomenology and Marxism in this chapter (see also n. 64,) even though the two are related. See presently.

106. Morris, *An Excursion into Creative Sociology*, p. 8.

107. "The group of social scientists with whom we shall be concerned in this book has been elsewhere called 'interpretive' ": ibid., p. 8.

108. Cf. end. of the section on Phenomenology and Marxism in this chapter (and n. 67).

109. Cf. n. 65 herein.

110. Cf. Morris, *An Excursion into Creative Sociology*, chap. 1.

111. Followed, thus solidified, by Thomas's *The Unadjusted Girl* (1923), and Thomas and Thomas's *The Child in America* (1928) [cf. Herbert Blumer, *An Appraisal of Thomas and Znaniecki's* The Polish Peasant in Europe and America (New York: Social Science Research Council, 1939)] and by Znaniecki's *The Laws of Social Psychology* (1925), *The Method of Sociology* (1934), *Social Actions* (1936), and *Cultural Sciences: Their Origin and Development* (1952); it seems safe to say, though, that next to and following their common seminal study, Thomas's work has had a far greater impact on the development and shape of American sociology than Znaniecki's.

112. This was not Weber's first work to appear in English but was preceded in 1927 by Frank H. Knight's translation of *General Economic History*, based, like most of Mead's works, on student notes (in this case from a course delivered by Weber in 1919–20). (The work, reprinted by the Free Press in 1950, has long been out-of-print, but is about to be reissued, with a new introduction by Paul Kecskemeti, by Transaction Books.)

113. *The Protestant Ethic* might also have played a role in the development of the much later "psychohistory," but seems not to have. It is interesting that although there is a whole chapter ("Asceticism and Mysticism," pp. 192–230) in Arthur Mitzman's "psychohistorical" study of Max Weber [*The Iron Cage: An Historical Interpretation of Max Weber* (New York: Knopf, 1970)] that deals with *The Protestant Ethic*, Mitzman does not mention it as of potential influence on the type of enterprise his own study is.

114. Once more attention should be called to the imminent publication, in English, of the Schutz-Parsons correspondence, which allows a finely attuned articulation of similarities and differences between—to put it into the present context—two representatives and facets of the subjective approach. (Cf. n. 66 herein.)

115. Goffman's first book (if not his first publication), *The Presentation of Self in Everyday Life*, appeared in 1956 (University of Edinburgh, Social Sciences Research Centre, monograph no. 2) and made him immediately well-known. Garfinkel took much longer, although his publications go back at least as far as 1959 ["Aspects of the Problem of Common-Sense Knowledge of Social Structures," in *Transactions of the Fourth World Congress of Sociology, vol. IV, The Sociology of Knowledge*, ed. Kurt H. Wolff (International Sociological Association, 1959) pp. 51–65].

116. Cf. Edmund Husserl, "Phänomenologie und Anthropologie" (a 1931 lecture), *Philosophy and Phenomenological Research*, vol. 2, no. 1 (1 September 1941) pp. 1–14; English trans. by Richard C. Schmitt, in R. M. Chisholm, ed., *Realism and the Background of Phenomenology* (Glencoe. Ill.: Free Press, 1960) pp. 129–42.

117. Jürgen Habermas. *Zur Logik der Sozialwissenschaften*, *Philosophische Rundschau*, *Beiheft* 5. (February 1967), "Der phänomenologische Ansatz," pp. 98–124.

118. Aaron V. Cicourel, *Method and Measurement in Sociology* (New York: Free Press, 1964).

119. Harold Garfinkel, *The Perception of the Other: A Study in Social Order*, unpublished Ph.D. dissertation (Cambridge: Harvard University, 1952); *A Conception of and Experiment with "Trust" as a Condition of Stable Concerted Action*, ms., 1957 [published as "A Conception of, and Experiments with, 'Trust' as a Condition of Stable Concerted Actions," in O. J. Harvey, ed., *Motivation and Social Interaction: Cognitive Determinants* (New York: Ronald Press, 1963) pp. 187–238].

120. Habermas refers to Erving Goffman's *Asylums: Essays on the Social Situation of Mental Patients and Other Inmates* (Garden City, N.Y.: Doubleday/Anchor, 1961); *Encounters: Two Studies in the Sociology of Interaction* (Indianapolis: Bobbs-Merrill, 1961); *Stigma: Notes on the Management of Spoiled Identity* (Englewood Cliffs, N. J.: Prentice-Hall, 1963); according to Habermas (*Zur Logik der Sozialwissenschaften*, p. 121), Goffman has been the one "actually to make the phenomenologically sharpened view respectable in sociology by means of his brilliant case studies."

121. Habermans, *Zur Logik*, p. 119.

122. Ibid., p. 123.

123. Ibid., pp. 123–24. "Today, the place of the traditional problematic of consciousness has been taken by the problematic of language": ibid., p. 124, the opening sentence of the section on

the linguistic approach (pp. 124–149), presumably Habermas's first publication in an area which he has since developed as "theory of communication."

124. Hans P. Neisser, "The Phenomenological Approach to Social Science," *Philosophy and Phenomenological Research,* vol. 20 (December 1959) pp. 198–212.

125. Neisser must mean *Ideas,* vol. III.

126. Neisser, "The Phenomenological Approach to Social Science," p. 207.

127. See, e.g., Alfred Schutz, "The Problem of Transcendental Intersubjectivity in Husserl" (1957), in Schutz *Collected Papers,* vol. III, pp. 51–84 (with comments by Eugen Fink, pp. 84–86, and Schutz's reply, pp. 87–91.

128. Neisser, "The Phenomenological Approach to Social Services," p. 210. In the following pages, Neisser shows failure to define the eidos, or efforts to present nonphenomenological as phenomenological definitions, of "community" [Edith Stein, *Jahrbuch für Philosophie und phänomenologische Forschung,* vol. V (1922)], "legal claim" [A. Reinach, *Die apriorischen Grundlagen des bürgerlichen Rechts,* vol. I (1913) p. 694] and "economic production" [J. Back, *Die Entwicklung der reinen Oekonomie zur nationalökonomischen Wesenswissenschaft* (1929) p. 189]. (Lest the reader should be misled: Neisser's observations have nothing to do with Alfred Schutz's illustrations, from economics and jurisprudence, of "subjective" and "objective" meaning: Schutz, *Phenomenology of the Social World,* pp. 242–48.)

129. Maurice Natanson, ed., *Phenomenology and the Social Sciences.* In addition to the editor's introduction, the work contains chapters on phenomenology and various social sciences: anthropology (two chapters, by Merleau-Ponty and David Bidney); sociology (two, by Luckmann and Tiryakian); psychology (two, by Kockelmans and Eugene T. Gendlin); linguistics (two, by Ernst Wolfgang Orth and John W. M. Verhaar); history (two, by Gerhard Funke and Donald M. Lowe); political science (three, by Hwa Yol Jung, Carl J. Friedrich, and John G. Gunnell); economics (two, by O'Neill and Murray N. Rothbard); legal theory (three, by Wolfgang Friedmann, Paul Amselek, and Mitchell Franklin). To do justice to this work would require its close study by a number of specialists.

130. Maurice Natanson, "Phenomenology and the Social Sciences," p. 28.

131. Ibid., p. 34.

132. Ibid., p. 28. The quotation is from Alfred Schutz, "Husserl's Importance for the Social Sciences" (1959), *Collected Papers,* vol. I, p. 149.

133. Natanson, "Phenomenology and the Social Sciences." p. 40.

134. Cf. ibid., p. 42.

135. Ibid., p. 43.

136. Ibid., p. 41. (Natanson reminds us that the phrase is part of the title of Husserl's last major work.)

137. Ibid., p. 41.

138. Cf. Heinrich von Kleist, "Essay on the Puppet Theater" (1810), trans. Eugene Jolas, *Partisan Review,* vol. 14 (1947) pp. 67–72; cf. Wolff, "This Is the Time for Radical Anthropology" (1973) in *Trying Sociology,* pp. 441–42.

139. Kleist, "Essay on the Puppet Theater," quoted in Wolff, *Trying Sociology,* p. 442.

140. It may be interesting that in his use of the term "puppet" as a synonym for the social scientist's ideal-types, Schutz nowhere refers to Kleist, whose essay—which is, or at least was for Schutz's generation, well-known in the German literary tradition—he is most likely to have known.

141. Cf. "being" (vs. "leading a life") in Wolff, "Beginning: In Hegel and Today" (1967), *Surrender and Catch,* p. 127.

142. In Husserl, "passive synthesis" is instanced by the "perceptual synthesis" of the various perceptions of the "same thing" (technically, "perceptual noema")—say, a house—that are yielded from various points of view. Cf. Gurwitsch, "The Kantian and Husserlian Conceptions of Consciousness" (1959) *Studies in Phenomenology and Psychology,* esp. p. 154.

143. Natanson, "Phenomenology and the Social Sciences," pp. 32–33.

144. The distinction made by Severyn T. Bruyn in his *Human Perspective in Sociology: The Methodology of Participant Observation* (Englewood Cliffs, N.J.: Prentice-Hall, 1966) between phenomenological and empirical observation (summarized on p. 277) is based on such a view of "empirical." But Bruyn's identification of the former (as well as of "participant observation") with Merton's "serendipity pattern" (pp. 277–78) shows that it actually refers to the difference between a relatively less and a relatively more received or preconceived conception of what is being observed. [On the difference between Husserlian and Weberian essences, with reference to Bruyn, see James L. Heap and Philip A. Roth, "On Phenomenological Sociology," *American Sociological Review,* vol. 38 (June 1973) p. 358.]

145. David Bidney, "Phenomenological Method and the Anthropological Science of the Life-World," in Natanson, ed., *Phenomenology and the Social Sciences,* pp. 109–40.

146. See Edmund Husserl, "Persönliche Aufzeichnungen," ed. Walter Biemel (and Herbert Spiegelberg), *Philosophy and Phenomenological Research,* vol. 16 (March 1956) pp. 292–302; on William James (25 September 1906), 294–95; this passage was translated and reprinted by Herbert Spiegelberg in *The Phenomenological Movement,* vol. 1, p. 114. Also cf. Spiegelberg, "What William James Knew about Edmund Husserl," in Lester E. Embree, ed., *Life-World and Consciousness: Essays for Aron Gurwitsch* (Evanston, Ill.: Northwestern University Press, 1972) pp. 407–22.

147. Bidney, "Phenomenological Method . . ." p. 123.

148. Michael Phillipson, "Phenomenological Philosophy and Sociology," in Paul Filmer, Michael Phillipson, David Silverman, and David Walsh, *New Directions in Sociological Theory* (Cambridge, Mass.: MIT Press, 1972) pp. 119–63.

149. Ibid., p. 146.

150. Ibid., p. 150. Cf. their mention herein.

151. Phillipson, "Phenomenological Philosophy and Sociology," p. 131.

152. Ibid., p. 131. The "simply" is apt to mislead—away from the painstaking difficulty of the reduction—and sounds as if no problem of intersubjectivity were involved. (Cf. Wolff, "The Possibility of Intersubjective Existential Truth," in Beginning: In Hegel and Today," pp. 128–132.)

153. Phillipson, "Phenomenological Philosophy and Sociology," p. 132.

154. David Silverman, "Some Neglected Questions about Social Reality," in Filmer, Phillipson, Silverman, and Walsh, *New Directions in Sociological Theory,* pp. 165–81.

155. Cf. ibid., pp. 167–69. (The last contribution is largely Harold Garfinkel's. See the next section of this chapter.)

156. Cf. ibid., pp. 172–81. Cf. Egon Bittner, "The Concept of Organization," *Social Research* vol. 32 (1965) pp. 230–55.

157. Cf. Aaron V. Cicourel, *Generative Semantics and the Structure of Social Interaction* (Rome: International Days of Sociolinguistics, 1969); Harold Garfinkel and Harvey Sacks, "On formal Structures of Practical Actions," in John C. McKinney and Edward A. Tiryakian, eds. *Theoretical Sociology: Perspectives and Developments* (New York: Appleton-Century-Crofts, 1970) pp. 337–66.

158. George Psathas, ed., *Phenomenological Sociology: Issues and Applications.* The introduction is on pp. 1–21.

159. Ibid., p. 13.

160. Furthermore, as some of the critics of phenomenology (see herein, e.g.,) have argued, there is the danger that the preoccupation with the subjective leads to the neglect of the objective—to the danger of replacing social science by ideology or service to ideology. The presentation of the problems of explicating ordinary "activities of knowing human subjects" and of "the impossibility of full explication" which they entail, however, is carefully and convincingly argued—cf. Psathas, *Phenomenological Sociology,* p. 11.

161. George Psathas and Frances C. Waksler, "Essential Features of Face-to-Face Interaction," in Psathas, ed., *Phenomenological Sociology,* pp. 159–83.

162. Psathas, introduction to *Phenomenological Sociology,* p. 10.

163. Cf. the section on Alfred Schutz herein esp. the paragraph containing n. 96 on page 520), and Schutz, *Phenomenology of the Social World,* pp. 43–44 ("appended [sic] note"), as well as chap. 4, pp. 176–214.

164. Helmut R. Wagner, "The Scope of Phenomenological Sociology: Considerations and Suggestions," in Psathas, *Phenomenological Sociology,* pp. 61–87.

165. Peter L. Berger and Thomas Luckmann, *The Social Construction of Reality.*

166. Wagner, "The Scope of Phenomenological Sociology," p. 70. (See n. 64 herein, and the quotation from Dilthey to which n. 64 refers.)

167. Such as are common and were experimentally induced by Harold Garfinkel (see the next section herein, esp. the passages to which nn. 217 and 218 refer).

168. Above all in one of his most famous papers, "Social Structure and Anomie" (1949) [also see "Continuities in the Theory of Social Structure and Anomie" (1957)], in Merton, *Social Theory and Social Structure,* 1968 enlarged ed., pp. 185–214, 215–48.

169. Egon Bittner, "Objectivity and Realism in Sociology," in Psathas, *Phenomenological Sociology,* pp. 109–25.

170. These are not Bittner's words, but those used in the fifth paragraph of this chapter, and in Wolff, "Sociology and History: Theory and Practice" (1959), in *Trying Sociology,* pp. 292–303,

esp. pp. 292–93.

171. Bittner, "Objectivity and Realism in Sociology," p. 114.

172. Ibid., p. 115. On ethnomethodology, see the next section of this chapter.

173. Bittner, "Objectivity and Realism in Sociology," p. 116.

174. See Wolff, "Ernst Grünwald and the Sociology of Knowledge," p. 593 and n. 5 (pp. 606–07.)

175. See throughout most of Mannheim's writing, especially during his German period, but most poignantly his letter of 1946 reproduced in Wolff, "The Sociology of Knowledge and Sociological Theory" (1959), in *Trying Sociology*, pp. 557–59.

176. Cf. Wolff, "The Unique and the General: Toward a Philosophy of Sociology" (1948), "The Sociology of Knowledge and the Study of Man" (1953), and "The Sociology of Knowledge and Sociological Theory," in *Trying Sociology*, pp. 498–501, 541–42, 561–62.

177. "I use the term 'realism' to refer to the field worker's efforts to discover and describe the full complexity and action import of the features of settings as they are appreciated by persons to whom these settings are the circumstances of their lives. The use is not intended to contain any implications linking it with the old nominalist-realist controversy": Bittner, "Objectivity and Realism in Sociology," p. 125, n. 13. In his pages on fieldwork (117–20), Bittner also pays homage to the Chicago School of the 1920s.

178. Two of them have figured before: Fred R. Dallmayr's "Phenomenology and Marxism" (cf. the passages herein to which nn. 43–46 refer), and John O'Neill's "On Simmel's 'Sociological Priorities' " (see n. 101); another—Peter K. Manning and Horacio Fabrega, Jr., "The Experience of Self and Body: Health and Illness in the Chiapas Highlands"—will figure in the next section (n. 237).

179. Fred R. Dallmayr, "Phenomenology and Social Science: An Overview and Appraisal," in David Carr and Edward S. Casey, eds., *Explorations in Phenomenology* (Papers of the Society for Phenomenology and Existential Philosophy), (The Hague: Nijhoff, 1973) pp. 133–66.

180. Ibid., p. 166.

181. Anthony Giddens, *New Rules of Sociological Method: A Positive Critique of Interpretative Sociologies* (New York: Basic Books, 1976).

182. Ibid., p. 53.

183. Ibid., pp. 159–60.

184. Ibid., pp. 160–62.

185. For informative reviews of Giddens's book, see Aaron V. Cicourel's and Thomas F. Gieryn's, *Contemporary Sociology*, vol. 6 (September 1977) pp. 533–37.

186. Such a distinction is, in fact, questioned by fieldwork, and by much of the literature on it, because of the problem of the student's "involvement" in the fellow human beings he or she more or less directly studies. [One of its most cogent presentations is found in George Devereux, *From Anxiety to Method in the Behavorial Sciences* (New York: Humanities Press, 1967).]

187. Cf. Karl Mannheim, "The Ideological and the Sociological Interpretation of Intellectual Phenomena."

188. Toward the end of the third section of this chapter, and see n. 63.

189. Heap and Roth, "On Phenomenological Sociology"; Burkart Holzner, "Comments on Heap and Roth 'On Phenomenology,' " *American Sociological Review*, vol. 39 (April 1964) pp. 286–89; James L. Heap, "Reply to Holzner," ibid., pp. 289–91.

190. Edward Tiryakian, "Existential Phenomenology and Sociology"; Jack Douglas, "Understanding Everyday Life," in Douglas, ed., *Understanding Everyday Life: Toward the Reconstruction of Sociological Knowledge* (Chicago: Aldine, 1970) pp. 3–44; Severyn Bruyn, *The Human Perspective in Sociology*.

191. Alfred Schutz, "Husserl's Importance for the Social Sciences" (1959).

192. Heap and Roth, "On Phenomenological Sociology," p. 361.

193. Ibid., p. 363.

194. Heap and Roth quote from Maurice Natanson, "A Study in Philosophy and the Social Sciences" (1958), in *Literature, Philosophy and the Social Sciences: Essays in Existentialism and Phenomenology* (The Hague: Nijhoff, 1962) pp. 155–77; the reference is to p. 165.

195. Berger and Luckmann, *The Social Construction of Reality;* Burkart Holzner, *Reality Construction in Society*.

196. Heap and Roth, "On Phenomenological Sociology," p. 362. The reference is to Alvin W. Gouldner, *The Coming Crisis of Western Sociology*.

197. Aaron V. Cicourel, *The Social Organization of Juvenille Justice* (New York: Wiley, 1968).

198. Heap and Roth, "On Phenomenological Sociology," p. 363.

199. Ibid. The reference is to Harold Garfinkel, *Studies in Ethnomethodology* (Englewood Cliffs, N.J.: Prentice-Hall, 1967); D. Lawrence Wieder, "On Meaning by Rule," pp. 107–35, and Don H. Zimmerman and Melvin Pollner, "The Everyday World as a Phenomenon," pp. 80–103, in Douglas, ed., *Understanding Everyday Life*.

200. Heap and Roth, "On Phenomenological Sociology," p. 364.

201. Holzner, "Comments on Heap and Roth 'On Phenomenology,' " p. 286.

202. Ibid., p. 287.

203. See esp. ibid., p. 288.

204. Heap's reference is to Aron Gurwitsch, "An Apparent Paradox in Leibnizianism," *Social Research*, vol. 33 (Spring 1966) pp. 47–64, esp. p. 47.

205. Cf. Heap, "Reply to Holzner," pp. 290–91.

206. The literature on the history of modern reason is considerable. See esp. Max Horkheimer, *Eclipse of Reason* (New York: Oxford University Press, 1947); and Reinhard Bendix, *Social Science and the Distrust of Reason* (Berkeley: University of California Press, 1951), and "Sociology and the Distrust of Reason" (1970), in Bendix and Roth, *Scholarship and Partisanship*, pp. 84–105; but also the undeservedly neglected *Tyranny of Progress: Reflections on the Origins of Sociology* (New York: Noonday Press, 1955) by Albert Salomon; and the recent *Enlightenment and Despair: A History of Sociology* (Cambridge: Cambridge University Press, 1976) by Geoffrey Hawthorn.

207. For Scheler, this applies only to his work in the sociology of knowledge, not to his work in ethics—which, however, he did not connect with the former such as to modify the problem of relativism.

208. Harold Garfinkel, "The Origin of the Term 'Ethnomethodology' " (1968), in Roy Turner, ed., *Ethnomethodology: Selected Readings*, Penquin Books, 1974, pp. 16–17. (The quotation is from pp. 5–11 of the source cited in the following note).

209. Harold Garfinkel in Richard J. Hill and Kathleen Stones Crittenden, eds., *Proceedings of the Purdue Symposium on Ethnomethodology* (Fayetteville, Ind.: Purdue Research Foundation, 1968) p. 3.

210. Ibid., p. 12. Eight years later, Garfinkel defined the concern of ethnomethodology as "materially grounded tasks of discovering the identifying issues of the problem of social order." Gisela J. Hinkle, chairperson of the panel on "When Is Phenomenology Sociological?" (1976), in *The Annals of Phenomenological Sociology*, vol. II (1977) p. 12.

211. See *Purdue Symposium*, pp. 140–41.

212. Harold Garfinkel, *Studies in Ethnomethodology*, p. 1.

213. Harold Garfinkel and Harvey Sacks, "On Formal Structures of Practical Actions," in John C. McKinney and Edward A. Tiryakian, eds., *Theoretical Sociology: Perspectives and Developments*, pp. 337–66.

214. Ibid., p. 345.

215. Ibid., p. 345.

216. *Purdue Symposium*, pp. 65, 66.

217. Harold Garfinkel, "Studies of the Routine Grounds of Everyday Activities" (1964), in David Sudnow, ed., *Studies in Social Interaction*, pp. 6, 7, 12, 17, 24, 27, 27.

218. Ibid., pp. 9, 13, 20. See a similar experiment in Peter McHugh, *Defining The Situation: The Organization of Meaning in Social Interaction* (Indianapolis and New York: Bobbs-Merrill, 1968) pp. 93–99.

219. Alvin Gouldner, *The Coming Crisis of Western Sociology* (New York, London: Basic Books, 1970) p. 393.

220. A related formulation is provided by Howard Brotz in "Theory and Practice: Ethnomethodology versus Humane Ethnography" (an extended review of Roy Turner, ed., *Ethnomethodology: Selected Readings*), *Jewish Journal of Sociology*, vol. 16 (December 1974), pp. 225–236, esp. 229.

221. Peter McHugh, *Defining the Situation*, p. 13. Or Don H. Zimmerman and Melvin Pollner, "The Everyday World as a Phenomenon," p. 83: "We propose to suspend conventional interest in the topics of members' practical investigations and urge the placing of exclusive emphasis on inquiry into practical investigations themselves, lay or professional. The topic then would consist not in the social order as ordinarily conceived, but rather in the ways in which members assemble particular scenes so as to provide for one another evidences of a social order as-ordinarily-conceived." and p. 95: "Thus, instead of an ethnography that inventories a setting's distinctive, substantive features, the research vehicle envisioned here is a *methodography* (to borrow Butcher's term) . . . that searches for the practices through which those substantive features are made observable."

222. Kurt H. Wolff, "Ernst Grünwald and the Sociology of Knowledge: A Collective Venture in Interpretation" (1965), in Wolff, *Trying Sociology,* p. 604. (Interestingly enough, H. Stuart Hughes makes a similar observation, though not using the terms used here, with regard to Ludwig Wittgenstein in *The Sea Change: The Migration of Social Thought, 1930–1965* (1975) (McGraw-Hill Paperback, 1977) pp. 59–62.

223. Cf. Wolff, *Trying Sociology,* pp. 604–06.

224. In this struggle, Weber passionately warned against false satisfactions: "And if Tolstoi's question recurs to you: as science does not, who is to answer the question: 'What shall we do, and, how shall we arrange our lives?' . . . then one can say that only a prophet or a savior can give the answers. . . . [But] The inward interest of a truly religiously 'musical' man can never be served by veiling to him and to others the fundamental fact that he is destined to live in a godless and prophetless time by giving him the *ersatz* of armchair prophecy": Max Weber, "Science as a Vocation" (1918), in *From Max Weber: Essays in Sociology,* trans., ed., and with an introduction by H. Gerth and C. Wright Mills (New York: Oxford University Press, 1946) pp. 152–53.

225. Harold Garfinkel, "Common Sense Knowledge of Social Structures: The Documentary Method of Interpretation in Lay and Professional Fact Finding" (1962), in *Studies in Ethnomethodology,* p. 78; Karl Mannheim, "On the Interpretation of '*Weltanschauung*' " (1921–22), trans. Paul Kecskemeti, in Mannheim, *Essays on the Sociology of Knowledge,* p. 57; Hans Peter Dreitzel, "Introduction: Patterns of Communicative Behavior," in Dreitzel, ed., *Recent Sociology No. 2: Patterns of Communicative Behavior,* (New York: Macmillan, 1970) p. xiv.

226. A few expressions of "no world" from only two sources may be found in McHugh, *Defining the Situation,* pp. 28, 43, and 53–54, and Peter McHugh, Stanley Raffel, Daniel C. Foss, and Alan F. Blum, *On the Beginning of Social Inquiry,* (London and Boston: Routledge & Kegan Paul, 1974) pp. 17, 26, 32, 34 (but see also pp. 8, 10, 12, 21, 25, 31, 33, 62, 182). Hugh Mehan and Houston Wood show an even more extreme lack of a world (and an epistemological unconcern in their panegyrical *The Reality of Ethnomethodology* (New York: Wiley, 1975), see esp. pp. 3, 114, 159, 216, 238. (It should be remembered that Garfinkel emphatically said that ethnomethodology is "not a cult"; he would undoubtedly disagree with a good many of Mehan and Wood's views and claims.)

227. See, e.g., *Purdue Symposium,* pp. 140–41, 255; Lewis A. Coser, "Two Methods in Search of a Substance," *American Sociological Review,* vol. 40, no. 6 (December 1975) pp. 691–700, esp. p. 698; but for rejoinders to Coser's overall attack on ethnomethodology, see Don H. Zimmerman, "A Reply to Professor Coser," *American Sociologist,* vol. 11, no. 1 (February 1976) pp. 4–13; Hugh Mehan and Houston Wood, "De-secting Ethnomethodology," ibid., pp. 13–21; and Helmut R. Wagner, "An Anti-Ethnomethodological Address," *Phenomenological Sociology Newsletter,* vol. 4, no. 2 (February 1976) pp. 3–5.

228. Georg Simmel, "The Ruin" (1911), trans. David Kettler, "The Handle" (1911), trans. Rudolph H. Weingartner, in Kurt H. Wolff, ed., *Georg Simmel, 1858-1918: A Collection of Essays, with Translations and a Bibliography* (Columbus: Ohio State University Press, 1959) pp. 259–66, 267–75.

229. Our topics being common, perhaps one could say that Simmel's resources also are his topics (in the terms used by Zimmerman and Pollner, "The Everyday World as a Phenomenon," p. 81, where they criticize traditional sociology for "confounding" the two).

230. "By 'cultural dope' I refer to the man-in-the-sociologist's-society who produces the stable features of the society by acting in compliance with preestablished and legitimate alternatives of action that the common culture provides. The 'psychological dope' is the man-in-the-psychologist's-society . . . [who does so] by choices among alternative courses of action that are compelled on the grounds of psychiatric biography, conditioning history, and the variables of mental functioning": Garfinkel, "Studies of the Routine Grounds of Everyday Activities," p. 24.

231. Ibid., p. 24.

232. These terms and their substantival forms, "achievement," "accomplishment," and the like, abound in the literature of ethnomethodology; e.g.—to use only one source—Melvin Pollner, quoting Garfinkel, in Roy Turner, ed., *Ethnomethodology: Selected Readings,* p. 27; Egon Bittner, ibid., p. 78 (here it is "skill and craftmanship"); Kenneth Stoddart, ibid., p. 174; Emmanuel Schegloff and Harvey Sacks, ibid., pp. 234, 236, 237, 238, 242, 252, 262; A. Lincoln Ryave and James N. Schenklein, ibid., pp. 265, 270.

233. Rainer Maria Rilke, "Der Panther (Im Jardin des Plantes, Paris)." I owe a reminder of its aptness here to Hans Mohr. It might be translated, roughly: "He feels as if there are a thousand bars/And back of a thousand bars no world." (Is there a connection between this cage and Max Weber's "Iron cage"? But unlike the late Puritan or Max Weber himself, who must carry his "iron cage," the panther's is a bit roomier: he paces round and round inside the thousand bars.)

234. To mention some which are readily available in collections of readings: in Douglas, ed., *Understanding Everyday Life,* the papers by Aron V. Cicourel [whose work, which has tended to move away from its beginnings in ethnomethodology, cannot be assessed here—see, particularly, from *Method and Measurement in Sociology* (1964), to *Cognitive Sociology* (1974) and Roy Turner; in Sudnow, ed., *Studies in Social Interaction,* the chapter by Cicourel; in Psathas, ed., *Phenomenological Sociology,* the contributions by Egon Bittner, and Peter K. Manning and Horacio Fabrega, Jr.; and in Turner, ed., *Ethnomethodology,* once more the pages by Cicourel. In addition, the following might be mentioned here: Egon Bittner, "Radicalism and the Organization of Radical Movements," *American Sociological Review,* vol. 28 (1963) pp. 928–40; "The Concept of Organization," *Social Research,* vol. 32 (1965) pp. 230–55; "The Police on Skid Row: A Study of Peace Keeping," *American Sociological Review,* vol. 32 (1967) pp. 699–715; "Radicalism," *International Encyclopedia of the Social Sciences* vol. 13 (1968) pp. 294–300; "Policing Juveniles: The Social Bases of Common Practice," in M. Rosenheim, ed., *Justice for the Child, Revisited* (Chicago: University of Chicago Press, 1975) pp. 69–93 (The nature and extent of the influence of ethnomethodology on Bittner's writing is often not clear); David Sudnow, *Passing On: The Social Organization of Dying* (Englewood Cliffs, N.J.: Prentice-Hall, 1967).]

For some commentaries on ethnomethodology: Review symposium on Harold Garfinkel, *Studies in Ethnomethodology* (James S. Coleman et al.), *American Sociological Review,* vol. 33 (February 1968) pp. 122–30, and Marvin Israel's comment, *American Sociologist,* vol. 4 (November 1969) pp. 333–34; George Psathas, "Ethnomethods and Phenomenology," *Social Research,* vol. 35 (Autumn 1968) pp. 500–20; Maurice Natanson, "Phenomenology and Social Role" (1972), in Natanson, *Phenomenology, Role, and Reason: Essays on the Coherence and Deformation of Social Reality* (Springfield, Ill.: Thomas, 1974) pp. 190–214, esp. pp. 203–06; Alvin W. Gouldner, "Sociology and the Everyday Life," in Lewis A. Coser, ed., *The Idea of Social Structure: Papers in Honor of Robert K. Merton* (New York: Harcourt Brace Jovanovich, 1975) pp. 417–32 (this is rather different in tone from Gouldner's earlier comments on ethnomethodology—cf. quotation to which n. 219 refers). The critical potential of ethnomethodology can be analyzed here as little as its substantive merits; the first topic is broached in interesting fashion by Dreitzel in his "Introduction: Patterns of Communicative Behavior," pp. xix–xxi.

235. Althought not exclusively: thus there is a recent anthology in German (which also includes related materials): Arbeitsgruppe Bielefelder Soziologen, eds., *Alltagswissen, Interaktion und gesellschaftliche Wirklichkeit,* vol. 1, *Symbolischer Interaktionismus und Ethnomethodologie;* vol. 2, *Ethnotheorie und Ethnographie des Sprechens* (Hamburg: Rowohlt, 1973; most of the material is translated from English (by the editors).

236. Natanson, "Phenomenology and Social Role," pp. 205–06.

237. It is the direction of "surrender and catch" (cf. Wolff, *Surrender and Catch*).

14

STRUCTURALISM

TOM BOTTOMORE AND ROBERT NISBET

STRUCTURAL INQUIRY in the social sciences and related areas as we know it today has deep roots in the history of Western thought. To discover the fundamental, constitutive, *structures* into which the sensory data of human observation and experience fall: this was a cardinal objective of the ancient Greeks, to go back no farther in time.[1] The Greek root of our word "idea" refers to pattern, configuration, or structure. When we speak of Plato's doctrine of Ideas, we might better speak of his doctrine of Forms, for this is precisely what they were. Granted that these were ideal, even heavenly entities in Plato's philosophy, it remains true, as Cornford has stressed, that Plato was also a cosmologist, keenly interested in the nature of the actual, empirical world, social as well as physical; and in Plato's cosmology there is a profound sense of reality as being constituted by not discrete data but shapes and forms mathematical in character.[2]

Nor was Plato's student and apostate Aristotle any less interested in structures. As all interpreters of Aristotle have stressed, it is the *organism,* and with it *growth,* that dominates Aristotle's mind as the fundamental model of structure. Organismic structure is, indeed, one of the very oldest and most persistent models to be found in Western philosophy and science. From Aristotle's day to our own, with scarcely any lapses, the philosophy of organism has been an influential one: sometimes with emphasis on the more static aspects, as in anatomy, but other times on the dynamic elements which are found to be constitutive, as in physiological processes, including growth. Structuralism, as we shall emphasize in this chapter, can be static in character, or it can be genetic and dynamic. In each instance the aim is ascertainment of the crucial patterns or shapes, whether at a given moment or over a period of time.[3]

Rivaling the purely organismic model of structure have been at least two others: the mathematical and the mechanical. Very probably the first is at least as old as the organismic. The ancient, pre-Socratic Pythagorean school of philosophy sought to demonstrate that reality is mathematical—that is, formed by irreducible geometrical patterns. As we know, the Pythagorean philosophy exerted great influence upon Plato, and much of his own cosmology consists of efforts to refine the Pythagorean view of the geometric structures which constitute the real. The notion that reality is ultimately mathematical in character is of course a very strong one at the present time. Underlying the notion is interest in the relationships, the connections, within which we find primal elements of matter and energy.[4]

The mechanical conception of structure, although also very old, enjoyed a renascence in the sixteenth and seventeenth centuries, the result in considerable degree of the influence on all thought of such physical philosophers as Kepler, Galileo, and Newton.[5] It was almost inevitable, given the great renown of these and other minds engaged in the search for laws, systems, and structures in the physical world, that the kind of systems and structures they set forth in astronomy, physics, and mechanics should have excited the interests of those concerned primarily with man and society. To see society as a great machine with patterns of equilibrium, action and reaction, and relationship of parts to the whole was tempting indeed, as so many of the ventures in "social physics" or "social mechanics" in the eighteenth century make evident. As with biology and the model of the organism, mechanics and its model of the machine provided both a statics and a dynamics.

Brief as the foregoing discussion is, it will suffice to impress upon the reader that structuralism in sociology and related disciplines has a long history insofar as its fundamental premises are concerned. As Raymond Williams has written: "We need to know this history if we are to understand the important and difficult development of *structural* and later *structuralist* as defining terms in the human sciences. . . ."[6] There are several major, and different, conceptions of structure to be found in the social sciences of the nineteenth and twentieth century, but at the roots of all of them lie in one relation or other the biological, mathematical, and mechanical models of reality which have exerted strong effect upon so many spheres of knowledge over the past several millennia in the West.

At the present time definitions and descriptions of structuralism are legion. They are to be found in the fields of literature, linguistics, art criticism, social anthropology, philosophy, psychology, and, of course, sociology. Unfortunately amid this number and diversity of conceptions a cultlike atmosphere, or rather a multiplicity of such cultatmospheres is to be found making even more difficult the problem of dealing historically with our subject.[7]

Our concern in this chapter will be largely sociological, and we shall hold to a simple but accurate and historically justifiable definition of structuralism as it is found in sociological and social-anthropological writing: "The relation is more important than the parts." There is much more than can be said, that will in appropriate context be said here, about sociological structuralism, but the gist is nevertheless contained in that brief definition.

It is our view that sociological structuralism arose in the works of Auguste Comte in France and Karl Marx in Germany. In France the preeminent *sociological* structuralist has been Emile Durkheim.[8] It is indeed in light of Durkheim's broad influence, extending beyond sociology, that we depart in some measure from a purely sociological canvas and turn to the social anthropologists A. R. Radcliffe-Brown and Claude Lévi-Strauss and also to the social psychologist Jean Piaget. For in one or other degree all three of these major figures were strongly influenced by Durkheim and his school. And just as they were influenced by Durkheim's sociology, so, in our own day, is sociology showing increasing marks of the thought of these three men. Such are the benefits of cross-disciplinary research!

French Structuralism

Auguste Comte (1798–1857) Although Comte's extraordinary and complex mind is properly regarded as the first systematic as well as self-styled sociologist, it would be negligent to deal with Comte without indicating immediately the profound influence that was exerted upon him by Saint-Simon (1760–1825). The researches of Henri Gouhier, among others, have established clearly the measure of Saint-Simon's contributions to Comte, although Comte himself was reluctant, to say the least, to acknowledge these contributions. Suffice it to say that well before Comte had even published his essays of the 1820s, Saint-Simon had, in article and book, set forth the most fundamental elements of systems theory, and his own structuralist bent of thought may be seen as easily in his philosophy of social development, where "organic" periods alternate with "critical" ages, as in his equilibrial approach to economy and society.

Nevertheless, this said, we begin with Comte. His entire sociology was built around the priority of relationships to individuals.

"According to a principle of general philosophy laid down in my Positive Philosophy," Comte writes in his *Positive Polity,* "a system can only be formed out of units similar to itself and differing only in magnitude. A *society* therefore can no more be decomposed into *individuals* than a geometric surface can be resolved into lines, or a line into points."[9] In a host of ways Comte exemplifies this general theory—including his treatments of family, government, city, and, not least, language. His chapter on the character and function of language in society is surprisingly acute in its distinctions among signs, symbols, and the like, and in their relation to the social order. Comte saw clearly the interactive relation between language and the social order. "The structure of language . . . is a matter of gradual development as the relations of society tend to improve, in the evolution and transformation of the collective activities of man." And it could be Piaget in our own century, rather than Comte, who wrote the following: "The essential laws of language are indeed much better observed by children, as they are by people, than they are by the great majority of philosophers. . . ."[10]

During the century following Comte's work, there would take place a somewhat more individualized, purely mental conception of structure than we find in Comte. This becomes the case especially after Durkheim. The social and presocial become fused; there is widening regard for unconscious as well as conscious forms in society and culture. What begins in Comte as a concern almost totally restricted to the "Grand Being," society—but also to the elemental structures, statical and dynamical, which Comte conceives as being conceptually antecedent to individuals—becomes in time less rigorously deterministic, more concerned with the interaction of the social or structural and the individual. But it would be grossly unjust to deprive Comte of his position as the first systematic structural thinker in French sociology.

His consuming antipathy is conceptual atomism or individualism in any form. What Comte refers to pejoratively as "metaphysical" thinking in the seventeenth and eighteenth centuries is at bottom the atomistic individualism along with the psychological associationism of the Age of Reason and the Enlightenment. His chief reason for the long treatment of the "hierarchy" and the "filiation" of the sciences given in *The Positive Philosophy* is to demonstrate that each science flows historically in structure and aims from its predecessor. "Social physics," or, as Comte came to call it, "sociology," is no exception.[11] It will possess a statics and a dynamics, each a means of structural analysis, just as each of the other sciences has.

Despite Comte's scientific (and in time religious) veneration for humanity or society as a whole, he was very much concerned with the smaller, component systems and structures which form the larger entity. This proved seminal in due time in France. We need only read Comte in detail on the inherently and irreducibly social character of the human mind, of language, of knowledge, as well as of family, marriage, and religion, to understand the influence Comte was to exert upon the greatest of the modern French structuralists, Durkheim. We shall come to Durkheim shortly. It is important to examine Comte somewhat more closely, for his influence upon not only the whole French tradition of sociology but that of England and in some degree Germany proved to be substantial.

We may go back to Comte's first work, *The Positive Philosophy*, for delineation of the statical and dynamical aspects of his structural inquiry. "Our real business," he writes, "is to analyze accurately the circumstances of phenomena *and to connect them by the natural relations of succession and resemblance* [italics added]." Relations of resemblance are the constitutive objects of what Comte called "statical" study.[12]

The statical study of sociology consists in the investigation of the laws of action and reaction of the different parts of the social system—apart, for the occasion, from the fundamental movement which is always gradually modifying them. . . . This view condemns the existing philosophical practice of contemplating social elements separately, as if they had an independent existence; it leads us to regard them as in mutual relation, and forming a whole which compels us to treat them in combination.[13]

"No social fact," he continues, "can have any scientific meaning till it is connected with some other social fact; with which connection it remains a mere anecdote, involving no rational utility."[14] The whole point of Comte's long and detailed account of the development of the sciences, commencing with astronomy among the ancients, is to show the logical emergence of each of the sciences—astronomy, physics, chemistry, and biology—over a three-thousand-year period, each successive science incorporating in itself the fundamental structural features of thought to be found in its predecessor, and thus be able to demonstrate what the character of a social physics or sociology must be in his own day.

All sciences, he notes, are divisible into a statics and a dynamics, and sociology is no exception. The great failure of social philosophies thus far has been their inability to combine into one general theory the laws of statics and the laws of dynamics—that is, evolution or progress. "The misfortune of our actual state is that the two ideas are set up in radical opposition to each other. . . ."[15] But the mission of Positivism will be that of demonstrating scientifically that there is no such opposition, that statics and dynamics are but two distinguishable modes of seeing the same thing: society in motion, but *structurally* in motion.

Social statics reveals to us the mechanics of solidarity, the connections, resemblances, and irreducibly social relationships in which human beings are always found in one kind of society or other. It is, Comte writes, when we turn to social dynamics that we see how in every form of social relationship there are the mechanisms for the emergence of other and higher forms of relationship. "The true spirit of social dynamics then consists in conceiving of each of these consecutive social states as the necessary result of the preceding, and the indispensable mover of the following, according to the axiom of Leibniz,—*the present is big with the future.*"[16]

What this means, obviously, is that within the "connections" and "resemblances" which social statics studies in human society there are motivations toward, and mechanisms of, the emergence of new forms of social order from the old. The normal condition of any society, in Comte's terms, is a *dynamic* condition. As he has told us, even though social order is the purpose of progress, there is always movement, and statics is simply a means of studying the nature of order while one *conceptually* suspends change, so to speak.

The structural nature of Comte's dynamics may best be observed in his famous "law of three states." History for Comte, despite its endless wealth of concrete detail, is ordered movement in time that may be charted as accurately as any movement of a physical or biological kind. "The function of sociology is to derive from the mass of unconnected material, information which, by the principles of the biological theory of man, may yield the laws of social life; each portion of this material being carefully prepared by stripping off from it whatever is peculiar or irrelevant—all circumstances, for instance, of climate locality, etc.—in order to transfer it from the concrete to the abstract."[17]

It is an abstract and generalized structuralism that Comte seeks in man's past and present. What he gives us its a law of three states—or periods or epochs. It is the nature of civilization to develop from a first period characterized by theological modes of thought to a second dominated by philosophical or "metaphysical" forms of thinking and eventually to the third stage where science, or Positive thinking, takes command. Moreover, it is the nature of social, in contrast to intellectual, development to move, in the same ordered sequence, from the "military" to the "feudal" to the "industrial-scientific." Not only do we see this structured movement in time in the large entity "civilization," but we see it in smaller unities: for example, each of the distinct bodies or spheres of thought. Physics passes from the theological through the metaphysical to the scientific; so does each of the other sciences. Finally, as one more indication of the systematic-structural approach Comte takes toward his subject matter, he stresses the marginal nature of each propulsion forward in the sciences. That is, *only* when the "lower" discipline in the hierarchy of knowledge attains positive or scientific status is it possible for the next higher discipline to become scientific in the true sense. Physics must reach the level of science before chemistry can become liberated from theological or metaphysical status; the same is true for biology and then, capping the hierarchy of sciences, sociology. The larger evolution of thought which underlies the evolution of society depends upon the separate evolutions of the several disciplines which together make up mankind's knowledge. Comte regarded his theory of evolution as the final systematization of the whole problem of order and change.

> It certainly appears to me that the whole course of human history affords so decisive a verification of my theory of evolution that no essential law of natural philosophy is more thoroughly documented. From the earliest beginnings . . . to the most advanced nations, this theory has explained, consistently and dispassionately, the character of all the great phases of humanity, . . . their precise filiation; so as to introduce perfect unity and rigorous continuity into this vast spectacle which otherwise appears altogether desultory and confused.[18]

No one ever worshiped system and structure more than Auguste Comte!

Giambattista Vico (1668-1744) It will no doubt seem strange for Vico's name to appear, not only under the heading of French structuralism but in the context of the nineteenth century. He was, after all, an Italian who wrote in the eighteenth century. His most famous work, *New Science,* was first published in 1725. But the fact remains that Vico was almost totally ignored in his own age. His deep opposition to Cartesianism in all its aspects helped him achieve that status. His book fell dead from the press upon publication, and even successive editions hardly helped his cause. Few minds have ever been as alien to their respective ages as was Vico. As Isaiah Berlin has written:

"No one understood the full originality of Vico in his lifetime or for nearly a century after his death, not even those few who actually read him."[19]

It was in the nineteenth century, and in France, that Vico finally acquired the luster that had been denied him during his life. The eminent French historian Michelet, having come upon Vico's writings in Italy in the 1820s, was so deeply impressed by them that he gave Vico a Newtonlike status. His full tribute to Vico appeared in the preface he wrote for his monumental *History of the Roman Republic*, which came out just as Comte's *Positive Philosophy* was making its appearance in France. In 1844 a French translation of *The New Science* was published, and this spread rapidly throughout Europe.

The fact is that Vico was critical of almost every major idea of his own time, starting with Cartesianism; and the equally unchallengeable truth, strange though it may seem, is that his own ideas are decidedly nineteenth century in character and thrust. It would be very hard indeed to find a mind in the nineteenth century more adapted to prevailing intellectual interests than Vico's. The nineteenth century's keen interests in social development, social origins, the conversion of conventional history and philosophy into a *science* of society, and the systematic effort to find rational-empirical causes to supplant those of theological or metaphysical nature—all these are clearly and forcefully adumbrated by Vico in his early-eighteenth-century work. The extent to which Vico actually stimulated or crucially influenced any of the greater figures of the nineteenth century is a matter for continuing scholarly investigation, but of the respect in which Vico was held throughout the nineteenth century—by minds as diverse as Michelet, Marx, Dilthey, Croce, and Sorel—there is no doubt.[20] For all the disorder of thought, the murkiness of style, and the fragmentary character of so much in Vico's *New Science*, it is nevertheless an extraordinary achievement for any age, and the more so for the age in which it was written, an age so largely governed by persisting ideas of medieval theology on the one hand and of natural law and Cartesianism on the other.

There are many areas of nineteenth-century thought within which Vico can be, and has been, considered. We shall confine ourselves here to Vico's structuralism; a form of inquiry every bit as distinct in his work as in any other figure of the nineteenth century. Moreover, as Edmund Leach has shown convincingly, there are interesting parallels between Vico and Lévi-Strauss (whom we shall come to later in the chapter) even though there is no evidence that Lévi-Strauss was ever directly influenced by Vico, as he was for example by Durkheim and especially Durkheim's student Mauss.[21]

There are several respects in which *New Science* may be seen as an expression of structural inquiry. First, in the early part of the book, there is the striking effort to find *recurrent patterns or structures* of events as these may be empirically inferred from the actual, concrete histories of a considerable number of peoples.[22] Vico's plea for, at one and the same time, an abandonment of conventional, unilinear historiography in which a great diversity of places and events is compressed into a unitary framework, and the subjection of historical materials to the comparative-empirical procedures of science rather than to the deductive, geometrylike propositions of Descartes, was not again to be seen in Western writing until George Cornewall Lewis's *Treatise on Methods of Observation*, a work that specifically cites Vico as forebear, appeared in England in 1851. In Vico's time—and later, for that matter—it was thought that similarities (what Comte was to call "connections" and "resemblances") in the human race were to be explained by a single origin of mankind. Vico disputes this, declaring that such similarities of belief and practice are perfectly reconcilable with polygenesis; that they bespeak instead certain embedded, if flexible, capacities in the human mind everywhere; and that when these capacities are challenged by more or less identical geographical, social, or economic stimuli, the results tend to be analogous.

A second structural aspect to Vico's thought, and one highly congenial to nineteenth-century interests, is the effort in *New Science* to discern the principal, and recurring, stages or phases through which peoples' histories tend to pass.[23] Not from any deistic or cosmic principle do these common stages emerge, but rather from the nature of the human mind—very much the same everywhere—and from the relation between mind and institutions. It is difficult to say whether Vico is more nearly a social or psychological thinker in his treatment of this relation. He can write in several contexts that institutions are ultimately the determinants of men's mental conceptions ("unable to attain all the utilities he wishes, he [man] is constrained by these institutions to seek those which are his due"), but Vico can also, as Werner Stark has emphasized, stress the intramental and its presocial, preinstitutional forces and patterns.[24] The essential point here is simply Vico's effort to combine the intramental and the extramental in patterns, the recurrence of which in human history should be the starting point for the science of mankind.

This takes us to a third and closely related use of the structural mode of inquiry, and one, as Edmund Leach suggests, very close to the structuralism of Lévi-Strauss. Like Lévi-Strauss, Vico was very much interested in mythology and the poetic imagination as these have affected the development of culture and human consciousness. Vico's general philosophy of history proceeded from his conviction that mankind and each of its peoples passes through, in order, an age of gods, an age of heroes, and finally an age of man. Vico's interest in myth came from his desire to uncover, as empirically as possible—and in strict contrast to Cartesian deduction—the primal nature of the human mind.

When we today "wish to give utterance to our understanding of spiritual things, we must seek aid from our imagination to explain them, and, like painters, form human images of them." But, Vico continues, it was very different at the beginning. Then, "theological poets, unable to make use of the understanding, did the opposite and more sublime thing: they attributed senses and passions . . . to bodies, and to bodies as vast as sky, sea, and earth.

Later as these vast imaginations shrank and the power of abstraction grew, the personifications were reduced to diminutive signs. . . ."

Vico understood fully the propensity of human beings, in modern as well as ancient times, to use the human body metaphorically. "It is noteworthy that in all known languages, the greater part of the expressions relating to inanimate things is formed by metaphor from the human body and its parts and from the human senses and passions. . . . All of which is a consequence of our axiom that wherever man is lost in ignorance he makes himself the measure of all things. Where rational metaphysics teaches that man becomes all things by understanding them, . . . this imaginative metaphysics shows that man becomes all things by *not* understanding them."[25]

There were many philologists, students of legend and folklore, and others in the nineteenth century for whom myth was a kind of "disease of language," without real roots in the human mind and its associations—more the consequence of linguistic confusion than of actual ratiocinative process. In these explanations of myth, the earliest human beings were like children—prelogical, prerational, and naturally given to a kind of nonsense.

But, as the passages just quoted make clear, Vico, early in the eighteenth century, had already reached a perspective that is very different from such explanations. It was Vico's merit to realize, in Edmund Leach's words, "that mythical stories do not exist as isolate units but as sets, and that the elements in the units of a set must somehow fit together."[26] The relation of all this to Lévi-Strauss is probably evident to all who have read this complex anthropologist with any care. As we know, Lévi-Strauss's avowedly structural interpretation of mythology and of other systems, including kinship, has its point of departure in linguistics. The structure of spoken languages gives Lévi-Strauss a kind of model from which he can move to other areas of culture. As Leach observes, the equivalent model for Vico was his interest in etymology, "which owed more to a vivid imagination than to sound knowledge of the facts, but which, even so, provided him with the wherewithal for many very shrewd observations."[27]

Emile Durkheim (1858–1917) Excepting only Comte (from whom Durkheim learned so much), Durkheim is France's preeminent sociologist, and he must also be regarded—at least prior to Lévi-Strauss—as the preeminent structuralist in French sociological thought. Different as Lévi-Strauss's structural analysis is from Durkheim's, Lévi-Strauss has never been other than outspoken in his admiration for Durkheim and in his declared indebtedness to not only Durkheim himself but to Durkheim's students, high among them Marcel Mauss and Maurice Halbwachs.[28]

There is no better way of introducing Durkheim's structural perspective than with a brief passage taken from an essay Durkheim wrote in 1900, "Sociology and Its Scientific Field." He is indicating the difficulty of making a sharp distinction between "statics" and "dynamics," much as Comte had seventy years earlier. "It is not a question of looking at society arrested at a given moment by abstraction (as has sometimes been said), but of analyzing its formation and accounting for it. Undoubtedly, the phenomena that have to do with structure have something more stable about them than have functional phenomena, but there are only differences of degree between these two orders of fact. Structure itself is encountered in *becoming*, and one cannot illustrate it except by pursuing this process of becoming. It forms and dissolves continually, it is life arrived at a certain measure of consolidation; to disconnect it from the life from which it derives or from that which it determines is equivalent to dissociating things that are inseparable."[29]

It is interesting to observe that when Lévi-Strauss took the chair in social anthropology at the College de France in 1960, he used that same quotation in his inaugural lecture, "The Scope of Anthropology," adding to it his conviction that Durkheim's words "seem to have been written today."

Even earlier, in his Latin dissertation on Montesquieu published in 1892, where he sought to define the scope and method of sociology, Durkheim had written: "If social science is really to exist, societies must be assumed to have a certain nature *which results from the nature and arrangement of the elements composing them,* and which is the source of social phenomena."[30]

Durkheim's reaction to analytical individualism was every bit as determined as Comte's had been, and every bit as passionate, we are obliged to say. Although Durkheim did not, as Comte had, expunge psychology from the world of true science, he expunged it and its type of explanation from the world of sociology. His famous declaration that every time a psychological explanation of a social phenomenon is made "we may be certain it is false" would have pleased Comte. There is in fact a psychology in Durkheim, but it is in every respect a social psychology, one that—in very considerable degree as the result of Durkheim's own nomenclature and intellectual style—led most of his readers for a long time to accuse him of creating a "group mind," of a limitless "social determinism," and of failing utterly to recognize the existence of individual human beings. These accusations are at very least distortions or exaggerations, but there can be no doubt that Durkheim accepted from Comte the idea that society is sui generis, independent of anything that exists solely in the discrete individual—that is, in individual drive, instinct, or affect. So also did Durkheim accept from Comte the view that society can be legitimately analyzed *only* into entities or structures which are themselves social, not individual or intraindividual, and that social facts have every bit as much reality so far as a social science is concerned as do physical facts.

As there is in Comte, there is a dynamics as well as a statics in Durkheim's work. This dynamic structuralism is evident in Durkheim's first major work, *The Division of Labor* (1893), and it is still present, if perhaps muted, in the last book to be published in his lifetime, *The Elementary Forms of Religious Life* (1912). In the earliest work the overriding objective was to demonstrate the evolutionary reality and importance of the two great types of solidarity: "mechanical" and "organic." These have the same temporal-structural reality for Durkheim that Comte's three stages had for him—or, for that matter,

Maine's "status" and "contract" or Marx's divisions of human history or Tönnies's *Gemeinschaft* and *Gesellschaft* had for their authors. That Durkheim did not ever again in his works use the typology of "mechanical" and "organic" in no way offsets the value it had in shaping his life's work or the latent dynamics we find in all his analyses of structure.

We confine ourselves here to a few of the more important instances of structural inquiry in Durkheim's writing. Descriptions of each must necessarily be brief but nevertheless sufficient to make clear the profoundly structuralist cast of his mind.

Perhaps the first signal example is that of Durkheim's treatment of contract in *The Division of Labor.* At one level this treatment is a repudiation of the whole contract mentality that had been ascendant since the reception of Roman Law in the Middle Ages, that had become a very canon of seventeenth- and eighteenth-century natural-law theory, to be seen at its height in Hobbes's *Leviathan.* But at a more relevant level today, Durkheim's criticism of contract may better be seen as an attack upon what we today call exchange theory. Herbert Spencer (to whom Durkheim is by no means always fair in his criticisms) had made the idea of contract, or exchange, fundamental, drawing heavily from utilitarian psychology. Beneath every social relationship, Spencer argued, there is, implicit at least, a contract resting upon the parties' recognition of their respective interests. It is the individual partner's perception of self-interest that in the end leads him to perception of the other's interest. In any event something approximating reciprocity—and perceived as such by the participants—is the core of all basic social relationships.

Durkheim, however, sees any contract as but a part of a larger system or structure. He takes us to what he calls the precontractual foundations of contract—that is, the whole web of inherited traditions, rules, and understandings which supply necessary background to modern contract. "In sum, a contract is not sufficient unto itself, but is possible only thanks to a regulation of the contract which is originally social."[31] The sanctity of contract does not—cannot—rest upon notions of self-interest. If left to an individual's interest alone, any contract would dissolve easily, for nothing is more fleeting than one's interest as one sees it from day to day. What makes contract a binding, respected instrument with derelictions from it punishable by law is that long before the idea of individual-to-individual contract appeared in our social development, there was the man's aboriginal "contract" or covenant with the gods, expressed ritually. The rise of modern contract is but a secularization of what was originally a very sacred ritual—hence the persisting power that inheres in contract.

Still another, and more radical, example of Durkheim's structural mode of thinking is to be seen in his treatment of the "categories of the mind": the ideas or categories of causation, space, force, time, and the like, all of which become means of assimilating, sifting, and ordering sensory impressions.[32] On the one hand, Durkheim is critical of Kant's view that these categories are innate, inseparable from mind itself. On the other hand, he is even more critical of Hume's earlier effort to explain men's ideas of cause, time, mass, and so on, in terms of the accumulation in the individual's life of experiences and observations, with the idea of cause resting upon innumerable experiences with one object having causal effect upon another. Durkheim denies that any number of mere experiences with external causation would ever create and give authority to the idea of cause that found in all human societies and that the child acquires early in life.

We must, Durkheim argues, see each of the categories as the outcome of society's dominance over the individual from the very earliest times. It is the social aspect of the mind that gives society and reason alike the exceptional authority each possesses. "This seems to be the origin of the exceptional authority which is inherent in the reason and which makes us accept its suggestions with confidence. It is the very authority of society, transferring itself to a certain mana of thought which is the indispensable condition of all thought. The necessity with which the categories are imposed upon us is not the effect of simple habits whose yoke we could easily throw off with little effort; nor is it a physical or metaphysical necessity. since the categories change in different places and times; it is a sort of moral necessity which is to the intellectual life what moral obligation is to the will."[33]

Note Durkheim's reference to the fact that "the categories change in different places and times." There is, he tells us, no universal idea of cause, for example—that is, no idea that is the same everywhere. The idea of cause we find in a given people or culture is part of a larger structure of ideas and preconceptions which are closely woven into the life of the people and into the day-to-day activities of individuals. There is nothing biological or genetically transmitted about the idea of cause. It stems from primitive man's experience with the force, the power, resident in community and its religion. Specifically, the idea of cause is the result of primitive man's subjection to certain totemic rituals where constant repetition of calculated sacred acts followed by foreseen results is the social basis of what in time becomes the more abstract and generalized notion of cause and effect. "Our analysis of facts has already enabled us to see that the prototype of the idea of force was the mana, the wakan, orenda, the totemic principle or any of the various names given to the collective force objectified and projected into things. The first power which men have thought of as such seems to have been that exercised by humanity over its members."[34]

So also for the categories of space and time. Each is, if we examine it in the context of a given culture, closely related to the fundamental "representations" of that culture. Thus, Durkheim notes, the Australian aborigine's conception of abstract space is one of concentric circles—reflecting the typical structure of an Australian village. The abstraction *time* is the result in mankind's earliest experience of the regular sequence of rites and festivals around the year.

It is not necessary to agree with Durkheim's account of the origin of the categories, and few scholars today concerned with the subject or anything related to it would give more than highly qualified assent. But Durkheim himself offered his social-structural explanations in the spirit of tentative hypothesis. "It is to be borne in mind . . . that we have never dreamed of offering the preceding observations as a complete theory of the concept of causality. The question is too complex to be resolved thus. . . . The views which we have set forth should be regarded as mere indications, which must be controlled and completed."[35]

One final example of Durkheim's structuralism will be given: his treatment of incest. He is as rigorously nonbiological and nonpsychological here as in the analyses of contract and the categories. The tabu on incest, almost universal among human societies, is not rooted in biology or in any fixed, inherited character of instinct, drive, or mind. After all, some of the most powerful of incest tabus have operated in degrees of relationship which are in no sense consanguineal, and moreover, a number of societies have made special exceptions for sexual relationships between close consanguineal relatives—even brothers and sisters, as in ancient Egyptian and also Hawaiian royalty, as the means of protecting purity of line. Nor, as Durkheim points out, can we be oblivious to the wide currency of themes of incest in world literature. Even though prohibited widely, even though capable of arousing reactions of horror and revulsion, incest has always had its fascination.

The origin of the tabu on incest is, for Durkheim, entirely social. He explores the origin and continuation of the tabu in two different, though related, ways. There is first the relation of the tabu to the ancient principle of exogamy, the original bond of which was totemic—that is, collective subordination of the members of the exogamic group to the sacred essence represented by the totemic plant or animal. In exogamy, Durkheim suggests, society in the real sense was founded, and the function of the incest tabu from the beginning was to prevent any profanation of the totem of the exogamic group by any form of uncleanness—whether pertaining to food, drink, or sex. Given the sacred character of the totemic group, relationships within it—of elders to the young, of the sexes to one another, and of peers within and between each of the sexes—were bound to become as sacred as the relation between the exogamic group and its totem.

Incest was, in short, no independent thing in human life, no simple object of abhorrence, but rather an element of a much wider network of relationships, as was the tabu against incest. Not from any inherent biological aversion to the single act of incest but from aversion to profanation of the totem and the group represented by the totem sprang in the first instance the prohibition against incest.

The structural character of tabu on incestuous relationships is just as evident, Durkheim tells us, in the modern family. Here Durkheim makes a sharp distinction between the kind of unit that is formed conjugally, from affection or analogous motivation, and the unit to which the word "kinship" more aptly applies—that is, the relation between parent and child, among siblings, and with others falling outside the conjugal bond as such. Affection or mutual attraction of some kind may form the essence of the husband-wife relation, but it is *duty* that lies at the heart of the kinship group proper.

Everything concerning the life of the family is dominated by the idea of duty. Our contacts with brothers, our sisters, our parents, are strictly regulated by morality; . . . Assuredly, sympathy and special inclination are far from being banished; however, the domestic affections always have the distinctive propriety that the sentiment of love is strongly colored with respect. Love in this instance is not simply a spontaneous movement of personal sensitivity; it is, in part, duty. . . ."[36]

Precisely because of the ancient and abiding sense of duty in relations between brothers and sisters or children and parents, it has been necessary from earliest times to prevent corruption or pollution of these relations. And any confusion of the kind of tie that exists in the purely conjugal relation with the tie of duty that exists in the kinship group is inevitably corruption or pollution. The problem of authority or jurisdiction immediately enters. We need only think of the chaos that would be introduced in kinship society by the presence of a child that was the issue of the father and one of his daughters or of a brother and sister. The whole structure of kinship, with its embedded lines of descent, its patterns of authority and function, would be thrown into hopeless confusion if such illicit liaisons and their issue were to be unchecked. It is of course more than a mere taxonomic problem in authority and function. For from earliest times the kinship relations of parents and children and of siblings have been invested with sacred character. Incest was no less a transgression of the sacred essence of kinship than parricide or fratricide. The tabu on incest thus remains, Durkheim stresses, by virtue of the deep if unstated belief that the effect of incest, widely carried on, would be destruction of the vital relationships in the kinship group.

. . . The dignity of the relationship which unites us with close kin thus excludes any other link which would not have the same value. One cannot court a person to whom one owes and who in turn owes you a respectful affection, with this latter feeling being corrupted or vanishing in one way or another. In a word, given our present ideas, a man cannot make a wife of his sister without her ceasing to be his sister. This is what makes us disapprove so strongly of incest.[37]

It is needless to offer additional examples of Durkheim's structural approach. For Durkheim, as for Comte, explanations which begin with biological aspects of race or individual; which take their departure from presumed drives or states whitin the individual; which have reference to the climatic, geographical, or other nonsocial areas of life; or which are based simply upon masses of particulars—all such explanations are useless to the sociologist. Only when the individual act, belief, or other element of human life is set properly by the investigator in the larger context of which it is a true part do we then begin scientific explanation properly defined. And for the sociologist this context must be at once social and structural. We must confine ourselves to the objective, visible aspects of social life, and we must ascertain what if any connections or relationships, static or dynamic, exist among these aspects.

One may, if he wishes, deal with the act of suicide as something utterly unique to the individual concerned, or the result of pathological disposition in the individual, or as contravention of God's law. But if a genuinely sociological explanation is to be offered, one must set this act of suicide in its relation to a large number of other data—economic, religious, kinship, and so on—and show why the rate and incidence of suicide is less in one pattern of such data than in another.

Precisely the same is true of religion. If we are to understand the original power of religion in human life, indeed its persisting power, we must find out what the real function is that religion serves and what religion's relation is to other dimensions of human life. Those who say that in the process of his setting religion in institutional focus Durkheim was neglectful of the problem of *meaning*—the meaning religion has for its adherents—have not read, or properly absorbed, the following passage: "The believer who has communicated with his god is not merely a man who sees new truths of which the unbeliever is ignorant; he is a man who is *stronger*. He feels within him more force, either to endure the trials of existence, or to conquer them."[38] Durkheim comes down hard on the rationalists who have thought they were explaining religion by simple reference to the ideas contained—ideas about the cosmos, the eternal, the ideal, the unknowable, about gods as distant beings, and the like. Such interpreters, being themselves outside religion, have failed to understand it. "Our entire study," Durkheim writes, "rests on the postulate that the unanimous sentiment of the believers of all times cannot be purely illusory."[39]

Not then as a complex of ideas *about* something external or internal, but as a structure involving community, authority, function, role, and status, does religion acquire and maintain its importance in human life. The *cult*—which is the social molecule, the smallest actual element of religion properly perceived, whether in primitive or modern religion—is vital. Anyone who has ever "really practised a religion knows very well that it is the cult which gives rise to those impressions of joy, of interior peace, of serenity, of enthusiasm, which are, for the believer, an experimental proof of his beliefs. The cult is not simply a system of signs by which the faith is outwardly translated; it is a collection of the means by which this is created and recreated periodically."[40]

Reading such a passage, one can only conclude that it is no wonder Durkheim throughout his life paid tribute to Comte. From Durkheim's acceptance of the reality of society as an entity sui generis all the way down to his most empirical studies, the spirit of Comte's own structural mode of inquiry is always visible.

Post-Durkheimian Structuralism

Had Durkheim himself never written a line, his contribution to structural analysis would still be great simply by virtue of those whom he taught, first at Bordeaux and then at Paris, whose own research contributions proved to be significant. Among these students, two warrant emphasis here: Marcel Mauss and Maurice Halbwachs. Both men worked well within Durkheim's major lines of sociological theory and method, but each carried structural analysis to new heights in France.

Marcel Mauss (1872–1950) A nephew of Durkheim, born in the same town and almost from the beginning the beneficiary of Durkheim's educational interest, Mauss is very probably foremost among Durkheim's students, not only in the intrinsic quality of his own work but in influence upon others, among them Radcliffe-Brown and Lévi-Strauss, whom we shall come to shortly.[41]

Deeply devoted though Mauss was, throughout his life, to Durkheim's methodological and theoretical canons, he yet managed to go beyond Durkheim in at least two important ways. In the first place he made use of a far greater diversity of ethnographical and historical materials than Durkheim had—drawing from a variety of living primitive peoples and also from civilizations of the past. Second, there is greater willingness in Mauss to enter the domain of psychology than there had been in Durkheim. Mauss does not hesitate to deal directly with psychological, as well as social and cultural, components of both subject and milieu.

The structuralist character of his work may be seen from the beginning: in the study of primitive classification systems he did in collaboration with Durkheim (1903); in the still earlier (1899) work *Sacrifice: Its Nature and Function*, done with another of Durkheim's students, Henri Hubert; and in his fascinating, multidimensional analysis of the Eskimos (1906), to mention but a few of Mauss's contributions.

But unquestionably the single most important and far-reaching of Mauss's studies was his *The Gift* (1925).[42] This is the work that so influenced Lévi-Strauss, producing in him, by his own account, emotions comparable to those which seized Malebranche upon first reading of Descartes. But Lévi-Strauss is by no means the only major figure in social anthropology and sociology to be so stimulated. It has been called the foremost work in French ethnology and to this day can serve as a model for the kind of research, analysis, and synthesis Mauss's book represents.

Mauss seized upon the gift—more accurately, the exchange of gifts—as the kind of social fact Durkheim had described in theoretical terms in his *The Rules of Sociological Method:* the kind that permits objective, empirical, and comparative analysis and that also serves as a focus for a broad and complex pattern of social, economic, religious, aesthetic, and psychological behavior. For Mauss the gift, as it is found throughout human society, past and present, illustrates admirably what Durkheim had called not simply a social fact but a fact of "total" or "typical" nature, one capable of casting broad illumination over many areas of behavior.

Taking his departure from the great variety of gift patterns in human history, with special emphasis upon the exchange of gifts, Mauss provides explanation of them all by reference to an archaic form of exchange in which the transfer of objects from one individual or one group to another can be seen as but the mere symbol of what is in fact a complicated interaction of social roles and statuses. This interaction, Mauss shows us, itself rests upon a three-dimensional *obligation* that is so deeply ingrained everywhere in human culture as to be accounted a part of the human mind itself. It is the obligation to *give,* to *receive,* and to *repay,* taking each of these in a sense wide enough to encompass social and psychological factors.

Just as Durkheim had made division of labor in economy the point of departure for a study of social solidarity—seeing the function of division of labor to be that of creating solidarity in the social system as a whole—so does Mauss see the basic function of gift exchange to be that of contributing to social solidarity. Gift exchanges, while "in theory voluntary, disinterested, and spontaneous . . . are in fact obligatory and interested." This is as true of the potlatch as it is of Christmas, of the ordinary gifts exchanged within a family or between friends as of the vaster gifts between peoples and nations. Granted that major moments of gift exchange often have behind them complex mythologies—as in Christmas—they are nevertheless inseparable from contexts of mutual aid, mutual understanding, reciprocity, and community which are the really crucial forces. "The lasting influence of the objects exchanged is a direct expression of the manner in which sub-groups within segmentary societies of an archaic type are constantly embroiled with, and feel themselves in debt to, each other."[43]

It would be hard to find a single meaning of structuralism as currently found in sociological and ethnological writing that is not present in some degree in Mauss's classic. There is not only the emphasis upon patterning of social relationships, upon the objective manifestations of recurrent human interaction, but also upon myths, states of mind, and other psychological components. Finally, there is in the book a profound—and altogether Durkheimian—moral thrust. Durkheim was himself deeply concerned with the moral condition of the age in which he lived; the final pages of both *The Division of Labor* and *Suicide* reveal this concern. Durkheim did not hesitate to propose, on moral grounds, such measures as the reinstituting of guildlike intermediate associations as the means of strengthening the social bond. Mauss too has a moral recommendation to make, one that he felt to be consonant with the humane socialism he was identified with politically. This is the deliberate recovery in contemporary society of the classic, archaic sense of obligation—to give, to receive, and to repay—that is the subject of his scientific analysis.

Maurice Halbwachs (1877–1945) Like Mauss, Halbwachs studied under Durkheim, collaborated with him in *L'Année sociologique,* and followed generally Durkheimian principles throughout his life (which ended in a Nazi execution for his role in the French Resistance during the Second World War). But, also as in Mauss, there is substantial enlargement of scope and method. Halbwachs wrote a perceptive study of social class (a subject Durkheim had almost completely ignored) in which he combined comparative and psychological analysis.[44] His study of suicide follows Durkheim's classic work fairly closely, but there is much greater sophistication of statistical method than was possible in Durkheim's day (Halbwachs's study was published in 1930). Perhaps even more important is Halbwachs's willingness to enter the domain of motivation. Durkheim had declared all preoccupation with motives out of bounds so far as science was concerned. But Halbwachs deals with motives, and it is on this ground that he makes his modification of Durkheim's types of suicide. Where Durkheim had referred to "altruistic" suicide, dealing with it as suicide in the full sense, though caused by hypercommitment to a group or culture rather than by "egoism" or "anomie," Halbwachs rejects the idea of altruistic suicide. The motive to such self-destruction, Halbwachs argues, removes it altogether from the category of suicide and places it instead in the psychologically and culturally different category of sacrifice. The interesting theoretical point is simply that Halbwachs, without abandoning Durkheim's structural approach to the study of suicide, expanded it and deepened it by his willingness to consider the psychological realm to a degree that Durkheim had not been.[45]

Perhaps the boldest of Halbwachs's structural inquiries was his *The Social Bases of Memory*. First published in 1925, it is a remarkable work by the standards of any age. It too is rooted in the ideas of Halbwachs's master, Durkheim; the book begins with a Durkheimian passage on dreams. From there, however, the book moves into detailed analyses of the social sources of individual memory. The function of language; the relation of family tradition to individual images, religion, and social class—all of these are dealt with by Halbwachs in his demonstration of the relation between the nature of individual memory and the social order.[46]

None of Halbwachs's works better illustrates the structural cast of his mind than his final one, *The Topography of Legend*, published in 1941 in France, at a time when other, more commanding matters must have been in the forepart of Halbwachs's mind. This remarkable work is the social-psychological study of a famous holy place and the fusion of tradition and legend into a collective memory of those who live there, or who make pilgrimages to it. We see how the very appearance of the holy-place changes with the shifting needs and motivations of the people concerned.

We cannot leave Halbwachs without mention, however brief, of the demographic and morphological interests which were becoming stronger all the time during his later years. In very loose and simple form, the concept of social morphology had appeared in Durkheim's works—notably in *The Division of Labor*. Halbwachs carried Durkheim's analysis to greater heights, and there are qualified scholars who believe that in the long run Halbwachs's largest significance as sociologist will flow from the ventures he made into morphological uses of population data.

A. R. Radcliffe-Brown (1881–1955) Some readers will regard as debatable, to say the least, our placing the name of this distinguished and influential British social anthropologist under the rubric of Durkheim. We are in no way unmindful of Radcliffe-Brown's originality and the strong, formative influence exerted upon his mind by his university teachers in England—W. H. R. Rivers, A. C. Haddon, and C. S. Myers, the first two being indeed the subjects of Radcliffe-Brown's dedication of his first major work, *The Andaman Islanders* (1922). And there were other strong influences upon his mind, ranging from ancient Greek philosophers to Herbert Spencer. Had he never read Durkheim it is clear that Radcliffe-Brown would have made his mark as social scientist.

The fact is, however, that he did encounter Durkheim's writing, and he was one of the very first outside France to hail not only its theoretical-philosophical importance but also its relevance to empirical study of social behavior. It was Radcliffe-Brown who, more than anyone else, really brought Durkheim into the position of intellectual authority he has held since the late 1930s in the United States. Earlier efforts by Americans to stimulate interest in Durkheim had failed. However, when Radcliffe-Brown went to the University of Chicago in 1931 for a six-year stay (he had been there briefly for a series of lectures slightly earlier), he was able to demonstrate, as no one else had, the greatness of Durkheim in the theoretical areas of social function and social structure. Critical though Radcliffe-Brown was of certain aspects of Durkheim's work, he nevertheless recognized the high value of Durkheim's persistent stress upon the structural character of social phenomena and upon the fact that the really crucial functions which we study in social life are functions, not of biological or psychological needs, but of the social structures themselves. It is, very probably, the relation in Durkheim between structure and function, along with Durkheim's fascination with social solidarity—its roots, forms, and influence upon the human mind—that exerted the greatest effect upon Radcliffe-Brown. He hailed Durkheim's treatment of function (in *The Rules*) as the first systematic and scientific application of the concept to the study of social phenomena.

And it is precisely Radcliffe-Brown's emphasis upon structure and function—an emphasis, as noted, that would be difficult to account for apart from his keen study of Durkheim—that places him among the post-Durkheimians. Radcliffe-Brown was what Durkheim was not, an accomplished field-worker; but this notwithstanding, his largest and undoubtedly most persisting influence has been and will continue to be in the more theoretical areas.

We cannot appreciate the full impact of Radcliffe-Brown on contemporary social thought except in light of his repudiation of the grand social evolutionism of which Spencer and Tylor had been exponents in England. Although Radcliffe-Brown began as a respectful reader of Spencer's works, he became alienated in time—just as Durkheim had—by Spencer's utilitarian individualism and by his construction of worldwide stages of the evolutionary development of institutions. Such construction, as Radcliffe-Brown was among the first to realize, led to a disregard for time, place, and circumstance, for the relation of individual traits to their contexts, and a disregard too for the elementary canons of what Radcliffe-Brown (again along with Durkheim) believed to be the true method of science. His work has been sometimes criticized as "unhistorical," even "antihistorical," but in fact it is not. Radcliffe-Brown was hostile to sweeping evolutionary explanations which all-too-often were labeled "historical," and also to those works which were premised on the feasibility of subjecting a tribe or people without written records to the same techniques used by historians. For peoples possessed of written records, the historian's approach is useful and clarifying, Radcliffe-

Brown declared; but for those not so possessed, efforts to portray episodes of history or development, to offer origins or causes of institutions for recordless peoples, leads only to what he called the "pseudohistorical" and the "pseudocausal." "The view taken here is that such speculations are not only useless but are worse than useless."[47]

Whereas in Radcliffe-Brown's judgment early anthropologists should have been in search of scientific laws of structure, function, and other cardinal elements of the primitive societies they studied, they entered instead into the vain search for "human origins" and stages of development presumably connected with the position of Western Europe in the world. In his famous essay "The Mother's Brother in South Africa," Radcliffe-Brown disputed theories which saw the preferred position of the brother in family life as a survival of some primordial matriarchal stage of existence. Such theories, he argued, can never be proved, given lack of records. What we can do, however, is demonstrate the perfectly logical relation this position of the mother's brother has to other ongoing aspects of tribal society, values, norms, and functions. And this Radcliffe-Brown did in exemplary fashion. For an inconclusive, basically impossible, effort at evolutionary origins, he substituted results rooted in the available data. It is in these terms that his structural-functional mode of analysis acquired the reputation of being purely static, oblivious to the facts of change and history.

Such a reputation is entirely undeserved. For peoples with histories—that is, recorded histories—historical methods can be used. For peoples without them, it is sheer pretension to talk about a "historical method," as did many American ethnologists, when there is no history being employed at all, only conjectural derivations set in time.

In his *Natural Science of Society,* Radcliffe-Brown wrote:

> One may say that the characteristics of a society are determined by two things: first, by the simple fact that the society is composed of human beings; and second, by the internal nature of those human beings. No amount of investigation can explain the characteristics of society by simple reference to the nature of human beings; but by an investigation of human beings *arranged in a certain order, yes. The social scientist is studying the structural arrangement of the units and takes the internal structure of the units for granted.*[48]

Durkheim could not have made the point more effectively!

It is by virtue of his structural approach to social phenomena that Radcliffe-Brown makes a highly important distinction relating to the nature of change, a distinction that too many students of the social process do not make. There is on the one hand "change within the structure," the kind that occurs, say, when two individuals previously unrelated marry, have children, and so on. This is, if we like, change in the life patterns of several individuals; but there is no change in the social structure—that is, marriage—within which *this* marriage, this "change," takes place. Very different, Radcliffe-Brown insists, is the kind of change that affects—alters or transforms—the structure of marriage itself. This second type is rarer, the result of internal or external disturbances made by impacts of one kind or other.[49] Just as we cannot, in Radcliffe-Brown's structuralism, ever legitimately deduce social relationships "from the simple nature of human beings" but only take and study those relationships as they are given, neither, he argues, can we take the first of the two types of "change" and use it, additively or cumulatively, to account for the second.

In no possible respect does this argue a bias on Radcliffe-Brown's part against the existence, or the study, of social change. Many of his students have given us valuable works on social change in Africa and other parts of the world. But they are, almost without exception, studies of observable changes occurring in primitive peoples as the results, say, of collision and contact with other peoples, phenomena in which the present century has been so rich as the result of the spread of Western society.

Radcliffe-Brown did not assume that study of social structure was the whole of anthropology, but he certainly accorded it a high, even the highest, place in the discipline. What so many American and other English anthropologists ascribed rather vaguely to "culture," Radcliffe-Brown ascribed—as Durkheim had—to those social connections, ties, bonds, and representations which effectively determine the role of individuals and of cultural traits alike. The so-called cultural school in anthropology (and also sociology) was born in the simple recognition of cultural traits, whether material or immaterial, whether external to the individual or a part of his personal makeup; and it was thought that the mere pointing-to culture and its component traits and to the type of inheritance leading to cultural continuity was a scientific explanation. It was Radcliffe-Brown's merit to dispute this, to show in detail the inadequacies and even distortions of the cultural school, especially as it existed in America. And it was his further merit, working chiefly from Durkheim and his immediate students, such as Mauss, to demonstrate the vital necessity of working in terms of social systems or structures.

As we have noted, it is to Radcliffe-Brown, more than anyone else, whether in anthropology or sociology, that American social scientists are indebted for the serious entry of Durkheimian thought into American sociology. Much of what is still called the Chicago school in anthropology and sociology alike flows directly from Radcliffe-Brown's visit to Chicago in 1929 and then his six-year residence there starting in 1931. It was he, more than anyone else, who set in motion the processes leading to American social anthropology.

The Annales School Here we turn to history, though remaining still in the post-Durkheimian tradition. We refer first to the notable journal in France, *Annales: Economies, sociētēs, civilisations,* founded in 1929 by two history professors at the University of Strasbourg, and second to the now famous "VI[e] section"—of the *Ecole pratique des hautes ētudes: Sciences ēconomiques et sociales.* The background of the founding of both the journal—by Professor Lucien Febvre and Professor Marc Bloch—and of the Sixth Section is substantially the same: a renunciation of what passed for history, what was regarded widely *as* history, in the official or establishment centers in France, chiefly at the Sorbonne. Such history was strictly political and diplomatic, written invariably and monotonously in terms of genealogies of events and personages, with each event or personage declared, explicitly or implicitly, absolutely unique and hence incapable of being legitimately fused with other events into a pattern or of being scientifically compared with other events or clusters of events.[50]

Before describing briefly the *Annales* conception of structure in history, it is useful as well as interesting to indicate that some of the inspiration for the founding by Febvre and Bloch—who would be joined in due time by Fernand Braudel, today the foremost figure in the school (Bloch was killed during the Second World War by the Gestapo in France; Febvre died in 1956)—of the journal *Annales* came from admiration for Durkheim's *L'année*. In *Annales's* creation, there was more than a simple desire to create a journal that would become a focal point for scholars of like minds. There was also a desire to employ in the study of history some of Durkheim's or Durkheim's followers' actual methods and concepts. And high among these was the concept of *structure*, whether used in static representation or dynamic.

The great difficulty with conventional historiography, Febvre, Bloch, and Braudel believed, was its affinity with what the French call *histoire évênementielle:* that is, history construed and constructed solely in terms of strings of events—"first this, and then, and then, . . ." as it has been characterized—not only linkage of events but overwhelmingly political, diplomatic, or military events—and so often with no more than passing effort to deal with contexts.

What the founders and successors in the Sixth Section achieved on a remarkable scale was the fusing of history and the social sciences. Nowhere else, so far as we are aware, has this fusion taken place so determinedly, imaginatively, and with such amplitude of sheer scholarship and research to give it footing. (For 1972–73 the program of instruction in the Sixth Section contained *forty-nine different research seminars* dealing with an immense diversity of social, economic, intellectual, and political matters, but within the common framework that Febvre, Bloch, and Braudel created. Where else in the world—certainly not in the wealthy United States—could such an imposing *mass* of historical teaching and research be found?)[51]

But in many ways the really striking aspect of *Annales* and the Sixth Section has less to do with the fusion of history and the social sciences than it does with the radical reconstituting of the nature of history, the structure of history, as the means of working toward genuinely scientific instead of merely humanistic or artistic results. Not history in the ancient, traditional, and conventional sense of *histoire évênementielle,* with its long genealogies of events, acts, and personages, with many time frames forced arbitrarily into one, but instead history conceived as the study of spatial and temporal structures.

There is no better way of succinctly describing the *Annales* treatment of history than to draw from Fernand Braudel's statement of intent and method in his monumental *The Mediterranean and the Mediterranean World in the*

Age of Philip II. Here are some revealing lines from the preface to the second edition, in which he describes the historian's problem:

> It is the problem confronting every historical undertaking. Is it possible somehow to convey simultaneously both that conspicuous history which holds our attention by its continual and dramatic changes—and that other, submerged, history, almost silent and always discreet, virtually unsuspected either by its observers or its participants, which is little touched by the obstinate erosion of time? This fundamental contradiction, which must always lie at the centre of our thought, can be a vital tool of knowledge and research. Relevant to every area of human life, it may take on a variety of forms according to the terms of the comparison.
>
> Historians have over the years grown accustomed to describing this contradiction in terms of *structure* and *conjuncture,* the former denoting long-term, the latter, short-term realities. Clearly there are different kinds of structure just as there are different kinds of conjuncture, and the duration of either structure or conjuncture may in turn vary. History accepts and discovers multidimensional explanations, reaching, as it were, vertically from one temporal plane to another. And on every plane there are also horizontal relationships and connections. . . .[52]

We take nothing away from the distinctiveness of Braudel's statement when we observe that Durkheim, in *The Rules of Sociological Method,* where he is describing the nature and importance of "social milieu," had reached substantially the same vision of history. For Durkheim, social milieu is at once a confluence of historical-temporal structures as well as those formed by geography, population, and the intersecting ties of human relationships.

Braudel's *Mediterranean,* which covers a half-century period in depth, deals with every possible aspect of its subject—the physical environment and long-term processes of change which may be discerned before and during the period at hand, coastlines, islands, the several climates in the area, the rhythms of the seasons, land and sea routes which have been important, the means of communication, mineral deposits, agriculture, mining, and all aspects of the economic, political, social, cultural, and intellectual life in the area for the period chosen. It is an astounding piece of historical work quite apart from methodological design and has of course been widely recognized as such. Braudel does for the half-century period of Mediterranean life what Marc Bloch had done earlier in his superb study of feudalism: he seeks to capture the long-term processes or structures of change and also the short-term ones and to weave into these a detailed analysis of "the ties of dependence"—including kinship, social class, village community, and parish church—as these affected and were affected by the *évênement* or *courte durée;* the "conjuncture," or *moyenne durée,* the "*structure,*" or *longue durée,* and of course the varied intersections of these.

Earlier Lucien Febvre, who was the guiding spirit of the *Annales* movement, had written his *Philippe II et la Fanche-Comtê,* in which much the same convergence, or fusion, of the geographic, social, cultural, and intellectual had been achieved, as well as synchronization of long-term trends and short, explosive events. Later Febvre's study of Rabelais and his epoch revealed the same set of talents and insights. We are given a first-rate portrait of Rabelais at the start of the book, then a detailed treatment of the "mental apparatus" of the period—the common words, feelings, and values, as they may be derived from contemporary documents, which form the social and intellectual structure of the period.

If there is a fault to be found in the *Annales* school thus far, it is the seeming preference for what may be called *histoire totale*—that is, the saturation approach to a given age or place, with literally every aspect touched upon—over what J. H. Hexter has called *histoire probléme*, with its manifold opportunities for not only intensive, multidimensional study of a single time and place in light of a recognized problem, but also for a comparative approach that allows for research, by a whole team when desired or required, into other places and times when an analogous problem existed.

But this said, it is still necessary to pay tribute to such a work as Braudel's *The Mediterranean*. Rarely—certainly not in the United States, despite all the financial resources which have gone into historical and social-scientific study—has so magnificent a synthesis of the historical and social-scientific approaches been achieved. It is a lesson in what can be accomplished by historians well versed in the social sciences and by social scientists versed in the techniques and perspectives of history. Hexter quotes Braudel tellingly: "I would wish that in the years of their apprenticeship young sociologists would take the time to study even in the most modest archive the simplest of historical questions; that once at least beyond the sterile manuals they might have contact with a craft that is simple but one that cannot be understood without practicing it."[53]

Claude Lévi-Strauss and Jean Piaget

Our final representatives of the French structuralist tradition manifest certain divergences in their respective works from that tradition as we have seen it develop from Comte through Durkheim and Mauss. But the roots of both Lévi-Strauss and Piaget are nevertheless deep in the work of Durkheim and his students—especially Mauss and Halbwachs. Lévi-Strauss is a social anthropologist—without question the most distinguished living French anthropologist—and Piaget is of course most famous for his studies of cognitive processes, especially in children. But, as noted, the impact of sociology upon the work of each is a matter of record, and, equally important, the impact of the works of each of these two scientists upon sociology is becoming more evident all the time.

Lêvi-Strauss (1908–) Born in Brussels, Lévi-Strauss studied philosophy and law at the University of Paris, 1927–32, was for a time associated with Jean-Paul Sartre's circle in Paris, and then went to South America, where he was professor of sociology at the University of São Paulo, Brazil, and commenced the fieldwork that was to yield some of his more notable writings and serve as the seedbed of reflections which would steadily develop during his entire life. For four years during the Second World War he was on the faculty of the New School of Social Research in New York. In 1950 he became head of studies at the *Ecole Pratique des Hautes Etudes* at the University of Paris. He was appointed to the chair in social anthropology at the Collège de France in 1959, a position that he has held to this day.

His first major work was *The Elementary Structures of Kinship* (1949), the very title of which will suggest the degree of influence that in fact emanated from Durkheim's classic. Primarily, however, it was Mauss's epochal study of the gift, with its emphasis upon reciprocity, that stimulated this work by Lévi-Strauss. What Lévi-Strauss did was apply Mauss's proposition concerning the circulation of types of valued commodities to the principal forms of kinship grouping found in the world and also to the incest prohibition—a subject that had been of keen interest to Durkheim and his students. Stated succinctly, Lévi-Strauss's reciprocity theory is that in the act of one man's denying to himself the use of a woman, thus making her available to another man, there is bound to be somewhere a woman who then becomes properly the possession of the man in question. This was certainly a novel theory of both kinship and of the totem taboo, and Lévi-Strauss's work aroused much attention, albeit controversial attention, when it was published in 1949.[54]

Perhaps most important, given the long succession of works and ideas that followed, is the thesis in his study of kinship that for explanation of the basic forms of reciprocity we find in kinship and totem systems, we must turn "to certain structures of the human mind." The dominant structures emerge from the relation of the individual self to others. There is a good deal of material on the behavior and thinking processes of children in this work, and it concludes that the aptitude for reciprocity that we find early on in the life of the child is in considerable part a reflection of the child's desire for closeness to the social group.

In later years in *The Savage Mind* (1962) Lévi-Strauss would apologize for certain characteristics of his earliest work, particularly those pertaining to "unconscious genesis" of kinship forms:

> I must confess to having myself unintentionally and unwittingly lent support to these erroneous ideas [he is referring to certain ideas of Sartre] by having seemed all toó often in *Les Structures êlêmentaires de la parentê* as if I were seeking out an unconscious genesis of matrimonial exchange. I should have made more distinction between exchange as it is expressed spontaneously and forcefully in the *praxis* of groups and the conscious and deliberate rules by which these same groups . . . spend their time codifying and controlling it.[55]

Nevertheless, it is hard to disagree with Edmund Leach's assessment of Lévi-Strauss [as one reads such Lévi-Straussian works as *Tristes Tropiques* (1955), translated into English as *A World on the Wane; Structural Anthropology* (1958); *The Savage Mind* (1962); *Totemism* (1962); and *Mythologiques*, a massive work that has appeared in four volumes over recent years] that Lévi-Strauss's consuming objective is to search out "the unconscious nature of collective phenomena." Leach writes:

> Like Freud, he seeks to discover principles of thought-formation which are universally

valid for all human minds. These universal principles . . . are operative in our brains just as much as in the brains of South American Indians. . . . If we are to get at the primitive universal logic in its uncontaminated form, we need to examine the thought processes of very primitive, technologically unsophisticated peoples (such as the South American Indians), and the study of myth is one way of achieving this end.[56]

Myth has become without doubt Lévi-Strauss's overriding interest; not, of course, in and for itself, but as a means of reaching the basic structures of thought and behavior throughout mankind. His distinction between "historical" and "mythic" peoples has been frequently criticized. According to Lévi-Strauss those people in whom the historical past is preserved use the past as the means of illuminating the present, whereas people without such historical consciousness, people in whom myth plays a major role, employ myths in the present as the instruments for creation of the past. Clearly "historical" peoples have their mythic structures also, structures indeed around which history writing tends to be done, and there must be few if any peoples utterly devoid of a historical sense, however permeated or overladen it may be by myths.

There are ambiguities and inconsistencies enough in Lévi-Strauss, as even his greatest admirers are obliged to concede, but surmounting all of these is a form of structural inquiry that is unique in contemporary thought, and one that bids fair to occupy the minds of more and more sociologists. There are assuredly long sections in Lévi-Strauss where his intellectual roots in Durkheim and Mauss are exceedingly hard to find. In such sections there is an appeal to the individual mind, to mental categories in general, and to configurations of thought which seem presocial, out of all keeping with Durkheim's rigorous objectivism and concentration upon the socially visible. Yet in his inaugural address on the occasion of taking the chair in social anthropology at the Collège de France, Lévi-Strauss is firm and eloquent on the indispensable role that Durkheim's method and theory played in his own development. Durkheim, Lévi-Strauss tells us there, "incarnates the essence of France's contribution to social anthropology. . . ."[57] And, as before noted, it was above all the experience of reading Marcel Mauss's *Essay on the Gift* that kindled in him "the gamut of emotions described by Malebranche upon his first reading of Descartes: the beating of the heart, the boiling up within the head. . . ."

Moreover, despite the claim of Leach and others that for Lévi-Strauss, "structure" refers to categories of the human mind universally held by mankind, there are sections in *Structural Anthropology* which plainly belie this neo-Kantian perspective. The following is eminently instructive:

. . . The term "social structure" has nothing to do with empirical reality but with *the models which are built up after it*. . . . Therefore social structure cannot claim a field of its own among others in the social studies. It is rather a method to be applied to any kind of social studies, similar to the structural analysis current in other disciplines. . . . Keeping this in mind we can say that a structure consists of a model meeting with several requirements.

First, the structure exhibits the characteristics of a system. It is made up of several elements, none of which can undergo a change without effecting changes in all the other elements.

Second, for any given model there should be a possibility of ordering a series of transformations resulting in a group of models of the same type.

Third, the above properties make it possible to predict how the model will react if one or more of its elements are submitted to certain modifications.

Finally, the model should be constituted so as to make immediately intelligible all the observed facts.[58]

The fact is inescapable that Lévi-Strauss, for all the richness of his ideas and results, does not present us with a rigorous and consistent notion of the method of structuralism. There are sections of his work, including those just quoted, in which little if anything is present that either Comte or Durkheim could fault. There are, however, other sections which deal with the mind and its properties as manifested in both logic and myth, in almost a Kantian way.

Probably our best hope in understanding Lévi-Strauss's view of structuralism lies in his treatment of myth as found in "the savage mind," a subject that has been a consuming one for him during the past two decades. First, what is meant by "the savage mind"?

The characteristic feature of the savage mind is its timelessness; its object is to grasp the world as both a synchronic and a diachronic totality, and the knowledge which it draws therefrom is like that afforded of a room by mirrors vised on opposite walls, which reflect each other. . . . The savage mind deepens its knowledge with the help of *imagines mundi*. It builds mental structures which facilitate an understanding of the world in as much as they resemble it. In this sense savage thought can be defined as analogical thought.[59]

Lévi-Strauss rejects completely Lévy-Bruhl's famous antinomy between civilized man's "logical" thought and primitive man's "prelogical" thinking. The primitive mind, Lévi-Strauss writes, "is logical in the same sense and the same fashion as ours, though as our own is only when it is applied to knowledge of a universe in which it recognizes physical and semantic properties simultaneously."

It is in his treatment of myth that we are best able to get at what Lévi-Strauss means by structure, though it would be false to imply that he is ever genuinely clear or free for the most part from a certain ambiguity. His distinction between art and myth is basic here. In works of art, Lévi-Strauss points out, "the starting point is a set of one or more objects and one or more events which aesthetic creation unifies by revealing a common structure. Myths travel the same road but start from the other end. They use a structure to produce what is itself an object consisting of a set of events (for all myths tell a story). Art thus proceeds from a set (object + event) to the *discovery* of its structure. Myth starts from a structure by means of which it constructs a set (object + event)."[60]

Myths for Lévi-Strauss are in no way "products" of man's asserted mythmaking capacity, his turning his back on "reality." Their principal value is indeed to preserve until the present time the remains of methods of observation and reflection which were and still are adapted to discoveries of a special kind: "those which nature authorised from the starting point of a speculative organization and exploitation of the sensible world in sensible terms."[61]

The increasing emphasis on myths that we find in Lévi-Strauss during the past two decades reflects the importance he gives to the collective unconsciousness of the universal human mind, rather than to the collective consciousness of a particular social organization. What Lévi-Strauss's interpreter, Edmund Leach, writes is illuminating here:

> The "general object of analysis" is conceived as a kind of algebraic matrix of possible permutations and combinations located in the unconscious "human mind"; the empirical evidence is merely an example of what is possible. . . . He conceives of the "human mind" as having objective existence; it is an attribute of human brains. We can ascertain attributes of the human mind by investigating and comparing the cultural products.[62]

Lévi-Strauss argues that man, by the very nature of his mind, views the world with binary concepts—for example, odd and even numbers. Through a development of algebraic matrices of these thought patterns, anthropologists can construct models of the possible formations of linguistic tendencies. Leach tells us that according to Lévi-Strauss, man's capacity to symbolize with his fellows requires that in the course of evolution the brain acquired the ability to make "plus/minus distinctions for treating the binary pairs thus formed as related couples, and for manipulating these relations as in a matrix algebra."

Without doubt, in Lévi-Strauss's general development of thought an enlarging neo-Kantianism is to be seen. As Leach has written: "Verbal categories provide the mechanism through which *universal* structural characteristics of human brains are transformed into *universal* structural characteristics of human culture."[63]

Jean Piaget (1896–) Piaget is perhaps the least obvious among the names listed here as falling in the post-Durkheimian structural tradition. In the first place Piaget is, and doubtless always will be, known primarily for his original and seminal studies in the psychology of learning, especially among children. Such works as *The Language and Thought of the Child* (1926) down through *The Early Growth of Logic in the Child* (1964) mark him, as do his long-continued researches and teachings in Geneva, first in the university, then (following a few years at the Sorbonne in Paris) in the International Center for Epistemology in Geneva, as preeminently the psychologist rather than the sociologist.

But a view limited strictly to that would be inadequate. As his *Sociological Studies* (1965) makes evident, his early readings in Durkheim, Mauss, and Lévy-Bruhl gave Piaget a sensitivity to sociological thought and method that has never deserted him. In the work just mentioned the long, opening essay, "Explanation in Sociology," is a detailed exploration of structural reasoning in biology, psychology, and sociology, with the largest emphasis upon the last, and it may be regarded as the logical forerunner of his better known and recent *Structuralism* (1970).[64]

In that work Piaget seeks to set forth a satisfactory and comprehensive definition of structuralism that would include all the uses found in contemporary psychology, linguistics, anthropology, philosophy, and sociology. Through an examination of what he calls "the affirmative ideal" in each of the structural systems of inquiry, Piaget works toward the fundamental nature of structuralism and "the common denominator" in all of these systems. There is, he tells us, "an ideal of intelligibility held in common, or at least inspired often, by all structuralists, even though their critical objectives vary enormously."[65]

As a beginning, Piaget writes, we may say "that a structure is a system of transformations. Inasmuch as it is a system and not a mere collection of elements and their properties, these transformations involve laws: the structure is preserved or enriched by the interplay of its transformation laws, which never yield results external to the system nor employ elements that are external to it. In short, the notion of structure is comprised by three key ideas: the idea of wholeness, the idea of transformation, and the idea of self-regulation."[66]

None of the French structuralists we have dealt with in this chapter, Auguste Comte included, would in all likelihood take issue with that definition, that designation of key elements. Nor would Comte and his successors demur at Piaget's declaration that the elements of a structure are subordinate to the laws governing the structure itself: "it is in terms of these laws that the structure qua whole or system is defined." For Piaget, as for Durkheim, Mauss, Radcliffe-Brown, and Lévi-Strauss, the whole has properties which are "distinct from the properties of its elements, which are again in some sense dependent upon the whole." Integers, he points out, "do not exist in isolation from one another, nor were they discovered one by one in some accidental sequence and then, finally, united into a whole."[67] If there is a major dispute between Piaget and Comte, and possibly also between Piaget and Durkheim in this respect, it lies in Piaget's repudiation of "totalities," meaning large-scale systems, along with "schemes of atomist association." In the aforementioned essay on the nature of sociological explication, Piaget writes critically of the two extremes, offering the intermediate way of attention to "natural" or "empirical" structures susceptible to actual study.

There is much evidence that Piaget has been influenced by Marx, especially the philosophic-humanistic Marx.[68] Certainly there are significant references to Marx and to the dynamic form of structuralism found in Marx's writings that we shall come to shortly. We think there is a substantial element of Marx in Piaget's treatment, or definition, of the idea of a "transformation" already referred to. For Piaget, "transformation" is the vital key to the understanding of structures as nonstatic systems:

"If the character of structured wholes depends on their laws of composition, these laws must of their very nature be *structuring;* it is the constant duality, or bipolarity, of always being simultaneously *structuring* and *struc-*

tured that accounts for the success of the notion of law or rule employed by structuralists. . . . Indeed all known structures—from mathematical groups to kinship systems—are without exception systems of transformation." Transformation, we are told, *need* not be a temporal process. Transforming is involved in the nontemporal succession of 1 + 1 = 2; or the number 3 following hard on 2. "On the other hand, transformation can be a temporal process: getting married 'takes time.' Were it not for the idea of transformation, structures would lose all explanatory import, since they would collapse into static forms."[69]

And yet, with all due credit given Marx for his influence upon Piaget, amply reflected in the passages just cited, it would be unfair to deny Durkheim his own full measure of continuing effect upon Piaget's thinking. After all, it was Durkheim who wrote the following words, as far back as 1900, words which have been quoted before in this chapter but merit quotation again:

> Without doubt, the phenomena which concern structure are somewhat more stable than functional phenomena, but between the two orders of facts there is only a difference of degree. Structure itself occurs in the process of becoming . . . it takes shape and breaks down ceaselessly, it is life which has reached a certain degree of consolidation; and to distinguish the life whence it derives from the life which it determines would be to dissociate inseparable things.[70] .

To be sure, there are very substantial differences between Piaget and Durkheim (as of course there are between Piaget and Marx), the greatest difference being a degree of theoretical concern for the individual in Piaget's work that is not often encountered in Durkheim's writings. Such differences notwithstanding, the impact of Durkheim on the young Piaget remains highly relevant to any understanding of the kind of thinking that lies behind the mature Piaget's work. His *Structuralism*, published in 1970, makes that fact evident enough.

German Structuralism

In Germany one principal source of a structuralist approach in the social sciences is Hegel's philosophy, in particular the concept of "totality." For Hegel the concept had a cosmic reference and included the whole historical process; but within this framework of a comprehensive totality, which was finally to be realized in Absolute Mind, Hegel devoted his attention to more limited totalities—the history of human society, especially in the Western world,[71] and the structure of modern "civil society" and the nation state.[72] Thus the Hegelian influence upon German social thought could take two different directions: one in which the main emphasis was placed upon the historical development of society, and hence upon the historical character of the social sciences (and at the same time their distinctive nature as "cultural sciences," or "sciences of the spirit"—*Geisteswissenschaften*); the other in which attention was concentrated upon the systematic interconnectedness, the structural order, of particular societies in distinct historical periods, or more generally, of human societies as such, regarded synchronically.

Both conceptions are present in Marx's work, which represents in many respects the most important development of Hegel's social thought in the nineteenth century. Especially in his early writings Marx was still largely preoccupied with Hegel's philosophy, and with Feuerbach's critical revision of it; and in his "Contribution to the Critique of Hegel's Philosophy of Right: Introduction" (1844) and the *Economic and Philosophical Manuscripts* (1844) he not only examines critically Hegel's analysis of the relation between civil society and the state and begins to outline his own conception of the mode of production of material life as the basis of civil society—subsequently formulated more precisely in the preface to *A Contribution to the Critique of Political Economy* (1859)—but he also expresses in a new form a philosophy of history derived from Hegel, the content of which is the self-creation of man through his action upon nature, upon himself, and upon his society. This philosophy of history, which is also a theory of progress,[73] is most vigorously expressed in the *Economic and Philosophical Manuscripts*, in a passage such as the following:

> *Communism* is the *positive* abolition of *private property*, of *human self-alienation*, and thus the real *appropriation* of *human* nature through and for man. It is, therefore, the return of man himself as a social, i.e. really human, being, a complete and conscious return which assimilates all the wealth of previous development. Communism as a fully developed naturalism is humanism and as a fully developed humanism is naturalism. It is the *definitive* resolution of the antagonism between man and nature, and between man and man. It is the true solution of the conflict between existence and essence, between objectification and self-affirmation, between freedom and necessity, between individual and species. It is the solution of the riddle of history and knows itself to be this solution.[74]

In his later work Marx plainly devoted himself principally to a profound analysis of one form of society, namely modern capitalist society and its roots in the capitalist mode of production, but the idea of a historical development toward socialism or communism was never absent from his thought. It is quite right to say, therefore, as does Althusser, that Marx's theory "reveals the existence of *two problems*. . . . Marx regards contemporary society (and every other past form of society) both as a *result* and as a *society*."[75] Nevertheless, among later Marxist thinkers there has been a fairly clear distinction between those who give preeminence to historical interpretation and those who concentrate their attention upon the structural analysis of the capitalist mode of production and capitalist society. In the former group, which is more strongly influenced by Hegelian philosophy, are to be counted Lukács, Gramsci, and the major thinkers of the Frankfurt School (Adorno, Horkheimer, and Marcuse); and one of the principal elements in their social theory is embodied in Lukács's conception of "totality":

Only in this context which sees the isolated facts of social life as aspects of the historical process and integrates them in a *totality,* can knowledge of the facts hope to become knowledge of *reality.* . . . It is not the primacy of economic motives in historical explanation that constitutes the decisive difference between Marxism and bourgeois thought; but the point of view of totality. The category of totality, the all-pervasive supremacy of the whole over the parts is the essence of the method which Marx took over from Hegel and brilliantly transformed into the foundations of a wholly new science."[76]

In contrast with this view, those Marxist thinkers who have been primarily concerned with analyzing the structure of modes of production and social formations, and more particularly the capitalist mode of production, have been inclined to conceive Marxist theory as political economy rather than history, as is the case, for example, in the later writings of Karl Korsch.[77] But it is during the past two decades in particular that Marxist structural analysis has developed most rapidly, leading to new interpretations of Marx's own theory, and it will be considered more fully in the next section. At an earlier time, it was the influence of Marx's thought upon other German sociologists which gave rise to a concentration of attention upon social structure, and above all, upon the structure of capitalist society. The best example is Ferdinand Tönnies, whose major work, *Gemeinschaft und Gesellschaft* (*Community and Association*) (1887),[78] is singled out by R. Bastide, in his introduction to a collective work on the uses of the term "structure" in the social sciences,[79] as the starting point for the contribution of German sociologists to the analysis of social structure. Tönnies himself, in the preface to the first edition of his book, referred to Marx as "the discoverer of the capitalist mode of production" and as "a thinker who had attempted to give expression to the same idea that I myself wanted to express in my own new conceptualization"; and the substance of his work is the contrast between two major types of social structure—"community" and "society"—and an analysis of the elements and relationships which constitute them. Tönnies's indebtedness to Marx is shown particularly in his analysis of *Gesellschaft,* which he largely identifies with modern capitalist society based upon commodity production:

If the retail market is considered only as the necessary consequence of commodity market, the essential structure of Gesellschaft is then described by three acts, all performed by the capitalist class. . . . The three acts are: (1) the purchase of labour, (2) the employment of labour, (3) the sale of labour in the form of value elements of the products.

Tönnies goes on to say that "the labouring class seemingly has its share only as an object; in reality all material which is apparently the causation of the second act lies with this labouring class, and only the formal causation lies with the capitalist class." And he concludes his analysis with the observation that: "The question of whether this dualistic construction of the concept of Gesellschaft is the only one possible does not concern us here. It is, at any rate, the construction which necessarily follows from the premise of commerce."[80]

According to Bastide, Tönnies's work was followed by several other attempts by German sociologists to distinguish the principal types of social and political structure; and this kind of analysis and classification may be seen as culminating, in certain respects, in the work of the French sociologist Georges Gurvitch, who not only critically reviewed the diverse efforts to define "social structure" and to produce a comprehensive typology of its forms,[81] but formulated his own concept of social structure (incorporating the notions of "destructuration" and "restructuration") and an elaborate classification of the principal types of "global societies."[82]

But there was also quite a different approach to the analysis of society as a structure or system, which emerged from the neo-Kantian revival in German philosophy in the later nineteenth century, best exemplified in the sociological writings of Georg Simmel. One important element in neo-Kantian philosophy, especially in the work of the Marburg school, was the concern with demarcating the spheres of scientific inquiry, establishing the logical foundations of the various sciences, and constructing rational models which could organize the data of experience. Thus Simmel in his essay "How is society possible?"[83] undertook, in Kantian fashion, to define the scope and subject matter of sociology and went on in numerous essays[84] and in his major sociological study, *Philosophy of Money*,[85] to construct models of the different forms of social relations, or "sociation," which characterized particular social groups or whole societies. "Society," according to Simmel, "is merely the name for a number of individuals, connected by interaction,"[86] and the analysis of society consists in specifying and elucidating the diverse forms of "interaction" or "sociation." For the most part the notion of a predominant form of interaction—that is, a distinctive structure—in a whole society remains somewhat vague in Simmel's writings, since he preferred to concentrate his own studies upon the interactions among the "atoms of society"; but in the *Philosophy of Money* he did examine, in a manner close to that of Marx and Tönnies, the all-pervading social relations engendered by the functions of money in modern capitalist society. It might be argued, indeed, that much of Simmel's sociological analysis has a greater affinity with recent structuralism than have the more empiricist conceptions of structure that are to be found in the works of Radcliffe-Brown, Gurvitch, and others,[87] because Simmel, like the recent structuralists, was primarily interested in the construction of models representing an inner logical structure behind appearances.

Simmel's ideas, as we have indicated, were communicated mainly in essays on particular, often quite limited, aspects of social life or on general methodological problems; except in his last comprehensive statement on sociology, *Grundfragen der Soziologie*, (*Fundamental Problems of Sociology*) they were not systematically expounded as a distinctive body of sociological thought. Later, however, they were systematized and at the same time modified by Leopold von Wiese, whose work established one of the types of sociology that Simmel distinguished and was most attracted by—"formal" or "systematic" sociology—as a distinct sociological approach.[88] Starting from the notion of individual interaction, von Wiese introduced, in the major exposition of his sociological system,[89] four basic concepts—social process, social distance, social space, and social formation—and in the second part of the book attempted to classify social formations in terms of their distance from the individual, arriving thus at a distinction between mass, group, and abstract collectivity. Social structure is conceived in this view as an abstract model of the relations between individuals and between groups, which nevertheless arises from and depends upon individual interaction, and constitutes only a representation of society as a whole that members themselves construct. Here there seems to be a marked divergence from Simmel's view of sociation, as well as a much more pronounced individualism—since for Simmel the "forms of sociation" or "societal forms" have an independent, objective existence and represent a specific "layer" of reality. As Tenbruck remarks: "Although [the forms] cannot—and are not meant to—account for interaction itself, they are operative in it; they account for its patterns. They exert constraint in the structuring of actions . . . in that they recurrently bring about typical situations and typical changes, forms provide a basis upon which predictions can be made."[90] From this we can see that Simmel's own "formal sociology" was, as Kurt Wolff has claimed, "close to the modern concern with 'social structure'; one does justice to a great portion of Simmel's sociology by saying that he attempted to throw light on the structure of society."[91] Still more, it can be said, as we have already suggested, that Simmel's conception is close to recent structuralist approaches, for as Aron has noted, citing the view of Theodor Geiger, one consequence of formal sociology was to give the concept of society an increasingly abstract and relational character.[92]

Recent Structuralism

In the preceding discussion we have shown that the concept of structure has had an important place in sociological analysis from the very beginnings of the discipline. R. Bastide, in the work previously mentioned, traces the use of the term "structure" from Herbert Spencer—in whose sociological system the structure of society is conceived by analogy with the structure of an organism—through Durkheim, to Radcliffe-Brown—who is quoted as saying that "there is a real and significant analogy between social structure and organic structure"; and from Marx to Tönnies and beyond.[93] Our own account, however, indicates that the concept can be found much earlier, in the work of Vico, Saint-Simon, and Comte, and later, in a particularly interesting form, in the writings of Simmel and of those who were influenced by him.

We have to ask, therefore, in what sense recent structuralism constitutes a distinctive type of sociological analysis, how it can be differentiated from the manifest, long-standing concern of sociologists with the depiction and investigation of social structures or social systems. Some commentators have regarded the structuralist movement as being, from one aspect, a new Parisian intellectual fashion which has taken the place of existentialism;[94] and they as well as others have insisted upon the fact that structural analysis has a longer history than is recognized by many adherents of the recent movement. Thus, Schaff cites the study by a Polish philosopher, J. Metallmann, published in 1933, which concludes that the concept of structure has become central and dominant in contemporary philosophical and scientific thought,[95] while Bastide argues, similarly, that the term "structure" underwent a transformation in the 1930s, with a movement from a biological to a mathematical conception of structure, and suggests that the development of Gestalt psychology was one important element in this revolution.[96]

A number of writers, taking a still longer view, have claimed that structuralism has not profoundly modified the notion of structure that was already employed by many nineteenth-century social scientists. Kolakowski, for example, in his critical essay on Althusser's Marxism, comments:

> Althusser stresses that instead of "expressing" the basic spiritual principle of the time (as in Hegelian doctrine), particular elements of the social whole are conceived in Marxism as being determined by ("over-determined") the structure of the whole and this "structure," which determines its elements, seems to him an especially innovatory methodological device. In reality, the concept of the "whole" which is not determined by the qualities of its elements and which, on the contrary, has qualities and "laws" of its own, determining qualities of the elements, this concept goes back to least to Aristotle. It was especially developed in Gestalt psychology and Gestalt theory which was able to endow it with empirical meaning. . . . To repeat now—as Althusser does—generalities about "structural determination" and the "irreducibility" of the whole to its elements does not lead us beyond common sense platitudes."[97]

In a similar vein, but on a more general level, Runciman suggests that his brief survey of structuralism leads to the conclusion that:

> "structuralism," whether in its Anglo-Saxon or Gallic version, should not be claimed to constitute a novel, coherent and comprehensive paradigm for sociological and anthropological theory. Whether viewed as a doctrine or a method . . . "structuralism" as such does not, on examination, stand for a more distinctive standpoint than a belief in the applicability of rigorous models to social behavior. . . .[98]

Nevertheless, it has been widely accepted that structuralism in its wider aspects does represent a new intellectual outlook, in philosophy, linguistics, and literary criticism as well as in the social sciences.[99] As a broad movement of thought, structuralism is characterized particularly, in the writings of Lévi-Strauss, Foucault, and Althusser—as Raymond Aron points out—by its antihumanism and/or antihistoricism.[100] What significance do these two features have for structuralism as a mode of sociological analysis?

By antihumanism is meant that the conscious and purposive actions of individuals and social groups (and particularly, in the case of Marxist writers, social classes) are excluded from the analysis, and sociological explanation is conceived in terms of "structural causality." This view is well formulated by Godelier when he distinguishes two kinds of conditions for the emergence, functioning, and evolution of any social system; namely (1) intentional activity and (2) the unintentional properties inherent in social relations; assigns a decisive importance to the latter; and argues that the ultimate reason or basis for the transformations that social systems undergo is to be found in the degree of compatibility or incompatibility between structures and in the development of contradictions within structures, especially within the *determining* structure, which is—from a Marxist standpoint—the mode of production of material life.[101] This aspect of the structuralist approach (in the case of Godelier, a Marxist structuralism) appears clearly when it is contrasted with Sartre's methodological investigations in *Critique de la raison dialectique*[102] the object of which is precisely to clarify the relation between structural conditions and the intentional actions—the "projects"—of individuals, and to introduce into Marxism some elements of the individualistic and humanist outlook of existentialism.

The antihistoricist orientation of structuralism may be expressed in different ways. In the work of Lévi-Strauss it appears as a general preference for synchronic as opposed to diachronic investigations, with the aim of discovering universal structural characteristics of human society, and more remotely, relating these characteristics to universal structures of the human mind itself. Here, the structuralist approach in anthropology and sociology shows a marked affinity with modern linguistic theory.[103] Among Marxist structuralists there are those, such as Hindess and Hirst, who are even more strongly antihistoricist and deny that Marxism is, or can be, a "science of history," since in their view all attempts to formulate historical explanations emerge as teleological doctrines, not scientific theories.[104] Others, however, adopt a more moderate, perhaps less rigorous, view. Althusser, as we have seen, considers that Marxist theory deals with two problems—society as a system and society as a result—and thus proffers two kinds of explanation, structural and historical. Godelier takes a similar attitude: structural analysis, he argues, has priority over historical inquiry, and it is only by defining the inner properties of particular structures and discovering the contradictions inherent in them that we shall be able eventually to establish the causes of historical transformations. Only when we know how ". . . to reconstruct, through scientific thought, the *limited* number of possible changes which any particular structure or particular combination of structures may carry out," shall we be in a position to *explain* history, instead of confronting it as an immense mass of unrelated facts.[105] From this standpoint he also criticizes Lévi-Strauss's structuralism, which, in spite of its claim to accept Marx's thesis of a law of order in social structures and their changes, reduces history to mere contingency and denies that historical processes are "analytical objects."[106]

It can scarcely be disputed that structuralism, by its rigorous criticism of and opposition to any analysis of society which is conceived primarily in terms either of the intentional actions of individuals or of the working out of historical processes, does constitute itself as a distinctive type of sociological analysis. But there are two other features of recent structuralism which also distinguish it, in important ways, from a general structural approach such as we have shown to be present in much nineteenth- and twentieth-century sociology and anthropology. In the first place, "structure" becomes a basic theoretical concept, to an extent that cannot be claimed for it as it was used in the sociological theories of Comte, Spencer, Durkheim, Radcliffe-Brown, or even perhaps (except by means of a structuralist reinterpretation) Marx. In recent structuralism the concept of structure occupies a central and dominant place and is the object of theoretical elaboration and refinement which goes far beyond the work of previous thinkers, with the possible exception, as we have suggested, of Simmel. Still more important is a second feature—namely, the insistence upon penetrating behind the immediately given, surface appearances of social phenomena to an inner, "hidden," or "deep" structure. This point of view is set out clearly by Godelier in his criticism of "classical empirical functionalism," which, he argues, has radical theoretical defects: ". . . by confusing social structure with external social relations, functionalist analysis is condemned to remain a prisoner of appearances within the social system studied, and there is no possibility of uncovering any below-surface logic, not evident in the system itself, still less the structural and consequential circumstances of their historical appearance and disappearance."[107] And Godelier defines the structuralist approach, which he grounds upon Marx's epistemology, in these terms: ". . . we must discover and examine, by ways yet to be found, the invisible network of causes linking together forms, functions, modes of articulation, and the hierarchy, appearance and disappearance of particular social structures."[108] Structuralism therefore emphasizes, as was noted earlier in the discussion of Lévi-Strauss, the unconscious causation of social events and situations.

From Godelier's presentation, as well as from the writings of modern linguistic theorists and of Lévi-Strauss and Althusser, it will be apparent that structuralism rests upon, or embodies, a general philosophy of science which is not only antihumanist (in the two senses that it rejects any account of social life in terms of subjective, conscious, intentional action, and that it refuses to assign a peculiar status to the human sciences) and antihistoricist, but also, in a specific sense, antiempiricist. Most prominently in the work of Althusser and of those influenced by him, structuralism adopts as its epistemological basis the "rational materialism" of Gaston Bachelard—which is also largely identified with the implicit epistemology of Marx—according to which the essential step in the constitution and development of any science is the theoretical construction of the object of scientific inquiry by the formation of concepts which refer to "hidden" realities, not to the immediately given data which provide the starting point for empiricist science. The structuralist movement, therefore, expresses a very general and distinctive orientation to scientific inquiry in any field, as well as a particular approach to the study of social systems.

This is not to say that structuralism, however wide-ranging its recent influence may have been in the social sciences, in linguistics, and in historical studies, has an entirely homogeneous orientation, or that it has the same degree of importance in all areas of inquiry. As we have seen, there are various disagreements between Marxist structuralists and others,[109] about whether there is an "ultimate" determining structural element in a social system, and about the existence and significance of "structural contradictions"; and a more general disagreement about the place of historical explanation within structuralist theory. Furthermore, it is clear that structuralism has so far been most influential and has made the most rapid progress in linguistics and in anthropology; in sociology its influence has been mediated by anthropology (through this is not perhaps of overriding significance, since very similar problems are raised, at least in social anthropology and sociology, and there is no longer any very precise line of demarcation between these two disciplines) and by Marxist thought. It could indeed be said that Marxist structuralism has been one of the principal intellectual factors in the recent revival of Marxist ideas in sociology.[110]

Our historical survey has shown, we believe, that while the concept of "structure" and the structural analysis of social systems have been important elements in the theoretical schemes of major sociological thinkers since the beginnings of the discipline, the structuralist movement—in spite of displaying, as various critics have observed, some of the features of a "cult" or intellectual "fashion"—does represent a new and distinctive orientation by its rejection of, and its formulation of an alternative to, humanist, historicist, and empiricist conceptions of the methodology of the social sciences. Whether this amounts to an "epistemological break" (to use Bachelard's expression) or the emergence of an entirely new paradigm following a "scientific revolution" (in Kuhn's terminology) is a matter of continuing controversy, but we can at least say that recent structuralist work in anthropology and sociology has introduced fruitful ideas and hypotheses and has raised the level of theoretical comprehension and debate to an extent that warrants our speaking of a genuine scientific advance in this sphere.

NOTES

1. See S. Sambursky, *Physical World of the Greeks,* Merton Dagut, trans. (New York: Macmillan, 1956) passim.

2. F. M. Cornford, *Principium Sapientiae: The Origins of Greek Scientific Thought.* (Cambridge: Cambridge University Press, 1952) especially pp. 179–81.

3. See Robert Nisbet, *Social Change and History* (New York: Oxford University Press, 1969) especially chaps. 1–3 but passim for an account of organism as image and model in Western thought.

4. For some interesting and revealing comments on how influential ancient Greek, and

especially Platonic, mathematical images of structure in the universe can be even at the present time, see Werner Heisenberg, *Physics and Beyond* (New York: Harper & Row, 1973)

5. F. A. Lange's classic *History of Materialism*, E. C. Thomas, trans. (Boston, 1881) vol. 3 remains the fullest treatment of this subject. See also Ernan McMullin, ed. *Galileo, Man of Science* (New York: Basic Books, 1967), in which all aspects of the role of physical science in the sixteenth and seventeenth centuries are dealt with authoritatively and usefully.

6. Raymond Williams, *Keywords: A Vocabulary of Culture and Society.* (New York: Oxford University Press, 1976) pp. 253–59.

7. See for example Raymond Boudon, *The Uses of Structuralism* (London: Heinemann, 1971); David Robey, ed., *Structuralism: An Introduction* (Oxford: Clarendon Press, 1973): Jean-Marie Benoist, *La Révolution Structurale* (Paris: Grasset, 1976); Philip Pettit, *The Concept of Structuralism* (London: Gill & Macmillan, 1976). We shall discuss Jean Piaget's fine overview of the subject later in this chapter.

8. We agree with Robert K. Merton "that structural analysis in sociology involves the confluence of ideas deriving principally from Durkheim and Marx," expressed in "Structural Analysis in Sociology" in Peter Blau, *Approaches to the Study of Social Structure* (New York: Free Press, 1976). The deep and far-reaching roots of Durkheim in Auguste Comte are, however, known to all students of Durkheim, as they were indeed to Durkheim himself.

9. Comte, *System of Positive Polity*, Frederick Harrison, trans. (1851–54) vol. 2, p. 153.

10. Ibid., pp. 216, 217.

11. See the *Outline of the Positive Philosophy* (1830–42), which is the first and most famous of Comte's major works, The final two volumes of the work deal with "social physics" and/or "sociology."

12. *Positive Philosophy*, vol. 1, chap. 1.

13. Ibid., vol. 3. book 6, chap. 1.

14. Ibid., vol. 3, book 6, chap. 3.

15. Ibid., vol. 3, book 6, chap. 3.

16. Ibid., vol. 3, book 6, chap. 3.

17. Ibid., vol. 3, book 6, chap. 7.

18. Ibid., vol. 3, book 6, chap. 12.

19. In Isaiah Berlin, "Vico's Concept of Knowledge," in Giorgio Tagliacozzo and Hayden V. White, eds., *Giambattista Vico: An International Symposium* (Baltimore: Johns Hopkins Press, 1969) p. 377. See also Isaiah Berlin, *Vico and Herder: Two Studies in the History of Ideas* (New York: Viking Press, 1976). The best and most succinct digest of Vico's philosophy is Leon Pompa, *Vico: A Study of the "New Science"* (Cambridge: Cambridge University Press, 1975). There has been, of course, an enormous amount of scholarship on Vico during recent years, but these works we have cited are a valuable representation of the scholarship so far done, and also a guide to the work of other scholars.

20. See especially Tagliacozzo and White, *Giambattista Vico*, part III, pp. 246–370, which deal with his impact upon nineteenth- and twentieth-century sociological and historical minds.

21. Edmund Leach, "Vico and Lévi-Strauss on the Origins of Humanity," in Tagliacozzo and White, *Giambattista Vico*, pp. 309–18.

22. See Pompa, *Vico*, chap. 1, on these recurrent structures.

23. Ibid., p. 26.

24. Werner Stark, "Giambattista Vico's Sociology of Knowledge" in Tagliacozzo and White, *Giambattista Vico*, p. 300.

25. Leach, "Vico and Lévi-Strauss," pp. 312–13.

26. Ibid., p. 314.

27. Ibid., p. 316.

28. See especially Lévi-Strauss's inaugural lecture at the Collège de France when he assumed the chair in social anthropology there: *The Scope of Anthropology* (London: Jonathan Cape, 1967) especially p. 8.

29. The passage is reprinted in Kurt Wolff, ed., *Emile Durkheim* (Columbus: Ohio State University Press, 1960) p. 362.

30. E. Durkheim, *Montesquieu and Rousseau*, R. Manheim trans. (Ann Arbor: University of Michigan Press, 1960) p. 13.

31. E. Durkheim, *The Division of Labor*, George Simpson, trans. (New York: Macmillan Co., 1933) p. 215.

32. See E. Durkheim, *The Elementary Forms of Religious Life*, Joseph Ward Swain, trans. (London: Allen & Unwin, 1915) pp. 9–18 and passim.

33. Ibid., pp. 17–18.

34. Ibid., p. 363.
35. Ibid., p. 369.
36. E. Durkheim, *Incest: The Nature and the Origin of the Taboo*, Edward Sagarin, trans. (New York: Lyle Stuart, 1963) p. 100.
37. Ibid., p. 103.
38. Durkheim, *Elementary Forms*, p. 416.
39. Ibid., p. 416.
40. Ibid., p. 417.
41. On Mauss's life and major works see Steven Lukes's excellent article in the *International Encyclopedia of the Social Sciences*, vol. 10, pp. 78–82. See also Marvin Harris, *The Rise of Anthropological Theory* (New York: Thomas Y. Crowell, 1968) pp. 482 ff.
42. Marcel Mauss, *The Gift*, I. Cunnison, trans. (New York: Free Press, 1954).
43. Mauss, *The Gift*, p. 31.
44. M. Halbwachs, *The Psychology of Social Class*, introduction by Georges Friedman, (Glencoe, Ill.: Free Press, 1959).
45. M. Halbwachs, *Les Causes du Suicide* (Paris: Alcan, 1930).
46. M. Halbwachs, *Les Cadres Sociaux de la Mêmoire* (Paris: Presses Universitaires de France, 1925, nouvelle ed., 1952; reprint ed. New York: Arno Press, 1975). See also Halbwachs's *Mêmoire Collective*, with its often brilliant follow-ups to earlier themes concerning memory, published posthumously in 1950, Jeanne Alexandre, ed.
47. Harris, *The Rise of Anthropological Theory*, p. 525.
48. A. R. Radcliffe-Brown, *A Natural Science of Society* (New York: Free Press, 1957) p. 49. (First published by the University of Chicago Press, 1948).
49. Ibid., p. 87.
50. See the detailed and superbly informative account of the *Annales* school, its principal figures and works, as well as major presuppositions and methods, in J. H. Hexter's long article in *The Journal of Modern History*, vol. 44, no. 4 (December 1972) pp. 480–539.
51. Ibid., p. 487 ff.
52. F. Braudel, *The Mediterranean*, Sian Reynolds, trans., 2 vols. (New York: Harper & Row, 1972) vol. I, p. 16. See also Braudel's fascinating *Capitalism and Material Life, 1400–1800*, Miriam Kochan, trans. (New York: Harper & Row, 1973).
53. Hexter, as cited, p. 538.
54. See the excellent account of the complex argument of this Lévi-Strauss work in Harris, *The Rise of Anthropological Theory*, p. 490–500.
55. C. Lévi-Strauss, *The Savage Mind* (Chicago: University of Chicago Press, 1966) p. 251.
56. Edmund Leach, *Claude Lêvi-Strauss* (New York: Viking Press. London: Fontana, 1970) p. 59.
57. C. Lévi-Strauss, *The Scope of Anthropology*, p. 8.
58. C. Lévi-Strauss *Structural Anthropology*. C. Jacobson and B. G. Schoepf, trans. (New York: Basic Books, 1963) pp. 15–16.
59. C. Lévi-Strauss, *The Savage Mind*, p. 263.
60. Ibid., p. 26.
61. Ibid., p. 16.
62. Leach, as cited, p. 43.
63. Ibid., p. 38.
64. Jean Piaget, *Etudes Sociologiques* (Geneva: Librairie Droz, 1965) pp. 15–99.
65. Piaget, *Structuralism*, Chaninah Maschler, trans. (New York: Basic Books, 1970) p. 4.
66. Ibid., p. 5.
67. Ibid., p. 7.
68. Ibid., p. 125: "That there is a structuralist strand in Marx, something just about halfway between what we called 'global' and 'analytic' structuralism, is obvious, since he distinguishes 'real infrastructures' from 'ideological superstructures' and describes the former in terms which, though remaining qualitative, are sufficiently precise to bring us close to directly observable relations."
69. Ibid., pp. 10–12, *passim*.
70. Wolff, *Emile Durkheim*, p. 362.
71. G. W. F. Hegel, *The Philosophy of History* (New York: Dover Publications, 1956).
72. G. W. F. Hegel, *The Philosophy of Right* (Oxford: Oxford University Press, 1942). For a general discussion of Hegel's theory of society and the state, see also Karl Löwith, *From Hegel to Nietzsche* (London: Constable, 1964) and Shlomo Avineri, *Hegel's Theory of the Modern State* (Cambridge: Cambridge University Press, 1972).

73. See Eric Hobsbawm, Introduction to Karl Marx, *Pre-Capitalist Economic Formations*, (London: Lawrence and Wishart, 1964), pp. 11–16.

74. T. B. Bottomore, ed., *Karl Marx: Early Writings* (London: Watts & Co. 1963) p. 155.

75. See chapter 4 herein.

76. G. Lukács, *History and Class Consciousness* (London: Merlin Press, 1971) pp. 8, 27. See also H. Marcuse, *Reason and Revolution* (New York: Oxford University Press, 1941) pp. 312–20. This Hegelian form of Marxist theory is discussed more fully in Bottomore, *Karl Marx: Early Writings*. See chapter 4 herein.

77. See especially Karl Korsch, *Karl Marx* (London: Chapman & Hall, 1938). Another instance of a more structural type of analysis is Rudolf Hilferding, *Das Finanzkapital*, (Vienna: Wiener Volksbuchhandlung, 1910).

78. F. Tönnies, *Community and Association* (London: Routledge & Kegan Paul, 1955).

79. Roger Bastide, ed., *Sens et usages du terme Structure* (The Hague: Mouton, 1962).

80. F. Tönnies, *Community and Association*, pp. 114–15.

81. G. Gurvitch, *La vocation actuelle de la Sociologie*, (Paris: Presses Universitaires de France, 2nd ed. 1957) vol. I, pp. 400–442.

82. G. Gurvitch, ed., *Traité de Sociologie* (Paris: Presses Universitaires de France, 1962) vol. I, chaps. 4 and 5.

83. In G. Simmel, *Soziologie* (1908); trans in Kurt H. Wolff, ed., *Georg Simmel 1858-1918* (Columbus: Ohio State University Press, 1959) pp. 337–56.

84. See especially the essays collected in G. Simmel, *Über soziale Differenzierung: Soziologische and psychologische Untersuchungen* (1890); and in *Soziologie: Untersuchungen über die Formen der Vergesellschaftung* (1908); and *Grundfragen der Soziologie (Individuum und Gesellschaft)* (1917).

85. G. Simmel, *Philosophie des Geldes* (1900); English trans. (London: Routledge & Kegan Paul, 1978.)

86. G. Simmel, *Grundfragen der Soziologie;* trans. in Kurt H. Wolff, ed., *The Sociology of Georg Simmel* (Glencoe: The Free Press, 1950) p. 10.

87. In addition to the works by Radcliffe-Brown and Gurvitch mentioned previously, see S. F. Nadel, *The Theory of Social Structure* (London: Cohen & West, 1957) and H. H. Gerth and C. Wright Mills, *Character and Social Structure* (London: Routledge & Kegan Paul, 1953).

88. See, for a general account of this approach, Raymond Aron, *German Sociology* (London: Heinemann, 1957) chap. 1; and F. H. Tenbruck, "Formal Sociology" in Wolff, *Georg Simmel, 1858-1918*, pp. 61–99.

89. Leopold von Wiese, *System der Soziologie als Lehre von den sozialen Prozessen und den sozialen Gebilden der Menschen (Beziehungslehre)*, 2d enlarged ed. (1933).

90. Tenbruck, "Formal Sociology," pp. 85–86.

91. Wolff, *The Sociology of Georg Simmel*, p. xxxvi.

92. Aron, *German Sociology*, p. 35.

93. Bastide, *Sens et usages du terme Structure*, pp. 10–12.

94. See for example, Raymond Aron, *Marxismes imaginaires* (Paris: Gallimard, 1970) note finale; and Adam Schaff, *Structuralisme et Marxisme* (Paris: Editions Anthropos, 1974) p. 11.

95. Ibid., pp. 9–10.

96. Bastide, *Sens et usage du terme Structure*, pp. 13–14.

97. Leszek Kolakowski, "Althusser's Marx," in *The Socialist Register*, (1971) p. 124.

98. W. G. Runciman, *Sociology in Its Place and Other Essays* (Cambridge: Cambridge University Press, 1970) p. 58.

99. For a general account of structuralism in diverse fields of inquiry, see David Robey, ed., *Structuralism: An Introduction;* and Jean Piaget, *Structuralism*

100. Aron, *Marxismes Imaginaires*, pp. 336–41.

101. Maurice Godelier, *Rationality and Irrationality in Economics* (London: New Left Books, 1974). See further the discussion in chapter 4 herein, p. 136.

102. Jean-Paul Sartre, *Critique de la raison dialectique* (Paris: Gallimard, 1960). Trans. of the prefatory essay as *Search for a Method* (New York: Alfred A. Knopf, 1963), and of the rest of the book as *Critique of Dialectical Reason* (London: New Left Books, 1976).

103. Notably that of Saussure, Jakobson, and most recently Chomsky, whose general view has been described as follows: "linguistics should determine the universal and essential properties of human language," cited in John Lyons, *Chomsky* (London: Fontana/Collins, 1970) p. 99.

104. See chapter 4 herein, p. 137.

105. M. Godelier, *Perspectives in Marxist Anthropology*, p. 7. See also the discussion in chapter 4 herein, p. 136.

106. Ibid., pp. 46–48.
107. Ibid., p. 35.
108. Ibid., p. 2.
109. Althusser, in his foreword to the Italian edition of *Reading Capital,* insists upon the difference between his own views and those expressed in what he calls the "structuralist ideology"; while Godelier, as we have shown in the text, criticizes some features of Lévi-Strauss's structuralism.
110. See chapter 4 herein, pp. 135–41.

15

SOCIAL STRATIFICATION

FRANK PARKIN

STRATIFICATION THEORY has no history in the sense of a cumulative body of knowledge showing a pattern of development from a primitive to a more sophisticated state of affairs. Anyone surveying the current literature would certainly be struck by its volume and diversity, but hardly by a sense of awe at the advances made over the work of the classical theorists. Alongside the growing refinements of technique and method, Western sociologists have shown a remarkable attachment to the conceptual building blocks provided by those who first analyzed the class structure of capitalism in the midnineteenth and early twentieth centuries. The implied tribute to this early stock of knowledge is all the more striking in view of the fact that it is the work of a fairly narrow circle within the founding family of the discipline. It is only the mildest exaggerations to say that most of what today counts as class or stratification theory has its origins almost exclusively in the writings of Marx and Engels, Max Weber, and the Mosca-Pareto school. This is not of course to deny that other classical theorists offered insights into and observations upon the structure and forms of inequality. The work of Saint-Simon, Tocqueville, Simmel, Durkheim, and the writers of the Scottish Enlightenment are replete with comments upon the newly emergent class structure of capitalism, the distribution of social honor, the strains imposed by new forms of inequality and recipes for their alleviation. But a diagnosis of the times or a series of brilliant aperçus is not equivalent to a corpus of ideas capable of surviving the context in which it was produced and thus establishing a *theoretical tradition*. It is no disparagement of the contribution to sociology in general made by Durkheim, Simmel, and the rest to ask the rhetorical question: what battery of concepts did they bequeath us for the analysis of modern class societies? The question is rhetorical because the answer is all too plain in the names missing from the roll call accompanying the bulk of contemporary work in this field. This might perhaps be due more to the failure of modern minds than to the shortcomings of the early writers; there may be rich seams in the work of these writers still waiting to be mined by intellectual prospectors. It would be unnecessarily dogmatic to deny the possibility of extracting a helpful framework of ideas for studying class or ethnic conflict from the contributions of, say, Tönnies or Comte or Spencer. Sociological imaginings must always be allowed for.

All this really amounts to is saying that most of the founding fathers of the discipline occupy a respectable place in the history of ideas about inequality, comparable to that of the social philosophers. Any such history would no doubt pay due respect to the observations of Plato, St. Augustine, Hobbes, Locke, Rousseau, Hegel—to name the obvious names. But, again, any importation of their ideas into the mainstream tradition of stratification theory is difficult to spot. Those frequent references to the Hobbesian problem of order, or to the social contract, or to the Hegelian conception of the state, and so forth, are wholly conventional embellishments upon the work in hand and play little part in actual analysis. Who would think it useful to confront the Hobbesian problem of order by reference to the ideas of Hobbes?

One possible reason why so much of classical sociology failed to make a greater impact upon what is in some respects the intellectual core of the discipline is that the writers of this early period were preoccupied above all else with the fateful transition from rural, agricultural society to urban, industrial society. Despite the differences in terminology, Durkheim's contrast between mechanical and organic forms of solidarity, Tönnies *Gemeinshaft* and *Gesellschaft*, Maine's status and contract, and so on, all refer to this great watershed in the moral and economic organization of European societies. So fundamental was this distinction between preindustrial and industrial systems thought to be that it tended to obscure a proper recognition of the variety of social and class formations encompassed under each of the general types. The classification of societies by one of the synonyms for preindustrial entailed the indiscriminate lumping together of a vast range of different systems, including tribal, slave, caste, feudal, absolutist, and Asiatic despotism; much in the way that in recent times the term industrial society has been employed as a catch-all for systems as unlike as welfare capitalism, fascism, state socialism, and military dictatorship. It was not so much that the different forms of stratification in preindustrial society were regarded as sufficiently similar in their fundamentals as to justify their inclusion in a single conceptual pigeonhole. Rather, the conceptual framework itself served to inhibit the recognition of historical and cultural variation as a matter for inquiry. It may not be altogether a coincidence that the wide-ranging interest in comparative class structures shown by both Marx and Weber was not accompanied by the common classificatory urge to capture the complexities of the social world in a handy, all-purpose dichotomy. Paradoxically, it was their unsociological respect for the historical record which gave their treatment of the processes of class formation, conflict, and change its distinctiveness and its staying power.

The all-pervasive influence of Marx and Weber upon stratification theory is, if anything, more pronounced today than at any other stage of the subject's development. This is to some extent due to two parallel tendencies in American sociology: first, the increased readiness to treat the work of Marx, and the Marxist tradition generally, with the same seriousness it has always been accorded in Europe, and not simply as a straw man constructed for the purpose of easy demolition; and second, the apparent disenchantment with those distinctively homegrown American varieties of class analysis which held sway in the immediate postwar period. Taken together, these two developments have brought American stratification theory more into line with its European counterpart, which never really strayed very far from the framework of inquiry and debate established by Marx and Weber.

In light of all this it may be convenient to begin a general assessment of stratification theory and its products by examining those contributions which have taken shape under the impress of specifically American concerns and conditions and which have no direct equivalent in the European branch of the discipline. It must at once be said that this should not be taken as an invitation to embark upon one more whirlwind tour of the mountainous literature on stratification research in the United States and elsewhere. Rather, the intention is to single out for examination a number of key themes and problems that pervade this literature, which for purposes of convenience will be considered under the following completely arbitrary headings: class and status, property, the state, ethnicity, and gender. Although this essay is neither a history nor a trend report, an attempt will be made to consider some of the most recent contributions to the subject without losing sight of the traditions they spring from.

Class and Status

It is in the use of the associated terms of class and status above all others in the stratification lexicon that a distinctively American approach having no clear parallels in European theory is most easily discernible. The special flavor of this approach is brought out sharply by the debate in the early postwar period over whether classes could be said to exist; that is, whether they could be regarded as real entities like the family or the church, or whether they were products of statistical fancy. The advocates of the latter view were impressed by the fact that the distribution of rewards in American society appeared to follow a more or less unbroken continuum from top to bottom, so that any decision to impose cut-off points separating a higher class or stratum from a lower one seemed an arbitrary and pointless procedure—arbitrary, because in the absence of natural breaks in the gradient an artificial line could be drawn almost anywhere; pointless, because the resulting classes would not correspond to genuine social groupings in the sense of a shared and recognized membership. As one of the earliest formulations of this view expressed it, "The researcher who goes into the field looking for a social class is hunting for something that is not there; he will find it only in his own mind as figments of the intellect."[1]

The theoretical defense of America as a classless society rested not only on the invisibility of any social cleavage but also on the associated claim that the criteria by which individuals and groups could be ranked in the reward hierarchy were too numerous and diverse for a consistent class pattern to emerge. It was suggested that clearly defined strata only occurred in societies in which the criteria of rank were strictly limited, as in the case of feudal systems where the right to bear arms or to possess land were among the few principles governing the distribution of honor. In advanced societies numerous other factors entered the picture, including education, income, occupation, religion, ethnicity, and so on. The fact that these criteria of rank were independent of each other meant that individuals who ranked high on one dimension could rank low on others, making it impermissible to speak of a coherent system of stratification at all.[2] In place of a model of structured inequality a picture emerged of a highly fragmented and inchoate social order comprised of loose aggregates of individuals having nothing in common other than a similar score in the measurement of ranked indices. Each individual was thus conceived of as a summation of his high and low statuses, rather as if these were separate items on a personal balance sheet which could be totted up to record the state of his moral and social credit in the Great Ledger of Society.

The intellectual origins of this "multidimensional" approach were usually traced to the work of Weber, and more especially to that Weber who inhabits the pages of student textbooks on stratification in which his ideas are presented as a refutation of Marx's theory of class. The multidimensional approach is there viewed as a corrective to, or displacement of, Marx's "economic determinism" by giving proper stress to the role of status factors which operate independently of class and dilute its social effects. Since it could easily be shown that income level did not necessarily correspond to status ranking, the clear inference was that the economic definition of class, and by extension Marxist theory in general, was of little use in understanding American reality. Numberless writers drove home the point that important discrepancies were to be found between status and class dimensions, usually simplistically understood as levels of income and prestige, and that consequently the notion of a class structure had to be approached with the greatest caution in so far as it could be entertained at all.[3]

Because Weber's contribution was seen to be the disentangling of a number of separate variables conflated in Marx's concept of class, the addition of a few more to the list could be defended as a procedure directly in line with

Weber's own reasoning. Whether because of the academic propriety conferred by the Weberian connection or not, American sociologists certainly warmed to this approach and virtually made it their own. According to Gordon, "The acceptance of the multidimensional approach and its elaboration and further clarification proceeded slowly but with gradually accelerated speed" in the postwar period.[4] "In fact, the entire period under review [1925–55] may be seen as one in which social class theorists were gradually and with increasing precision engaged in the process of making analytical distinctions among the numerous factors or variables which may be subsumed under the rubric of social stratification." Gordon goes on to suggest that "the multidimensional approach itself may be seen as part of an analytical operation which is fundamental to all research and scientific understanding: the specification of variables inherent in a given problem area."[5]

It would be incorrect to suggest that the attraction of the multidimensional model was due solely, or even mainly, to the need for an alternative to Marxist class analysis. The more obvious alternative was nearer at hand in the shape of Warner's work on the class structure of the local community. The Warner School and its offshoots had sought to apply the investigatory techniques of social anthropology to demonstrate the existence of a formalized class structure in typical American townships. It was argued that the population of these towns was clearly conscious of a ranked order of discrete classes, each displaying its own characteristic pattern of conduct and values and organized around different interests. It seemed the anthropologists had succeeded in unmasking a class system where sociologists had failed. The main point on which these various studies differed was the not unimportant one of the actual number of classes they had managed to identify. The Lynds, in one of the earliest investigations, had settled for two in Middletown; West discovered four in Plainville; Hollingshead, five in Elmtown; and Warner, six in Yankee City.[6] The advocates of the classless-continuum thesis could hardly have asked for more conclusive evidence for their case.

The main reason for this chaos of course did not have to do with the basic differences in the communities being investigated but with the nature of the methodology employed. The technique of ranking individuals or their families into social clusters according to their vaguely defined social standing in the community is one which allows almost unfettered play to the observer's whims; when the classification is dependent upon an apparently random mixture of the observer's criteria with the assessments made by panels of local worthies, confusion is the only possible outcome.[7] Nowhere is the electicism of the Warner School more tellingly demonstrated than in the folksy terminology by which classes are categorized. "Good lower-class people," "the people who live like animals," "the common-level man," "the tops and the bottoms," are the typical formulations. It is a terminology based wholly on invidious status distinctions, and it conveys no real sense of a formal class system of antagonistic groups engaged in a struggle for resources and opportunities. Notwithstanding Warner's insistence to the contrary, an evaluative system of ranking can hardly be said to constitute a model of class relations. This is not simply because class entails considerably more than a set of subjective estimates of social worth, but more importantly because it is a *societal*, not a community, phenomenon. Class relations are played out within a context of social and legal arrangements, such as those surrounding private property, the market, the division of labor, and so forth, which are controlled by groups and agencies external to any local community. To confine the analysis of class to the circumscribed arena of the small town is justifiable only on the assumption that this social unit is a miniature version of the nation state—an assumption which Warner does in fact make in his well-known aphorism, "To study Jonesville is to study America."[8] Perhaps this is a natural extension of the anthropological tradition of turning a blind eye to the colonial system when studying the tribal societies exploited within this larger system.

As various critics have pointed out, the activities of the Warner School were designed more to elaborate the differences among local status groups than to yield a model of class structure. (Warner's manual, *Social Class in America,* is in fact subtitled *The Evaluation of Status*). Not surprisingly in view of this, the affinity with Weber is once again alluded to in conjunction with a strict dissociation from the ideas of Marx. Warner's familiarity with Weber's work might well have fostered the belief that his own study of status groups was part of this same tradition, much in the way that the advocates of the multidimensional approach felt theirs to be. The crucial difference was of course that Weber generally understood status groups to be social formations which arose *within* broad class categories; they were never thought of as equivalent to classes in their own right. In the Warner studies, status groups are constructed in a complete class vacuum, so that instead of being treated as a refinement upon class analysis, they turn out to be a substitute for it.

The burden of the foregoing remarks seems to indicate that some of Weber's key ideas have undergone a strange metamorphosis in the process of being incorporated into American stratification theory. The Weber who emerges from this theory is hardly recognizable as the author of *Economy and Society,* a disfigurement due largely to his being called upon as main standard-bearer of the movement against materialism or economic determinism or the monocausal interpretation of class, or some equivalent term for what passed as Marxism during this period. It is a Weber who has been thoroughly de-Marxified and so rendered fit to assume duties as the ideological champion of the classless society of American capitalism. Thus one searches these various offerings in vain for any trace of the persistent Weberian concerns with property or state bureaucracy or class antagonisms and structural change; or for any small recognition that for Weber the "dimensions" of stratification were never regarded as aggregates of individual attributes but as "phenomena of the distribution of power." Instead, the American reality portrayed gives every appearance of a society in which property has been liquidated, classes have dissolved, and the state has withered away. It is a sociological portrait of America as drawn by Norman Rockwell for the *Saturday Evening Post.* One can only surmise whether Weber, if confronted with the knowledge of the things said and written in his name, would take a leaf out of his predecessor's book and declare, "*Je ne suis pas Weberien.*"

It is permissible to speak of a strictly domestic, American brand of stratification theory and research in so far as the concepts and assumptions informing it have never really traveled well beyond the United States, at least compared with the intellectual exports in so many other branches of sociology. Within the European tradition, for example, the issue of whether classes can really be said to exist has never been regarded as much of a problem. Nor has there been a noticeable tendency to conflate the definition of class with that of status. Perhaps more surprisingly, it is not even possible to speak of a controversy over the number of social classes conventionally identified. The prevailing consensus has been that a dichotomous model of some kind is the most fruitful device for analyzing class relations; disagreement centers largely on the choice of criteria by which the line of cleavage is revealed. Although retaining Marx's general scheme of a dualistic conflict model, most academic social theorists have felt it necessary to replace the original protagonists by a different pair. Thus the proposed distinctions between possession and non-possession of authority, or between political classes and masses, or between manual and nonmanual labor, and so on, may all be seen as part of a common response to the felt inadequacies of the classic distinction between capital and labor as the primary source of conflict and cleavage.

The objection to the Marxist definition has been twofold. First is that the existence of a distinct class of capitalist entrepreneurs no longer holds, following the rise of the modern corporation and the separation of ownership and control. This development has itself inspired the production of various theories which assert the primacy of managerial authority, as opposed to the mere rights of ownership, as the basic fact of class domination—most notably in the work of Burnham and Dahrendorf. Seen from this perspective, the very idea of a capitalist society loses much of its meaning, since all industrial societies, whatever their political coloration, will exhibit a similar conflict between managers and managed. The second objection to the Marxist model, loosely related to this but by no means dependent on it, is that the general category "labor" is far too inclusive to capture the variations in market position and life chances of those who sell their labor services. Such a catholic definition of proletariat not only minimizes important differences in the politics and ideology of white-collar professionals on the one hand and industrial laborers on the other, but it also bears a curious resemblance to the familiar conservative claim that "today we are *all* working class."

The rejection of the Marxist class model thus sprang more than anything else from its apparent inability to cope with the rise of those intermediate white-collar groups which, though sharing certain conditions with the "common wage laborer," nevertheless enjoy sufficient tangible and intangible advantages over them to inhibit any sense of common identity. It was the rapid growth of the white-collar sector which in the view of most critics effectively demolished Marx's polarization thesis, and hence the general theory of class transformation which hinged upon it. Instead of the social space between bourgeoisie and proletariat becoming increasingly uninhabitable as the centrifugal forces of class conflict flung all intermediate strata to one side or the other, precisely the opposite appeared to happen. The no-man's-land between the entrenched classes proved to be extremely hospitable to the new occupational groups. Not only did they give no indication of being temporary residents, their frontiers extended in both direction to encroach upon the positions of the two great "armed camps."

The significance of all this for Marxism, and for class analysis generally, was first raised in the context of the revisionist debates in the German Social Democratic Party, and subsequently by German scholars engaged in the sociology of the *Angestellten*.[9] The aim in each case was similar: to assess the extent to which a working class in the process of changing the color of its collar would change the nature of its political demands also. The continuing fascination of the topic is illustrated by the fact that this and the associated *Verbürgerlichung* debate of the 1920s and 1930s resurfaced in somewhat different form in the 1960s as the *embourgeoisement* debate. Whereas the former was addressed to the problem of potential white-collar incorporation into the working class, the latter was concerned with the likelihood or otherwise of blue-collar absorption into the middle class. In both cases it was naturally assumed that the nature of occupations themselves, their job characteristics, their nonpecuniary rewards, and so on, were crucial factors in shaping class attitudes and behavior. In other words, it was within the division of labor, rather than in property relations, that the behaviorally relevant divisions of class were to be found.

This proposition has reached its most formalized expression in the one model of social class which can claim to enjoy almost universal acceptance by Western sociologists; namely, the manual/nonmanual model. No other definition of class has shown itself to be so adaptable to the investigations and surveys of political choice, family structure, consumption patterns, children's educational attainments, social imagery, and similar inquiries which keep the wheels of empirical sociology endlessly turning. However much the terminology of "working class" and "middle class" is preferred in the discussion of findings and in theoretical writings, the operational definition is almost always based on the familiar distinction. For some reason sociologists do not like to speak of manual and nonmanual classes, or of blue-collar and white-collar classes, a reluctance which possibly indicates a sense of unease about the use of this model as a representation of the class structure and its major line of cleavage.

However this may be, it is somewhat surprising that Western sociologists have never really exposed the manual/non-manual model to the same careful examination as that given to the Marxist alternative, despite its obvious shortcomings. For example, it cannot properly be construed as a model which emphasizes the conflictual character of class relations, even though many of those who adopt it would not wish to conceive of such relations in consensual terms. It is certainly true that within the sphere of industry the white-collar/blue-collar divide is one which corresponds fairly closely to the line of confrontation, particularly insofar as even the lower grades of white-collar staff play the part of managerial subalterns. But there is a vast and ever-expanding array of white-collar occupations, especially in state and local government and the service professions, which cannot in any real sense be thought of as standing in opposition to a blue-collar work force as part of a broad managerial apparatus. Frequently there is no blue-collar workforce to confront in the occupational settings in which these groups are employed. If nonmanual groups in the large public sector are not typically in conflict with manual workers in their own occupational setting, it could perhaps be argued that conflict is displaced to the national level. Again though, it is less than convincing to claim that there is a fundamental antagonism between dockers, railwaymen, miners, and so forth, on the one hand and nurses, teachers, social workers, and so forth, on the other. At any rate, there is no evidence to suggest that these two broad categories have attempted to organize along lines which declare that manual and nonmanual workers have opposing interests. Indeed, all the evidence points in the other direction. White-collar trade unions have shown an increasing tendency in recent years to overcome their traditional sense of status superiority over manual unions and to enter into alliance with them for bargaining purposes. When both sets of workers are formally represented in the industrial wing of the labor movement, as they now are in many countries, it seems something of a theoretical conceit for sociologists to continue regarding them as occupying different sides of the class divide.

The rationale for treating the lower and intermediate white-collar groups as a constituent part of the middle class is that within the sphere of private industry they have identified with those above them in the organization rather than with those below. In the public sector, on the other hand, not only is there frequently no subordinate manual group to issue commands to, but the identification with managerial superiors is less easy to accomplish when the chain of authority extends upward and out of sight into the amorphous body of the state. Moreover, public-sector employees do not usually have the opportunities for transferring their skills and services to another enterprise, comparable to those in private industry and commerce; all improvements in pay and conditions must be negotiated with a monopoly employer, and one who is under close budgetary scrutiny. All this makes for a condition of potential and increasingly manifest hostility between white-collar employees and the state *qua* employer—a condition not dissimilar to that between management and workers in private industry. As state and welfare services fall under the ax of government spending cuts, the collective responses of the employees affected are a direct replica of the protest demonstrations, strikes, picketings, and other forms of militancy which were once felt to be the preserve of the blue-collar work force. The sociologists' model of class has yet to adjust itself to this change.

Another characteristic of this model is that it does not represent the relations between classes as aspects of the distribution of power. Manual and nonmanual groups are conceived of as socially differentiated from each other, but not as standing in a relationship of exploiter and exploited, of dominance and subordination, in the manner in which a genuine power model would seek to represent class relations. It is therefore misleading to assume that the two main class groupings identified by contemporary sociology are in some way analogous to the classical distinction between bourgeoisie and proletariat. The conceptual alteration has been accompanied by a radical change from a theoretical framework organized around the central ideas of mutual antagonism and the incompatibility of interests to one organized around the empirical facts of mere social differentiation.

Property

The main consequence of this conceptual shift is that the sociological model requires that the entire weight of class analysis be borne by the consideration of those inequalities stemming from the division of labor. Thus there is no obvious place into which the facts and consequences of private property ownership can be incorporated into the schema. Originating as an attempt to break down the portmanteau concept of "labor" by focusing sharply on the diversities produced by the occupational structure, the manual/nonmanual model has succeeded unwittingly in abolishing the sister concept of "capital" from the class lexicon. The power and privileges emanating from the possession of wealth and capital are analytically separate from those which stem directly from the division of labor. A model of class which addresses itself only to the latter is a lopsided one indeed. In so far as it is even recognized that property ownership sets up class interests of its own, the general assumption appears to be that these are broadly in line with the interests of the nonmanual class or at least its upper echelons. Empirically this may often be the case, but it is difficult to explain this connection *theoretically* within the logic of a model based purely upon occupationally linked differences. If those who live off inherited wealth and ownership of capital are normally able to make common cause with those who live well purely from the sale of their labor services, this is a puzzling feature of capitalism which needs to be explained. It cannot even be properly posed within a model of class in which property is an absentee concept.

It is not of course only the reigning orthodox model of social class of which this is true. A great deal of general theorizing about changes in the stratification system occurs without reference to the institution which both Marx and Weber held to be the foundation stone of all class structures. No one could possibly quibble with Parsons's assertion that "In recent, non-Marxian discussions of class, the specific reference to the ownership of the means of production has virtually disappeared."[10] Parsons's obvious approval of this state of affairs stems from his belief that the disappearance of the concept is due directly to the dissolution of property itself as a significant factor in the maintenance of class inequality. This has come about not only through the separation of ownership from control in the joint-stock company, but also because of the "immense extent to which household income has come from occupational rather than property sources, extending upward in status terms from the proletarian wage worker to the very top of the occupational scale."[11] Given that we "can clearly no longer speak of a 'capitalistic' propertied class which has replaced the earlier 'feudal' landed class," Parsons recommends "divorcing the concept of social class from its historic relation to both kinship and property as such."[12]

Curiously, it seems to be the very fact that property is so highly concentrated in a few hands that persuades Parsons of its irrelevance. This is a strange position to adopt on the part of a theorist who normally equates the benign effect of a resource with its wide distribution. Power, for example, loses its association with dominance and coercion and all things unpleasant by virtue of its dispersal throughout the social order; property, it seems, loses its association with power and privilege on precisely the opposite grounds.

Parsons is more faithful to his usual mode of reasoning when he conflates property, in the manner of various other sociologists, with "possessions"; that is, as an "entity which is transferable from one actor to another, which can change hands through a process of exchange."[13] If property is simply a specific form of possession, then everyone in society is a proprietor to some degree. On this reckoning there can be no clear social division between owners and nonowners, only a gradually descending scale from those with a lot to those with a little. The possession of an oil field or a toothbrush confers similar rights and obligations upon their owners, so that property laws cannot be understood as class laws. As Rose and his colleagues have suggested:

> . . . the ideological significance of such a universalistic and disinterested legal interpretation of property in modern capitalist society is two-fold. First, as the law protects and recognises *all* private property, and as virtually all members of the society can claim title to *some* such property, it may be claimed that all members of society have some vested interest in the *status quo*. From such a perspective, therefore, it can be argued that, far from representing an irreconcilable conflict of interests, the distribution of property in modern capitalist society gives rise to a commensurability of interests, any differences being variations of degree rather than kind. The office developer, the shareholder, the factory owner, the householder and even the second-hand car owner may thus be represented as sharing fundamentally common interests, if not identities.[14]

What the sociological definition of property interestingly fails to ask is why only *certain* forms of possession are legally admissible. For example, it is not the case that workers are permitted to enjoy legal rights in their jobs; or tenants, rights of possession to their homes; or welfare claimants, rights to benefits. Possession in all these cases is preempted by the conflicting claims of employers, landlords, and the state respectively, which are accorded legal priority. Although the law may treat the rights of property in true universalistic fashion, it is naturally silent on the manner of the arrangement by which only some "expectations" are successfully converted to the status of proprietory right and others are not. It is a poor sociology which remains equally silent.

The apparent desire to think property away as a factor in modern stratification is especially understandable in the case of those committed to a functionalist position. Given a belief in the sweeping victory of achievement values over ascriptive criteria, and the establishment of a merit system of reward, the persistence of property as a major institution is bound to appear anomalous. The inheritance of wealth, after all, requires notably little expenditure of those talents and efforts which are said to be the only keys to the gates of fortune. Yet the only acknowledgement of this peculiar institution in Davis and Moore's functionalist manifesto is a brief reference to the fact that "strictly legal and functionless ownership . . . is open to attack" as capitalism develops.[15] Inheritance and estate taxes may undoubtedly have provided a useful source of exchequer revenue; but the institution of inheritance seems to have emerged remarkably unscathed from these "attacks." To propose that legal reforms of this kind are evidence of the erosion of inheritance rights is somewhat like suggesting that the introduction of divorce laws is evidence for the erosion of the family. Property in this scheme of things can only be understood as a case of cultural lag—one of those quaint institutional remnants from an earlier epoch which survives by the grace of social inertia.[16]

The dismissal of property from the functionalist theory of stratification is made possible, or even necessary, by the belief that occupational rewards under capitalism are determined by their presumed importance to the system rather than by market forces. Once it is accepted that the laws of supply and demand exert a powerful influence on income distribution, quite independently of functional importance, then the role of property would have to be taken less lightly. This is because a system of reward allocation in which market forces are given extensive leeway can only operate effectively in an economic climate which is friendly to the rights of property—not as mere possession, but as "rights of appropriation." Private property and market forces require one another in the way that central planning and state control require one another in the main alternative to capitalism. Any serious dismemberment of private rights of appropriation would throw a market system of reward into jeopardy; property is not some optional extra for the system, but its very *raison d'etre*. The determinate role of property can only be denied if inequalities associated with the occupational system of Western society are regarded as an inherent feature of the division of labor. Yet, quite clearly, the same division of labor can yield different distributive systems in different legal and political contexts. Societies which give legal backing to rights of private appropriation are far more likely to give rise to a system of rewards spanning the entire range from millionaire status to pauperdom than are societies in which private property in the means of production is disallowed.

It is not difficult to see why the concept of property should have caused some difficulties for interpretations of the social order as a united and peaceful moral community, given its historic associations with bloodshed and strife, particularly over the ownership of land. It is when property as land gives way to property as industrial capital that it is felt to undergo a transformation from a potentially malignant to a beneficent or harmless resource. Even the most committed functionalist would no doubt be prepared to concede that the relationship between lord and serf could not be understood as one of harmonious exchange. The bland vocabulary of exchange and reciprocity, rights and duties, only becomes applicable, it seems, to the relationship between the social embodiments of capital and labor. The domestication of property, in the literal as well as the figurative sense, is marked by the transition from the capitalist firm to the modern corporation, a change bringing with it a new force for good in society in the shape of a managerial stratum. In managerial hands, property finds its soul, as well as its final resting place. From now on, it is those who control property rather than own it who command the stage; and since they are themselves paid employees, sellers of labor power, their class interests and allegiances are determined in the same way as everyone else's—by their position in the division of labor. It is at this point that functionalism joins forces with the rest of sociology in eliminating property from the conceptual storehouse of stratification theory.

The most explicit and closely reasoned case for abandoning the notion of property from class analysis was advanced not by Parsons, but by Dahrendorf.[17] His argument was unusual mainly in so far as it was presented as a defense of the conflict model of class, in opposition to Parsonian and other consensualist varieties. Marx's cardinal error, it was suggested, was to confuse the part for the whole by failing to see that property was but a specific form of authority; authority itself is the generic form of class domination and the source of conflict. The antagonism between classes under modern industrialism arises not mainly from the maldistribution of resources and opportunities, but because of the incompatibility of interests between those who command and those who obey. By dissolving property into authority relations, a large volume of cold water can be thrown over any lingering hopes for a possible classless society. It is of course water drawn from the wellsprings of Weberian theory and polemic concerning the impossibility of socialism in a world dominated by bureaucracy. At the same time it is a bid to cast the explanatory net over a wider range of societies than those of the capitalist bloc; authority holds no respect for political and ideological boundaries.

One of the harmful theoretical side effects of reconstituting property as authority is that the notion of a social class is wrenched from its usual societal setting and placed into a much more narrow organizational one. A "subordinate class" now exists only within the confines of a bureaucratic locale, be it an industrial firm, prison, trade union, hospital organization, or whatever. In other words, there are *many* subordinate classes, institutionally isolated from each other, rather than a single class created by a common exclusion from authority. The image is more one of a "sack of potatoes" than a collectivity. In Marx's schema, the propertyless are a class in the full sense in that the entire political and legal apparatus bears down upon them in whatever particular social setting they are found. In Dahrendorf's schema, the authorityless are a class only in a partial and limited sense, insofar as they shed their subordinate status immediately upon leaving the physical location in which the rules of obedience and authority operate. A worker ceases to be a member of a subordinate class the moment he steps outside the factory; from then on he is at liberty to assume other roles, including those invested with their own authority. Authority relations do not penetrate into the very pores of society, leaving no place for respite, concealment, and escape, in the way that property relations do. Marx's proletariat has no means of escape from its condition because the effects of property cannot be contained within restricted social zones any more than the effects and consequences of the market can. It is as a result of this that class is universalized. Redefining property as authority *particularizes* class by presenting it as a function of organizational forms which are too diverse to yield a common class situation.

The question never seriously posed by Dahrendorf is: for what *purpose* is authority exercised and occasionally challenged? The command structure of a business enterprise is geared directly to the pursuit of profit, so that those who staff the key posts are in effect the guardians of capital; they are not concerned with the enforcement of obedience as an end in itself. Similarly, any challenge to managerial authority by organized labor is usually for the specific purpose of redistributing the share between capital and labor, and not for a romantic belief in the psychic benefits of insubordination. In other words, the authority exercised in an organization could be said to take its significance from the ends to which the organization is dedicated; it is not something which is properly understood independently of its uses. The claim that property is but a special instance of authority rides roughshod over the differences between forms of authority which serve to maintain rights of appropriation from those which do not. As Etzioni's classification of complex organization showed, there are many types of hierarchical authority which do not produce the alienative and oppositional responses among the subordinate which Dahrendorf takes to be universal.[18] Responses of this type occur largely in reaction to systems of command which deny access to rewards and opportunities to "lower participants"; where no such exclusion is entailed, authority is usually uncontested. The fact that Dahrendorf should select the industrial firm as the paradigm case for his theory really proves the point, because this is the one locus above all others where authority relations are inseparable from property rights. When workers occupy their factory and lock out management, it is instructive to bear in mind the offense with which they are liable to be arraigned before the courts. It is not disobedience, which is merely an offense against authority; it is unlawful trespass, which is an offense against property.

The fact that class conflict between managers and managed is ultimately not containable or resolvable within the walls of the organization really removes the ground from beneath Dahrendorf's theory. When the chips are down and conflict assumes a less benign character from its rountinized version, authority is seen not to reside in the "incumbency of positions" within the organization, but in the state--an external body charged with the duty of protecting the rights of private ownership. Managerial command over labor therefore takes place within a legal framework in which property is already guaranteed its sacred character. In other words, the exercise of authority may be thought of more as an activity which is licensed, as it were, by the state, than as something which draws its own legitimacy from the logic of organization. The background reality of the state is far more easily overlooked in the matter of authority than in the matter of private property. Clearly, no one would ever imagine otherwise than that the state, not the proprietors themselves, would be the main line of defense behind property. The images of the policeman, the courthouse, and the prison are almost inseparable from the idea of property. These images tend to recede when authority displaces property as the leading idea, because it so often appears that industrial and other bureaucracies are self-regulating. It is only on those dramatic occasions which organizations themselves cannot handle that the wholly derivative nature of managerial authority is revealed with great clarity by the activity of that agency which houses the very substance of power, and which puts that power in the service of property.

The one branch of stratification theory which has traditionally accorded property a central place is of course Marxism. At one time it might have been reasonable to claim that the full recognition of this institution provided the major point of contrast between the Marxist and sociological accounts of class structure. If this claim is a considerably weaker one today, it is due not to a renewed awareness of property among academic theorists, but to the fact that contemporary Marxism has moved unexpectedly closer to the sociological position. This shift has occured as part of a more general attempt by Western Marxists to reconsider the classical or orthodox model of class under the new conditions of "monopoly capitalism." More specifically, the intention has been to repair the Marxist definition at what has always appeared to be its weakest point: namely, in the equation of the formal categories of capital and labor with the social classes of bourgeoisie and proletariat. The starting point here has been to concede that the association between propertylessness and class position is a more complex one, and that the status of wage laborer is only a necessary and not a sufficient condition of working-class membership. Since not all those who sell their labor meet these additional criteria, it follows that the proletariat, as now conceived, is but a subgroup of this general category, which also comprises that theoretically troublesome grouping known to Marxists as the "new petty bourgeoisie"—that is, the white-collar employees. Much of the current debate centers upon the correct location of the primary class cleavage under monopoly capitalism, and in particular the place of the new petty bourgeoisie in the scheme of things—what Poulantzas has referred to as the "boundary problem."[19]

Poulantzas's strategy for coming to grips with this problem has been to introduce two separate classificatory devices, drawn from Marx's own work, which have the effect of paring down the unwieldy construct of exploited wage labor until the lean forms of the proletariat are finally made clear. The first step in this enterprise is the resurrection of Marx's neglected distinction between productive and unproductive labor as a criterion of class standing. Here it should be recalled that in Marxist theory this distinction bears not upon the nature of the work performed, but upon the social context of its performance. Very simply, productive labor is that which yields surplus value; unproductive labor is that which does not. Expressed more formally, productive labor is that which is exchanged against capital to produce surplus, whereas unproductive labor is a charge against revenue. The barber who trims Marx's beard is performing unproductive labor if he is working on his own account, since the service given is essentially no different from that provided by a household servant. Each entails a direct charge against revenue and, as such, makes no direct contribution to capital accumulation. If, on the other hand, Marx's barber is a paid employee of the barbershop owner, he is performing productive labor by creating surplus value on behalf of his master. On a more elevated plane, the unproductive category comprises not only those who perform services against revenue, but also those employed in the state sector whose incomes are met from taxation. Taxes are siphoned off from the wages of productive workers or from surplus value in the shape of taxes on profits, so that in effect the labor of "state servants," like that of household servants, is an exchange against revenue.

The crucial point of all this is that only those whose labor is productive can be regarded as a constituent part of the proletariat. Unproductive wage laborers are consigned to the ranks of the "new petty bourgeoisie." This means that the line of class demarcation is drawn considerably lower in the stratification hierarchy than it is in the orthodox model. And this invisible line is pushed down still farther by the addition of Poulantzas's second classification, in the form of a distinction between mental and manual labor. Mental labor is conceptual shorthand for those occupations which include elements of a supervisory or disciplinary nature (what Marx occasionally refers to as "the labor of superintendance"), as well as professional occupations which claim special privileges by virtue of their monopoly of secret knowledge. The supervisory component of mental labor is especially prominent in occupations within the technical sphere of production, where the need for direct surveillance of the work force is essential to the exploitation process. Now, those who perform supervisory functions are usually not only wage workers but productive laborers to boot, insofar as they are just as instrumental in producing surplus value as the men whose activities they oversee. However, the activity of mental labor is automatic grounds for exclusion from the category of working class and inclusion in the ranks of the new petty bourgeoisie. Combining these two sets of variables, we arrive at four distinct types of wage labor: productive mental; productive manual; unproductive mental; and unproductive manual. In Poulantzas's reckoning only the productive manual category counts as working class; it is the only form of labor which contributes to surplus value while not at the same time being implicated in the apparatus of control.

One of the theoretical effects of this schema is to posit a concealed conflict of interests between productive and unproductive workers, on the grounds that the latter are in some ultimate sense parasitic upon those who create value. This is a position advanced some time ago by Sweezy. Sweezy suggested that unproductive groups such as teachers, professionals, and state employees "constitute, so to speak, a mass army which readily accepts the leadership of capitalist generals." The chief reason for this is that, "since under capitalism a large proportion of them derive their incomes directly or indirectly from surplus value, so that a diminution of surplus value would necessarily react upon them unfavourably, there . . . exists an objective bond linking their fortunes with those of the ruling class."[20]

It should at once be said that many Western Marxists would reject this attempt to revive the distinction between productive and unproductive labor as a determinant of class. One practical reason why is that the use of such stringent criteria in defining class membership reduces the proletariat to pygmy proportions. As one of Poulantzas's sympathetic critics plaintively remarks, the strict application of these criteria "reduces the American working class to a small minority. It is hard to imagine a viable socialist movement developing in an advanced capitalist country in which less than one in five people are workers."[21] It is ironic that a theory intended, among other things, as a critique of those bourgeois conceptions which present the working class as historically doomed should itself end up with a set of propositions which lead to a similar conclusion.

The issue on which latter-day Marxists display a much greater degree of consensus is on the social location of the technical and managerial cadres of capitalist enterprise; and it is on this point that the extent of departure from the classical model is most apparent. The dilemma is that these groups are sellers of labor power and productive workers in the accepted Marxist sense. Yet theorists within this tradition are understandably reluctant to include them as part of the working class, if only for the reason that it is professional management which more than any other group stands in blatant opposition to the demands of the industrial proletariat. Consequently, the need has been for some criterion which locates the managerial cadres on the opposite side of the class boundary from the proletariat, notwithstanding the fact that they are not themselves an ownership class. Poulantzas has singled out the "mental" status of their labor to account for their incorporation into the bourgeoisie; in a similar vein, the Italian Marxist Carchedi has proposed that all groups which perform the "global functions of capital," that is, carry out supervisory or control tasks, are to be understood as an integral part of the capitalist class, notwithstanding their status as employees. Carchedi pursues this line of reasoning *á l'outrance* by arguing that under monopoly capitalism ". . . the manager rather than the capitalist rentier is the central figure . . . . He rather than the capitalist is capital personified."[22]

Interestingly enough, by insisting that the performance of supervisory and disciplinary functions is a hallmark of bourgeois status, Marxist theorists have come surprisingly close to endorsing Dahrendorf's argument regarding the determinate role of *authority* in establishing the class boundary. Their strict avoidance of the actual term authority in favor of some synonym or circumlocution is perhaps a tacit admission of the embarrassing affinity to neo-Weberian analyses which treat the distribution of power as a function of organizational hierarchy. At any rate, if the manager is now "capital personified," then it would seem to follow that authority has superseded property as the primary attribute of class and the focus of conflict. The concept of "rights of appropriation" recedes in favor of one stressing the "rights of superintendance." Differences in terminology can hardly conceal the extent to which the sociological assessment of property has begun to find its unexpected parallel in Marxist theory.

State

It is only within the last decade or so that the concept of the state has penetrated into the sociology of inequality. Both functionalist-cum-pluralist and class models of stratification have sought to map out a terrain called society; but because the state has conventionally been thought of as something separate from or "above" society, it could not easily be incorporated into the general model. Pluralism could, in any case, dispense with the idea of the state altogether because it dispenses with the idea of a concentrated locus of power. The state implies the existence of a power which is something more than an amalgam of competing interest groups, and there could be no place for such an agency in a model that treats power as a resource which is not so much accumulated as canceled out by the pull of opposites. Moreover, to suggest that power resides in the state is to cast some doubt on the democratic credentials of modern society; governments are elected by the people, the state is not. The pluralist preference is for that political imagery which pictures a clear *separation* of powers among executive, judiciary, and administration, such that no group monopolizes power to the detriment of the people. The image of the state, on the other hand, is of a cohesive and unified agency not directly responsive to the popular will and capable of unleashing violence. The term has thus tended to be avoided by those who have learned to love their governments and their social structures.

Class theories, on the other hand, have paid little attention to the state because the distribution of power is usually conceived of as a function of the division of labor, in which the state dissolves into a series of occupational positions. Or, alternately, power is seen as a function of the relation between dominant and subordinate classes in which there is no obvious place for a "third force." For Marx the state was simply the executive committee of the ruling class at any particular epoch and as such, required no special theoretical treatment. Weber, too, was more concerned with treating the state in its capacity as the guardian of national boundaries than as a collective force impinging upon the inner workings of class society. The state was decidedly not one of the three elements in the distribution of power. This suggests that the neglect of the state by stratification theorists and political sociologists is by no means a departure from established tradition. If anything, it is the recent upsurge of interest in the state which is a novel feature of the discipline. Suddenly everyone seems to be talking about the state; it has become the latest of those neglected problems crying out for theoretical solution.

No doubt one of the main reasons for this is that the agencies of the state are much more with us, and palpably so, than in any previous era. All the ills to which society is heir are frequently attributed to the activity, or inactivity, of the central power, and a remedy demanded from the same quarter. Welfare and punishment, schooling and manipulation, taxation and public spending are now felt to be on a scale too vast to ignore by taking refuge in the conventional dichotomy between state and society. The state, it seems, no longer occupies that curious limbo of the liberal imagination; it has descended into society and absorbed great tracts of it. On this point modern Marxist and conservative theorists are in unaccustomed unanimity. The question which naturally arises is whether the introduction of the concept of the state can be accommodated into existing class theories or whether some modifications are now called for.

The answer offered by contemporary Marxism is that the orthodox class model of bourgeois society is too simplistic, given the interventionist character of the state under the monopoly stage of capitalism. There is widespread dissatisfaction among Western Marxists at the uncomplicated formula in the *Communist Manifesto* which relegates the state to the role of a mere instrument wielded by a dominant bourgeois class. Although all contemporary Marxists endorse the view of the state as an agency which serves the interests of an exploiting few over the exploited many, the manner in which this is accomplished is felt to be quite unlike that of an "executive committee." The organizing concept around which the current debate revolves is that of the "relative autonomy" of the state from the class which it ultimately serves.[23] This social distancing between state and bourgeoisie is believed to serve two essential functions. First, it enables conflicts between different segments of the ruling class to be settled and mediated by an external body not itself implicated in the struggle. Only an institution which had some degree of independence of the warring factions could bring to bear the necessary judgment and dispassion to settle conflicts of interest in such a way as to benefit the entire bourgeoisie. The ruling class cannot operate effectively and maintain its dominance over time not only because it is internally divided, but also because it is too caught up in the day-to-day struggles against the working class to be able to distinguish properly between its short-term, immediate interests and its long-term interests. The state, on the other hand, by being removed from the front line of the class struggle, is better placed to organize the general plan of campaign on behalf of the bourgeoisie, so guaranteeing its survival. The state acts as the intelligence of the bourgeoisie rather in the way that the Leninist vanguard party acts as the intelligence of the proletariat. In each case the need is for a political organ which is *for* a particular class, but not directly *of* it.

The second purpose of the state's relative autonomy is to facilitate the task of self-legitimation. If the state was seen to be acting directly as a committee of the ruling class, blatantly favoring this class in fiscal and legal matters, the support of other groups and classes would be impossible to maintain other than by the wasteful and inefficient means of coercion. Hence it is necessary for the state to cultivate an aura of independence from and impartiality toward any particular interest group in society by introducing occasional reforms which benefit the underprivileged at the immediate expense of the privileged. In this manner, the state can be held up as the champion of the underdog against the battalions of wealth and arrogance. Left to themselves, the argument suggests, the bourgeoisie would tend to resist those reforms and concessions which have been so important in contributing to their continued survival as a class. The state's relative autonomy insures that it can push through those changes which protect the bourgeoisie from itself.

The prototype upon which this analysis is based is the Bonapartist state—that peculiar system characterized by Marx as one in which a weak and disorganized bourgeoisie is willing to relinquish political power to a petty dictator in order to hold on to the vestiges of economic power. The attraction of the Bonapartist model for contemporary Marxists is that it appears to provide a more sophisticated account of the complex relations between state and ruling class which prevail under modern capitalism. However, it is extremely doubtful whether Marxism requires, or can accommodate, a distinct theory of this type. Once it is suggested that the state is capable of attaining a measure of autonomy from the dominant class, then the inescapable conclusion is that a new force has arisen in society whose power is not directly rooted in the system of productive relations. As a result, the state would be in a position to affect the distributive system in such a way as to alter the balance of rewards and privileges which would normally be expected to prevail under conditions of pure class conflict and struggle. But the question for Marxism must be: what is the *source* of the state's power? Within this theoretical tradition the distribution of power is usually regarded as synonymous with the balance of forces between social classes, and there is no room for the introduction of some other formation which could usurp the power invested in social classes and which could possibly harbor specific interests of its own. For Marx the state is typically an arena in which the antagonisms between classes are given political expression; it is in no sense a prime mover in these events.

The notion of the state as a relatively autonomous entity with a power base separate from that of class power really owes more to nineteenth-century liberal theory than to classical Marxism. The critique of the state offered from this quarter has usually been couched in terms of the erosion of solid bourgeois virtues, such as individualism, self-help, and market competition, and their replacement by their very opposites—collectivism, welfare, and central planning. On this reckoning, not only is the state independent of the bourgeois class, it is its mortal enemy. It is the great Leviathan, trampling roughshod over the carefully constructed foundations of civil liberties and public virtue in pursuit of a mindless and squalid egalitarianism. It is only a short step from this portrayal of the state to the possibility, outlined by writers such as Plamenatz, of the state as an agency in and for itself, dedicated to serving the interests of its own members in opposition to those of all other classes, including the dominant one. This is the state broken completely free of all class moorings to become a predator upon society.[24]

Marxist writers, of course, do not go as far as to suggest that the state could follow this path to complete autonomy. But neither is any indication given as to why the process of separation between state and ruling class should freeze at the stage of *relative* autonomy. Once it is accepted that a form of power can be generated on a different social basis than that of class organization, then the ability of a dominant class to check the growth and the usurpationary potential of the state must be at the very least posed as a serious problem for the theory. The failure of contemporary Marxism to confront, let alone resolve, this tension at the heart of the theory may have something to do with the fact that the notion of an emergent power in society distinct from class power has all the hallmarks of Weberian sociology, and in particular the theory of bureaucracy. Weber's model of bureaucracy is commonly regarded as an alternative to Marx's theory insofar as it suggests that the very fact of organization itself provides a locus of power independent of that generated by the productive system. In other words, an explanation for the state's relative autonomy is disturbingly at hand in the shape of that very theory of bureaucracy which Marxism has traditionally rejected.

Part of the difficulty in theorizing about the state arises from a deep-seated uncertainty about its phenomenal status. On the one hand, there is an inclination to regard it not so much as an object or thing as a relationship or an "effect" of class forces. On the other hand, there is a parallel tendency to insist upon the concrete nature of the state as part of a general political strategy which has as its goal the seizure or the destruction of the state. Revolutionaries cannot be enjoined to seize or smash a "relationship." Marxism thus perpetually vacillates between the representation of the state as corporeal entity and as conceptual abstraction.[25]

The surprising thing about the current attempts to update the theory of the state is how well Marx's original dictum manages to survive in the face of it all. Very little in fact is added to the central idea that state legislation, budgetary and fiscal policies, and welfare and social reforms are the outcome of a struggle between organized interest groups and so reflect the ever-changing balance of class forces. The fact that in almost all Western societies in the postwar period governments have introduced policies beneficial to the working class need not therefore be accounted for in terms of a strategy to save the skins of the bourgeoisie. It can be seen more simply as a direct outcome of the increased power of organized labor. Indeed, it could be argued that the reason why the state has now become a "problem" is that the changing balance of class forces has resulted in greater pressures being exerted upon the central power to provide an ever-extending range of services designed to benefit those who could not possibly acquire them at market rates. If, then, there is a crisis facing Western capitalist societies—be it fiscal or ideological—it is not a crisis of the state, but of the dominant class. The very theory which might have been expected to be especially sensitive to these developments has obscured the dynamics of class struggle by a misplaced emphasis upon the separate reality of the capitalist state.[26]

Paradoxically, the type of social system in which the notion of state autonomy would seem to have some explanatory value is one which has always presented difficulties for Marxist analysis—namely, the Soviet system. This is a social order in which the state cannot plausibly be represented as an instrument of a ruling class, as conventionally understood. Domination and privilege in socialist societies flow from the monopolization of power by the party, not by any identifiable social class. Even a reformulation of the classical thesis to the effect that the state is the executive committee of the ruling party would not be especially helpful or illuminating because, under this type of system, state and party are so intertwined at every level as to be distinguishable only in a purely formal or legal sense. To all intents and purposes, state and party are one, and there is no dominant group or class whose interests they conjointly represent and defend. Where a hegemonic party is in control, the party-state complex alone determines the distribution of rewards and the general pattern of inequality. Although the intelligentsia and the managerial cadres may absorb a disproportionately bigger share of resources than workers, this is not the outcome of a class struggle but of administrative fiat. Indeed, the chief characteristic of this distributive system is that the pattern of rewards is markedly different from that which would normally obtain under conditions of open class conflict. That is the true measure of the state's relative autonomy. It is a condition which prevails only where the state is not directly susceptible to the pressures and demands emanating from civil society. Under Western capitalism the state enjoys no such immunity from these pressures; on the contrary, it is the very locus in which class tensions are made politically manifest. Where, on the other hand, the hegemonic party is virtually fused with the state, the state is not an arena of conflict but the moving force of the entire reward system. The state is the independent, not the dependent, variable. It is precisely this assumption which has inspired those various interpretations of the party bureaucracy as a "new class," having a similar exploitative relationship to the working masses as a capitalist, propertied class. Although Western Marxists critical of the Soviet Union and its offshoots have frequently flirted with this idea, they have always stopped short of accepting it fully, for the reasons already alluded to. It is largely because of this inability of the theory to incorporate the facts of bureaucratic power that a convincing analysis of the Soviet state still awaits its Marxist author.

Ethnicity

Until very recently any conspectus of the general condition of stratification theory could quite easily have omitted discussion of ethnicity without being guilty of dereliction. Although some discussion of the field of race relations would have been called for, the same would not have been true of an area of inquiry concerned with inequality and conflict based upon "communal" divisions in general. European theorists in particular have long been accustomed to analyzing class relations within a framework of assumed ethnic and racial homogeneity. One of the widely shared expectations of the classical and social theorists was that ascriptively based identities such as those of language, race, religion, and culture would progressively give way under the homogenizing influence of the modern industrial order. It was felt that the gradual incorporation of previously excluded groups into civil society would undermine those traditionalistic and narrower "tribal" loyalties which flourished under agrarian systems. This is one respect in which liberal theory and Marxism seem to be in agreement. Capitalism in its great epoch of ascendency was portrayed as a corrosive force upon status group attachments, replacing them by the highly instrumental and impersonal relations of the marketplace. The final showdown between the two great contending classes could not really take place until this historically prior clearing operation, capitalism's "civilizing mission," had been accomplished.

This reluctance to take seriously the extent of cultural or ethnic diversity, and its persistence, could partly be defended on theoretical grounds. One of the distinctive features of ethnic differentiation and conflict is the sheer variety of forms it assumes in each society. It emerges under conditions which are highly specific to a given society; there appear to be few common historical antecedents to explain political cleavage based upon color, language, faith, and the like. This may partly be due to the fact that ethnicity, unlike class, cannot be regarded as an inherent feature of a capitalist or industrial system. It is a purely contingent feature in the sense that it is perfectly possible to construct a model of capitalism from which ethnic factors are totally excluded. Because ethnicity was never really regarded by earlier sociologists as one of the defining attributes of the social system—that is, as a necessary and universal feature—the possibility, or even the need for, a general theory of ethnic conflict was not seriously considered. As Lockwood has pointed out, the usual strategy was to treat the existence of ethnic divisions as a "complicating" factor in class analysis; that is, as an acknowledged social fact which simply disturbs the pure class model, but not as something to be accorded the same theoretical weighting as class, and certainly not to be regarded as a phenomenon *sui generis*.[27]

Thus, one of the less welcome legacies bequeathed by the classical writers has been to render contemporary sociology theoretically unprepared to deal with the renaissance of ethnic identity and conflict in the very heartlands of

Western capitalism. Societies within this orbit which are wholly free of political troubles between communal groups are rapidly approaching the status of deviant cases. Ethnic conflict would now appear to be as normal a feature of advanced industrial societies as class conflict, even though its theoretical treatment is still at a relatively primitive stage. The emergence of these "archaic" forms of cleavage and antagonism in Western Europe is partly the result of the migration of workers from the poorer lands of the southern perimeter into the heavily industrialized countries of the north, as well as the flow of labor from the old colonial territories into the former imperial motherlands. In addition, however, the picture has been complicated by the eruption of political antagonisms among religious and language groups which have been part of a single nation state for centuries. Stratification theory has thus been faced with two interlocking problems: how to account for the synchronization, as it were, of obviously disconnected conflicts, especially in societies where such conflicts have been fairly dormant over a long period; and how to consider the nature of the connection, if any, between ethnic or communal relations and the more familiar pattern of class inequality.

A general approach to the problem which makes the cleanest break with the orthodox tradition is advocated by those theorists who see the new ethnicity not simply as a factor to be explained within some larger class context, but rather as one which has virtually *displaced* class as the major form of social cleavage and political identity. In Glazer and Moynihan's most recent formulation, "the preoccupation with property relations obscured ethnic ones," but now "it is *property* that begins to seem derivative, and ethnicity that seems to become a more fundamental source of stratification."[28] Not the least of the reasons adduced in support of this view is that the nature of collective action mounted by ethnic groups has undergone a significant change in recent times. Originally dedicated to fighting rear-guard actions of cultural preservation, ethnic groups have now adopted more combative forms of activity expressly designed to alter the distribution of rewards in their members' favor. It is not simply that ethnic groups have assumed political functions comparable to those of a subordinate class; they have in important respects become more effective than social classes in mobilizing their forces in pursuit of collective ends. The reason for this is suggested by Bell, as an extension of his thesis on the character of the postindustrial society. In this type of society the increasingly white-collar composition of the working class leads to its gradual demoralization, in the sense of a weakened ability to mount forms of activity which combine both instrumental and effective appeals. The new working class of the modern industrial state has been severed from the history, ideology, and symbolism of the old labor movement, leaving it with only the most narrowly defined economic goals as a motive for action. It is into this moral vacuum that ethnic groups are drawn. They *can* provide the badge of moral identification and the yearning for collective dignity which fuel the engines of political action among the dispossessed.[29] If the period of quiet calm following the end of ideology has now abruptly expired, it appears to be succeeded by one in which entirely new political banners are raised aloft and inscribed with insignia quite unrecognizable to any surviving warriors of the class struggle.

The theoretical grounding for this type of analysis is to be found in Weber's well-known thesis concerning the periodic oscillations between class politics and status-group politics. In Weber's capsule statement of the matter, classes are more likely to be the primary or politically significant social formations under conditions of general economic dislocation or crisis, whereas status groups flourish during periods of relative stability and social peace. Since ethnic groups are, in Weber's own writings, virtually the paradigm case of status organizations, their period of ascendency would naturally be expected to coincide more or less with the relative decline in the salience of class. (As if with Weber's schema in mind, Bell does in fact add a cautious rider to his analysis, suggesting that class organization and conflict could again come to the fore in the event of a worsening in the economic climate). The assumption quietly at work here is that the sense of identity with, or membership in, a class or ethnic group is essentially an either/or affair, such that a moral commitment to one precludes involvement in the other.[30] It is a conception of political and social identity that yields little to those notions of situational choice and context which, as Marx might have put it, allow a man to think of himself as an industrial worker in the morning, a black in the afternoon, and an American in the evening, without ever thinking of himself wholly as a worker, a black, or an American. Insofar as class and ethnic identities can be held *simultaneously* and activated, as it were, according to situational exigencies, then the less persuasive are those models of Weberian origin which emphasize instead periodic alternations of class and status groups according to the severity of the economic climate. It would in any case tax all Weber's ingenuity to convince a modern audience that the new wave of ethnic consciousness and communal disturbance has occurred under conditions of economic tranquility and peaceful coexistence between the classes.

Theories which proclaim that ethnic stratification has now displaced class stratification as the central fact of inequality under advanced capitalism would seem to fall squarely outside the Marxist pale. However, the powers of innovation within this camp are again demonstrated by the attempt to harness the notion of ethnic primacy to a theory of political conflict which owes as much to Marx as to Weber, in its moral overtones at least. This is the analysis of communal minorities as "internal colonies" within the body politic of the nation state. Viewed from this angle, ethnic minorities are to be understood as embryonic nations subjected to similar forms of material and cultural exploitation as those experienced by subject nations under imperial rule. Ethnic minorities are in effect Third World contingents in the heartlands of the First World. In Hechter's presentation of the thesis, the transition from backwardness to modernity occurs as a series of uneven waves moving across state territory and conferring special benefits on the core regions first affected and corresponding deficits on the peripheral areas.[31] This pattern of uneven development takes on special significance where spatial units correspond to distinct cultural units and where, in particular, the people of the core are ethnically distinguishable from those of the periphery. The outcome is a "cultural division of labor" based on an unequal exchange relationship which has all the hallmarks of a colonial situation.

Although the model of internal colonialism would appear to be applicable largely to conditions of ethnic conflict in which a clear territorial component is present, its earliest formulations arose as an account of racial cleavages in the United States, where the prospects of "colonial liberation" by the black minority seemed especially unpromising. As Blauner points out, the model of the internal colony was suggested by black activists as an alternative to the race-relations approach of academic sociology, which tended to locate the problem of racism in the defective attitudes of individuals rather than in a formal system of power and dominance.[32] It has thus been the American rather than the European experience which has inspired a fundamental restatement of the relationship between class and ethnicity by use of the colonial analogy, even though on the face of it the analogy seems more applicable to the European context.

Now, once the dominant ethnic group has been defined as a kind of occupying power, there is very little theoretical temptation to uncover differences and conflicts within this power, along the lines of class. For all practical intents and purposes, the white working class can be assumed to be an integral part of the exploiting racial group, politically indistinct from the white bourgeoisie. Indeed, in some versions of the argument the white working class is identified as the principal beneficiary of the system, so furnishing the "bulk of the counter-revolutionary force against the Negro revolt."[33]

The exploitative nature of the "white proletariat," or its counterpart under different ethnic systems, is a recurring theme in radical interpretations of communal conflict. While there is nothing inherently contradictory about such a notion, it is somewhat bizarre to find it being advanced from an avowedly Marxist perspective, with specific reference to Marxist economic doctrine, as in Davies's account of the process by which white South African mine workers are said to extract surplus value from their fellow blacks.[34] In a similar, if more muted vein, Hechter suggests that the working-class movement in Britain served to strengthen the grip of the English upon the Celtic minorities by furthering the "negative integration" of the latter in the United Kingdom.[35] The clear implication is that by organizing itself along the lines of pure class action, the labor movement has succeeded in diverting attention away from those injustices and inequalities which are directly attributable to the subordination of the Scots, Welsh, and Irish minorities, from which English workers have indirectly benefited. The central moral strand in this entire thesis is that exploitation and its accompanying degradations arising on the basis of ethnic differences have a *prior* claim to remedial action over the large and small injustices of class. Seen from this angle, any argument to the effect that class exploitation is the foundation of all other forms, including ethnic, and that therefore the political unity of the class is the first item on the agenda, can easily be made to appear as a subtle defense of the racial and cultural status quo. Thus, if stratification theory in its beginnings is marked by a reluctance to treat ethnicity as little more than a ripple across the surface of the class structure, there are now indications from several quite different quarters of a complete theoretical reversal; it is now class which is just as likely to be treated as a complicating feature of a social system molded largely by the realities of ethnic forces.

It might perhaps have been anticipated that some resistance to this tendency would have been registered on the part of those theorists for whom the notion of an exploitative proletariat would be a hopeless contradiction in terms. Yet orthodox Marxism has been noticeably unproductive in this entire sphere. There has in fact been very little advance beyond that line of approach which presents ethnic conflict either as a joint product of bourgeois cunning and proletarian gullibility (the *impera et divide* thesis) or as a "displacement" of social antagonisms whose origins are buried in the deep, mysterious layers of the capitalist mode of production.[36] On current evidence one could be forgiven for concluding that the preferred Marxist response to the fact of racial or communal strife is to ignore it. Not one of the various reformulations of class theory already referred to makes any serious attempt to consider how the division between blacks and whites, Catholics and Protestants, Flemings and Walloons, Francophones and Anglophones, or between indigenous and immigrant workers affects their general analysis. It is especially difficult to see what kind of explanation could in any case be expected from those formulations which draw heavily upon the conceptual storehouse of political economy. Notions such as the mode of production make their claims to explanatory power precisely on the grounds of their indifference to the nature of the human material whose activities they determine. To introduce questions such as the ethnic composition of the work force is to clutter up the analysis by laying stress upon the quality of *social actors*, a conception diametrically opposed to the notion of human agents as *träger* or "embodiments" of systemic forces. Presumably for Marxists operating within this schema, the existence of communal divisions within a class need be thought of as no more a hindrance to the theory than the equally important divisions along the lines of skill. The expectation is that the growing tension between capital and labor serves to reduce the importance of purely internal class differences. In this respect, ethnic cleavages could be expected to undergo the same healing process as that which gradually eroded the historic antagonism between the labor aristocracy and the laboring poor.

One additional reason why communal conflicts might be thought not to merit the same importance for stratification theory as class conflict is that the former, however socially disruptive, are felt to lack the capacity for transforming the social system. Only class actions are capable of translating violence into the creative act of political renewal. Communal conflict, in Lockwood's words, is not first and foremost directed at an alteration in the structure of power and deference but rather at the usurpation of power and deference by one section of the community to the disadvantage of the other. Ethnic and racial conflict has this orientation primarily because it is in the nature of the experience of the relationships of the majority and minority groups that the salient "cause" of disaffection inheres in the given and unalterable properties of individual actors and not in the contingent properties of social systems. Because of this, racial and ethnic conflict is more akin to rebellion in ethnically and racially homogenous societies in which the social order is likewise regarded as ineluctable. Thus revolutionary goals are unlikely to emerge from the antagonisms of groups in plural societies unless ethnic and racial divisions happen to coincide with lines of economic and other power relationships.[37]

To the extent, then, that communal conflicts are seen to have more in common with rituals of rebellion than with revolutionary politics, it would seem that Marxists at least could be excused duties in this field, abandoning it perhaps to social anthropology or the sociology of religion. Of course, such a position implies not only that classes under advanced capitalism still retain their explosive potential, but that they are also a greater threat to the survival of the state than the forces unleashed by communal disturbances and grievances. However, it should be pointed out that whereas the modern proletariat appears to have a purely theoretical capacity to reconstitute the social order in its own image, ethnic groups have frequently displayed a more than abstract commitment to dissolving the boundaries of the nation state and redrawing them anew. Given the aura of sanctity and omnipotence surrounding the state in current social theory, it should surely follow that any threat to its sovereignty from within would qualify as a supremely political act. The fact that the breakaway state might continue to be a version of capitalism does not make its activities any less political. Leviathan does not take more kindly to the prospect of its dismemberment simply because the reconstituted part may share a natural affinity to it. One possible conclusion to be drawn from this is that ethnic politics is often more explicable by reference to the concept of nationalism than by reference to stratification theory. At any rate, wherever a strong territorial component is present, it seems unlikely that explanations of ethnicity couched wholly or largely in terms of distributive injustice will capture the special significance of those actions and sentiments by which a group seeks to win for itself the status of a separate people.[38]

Gender

The difficulties and confusions which the resurgence of ethnicity in all its forms have created for social theory are not surprisingly matched by those thrown up by the belated recognition accorded to inequalities between the sexes. Once again it is a case of ascribed characteristics taking on an importance quite out of keeping with the confident expectations of social theory. In both cases, too, sociology has been forced to reconsider its traditional stance, not as a result of developments internal to the discipline, but as a result of explanatory efforts made by those outside the magic circle. One of the consequences of the professional theorists' unpreparedness has been that those directly involved in the new movements have themselves largely set the terms of the debate, and in a manner not always congenial to standard approaches.

In some respects the attempts to incorporate the idea of sexual inequality into the familiar formulas have posed more difficulties than the attempts to come to grips with the problem of ethnicity. The reason for this is that the analysis of ethnic factors can be undertaken without abandoning one of the central tenets of stratification theory: namely, that the family is the basic unit of study, not the individual. Whereas the communities of color, faith, language, and the like are perfectly hospitable to notions of family, kinship, and descent, the assertion of inequality between the sexes is one which naturally plays havoc with traditional ideas of the "family unit."

The theoretical rationale of taking the family rather than the individual as the appropriate unit of analysis has been the need to demonstrate the mechanism by which privileges and advantages are transmitted from generation to generation. The distinguishing feature of a class or other stratified order, as opposed to a mere system of inequality, is the tendency toward the reproduction of social statuses through the kinship line. It would be difficult to account for the process of class formation and reproduction, especially in the higher reaches of the order, if social attainments were held to be a function of the individual's own capacities and attributes rather than of collective family resources. Indeed, one of the main reasons for insisting upon the kinship connection was to combat those optimistic liberal beliefs about the open society and the attainment of equal opportunity. As part of this critique the family was held up, not as an idyllic refuge from the stresses of bureaucratic rationality as it is commonly presented in the functionalist literature, but as the discreet saboteur of all programs with equality as their goal. The family was the indirect agent of class rule, the medium through which the remote forces of institutional dominance and privilege entered the life stream of the individual.

Paradoxically, then, it was this very strategy of focusing upon the family in order to construct a radical alternative to the liberal individualist view which called forth in turn the charge of "intellectual sexism."[39] Those who leveled this charge could easily show that the concept of the family had been interpreted to mean the male head of the household; insofar as women occupied a place in the class structure at all, it was as the pale reflection of their husbands' or fathers' status. Generalizations about class behavior, social mobility, and the like, thus came to be based almost exclusively upon the activity of that minority sex which, so it happens, also provided most of the theorists. All this seemed to be a direct outcome of the collective agreement signed by functionalists, Marxists, and many others at ideological points in between, to exclude from the class picture those without an assignable place in the labor and property markets. A large proportion of women hence were cast into the same residual category as pensioners, children, and the unemployed. Even those women who were "gainfully employed" could not be treated as having an unambiguous class position of their own, because their occupational status suffered from contamination with the general status of female, which was one indelibly marked by the classless condition known as housewife.

The attack on this position has been two-pronged. First, it has been pointed out that a very large proportion of households do not have a male head, as this term is generally understood. (Acker reports a figure as high as two-fifths in the United States).[40] Moreover, female-headed households account for almost 40 percent of those below the poverty line, suggesting that "When stratification theorists talk about some classes, they are talking about women to a large extent."[41] Now, of course, the sex composition of a class or stratum need not be thought to have much bearing upon the nature of class conduct, and in particular the capacity for collective action. If an actor's position in the division of labor is taken as the independent variable, then it matters not at all if the actor is male or female. To argue otherwise by suggesting, for example, that a preponderance of women in a class has an immobilizing effect upon it, would be to fall prey to those unacceptable ideas about the innate social differences between the sexes. All that needs to be said here is that this defense of sex-blindness would be more persuasive if it were consistently applied. The evidence is, however, that the vocabulary of class is one which still lacks a feminine gender, indicating no doubt the persistence of subterranean beliefs that women workers are not quite the genuine article.

A second set of objections has been directed explicitly against the view of women as "non-workers" by way of a fundamental reevaluation of the meaning of housework. The orthodox view of housework as a nonoccupational activity external to the division of labor has been challenged by the interpretation of "domestic labor" as a vital link in the productive chain. On this reckoning, the chief functions of domestic labor are "first, the daily reproduction of the labor power of those members of the family who work in the market economy, and, second, the reproduction of new generations of laborers."[42] The domestic unit is thereby dramatically transformed from a haven of tranquility far removed from the world of work into a silent wheel in the complex machinery of capitalist production and exploitation. The status of those who do housework presumably also undergoes alteration from the linguistically absurd "housewife" to the more politically euphonious "houseworker."

Once the position is adopted that women not directly employed in the economy have a class position determined by their domestic labor, a point of conflict is reached with those theories which locate the source of women's subjugation not in their status as particular kinds of producers but in their status as women. The latter view is that the peculiar forms of humiliation and degradation to which women are subjected arise quite independently of their class situation. Expressed somewhat differently, male and female statuses *are* the basic components of class around which other types of social and material inequality tend to crystallize. The moving force of history thus undergoes revision as the "division of society into two distinct biological classes" and the "struggle of those classes with one another."[43] On this reckoning it is not so much capitalism which is the root of the problem, but men.

The appeal of the radical feminist critique undoubtedly lies in its emphasis on the fact that the subordination of women is a feature of almost all known types of society and is not a unique product of one specific mode of production. Clearly, the form that this subordination assumes under capitalism will be different from that typical of feudal or tribal systems; but it is the *universality* of male dominance which is felt to require explanation, not the variations in its institutional expression. Moreover, it could be thought that one of the practical, political implications of singling out capitalism rather than men as the source of the problem would be to lower women's guard against the possible reassertion of male dominance in the new social order. The effort to harness Marxist theory to the understanding of the "women problem" could all too easily be made to look like an attempt by radical men to stave off the unfamiliar charge of being members of an exploiting class, however scrupulous their own conduct as individuals toward members of the oppressed sex. Perhaps the true measure of radical man's discomfort at being informed that his gender is not as separable from "the system" as his theory led him to believe could only really be appreciated by a radical feminist confronted with the knowledge that a white skin is sufficient to define *her* in turn, as a member of an oppressive and exploiting race.

The recent discussions of ethnicity and gender show with particular clarity the extent to which Marxist categories of thought and argument have penetrated into academic stratification theory. The fact that Marxism has made so much of the running in the past decade or so is partly attributable to the virtual disintegration of the inner core of sociological theory in general. With the collapse of structural-functionalism, and the much more serious erosion of the old positivist certainties, the field was open for the acceptance of another theory which seemed to offer the same all-purpose explanatory coverage as the old schema without being sullied by association with it. One of the consequences of this has been that American and European approaches to the study of class and other stratified systems have shed some of their more glaring contrasts. It is difficult to envisage the rise of any new equivalent to the Warner school of stratification in an intellectual climate increasingly open to the currents of Althusserian and Frankfurt Marxism and their prolific offshoots. Although the explanatory yield of these new ideas may not be all that impressive, they have at least had the beneficial side effects of pitching the discussion to a new level of seriousness, and of bringing substantive issues to the fore, in a way not always matched by more orthodox approaches in which methodological concerns often seem to have outweighed all others. Sociology's contribution to the subject over the next decade or so is almost sure to be judged in terms of the quality of its response to the claims of its old and irrepressible rival.

NOTES

1. Oliver Cromwell Cox, *Caste, Class and Race* (New York: Monthly Review Press, 1970 ed.) p. 306.

2. The clearest statement of this position is by Gerhard E. Lenski, "American Social Classes: Statistical Strata or Social Groups?" *American Journal of Sociology,* LVIII: 2 (September 1952) pp. 139–44.

3. Various examples of this procedure are given in Frank Parkin, *Class Inequality and Political Order* (London: MacGibbon & Kee, 1971) pp. 28–34.

4. Milton M. Gordon, *Social Class in American Sociology,* (New York: McGraw-Hill, 1963) p. 15.

5. Gordon, *Social Class in American Sociology,* p. 16. According to Bernard Barber, "It is fundamental that social stratification is multidimensional." Moreover, those who question this assumption do so because "for ideological reasons they want the term 'class' to refer to some single, simple and all-explanatory notion." Bernard Barber, "Social Stratification," *International Encyclopedia of the Social Sciences,* vol. 15, 1968, p. 292.

6. Robert S. Lynd and Helen M. Lynd, *Middletown* (New York: Harcourt, Brace, 1929); *Middletown in Transition* (New York: Harcourt, Brace, 1937); James West, *Plainville, U.S.A.* (New York: Columbia University Press, 1945); A. B. Hollingshead, *Elmtown's Youth,* (New York: John Wiley, 1949); W. Lloyd Warner and Paul S. Lunt, *The Social Life of a Modern Community* (New Haven: Yale University Press, 1941).

7. For general appraisals of the Warner School and its methods see Gordon, *Social Class in American Sociology;* H. W. Pfautz and O. D. Duncan, "A Critical Review of Warner's Work in Community Stratification," *American Sociological Review,* vol. 15 (April 1950) pp. 205–15; Reinhard Bendix and S. M. Lipset, "Social Status and Social Structure: A Reexamination of Data and Interpretations," *British Journal of Sociology,* II: 2 (June 1951) pp. 150–168 and II: 3 (September 1951) pp. 230–254.

8. W. Lloyd Warner, et al., *Democracy in Jonesville* (New York: Harper & Brothers, 1949) p. XV.

9. See Peter Gay, *The Dilemma of Democratic Socialism* (New York: Columbia University Press, 1952) pp. 204–19; Hans Speier, "The Salaried Employee in Modern Society," *Social Research* (February 1934), reprinted in Hans Speier, *Social Order and the Risks of War,* (Cambridge: M. I. T. Press, 1952); Emil Lederer, *Die Privatangestellten in der modernen Wirtschaftsentwicklung* (1912).

10. Talcott Parsons, "Equality and Inequality in Modern Society, or Social Stratification Revisited," *Sociological Inquiry,* 40: 2 (Spring 1970) p. 22.

11. Ibid., p. 23.

12. Ibid., p. 24.

13. Talcott Parsons, *The Social System* (London: Routledge, 1951) p. 119. The entry in the index under "Property," invites the reader to "see Possessions."

14. David Rose, et. al., "Ideologies of Property: A Case Study," *Sociological Review,* 24: 4 (November 1976) p. 703.

15. Kingsley Davis and Wilbert E. Moore, "Some Principles of Social Stratification," in Reinhard Bendix and S. M. Lipset, eds., *Class, Status and Power* (London: Routledge, 1967) p. 51.

16. Durkheim, too, felt that because property inheritance "offends the spirit of justice" and

the tenets of true individualism, it would gradually wither away and survive only "in a weakened form." Emile Durkheim, *Professional Ethics and Civic Morals* (London: Routledge, 1957) pp. 216–17.

17. Ralf Dahrendorf, *Class and Class Conflict in Industrial Society* (London: Routledge, 1959).

18. A. Etzioni, *A Comparative Analysis of Complex Organizations* (Glencoe: Free Press, 1961).

19. Nicos Poulantzas, *Classes in Contemporary Capitalism* (London: New Left Books, 1975).

20. Paul Sweezy, *The Theory of Capitalist Development* (London: Dobson, 1946) p. 284.

21. Erik Olin Wright, "Class Boundaries in Advanced Capitalist Societies," *New Left Review*, no. 98 (July–August 1976) p. 23.

22. G. Carchedi, "On the Economic Identification of the New Middle Class," *Economy and Society*, vol. IV, no. 1 (1975) p. 48.

23. Ralph Miliband, *The State in Capitalist Society* (London: Weidenfeld & Nicholson, 1969); Nicos Poulantzas, *Political Power and Social Classes* (London: New Left Books, 1973); see also the protracted exchanges between these two writers in the pages of the *New Left Review*, no. 58 (1969), no. 59 (1970), no. 82 (1973), and no. 95 (1976).

24. John Plamenatz, *Man and Society*, vol. II (London: Longman, 1963) pp. 369–72.

25. Miliband, for example, acknowledges that " . . . 'the state' is not a thing, that it does not, as such, exist." Miliband, *The State in Capitalist Society*, p. 49.

26. This is partly due to the sloppy way that the term state is often used when all that is meant is "government." James O'Connor's analysis of the *Fiscal Crisis of the State* (New York: St. Martin's Press, 1973) is in fact about the fiscal crisis of government. Contrast the current usage with Laski's clear-minded statement that the citizen " . . . infers . . . the nature of the state from the character of its governmental acts; and he cannot know it otherwise. That is why no theory of the state is adequate that does not make the governmental act central to the explanation it offers. A state is what its government does." Harold Laski, *The State in Theory and Practice* (London: Allen & Unwin, 1935) pp. 73–74. Current Marxist theory seem to start from the very opposite assumption, namely, that "the treatment of one part of the state—usually the government—as the state itself introduces a major element of confusion in the discussion of the nature and incidence of state *power*." Miliband, *The State in Capitalist Society*, p. 49.

27. David Lockwood, "Race, Conflict and Plural Society," in Sami Zubaida, ed., *Race and Racialism* (London: Tavistock, 1970). pp. 57–72.

28. Nathan Glazer and Daniel P. Moynihan, eds., *Ethnicity* (Cambridge: Harvard University Press, 1975) pp. 16–17.

29. Daniel Bell, "Ethnicity and Social Change," in Glazer and Moynihan, *Ethnicity*.

30. As Bell puts it, " . . . it is clear that 'class' and 'ethnicity' have been the two . . . dominant modes of coherent group feeling and action, and we can raise the general question, under what conditions has *one or the other* [my italic] become most salient for action, or under what conditions might the two be fused." Bell, "Ethnicity and Social Change," pp. 165–66 This way of posing the question seems to rule out the possibility of the *equal* salience of class and ethnicity, without any "fusion" of the two. It must be said, however, that Bell, unlike many writers, does emphasize the fact of *choice* between political identities.

31. Michael Hechter, *Internal Colonialism* (London: Routledge, 1975).

32. Robert Blauner, *Racial Oppression in America* (New York: Harper & Row, 1972). Also see, in particular, Stokely Carmichael and Charles V. Hamilton, *Black Power* (New York: Random House, 1967).

33. James Boggs, *Racism and the Class Struggle* (New York: Monthly Review Press, 1970) p. 14.

34. Robert Davies, "The White Working Class in South Africa," *New Left Review*, no. 82 (November–December 1973).

35. Hechter, *Internal Colonialism*, p. 292.

36. See, for example, Boserup's account of the Ulster crisis as a "manifestation at the political level of the transition from one variant of a capitalist social formation to another." The specific contradiction is here said to be between a "clientalist" form of capitalism and monopoly capitalism. Anders Boserup, "Contradictions and Struggles in Northern Ireland," *Socialist Register* (London: Merlin Press, 1972) p. 173.

37. Lockwood, "Race, Conflict and Plural Society," p. 64.

38. It is curious that Glazer and Moynihan should regard ethnicity as a social and political fact which is " . . . troublesome both to those who wish to emphasize the primacy of class, and those

who wish to emphasize the primacy of nation." Glazer and Moynihan, *Ethnicity,* p. 18. Ethnicity poses no problem for the concept of nation; it takes on its special significance precisely *because* of its affiliation to it.

39. Joan Acker, "Women and Social Stratification: A Case of Intellectual Sexism," *American Journal of Sociology,* 78: 4, (January 1973) 936–45.

40. Ibid.

41. Ibid., pp. 939–40.

42. Chris Middleton, "Sexual Inequality and Stratification Theory," in Frank Parkin, ed., *The Social Analysis of Class Structure* (London: Tavistock, 1974) p. 197.

43. Shulamith Firestone, *The Dialectic of Sex* (London: Paladin, 1972) p. 13. For a general critique of the feminist position from a Marxist viewpoint, see Juliet Mitchell, *Woman's Estate* (Harmondsworth: Penguin Books, 1971); also, Middleton, "Sexual Inequality and Stratification Theory." For an interesting collection of recent papers on sexual inequality, see the companion volumes by Sheila Allen and Diana Leonard Barker, *Sexual Divisions and Society: Process and Change* (London: Tavistock, 1976); and *Dependence and Exploitation in Work and Marriage* (London: Longman, 1976).

16

POWER AND AUTHORITY

STEVEN LUKES

TRACING the history of power and authority poses peculiar problems. The history of political theory and of sociology is in part a history of unending disagreement as to how power and authority are to be conceptualized and how they relate to one another. Moreover, that disagreement is endemic, and it is so for deep reasons. These concepts are not labels for discrete phenomena: they have distinct roles in social and political theorizing and in social and political life. Different and contending theories and world views yield different ways of conceiving power and authority and the relations between them. Thus an adequate history of power and authority would have to include an account of those theories and world views and their basis in social and political life.

Consider the following questions. Is power a property or a relationship? Is it potential or actual, a capacity or the exercise of a capacity? By whom, or what, is it possessed or exercised: by agents (individual or collective?) or by structures or systems? Over whom or upon what is it exercised: agents (individual or collective?) or structures or systems? Is it, by definition, intentional, or can its exercise be partly intended or unintended? Must it be (wholly or partly) effective? What *kinds* of outcomes does it produce: does it modify interests, options, preferences, policies, or behavior? Is it a relation which is reflexive or irreflexive, transitive or intransitive, complete or incomplete? Is it asymmetrical? Does exercising power by some reduce the power of others? (Is it a zero-sum concept?) Or can its exercise maintain or increase the total of power? Is it demonic or benign? Must it rest on or employ force or coercion, or the threat of sanctions or deprivations? (And, if so, what balance of costs and rewards must there be between the parties for power to exist?) Does the concept only apply where there is conflict of some kind, or resistance? If so, must the conflict be manifest, or may it be latent: must it be between revealed preferences or can it involve real interests (however defined)? Is it a behavioral concept, and, if so, in what sense? Is it a causal concept?

Parallel questions arise in relation to authority, along with others such as these: Is authority by definition legitimate? Is it by definition consensual? (And are these two questions the same question?) Can it (or must it) be coercive? Is it exercised over belief or over conduct or both? Is it a concept whose use is "normative" or "empirical"; is it "quasi—performative" or "neutral"? Is it de jure or de facto or both? Does it indicate a causal or an "internal" relation? Does it presuppose a normative relationship? Can it be accounted for in individualist and behavioral or influence terms? Does it presuppose inequality? Is submission to authority compatible with the exercise of reason? Is it a denial, or sometimes a condition, of freedom and autonomy?

And what of the relationship between power and authority? Is authority a form of power? Or are only some forms of authority forms of power? Or does power (always or sometimes?) underlie authority? Or is there a radical opposition between power and authority? Or perhaps "power is essentially tied to the personality of individuals" whereas "authority is always associated with social positions or roles"?[1]

The alternative answers offered to questions such as these have wider theoretical and often philosophical import and they cannot be systematically treated here. What I propose to do instead is to offer a formal and abstract account of the *concepts* of power and authority respectively which inhere within the many *conceptions* of power and authority that have been used by particular thinkers within specific contexts, in development from and in reaction to one another. Any given conception of power and of authority (and of the relation between them) can be seen as an interpretation and application of its concept. The various conceptions of power and authority are, as John Rawls writes of conceptions of justice, "the outgrowth of different notions of society against the background of opposing views of the natural necessities and opportunities of human life." To understand any such conception fully, "We must make explicit the conception of social co-operation from which it derives."[2] I shall classify and indicate something of the range of alternative conceptions. I shall then sketch the outlines of a number of traditions of conceptualizing power and authority, and the relations between them, within political and social theory. I shall conclude by indicating a number of contemporary controversies in which alternative conceptions are at issue.

I

First, the concept of power. The absolutely basic common core to all conceptions of power is the notion of the bringing about of consequences, with no restriction on what the consequences might be or what brings them about. When used in relation to human beings in social relations with one another, it is attributed to persons or collectivities or, sometimes, to systems or structures within which they act. It is, therefore, no surprise that any given conception of power will necessarily incorporate a theory of that to which it is attributed: to identify the power of an individual, or a class, or a social system, one must, consciously or unconsciously, have a theory of the nature—that is, the causal powers—of individuals, classes, or social systems. In applying this basic notion to the understanding of social and political life, however, something further is required than the mere idea that persons, groups, or systems generate causal consequences: namely, the idea that such consequences are nontrivial or significant in some way. Clearly, we all affect the world and one another in countless ways all the time; any given use of the concept of power—and related concepts such as authority, influence, coercion, force, violence, manipulation, and so on—picks out ranges of such consequences that are held to be significant in specific (and related) ways. A conception of power useful for understanding social relationships must incorporate a criterion of significance—that is, it must imply an answer to the question: What makes the consequences brought about by *A* significant in such a way as to count as power?

A wide range of answers is to be found—answers which dictate specific responses to some or all of the questions raised in the second paragraph of this chapter. For some, what is essential to power is the realization of a will or desire. This will yield an intentional conception of power, which may be *potential,* as in Hobbes's view that "the POWER *of a man*" is "his present means to obtain some future apparent good";[3] or *actual,* as in Voltaire's view that "power consists in making others act as I choose,"[4] or, even more simply, Bertrand Russell's "the production of intended effects."[5] In intentional conceptions, the focus is on individual agents, and on collective agents only insofar as intentions can be attributed to them (hence, in this view, groups such as elites will not have or exercise power unless they are united and consciously pursue their goals). Other conceptions do not take intention, or the realization of will, to be essential to power; such conceptions broaden the application of the concept to cover the actions, and perhaps inaction, of (individual or collective) agents which further their interests (which may or may not coincide with their intentions, if such they have).

Such an approach allows in not just unintended effects but of various forms of individual and collective power (class power, state power) which the former conceptions do not. Some writers go so far as to see power as a variant of systemic or structural determinism (whether this be in the context of structural functionalism, systems theory, or structuralist Marxism). However, there is, it seems to me, much to be said for the view that this is an overextended and confusing use of the concept: power (and its cognate concepts) would seem to be an "agency" notion (though, of course, views differ about what constitutes an "agent"). Thus it is held and exercised by agents (individual or collective) within systems and structural determinants.[6]

There are, however, as we shall see, conceptions of power that deny this (or appear to).

It seems that conceptions of power may be divided into two very broad categories. On the one hand, there are those which are asymmetrical and tend to involve (actual or potential) conflict and resistance.[7] Such conceptions appear to presuppose a view of social or political relations as competitive and inherently conflictual; as Hobbes remarked, "because the power of a man resisteth and hindereth the effects of the power of another: power simply is no more, but the excess of the power of one above that of another."[8] On the other hand, there are those conceptions which do not imply that some gain at others' expense but rather that all may gain: power is a collective capacity or achievement. Such conceptions appèar to rest on a view of social or political relations as at least potentially harmonious and communal. As Montesquieu observed, quoting the seventeenth-century Italian jurist Gravina, "the combining of all power held by individuals . . . constitutes what is called the political state"; the "power of individuals," he maintained, "cannot be united without the conjunctions of all their wills."[9]

The first category may, in turn, be seen as composed of three closely related but analytically distinct ways of conceiving power. First are those conceptions which focus on the *securing of compliance*, on the (attempted or successful) *control* by some of others.[10] Among these, some take the prevailing of some men's wills over others', and thus overt conflict and resistance, as essential to power. From Hobbes to those behaviorist political scientists in the contemporary community-power debate who identify power by discovering "who prevails in decision making," this is the most clear-cut and also the narrowest of all conceptions of power. Some writers analyze power in terms of the concept of force (Cartwright[11]); others follow Georg Simmel in stressing the aspect of voluntary compliance in all superordinate-subordinate relations, the "spontaneity and coefficiency of the subordinate subject"[12] (force, unlike power, being a nonsocial relation which destroys the subordinate's freedom). Some see the securing of compliance as achieved by the manipulation of utility functions or incentive systems (Karlsson[13]; others (Riker, Shapley, and Shubik[14]) locate power by identifying the last-added member of a minimum winning coalition. Within systems theory, power as control can be conceptualized (as by Niklas Luhmann[15]) as a medium of communication by means of which one party makes more probable selections of action alternatives by another party than would otherwise be less probable. Among those who stress the conflict of wills, it is commonly assumed that power must involve the use or threat of deprivations. This for Lasswell and Kaplan, power is "the process of affecting the policies of others with the help of (actual or threatened) deprivations for nonconformity with the policies intended."[16] Blau is even more specific, defining power as "the ability of persons or groups to impose their will on others despite resistance through deterrence either in the form of withholding regularly supplied rewards or in the form of punishment inasmuch as the former, as well as the latter, constitute, in effect, a negative sanction."[17] Others follow Machiavelli, seeing power as social control that is made the more effective by the averting of conflict and the economizing of the use and the threat of sanctions. For such writers, power is asymmetrical but need not involve manifest conflict and resistance.

Distinct from the notion of securing compliance by exercising power is the closely related idea of power as *a relation of dependence,* in which *B* conforms to *A*'s will or interests not by virtue of any discernible actions or threats of *A*, but by reason of the very relationship between *A* and *B*. This way of conceiving power could be seen as a variant of the first, on the argument that it is simply a matter of *A* securing *B*'s compliance *indirectly* and at low cost to himself. But it seems more perspicuous to see it as constituting a distinct range of conceptions, since there are many cases where *B* may be dependent on *A*, irrespective of *A*'s actions, purposes, or even knowledge. James Mill had this idea in mind when he defined power as "security for the conformity between the will of one man and the acts of other men."[18] Such security is typically a function of social and economic relations and institutional arrangements rather than, or as well as, the action, and inaction, of individuals and groups. Perhaps the most clearly articulated and worked-out version of this idea is to be found in the literature on dependency theory, which pictures development and underdevelopment as interdependent within a single global system. Thus, Dos Santos writes:

> . . . dependence is a *conditioning situation* in which the economies of one group of countries are conditioned by the development and expansion of others. A relationship of interdependence between two or more economies or between such economies and the world trading system becomes a dependent relationship when some countries can expand through self-impulsion while others, being in a dependent position, can only expand as a reflection of the expansion of the dominant countries, which may have positive or negative effects on their immediate development.[19]

A third way of conceiving asymmetric power is again very closely related to the second, but distinct from it; this is the notion of power as *inequality*—that is, a distributive notion which focuses on the differential capacities of actors within a system to secure valued but scarce advantages and resources. Power as control and as dependence are measured by determining *A*'s net advantage and *B*'s net loss from *B*'s compliance; power as inequality is measured by determining who gains and who loses—that is, *A*'s ability to gain at *B*'s expense.[20] Power in this sense may be held or exercised without *A* securing *B*'s compliance and with *B* being dependent on *A*: consider the power of organized vis-à-vis unorganized workers (though, of course, inequality, dependence, and control are very often likely to coexist empirically. It is in this sense that power is often used by stratification theorists. Max Weber evidently had this conception of power in mind when he observed that " 'classes,' 'status groups' and 'parties' *are phenomena of the distribution of power within a community.*" '[21] Lenski argues that "if we can establish the pattern of [the distribution of power] in a given society, we have largely established the pattern for the distribution of privilege, and if we can discover the causes of a given distribution of power we have also discovered the causes of the distribution of privilege linked with it."[22] Frank Parkin has articulated this conception of power as inequality with the greatest clarity:

> . . . to speak of the distribution of power could be understood as another way of describing the flow of rewards; the very fact that the dominant class can successfully claim a disproportionate share of rewards vis-à-vis the subordinate class, is in a sense a *measure* of the former's power over the latter. In other words, power need not be thought of as something which exists over and above the system of material and social rewards; rather it can be thought of as a concept or metaphor which is used to depict the flow of resources which constitutes the system. And as such it is not a separate dimension of stratification at all.[23]

In sum, control, dependence, and inequality represent three major ways of conceptualizing power, understood as an asymmetric relation. It is, perhaps, worth noting that Max Weber's celebrated definition of power as "the probability that one actor within a social relationship will be in a position to carry out his own will despite resistance, regardless of the basis on which this probability rests"[24] is compatible with all three.

Conceptions of power as a collective capacity or achievement tend to stress the benign and communal rather than the demonic and competitive aspect of power: power is exercised with rather than over others. Benjamin Constant remarked that the ancient, as opposed to the modern, citizen engaged in "the active and constant participation in collective power."[25] For Plato and Aristotle, according to Franz Neumann, "political power is the total power of the community."[26] Cicero said that "in no other city except in one where the people has the supreme power, can liberty find its abode," and he distinguished between "*potestas in populo*" and "*auctoritas in senatu*."[27] Similarly, the *Digest* of Justinian's code of Roman Law *(Corpus Iuris Civilis)* derives the legal force of the prince's decision from the fact that "the people has conferred to him and upon him the whole of its government and power."[28] These republican and imperial conceptions of collective power were succeeded in the Middle Ages by more hierarchical conceptions; for Aquinas "order principally denotes power" and "power properly denotes active potentiality, together with some kind of pre-eminence."[29] There is Burke's Whiggish conception that "liberty, when men act in bodies, is *power*"[30] and the distinctive liberal conception of collective power according to which reciprocal and complementary activities promote the individual good as part of the common good. Thus, for Humboldt, human powers are to be cultivated and developed through "the mutual freedom of activity among all the members of a nation" (an idea taken up by Rawls[31]), while T. H. Green defined "freedom in the positive sense" as "the liberation of powers of all men equally for contributions to a common good" and "a power which each man exercises through the help or security given him by his fellow-men."[32] Marxism also contains a collective conception in application to the task of building socialism: Soviet power, wrote Lenin, "paves the way to socialism. It gives those who were formerly oppressed the chance to straighten their backs and to an ever-increasing degree to take the whole government of the country, the whole administration of the economy, the whole management of production, into their own hands."[33] Among contemporary theorists, as we shall see, Hannah Arendt and Talcott Parsons advance collective conceptions, the former by reference to a classical, republican conception of politics in which the essence of power does "not rely on the command-obedience relationship" but corresponds rather to "the human ability to . . . act in concert";[34] while for the latter power is a system resource, being the "capacity to mobilize the resources of the society for the attainment of goals for which a general "public" commitment has been made, or may be made."[35] Conceptions such as these are, it will be clear, at the other end of the spectrum from the Hobbesian and the Weberian.

Of course, asymmetric and collective conceptions of power are not, in any simple way, exclusive of one another. What some may see as an asymmetric relation, others may see merely as a collective capacity, simply by confining their analytic focus to a given collectivity abstracted from its relations with others. Conversely, a system (such as capitalism) may be seen as having certain collective capacities (for instance, productive power) in virtue, at least in part, of its internal and conflictual power relations.

The concept of authority, as the common core to all the various conceptions of authority, has a more complex structure than the concept of power. That structure is basically two tiered.[36] On the one hand, authority involves the nonexercise of private judgment. He who accepts authority accepts as a sufficient reason for acting or believing something the fact that he has been so instructed by someone whose claim to do so he acknowledges. To accept authority is precisely to refrain from examining what one is being told to do or believe. It is to act or believe not on the balance of reasons, but rather on the basis of a second-order reason that precisely requires that one disregard the balance of reasons as one sees it. Likewise, to exercise authority is precisely not to have to offer reasons, but to be obeyed or believed because one has a recognized claim to be. Aquinas made the point in relation to authority over belief as follows: the "decisive factor is who it is whose statement is assented to; by comparison the subject matter which is assented to is in a certain sense secondary."[37] And Hobbes made the point in relation to authority over conduct by drawing the following distinction between advice (counsel) and authority (command):

> . . . counsel is a precept, in which the reason of my obeying it is taken from the thing itself which is advised; but command is a precept, in which the cause of my obedience depends on the will of commander. For it is not properly said . . . I command, except the will stands for reason. Now when obedience is yielded to the laws, not for the thing itself, but by reason of the advisor's will, the law is not a counsel but a command. . . .[38]

The first component of the concept of authority, then, is the giving and acceptance of a reason which is both a first-order reason for action and/or belief and a second-order reason for disregarding conflicting reasons. A number of points are worth noting here. First, the giving of such a reason (i.e., the exercise of authority) need not be intentional: I may accept as authoritative what you intend, say, as advice. Second, whether a given case counts as an instance of authority will depend on the point of view from which it is being identified. I may be using the term in a "normative" or nonrelativized way: in such a case I am judging whether an authoritative reason has been given (against standards which, however, I may claim to be objective). Alternatively, I may (as a sociologist, say) be using the term in a "descriptive" or relativized way. Here there are at least two possibilities. I may identify which reasons are authoritative by reference to the beliefs and attitudes of those subject to authority (this being what is called de facto authority), or I may do so by reference to a set of rules prevalent in a given society, whatever the parties to a particular relationship might believe (this being de jure authority).[39] This is the standpoint of legal theorists—and also that of Max Weber. "In a concrete case," Weber writes, "the performance of the command may have been motivated by the ruled's own conviction of its propriety, or by his sense of duty, or by fear, or by "dull" custom, or by a desire to obtain some benefit for himself. Sociologically these differences are not necessarily relevant." The sociologist "will normally start from the observation that "factual" powers of command usually claim to exist "by virtue of law." It is exactly for this reason that the sociologist cannot help operating with the conceptual apparatus of the law."[40]

The third point worth noting is that a considerable range of variation is possible with respect to the *range* of conflicting reasons which the authoritative reason excludes. If subject to authority, I might be permitted to act on my conscience or on certain of my interests (e.g., survival, as in Hobbes, or self-regarding actions, as in J. S. Mill) or indeed on the basis of another authority, as for instance that of the king should he be present within a feudal lord's jurisdiction. Authority, in this analysis, is not a matter of one reason *overriding* other, conflicting reasons because it is weightier; rather, it excludes them by kind not weight.[41] Some very weighty reasons might be excluded: the point is that authority excludes action or belief on the balance of reasons. Of course, those who accept authority assume that authoritative utterances contain, as Friedrich puts it, "the potentiality of reasoned elaboration."[42] Authority, like intuition, is thus seen as a shortcut to where reason is presumed to lead. The point is that authority dispenses with the elaboration of the reasons; the shortcut is taken (sometimes on entirely rational grounds, as when one accepts the authority of an expert). With every attribution of authority there goes an assumption about the circumstances under which it applies and the kinds of reasons which it excludes. (Accordingly, authority can be absolute in two ways: applying to all circumstances and excluding all conflicting reasons).

This first component of authority is sometimes described as the "surrender of private judgment." This, however, supposes that a distinction already exists between the "individual's private judgment" and the dictates of authority. But in some traditional authority relationships, such a distinction, which presupposes that the individual is able to stand outside custom and tradition in order to apply critical standards to them, may not, or may not yet, exist.

Authority may be accepted unconditionally and uncritically because the culture may not provide the individual with alternatives to the established mode of thought: the preconditions for moral autonomy and independent "private" judgment may not have appeared. Moreover, one could say that what counts as "private judgment" does not relate to a distinction between "private" and "public" drawn elsewhere but is itself determined by the scope of authority—private judgment being precisely that judgment which is nonauthoritative—that is, based on reasons that are excluded when authority prevails. When authority goes unquestioned, private judgment does not exist.[43]

The second component of the concept of authority is the identification of the possessor or exerciser of authority as having a claim to do so. Any use of the concept must presuppose some criterion for identifying the source (as opposed to the content) of authoritative utterances. Since accepting authority excludes evaluation of the *content* of an utterance as the method of identifying whether it is authoritative, there (logically) must be some means of identifying its source as authoritative—a criterion which picks out, in Hobbes's words, not "the saying of a man" but "his virtue." Thus Hobbes wrote of "marks whereby a man may discern in what men, or assembly of men, the sovereign power is placed and resideth,"[44] and Bentham, of "a common signal . . . notorious and visible to all."[45] It is instructive to consider the wide ranges of such marks or signals there have been in different historical periods and kinds of community. These may be age; gender; status, whether of kinship, occupation, caste, or race; wealth; property; military prowess; religious claims, whether traditional or charismatic; honor or esteem of all kinds; credentials; functional role; office—and, not least, power itself. Such an identifying criterion for designating the source of authoritative utterances requires that there must be some mutually recognized norms or "rules of recognition" (in H. L. A. Hart's phrase[46]) which enable the parties to distinguish who is authoritative from who is not. Such accepted rules of recognition need not be formalized; they may indeed amount to unarticulated norms that are subject to highly personal interpretation. So in *King Lear* there is this exchange:

KENT: . . . you have that in your countenance which I would fain call master.
LEAR: What's that?
KENT: Authority.[47]

And sometimes the interpretation may be innovative, even revolutionary, as in Weber's case of charismatic authority.

The ways in which alternative conceptions of authority derive from alternative "notions of society" and "conceptions of social cooperation" and indeed philosophical presuppositions may be briefly illustrated. We may distinguish three broad ways of conceptualizing authority.

In the first place, authority may be seen as exercised *over belief*, as opposed to conduct (a distinction often indicated by contrasting being "an authority" and "in authority"). To accept authority understood this way is to assent to propositions as true or valid because their source is recognized as an authority. This covers a continuum of cases from that blind faith (as in priests or prophets) to rationally grounded acceptance (as of expert opinion).

Originally, *auctoritas* for the Romans and throughout the Middle Ages signified the possession by some of some special status or quality or claim that added a compelling ground for trust or obedience, and this could derive from some special relation to some founding act or past beginning or to a sacred being, or some special access to or knowledge of some set of truths. The Roman senate had authority in this sense, as did Augustus.[48] In Matthew it says that Jesus taught the people "as one having authority and not as the scribes."[49] Augustine distinguished God's "divine authority," "Christ's authority," "scriptural authority," "patristic authority," and "church authority," observing in relation to the last that "I would not believe the Gospel if the authority of the Catholic Church did not impel me to it."[50] And Hooker wrote that by "a man's authority we here understand the force which his word hath for the assurance of another's mind that buildeth upon it."[51]

In all these cases, authority is claimed over belief on the grounds of some special wisdom, revelation, skill, insight or knowledge. This, of course, requires the epistemological assumption that such knowledge is to be had. Pre-Reformation Christians and, say, nineteenth-century positivists and twentieth-century technocrats have supposed that such knowledge is available but that access to it is restricted—for medieval Christians, to the papacy or the Church; for August Comte and his followers, to the spiritual leaders of society; for modern technocrats, to the scientific and administrative elites. It is evident that such conceptions are inherently inegalitarian, since those who have restricted access to such knowledge are, by virtue of that very fact, superior to others and entitled to their deference and submission. On the other hand, where there is no assumption of restricted access to religious or scientific truths (whether on grounds of revelation or status or office or natural ability) authority may be accepted as a pragmatic matter of convenience or economy of effort, as in the intellectual division of labor. The notion of "moral authority" perhaps only makes sense in a community which shares values and principles about which some persons are assumed to be capable of greater knowledge than others; such a notion loses its sense where such values and principles come to be seen not as objects of knowledge but as subject to individual choice.[52]

One may contrast with authority as a compelling ground for belief, based on special and accepted claims, two further broad ways of conceiving authority.

The first of these is authority *by convention*. Here authority is seen as a matter of binding decisions compelling obedience, the source of which is assumed to be voluntarily accepted as authoritative by those subject to it. Here authority is the solution to a predicament: a collectivity of individuals wish to engage in some common activity or activities but cannot agree on what is to be done. Coordinated action is necessary but unachievable if everyone follows his own judgment. As James Fitzjames Stephen put it: "No case can be specified in which people unite for a common object from making a pair of shoes up to governing an empire in which the power to decide does not rest somewhere; and what is this but command and obedience?"[53] The claim to obedience by a person or persons *in authority* does not rest of any claim to connection with traditional origins or sacred beings or special knowledge, but rather on their having been put in authority by some agreed procedure. Those subject to such authority are obliged by individual decisions (within given limits), whatever their merits in any given case, because the pursuit of their common activity requires this sacrifice of their individual private judgments. Note, however, that unlike authority over belief, which necessarily compels the assent of those subject to it (i.e., if I believe an opinion on authority, I cannot at the same time dissent from it), this kind of authority simply requires that the subject refrains from *acting* on his own judgment: he remains free to dissent privately from the particular command whose authority he accepts.

Conceptions of voluntarily accepted authority by convention are, of course, extremely widespread in the postmedieval world. For Hobbes and Spinoza, the very existence of society was held to require the acceptance of such authority in order to provide the requisite security for social life to be possible, while the liberal tradition from Locke onward has taken the requirements of coordination to be more specific, imposing a more limited sacrifice of individuals' right to follow their own judgment. Sometimes, as in social-contract and state-of-nature theories, the predicament and its solution are hypothetical (people are to be regarded "as if" they had accepted authority); alternatively, people are assumed to have registered their voluntary acceptance by, for instance, voting, possessing property, etc. For others—radical democrats since Rousseau, anarchists, Marxists, and socialists of many kinds—authority by convention, at least in society as a whole and in particular the political sphere, has yet to be achieved.

The third way of conceiving authority is as authority *by imposition*—and that is how these last thinkers tend to see authority in the past and present though not in possible future societies. In this view, the acceptance of both authoritative reasons and the rules of recognition is imposed by means of power. Notions such as "hegemony," "legitimation," and indeed "ideology" as used by neo-Marxist writers and "the mobilization of bias" and "false consensus" as used by radical critics of liberal democracy all signify the idea that in contemporary societies authority is (at least in part) imposed by power, either directly by control, or indirectly, through dependence relations.

More generally, "realist" thinkers from Thrasymachus to Machiavelli to the neo-Machiavellian elite theorists and beyond have argued as though authority over belief and the voluntary acceptance of authority by convention are *always* largely illusory, and that behind the authoritative reasons and rules of recognition ("derivations," "political formulas") there always lies the *force majeure* of the ruler or rulers.[54] Hobbes is a key figure here too, since his view ingeniously straddles the views of authority by convention and authority by imposition. (Compare Hobbes's own distinction between sovereignty by institution and sovereignty by acquisition.[55] For he assumed that the sovereign, once voluntarily established as the solution to the predicament of the war of all against all, would thereafter be the continuing source of all authority relations through the exercise of will: hence his theory of law as command (taken up by Bentham and Austin) and his view of the sovereign as the Great Definer, whose power extends to assigning the very meanings of words and the enforcement of their definitions.[56] Combining a voluntarist and a power analysis of authority, he thus stands both in the liberal and the "realist" traditions.

II

I now turn to a sketch of various broad traditions within political theory and sociology. Such categorization is not, of course, intended to capture the total positions of the thinkers referred to, only the background and the thrust of their ways of conceiving power and authority and the relations between them.

First are all those who take it for granted that social order is constituted, largely or wholly, by shared beliefs, held for the most part on authority—whether divinely inspired, as for the French counterrevolutionary theocrats; or traditional, "as if in the presence of canonized forefathers," as for Burke;[57] or anchored in science, as for Saint-Simon and Comte; or in a central value system, as for normative functionalists. In such conceptions, authority over belief is central to the explanation both of social cohesion and political order; power is conceptualized in relation to this central role of authority—partly as functional, even integral to it, and partly as threatening, insofar as it is abused or diffused in such a way as to jeopardize its continuance.

In medieval thought, authority and power (seen as institutionalized social control involving coercion) became ever more closely linked. Aquinas used the term "the authorities" to refer both to "the principle of origins . . . in divine matters" and to the agency of "coercive force" in public affairs: "all those who govern" follow a plan derived from "the eternal law" and are part of the order "Divine Providence" imposes "on all things."[58] Within the Church, *auctoritas* and *potestas* came to be used interchangeably, conflating the right to evoke assent and the right to compel obedience. And from the thirteenth century onward, authority, both within and without the Church, came to be seen as the basis for coercive power; thus, for both the papalists and the conciliarists, "the idea of authority in Church-State relations . . . became inseparable from coercive dominion."[59] Similarly, the main Protestant reformers (as opposed to the radical sects) preached individual submission to the authority of the churches and, unless they grossly violated God's word, to the temporal authorities, who facilitated the operation of the true Church.

Perhaps the most pronounced linkage of divinely inspired authority over belief and power in the modern era is to be found among the Catholic counterrevolutionaries of the early nineteenth century. For de Maistre, "religion and patriotism" are "the great and solid bases of all possible institutions" and a "powerful binding force . . . in the state"; they know "only two words, *submission and belief;* with these two levers they raise the world." What is more, in politics, "we *know* that it is necessary to respect those powers established we know not how or by whom"; indeed, the most extreme form of coercive power becomes integral to political authority and social cohesion:

> . . . all grandeur, all power, all subordination rests on the executioner: he is the horror and bond of human association. Remove this incomprehensible agent from the world, and at that very moment order gives way to chaos, thrones topple, and society disappears.[60]

For Bonald, bitter opponent of "atheism and anarchy" and of "that doctrine which substituted the reason of each for the religion of all, and the calculations of personal interest for the love of the Supreme Being and of one's fellows," there was "a religion for social man, just as there is a political constitution for society": the "power and force of religion" achieving "the repression of [man's] depraved desires" and "the power and force of political society" achieving the "repression of the external acts arising from those same desires." Authority, in the form of the "power of God" and power in the form of the "power of man" formed an "intimate, indissoluble union."[61] Thomas Carlyle, similarly, proclaimed that, man being "necessitated to obey superiors,"

> Aristocracy and Priesthood, a Governing Class and a Teaching Class: these two, sometimes separate, and endeavouring to harmonise themselves, sometimes conjoined as one, and the King a Pontiff-King:—there did no Society exist without these two vital elements, there will none exist.[62]

Other conservatives, reacting to the ideas, practice and consequences of the French Revolution, identified authority over belief at least as much in terms of submission to precedent and tradition as to divinely revealed truths. For Burke, "we procure reverence to our civil institutions . . . on account of their age, and on account of those from whom they are descended"; the bond which "holds all physical and moral natures, each in their appointed place" and prevents society dissolving into "an unsocial, uncivil, unconnected chaos of elementary principles" is "a necessity to which men must be obedient by consent or force." Accordingly, "We fear God; we look up with awe to Kings: with affection to Parliaments; with duty to magistrates; with reverence to priests; and with respect to nobility." Such social authority, inculcating "this mixed system of opinion and sentiment," all these "pleasing illusions" made "power gentle and obedience liberal." This was a much less harsh doctrine than de Maistre's. Authority restrained the use of power: "All persons possessing any portion of power ought to be strongly and awfully impressed with an idea that they act in trust" on behalf of "the one great Master, Author and Founder of Society." On the other hand, when "ancient opinions and rules of life are taken away," power will "find other and worse means of its support"; the "present French power is the very first body of citizens, who, having obtained full authority to do with their country what they pleased, have chosen to dissever it," acting "as conquerors" of the French and destroying "the bonds of their union." Power thus escapes from the gentling constraints of traditional authority.[63]

These conservative and traditionalist ideas lead support to R. A. Nisbet's claim that the French Revolution's impact upon traditional society generated a "seminal distinction between authority and power": "the image of *social authority* is cast from materials drawn from the old regime; the image of *political power*—rational, centralized and popular—from the legislative pattern of the Revolution."[64] Thus, as Carlyle said, "we worship and follow after Power," and Burckhardt attributed to the diffusion of the doctrine of human perfectibility "the complete disintegration of the idea of authority in the hands of mortal men, whereupon, of course, we periodically fall victims to sheer power."[65]

On the other hand, nineteenth- and twentieth-century thinkers developed a very wide range of conceptions of authority over belief which were not, as Nisbet seems to suppose, exclusively, or even primarily, tied to traditional conceptions. Nisbet writes:

> Social authority *versus* political power is precisely the way in which the issue was drawn, first by the conservatives and then all the way through the century to Durkheim's reflections on centralization and social groups and Weber's on rationalization and tradition. The vast and continuing interest in social constraint, social control and normative authority that the history of sociology reveals, as well as its own special distinction between authority and power, has its roots in the same soil that produced its interest in community.

Although Nisbet acknowledges that it "would be false to think of this distinction between social authority and political power as one resting solely in conservative thought," his account of nineteenth-century sociological theories of authority focuses entirely on "the rediscovery of custom and tradition, of patriarchal and corporate authority, all of which, it is argued, are the fundamental (and continuing) sources of social and political order."[66]

Here, on the contrary, it is argued that a range of alternative conceptions to traditional authority over belief form a central part of the history of nineteenth- and twentieth-century sociology. Montesquieu had already treated the "Spirit of the Laws" under republican, monarchical, and despotic governments as distinct. Republican governments and monarchies were "moderate" forms, but only the latter involved "preeminence and ranks"; despotism, by contrast, put "mankind . . . all upon a level," so that "all are slaves." As these types of government differed, so also did "the manner of obeying."[67]

In the nineteenth and twentieth centuries, authority over belief came to be seen in a number of nontraditionalist ways and in ways that combined the traditional and the modern in a number of different mixtures, relating both the nature of authoritative utterances and the rules of recognition to specifically modern conditions of life. For Saint-Simon, the new political system suitable for an industrial society would be based on "positive knowledge," on "a state of enlightenment with the consequence that Society, aware of the means it must employ to improve its lot, can be guided by principles, and no longer has any need to give arbitrary powers to those whom it entrusts with the tasks of administering its affairs." No longer need society find its leaders among the "nobility and the clergy"; the new system would be "conceived and organized according to principles derived from a healthy morality and a true philosophy." This would consist in "scientific opinions clothed in forms which make them sacred." It would be recognized that "all government will be arbitrary so long as its leaders are taken from military men and metaphysicians"; by contrast, "scientists, artists and industrialists and the heads of industrial concerns are the men who possess the most eminent, varied and most positively useful ability for the guidance of men's minds at the present time." These would henceforth exercise authority over men's minds, administration would replace "the governmental machine" and the functions of government would be "limited to maintaining public order." A wholly new principle of authority and type of social integration, a quite new social structure, based on the functional requirements of industrial production, would replace the old system of hierarchy and subordination. The government of men would give way to the administration of things, and power, in the form of political action, would be "reduced to what is necessary for establishing a hierarchy of functions in the general action of men on nature." Thus "the desire to dominate" would be "harnessed to the collective good."[68]

Auguste Comte saw the new "positive philosophy" as justifying a new form of "social subordination," a "positive hierarchy" to replace the old order. The new "spiritual power" would "set up morality" to guide society: its role would be "the government of opinion, that is the establishment and maintenance of the principles that must govern the various social relations." It would exercise an authority which would be effective "on account both of its educational function and of its regular intervention in social conflicts." "Moral" would prevail over "political solutions." Comte clearly believed that this would be a *new* principle of authority, a "modern spiritual power." T. H. Huxley was to call this "Catholicism without Christianity," but Comte wrote that "the allegiance of the people to their new scientific leaders would be of quite a different character from the unreasoning obedience to priests in the theological phase." Comte's motto was, after all, "order and progress"; we need, he argued, "equally the inheritance of de Maistre and Condorcet . . . a doctrine equally progressive and hierarchic." The *savants* "alone as regards theory exercise an uncontested authority"; they are "exclusively invested with the moral force essential to secure [the new organic doctrine's] recognition." The "*savants* in our day possess, to the exclusion of all other classes, the two fundamental elements of spiritual government, capacity and authority in matters of theory."[69]

Tocqueville likewise contrasted traditional and modern forms of social authority, though for him the latter was democratic and based on equality. All societies needed "common belief"—"opinions that men receive on trust and without discussion." In aristocratic periods, men are "naturally inclined to shape their opinions by the superior standard of a person or class of persons"; in "ages of equality," the individual's "readiness to believe the multitude increases" and "common opinion" becomes "the only guide which private judgment retains among a democratic people." Tocqueville's contrast was not, as Nisbet claims, between traditional authority and political power, but between traditional and democratic authority. The former imposed all kinds of obligations, responsibilities and constraints upon superiors in their relations to inferiors, thus limiting their power and directing it to the national interest. In a democracy, the links of the chain binding all "from the peasant to the King" were broken, the individual turned in on himself and was threatened by the tyranny of public opinion ("acting on the will as much as on the actions of men and preventing both opposition and the desire to oppose") and by the political coercion of a centralizing state—a new kind of despotism or "democratic dictatorship," which "cramps, represses, enervates, deadens, dulls and finally reduces every nation to a flock of timid and industrious animals, whose shepherd is the government." For Tocqueville, this form of authority, backed by centralized power and ramifying administration, was a real danger. It could be contained by institutional safeguards, regional diversity and, above all, by "the gradual development of democratic institutions and attitudes," by freedom of association and "democratic liberty." One of Tocqueville's aims was precisely to show traditionalists that "society was advancing and sweeping them each day toward the equalization of conditions": the task was to find ways to achieve "a democratic society advancing . . . with order and morality."[70]

Durkheim similarly came to see all societies as integrated, indeed partially constituted by shared beliefs authoritatively communicated—*représentations collectives* whose content and manner of transmission varied with different types of social order. The components of authority—authoritative reasons for belief and action and rules of recognition—in modern societies were distinctive. Modern society required a "religion" in the sense of a "system of collective beliefs and practices that have a special authority." Its priests were to be the schoolteachers of the nation and, more generally, the intellectuals, who would themselves be brought by instruction to an understanding of the morality determined and required by society. Its content was, in a word, "individualism—a "social product, like all moralities and all religions." Individualism, Durkheim maintained, against the anti-Dreyfusards, was "henceforth the only system of beliefs which ensure the moral unity of the country." It was a religion of which man is "both believer and God," in which the "rights of the person are placed above the State," glorifying "not the self" but "the individual in general," committed to "sympathy for all that is human" and to economic and social justice. Interestingly, Durkheim claimed that this "religion," "faith," or "cult" whose social authority was necessary to modern society's cohesion was entirely compatible with reason and autonomy. Indeed, it had "for its first rite freedom of thought." Liberty of thought, he argued, was entirely compatible with respect for authority when that authority was rationally grounded. Conversely, and in a neat circle, he saw liberty as "the fruit of regulation," defining it as self-mastery—"the ability to act rationally and do one's duty"; while he defined autonomy as having "as clear and complete an awareness as possible of the reasons for our conduct" when "deferring to a rule or devoting ourselves to a collective ideal." As for power, Durkheim (in contrast to Weber) had nothing to say about power as an asymmetric relation between individuals and groups. Like Saint-Simon, he saw not class conflict, but an emerging functional hierarchy, and, like Comte, he foresaw the prevalance of "moral" over "political" solutions.[71]

These various visions of authority over belief under modern conditions—technocratic, democratic, individualist—could be supplemented by many others advanced in the nineteenth and twentieth centuries. There are, for instance, those forms of nationalist doctrine which identified authority with the expression of the national culture, or the *Volksgeist*, or the "spirit of the people." From Herder onward, the idealist background of such theories provided the assumption that there was something to be known and authoritatively transmitted by those able to discern and interpret it; as Savigny, the leader of the German historical school of law, observed, "the common consciousness of the people is the peculiar seat of law."[72] Various forms of socialist doctrine have likewise implied the dependence of social order and progress upon the authoritative transmission of certain beliefs taken to be true. Thus, for example, Fabian socialists supposed the "nascent science of and art of democratic institutions," offering "greater knowledge of the successful working of social institutions," gave authority to the public-spirited leaders of the socialist commonwealth.[73] And the state socialist societies of Eastern Europe since Lenin have, of course, been ruled on the unquestionable assumption that the Party is the authoritative interpreter and inculcator of the truths that Marxist-Leninst theory has discovered.

Again, technocratic theorists of all kinds see authority as deriving from newly indispensable knowledge and skills. Thus, for Daniel Bell, the "axial principle" of "postindustrial society" is "the centrality of and codification of theoretical knowledge." "Engineering and economics become central to the technical decisions of the society," and we see "a new social order based, in principle, on the priority of educated talent." Bell defines authority as

> . . . a competence based upon skill, learning, talent, artistry, or some similar attribute. Inevitably it leads to distinctions between those who are superior and those who are not. A meritocracy is made up of those who have earned their authority. An unjust meritocracy is one which makes these distinctions invidious and demeans those below.

Power, by contrast, is "the ability to command, which is backed up, either implicitly or explicitly, by force"; it "allows some men to exercise domination over others"; but, says Bell, "in the polity at large, and in most institutions, such unilateral power is increasingly checked."[74]

The functionalist consensus theories of recent American sociology and political science are simply the generalized and relativized form of all these conceptions of authority over belief. Here what counts as authoritative or "legitimate" is simply what any given society's value system is taken (or imputed) to be. Thus Parsons writes: "Without the attachment to the constitutive common values the collectivity tends to dissolve"; these values are "the commitments of individual persons to pursue and support certain *directions* or types of action for the collectivity as a system and hence derivatively for their own roles in the collectivity."[75] (Lipset similarly defines legitimacy as "the capacity of the system to engender and maintain the belief that the existing political institutions are the most appropriate ones for the society.")[76] For Parsons, the shared values and norms specify what and who is authoritative: authority amounts to "the complex of instututionalized rights to control the actions of members of the society with reference to their bearing on the attainment of collective goals"—the rights being those of "leaders to expect support from the members of the collectivity." Given Parsons's view of power as the "*generalized capacity of a social system to get things done in the interest of collective goals,*"[77] it will be clear how for him power derives from authority.

In general, it may be said of all these conceptions of authority over belief that they take the authority relation as primary. Power is seen as integral to or derivative from it but also as a threat when abused so as to weaken or destroy consensual beliefs and thus social and political order. Under consensual conditions, power tends to assume a nonasymmetric, nonconflictual form, at least internally to the society in question, and the notion of "leadership" is emphasized. Individuals are seen as molded, even constituted, by the authority relation. Their role identifications, their self-perceptions, indeed their very identity is seen as dependent on it. Conflicts of interest between individuals and groups, at least in a well-functioning society, are understressed—partly because the very existence of authority is taken to create and promote an identity of interests between those exercising it and those subject to it.

A quite different tradition of conceptualizing authority developed in reaction to the early forms of the first tradition, the later form of which in turn reacted against it. This tradition sees authority as conventional and power as asymmetric, indeed coercive. It assumes a natural conflict of interests between individuals, whose identities are unaffected and whose freedom is limited by authority, which is, in turn, seen as exercised over conduct, even in the absence of shared beliefs and values. Their ends are private and conflicting, and the task of authority is to coordinate their actions so that common enterprises are possible. This view tends to focus on the authority of the state vis-à-vis individuals, who are taken to be given, with (conflicting) private ends, values, and opinions; rules of conduct are needed to enable such individuals to pursue their respective ends. Authority does not produce shared beliefs but rather a common framework within which individuals pursue their interests—and neither the identity of the individuals nor that of their interests is modified by the exercise of authority.[78] Authority in this sense produces coordinated action rather than common belief. Indeed, it allows for a gap to open up between private belief and public action. The individual may submit to authority while privately dissenting. As Hobbes saw it, though men obey the sovereign, "belief and unbelief never follow men's commands,"[79] and as Spinoza said, "No man's mind can possibly lie wholly at the disposition of another, for no man can willingly transfer his natural right of free reason and judgment, or be compelled to do so."[80]

"What manner of life would there be," asked Hobbes, "where there were no common power to fear?" The Hobbesian predicament, the state of nature, consists in the equal powers of individuals with irreducibly conflicting interests: "equal powers opposed, destroy one another; and such this opposition is called contention." The price of peace is to erect a "common power," for men "to confer all their strength and power upon one man, or upon one assembly of men that may reduce all their wills, by plurality of voices, unto one will." Thus a "multitude of men, are made *one* person, when they are by one man, or one person represented; so that it be done with the consent of every one of that multitude in particular." Here lies Hobbes's innovatory theory of authority. The covenant is an agreement of "every one with every one" to obey the commands of the sovereign as if they were his own; the sovereign is "authorized" to command them as he wills, since they have, given their irreducibly conflicting interests, agreed to "own and be reputed author" of all the sovereign's decisions. Authority is "a right of doing any act; and *done by authority*, done by commission, or licence from him whose right it is." Thus: "Every particular man is author of all the sovereign doth."[81]

Two points are to be noted here. First, though the sovereign's authorized power is (almost) absolute, in the sense of excluding all conflicting reasons for action (save self-preservation), it is only applicable in a selected range of human activities: "In all kinds of actions by the laws praetermitted, men have the liberty of doing what their own reasons shall suggest, for the most profitable to themselves," such as "the liberty to buy and sell, and otherwise contract with one another. "Second, and relatedly, in contrast with the claims of tradition and divine right, and indeed all the views of authority so far considered, Hobbes did not require any sense of public involvement or active support by the citizen for the sovereign, nor did the latter's authority confer any communal or collective benefits upon the citizens—their nature and purposes were unaffected by it. The "body politic" was simply a "multitude of men, united as one person by a common power, for their common peace, defence and benefit." Fear and insecurity held them together and authority was exercised simply to secure a framework within which they could pursue their unending search for "felicity":

> The use of laws, which are but rules authorised, is not to bind the people from all voluntary actions; but to direct and keep them in such a motion, as not to hurt themselves by their own impetuous desires, rashness or indiscretion; as hedges are set, not to stop travellers, but to keep them in their way.[82]

This conception of authority by convention, as derived from the consent of individuals with conflicting interests who agree to obey a public power whose role is to guarantee their continued pursuit of private interests, runs like a thread through the whole history of liberalism. It was Locke's theory of contract, however, which pointed the direction in which liberal theories developed, by drawing tighter bounds around the scope of authority. The Lockean predicament to which authority is the solution was less drastic than the Hobbesian: it was a matter of "inconveniences," the "fears and continual dangers" caused by "the corruption and viciousness of degenerate men." The "remedy" of "civil government" had as its "chief and great end" the "preservation of property." As with Hobbes, the new authority had no communal or integrative function; on the contrary, "the commonwealth" was "a society of men constituted only for the procuring, preserving and advancing their own civil interests." Political authority was bounded by the terms of the original compact: "there remains still in the people a supreme power to remove or alter the legislative, when they find the legislative act contrary to the trust reposed in them."

This should, however, not be misunderstood. Men are described as agreeing in the contract to resign their natural powers to the community which in turn puts the legislative power into the hands of those it trusts; moreover, each agrees to submit to "the determination of the majority." Furthermore, the language of "express consent" shifts to that of "tacit consent," and this comes to be seen as registered by the mere possession of property.[83] Authority based on consent thus becomes inverted into the imposition of authority over the holders of property. There was no recurrent renewal of consent, but rather the establishment of a way of thinking about government and authority which suggested a basis of consent, setting indeterminate and flexible limits to the power of governments. Society came to be seen as "civil society"—the "natural" arena in which individuals pursued their "civil interests," which it was the function of authority to secure. And power was seen by Locke, as by Hobbes, as personal and coercive control. Hence the liberal project of both restraining the coercive power of government while claiming its authority to be based on consent and to promote the general interest.

The history of liberalism has been the history, among other things, of this combination of ideas. Authority is granted by individuals whose conflicting interests have free play in the economic sphere (society) but which require coordination and control (whose extent varies with different thinkers and periods) from the political. Government maintains the conditions for an effectively competitive order, maintaining "law and order." Authority is based on voluntary consent to this necessary coordination and control; the resulting coercions are seen as "interferences" to be minimized. As Locke put it, "the community comes to be umpire by setting standing rules, indifferent and the same to all parties,"[84] though Adam Smith was nearer the bone when he observed that "Civil government, so far as it is instituted for the security of property, is in reality instituted for the defence of the rich against the poor, or of those who have some property against those who have none at all."[85] Scottish classical economists, French liberals, English radicals and utilitarians, and American constitutional democrats all reasoned in this way. In Paine's words, "Society is produced by our wants and government by our wickedness- . . . . Society, in every state, is a blessing, Government, even in its best state is but a necessary evil."[86] While for Bastiat the choice lay between "*société libre, gouvernement simple*" and "*société constrainte, gouvernement compliqué*."[87] Smith advocated leaving "nature"—that is, the economic life of society (whose constraints were, unlike the government's, impersonal)—alone, as did Jefferson and liberals of all kinds down to Herbert Spencer and beyond to von Mises, Hayek, and Milton Friedman.

All these views offer a contrast between authority and power different from those previously considered. Authority is here restricted to the "standing rules" of Locke's umpire and rests on consent; power is coercive and personal and threatens the "natural" order of society. As Diderot's *Encyclopédie* put it, "*authority* is communicated by the laws; power by those in whose hands they are placed." Thus:

> The prince derives from his subjects the authority he holds over them; and this authority is limited by the laws of nature and of the state. The laws of nature and of the state are the conditions under which they have or are supposed to have submitted themselves to his rule. One of these conditions is that, having no power or authority over them except by their choice and their consent, he can never use this authority to break the act or contract by which it has been conferred on him. . . .

His "authority can only subsist by the entitlement that established it," and he "cannot therefore dispose of his power or his subjects without the consent of the nation and independently of the choices indicated in the contract of submission."[88]

This did not, however, mean that authority set any determinate limits to power's exercise. The story of how consent, seen as self-assumed obligation, was actually registered was always sufficiently mysterious for the limits it set upon the exercise of power to be very flexible.[89] We have already noticed Locke's shift from express to tacit consent. Adam Ferguson offered an even less constraining account of how consent was registered:

> The consent, upon which the right to command is founded may not be prior to the establishment of government; but may be obtained under the reasonable exercise of an actual power, to which every person within the community, by accepting of a customary protection, becomes bound to pay the customary allegiance and submission. Here is a compact ratified by the least ambiguous of all signs, the whole practice, or continued observance of an ordinary life.[90]

All liberal-democratic thinkers assume that authority is, in one way or another, a form of voluntary, self-assumed obligation. But *who* assumes it and how is it assumed? The social-contract tradition offered an account of the *creation* of such obligations by voluntary agreement, and the various forms of consent theory an account of how individuals' action, or inaction, might be taken to signify continuing consent to them. Thus for Madison, the "people" are the sole legitimate source of political power, its authority grounded through the "elective mode" (and its power limited through checks and balances, federalism, and the "vigilant and manly spirit" of the American people).[91] Bentham likewise sought to prevent the abuse of power by government, the "exercise of its powers" consisting in "the giving of directions or commands, positive and prohibitive, and incidentally in securing compliance through the application of rewards and punishments," and the basis of its authority lying in the expression of "the will of the governed" manifested at periodic elections.[92] James Mill took a similar view.[93]

John Stuart Mill's views, however, were more complex. He had learnt much from Comte, Tocqueville, and Coleridge. A "permanent political society" required "the feeling of allegiance or loyalty," "*something* which is settled, something permanent, and not to be called in question." There was not, and had never been "any state of society in which collisions did not occur between immediate interests and passions of powerful sections of the people." "What, then, enables society to weather these storms . . . that however important the interests about which men fall out, the conflict did not affect the fundamental principles of the system of social union which happened to exist; nor threaten large portions of the community with the subversion of that on which they had built their calculations, and with which their hopes and aims had become identified."

Mill, like other liberals, naturally saw power as coercive and associated it with the deprivation of liberty, but he also, like Tocqueville, saw the individual as needing protection against "the tyranny of the prevailing opinion and feeling." As for the basis of political authority, his views were similarly complex. Democratic authority was based on consent but, ideally, consent in the form of universal participation, in other words, "the whole people participate." Moreover, as with Hobbes, Locke, Madison, and Bentham, government must not merely provide the framework for the pursuit of individual interests; the government must seek to "promote the general mental advancement of the community" and "organise the moral, intellectual and active worth already existing." Mill himself recognized that he was thus led toward a "qualified socialism," as were his successors in the Anglo-Saxon tradition, such as Green and Hobhouse.[94]

The entire liberal-democratic tradition gave a voluntarist account of authority by convention and a coercive account of asymmetric power. Liberal demorcracy, as Rawls has put it, comes "as close as society can to being a voluntary scheme . . . its members are autonomous and the obligations they recognise self-imposed."[95] The "selves" who impose such obligations upon themselves are mutually disinterested and conflicting, and the authority over their conduct to which they are said to consent sets them free to pursue their otherwise mutually incompatible and unrealizable interests.

An alternative tradition begins exactly at this point, similarly aiming at a reconciliation of autonomy and authority, but rejecting the picture of conflicting, mutually disinterested selves as given. Thus Rousseau transformed the notion of the social contract and the idea of authority as based upon consent into a wholly new perspective. Ancient and medieval thinkers had often derived political authority from the consent of subjects, alongside traditional and divine sources. With the rise of individualistic theories of contract and consent and opposition to divine-right theories of absolutism in the sixteenth and seventeenth centuries, authority came to be seen as based on an agreement to protect the rights and pursuit of the conflicting interests of autonomous individuals.

Rousseau's view of authority was a new departure, aiming to retain the gains of individualism—the autonomous individual—while uniting him in community with others to achieve a collective will, as among the ancients. The basic problem to which the social contract provides the solution is to find "a form of association" as a result of which "the whole strength of the community will be enlisted for the protection of the person and property of each constituent member, in such a way that each, when united to his fellows, renders obedience to his own will, and remains as free as he was before." Citizenship confers "moral freedom," which "alone makes a man his own master": "to obey the laws laid down by society is to be free." The key to Rousseau's notion of community-with-autonomy is the idea of freedom from the *power* of others: "dependence on men, being out of order, gives rise to every kind of vice, and through this master and slave become mutually depraved." The *impersonal authority* of a community of individuals, whose identity and interests have become moralized and harmonized, derives from the expression of those individuals' general will. "Each in giving himself to all gives himself to none"; in conditions of social equality and direct democracy, everyone becomes both ruler and subject. Asymmetric power, as control, dependence, and inequality, is abolished, and authority, being self-prescribed, is compatible with equality, autonomy, and reason.[96]

Hegel took this explosive combination of ideas further. Like Rousseau's, Hegel's idea of the state implies that its laws

> . . . are not something alien to the subject. On the contrary, his spirit bears witness to them as to its own essence, the essence in which he has a feeling of own self-hood, and in which he lives on in his own element which is not distinguished from himself. The subject is thus directly linked to the ethical order by a relation which is more like an identity than even the relation of faith or trust.

The state unites subjective consciousness and objective order, and in such conditions, "to say that men allow themselves to be ruled counter to their own interests, ends and intentions is preposterous." In a manner strongly recalling Rousseau, Hegel observed that "in the state, as something ethical, as the interpenetration of the substantive and the particular, my obligation to what is substantive is at the same time the embodiment of my particular freedom." The "essence of the modern state is that the universal is bound up with the complete freedom of its particular members and with private well-being." Hegel rejected the restoration thinkers (Haller, Müller, Savigny) who had sought to rest the authority of the state on tradition and on power. He also disagreed with the liberal view of the state as inherently coercive and at best providing a framework for the pursuit of self-interest. On the contrary, he saw the state as the positive embodiment of man's self-consciousness—the "actuality of the substantial will"—the basis of the state's authority being the rational wills of individuals who are precisely not mutually disinterested in that they will each others' goals—that is, the common good. For Hegel, the "individual finds his liberation" in the differentiated spheres of "ethical life"—the family, civil society (the interdependent sphere of economic self-interest) and the state. Civil society, left to itself, leads to "physical and ethical degeneration." However, the state can only fulfill its role as the concrete rational manifestation of human will by containing within itself a differentiated civil society.[97]

Rousseau envisaged the self-annihilating authority of consensual rational wills in an ideal community, fit, as he remarked, only for gods. For Hegel, such authority was to be exercised in the public domain in the post-Napoleonic constitutional state.[98] Others—from Fichte onward—saw such authority, arising from united, rational wills, in the context of the nation. Most varieties of nationalism have made use of this idea in some form.[99] Power is seen as derivative from such authority—a collective capacity harnessed to transcendent ends. Fascist doctrine carried this idea further. Elaborating "the facscist theory of authority," Mussolini proclaimed the fascist state to be "a will to power and to government." It has "a consciousness of its own, a will of its own;" on this account it is called an "ethical state" and it is "strong, organic and at the same time founded on a wide popular basis."[100]

Ideas of authority and power (deriving from interpretations and misinterpretations of Rousseau and Hegel) basing the former on united rational wills and the latter on the former had a very wide impact in the nineteenth century. Apart from the history of nationalism, they entered into liberalism at various points (notably with Green in England and Croce in Italy) and into both conservative and socialist thought. The anarchist tradition too sought to transcend both the tradition of authoritative belief and the liberal tradition of conventional authority guaranteeing a market society by postulating an ideal community of consensual wills. But the anarchists saw this not as the realization of authority but rather as its removal.

Proudhon's project was "to live without government, to abolish all authority, absolutely and unreservedly"; "industrial organization" would be substituted for government, contracts for laws, "economic forces" for "political powers," and "identity of interests" for police.[101] Bakunin, aiming at "the most complete liberty of individuals and associations," rejected "the establishment of regulative authority of whatever kind";[102] and Kropotkin similarly saw progress as "*the abolition of all the authority of government,* as *a development of free agreement* for all that was formerly a function of church and state, and as *a development of free initiative* in every individual and every group."[103] It is distinctive of the anarachist tradition to denounce both authority over belief) ("the old system," said Proudhon, stood on "authority and Faith")[104] and *political* authority over conduct. Anarchist society would be free of politics, though it would still require coordination and thus the performance of administrative functions. Also, anarchists have tended to respect the authority of science. They see power in all hitherto existing societies as asymmetrical and inherently coercive, and as having its natural home in the state; as Rudolph Rocker said, "the modern state" was "the organ of political power for the forcible subjugation and aggression of the nonpossessing classes."[105] However, power was also potentially collective and benign: as Bakunin put it, in the people "there is a great deal of elemental power, more power indeed than in the government, taken together with all the ruling classes; but an elemental force lacking organisation is not a real power."[106]

The Marxist tradition also sees the authority and power typical of class societies as destined to be historically surpassed, though it offers a much more complex account of their nature and interrelation. In the first place, power is class power (political power Marx and Engels defined as "merely the organised power of one class for oppressing another"), and authority is a form of it. Both are exercised within, and in turn reinforce, the economic constraints set by the mode of production. these are imposed by economic relations whose "dull compulsion . . . completes the subjection of the labourer to the capitalist." The nature of these exploitative relations of production is concealed from the agents of production by ideology—a whole web of "conceptions which arise about the laws of production in the minds of agents of capitalist production and circulation" which "will diverge drastically from the real laws."[107] In general, the dynamics and possibilities of transformation of class society are concealed from subordinate classes by the ruling ideas of any age, these being "the ideas of the ruling class." In this way, authority over belief—whether it be religion or political economy or social science—is successfully imposed by class power. Moreover, the illusion of authority by convention, voluntarily granted to the government by free and equal citizens, is similarly imposed as the ideology of bourgeois democracry. To this must be added a whole arsenal of instruments of rule—though it must be said that Marxism in general lacks a properly worked out theory of domination. The most one has is a series of historically located aperçus in Marx and Engels, a few rudimentary generalizations in Engels and Lenin, and the only (flawed) attempt at a more developed theory in Gramsci.

For Marx and Engels, class power (of its very nature asymmetric) is exercised by superordinate over subordinate classes in a variety of ways, ranging from ideological mystification through all the various forms of inducement, persuasion, influence, and control—through the family, in the educational and legal system, in the labor market and the labor process—to outright coercion and force, typically exercised by the state. There are of course considerable variations among capitalist states, with respect both to the extent of the state's control of civil society and to the state's relative autonomy from class control. This has posed a crux for Marxist thinkers. Were these just different forms of class domination, or were certain forms—namely, bourgeois parliamentary democracy—based on the (genuine rather than imposed) consent of the working class to advanced capitalism? If so, clearly the "parliamentary road to socialism" was in the cards. In other words, was bourgeois democracy merely a way of keeping people in subjection by deception and concession, as Lenin thought ("concessions of the unessential, while retaining the essential")[108] or was it, as Engels and at times Marx came to suspect, a framework within which class power could be peacefully transferred to the working class?

Central to this discussion has been the work of Gramsci, whose theorizing about power and authority is encapsulated in his much-discussed concept of "hegemony," the suggestive complexities of which can only be hinted at here. Beginning from a traditional, if rather simple, dichotomy between "force and consent" characteristic of Italian thought (found in Machiavelli, in the elitist Machiavellians, and in Gentile), Gramsci added the parallel contrasts "domination and hegemony," "violence and civilization," and he spoke of hegemony as "intellectual and moral direction." and also as "the moment of consent, of cultural direction" as opposed to "the moment of force, of constraint, or of state-legislative or police intervention." When speaking thus, he was thinking of class power as cultural and ideological and exercised within civil society ("through so-called private organisations, like the church, trade unions, schools, and so on"). Elsewhere, he spoke of hegemony as "a combination of force and consent which form variable equilibria, without force ever prevailing too much over consent." In this sense, hegemony was exercised both within the state and civil society; this allowed him to take account of the ideological functions of the state and corrected the earlier exclusive focus on cultural hegemony. In a third version, hegemony is again seen as a mixture of force and consent, but exercised within the state, which is now seen as incorporating both political and civil society—"not merely the govermental apparatus, but also the 'private' apparatus of hegemony or civil society."[109] This last, expanded notion of the state has been taken over by Louis Althusser, who speaks of the state's "repressive" and "ideological" apparatuses.[110] Gramsci's original insight into the consensual dimension of class power operating *outside* the state, and indeed the crucial differences between cases where it lies outside and inside the state, is lost. At all events, Gramsci's inconclusive and shifting treatment of hegemony raised the discussion of the relations between power and authority to a new level within the Marxist tradition. In particular, he raised (though he did not answer) the closely related questions of the relation between the legitimacy of parliamentary institutions in the West and the state's monopoly of force and of the role of consensual direction and coercion in the struggle of the working class, in alliance with others, for power.

The Marxist tradition, like the anarchist, is committed to the proposition that power, as control, dependency and inequality, and authority—insofar as it conflicts with equality, freedom, and reason—are to be eliminated. (This, doubtless, must occur within communist rather than socialist society, though Marx never faced the issue of what power and authority would be like in the latter). In their futuristic projections, there are interesting differences between the Marxist founding fathers.

Marx (especially the early Marx) often spoke as though all forms of superordination and subordination would be abolished. Communism would deprive men of "the power to subjugate the labour of others by means of . . . appropriation"; and when "class distinctions have disappeared, and all production has been concentrated in the hands of a vast association of the whole nation, the public power will lose its political character."[111] Engels echoed this, claiming that "the political state, and with it political authority, will disappear as the result of the coming social revolution, that is . . . public functions will lose their political character and be transformed into the simple administrative functions of watching over the true interests of society."[112] Here Engels and Lenin, who followed up these thoughts in *State and Revolution,* rejoin Saint-Simon. As Lenin wrote:

> From the moment all members of society, or at least the vast majority, have learned to administer the state *themselves*, have taken this work into their own hands, have organised control over the insignificant capitalist minority, over the gentry who wish to preserve their capitalist habits and over the workers who have been thoroughly corrupted by capitalism—from this moment the need for government of any kind begins to disappear altogether. The more complete the democracy, the nearer the moment when it becomes unnecessary.[113]

But Marx's image of the dissolution of power and authority extended (at times) even to the labor process itself. Under capitalism "the mass of direct producers is confronted by the social character of their production in the form of strictly regulating authority and a social mechanism of the labour process organised as a complete hierarchy." Though "physical necessity"—that is, nature—set constraints, Marx's image of freedom was of "socialised man, the associated producers, rationally regulating their interchange with Nature, bringing it under their control, instead of being ruled by it as by the blind forces of Nature." The need to "coordinate and unify the labor process in the workshops of the future would be met as if by "an orchestra conductor." Eventually,

> . . . the human being comes to relate more as a watchman and regulator to the production process itself . . . He steps to the side of the production process, instead of being its chief actor. In this transformation, it is neither the direct human labour he himself performs, nor the time during which he works, but rather the appropriation of his own general productive power, his understanding of nature and his mastery over it by virture of his presence as a social body—it is, in a word, the development of the social individual which appears as the great foundation-stone of production and of wealth.[114]

Engels, however, struck a more "realistic" note, arguing in opposition to the anarchists that it was not possible to have organization without authority (by "authority" he meant "the imposition of the will of another upon ours") and claimed that it "presupposes subordination." The forces of nature, he argued, require the organization of labor to be settled "in an authoritarian way." Thus, "a certain authority, no matter how delegated, and . . . a certain subordination, are things which, independently of all social organization, are imposed upon us, together with the material conditions under which we produce and make products circulate." Hence:

> . . . it is absurd to speak of the principle of authority as being absolutely evil, and of the principle of autonomy as being absolutely good. Authority and autonomy are relative things whose spheres vary with the various phases of the development of society. If the autonomists confined themselves to saying that the social organisation of the future would restrict authority solely to the limits within which the conditions of production render it inevitable, we would understand each other . . .[115]

Thus Engels rejected the anarcho-syndicalist dream (of which there are more than hints in Marx) of the abolition of power (as control) and authority (by imposition) within the sphere of production itself. However, he shared with Marx and all other classical Marxists the belief that elsewhere, especially in the political sphere, such power and authority would disappear—however authoritarian and coercive might be the means necessary to achieve that happy end state.

In contrast with all those—radical democrats, anarchists, Marxists, and others—who contemplate the possibility of such an end state of benign collective power and consensual authority, we may identify what might be called a "realist" tradition of viewing power and authority, whose prime modern exponents are the neo-Machiavellian elite theorists, notably Pareto, Mosca, and Michels. However, this tradition stands no less in opposition to liberal democracy, lacking its distrust of power and debunking its justification of authority. Again, its attitude to doctrines of authoritative belief, whether traditionalist, religious, or secular, is reductionist: "ruling classes," Mosca observed, "do not justify their power solely by de facto possession of it, but try to find a moral and legal basis for it, representing it as the logical and necessary consequence of doctrines and beliefs that are generally recognised and accepted"—though for Mosca such political formulas are not "mere quackeries aptly invented to trick the masses into obedience"; they answer "a real need in man's social nature . . . of governing and knowing that one is governed not on the basis of mere material or intellectual force, but on the basis of a moral principle." "Every governing class," he remarked, "tends to justify its actual exercise of power by resting it on some universal moral principle" which "has come forward in our time in scientific trappings." Indeed, Mosca asked whether "a society can hold together without one of these 'great superstitions'—whether a universal illusion is not a social force that contributes powerfully to consolidating political organization and unifying peoples or even whole civilizations.[116]

Likewise, Pareto has some splendid debunking paragraphs on authority as a tool of proof and a tool of persuasion. It is "an instrument for logicalizing nonlogical actions and the sentiments in which they originate"; it is appealed to by the Protestant, the Catholic, "the humanitarian who swoons over a passage of Rousseau," the "socialist who swears by the Word of Marx and Engels," and "the devout democrat who bows reverent head and submits judgment and will to the oracles of suffrage, universal or limited, or what is worse to the pronouncements of parliaments and legislatures." It holds "in our present-day societies, not only for the ignorant, and not only touching matters of religion and morality, but even in the sciences, especially in those branches with which a person is not directly familiar."[117]

Such realist writers agree with Marxists and anarchists in uncovering the asymmetric power dimension behind authority over belief and by convention, and in debunking liberal illusions, but they generalize the attack, seeing control, dependence, and inequality, and authority by imposition as inevitable and ineradicable features of all societies, not least those which purport to be socialist and democratic. Hence Michels's claim that "the formation of oligarchies within the various forms of democracy is the outcome of organic necessity, and consequently affects every organization, be it socialist or even anarchist," The government or state "cannot be anything other than the organization of a minority." As for the majority, it is "permanently incapable of self-government":

> Even when the discontent of the masses culminates in a successful attempt to deprive the bourgeoisie of power, this is after all, as Mosca contends, effected only in appearance; always and necessarily there springs from the masses a new organized minority which raises itself to the rank of a governing class. Thus the majority of human beings, in a condition of eternal tutelage, are predestined by tragic necessity to submit to the dominion of a small minority, and must be content to constitute the pedestal of an oligarchy.[118]

Pareto is harsher still:

> All governments use force and all assert that they are founded on reason. In the fact, whether universal suffrage prevails or not, it is always an oligarchy that governs, finding ways to give to "the will of the people" the expression which the few desire. . . .

He argued that "one finds everywhere a governing class of relatively few individuals that keeps itself in power partly by force and partly by the consent of the subject class, which is much more populous. The difference lies principally, as regards substance, in the relative proportions of force and consent; and as regards forms, in the manners in which the force is used and the consent obtained." But Pareto had a most cynical, "realistic" view of the nature of consent: consent is always manipulated, authority always imposed by means of power. Both consent and force were for Pareto "instruments of governing"—consent being achieved by the skillful manipulation of "sentiments and interests."[119]

Others can be included within the "realist" tradition who, no less wary of what Michels called "excessive optimism," offered a more rounded, less reductionist account of power and authority. Thus Simmel sensitively explored the forms of superordination and subordination (under an individual, under a plurality, under a principle), commenting on the "sociological error of socialism and anarchism."[120] Freud, too, can be seen as exploring, at the level of the individual, the many forms that social control may take of coercion and dependence and the acceptance of authority, in the face of "the human instinct of aggression and self-destruction."[121]

It was, however, unquestionably Max Weber who was the "realist" who offered the subtlest and richest account of power and authority in the whole history of social and political theorizing. We have already seen that Weber's view of power as asymmetrical covers control, dependence, and inequality—power being "the probability that one actor within a social relationship will be in a position to carry out his own will despite resistance, regardless of the basis on which this probability rests." Weber stressed that there was an extremely wide variety of such bases: "All conceivable qualities of a person and all conceivable combinations of circumstances may put him in a position to impose his will in a given situation." For this reason, Weber regarded the concept of power as "sociologically amorphous" and proposed the "more precise" concept of *Herrschaft,* or domination, which he saw as a "special case of power." What, then, did he mean by *Herrschaft?*[122]

He distinguished between "the most general" and a "narrower sense." The former simply designated all structures of power relations: on such a broad definition, dominant positions could "emerge from the social relations in a drawing room as well as in the market, from the rostrum of a lecture hall as well as from the command post of a regiment, from an erotic or charitable relationship as well as from scholarly discussion or athletics."[123]

Weber therefore drew a distinction between "domination by virtue of a constellation of interests (in particular: by virtue of a position of monopoly)" and "domination by virtue of authority, i.e., power to command and duty to obey." Domination in the narrower sense excluded the former—that is "domination which originates in the market or other interest constellations" (even though this may "because of the very absence of rules . . . be felt to be much more oppressive") and was equated with *"authoritarian power of command."* More specifically, he wrote:

> . . . *domination* will thus mean the situation in which the manifested will (*command*) of the *ruler* or rulers is meant to influence the conduct of one or more others (the *ruled*) and actually does influence it in such a way that their conduct to a socially relevant degree occurs as if the ruled had made the content of the command the maxim of their conduct for its very own sake.[124]

These are, of course, Weberian "types," and in reality the borderline between them is fluid: "the transitions are gradual," since "sharp differentiation in concrete fact is often impossible" (this making "clarity in the analytical distinctions all the more important"). Hence, "Any type of domination by virtue of constellation of interests may . . . be transformed into domination by authority," as when economic, market-based dependencies are formalized into norm-governed authority relations; thus a vassal freely enters into the relation of fealty with a feudal lord, who thenceforth acquires authority over him; or contracts "concluded in the labor market by formally "equal" parties through the "voluntary" acceptance of the terms offered by the employer "become transformed into formalized positions in (public or private) corporate hierarchies. Moreover, "a certain minimum interest of the subordinate in his own obeying will normally constitute one of the indispensable motives of obedience even in the completely authoritarian duty-relationship."[125]

There has been much scholarly debate about how *Herrschaft* is to be understood. Parsons (typically interpreting Weber as a pre-Parsonian) translates it (in the narrower sense) as "authority" rather than "domination" on the grounds that the latter term suggests that the fact that "a leader has power over his followers . . . rather than the integration of the collectivity in the interest of effective functioning . . . is the critical factor from Weber's point of view."[126] By contrast, Bendix, who rightly prefers "domination," argues that "as a realist in the analysis of power, [Weber] would have been critical of any translation that tended to obscure the "threat of force" present in all relations between superiors and subordinates."[127]

It is clear that by *Herrschaft* (in the narrower sense) Weber meant to identify such structured relations between superiors and subordinates in which compliance could be based on a wide variety of motives ("all the way from simple habituation to the most purely rational calculation of advantage") and achieved by a wide variety of means. The primary virtue of his whole approach is its sensitivity to this variety, and the resultant questions it opens up about how such relations are established and maintained. His general hypothesis was that:

> . . . in no instance does domination voluntarily limit itself to the appeal to material or affectual or ideal motives as a basis for its continuance. In addition every such system attempts to establish and to cultivate the belief in its legitimacy. But according to the kind of legitimacy which is claimed, the type of obedience, the kind of administrative staff developed to guarantee it, and the mode of exercising authority will all differ fundamentally.

Hence Weber's decision to classify the types of domination according to the kind of claim to legitimacy typically made by each, since the differences between kinds of claims were held to be basic to, to vary with, and to be explanatory of power relations and forms of administration. In other words, "the sociological character of domination will differ according to the basic differences in the major modes of legitimation."[128]

Parsons is therefore quite mistaken in translating *Herrschaft* as "authority." Rather, the celebrated "three pure types of authority" single out prevailing rationales for obedience to authority *within* structures of domination.[129] They do not, moreover, refer to motives of obedience or to structures of power. People, according to Weber, may obey hypocritically, opportunistically, out of material self-interest, or "from individual weakness or helplessness, because there is no acceptable alternative." What is important is "the fact that in a given case the particular claim to legitimacy is to a significant degree and according to its type treated as 'valid': that this fact confirms the position of the person claiming authority and that it helps to determine the choice of means of its exercise."[130]

The types of authority invoke types of norms which specify who and what is to count as authoritative. Thus traditional, rational or legal, and charismatic authority signify publicly advanced types of reasons or "grounds" for obeying, each of which, according to Weber, tends to prevail under certain conditions and is in turn associated with and explanatory of power relations and forms of administration. Weber postulated that one or another type tends to predominate in any given political association or institutional order: rational-legal authority in the modern state and in bureaucratic forms of organization, private and public; traditional authority in patriarchal, patrimonial, and feudal societies and in the medieval manor; while charismatic authority erupts (only to be subsequently routinized) in all communities up to the modern world in periods of transition. However, although one type of authority will predominate in any given structure of domination, "the forms of domination occurring in historical reality constitute combinations, mixtures, adaptations or modifications of these 'pure' types."[131]

What, then, was Weber's ultimate view of the relations between power and authority? No simple answer can be given, but four remarks may serve to indicate the essence of his way of seeing the issues.

First, he saw power as extending much further than authority, and, in particular, as covering all cases of domination excluded by the more narrow sense—that is, "forms of power . . . based upon constellations of interests," of which the "purest type" is "monopolistic domination in the market," but which include "all relationships of exchange, including those of intangibles." Thus Weber listed, apart from market relations, those produced by "society"—as, for instance, the position of a *salon*—and those between political entities—as in the role of Prussia within the German Customs Union or New York within the United States. (He might well have included all patron-client relations). Certainly, Weber was keenly sensitive to the exertion of economic power within "civil society," through the dictation of the terms of exchange to contractual partners: "influence derived exclusively from the possessions of goods or marketable skills guaranteed in some way and acting upon the conduct of those dominated, who remain, however, formally free and are motivated simply by the pursuit of their own interests." His theory of classes was based on this idea.[132]

Second, he did not, as did the neo-Machiavellians, see all consent to authority as imposed by rulers. Thus, for example:

> As a rule . . . the political patrimonial ruler is linked with the ruled through a consensual community which also exists apart from his independent military force and which is rooted in the belief that the ruler's powers are legitimate insofar as they are traditional.

On the other hand, he naturally inclined to a "realistic" power analysis, especially of "democratic" forms of authority. "Direct democratic administration" he saw as a "marginal type case," "unstable," and manifesting a tendency "to turn into rule by notables," and, like Michels and the other elite theorists, he accepted "the law of the small number"—namely, the principle that (because of complexity, the need for specialized skills and organizational dynamics) ruling minorities, whether collegial or monocratic, are indispensable to the very existence of organization. Thus he was systematically doubtful about the claims of democracy, direct or indirect: "the fact that the chief and his administrative staff often appear formally as servants or agents of those they rule does nothing whatever to disprove the quality of dominance . . . a certain minimum of assured power to issue commands, thus of domination, must be provided for in nearly every conceivable case." And, more generally, he spoke of the acceptance of the "myth" of the natural superiority of the highly privileged by negatively privileged strata "under conditions of stable distribution of power and, consequently [sic], of status order." Indeed, "the continued exercise of every domination . . . always has the strongest need of self-justification through appealing to the principles of its legitimation."[133]

Third, as we have seen, he assumed that the type of authority ("the ultimate grounds of the validity of a domination") is, in any particular case of domination, basic to, and to a significant extent explanatory of, "the kind of relationship between the master or masters and the apparatus, the kind of relationship of both to the ruled, and . . . its specific *organizational* structure, i.e. its specific way of distributing the powers of command."[134]

Finally, Weber stressed the ultimate role of power, in the form of coercion, or the threat of force, as an indispensable underpinning for the exercise of authority: for "the political community, even more than other institutionally organized communities, is so constituted that it imposes obligations on the individual which many of them fulfill only because they are aware of the probability of physical coercion backing up such obligations."[135]

III

There is little in modern debates about the concepts of power and authority that is not implicit in their history. I shall here refer to four such debates, the first of which is between a collective and an asymmetric conception of power; the second and third, between different asymmetric conceptions; and the fourth, between alternative collective conceptions.

The disagreement between Talcott Parsons and C. Wright Mills is a double disagreement. Its two aspects are contained in Parsons's statement that "to Mills, power is not a facility for the performance of function in, and on behalf of, the society as a system, but is interpreted exclusively as a facility for getting what one group, the holders of power, wants by preventing another group, the 'outs,' from getting what it wants."[136]

The first disagreement centers on the very question of whether power is or is not asymmetric—or, as Parsons (but not Mills) puts it, "zerosum." Here Mills follows Weber and other asymmetric theorists of power, identifying it with control, dependence, and inequality; "By the powerful," he writes, "we mean, of course, those who are able to realize their will, even if others resist it."[137] For Parsons, by contrast, this view is "highly selective" and serves to "elevate a secondary and derived aspect of a total phenomenon into the central place."[138] Power is comparable to money: it becomes a facility for the achievement of collective goals through the agreement of members of a society to legitimize leadership positions whose incumbents further the goals of the system. Thus the amount of power in the system can be increased by analogy with credit creation in the economy. This view of power and authority deflects attention from all cases where power is exercised over and authority imposed upon others, and in general from power differentials and conflicts of interest. It is not a relation between individuals and groups, but a system property—the capacity to use authoritative decisions to further agreed-upon, collective goals.

This leads to the second disagreement, which is over whether power is attributed to systems or to social actors. Parsons sees power as a system resource—"a generalized facility or resource in the society."[139] Authority is "the institutionalization of the 'rights' of leaders to expect support from the members of the collectivity." It is, in other words, the set of rights enabling leaders to command support and hence the precondition for the system's power to be exercised. Thus authority is not a form of power (e.g., legitimate power), but rather a *basis* of power, indeed the *only* basis of power. There is therefore no such thing as "illegitimate power"; power is by definition legitimate. Thus, ". . . the threat of coercive measure, or of compulsion, without legitimation or justification, should not properly be called the use of power at all. . . ."[140]

By contrast, Mills attributes power to social actors. "Power," he writes, "has to do with whatever decisions men make about the arrangements under which they live, and about the events which make up the history of their times . . . in so far as such decisions are made, the problem of who is involved in the making of them is the basic problem of power. In so far as they could be made but are not, the problem becomes who fails to make them." Like other elite theorists, Mills sees power as exercised by individual or collective actors—who today "have the power to manipulate and manage the consent of men." Authority, in this view, is one of the forms of power—"power that is justified by the beliefs of the voluntarily obedient," alongside manipulation ("power that is wielded unknown to the powerless") and coercion.[141]

The debate within the Marxist tradition between Nicos Poulantzas and Ralph Miliband is in some ways parallel to that between Parsons and Mills. In this debate too, the disagreement is partly over whether power is attributable to agents or to the structures and systems within which they act. According to Poulantzas, Miliband had

> . . . difficulties . . . in comprehending social classes and the State as *objective structures,* and their relations as an *objective system of regular connections,* a structure and a system whose agents, "men," are in the words of Marx, "bearers" of it—*Träger.*

Miliband constantly gives the impression that for him social classes or "groups" are in some way reducible to *inter-personal relations,* that the State is reducible to inter-personal relations of the members of the diverse "groups" that constitute the State apparatus, and finally that the relation between social classes and the State is itself reducible to inter-personal relations of "individuals" composing social groups and "individuals" composing the State apparatus.

This conception, Poulantzas continues,

. . . seems to me to derive from a *problematic of the subject* which has had constant repercussions in the history of Marxist thought. According to this problematic, the agents of a social formation, "men," are not considered as the "bearers" of objective instances (as they are for Marx), but as the genetic principle of the levels of the social whole. This is a problematic of *social actors,* of individuals as the origin of *social action:* sociological research thus leads finally, not to the study of the objective co-ordinates that determine the distribution of agents into social classes and the contradictions between these classes, but to the search for *finalist* explanations founded on the *motivations of conduct* of the individual actors.[142]

Miliband, in response to this, maintains that Poulantzas

. . . is here rather one-sided and that he goes much too far in dismissing the nature of the state elite as of altogether no account. For what his *exclusive* stress on "objective relations" suggests is that what the state does is in every particular and at all times *wholly* determined by these "objective relations": in other words, that the structural constraints of the system are so absolutely compelling as to turn those who run the state into the merest functionaries and executants of policies imposed upon them by "the system."

Poulantzas, writes Miliband, substitutes "the notion of 'objective structures' for the notion of a 'ruling' class," and he falls into

. . . a "hyperstructuralist" trap, which deprives "agents" of any freedom of choice and maneouvre and turns them into the "bearers" of objective forces which they are unable to affect. This perspective is but another form of determinism—which is alien to Marxism and in any case false, which is much more serious. Governments can and do press against the "structural constraints" by which they are beset.[143]

Also at issue between Poulantzas and Miliband is whether all power is class power. Indeed, Poulantzas *defines* power as "*the capacity of a social class to realise its specific objective interests.*"[144] Miliband, on the other hand, seeks to allow a (historically variable) place for (relatively autonomous) state power: he seeks to avoid any "confusion between *class power* and *state power,* a distinction which it is important not to blur."[145] Both writers, however, agree in seeing the "legitimation" of authority as a form of power, though Poulantzas follows Althusser and Gramsci's third model of hegemony in speaking of this as occurring within the "state ideological apparatuses," while Miliband argues that

. . . there is absolutely no warrant for speaking of "state ideological apparatuses" in regard to institutions which, in bourgeois democratic societies, are not part of the state; and much which is important about the life of these societies is lost in the obliteration of the distinction between ideological apparatuses which are mainly the product of "civil society" and those which are the product and part of the state apparatus.[146]

The "community power debate" within recent American political science is a debate between disputants who share a general conception of asymmetric power as control, or the securing of compliance, but who disagree about how it is to be identified and measured. More specifically, they agree in seeing power as exercised when *A* affects *B* in *A*'s but against *B*'s interests, but they disagree about how this idea is properly to be understood and applied in research—and this disagreement largely stems from differing conceptions of what are to count as interests and how they may be adversely affected, which stems from fundamental differences of philosophical and methodological positions and ultimately of world view.

Robert Dahl, Nelson Polsby, and their colleagues employ a "one-dimensional" view of power which involves a focus on behavior in the making of decisions on (key) issues over which there is an observable conflict of (subjective) interests, seen as express policy preferences revealed by political participation. Thus Polsby writes that

> . . . one can conceive of "power"—"influence" and "control" are serviceable synonyms—as the capacity of one actor to do something affecting another actor, which changes the probable pattern of specified future events. This can be envisaged most easily in a decision-making situation.

And he argues that identifying "who prevails in decision-making" seems "the best way to determine which individuals and groups have "more" power in social life, because direct conflict between actors presents a situation most closely approximating an experimental test of their capacities to affect outcomes."[147] Thus Dahl's central method in *Who Governs?* was to

> . . . determine for each decision which participants had initiated alternatives that were finally adopted, had vetoed alternatives initiated by others, or had proposed alternatives that were turned down. Their actions were then tabulated as individual "successes" or "defeats." The participants with the greatest proportion of success out of the total number of successes were then considered to be the most influential.[148]

Peter Bachrach and Morton Baratz criticize this view of power as restrictive and, by virtue of that fact, as giving a misleadingly sanguine pluralist picture of American politics. Power, they claim, has two faces. The first face is that examined by Dahl and his colleagues, according to which "power is totally embodied and fully reflected in 'concrete decisions' or in activity bearing upon their making." But, they maintain, it is also exercised

> . . . when A devotes his energies to creating or reinforcing social and political values and institutional practices that limit the scope of the political process to public consideration of only those issues which are comparatively innocuous to A. To the extent that A succeeds in doing this, B is prevented, for all practical purposes, from bringing to the fore any issues that might in their resolution be seriously detrimental to A's set of preferences.

The second face of power exists "to the extent that a person or group—

consciously or unconsciously—creates or reinforces barriers to the public airing of policy conflicts" by "non-decision making"—that is, decision making that "results in suppression or thwarting of a latent or manifest challenge to the values or interests of the decision-maker." Such power, however, only shows up where there is conflict, overt or covert; in the absence of such conflict, "the presumption must be that there is consensus on the prevailing allocation of values."[149] In sum, the two-dimensional view of power involves a qualified critique of the behavioral focus of the one-dimensional (qualified because it still assumes that non-decision making is a form of decision making), and it allows for consideration of the ways in which decisions are prevented from being taken on potential issues over which there is an observable conflict of (subjective) interests, seen as embodied either in express policy preferences revealed by political participation, or in covert or deflected subpolitical grievances.

I have, in turn, criticized this two-dimensional view[150] as being both too behaviorist and too individualistic, and because of its insistence that for power to exist there must be observable conflict and the existence of grievances, albeit covert. A three-dimensional view of power can be elaborated which incorporates the first two but allows for consideration of the subtler and less visible ways in which potential issues are kept out of politics through the behavior of groups and practices of institutions (which may not be analyzable in terms of individuals' decision making and may indeed be manifested by individuals' inaction). Moreover, such power may be exercised in the absence of observable conflict and grievances; is it not the supreme exercise of power to avert conflict and grievance by influencing, shaping, and determining the perceptions and preferences of others? Such a view requires the hypothesis of a contradiction between the interests of those exercising power and the real interests of those who silently acquiesce. Doubtless, such a hypothesis raises several acute difficulties of theory and research; but such difficulties are not solved by adopting the alternative, and methodologically easier, hypothesis that power of this kind cannot exist.

As for authority, proponents of the first view tend to see political authority as authority by convention in classical liberal-democratic terms: it is voluntarily given in the form of renewed consent at regular elections (which also enable the electorate to exercise "indirect influence on the decisions of leaders").[151] Bachrach and Baratz, however, are equivocal on the topic of authority. They see it as one of the means of control, or securing compliance (along with the threat of sanctions, influence, force, and manipulation), where "B complies because he recognises that [A's] command is reasonable in terms of his own values," because either its content or the procedure by which it is reached is legitimate and reasonable. Yet they seem unsure about whether it is a form of power, involving a "possible conflict of values," or an "agreement based upon reason."[152] Consideration of the third dimension of power opens up the whole question of how and to what extent the internal acceptance of rules of authoritative reasons and rules of recognition may be imposed by the superordinate upon the subordinate.

Finally we may refer to an interesting difference of view between two thinkers with much in common by way of intellectual background—Hannah Arendt, who is a postclassical political theorist and Jürgen Habermas, a neo-Marxist social philosopher. This dispute occurs within the collective or communal family of conceptions of power.

Arendt denies that "Power, strength, force, authority, violence . . . are but words to indicate the means by which man rules over man." She rejects the tradition of thinking that reduces "public affairs to the business of domination" and appeals rather to "another tradition and another vocabulary no less old and time honoured," common to the Athenians, the Romans, and the eighteenth-century revolutionaries, a tradition which employed "a concept of power and law whose essence did not rely on the command-obedience relationship and which did not identify power and rule or law and command." For Arendt, power

> . . . corresponds to the human ability not just to act but to act in concert. Power is never the property of the individual; it belongs to a group and remains in existence only so long as the group keeps together. When we say of somebody that he is "in power" we actually refer to his being empowered by a certain number of people to act in their name.[153]

Authority, Arendt believes, "has vanished from the modern world"; it "grew out of the Roman experience of foundation and was understood in the light of Greek political philosophy," and it has "nowhere been re-established," indeed, all modern revolutions since the French are failed attempts to reestablish it. It involved "the religious trust in a sacred beginning" and "the protection of tradition and therefore self-evident standards of behavior." Its hallmark was "unquestioning recognition by those who are asked to obey; neither coercion nor persuasion is needed."[154]

Habermas recognizes Arendt's conception of power as denoting "not the instrumentalisation of *another's* will, but the formation of a *common* will directed to reaching agreement"—the "power of agreement-oriented communication to produce consensus." This is reminiscent of Habermas's own notion of "consensus brought about in unconstrained communication," in which "those involved are oriented to reaching agreement and not primarily to their respective individual successes." But he differs from Arendt with respect to the way he grounds this "communications concept of power" and the historical and political significance he attaches to it. For Arendt, such power derives from a view of a nondeformed "public realm" based on classical political models, which in the modern world finds its expression in revolutionary attempts to establish political liberty (American town-hall meetings in 1776, the Parisian *sociétés populaires* between 1789 and 1793, sections of the Paris Commune in 1871, the Russian Soviets in 1905 and 1917, the *Rätedemokratie* in Germany in 1918) and its antithesis in totalitarian rule. Habermas sees this position as based on an anachronistic image of the Greek polis, "inapplicable to modern conditions." Arendt's view of politics excludes "strategic action," the "struggle for political power," and is unconnected to the economic and social environment in which it is embedded through the administrative system. For her, politics is identified with "the praxis of those who talk together in order to act in common." On the other hand, Habermas values in her thesis the idea that legitimate power is generated (as opposed to acquired, maintained, and employed) through "common convictions in unconstrained communication."[155]

For Habermas, political rule has rarely been the expression of such unconstrained consensus. Rather, systematically restricted communication and illusory ideologies have served to legitimate power, through "convictions subjectively free from constraint, convictions which are however illusionary.[156] This neo-Marxist twist to the old tale of power and authority comes as no surprise. For a complex set of reasons, Habermas holds that late capitalism faces a legitimation crisis as the state, whose class character becomes increasingly transparent, is increasingly unable to maintain its legitimacy. For him, legitimate power, based on undistorted communication, represents a counterfactual ideal of emancipation at the basis of critical theory.[157] Like other contemporary conceptions of power and authority, this embodies a view of "the natural necessities and opportunities of human life" and a "conception of social cooperation" whose roots lie deep in the history of social and political theory.

NOTES

1. R. Dahrendorf, *Class and Class Conflict in an Industrial Society* (London: Routledge & Kegan Paul, 1959) p. 166.
2. J. Rawls, *A Theory of Justice* (Oxford: Clarendon Press, 1972) pp. 9–10.
3. T. Hobbes, *Leviathan*, part I, chap. X.
4. Cited in H. Arendt, *On Violence* (London: The Penguin Press, 1970) p. 36.
5. B. Russell, *Power: A New Social Analysis* (London: Allen & Unwin, 1938) p. 35.
6. See S. Lukes, "Power and Structure" in *Essays in Social Theory* (London: Macmillan and New York: Columbia University Press, 1977).
7. This is sometimes described, as by Talcott Parsons, as a zero-sum notion of power. This is, however, confusing, since "zero-sum" is a term from the theory of games, where its use presupposes a closed system confined to the players and the measurability of power on a single scale. It is, moreover, unclear *what* is supposed to sum to zero—the payoffs to the players or their power. By "asymmetrical" I mean simply that, in virtue of his power, *A* can or does affect *B*, in some given respect, more than *B* affects *A*.
8. T. Hobbes, *Elements of Law, Natural and Politic*, part I, chap. 8, sections 3 and 4.
9. Montesquieu, *L'Esprit des Lois*, book I, chap. III.
10. Cf. A. Etzioni's definition of compliance as "a relationship consisting of the power employed by superiors to control subordinates and the orientation of subordinates to this power" in his *A Comparative Analysis of Complex Organizations* (New York: Free Press, 1961) p. xv. This work advances a comprehensive typology of compliance relations.
11. D. Cartwright, "A Field Theoretical Conception of Power" in Cartwright, ed., *Studies in Social Power* (Ann Arbor: University of Michigan Press, 1959).
12. G. Simmel, *The Sociology of Georg Simmel*, K. H. Wolff, ed. (Glencoe, Ill.: Free Press, 1950) p. 183.

13. G. Karlsson, "Some Aspects of Power in Small Groups" J. H. Criswell, H. Salomon, and P. Suppes, eds., in *Mathematical Methods in Small Group Processes* (Stanford: Stanford University Press, 1962) pp. 193–202.

14. W. Riker, "Some Ambiguities in the Notion of Power," *American Political Science Review*, vol. 58 (1964) pp. 341–49; L. S. Shapley and M. Shubik, "A Method for Evaluating the Distribution of Power in a Committee System," *American Political Science Review*, vol. 48 (1954) pp. 787–92.

15. N. Luhmann, *Macht* (Stuttgart: Enke, 1975).

16. H. Lasswell and A. Kaplan, *Power and Society* (New Haven: Yale University Press, 1950) p. 76.

17. P. M. Blau, *Exchange and Power in Social Life* (New York: John Wiley & Sons, 1967) p. 117.

18. James Mill, *An Essay on Government*, section IX, E. Barker, ed. (Cambridge: Cambridge University Press, 1937) p. 17.

19. T. Dos Santos, "The Crisis of Development Theory and the Problem of Dependence in Latin America," in H. Bernstein, ed., *Underdevelopment and Development*, (Harmondsworth: Penguin, 1973) p. 76. "In either case," writes Dos Santos, "the basic situation of dependence causes these countries to be both backward and exploited. Dominant countries are endowed with technological, commercial, capital and socio-political predominance over dependent countries—the form of this predominance varying according to the particular historical moment—and can therefore exploit them, and extract part of the locally produced surplus. Dependence, then, is based upon an international division of labour which allows industrial development to take place in some countries while restricting it in others, whose growth is conditioned by and subjected to the power centres of the world" (pp. 76–77).

20. See Brian Barry, "Power: An Economic Analysis," in B. Barry, ed., *Power and Political Theory: Some European Perspectives* (London: John Wiley, 1976) pp. 67–101.

21. M. Weber, *Economy and Society*, G. Roth and C. Wittich, eds. (New York: Bedminster, 1968) vol. 2, p. 927.

22. G. Lenski, *Power and Privilege* (New York: McGraw-Hill, 1966) p. 45.

23. F. Parkin, *Class, Inequality and Political Order* (London: MacGibbon & Kee, 1971) p. 46.

24. Weber, *Economy and Society*, vol. 1, p. 53.

25. B. Constant, *De la liberté des anciens comparée á celle des modernes*, in his *Oeuvres Politiques*, C. Louandre, ed. (Paris, 1874) p. 260.

26. F. Neumann, "Approaches to the Study of Political Power" in *The Democratic and Authoritarian State* (New York: Free Press, 1964) p. 5.

27. Cicero, *De Re Publica*, Book 1, art. 31.

28. *Digesta Justiniani Augusti*, book 1, Ch. 4, Sect. 1.

29. Aquinas, *Summa Theologica*, part III (suppl.), q. 34, art. I.

30. E. Burke, *Reflections on the Revolution in France*, Everyman edition, (London: Dent, 1910) p. 7.

31. W. von Humboldt, *The Sphere and Duties of Government*, trans. J. Coulthard (London: Trubner, 1854) pp. 189–90. Rawls refers to Humboldt on pp. 523–24 of his *Theory of Justice*.

32. T. H. Green, "Lecture on Liberal Legislation and Freedom of Contract" in *Works*, 6th imp. (London: Longmans Green, 1911) vol. III, pp. 370–73.

33. V. I. Lenin, "What is Soviet Power?" in *Selected Works* (in one vol.) (London: Lawrence & Wishart, 1969) pp. 476–77.

34. Arendt, *On Violence*, pp. 40, 44.

35. T. Parsons, *Structure and Process in Modern Societies* (New York: Free Press, 1960) p. 221.

36. I owe much in the following analysis to the very fine paper by R. Friedmann, "On the Concept of Authority in Political Philosophy" in R. Flathman, ed., *Concepts in Social and Political Philosophy*, (New York: Macmillan, 1973) pp. 121–46, and to my colleague Joseph Raz, who let me see his unpublished paper, "On Legitimate Authority," from which I derived much profit.

37. Aquinas, *Summa Theologica*, second part of the second part, II, i, cited in Friedmann, "On the Concept of Authority in Political Philosophy."

38. Hobbes, *De Cive*, chap. 14, part 1, cited in ibid.

39. See R. S. Peters, "Authority," *Proceedings of the Aristotelian Society*, supp. vol. 32 (1958).

40. Weber, *Economy and Society*, vol. 3, pp. 946–47, 948.

41. This is Raz's formulation.

42. C. J. Friedrich, "Authority, Reason and Disaction" in C. J. Friedrich, ed., *Authority*.

Nomos I, The American Society of Political and Legal Philosophy (Cambridge: Harvard University Press, 1958) p. 35. Diderot's *Encyclopédie* gives a more graphic picture of authority as a useful human contrivance for leading us to rational ends: reason is "a torch lit by nature, and destined to enlighten us"; authority is "no more than a walking-stick made by human hands, which has the virtue of helping us, when weak, along the road shown us by reason" (article on "*Autorité*").

43. See Friedmann, "On the Concept of Authority in Political Philosophy," and Robin Horton, "African Traditional Thought and Western Science," *Africa*, vol. XXXVII (1967) pp. 50–71 and 155–87, reprinted (in abridged form) in B. R. Wilson, ed., *Rationality*, (Oxford: Blackwell, 1970).

44. Hobbes, *Leviathan*, chap. 7, Oakeshott ed., (Oxford: Oxford University Press, n.d. pp. 41–42; chap. 18, ibid., p. 118; Cf. ibid, chap. 26, p. 178. Cited in Friedmann, "On the Concept of Authority in Political Philosophy."

45. J. Bentham, *A Fragment on Government*, W. Harrison, ed. (Oxford: Oxford University Press, 1948) p. 99. Cited in Friedmann, "On the Concept of Authority in Political Philosophy."

46. *The Concept of Law* (Oxford: Clarendon Press, 1961) chap. VI.

47. Act I, scene IV.

48. See L. Krieger, "Authority," in P. P. Wiener, ed., *Dictionary of the History of Ideas* (New York: Scribners, 1973) vol. I, pp. 141–62.

49. Matt. 7: 29.

50. St. Augustine, *Contra epistolam quam vocat fundamenti*, cited in Krieger, "Authority."

51. Hooker, *Laws of Ecclesiastical Polity* vol. II, chap. VII, book 2, cited in Friedmann, "On the Concept of Authority in Political Philosophy."

52. See A. MacIntyre, *Secularisation and Moral Change* (London: Oxford University Press for the University of Newcastle upon Tyne, 1967).

53. J. F. Stephen, *Liberty, Equality, Fraternity*, (London: Smith, Elder & Co., 1874) p. 234.

54. See R. Dahrendorf, "In Praise of Thrasymachus," in *Essays in the Theory of Society* (London: Routledge & Kegan Paul, 1968).

55. Hobbes, *Leviathan*, part II, chap. XVII.

56. See S. S. Wolin, *Politics and Vision* (London: Allen & Unwin, 1961) pp. 265–72.

57. E. Burke, *Reflections on the Revolution in France* (London: Dent, 1910) p. 32.

58. Aquinas, *Summa Theologica*, part III (suppl.) q. 34, art. 2, ad. 2.

59. L. Krieger, "*Authority*," p. 149.

60. J. de Maistre, *Essai sur le principe générateur des constitutions politiques et des autres institutions humaines*, bk. I, chap. X, XII, trans. in J. Lively, ed., *The Works of Joseph de Maistre* (London: Allen & Unwin, 1965) pp. 108–11; and *Les Soirées de Saint-Petersbourg, ler. Entretien*, trans. in ibid., p. 192.

61. L. de Bonald, *Théorie du pouvoir politique et religieux, Oeuvres*, (Paris, 1854) vol. I, pp. 122, 494–95, 157, 159.

62. T. Carlyle, *Past and Present* (London: Chapman & Hall, 1888) p. 207.

63. E. Burke, *Reflections on the Revolution in France*, pp. 32, 93–94, 83, 73, 74, 89–90, 75, 179. According to Burke, "Society requires not only that the passions of individuals should be subjected, but that even in the mass and body, as well as in the individuals, the inclinations of men shall frequently be thwarted, their will controlled, and their passions brought into subjection. This can only be done by *a power out of themselves;* and not, in the exercise of its function, subject to that will and to those passions which it is its office to bridle and subdue. In this sense the restraints on men, as well as their liberties, are to be reckoned among their rights" (ibid., pp. 57–58).

64. R. A. Nisbet, *The Sociological Tradition* (New York: Basic Books, 1966) p. 112.

65. Cited in Nisbet, ibid. pp. 109, 108.

66. Nisbet, ibid., pp. 112, 114, 116.

67. Montesquieu, *L'Esprit des Lois*, book III.

68. Saint-Simon, *Oeuvres de Saint-Simon et d'Enfantin* (Paris: Dentu, 1865–78) vol. XX, pp. 38–43; vol. I, p. 219; vol. XXXIX, pp. 125–32.

69. *The Positive Philosophy of Auguste Comte*, H. Martineau, trans. (London: Trubner, n.d.) vol. II, pp. 480–83, 485–87; Saint-Simon, *Oeuvres*, vol. XX, p. 156; Wolin, *Politics and Vision*, p. 397; G. Lenzer, ed., *Auguste Comte and Positivism; The Essential Writings* (New York: Harper Torchbooks, 1975) pp. 26–27.

70. A. de Tocqueville, *La Démocratie en Amérique*, book II, part I, chap. II; book II, part II, chap. II; book II, part III, chap. XXI; book I, part I, chap. III; book II, part IV, chap. VI; "Lettre à Eugene Stoffels" in *Oeuvres et Correspondance Inédite*, G. de Beaumont, ed. (Paris, 1861) vol. I, pp. 427–49.

71. E. Durkheim, "L'Individualism et les Intellectuels" *Revue bleue*, 4e série, vol. X (1898) pp. 7–13; *L'Education morale*, (Paris, 1925) pp. 62, 136–37.

72. F. C. von Savigny, *Vom Beruf unserer Zeit für Gesetzgebung*, J. Stern, ed. (Berlin: Thibaut & Savigny, 1914) p. 78.

73. Sidney and Beatrice Webb, *A Constitution for the Socialist Commonwealth of Great Britain* (London: Longmans, Green & Co., 1920) pp. 350–56.

74. D. Bell, *The Coming of Post-Industrial Society* (New York: Basic Books, 1973) pp. 118, 426, 453, 455.

75. T. Parsons, *The Social System* (London: Routledge & Kegan Paul, 1951) p. 41; "Authority, Legitimation and Political Action" in C. J. Friedrich, ed., *Authority, Nomos I*, The American Society of Political and Legal Philosophy (Cambridge: Harvard University Press, 1958) p. 199.

76. S. M. Lipset, *Political Man* (Garden City, N.Y.: Doubleday, 1960) p. 77.

77. Parsons, "Authority, Legitimation and Political Action," pp. 210, 206.

78. See Wolin, *Politics and Vision*, chap. IX, and S. Lukes, *Individualism* (Oxford: Blackwell, and New York: Harper & Row, 1973).

79. Hobbes, *Leviathan* chap. XLII.

80. Spinoza, *Tractatus Theologico-Politicus*, chap. XX.

81. Hobbes, *Leviathan*, XIII; *The Elements of Law*, I, VIII, 4; *Leviathan*, XVII, XVI.

82. Hobbes, XXI; *Elements of Law*, I, XIX, 8; *Leviathan*, XXX. Spinoza took this authority conferred by consent to be more absolute (with regard to its circumstances of application) than did Hobbes: the individual "has determined to obey" the sovereign "in everything without exception." Authority, in his view, yields "supreme power to coerce all," though with the ultimate aim of freeing men from fear, thereby enabling them "to develop their minds and bodies in security, and to employ their reason unshackled" (*Tractatus Theologico-Politicus*, chap. XVI).

83. J. Locke, *Two Treatises of Government: Second Treatise*.

84. Ibid.

85. A. Smith, *Wealth of Nations*, Everyman edition (London: Dent 1961) vol. II, p. 203.

86. T. Paine, *Common Sense*, in *The Political and Miscellaneous Works of Thomas Paine in Two Volumes*, (London: R. Carlile, 1819) vol. 1, p. 5.

87. F. Bastiat, *Oeuvres complètes* (Paris, 1862–78) vol. I, p. 427, cited in Wolin, *Politics and Vision*, q.v. for an excellent discussion of this mode of thinking.

88. Diderot, *Encyclopédie, ou Dictionnaire raisonné des sciences, des arts et des métiers* (Paris, 1752–72) vol. I.

89. I have been much helped on this topic by an as yet unpublished manuscript by Carole Pateman on the "problem of political obligation."

90. A. Ferguson, *Principles of Moral and Political Science* (London, 1792) vol. II, pp. 245–46.

91. A. Hamilton, J. Madison, and J. Jay, *The Federalist, passim*.

92. J. Bentham, "The Constitutional Code" in *The Works of Jeremy Bentham*, J. Bowring, ed. (Edinburgh, 1843) vol. IX.

93. See James Mill, *Essay on Government*. In fact, it is most plausible to date Bentham's conversion to democracy from about 1809, when he came under the influence of James Mill.

94. See *Mill on Bentham and Coleridge*, F. R. Leavis, ed. (London: Chatto & Windus, 1959) p. 123; J. Mill, *On Liberty: Principles of Political Economy*, 3rd ed.

95. J. Rawls, *A Theory of Justice*, p. 13.

96. J. J. Rousseau, *Le Contrat Social*, passim.; *Emile*, B. Foxley, trans. (London and New York: Dutton, 1911) p. 149.

97. G. W. F. Hegel, *Philosophy of Right* § 147, Addition to § 281, § 261, § 260 and Addition.

98. See *Hegel's Political Writings*, Z. A. Pelczynski, ed. (Oxford: Oxford University Press, 1964).

99. See E. Kedourie, *Nationalism* (London: Hutchinson, 1960).

100. B. Mussolini, "The Doctrine of Fascism" trans. in *The Social and Political Doctrines of Contemporary Europe*, M. Oakeshott, ed. (London: Cambridge University Press, 1940) pp. 175–79.

101. P. J. Proudhon, *General Idea of the Revolution in the Nineteenth Century*, J. B. Robinson, trans. (London: Freedom Press, 1923) pp. 245–77.

102. M. Bakunin, *Oeuvres*, (Paris: P. V. Stock, 1895) pp. 54–59.

103. P. Kropotkin, *Modern Science and Anarchism* (London: Freedom Press, 1912) reprinted in I. L. Horowitz, ed., *The Anarchists* (New York: Dell, 1964) p. 163.

104. Proudhon, *General Idea of the Revolution*, pp. 245–47.

105. R. Rocker, "Anarchism and Anarcho-Syndicalism," reprinted in Horowitz, *The Anarchists*, p. 190.

106. M. Bakunin, "Science and the Urgent Revolutionary Task," reprinted in Horowitz, *The Anarchists*, p. 132.

107. K. Marx and F. Engels, *The Communist Manifesto;* K. Marx, *Capital* (Moscow: Foreign Language Publishing House, 1962) vol. I, p. 737; vol. III, p. 307.

108. V. I. Lenin, *Collected Works* (London: Lawrence & Wishart, 1960–1970) vol. 24, pp. 63–64.

109. A. Gramsci, *Selections from the Prison Notebooks*, Q. Hoare and G. Nowell-Smith, eds. (London: New Left Books, 1971) pp. 169–70, 57; *Lettere del Carcere*, Turin, 1965, pp. 616, 481; *Selections from the Prison Notebooks*, pp. 80 n., 242. These quotations are cited by Perry Anderson in his extremely valuable essay, "The Antinomies of Antonio Gramsci, *New Left Review*, 100 (1976–77), pp. 5–78.

110. See L. Althusser, *Lenin and Philosophy, and Other Essays*, (London: New Left Books, 1971).

111. K. Marx and F. Engels, *The Communist Manifesto*, section II.

112. F. Engels, "On Authority" in Marx and Engels, *Selected Works*, 2 vols., (Moscow: Foreign Languages Publishing House, 1962) vol. I, p. 639.

113. V. I. Lenin, *State and Revolution* in *Selected Works* (London: Lawrence and Wishart, 1969) p. 337.

114. K. Marx, *Capital*, vol. III, pp. 859, 800, 376; *Grundrisse*, Martin Nicolaus, trans. (Harmondsworth: Penguin Books in association with *New Left Review*, 1973) p. 705.

115. F. Engels, "On Authority," pp. 635–39. "Wanting to abolish authority in large-scale industry," wrote Engels, "is tantamount to wanting to abolish industry itself, to destroy the power loom in order to return to the spinning wheel" (p. 637).

116. G. Mosca, *The Ruling Class (Elementi de Scienza Politica)*, H. D. Kahn, trans., A. Livingston, ed. (New York: McGraw-Hill, 1939) pp. 70, 71, 62, 71.

117. V. Pareto, *The Mind and Society: A Treatise on General Sociology* (New York: Dover, 1963) §§ 583, 585, 590.

118. R. Michels, *Political Parties*, E. and C. Paul, trans. (New York: Dover, 1959) pp. 402, 390.

119. Pareto, *Mind and Society*, §§ 2183, 2244, 2251, 2252.

120. G. Simmel, "Superordination and Subordination," in K. H. Wolff, ed., *The Sociology of Georg Simmel* (Glencoe, Ill.: Free Press, 1950) pp. 282–83.

121. See S. Freud, *Civilisation and its Discontents* (London: Hogarth Press, 1961).

122. Weber, *Economy and Society*, pp. 53, 941.

123. Ibid., pp. 941, 946, 943.

124. Ibid., pp. 943, 946.

125. Ibid., 944, 214, 943, 944–45.

126. T. Parsons, review article of R. Bendix's *Max Weber: An Intellectual Portrait, American Sociological Review*, vol. 25 (1960) p. 752.

127. R. Bendix, *Max Weber: An Intellectual Portrait* (Garden City, N.Y.: Anchor Books, Doubleday, 1962) p. 482.

128. Weber, *Economy and Society*, pp. 212, 213, 947.

129. See Denis Wrong, introduction to *Max Weber*, D. Wrong, ed. (Englewood Cliffs, N.J. Prentice-Hall, 1976) p. 50.

130. Weber, *Economy and Society*, p. 214.

131. Ibid., p. 954.

132. Ibid., pp. 946, 943, 947, 943.

133. Ibid., pp. 1020, 949, 950, 952, 215, 953, 954.

134. Ibid., p. 953.

135. Ibid., p. 903.

136. T. Parsons, "The Distribution of Power in American Society," a review of C. Wright Mills's *The Power Elite*, *World Politics* (Oct. 1957) reprinted in *C. Wright Mills and The Power Elite*, G. W. Domhoff and H. B. Ballard, eds. (Boston: Beacon, 1968) p. 82.

137. C. Wright Mills, *The Power Elite* (New York and London: Oxford University Press, 1956) p. 9.

138. Parsons, "The Distribution of Power in American Society," pp. 82 et seq. Cf. A. Giddens, "Power" on the writings of Talcott Parsons in his *Studies in Social and Political Theory* (London: Hutchinson, 1977).

139. Parsons, "The Distribution of Power in American Society," p. 83.

140. T. Parsons, "Authority, Legitimation and Political Action," p. 181; "On the Concept of Political Power," *Proceedings of the American Philosophical Society*, vol. 107 (1963) p. 250.

141. C. Wright Mills, "The Structure of Power in American Society" in *Power, Politics and People: The Collected Essays of C. Wright Mills*, I. L. Horowitz, ed. (New York and London: Oxford University Press, 1963) p. 23.

142. N. Poulantzas, "The Problem of the Capitalist State," *New Left Review*, vol. 58 (Nov.–Dec. 1969) p. 70.

143. R. Miliband, "The Capitalist State: Reply to Nicos Poulantzas," *New Left Review*, vol. 59 (Jan.–Feb. 1970) p. 57; and *Marxism and Politics* (Oxford: Oxford University Press, 1977) p. 73. Cf. S. Lukes, "Power and Structure."

144. N. Poulantzas, *Political Power and Social Classes*, T. O'Hagan, trans. (London: New Left Books and Sheed & Ward, 1973) p. 104.

145. R. Miliband, *Marxism and Politics*, p. 54.

146. Ibid., p. 57.

147. N. W. Polsby, *Community Power and Political Theory* (New Haven and London: Yale University Press, 1963) pp. 3–4.

148. R. A. Dahl, *Who Governs?: Democracy and Power in an American City* (New Haven and London: Yale University Press, 1961) p. 336.

149. P. Bachrach and M. S. Baratz, *Power and Poverty in Theory and Practice* (New York: Oxford University Press, 1970) pp. 7, 8, 44, 49.

150. S. Lukes, *Power: A Radical View* (London: Macmillan, and Atlantic Highlands, N.J.: Humanities Press, 1974).

151. R. A. Dahl, *Who Governs?* p. 101.

152. Bachrach and Baratz, *Power and Poverty*, pp. 34, 37, 20.

153. Arendt, *On Violence*, pp. 43, 44, 40, 44.

154. H. Arendt, "What Is Authority?" in H. Arendt, *Between Past and Future* (New York: Viking Press, 1968 ed.) pp. 91, 141; *On Violence*, p. 45. Arendt remarks that if authority is to be defined, "it must be in contradistinction to both coercion by force and persuasion through arguments" ("What Is Authority?" p. 93).

155. J. Habermas, "Hannah Arendt's Communications Concept of Power," *Social Research*, vol. 44, no. 1 (Spring 1977) pp. 4, 5, 6, 14, 17, 21, 18.

156. Ibid., p. 22.

157. See J. Habermas, *Legitimation Crisis*, T. McCarthy, trans. (London: Heinemann, 1975).

17

SOCIOLOGICAL ANALYSIS AND SOCIAL POLICY

JAMES COLEMAN

IN THIS CHAPTER I will try to trace two kinds of development. One is the development of actual sociological inquiry designed to have some impact on the functioning of society. Such inquiry may be termed "social policy research"—that is, social research designed to inform policy in a narrow sense or to inform societal actions in a broader sense. The most prominent recent examples of such research are social experiments such as the negative income tax, and housing allowance, and health insurance experiments in the United States [see Pechman and Timpane (1975)].[1] The other is the development of ideas about the appropriate or possible role for sociology in social policy. The first is a history of social policy research, the second is a history of theories about the way in which sociology can inform action in society.

Perhaps the best way to explicate what is meant by the second of these developments is to sketch the components of rational action as if society were a single actor. Although this is admittedly a simplistic view (and, as will be evident later, can introduce a systematic bias), it will illustrate where ideas about policy research fit into social theory generally. Rational action can be seen as a sequence in which action is directed toward a goal, then informed about its deviations from this goal, redirected on the basis of this information, and so on.

Thus, if we saw "society" or "government" as a rational actor, its actions should include these components. The place of sociological analysis in such a sequence—insofar as sociological analysis is seen as having a role in the functioning of society—is in providing the feedback information that allows redirection of social action. Thus, insofar as social theory contains a theory of rational societal action, it must include statements about the process through which information is provided and used to reshape social action. That is, it must include either a positive or normative theory about the role of sociological analysis in informing social policy. Therefore, in reviewing this history of ideas or theories, I will be reviewing what social theorists have had to say about the social role of sociological knowledge. I will call this the history of theories of the social role of sociology.

Theories of the Social Role of Sociology

The first point that strikes one in reviewing what early sociologists and social philosophers have had to say in their theoretical work about the social role of sociological knowledge is how little they had to say. They had much to say about what was wrong with society, or what was right about it; value orientations were not missing from this early work. The work of most was apparently motivated by a desire to affect the functioning of society, but they seldom had much to say about the process through which that effect would occur. They devoted little time to the reflexive act of asking how sociological investigation itself might enter into and become a part of the process of social change.

Auguste Comte, however, did have a rather explicit theory of the social role of sociology. Comte was motivated, as were nearly all early social theorists, by a desire to influence the course of society—as reflected in his famous statement, "*Savoir pour prêvoir, pour pouvoir*"—and, to a greater degree than most of those who followed him, his philosophy of history contained a place for sociological knowledge. He had a conception of that knowledge and the prediction it would allow as leading to a "scientific humanism." But his conception of how this would take place was primitive. He naively conceived of a utopia which was little different from that which Plato conceived two millennia earlier. Comte believed that positive knowledge (as distinct from normative or ideologically inspired beliefs) about social functioning would provide the basis for rational social planning, with social scientists as the guiding elite. In the final phase of Comte's work—his vision of a "religion of humanism"—the social scientists constituted the high priests of the religion. Thus, in Comte's overall conception of the society of the future, the role of positive knowledge about societal functioning was a central one; but there were only simple assumptions about how that knowledge would have its effect.

Other early sociologists actually carried out research designed to affect policy—they were the forebears of modern "policy researchers"—but their theories did not contain a place for the role of such research as an element of social change. Frederick Le Play provides a good illustration of the separation of social theory and social research, for Le Play was both a theorist and an initiator of systematic empirical research. His theory of social change included both notions about the effects of beliefs and ideas (particularly religious beliefs) and notions of geographical and technological determinism. The family was the central institution of society for Le Play, both in his observation of current reality and in his exhortation about the desirable future social structure.

In addition, Le Play carried out research on the family, with groundbreaking studies of family budgets at different social levels and in different countries.[2] Le Play intended this research to have demonstration value perhaps not precisely for social policy but for increasing knowledge about the "basic moral laws" of society.

But of central importance for us to note is that although Le Play's research was both more advanced and more closely related to his theoretical work than was true for most of his contemporaries, there was no place in his theory for social research or sociological knowledge itself to play a part in social change. Unlike Comte, he did not have a place for the role of sociological knowledge in his philosophy of history. Consequently, for our purposes, he must be remembered as a forerunner of modern systematic quantitative research at the individual or household level, and not as a theorist of the social role of those research results.

In a different way, Karl Marx exhibits the absence of attention to the social role of social science. His work shows a curious paradox in the conception of how social science would shape society. As an activist radical, he devoted a portion of his life to an attempt to bring about the next stage, as he saw it, in the historical development of society.[3] Yet his theory of historical development, perhaps the most complete of any social theorist's, was one in which only material factors played a part. Put in oversimplified terms, the technology determined the mode of economic production; the mode of production determined the structure of classes and their relation to the means of production and thus to one another; and this in turn generated, over time, their orientation to (e.g., alienation from) the system of production and led to their action which would transform it. The place of ideas and social knowledge in Marx's theory of history was as dependent or derivative phenomena, as a superstructure generated by the conditions of material existence in which men found themselves. In this respect, Marx was the originator of the sociology of knowledge, with a specific theory about the way in which social conditions of existence brought about knowledge, beliefs, and values concerning social functioning—but without a theory about the way knowledge, beliefs, and values might affect social conditions.

Perhaps the place to look most carefully for the role of sociological knowledge in Marx's theory of the course of social change is in the transformation of a class from a class in itself to a class for itself, the development of class-consciousness. Certainly it was at this point that Marx's own activist efforts were directed, in the attempt to arouse the working classes of nineteenth-century Europe to self-consciousness. Yet even here, his theoretical statements gave the principal role to the structural conditions in which men found themselves. The general pattern by which a class came to gain class-consciousness and the subsidiary role of ideas are perhaps most evident in Marx's discussion of the role of theory in the process:

> Just as *economists* are the scientific representatives of the bourgeois class, so the *Socialists* and the *Communists* are the theoreticians of the proletarian class. So long as the proletariat is not sufficiently developed to constitute itself as a class, . . . these theoreticians are merely utopians who, to meet the wants of the oppressed classes, improvise systems and go in search of a regenerating science. But in the measure that history moves forward, and with it the struggle of the proletariat assumes clearer outlines, they no longer need to seek science in their minds; they have only to take note of what is happening before their eyes and become its mouthpiece.[4]

Note that in this statement, the "theoreticians" role is circumscribed by the state of the proletariat's consciousness, and they constitute merely a "mouthpiece" describing the drama as it unfolds.

At one point there is a recognition by Marx of the role of knowledge and ideas in social change. This is in his *Grundrisse:*

> . . . locomotives, railways, electric telegraphs . . . are products of human industry . . . the power of knowledge objectified. The development of fixed capital indicates to what degree general social knowledge has become *a direct force of production*, and to what degree, hence, the conditions of the process of social life itself have come under the general control of intellect and been transformed in accordance with it.[5]

Here, however, Marx is discussing the role of technological knowledge in changing industry; he seems not to have addressed the question of the role of sociological knowledge in changing social policy. Insofar as there is any nonmaterial force in Marx's theory of social change, it is here.

Yet this is wholly undeveloped and gives no real point of departure for a theory of the social role of sociology. There is not, in his work, any conception of the role of the ideas and leadership provided by the disaffected higher classes (such as himself, Engels, and others) in moving the working classes toward class-consciousness and socialism. Marx envisioned a rational or planned society but had no theory about the place of sociological knowledge in informing that rational action, just as he had no developed ideas about how that "classless" society would function.

Max Weber was another major theoretician without a theory of the social role of social science. Weber was motivated in his sociological investigations, no less than Comte or Marx, by an interest in influencing social change. And the content of his theoretical writings about social change provides a far more hospitable environment for a theory of the social role of sociology than does that of Marx. Weber seems to have had two divergent theses about social change, and each provides, in different ways, a potential foothold for such ideas. One side of Weber is manifested in his study of the world's religions and is best seen in the most famous of these, his study of Protestantism and the rise of capitalism. Weber saw ideas, beliefs, and values, as embodied in a religion, providing the basis which (in the case of Protestantism) could counter communal bonds and generate the individualistic spirit that would allow capitalism and industrial development to take place.

But Weber did not extend his conception of the role of these "ideal" forces (as opposed to Marx's material forces) to a consideration of how sociological analysis might become an element in social change. He carried out sociological analysis, and he was motivated in his selection of problems by the values he held about society; but he, like his contemporaries, did not allow a role for sociological analysis in social change.

The other side of Weber's theses about social change was his belief in the progressive rationalization of society. His study of authority systems showed a progression from traditional authority to rational authority (with charismatic authority as an unstable "filler" between stable authority systems), and he expressed in several places the conception of an increasing rationalization of markets (e.g., in his discussion of the expanding role of money[6]) and of authority systems. In fact, at one point he expressed a despair about the future as he sees the continuation of this rationalization:

> It is as if . . . we were deliberately to become men who need "order" and nothing but order, who become nervous and cowardly if for one moment the order wavers, and helpless if they are torn away from their total incorporation in it. That the world should know no men but these: it is in such an evolution that we are already caught up, and the great question is therefore not how we can promote and hasten it, but what we can oppose to this machinery in order to keep a portion of mankind free from this parcelling-out of the soul, from this supreme mastery of the bureaucratic way of life.[7]

This conception of social change held by Weber has in principle a place for the role of sociological analysis in social change. For a component of rational action (whether of a person, a bureaucratic corporation, or a bureaucratic government) is, as indicated earlier, the provision of information to redirect action. And indeed, this is the way in which social policy research has been used by organizations, as we shall see. But Weber never included in his theory of rational authority a feedback mechanism to provide information for action. Perhaps this was because his conception of rational or bureaucratic authority was a wholly static one. It was a conception of a fixed structure of positions, occupied by persons functioning like a machine, with no mechanism for change. But whatever the reason, there was nowhere in this theory of rational authority a role for information as a guide to policy.

In the work of another classical social theorist, Emile Durkheim, far less room for such a theoretical direction can be found. Where Marx saw economic conditions as the prime movers of change, and Weber (in part of his work) saw values, Durkheim saw social and demographic conditions (as well as technological developments, leading to an increasing division of labor). As with the other classical theorists, and perhaps to an even greater extent, Durkheim was a student of society, and he did not raise the question of how his and others' sociological analyses might enter into the course of social change—or how, in the future, sociological analysis might constitute an intrinsic component of social action. He did conjecture about future social development, and even advocated certain developments (most prominently in the preface to the second edition of the *Division of Labor*, where he proposed the formation of occupational groups to replace the mechanical solidarity of the primitive community), but his conception of social change had no place for sociological analysis.

A more extended examination of the work of classical social theorists might show more ideas about the social role of sociological analysis. But on the whole, there seems to be little of this in the work of early sociologists. Perhaps this should not be surprising; when sociological analysis was in its infancy, it would have been either presumptuous or visionary to assign an important role in the functioning of society to such analysis. Today, when policy research is widespread, questions about its social role arise naturally; it is no longer so small or weak that its role can be ignored. But at the time of the classical theorists, social theory had little reason to incorporate a reflexive element.

The beginnings of American sociology, almost contemporary with the European classical theorists, present a somewhat different orientation to the social role of sociology. American sociologists were pragmatic reformers: while in Europe, sociology and socialism sometimes seemed indistinguishable, in America, sociology was intertwined with social problems and social reform.

These early American sociologists—like Ross, Ward, and Small—were not only reformers, they were nonresearchers. Many of them came from ministerial training and inherited from it a style of work—lectures, writing, exhortations—which was wholly distinct from systematic research. The investigations initiated by the men who followed them—in particular, Park and his students—were focused on social problems, particularly those associated with the city. This work, like that of a few European social-reform sociologists such as Charles Booth,[8] and earlier, Henry Mayhew,[9] was far more empirically grounded than that of most of the Europeans. As such, it began to provide the concrete investigations which could constitute inputs to policy. However, the theoretical assumptions that accompanied this work included only a simple conception about the way its results would influence policy. The implicit theory of directed change behind these efforts was that of the exposé: the notion that exposing an evil condition would set into motion the forces to correct it.

Thus, in a different way and for different reasons, early American sociology did not come any closer than did European sociology to a theory which specified the social role of sociological analysis.

The phase of American social theory between the early period and the recent past (that is, roughly between 1930 and 1960) constituted an attempt to reject the social-problem and social-reform orientation of sociology, and to ingest more of the intellectually rich European tradition. [The most important events in this reorientation were Sorokin's appointment at Harvard (1930) and Parsons's publication of *The Structure of Social Action*. (1937).[10]] With this increased intellectualization of sociology came the embrace of a scientific self-image, which, in rejecting a social-problem orientation, had no place for theory about the social role of sociological analysis.

At the same time, the scientific self-image of sociology led to empirical investigations which had as their goal the enrichment of knowledge *within* the discipline. This meant an implicit rejection of a policy role for sociological analysis as out of keeping with the task of constructing a scientific edifice. No matter if the empirical investigations were microsociological, while the theoretical work was largely macrosociological; although the divergence between research and theory was pronounced, both were concerned with the internal task of creating the discipline, with little time for the question—a fundamental *sociological* question, as it happens—of how the knowledge of that discipline would shape developments in society.

During this period, one branch of sociology pursued a different path (and for this reason was largely disregarded by the mainstream of the discipline). This was rural sociology in the United States, engaged in the practical task—primarily at the behest of the Department of Agriculture and its affiliated schools of agriculture in state universities—of determining how new agricultural developments came to be put into practice. The knowledge and information designed to affect policy was not in this case sociological, but technical: developments in fertilizers, in land-use practices, in hybrid grain, in scientific breeding. But the sociological question of how these policy-relevant research results were to influence social change was the same as that I have been raising throughout.

The studies of these rural sociologists began to throw some light on a particular process in planned social change, that of social diffusion [see Rogers and Shoemaker (1971)].[11] In agriculture, the "policy makers" in question were dispersed farmers, not a single central authority, and for such a structure of social decision making, the rural sociologists developed extensive knowledge about the social processes through which information came to affect practice. The differing roles of persons of different status in the local community, of change agents and "experts," and of communication media were discovered.

The results of this work have obvious relevance not merely for the translation of agricultural innovations into planned change, but in other areas as well, wherever policy-relevant research (whether social, economic, or technical) is to be implemented by dispersed decision makers rather than a single authority. The results have been extended and applied in developing countries, in areas of health practice, agricultural change, and other phenomena,[12] as well as in modern societies.[13] The work stands as probably the most fully developed and widely used sociological knowledge about the translation of new ideas and new information into social action.

It is apparent at the same time that such work is far from a full-scale theoretical attack on the problem of the role of systematic information in social policy. It is obviously limited to areas in which the implementation of policy is rather widely dispersed. At the same time, it is not specific to the diffusion of social research results. Thus, it is more narrow in one sense than a theory of the social role of sociological knowledge, and broader in another.

Most recently, there has come to be a rather different orientation to the role of social research in society, an orientation most akin to the conceptions of those utopian socialists of the nineteenth century with visions of a planned society. The orientation has been taken over from control theory in physical systems, and uses the following general imagery: the government makes decisions; the consequences of the policy are systematically observed and fed back to the decision center, which modifies policies on the basis of the feedback. Social policy research is then one portion of the feedback loop.

This orientation has been present in economics at least since Keynes. Macroeconomic policies include government spending when unemployment reaches a certain level, changes in money supply by the central bank, and so on. Economic indicators, the most prominent of which are price indicators and measures of unemployment, are regularly obtained in most countries (in the U.S., by the Bureau of Labor Statistics). In addition, the Federal Reserve Board has conducted research on consumer expectations[14] designed to inform its policies of tightening or loosening the money supply. These informational needs for economic policy have generated some of the earliest research which is explicitly policy related.

For social policy more broadly, however, this orientation is a relatively recent one. A social philosopher most explicit about this is Haworth, who has developed a notion of the "experimenting society" in which social policies would be arrived at not through the usual interplay of interests, but as a result of explicit social experimentation.[15] The idea is that of a society in which social experiments and pilot studies would constitute a continuing feedback to policy makers, providing the information base upon which social policies would rest. It is a vision of society as a rational actor, engaged in a process of optimum search, using social-science research methods, to arrive at appropriate policies. Donald Campbell has expanded upon this orientation, giving both examples of and methods for social experimentation which can fulfill the role Haworth envisioned.[16]

Jürgen Habermas, writing not about the role of social-science knowledge alone, but about the role of all policy-relevant knowledge generated by scientific procedures, has a conception very similar to Haworth's regarding the emergent feedback process in social policy. Habermas, however, sees this not as a benign vision of future society, but as a threatening one. He says (and I quote at length, because Habermas's vision of the future is a complex one, requiring an extensive passage to give even a glimpse):

> The model according to which the planned reconstruction of society is to proceed is taken from systems analysis. It is possible in principle to comprehend and analyze individual enterprises and organizations, even political or economic subsystems and social systems as a whole, according to the pattern of self-regulated systems. It makes a difference, of course, whether we use a cybernetic frame of reference for analytic purposes or organize a given social system in accordance with this pattern as a man-

machine system. But the transferral of the analytic model to the level of social organization is implied by the very approach taken by systems analysis. Carrying out this intention of an instinct-like self-stabilization of social systems yields the peculiar perspective that the structure of one of the two types of action, namely the behavioral system of purposive-rational action, not only predominates over the institutional framework but gradually absorbs communicative action as such. According to this idea the institutional framework of society—which previously was rooted in a different type of action—would now, in a fundamental reversal, be absorbed by the subsystems of purposive-rational action, which were embedded in it.

Of course this technocratic intention has not been realized anywhere even in its beginnings. But it serves as an ideology for the new politics, which is adapted to technical problems and brackets out practical questions. Furthermore it does correspond to certain developmental tendencies that could lead to a creeping erosion of what we have called the institutional framework. The manifest domination of the authoritarian state gives way to the manipulative compulsions of technical-operational administration. The moral realization of a normative order is a function of communicative action oriented to shared cultural meaning and presupposing the internalization of values. It is increasingly supplanted by conditioned behavior, while large organizations as such are increasingly patterned after the structure of purposive-rational action.[17]

Habermas, then, sees the possible society of the future as using social-science research in a feedback process for self-regulation, just as does Haworth. However, he sees in this transformation of social governing processes a source of central control, a means for eliminating dissent and its creative force in social reorganization.[18]

Whether one holds this vision of a future society as seen (but evaluated differently) by Haworth and Habermas, precisely some such vision of the future, philosophy of history, or theory of social change is necessary as a framework for embedding the social policy research which is increasingly a part of society. This, of course, is only one component of the framework, the most macrosociological. In addition, more microsociological work—that is, a social structural analysis of the generation and disposition of social-policy research—is necessary. The microsociological work would show how the results and utilization of policy research are affected by the social structure within which it is generated, executed, and utilized. For example, it is necessary to know how the social position of the problem originator, relative to the position of the ultimate decision maker, affects the disposition of the research. Or it is important to understand the conditions which lead an interested party to initiate social policy research, to determine which side of a conflict is likely to be more fully equipped with social science information.

Some work on this second component has been done. In the last few years before his death, Paul Lazarsfeld was at work on what he called a "theory of utilization" of social research. This work has generated some ideas and generalizations about utilization,[19] though only a beginning has been made.

To return to macrosociological theories about the future role of social science, the vision of an "experimenting society" or the "cybernetically controlled society" is not the only possible vision and perhaps not even a very sociologically sophisticated one. To show the possible deficiencies, and to show also that there are alternative visions, it is useful to sketch what an alternative vision might look like.

First, we may note that the notion of an "experimenting society" has, as Habermas makes clear, a monolithic or unitary quality, as if society were indeed a single rational actor with unitary goals. Social policy research is explicitly or unwittingly an agent of this monolithic society or (more likely) centralized state. There is no sense of an interplay of interests in society. In contrast to this notion, of course, society is in fact composed of distinct actors with differing interests and often conflicting goals—what Habermas calls the institutional framework. Some of these actors are persons and others are corporate bodies, like trade unions; business firms; professional associations; consumer organizations; racial, ethnic, and religious organizations; and so on.

Social policies may be made by a "decision maker" insulated from pressures by interested parties, they may be made in direct proximity to those interests (as in the case of congressmen), or at the extreme, they may be an aggregate outcome of the actions of the interested parties themselves. (To give an example of the latter, if families had complete choice among schools, public and private, to which to send their children, as in a voucher system, then school policies would be an outcome of the aggregate choices of parents choosing those schools with policies they prefer.) Only in the first of these cases, that of the fully insulated decision maker, is the model of an experimenting society an appropriate one.[20] In the others, the appropriate model is that of multiple decision makers, multiple rational actors requiring feedback in order to know what policies would best implement their interests. In such a model, the notion of social experimentation and social-science-generated feedback to decision makers does not replace the political process by value-free, disinterested social policy research, as in the model of the experimenting society. Rather, it complements the political process, providing for each of the actors the information base which will allow him to better relate his interests to specific policies. Political conflict is not thereby reduced, as in the sanitary conception of the experimenting society, but only better informed. Recently, orientations like that outlined here have begun to emerge and take shape. Perhaps the most fully developed conception is that of Duncan MacRae, in *The Social Function of Social Science*.[21] MacRae's book can perhaps be seen as the first of a genre which will move social science into a new era of self-consciousness about its social role.

But if this vision or model of the policy process in society is not to lead to distortions of the political process by the policy research itself, then attention is necessary to some of the more fine-grain theories of policy research. In particular, it is necessary to know those factors which lead interested parties to make more or less use of policy research. For example, the fact that policy research results are public goods (like information generally) means that the size and the degree of unitary organization of an interested party are important factors in the genesis of policy research. An example of this is the extensive use by the federal government of research relating to school desegregation and the absence of its use by cities, who are often the opponents of the federal government (i.e., HEW) in school-desegregation conflicts. Another example is the near absence of consumer research on consumer products to inform consumers' decisions, as compared with the extensive use of market research to inform producers, who are generally larger and better organized.

Although it is not possible to examine work on this fine-grain or microsociological theory of social research in detail, there has been some work which addresses it,[22] and it is useful to outline a few points.

Points for the Microsociological Theory of the Social Role of Social Research

It is useful to conceive of two worlds governed by different norms and having different properties. One is the world of the discipline or, alternatively, the world of sociological knowledge, in which sociological research is carried out and social theory is developed. The other is the world of action, in which policies are made and consequential events occur.

The world of action consists of a sequence of actions and responses among a variety of parties. As such, it has two properties not shared by the world of the discipline: *interested parties,* whose interests in a given action differ, and sometimes conflict; and *time,* since the actions are embedded in a sequence, with those later in the sequence dependent on those earlier. The disciplinary world is a world of knowledge abstracted from the world of action, but having a separate existence and a separate structure.[23] The norms or values of the discipline favor disinterested inquiry, a search for truth, and full communication of information. The world of action tolerates secrecy, privacy, pursuit of interests, and diversity of values.

The utility of this distinction lies in the fact that while sociological analysis related to policy is executed in the world of the discipline, the problems arise from the world of action, and the information obtained in the sociological analysis returns to the world of action, if it is to have any impact on policy. Policy research, then, as distinct from "pure" or "disciplinary" research, involves both of these worlds and the transitions between them. This has a number of implications. One of the most important concerns the relation between the social policy researcher and the world of action. Because the world of action contains interested parties, the policy researcher is ordinarily an *agent* of one of those parties, though in some cases he may be acting independently. Characteristically, the policy researcher has been in one of three roles:

a) An agent (either employee, contractor, or consultant) of the party whose policy is in question. This is ordinarily the case in market research, and it is also the case in public policy research when the client is the agency which will implement the policy (for example, the Department of Housing and Urban Development as client for the housing-allowance experiments, or the

Department of Health, Education, and Welfare as client for income-maintenance or health-insurance experiments).

b) An agent of a "third party" which is not the policy-making party but represents in some fashion the interests of those persons whom the policies affect. Foundations have often been in this role. For example, the Vera Foundation initiated research to discover the effect of the size of bail bonds on appearance in court, with the hope that the results would lead to a reduction in the size of bonds.

In some cases, the federal government is a third-party client, representing interests of citizens for research on policies of local government authorities or policies of private firms. This is particularly true when the client is an agency like NIMH (National Institute of Mental Health) or NIE, (National Institute of Education) which has no administrative authority but is only a funding agency for research and development. For example, NIE provides funds for research on the effects of educational programs, classroom organization, school financing, desegregation, and career education with the hope that the research results will bring about local educational policies more beneficial to children (or in a few cases, teachers). Analogously, NIMH funded a study of retail stores in Harlem, resulting in a book, *The Poor Pay More.*[24] The implicit aim of NIMH was to benefit the residents of Harlem through such research. It is interesting to note that the very organization of these research activities through agencies such as NIE or NIMH carries an implicit theory about the way social research can best inform social action. If this implicit theory is incorrect, then the value of such research for policy is destined to be low.

c) An independent researcher. In this case, the researcher's own values ordinarily dictate the research problem and the specific issues examined.

This classification of the auspices under which policy research is undertaken is very rough, obscuring a number of variations. For example, the policy researcher is often an agent of the policy-making organization, but the direct client is the research department of that organization, not the policy maker himself. Or in an area of dispersed rather than centralized policy making, the researcher may be an agent of an interested party not in control of policy but hoping to influence policy through the research results. For example, research was commissioned by the New York Federation of Teachers (NYFT) to analyze data from the More Effective Schools program in New York, a pilot program initiated with the support of the NYFT. The teachers' union hoped to influence school policy through this pilot program and associated research.

But even this rough classification suggests the difficulties created by these different kinds of relations between the world of action and the world of discipline. In situation *a*, the research problems are those perceived by the policy-making body, and the implications drawn from the research are likely to be differentially attentive to the policy maker's interests. In addition, the issue of secrecy of research results has often arisen in such a situation. In situations *b* and *c*, the research problems are those perceived by a different interested party (or by his supposed representative, which may be a different thing), and the implications drawn are likely to favor that party's interests.[25] Apart from the biases resulting from the researcher's social position, it is evident that the research is less likely to be utilized by the policy maker in situation *b* or *c*, because the researcher's information is not directed toward the perceived policy needs of the policy maker. This does not mean, as will be emphasized later, that the research in situations *b* and *c* is less likely to be utilized altogether, for when available to others, it has often been widely used by them.

The examples presented in this section, and the inferences we can draw from them, indicate that there is a potential for the development of theory about the social role of social research. That theory is now in its infancy, but the continuing growth of policy research gives an indication that it will not be so for long.

One element of this theory as it emerges is related to a debate which has preoccupied a number of sociologists for a long time. Because this debate has been central to sociological self-definition, it is important to review the positions.

The Relation of Values to Sociological Analysis

Whenever sociological analysis has been addressed to questions that have potential impact on social policy, the issue of values in sociological analysis has arisen. Should sociology be "value-free"? And in such a question, what is meant by "value-free"? It turns out that, in principle, there has been a considerable degree of consensus among sociologists on this issue, though in practice, the differing emphases on different parts of the answer have provoked extensive controversy.

Weber was among the most explicit of early sociologists in his statements about values in the relation of social science to social policy. The occasion which prompted these statements was his assumption of editorship of the *Archiv für Sozialwissenschaft und Sozialpolitik*, which led to an extended editorial statement by Weber on behalf of the editors. The *Archiv* had been under editorship sympathetic to socialist doctrine, and this change constituted an important change in direction for the journal.

In his statement of editorial policy, Weber first made an effort to dispel the confusion that existed over the relation of sociological analysis to values, goals, and policy prescriptions. I will examine his perspective in some detail because I believe it contains elements that were not only relevant to the sociological essays and historical analysis of Weber's time but to the empirical research related to policy which is carried out today. Weber outlines the sociologist's role as one of providing a technical analysis which would supply information but not go further. He says:

> To apply the results of this analysis in the making of a decision, however, is not a task which science can undertake; it is rather the task of the acting, willing person: he weighs and chooses from among the values involved according to his own conscience

and his personal view of the world. Science can make him realize that all action and naturally, according to the circumstances, inaction imply in their consequences the espousal of certain values—and . . . the rejection of certain others.[26]

Weber here sharply distinguishes the role of the social scientist in providing knowledge from that of the acting person (the "policy maker") who uses this knowledge. But although he limits *social science* to this informative, nonevaluative role, he recognizes that *social scientists* may go beyond such scientific statements. In outlining the character that the *Archiv* will take, he says:

In the pages of this journal, there will inevitably be found social *policy*, i.e., the statement of ideals, in addition to social *science*, i.e., the analysis of facts. But we do not by any means intend to present such discussions as "science" and we will guard as best we can against allowing these two to be confused with one another. For that reason, the second fundamental imperative of scientific freedom is that in such cases it should constantly be made clear to the readers (and—again we say it—above all to one's self!) exactly at which point the scientific investigator becomes silent and the evaluating and acting person begins to speak. . . . The foregoing arguments are directed against this confusion, and not against the clear-cut introduction of one's own ideals into the discussion.[27]

Thus Weber makes a distinction between the "scientific investigator" and the "evaluating and acting person," though those activities may be lodged in the same physical person. But Weber argues that there is a specific additional way in which the nonscientific values may properly enter investigation in social science. He says, "In social sciences, the stimulus to the posing of scientific problems is in actuality always given by *practical* questions."[28] The social scientists' values concerning which practical questions are important for policy decisions obviously affect the selection of problems—assuming that it is the social scientist who selects the problems, a circumstance which is wholly true only in case *c* of the earlier classification.

Weber sees the social scientist as occupying two quite different positions, and functioning differently in the two. One is as scientific investigator, a role from which values should be excluded. The other is as selector of the problem, where one makes recommendations or arguments about policies to be taken, activities which may properly be guided by the social scientist's values.

This conception is compatible with, and further extends, the conceptual distinction made earlier between the world of the discipline and the world of action. As a scientific investigator, the social scientist is within the world of the discipline and should be governed by its norms. In selecting the problem and in stating implications of the results, that same person may be in the world of action, and is governed by his own values or interests in that world.

The distinction between these two roles of the social scientist is still very problematic in the application of social science to social policy. And there is a further point which compounds the problem: the social scientist (or for that matter, the natural scientist) who has contributed to the knowledge related to an issue gains credibility in the eyes of others which give his value statements unwarranted power. For example, in the period immediately after the explosion of the first atomic bomb, physicists were sought out extensively for their opinions and advice about the use of the bomb, and a number of physicists gave extensive advice. The *Bulletin of the Atomic Scientists* was born out of a desire by physicists to have a forum for expressing this policy advice.

More recently, attention similarly has been paid to opinions of social scientists in policy issues related to their research: What policies are best in dealing with crime? What about busing for school desegregation? How can juvenile delinquency be reduced? What is the best way of providing housing for the poor?

There has been strong evidence that social scientists who have carried out policy research have gained credibility in the world of action that has given their value statements power which may be unwarranted.[29] For example, social scientists have been called to give testimony in legislatures on child-care policy, health policy, crime prevention, school desegregation, welfare programs, housing policies, transportation systems, environmental issues, employment practices, and many others. In many of these cases, the legislators ask for, and get, not only factual information but also statements about the implications of these results for policy.

To an even greater extent, this mixture of facts and value premises occurs when social scientists' statements appear in the media. This has even led, in the issue of school desegregation, to a newspaper article in the *Washington Post* with the headline "Social Scientist as Confuser."[30]

Altogether, though the analytical distinction made by Weber between the two roles of the social scientist who carries out policy research is a clear-cut and precise one, the empirical separation of these two roles is exceedingly difficult. As a consequence, elimination of the special influence of the investigator's values on policy may not be possible. It may be more feasible to create a social structure for the initiation and reporting of research which can counter such bias.[31]

In sociological discourse, the issue of values in sociology has continued to arise. The sharpest cleavage has placed on one side those who see their tasks as technical and themselves as scientific investigators who need not be concerned with the values that generated the problem or with the societal implications of the results, so long as the problem is intellectually exciting. The prototype of this investigator, at least in the eyes of the other side, was Paul Lazarsfeld; and "American empirical sociology" since the Second World War as a whole has been seen as prototypical.

Opposed to this orientation have been those who emphasize the other part of the social scientist, the values which shape (or should shape, as they see it) the problems he selects and the policy positions he takes. These persons have characteristically been on the sociological left, often Europeans from a Marxist tradition but sometimes American sociologists as well. C. Wright Mills, an American example of this kind of social scientist, makes the argument against the technicians in his polemical *The Sociological Imagination*.[32] Robert S. Lynd perhaps stated the position best in his influential

Knowledge for What?, a plea for the explicit introduction of values into sociological enterprise. Lynd, however, saw as clearly as Weber the distinction between value-laden and value-free activities of the social scientist. He says, "Values may be and are properly and necessarily applied in the preliminary selection of 'significant,' 'important' problems for research. They may but should not be applied thereafter to bias one's analysis or the interpretation of the meanings inherent in one's data."[33]

However, a somewhat stronger role for values has been proposed by some. Howard Becker, in "Whose Side Are We On?", a presidential address of the Society for the Study of Social Problems,[34] argues strongly not just for the introduction of values, but for a *particular* set of values to be held by social scientists generally—values favoring the underdog or the subordinate in a social situation. Lynd comes close to that same position when he emphasizes that the lack of concern with values in selecting a problem often reinforces existing institutional values: "By refusing commerce with such inclusive values, the social scientist does not escape them. What he does is, rather, to accept tacitly the inclusive value-judgment of the culture as to the rightness of the 'American way' and the need for only minor remedial changes."[35]

It has been a general argument of the antitechnicians that the lack of explicit attention to values in selecting a problem and in stating the implications of research results leads to support, implicit or explicit, of the status quo.

Yet there has been more complexity in the injection of policy research results into a social system than the fears of Lynd or the paradigm of rational action I presented earlier would suggest. Some examples show this: the Equality of Educational Opportunity Survey[36] was mandated by Congress and carried out by the U.S. Office of Education. But its results were not used by either of these bodies, or by local school administrations. Instead, they were used by parties outside the educational establishment: by the NAACP in pursuing school-desegregation cases; by advocates of change in school-board conflicts; by opponents of increased school budgets; and in general, more by parties outside school administration and opposing their policies than by those inside and favoring their policies. Similarly, results of research on Head Start by Cicarelli[37] were little used by, and of little use to, Head Start administrators, even though they initiated the research; the results were used by opponents of Head Start. Recent research on white flight from cities as a result of desegregation policies[38] has been used by city school systems opposing those policies, not by HEW or the NAACP, which are pursuing them. Research by economists on the effect of the minimum wage[39] is used more by opponents to the current minimum-wage policy than by its advocates. Research on the results of performance contracting in education was similarly used more by opponents of the policy than by its advocates.[40] Research by criminologists, their questions guided by rehabilitative theories, has been a major tool for opponents of deterrence policies in American penal institutions. At present, when rehabilitative principles have replaced deterrence principles in practice, research by a different set of sociologists and economists, guided by deterrence theories, has come to be used by opponents of present practices. In Sweden, results of a study of levels of living commissioned by the government in the late 1960s were used by the news media to attack the government and ultimately brought about the resignation of a government minister.

These examples raise a question: What is it about policy research that sometimes makes it, despite its initiation by administrative authorities, often more useful to, or at least more used by, opponents of an administrative authority than by the authority? There seem to be at least two parts to the answer. First, certain kinds of policy research, such as program evaluation or a status survey of existing conditions, examine effects of policies currently in force—either on a pilot basis or as a general policy. Such effects are seldom as strong and as beneficial as planned, intended, and claimed by those who instituted them. If the research results show this, they show a "failure" of policy, or a "gap" between claims and outcomes. This is obviously useful to those who want to attack or change the policy. They legitimate opposition to the policy.

Second, even more fundamentally, there is an implicit conflict in principle between research results and authoritative policy. Policy as laid down by the authorities gains its legitimacy from the authority of their position. In the case of elected authorities, legitimacy derives ultimately from the constituents, who implicitly endorsed the policies. But research gains *its* legitimacy from its claim to present the objective facts. If the research results do not support the policy, they challenge not only the policy, but the base of legitimacy on which it rests. Even if the results are largely favorable to the policy, the alternative basis of legitimacy they offer presents an opportunity for parties opposed to the policy to challenge its legitimacy.

One can see this in education. As research results show ineffectiveness of educational programs, they challenge the legitimacy of educational authorities—superintendents, principals, teachers—who devise and carry out these policies. A teacher's authority to determine what children will learn and how they will be taught is an element in the teacher's effectiveness; that authority can be undermined by policy research which reopens these questions. In certain areas, such as education or health, such loss of confidence in authorities may reduce the effectiveness of *whatever* policies they institute.

These results suggest that policy research may, like investigative reporting in news media, have negative side effects on the functioning of a social system which contains authority structures (as all social systems do). The element in all authority of mystical, unchallengeable, essential "rightness," which induces obedience to that authority, is destroyed by much social policy research.

The question then arises: Is policy research, by its very nature, inimical to an authority structure when its results are openly published? The answer is unclear. Policy research may only be inimical to certain stances taken by those in authority, just as democratic elections and political campaigns are inimical to paternalistic or charismatic authority. But just as democratic elections can strengthen an authority structure by keeping it responsible, policy research may, through the changes it induces or provokes, make an authority system more resilient.

The overall effect of policy research on authority systems is, however, uncertain. This uncertainty illustrates the absence of theory concerning the role of policy research in a social system. Yet as policy research plays an increasingly important role in shaping policy, the question becomes an important one for the student of social change.

The examples I have cited indicate that the matter is more complex than argued by Lynd or Mills or others who fear that social research will support the status quo unless sociologists' values determine the selection of problems and statement of implications. Indeed, they indicate that something close to the reverse may be true: that social research results, even when sponsored by those in authority, are very often more useful to those challenging that authority. At the same time, this usefulness depends upon open publication of results, making them available to opponents as well as proponents of the existing policy.

These examples suggest, then, that we may be in a better situation than feared by Lynd and others: the use to which social policy research is put may depend less on the sociologist's values than on the social context within which the results of social research are expressed. The examples suggest that if those results are available to a wide range of interested parties with access to communication media or arenas within which policy issues are decided (such as courts and legislatures), their impact will be far from that envisioned (with differing evaluations of that impact) by Lynd, Haworth, Habermas, and others.

Modern Social Policy Research

The modern period in the history of social policy research began with the development of systematic sample survey research in the late 1930s and the 1940s. The creation of this instrument allowed what had been an art in the hands of Charles Booth in London to become a technical skill based on codified methods with which ordinary social researchers could provide policy-relevant information. Sample survey research was developed in the United States in the thirties and forties, but only after the Second World War was it used in Europe. The early uses in the U.S. were for four kinds of clients: as audience research for radio and magazines; as market research for manufacturing firms; as research on soldiers' attitudes and behavior for the armed forces in the Second World War; and as public-opinion polls for politicians. It is perhaps an extension of the term "policy" to include business decisions which used audience research and market research. But if so, it is an extension useful for our purposes here, because the current social policy research for government agencies or foundations is a direct outgrowth of that work, in which both its methodological and conceptual roots lie. In another sense, market research can hardly be seen as different from other social policy research, for in socialist economic systems, marketing of goods and services is part of government policy, just as is education. The fact that in capitalist economies it is private firms which make these policies does not fundamentally affect the research or its utilization.

The early audience research is exemplified by Lazarsfeld and Stanton;[41] the market research mostly has taken the form of unpublished reports to clients, though some work has been published in journals such as the *Journal of Marketing Research*; and the armed-forces research was published after the war in the monumental four volumes of *The American Soldier*;[42] though further research has continued [see Janowitz (1964)].[43]

Public-opinion research for political clients, although presented to clients in private reports, sometimes made its way into *Public Opinion Quarterly*. POQ, in fact, was the principal organ in the forties and fifties by which the developing technique of survey research used for applied purposes found academic expression. AAPOR (American Association of Public Opinion Research), of which POQ was the official journal, was the organization of pioneers in the survey-research field, with members from applied-research groups in universities and from commerical market-research organizations. Most showed common intellectual origins, having done graduate work or apprenticeships in one of the survey-research organizations, such as the National Opinion Research Center (first in Denver, then at the University of Chicago); the Gallup Organization; Elmo Roper, Stouffer's wartime research unit; or Lazarsfeld's Bureau of Applied Social Research at Columbia. The latter was probably most important in providing the manpower for the market-research organizations which grew up in the forties and fifties, principally in New York.

The institutional locus of this work is important to note, in view of the developments occurring in current social policy research. The work began principally in universities—at Columbia, Princeton, and elsewhere. But within a few years, the majority of the most directly policy-related work was carried out in commercial market-research organizations. The academic research institutes appeared to be most capable of developing the new technique and of training persons in it. But as it became regularized, the universities were either not sufficiently efficient or not sufficiently responsive to client interests to successfully compete with commercial organizations.

Sharing the common intellectual origins of the market-research and public-opinion research of the thirties and forties was the massive body of work carried out within the armed forces during the Second World War in the Research Branch of the Information and Education Division of the War Department. Although the work included experimentation in mass communications[44] which had a strong impact on work in social psychology, the field survey work of samples of military personnel, carried out under the general supervision of Samuel Stouffer and reported in *The American Soldier*,[45] has had most descendents in modern policy research.

Not all the work done by the Research Branch informed policy; however, much of it did, and there were some striking examples of its use. For instance, the point system for release of military personnel after the end of the war was based upon survey results showing the potential reaction of these persons to different release policies.

Concurrent with the market, communications, and armed-forces research, another body of research, related to policy in a different way, was being carried out [see Lionberger (1960)[46] for a discussion and review of this work]. This was research in rural sociology, mentioned earlier in this chapter (page 683), which focused on how technological innovations in farming might be translated into policy through their adoption by farmers. The results of this research are of aid in developing a theory about the role of information in directed social change, as discussed on page 683. Yet the research itself was social policy research, a precursor, both in method and in intent, to current policy research. For it was designed to inform policies about introducing agricultural innovations in such a way that they would be widely and speedily adopted. And its methods were like those emerging in public opinion and market research: sample surveys, followed by statistical analysis of survey responses. Rensis Likert, one of the men who developed these methods in the Department of Agriculture, moved to the Survey Research Center at the University of Michigan and brought with him these methods for use more broadly in social policy research. The policy research initiated there ranged widely in areas unrelated to agriculture: consumer expectations of economic conditions for the Federal Reserve Board [see Katona (1960)],[47] work in industrial sociology for employers [see Kahn (1964)],[48] and others.

Social Policy Research in the 1960s and 1970s

Applied social research, primarily survey research, which first had commercial applications in market and audience research, began to be seen in the 1950s as a potential instrument for solving various "public" social problems. The "clients" this time were foundations such as the Ford Foundation, Russell Sage Foundation, and Carnegie Corporation, and agencies such as NIMH and the U.S. Office of Education. The general notion was that the same systematic techniques of sample surveys and data analysis could be applied to various social problems, such as delinquency, community disorganization, social pathologies associated with poverty, and educational problems. There was a difference, however: these organizations were not truly clients, for they were in no position to implement any policies making use of research results. They were a peculiar type of organization known as "funding organizations," without any policies to implement; they merely funded research grants or contracts.

As a consequence, there developed a major delusion and a diversion of funds. The delusion was on the part of the agencies, in thinking that their research funding might in some way aid policy. The diversion of funds was by academic social scientists, who proceeded to design research not to inform social policy but to lead to academic publication. This period and its research, much of which was valuable neither as academic research nor as social policy research, suggest that such nonoperating organizations may be inappropriate originators of social policy research. But this may not be so, if the organizations approach their task in a somewhat different way. I will return to this question subsequently.

Evaluation Research, Social Experiments, and Related Work

In the mid-1960s, social policy research in its present form began to take shape, spearheaded by a few prototypes. The most important change was that operating agencies with responsibilities for policy began to commission research. Head Start evaluation[49] sponsored by its parent agency, the Office of Economic Opportunity (OEO), was one example; the Equality of Educational Opportunity Survey,[50] carried out under a directive from Congress—the Civil Rights Act of 1964—was another. The operative consequences of this change were: (a) the research was sufficiently large-scale so that the results would be meaningful for national policy; (b) the research questions were set by the agency, not by the researcher via an unsolicited proposal; and (c) the client agency was interested in the research results, a somewhat new experience for social researchers outside commercial organizations.

With OEO as the most innovative agency for social policy research, a number of types of policy research began to emerge. They are as follows:

a) Review of Research: Not new research at all, but a review and synthesis of existing research brought to bear on policy questions. Example: *Youth: Transition to Adulthood*.[51]

b) Status Survey: A survey of the situation in a particular area, not designed to evaluate a specific existing or pilot program but to provide an information base for future policies. Such surveys not only occur in research on public policy but are widespread in market research as well, as studies of purchasing behavior and attitudes toward items in the market. Examples: *Equality of Educational Opportunity*,[52] *The End of Growth*,[53] *Reports* to the National Commission on the Causes and Prevention of Violence.[54]

c) Evaluation Research: Evaluation of a specific program, either a full-scale one (as in Head Start) or a pilot program (as in various local evaluations of Experimental Schools, a program initiated by the U.S. Office of Education). Ordinarily the term "evaluation research" implies that no experimental design is used in the initial policy and any experimental controls are introduced after the program is in effect. Various research designs are used, including a number of pseudoexperimental designs [see Campbell and Stanley (1963)].[55] *Formative* or *process* evaluation is designed to evaluate the process through which the program is implemented and is ordinarily intended to provide rapid feedback to a program director to facilitate modification of the program. *Summative* or *product* evaluation is designed to evaluate the outcomes of a program, generally to discover whether it achieved its intended goals and what any side effects were. It is ordinarily intended to provide information to an operating agency about whether or not to continue a program. Examples: Head Start,[56] Sesame Street,[57] Follow Through,[58] Abt Associates,[59] School Vouchers.[60]

d) Social Experiments: A pilot program carried out with explicit use of experimental design, including data collection in conjunction with the ongoing program. In social experiments, the explicit purpose of the program is to obtain policy-relevant information, while in evaluation research, the program is initiated for its presumed benefits and the evaluation is not an intrinsic part of the program. Examples: income-maintenance experiment,[61] housing-allowance experiments,[62] health-insurance experiments.[63]

e) Secondary Analysis: Analysis of data gathered by other parties, often for other purposes. Such secondary analysis is sometimes reanalysis of data gathered for research of the sorts described in *a* through *d* above. For example Cook reanalyzed the Sesame Street data and arrived at different policy recommendations than did Ball and Bogatz.[64] And there were many reanalyses of the Equality of Educational Opportunity data, including Bowles and Levin,[65] several found in Moynihan and Mosteller,[66] and Cain and Watts.[67] These also arrived at results differing in some respects from those of the original investigators. Rossi and Lyall carried out a secondary analysis of a somewhat different sort of the New Jersey income-maintenance experiments.[68] Their aim was not so much to dispute the original results as to explicate them for a broader audience and examine their implications.

In some cases, the secondary analysis uses data gathered for other purposes, such as administrative data, examining them to answer certain policy-related questions. For example, data on racial composition of schools throughout the country from 1967–73 were examined by Farley,[69] Coleman, Kelly and Moore,[70] and Clotfelter[71] to examine changes in school integration and to draw inferences about effects of desegregation policies on resegregation between city and suburbs. Similarly, data on school financing from administrative sources were used by Coons, Clune, and Sugarman[72] to examine the inequalities of financing within various states.

Institutional Differentiation

This description of types of social policy research suggests a relatively high level of development of the field, compared to the undifferentiated state forty years ago when market research had its beginnings. (In this listing of types of policy research, I have emphasized research on public policy. There have developed analogous types of market and audience research, including surveys, test marketing, product-preference testing, consumer panels, and the use of experimental designs in the study of shopping habits and in-store patterns of activity.)

Another differentiation has developed as well. Just as market research moved in large part (though never entirely) outside academic institutions to commercial organizations, public-policy research has begun to move outside universities to nonprofit and profit-making organizations, each having its own distinct character. I will mention a few of the most prominent. Rand Corporation, building upon its economic expertise in foreign-policy analyses, began in the late 1960s to study problems of (domestic) social and economic policy, emphasizing its design and analytical capacities, with a strong emphasis on social experimentation (the housing-allowance and health-insurance experiments constituting the most massive). The Urban Institute has developed similarly, with a high concentration of economic analyses, but focusing more specifically on urban problems and policies, and more nearly using secondary analysis. Brookings Institution's work has been similar, but with a higher component of political science, closer ties to federal-government policy, and more emphasis on reviews of research. Abt Associates, a profit-making organization, has a higher component of sociological skills and backgrounds and has focused on more "social" problems such as education, health care, housing, and employment. Mathematica, which in conjunction with the Poverty Institute at the University of Wisconsin carried out the income-maintenance experiment, lies somewhere between Rand and Abt in the kind of work it has done. SRI (formerly Stanford Research Institute, but now without ties to Stanford) carries out a broad range of activities, having like Abt, a more sociological orientation than Rand or Mathematica. Westat, with a national field staff of interviewers, is principally a data-collection organization, complementing the skills of the organizations named earlier, which do not maintain national field staffs. In addition to these social policy research organizations, there are many others, mostly at a local level, principally engaged in program evaluation.

There remain, to be sure, policy research organizations affiliated with universities: the Poverty Institute at the University of Wisconsin, the Institute for Social Research at the University of Michigan, NORC at the University of Chicago, the Research Triangle Institute in North Carolina, and others. The rapid growth in policy research, however, has been in the nonuniversity organizations. The general pattern, as evidenced in market, audience, and now public policy research, seems to be for the new type of activity to develop within the shelter of a university but then to move outside. This suggests that the relatively unstructured and nondirective university setting facilitates the exploratory activity and can sustain it in its early stages, but is too irregular, irresponsible, and unpredictable for the most efficient execution of policy research once it is regularized. This suggestion is strenthened by the fact that the university-related policy-research organizations that have been most successful, such as those mentioned above, have come to be structured much like the independent organizations referred to earlier.

Another aspect of the institutional structure through which policy research is generated concerns the funding agencies for research. In the U.S. government there exist agencies such as NIMH and NIE which do not make policy, but merely fund social policy research. Their early mode of operation was to fund investigator-initiated research. Their present mode is to fund research that can directly inform government policy, implicitly following the conception of the monolithic "experimenting society." But there has not yet developed a conception within these agencies that their role is to inform the policy-relevant decisions of all legitimate parties in a given area, in and out of government. As a consequence, there has not come to be a rationale or an institutional mechanism related to the structure of society, through which research is initiated in a pluralistic fashion.

Conclusion

The rapid growth of social policy research and its increasing importance for social policy have begun in recent years to push social scientists and social philosophers toward what both the classical and the modern theorists have neglected: the development of a theory of purposive or directed social change. Haworth's conception of an experimenting society is one move in that direction; Lazarsfeld's attempt to develop a theory of utilization is another.

One major aspect of such theory, at the more macrosociological level, must be, in effect, political theory: the way in which diverse interested parties, not all sufficiently well organized to initiate research, can nevertheless obtain feedback to inform their decisions and thus their politically relevant actions. Another aspect must concern the relation between authority and research-generated information. Under what conditions does that information strengthen authority, and under what conditions does it strengthen opposing interests? In addition to these political or macrosociological questions, there is a microsociological theory of social policy research to be developed as well: How does the position of the investigator affect the initiation and utilization of the research? How do the differences between the world of the discipline and the world of action affect the execution of the research? How does the social structure within which the policy decision is to be made (e.g., centralized decision versus dispersed decision) affect the utilization of the research?

It can be expected, as the quantity of social policy research expands and as its impact on social policy increases, that such theory, nearly absent in sociology until now, will develop with some rapidity. And because of its intimate relation to political theory, it is likely to have an impact on the way social policy research is institutionalized in society.

NOTES

1. J. A. Pechman, and Michael Timpane, *Work Incentives and Income Guarantees* (Washington: The Brookings Institution, 1975).

2. Frederick Le Play, *Les ouvriers européens*, 2d ed. (1855; Tours: Mame, 1855–79) 6 vols.

3. Though Marx did not devote his time to policy research, it is interesting to note that he did once create a questionnaire, distributed to workers through the *Revue Socialiste* in 1880. This attempt, however, was a dismal failure. The questionnaire, composed of 101 questions which even the most literate and informed person would find difficult to answer, was returned by only a few workers, and never mentioned again. See Thomas Bottomore, and M. Rubel, *Karl Marx: Selected Writings in Sociology and Social Philosophy* (London: C. A. Watts and Co., 1956), p. 203.

4. Karl Marx, *The Poverty of Philosophy* (1847; New York: International Publishers, 1963) p. 125.

5. Karl Marx, *Grundrisse*, trans. Martin Nicolaus (orig. German ed., 1858; London: Allan Lane, 1973) p. 706.

6. Max Weber, *The Theory of Social and Economic Organization*, trans. A. M. Henderson and T. Parsons (New York: Oxford University Press, 1947).

7. Max Weber, in P. J. Mayer, *Max Weber and German Politics* (London: Faber and Faber, 1944) p. 97.

8. Charles Booth, *Life and Labour of the People* (1889–91; London: Macmillan, 1902–03) 12 vols.

9. Henry Mayhew, *London Labour and the London Poor (1851;* London: Griffin, 1861).

10. Talcott Parsons, *The Structure of Social Action* (Glencoe, Illinois: Free Press, 1937).

11. Everett M. Rogers and F. Floyd Shoemaker, *Communication of Innovation* (New York: Free Press, 1971).

12. Ibid.

13. Elihu Katz and Paul F. Lazarsfeld, *Personal Influence*, (Glencoe, Illinois: Free Press, 1955).

14. George Katona, *The Powerful Consumer: Psychological Studies of the American Economy* (New York: McGraw-Hill, 1960).

15. L. Haworth, "The Experimenting Society: Dewey and Jordan," *Ethics* 71 (1960), pp. 27–40.

16. Donald Campbell, "Methods for the Experimenting Society," (paper presented at the meeting of the American Psychological Association; Washington, D.C., September 1971). Forthcoming.

17. Jürgen Habermas, *Toward a Rational Society* (London: Heinemann, 1971) pp. 106–07.

18. Habermas, recognizing the absence in Marx's social theory of any such process as he describes, attempts to modify or correct Marxist theory to incorporate it.

19. Paul F. Lazarsfeld, W. H. Sewell, and Harold Wilensky, eds., *The Uses of Sociology* (New York: Basic Books, 1967) pp. ix–xxxiii.

20. It is useful to note that procedures moving in the direction of the experimenting society were initiated by Robert McNamara when he was secretary of defense. He instituted, for example, a procedure of competing prototypes of weapons built by two or more firms, to inform the decision about what contract to let. This procedure has been used on even large weapons such as airplanes and tanks. It is hardly an accident that such a procedure orginated in the Defense Department, for in contrast to most (though not all) domestic social policies, the decision is highly centralized. McNamara seems to have instituted this procedure in part as a way of insulating the defense weapons decisions from interested parties among manufacturing firms, their congressional representatives, and their service advocates.

21. Duncan MacRae, Jr. *The Social Function of Social Science* (New Haven: Yale University Press, 1976).

22. Lazarsfeld et al., *The Uses of Sociology*, 1967; James S. Coleman, *Methods of Policy Research* (Morristown, New Jersey: General Learning Press, 1972); MacRae, *The Social Function of Social Science*, 1976.

23. There is a sense, of course, in which time is important in the world of the discipline, since knowledge accumulates over time. But it is a sequence that is cut off from, independent of the sequence of actions outside the discipline.

24. David Caplovitz, *The Poor Pay More* (New York: Free Press, 1963).

25. This is not merely conjecture. In a review of thirty-eight cases of policy research [James S.

Coleman, *Utilization of Policy Research and the Social Location of the Researcher* (mimeographed; Chicago: U. of Chicago, 1973.], I found that the recommendations or implications drawn from the research by the policy researcher showed this relation to his social position:

	Researcher's position	
Implications drawn were from point of view of:	Policy-maker's agent	Third-party agent or independent
Policy maker	(a)	(b), (c)
Persons subject to policy	11	2
	12	13

26. Max Weber, *On the Methodology of the Social Sciences,* tr. by E. A. Shils and H. A. Finch (Glencoe, Ill.: The Free Press, 1949) p. 53. The essay "Objectivity" in *Social Science and Social Policy* from which this quotation is taken, was first published in *Archiv für Sozialwissenschaft und Sozialpolitik* in 1904.

27. Ibid., p. 60.

28. Ibid., p. 61.

29. The social scientist's recommendations about policy contain a combination of factual information based on research results, *together with* a value premise, which is often implicit. A major part of the problem lies in the difficulty of untangling the facts from the value premise, and of making the latter explicit.

30. Epstein

31. For example, a structure in which *more than one* research activity is initiated in a given policy area, explicitly addressing questions of interest to different interested parties, might be appropriate. And in reporting the research results, some forumlike structure involving other social scientists may be appropriate. For policy-related natural science, a "science court" has been proposed, in response to this same problem. See the Task Force of the Presidential Advisory Group on Anticipated Advances in Science and Technology, "The Science Court Experiment: An Interim Report," *Science* 193: (August 20, 1976) pp. 653–56.

32. C. Wright Mills, *The Sociological Imagination* (New York: Oxford University Press, 1959).

33. Robert S. Lynd, *Knowledge for What?* (Princeton: Princeton University Press, 1939) p. 183.

34. Howard Becker, "Whose Side Are We On?" *Social Problems* 14 (1967) pp. 239–47.

35. Lynd, *Knowledge for What?*, p. 185.

36. James S. Coleman et al., *Equality of Educational Opportunity* (Washington: U.S. Government Printing Office, 1966).

37. Victor Cicarelli, et al., *The Impact of Head Start* (Springfield, Virginia: U.S. Clearinghouse for Federal Scientific and Technical Information, 1969).

38. James S. Coleman, Sara Kelly, and John Moore, *Trends in School Segregation 1968–73* (Washington: Urban Institute, 1975); Charles T. Clotfelter, "School Desegregation, 'Tipping' and Private School Enrollment," *Journal of Human Resources* 11 (1976) pp. 28–50.

39. Jacob Mincer, "Effects of Minimum Wages on Employment, Unemployment, and Skill Formation of Youths" (mimeographed; New York: Columbia University, 1977).

40. Edward M. Gramlich and Patricia P. Koshel, *Educational Performance Contracting* (Washington: The Brookings Institution, 1975).

41. Paul F. Lazarsfeld and Frank Stanton, *Radio Research 1942–43* (New York: Duell, Sloan, and Pearce, 1944).

42. S. A. Stouffer et al., *The American Soldier,* vol. I–IV (Princeton: Princeton University Press, 1948–50).

43. Morris Janowitz, ed., *The New Military: Changing Patterns of Organization* (New York: Russell Sage, 1964).

44. C. I. Hovland, Arthur Lumsdaine, and Fred Sheffield, *Experiments on Mass Communication* (Princeton: Princeton University Press, 1949).

45. Stouffer et al., *The American Soldier,* 1948.

46. Herbert F. Lionberger, *Adoption of New Ideas and Practices: A Summary of the Research Dealing with the Acceptance of Technological Change in Agriculture, with Implications for Action in Facilitating Social Change* (Ames, Iowa: Iowa State University Press, 1960).

47. Katona, *The Powerful Consumer.*

48. Robert L. Kahn, *Organizational Stress: Studies in Role Conflict and Ambiguity* (New York: John Wiley, 1964).

49. Cicarelli et al., *The Impact of Head Start.*

50. Coleman et al., *Equality of Educational Opportunity.*

51. Panel on Youth, *Youth: Transition to Adulthood* (Chicago: University of Chicago Press, 1974).

52. Coleman et al., *Equality of Educational Opportunity.*

53. U.S. Commission on Population Growth and the American Future, *Population and the American Future* (Washington: U.S. Government Printing Office, 1972).

54. National Commission on the Causes and Prevention of Violence, *Reports to the Commission* (Washington: U. S. Government Printing Office, 1969) 13 vols.

55. Donald Campbell and Julian Stanley, *Experimental and Quasi-Experimental Designs for Research* (Chicago: Rand McNally, 1963).

56. Cicarelli et al., *The Impact of Head Start.*

57. S. Ball and G. A. Bogatz, *The First Year of Sesame Street: An Evaluation* (Princeton, New Jersey: Educational Testing Service, 1969).

58. Alice M. Rivlin, and P. Michael Timpane, eds., *Planned Variation in Education* (Washington: The Brookings Institution, 1975).

59. Abt Associates, *Education as Experimentation: A Planned Variation Model, Reports of the Project* (Cambridge, Massachusetts: Abt Associates, 1977).

60. D. Weiler, *A Public School Voucher Demonstration: The First Year at Alum Rock* (Santa Monica, California: Rand, 1974.)

61. David Kershaw et al., *Final Report of the New Jersey Graduated Work Incentive Experiment,* (New York: Academic Press, 1976) vol. I–IV.

62. Rand Corporation, *Third Annual Report of the Housing Assistance Supply Experiment* (Santa Monica, California: Rand, 1977).

63. J. P. Newhouse, *The Health Insurance Study—A Summary* (Santa Monica, California: Rand, 1974).

64. Thomas D. Cook et al., *"Sesame Street" Revisited* (New York: Russell Sage Foundation, 1975).

65. S. Bowles and Henry Levin, "The Determinants of Scholastic Achievement—An Appraisal of Some Recent Evidence," *Journal of Human Resources* 3 (Winter 1968) pp. 3–24.

66. Eric Hanushek and John F. Kain, "On the Value of *Equality of Educational Opportunity* as a Guide to Public Policy," in F. Mosteller and D. P. Moynihan, eds., *On Equality of Educational Opportunity* (New York: Random House, 1972) pp. 116–45.

67. Glen Cain, and Harold Watts, "Problems in Making Policy Inferences from the Coleman Report," *American Sociological Review* 35 (1970), pp. 228–42.

68. Peter H. Rossi and Katharine C. Lyall, *Reforming Public Welfare* (New York: Russell Sage Foundation, 1976).

69. Reynolds Farley, "Can Government Policies Integrate Public Schools" (unpublished manuscript, University of Michigan, 1977).

70. Coleman, Kelly, and Moore, *Trends in School Segregation 1968–73.*

71. Charles T. Clotfelter, "Urban School Desegregation and Declines in White Enrollment: A Reexamination," mimeographed (Baltimore: University of Maryland, 1977).

72. John Coons et al., *Private Wealth and Public Education* (Cambridge: Harvard University Press, 1970).

NAME INDEX

SUBJECT INDEX